ST/ESA/STAT/SER.X/18

Department for Economic and Social Information and Policy Analysis
Statistical Division

WITHDRAWN

National Accounts Statistics     Series X, No. 18
**Special Issue**

# Trends in International Distribution of Gross World Product

Harry C. Trexler Library
Muhlenberg College

United Nations   New York, 1993

NOTE

Symbols of United Nations documents are composed of capital letters combined with figures.

The designations employed and the presentation of material in this publication do not imply the expression of any opinion whatsoever on the part of the Secretariat of the United Nations concerning the legal status of any country, territory, city or area or of its authorities, or concerning the delimitation of its frontiers or boundaries.

Where the designation "country or area" appears in the heading of tables, it covers countries, territories or areas.

The time period covered in this volume is 1970-1989. Accordingly, the countries and areas reported on and the designations used are those pertaining at the end of 1989. Subsequent delimitations with regard to unification or emergence of new countries or areas are not reflected in the text, tables or charts presented herein.

ST/ESA/STAT/SER.X/18
United Nations publication
Sales No. E.93.XVII.7
ISBN 92-1-161346-9
Copyright © United Nations, 1993

# Contents

## Tables

## Annex tables

# Figures

# Overview

The present study analyses the effects of using alternative conversion rates on the changes in the distribution of gross world product (i.e., the total of gross domestic product (GDP) for 178 countries) between countries and regions over time. The period covered is 1970–1989. The study uses four types of conversion rates: market exchange rates (MERs) as published by the International Monetary Fund, purchasing power parities (PPPs) estimates from Penn World Tables, *World Bank Atlas* (WA) conversion rates used by the World Bank and price adjusted rates of exchange (PAREs) developed by the Statistical Division of the United Nations Secretariat. Measures and graphs which are similar to those traditionally used in the measurement of income distribution within a country are used to carry out the analysis. These include Lorenz curves, Gin-coefficients, percentage of income received by quarters and eighths of the population, ranking of countries and standard deviation measures. Some of the conclusions drawn from the study are summarized below.

Increases in the inequality of the distribution of gross world product are observed when using MER or WA rates; however, GDP data converted on the basis of PAREs do not indicate substantial change in the level of inequality in the world during the period of study. Data based on PPPs demonstrate much less inequality in the distribution of gross world product than do data based on any of the other conversion rates but indicate a slight increase in inequality between 1970 and 1989.

When using MER and WA rates, the proportion of the richest quarter of the population increased from 80 per cent to almost 87 per cent of the gross world product. The third quarter—and not the poorest half of the world—is the group whose relative position worsened. Similarly, the pattern described by data based on PAREs show that the richest eighth of the world population became relatively richer while the shares of the sixth and the seventh eighths just below decreased the most and decreased continuously. The composition of the group of richest countries also changed.

The ranks of countries based on per capita GDP remained fairly stable during the last two decades based on each conversion rate. Comparing the first and last years, the typical correlation coefficient between rank structures was 0.90–0.94. Also, the country ranks based on the same conversion rates did not change significantly during the period. The least change in the ranks was observed when using PPPs. In the case of PAREs, the rank of the countries changed, even though Lorenz curves and Gini indices did not indicate substantial change in the GDP distribution. The directions of the changes (i.e. increases or decreases) in country ranks were mostly

1

stable during the whole period in the case of PAREs; they varied considerably in the case of MER and WA rates.

Two types of regionalization were carried out for the purpose of the study. Eight regions were identified first; then—to carry the analysis further—these regions were subdivided into 14 more homogeneous subregions. Calculations based on different regionalizations sometimes lead to different conclusions, but the results of both analyses show that differences between the regions were always more dominant than the differences within them.

In line with findings for individual countries, the regional analysis shows that patterns for MER and WA conversions are very similar to each other as well as to the main trends based on pare conversions. Furthermore, trends based on PAREs are smoother than those based on MER and WA conversions.

# Introduction

The present publication is a special supplement to the National Accounts Statistics series.[1] It is the first of several specialized publications designed to apply a variety of analyses to the integrated national accounts database maintained by the Statistical Division of the United Nations Secretariat. This database currently covers the period 1970–1989 and includes national accounts data for 178 countries or areas of the world. The objective of this special issue is to assess the changes in the distribution of gross world product (i.e., the total of gross domestic product (GDP) for all 178 countries or areas) between countries and regions of the world during the period covered by the database of the Statistical Division.

The data used for this assessment are the latest GDP and per capita GDP data available to the Statistical Division of the United Nations Secretariat as of mid–1992.[2] They are converted to United States dollars using alternative conversion rates. Traditional income distribution measures are applied to assess the distribution of gross world product and the changes therein during the period 1970–1989. A number of considerations should be taken into account in evaluating the results of the study.

The first one is that GDP is a measure of product produced on the territory of a country or area but not the income earned by the nation. GDP was selected for distribution study as it was the only principal national accounts aggregate that is available or can be estimated for a majority of countries on a comparable basis. Using GDP as the key for the distribution implies that the distribution reflects in principle only differences in economic development between countries. However, as the differences between GDP and such income measures as national income and national disposable income are generally small, the distribution of gross world product between countries could be considered as an approximation of the distribution of income between countries.

Secondly, the study deals only with the distribution of gross world product between countries. The distribution of GDP between regions of a country is not considered here as few countries compile such data. Also, the distribution of income within a country is not dealt with—first because of the focus of the study on GDP and, secondly, because no compatible income distribution data are available for a large number of countries.

Finally, the emphasis of the study is not on the distribution of world gross domestic product, but rather on the effects of using alternative conversion rates in measuring the distribution of gross world product between countries and regions and its changes over time. The conversion rates include market exchange rates (MERs) published by the International Monetary Fund,[3] purchasing power parities (PPPs),[4] conversion rates used by the World Bank in its *World Bank Atlas* (WA)[5] and price adjusted rates of exchange (PAREs) developed by the Statistical Division of the United Nations Secretariat for administrative use by the Committee on Contributions of the United Nations General Assembly.

The study is presented in two chapters. Chapter I deals with the GDP data and United States dollar conversion rates used in the study. Chapter II analyses changes in the distribution of gross world product over time using graphs and summary tables.

Two detailed country tables are included in annex A to this volume. Annex table A.1 incorporates the percentage distribution of gross world product between countries according to the four principal conversion rates used in the study. It presents annual data on total and per capita GDP for each of the 178 countries, covering each year of the 1970–1989 period, as well as averages for 1970–1989, 1970–1979 and 1980–1989. Annex table A.2 includes the conversion rates for the same countries, years and periods that were used in the study. In discussing the data, most of the emphasis is on the four conversion rates that were used to translate local currency data into United States dollars. Only a summary description is included on the sources and methods used to calculate GDP and per capita GDP data; for more detailed information, the reader is referred to *National Accounts Statistics: Analysis of Main Aggregates, 1988–1989.*[6]

The analysis in chapter II is presented in two sections. Section A provides an analysis of changes over time in total and per capita gross world product based on different conversion rates. It includes an analysis of the changes in the distribution of gross world product between countries, alternatively measured on the basis of the different conversion rates. In the context of this specialized analysis, measures and graphs which are similar to those traditionally used in the measurement of income distribution within a country are applied. These include Lorenz curves, Gini-coefficients, percentage of income received by quarters and eighths of the population, ranking of countries or areas and standard deviation measures.

Section B of chapter II carries out a similar analysis focusing on regions. The distribution of gross world product in the different regions and subregions of the world is shown in annex table A.6. Special attention has been paid to whether the per capita GDP data of countries are correlated with the per capita gross regional product of the region where they are located.

The present study is an example of how the comprehensive national accounts database developed by the Statistical Division of the United Nations Secretariat can be used for analysis. In order to facilitate analytical use beyond the orientation suggested in this volume, readers may contact the Statistical Division to obtain access to the database in one of the following ways. A computer magnetic tape containing a comprehensive set of official national accounts data covering, in principle, all data elements of the System of National Accounts (SNA) may be purchased. Alternatively, interested users may purchase a tape comprising all official data and Statistical Division estimates covering, at present, only GDP and its activity and expenditure components at current and constant prices. This is the tape used as the basis for the present study. Finally, the Statistical Division can provide diskettes that include data on GDP and per capita GDP and the complete set, including estimates, of the variant conversion factors of individual countries, as contained in annex tables A.1 and A.2 of the present publication.

## Notes

1.    The most recent publications in the series are *National Accounts Statistics: Analysis of Main Aggregates, 1988–1989* (United Nations publication, Sales No. E.91.XVII.17) and *National Accounts Statistics: Main Aggregates and Detailed Tables, 1989*, Parts I and II (United Nations publication, Sales No. E.91.XVII.16, Part I and Part II).

2.    The figures shown are the most recent estimates and revisions available at the time of compilation.  In general, figures for the most recent year are to be regarded as provisional.  For more up-to-date information, reference is made to selected issues of the *Monthly Bulletin of Statistics*, prepared by the Statistical Division, United Nations Secretariat (United Nations sales publication, Series Q).

3.    IMF, *International Financial Statistics* (Washington, D.C., various editions).

4.    Robert Summers and Alan Heston, "A new set of international comparisons of real products and prices: estimates for 130 countries", *The Review of Income and Wealth*, 1988, pp. 1–25.

5.    World Bank, *The World Bank Atlas* (Washington, D.C., various editions).

6.    *Op. cit.*

# I. Gross domestic product data and United States dollar conversion rates

The study uses GDP, per capita GDP and four principal conversion rates: market exchange rates (MERs), purchasing power parities (PPPs), *World Bank Atlas* (WA) conversion rates, and three different versions of the price adjusted rate of exchange (PARE). The latter include a "relative" 1970–1989 PARE, which is based on extrapolation of average exchange rates for the base period 1970–1989 for each country, except the United States, with the help of relative price indices that reflect domestic inflation relative to the United States; an "absolute" 1970–1989 PARE, which is based for each country, including the United States, on extrapolation of average exchange rates for the same base period with absolute price indices; and finally, an "absolute" 1980–1989 PARE, which takes the average exchange rates for the base period 1980–1989 as the point of departure for the extrapolation. More detailed conceptual and compilation aspects of each are described below. Average annual market exchange rates were obtained from the International Monetary Fund (IMF). Population information is based on official data and estimates published in the United Nations *Demographic Yearbook*.

## A. GDP and per capita GDP

Data on GDP and per capita GDP are presented in annex table A.1. It includes annual data and averages for the years 1970–1989 for 178 countries or areas. The data are expressed in United States dollars, using the four alternative methods of conversion (presented in annex table A.2 and discussed below). Additionally, table A.1 shows the percentage changes in each country's share of gross world product in relation to the total gross world product with each application of the alternative conversion rates.

The left-most column of annex table A.1 lists, for each country or area, the type of conversion rate, numbered in rows as follows: (1) MER; (2) PPPs; (3) absolute 1970–1989 PARE; (4) relative 1970–1989 PARE; (5) absolute 1980–1989 PARE; and (6) WA conversion rates. Each conversion rate is subdivided into subscripts a, b and c, corresponding to per capita GDP in United States dollars, total GDP in millions of United States dollars and the percentage share of each country's GDP in the gross world product.

Columns 1–20 show the individual years 1970–1989. The last three columns present the averages of each item and country or area for three periods: 1970–1989, the entire period covered by the study; the decade 1970–1979; and the decade 1980–1989.

In interpreting the levels of GDP and per capita GDP for each country or area in annex table A.1, the reader should keep in mind that the central focus of the present study is on gross world product distribution and less on GDP levels. As will be clearly evident from the explanation and elaboration of the conversion rates below, comparison of GDP levels between different conversion rates is more difficult to assess because alternative conversion factors are based implicitly on different units of measurement.

For example, for Algeria in 1970, as shown in column 1, per capita GDP ranges from a low of US$376 when using both the MER and WA rates (rows 1a and 6a), to US$505 when using PPPs (row 2a), increasing to US$678 and US$1,392 with the application of the relative and absolute 1970–1989 PARE rates (rows 4a and 3a, respectively). In the same context, total GDP amounts to US$5,167 million when translated by the MER and WA rates (rows 1b and 6b), to US$6,943 million (row 2b) using PPPs and, with relative and absolute 1970–1979 PARE applications, rises to US$9,327 million and US$19,130 million respectively (rows 4b and 3b). The derived GDP amounts result in distributive shares of gross world product of 0.16 per cent for MER and WA rates (rows 1c and 6c) and 0.27 per cent for both PARE calculations (rows 4c and 3c). PPP shares of gross world product are not shown because PPP rates are not completely available for all the constituent countries of the world (see section B below). While the GDP dollar amounts based on MER and WA rates are identical, the PPP and PARE conversions bring about increased GDP levels. On the other hand, in 1986 (column 17), the results generated by dollar conversions using the corresponding rates mentioned above disclose a reversed trend, showing higher GDP levels when based on MER and WA rates than when using PPPs and PAREs and bigger shares of gross world product in comparison with PARE applications.

Turning to another example, for India in 1989 (column 20), total GDP ranges between US$200,000 million and US$350,000 million based on the application of all conversion rates except PPPs (rows 1,3,4,5 and 6, subscript b). When PPPs are used the total GDP increases to more than US$1,000,000 (row 2b). On this basis, India's share of gross world product in 1989 starts at around 1.35 per cent using MER and WA rates and increases to 1.77 per cent with both types of 1970–1989 PARE calculations. In contrast, during the early 1970s, the GDP shares in the world total are higher according to MER and WA rates—roughly 1.8 per cent—than are the GDP shares produced by PARE rates, which amount only to about 1.5 per cent of the world total.

As cited in the examples above, the divergences apparent in the derived data when comparing GDP levels and distribution based on different conversion rates merely highlight the unique qualities of each type of conversion rate without explaining the reasons for these divergences. For a more thorough discussion and analysis of inherent characteristics, features and effects generated by each conversion rate which are not easily discernible from the above examples, the reader is referred to the description in section B and to the discussion of the gross world product distribution measures in chapter II.

The GDP data used in annex table A.1 are obtained through a national accounts questionnaire that is sent by the Statistical Division of the United Nations Secretariat to statistical organizations in each country. The data are submitted in accordance with GDP definitions contained in the 1968 System of National Accounts (SNA). In the cases of countries in transition, for which GDP data are not available for most years, estimates of net material product (NMP) based on the System of Material Product Balances (MPS) were adjusted to GDP by adding the value added of non-material services and the consumption of fixed capital and then deducting material services used as inputs in the production of non-material services. Recent studies have shown that these estimates of GDP for countries in transition have deficiencies and may need to be revised in the future.

The resulting data series are not complete for all countries and years and likewise include multiple series for countries that have changed statistical definitions and compilation methodology during the period covered by the time series, resulting in modifications of GDP. Therefore adjustments were made to the basic data. First, estimates were prepared by the Statistical Division of the United Nations Secretariat in order to fill data gaps. Subsequently, multiple series were merged into one homogeneous time series by extrapolating backwards from the latest time series with the use of growth rates of earlier series.

In preparing estimates to supplement the official data, the order or priority of data sources used is as follows: national publications, regional economic surveys, studies and estimates prepared by the United Nations regional commissions; various international publications, such as those issued by the IMF, the World Bank and other international institutions. For countries which are members of specialized intergovernmental organizations, such as the Organization of Petroleum Exporting Countries (OPEC) and the former Council for Mutual Economic Assistance (CMEA), the publications issued by these organizations are given priority over those of other non-United Nations international sources.

## B. Conversion of local currency data to United States dollars

The conversion rates used in annex table A.1 to translate local currency units of GDP and per capita GDP into United States dollars are presented in annex table A.2. The table lists, for each country and for each year of available information, the different conversion rates in the following sequence: (1) MERs; (2) PPPs; (3) absolute 1970–1989 PAREs; (4) relative 1970–1989 PAREs; (5) absolute 1980–1989 PAREs; (6) WA rates.

It should be noted that conversion rates shown for countries and years include two types—those that were available from the original source (as described below) and rates which were estimated by the Statistical Division of the United Nations Secretariat in order to complete the entire period (1970–1989) for which analysis was carried out. For example, WA conversion rates include not only those countries whose data were directly obtained from the World Bank, but also the rates estimated by the Statistical Division of the United Nations Secretariat for 40 or so countries on the basis of the *World Bank Atlas* methodology. Likewise, PPP rates cover those countries and years included in the Penn World Tables (PWT) and also those rates estimated by the Statistical Division for later years for the same countries in order to complete the time series. Countries for which the WA rates were estimated by the Statistical Division are footnoted in annex table A.2; PPPs that were estimated cover the years 1986–1989 and have also been denoted. No PPP estimates were made for countries not included in the PWT. For the MER and the derived PARE conversions, however, the period and country coverage is complete for each year and all three base periods.

The conversion rates presented in annex table A.2 are expressed in terms of units of local currencies per United States dollar. Thus for Bahrain in 1981, for example, it shows that US$1 is equivalent to 0.376 dinars based on the MER and WA rates (rows 1 and 6), 0.433 dinars per PPPs (row 2), 0.551 and 0.508 dinars based on absolute and relative 1970–1989 PARE rates respectively (rows 3 and 4), and 0.395 dinars when absolute 1980–1989 PAREs (row 5) are used. It should be noted however, that when absolute and relative PAREs are applied, the United States dollar (the measurement unit) corresponds to a base period and not to the current year.

Continuing the example of Bahrain, in the following year, one sees in row 3 that, after eliminating the absolute price changes of the period, US$1 of 1982 was equal to 0.627 dinar when converted by absolute 1970–1989 PARE. This rate represents the highest value of the United States dollar relative to the dinar among all the other conversion rates for any year within the whole period. When the relative 1970–1989 PARE is used (i.e., the relative price changes of the period are excluded in addition to absolute price changes) the dinar in 1982 is equivalent to 0.543 per US$1. The difference between these two PAREs corresponds to the effects of inflation in the United States for the period in question.

Meanwhile in the case of Zaire, the local currency, called the zaire, likewise exhibits a continuing depreciating value in its MER and WA rates relative to the United States dollar. Starting from the equivalent of 0.50 zaire per US$1 during the years 1970–1975 (rows 1 and 6, columns 1–6), it culminates in a rate of more than 380 zaires per US$1 in 1989 (column 20). Both absolute PARE rates show that in 1970 the currency was valued at approximately 0.25 zaire per US$1 but that in 1989 its value depreciated to more than 300 zaires to US$1. Implicit in these PARE calculations is the magnitude of inflation, which greatly reduced the value of this currency. The average rates listed in the last two columns of the table also mirror this decline as they show the higher value of the zaire during the first part of the period 1970–1989 in comparison with later years, when its value begins to diminish.

## 1.   Market exchange rates (MERs)

The most frequently used conversion rates are the average market exchange rates that are regularly published by the IMF in *International Financial Statistics*. These are annual averages based on the exchange rates communicated to the IMF by the monetary authority of each member country and agreed to by the Fund. As used by the IMF, the term "market rate"[1] refers to the principal exchange rate used for the majority of transactions. Market exchange rates are the rates that are either (a) determined by the market, as for countries with convertible currencies; (b) pegged or fixed in relation to another currency, as in the cases of the majority of the francophone nations in Africa, which peg their currencies to the French franc, and the British Commonwealth nations, whose currencies are pegged to the pound sterling; or (c) fixed by government decree or directed by some form of government control largely depending on movements of market forces in parallel markets. This latter category applies to a number of national currencies in Latin American countries and to some Middle Eastern ones as well.

For countries that were not members of the IMF during some or all of the years under study—the majority of which are the so-called economies in transition—the conversion rates used are the averages of United Nations operational rates of exchange, which were primarily established for accounting purposes and which are applied to all official transactions of the United Nations with those countries, including payments of local salaries and wages, standard subsistence allowances, pension payments, etc. These rates may take the form of the official, commercial or tourist rates of exchange in those countries.

The essential condition for comparing GDP data expressed in different currencies is the availability of conversion rates that are neutral in the sense that they do not distort the results of the comparison. For the specific purpose of the present study the conversion rates should adequately reflect the relative price changes over time. Exchange rates are adequate conversion rates, reflecting relative price levels between trading countries, only if they keep a close correlation with changes in the relative prices in these countries over time. This situation, however, rarely happens. One reason is that exchange rates—even if determined directly by the market, as for countries with convertible currencies—are based on the relative prices of only those goods and services that are traded internationally and exclude a number of other products and activities. On the other hand, the exchange rates are not determined only by international trade but are also influenced by other international transactions, such as foreign investments and loans, incomes and remittances, and current and capital transfers. Interest rates, expectations of the financial markets and several other factors determine the actual changes in market exchange rates. These additional transactions may result in exchange rate levels that do not necessarily reflect price relatives of goods and services and may continue to do so for long periods of time, or for as long as resulting trade deficits could be financed by

other current or capital inflows which make up for the reduction in
the foreign currency reserves.

Exchange rates may furthermore not adequately reflect price
relatives when one or more of the countries compared heavily subsidize their export products or levy duties on selected imports. Moreover, administrative regulations may likewise serve to distort the
link between prices and exchange rates in countries which require
that licenses be obtained by institutions other than government-ap-
proved entities in order to export oil or other products or to import
selected merchandise, in an attempt to balance foreign trade or pro-
tect the domestic producers.

It is precisely because exchange rates do not adequately reflect
differences in price levels of internationally traded goods and services and, moreover, might be even less effective as a means of
comparing price levels of goods and services that are not traded internationally, that alternative conversion rates such as PPPs and
PARE rates were and continue to be explored.

## 2.    PARE rates developed by the Statistical Division, United Nations Secretariat

PARE rates are derived by extrapolating the exchange rate of a base
year or period to past and future years by using price indices for
each of the countries concerned. Price adjustments of exchange rates
are not new. The World Bank has for some time been applying adjustments to the exchange rates of all countries included in the
*World Bank Atlas*. Also, the Statistical Division of the United Nations Secretariat has in the past applied exchange rate adjustments
on an ad hoc basis to convert national currency data to United States
dollars for a limited number of countries with severe inflation and
exchange rate movements that did not adequately reflect domestic
price changes. More recently, the Statistical Division has system-
atized the use of this method in the development of PARE rates for
administrative use by United Nations organs. While the PARE
method developed by the Statistical Division and the WA conversion
method are similar in nature, each applies the price adjustments to
exchange rates very differently and thus may result, under certain
conditions, in conversion rates that are quantitatively very divergent.

The PARE rate as developed by the Statistical Division of the
United Nations Secretariat is derived for each year by extrapolating
the exchange rate for a fixed base year or base period by using price
movements based on GDP implicit price deflators. The latter are obtained by dividing the constant values into the current values of GDP
for each year and adjusting the result to index number form by at-
tributing a value equal to 100 to the base year and calculating the index numbers for previous and subsequent years of the series, using
the rates of price change implicit in the deflators. The base-year or
base-period exchange rates play a very important role in the PARE
calculations. Their use is based on the assumption that the base-year
or base-period exchange rates are close to the price relatives of
goods and services between the countries that are compared.

The use of a fixed base-year or base-period application is one of the principal features of PARE. The base-year exchange rate for the fixed base year or period is the one which is assumed to be an adequate measure of price relatives between the United States and other countries at that time. As base years may differ between groups of countries, the present study applies average exchange rates for longer base periods as bases in the calculation of the PARE rates. This assumes that for such base periods, average exchange rates and price relatives coincide.

If the PARE rates as described above were applied in the calculations to the local currency values of GDP, they would eliminate all price changes from the GDP data and express those data in United States dollars using the conversion rate of the base period. The growth rate of GDP for each country expressed in United States dollars thus would be the same as the real growth of GDP in national currency. The level of GDP for individual countries, regions and the world would vary with the base year of PARE.

At this point, it should be mentioned that the Statistical Division of the United Nations Secretariat has developed two versions of PARE for the purposes of the present study. They have been referred to earlier as absolute and relative PAREs. In the case of the absolute PARE, adjustments based on price movements are applied to all countries, including the United States, while derivation of the relative PARE involves adjustments to the exchange rates of all countries except the United States. The advantage of the absolute PARE is that it eliminates inflation in all countries, while the advantage of the relative PARE is that it simulates exchange rates which perfectly respond to the changes in relative price levels. The absolute PARE conversion would thus result in growth of gross world or regional product expressed in United States dollars which would equal the real growth of gross world and regional product, while growth of gross world and regional product based on the relative PARE would still reflect United States inflation. There is no difference between the relative and absolute PAREs when they are used in chapter II to analyse the gross world product distribution; therefore, in those types of analyses they are not distinguished and the only reference made is to PARE without any further qualification.

There are no general criteria to determine which PARE is analytically more appropriate. An evaluation of the different PAREs must take into account the purpose of the analysis. When the focus in GDP studies is on real growth, the absolute PARE is the most appropriate conversion rate. However, if a comparison is being made between the aggregates converted according to PARE and those based on other conversion rates, such as MER, WA or current PPPs, the relative PARE, which reflects United States inflation, is more appropriate as all other conversion rates include United States inflation. There is no difference between relative and absolute PAREs when they are used to analyse the GDP distribution in a particular year; in those types of analyses they provide the same results since the absolute PARE is derived for each country from the relative PARE through simple division by the United States dollar price index (which is equal to the absolute PARE belonging to the United States).

The PARE calculations in this study use as price relatives between the United States and other countries the average exchange rates for two alternative base periods—for the entire period 1970–1989 and the period 1980–1989. The average rates were derived by dividing the aggregate GDP in United States dollars for the respective base periods, using each year's exchange rate, by the aggregate GDP expressed in national currency.

The use of PARE rates eliminates most of the distorting effects mentioned when discussing MER and other conversion rates. In particular, PARE rates are applicable to a larger number of transactions as the GDP implicit price deflators which are used in the calculation of PARE not only reflect internationally tradeable goods and services—as is the case with MER—but also cover all goods and services produced by the economy of each country. Besides, PARE calculations are mostly free of the speculation and other effects of the international capital markets.

However, the problems are not eliminated entirely by the PARE calculation because the base-year or base-period exchange rates play a very important role in the PARE calculations. Their use is based on the assumption that such exchange rates are close to the relative prices of goods and services between the countries that are compared. In practice, it is very difficult to find a base year or period which meets this requirement. In-depth historical examination of the trade balance in the current account of the balance of payments, as contained in the IMF *Balance of Payments Statistics Yearbook*, was abandoned because it failed to produce a single year in which the exchange rates were closer to the equilibrium foreign exchange rates than in any other years. In addition, it became evident that investigation of the trade balance alone could not adequately identify such a base year, particularly because services which should have been an important factor, could not be compared because of the dearth of comparable and consistent information on them. In short, the base year may show any of the distorting factors. This is why base periods longer than one year were identified and why more than one of them was tested.

While eliminating several disturbing effects, some new difficulties emerge in the use of PAREs. For example, Governments may control not only exchange rates but also prices and may subsidize not only exports and imports but also domestic production of goods and services. Furthermore, government control of exchange rates and of prices often go hand in hand. Since prices may also be distorted, these are distortive factors pertaining to international comparison in the case of PAREs and WA rates, as well as PPPs. Another question is whether prices reflect quality, or in other words, whether prices are directly comparable. Additionally, price statistics may be of poor quality in some countries.

## 3. *World Bank Atlas* conversion rates

**Conversion method used by
the World Bank**

I.  Fiscal year conversion factors

| | |
|---|---|
| Australia | 1970–89 |
| Bangladesh | 1970–90 |
| Botswana | 1970–90 |
| Cameroon | 1970–90 |
| Gambia, The | 1970–90 |
| Haiti | 1970–90 |
| India | 1970–90 |
| Iran | 1970–84 |
| Nepal | 1970–89 |
| Nigeria | 1970–79 |
| New Zealand | 1970–90 |
| Pakistan | 1970–90 |
| Sierra Leone | 1970–90 |
| Sudan | 1976–90 |
| Tonga | 1970–90 |

II.  Trade–weighted conversion factors

| | |
|---|---|
| Dominican Republic | 1982–84 |
| Ecuador | 1982–85 |
| Egypt,Arab Republic | 1974–90 |
| El Salvador | 1982–85 |
| | 1989–90 |
| Guatemala | 1985–86 |
| Honduras | 1988–90 |
| Iran | 1985–90 |
| Jamaica | 1981–83 |
| Nicaragua | 1982–87 |
| Paraguay | 1982–86 |
| Peru | 1986–89 |
| Romania | 1973–90 |
| Sudan | 1988–89 |
| Suriname | 1989–90 |
| Syria | 1981–90 |
| Uganda | 1988–90 |
| Zambia | 1990 |

III.  Other conversion factors estimated
by World Bank

| | |
|---|---|
| Argentina | 1970–81 |
| Bolivia | 1974–85 |
| Ghana | 1973–87 |
| Guinea–Bissau | 1970–86 |
| Somalia | 1977–90 |

Source: *World Tables*, 1991 edition, World Bank

The *World Bank Atlas* (WA) conversion method does not use a fixed base period but is based on a moving average of three types of conversion rates, each linked to a specific base year. For a specific year, it is calculated as a simple average of the exchange rate of the present year, a PARE rate for the present year using the previous year as base year, and a PARE rate for the present year using the exchange rate of two years ago as a base. The method assumes that exchange rates adjust themselves to price changes within a period of three years.

The World Bank applies different variants to its type of conversion method for some countries in which, for a number of specific reasons, the basic methodology does not adjust adequately. Three types of variants are used: (a) fiscal year conversion factors, by which conversion rates are adjusted in accordance with fiscal year compilations of accounts; (b) conversion factors for Member States with multiple market exchange rates, which are calculated averages of individual rates, using external trade transactions as weights; and (c) conversion factors estimated by the Bank for countries that are either beset by considerable inflation or whose exchange rate has been fixed for many years while ignoring movements of market forces and thereby resulting in highly improbable and unrealistic dollar conversions; their exchange rates are "corrected" in order to reflect comparable levels of GDP. On the basis of the most recent calculations of the WA rates, 15 members of the World Bank are adjusted according to variant (a), 17 are affected by variant (b) and five countries by variant (c), as shown at left.

Since the WA rate is an average of the actual exchange rate and two PARE rates, it is generally much closer to the MER conversion than the PARE rate developed by Statistical Division of the United Nations Secretariat. As a consequence of incorporating the exchange rate as one of the components in the calculation of the WA conversion rate, the latter does not entirely eliminate domestic inflation in each country, as does the PARE rate developed by Statistical Division of the United Nations Secretariat. This implies that when the WA conversion rate is applied to GDP data in national currency, the growth rate of GDP in United States dollars for each country does not coincide with the growth rate of its real GDP. As in the application of the relative PARE, the WA conversion is not applied to the United States. Therefore, when the WA rates are used in the aggregation of countries' GDP to arrive at gross world and regional product, the growth rate of the latter reflects not only real growth but also inflation in the United States and some inflation in other countries.

The WA conversion rates were obtained from the World Bank for 137 countries covering the years 1970–1989. Comparable rates for the missing 41 countries were arrived at by using the basic methodology used in the *World Bank Atlas* calculations—that is, by averaging the current year exchange rate and PARE rates for the two immediately preceding years. However, special corrections based on

the variant *World Bank Atlas* methodology were not applied to any
of these estimated rates.

## 4.   Purchasing power parities (PPPs)

PPPs are derived from the price relatives of common baskets of
goods and services expressed in the currencies of each of the partici-
pating countries. The PPPs applied to GDP for each country are obtained as weighted averages of the price relatives of individual baskets of goods and services, using as weights the total expenditures
on those goods and services included in GDP. Unlike the PARE rates
as used by the World Bank and the Statistical Division of the United
Nations Secretariat, PPPs are not derived from actual exchange rates;
they are obtained as independent measures based on information obtained through price surveys.

The PPP conversion rates used in this study are based on the
Penn World Tables (PWT) data bank, which was developed by Summers and Heston of the University of Pennsylvania.[2] They are the result of merging, and further extending to other years and countries,
direct benchmark estimates for a limited number of countries for the
benchmark years 1970, 1975 and 1980 obtained during phases II, III
and IV of the International Comparison Project (ICP) of the United
Nations. While the PWT data bank developed PPPs for 130 countries
covering the period up to 1985, the number of direct estimates was
actually relatively small in terms of countries and years. Phase III
included direct benchmark estimates for 1975 for 34 countries, while
in phase IV, the number of benchmark estimates for base year 1980
covered 60 countries, with 27 common countries in both phases. In
extending benchmark studies to non-reporting countries, one method
used was to apply information from less comprehensive price and
expenditure surveys carried out by the World Bank for 14 non-ICP
countries for the years 1980 and 1982. One other way in which the
direct benchmark estimates were expanded to other countries was by
applying the ratios between PPP conversions and exchange rates for
GDP and components of GDP for countries with direct PPP measure-
ments to non-participants. Inter-temporal annual updates of the PPPs
for the benchmark years 1975, 1980 and 1985 were prepared for all
countries on the basis of price indices for GDP components of individual countries relative to the corresponding price indices of the
United States. Finally, the three benchmark estimates as expanded in
time and space were then made mutually consistent by reconciling
for one selected year (1987) the three annual inter-temporal expan-
sions for all countries, with each based on one of the three benchmark estimates.

Since no information later than the 1985 PPPs was available to
Statistical Division of the United Nations Secretariat when the present study was prepared, PPP rates for the missing years 1986–1989
were derived by applying the trend of relative 1980–1989 PARE
rates to the level of PPPs in 1985. No estimates were made for countries without any PPPs and as a result gross regional and world product totals were not calculated on the basis of PPPs. In the meantime,

new Penn World Tables have been published. The new estimates are based on the cost-of-living indexes derived from various surveys on international living costs.[3] The new PWT data were not taken into account in the present study as the latest PPP rates resulting from the present International Price Comparison will be published shortly and it is expected that the PWT tables will be adjusted accordingly.

It is apparent that PPPs are dependent on base year information in the same manner as PAREs. However, the PPP rates for a base year are price relatives that have been measured on the basis of actual prices in pairs of countries and are therefore independent of exchange rates. On the other hand, changes in the PPPs over time may be closely related to changes in PARE rates, as both PARE and PPP rates are extrapolated over time with the help of price indices in the countries concerned. As the PPP price relatives applied in the present study are calculated in relation to United States prices, United States inflation is reflected in the GDP data when PPPs are used as conversion rates.

Notes

1.    The preference is the period average rate determined in the market of each country.  If these rates are not available, the list of priorities of other types of rates is as follows: the period average rates in New York, estimated rates derived on the basis of a simple average of the end-of-period market rates in the markets of the country and, finally, official rates.  Thus, only in cases where market rates are missing do the published IMF rates refer to official rates.

2.    Summers and Heston, loc. cit.

3.    *Quarterly Journal of Economics* May 1991.

# II. Measures of gross world product distribution

Using the GDP data and conversion rates presented in chapter I, chapter II measures the effects of alternative conversion rates on the distribution of gross world product between countries and regions and changes therein over time, using measures and graphs which are similar to those traditionally used in the measurement of income distribution within a country. These include Lorenz curves, Gini coefficients, percentage of gross world product received by quarters and eighths of the population, ranking of the countries or areas and standard deviation measures. Section A deals with the gross world product distribution between individual countries and section B focuses on the distribution of the gross regional product and, in particular, on the link between the per capita GDP of each country and the per capita gross regional product of the corresponding region. Both sections start with the measurement of total and per capita gross world and regional product, respectively, as these are the frames of reference for the distribution of gross world product between countries.

## A. Measures of the level and distribution of gross world product and per capita gross world product

Table 1 summarizes, for the world as a whole, the country data presented in annex table A.1. The country data have been aggregated for each year to arrive at a gross world product level expressed in United States dollars, using the six alternative conversion rates, and are shown respectively along rows 1–6 under subscript b. The gross world product dollar totals were then divided by corresponding population estimates for the world, covering the same constituent 178 countries or areas, in order to derive per capita gross world product, this time listed along each of the rows with subscript a. World totals for the individual years 1970 to 1989 presented in columns 1 through 20 and world averages for the periods 1970–1989, 1970–1979 and 1980–1989 are shown in columns 21–23, respectively. A similar format is used in annex tables A.1 and A.2.

The table includes six alternative estimates of total and per capita gross world product based on the corresponding conversion rates presented in annex table A.2. However, since data based on PPPs are not available for all countries, total and per capita gross world product could not be calculated on the basis of PPPs; in this case, the totals for PPPs shown in the table only refer to the 117 countries or areas with available data. The table demonstrates that the type of conversion rate influences the level of gross world product. For example, for the entire 1970–1989 period, the average of

**Table 1**
Gross world product and per capita gross world product, based on alternative conversion rates, 1970–89

|  |  | 1970<br>(1) | 1971<br>(2) | 1972<br>(3) | 1973<br>(4) | 1974<br>(5) | 1975<br>(6) | 1976<br>(7) | 1977<br>(8) | 1978<br>(9) | 1979<br>(10) |
|---|---|---|---|---|---|---|---|---|---|---|---|
| 1. | **Market exchange rate** | | | | | | | | | | |
| 1a. | Per capita gross world product | 867 | 931 | 1 049 | 1 255 | 1 393 | 1 530 | 1 623 | 1 798 | 2 099 | 2 367 |
| 1b. | Gross world product | 3 190 | 3 499 | 4 022 | 49 077 | 5 554 | 6 211 | 6 709 | 7 564 | 8 985 | 10 305 |
| 2. | **PPPs (117 countries)** | | | | | | | | | | |
| 2a. | Per capita gross world product | 1 403 | 1 501 | 1 630 | 1 819 | 2 014 | 2 187 | 2 383 | 2 595 | 2 844 | 3 160 |
| 2b. | Gross world product | 3 315 | 3 620 | 4 013 | 45 704 | 5 165 | 5 722 | 6 361 | 7 064 | 7 895 | 8 945 |
| 3. | **Absolute 1970–1989 PARE** | | | | | | | | | | |
| 3a. | Per capita gross world product | 1 930 | 1 970 | 2 034 | 2 121 | 2 126 | 2 118 | 2 189 | 2 243 | 2 297 | 2 336 |
| 3b. | Gross world product | 7 105 | 7 403 | 7 801 | 82 969 | 8 476 | 8 601 | 9 049 | 9 437 | 9 833 | 10 167 |
| 4. | **Relative 1970–1989 PARE** | | | | | | | | | | |
| 4a. | Per capita gross world product | 941 | 1 010 | 1 091 | 1 213 | 1 326 | 1 451 | 1 593 | 1 743 | 1 915 | 2 121 |
| 4b. | Gross world product | 3 464 | 3 795 | 4 182 | 47 434 | 5 286 | 5 893 | 6 587 | 7 333 | 8 198 | 9 233 |
| 5. | **Absolute 1980–1989 PARE** | | | | | | | | | | |
| 5a. | Per capita gross world product | 2 364 | 2 412 | 2 493 | 2 598 | 2 602 | 2 587 | 2 675 | 2 740 | 2 803 | 2 848 |
| 5b. | Gross world product | 8 702 | 9 066 | 9 558 | 101 620 | 10 373 | 10 506 | 11 060 | 11 529 | 11 997 | 12 399 |
| 6. | *World Bank Atlas* | | | | | | | | | | |
| 6a. | Per capita gross world product | 867 | 928 | 1 045 | 1 243 | 1 399 | 1 517 | 1 623 | 1 792 | 2 075 | 2 350 |
| 6b. | Gross world product | 3 192 | 3 488 | 4 005 | 48 635 | 5 579 | 6 162 | 6 710 | 7 540 | 8 881 | 10 229 |

Note:   Gross world product is expressed in billions (thousand millions) of United States dollars.

gross world product varies between US$10.1 and US$12.4 billion, and per capita gross world product between approximately US$2,300 and US$2,800, depending on which conversion rate is applied.

## 1.   Level of gross world product

The movement over time of gross world product by different conversion rates is presented in figure 1. The figure shows that although the WA rate is an adjusted market exchange rate, time series based on MER and WA rates are almost identical. Both indicate a very large—more than six-fold—increase in gross world product. The growth rates based on these two conversion rates varied considerably over time. They were sometimes close to zero and once, in 1982, were even negative.

The curve based on the relative 1970–1989 PARE shows a steady growth of gross world product over time. Due to the choice of the base period, the beginning and end points of the curve are identical with those corresponding to gross world product levels based on MER conversion. Since the PARE curve eliminates real appreciations and depreciations of the currencies of all countries relative to the United States dollar, the differences in the trends based on the relative PARE and MER reflect changes in exchange rates between the currencies of different countries. Sudden changes in the growth of gross world product based on MER conversion are caused

| 1980 (11) | 1981 (12) | 1982 (13) | 1983 (14) | 1984 (15) | 1985 (16) | 1986 (17) | 1987 (18) | 1988 (19) | 1989 (20) | 1970-89 average (21) | 1970-79 average (22) | 1980-89 average (23) | |
|---|---|---|---|---|---|---|---|---|---|---|---|---|---|
| | | | | | | | | | | | | | 1. |
| 2 617 | 2 597 | 2 533 | 2 539 | 2 568 | 2 608 | 3 030 | 3 437 | 3 756 | 3 872 | 2 320 | 1 515 | 2 981 | 1a. |
| 11 589 | 11 708 | 11 626 | 11 855 | 12 197 | 12 595 | 14 890 | 17 186 | 19 106 | 20 052 | 10 188 | 6 095 | 14 280 | 1b. |
| | | | | | | | | | | | | | 2. |
| 3 507 | 3 816 | 3 953 | 4 075 | 4 331 | 4 458 | 4 609 | 4 848 | 5 174 | 5 522 | 3 464 | 2 188 | 4 468 | 2a. |
| 10 128 | 11 245 | 11 890 | 12 510 | 13 570 | 14 254 | 15 033 | 16 128 | 17 554 | 19 106 | 9 904 | 5 667 | 14 142 | 2b. |
| | | | | | | | | | | | | | 3. |
| 2 346 | 2 349 | 2 323 | 2 349 | 2 414 | 2 457 | 2 485 | 2 527 | 2 593 | 2 627 | 2 320 | 2 141 | 2 455 | 3a. |
| 10 388 | 10 588 | 10 662 | 10 969 | 11 466 | 11 866 | 12 213 | 12 635 | 13 191 | 13 604 | 10 188 | 8 617 | 11 758 | 3b. |
| | | | | | | | | | | | | | 4. |
| 2 325 | 2 548 | 2 683 | 2 805 | 2 986 | 3 121 | 3 221 | 3 369 | 3 573 | 3 769 | 2 341 | 1 459 | 3 065 | 4a. |
| 10 297 | 11 488 | 12 316 | 13 099 | 14 183 | 15 075 | 15 828 | 16 846 | 18 178 | 19 515 | 10 277 | 5 871 | 14 683 | 4b. |
| | | | | | | | | | | | | | 5. |
| 2 856 | 2 858 | 2 825 | 2 855 | 2 933 | 2 983 | 3 015 | 3 065 | 3 144 | 3 185 | 2 826 | 2 618 | 2 981 | 5a. |
| 12 649 | 12 884 | 12 967 | 13 335 | 13 932 | 14 410 | 14 819 | 15 326 | 15 991 | 16 491 | 12 408 | 10 535 | 14 280 | 5b. |
| | | | | | | | | | | | | | 6. |
| 2 601 | 2 616 | 2 539 | 2 538 | 2 574 | 2 618 | 2 993 | 3 332 | 3 680 | 3 790 | 2 301 | 1 507 | 2 952 | 6a. |
| 11 518 | 11 793 | 11 655 | 11 854 | 12 226 | 12 644 | 14 707 | 16 662 | 18 718 | 19 625 | 10 102 | 6 065 | 14 140 | 6b. |

by overall changes in the value of the United States dollar relative to all other currencies.

For instance, the curve based on MER conversion (figure 1) suggests that United States currency gradually depreciated in real terms between 1977 and 1980, and between 1980 and 1985 the dollar continuously appreciated. Since the main causes of the depreciation and appreciation were relatively high interest rates and positive expectations, and not differences in inflation rates, the United States dollar was relatively undervalued before and overvalued after 1981.

Consequently, gross world product based on MER conversion was relatively lower in the later period than in the earlier years. This reversed after 1985, due to such factors as large trade deficits and changes in expectations, and the United States dollar was continuously depreciated. As a consequence, gross world product expressed in United States dollars was relatively higher than before. In 1986 gross world product based on MER and relative PARE conversions were equal, which implies that the PARE rate and exchange rate in that year were the same.

The growth rates of gross world product based on PPPs and relative 1970–1989 PARE are very similar. One reason is that conversion methods attempt to link the prices of different countries directly, without using the links of actual MER rates. The other reason is that the method used to update PPPs between benchmark years is similar to the method used to derive relative PAREs. The reader should keep in mind that the PPP data only cover 117 countries or areas, while gross world product data based on PARE and MER conversions cover all 178 countries or areas.

One of the reasons for the large difference between gross world product growth based on absolute PAREs and other conversion rates is that the trends based on the latter reflect inflation in the United States, while the trend based on the absolute PAREs excludes United States inflation. Growth of gross world product based on absolute PARE conversion, which could be considered as growth at constant prices, using 1980–1989 and 1970–1989 base periods, was almost twice as high in 1989 as it was in 1970. The growth was steady during the whole period. While the trends of gross world product based on the two different absolute PARE conversions both reflect real growth, they are slightly different because of a different structure of average MERs between countries for the 1970–1979 and 1980–1989 base periods.

Alternative absolute PARE conversions resulted in a lower level of gross world product based on the absolute 1970–1989 PARE than when gross world product was calculated on the basis of the absolute 1980–1989 PARE. The reason is that both level and structure of base-period average exchange rates, which are the starting points of the PARE calculation, differ between the two base periods.

## 2.   Per capita gross world product

Table 1 and figure 2 show that the changes in per capita gross world product were more moderate than the growth of total gross world product, because the world population grew by almost 50 per cent during the period of 1970–1989. However, as the growth rate of the world population was quite steady every year, a comparison between figures 1 and 2 shows that the trends of per capita and total gross world product are similar to each other. However, the slopes of the curves in figures 1 and 2 are not the same and this is explained by the growth rate of the population.

Per capita real gross world product based on the absolute PARE conversion grew steadily by 35 to 40 per cent within 20 years. In line with what was found in the previous analysis of total gross world product, time series of per capita gross world product based on MER and WA conversions show the highest increase—more than four-fold—during the period of study. The growth rates, however, varied considerably and sometimes were even negative. Time series based on the relative PARE show a four-fold increase during the period, which is similar to the high increase based on MER and WA.

Per capita gross world product data based on PPPs are much higher than those based on any other conversion rate. However, there is not only a difference in the level but also in the trend; the curve based on PPPs has a steeper slope than any of the other curves in figure 2. All of this suggests that on the basis of PPPs, the United States dollar has been gradually appreciated—or other currencies depreciated—in real terms during the period. It was overvalued even in 1970 on the basis of the figures presented, which conflicts with results of the PARE calculation. One may assume either that the PARE base-period exchange rate does not well reflect price relatives or that PPPs underestimate the value of the United States dollar.

**Figure 1**
Gross world product, 1970–1989

Trillion US$

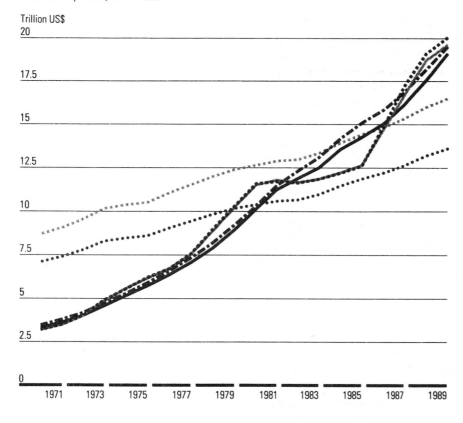

Source: Statistical Division, United Nations Secretariat.

........ Market exchange rate
———— *World Bank Atlas* rate
———— PPPs (117 countries)
—·—·— Relative 1970–1989 PARE
........ Absolute 1970–1989 PARE
........ Absolute 1980–1989 PARE

**Figure 2**
Per capita gross world product, 1970–1989

Thousand US$

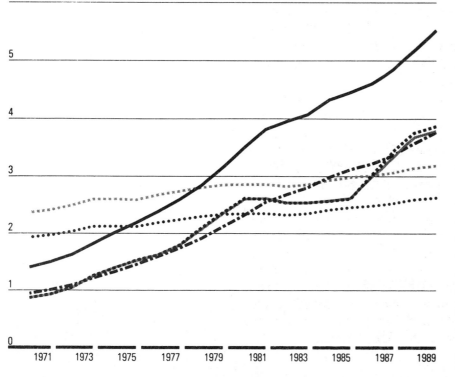

Source: Statistical Division, United Nations Secretariat.

........ Market exchange rate
———— *World Bank Atlas* rate
———— PPPs (117 countries)
—·—·— Relative 1970–1989 PARE
........ Absolute 1970–1989 PARE
........ Absolute 1980–1989 PARE

## 3.  Income distribution measures applied to distribution of gross world product

Various measures similar to those traditionally used in the measurement of income distribution within a country, such as Lorenz curves, Gini indices and quartile distribution of gross world product, are used below to measure the distribution of gross world product between countries. Analysis in the following paragraphs focuses in particular on GDP data converted on the basis of MER and 1970–1989 PARE rates, as these are the conversion rates that generate the most dramatic differences. As PPPs were available only for a limited number of countries, the analysis based on this conversion rate was less conclusive. The WA method generates results that are close to those based on MER and the results of the 1980–1989 PARE conversion are close to those based on the 1970–1989 PARE. As there is no difference between the results of the absolute and relative PAREs in gross world product distribution analysis, this distinction will not be made here.

### Ranking of countries

The structure of the distribution of gross world product is reflected in the ranks of countries on the basis of their per capita GDP, as presented for the years 1970, 1980 and 1989 in annex tables A.3, A.4 and A.5.

The tables include separate columns for the country ranks corresponding to each conversion rate. The double lines in each column of the table identify approximately population quarters. Since the poorer half of the world (the upper half of the table) includes some countries with large populations, such as China and India, some countries (the shaded ones in the table) were divided into two parts in order to make each group equal to 25 per cent of the world population. The poorer half of the world consists of only 34 to 66 countries. As the richer half of the world consists of a much larger number of countries, single lines at 62.5 per cent and the 87.5 per cent of the world population introduce a further split in the lower (richer) half of the table, each containing one eighth of the world population. Significant changes in the ranks of four of the very large countries— China, India, the USSR and the United States—are affected by relative changes in their population and gross world product shares.

Country data based on MER conversion as presented in annex table A.1 demonstrate that 15 per cent of the world population lived in India in 1970 and the Indian GDP was 1.8 per cent of the gross world product at that time. Twenty years later the country's share of world population was higher, 16 per cent, while its share of gross world product had declined to only 1.4 per cent. China's share of world population decreased from 22 per cent to 21 per cent and its share of gross world product decreased even more, from 2.8 per cent to 2.1 per cent during the two decades.

The per capita GDP of both India and China increased—the Indian per capita GDP increased from US$104 to US$326 and the Chinese per capita GDP increased from US$112 to US$377. Even though China and India have a higher rank number in 1989 than in 1970, their relative situations in the world (on the basis of GDPs calculated by MER conversion) worsened between the two years because their per capita GDP grew less than the world per capita GDP did.

The USSR is another large country whose relative situation worsened. Ranked 145th in 1970, it fell to 130th 20 years later. (In each case, 178 is the highest rank.)

The relative situation of the richest group of countries did not change much but their rank structure changed. While the United States had the highest GDP in 1970, there were six countries ahead of the United States 20 years later. The relative situation of the United States worsened while the relative position of Japan improved.

## Lorenz curves

The *Lorenz curve* used in this study plots the cumulative percentage of aggregate GDP received (ranked from the lowest to the highest per capita income) against the cumulative percentage of the population. The cumulative percentage of the population is presented on the horizontal axis while the cumulative percentage of GDP is shown on the vertical axis. The cumulative percentages of the population and GDP do not refer in the present study to individuals but correspond to countries, as population and GDP data are only available by countries.

With complete equality, the Lorenz curve lies on the 45–degree line from the origin to the point defined by 100 per cent of the total gross world product and 100 per cent of the world population. With complete inequality, the Lorenz curve runs along the horizontal axis and then jumps up to the point defined by 100 per cent of the total gross world product and 100 per cent of the world population. The closer the Lorenz curve lies to the 45–degree equality line, the more equally is GDP distributed between countries. A greater curve in the Lorenz curve reflects a more unequal distribution of GDP between countries.

Inequalities in the distribution of gross world product based on alternative conversion factors are reflected in the Lorenz curves presented in figures 3–7. Each graph corresponds to one conversion rate and includes pairs of Lorenz curves related to the beginning (1970) and end (1989) of the period under study. Since Lorenz curves are constructed by first ranking the countries on the basis of their per capita GDP, the location of individual countries—particularly the large ones mentioned above—can be identified in the Lorenz curves with the help of annex tables A.3, A.4 and A.5. It is important to keep in mind that the study does not deal with income distribution within countries, as no comparable data are available for most countries.

Lorenz curves have been elaborated for each year and each conversion rate, but are not included in this volume. A detailed study of these curves shows that curves for in-between years based on data converted on the basis MER, WA rates and PPPs for each year were located between the curves belonging to the first and last years of the two-decade period. Annual curves based on PAREs are almost identical to each other.

The shapes of all the curves, except those based on PPPs, demonstrate similar patterns of gross world product distribution for 1970 and 1989. Lorenz curves based on PPPs show a more equal distribution of gross world product for both years than the others. Three of the figures show that the inequality among countries increased, while the remaining two show that the inequality of the gross world product distribution was similar in 1970 and 1989.

According to the Lorenz curves based on PPPs, MER and WA rates, the general level of inequality in the distribution of gross world product increased between 1970 and 1989. The shapes of the curves based on MER and WA conversions are very similar to each other. Although the figure based on PPPs also shows an increase in inequality in the distribution of gross world product, the nature of this change is different.

Lorenz curves corresponding to data converted on the basis of 1980–1989 and 1970–1989 PARE rates do not indicate essential changes in the level of inequality in the distribution of gross world product between countries. However, the slight change in the shape of the curves between 1970 and 1989 means that the structure of inequality changed.

The basic GDP data in national currencies are the same for each calculation. The differences in the shapes of Lorenz curves are therefore the consequences of using different conversion rates, each of which has its own features. The fact that the curves based on PAREs do not show any substantial change in the general level of inequality indicates that the differences in the gross world product distribution among countries in real terms did not change much. If this lack of change in the distribution of gross world product in real terms based on PARE conversion is correct, the increase in inequality shown by the curves based on MER and WA rates only reflect what will be called real changes in the exchange rates—that is, appreciation or depreciation of the market exchange rates over and above the relative price changes in the countries concerned.

The lesser inequality implied by the shape of the curves based on PPPs as compared with the curves based on all other conversion rates is partly because PPPs cover only 117 out of 178 countries. Since not one of the missing countries belongs to the richest group and several belong to the poorer half of the world, the inequality of gross world product seems to be smaller. Furthermore, GDP data in

**Figure 3**

Lorenz curve presentations of world population and gross world product shares of countries, based on market exchange rate conversion

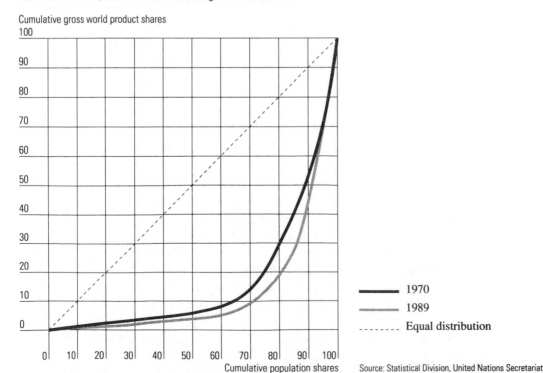

Source: Statistical Division, United Nations Secretariat.

**Figure 4**

Lorenz curve presentations of world population and gross world product
shares of countries, based on *World Bank Atlas* conversion

Cumulative gross world product shares

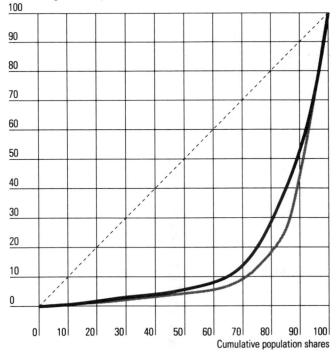

Cumulative population shares

1970
1989
Equal distribution

Source: Statistical Division, United Nations Secretariat.

**Figure 5**

Lorenz curve presentations of world population and gross world product
shares of countries, based on PPP conversion

Cumulative gross world product shares

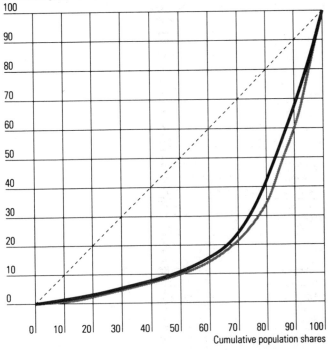

Cumulative population shares

1970
1989
Equal distribution

Source: Statistical Division, United Nations Secretariat.

**Figure 6**

Lorenz curve presentations of world population and gross world product
shares of countries, based on 1970–1989 PARE conversion

Cumulative gross world product shares

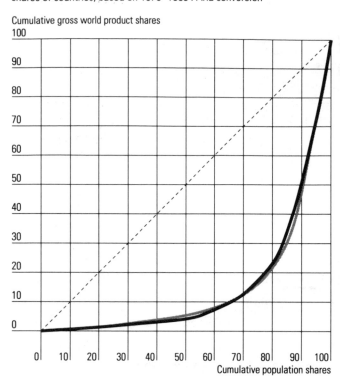

Cumulative population shares          Source: Statistical Division, United Nations Secretariat.

——— 1970
——— 1989
------- Equal distribution

**Figure 7**

Lorenz curve presentations of world population and gross world product
shares of countries, based on 1980–1989 PARE conversion

Cumulative gross world product shares

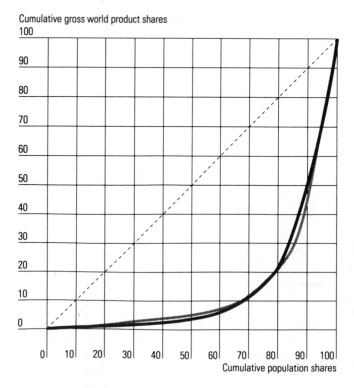

Cumulative population shares          Source: Statistical Division, United Nations Secretariat.

——— 1970
——— 1989
------- Equal distribution

United States dollars of poor countries converted on the basis of PPPs are usually higher and those of richer countries are usually lower than the corresponding GDP data based on MER conversion.

## Gini indices

The *Gini index* is a numerical measure of inequality. It is the ratio of the area between the Lorenz curve and the complete equality line (45–degree line) to the entire area between the complete equality line and the complete inequality line (right–hand x and y–axes). The value of the Gini index will lie between zero (complete equality, with the Lorenz curve on the complete equality line) and 1 (complete inequality, with the Lorenz curve on the complete inequality line). The formula is given in annex C.

In order to obtain a numerical measure of inequality, Gini indices were calculated for data based on each conversion rate in each year. The results are presented in table 2. The average values of Gini indices presented at the bottom of the table represent the general level of inequality for the whole period. Like the results of the analysis based on Lorenz curves, GDP data converted with help of PPPs show the most equal distribution of gross world product, since the average of the Gini index is only 0.564 . Gini indices corresponding to other conversion factors range between 0.69 and 0.71. Differences among the values of the two Gini indices based on the 1970–1989 and 1980–1989 PAREs are a consequence of using different base periods with different exchange rate structures between countries. Even though inequality did not change over time according to any of the PARE calculations, different exchange rate structures between the two halves of the period caused changes in the gross world product distribution.

Table 2 presents a time series of Gini coefficients reflecting changes in the gross world product distribution over time, according to different conversion rates. The higher the index, the higher the inequality in gross world product distribution.

The changes of Gini indices during the period are the largest in the case of both MER and WA rates, somewhat smaller in the case of PPPs and very small in the case of all PAREs. While the data calculated by either the MER or WA rates indicate an essential increase in inequality of the gross world product distribution (Gini indices increased from 0.67 to 0.73 for the data based on MER conversion), data calculated by PAREs show that there were no substantial changes in the level of inequality in the world. Data based on PPPs demonstrate much less inequality in the distribution of gross world product than any of the other alternative conversion rates. The Gini coefficients corresponding to PPPs show a slight increase between 1970 and 1989.

Figure 8 is based on annex table 2. It shows graphically the differences between and changes over time of the Gini coefficients representing the gross world product distribution, corresponding to alternative conversion rates.

Figure 8 shows that there is an almost perfect correlation between the time series based on the MER and WA rates. Even though the data are not identical every year, both their average and standard deviation are equal. Time series based on the 1970–1989 and 1980–1989 PAREs are also strongly correlated. Gini index series based on MER and WA rates are not correlated with the ones based on PAREs, which implies that changes in exchange rates in real terms significantly affected the gross world product distribution. During the periods of oil price changes, i.e. between 1973 and 1975

**Table 2**
Gini indices measuring the inequality of distribution of gross world product, based on alternative conversion rates, 1970–1989

| Year | MER | WA | PPPs | PARE 1970–89 | PARE 1980–89 |
|------|------|------|------|------|------|
| 1970 | 0.669 | 0.669 | 0.554 | 0.697 | 0.708 |
| 1971 | 0.676 | 0.675 | 0.558 | 0.697 | 0.709 |
| 1972 | 0.677 | 0.676 | 0.563 | 0.700 | 0.711 |
| 1973 | 0.675 | 0.676 | 0.566 | 0.700 | 0.712 |
| 1974 | 0.670 | 0.671 | 0.561 | 0.697 | 0.709 |
| 1975 | 0.674 | 0.675 | 0.556 | 0.693 | 0.704 |
| 1976 | 0.681 | 0.682 | 0.560 | 0.696 | 0.707 |
| 1977 | 0.681 | 0.682 | 0.559 | 0.695 | 0.707 |
| 1978 | 0.682 | 0.685 | 0.563 | 0.695 | 0.707 |
| 1979 | 0.684 | 0.685 | 0.567 | 0.696 | 0.708 |
| 1980 | 0.679 | 0.681 | 0.562 | 0.694 | 0.706 |
| 1981 | 0.683 | 0.682 | 0.563 | 0.694 | 0.706 |
| 1982 | 0.685 | 0.686 | 0.563 | 0.690 | 0.702 |
| 1983 | 0.691 | 0.692 | 0.564 | 0.690 | 0.703 |
| 1984 | 0.699 | 0.700 | 0.566 | 0.693 | 0.705 |
| 1985 | 0.706 | 0.706 | 0.568 | 0.692 | 0.704 |
| 1986 | 0.720 | 0.722 | 0.570 | 0.692 | 0.705 |
| 1987 | 0.726 | 0.731 | 0.573 | 0.693 | 0.705 |
| 1988 | 0.729 | 0.734 | 0.575 | 0.693 | 0.706 |
| 1989 | 0.729 | 0.733 | 0.577 | 0.695 | 0.708 |
| Average | 0.691 | 0.692 | 0.564 | 0.695 | 0.707 |

**Figure 8**
Gini indices measuring inequality of gross world product distribution, based on alternative conversion rates, 1970–1989

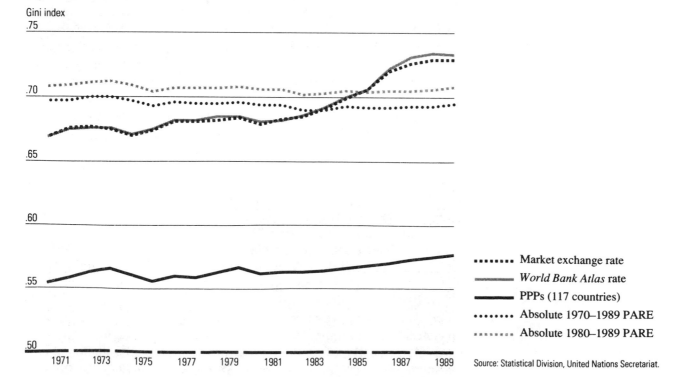

Gini index

Source: Statistical Division, United Nations Secretariat.

and in 1980, inequalities in gross world product distribution decreased according to all of the conversion rates. After 1980 the different curves represented different trends. Gini index series based on PPPs are not compared because they cover fewer countries.

A weakness of the Gini index as a measure of the level of inequality is that it does not reflect changes in the structure of inequality. Since the Gini index is the ratio of two areas, it can not measure changes in the shape of the Lorenz curve. Different Lorenz curves can be drawn which have the same area but correspond to different patterns of gross world product distribution and levels of inequality. Figures showed that, particularly in the case of PARE, the shape of the Lorenz curve changed without any essential change in the area covered by the curve.

## Correlation of country ranks over time and using different conversion rates

*Spearman's coefficient of rank correlation* measures the level of correlation between two rank orders. The result is a number between –1 and 1. A coefficient of 1 means perfect positive correlation, –1 perfect negative correlation, and 0 no correlation. The formulas are given in annex C.

Returning to annex tables A.3, A.4 and A.5, which rank countries by per capita GDP, and to the analysis which was started above in section 1, it can be observed that country ranks differ over time and vary by conversion rates. The following two subsections analyse first the changes between selected years and then compare the country ranks when different conversion rates are applied. Both analyses are based on the use of the Spearman rank coefficient.

### Correlation of country ranks over time

Table 3 contains correlation coefficients for alternative conversion rates between country ranks corresponding to the first and last year of the period indicated in each row. The table shows that the rank of the countries was stable during the last two decades. Comparing the first and last years, the typical coefficient is 0.90–0.94. This means that the country ranks based on the same conversion rates did not change significantly during the period. The highest rank correlation coefficient corresponds to PPPs, which may imply that country ranks based on PPPs changed less than country ranks based on any other conversion rate. In the case of PAREs the rank of the countries changed, even though Lorenz curves and Gini indices do not indicate any substantial change in the gross world product distribution.

**Table 3**

Correlation coefficients of country ranks, based on per capita gross domestic product between selected years

| Period | Market exchange rate | WA rate | PPPs | PARE 1970–1989 | PARE 1980–1989 |
|---|---|---|---|---|---|
| 1970–1989 | 0.910 | 0.903 | 0.938 | 0.911 | 0.911 |
| 1970–1980 | 0.941 | 0.929 | 0.957 | 0.955 | 0.954 |
| 1980–1989 | 0.936 | 0.939 | 0.966 | 0.974 | 0.975 |
| 1970–1975 | 0.967 | 0.961 | 0.971 | 0.976 | 0.978 |
| 1975–1980 | 0.972 | 0.969 | 0.988 | 0.978 | 0.978 |
| 1980–1985 | 0.963 | 0.967 | 0.978 | 0.988 | 0.990 |
| 1985–1989 | 0.967 | 0.969 | 0.992 | 0.994 | 0.993 |

**Table 4**
Countries with 20 or more rank increases between 1970 and 1989

| Market rate | | 1970-1989 PARE | | PPPs[a] | |
|---|---|---|---|---|---|
| Maldives | 20 | United Arab Emirates | 20 | Barbados | 13 |
| Rwanda | 21 | Singapore | 21 | Swaziland | 15 |
| Japan | 23 | Bulgaria | 21 | Thailand | 15 |
| Malaysia | 23 | Swaziland | 22 | Saudi Arabia | 15 |
| Cameroon | 24 | Tonga | 24 | Iran (Islamic Rep. of) | 15 |
| Saint itts-Nevis | 24 | Malaysia | 24 | Tunisia | 15 |
| Cape Verde | 26 | Mauritius | 28 | Malaysia | 18 |
| Egypt | 27 | Indonesia | 28 | Bangladesh | 19 |
| Afghanistan | 28 | Yemen | 28 | Gambia | 20 |
| Thailand | 29 | Thailand | 31 | Indonesia | 33 |
| Mauritius | 30 | Guinea-Bissau | 31 | Botswana | 34 |
| Haiti | 31 | Korea, Republic of | 34 | Lesotho | 35 |
| Grenada | 32 | China | 36 | Oman | 39 |
| Barbados | 32 | Egypt | 38 | | |
| St. Vincent-Grenadines | 33 | Norway | 42 | | |
| Seychelles | 33 | Maldives | 45 | | |
| Iraq | 33 | Botswana | 47 | | |
| Indonesia | 34 | Korea, D.P.R. of | 51 | | |
| Lao People's Dem. Rep. | 35 | Anguilla | 71 | | |
| Oman | 37 | Seychelles | 86 | | |
| Anguilla | 41 | | | | |
| Tonga | 44 | | | | |
| Yemen | 45 | | | | |
| Iran (Islamic Rep. of) | 48 | | | | |
| Korea, Republic of | 57 | | | | |
| Botswana | 67 | | | | |

[a] Countries with 13 or more rank increases.

The ranks of the countries based on MER and WA rates changed more in each five-or ten-year period than the ranks based on PAREs. However, the changes in rank of countries for the whole period, based on PAREs were not smaller than in the case of MER and WA rates. This implies that while the directions of the changes (i.e., increase or decrease) in the country ranks were mostly stable during the whole period in the case of PAREs, they varied considerably in the case of MER and WA rates.

The ranks of the countries changed somewhat more during the first decade than during the second one. In the first decade the rank based on the WA rates changed the most, while the country rank based on PPPs changed the least. The latter is partly a consequence of the fact that the PPP list is shorter than the others. Although the rank of the countries was more stable during the second than the first decade, there is an exception with regard to the rank changes based on the MER conversion, which changed more during the second decade than during the first decade. This confirms what was observed previously in the analyses based on the Lorenz curves and the Gini indices, which showed that GDP data based on MER conversion showed an increase in the inequality of gross world product distribution during the second decade.

When splitting the second decade into two five year periods, the ranks based on MER and WA rates changed the most in each of them. The country ranks based on PAREs hardly changed at all. The rank in the first half of the decade was less stable than in the second half. Ranks of countries based on PAREs and PPPs hardly changed between 1985 and 1989.

To supplement the analysis of table 3 with greater detail, tables 4 and 5 identify for MER, 1970–1989 PARE and PPPs, those countries with 20 or more rank increases and decreases between 1970 and 1989. As the country coverage of PPPs is more limited, the threshold was reduced to 13. The dividing line in each column is between countries whose rank increased (table 4) or decreased (table 5) by more than 30 steps, and for PPPs by more than 20 steps.

Table 4 shows that based on MER conversion, there are 26 countries which increased in rank by more than 20 steps between 1970 and 1989. Botswana is the country that increased the most, by 67 steps from 33rd to 100th place (with 178 the highest). The Republic of Korea, Yemen, Indonesia, Thailand, Egypt, Malaysia and Japan are other examples of countries whose rank increased considerably over time. Table 5 shows that Nicaragua is the country which decreased in rank the most, by 70 steps. Argentina, Poland, Uganda, Nigeria, Venezuela and Ghana are other examples of countries that fell considerably in rank. Both lists of countries are heterogenous in terms of country types; there are countries of large and small population from different continents, as well as countries with high and low per capita GDP in 1970.

Japan is the country which had the highest rank (152 out of 178) and Rwanda had the lowest rank (3, that is, third from the lowest) in 1970 among the countries which improved their position the most. Japan is the only developed country in this country group; most are developing countries, such as Barbados, Iran (Islamic Republic of),

**Table 5**

Countries with 20 or more rank decreases between 1970 and 1989

| Market exchange rate | | 1970-1989 PARE | | PPPs[a] | |
|---|---|---|---|---|---|
| Guatemala | -20 | Bolivia | -20 | Sierra Leone | -13 |
| Kuwait | -21 | Guatemala | -20 | Guatemala | -13 |
| Samoa | -21 | Madagascar | -20 | Nigeria | -15 |
| Zimbabwe | -21 | US Virgin Islan | -20 | Bolivia | -15 |
| Albania | -23 | French Guiana | -22 | El Salvador | -16 |
| US Virgin Islan | -23 | Liberia | -22 | Sudan | -17 |
| Vietnam | -24 | Zambia | -22 | Guyana | -18 |
| Madagascar | -25 | Mozambique | -23 | Peru | -18 |
| Mongolia | -25 | Peru | -23 | Argentina | -19 |
| Mozambique | -25 | Iraq | -24 | Jamaica | -20 |
| Sierra Leone | -25 | Jamaica | -24 | Madagascar | -22 |
| Hungary | -26 | Bahrain | -25 | Angola | -23 |
| Namibia | -26 | Gabon | -27 | Zambia | -24 |
| Chile | -30 | Kuwait | -27 | Papua New Guine | -24 |
| Kiribati | -30 | Papua New Guine | -27 | Nicaragua | -26 |
| Jamaica | -31 | Uganda | -31 | | |
| Ghana | -35 | Namibia | -32 | | |
| Guinea-Bissau | -35 | Kiribati | -34 | | |
| Venezuela | -35 | Sao Tome-Princi | -39 | | |
| Nigeria | -37 | Angola | -43 | | |
| Uganda | -37 | Djibouti | -43 | | |
| Poland | -38 | Nicaragua | -45 | | |
| Argentina | -39 | Equatorial Guin | -49 | | |
| Vanuatu | -42 | Lebanon | -97 | | |
| Zambia | -61 | | | | |
| Lebanon | -65 | | | | |
| Guyana | -70 | | | | |
| Nicaragua | -70 | | | | |

[a] Countries with 13 or more rank decreases.

Haiti and Laos. Most of the countries are from Africa, the
Caribbean, the Middle East and south-eastern Asia. The United
States Virgin Islands had the highest (177 out of 178) and Mozam-
bique had the lowest (27) per capita GDP in 1970 among the countries whose position worsened the most. There is no developed country among this group, which includes a variety of countries from different regions and backgrounds such as Kuwait, Chile, Poland and
Argentina, as well as Viet Nam, Madagascar and Sierra Leone. Most
of the countries are from sub-Saharan Africa and Latin America, although there are some from Oceania, eastern Europe and the
Caribbean.

More detailed analysis shows that the increase in the ranks was
not continuous in the case of more than the half of the 26 countries
whose position improved substantially between 1970 and 1989.
Some oil-producing countries, such as Iraq, Indonesia and Oman, after a continuous increase, decreased in rank between 1985 and 1989.
Others, such as Egypt and Thailand, decreased first and started to go
up only in the second half of the period. There are other countries
with volatile rank movements, such as Iran and Mauritius. Twenty of
the 28 countries whose position worsened showed some temporary
improvement within the period; Chile, Argentina, Ghana, Nigeria
and Poland are examples.

Comparing the country ranks between 1970 and 1989 on the basis of the 1970–1989 PARE, 39 countries changed their rank by more
than 20 steps. Nineteen of them improved their situation, while the
remaining 20 countries' position worsened. The scale is wide: Sey-
chelles improved by 86 steps, while Lebanon at the other extreme,
fell by 97 steps. The composition of the two country groups is quite
similar to the one based on MER, although Japan, for example, is not
included here. What is different from the data based on MER is that
the increases or decreases were stable for the majority of the countries during the whole period. This implies that frequent and volatile
changes (real appreciations and depreciations) in the exchange rates
were the reason for the volatile changes in the rank of the countries
based on the exchange rate.

When analysing the rank change with regard to PPPs, one
should keep in mind that these data are not entirely comparable because of different country coverage and threshold selection. There
were only 13 countries that increased and 15 which decreased in
rank by 13 or more steps. Most of the countries are from Africa,
south-eastern Asia and the Middle East. Saudi Arabia had the highest rank (104 of 178) and Lesotho had the lowest rank (16) in 1970
among the countries which improved their position the most. Argentina had the highest rank in 1970 and Sierra Leone had the lowest rank (32) among the countries which decreased in rank the most.
Eight countries with rank decreases out of the 15 are from Latin
America, and five of them are from sub-Saharan Africa.

*Correlation of country ranks using*
*different conversion rates*
The ranks of the countries also differ from each other in the same
year according to the different conversion rates. This analysis is car-

**Table 6**
Correlation coeeficients of country ranks based on per capita gross domestic product, using alternative conversion rates

| 1970 | MER | WA | 1970-89 PARE | 1980-89 PARE |
|---|---|---|---|---|
| MER | 1.000 | 0.986 | 0.948 | 0.932 |
| WA | 0.986 | 1.000 | 0.934 | 0.923 |
| 1970-89 PARE | 0.948 | 0.934 | 1.000 | 0.996 |
| 1980-89 PARE | 0.932 | 0.923 | 0.996 | 1.000 |

| 1975 | MER | WA | 1970-89 PARE | 1980-89 PARE |
|---|---|---|---|---|
| MER | 1.000 | 0.989 | 0.983 | 0.972 |
| WA | 0.989 | 1.000 | 0.979 | 0.974 |
| 1970-89 PARE | 0.983 | 0.979 | 1.000 | 0.996 |
| 1980-89 PARE | 0.972 | 0.974 | 0.996 | 1.000 |

| 1980 | MER | WA | 1970-89 PARE | 1980-89 PARE |
|---|---|---|---|---|
| MER | 1.000 | 0.984 | 0.988 | 0.983 |
| WA | 0.984 | 1.000 | 0.984 | 0.983 |
| 1970-89 PARE | 0.988 | 0.984 | 1.000 | 0.997 |
| 1980-89 PARE | 0.983 | 0.983 | 0.997 | 1.000 |

| 1985 | MER | WA | 1970-89 PARE | 1980-89 PARE |
|---|---|---|---|---|
| MER | 1.000 | 0.997 | 0.988 | 0.993 |
| WA | 0.997 | 1.000 | 0.988 | 0.991 |
| 1970-89 PARE | 0.988 | 0.988 | 1.000 | 0.996 |
| 1980-89 PARE | 0.993 | 0.991 | 0.996 | 1.000 |

| 1989 | MER | WA | 1970-89 PARE | 1980-89 PARE |
|---|---|---|---|---|
| MER | 1.000 | 0.994 | 0.981 | 0.984 |
| WA | 0.994 | 1.000 | 0.983 | 0.986 |
| 1970-89 PARE | 0.981 | 0.983 | 1.000 | 0.997 |
| 1980-89 PARE | 0.984 | 0.986 | 0.997 | 1.000 |

ried out in table 6, which presents the correlation coefficients between the ranks of countries for pairs of alternative conversion rates in 1970, 1975, 1980, 1985 and 1989. Since the country list based on PPPs is considerably shorter, PPPs are not included in this analysis.

The rank correlation coefficient between the ranks of countries for pairs of alternative conversion rates is very high (between 0.923 and 0.997) for each year. The ranks of countries were less correlated in 1970 and were closest to each other in 1985. This implies that in 1970 the conversion rate structures were the least similar while in 1985 they were the closest to each other.

The ranks based on the MER and WA rates were very similar in all years, which means that the adjustment applied in the case of the WA rate did not affect the rank of the countries too much (the lowest coefficient is 0.984). The similarity between the ranks based on MER and the 1970–1989 and 1980–1989 PARE rates increased during the period; the coefficients were higher than 0.98 in 1980 and afterwards. In the case of the 1980–1989 PARE, this is a consequence of the fact that the 1980–1989 PARE is based on the average exchange rate of the second decade.

The ranks of the countries based on different PAREs were very similar to each other in all years.

## Share of population quarters in gross world product

The percentage share of gross world product contributed by countries with the first (poorest), second, third and fourth (richest) quarters of the world population is another way of analysing the structure of the gross world product distribution between countries. Table 7 and figures 9 and 10 reflect this type of analysis based on data for 1970, 1980 and 1989, corresponding to two of the six conversion rates.

Table 7 shows the share of four population quarters in gross world product in 1970, 1980 and 1989; the third and fourth quarters for the MER and PARE rates are divided further into two eighths. The population quarters and eighths are constructed by ranking the countries on the basis of their per capita GDP in each of the years presented in the table, as was done in annex tables A.3, A.4 and A.5. Calculations were carried out for each conversion rate but not for PPPs. In the case of MER and PARE, the analysis is more detailed than for the other conversion rates. The first row in each box shows the percentage distribution of gross world product by population quarter and eighth in 1970. The following two rows present the changes in the population quarter's share between 1970 and 1979 and between 1980 and 1989. The fourth row in each box shows their percentage share in 1989. In the case of MER and 1970–1989 PARE a fifth and sixth row are incorporated. The fifth row shows the percentage distribution of gross world product by population quarters based on the country rank of 1970 and the last row presents the difference between the percentage share of gross world product belonging to the population quarters based on 1970 and 1989 per capita rankings.

**Figure 9**

Shares of gross world product by quarters and eighths of the population,
based on 1970–1989 PARE conversion

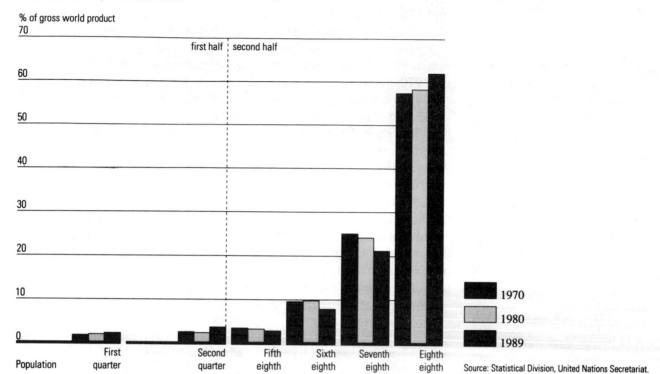

Source: Statistical Division, United Nations Secretariat.

**Figure 10**

Shares of gross world product by quarters and eighths of the population,
based on market exchange rate conversion

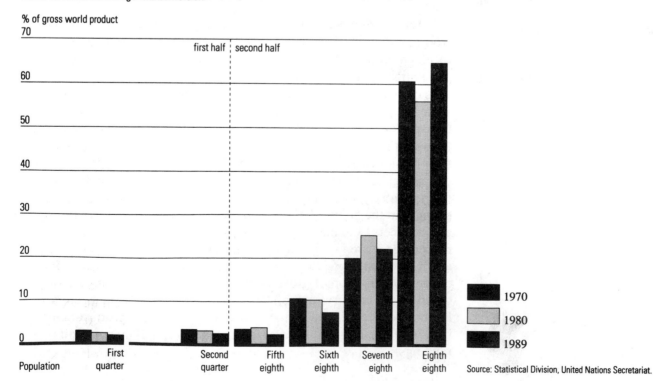

Source: Statistical Division, United Nations Secretariat.

**Table 7**

Changes in share of gross world product by quarters and eighths of the population,
classified by per capita gross domestic product

| Conversion rate and year | Population groups | | | | | | | |
|---|---|---|---|---|---|---|---|---|
| | Poorest quarter | Second quarter | Third quarter | Fourth eighth | Fifth eighth | Richest quarter | Seventh eighth | Eighth eighth |
| **Market rate** | | | | | | | | |
| 1  1970 (share) | 2.7 | 3.3 | 13.8 | 3.4 | 10.4 | 80.2 | 19.8 | 60.4 |
| 2  1970 minus 1979 | −0.51 | −0.28 | 0.04 | 0.3 | −0.3 | 0.8 | 5.3 | −4.6 |
| 3  1980 minus 1989 | −0.50 | −0.63 | −4.47 | −1.6 | −2.8 | 5.6 | −3.1 | 8.7 |
| 4  1989 (base: 1989) | 1.7 | 2.4 | 9.4 | 2.2 | 7.2 | 86.6 | 22.0 | 64.6 |
| 5  1989 (base: 1970) | 2.3 | 2.3 | 16.2 | 4.0 | 12.2 | 79.2 | 28.8 | 50.4 |
| 6  Rows 5-4 | 0.6 | −0.1 | 6.9 | 1.8 | 5.0 | −7.4 | 6.8 | −14.2 |
| **PARE 1970-1989** | | | | | | | | |
| 7  1970 (share) | 1.8 | 2.6 | 13.1 | 3.5 | 9.6 | 82.5 | 25.1 | 57.4 |
| 8  1970 minus 1979 | 0.20 | −0.14 | 0.00 | −0.2 | 0.2 | −0.1 | −0.9 | 0.9 |
| 9  1980 minus 1989 | 0.26 | 1.31 | −2.28 | −0.4 | −1.9 | 0.7 | −3.0 | 3.7 |
| 10  1989 (base: 1989) | 2.3 | 3.7 | 10.8 | 2.9 | 7.9 | 83.2 | 21.2 | 62.0 |
| 11  1989 (base: 1970) | 3.6 | 3.0 | 12.1 | 4.3 | 7.8 | 81.3 | 24.7 | 56.6 |
| 12  Rows 11-10 | 1.3 | −0.7 | 1.3 | 1.4 | −0.1 | −1.9 | 3.5 | −5.4 |
| **PARE 1980-1989** | | | | | | | | |
| 23  1970 (share) | 1.5 | 2.4 | 12.2 | | | 83.9 | | |
| 24  1970 minus 1979 | 0.20 | −0.15 | 0.31 | | | −0.4 | | |
| 25  1980 minus 1989 | 0.51 | 0.85 | −2.18 | | | 0.8 | | |
| 26  1989 (base: 1989) | 2.2 | 3.1 | 10.4 | | | 84.3 | | |
| ***World Bank Atlas*** | | | | | | | | |
| 27  1970 (share) | 2.7 | 3.3 | 13.8 | | | 80.2 | | |
| 28  1970 minus 1979 | −0.56 | −0.27 | −0.14 | | | 1.0 | | |
| 29  1980 minus 1989 | −0.48 | −0.54 | −4.68 | | | 5.7 | | |
| 30  1989 (base: 1989) | 1.7 | 2.5 | 9.0 | | | 86.8 | | |

Note:  Highlighted figures are discussed in the text.

When analysing table 7, one should keep in mind that the same groups may consist of different countries, depending on the time period and the type of conversion rate. For example, although the first two groups are dominated by China and India, their rank is not always the same. On the basis of MER conversion, the Indian per capita GDP is lower than the Chinese one and India belongs to the poorest quarter of the world, while China is included in the second quarter, for all three years. However, PARE calculations show that the rank of the two countries changed within the period and China overtook India between 1980 and 1989. Therefore, although China belonged to the poorest quarter of the population at the beginning of the period, it became part of the second group 20 years later and India was relocated to the poorest quarter.

In the case of MER, the table shows that while the poorest quarter's share of gross world product was 2.7 per cent (see row 1), it decreased to 1.7 per cent (see row 4) in 1989. However, if the ranking of countries is based on 1970 per capita GDP, the poorest quarter in 1970 received 2.3 per cent of gross world product in 1989 (row 5). As row 6 indicates, the country group that was the poorest in 1970 had a higher share of gross world product than the group which was

the poorest in 1989. This means that some of the countries which
were the poorest in 1970 improved their position, while other countries were reclassified to the poorest group between 1970 and 1989.

The table clearly illustrates the inequality in the distribution of
gross world product. While the share of gross world product of the
poorest quarter of the population was between 1.5 and 2.7 per cent,
the share of the richest quarter was between 80 and 87 per cent during the last two decades. The share in gross world product of the
second group was between around 3 per cent and the share of the
third quarter was between 9 and 16 per cent. Some of the information in table 7 is graphically represented in figures 9 and 10. The bar
charts show the shares in gross world product of each of the population quarters and eighths in 1970, 1980 and 1989, based on MER and
1970–1989 PARE conversions. Since MER often produced results
closely correlated with the WA rates, in the same manner that all
PARE conversions do, figures 9 and 10 are presented only in terms
of the MER and 1970–1989 PARE rates, with the implicit assumption
that these two rates characteristically represent the effects generated
by each of the other applications.

When analysing the changes over time shown in the figures and
in annex table 7 for MER and WA conversions, it is clear that both
indicate an increase in inequality in the gross world product distribution. This confirms what was concluded on the basis of earlier
analyses of Lorenz curves and Gini indices. For these two rates the
proportion of the richest quarter of the population increased from 80
per cent to almost 87 per cent of the gross world product. The group
that lost the greatest share is the third (second richest) quarter, and
not the poorest half of the world.

Data based on MER and WA conversions indicate that although
the richest group became richer, the group which became relatively
poorer is the third quarter of the population and not the poorest
quarter. The share of the poorer half of the population also decreased. However, these countries account for only 30 per cent of
the negative changes, while the decline in the proportion of the third
quarter accounts for 70 per cent. The relatively smaller decrease in
the proportion from the total means a larger-scale decrease for a
poor country than for a richer one. A 1.1 per cent decrease for example, means for the poorest group that its share decreased to less than
two thirds of its 1970 share.

When focusing on eighths of the population, figures based on
MER indicate that both of the two richest groups' shares increased,
but this increase was not steady. All other groups' shares decreased
continuously during the period. The largest loser is the sixth eighth
of the population. As was mentioned before, a relatively slight decrease in the share of gross world product may mean a sharper fall
for a poorer country in relative terms than for a richer one.

The pattern of the data based on PAREs also shows that the richest eighth of the world became relatively richer, but it does not indicate any temporary decrease in their shares, as was observed for the
MER-converted gross world product. Since almost the same countries constitute the group for which a decline was shown by data

based on MER conversion, it seems to indicate that real changes in exchange rates were the cause. The sixth and the seventh eighths' share decreased the most and continuously according to the PARE calculations, although the seventh eighth's proportion increased between 1970 and 1980 on the basis of MER conversion.

Table 7 shows that according to the MER conversion, the countries which formed the richest eighth of the world in 1970 and whose proportion was 60.4 per cent of the total gross world product at that time, had a share of 50.4 per cent (row 5) of the gross world product in 1989. The countries which made up the richest eighth in 1989 had a share of 64.6 per cent of the total. This means that the composition of the richest countries' group changed. Some of the countries that were the richest ones at the beginning of the period could not keep their relative advantage and other countries overtook them.

The United Kingdom, New Zealand and Kuwait are examples of countries whose position worsened relatively, while Italy and Japan are the new members of the richest group of countries. Since the groups are identified on the basis of the size of the population, it can be observed that the United Kingdom left the richest group even though it improved its rank position among the countries. Although it is the 158th country in the list according to annex table A.5 (with 178 the highest), the fact that Japan, with a large population (almost 123 million people), is one of the new members, decreased the number of the countries in the group.

The last rows in table 7, under MER, indicate that the countries which constituted the third quarter in 1970 became richer in total than the third quarter in 1989. Therefore, some of these countries were re-allocated to the richest population quarter in 1989. The same applies to the seventh eighth, while the reverse happened to the richest eighth: some of the richest countries became relatively poorer, as was shown above.

The same analysis based on PARE shows a similar pattern. It indicates that countries that used to belong to the first and the third population quarters and the seventh eighth became relatively richer than the corresponding group in 1989. Although the second quarter became a bit poorer than the corresponding group in 1989, their share in absolute terms increased somewhat. The only group which decreased its share in both absolute and relative terms is the richest eighth of the population.

## B. Measures of inequality of gross world product distribution between regions

Annex table A.6 presents, for the principal geographical regions of the world, the total and per capita gross regional product after conversion to United States dollars based on the alternative methods of conversion. It also shows the percentage changes in the regional share of gross world product with each application of the alternative conversion rates. The regional classifications and country groupings are presented in annex B.

The format and orientation of the table are identical to annex table A.1, differing only along the region/country basis. The left-most column of table A.6 lists the individual regions and the types of conversion rates, which are presented in numbered rows in the same sequence as in table A.1: (1) MER; (2) PPPs; (3) absolute 1970–1989 PARE; (4) relative 1970–1989 PARE; (5) absolute 1980–1989 PARE; and (6) WA rates. Each conversion rate is likewise subdivided into subscripts a, b and c, corresponding to the per capita gross regional product in United States dollars, total gross regional product in millions of United States dollars and percentage shares of gross world product, respectively. Columns 1 to 20 show the individual years from 1970 to 1989, while the last three columns (21 to 23) list the three period averages of 1970–1989, 1970–1979 and 1980–1989.

In reviewing the table, the reader should keep in mind that data based on PPPs are not available for all countries. In particular, data are missing altogether for two regions: eastern Europe and eastern Asia, excluding Japan. In the case of the Caribbean, data for distribution of gross world product of each region as relative shares of gross world product are missing for more than 50 per cent of the countries; for other regions, data are available for 75 to 100 per cent of the countries. In view of this, gross world product based on PPPs is not available and regional shares could not be calculated.

The reader should also recognize that the average per capita GDP for the periods 1970–1989 and 1980–1989 based on MER and the average per capita GDP converted on the basis of the 1970–1989 and 1980–1989 PARE, respectively, are equal because the price relatives used in the PAREs are calculated as period averages of market exchange rates.

## 1. Gross regional product

The data in annex table A.6 on regional shares of gross world product are graphically presented in figures 11–14. They include data for 14 regions based on each conversion rate except PPPs. Years between 1970 and 1989 are shown on the horizontal axis and the share of regions expressed as a percentage of gross world product are shown on the vertical axis. Since the range is wide (from almost 0 to 35 per cent), the figures are printed in three parts (regions with more than 5 per cent share, regions between 3 per cent and 5 per cent share and regions with less than 3 per cent share) in order to give a clearer view of the level and changes in the share of each region.

In line with previous findings, the figures show that patterns for MER and WA conversions are very similar to each other as well as to the main trends based on PARE conversions. Furthermore, trends in PARE related figures show smoother changes over time than do the figures based on MER and WA conversions.

Even though the trends of PARE related curves are mostly similar, there are substantial differences between them in the proportion of some regions. These differences result from two factors. One is that the measurement unit is different. In the case of the 1970–1989

**Figure 11**

Gross world product distribution by region, based on market exchange rate

Regions with more than 5% share

35%

Northern America
Japan
Western Europe
Eastern Europe

Regions between 3% and 5% share

5%

Latin America
Middle East
Eastern-Asia exc. Japan

Regions with less than 3% share

3%

Sub-Saharan Africa
Northern Africa
Caribbean
South-eastern Asia
Southern Asia
Australia, New Zealand
Other Oceania

Source: Statistical Division, United Nations Secretariat.

**Figure 12**
Gross world product distribution by region, based on *World Bank Atlas* conversion

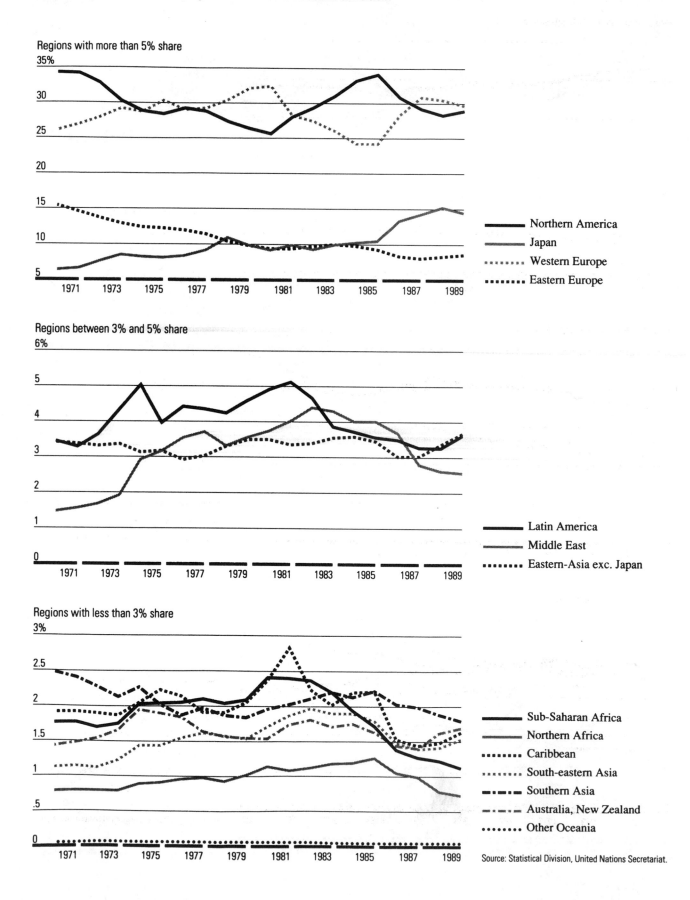

Regions with more than 5% share

Northern America
Japan
Western Europe
Eastern Europe

Regions between 3% and 5% share

Latin America
Middle East
Eastern-Asia exc. Japan

Regions with less than 3% share

Sub-Saharan Africa
Northern Africa
Caribbean
South-eastern Asia
Southern Asia
Australia, New Zealand
Other Oceania

Source: Statistical Division, United Nations Secretariat.

**Figure 13**
Gross world product distribution by region, based on 1970–1989 PARE conversion

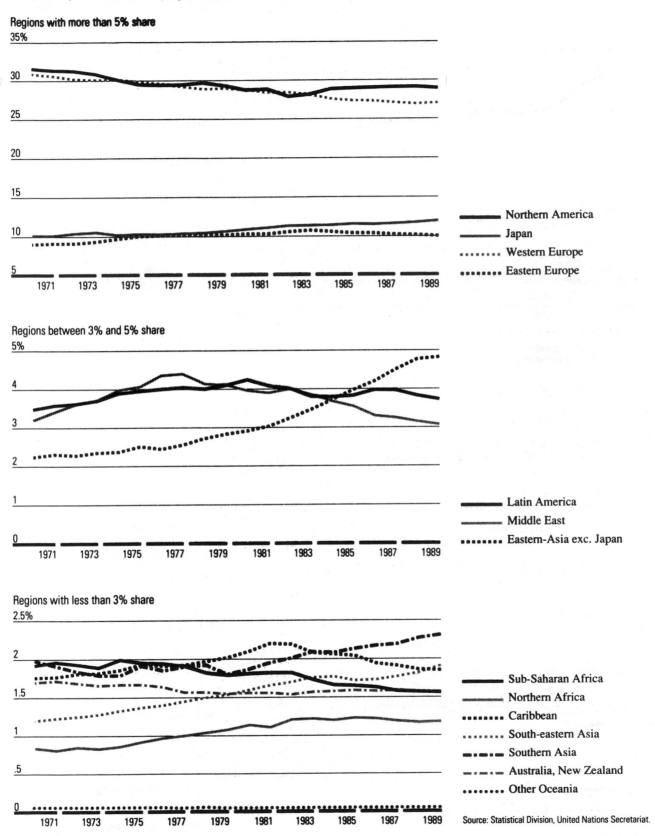

Regions with more than 5% share

Northern America
Japan
Western Europe
Eastern Europe

Regions between 3% and 5% share

Latin America
Middle East
Eastern-Asia exc. Japan

Regions with less than 3% share

Sub-Saharan Africa
Northern Africa
Caribbean
South-eastern Asia
Southern Asia
Australia, New Zealand
Other Oceania

Source: Statistical Division, United Nations Secretariat.

**Figure 14**

Gross world product distribution by region, based on 1980–1989 PARE conversion

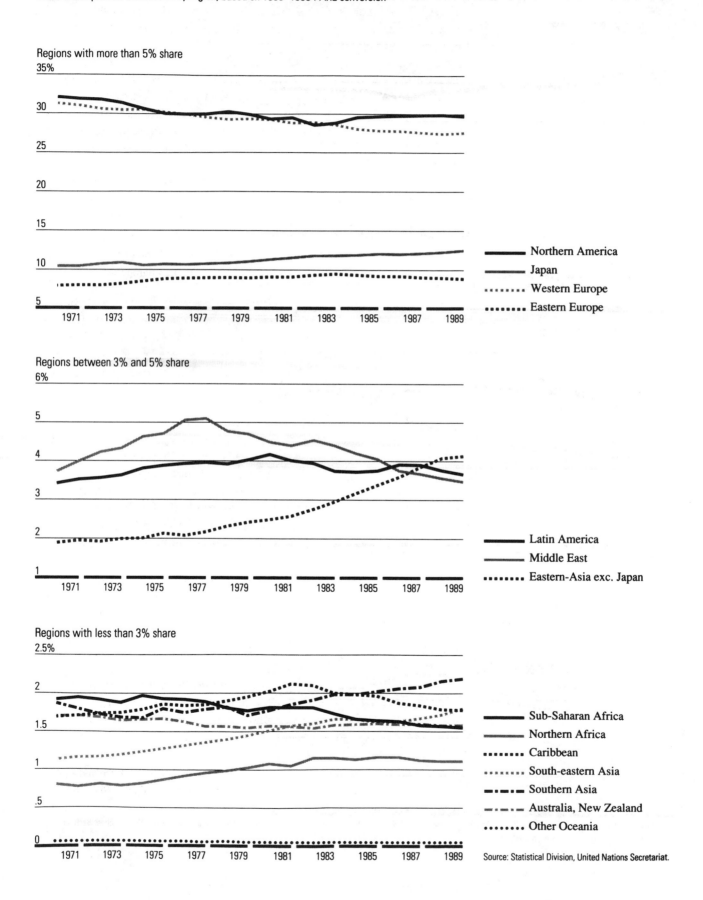

Regions with more than 5% share

Northern America
Japan
Western Europe
Eastern Europe

Regions between 3% and 5% share

Latin America
Middle East
Eastern-Asia exc. Japan

Regions with less than 3% share

Sub-Saharan Africa
Northern Africa
Caribbean
South-eastern Asia
Southern Asia
Australia, New Zealand
Other Oceania

Source: Statistical Division, United Nations Secretariat.

PARE it is the average United States dollar for the whole period, while in the case of the 1980–1989 PARE, the measurement unit is the average United States dollar during the period 1980–1989. The second factor is that the structure of the exchange rates differs between the two periods.

Comparing the data of the first and last years of the period based on MER and WA conversions, one observes a notable decline in the share of gross world product of the regions of northern America and eastern Europe and the USSR and some decrease in the proportion of southern Asia, sub-Saharan Africa and the Caribbean. The slack is taken up primarily by Japan, the Middle East and western Europe.

According to PARE calculations, the shares of most of the regions decreased or stagnated. The exceptions are eastern Asia and Japan, south-eastern and southern Asia, and north Africa. The most remarkable increase is registered by eastern Asia, excluding Japan; this region doubled its share of gross world product.

The two regions that had the highest share of gross world product based on any conversion rate are northern America and western Europe. With the application of the MER and WA conversions, their shares vary considerably over time, at the expense of each other, as a consequence of changes in the exchange rates between the United States dollar and currencies in western Europe. PARE calculations indicate that the share of the two regions together steadily decreased for several years and than stabilized in the middle of the second decade.

The changes in the shares of the next two regions—Japan and eastern Europe—were the reverse of each other calculated on the basis of MER, WA and 1970–1989 PARE: Japan increased and eastern Europe decreased its share. The trend based on the 1980–1989 PARE is a good example of the effect of the base period. Since the eastern European share based on MER declined during the period, while the GDP share of Japan was increasing at the same time, the share of eastern Europe is higher than the Japanese share as calculated by the 1980–1989 PARE.

When reviewing the figures corresponding to the regions of less than 5 per cent share, one can observe that the percentage data based on MER and WA conversions are sometimes substantially different. The most obvious examples are the Latin American data in the first 13 years and the Middle Eastern data for the last three years.

Trends based on MER and WA conversions differ considerably from those calculated by different PAREs in the case of eastern Asia, excluding Japan. These differences indicate that the currencies of these countries were more depreciated than justified by relative price changes during the period. This is also reflected in the relative position of curves based on different PAREs. While the share of eastern Asia, excluding Japan, exceeded the shares of all others after 1985 based on the 1970–1989 PARE, it did so only after 1987 based on the 1980–1989 PARE.

## 2.   Per capita gross regional product

In order to show to what extent development of GDP is offset by
population changes, per capita gross regional product data were calculated. Figures 15–19 present in graphical form the data from annex table A.6 on per capita gross regional product, for 14 regions
and for each of the conversion rates, including PPPs. PPP data in
some cases do not cover the whole region. Years between 1970 and
1989 are presented horizontally and per capita gross regional product data are shown vertically. Since the per capita gross regional
product range is wide (from almost 0 to approximately US$25,000),
the figures are printed in three sections for regions with high, medium and low per capita gross regional product.

On the basis of annex table A.6 and in terms of average per
capita gross regional product for the period as a whole (column 21),
four groups of regions can be distinguished. The richest region was
northern America, with an average per capita gross regional product
for the period 1970-1989 that was higher than US$10,000 on aver-
age for the period. The next richest regions were Australia and New
Zealand, which are treated as subregions of Oceania, and Japan,
which is identified as a subregion of eastern Asia. Their average per
capita gross regional product was almost US$10,000 based on MER
conversion. The data based on PPPs indicate a lower level of per
capita gross regional product for these subregions of around
US$8,000. The fourth richest region, according to MER conversion,
was western Europe, with an average per capita gross regional product of almost US$7,500.

When analysing the changes over time, gross regional product
data based on PARE conversion show an almost steady real growth
during the whole period for all four regions mentioned. The trends
of per capita gross regional product based on MER conversion are
less similar for the four regions. The growth is steady only in the
case of the United States. All the other three regions were affected
by changes in the United States dollar exchange rate relative to other
currencies between 1980 and 1989. When the United States dollar
appreciated, per capita GDP data of the countries expressed in United States dollars were relatively low, but when the United States
dollar depreciated, their data in terms of United States dollars
showed rapid increases. Japan is the country in these richest groups
which had the fastest growth between 1970 and 1989 based on any
conversion rate except PPPs.

The above-mentioned groups are very different from the other
regions, not only because of their exceptionally high average per
capita gross regional product, but also because of their large increases over time.

The Middle East and eastern Europe were the next richest regions, with a per capita gross regional product of almost US$3,000
on average—2.5 to 3 times lower than the per capita gross regional
product of the richer regions and subregions. Data for the Middle
East based on PPPs give a higher per capita gross regional product

**Figure 15**
Per capita gross regional product, based on market exchange rate

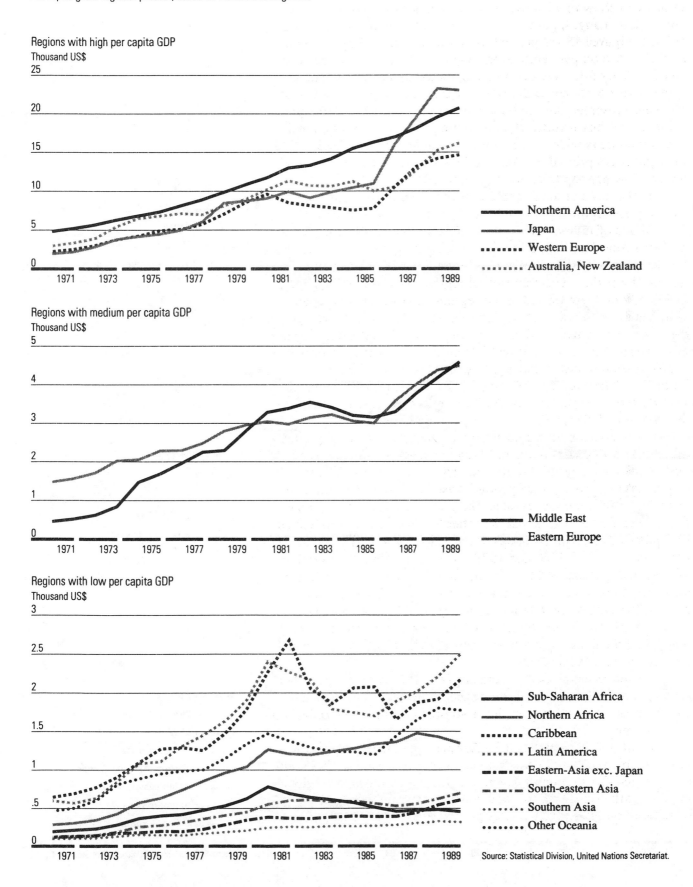

Regions with high per capita GDP
Thousand US$

— Northern America
— Japan
...... Western Europe
······· Australia, New Zealand

Regions with medium per capita GDP
Thousand US$

— Middle East
— Eastern Europe

Regions with low per capita GDP
Thousand US$

— Sub-Saharan Africa
— Northern Africa
...... Caribbean
······· Latin America
–·–·– Eastern-Asia exc. Japan
–·–·– South-eastern Asia
······· Southern Asia
...... Other Oceania

Source: Statistical Division, United Nations Secretariat.

**Figure 16**
Per capita gross regional product, based on *World Bank Atlas* conversion

Regions with high per capita GDP
Thousand US$

— Northern America
— Japan
••••••• Western Europe
········ Australia, New Zealand

Regions with medium per capita GDP
Thousand US$

— Middle East
— Eastern Europe

Regions with low per capita GDP
Thousand US$

— Sub-Saharan Africa
— Northern Africa
••••••• Caribbean
········ Latin America
–••–•• Eastern-Asia exc. Japan
–•–•– South-eastern Asia
········ Southern Asia
••••••• Other Oceania

Source: Statistical Division, United Nations Secretariat.

**Figure 17**
Per capita gross regional product, based on PPP conversion

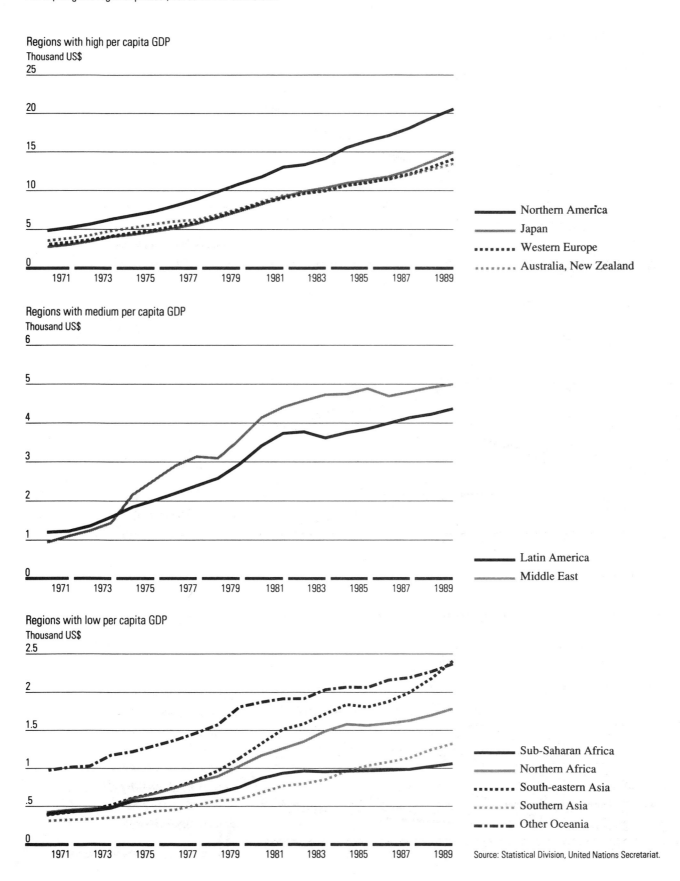

Regions with high per capita GDP
Thousand US$

Northern America
Japan
Western Europe
Australia, New Zealand

Regions with medium per capita GDP
Thousand US$

Latin America
Middle East

Regions with low per capita GDP
Thousand US$

Sub-Saharan Africa
Northern Africa
South-eastern Asia
Southern Asia
Other Oceania

Source: Statistical Division, United Nations Secretariat.

**Figure 18**
Per capita gross regional product, based on 1970–1989 PARE conversion

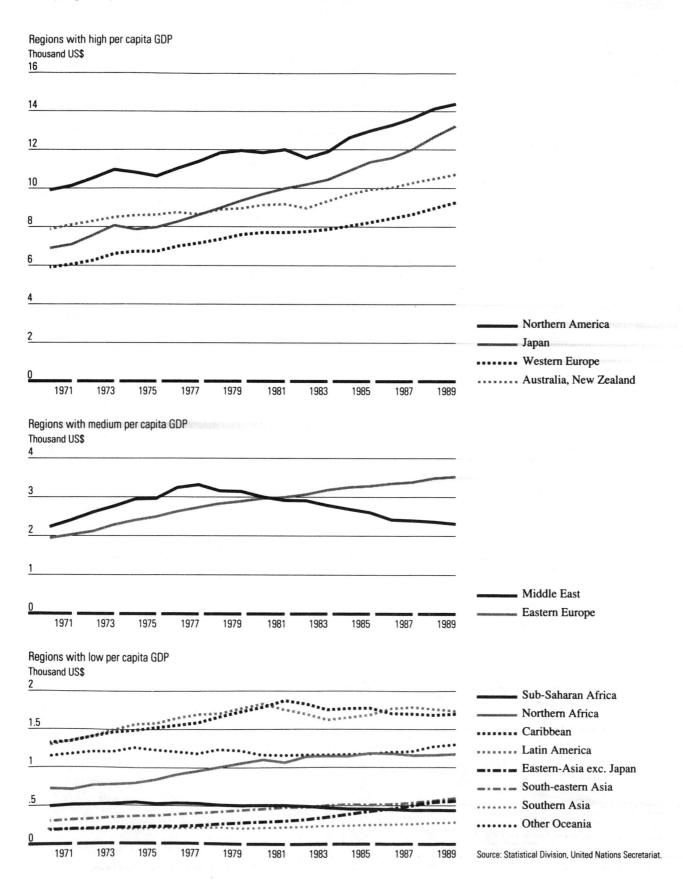

Regions with high per capita GDP
Thousand US$

— Northern America
— Japan
...... Western Europe
...... Australia, New Zealand

Regions with medium per capita GDP
Thousand US$

— Middle East
— Eastern Europe

Regions with low per capita GDP
Thousand US$

— Sub-Saharan Africa
— Northern Africa
...... Caribbean
...... Latin America
–·–·– Eastern-Asia exc. Japan
–·–·– South-eastern Asia
...... Southern Asia
...... Other Oceania

Source: Statistical Division, United Nations Secretariat.

**Figure 19**
Per capita gross regional product, based on 1980–1989 PARE conversion

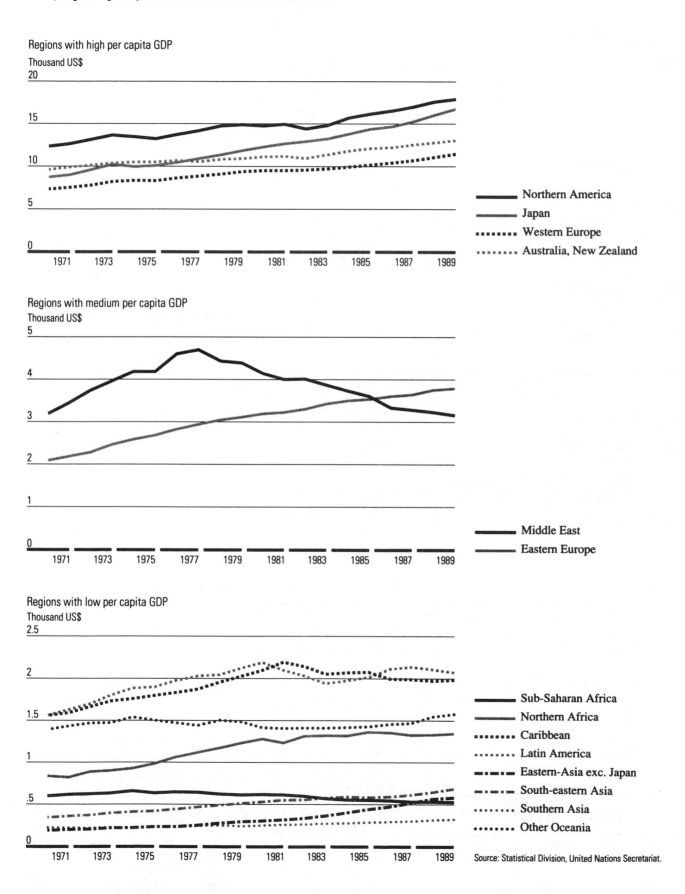

Regions with high per capita GDP
Thousand US$

——— Northern America
——— Japan
••••••• Western Europe
•••••••• Australia, New Zealand

Regions with medium per capita GDP
Thousand US$

——— Middle East
——— Eastern Europe

Regions with low per capita GDP
Thousand US$

——— Sub-Saharan Africa
——— Northern Africa
••••••• Caribbean
•••••••• Latin America
—•—•— Eastern-Asia exc. Japan
—••—••— South-eastern Asia
•••••••• Southern Asia
••••••• Other Oceania

Source: Statistical Division, United Nations Secretariat.

figure of US$3,600. Similar data for eastern Europe are not available.

Per capita gross regional product data based on PAREs indicate a turning point in 1977 in the case of the Middle East. The figures suggest that real per capita gross regional product was not substantially higher in the Middle East in 1989 than in 1970 even though there was a considerable increase between 1970 and 1979. Data based on MER conversion do not follow the decrease indicated by data based on PAREs before 1982. This suggests that the currencies of the countries in the Middle East were gradually appreciated in real terms between 1977 and 1982. The Middle East shows one of the rare examples where MER and WA conversions substantially differ from each other. Data based on the latter indicate a decrease in per capita gross regional product after 1986.

Per capita gross regional product data based on PAREs show a continuous growth in eastern Europe. Data based on MER conversion show an almost steady increase of per capita gross regional product in the region, except for the years when considerable increases in the United States dollar exchange rate occurred. Latin America, the Caribbean, other Oceania and North Africa are four regions which constitute a third group. Their per capita gross regional product data on the average was US$1,000 to US$1,800 based on the MER conversion and US$1,300 to US$3,000 based on PPPs. The per capita gross regional product data based on MER conversion were similar in the case of Latin America and the Caribbean (US$1,600 to US$1,800). Data based on PPPs for Latin America are substantially higher than the ones based on MER conversion. Per capita gross regional product in other Oceania and North Africa was between US$1,000 and US$1,200 based on MER; data based on PPPs show the figures to be relatively higher.

Per capita gross regional product in Latin America and the Caribbean increased steadily in real terms when based on PAREs. The trend based on MER conversion shows a different pattern for the two regions. The changes in the United States dollar exchange rates did not affect the Caribbean data very much, which implies that the currencies of the countries in that region were appreciated and depreciated in parallel with the United States dollar. On the other hand, changes in the United States dollar were reflected in the Latin American per capita gross regional product data for all years except the period 1983 to 1986. Although data based on PPPs show Latin America as the fifth region in the rank of countries, growth there slowed considerably after 1981.

Data based on PAREs do not show any substantial change in per capita gross regional product in Other Oceania, while data based on MER clearly reflect the changes in the United States dollar exchange rate. North Africa shows a real increase during the first period but stagnation in the second decade. The exchange rates of the currencies of this region, however, seem to be appreciated in parallel with the United States dollar between 1982 and 1985. At the end of the period though, a significant real depreciation is indicated by the data.

In terms of per capita gross regional product, the poorest regions are sub-Saharan Africa, south-eastern Asia, eastern Asia and southern Asia. The per capita GDP of countries in these regions was between US$200 and to US$500 on average based on the MER conversion. According to data based on PPPs the range is between US$700 and US$1,400.

Two regions—eastern Asia (excluding Japan) and south-eastern Asia—show a steady increase in their per capita gross regional product in real terms. Southern Asia's per capita gross regional product stagnated, while the per capita gross regional product decreased in real terms in sub-Saharan Africa. Data based on MER conversion show a slight increase in per capita gross regional product in southern Asia and south-eastern Asia and also indicate that the exchange rates changed in parallel with the United States dollar. Per capita gross regional product data for eastern Asia show more rapid changes, while data for sub-Saharan Africa suggest that the currencies of these countries were significantly depreciated in real terms in later years.

## 3. Distribution of gross world product within and between regions

*Decomposition of standard deviation* is the separate calculation of the standard deviation within and between groups of data. The square standard deviation corresponding to the total universe is equal to the sum of the square standard deviations between and within the groups (see formulas in annex C). The ratio of the square standard deviation between the groups and the total standard deviation corresponding to the population as a whole shows the relative importance of the grouping variable. If the ratio is high, the variations within the groups are small and they are homogeneous; when the ratio is low, there is more variation within the groups and they are more heterogeneous.

As observed so far, there are considerable differences in the average per capita gross regional product of the 14 regions. However, within each of those regions, there are also differences between the per capita GDP of the constituent countries. The question that is dealt with below is whether the differences in per capita GDP between the regions are quantitatively more important than the differences within each region or vice versa.

In order to quantify the importance of the "within-region" differences of per capita gross product relative to the "between-region" differences, ratios were calculated between the square standard deviations of the average per capita gross regional product and the square standard deviation of per capita GDP for all countries in the world. The calculated ratio is an indication of the extent to which variations in per capita gross product in the world can be explained by variations in per capita gross regional product averages.

Changes over time in these ratios for each region are presented in figure 20 for per capita GDP based on the MER, WA, and the 1970–1989 and 1980–1989 PAREs. The ratios expressed as percentages of the square standard deviation of per capita GDP for all countries in the world are presented vertically and the years are presented horizontally.

As the figure indicates, the differences between the regions were always more dominant than the differences within the regions. Even though trends and levels differ between conversion rates, the ratio was always higher than 86 per cent. The PARE curves show that the importance of the between-region differences increased almost steadily, except for the period between 1978 and 1980. Results based on the MER and WA conversions indicate that the ratio varied over time almost in the same range (i.e., between 87 per cent and 95 per cent).

When focusing on the curves corresponding to the MER and
WA, the first substantial decrease in the ratio representing the relative importance of differences between the regions took place in the
years 1973 and 1974, the second one occurred between 1978 and
1980 and a much less pronounced change can be observed between
1985 and 1987; the ratio was lowest in 1980. The figures indicate
that at the time of the increase in oil prices the relative importance
of the regional differences decreased. Further analysis shows that
the changes in the ratios were a consequence of two factors—
changes in the total standard deviation of per capita GDP for all
countries in the world and changes in the standard deviation of the
regional averages of per capita GDP. The total standard deviation decreased sharply between 1970 and 1974, and much less so between
1978 and 1980. On the other hand, the standard deviation of average
per capita GDP of regions increased sharply between 1980 and 1985
and changed very little afterwards.

The differences between the changes over time in the ratios
based on MER, WA and PAREs indicate that most of the ratio changes
were a consequence of changes in prices and exchange rates. However, the PARE curves show that regional differences are becoming
relatively more important. These results are mostly a consequence of
further subdividing the eight main regions into a larger number (i.e.,
14 regions) of more homogeneous subregions, in which Asia, for example was subdivided into five subregions, Japan was split off from
the rest of Asia, and Africa was split into two subregions. When applying the same analysis to the less homogeneous eight regional
groupings, results indicated a contrary conclusion, namely that regional differences were becoming relatively less important.

Further to the analysis of figure 20, annex table A.7 carries out
a more detailed complementary analysis measuring the extent to
which within-region differences in per capita GDP explain the overall distribution of gross world product. In order to accomplish this,
the table cross-classifies countries by the 14 regions and subregions
and by the population quarters and eighths that identify per capita
GDP groups and that were used earlier in the section on country
ranks. The data in the table refer to the number of countries in each
cell of the table, covering 1970, 1980 and 1989, based on per capita
GDP converted by MER and 1970–1989 PARE. A comparison between the years shows how per capita GDP groups per region
changed over time.

Starting with the regions having the highest per capita gross regional product, the table shows that the countries of northern America belonged to the richest eighths of the world at all times, whether
calculated on the basis of MER or PARE. Australia also belonged to
the richest group at all times, while New Zealand mostly belonged to
the second eighth. Japan, except at beginning of the period, also belonged to the richest population quarter. Western Europe was the
most heterogeneous region in this group, although it became more
homogeneous later on. While three to five countries from western
Europe belonged to the third population quarter in 1970 and 1980,
all belonged to the richest quarter in 1989 based on both conversion

rates. Nine to 14 countries of the 21 belonged to the richest eighth during the entire period.

Eastern Europe was very homogeneous at all times; most of the countries belonged to the second half of the third quarter during the entire period. The Middle East was more heterogeneous. According to the calculations based on the MER conversion for the year of 1970, countries from the region were included in each per capita GDP group, even in the poorest and the richest ones. Most countries belonged to the second half of the third population quarter. The position of these countries, however, steadily improved afterwards; most of them belonged to the first half of the richest quarter in 1989. However, data based on PARE show a somewhat different pattern, indicating that the region became more heterogeneous than it was at the beginning.

The position of Latin America did not change much over time according to the MER conversion. Most countries belonged to the second population quarter, and the majority to the richer part of it. Although the situation of the Latin American countries improved a bit by 1980, their relative position was almost the same at the end of the period. Data based on PARE indicate that there were more countries from the region among the relatively rich ones in 1980 and 1989 as compared with groupings based on MER conversion. Most of the Caribbean countries belonged to the third quarter during the entire period, as calculated by both conversion rates. However, the position of these countries improved, because there were more coun-

**Figure 20**

Ratio between standard deviation of per capita gross regional product and standard deviation of per capita gross domestic product of all countries

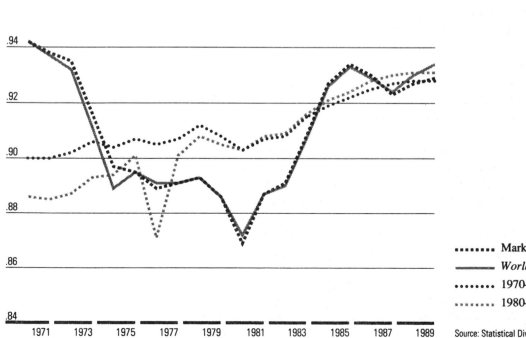

········ Market exchange rate

———— *World Bank Atlas* rate

········ 1970–1989 PARE

········ 1980–1989 PARE

Source: Statistical Division, United Nations Secretariat.

tries in the richest quarter in 1989 than 20 years before. The relative position of the Caribbean countries in 1970 and 1980 was better when based on PARE than when using MER conversions, but this situation was reversed by 1989.

Most of the countries of other Oceania belonged to the third quarter, mainly to the first half. The pattern shown by the different conversion rates is very similar. The position of the North African countries improved slightly as calculated by all conversion rates, but they still belonged only to the third quarter at the end of the period.

Some of the countries of eastern Asia (excluding Japan) improved their position and entered the richest population quarter, while others were still poor at the end of the period. The differences also grew in south-eastern Asia, although the general situation improved. Data based on PARE indicate larger differences between the countries than are evident from the MER conversion.

Southern Asia and sub-Saharan Africa were in the worst position during the entire period according to all conversion rates. When using PARE, Southern Asia's per capita gross regional product is reduced even further as compared with per capita gross regional product converted on the basis of MER. The per capita gross regional product was the lowest in this region in 1980, when all countries of the region belonged to the poorest half of the world. In the case of the 47 sub-Saharan countries of Africa, per capita GDP data based on PARE conversion, as compared with MER conversion, show a better position for these countries in 1970 and 1980 and a worse situation in 1989. Differences grew within the region.

Annex A    **Detailed tables**

**Table A.1**  Total and per capita gross domestic product of individual countries or areas, expressed in United States dollars, and their individual shares of gross world product, based on alternative conversion rates, 1970–1989

| Country or area | 1970 (1) | 1971 (2) | 1972 (3) | 1973 (4) | 1974 (5) | 1975 (6) | 1976 (7) | 1977 (8) | 1978 (9) | 1979 (10) |
|---|---|---|---|---|---|---|---|---|---|---|
| **Afghanistan** | | | | | | | | | | |
| **1. MER** | | | | | | | | | | |
| 1a. Per capita GDP | 102 | 103 | 124 | 125 | 147 | 160 | 168 | 173 | 198 | 248 |
| 1b. GDP | 1 389 | 1 436 | 1 778 | 1 844 | 2 211 | 2 467 | 2 633 | 2 756 | 3 189 | 4 002 |
| 1c. % of GWP | 0.04 | 0.04 | 0.04 | 0.04 | 0.04 | 0.04 | 0.04 | 0.04 | 0.04 | 0.04 |
| **2. PPPs** | | | | | | | | | | |
| 2a. Per capita GDP | 257 | 246 | 341 | 359 | 397 | 450 | 480 | 484 | 553 | 638 |
| 2b. GDP | 3 497 | 3 434 | 4 894 | 5 285 | 5 986 | 6 915 | 7 509 | 7 697 | 8 895 | 10 307 |
| 2c. % of GWP | ... | ... | ... | ... | ... | ... | ... | ... | ... | ... |
| **3. Absolute 1970–1989 PARE** | | | | | | | | | | |
| 3a. Per capita GDP | 239 | 222 | 212 | 230 | 236 | 243 | 251 | 234 | 247 | 242 |
| 3b. GDP | 3 259 | 3 101 | 3 047 | 3 392 | 3 554 | 3 741 | 3 928 | 3 730 | 3 981 | 3 903 |
| 3c. % of GWP | 0.05 | 0.04 | 0.04 | 0.04 | 0.04 | 0.04 | 0.04 | 0.04 | 0.04 | 0.04 |
| **4. Relative 1970–1989 PARE** | | | | | | | | | | |
| 4a. Per capita GDP | 117 | 114 | 114 | 132 | 147 | 167 | 183 | 182 | 206 | 219 |
| 4b. GDP | 1 589 | 1 590 | 1 633 | 1 939 | 2 216 | 2 563 | 2 859 | 2 898 | 3 319 | 3 545 |
| 4c. % of GWP | 0.05 | 0.04 | 0.04 | 0.04 | 0.04 | 0.04 | 0.04 | 0.04 | 0.04 | 0.04 |
| **5. Absolute 1980–1989 PARE** | | | | | | | | | | |
| 5a. Per capita GDP | 312 | 289 | 277 | 301 | 308 | 317 | 327 | 306 | 323 | 315 |
| 5b. GDP | 4 252 | 4 046 | 3 976 | 4 426 | 4 638 | 4 882 | 5 126 | 4 867 | 5 195 | 5 093 |
| 5c. % of GWP | 0.05 | 0.04 | 0.04 | 0.04 | 0.04 | 0.05 | 0.05 | 0.04 | 0.04 | 0.04 |
| **6. WA[a]** | | | | | | | | | | |
| 6a. Per capita GDP | 93 | 94 | 102 | 121 | 137 | 147 | 163 | 161 | 181 | 203 |
| 6b. GDP | 1 263 | 1 314 | 1 469 | 1 781 | 2 066 | 2 261 | 2 553 | 2 565 | 2 917 | 3 273 |
| 6c. % of GWP | 0.04 | 0.04 | 0.04 | 0.04 | 0.04 | 0.04 | 0.04 | 0.03 | 0.03 | 0.03 |
| **Albania** | | | | | | | | | | |
| **1. MER** | | | | | | | | | | |
| 1a. Per capita GDP | 421 | 505 | 551 | 601 | 657 | 722 | 748 | 779 | 809 | 843 |
| 1b. GDP | 900 | 1 109 | 1 241 | 1 390 | 1 557 | 1 751 | 1 853 | 1 967 | 2 081 | 2 208 |
| 1c. % of GWP | 0.03 | 0.03 | 0.03 | 0.03 | 0.03 | 0.03 | 0.03 | 0.03 | 0.02 | 0.02 |
| **2. PPPs** | | | | | | | | | | |
| 2a. Per capita GDP | ... | ... | ... | ... | ... | ... | ... | ... | ... | ... |
| 2b. GDP | ... | ... | ... | ... | ... | ... | ... | ... | ... | ... |
| 2c. % of GWP | ... | ... | ... | ... | ... | ... | ... | ... | ... | ... |
| **3. Absolute 1970–1989 PARE** | | | | | | | | | | |
| 3a. Per capita GDP | 598 | 623 | 661 | 716 | 684 | 708 | 742 | 774 | 811 | 842 |
| 3b. GDP | 1 279 | 1 369 | 1 491 | 1 655 | 1 621 | 1 716 | 1 838 | 1 955 | 2 085 | 2 205 |
| 3c. % of GWP | 0.02 | 0.02 | 0.02 | 0.02 | 0.02 | 0.02 | 0.02 | 0.02 | 0.02 | 0.02 |
| **4. Relative 1970–1989 PARE** | | | | | | | | | | |
| 4a. Per capita GDP | 292 | 320 | 355 | 409 | 427 | 485 | 540 | 602 | 676 | 764 |
| 4b. GDP | 624 | 702 | 799 | 946 | 1 011 | 1 176 | 1 338 | 1 519 | 1 738 | 2 003 |
| 4c. % of GWP | 0.02 | 0.02 | 0.02 | 0.02 | 0.02 | 0.02 | 0.02 | 0.02 | 0.02 | 0.02 |
| **5. Absolute 1980–1989 PARE** | | | | | | | | | | |
| 5a. Per capita GDP | 624 | 650 | 690 | 746 | 713 | 738 | 774 | 808 | 846 | 878 |
| 5b. GDP | 1 334 | 1 428 | 1 555 | 1 726 | 1 691 | 1 790 | 1 917 | 2 039 | 2 175 | 2 300 |
| 5c. % of GWP | 0.02 | 0.02 | 0.02 | 0.02 | 0.02 | 0.02 | 0.02 | 0.02 | 0.02 | 0.02 |
| **6. WA[a]** | | | | | | | | | | |
| 6a. Per capita GDP | 389 | 447 | 514 | 592 | 598 | 661 | 739 | 783 | 814 | 843 |
| 6b. GDP | 833 | 981 | 1 160 | 1 369 | 1 417 | 1 603 | 1 830 | 1 977 | 2 094 | 2 209 |
| 6c. % of GWP | 0.03 | 0.03 | 0.03 | 0.03 | 0.03 | 0.03 | 0.03 | 0.03 | 0.02 | 0.02 |

| | | | | | | | | | | Averages | | |
|---|---|---|---|---|---|---|---|---|---|---|---|---|
| 1980 (11) | 1981 (12) | 1982 (13) | 1983 (14) | 1984 (15) | 1985 (16) | 1986 (17) | 1987 (18) | 1988 (19) | 1989 (20) | 1970–89 (21) | 1970–79 (22) | 1980–89 (23) |
| 240 | 233 | 248 | 263 | 294 | 335 | 348 | 371 | 453 | 588 | 232 | 156 | 350 |
| 3 852 | 3 678 | 3 834 | 3 945 | 4 318 | 4 862 | 5 059 | 5 455 | 6 840 | 9 233 | 3 739 | 2 370 | 5 108 |
| 0.03 | 0.03 | 0.03 | 0.03 | 0.04 | 0.04 | 0.03 | 0.03 | 0.04 | 0.05 | 0.04 | 0.04 | 0.04 |
| 677 | 676 | 706 | 761 | 793 | 804 | 845 | 770 | 719 | 670 | 548 | 423 | 768 |
| 10 877 | 10 686 | 10 904 | 11 438 | 11 648 | 11 672 | 12 271 | 11 328 | 10 849 | 10 523 | 8 831 | 6 442 | 11 220 |
| ... | ... | ... | ... | ... | ... | ... | ... | ... | ... | ... | ... | ... |
| 234 | 243 | 254 | 273 | 285 | 289 | 297 | 264 | 238 | 213 | 232 | 234 | 268 |
| 3 758 | 3 839 | 3 917 | 4 110 | 4 185 | 4 193 | 4 322 | 3 878 | 3 593 | 3 348 | 3 739 | 3 564 | 3 914 |
| 0.04 | 0.04 | 0.04 | 0.04 | 0.04 | 0.04 | 0.04 | 0.03 | 0.03 | 0.02 | 0.04 | 0.04 | 0.03 |
| 232 | 263 | 293 | 327 | 352 | 367 | 385 | 351 | 328 | 306 | 225 | 159 | 331 |
| 3 725 | 4 165 | 4 525 | 4 908 | 5 177 | 5 327 | 5 601 | 5 170 | 4 952 | 4 803 | 3 625 | 2 415 | 4 835 |
| 0.04 | 0.04 | 0.04 | 0.04 | 0.04 | 0.04 | 0.04 | 0.03 | 0.03 | 0.02 | 0.04 | 0.04 | 0.03 |
| 305 | 317 | 331 | 357 | 372 | 377 | 388 | 344 | 311 | 278 | 303 | 305 | 350 |
| 4 904 | 5 009 | 5 111 | 5 362 | 5 461 | 5 472 | 5 639 | 5 060 | 4 689 | 4 369 | 4 879 | 4 650 | 5 108 |
| 0.04 | 0.04 | 0.04 | 0.04 | 0.04 | 0.04 | 0.04 | 0.03 | 0.03 | 0.03 | 0.04 | 0.04 | 0.04 |
| 219 | 243 | 250 | 264 | 282 | 302 | 332 | 326 | 342 | 400 | 206 | 141 | 307 |
| 3 524 | 3 846 | 3 864 | 3 968 | 4 140 | 4 378 | 4 827 | 4 792 | 5 157 | 6 282 | 3 312 | 2 146 | 4 478 |
| 0.03 | 0.03 | 0.03 | 0.03 | 0.03 | 0.03 | 0.03 | 0.03 | 0.03 | 0.03 | 0.03 | 0.04 | 0.03 |
| 888 | 896 | 904 | 919 | 952 | 964 | 978 | 1 001 | 1 005 | 1 038 | 834 | 670 | 957 |
| 2 373 | 2 444 | 2 518 | 2 614 | 2 766 | 2 855 | 2 955 | 3 080 | 3 150 | 3 310 | 2 206 | 1 606 | 2 807 |
| 0.02 | 0.02 | 0.02 | 0.02 | 0.02 | 0.02 | 0.02 | 0.02 | 0.02 | 0.02 | 0.02 | 0.03 | 0.02 |
| ... | ... | ... | ... | ... | ... | ... | ... | ... | ... | ... | ... | ... |
| ... | ... | ... | ... | ... | ... | ... | ... | ... | ... | ... | ... | ... |
| ... | ... | ... | ... | ... | ... | ... | ... | ... | ... | ... | ... | ... |
| 877 | 885 | 894 | 901 | 909 | 904 | 947 | 947 | 949 | 951 | 834 | 718 | 917 |
| 2 345 | 2 414 | 2 488 | 2 561 | 2 639 | 2 678 | 2 860 | 2 916 | 2 973 | 3 034 | 2 206 | 1 721 | 2 691 |
| 0.02 | 0.02 | 0.02 | 0.02 | 0.02 | 0.02 | 0.02 | 0.02 | 0.02 | 0.02 | 0.02 | 0.02 | 0.02 |
| 870 | 960 | 1 032 | 1 076 | 1 124 | 1 148 | 1 227 | 1 263 | 1 307 | 1 364 | 859 | 494 | 1 145 |
| 2 324 | 2 619 | 2 873 | 3 059 | 3 265 | 3 402 | 3 706 | 3 888 | 4 096 | 4 352 | 2 272 | 1 186 | 3 359 |
| 0.02 | 0.02 | 0.02 | 0.02 | 0.02 | 0.02 | 0.02 | 0.02 | 0.02 | 0.02 | 0.02 | 0.02 | 0.02 |
| 915 | 923 | 932 | 939 | 948 | 943 | 987 | 988 | 989 | 992 | 870 | 749 | 957 |
| 2 445 | 2 517 | 2 595 | 2 672 | 2 753 | 2 793 | 2 983 | 3 042 | 3 101 | 3 165 | 2 301 | 1 796 | 2 806 |
| 0.02 | 0.02 | 0.02 | 0.02 | 0.02 | 0.02 | 0.02 | 0.02 | 0.02 | 0.02 | 0.02 | 0.02 | 0.02 |
| 881 | 893 | 905 | 914 | 933 | 944 | 993 | 996 | 996 | 1 016 | 818 | 645 | 949 |
| 2 353 | 2 434 | 2 518 | 2 600 | 2 710 | 2 797 | 3 000 | 3 067 | 3 120 | 3 243 | 2 166 | 1 547 | 2 784 |
| 0.02 | 0.02 | 0.02 | 0.02 | 0.02 | 0.02 | 0.02 | 0.02 | 0.02 | 0.02 | 0.02 | 0.03 | 0.02 |

**Table A.1** Total and per capita gross domestic product of individual countries or areas, expressed in United States dollars, and their individual shares of gross world product, based on alternative conversion rates, 1970−1989 [*cont.*]

| Country or area | 1970 (1) | 1971 (2) | 1972 (3) | 1973 (4) | 1974 (5) | 1975 (6) | 1976 (7) | 1977 (8) | 1978 (9) | 1979 (10) |
|---|---|---|---|---|---|---|---|---|---|---|
| **Algeria** | | | | | | | | | | |
| **1.    MER** | | | | | | | | | | |
| 1a.   Per capita GDP | 376 | 379 | 492 | 615 | 856 | 973 | 1 076 | 1 233 | 1 502 | 1 832 |
| 1b.   GDP | 5 167 | 5 375 | 7 187 | 9 259 | 13 289 | 15 592 | 17 789 | 21 037 | 26 433 | 33 279 |
| 1c.   % of GWP | 0.16 | 0.15 | 0.18 | 0.19 | 0.24 | 0.25 | 0.27 | 0.28 | 0.29 | 0.32 |
| **2.    PPPs** | | | | | | | | | | |
| 2a.   Per capita GDP | 505 | 520 | 593 | 656 | 969 | 1 009 | 1 134 | 1 243 | 1 321 | 1 638 |
| 2b.   GDP | 6 943 | 7 367 | 8 658 | 9 879 | 15 050 | 16 158 | 18 743 | 21 209 | 23 254 | 29 758 |
| 2c.   % of GWP | ... | ... | ... | ... | ... | ... | ... | ... | ... | ... |
| **3.    Absolute 1970−1989 PARE** | | | | | | | | | | |
| 3a.   Per capita GDP | 1 392 | 1 222 | 1 449 | 1 466 | 1 475 | 1 513 | 1 557 | 1 651 | 1 763 | 1 831 |
| 3b.   GDP | 19 130 | 17 308 | 21 159 | 22 074 | 22 905 | 24 240 | 25 740 | 28 163 | 31 028 | 33 264 |
| 3c.   % of GWP | 0.27 | 0.23 | 0.27 | 0.27 | 0.27 | 0.28 | 0.28 | 0.30 | 0.32 | 0.33 |
| **4.    Relative 1970−1989 PARE** | | | | | | | | | | |
| 4a.   Per capita GDP | 678 | 626 | 777 | 838 | 920 | 1 037 | 1 134 | 1 283 | 1 469 | 1 663 |
| 4b.   GDP | 9 327 | 8 872 | 11 343 | 12 620 | 14 284 | 16 607 | 18 737 | 21 883 | 25 868 | 30 208 |
| 4c.   % of GWP | 0.27 | 0.23 | 0.27 | 0.27 | 0.27 | 0.28 | 0.28 | 0.30 | 0.32 | 0.33 |
| **5.    Absolute 1980−1989 PARE** | | | | | | | | | | |
| 5a.   Per capita GDP | 1 686 | 1 480 | 1 756 | 1 776 | 1 787 | 1 834 | 1 887 | 2 000 | 2 136 | 2 219 |
| 5b.   GDP | 23 179 | 20 972 | 25 638 | 26 746 | 27 754 | 29 371 | 31 189 | 34 124 | 37 596 | 40 305 |
| 5c.   % of GWP | 0.27 | 0.23 | 0.27 | 0.26 | 0.27 | 0.28 | 0.28 | 0.30 | 0.31 | 0.33 |
| **6.    WA** | | | | | | | | | | |
| 6a.   Per capita GDP | 376 | 379 | 492 | 615 | 856 | 973 | 1 076 | 1 233 | 1 502 | 1 832 |
| 6b.   GDP | 5 167 | 5 376 | 7 187 | 9 258 | 13 290 | 15 591 | 17 790 | 21 038 | 26 433 | 33 276 |
| 6c.   % of GWP | 0.16 | 0.15 | 0.18 | 0.19 | 0.24 | 0.25 | 0.27 | 0.28 | 0.30 | 0.33 |
| **Angola** | | | | | | | | | | |
| **1.    MER** | | | | | | | | | | |
| 1a.   Per capita GDP | 162 | 169 | 188 | 254 | 307 | 229 | 255 | 267 | 305 | 347 |
| 1b.   GDP | 904 | 968 | 1 107 | 1 550 | 1 935 | 1 494 | 1 719 | 1 867 | 2 213 | 2 601 |
| 1c.   % of GWP | 0.03 | 0.03 | 0.03 | 0.03 | 0.03 | 0.02 | 0.03 | 0.02 | 0.02 | 0.03 |
| **2.    PPPs** | | | | | | | | | | |
| 2a.   Per capita GDP | 296 | 306 | 305 | 356 | 391 | 276 | 250 | 265 | 285 | 306 |
| 2b.   GDP | 1 654 | 1 755 | 1 797 | 2 170 | 2 464 | 1 801 | 1 690 | 1 853 | 2 066 | 2 296 |
| 2c.   % of GWP | ... | ... | ... | ... | ... | ... | ... | ... | ... | ... |
| **3.    Absolute 1970−1989 PARE** | | | | | | | | | | |
| 3a.   Per capita GDP | 746 | 736 | 726 | 751 | 690 | 411 | 356 | 351 | 354 | 350 |
| 3b.   GDP | 4 170 | 4 219 | 4 282 | 4 574 | 4 345 | 2 679 | 2 404 | 2 460 | 2 565 | 2 624 |
| 3c.   % of GWP | 0.06 | 0.06 | 0.05 | 0.06 | 0.05 | 0.03 | 0.03 | 0.03 | 0.03 | 0.03 |
| **4.    Relative 1970−1989 PARE** | | | | | | | | | | |
| 4a.   Per capita GDP | 364 | 377 | 389 | 429 | 430 | 281 | 259 | 273 | 295 | 318 |
| 4b.   GDP | 2 033 | 2 163 | 2 295 | 2 615 | 2 710 | 1 835 | 1 750 | 1 912 | 2 139 | 2 383 |
| 4c.   % of GWP | 0.06 | 0.06 | 0.05 | 0.06 | 0.05 | 0.03 | 0.03 | 0.03 | 0.03 | 0.03 |
| **5.    Absolute 1980−1989 PARE** | | | | | | | | | | |
| 5a.   Per capita GDP | 1 173 | 1 157 | 1 141 | 1 180 | 1 084 | 646 | 560 | 553 | 556 | 551 |
| 5b.   GDP | 6 555 | 6 632 | 6 730 | 7 190 | 6 831 | 4 211 | 3 779 | 3 867 | 4 032 | 4 125 |
| 5c.   % of GWP | 0.08 | 0.07 | 0.07 | 0.07 | 0.07 | 0.04 | 0.03 | 0.03 | 0.03 | 0.03 |
| **6.    WA**[a] | | | | | | | | | | |
| 6a.   Per capita GDP | 137 | 154 | 170 | 202 | 228 | 176 | 196 | 234 | 274 | 301 |
| 6b.   GDP | 765 | 881 | 1 000 | 1 228 | 1 438 | 1 150 | 1 327 | 1 637 | 1 986 | 2 259 |
| 6c.   % of GWP | 0.02 | 0.03 | 0.02 | 0.03 | 0.03 | 0.02 | 0.02 | 0.02 | 0.02 | 0.02 |

|  |  |  |  |  |  |  |  |  |  | Averages | | |
| 1980 (11) | 1981 (12) | 1982 (13) | 1983 (14) | 1984 (15) | 1985 (16) | 1986 (17) | 1987 (18) | 1988 (19) | 1989 (20) | 1970−89 (21) | 1970−79 (22) | 1980−89 (23) |
|---|---|---|---|---|---|---|---|---|---|---|---|---|
| 2 259 | 2 295 | 2 267 | 2 375 | 2 464 | 2 623 | 2 721 | 2 786 | 2 294 | 2 027 | 1 824 | 979 | 2 414 |
| 42 342 | 44 363 | 45 199 | 48 810 | 52 157 | 57 160 | 60 957 | 64 146 | 54 237 | 49 233 | 33 651 | 15 441 | 51 860 |
| 0.37 | 0.38 | 0.39 | 0.41 | 0.43 | 0.45 | 0.41 | 0.37 | 0.28 | 0.25 | 0.33 | 0.25 | 0.36 |
| 2 001 | 2 172 | 2 174 | 2 136 | 2 516 | 2 548 | 2 604 | 2 511 | 2 595 | 2 708 | 1 831 | 995 | 2 415 |
| 37 494 | 41 978 | 43 339 | 43 898 | 53 271 | 55 522 | 58 337 | 57 812 | 61 369 | 65 767 | 33 790 | 15 702 | 51 879 |
| ... | ... | ... | ... | ... | ... | ... | ... | ... | ... | ... | ... | ... |
| 1 909 | 1 897 | 1 957 | 1 997 | 2 048 | 2 093 | 2 096 | 1 965 | 1 965 | 1 969 | 1 824 | 1 553 | 1 993 |
| 35 782 | 36 675 | 39 023 | 41 049 | 43 351 | 45 600 | 46 968 | 45 246 | 46 469 | 47 838 | 33 651 | 24 501 | 42 800 |
| 0.34 | 0.35 | 0.37 | 0.37 | 0.38 | 0.38 | 0.38 | 0.36 | 0.35 | 0.35 | 0.33 | 0.28 | 0.36 |
| 1 893 | 2 059 | 2 261 | 2 385 | 2 533 | 2 659 | 2 717 | 2 620 | 2 708 | 2 825 | 1 909 | 1 076 | 2 490 |
| 35 469 | 39 795 | 45 077 | 49 020 | 53 623 | 57 933 | 60 871 | 60 323 | 64 034 | 68 623 | 35 226 | 16 975 | 53 477 |
| 0.34 | 0.35 | 0.37 | 0.37 | 0.38 | 0.38 | 0.38 | 0.36 | 0.35 | 0.35 | 0.34 | 0.29 | 0.36 |
| 2 313 | 2 299 | 2 372 | 2 420 | 2 481 | 2 536 | 2 540 | 2 381 | 2 381 | 2 386 | 2 210 | 1 882 | 2 414 |
| 43 357 | 44 439 | 47 284 | 49 738 | 52 527 | 55 253 | 56 911 | 54 824 | 56 306 | 57 965 | 40 774 | 29 688 | 51 860 |
| 0.34 | 0.34 | 0.36 | 0.37 | 0.38 | 0.38 | 0.38 | 0.36 | 0.35 | 0.35 | 0.33 | 0.28 | 0.36 |
| 2 260 | 2 295 | 2 267 | 2 375 | 2 464 | 2 624 | 2 720 | 2 758 | 2 288 | 2 024 | 1 821 | 979 | 2 410 |
| 42 347 | 44 365 | 45 197 | 48 812 | 52 153 | 57 162 | 60 932 | 63 485 | 54 102 | 49 175 | 33 607 | 15 441 | 51 773 |
| 0.37 | 0.38 | 0.39 | 0.41 | 0.43 | 0.45 | 0.41 | 0.38 | 0.29 | 0.25 | 0.33 | 0.25 | 0.37 |
| 449 | 462 | 495 | 508 | 556 | 554 | 583 | 633 | 663 | 717 | 432 | 255 | 571 |
| 3 467 | 3 671 | 4 032 | 4 235 | 4 746 | 4 853 | 5 240 | 5 843 | 6 291 | 6 990 | 3 286 | 1 636 | 4 937 |
| 0.03 | 0.03 | 0.03 | 0.04 | 0.04 | 0.04 | 0.04 | 0.03 | 0.03 | 0.03 | 0.03 | 0.03 | 0.03 |
| 375 | 386 | 408 | 417 | 387 | 299 | 309 | 320 | 334 | 342 | 332 | 305 | 358 |
| 2 894 | 3 066 | 3 325 | 3 475 | 3 306 | 2 617 | 2 779 | 2 953 | 3 164 | 3 336 | 2 523 | 1 955 | 3 092 |
| ... | ... | ... | ... | ... | ... | ... | ... | ... | ... | ... | ... | ... |
| 359 | 342 | 352 | 349 | 356 | 365 | 370 | 372 | 375 | 370 | 432 | 535 | 363 |
| 2 771 | 2 718 | 2 862 | 2 908 | 3 039 | 3 191 | 3 323 | 3 432 | 3 558 | 3 604 | 3 286 | 3 432 | 3 140 |
| 0.03 | 0.03 | 0.03 | 0.03 | 0.03 | 0.03 | 0.03 | 0.03 | 0.03 | 0.03 | 0.03 | 0.04 | 0.03 |
| 356 | 371 | 406 | 416 | 440 | 463 | 479 | 496 | 517 | 530 | 401 | 341 | 454 |
| 2 747 | 2 949 | 3 306 | 3 472 | 3 759 | 4 054 | 4 306 | 4 575 | 4 903 | 5 169 | 3 054 | 2 183 | 3 924 |
| 0.03 | 0.03 | 0.03 | 0.03 | 0.03 | 0.03 | 0.03 | 0.03 | 0.03 | 0.03 | 0.03 | 0.04 | 0.03 |
| 564 | 538 | 553 | 548 | 559 | 573 | 581 | 585 | 590 | 581 | 679 | 842 | 571 |
| 4 356 | 4 272 | 4 498 | 4 571 | 4 778 | 5 016 | 5 223 | 5 395 | 5 593 | 5 665 | 5 166 | 5 395 | 4 937 |
| 0.03 | 0.03 | 0.03 | 0.03 | 0.03 | 0.03 | 0.04 | 0.04 | 0.03 | 0.03 | 0.04 | 0.05 | 0.03 |
| 363 | 403 | 469 | 490 | 524 | 551 | 574 | 594 | 630 | 665 | 394 | 213 | 535 |
| 2 802 | 3 200 | 3 817 | 4 082 | 4 477 | 4 824 | 5 159 | 5 479 | 5 973 | 6 479 | 2 998 | 1 367 | 4 629 |
| 0.02 | 0.03 | 0.03 | 0.03 | 0.04 | 0.04 | 0.04 | 0.03 | 0.03 | 0.03 | 0.03 | 0.02 | 0.03 |

**Table A.1**    Total and per capita gross domestic product of individual countries or areas,
expressed in United States dollars, and their individual shares of gross world
product, based on alternative conversion rates, 1970–1989 [*cont.*]

| Country or area | 1970 (1) | 1971 (2) | 1972 (3) | 1973 (4) | 1974 (5) | 1975 (6) | 1976 (7) | 1977 (8) | 1978 (9) | 1979 (10) |
|---|---|---|---|---|---|---|---|---|---|---|
| **Anguilla** | | | | | | | | | | |
| **1.   MER** | | | | | | | | | | |
| 1a.   Per capita GDP | 343 | 402 | 475 | 537 | 591 | 646 | 618 | 691 | 798 | 920 |
| 1b.   GDP | 2 | 3 | 3 | 4 | 4 | 5 | 4 | 5 | 6 | 6 |
| 1c.   % of GWP | 0.00 | 0.00 | 0.00 | 0.00 | 0.00 | 0.00 | 0.00 | 0.00 | 0.00 | 0.00 |
| **2.   PPPs** | | | | | | | | | | |
| 2a.   Per capita GDP | ... | ... | ... | ... | ... | ... | ... | ... | ... | ... |
| 2b.   GDP | ... | ... | ... | ... | ... | ... | ... | ... | ... | ... |
| 2c.   % of GWP | ... | ... | ... | ... | ... | ... | ... | ... | ... | ... |
| **3.   Absolute 1970–1989 PARE** | | | | | | | | | | |
| 3a.   Per capita GDP | 486 | 542 | 598 | 673 | 729 | 822 | 916 | 1 009 | 1 121 | 1 252 |
| 3b.   GDP | 3 | 4 | 4 | 5 | 5 | 6 | 6 | 7 | 8 | 9 |
| 3c.   % of GWP | 0.00 | 0.00 | 0.00 | 0.00 | 0.00 | 0.00 | 0.00 | 0.00 | 0.00 | 0.00 |
| **4.   Relative 1970–1989 PARE** | | | | | | | | | | |
| 4a.   Per capita GDP | 237 | 278 | 321 | 385 | 454 | 563 | 666 | 784 | 935 | 1 137 |
| 4b.   GDP | 2 | 2 | 2 | 3 | 3 | 4 | 5 | 5 | 7 | 8 |
| 4c.   % of GWP | 0.00 | 0.00 | 0.00 | 0.00 | 0.00 | 0.00 | 0.00 | 0.00 | 0.00 | 0.00 |
| **5.   Absolute 1980–1989 PARE** | | | | | | | | | | |
| 5a.   Per capita GDP | 530 | 591 | 652 | 734 | 795 | 897 | 999 | 1 101 | 1 223 | 1 366 |
| 5b.   GDP | 4 | 4 | 5 | 5 | 6 | 6 | 7 | 8 | 9 | 10 |
| 5c.   % of GWP | 0.00 | 0.00 | 0.00 | 0.00 | 0.00 | 0.00 | 0.00 | 0.00 | 0.00 | 0.00 |
| **6.   WA[a]** | | | | | | | | | | |
| 6a.   Per capita GDP | 329 | 383 | 446 | 523 | 584 | 656 | 689 | 718 | 774 | 889 |
| 6b.   GDP | 2 | 3 | 3 | 4 | 4 | 5 | 5 | 5 | 5 | 6 |
| 6c.   % of GWP | 0.00 | 0.00 | 0.00 | 0.00 | 0.00 | 0.00 | 0.00 | 0.00 | 0.00 | 0.00 |
| **Antigua and Barbuda** | | | | | | | | | | |
| **1.   MER** | | | | | | | | | | |
| 1a.   Per capita GDP | 739 | 775 | 890 | 930 | 977 | 985 | 807 | 907 | 1 012 | 1 230 |
| 1b.   GDP | 49 | 52 | 60 | 64 | 68 | 70 | 58 | 66 | 75 | 92 |
| 1c.   % of GWP | 0.00 | 0.00 | 0.00 | 0.00 | 0.00 | 0.00 | 0.00 | 0.00 | 0.00 | 0.00 |
| **2.   PPPs** | | | | | | | | | | |
| 2a.   Per capita GDP | ... | ... | ... | ... | ... | ... | ... | ... | ... | ... |
| 2b.   GDP | ... | ... | ... | ... | ... | ... | ... | ... | ... | ... |
| 2c.   % of GWP | ... | ... | ... | ... | ... | ... | ... | ... | ... | ... |
| **3.   Absolute 1970–1989 PARE** | | | | | | | | | | |
| 3a.   Per capita GDP | 1 451 | 1 393 | 1 461 | 1 388 | 1 415 | 1 319 | 1 184 | 1 253 | 1 279 | 1 398 |
| 3b.   GDP | 96 | 93 | 99 | 96 | 99 | 94 | 85 | 91 | 95 | 105 |
| 3c.   % of GWP | 0.00 | 0.00 | 0.00 | 0.00 | 0.00 | 0.00 | 0.00 | 0.00 | 0.00 | 0.00 |
| **4.   Relative 1970–1989 PARE** | | | | | | | | | | |
| 4a.   Per capita GDP | 708 | 714 | 783 | 794 | 882 | 903 | 862 | 973 | 1 067 | 1 270 |
| 4b.   GDP | 47 | 48 | 53 | 55 | 62 | 64 | 62 | 71 | 79 | 95 |
| 4c.   % of GWP | 0.00 | 0.00 | 0.00 | 0.00 | 0.00 | 0.00 | 0.00 | 0.00 | 0.00 | 0.00 |
| **5.   Absolute 1980–1989 PARE** | | | | | | | | | | |
| 5a.   Per capita GDP | 1 747 | 1 676 | 1 759 | 1 671 | 1 703 | 1 587 | 1 425 | 1 508 | 1 540 | 1 683 |
| 5b.   GDP | 115 | 112 | 120 | 115 | 119 | 113 | 103 | 110 | 114 | 126 |
| 5c.   % of GWP | 0.00 | 0.00 | 0.00 | 0.00 | 0.00 | 0.00 | 0.00 | 0.00 | 0.00 | 0.00 |
| **6.   WA** | | | | | | | | | | |
| 6a.   Per capita GDP | 739 | 771 | 890 | 930 | 977 | 985 | 808 | 907 | 1 012 | 1 230 |
| 6b.   GDP | 49 | 52 | 61 | 64 | 68 | 70 | 58 | 66 | 75 | 92 |
| 6c.   % of GWP | 0.00 | 0.00 | 0.00 | 0.00 | 0.00 | 0.00 | 0.00 | 0.00 | 0.00 | 0.00 |

| | | | | | | | | | | Averages | | |
|---|---|---|---|---|---|---|---|---|---|---|---|---|
| 1980 | 1981 | 1982 | 1983 | 1984 | 1985 | 1986 | 1987 | 1988 | 1989 | 1970–89 | 1970–79 | 1980–89 |
| (11) | (12) | (13) | (14) | (15) | (16) | (17) | (18) | (19) | (20) | (21) | (22) | (23) |
| 1 062 | 1 226 | 1 414 | 1 632 | 1 884 | 2 406 | 3 039 | 3 189 | 3 746 | 4 279 | 1 575 | 602 | 2 548 |
| 7 | 9 | 10 | 11 | 13 | 17 | 21 | 26 | 30 | 34 | 11 | 4 | 18 |
| 0.00 | 0.00 | 0.00 | 0.00 | 0.00 | 0.00 | 0.00 | 0.00 | 0.00 | 0.00 | 0.00 | 0.00 | 0.00 |
| ... | ... | ... | ... | ... | ... | ... | ... | ... | ... | ... | ... | ... |
| ... | ... | ... | ... | ... | ... | ... | ... | ... | ... | ... | ... | ... |
| ... | ... | ... | ... | ... | ... | ... | ... | ... | ... | ... | ... | ... |
| 1 383 | 1 551 | 1 719 | 1 906 | 2 111 | 2 317 | 2 634 | 2 583 | 2 894 | 3 041 | 1 575 | 815 | 2 335 |
| 10 | 11 | 12 | 13 | 15 | 16 | 18 | 21 | 23 | 24 | 11 | 6 | 16 |
| 0.00 | 0.00 | 0.00 | 0.00 | 0.00 | 0.00 | 0.00 | 0.00 | 0.00 | 0.00 | 0.00 | 0.00 | 0.00 |
| 1 371 | 1 683 | 1 986 | 2 276 | 2 612 | 2 943 | 3 414 | 3 444 | 3 987 | 4 362 | 1 776 | 576 | 2 976 |
| 10 | 12 | 14 | 16 | 18 | 21 | 24 | 28 | 32 | 35 | 12 | 4 | 21 |
| 0.00 | 0.00 | 0.00 | 0.00 | 0.00 | 0.00 | 0.00 | 0.00 | 0.00 | 0.00 | 0.00 | 0.00 | 0.00 |
| 1 508 | 1 692 | 1 875 | 2 079 | 2 303 | 2 528 | 2 874 | 2 818 | 3 157 | 3 317 | 1 718 | 889 | 2 548 |
| 11 | 12 | 13 | 15 | 16 | 18 | 20 | 23 | 25 | 27 | 12 | 6 | 18 |
| 0.00 | 0.00 | 0.00 | 0.00 | 0.00 | 0.00 | 0.00 | 0.00 | 0.00 | 0.00 | 0.00 | 0.00 | 0.00 |
| 1 020 | 1 185 | 1 363 | 1 567 | 1 808 | 2 138 | 2 678 | 2 936 | 3 544 | 3 978 | 1 485 | 599 | 2 371 |
| 7 | 8 | 10 | 11 | 13 | 15 | 19 | 23 | 28 | 32 | 10 | 4 | 17 |
| 0.00 | 0.00 | 0.00 | 0.00 | 0.00 | 0.00 | 0.00 | 0.00 | 0.00 | 0.00 | 0.00 | 0.00 | 0.00 |
| 1 253 | 1 410 | 1 545 | 1 735 | 1 966 | 2 265 | 2 561 | 3 002 | 3 562 | 3 810 | 1 602 | 929 | 2 321 |
| 95 | 107 | 117 | 132 | 149 | 172 | 195 | 228 | 274 | 293 | 121 | 66 | 176 |
| 0.00 | 0.00 | 0.00 | 0.00 | 0.00 | 0.00 | 0.00 | 0.00 | 0.00 | 0.00 | 0.00 | 0.00 | 0.00 |
| ... | ... | ... | ... | ... | ... | ... | ... | ... | ... | ... | ... | ... |
| ... | ... | ... | ... | ... | ... | ... | ... | ... | ... | ... | ... | ... |
| ... | ... | ... | ... | ... | ... | ... | ... | ... | ... | ... | ... | ... |
| 1 473 | 1 545 | 1 551 | 1 658 | 1 781 | 1 919 | 2 081 | 2 262 | 2 402 | 2 551 | 1 602 | 1 352 | 1 929 |
| 112 | 117 | 118 | 126 | 135 | 146 | 158 | 172 | 185 | 196 | 121 | 95 | 147 |
| 0.00 | 0.00 | 0.00 | 0.00 | 0.00 | 0.00 | 0.00 | 0.00 | 0.00 | 0.00 | 0.00 | 0.00 | 0.00 |
| 1 460 | 1 677 | 1 792 | 1 979 | 2 203 | 2 438 | 2 696 | 3 016 | 3 309 | 3 659 | 1 645 | 902 | 2 432 |
| 111 | 127 | 136 | 150 | 167 | 185 | 205 | 229 | 255 | 282 | 124 | 64 | 185 |
| 0.00 | 0.00 | 0.00 | 0.00 | 0.00 | 0.00 | 0.00 | 0.00 | 0.00 | 0.00 | 0.00 | 0.00 | 0.00 |
| 1 772 | 1 860 | 1 867 | 1 995 | 2 143 | 2 309 | 2 504 | 2 722 | 2 890 | 3 069 | 1 928 | 1 627 | 2 321 |
| 135 | 141 | 142 | 152 | 163 | 176 | 190 | 207 | 223 | 236 | 146 | 115 | 176 |
| 0.00 | 0.00 | 0.00 | 0.00 | 0.00 | 0.00 | 0.00 | 0.00 | 0.00 | 0.00 | 0.00 | 0.00 | 0.00 |
| 1 253 | 1 410 | 1 545 | 1 735 | 1 966 | 2 265 | 2 561 | 3 002 | 3 562 | 3 810 | 1 602 | 929 | 2 321 |
| 95 | 107 | 117 | 132 | 149 | 172 | 195 | 228 | 274 | 293 | 121 | 65 | 176 |
| 0.00 | 0.00 | 0.00 | 0.00 | 0.00 | 0.00 | 0.00 | 0.00 | 0.00 | 0.00 | 0.00 | 0.00 | 0.00 |

**Table A.1** Total and per capita gross domestic product of individual countries or areas, expressed in United States dollars, and their individual shares of gross world product, based on alternative conversion rates, 1970–1989 [*cont.*]

| Country or area | 1970 (1) | 1971 (2) | 1972 (3) | 1973 (4) | 1974 (5) | 1975 (6) | 1976 (7) | 1977 (8) | 1978 (9) | 1979 (10) |
|---|---|---|---|---|---|---|---|---|---|---|
| **Argentina** | | | | | | | | | | |
| **1. MER** | | | | | | | | | | |
| 1a. Per capita GDP | 939 | 1 068 | 1 060 | 1 544 | 2 125 | 1 372 | 2 047 | 1 896 | 2 391 | 3 883 |
| 1b. GDP | 22 500 | 26 000 | 26 250 | 38 889 | 54 444 | 35 750 | 54 214 | 51 049 | 65 425 | 107 962 |
| 1c. % of GWP | 0.71 | 0.74 | 0.65 | 0.79 | 0.98 | 0.58 | 0.81 | 0.67 | 0.73 | 1.05 |
| **2. PPPs** | | | | | | | | | | |
| 2a. Per capita GDP | 1 995 | 2 219 | 2 265 | 2 360 | 2 762 | 2 942 | 3 010 | 3 331 | 3 336 | 3 869 |
| 2b. GDP | 47 803 | 54 026 | 56 076 | 59 441 | 70 748 | 76 634 | 79 742 | 89 701 | 91 299 | 107 578 |
| 2c. % of GWP | ... | ... | ... | ... | ... | ... | ... | ... | ... | ... |
| **3. Absolute 1970–1989 PARE** | | | | | | | | | | |
| 3a. Per capita GDP | 2 391 | 2 442 | 2 451 | 2 500 | 2 591 | 2 532 | 2 490 | 2 606 | 2 482 | 2 614 |
| 3b. GDP | 57 301 | 59 456 | 60 690 | 62 963 | 66 365 | 65 973 | 65 967 | 70 179 | 67 913 | 72 680 |
| 3c. % of GWP | 0.81 | 0.80 | 0.78 | 0.76 | 0.78 | 0.77 | 0.73 | 0.74 | 0.69 | 0.71 |
| **4. Relative 1970–1989 PARE** | | | | | | | | | | |
| 4a. Per capita GDP | 1 166 | 1 252 | 1 314 | 1 429 | 1 616 | 1 735 | 1 813 | 2 025 | 2 069 | 2 374 |
| 4b. GDP | 27 938 | 30 476 | 32 536 | 35 996 | 41 385 | 45 199 | 48 019 | 54 530 | 56 619 | 66 003 |
| 4c. % of GWP | 0.81 | 0.80 | 0.78 | 0.76 | 0.78 | 0.77 | 0.73 | 0.74 | 0.69 | 0.71 |
| **5. Absolute 1980–1989 PARE** | | | | | | | | | | |
| 5a. Per capita GDP | 2 971 | 3 034 | 3 046 | 3 107 | 3 219 | 3 147 | 3 095 | 3 238 | 3 084 | 3 248 |
| 5b. GDP | 71 206 | 73 883 | 75 417 | 78 241 | 82 469 | 81 982 | 81 974 | 87 208 | 84 392 | 90 316 |
| 5c. % of GWP | 0.82 | 0.81 | 0.79 | 0.77 | 0.80 | 0.78 | 0.74 | 0.76 | 0.70 | 0.73 |
| **6. WA** | | | | | | | | | | |
| 6a. Per capita GDP | 991 | 1 181 | 1 696 | 2 780 | 3 826 | 1 501 | 2 047 | 1 907 | 2 403 | 3 892 |
| 6b. GDP | 23 736 | 28 750 | 42 000 | 70 000 | 98 000 | 39 098 | 54 220 | 51 345 | 65 774 | 108 211 |
| 6c. % of GWP | 0.74 | 0.82 | 1.05 | 1.44 | 1.76 | 0.63 | 0.81 | 0.68 | 0.74 | 1.06 |
| **Australia** | | | | | | | | | | |
| **1. MER** | | | | | | | | | | |
| 1a. Per capita GDP | 3 133 | 3 495 | 4 109 | 5 765 | 6 936 | 7 347 | 7 728 | 7 482 | 8 662 | 9 462 |
| 1b. GDP | 39 324 | 44 651 | 53 378 | 76 118 | 93 049 | 100 127 | 106 964 | 105 155 | 123 593 | 137 032 |
| 1c. % of GWP | 1.23 | 1.28 | 1.33 | 1.55 | 1.68 | 1.61 | 1.59 | 1.39 | 1.38 | 1.33 |
| **2. PPPs** | | | | | | | | | | |
| 2a. Per capita GDP | 3 651 | 3 938 | 4 364 | 4 895 | 5 341 | 5 861 | 6 203 | 6 404 | 7 133 | 7 944 |
| 2b. GDP | 45 826 | 50 305 | 56 694 | 64 631 | 71 657 | 79 878 | 85 860 | 90 007 | 101 781 | 115 047 |
| 2c. % of GWP | ... | ... | ... | ... | ... | ... | ... | ... | ... | ... |
| **3. Absolute 1970–1989 PARE** | | | | | | | | | | |
| 3a. Per capita GDP | 8 265 | 8 566 | 8 767 | 8 984 | 9 013 | 9 079 | 9 196 | 9 147 | 9 460 | 9 542 |
| 3b. GDP | 103 743 | 109 430 | 113 892 | 118 623 | 120 916 | 123 732 | 127 278 | 128 554 | 134 983 | 138 190 |
| 3c. % of GWP | 1.46 | 1.48 | 1.46 | 1.43 | 1.43 | 1.44 | 1.41 | 1.36 | 1.37 | 1.36 |
| **4. Relative 1970–1989 PARE** | | | | | | | | | | |
| 4a. Per capita GDP | 4 030 | 4 391 | 4 700 | 5 136 | 5 620 | 6 220 | 6 694 | 7 107 | 7 887 | 8 665 |
| 4b. GDP | 50 582 | 56 092 | 61 057 | 67 818 | 75 403 | 84 770 | 92 649 | 99 889 | 112 536 | 125 496 |
| 4c. % of GWP | 1.46 | 1.48 | 1.46 | 1.43 | 1.43 | 1.44 | 1.41 | 1.36 | 1.37 | 1.36 |
| **5. Absolute 1980–1989 PARE** | | | | | | | | | | |
| 5a. Per capita GDP | 9 987 | 10 351 | 10 594 | 10 856 | 10 891 | 10 971 | 11 112 | 11 052 | 11 431 | 11 530 |
| 5b. GDP | 125 359 | 132 232 | 137 623 | 143 340 | 146 111 | 149 514 | 153 799 | 155 341 | 163 109 | 166 984 |
| 5c. % of GWP | 1.44 | 1.46 | 1.44 | 1.41 | 1.41 | 1.42 | 1.39 | 1.35 | 1.36 | 1.35 |
| **6. WA** | | | | | | | | | | |
| 6a. Per capita GDP | 3 133 | 3 445 | 4 027 | 5 199 | 7 104 | 7 654 | 7 949 | 7 740 | 8 538 | 9 619 |
| 6b. GDP | 39 330 | 44 008 | 52 314 | 68 651 | 95 303 | 104 315 | 110 019 | 108 790 | 121 832 | 139 312 |
| 6c. % of GWP | 1.23 | 1.26 | 1.31 | 1.41 | 1.71 | 1.69 | 1.64 | 1.44 | 1.37 | 1.36 |

| | | | | | | | | | | Averages | | |
|---|---|---|---|---|---|---|---|---|---|---|---|---|
| 1980 (11) | 1981 (12) | 1982 (13) | 1983 (14) | 1984 (15) | 1985 (16) | 1986 (17) | 1987 (18) | 1988 (19) | 1989 (20) | 1970−89 (21) | 1970−79 (22) | 1980−89 (23) |
| 5 454 | 4 341 | 1 959 | 2 197 | 2 608 | 2 169 | 2 572 | 2 647 | 2 828 | 1 894 | 2 437 | 1 963 | 2 850 |
| 154 005 | 124 436 | 56 993 | 64 829 | 78 049 | 65 785 | 79 053 | 82 433 | 89 181 | 60 473 | 66 886 | 48 248 | 85 524 |
| 1.33 | 1.06 | 0.49 | 0.55 | 0.64 | 0.52 | 0.53 | 0.48 | 0.47 | 0.30 | 0.66 | 0.79 | 0.60 |
| 4 353 | 4 303 | 3 945 | 3 974 | 4 465 | 4 182 | 4 444 | 4 611 | 4 579 | 4 499 | 3 640 | 2 838 | 4 338 |
| 122 924 | 123 353 | 114 748 | 117 253 | 133 599 | 126 851 | 136 610 | 143 593 | 144 398 | 143 652 | 102 002 | 73 305 | 130 698 |
| ... | ... | ... | ... | ... | ... | ... | ... | ... | ... | ... | ... | ... |
| 2 611 | 2 403 | 2 251 | 2 286 | 2 314 | 2 183 | 2 274 | 2 294 | 2 204 | 2 080 | 2 437 | 2 642 | 2 293 |
| 73 737 | 68 873 | 65 470 | 67 442 | 69 232 | 66 221 | 69 911 | 71 432 | 69 499 | 66 417 | 66 886 | 64 949 | 68 824 |
| 0.71 | 0.65 | 0.61 | 0.61 | 0.60 | 0.56 | 0.57 | 0.57 | 0.53 | 0.49 | 0.66 | 0.75 | 0.59 |
| 2 588 | 2 607 | 2 600 | 2 729 | 2 862 | 2 774 | 2 948 | 3 058 | 3 037 | 2 984 | 2 301 | 1 698 | 2 824 |
| 73 093 | 74 730 | 75 627 | 80 538 | 85 636 | 84 132 | 90 604 | 95 236 | 95 770 | 95 275 | 64 467 | 43 870 | 85 064 |
| 0.71 | 0.65 | 0.61 | 0.61 | 0.60 | 0.56 | 0.57 | 0.57 | 0.53 | 0.49 | 0.63 | 0.75 | 0.58 |
| 3 245 | 2 986 | 2 797 | 2 840 | 2 875 | 2 713 | 2 826 | 2 851 | 2 739 | 2 585 | 3 028 | 3 284 | 2 850 |
| 91 630 | 85 585 | 81 357 | 83 808 | 86 031 | 82 290 | 86 875 | 88 766 | 86 364 | 82 534 | 83 116 | 80 709 | 85 524 |
| 0.72 | 0.66 | 0.63 | 0.63 | 0.62 | 0.57 | 0.59 | 0.58 | 0.54 | 0.50 | 0.67 | 0.77 | 0.60 |
| 5 462 | 4 338 | 1 958 | 2 197 | 2 608 | 2 169 | 2 564 | 2 593 | 2 843 | 1 892 | 2 614 | 2 364 | 2 845 |
| 154 243 | 124 360 | 56 944 | 64 829 | 78 050 | 65 785 | 78 799 | 80 730 | 89 664 | 60 425 | 71 748 | 58 113 | 85 383 |
| 1.34 | 1.05 | 0.49 | 0.55 | 0.64 | 0.52 | 0.54 | 0.48 | 0.48 | 0.31 | 0.71 | 0.96 | 0.60 |
| 10 836 | 12 079 | 11 397 | 11 344 | 12 136 | 10 644 | 10 951 | 13 083 | 15 753 | 17 039 | 9 770 | 6 503 | 12 597 |
| 159 241 | 180 059 | 172 306 | 173 875 | 188 625 | 167 737 | 174 993 | 212 006 | 258 835 | 283 765 | 142 542 | 87 939 | 197 144 |
| 1.37 | 1.54 | 1.48 | 1.47 | 1.55 | 1.33 | 1.18 | 1.23 | 1.35 | 1.42 | 1.40 | 1.44 | 1.38 |
| 8 920 | 9 688 | 9 868 | 10 392 | 10 942 | 11 417 | 11 737 | 12 461 | 13 160 | 14 002 | 8 686 | 5 633 | 11 328 |
| 131 085 | 144 417 | 149 186 | 159 285 | 170 055 | 179 918 | 187 552 | 201 929 | 216 227 | 233 195 | 126 727 | 76 169 | 177 285 |
| ... | ... | ... | ... | ... | ... | ... | ... | ... | ... | ... | ... | ... |
| 9 722 | 9 735 | 9 467 | 9 854 | 10 244 | 10 563 | 10 645 | 10 986 | 11 225 | 11 474 | 9 770 | 9 017 | 10 425 |
| 142 871 | 145 116 | 143 129 | 151 047 | 159 220 | 166 458 | 170 103 | 178 027 | 184 441 | 191 080 | 142 542 | 121 934 | 163 149 |
| 1.38 | 1.37 | 1.34 | 1.38 | 1.39 | 1.40 | 1.39 | 1.41 | 1.40 | 1.40 | 1.40 | 1.42 | 1.39 |
| 9 637 | 10 563 | 10 936 | 11 768 | 12 672 | 13 420 | 13 796 | 14 647 | 15 468 | 16 459 | 9 821 | 6 111 | 13 030 |
| 141 623 | 157 458 | 165 333 | 180 377 | 196 948 | 211 479 | 220 453 | 237 351 | 254 158 | 274 103 | 143 279 | 82 629 | 203 928 |
| 1.38 | 1.37 | 1.34 | 1.38 | 1.39 | 1.40 | 1.39 | 1.41 | 1.40 | 1.40 | 1.39 | 1.41 | 1.39 |
| 11 747 | 11 763 | 11 440 | 11 908 | 12 379 | 12 764 | 12 863 | 13 275 | 13 564 | 13 864 | 11 806 | 10 896 | 12 597 |
| 172 641 | 175 354 | 172 952 | 182 521 | 192 396 | 201 143 | 205 547 | 215 122 | 222 872 | 230 894 | 172 243 | 147 341 | 197 144 |
| 1.36 | 1.36 | 1.33 | 1.37 | 1.38 | 1.40 | 1.39 | 1.40 | 1.39 | 1.40 | 1.39 | 1.40 | 1.38 |
| 10 599 | 12 200 | 12 449 | 11 763 | 12 497 | 11 651 | 11 489 | 12 119 | 16 000 | 17 516 | 9 947 | 6 537 | 12 898 |
| 155 768 | 181 860 | 188 204 | 180 300 | 194 226 | 183 603 | 183 600 | 196 396 | 262 897 | 291 708 | 145 122 | 88 388 | 201 856 |
| 1.35 | 1.54 | 1.61 | 1.52 | 1.59 | 1.45 | 1.25 | 1.18 | 1.40 | 1.49 | 1.44 | 1.46 | 1.43 |

**Table A.1** Total and per capita gross domestic product of individual countries or areas, expressed in United States dollars, and their individual shares of gross world product, based on alternative conversion rates, 1970–1989 [*cont.*]

| Country or area | 1970 (1) | 1971 (2) | 1972 (3) | 1973 (4) | 1974 (5) | 1975 (6) | 1976 (7) | 1977 (8) | 1978 (9) | 1979 (10) |
|---|---|---|---|---|---|---|---|---|---|---|
| **Austria** | | | | | | | | | | |
| 1. **MER** | | | | | | | | | | |
| 1a. Per capita GDP | 1 936 | 2 246 | 2 756 | 3 675 | 4 372 | 4 970 | 5 329 | 6 359 | 7 665 | 9 092 |
| 1b. GDP | 14 457 | 16 843 | 20 746 | 27 756 | 33 090 | 37 671 | 40 399 | 48 175 | 58 004 | 68 712 |
| 1c. % of GWP | 0.45 | 0.48 | 0.52 | 0.57 | 0.60 | 0.61 | 0.60 | 0.64 | 0.65 | 0.67 |
| 2. **PPPs** | | | | | | | | | | |
| 2a. Per capita GDP | 2 832 | 3 159 | 3 523 | 3 994 | 4 509 | 4 908 | 5 390 | 6 002 | 6 446 | 7 364 |
| 2b. GDP | 21 151 | 23 688 | 26 519 | 30 163 | 34 131 | 37 195 | 40 864 | 45 470 | 48 779 | 55 653 |
| 2c. % of GWP | ... | ... | ... | ... | ... | ... | ... | ... | ... | ... |
| 3. **Absolute 1970–1989 PARE** | | | | | | | | | | |
| 3a. Per capita GDP | 6 054 | 6 337 | 6 705 | 7 010 | 7 270 | 7 234 | 7 563 | 7 912 | 7 926 | 8 313 |
| 3b. GDP | 45 212 | 47 524 | 50 474 | 52 941 | 55 028 | 54 829 | 57 339 | 59 942 | 59 977 | 62 821 |
| 3c. % of GWP | 0.64 | 0.64 | 0.65 | 0.64 | 0.65 | 0.64 | 0.63 | 0.64 | 0.61 | 0.62 |
| 4. **Relative 1970–1989 PARE** | | | | | | | | | | |
| 4a. Per capita GDP | 2 952 | 3 248 | 3 594 | 4 008 | 4 534 | 4 956 | 5 506 | 6 148 | 6 608 | 7 549 |
| 4b. GDP | 22 044 | 24 360 | 27 059 | 30 267 | 34 315 | 37 564 | 41 738 | 46 576 | 50 003 | 57 050 |
| 4c. % of GWP | 0.64 | 0.64 | 0.65 | 0.64 | 0.65 | 0.64 | 0.63 | 0.64 | 0.61 | 0.62 |
| 5. **Absolute 1980–1989 PARE** | | | | | | | | | | |
| 5a. Per capita GDP | 7 638 | 7 995 | 8 459 | 8 844 | 9 172 | 9 127 | 9 542 | 9 982 | 10 000 | 10 488 |
| 5b. GDP | 57 040 | 59 956 | 63 678 | 66 790 | 69 424 | 69 173 | 72 339 | 75 624 | 75 668 | 79 256 |
| 5c. % of GWP | 0.66 | 0.66 | 0.67 | 0.66 | 0.67 | 0.66 | 0.65 | 0.66 | 0.63 | 0.64 |
| 6. **WA** | | | | | | | | | | |
| 6a. Per capita GDP | 1 936 | 2 242 | 2 756 | 3 675 | 4 372 | 4 970 | 5 329 | 6 359 | 7 666 | 9 093 |
| 6b. GDP | 14 457 | 16 811 | 20 746 | 27 756 | 33 091 | 37 671 | 40 399 | 48 175 | 58 005 | 68 714 |
| 6c. % of GWP | 0.45 | 0.48 | 0.52 | 0.57 | 0.59 | 0.61 | 0.60 | 0.64 | 0.65 | 0.67 |
| **Bahamas** | | | | | | | | | | |
| 1. **MER** | | | | | | | | | | |
| 1a. Per capita GDP | 2 897 | 3 008 | 3 031 | 3 385 | 3 592 | 4 327 | 4 546 | 4 825 | 5 437 | 6 233 |
| 1b. GDP | 495 | 526 | 543 | 616 | 668 | 822 | 882 | 955 | 1 098 | 1 284 |
| 1c. % of GWP | 0.02 | 0.02 | 0.01 | 0.01 | 0.01 | 0.01 | 0.01 | 0.01 | 0.01 | 0.01 |
| 2. **PPPs** | | | | | | | | | | |
| 2a. Per capita GDP | ... | ... | ... | ... | ... | ... | ... | ... | ... | ... |
| 2b. GDP | ... | ... | ... | ... | ... | ... | ... | ... | ... | ... |
| 2c. % of GWP | ... | ... | ... | ... | ... | ... | ... | ... | ... | ... |
| 3. **Absolute 1970–1989 PARE** | | | | | | | | | | |
| 3a. Per capita GDP | 7 596 | 7 538 | 7 196 | 7 504 | 6 133 | 5 146 | 5 280 | 5 636 | 5 870 | 5 921 |
| 3b. GDP | 1 299 | 1 319 | 1 288 | 1 366 | 1 141 | 978 | 1 024 | 1 116 | 1 186 | 1 220 |
| 3c. % of GWP | 0.02 | 0.02 | 0.02 | 0.02 | 0.01 | 0.01 | 0.01 | 0.01 | 0.01 | 0.01 |
| 4. **Relative 1970–1989 PARE** | | | | | | | | | | |
| 4a. Per capita GDP | 3 704 | 3 864 | 3 858 | 4 290 | 3 824 | 3 525 | 3 843 | 4 379 | 4 894 | 5 378 |
| 4b. GDP | 633 | 676 | 691 | 781 | 711 | 670 | 746 | 867 | 989 | 1 108 |
| 4c. % of GWP | 0.02 | 0.02 | 0.02 | 0.02 | 0.01 | 0.01 | 0.01 | 0.01 | 0.01 | 0.01 |
| 5. **Absolute 1980–1989 PARE** | | | | | | | | | | |
| 5a. Per capita GDP | 9 666 | 9 591 | 9 156 | 9 548 | 7 803 | 6 548 | 6 718 | 7 171 | 7 469 | 7 534 |
| 5b. GDP | 1 653 | 1 678 | 1 639 | 1 738 | 1 451 | 1 244 | 1 303 | 1 420 | 1 509 | 1 552 |
| 5c. % of GWP | 0.02 | 0.02 | 0.02 | 0.02 | 0.01 | 0.01 | 0.01 | 0.01 | 0.01 | 0.01 |
| 6. **WA** | | | | | | | | | | |
| 6a. Per capita GDP | 2 892 | 3 008 | 3 031 | 3 385 | 3 592 | 4 327 | 4 546 | 4 825 | 5 437 | 6 233 |
| 6b. GDP | 495 | 526 | 543 | 616 | 668 | 822 | 882 | 955 | 1 098 | 1 284 |
| 6c. % of GWP | 0.02 | 0.02 | 0.01 | 0.01 | 0.01 | 0.01 | 0.01 | 0.01 | 0.01 | 0.01 |

| | | | | | | | | | | Averages | | |
|---|---|---|---|---|---|---|---|---|---|---|---|---|
| 1980 (11) | 1981 (12) | 1982 (13) | 1983 (14) | 1984 (15) | 1985 (16) | 1986 (17) | 1987 (18) | 1988 (19) | 1989 (20) | 1970–89 (21) | 1970–79 (22) | 1980–89 (23) |
| 10 183 | 8 785 | 8 805 | 8 857 | 8 447 | 8 623 | 12 261 | 15 457 | 16 798 | 16 727 | 8 175 | 4 830 | 11 503 |
| 76 882 | 66 301 | 66 448 | 66 872 | 63 810 | 65 173 | 92 729 | 116 976 | 127 210 | 126 775 | 61 751 | 36 585 | 86 917 |
| 0.66 | 0.57 | 0.57 | 0.56 | 0.52 | 0.52 | 0.62 | 0.68 | 0.67 | 0.63 | 0.61 | 0.60 | 0.61 |
| 8 216 | 8 811 | 9 495 | 9 999 | 10 742 | 11 121 | 11 466 | 12 017 | 12 900 | 13 952 | 7 848 | 4 801 | 10 878 |
| 62 032 | 66 493 | 71 657 | 75 494 | 81 142 | 84 050 | 86 718 | 90 947 | 97 688 | 105 741 | 59 279 | 36 361 | 82 196 |
| ... | ... | ... | ... | ... | ... | ... | ... | ... | ... | ... | ... | ... |
| 8 563 | 8 542 | 8 633 | 8 802 | 8 917 | 9 132 | 9 230 | 9 403 | 9 766 | 10 147 | 8 175 | 7 210 | 9 118 |
| 64 654 | 64 467 | 65 157 | 66 456 | 67 360 | 69 018 | 69 806 | 71 165 | 73 957 | 76 901 | 61 751 | 54 609 | 68 894 |
| 0.62 | 0.61 | 0.61 | 0.61 | 0.59 | 0.58 | 0.57 | 0.56 | 0.56 | 0.57 | 0.61 | 0.63 | 0.59 |
| 8 489 | 9 269 | 9 973 | 10 511 | 11 030 | 11 602 | 11 962 | 12 537 | 13 457 | 14 555 | 8 130 | 4 898 | 11 345 |
| 64 089 | 69 950 | 75 265 | 79 360 | 83 321 | 87 685 | 90 468 | 94 880 | 101 912 | 110 314 | 61 411 | 37 098 | 85 724 |
| 0.62 | 0.61 | 0.61 | 0.61 | 0.59 | 0.58 | 0.57 | 0.56 | 0.56 | 0.57 | 0.60 | 0.63 | 0.58 |
| 10 804 | 10 777 | 10 892 | 11 105 | 11 250 | 11 521 | 11 645 | 11 864 | 12 321 | 12 801 | 10 314 | 9 096 | 11 503 |
| 81 568 | 81 333 | 82 203 | 83 841 | 84 982 | 87 074 | 88 068 | 89 783 | 93 305 | 97 019 | 77 906 | 68 895 | 86 917 |
| 0.64 | 0.63 | 0.63 | 0.63 | 0.61 | 0.60 | 0.59 | 0.59 | 0.58 | 0.59 | 0.63 | 0.65 | 0.61 |
| 10 183 | 8 785 | 8 804 | 8 857 | 8 447 | 8 623 | 12 263 | 15 405 | 16 733 | 16 688 | 8 167 | 4 830 | 11 488 |
| 76 882 | 66 301 | 66 447 | 66 871 | 63 809 | 65 174 | 92 746 | 116 583 | 126 718 | 126 481 | 61 692 | 36 583 | 86 801 |
| 0.67 | 0.56 | 0.57 | 0.56 | 0.52 | 0.52 | 0.63 | 0.70 | 0.68 | 0.64 | 0.61 | 0.60 | 0.61 |
| 6 255 | 7 011 | 6 923 | 6 666 | 7 084 | 8 018 | 8 852 | 9 644 | 10 032 | 10 787 | 6 424 | 4 197 | 8 198 |
| 1 320 | 1 507 | 1 516 | 1 493 | 1 615 | 1 868 | 2 098 | 2 324 | 2 458 | 2 697 | 1 339 | 789 | 1 890 |
| 0.01 | 0.01 | 0.01 | 0.01 | 0.01 | 0.01 | 0.01 | 0.01 | 0.01 | 0.01 | 0.01 | 0.01 | 0.01 |
| ... | ... | ... | ... | ... | ... | ... | ... | ... | ... | ... | ... | ... |
| ... | ... | ... | ... | ... | ... | ... | ... | ... | ... | ... | ... | ... |
| ... | ... | ... | ... | ... | ... | ... | ... | ... | ... | ... | ... | ... |
| 5 575 | 6 505 | 6 439 | 5 820 | 5 887 | 6 538 | 6 662 | 6 893 | 6 916 | 7 049 | 6 424 | 6 349 | 6 443 |
| 1 176 | 1 399 | 1 410 | 1 304 | 1 342 | 1 523 | 1 579 | 1 661 | 1 694 | 1 762 | 1 339 | 1 194 | 1 485 |
| 0.01 | 0.01 | 0.01 | 0.01 | 0.01 | 0.01 | 0.01 | 0.01 | 0.01 | 0.01 | 0.01 | 0.01 | 0.01 |
| 5 526 | 7 059 | 7 438 | 6 950 | 7 282 | 8 307 | 8 633 | 9 190 | 9 530 | 10 111 | 6 345 | 4 187 | 8 065 |
| 1 166 | 1 518 | 1 629 | 1 557 | 1 660 | 1 935 | 2 046 | 2 215 | 2 335 | 2 528 | 1 323 | 787 | 1 859 |
| 0.01 | 0.01 | 0.01 | 0.01 | 0.01 | 0.01 | 0.01 | 0.01 | 0.01 | 0.01 | 0.01 | 0.01 | 0.01 |
| 7 094 | 8 277 | 8 194 | 7 406 | 7 490 | 8 319 | 8 476 | 8 770 | 8 800 | 8 969 | 8 174 | 8 078 | 8 198 |
| 1 497 | 1 780 | 1 794 | 1 659 | 1 708 | 1 938 | 2 009 | 2 114 | 2 156 | 2 242 | 1 704 | 1 519 | 1 890 |
| 0.01 | 0.01 | 0.01 | 0.01 | 0.01 | 0.01 | 0.01 | 0.01 | 0.01 | 0.01 | 0.01 | 0.01 | 0.01 |
| 6 255 | 7 011 | 6 923 | 6 666 | 7 084 | 8 018 | 8 852 | 9 644 | 10 032 | 10 787 | 6 424 | 4 197 | 8 198 |
| 1 320 | 1 507 | 1 516 | 1 493 | 1 615 | 1 868 | 2 098 | 2 324 | 2 458 | 2 697 | 1 339 | 789 | 1 890 |
| 0.01 | 0.01 | 0.01 | 0.01 | 0.01 | 0.01 | 0.01 | 0.01 | 0.01 | 0.01 | 0.01 | 0.01 | 0.01 |

**Table A.1**    Total and per capita gross domestic product of individual countries or areas, expressed in United States dollars, and their individual shares of gross world product, based on alternative conversion rates, 1970–1989 [*cont.*]

| Country or area | 1970 (1) | 1971 (2) | 1972 (3) | 1973 (4) | 1974 (5) | 1975 (6) | 1976 (7) | 1977 (8) | 1978 (9) | 1979 (10) |
|---|---|---|---|---|---|---|---|---|---|---|
| **Bahrain** | | | | | | | | | | |
| **1. MER** | | | | | | | | | | |
| 1a. Per capita GDP | 1 060 | 1 099 | 1 220 | 1 425 | 2 921 | 3 549 | 4 859 | 5 807 | 6 331 | 7 189 |
| 1b. GDP | 233 | 251 | 290 | 353 | 759 | 965 | 1 390 | 1 748 | 2 001 | 2 387 |
| 1c. % of GWP | 0.01 | 0.01 | 0.01 | 0.01 | 0.01 | 0.02 | 0.02 | 0.02 | 0.02 | 0.02 |
| **2. PPPs** | | | | | | | | | | |
| 2a. Per capita GDP | 1 768 | 1 802 | 1 771 | 1 731 | 2 858 | 3 575 | 4 629 | 5 011 | 5 667 | 6 426 |
| 2b. GDP | 389 | 411 | 422 | 429 | 743 | 972 | 1 324 | 1 508 | 1 791 | 2 134 |
| 2c. % of GWP | ... | ... | ... | ... | ... | ... | ... | ... | ... | ... |
| **3. Absolute 1970–1989 PARE** | | | | | | | | | | |
| 3a. Per capita GDP | 7 799 | 8 003 | 7 824 | 7 662 | 7 612 | 5 540 | 7 241 | 7 652 | 7 598 | 7 503 |
| 3b. GDP | 1 716 | 1 825 | 1 862 | 1 900 | 1 979 | 1 507 | 2 071 | 2 303 | 2 401 | 2 491 |
| 3c. % of GWP | 0.02 | 0.02 | 0.02 | 0.02 | 0.02 | 0.02 | 0.02 | 0.02 | 0.02 | 0.02 |
| **4. Relative 1970–1989 PARE** | | | | | | | | | | |
| 4a. Per capita GDP | 3 802 | 4 102 | 4 194 | 4 381 | 4 747 | 3 795 | 5 271 | 5 946 | 6 334 | 6 814 |
| 4b. GDP | 837 | 935 | 998 | 1 086 | 1 234 | 1 032 | 1 507 | 1 790 | 2 002 | 2 262 |
| 4c. % of GWP | 0.02 | 0.02 | 0.02 | 0.02 | 0.02 | 0.02 | 0.02 | 0.02 | 0.02 | 0.02 |
| **5. Absolute 1980–1989 PARE** | | | | | | | | | | |
| 5a. Per capita GDP | 10 887 | 11 172 | 10 922 | 10 696 | 10 626 | 7 734 | 10 108 | 10 683 | 10 606 | 10 475 |
| 5b. GDP | 2 395 | 2 547 | 2 599 | 2 653 | 2 763 | 2 104 | 2 891 | 3 215 | 3 352 | 3 478 |
| 5c. % of GWP | 0.03 | 0.03 | 0.03 | 0.03 | 0.03 | 0.02 | 0.03 | 0.03 | 0.03 | 0.03 |
| **6. WA** | | | | | | | | | | |
| 6a. Per capita GDP | 1 060 | 1 099 | 1 221 | 1 423 | 2 923 | 3 554 | 4 864 | 5 812 | 6 323 | 7 177 |
| 6b. GDP | 233 | 251 | 291 | 353 | 760 | 967 | 1 391 | 1 750 | 1 998 | 2 383 |
| 6c. % of GWP | 0.01 | 0.01 | 0.01 | 0.01 | 0.01 | 0.02 | 0.02 | 0.02 | 0.02 | 0.02 |
| **Bangladesh** | | | | | | | | | | |
| **1. MER** | | | | | | | | | | |
| 1a. Per capita GDP | 64 | 52 | 94 | 139 | 218 | 122 | 94 | 124 | 148 | 159 |
| 1b. GDP | 4 242 | 3 574 | 6 594 | 10 035 | 16 240 | 9 322 | 7 414 | 10 018 | 12 381 | 13 642 |
| 1c. % of GWP | 0.13 | 0.10 | 0.16 | 0.20 | 0.29 | 0.15 | 0.11 | 0.13 | 0.14 | 0.13 |
| **2. PPPs** | | | | | | | | | | |
| 2a. Per capita GDP | 223 | 201 | 224 | 261 | 268 | 321 | 355 | 432 | 479 | 501 |
| 2b. GDP | 14 877 | 13 753 | 15 781 | 18 873 | 19 961 | 24 603 | 27 972 | 35 002 | 39 964 | 42 961 |
| 2c. % of GWP | ... | ... | ... | ... | ... | ... | ... | ... | ... | ... |
| **3. Absolute 1970–1989 PARE** | | | | | | | | | | |
| 3a. Per capita GDP | 138 | 117 | 134 | 145 | 144 | 151 | 149 | 154 | 157 | 155 |
| 3b. GDP | 9 221 | 7 993 | 9 426 | 10 534 | 10 702 | 11 562 | 11 767 | 12 494 | 13 129 | 13 256 |
| 3c. % of GWP | 0.13 | 0.11 | 0.12 | 0.13 | 0.13 | 0.13 | 0.13 | 0.13 | 0.13 | 0.13 |
| **4. Relative 1970–1989 PARE** | | | | | | | | | | |
| 4a. Per capita GDP | 67 | 60 | 72 | 83 | 90 | 103 | 109 | 120 | 131 | 140 |
| 4b. GDP | 4 496 | 4 097 | 5 053 | 6 022 | 6 674 | 7 921 | 8 565 | 9 708 | 10 946 | 12 038 |
| 4c. % of GWP | 0.13 | 0.11 | 0.12 | 0.13 | 0.13 | 0.13 | 0.13 | 0.13 | 0.13 | 0.13 |
| **5. Absolute 1980–1989 PARE** | | | | | | | | | | |
| 5a. Per capita GDP | 152 | 129 | 147 | 160 | 158 | 166 | 165 | 170 | 173 | 170 |
| 5b. GDP | 10 158 | 8 806 | 10 384 | 11 604 | 11 789 | 12 737 | 12 963 | 13 764 | 14 464 | 14 603 |
| 5c. % of GWP | 0.12 | 0.10 | 0.11 | 0.11 | 0.11 | 0.12 | 0.12 | 0.12 | 0.12 | 0.12 |
| **6. WA** | | | | | | | | | | |
| 6a. Per capita GDP | 97 | 85 | 118 | 138 | 222 | 165 | 97 | 123 | 147 | 162 |
| 6b. GDP | 6 485 | 5 825 | 8 305 | 9 985 | 16 539 | 12 623 | 7 661 | 9 962 | 12 295 | 13 937 |
| 6c. % of GWP | 0.20 | 0.17 | 0.21 | 0.21 | 0.30 | 0.20 | 0.11 | 0.13 | 0.14 | 0.14 |

| | | | | | | | | | | Averages | | |
|---|---|---|---|---|---|---|---|---|---|---|---|---|
| 1980 (11) | 1981 (12) | 1982 (13) | 1983 (14) | 1984 (15) | 1985 (16) | 1986 (17) | 1987 (18) | 1988 (19) | 1989 (20) | 1970–89 (21) | 1970–79 (22) | 1980–89 (23) |

| 8 827 | 9 527 | 9 594 | 9 432 | 9 527 | 8 615 | 7 054 | 6 421 | 6 550 | 6 549 | 6 543 | 3 901 | 8 094 |
|---|---|---|---|---|---|---|---|---|---|---|---|---|
| 3 072 | 3 468 | 3 646 | 3 735 | 3 935 | 3 705 | 3 153 | 2 980 | 3 157 | 3 268 | 2 225 | 1 038 | 3 412 |
| 0.03 | 0.03 | 0.03 | 0.03 | 0.03 | 0.03 | 0.02 | 0.02 | 0.02 | 0.02 | 0.02 | 0.02 | 0.02 |
| 7 765 | 8 271 | 7 678 | 7 414 | 7 862 | 7 338 | 7 690 | 7 407 | 7 862 | 8 102 | 6 294 | 3 805 | 7 752 |
| 2 702 | 3 011 | 2 918 | 2 936 | 3 247 | 3 155 | 3 437 | 3 437 | 3 789 | 4 043 | 2 140 | 1 012 | 3 268 |
| ... | ... | ... | ... | ... | ... | ... | ... | ... | ... | ... | ... | ... |
| 7 175 | 6 495 | 5 751 | 5 870 | 5 945 | 5 485 | 5 635 | 5 276 | 5 418 | 5 364 | 6 543 | 7 539 | 5 798 |
| 2 497 | 2 364 | 2 186 | 2 324 | 2 455 | 2 359 | 2 519 | 2 448 | 2 611 | 2 676 | 2 225 | 2 005 | 2 444 |
| 0.02 | 0.02 | 0.02 | 0.02 | 0.02 | 0.02 | 0.02 | 0.02 | 0.02 | 0.02 | 0.02 | 0.02 | 0.02 |
| 7 112 | 7 048 | 6 644 | 7 010 | 7 354 | 6 969 | 7 303 | 7 034 | 7 466 | 7 694 | 6 474 | 5 144 | 7 198 |
| 2 475 | 2 565 | 2 525 | 2 776 | 3 037 | 2 997 | 3 264 | 3 264 | 3 598 | 3 839 | 2 201 | 1 368 | 3 034 |
| 0.02 | 0.02 | 0.02 | 0.02 | 0.02 | 0.02 | 0.02 | 0.02 | 0.02 | 0.02 | 0.02 | 0.02 | 0.02 |
| 10 016 | 9 067 | 8 029 | 8 194 | 8 299 | 7 657 | 7 866 | 7 365 | 7 563 | 7 487 | 9 134 | 10 525 | 8 094 |
| 3 485 | 3 301 | 3 051 | 3 245 | 3 428 | 3 293 | 3 516 | 3 417 | 3 645 | 3 736 | 3 106 | 2 800 | 3 412 |
| 0.03 | 0.03 | 0.02 | 0.02 | 0.02 | 0.02 | 0.02 | 0.02 | 0.02 | 0.02 | 0.03 | 0.03 | 0.02 |
| 8 827 | 9 527 | 9 594 | 9 432 | 9 527 | 8 615 | 7 129 | 6 831 | 6 968 | 6 967 | 6 636 | 3 901 | 8 245 |
| 3 072 | 3 468 | 3 646 | 3 735 | 3 935 | 3 705 | 3 187 | 3 170 | 3 359 | 3 476 | 2 256 | 1 038 | 3 475 |
| 0.03 | 0.03 | 0.03 | 0.03 | 0.03 | 0.03 | 0.02 | 0.02 | 0.02 | 0.02 | 0.02 | 0.02 | 0.02 |

| 179 | 168 | 149 | 156 | 178 | 174 | 181 | 189 | 199 | 217 | 157 | 124 | 180 |
|---|---|---|---|---|---|---|---|---|---|---|---|---|
| 15 806 | 15 214 | 13 879 | 14 979 | 17 488 | 17 649 | 18 797 | 20 168 | 21 772 | 24 381 | 13 680 | 9 346 | 18 013 |
| 0.14 | 0.13 | 0.12 | 0.13 | 0.14 | 0.14 | 0.13 | 0.12 | 0.11 | 0.12 | 0.13 | 0.15 | 0.13 |
| 567 | 599 | 667 | 760 | 775 | 849 | 872 | 893 | 923 | 997 | 606 | 336 | 802 |
| 50 020 | 54 298 | 62 206 | 72 843 | 76 343 | 85 834 | 90 608 | 95 329 | 101 088 | 112 259 | 52 729 | 25 375 | 80 083 |
| ... | ... | ... | ... | ... | ... | ... | ... | ... | ... | ... | ... | ... |
| 158 | 155 | 158 | 160 | 163 | 166 | 167 | 166 | 166 | 172 | 157 | 146 | 164 |
| 13 911 | 14 063 | 14 729 | 15 297 | 16 063 | 16 759 | 17 343 | 17 737 | 18 197 | 19 412 | 13 680 | 11 008 | 16 351 |
| 0.13 | 0.13 | 0.14 | 0.14 | 0.14 | 0.14 | 0.14 | 0.14 | 0.14 | 0.14 | 0.13 | 0.13 | 0.14 |
| 156 | 168 | 182 | 191 | 202 | 211 | 216 | 222 | 229 | 247 | 161 | 100 | 205 |
| 13 790 | 15 259 | 17 014 | 18 268 | 19 869 | 21 292 | 22 476 | 23 648 | 25 076 | 27 847 | 14 003 | 7 552 | 20 454 |
| 0.13 | 0.13 | 0.14 | 0.14 | 0.14 | 0.14 | 0.14 | 0.14 | 0.14 | 0.14 | 0.13 | 0.13 | 0.14 |
| 174 | 171 | 174 | 176 | 180 | 183 | 184 | 183 | 183 | 190 | 173 | 161 | 180 |
| 15 325 | 15 493 | 16 227 | 16 852 | 17 695 | 18 463 | 19 106 | 19 540 | 20 047 | 21 386 | 15 070 | 12 127 | 18 013 |
| 0.12 | 0.12 | 0.13 | 0.13 | 0.13 | 0.13 | 0.13 | 0.13 | 0.13 | 0.13 | 0.12 | 0.12 | 0.13 |
| 179 | 185 | 164 | 162 | 181 | 188 | 184 | 191 | 202 | 218 | 167 | 137 | 187 |
| 15 782 | 16 743 | 15 318 | 15 522 | 17 772 | 19 004 | 19 126 | 20 342 | 22 089 | 24 501 | 14 491 | 10 362 | 18 620 |
| 0.14 | 0.14 | 0.13 | 0.13 | 0.15 | 0.15 | 0.13 | 0.12 | 0.12 | 0.12 | 0.14 | 0.17 | 0.13 |

**Table A.1**    Total and per capita gross domestic product of individual countries or areas,
expressed in United States dollars, and their individual shares of gross world
product, based on alternative conversion rates, 1970–1989 [*cont.*]

| Country or area | 1970 (1) | 1971 (2) | 1972 (3) | 1973 (4) | 1974 (5) | 1975 (6) | 1976 (7) | 1977 (8) | 1978 (9) | 1979 (10) |
|---|---|---|---|---|---|---|---|---|---|---|
| **Barbados** | | | | | | | | | | |
| 1.   **MER** | | | | | | | | | | |
| 1a.   Per capita GDP | 553 | 856 | 970 | 1 178 | 1 397 | 1 635 | 1 765 | 1 996 | 2 230 | 2 693 |
| 1b.   GDP | 132 | 206 | 235 | 286 | 342 | 402 | 436 | 495 | 553 | 671 |
| 1c.   % of GWP | 0.00 | 0.01 | 0.01 | 0.01 | 0.01 | 0.01 | 0.01 | 0.01 | 0.01 | 0.01 |
| 2.   **PPPs** | | | | | | | | | | |
| 2a.   Per capita GDP | 1 094 | 1 563 | 1 807 | 1 962 | 2 152 | 2 623 | 2 733 | 3 145 | 3 258 | 3 757 |
| 2b.   GDP | 261 | 377 | 437 | 477 | 527 | 645 | 675 | 780 | 808 | 936 |
| 2c.   % of GWP | ... | ... | ... | ... | ... | ... | ... | ... | ... | ... |
| 3.   **Absolute 1970–1989 PARE** | | | | | | | | | | |
| 3a.   Per capita GDP | 2 490 | 2 565 | 2 716 | 2 786 | 2 698 | 2 634 | 2 741 | 2 836 | 3 187 | 3 419 |
| 3b.   GDP | 595 | 618 | 657 | 677 | 661 | 648 | 677 | 703 | 790 | 851 |
| 3c.   % of GWP | 0.01 | 0.01 | 0.01 | 0.01 | 0.01 | 0.01 | 0.01 | 0.01 | 0.01 | 0.01 |
| 4.   **Relative 1970–1989 PARE** | | | | | | | | | | |
| 4a.   Per capita GDP | 1 214 | 1 315 | 1 456 | 1 593 | 1 682 | 1 804 | 1 995 | 2 204 | 2 657 | 3 105 |
| 4b.   GDP | 290 | 317 | 352 | 387 | 412 | 444 | 493 | 547 | 659 | 773 |
| 4c.   % of GWP | 0.01 | 0.01 | 0.01 | 0.01 | 0.01 | 0.01 | 0.01 | 0.01 | 0.01 | 0.01 |
| 5.   **Absolute 1980–1989 PARE** | | | | | | | | | | |
| 5a.   Per capita GDP | 3 343 | 3 444 | 3 647 | 3 741 | 3 623 | 3 537 | 3 680 | 3 808 | 4 280 | 4 591 |
| 5b.   GDP | 799 | 830 | 883 | 909 | 888 | 870 | 909 | 944 | 1 061 | 1 143 |
| 5c.   % of GWP | 0.01 | 0.01 | 0.01 | 0.01 | 0.01 | 0.01 | 0.01 | 0.01 | 0.01 | 0.01 |
| 6.   **WA** | | | | | | | | | | |
| 6a.   Per capita GDP | 553 | 851 | 970 | 1 178 | 1 397 | 1 635 | 1 765 | 1 996 | 2 230 | 2 692 |
| 6b.   GDP | 132 | 205 | 235 | 286 | 342 | 402 | 436 | 495 | 553 | 670 |
| 6c.   % of GWP | 0.00 | 0.01 | 0.01 | 0.01 | 0.01 | 0.01 | 0.01 | 0.01 | 0.01 | 0.01 |
| **Belgium** | | | | | | | | | | |
| 1.   **MER** | | | | | | | | | | |
| 1a.   Per capita GDP | 2 597 | 2 916 | 3 589 | 4 591 | 5 375 | 6 283 | 6 801 | 7 910 | 9 660 | 11 069 |
| 1b.   GDP | 25 075 | 28 248 | 34 880 | 44 758 | 52 540 | 61 559 | 66 743 | 77 740 | 95 033 | 108 990 |
| 1c.   % of GWP | 0.79 | 0.81 | 0.87 | 0.91 | 0.95 | 0.99 | 0.99 | 1.03 | 1.06 | 1.06 |
| 2.   **PPPs** | | | | | | | | | | |
| 2a.   Per capita GDP | 3 369 | 3 664 | 4 065 | 4 623 | 5 263 | 5 600 | 6 243 | 6 706 | 7 409 | 8 308 |
| 2b.   GDP | 32 536 | 35 495 | 39 507 | 45 066 | 51 449 | 54 862 | 61 265 | 65 902 | 72 887 | 81 800 |
| 2c.   % of GWP | ... | ... | ... | ... | ... | ... | ... | ... | ... | ... |
| 3.   **Absolute 1970–1989 PARE** | | | | | | | | | | |
| 3a.   Per capita GDP | 6 628 | 6 851 | 7 196 | 7 602 | 7 898 | 7 769 | 8 197 | 8 233 | 8 459 | 8 634 |
| 3b.   GDP | 64 000 | 66 375 | 69 935 | 74 111 | 77 199 | 76 118 | 80 444 | 80 909 | 83 217 | 85 014 |
| 3c.   % of GWP | 0.90 | 0.90 | 0.90 | 0.89 | 0.91 | 0.88 | 0.89 | 0.86 | 0.85 | 0.84 |
| 4.   **Relative 1970–1989 PARE** | | | | | | | | | | |
| 4a.   Per capita GDP | 3 232 | 3 512 | 3 858 | 4 346 | 4 925 | 5 323 | 5 967 | 6 397 | 7 052 | 7 841 |
| 4b.   GDP | 31 205 | 34 022 | 37 492 | 42 370 | 48 141 | 52 149 | 58 557 | 62 868 | 69 378 | 77 205 |
| 4c.   % of GWP | 0.90 | 0.90 | 0.90 | 0.89 | 0.91 | 0.88 | 0.89 | 0.86 | 0.85 | 0.84 |
| 5.   **Absolute 1980–1989 PARE** | | | | | | | | | | |
| 5a.   Per capita GDP | 7 781 | 8 043 | 8 447 | 8 924 | 9 271 | 9 121 | 9 623 | 9 664 | 9 930 | 10 136 |
| 5b.   GDP | 75 133 | 77 920 | 82 099 | 87 002 | 90 627 | 89 358 | 94 437 | 94 983 | 97 692 | 99 802 |
| 5c.   % of GWP | 0.86 | 0.86 | 0.86 | 0.86 | 0.87 | 0.85 | 0.85 | 0.82 | 0.81 | 0.80 |
| 6.   **WA** | | | | | | | | | | |
| 6a.   Per capita GDP | 2 597 | 2 899 | 3 589 | 4 591 | 5 375 | 6 283 | 6 802 | 7 910 | 9 660 | 11 070 |
| 6b.   GDP | 25 075 | 28 088 | 34 880 | 44 759 | 52 541 | 61 559 | 66 751 | 77 741 | 95 033 | 108 991 |
| 6c.   % of GWP | 0.79 | 0.81 | 0.87 | 0.92 | 0.94 | 1.00 | 0.99 | 1.03 | 1.07 | 1.07 |

| | | | | | | | | | | Averages | | |
|---|---|---|---|---|---|---|---|---|---|---|---|---|
| 1980 | 1981 | 1982 | 1983 | 1984 | 1985 | 1986 | 1987 | 1988 | 1989 | 1970–89 | 1970–79 | 1980–89 |
| (11) | (12) | (13) | (14) | (15) | (16) | (17) | (18) | (19) | (20) | (21) | (22) | (23) |
| 3 442 | 3 788 | 3 942 | 4 169 | 4 526 | 4 737 | 5 183 | 5 736 | 6 075 | 6 694 | 3 202 | 1 531 | 4 830 |
| 861 | 947 | 990 | 1 051 | 1 145 | 1 198 | 1 316 | 1 457 | 1 549 | 1 707 | 799 | 376 | 1 222 |
| 0.01 | 0.01 | 0.01 | 0.01 | 0.01 | 0.01 | 0.01 | 0.01 | 0.01 | 0.01 | 0.01 | 0.01 | 0.01 |
| 4 436 | 4 900 | 4 858 | 5 050 | 5 654 | 6 291 | 7 048 | 7 744 | 8 250 | 8 884 | 4 388 | 2 413 | 6 314 |
| 1 109 | 1 225 | 1 219 | 1 272 | 1 430 | 1 592 | 1 790 | 1 967 | 2 104 | 2 266 | 1 095 | 592 | 1 597 |
| ... | ... | ... | ... | ... | ... | ... | ... | ... | ... | ... | ... | ... |
| 3 526 | 3 433 | 3 273 | 3 260 | 3 324 | 3 347 | 3 676 | 3 926 | 4 047 | 4 186 | 3 202 | 2 802 | 3 597 |
| 881 | 858 | 821 | 821 | 841 | 847 | 934 | 997 | 1 032 | 1 067 | 799 | 688 | 910 |
| 0.01 | 0.01 | 0.01 | 0.01 | 0.01 | 0.01 | 0.01 | 0.01 | 0.01 | 0.01 | 0.01 | 0.01 | 0.01 |
| 3 495 | 3 725 | 3 780 | 3 893 | 4 112 | 4 252 | 4 764 | 5 234 | 5 576 | 6 005 | 3 210 | 1 904 | 4 484 |
| 874 | 931 | 949 | 981 | 1 040 | 1 076 | 1 210 | 1 330 | 1 422 | 1 531 | 801 | 467 | 1 134 |
| 0.01 | 0.01 | 0.01 | 0.01 | 0.01 | 0.01 | 0.01 | 0.01 | 0.01 | 0.01 | 0.01 | 0.01 | 0.01 |
| 4 734 | 4 610 | 4 395 | 4 377 | 4 464 | 4 494 | 4 936 | 5 272 | 5 434 | 5 621 | 4 300 | 3 762 | 4 830 |
| 1 184 | 1 152 | 1 103 | 1 103 | 1 129 | 1 137 | 1 254 | 1 339 | 1 386 | 1 433 | 1 073 | 924 | 1 222 |
| 0.01 | 0.01 | 0.01 | 0.01 | 0.01 | 0.01 | 0.01 | 0.01 | 0.01 | 0.01 | 0.01 | 0.01 | 0.01 |
| 3 442 | 3 788 | 3 942 | 4 168 | 4 525 | 4 736 | 5 179 | 5 703 | 6 041 | 6 656 | 3 196 | 1 530 | 4 819 |
| 860 | 947 | 989 | 1 050 | 1 145 | 1 198 | 1 316 | 1 449 | 1 540 | 1 697 | 797 | 376 | 1 219 |
| 0.01 | 0.01 | 0.01 | 0.01 | 0.01 | 0.01 | 0.01 | 0.01 | 0.01 | 0.01 | 0.01 | 0.01 | 0.01 |
| 11 979 | 9 775 | 8 633 | 8 177 | 7 774 | 8 094 | 11 320 | 14 188 | 15 307 | 15 537 | 8 566 | 6 086 | 11 072 |
| 118 016 | 96 348 | 85 117 | 80 622 | 76 653 | 79 798 | 111 580 | 139 789 | 150 774 | 152 992 | 84 363 | 59 557 | 109 169 |
| 1.02 | 0.82 | 0.73 | 0.68 | 0.63 | 0.63 | 0.75 | 0.81 | 0.79 | 0.76 | 0.83 | 0.98 | 0.76 |
| 9 291 | 9 720 | 10 488 | 10 568 | 11 306 | 11 675 | 12 085 | 12 717 | 13 752 | 14 875 | 8 573 | 5 526 | 11 642 |
| 91 537 | 95 812 | 103 404 | 104 203 | 111 480 | 115 099 | 119 122 | 125 301 | 135 456 | 146 471 | 84 433 | 54 077 | 114 788 |
| ... | ... | ... | ... | ... | ... | ... | ... | ... | ... | ... | ... | ... |
| 8 987 | 8 894 | 9 020 | 9 059 | 9 254 | 9 330 | 9 468 | 9 685 | 10 133 | 10 529 | 8 566 | 7 739 | 9 432 |
| 88 542 | 87 666 | 88 929 | 89 325 | 91 245 | 91 989 | 93 328 | 95 427 | 99 810 | 103 675 | 84 363 | 75 732 | 92 994 |
| 0.85 | 0.83 | 0.83 | 0.81 | 0.80 | 0.78 | 0.76 | 0.76 | 0.76 | 0.76 | 0.83 | 0.88 | 0.79 |
| 8 909 | 9 650 | 10 419 | 10 818 | 11 447 | 11 854 | 12 271 | 12 913 | 13 963 | 15 103 | 8 477 | 5 246 | 11 729 |
| 87 768 | 95 122 | 102 725 | 106 670 | 112 866 | 116 868 | 120 953 | 127 227 | 137 538 | 148 722 | 83 492 | 51 339 | 115 646 |
| 0.85 | 0.83 | 0.83 | 0.81 | 0.80 | 0.78 | 0.76 | 0.76 | 0.76 | 0.76 | 0.81 | 0.87 | 0.79 |
| 10 550 | 10 441 | 10 589 | 10 635 | 10 864 | 10 953 | 11 115 | 11 370 | 11 896 | 12 360 | 10 056 | 9 085 | 11 072 |
| 103 943 | 102 914 | 104 397 | 104 863 | 107 116 | 107 989 | 109 562 | 112 026 | 117 171 | 121 709 | 99 037 | 88 905 | 109 169 |
| 0.82 | 0.80 | 0.81 | 0.79 | 0.77 | 0.75 | 0.74 | 0.73 | 0.73 | 0.74 | 0.80 | 0.84 | 0.76 |
| 11 979 | 9 775 | 8 634 | 8 177 | 7 774 | 8 094 | 11 319 | 14 175 | 15 320 | 15 535 | 8 565 | 6 084 | 11 072 |
| 118 022 | 96 353 | 85 118 | 80 622 | 76 653 | 79 798 | 111 575 | 139 662 | 150 904 | 152 977 | 84 355 | 59 542 | 109 168 |
| 1.02 | 0.82 | 0.73 | 0.68 | 0.63 | 0.63 | 0.76 | 0.84 | 0.81 | 0.78 | 0.83 | 0.98 | 0.77 |

**Table A.1**     Total and per capita gross domestic product of individual countries or areas,
expressed in United States dollars, and their individual shares of gross world
product, based on alternative conversion rates, 1970–1989 [*cont.*]

| Country or area | 1970 (1) | 1971 (2) | 1972 (3) | 1973 (4) | 1974 (5) | 1975 (6) | 1976 (7) | 1977 (8) | 1978 (9) | 1979 (10) |
|---|---|---|---|---|---|---|---|---|---|---|
| **Belize** | | | | | | | | | | |
| **1.   MER** | | | | | | | | | | |
| 1a.   Per capita GDP | 397 | 430 | 486 | 540 | 710 | 809 | 623 | 784 | 869 | 994 |
| 1b.   GDP | 48 | 52 | 60 | 68 | 90 | 104 | 82 | 106 | 121 | 141 |
| 1c.   % of GWP | 0.00 | 0.00 | 0.00 | 0.00 | 0.00 | 0.00 | 0.00 | 0.00 | 0.00 | 0.00 |
| **2.   PPPs** | | | | | | | | | | |
| 2a.   Per capita GDP | ... | ... | ... | ... | ... | ... | ... | ... | ... | ... |
| 2b.   GDP | ... | ... | ... | ... | ... | ... | ... | ... | ... | ... |
| 2c.   % of GWP | ... | ... | ... | ... | ... | ... | ... | ... | ... | ... |
| **3.   Absolute 1970–1989 PARE** | | | | | | | | | | |
| 3a.   Per capita GDP | 854 | 872 | 918 | 948 | 1 020 | 1 011 | 981 | 999 | 1 047 | 1 064 |
| 3b.   GDP | 103 | 106 | 114 | 118 | 129 | 130 | 129 | 135 | 146 | 151 |
| 3c.   % of GWP | 0.00 | 0.00 | 0.00 | 0.00 | 0.00 | 0.00 | 0.00 | 0.00 | 0.00 | 0.00 |
| **4.   Relative 1970–1989 PARE** | | | | | | | | | | |
| 4a.   Per capita GDP | 416 | 447 | 492 | 542 | 636 | 692 | 714 | 776 | 873 | 966 |
| 4b.   GDP | 50 | 55 | 61 | 68 | 81 | 89 | 94 | 105 | 121 | 137 |
| 4c.   % of GWP | 0.00 | 0.00 | 0.00 | 0.00 | 0.00 | 0.00 | 0.00 | 0.00 | 0.00 | 0.00 |
| **5.   Absolute 1980–1989 PARE** | | | | | | | | | | |
| 5a.   Per capita GDP | 1 044 | 1 066 | 1 122 | 1 159 | 1 247 | 1 236 | 1 199 | 1 222 | 1 280 | 1 301 |
| 5b.   GDP | 126 | 130 | 139 | 145 | 158 | 159 | 158 | 165 | 178 | 185 |
| 5c.   % of GWP | 0.00 | 0.00 | 0.00 | 0.00 | 0.00 | 0.00 | 0.00 | 0.00 | 0.00 | 0.00 |
| **6.   WA** | | | | | | | | | | |
| 6a.   Per capita GDP | 397 | 430 | 486 | 540 | 710 | 809 | 624 | 784 | 869 | 994 |
| 6b.   GDP | 48 | 53 | 60 | 68 | 90 | 104 | 82 | 106 | 121 | 141 |
| 6c.   % of GWP | 0.00 | 0.00 | 0.00 | 0.00 | 0.00 | 0.00 | 0.00 | 0.00 | 0.00 | 0.00 |
| **Benin** | | | | | | | | | | |
| **1.   MER** | | | | | | | | | | |
| 1a.   Per capita GDP | 93 | 97 | 117 | 140 | 147 | 174 | 181 | 193 | 228 | 270 |
| 1b.   GDP | 251 | 266 | 329 | 404 | 434 | 528 | 562 | 615 | 747 | 910 |
| 1c.   % of GWP | 0.01 | 0.01 | 0.01 | 0.01 | 0.01 | 0.01 | 0.01 | 0.01 | 0.01 | 0.01 |
| **2.   PPPs** | | | | | | | | | | |
| 2a.   Per capita GDP | 319 | 333 | 370 | 395 | 424 | 438 | 450 | 431 | 438 | 470 |
| 2b.   GDP | 859 | 918 | 1 042 | 1 140 | 1 253 | 1 329 | 1 399 | 1 375 | 1 436 | 1 584 |
| 2c.   % of GWP | ... | ... | ... | ... | ... | ... | ... | ... | ... | ... |
| **3.   Absolute 1970–1989 PARE** | | | | | | | | | | |
| 3a.   Per capita GDP | 278 | 276 | 317 | 313 | 322 | 299 | 299 | 259 | 249 | 248 |
| 3b.   GDP | 748 | 760 | 893 | 903 | 953 | 906 | 930 | 827 | 815 | 834 |
| 3c.   % of GWP | 0.01 | 0.01 | 0.01 | 0.01 | 0.01 | 0.01 | 0.01 | 0.01 | 0.01 | 0.01 |
| **4.   Relative 1970–1989 PARE** | | | | | | | | | | |
| 4a.   Per capita GDP | 135 | 141 | 170 | 179 | 201 | 205 | 218 | 201 | 207 | 225 |
| 4b.   GDP | 365 | 390 | 479 | 516 | 594 | 621 | 677 | 642 | 680 | 757 |
| 4c.   % of GWP | 0.01 | 0.01 | 0.01 | 0.01 | 0.01 | 0.01 | 0.01 | 0.01 | 0.01 | 0.01 |
| **5.   Absolute 1980–1989 PARE** | | | | | | | | | | |
| 5a.   Per capita GDP | 379 | 377 | 432 | 427 | 440 | 408 | 408 | 353 | 339 | 338 |
| 5b.   GDP | 1 022 | 1 038 | 1 219 | 1 233 | 1 301 | 1 237 | 1 269 | 1 128 | 1 113 | 1 138 |
| 5c.   % of GWP | 0.01 | 0.01 | 0.01 | 0.01 | 0.01 | 0.01 | 0.01 | 0.01 | 0.01 | 0.01 |
| **6.   WA** | | | | | | | | | | |
| 6a.   Per capita GDP | 93 | 97 | 117 | 140 | 147 | 174 | 181 | 193 | 228 | 270 |
| 6b.   GDP | 251 | 266 | 329 | 404 | 434 | 528 | 562 | 615 | 747 | 910 |
| 6c.   % of GWP | 0.01 | 0.01 | 0.01 | 0.01 | 0.01 | 0.01 | 0.01 | 0.01 | 0.01 | 0.01 |

| 1980 (11) | 1981 (12) | 1982 (13) | 1983 (14) | 1984 (15) | 1985 (16) | 1986 (17) | 1987 (18) | 1988 (19) | 1989 (20) | Averages 1970–89 (21) | 1970–79 (22) | 1980–89 (23) |
|---|---|---|---|---|---|---|---|---|---|---|---|---|
| 1 173 | 1 195 | 1 119 | 1 110 | 1 185 | 1 167 | 1 243 | 1 445 | 1 540 | 1 699 | 1 046 | 682 | 1 297 |
| 171 | 179 | 172 | 175 | 193 | 195 | 213 | 253 | 276 | 313 | 151 | 87 | 214 |
| 0.00 | 0.00 | 0.00 | 0.00 | 0.00 | 0.00 | 0.00 | 0.00 | 0.00 | 0.00 | 0.00 | 0.00 | 0.00 |
| ... | ... | ... | ... | ... | ... | ... | ... | ... | ... | ... | ... | ... |
| ... | ... | ... | ... | ... | ... | ... | ... | ... | ... | ... | ... | ... |
| ... | ... | ... | ... | ... | ... | ... | ... | ... | ... | ... | ... | ... |
| 1 080 | 1 066 | 1 038 | 988 | 1 009 | 1 007 | 1 019 | 1 125 | 1 122 | 1 153 | 1 046 | 987 | 1 061 |
| 158 | 160 | 160 | 156 | 164 | 168 | 174 | 197 | 201 | 212 | 151 | 126 | 175 |
| 0.00 | 0.00 | 0.00 | 0.00 | 0.00 | 0.00 | 0.00 | 0.00 | 0.00 | 0.00 | 0.00 | 0.00 | 0.00 |
| 1 071 | 1 157 | 1 199 | 1 180 | 1 248 | 1 280 | 1 320 | 1 500 | 1 545 | 1 654 | 1 059 | 673 | 1 326 |
| 156 | 174 | 185 | 186 | 203 | 214 | 226 | 262 | 277 | 304 | 152 | 86 | 219 |
| 0.00 | 0.00 | 0.00 | 0.00 | 0.00 | 0.00 | 0.00 | 0.00 | 0.00 | 0.00 | 0.00 | 0.00 | 0.00 |
| 1 321 | 1 304 | 1 269 | 1 208 | 1 234 | 1 231 | 1 245 | 1 375 | 1 371 | 1 410 | 1 279 | 1 206 | 1 297 |
| 193 | 196 | 195 | 191 | 201 | 206 | 213 | 241 | 245 | 259 | 184 | 154 | 214 |
| 0.00 | 0.00 | 0.00 | 0.00 | 0.00 | 0.00 | 0.00 | 0.00 | 0.00 | 0.00 | 0.00 | 0.00 | 0.00 |
| 1 173 | 1 195 | 1 119 | 1 110 | 1 185 | 1 167 | 1 243 | 1 445 | 1 540 | 1 699 | 1 046 | 682 | 1 297 |
| 171 | 179 | 172 | 175 | 193 | 195 | 213 | 253 | 276 | 313 | 151 | 87 | 214 |
| 0.00 | 0.00 | 0.00 | 0.00 | 0.00 | 0.00 | 0.00 | 0.00 | 0.00 | 0.00 | 0.00 | 0.00 | 0.00 |
| 336 | 312 | 343 | 307 | 276 | 279 | 354 | 380 | 384 | 355 | 267 | 168 | 335 |
| 1 163 | 1 108 | 1 253 | 1 153 | 1 067 | 1 113 | 1 452 | 1 608 | 1 672 | 1 593 | 911 | 505 | 1 318 |
| 0.01 | 0.01 | 0.01 | 0.01 | 0.01 | 0.01 | 0.01 | 0.01 | 0.01 | 0.01 | 0.01 | 0.01 | 0.01 |
| 557 | 634 | 798 | 792 | 756 | 770 | 757 | 726 | 777 | 773 | 607 | 412 | 741 |
| 1 926 | 2 256 | 2 917 | 2 981 | 2 929 | 3 070 | 3 109 | 3 070 | 3 384 | 3 474 | 2 073 | 1 234 | 2 912 |
| ... | ... | ... | ... | ... | ... | ... | ... | ... | ... | ... | ... | ... |
| 266 | 269 | 273 | 263 | 256 | 243 | 234 | 218 | 226 | 216 | 267 | 286 | 246 |
| 918 | 956 | 997 | 991 | 992 | 968 | 960 | 922 | 983 | 970 | 911 | 857 | 966 |
| 0.01 | 0.01 | 0.01 | 0.01 | 0.01 | 0.01 | 0.01 | 0.01 | 0.01 | 0.01 | 0.01 | 0.01 | 0.01 |
| 263 | 292 | 315 | 314 | 317 | 308 | 303 | 291 | 311 | 310 | 259 | 191 | 304 |
| 910 | 1 037 | 1 152 | 1 183 | 1 227 | 1 229 | 1 245 | 1 229 | 1 355 | 1 391 | 884 | 572 | 1 196 |
| 0.01 | 0.01 | 0.01 | 0.01 | 0.01 | 0.01 | 0.01 | 0.01 | 0.01 | 0.01 | 0.01 | 0.01 | 0.01 |
| 362 | 367 | 372 | 359 | 350 | 331 | 319 | 298 | 308 | 295 | 364 | 390 | 335 |
| 1 254 | 1 305 | 1 361 | 1 352 | 1 354 | 1 321 | 1 311 | 1 259 | 1 342 | 1 323 | 1 244 | 1 170 | 1 318 |
| 0.01 | 0.01 | 0.01 | 0.01 | 0.01 | 0.01 | 0.01 | 0.01 | 0.01 | 0.01 | 0.01 | 0.01 | 0.01 |
| 336 | 312 | 343 | 306 | 276 | 279 | 354 | 380 | 384 | 355 | 267 | 168 | 335 |
| 1 163 | 1 108 | 1 253 | 1 153 | 1 067 | 1 113 | 1 452 | 1 608 | 1 672 | 1 593 | 911 | 505 | 1 318 |
| 0.01 | 0.01 | 0.01 | 0.01 | 0.01 | 0.01 | 0.01 | 0.01 | 0.01 | 0.01 | 0.01 | 0.01 | 0.01 |

**Table A.1**    Total and per capita gross domestic product of individual countries or areas, expressed in United States dollars, and their individual shares of gross world product, based on alternative conversion rates, 1970–1989 [*cont.*]

| Country or area | 1970 (1) | 1971 (2) | 1972 (3) | 1973 (4) | 1974 (5) | 1975 (6) | 1976 (7) | 1977 (8) | 1978 (9) | 1979 (10) |
|---|---|---|---|---|---|---|---|---|---|---|
| **Bermuda** | | | | | | | | | | |
| 1.   **MER** | | | | | | | | | | |
| 1a.  Per capita GDP | 3 841 | 4 352 | 4 852 | 5 556 | 6 444 | 7 281 | 8 424 | 8 970 | 9 750 | 11 561 |
| 1b.  GDP | 207 | 235 | 262 | 300 | 348 | 393 | 455 | 484 | 527 | 624 |
| 1c.  % of GWP | 0.01 | 0.01 | 0.01 | 0.01 | 0.01 | 0.01 | 0.01 | 0.01 | 0.01 | 0.01 |
| 2.   **PPPs** | | | | | | | | | | |
| 2a.  Per capita GDP | ... | ... | ... | ... | ... | ... | ... | ... | ... | ... |
| 2b.  GDP | ... | ... | ... | ... | ... | ... | ... | ... | ... | ... |
| 2c.  % of GWP | ... | ... | ... | ... | ... | ... | ... | ... | ... | ... |
| 3.   **Absolute 1970–1989 PARE** | | | | | | | | | | |
| 3a.  Per capita GDP | 10 965 | 11 362 | 11 551 | 11 710 | 11 817 | 12 790 | 13 541 | 13 743 | 14 045 | 15 168 |
| 3b.  GDP | 592 | 614 | 624 | 632 | 638 | 691 | 731 | 742 | 758 | 819 |
| 3c.  % of GWP | 0.01 | 0.01 | 0.01 | 0.01 | 0.01 | 0.01 | 0.01 | 0.01 | 0.01 | 0.01 |
| 4.   **Relative 1970–1989 PARE** | | | | | | | | | | |
| 4a.  Per capita GDP | 5 346 | 5 824 | 6 192 | 6 695 | 7 369 | 8 762 | 9 857 | 10 678 | 11 710 | 13 774 |
| 4b.  GDP | 289 | 314 | 334 | 362 | 398 | 473 | 532 | 577 | 632 | 744 |
| 4c.  % of GWP | 0.01 | 0.01 | 0.01 | 0.01 | 0.01 | 0.01 | 0.01 | 0.01 | 0.01 | 0.01 |
| 5.   **Absolute 1980–1989 PARE** | | | | | | | | | | |
| 5a.  Per capita GDP | 14 865 | 15 403 | 15 659 | 15 875 | 16 020 | 17 339 | 18 358 | 18 631 | 19 041 | 20 562 |
| 5b.  GDP | 803 | 832 | 846 | 857 | 865 | 936 | 991 | 1 006 | 1 028 | 1 110 |
| 5c.  % of GWP | 0.01 | 0.01 | 0.01 | 0.01 | 0.01 | 0.01 | 0.01 | 0.01 | 0.01 | 0.01 |
| 6.   **WA**[a] | | | | | | | | | | |
| 6a.  Per capita GDP | 3 494 | 3 966 | 4 416 | 4 948 | 5 608 | 6 734 | 7 816 | 8 421 | 9 200 | 10 620 |
| 6b.  GDP | 189 | 214 | 238 | 267 | 303 | 364 | 422 | 455 | 497 | 573 |
| 6c.  % of GWP | 0.01 | 0.01 | 0.01 | 0.01 | 0.01 | 0.01 | 0.01 | 0.01 | 0.01 | 0.01 |
| **Bhutan** | | | | | | | | | | |
| 1.   **MER** | | | | | | | | | | |
| 1a.  Per capita GDP | 44 | 49 | 59 | 61 | 67 | 91 | 97 | 94 | 103 | 108 |
| 1b.  GDP | 46 | 52 | 64 | 67 | 75 | 104 | 113 | 111 | 124 | 133 |
| 1c.  % of GWP | 0.00 | 0.00 | 0.00 | 0.00 | 0.00 | 0.00 | 0.00 | 0.00 | 0.00 | 0.00 |
| 2.   **PPPs** | | | | | | | | | | |
| 2a.  Per capita GDP | ... | ... | ... | ... | ... | ... | ... | ... | ... | ... |
| 2b.  GDP | ... | ... | ... | ... | ... | ... | ... | ... | ... | ... |
| 2c.  % of GWP | ... | ... | ... | ... | ... | ... | ... | ... | ... | ... |
| 3.   **Absolute 1970–1989 PARE** | | | | | | | | | | |
| 3a.  Per capita GDP | 67 | 69 | 69 | 74 | 75 | 78 | 81 | 85 | 82 | 100 |
| 3b.  GDP | 70 | 73 | 75 | 82 | 84 | 90 | 94 | 101 | 99 | 122 |
| 3c.  % of GWP | 0.00 | 0.00 | 0.00 | 0.00 | 0.00 | 0.00 | 0.00 | 0.00 | 0.00 | 0.00 |
| 4.   **Relative 1970–1989 PARE** | | | | | | | | | | |
| 4a.  Per capita GDP | 33 | 35 | 37 | 42 | 47 | 54 | 59 | 66 | 69 | 91 |
| 4b.  GDP | 34 | 37 | 40 | 47 | 53 | 61 | 69 | 79 | 83 | 111 |
| 4c.  % of GWP | 0.00 | 0.00 | 0.00 | 0.00 | 0.00 | 0.00 | 0.00 | 0.00 | 0.00 | 0.00 |
| 5.   **Absolute 1980–1989 PARE** | | | | | | | | | | |
| 5a.  Per capita GDP | 67 | 69 | 69 | 74 | 75 | 78 | 81 | 85 | 83 | 100 |
| 5b.  GDP | 70 | 73 | 75 | 82 | 84 | 90 | 94 | 101 | 99 | 122 |
| 5c.  % of GWP | 0.00 | 0.00 | 0.00 | 0.00 | 0.00 | 0.00 | 0.00 | 0.00 | 0.00 | 0.00 |
| 6.   **WA** | | | | | | | | | | |
| 6a.  Per capita GDP | 44 | 49 | 59 | 59 | 67 | 91 | 97 | 94 | 103 | 108 |
| 6b.  GDP | 46 | 52 | 64 | 65 | 75 | 104 | 113 | 111 | 124 | 133 |
| 6c.  % of GWP | 0.00 | 0.00 | 0.00 | 0.00 | 0.00 | 0.00 | 0.00 | 0.00 | 0.00 | 0.00 |

|  |  |  |  |  |  |  |  |  |  | Averages |  |  |
| 1980 (11) | 1981 (12) | 1982 (13) | 1983 (14) | 1984 (15) | 1985 (16) | 1986 (17) | 1987 (18) | 1988 (19) | 1989 (20) | 1970–89 (21) | 1970–79 (22) | 1980–89 (23) |
|---|---|---|---|---|---|---|---|---|---|---|---|---|
| 13 678 | 14 538 | 16 460 | 17 918 | 19 041 | 20 684 | 22 475 | 24 518 | 25 860 | 27 098 | 14 029 | 7 103 | 20 276 |
| 752 | 800 | 905 | 1 003 | 1 066 | 1 179 | 1 281 | 1 398 | 1 500 | 1 572 | 765 | 384 | 1 146 |
| 0.01 | 0.01 | 0.01 | 0.01 | 0.01 | 0.01 | 0.01 | 0.01 | 0.01 | 0.01 | 0.01 | 0.01 | 0.01 |
| ... | ... | ... | ... | ... | ... | ... | ... | ... | ... | ... | ... | ... |
| ... | ... | ... | ... | ... | ... | ... | ... | ... | ... | ... | ... | ... |
| ... | ... | ... | ... | ... | ... | ... | ... | ... | ... | ... | ... | ... |
| 15 265 | 14 429 | 14 726 | 14 532 | 14 193 | 14 721 | 15 115 | 15 728 | 15 572 | 15 490 | 14 029 | 12 669 | 14 957 |
| 840 | 794 | 810 | 814 | 795 | 839 | 862 | 897 | 903 | 898 | 765 | 684 | 845 |
| 0.01 | 0.01 | 0.01 | 0.01 | 0.01 | 0.01 | 0.01 | 0.01 | 0.01 | 0.01 | 0.01 | 0.01 | 0.01 |
| 15 132 | 15 656 | 17 010 | 17 354 | 17 556 | 18 702 | 19 589 | 20 969 | 21 458 | 22 221 | 13 899 | 8 621 | 18 575 |
| 832 | 861 | 936 | 972 | 983 | 1 066 | 1 117 | 1 195 | 1 245 | 1 289 | 758 | 466 | 1 050 |
| 0.01 | 0.01 | 0.01 | 0.01 | 0.01 | 0.01 | 0.01 | 0.01 | 0.01 | 0.01 | 0.01 | 0.01 | 0.01 |
| 20 695 | 19 561 | 19 963 | 19 700 | 19 241 | 19 956 | 20 491 | 21 322 | 21 111 | 21 000 | 19 019 | 17 175 | 20 276 |
| 1 138 | 1 076 | 1 098 | 1 103 | 1 078 | 1 138 | 1 168 | 1 215 | 1 224 | 1 218 | 1 037 | 927 | 1 146 |
| 0.01 | 0.01 | 0.01 | 0.01 | 0.01 | 0.01 | 0.01 | 0.01 | 0.01 | 0.01 | 0.01 | 0.01 | 0.01 |
| 11 838 | 12 655 | 14 710 | 16 158 | 17 372 | 19 471 | 21 293 | 23 293 | 24 380 | 25 600 | 12 941 | 6 522 | 18 733 |
| 651 | 696 | 809 | 905 | 973 | 1 110 | 1 214 | 1 328 | 1 414 | 1 485 | 705 | 352 | 1 058 |
| 0.01 | 0.01 | 0.01 | 0.01 | 0.01 | 0.01 | 0.01 | 0.01 | 0.01 | 0.01 | 0.01 | 0.01 | 0.01 |
| 114 | 119 | 125 | 130 | 139 | 142 | 160 | 195 | 195 | 196 | 120 | 78 | 154 |
| 142 | 150 | 161 | 170 | 185 | 193 | 222 | 278 | 284 | 291 | 148 | 89 | 208 |
| 0.00 | 0.00 | 0.00 | 0.00 | 0.00 | 0.00 | 0.00 | 0.00 | 0.00 | 0.00 | 0.00 | 0.00 | 0.00 |
| ... | ... | ... | ... | ... | ... | ... | ... | ... | ... | ... | ... | ... |
| ... | ... | ... | ... | ... | ... | ... | ... | ... | ... | ... | ... | ... |
| ... | ... | ... | ... | ... | ... | ... | ... | ... | ... | ... | ... | ... |
| 115 | 125 | 129 | 137 | 144 | 146 | 158 | 182 | 184 | 195 | 120 | 79 | 154 |
| 144 | 158 | 166 | 180 | 192 | 199 | 220 | 259 | 267 | 289 | 148 | 89 | 207 |
| 0.00 | 0.00 | 0.00 | 0.00 | 0.00 | 0.00 | 0.00 | 0.00 | 0.00 | 0.00 | 0.00 | 0.00 | 0.00 |
| 114 | 135 | 149 | 164 | 178 | 186 | 205 | 243 | 254 | 280 | 131 | 54 | 194 |
| 142 | 171 | 192 | 215 | 238 | 253 | 285 | 345 | 368 | 415 | 162 | 61 | 262 |
| 0.00 | 0.00 | 0.00 | 0.00 | 0.00 | 0.00 | 0.00 | 0.00 | 0.00 | 0.00 | 0.00 | 0.00 | 0.00 |
| 115 | 125 | 129 | 137 | 144 | 146 | 158 | 182 | 184 | 195 | 120 | 79 | 154 |
| 144 | 158 | 167 | 180 | 192 | 199 | 220 | 259 | 268 | 289 | 148 | 89 | 208 |
| 0.00 | 0.00 | 0.00 | 0.00 | 0.00 | 0.00 | 0.00 | 0.00 | 0.00 | 0.00 | 0.00 | 0.00 | 0.00 |
| 114 | 119 | 125 | 135 | 139 | 142 | 160 | 196 | 195 | 196 | 120 | 78 | 154 |
| 142 | 150 | 161 | 177 | 185 | 193 | 222 | 278 | 283 | 290 | 148 | 89 | 208 |
| 0.00 | 0.00 | 0.00 | 0.00 | 0.00 | 0.00 | 0.00 | 0.00 | 0.00 | 0.00 | 0.00 | 0.00 | 0.00 |

**Table A.1**   Total and per capita gross domestic product of individual countries or areas, expressed in United States dollars, and their individual shares of gross world product, based on alternative conversion rates, 1970−1989 [*cont.*]

| Country or area | 1970 (1) | 1971 (2) | 1972 (3) | 1973 (4) | 1974 (5) | 1975 (6) | 1976 (7) | 1977 (8) | 1978 (9) | 1979 (10) |
|---|---|---|---|---|---|---|---|---|---|---|
| **Bolivia** | | | | | | | | | | |
| **1.   MER** | | | | | | | | | | |
| 1a.   Per capita GDP | 234 | 266 | 283 | 279 | 450 | 501 | 558 | 631 | 709 | 813 |
| 1b.   GDP | 1 010 | 1 178 | 1 285 | 1 300 | 2 150 | 2 450 | 2 800 | 3 250 | 3 750 | 4 413 |
| 1c.   % of GWP | 0.03 | 0.03 | 0.03 | 0.03 | 0.04 | 0.04 | 0.04 | 0.04 | 0.04 | 0.04 |
| **2.   PPPs** | | | | | | | | | | |
| 2a.   Per capita GDP | 589 | 672 | 682 | 758 | 864 | 978 | 1 039 | 1 163 | 1 205 | 1 314 |
| 2b.   GDP | 2 547 | 2 977 | 3 099 | 3 530 | 4 124 | 4 787 | 5 215 | 5 990 | 6 370 | 7 128 |
| 2c.   % of GWP | ... | ... | ... | ... | ... | ... | ... | ... | ... | ... |
| **3.   Absolute 1970−1989 PARE** | | | | | | | | | | |
| 3a.   Per capita GDP | 651 | 667 | 703 | 725 | 728 | 762 | 777 | 795 | 791 | 772 |
| 3b.   GDP | 2 816 | 2 958 | 3 194 | 3 377 | 3 476 | 3 731 | 3 903 | 4 097 | 4 181 | 4 186 |
| 3c.   % of GWP | 0.04 | 0.04 | 0.04 | 0.04 | 0.04 | 0.04 | 0.04 | 0.04 | 0.04 | 0.04 |
| **4.   Relative 1970−1989 PARE** | | | | | | | | | | |
| 4a.   Per capita GDP | 317 | 342 | 377 | 415 | 454 | 522 | 566 | 618 | 659 | 701 |
| 4b.   GDP | 1 373 | 1 516 | 1 712 | 1 931 | 2 168 | 2 556 | 2 841 | 3 183 | 3 486 | 3 802 |
| 4c.   % of GWP | 0.04 | 0.04 | 0.04 | 0.04 | 0.04 | 0.04 | 0.04 | 0.04 | 0.04 | 0.04 |
| **5.   Absolute 1980−1989 PARE** | | | | | | | | | | |
| 5a.   Per capita GDP | 860 | 882 | 929 | 959 | 962 | 1 007 | 1 027 | 1 051 | 1 045 | 1 020 |
| 5b.   GDP | 3 721 | 3 909 | 4 221 | 4 463 | 4 594 | 4 930 | 5 157 | 5 414 | 5 525 | 5 532 |
| 5c.   % of GWP | 0.04 | 0.04 | 0.04 | 0.04 | 0.04 | 0.05 | 0.05 | 0.05 | 0.05 | 0.04 |
| **6.   WA** | | | | | | | | | | |
| 6a.   Per capita GDP | 234 | 266 | 282 | 279 | 450 | 500 | 557 | 631 | 709 | 813 |
| 6b.   GDP | 1 010 | 1 178 | 1 279 | 1 299 | 2 149 | 2 449 | 2 799 | 3 248 | 3 748 | 4 411 |
| 6c.   % of GWP | 0.03 | 0.03 | 0.03 | 0.03 | 0.04 | 0.04 | 0.04 | 0.04 | 0.04 | 0.04 |
| **Botswana** | | | | | | | | | | |
| **1.   MER** | | | | | | | | | | |
| 1a.   Per capita GDP | 134 | 169 | 198 | 311 | 375 | 373 | 396 | 455 | 509 | 710 |
| 1b.   GDP | 84 | 109 | 133 | 217 | 272 | 282 | 310 | 369 | 428 | 619 |
| 1c.   % of GWP | 0.00 | 0.00 | 0.00 | 0.00 | 0.00 | 0.00 | 0.00 | 0.00 | 0.00 | 0.01 |
| **2.   PPPs** | | | | | | | | | | |
| 2a.   Per capita GDP | 349 | 393 | 415 | 522 | 596 | 613 | 719 | 804 | 800 | 1 041 |
| 2b.   GDP | 218 | 254 | 278 | 365 | 433 | 464 | 564 | 653 | 673 | 907 |
| 2c.   % of GWP | ... | ... | ... | ... | ... | ... | ... | ... | ... | ... |
| **3.   Absolute 1970−1989 PARE** | | | | | | | | | | |
| 3a.   Per capita GDP | 383 | 392 | 486 | 513 | 526 | 500 | 559 | 553 | 632 | 678 |
| 3b.   GDP | 239 | 253 | 326 | 359 | 383 | 378 | 438 | 449 | 531 | 591 |
| 3c.   % of GWP | 0.00 | 0.00 | 0.00 | 0.00 | 0.00 | 0.00 | 0.00 | 0.00 | 0.01 | 0.01 |
| **4.   Relative 1970−1989 PARE** | | | | | | | | | | |
| 4a.   Per capita GDP | 187 | 201 | 261 | 293 | 328 | 342 | 407 | 429 | 527 | 616 |
| 4b.   GDP | 116 | 130 | 175 | 205 | 239 | 259 | 319 | 349 | 443 | 536 |
| 4c.   % of GWP | 0.00 | 0.00 | 0.00 | 0.00 | 0.00 | 0.00 | 0.00 | 0.00 | 0.01 | 0.01 |
| **5.   Absolute 1980−1989 PARE** | | | | | | | | | | |
| 5a.   Per capita GDP | 420 | 430 | 534 | 563 | 578 | 549 | 613 | 607 | 693 | 745 |
| 5b.   GDP | 262 | 278 | 358 | 394 | 420 | 415 | 481 | 493 | 583 | 649 |
| 5c.   % of GWP | 0.00 | 0.00 | 0.00 | 0.00 | 0.00 | 0.00 | 0.00 | 0.00 | 0.00 | 0.01 |
| **6.   WA** | | | | | | | | | | |
| 6a.   Per capita GDP | 134 | 169 | 208 | 285 | 379 | 403 | 412 | 444 | 511 | 699 |
| 6b.   GDP | 84 | 109 | 140 | 199 | 276 | 305 | 323 | 360 | 430 | 609 |
| 6c.   % of GWP | 0.00 | 0.00 | 0.00 | 0.00 | 0.00 | 0.00 | 0.00 | 0.00 | 0.00 | 0.01 |

| 1980 (11) | 1981 (12) | 1982 (13) | 1983 (14) | 1984 (15) | 1985 (16) | 1986 (17) | 1987 (18) | 1988 (19) | 1989 (20) | Averages 1970−89 (21) | 1970−79 (22) | 1980−89 (23) |
|---|---|---|---|---|---|---|---|---|---|---|---|---|
| 901 | 1 106 | 1 067 | 992 | 956 | 764 | 556 | 601 | 618 | 609 | 675 | 488 | 806 |
| 5 018 | 6 324 | 6 271 | 5 989 | 5 928 | 4 866 | 3 639 | 4 044 | 4 277 | 4 334 | 3 714 | 2 359 | 5 069 |
| 0.04 | 0.05 | 0.05 | 0.05 | 0.05 | 0.04 | 0.02 | 0.02 | 0.02 | 0.02 | 0.04 | 0.04 | 0.04 |
| 1 461 | 1 418 | 1 408 | 1 080 | 1 185 | 1 248 | 1 203 | 1 229 | 1 270 | 1 318 | 1 150 | 947 | 1 283 |
| 8 139 | 8 111 | 8 270 | 6 519 | 7 344 | 7 953 | 7 875 | 8 273 | 8 790 | 9 374 | 6 321 | 4 577 | 8 065 |
| ... | ... | ... | ... | ... | ... | ... | ... | ... | ... | ... | ... | ... |
| 741 | 729 | 678 | 617 | 599 | 582 | 550 | 546 | 546 | 544 | 675 | 743 | 610 |
| 4 129 | 4 167 | 3 986 | 3 726 | 3 715 | 3 709 | 3 601 | 3 677 | 3 780 | 3 872 | 3 714 | 3 592 | 3 836 |
| 0.04 | 0.04 | 0.04 | 0.03 | 0.03 | 0.03 | 0.03 | 0.03 | 0.03 | 0.03 | 0.04 | 0.04 | 0.03 |
| 735 | 790 | 784 | 737 | 741 | 740 | 713 | 728 | 753 | 781 | 654 | 508 | 753 |
| 4 093 | 4 522 | 4 604 | 4 449 | 4 595 | 4 712 | 4 666 | 4 902 | 5 208 | 5 554 | 3 594 | 2 457 | 4 731 |
| 0.04 | 0.04 | 0.04 | 0.03 | 0.03 | 0.03 | 0.03 | 0.03 | 0.03 | 0.03 | 0.03 | 0.04 | 0.03 |
| 979 | 963 | 896 | 816 | 792 | 769 | 727 | 722 | 722 | 719 | 893 | 982 | 806 |
| 5 456 | 5 507 | 5 267 | 4 924 | 4 909 | 4 902 | 4 758 | 4 859 | 4 995 | 5 117 | 4 908 | 4 747 | 5 069 |
| 0.04 | 0.04 | 0.04 | 0.04 | 0.04 | 0.03 | 0.03 | 0.03 | 0.03 | 0.03 | 0.04 | 0.05 | 0.04 |
| 900 | 1 105 | 1 068 | 992 | 956 | 767 | 555 | 601 | 618 | 609 | 675 | 488 | 807 |
| 5 016 | 6 321 | 6 274 | 5 988 | 5 928 | 4 887 | 3 635 | 4 045 | 4 277 | 4 334 | 3 714 | 2 357 | 5 071 |
| 0.04 | 0.05 | 0.05 | 0.05 | 0.05 | 0.04 | 0.02 | 0.02 | 0.02 | 0.02 | 0.04 | 0.04 | 0.04 |
| 1 012 | 1 006 | 794 | 952 | 959 | 806 | 1 057 | 1 333 | 1 558 | 1 982 | 869 | 381 | 1 183 |
| 913 | 941 | 770 | 958 | 1 002 | 874 | 1 189 | 1 557 | 1 888 | 2 494 | 770 | 282 | 1 259 |
| 0.01 | 0.01 | 0.01 | 0.01 | 0.01 | 0.01 | 0.01 | 0.01 | 0.01 | 0.01 | 0.01 | 0.00 | 0.01 |
| 1 361 | 1 628 | 1 529 | 1 758 | 1 917 | 2 401 | 2 688 | 2 781 | 3 019 | 3 438 | 1 673 | 648 | 2 337 |
| 1 228 | 1 522 | 1 483 | 1 768 | 2 002 | 2 602 | 3 024 | 3 248 | 3 659 | 4 325 | 1 484 | 481 | 2 486 |
| ... | ... | ... | ... | ... | ... | ... | ... | ... | ... | ... | ... | ... |
| 772 | 810 | 763 | 912 | 1 054 | 1 097 | 1 205 | 1 211 | 1 272 | 1 392 | 869 | 532 | 1 077 |
| 697 | 757 | 740 | 917 | 1 100 | 1 189 | 1 355 | 1 415 | 1 542 | 1 751 | 770 | 395 | 1 146 |
| 0.01 | 0.01 | 0.01 | 0.01 | 0.01 | 0.01 | 0.01 | 0.01 | 0.01 | 0.01 | 0.01 | 0.00 | 0.01 |
| 766 | 879 | 881 | 1 089 | 1 303 | 1 394 | 1 561 | 1 615 | 1 753 | 1 996 | 980 | 374 | 1 373 |
| 690 | 822 | 855 | 1 095 | 1 361 | 1 511 | 1 756 | 1 886 | 2 125 | 2 511 | 869 | 277 | 1 461 |
| 0.01 | 0.01 | 0.01 | 0.01 | 0.01 | 0.01 | 0.01 | 0.01 | 0.01 | 0.01 | 0.01 | 0.00 | 0.01 |
| 848 | 889 | 837 | 1 001 | 1 157 | 1 205 | 1 322 | 1 330 | 1 397 | 1 528 | 954 | 584 | 1 183 |
| 765 | 832 | 812 | 1 007 | 1 208 | 1 306 | 1 488 | 1 553 | 1 693 | 1 922 | 846 | 433 | 1 259 |
| 0.01 | 0.01 | 0.01 | 0.01 | 0.01 | 0.01 | 0.01 | 0.01 | 0.01 | 0.01 | 0.01 | 0.00 | 0.01 |
| 990 | 1 086 | 888 | 959 | 1 090 | 952 | 1 039 | 1 245 | 1 661 | 1 989 | 895 | 382 | 1 226 |
| 893 | 1 015 | 861 | 964 | 1 138 | 1 032 | 1 169 | 1 454 | 2 013 | 2 503 | 794 | 283 | 1 304 |
| 0.01 | 0.01 | 0.01 | 0.01 | 0.01 | 0.01 | 0.01 | 0.01 | 0.01 | 0.01 | 0.01 | 0.00 | 0.01 |

**Table A.1**     Total and per capita gross domestic product of individual countries or areas,
expressed in United States dollars, and their individual shares of gross world
product, based on alternative conversion rates, 1970−1989 [*cont.*]

| Country or area | 1970 (1) | 1971 (2) | 1972 (3) | 1973 (4) | 1974 (5) | 1975 (6) | 1976 (7) | 1977 (8) | 1978 (9) | 1979 (10) |
|---|---|---|---|---|---|---|---|---|---|---|
| **Brazil** | | | | | | | | | | |
| **1.    MER** | | | | | | | | | | |
| 1a.   Per capita GDP | 522 | 407 | 497 | 809 | 948 | 1 143 | 1 315 | 1 514 | 1 678 | 1 631 |
| 1b.   GDP | 50 000 | 40 000 | 50 000 | 83 333 | 100 000 | 123 457 | 145 455 | 171 429 | 194 444 | 193 333 |
| 1c.   % of GWP | 1.57 | 1.14 | 1.24 | 1.70 | 1.80 | 1.99 | 2.17 | 2.27 | 2.16 | 1.88 |
| **2.    PPPs** | | | | | | | | | | |
| 2a.   Per capita GDP | 902 | 783 | 1 010 | 1 419 | 1 591 | 1 801 | 2 047 | 2 230 | 2 366 | 2 673 |
| 2b.   GDP | 86 465 | 76 935 | 101 620 | 146 243 | 167 849 | 194 602 | 226 417 | 252 392 | 274 078 | 316 922 |
| 2c.   % of GWP | ... | ... | ... | ... | ... | ... | ... | ... | ... | ... |
| **3.    Absolute 1970−1989 PARE** | | | | | | | | | | |
| 3a.   Per capita GDP | 1 030 | 1 119 | 1 224 | 1 362 | 1 451 | 1 491 | 1 599 | 1 634 | 1 674 | 1 754 |
| 3b.   GDP | 98 770 | 109 934 | 123 180 | 140 392 | 153 082 | 161 069 | 176 828 | 184 976 | 193 897 | 207 878 |
| 3c.   % of GWP | 1.39 | 1.49 | 1.58 | 1.69 | 1.81 | 1.87 | 1.95 | 1.96 | 1.97 | 2.04 |
| **4.    Relative 1970−1989 PARE** | | | | | | | | | | |
| 4a.   Per capita GDP | 502 | 574 | 656 | 779 | 905 | 1 021 | 1 164 | 1 270 | 1 395 | 1 592 |
| 4b.   GDP | 48 157 | 56 350 | 66 037 | 80 263 | 95 461 | 110 349 | 128 717 | 143 730 | 161 652 | 188 783 |
| 4c.   % of GWP | 1.39 | 1.48 | 1.58 | 1.69 | 1.81 | 1.87 | 1.95 | 1.96 | 1.97 | 2.04 |
| **5.    Absolute 1980−1989 PARE** | | | | | | | | | | |
| 5a.   Per capita GDP | 1 198 | 1 301 | 1 423 | 1 584 | 1 686 | 1 733 | 1 858 | 1 899 | 1 945 | 2 038 |
| 5b.   GDP | 114 797 | 127 773 | 143 168 | 163 174 | 177 922 | 187 205 | 205 521 | 214 992 | 225 360 | 241 611 |
| 5c.   % of GWP | 1.32 | 1.41 | 1.50 | 1.61 | 1.72 | 1.78 | 1.86 | 1.86 | 1.88 | 1.95 |
| **6.    WA** | | | | | | | | | | |
| 6a.   Per capita GDP | 454 | 385 | 502 | 792 | 977 | 1 139 | 1 356 | 1 499 | 1 672 | 1 816 |
| 6b.   GDP | 43 540 | 37 825 | 50 556 | 81 623 | 103 094 | 123 052 | 149 914 | 169 683 | 193 694 | 215 252 |
| 6c.   % of GWP | 1.36 | 1.08 | 1.26 | 1.68 | 1.85 | 2.00 | 2.23 | 2.25 | 2.18 | 2.10 |
| **British Virgin Islands** | | | | | | | | | | |
| **1.    MER** | | | | | | | | | | |
| 1a.   Per capita GDP | 1 803 | 1 556 | 1 625 | 1 839 | 2 199 | 2 416 | 2 634 | 2 723 | 3 163 | 3 945 |
| 1b.   GDP | 20 | 17 | 18 | 20 | 24 | 27 | 29 | 30 | 35 | 43 |
| 1c.   % of GWP | 0.00 | 0.00 | 0.00 | 0.00 | 0.00 | 0.00 | 0.00 | 0.00 | 0.00 | 0.00 |
| **2.    PPPs** | | | | | | | | | | |
| 2a.   Per capita GDP | ... | ... | ... | ... | ... | ... | ... | ... | ... | ... |
| 2b.   GDP | ... | ... | ... | ... | ... | ... | ... | ... | ... | ... |
| 2c.   % of GWP | ... | ... | ... | ... | ... | ... | ... | ... | ... | ... |
| **3.    Absolute 1970−1989 PARE** | | | | | | | | | | |
| 3a.   Per capita GDP | 3 839 | 3 456 | 3 461 | 3 653 | 4 006 | 4 186 | 4 174 | 4 251 | 4 576 | 4 831 |
| 3b.   GDP | 42 | 38 | 38 | 40 | 44 | 46 | 46 | 47 | 50 | 53 |
| 3c.   % of GWP | 0.00 | 0.00 | 0.00 | 0.00 | 0.00 | 0.00 | 0.00 | 0.00 | 0.00 | 0.00 |
| **4.    Relative 1970−1989 PARE** | | | | | | | | | | |
| 4a.   Per capita GDP | 1 872 | 1 772 | 1 855 | 2 089 | 2 498 | 2 868 | 3 039 | 3 303 | 3 815 | 4 387 |
| 4b.   GDP | 21 | 19 | 20 | 23 | 27 | 32 | 33 | 36 | 42 | 48 |
| 4c.   % of GWP | 0.00 | 0.00 | 0.00 | 0.00 | 0.00 | 0.00 | 0.00 | 0.00 | 0.00 | 0.00 |
| **5.    Absolute 1980−1989 PARE** | | | | | | | | | | |
| 5a.   Per capita GDP | 4 773 | 4 297 | 4 302 | 4 542 | 4 980 | 5 204 | 5 189 | 5 285 | 5 689 | 6 006 |
| 5b.   GDP | 53 | 47 | 47 | 50 | 55 | 57 | 57 | 58 | 63 | 66 |
| 5c.   % of GWP | 0.00 | 0.00 | 0.00 | 0.00 | 0.00 | 0.00 | 0.00 | 0.00 | 0.00 | 0.00 |
| **6.    WA**[a] | | | | | | | | | | |
| 6a.   Per capita GDP | 1 406 | 1 540 | 1 602 | 1 730 | 2 024 | 2 267 | 2 437 | 2 614 | 2 989 | 3 424 |
| 6b.   GDP | 15 | 17 | 18 | 19 | 22 | 25 | 27 | 29 | 33 | 38 |
| 6c.   % of GWP | 0.00 | 0.00 | 0.00 | 0.00 | 0.00 | 0.00 | 0.00 | 0.00 | 0.00 | 0.00 |

| | | | | | | | | | | Averages | | |
|---|---|---|---|---|---|---|---|---|---|---|---|---|
| 1980 | 1981 | 1982 | 1983 | 1984 | 1985 | 1986 | 1987 | 1988 | 1989 | 1970–89 | 1970–79 | 1980–89 |
| (11) | (12) | (13) | (14) | (15) | (16) | (17) | (18) | (19) | (20) | (21) | (22) | (23) |
| 1 979 | 2 239 | 2 233 | 1 581 | 1 606 | 1 681 | 1 960 | 2 146 | 2 426 | 3 270 | 1 670 | 1 078 | 2 129 |
| 240 000 | 277 778 | 283 333 | 205 172 | 212 973 | 227 903 | 271 523 | 303 571 | 350 427 | 482 004 | 200 307 | 115 145 | 285 468 |
| 2.07 | 2.37 | 2.44 | 1.73 | 1.75 | 1.81 | 1.82 | 1.77 | 1.83 | 2.40 | 1.97 | 1.89 | 2.00 |
| 3 059 | 3 389 | 3 629 | 3 527 | 3 662 | 3 860 | 4 166 | 4 317 | 4 370 | 4 592 | 2 943 | 1 727 | 3 888 |
| 371 057 | 420 492 | 460 480 | 457 590 | 485 760 | 523 314 | 577 003 | 610 715 | 631 220 | 676 826 | 352 899 | 184 352 | 521 446 |
| ... | ... | ... | ... | ... | ... | ... | ... | ... | ... | ... | ... | ... |
| 1 870 | 1 767 | 1 744 | 1 662 | 1 719 | 1 820 | 1 926 | 1 940 | 1 900 | 1 918 | 1 670 | 1 452 | 1 831 |
| 226 850 | 219 258 | 221 268 | 215 668 | 227 963 | 246 790 | 266 749 | 274 449 | 274 449 | 282 687 | 200 307 | 155 001 | 245 613 |
| 2.18 | 2.07 | 2.08 | 1.97 | 1.99 | 2.08 | 2.18 | 2.17 | 2.08 | 2.08 | 1.97 | 1.80 | 2.09 |
| 1 854 | 1 917 | 2 014 | 1 985 | 2 126 | 2 313 | 2 496 | 2 587 | 2 619 | 2 751 | 1 729 | 1 011 | 2 287 |
| 224 867 | 237 905 | 255 594 | 257 546 | 281 979 | 313 538 | 345 706 | 365 904 | 378 189 | 405 513 | 207 312 | 107 950 | 306 674 |
| 2.18 | 2.07 | 2.08 | 1.97 | 1.99 | 2.08 | 2.18 | 2.17 | 2.08 | 2.08 | 2.02 | 1.84 | 2.09 |
| 2 174 | 2 054 | 2 027 | 1 932 | 1 997 | 2 116 | 2 238 | 2 255 | 2 209 | 2 229 | 1 941 | 1 687 | 2 129 |
| 263 661 | 254 836 | 257 173 | 250 664 | 264 954 | 286 837 | 310 034 | 318 984 | 318 984 | 328 559 | 232 810 | 180 152 | 285 469 |
| 2.08 | 1.98 | 1.98 | 1.88 | 1.90 | 1.99 | 2.09 | 2.08 | 1.99 | 1.99 | 1.88 | 1.71 | 2.00 |
| 1 877 | 2 164 | 2 239 | 1 589 | 1 607 | 1 681 | 1 961 | 2 144 | 2 426 | 3 270 | 1 669 | 1 094 | 2 114 |
| 227 643 | 268 458 | 284 100 | 206 224 | 213 201 | 227 890 | 271 602 | 303 351 | 350 450 | 482 018 | 200 158 | 116 823 | 283 494 |
| 1.98 | 2.28 | 2.44 | 1.74 | 1.74 | 1.80 | 1.85 | 1.82 | 1.87 | 2.46 | 1.98 | 1.93 | 2.00 |
| 4 514 | 4 936 | 5 810 | 6 548 | 7 192 | 7 490 | 7 525 | 8 974 | 10 103 | 11 235 | 5 186 | 2 390 | 7 748 |
| 54 | 59 | 70 | 79 | 86 | 90 | 98 | 117 | 131 | 146 | 60 | 26 | 93 |
| 0.00 | 0.00 | 0.00 | 0.00 | 0.00 | 0.00 | 0.00 | 0.00 | 0.00 | 0.00 | 0.00 | 0.00 | 0.00 |
| ... | ... | ... | ... | ... | ... | ... | ... | ... | ... | ... | ... | ... |
| ... | ... | ... | ... | ... | ... | ... | ... | ... | ... | ... | ... | ... |
| ... | ... | ... | ... | ... | ... | ... | ... | ... | ... | ... | ... | ... |
| 5 342 | 5 376 | 5 498 | 5 820 | 6 157 | 6 158 | 5 966 | 6 157 | 6 706 | 6 992 | 5 186 | 4 044 | 6 232 |
| 64 | 65 | 66 | 70 | 74 | 74 | 78 | 80 | 87 | 91 | 60 | 44 | 75 |
| 0.00 | 0.00 | 0.00 | 0.00 | 0.00 | 0.00 | 0.00 | 0.00 | 0.00 | 0.00 | 0.00 | 0.00 | 0.00 |
| 5 295 | 5 833 | 6 350 | 6 950 | 7 615 | 7 823 | 7 732 | 8 209 | 9 241 | 10 031 | 5 385 | 2 750 | 7 802 |
| 64 | 70 | 76 | 83 | 91 | 94 | 101 | 107 | 120 | 130 | 62 | 30 | 94 |
| 0.00 | 0.00 | 0.00 | 0.00 | 0.00 | 0.00 | 0.00 | 0.00 | 0.00 | 0.00 | 0.00 | 0.00 | 0.00 |
| 6 641 | 6 683 | 6 834 | 7 236 | 7 654 | 7 655 | 7 417 | 7 655 | 8 337 | 8 693 | 6 446 | 5 027 | 7 748 |
| 80 | 80 | 82 | 87 | 92 | 92 | 96 | 100 | 108 | 113 | 74 | 55 | 93 |
| 0.00 | 0.00 | 0.00 | 0.00 | 0.00 | 0.00 | 0.00 | 0.00 | 0.00 | 0.00 | 0.00 | 0.00 | 0.00 |
| 4 157 | 4 612 | 5 124 | 5 971 | 6 863 | 7 196 | 7 243 | 8 027 | 9 388 | 10 636 | 4 819 | 2 203 | 7 216 |
| 50 | 55 | 61 | 72 | 82 | 86 | 94 | 104 | 122 | 138 | 55 | 24 | 87 |
| 0.00 | 0.00 | 0.00 | 0.00 | 0.00 | 0.00 | 0.00 | 0.00 | 0.00 | 0.00 | 0.00 | 0.00 | 0.00 |

**Table A.1**    Total and per capita gross domestic product of individual countries or areas,
expressed in United States dollars, and their individual shares of gross world
product, based on alternative conversion rates, 1970–1989 [*cont.*]

| Country or area | 1970 (1) | 1971 (2) | 1972 (3) | 1973 (4) | 1974 (5) | 1975 (6) | 1976 (7) | 1977 (8) | 1978 (9) | 1979 (10) |
|---|---|---|---|---|---|---|---|---|---|---|
| **Brunei Darussalam** | | | | | | | | | | |
| **1.    MER** | | | | | | | | | | |
| 1a.    Per capita GDP | 1 362 | 1 463 | 1 929 | 2 736 | 7 198 | 7 346 | 8 538 | 10 223 | 11 020 | 15 568 |
| 1b.    GDP | 178 | 199 | 272 | 400 | 1 087 | 1 153 | 1 383 | 1 718 | 1 906 | 2 787 |
| 1c.    % of GWP | 0.01 | 0.01 | 0.01 | 0.01 | 0.02 | 0.02 | 0.02 | 0.02 | 0.02 | 0.03 |
| **2.    PPPs** | | | | | | | | | | |
| 2a.    Per capita GDP | ... | ... | ... | ... | ... | ... | ... | ... | ... | ... |
| 2b.    GDP | ... | ... | ... | ... | ... | ... | ... | ... | ... | ... |
| 2c.    % of GWP | ... | ... | ... | ... | ... | ... | ... | ... | ... | ... |
| **3.    Absolute 1970–1989 PARE** | | | | | | | | | | |
| 3a.    Per capita GDP | 9 949 | 10 349 | 10 781 | 11 245 | 11 742 | 11 334 | 13 198 | 14 116 | 14 640 | 17 338 |
| 3b.    GDP | 1 303 | 1 407 | 1 520 | 1 642 | 1 773 | 1 779 | 2 138 | 2 371 | 2 533 | 3 104 |
| 3c.    % of GWP | 0.02 | 0.02 | 0.02 | 0.02 | 0.02 | 0.02 | 0.02 | 0.03 | 0.03 | 0.03 |
| **4.    Relative 1970–1989 PARE** | | | | | | | | | | |
| 4a.    Per capita GDP | 4 851 | 5 305 | 5 780 | 6 429 | 7 322 | 7 765 | 9 607 | 10 968 | 12 205 | 15 746 |
| 4b.    GDP | 635 | 721 | 815 | 939 | 1 106 | 1 219 | 1 556 | 1 843 | 2 111 | 2 818 |
| 4c.    % of GWP | 0.02 | 0.02 | 0.02 | 0.02 | 0.02 | 0.02 | 0.02 | 0.03 | 0.03 | 0.03 |
| **5.    Absolute 1980–1989 PARE** | | | | | | | | | | |
| 5a.    Per capita GDP | 13 508 | 14 052 | 14 638 | 15 268 | 15 943 | 15 389 | 17 920 | 19 166 | 19 877 | 23 541 |
| 5b.    GDP | 1 770 | 1 911 | 2 064 | 2 229 | 2 407 | 2 416 | 2 903 | 3 220 | 3 439 | 4 214 |
| 5c.    % of GWP | 0.02 | 0.02 | 0.02 | 0.02 | 0.02 | 0.02 | 0.03 | 0.03 | 0.03 | 0.03 |
| **6.    WA[a]** | | | | | | | | | | |
| 6a.    Per capita GDP | 975 | 1 279 | 1 620 | 2 012 | 3 109 | 4 668 | 8 389 | 9 475 | 10 322 | 13 606 |
| 6b.    GDP | 128 | 174 | 228 | 294 | 470 | 733 | 1 359 | 1 592 | 1 786 | 2 435 |
| 6c.    % of GWP | 0.00 | 0.00 | 0.01 | 0.01 | 0.01 | 0.01 | 0.02 | 0.02 | 0.02 | 0.02 |
| **Bulgaria** | | | | | | | | | | |
| **1.    MER** | | | | | | | | | | |
| 1a.    Per capita GDP | 771 | 842 | 880 | 1 041 | 1 187 | 1 699 | 1 793 | 1 828 | 1 721 | 1 913 |
| 1b.    GDP | 6 550 | 7 193 | 7 561 | 8 997 | 10 310 | 14 817 | 15 704 | 16 058 | 15 172 | 16 908 |
| 1c.    % of GWP | 0.21 | 0.21 | 0.19 | 0.18 | 0.19 | 0.24 | 0.23 | 0.21 | 0.17 | 0.16 |
| **2.    PPPs** | | | | | | | | | | |
| 2a.    Per capita GDP | ... | ... | ... | ... | ... | ... | ... | ... | ... | ... |
| 2b.    GDP | ... | ... | ... | ... | ... | ... | ... | ... | ... | ... |
| 2c.    % of GWP | ... | ... | ... | ... | ... | ... | ... | ... | ... | ... |
| **3.    Absolute 1970–1989 PARE** | | | | | | | | | | |
| 3a.    Per capita GDP | 1 171 | 1 244 | 1 334 | 1 433 | 1 534 | 1 661 | 1 764 | 1 871 | 1 965 | 2 090 |
| 3b.    GDP | 9 939 | 10 622 | 11 462 | 12 380 | 13 316 | 14 488 | 15 444 | 16 444 | 17 319 | 18 471 |
| 3c.    % of GWP | 0.14 | 0.14 | 0.15 | 0.15 | 0.16 | 0.17 | 0.17 | 0.17 | 0.18 | 0.18 |
| **4.    Relative 1970–1989 PARE** | | | | | | | | | | |
| 4a.    Per capita GDP | 571 | 637 | 715 | 819 | 956 | 1 138 | 1 284 | 1 454 | 1 638 | 1 898 |
| 4b.    GDP | 4 846 | 5 445 | 6 145 | 7 078 | 8 304 | 9 925 | 11 242 | 12 777 | 14 439 | 16 774 |
| 4c.    % of GWP | 0.14 | 0.14 | 0.15 | 0.15 | 0.16 | 0.17 | 0.17 | 0.17 | 0.18 | 0.18 |
| **5.    Absolute 1980–1989 PARE** | | | | | | | | | | |
| 5a.    Per capita GDP | 1 274 | 1 353 | 1 452 | 1 559 | 1 669 | 1 808 | 1 919 | 2 037 | 2 138 | 2 274 |
| 5b.    GDP | 10 816 | 11 560 | 12 474 | 13 473 | 14 492 | 15 767 | 16 808 | 17 896 | 18 848 | 20 102 |
| 5c.    % of GWP | 0.12 | 0.13 | 0.13 | 0.13 | 0.14 | 0.15 | 0.15 | 0.16 | 0.16 | 0.16 |
| **6.    WA[a]** | | | | | | | | | | |
| 6a.    Per capita GDP | 735 | 811 | 887 | 984 | 1 100 | 1 367 | 1 627 | 1 881 | 1 872 | 1 924 |
| 6b.    GDP | 6 242 | 6 926 | 7 624 | 8 501 | 9 549 | 11 923 | 14 244 | 16 525 | 16 499 | 17 008 |
| 6c.    % of GWP | 0.20 | 0.20 | 0.19 | 0.17 | 0.17 | 0.19 | 0.21 | 0.22 | 0.19 | 0.17 |

| | | | | | | | | | | Averages | | |
|---|---|---|---|---|---|---|---|---|---|---|---|---|
| 1980 (11) | 1981 (12) | 1982 (13) | 1983 (14) | 1984 (15) | 1985 (16) | 1986 (17) | 1987 (18) | 1988 (19) | 1989 (20) | 1970–89 (21) | 1970–79 (22) | 1980–89 (23) |
| 26 063 | 20 745 | 19 541 | 16 828 | 15 936 | 14 352 | 9 600 | 9 852 | 9 284 | 9 101 | 11 861 | 7 197 | 14 608 |
| 4 848 | 4 004 | 3 908 | 3 500 | 3 442 | 3 229 | 2 237 | 2 374 | 2 321 | 2 348 | 2 165 | 1 108 | 3 221 |
| 0.04 | 0.03 | 0.03 | 0.03 | 0.03 | 0.03 | 0.02 | 0.01 | 0.01 | 0.01 | 0.02 | 0.02 | 0.02 |
| ... | ... | ... | ... | ... | ... | ... | ... | ... | ... | ... | ... | ... |
| ... | ... | ... | ... | ... | ... | ... | ... | ... | ... | ... | ... | ... |
| ... | ... | ... | ... | ... | ... | ... | ... | ... | ... | ... | ... | ... |
| 15 518 | 11 990 | 12 028 | 11 624 | 11 260 | 10 889 | 9 225 | 9 016 | 8 880 | 8 820 | 11 861 | 12 708 | 10 759 |
| 2 886 | 2 314 | 2 406 | 2 418 | 2 432 | 2 450 | 2 149 | 2 173 | 2 220 | 2 276 | 2 165 | 1 957 | 2 372 |
| 0.03 | 0.02 | 0.02 | 0.02 | 0.02 | 0.02 | 0.02 | 0.02 | 0.02 | 0.02 | 0.02 | 0.02 | 0.02 |
| 15 383 | 13 010 | 13 894 | 13 881 | 13 929 | 13 834 | 11 955 | 12 020 | 12 237 | 12 652 | 11 761 | 8 938 | 13 227 |
| 2 861 | 2 511 | 2 779 | 2 887 | 3 009 | 3 113 | 2 786 | 2 897 | 3 059 | 3 264 | 2 146 | 1 376 | 2 917 |
| 0.03 | 0.02 | 0.02 | 0.02 | 0.02 | 0.02 | 0.02 | 0.02 | 0.02 | 0.02 | 0.02 | 0.02 | 0.02 |
| 21 070 | 16 280 | 16 331 | 15 782 | 15 289 | 14 784 | 12 525 | 12 241 | 12 057 | 11 976 | 16 105 | 17 255 | 14 608 |
| 3 919 | 3 142 | 3 266 | 3 283 | 3 302 | 3 326 | 2 918 | 2 950 | 3 014 | 3 090 | 2 939 | 2 657 | 3 221 |
| 0.03 | 0.02 | 0.03 | 0.02 | 0.02 | 0.02 | 0.02 | 0.02 | 0.02 | 0.02 | 0.02 | 0.03 | 0.02 |
| 15 326 | 15 727 | 20 170 | 18 506 | 16 783 | 15 151 | 11 406 | 10 266 | 9 405 | 9 315 | 10 928 | 5 973 | 13 918 |
| 2 851 | 3 035 | 4 034 | 3 849 | 3 625 | 3 409 | 2 658 | 2 474 | 2 351 | 2 403 | 1 994 | 920 | 3 069 |
| 0.02 | 0.03 | 0.03 | 0.03 | 0.03 | 0.03 | 0.02 | 0.01 | 0.01 | 0.01 | 0.02 | 0.02 | 0.02 |
| 2 256 | 2 252 | 2 231 | 2 288 | 3 576 | 3 601 | 3519 | 3201 | 2 900 | 2 566 | 2 109 | 1 371 | 2 838 |
| 19 993 | 20 013 | 19 872 | 20 421 | 31 991 | 32 272 | 31 582 | 28 765 | 26 085 | 23 104 | 18 668 | 11 927 | 25 410 |
| 0.17 | 0.17 | 0.17 | 0.17 | 0.26 | 0.26 | 0.21 | 0.17 | 0.14 | 0.12 | 0.18 | 0.20 | 0.18 |
| ... | ... | ... | ... | ... | ... | ... | ... | ... | ... | ... | ... | ... |
| ... | ... | ... | ... | ... | ... | ... | ... | ... | ... | ... | ... | ... |
| ... | ... | ... | ... | ... | ... | ... | ... | ... | ... | ... | ... | ... |
| 2 203 | 2 307 | 2 398 | 2 465 | 2 574 | 2 615 | 2 750 | 2 886 | 2 952 | 2 940 | 2 109 | 1 607 | 2 608 |
| 19 525 | 20 502 | 21 360 | 22 005 | 23 021 | 23 430 | 24 680 | 25 929 | 26 555 | 26 476 | 18 668 | 13 988 | 23 348 |
| 0.19 | 0.19 | 0.20 | 0.20 | 0.20 | 0.20 | 0.20 | 0.21 | 0.20 | 0.19 | 0.18 | 0.16 | 0.20 |
| 2 184 | 2 504 | 2 771 | 2 944 | 3 183 | 3 322 | 3 564 | 3 847 | 4 068 | 4 218 | 2 197 | 1 114 | 3 261 |
| 19 354 | 22 245 | 24 674 | 26 278 | 28 476 | 29 767 | 31 986 | 34 570 | 36 593 | 37 980 | 19 445 | 9 698 | 29 192 |
| 0.19 | 0.19 | 0.20 | 0.20 | 0.20 | 0.20 | 0.20 | 0.21 | 0.20 | 0.19 | 0.19 | 0.17 | 0.20 |
| 2 398 | 2 511 | 2 610 | 2 683 | 2 801 | 2 846 | 2 993 | 3 140 | 3 213 | 3 200 | 2 296 | 1 749 | 2 838 |
| 21 249 | 22 312 | 23 246 | 23 948 | 25 053 | 25 499 | 26 859 | 28 219 | 28 899 | 28 813 | 20 317 | 15 223 | 25 410 |
| 0.17 | 0.17 | 0.18 | 0.18 | 0.18 | 0.18 | 0.18 | 0.18 | 0.18 | 0.17 | 0.16 | 0.14 | 0.18 |
| 2 059 | 2 238 | 2 339 | 2 328 | 2 688 | 3 109 | 3 705 | 3 594 | 3 279 | 2 878 | 2 077 | 1 322 | 2 821 |
| 18 245 | 19 883 | 20 833 | 20 780 | 24 046 | 27 858 | 33 245 | 32 292 | 29 495 | 25 911 | 18 382 | 11 504 | 25 259 |
| 0.16 | 0.17 | 0.18 | 0.18 | 0.20 | 0.22 | 0.23 | 0.19 | 0.16 | 0.13 | 0.18 | 0.19 | 0.18 |

**Table A.1** Total and per capita gross domestic product of individual countries or areas, expressed in United States dollars, and their individual shares of gross world product, based on alternative conversion rates, 1970–1989 [*cont.*]

| Country or area | 1970 (1) | 1971 (2) | 1972 (3) | 1973 (4) | 1974 (5) | 1975 (6) | 1976 (7) | 1977 (8) | 1978 (9) | 1979 (10) |
|---|---|---|---|---|---|---|---|---|---|---|
| **Burkina Faso** | | | | | | | | | | |
| **1. MER** | | | | | | | | | | |
| 1a. Per capita GDP | 54 | 54 | 67 | 76 | 82 | 96 | 90 | 106 | 133 | 175 |
| 1b. GDP | 298 | 306 | 390 | 453 | 498 | 592 | 568 | 686 | 885 | 1 187 |
| 1c. % of GWP | 0.01 | 0.01 | 0.01 | 0.01 | 0.01 | 0.01 | 0.01 | 0.01 | 0.01 | 0.01 |
| **2. PPPs** | | | | | | | | | | |
| 2a. Per capita GDP | 109 | 154 | 162 | 164 | 188 | 201 | 207 | 234 | 238 | 300 |
| 2b. GDP | 606 | 873 | 939 | 974 | 1 139 | 1 250 | 1 314 | 1 522 | 1 581 | 2 038 |
| 2c. % of GWP | ... | ... | ... | ... | ... | ... | ... | ... | ... | ... |
| **3. Absolute 1970–1989 PARE** | | | | | | | | | | |
| 3a. Per capita GDP | 122 | 119 | 143 | 132 | 136 | 137 | 132 | 138 | 151 | 149 |
| 3b. GDP | 678 | 675 | 827 | 784 | 827 | 847 | 839 | 898 | 1 003 | 1 009 |
| 3c. % of GWP | 0.01 | 0.01 | 0.01 | 0.01 | 0.01 | 0.01 | 0.01 | 0.01 | 0.01 | 0.01 |
| **4. Relative 1970–1989 PARE** | | | | | | | | | | |
| 4a. Per capita GDP | 60 | 61 | 76 | 76 | 85 | 94 | 96 | 108 | 126 | 135 |
| 4b. GDP | 331 | 346 | 443 | 448 | 516 | 580 | 610 | 698 | 836 | 917 |
| 4c. % of GWP | 0.01 | 0.01 | 0.01 | 0.01 | 0.01 | 0.01 | 0.01 | 0.01 | 0.01 | 0.01 |
| **5. Absolute 1980–1989 PARE** | | | | | | | | | | |
| 5a. Per capita GDP | 150 | 146 | 175 | 162 | 168 | 168 | 162 | 170 | 186 | 183 |
| 5b. GDP | 834 | 830 | 1 016 | 964 | 1 017 | 1 041 | 1 031 | 1 104 | 1 232 | 1 240 |
| 5c. % of GWP | 0.01 | 0.01 | 0.01 | 0.01 | 0.01 | 0.01 | 0.01 | 0.01 | 0.01 | 0.01 |
| **6. WA** | | | | | | | | | | |
| 6a. Per capita GDP | 54 | 54 | 67 | 76 | 82 | 96 | 90 | 106 | 133 | 175 |
| 6b. GDP | 298 | 304 | 390 | 452 | 498 | 592 | 568 | 686 | 885 | 1 187 |
| 6c. % of GWP | 0.01 | 0.01 | 0.01 | 0.01 | 0.01 | 0.01 | 0.01 | 0.01 | 0.01 | 0.01 |
| **Burundi** | | | | | | | | | | |
| **1. MER** | | | | | | | | | | |
| 1a. Per capita GDP | 70 | 71 | 69 | 85 | 95 | 113 | 122 | 142 | 156 | 197 |
| 1b. GDP | 245 | 253 | 246 | 308 | 346 | 415 | 457 | 543 | 614 | 793 |
| 1c. % of GWP | 0.01 | 0.01 | 0.01 | 0.01 | 0.01 | 0.01 | 0.01 | 0.01 | 0.01 | 0.01 |
| **2. PPPs** | | | | | | | | | | |
| 2a. Per capita GDP | 161 | 170 | 164 | 179 | 189 | 204 | 241 | 287 | 296 | 316 |
| 2b. GDP | 566 | 605 | 588 | 644 | 687 | 750 | 903 | 1 099 | 1 160 | 1 273 |
| 2c. % of GWP | ... | ... | ... | ... | ... | ... | ... | ... | ... | ... |
| **3. Absolute 1970–1989 PARE** | | | | | | | | | | |
| 3a. Per capita GDP | 158 | 162 | 151 | 160 | 158 | 156 | 169 | 181 | 185 | 183 |
| 3b. GDP | 557 | 575 | 541 | 578 | 575 | 575 | 635 | 692 | 726 | 738 |
| 3c. % of GWP | 0.01 | 0.01 | 0.01 | 0.01 | 0.01 | 0.01 | 0.01 | 0.01 | 0.01 | 0.01 |
| **4. Relative 1970–1989 PARE** | | | | | | | | | | |
| 4a. Per capita GDP | 77 | 83 | 81 | 92 | 99 | 107 | 123 | 141 | 154 | 166 |
| 4b. GDP | 272 | 295 | 290 | 330 | 359 | 394 | 462 | 538 | 605 | 670 |
| 4c. % of GWP | 0.01 | 0.01 | 0.01 | 0.01 | 0.01 | 0.01 | 0.01 | 0.01 | 0.01 | 0.01 |
| **5. Absolute 1980–1989 PARE** | | | | | | | | | | |
| 5a. Per capita GDP | 193 | 198 | 184 | 196 | 193 | 191 | 207 | 221 | 226 | 224 |
| 5b. GDP | 680 | 703 | 661 | 706 | 702 | 703 | 776 | 846 | 887 | 901 |
| 5c. % of GWP | 0.01 | 0.01 | 0.01 | 0.01 | 0.01 | 0.01 | 0.01 | 0.01 | 0.01 | 0.01 |
| **6. WA** | | | | | | | | | | |
| 6a. Per capita GDP | 70 | 71 | 69 | 85 | 95 | 113 | 122 | 142 | 156 | 197 |
| 6b. GDP | 245 | 253 | 246 | 305 | 346 | 415 | 457 | 543 | 614 | 793 |
| 6c. % of GWP | 0.01 | 0.01 | 0.01 | 0.01 | 0.01 | 0.01 | 0.01 | 0.01 | 0.01 | 0.01 |

| | | | | | | | | | | Averages | | |
|---|---|---|---|---|---|---|---|---|---|---|---|---|
| 1980 (11) | 1981 (12) | 1982 (13) | 1983 (14) | 1984 (15) | 1985 (16) | 1986 (17) | 1987 (18) | 1988 (19) | 1989 (20) | 1970–89 (21) | 1970–79 (22) | 1980–89 (23) |
| 185 | 167 | 150 | 134 | 116 | 133 | 180 | 216 | 223 | 216 | 141 | 96 | 174 |
| 1 287 | 1 193 | 1 094 | 1 000 | 894 | 1 045 | 1 454 | 1 788 | 1 900 | 1 890 | 971 | 586 | 1 355 |
| 0.01 | 0.01 | 0.01 | 0.01 | 0.01 | 0.01 | 0.01 | 0.01 | 0.01 | 0.01 | 0.01 | 0.01 | 0.01 |
| 320 | 371 | 394 | 401 | 391 | 446 | 461 | 469 | 482 | 503 | 332 | 199 | 429 |
| 2 225 | 2 645 | 2 874 | 3 004 | 3 000 | 3 514 | 3 727 | 3 890 | 4 103 | 4 399 | 2 281 | 1 224 | 3 338 |
| ... | ... | ... | ... | ... | ... | ... | ... | ... | ... | ... | ... | ... |
| 143 | 149 | 148 | 137 | 131 | 141 | 143 | 141 | 140 | 140 | 141 | 137 | 142 |
| 995 | 1 063 | 1 079 | 1 027 | 1 005 | 1 109 | 1 153 | 1 170 | 1 194 | 1 229 | 971 | 839 | 1 102 |
| 0.01 | 0.01 | 0.01 | 0.01 | 0.01 | 0.01 | 0.01 | 0.01 | 0.01 | 0.01 | 0.01 | 0.01 | 0.01 |
| 142 | 162 | 171 | 164 | 162 | 179 | 185 | 188 | 193 | 201 | 141 | 93 | 176 |
| 986 | 1 154 | 1 246 | 1 226 | 1 243 | 1 409 | 1 494 | 1 559 | 1 645 | 1 763 | 973 | 573 | 1 373 |
| 0.01 | 0.01 | 0.01 | 0.01 | 0.01 | 0.01 | 0.01 | 0.01 | 0.01 | 0.01 | 0.01 | 0.01 | 0.01 |
| 176 | 183 | 181 | 169 | 161 | 173 | 175 | 173 | 172 | 173 | 173 | 168 | 174 |
| 1 222 | 1 307 | 1 326 | 1 262 | 1 235 | 1 363 | 1 417 | 1 437 | 1 467 | 1 511 | 1 193 | 1 031 | 1 355 |
| 0.01 | 0.01 | 0.01 | 0.01 | 0.01 | 0.01 | 0.01 | 0.01 | 0.01 | 0.01 | 0.01 | 0.01 | 0.01 |
| 185 | 167 | 150 | 134 | 116 | 133 | 180 | 216 | 223 | 216 | 141 | 96 | 174 |
| 1 287 | 1 193 | 1 094 | 1 000 | 894 | 1 045 | 1 454 | 1 788 | 1 900 | 1 890 | 970 | 586 | 1 355 |
| 0.01 | 0.01 | 0.01 | 0.01 | 0.01 | 0.01 | 0.01 | 0.01 | 0.01 | 0.01 | 0.01 | 0.01 | 0.01 |
| 230 | 234 | 240 | 247 | 219 | 248 | 253 | 232 | 211 | 207 | 185 | 115 | 233 |
| 951 | 993 | 1 045 | 1 107 | 1 006 | 1 171 | 1 234 | 1 162 | 1 090 | 1 102 | 754 | 422 | 1 086 |
| 0.01 | 0.01 | 0.01 | 0.01 | 0.01 | 0.01 | 0.01 | 0.01 | 0.01 | 0.01 | 0.01 | 0.01 | 0.01 |
| 354 | 369 | 373 | 375 | 421 | 457 | 470 | 489 | 501 | 514 | 352 | 226 | 439 |
| 1 465 | 1 564 | 1 623 | 1 678 | 1 936 | 2 162 | 2 289 | 2 451 | 2 584 | 2 730 | 1 438 | 827 | 2 048 |
| ... | ... | ... | ... | ... | ... | ... | ... | ... | ... | ... | ... | ... |
| 175 | 189 | 184 | 184 | 179 | 195 | 196 | 199 | 197 | 194 | 185 | 169 | 191 |
| 724 | 803 | 800 | 825 | 824 | 920 | 955 | 995 | 1 014 | 1 029 | 754 | 619 | 889 |
| 0.01 | 0.01 | 0.01 | 0.01 | 0.01 | 0.01 | 0.01 | 0.01 | 0.01 | 0.01 | 0.01 | 0.01 | 0.01 |
| 174 | 205 | 212 | 220 | 222 | 247 | 254 | 265 | 271 | 278 | 188 | 115 | 238 |
| 718 | 872 | 924 | 985 | 1 019 | 1 169 | 1 238 | 1 326 | 1 398 | 1 476 | 767 | 421 | 1 113 |
| 0.01 | 0.01 | 0.01 | 0.01 | 0.01 | 0.01 | 0.01 | 0.01 | 0.01 | 0.01 | 0.01 | 0.01 | 0.01 |
| 214 | 231 | 224 | 225 | 219 | 238 | 240 | 243 | 240 | 237 | 226 | 207 | 233 |
| 885 | 981 | 977 | 1 008 | 1 007 | 1 124 | 1 167 | 1 215 | 1 239 | 1 257 | 921 | 756 | 1 086 |
| 0.01 | 0.01 | 0.01 | 0.01 | 0.01 | 0.01 | 0.01 | 0.01 | 0.01 | 0.01 | 0.01 | 0.01 | 0.01 |
| 230 | 234 | 240 | 247 | 219 | 248 | 253 | 232 | 211 | 207 | 185 | 115 | 233 |
| 951 | 993 | 1 045 | 1 107 | 1 006 | 1 171 | 1 234 | 1 162 | 1 090 | 1 102 | 754 | 422 | 1 086 |
| 0.01 | 0.01 | 0.01 | 0.01 | 0.01 | 0.01 | 0.01 | 0.01 | 0.01 | 0.01 | 0.01 | 0.01 | 0.01 |

**Table A.1**     Total and per capita gross domestic product of individual countries or areas, expressed in United States dollars, and their individual shares of gross world product, based on alternative conversion rates, 1970–1989 [*cont.*]

| Country or area | 1970 (1) | 1971 (2) | 1972 (3) | 1973 (4) | 1974 (5) | 1975 (6) | 1976 (7) | 1977 (8) | 1978 (9) | 1979 (10) |
|---|---|---|---|---|---|---|---|---|---|---|
| **Cambodia** | | | | | | | | | | |
| **1.** **MER** | | | | | | | | | | |
| 1a. Per capita GDP | 103 | 138 | 71 | 96 | 82 | 83 | 84 | 85 | 86 | 87 |
| 1b. GDP | 718 | 970 | 506 | 689 | 588 | 592 | 585 | 577 | 568 | 563 |
| 1c. % of GWP | 0.02 | 0.03 | 0.01 | 0.01 | 0.01 | 0.01 | 0.01 | 0.01 | 0.01 | 0.01 |
| **2.** **PPPs** | | | | | | | | | | |
| 2a. Per capita GDP | ... | ... | ... | ... | ... | ... | ... | ... | ... | ... |
| 2b. GDP | ... | ... | ... | ... | ... | ... | ... | ... | ... | ... |
| 2c. % of GWP | ... | ... | ... | ... | ... | ... | ... | ... | ... | ... |
| **3.** **Absolute 1970–1989 PARE** | | | | | | | | | | |
| 3a. Per capita GDP | 159 | 149 | 140 | 112 | 107 | 106 | 108 | 95 | 97 | 87 |
| 3b. GDP | 1 106 | 1 051 | 994 | 805 | 763 | 752 | 752 | 642 | 642 | 560 |
| 3c. % of GWP | 0.02 | 0.01 | 0.01 | 0.01 | 0.01 | 0.01 | 0.01 | 0.01 | 0.01 | 0.01 |
| **4.** **Relative 1970–1989 PARE** | | | | | | | | | | |
| 4a. Per capita GDP | 78 | 76 | 75 | 64 | 66 | 73 | 79 | 74 | 81 | 79 |
| 4b. GDP | 539 | 538 | 533 | 460 | 476 | 515 | 548 | 499 | 536 | 509 |
| 4c. % of GWP | 0.02 | 0.01 | 0.01 | 0.01 | 0.01 | 0.01 | 0.01 | 0.01 | 0.01 | 0.01 |
| **5.** **Absolute 1980–1989 PARE** | | | | | | | | | | |
| 5a. Per capita GDP | 216 | 202 | 189 | 152 | 144 | 144 | 146 | 128 | 132 | 118 |
| 5b. GDP | 1 498 | 1 423 | 1 346 | 1 091 | 1 033 | 1 019 | 1 019 | 870 | 870 | 759 |
| 5c. % of GWP | 0.02 | 0.02 | 0.01 | 0.01 | 0.01 | 0.01 | 0.01 | 0.01 | 0.01 | 0.01 |
| **6.** **WA**[a] | | | | | | | | | | |
| 6a. Per capita GDP | 94 | 104 | 91 | 80 | 72 | 85 | 84 | 77 | 83 | 80 |
| 6b. GDP | 654 | 731 | 650 | 573 | 517 | 604 | 586 | 525 | 546 | 519 |
| 6c. % of GWP | 0.02 | 0.02 | 0.02 | 0.01 | 0.01 | 0.01 | 0.01 | 0.01 | 0.01 | 0.01 |
| **Cameroon** | | | | | | | | | | |
| **1.** **MER** | | | | | | | | | | |
| 1a. Per capita GDP | 173 | 172 | 203 | 252 | 280 | 360 | 356 | 405 | 525 | 641 |
| 1b. GDP | 1 146 | 1 166 | 1 411 | 1 798 | 2 048 | 2 707 | 2 750 | 3 215 | 4 290 | 5 387 |
| 1c. % of GWP | 0.04 | 0.03 | 0.04 | 0.04 | 0.04 | 0.04 | 0.04 | 0.04 | 0.05 | 0.05 |
| **2.** **PPPs** | | | | | | | | | | |
| 2a. Per capita GDP | 329 | 332 | 334 | 343 | 391 | 434 | 417 | 485 | 539 | 625 |
| 2b. GDP | 2 176 | 2 251 | 2 325 | 2 446 | 2 863 | 3 267 | 3 223 | 3 852 | 4 405 | 5 251 |
| 2c. % of GWP | ... | ... | ... | ... | ... | ... | ... | ... | ... | ... |
| **3.** **Absolute 1970–1989 PARE** | | | | | | | | | | |
| 3a. Per capita GDP | 534 | 541 | 550 | 544 | 554 | 567 | 562 | 578 | 589 | 632 |
| 3b. GDP | 3 527 | 3 668 | 3 826 | 3 882 | 4 055 | 4 264 | 4 346 | 4 592 | 4 815 | 5 311 |
| 3c. % of GWP | 0.05 | 0.05 | 0.05 | 0.05 | 0.05 | 0.05 | 0.05 | 0.05 | 0.05 | 0.05 |
| **4.** **Relative 1970–1989 PARE** | | | | | | | | | | |
| 4a. Per capita GDP | 260 | 277 | 295 | 311 | 345 | 388 | 409 | 449 | 491 | 574 |
| 4b. GDP | 1 719 | 1 880 | 2 051 | 2 219 | 2 529 | 2 921 | 3 163 | 3 568 | 4 014 | 4 823 |
| 4c. % of GWP | 0.05 | 0.05 | 0.05 | 0.05 | 0.05 | 0.05 | 0.05 | 0.05 | 0.05 | 0.05 |
| **5.** **Absolute 1980–1989 PARE** | | | | | | | | | | |
| 5a. Per capita GDP | 649 | 659 | 670 | 662 | 674 | 690 | 684 | 704 | 717 | 769 |
| 5b. GDP | 4 293 | 4 464 | 4 658 | 4 725 | 4 936 | 5 190 | 5 290 | 5 590 | 5 861 | 6 464 |
| 5c. % of GWP | 0.05 | 0.05 | 0.05 | 0.05 | 0.05 | 0.05 | 0.05 | 0.05 | 0.05 | 0.05 |
| **6.** **WA** | | | | | | | | | | |
| 6a. Per capita GDP | 175 | 171 | 193 | 233 | 292 | 347 | 378 | 401 | 497 | 629 |
| 6b. GDP | 1 160 | 1 157 | 1 341 | 1 662 | 2 141 | 2 609 | 2 920 | 3 188 | 4 058 | 5 290 |
| 6c. % of GWP | 0.04 | 0.03 | 0.03 | 0.03 | 0.04 | 0.04 | 0.04 | 0.04 | 0.05 | 0.05 |

| | 1980 (11) | 1981 (12) | 1982 (13) | 1983 (14) | 1984 (15) | 1985 (16) | 1986 (17) | 1987 (18) | 1988 (19) | 1989 (20) | Averages 1970-89 (21) | 1970-79 (22) | 1980-89 (23) |
|---|---|---|---|---|---|---|---|---|---|---|---|---|---|
| | 88 | 88 | 83 | 96 | 97 | 89 | 83 | 81 | 97 | 106 | 100 | 89 | 91 |
| | 563 | 570 | 550 | 658 | 685 | 650 | 620 | 625 | 765 | 850 | 645 | 636 | 654 |
| | 0.00 | 0.00 | 0.00 | 0.01 | 0.01 | 0.01 | 0.00 | 0.00 | 0.00 | 0.00 | 0.01 | 0.01 | 0.00 |
| | ... | ... | ... | ... | ... | ... | ... | ... | ... | ... | ... | ... | ... |
| | ... | ... | ... | ... | ... | ... | ... | ... | ... | ... | ... | ... | ... |
| | ... | ... | ... | ... | ... | ... | ... | ... | ... | ... | ... | ... | ... |
| | 82 | 82 | 78 | 72 | 68 | 63 | 58 | 56 | 61 | 59 | 100 | 113 | 67 |
| | 527 | 532 | 512 | 492 | 480 | 460 | 436 | 431 | 481 | 471 | 645 | 807 | 482 |
| | 0.01 | 0.01 | 0.00 | 0.00 | 0.00 | 0.00 | 0.00 | 0.00 | 0.00 | 0.00 | 0.01 | 0.01 | 0.00 |
| | 82 | 89 | 90 | 86 | 84 | 80 | 75 | 75 | 84 | 84 | 86 | 72 | 83 |
| | 522 | 577 | 592 | 588 | 594 | 585 | 565 | 575 | 663 | 676 | 555 | 515 | 594 |
| | 0.01 | 0.01 | 0.00 | 0.00 | 0.00 | 0.00 | 0.00 | 0.00 | 0.00 | 0.00 | 0.01 | 0.01 | 0.00 |
| | 112 | 112 | 105 | 98 | 92 | 86 | 79 | 76 | 83 | 79 | 136 | 153 | 91 |
| | 714 | 721 | 694 | 667 | 651 | 624 | 591 | 584 | 652 | 639 | 873 | 1 093 | 654 |
| | 0.01 | 0.01 | 0.01 | 0.01 | 0.00 | 0.00 | 0.00 | 0.00 | 0.00 | 0.00 | 0.01 | 0.01 | 0.00 |
| | 81 | 86 | 83 | 83 | 86 | 88 | 83 | 80 | 91 | 94 | 94 | 83 | 86 |
| | 516 | 557 | 549 | 565 | 605 | 640 | 619 | 615 | 714 | 755 | 602 | 590 | 614 |
| | 0.00 | 0.00 | 0.00 | 0.00 | 0.00 | 0.01 | 0.00 | 0.00 | 0.00 | 0.00 | 0.01 | 0.01 | 0.00 |
| | 771 | 742 | 721 | 727 | 750 | 850 | 1 151 | 1 244 | 1 143 | 975 | 689 | 349 | 927 |
| | 6 674 | 6 611 | 6 612 | 6 871 | 7 312 | 8 545 | 11 941 | 13 327 | 12 659 | 11 160 | 5 882 | 2 592 | 9 171 |
| | 0.06 | 0.06 | 0.06 | 0.06 | 0.06 | 0.07 | 0.08 | 0.08 | 0.07 | 0.06 | 0.06 | 0.04 | 0.06 |
| | 730 | 888 | 982 | 1 025 | 1 151 | 1 249 | 1 323 | 1 253 | 1 162 | 1 101 | 829 | 432 | 1 104 |
| | 6 313 | 7 909 | 9 005 | 9 686 | 11 211 | 12 551 | 13 729 | 13 422 | 12 870 | 12 601 | 7 068 | 3 206 | 10 930 |
| | ... | ... | ... | ... | ... | ... | ... | ... | ... | ... | ... | ... | ... |
| | 656 | 709 | 740 | 768 | 800 | 839 | 871 | 802 | 720 | 655 | 689 | 570 | 761 |
| | 5 676 | 6 312 | 6 790 | 7 255 | 7 796 | 8 428 | 9 038 | 8 589 | 7 968 | 7 494 | 5 882 | 4 229 | 7 535 |
| | 0.05 | 0.06 | 0.06 | 0.07 | 0.07 | 0.07 | 0.07 | 0.07 | 0.06 | 0.06 | 0.06 | 0.05 | 0.06 |
| | 650 | 769 | 855 | 917 | 990 | 1 065 | 1 129 | 1 069 | 992 | 939 | 722 | 389 | 952 |
| | 5 626 | 6 849 | 7 843 | 8 664 | 9 644 | 10 708 | 11 713 | 11 451 | 10 980 | 10 751 | 6 156 | 2 889 | 9 423 |
| | 0.05 | 0.06 | 0.06 | 0.07 | 0.07 | 0.07 | 0.07 | 0.07 | 0.06 | 0.06 | 0.06 | 0.05 | 0.06 |
| | 798 | 862 | 901 | 934 | 974 | 1 021 | 1 060 | 976 | 876 | 797 | 839 | 694 | 927 |
| | 6 908 | 7 683 | 8 265 | 8 831 | 9 490 | 10 259 | 11 001 | 10 454 | 9 699 | 9 122 | 7 159 | 5 147 | 9 171 |
| | 0.05 | 0.06 | 0.06 | 0.07 | 0.07 | 0.07 | 0.07 | 0.07 | 0.06 | 0.06 | 0.06 | 0.05 | 0.06 |
| | 779 | 857 | 798 | 781 | 801 | 811 | 1 031 | 1 173 | 1 167 | 986 | 692 | 344 | 935 |
| | 6 740 | 7 636 | 7 324 | 7 382 | 7 802 | 8 148 | 10 696 | 12 568 | 12 923 | 11 289 | 5 902 | 2 552 | 9 251 |
| | 0.06 | 0.06 | 0.06 | 0.06 | 0.06 | 0.06 | 0.07 | 0.08 | 0.07 | 0.06 | 0.06 | 0.04 | 0.07 |

**Table A.1**     Total and per capita gross domestic product of individual countries or areas,
expressed in United States dollars, and their individual shares of gross world
product, based on alternative conversion rates, 1970–1989 [*cont.*]

| Country or area | 1970 (1) | 1971 (2) | 1972 (3) | 1973 (4) | 1974 (5) | 1975 (6) | 1976 (7) | 1977 (8) | 1978 (9) | 1979 (10) |
|---|---|---|---|---|---|---|---|---|---|---|
| **Canada** | | | | | | | | | | |
| 1. **MER** | | | | | | | | | | |
| 1a. Per capita GDP | 3 973 | 4 421 | 4 964 | 5 698 | 6 873 | 7 360 | 8 658 | 8 733 | 8 929 | 9 844 |
| 1b. GDP | 84 734 | 95 594 | 108 764 | 126 420 | 154 352 | 167 263 | 199 079 | 203 090 | 209 974 | 234 067 |
| 1c. % of GWP | 2.66 | 2.73 | 2.70 | 2.58 | 2.78 | 2.69 | 2.97 | 2.68 | 2.34 | 2.27 |
| 2. **PPPs** | | | | | | | | | | |
| 2a. Per capita GDP | 4 168 | 4 565 | 5 042 | 5 754 | 6 634 | 7 198 | 7 947 | 8 439 | 9 170 | 10 406 |
| 2b. GDP | 88 872 | 98 713 | 110 464 | 127 671 | 149 003 | 163 598 | 182 725 | 196 255 | 215 635 | 247 428 |
| 2c. % of GWP | ... | ... | ... | ... | ... | ... | ... | ... | ... | ... |
| 3. **Absolute 1970–1989 PARE** | | | | | | | | | | |
| 3a. Per capita GDP | 8 102 | 8 450 | 8 814 | 9 375 | 9 666 | 9 800 | 10 283 | 10 531 | 10 890 | 11 179 |
| 3b. GDP | 172 769 | 182 719 | 193 112 | 208 005 | 217 094 | 222 730 | 236 430 | 244 888 | 256 090 | 265 808 |
| 3c. % of GWP | 2.43 | 2.47 | 2.48 | 2.51 | 2.56 | 2.59 | 2.61 | 2.59 | 2.60 | 2.61 |
| 4. **Relative 1970–1989 PARE** | | | | | | | | | | |
| 4a. Per capita GDP | 3 950 | 4 331 | 4 725 | 5 360 | 6 028 | 6 714 | 7 485 | 8 182 | 9 079 | 10 152 |
| 4b. GDP | 84 237 | 93 658 | 103 527 | 118 918 | 135 379 | 152 594 | 172 102 | 190 283 | 213 503 | 241 390 |
| 4c. % of GWP | 2.43 | 2.47 | 2.48 | 2.51 | 2.56 | 2.59 | 2.61 | 2.59 | 2.60 | 2.61 |
| 5. **Absolute 1980–1989 PARE** | | | | | | | | | | |
| 5a. Per capita GDP | 9 725 | 10 144 | 10 580 | 11 254 | 11 603 | 11 764 | 12 343 | 12 641 | 13 072 | 13 419 |
| 5b. GDP | 207 392 | 219 336 | 231 811 | 249 688 | 260 600 | 267 365 | 283 810 | 293 963 | 307 410 | 319 075 |
| 5c. % of GWP | 2.38 | 2.42 | 2.43 | 2.46 | 2.51 | 2.54 | 2.57 | 2.55 | 2.56 | 2.57 |
| 6. **WA** | | | | | | | | | | |
| 6a. Per capita GDP | 3 960 | 4 422 | 4 969 | 5 697 | 6 872 | 7 358 | 8 658 | 8 738 | 8 932 | 9 840 |
| 6b. GDP | 84 438 | 95 614 | 108 881 | 126 410 | 154 347 | 167 236 | 199 074 | 203 195 | 210 034 | 233 983 |
| 6c. % of GWP | 2.65 | 2.74 | 2.72 | 2.60 | 2.77 | 2.71 | 2.97 | 2.69 | 2.36 | 2.29 |
| **Cape Verde** | | | | | | | | | | |
| 1. **MER** | | | | | | | | | | |
| 1a. Per capita GDP | 145 | 157 | 170 | 217 | 280 | 348 | 324 | 311 | 421 | 461 |
| 1b. GDP | 39 | 43 | 47 | 60 | 78 | 97 | 91 | 87 | 119 | 132 |
| 1c. % of GWP | 0.00 | 0.00 | 0.00 | 0.00 | 0.00 | 0.00 | 0.00 | 0.00 | 0.00 | 0.00 |
| 2. **PPPs** | | | | | | | | | | |
| 2a. Per capita GDP | ... | ... | ... | ... | ... | ... | ... | ... | ... | ... |
| 2b. GDP | ... | ... | ... | ... | ... | ... | ... | ... | ... | ... |
| 2c. % of GWP | ... | ... | ... | ... | ... | ... | ... | ... | ... | ... |
| 3. **Absolute 1970–1989 PARE** | | | | | | | | | | |
| 3a. Per capita GDP | 439 | 400 | 379 | 374 | 362 | 373 | 382 | 379 | 381 | 393 |
| 3b. GDP | 117 | 109 | 104 | 103 | 100 | 104 | 107 | 106 | 108 | 113 |
| 3c. % of GWP | 0.00 | 0.00 | 0.00 | 0.00 | 0.00 | 0.00 | 0.00 | 0.00 | 0.00 | 0.00 |
| 4. **Relative 1970–1989 PARE** | | | | | | | | | | |
| 4a. Per capita GDP | 214 | 205 | 203 | 214 | 225 | 255 | 278 | 294 | 318 | 357 |
| 4b. GDP | 57 | 56 | 56 | 59 | 62 | 71 | 78 | 83 | 90 | 102 |
| 4c. % of GWP | 0.00 | 0.00 | 0.00 | 0.00 | 0.00 | 0.00 | 0.00 | 0.00 | 0.00 | 0.00 |
| 5. **Absolute 1980–1989 PARE** | | | | | | | | | | |
| 5a. Per capita GDP | 518 | 473 | 448 | 442 | 427 | 440 | 451 | 447 | 450 | 464 |
| 5b. GDP | 138 | 129 | 123 | 122 | 118 | 122 | 126 | 126 | 127 | 133 |
| 5c. % of GWP | 0.00 | 0.00 | 0.00 | 0.00 | 0.00 | 0.00 | 0.00 | 0.00 | 0.00 | 0.00 |
| 6. **WA** | | | | | | | | | | |
| 6a. Per capita GDP | 145 | 157 | 170 | 217 | 280 | 348 | 324 | 311 | 421 | 461 |
| 6b. GDP | 39 | 43 | 47 | 60 | 78 | 97 | 91 | 87 | 119 | 132 |
| 6c. % of GWP | 0.00 | 0.00 | 0.00 | 0.00 | 0.00 | 0.00 | 0.00 | 0.00 | 0.00 | 0.00 |

|  |  |  |  |  |  |  |  |  |  | Averages | | |
| 1980 (11) | 1981 (12) | 1982 (13) | 1983 (14) | 1984 (15) | 1985 (16) | 1986 (17) | 1987 (18) | 1988 (19) | 1989 (20) | 1970–89 (21) | 1970–79 (22) | 1980–89 (23) |
|---|---|---|---|---|---|---|---|---|---|---|---|---|
| 10 949 | 12 125 | 12 256 | 13 135 | 13 564 | 13 682 | 14 078 | 16 258 | 19 111 | 20 462 | 11 031 | 7 008 | 14 620 |
| 263 242 | 294 791 | 301 313 | 326 485 | 340 781 | 347 247 | 360 738 | 420 398 | 498 482 | 538 245 | 263 753 | 158 334 | 369 172 |
| 2.27 | 2.52 | 2.59 | 2.75 | 2.79 | 2.76 | 2.42 | 2.45 | 2.61 | 2.68 | 2.59 | 2.60 | 2.59 |
| 11 509 | 12 662 | 12 614 | 13 165 | 14 272 | 14 780 | 15 420 | 16 346 | 17 496 | 18 596 | 11 081 | 6 995 | 14 728 |
| 276 718 | 307 843 | 310 120 | 327 237 | 358 566 | 375 109 | 395 111 | 422 676 | 456 363 | 489 160 | 264 963 | 158 037 | 371 890 |
| ... | ... | ... | ... | ... | ... | ... | ... | ... | ... | ... | ... | ... |
| 11 232 | 11 517 | 11 024 | 11 250 | 11 841 | 12 277 | 12 556 | 12 938 | 13 399 | 13 680 | 11 031 | 9 736 | 12 179 |
| 270 047 | 280 010 | 271 017 | 279 647 | 297 491 | 311 577 | 321 726 | 334 558 | 349 488 | 359 850 | 263 753 | 219 964 | 307 541 |
| 2.60 | 2.64 | 2.54 | 2.55 | 2.59 | 2.63 | 2.63 | 2.65 | 2.65 | 2.65 | 2.59 | 2.55 | 2.62 |
| 11 134 | 12 496 | 12 734 | 13 435 | 14 647 | 15 597 | 16 272 | 17 250 | 18 463 | 19 625 | 11 185 | 6 664 | 15 220 |
| 267 687 | 303 824 | 313 061 | 333 949 | 367 983 | 395 847 | 416 955 | 446 044 | 481 593 | 516 203 | 267 437 | 150 559 | 384 315 |
| 2.60 | 2.64 | 2.54 | 2.55 | 2.59 | 2.63 | 2.63 | 2.65 | 2.65 | 2.65 | 2.60 | 2.56 | 2.62 |
| 13 483 | 13 825 | 13 233 | 13 505 | 14 214 | 14 737 | 15 072 | 15 531 | 16 084 | 16 422 | 13 241 | 11 687 | 14 620 |
| 324 164 | 336 123 | 325 328 | 335 688 | 357 108 | 374 017 | 386 199 | 401 603 | 419 526 | 431 964 | 316 609 | 264 045 | 369 172 |
| 2.56 | 2.61 | 2.51 | 2.52 | 2.56 | 2.60 | 2.61 | 2.62 | 2.62 | 2.62 | 2.55 | 2.51 | 2.59 |
| 10 947 | 12 126 | 12 259 | 13 130 | 13 564 | 13 688 | 14 083 | 15 939 | 18 634 | 20 739 | 11 003 | 7 008 | 14 568 |
| 263 193 | 294 813 | 301 379 | 326 373 | 340 762 | 347 379 | 360 868 | 412 158 | 486 043 | 545 523 | 263 085 | 158 321 | 367 849 |
| 2.29 | 2.50 | 2.59 | 2.75 | 2.79 | 2.75 | 2.45 | 2.47 | 2.60 | 2.78 | 2.60 | 2.61 | 2.60 |
| 491 | 473 | 484 | 448 | 418 | 425 | 575 | 711 | 775 | 813 | 455 | 285 | 572 |
| 142 | 139 | 146 | 139 | 132 | 138 | 191 | 242 | 271 | 292 | 131 | 79 | 183 |
| 0.00 | 0.00 | 0.00 | 0.00 | 0.00 | 0.00 | 0.00 | 0.00 | 0.00 | 0.00 | 0.00 | 0.00 | 0.00 |
| ... | ... | ... | ... | ... | ... | ... | ... | ... | ... | ... | ... | ... |
| ... | ... | ... | ... | ... | ... | ... | ... | ... | ... | ... | ... | ... |
| ... | ... | ... | ... | ... | ... | ... | ... | ... | ... | ... | ... | ... |
| 401 | 427 | 431 | 459 | 466 | 494 | 496 | 519 | 541 | 557 | 455 | 386 | 485 |
| 116 | 126 | 130 | 142 | 147 | 160 | 165 | 177 | 189 | 200 | 131 | 107 | 155 |
| 0.00 | 0.00 | 0.00 | 0.00 | 0.00 | 0.00 | 0.00 | 0.00 | 0.00 | 0.00 | 0.00 | 0.00 | 0.00 |
| 397 | 464 | 497 | 549 | 577 | 628 | 643 | 692 | 746 | 799 | 463 | 257 | 611 |
| 115 | 137 | 150 | 170 | 182 | 203 | 213 | 236 | 261 | 287 | 133 | 71 | 195 |
| 0.00 | 0.00 | 0.00 | 0.00 | 0.00 | 0.00 | 0.00 | 0.00 | 0.00 | 0.00 | 0.00 | 0.00 | 0.00 |
| 473 | 504 | 508 | 542 | 550 | 583 | 585 | 613 | 639 | 657 | 537 | 455 | 572 |
| 137 | 149 | 153 | 168 | 174 | 189 | 194 | 209 | 224 | 236 | 155 | 126 | 183 |
| 0.00 | 0.00 | 0.00 | 0.00 | 0.00 | 0.00 | 0.00 | 0.00 | 0.00 | 0.00 | 0.00 | 0.00 | 0.00 |
| 491 | 473 | 467 | 448 | 418 | 425 | 574 | 711 | 776 | 813 | 455 | 285 | 571 |
| 142 | 139 | 141 | 139 | 132 | 138 | 191 | 243 | 271 | 292 | 131 | 79 | 183 |
| 0.00 | 0.00 | 0.00 | 0.00 | 0.00 | 0.00 | 0.00 | 0.00 | 0.00 | 0.00 | 0.00 | 0.00 | 0.00 |

**Table A.1**  Total and per capita gross domestic product of individual countries or areas,
expressed in United States dollars, and their individual shares of gross world
product, based on alternative conversion rates, 1970–1989 [*cont.*]

| Country or area | 1970 (1) | 1971 (2) | 1972 (3) | 1973 (4) | 1974 (5) | 1975 (6) | 1976 (7) | 1977 (8) | 1978 (9) | 1979 (10) |
|---|---|---|---|---|---|---|---|---|---|---|
| **Central African Republic** | | | | | | | | | | |
| **1.   MER** | | | | | | | | | | |
| 1a.  Per capita GDP | 97 | 101 | 114 | 130 | 149 | 183 | 213 | 233 | 274 | 313 |
| 1b.  GDP | 179 | 191 | 220 | 256 | 299 | 376 | 448 | 503 | 604 | 709 |
| 1c.  % of GWP | 0.01 | 0.01 | 0.01 | 0.01 | 0.01 | 0.01 | 0.01 | 0.01 | 0.01 | 0.01 |
| **2.   PPPs** | | | | | | | | | | |
| 2a.  Per capita GDP | 236 | 247 | 248 | 247 | 309 | 323 | 406 | 413 | 451 | 467 |
| 2b.  GDP | 436 | 466 | 478 | 486 | 622 | 664 | 854 | 890 | 995 | 1 057 |
| 2c.  % of GWP | ... | ... | ... | ... | ... | ... | ... | ... | ... | ... |
| **3.   Absolute 1970–1989 PARE** | | | | | | | | | | |
| 3a.  Per capita GDP | 306 | 290 | 279 | 285 | 271 | 270 | 275 | 290 | 292 | 276 |
| 3b.  GDP | 565 | 548 | 537 | 562 | 545 | 555 | 579 | 626 | 645 | 626 |
| 3c.  % of GWP | 0.01 | 0.01 | 0.01 | 0.01 | 0.01 | 0.01 | 0.01 | 0.01 | 0.01 | 0.01 |
| **4.   Relative 1970–1989 PARE** | | | | | | | | | | |
| 4a.  Per capita GDP | 149 | 149 | 149 | 163 | 169 | 185 | 200 | 226 | 243 | 251 |
| 4b.  GDP | 276 | 281 | 288 | 321 | 340 | 380 | 422 | 486 | 538 | 568 |
| 4c.  % of GWP | 0.01 | 0.01 | 0.01 | 0.01 | 0.01 | 0.01 | 0.01 | 0.01 | 0.01 | 0.01 |
| **5.   Absolute 1980–1989 PARE** | | | | | | | | | | |
| 5a.  Per capita GDP | 400 | 380 | 365 | 373 | 354 | 353 | 360 | 380 | 382 | 362 |
| 5b.  GDP | 740 | 717 | 703 | 735 | 713 | 726 | 758 | 819 | 844 | 818 |
| 5c.  % of GWP | 0.01 | 0.01 | 0.01 | 0.01 | 0.01 | 0.01 | 0.01 | 0.01 | 0.01 | 0.01 |
| **6.   WA** | | | | | | | | | | |
| 6a.  Per capita GDP | 97 | 101 | 114 | 130 | 149 | 183 | 213 | 233 | 274 | 313 |
| 6b.  GDP | 179 | 190 | 220 | 256 | 299 | 376 | 448 | 503 | 604 | 709 |
| 6c.  % of GWP | 0.01 | 0.01 | 0.01 | 0.01 | 0.01 | 0.01 | 0.01 | 0.01 | 0.01 | 0.01 |
| **Chad** | | | | | | | | | | |
| **1.   MER** | | | | | | | | | | |
| 1a.  Per capita GDP | 89 | 96 | 98 | 106 | 122 | 172 | 158 | 157 | 180 | 202 |
| 1b.  GDP | 326 | 357 | 371 | 412 | 480 | 693 | 651 | 658 | 771 | 886 |
| 1c.  % of GWP | 0.01 | 0.01 | 0.01 | 0.01 | 0.01 | 0.01 | 0.01 | 0.01 | 0.01 | 0.01 |
| **2.   PPPs** | | | | | | | | | | |
| 2a.  Per capita GDP | 231 | 246 | 231 | 224 | 268 | 321 | 331 | 334 | 334 | 329 |
| 2b.  GDP | 845 | 918 | 877 | 869 | 1 059 | 1 293 | 1 362 | 1 402 | 1 432 | 1 439 |
| 2c.  % of GWP | ... | ... | ... | ... | ... | ... | ... | ... | ... | ... |
| **3.   Absolute 1970–1989 PARE** | | | | | | | | | | |
| 3a.  Per capita GDP | 192 | 192 | 175 | 163 | 182 | 209 | 202 | 183 | 172 | 161 |
| 3b.  GDP | 700 | 714 | 665 | 633 | 719 | 843 | 830 | 768 | 740 | 704 |
| 3c.  % of GWP | 0.01 | 0.01 | 0.01 | 0.01 | 0.01 | 0.01 | 0.01 | 0.01 | 0.01 | 0.01 |
| **4.   Relative 1970–1989 PARE** | | | | | | | | | | |
| 4a.  Per capita GDP | 93 | 98 | 94 | 93 | 114 | 143 | 147 | 142 | 144 | 146 |
| 4b.  GDP | 342 | 366 | 356 | 362 | 448 | 578 | 604 | 597 | 617 | 639 |
| 4c.  % of GWP | 0.01 | 0.01 | 0.01 | 0.01 | 0.01 | 0.01 | 0.01 | 0.01 | 0.01 | 0.01 |
| **5.   Absolute 1980–1989 PARE** | | | | | | | | | | |
| 5a.  Per capita GDP | 250 | 250 | 228 | 213 | 237 | 273 | 263 | 238 | 225 | 209 |
| 5b.  GDP | 913 | 930 | 866 | 824 | 937 | 1 099 | 1 082 | 1 001 | 964 | 917 |
| 5c.  % of GWP | 0.01 | 0.01 | 0.01 | 0.01 | 0.01 | 0.01 | 0.01 | 0.01 | 0.01 | 0.01 |
| **6.   WA** | | | | | | | | | | |
| 6a.  Per capita GDP | 89 | 95 | 98 | 106 | 121 | 172 | 158 | 157 | 180 | 202 |
| 6b.  GDP | 326 | 355 | 371 | 412 | 480 | 693 | 651 | 658 | 771 | 886 |
| 6c.  % of GWP | 0.01 | 0.01 | 0.01 | 0.01 | 0.01 | 0.01 | 0.01 | 0.01 | 0.01 | 0.01 |

| | | | | | | | | | | Averages | | |
|---|---|---|---|---|---|---|---|---|---|---|---|---|
| 1980 (11) | 1981 (12) | 1982 (13) | 1983 (14) | 1984 (15) | 1985 (16) | 1986 (17) | 1987 (18) | 1988 (19) | 1989 (20) | 1970–89 (21) | 1970–79 (22) | 1980–89 (23) |
| 343 | 292 | 306 | 263 | 248 | 265 | 351 | 385 | 390 | 374 | 268 | 186 | 325 |
| 797 | 695 | 748 | 659 | 638 | 702 | 956 | 1 077 | 1 119 | 1 105 | 614 | 379 | 850 |
| 0.01 | 0.01 | 0.01 | 0.01 | 0.01 | 0.01 | 0.01 | 0.01 | 0.01 | 0.01 | 0.01 | 0.01 | 0.01 |
| 479 | 516 | 617 | 573 | 550 | 588 | 592 | 598 | 610 | 640 | 483 | 342 | 581 |
| 1 112 | 1 228 | 1 507 | 1 436 | 1 416 | 1 556 | 1 609 | 1 671 | 1 753 | 1 892 | 1 107 | 695 | 1 518 |
| ... | ... | ... | ... | ... | ... | ... | ... | ... | ... | ... | ... | ... |
| 259 | 247 | 259 | 235 | 249 | 252 | 249 | 244 | 241 | 243 | 268 | 284 | 249 |
| 602 | 589 | 633 | 590 | 642 | 667 | 676 | 683 | 693 | 719 | 614 | 579 | 649 |
| 0.01 | 0.01 | 0.01 | 0.01 | 0.01 | 0.01 | 0.01 | 0.01 | 0.01 | 0.01 | 0.01 | 0.01 | 0.01 |
| 257 | 268 | 299 | 281 | 308 | 320 | 322 | 326 | 332 | 349 | 261 | 192 | 310 |
| 597 | 639 | 731 | 705 | 795 | 847 | 876 | 910 | 955 | 1 031 | 599 | 390 | 809 |
| 0.01 | 0.01 | 0.01 | 0.01 | 0.01 | 0.01 | 0.01 | 0.01 | 0.01 | 0.01 | 0.01 | 0.01 | 0.01 |
| 339 | 323 | 339 | 308 | 326 | 330 | 325 | 320 | 316 | 318 | 351 | 372 | 325 |
| 788 | 770 | 828 | 772 | 840 | 873 | 885 | 893 | 907 | 940 | 803 | 757 | 850 |
| 0.01 | 0.01 | 0.01 | 0.01 | 0.01 | 0.01 | 0.01 | 0.01 | 0.01 | 0.01 | 0.01 | 0.01 | 0.01 |
| 343 | 292 | 306 | 263 | 248 | 265 | 351 | 385 | 389 | 374 | 268 | 186 | 325 |
| 797 | 695 | 748 | 659 | 638 | 702 | 956 | 1 077 | 1 119 | 1 105 | 614 | 378 | 849 |
| 0.01 | 0.01 | 0.01 | 0.01 | 0.01 | 0.01 | 0.01 | 0.01 | 0.01 | 0.01 | 0.01 | 0.01 | 0.01 |
| 205 | 161 | 134 | 124 | 108 | 131 | 134 | 140 | 176 | 165 | 146 | 140 | 148 |
| 920 | 736 | 626 | 594 | 528 | 659 | 690 | 737 | 948 | 914 | 648 | 561 | 735 |
| 0.01 | 0.01 | 0.01 | 0.01 | 0.00 | 0.01 | 0.00 | 0.00 | 0.00 | 0.00 | 0.01 | 0.01 | 0.01 |
| 323 | 319 | 300 | 303 | 307 | 423 | 443 | 453 | 496 | 508 | 350 | 288 | 394 |
| 1 446 | 1 462 | 1 402 | 1 453 | 1 503 | 2 122 | 2 277 | 2 387 | 2 676 | 2 812 | 1 552 | 1 150 | 1 954 |
| ... | ... | ... | ... | ... | ... | ... | ... | ... | ... | ... | ... | ... |
| 146 | 130 | 117 | 107 | 100 | 104 | 107 | 106 | 112 | 110 | 146 | 183 | 114 |
| 652 | 593 | 550 | 511 | 488 | 521 | 548 | 559 | 606 | 612 | 648 | 732 | 564 |
| 0.01 | 0.01 | 0.01 | 0.00 | 0.00 | 0.00 | 0.00 | 0.00 | 0.00 | 0.00 | 0.01 | 0.01 | 0.00 |
| 144 | 141 | 136 | 128 | 123 | 132 | 138 | 141 | 155 | 158 | 134 | 123 | 141 |
| 646 | 644 | 635 | 611 | 603 | 662 | 711 | 745 | 835 | 878 | 594 | 491 | 697 |
| 0.01 | 0.01 | 0.01 | 0.00 | 0.00 | 0.00 | 0.00 | 0.00 | 0.00 | 0.00 | 0.01 | 0.01 | 0.00 |
| 190 | 169 | 153 | 139 | 130 | 135 | 139 | 138 | 146 | 144 | 191 | 239 | 148 |
| 849 | 773 | 717 | 666 | 636 | 679 | 715 | 728 | 790 | 797 | 844 | 953 | 735 |
| 0.01 | 0.01 | 0.01 | 0.00 | 0.00 | 0.00 | 0.00 | 0.00 | 0.00 | 0.00 | 0.01 | 0.01 | 0.01 |
| 205 | 161 | 134 | 124 | 108 | 131 | 134 | 140 | 175 | 165 | 146 | 140 | 148 |
| 920 | 736 | 626 | 594 | 528 | 659 | 690 | 737 | 948 | 914 | 648 | 560 | 735 |
| 0.01 | 0.01 | 0.01 | 0.01 | 0.00 | 0.01 | 0.00 | 0.00 | 0.01 | 0.00 | 0.01 | 0.01 | 0.01 |

**Table A.1**   Total and per capita gross domestic product of individual countries or areas, expressed in United States dollars, and their individual shares of gross world product, based on alternative conversion rates, 1970–1989 [*cont.*]

| Country or area | 1970 (1) | 1971 (2) | 1972 (3) | 1973 (4) | 1974 (5) | 1975 (6) | 1976 (7) | 1977 (8) | 1978 (9) | 1979 (10) |
|---|---|---|---|---|---|---|---|---|---|---|
| **Chile** | | | | | | | | | | |
| **1. MER** | | | | | | | | | | |
| 1a. Per capita GDP | 859 | 820 | 950 | 318 | 483 | 403 | 703 | 965 | 1 328 | 1 804 |
| 1b. GDP | 8 167 | 7 938 | 9 360 | 3 186 | 4 919 | 4 170 | 7 387 | 10 292 | 14 360 | 19 800 |
| 1c. % of GWP | 0.26 | 0.23 | 0.23 | 0.06 | 0.09 | 0.07 | 0.11 | 0.14 | 0.16 | 0.19 |
| **2. PPPs** | | | | | | | | | | |
| 2a. Per capita GDP | 1 777 | 1 903 | 1 935 | 1 941 | 2 478 | 2 012 | 2 262 | 2 598 | 3 088 | 3 620 |
| 2b. GDP | 16 894 | 18 422 | 19 065 | 19 456 | 25 253 | 20 825 | 23 773 | 27 697 | 33 399 | 39 735 |
| 2c. % of GWP | ... | ... | ... | ... | ... | ... | ... | ... | ... | ... |
| **3. Absolute 1970–1989 PARE** | | | | | | | | | | |
| 3a. Per capita GDP | 1 387 | 1 484 | 1 440 | 1 337 | 1 328 | 1 138 | 1 161 | 1 257 | 1 341 | 1 431 |
| 3b. GDP | 13 183 | 14 363 | 14 189 | 13 399 | 13 530 | 11 783 | 12 198 | 13 400 | 14 502 | 15 703 |
| 3c. % of GWP | 0.19 | 0.19 | 0.18 | 0.16 | 0.16 | 0.14 | 0.13 | 0.14 | 0.15 | 0.15 |
| **4. Relative 1970–1989 PARE** | | | | | | | | | | |
| 4a. Per capita GDP | 676 | 760 | 772 | 764 | 828 | 780 | 845 | 977 | 1 118 | 1 299 |
| 4b. GDP | 6 428 | 7 362 | 7 607 | 7 661 | 8 437 | 8 073 | 8 879 | 10 412 | 12 090 | 14 260 |
| 4c. % of GWP | 0.19 | 0.19 | 0.18 | 0.16 | 0.16 | 0.14 | 0.13 | 0.14 | 0.15 | 0.15 |
| **5. Absolute 1980–1989 PARE** | | | | | | | | | | |
| 5a. Per capita GDP | 1 755 | 1 877 | 1 822 | 1 691 | 1 680 | 1 440 | 1 469 | 1 590 | 1 696 | 1 810 |
| 5b. GDP | 16 678 | 18 171 | 17 951 | 16 952 | 17 117 | 14 907 | 15 432 | 16 953 | 18 346 | 19 865 |
| 5c. % of GWP | 0.19 | 0.20 | 0.19 | 0.17 | 0.17 | 0.14 | 0.14 | 0.15 | 0.15 | 0.16 |
| **6. WA** | | | | | | | | | | |
| 6a. Per capita GDP | 858 | 1 058 | 1 219 | 1 033 | 1 085 | 697 | 938 | 1 254 | 1 424 | 1 889 |
| 6b. GDP | 8 153 | 10 242 | 12 012 | 10 352 | 11 058 | 7 219 | 9 857 | 13 367 | 15 400 | 20 732 |
| 6c. % of GWP | 0.26 | 0.29 | 0.30 | 0.21 | 0.20 | 0.12 | 0.15 | 0.18 | 0.17 | 0.20 |
| **China** | | | | | | | | | | |
| **1. MER** | | | | | | | | | | |
| 1a. Per capita GDP | 112 | 117 | 129 | 154 | 155 | 172 | 157 | 176 | 223 | 266 |
| 1b. GDP | 91 057 | 98 171 | 110 400 | 135 427 | 139 164 | 156 398 | 145 286 | 165 339 | 213 064 | 257 106 |
| 1c. % of GWP | 2.85 | 2.81 | 2.75 | 2.76 | 2.51 | 2.52 | 2.17 | 2.19 | 2.37 | 2.50 |
| **2. PPPs** | | | | | | | | | | |
| 2a. Per capita GDP | ... | ... | ... | ... | ... | ... | ... | ... | ... | ... |
| 2b. GDP | ... | ... | ... | ... | ... | ... | ... | ... | ... | ... |
| 2c. % of GWP | ... | ... | ... | ... | ... | ... | ... | ... | ... | ... |
| **3. Absolute 1970–1989 PARE** | | | | | | | | | | |
| 3a. Per capita GDP | 143 | 149 | 149 | 158 | 157 | 167 | 160 | 170 | 188 | 198 |
| 3b. GDP | 116 468 | 124 642 | 128 206 | 138 850 | 140 418 | 152 060 | 148 021 | 159 568 | 179 241 | 191 738 |
| 3c. % of GWP | 1.64 | 1.68 | 1.64 | 1.67 | 1.66 | 1.77 | 1.64 | 1.69 | 1.82 | 1.89 |
| **4. Relative 1970–1989 PARE** | | | | | | | | | | |
| 4a. Per capita GDP | 70 | 76 | 80 | 90 | 98 | 114 | 116 | 132 | 157 | 180 |
| 4b. GDP | 56 786 | 63 889 | 68 731 | 79 382 | 87 564 | 104 177 | 107 748 | 123 987 | 149 434 | 174 125 |
| 4c. % of GWP | 1.64 | 1.68 | 1.64 | 1.67 | 1.66 | 1.77 | 1.64 | 1.69 | 1.82 | 1.89 |
| **5. Absolute 1980–1989 PARE** | | | | | | | | | | |
| 5a. Per capita GDP | 141 | 147 | 148 | 157 | 155 | 165 | 158 | 168 | 186 | 196 |
| 5b. GDP | 115 276 | 123 366 | 126 893 | 137 429 | 138 981 | 150 504 | 146 506 | 157 935 | 177 406 | 189 776 |
| 5c. % of GWP | 1.32 | 1.36 | 1.33 | 1.35 | 1.34 | 1.43 | 1.32 | 1.37 | 1.48 | 1.53 |
| **6. WA** | | | | | | | | | | |
| 6a. Per capita GDP | 111 | 117 | 129 | 154 | 155 | 172 | 157 | 176 | 223 | 266 |
| 6b. GDP | 90 990 | 98 099 | 110 642 | 135 467 | 139 150 | 156 415 | 145 256 | 165 357 | 213 115 | 257 106 |
| 6c. % of GWP | 2.85 | 2.81 | 2.76 | 2.79 | 2.49 | 2.54 | 2.16 | 2.19 | 2.40 | 2.51 |

| | | | | | | | | | | Averages | | |
|---|---|---|---|---|---|---|---|---|---|---|---|---|
| 1980 | 1981 | 1982 | 1983 | 1984 | 1985 | 1986 | 1987 | 1988 | 1989 | 1970–89 | 1970–79 | 1980–89 |
| (11) | (12) | (13) | (14) | (15) | (16) | (17) | (18) | (19) | (20) | (21) | (22) | (23) |
| 2 474 | 2 882 | 2 114 | 1 687 | 1 610 | 1 320 | 1 364 | 1 511 | 1 732 | 1 958 | 1 412 | 872 | 1 853 |
| 27 571 | 32 644 | 24 339 | 19 758 | 19 191 | 15 996 | 16 817 | 18 951 | 22 086 | 25 372 | 15 615 | 8 958 | 22 273 |
| 0.24 | 0.28 | 0.21 | 0.17 | 0.16 | 0.13 | 0.11 | 0.11 | 0.12 | 0.13 | 0.15 | 0.15 | 0.16 |
| 4 255 | 4 706 | 3 878 | 3 846 | 4 061 | 4 022 | 4 262 | 4 559 | 4 975 | 5 603 | 3 516 | 2 381 | 4 437 |
| 47 424 | 53 297 | 44 660 | 45 058 | 48 391 | 48 753 | 52 549 | 57 159 | 63 425 | 72 622 | 38 893 | 24 452 | 53 334 |
| ... | ... | ... | ... | ... | ... | ... | ... | ... | ... | ... | ... | ... |
| 1 519 | 1 577 | 1 332 | 1 301 | 1 360 | 1 369 | 1 423 | 1 479 | 1 562 | 1 689 | 1 412 | 1 327 | 1 465 |
| 16 924 | 17 861 | 15 345 | 15 236 | 16 202 | 16 598 | 17 538 | 18 544 | 19 909 | 21 898 | 15 615 | 13 625 | 17 605 |
| 0.16 | 0.17 | 0.14 | 0.14 | 0.14 | 0.14 | 0.14 | 0.15 | 0.15 | 0.16 | 0.15 | 0.16 | 0.15 |
| 1 505 | 1 711 | 1 539 | 1 553 | 1 682 | 1 740 | 1 844 | 1 972 | 2 152 | 2 424 | 1 405 | 888 | 1 826 |
| 16 776 | 19 380 | 17 725 | 18 194 | 20 041 | 21 088 | 22 729 | 24 724 | 27 434 | 31 412 | 15 536 | 9 121 | 21 950 |
| 0.16 | 0.17 | 0.14 | 0.14 | 0.14 | 0.14 | 0.14 | 0.15 | 0.15 | 0.16 | 0.15 | 0.16 | 0.15 |
| 1 921 | 1 995 | 1 686 | 1 645 | 1 720 | 1 732 | 1 800 | 1 871 | 1 976 | 2 137 | 1 786 | 1 678 | 1 853 |
| 21 411 | 22 595 | 19 413 | 19 275 | 20 497 | 20 999 | 22 188 | 23 460 | 25 186 | 27 703 | 19 755 | 17 237 | 22 273 |
| 0.17 | 0.18 | 0.15 | 0.14 | 0.15 | 0.15 | 0.15 | 0.15 | 0.16 | 0.17 | 0.16 | 0.16 | 0.16 |
| 2 474 | 2 882 | 2 114 | 1 687 | 1 610 | 1 320 | 1 364 | 1 511 | 1 732 | 1 958 | 1 542 | 1 153 | 1 853 |
| 27 571 | 32 644 | 24 340 | 19 757 | 19 192 | 15 996 | 16 817 | 18 948 | 22 081 | 25 376 | 17 056 | 11 839 | 22 272 |
| 0.24 | 0.28 | 0.21 | 0.17 | 0.16 | 0.13 | 0.11 | 0.11 | 0.12 | 0.13 | 0.17 | 0.20 | 0.16 |
| 305 | 282 | 271 | 287 | 290 | 279 | 266 | 286 | 349 | 377 | 238 | 167 | 301 |
| 298 398 | 280 059 | 273 745 | 292 864 | 298 621 | 290 330 | 280 568 | 305 595 | 378 108 | 415 632 | 231 267 | 151 141 | 311 392 |
| 2.57 | 2.39 | 2.35 | 2.47 | 2.45 | 2.31 | 1.88 | 1.78 | 1.98 | 2.07 | 2.27 | 2.48 | 2.18 |
| ... | ... | ... | ... | ... | ... | ... | ... | ... | ... | ... | ... | ... |
| ... | ... | ... | ... | ... | ... | ... | ... | ... | ... | ... | ... | ... |
| ... | ... | ... | ... | ... | ... | ... | ... | ... | ... | ... | ... | ... |
| 209 | 215 | 230 | 250 | 280 | 314 | 335 | 365 | 400 | 408 | 238 | 164 | 304 |
| 204 093 | 214 024 | 231 701 | 254 510 | 288 819 | 326 739 | 352 827 | 389 749 | 433 371 | 450 287 | 231 267 | 147 921 | 314 612 |
| 1.96 | 2.02 | 2.17 | 2.32 | 2.52 | 2.75 | 2.89 | 3.08 | 3.29 | 3.31 | 2.27 | 1.72 | 2.68 |
| 207 | 234 | 265 | 298 | 347 | 399 | 434 | 486 | 551 | 586 | 258 | 112 | 386 |
| 202 309 | 232 227 | 267 646 | 303 931 | 357 256 | 415 110 | 457 261 | 519 626 | 597 182 | 645 935 | 250 715 | 101 582 | 399 848 |
| 1.96 | 2.02 | 2.17 | 2.32 | 2.52 | 2.75 | 2.89 | 3.08 | 3.29 | 3.31 | 2.44 | 1.73 | 2.72 |
| 206 | 213 | 227 | 247 | 277 | 311 | 331 | 361 | 396 | 404 | 235 | 162 | 301 |
| 202 004 | 211 834 | 229 330 | 251 905 | 285 863 | 323 395 | 349 215 | 385 759 | 428 935 | 445 679 | 228 899 | 146 407 | 311 392 |
| 1.60 | 1.64 | 1.77 | 1.89 | 2.05 | 2.24 | 2.36 | 2.52 | 2.68 | 2.70 | 1.84 | 1.39 | 2.18 |
| 305 | 282 | 272 | 287 | 290 | 279 | 266 | 284 | 347 | 381 | 238 | 167 | 301 |
| 298 318 | 280 134 | 273 812 | 292 913 | 298 616 | 290 364 | 280 585 | 303 780 | 375 863 | 419 483 | 231 273 | 151 160 | 311 387 |
| 2.59 | 2.38 | 2.35 | 2.47 | 2.44 | 2.30 | 1.91 | 1.82 | 2.01 | 2.14 | 2.29 | 2.49 | 2.20 |

**Table A.1**     Total and per capita gross domestic product of individual countries or areas, expressed in United States dollars, and their individual shares of gross world product, based on alternative conversion rates, 1970−1989 [*cont.*]

| Country or area | 1970 (1) | 1971 (2) | 1972 (3) | 1973 (4) | 1974 (5) | 1975 (6) | 1976 (7) | 1977 (8) | 1978 (9) | 1979 (10) |
|---|---|---|---|---|---|---|---|---|---|---|
| **Colombia** | | | | | | | | | | |
| **1. MER** | | | | | | | | | | |
| 1a. Per capita GDP | 337 | 368 | 387 | 449 | 527 | 546 | 625 | 775 | 905 | 1 062 |
| 1b. GDP | 7 200 | 8 064 | 8 670 | 10 286 | 12 369 | 13 098 | 15 342 | 19 471 | 23 264 | 27 935 |
| 1c. % of GWP | 0.23 | 0.23 | 0.22 | 0.21 | 0.22 | 0.21 | 0.23 | 0.26 | 0.26 | 0.27 |
| **2. PPPs** | | | | | | | | | | |
| 2a. Per capita GDP | 843 | 943 | 1 017 | 1 127 | 1 299 | 1 398 | 1 548 | 1 715 | 1 934 | 2 144 |
| 2b. GDP | 18 012 | 20 659 | 22 804 | 25 842 | 30 470 | 33 531 | 37 997 | 43 088 | 49 730 | 56 406 |
| 2c. % of GWP | ... | ... | ... | ... | ... | ... | ... | ... | ... | ... |
| **3. Absolute 1970−1989 PARE** | | | | | | | | | | |
| 3a. Per capita GDP | 744 | 769 | 809 | 844 | 872 | 873 | 893 | 909 | 963 | 992 |
| 3b. GDP | 15 891 | 16 838 | 18 129 | 19 348 | 20 460 | 20 935 | 21 925 | 22 837 | 24 771 | 26 103 |
| 3c. % of GWP | 0.22 | 0.23 | 0.23 | 0.23 | 0.24 | 0.24 | 0.24 | 0.24 | 0.25 | 0.26 |
| **4. Relative 1970−1989 PARE** | | | | | | | | | | |
| 4a. Per capita GDP | 363 | 394 | 434 | 482 | 544 | 598 | 650 | 706 | 803 | 901 |
| 4b. GDP | 7 748 | 8 631 | 9 719 | 11 061 | 12 759 | 14 343 | 15 960 | 17 744 | 20 651 | 23 705 |
| 4c. % of GWP | 0.22 | 0.23 | 0.23 | 0.23 | 0.24 | 0.24 | 0.24 | 0.24 | 0.25 | 0.26 |
| **5. Absolute 1980−1989 PARE** | | | | | | | | | | |
| 5a. Per capita GDP | 892 | 922 | 970 | 1 012 | 1 046 | 1 047 | 1 071 | 1 090 | 1 155 | 1 190 |
| 5b. GDP | 19 058 | 20 194 | 21 743 | 23 204 | 24 538 | 25 108 | 26 295 | 27 388 | 29 708 | 31 306 |
| 5c. % of GWP | 0.22 | 0.22 | 0.23 | 0.23 | 0.24 | 0.24 | 0.24 | 0.24 | 0.25 | 0.25 |
| **6. WA** | | | | | | | | | | |
| 6a. Per capita GDP | 337 | 357 | 387 | 449 | 527 | 546 | 625 | 775 | 905 | 1 062 |
| 6b. GDP | 7 199 | 7 821 | 8 672 | 10 287 | 12 369 | 13 098 | 15 342 | 19 471 | 23 264 | 27 939 |
| 6c. % of GWP | 0.23 | 0.22 | 0.22 | 0.21 | 0.22 | 0.21 | 0.23 | 0.26 | 0.26 | 0.27 |
| **Comoros** | | | | | | | | | | |
| **1. MER** | | | | | | | | | | |
| 1a. Per capita GDP | 122 | 139 | 157 | 192 | 260 | 252 | 186 | 192 | 239 | 307 |
| 1b. GDP | 33 | 39 | 46 | 57 | 80 | 81 | 62 | 67 | 87 | 116 |
| 1c. % of GWP | 0.00 | 0.00 | 0.00 | 0.00 | 0.00 | 0.00 | 0.00 | 0.00 | 0.00 | 0.00 |
| **2. PPPs** | | | | | | | | | | |
| 2a. Per capita GDP | ... | ... | ... | ... | ... | ... | ... | ... | ... | ... |
| 2b. GDP | ... | ... | ... | ... | ... | ... | ... | ... | ... | ... |
| 2c. % of GWP | ... | ... | ... | ... | ... | ... | ... | ... | ... | ... |
| **3. Absolute 1970−1989 PARE** | | | | | | | | | | |
| 3a. Per capita GDP | 336 | 359 | 357 | 345 | 372 | 316 | 245 | 244 | 240 | 253 |
| 3b. GDP | 92 | 102 | 104 | 103 | 115 | 102 | 82 | 85 | 87 | 96 |
| 3c. % of GWP | 0.00 | 0.00 | 0.00 | 0.00 | 0.00 | 0.00 | 0.00 | 0.00 | 0.00 | 0.00 |
| **4. Relative 1970−1989 PARE** | | | | | | | | | | |
| 4a. Per capita GDP | 164 | 184 | 191 | 197 | 232 | 217 | 178 | 189 | 200 | 230 |
| 4b. GDP | 45 | 52 | 56 | 59 | 72 | 70 | 59 | 66 | 73 | 87 |
| 4c. % of GWP | 0.00 | 0.00 | 0.00 | 0.00 | 0.00 | 0.00 | 0.00 | 0.00 | 0.00 | 0.00 |
| **5. Absolute 1980−1989 PARE** | | | | | | | | | | |
| 5a. Per capita GDP | 418 | 446 | 443 | 428 | 462 | 393 | 304 | 303 | 299 | 315 |
| 5b. GDP | 115 | 126 | 129 | 128 | 143 | 126 | 101 | 105 | 108 | 119 |
| 5c. % of GWP | 0.00 | 0.00 | 0.00 | 0.00 | 0.00 | 0.00 | 0.00 | 0.00 | 0.00 | 0.00 |
| **6. WA** | | | | | | | | | | |
| 6a. Per capita GDP | 122 | 139 | 157 | 192 | 260 | 252 | 186 | 192 | 239 | 307 |
| 6b. GDP | 33 | 39 | 46 | 57 | 80 | 81 | 62 | 67 | 87 | 116 |
| 6c. % of GWP | 0.00 | 0.00 | 0.00 | 0.00 | 0.00 | 0.00 | 0.00 | 0.00 | 0.00 | 0.00 |

| | | | | | | | | | | Averages | | |
|---|---|---|---|---|---|---|---|---|---|---|---|---|
| 1980 (11) | 1981 (12) | 1982 (13) | 1983 (14) | 1984 (15) | 1985 (16) | 1986 (17) | 1987 (18) | 1988 (19) | 1989 (20) | 1970–89 (21) | 1970–79 (22) | 1980–89 (23) |
| 1 241 | 1 323 | 1 387 | 1 350 | 1 307 | 1 168 | 1 146 | 1 169 | 1 225 | 1 219 | 970 | 614 | 1 252 |
| 33 400 | 36 388 | 38 965 | 38 734 | 38 252 | 34 895 | 34 943 | 36 374 | 38 877 | 39 438 | 25 798 | 14 570 | 37 026 |
| 0.29 | 0.31 | 0.34 | 0.33 | 0.31 | 0.28 | 0.23 | 0.21 | 0.20 | 0.20 | 0.25 | 0.24 | 0.26 |
| 2 456 | 2 663 | 2 866 | 2 963 | 3 063 | 3 123 | 3 304 | 3 511 | 3 690 | 3 895 | 2 404 | 1 427 | 3 181 |
| 66 086 | 73 214 | 80 508 | 84 983 | 89 670 | 93 326 | 100 746 | 109 205 | 117 056 | 126 013 | 63 967 | 33 854 | 94 081 |
| ... | ... | ... | ... | ... | ... | ... | ... | ... | ... | ... | ... | ... |
| 1 010 | 1 011 | 999 | 993 | 1 006 | 1 016 | 1 054 | 1 089 | 1 107 | 1 122 | 970 | 874 | 1 044 |
| 27 170 | 27 789 | 28 052 | 28 494 | 29 449 | 30 364 | 32 132 | 33 857 | 35 112 | 36 310 | 25 798 | 20 723 | 30 873 |
| 0.26 | 0.26 | 0.26 | 0.26 | 0.26 | 0.26 | 0.26 | 0.27 | 0.27 | 0.27 | 0.25 | 0.24 | 0.26 |
| 1 001 | 1 097 | 1 154 | 1 186 | 1 244 | 1 291 | 1 366 | 1 451 | 1 525 | 1 610 | 992 | 600 | 1 304 |
| 26 933 | 30 152 | 32 404 | 34 027 | 36 427 | 38 576 | 41 643 | 45 139 | 48 384 | 52 087 | 26 405 | 14 232 | 38 577 |
| 0.26 | 0.26 | 0.26 | 0.26 | 0.26 | 0.26 | 0.26 | 0.27 | 0.27 | 0.27 | 0.26 | 0.24 | 0.26 |
| 1 211 | 1 212 | 1 198 | 1 191 | 1 206 | 1 219 | 1 264 | 1 305 | 1 327 | 1 346 | 1 163 | 1 048 | 1 252 |
| 32 586 | 33 328 | 33 644 | 34 173 | 35 318 | 36 416 | 38 537 | 40 606 | 42 111 | 43 548 | 30 940 | 24 854 | 37 026 |
| 0.26 | 0.26 | 0.26 | 0.26 | 0.25 | 0.25 | 0.26 | 0.26 | 0.26 | 0.26 | 0.25 | 0.24 | 0.26 |
| 1 241 | 1 323 | 1 387 | 1 350 | 1 307 | 1 168 | 1 146 | 1 169 | 1 226 | 1 219 | 969 | 613 | 1 252 |
| 33 400 | 36 388 | 38 969 | 38 732 | 38 252 | 34 895 | 34 943 | 36 373 | 38 880 | 39 441 | 25 787 | 14 546 | 37 027 |
| 0.29 | 0.31 | 0.33 | 0.33 | 0.31 | 0.28 | 0.24 | 0.22 | 0.21 | 0.20 | 0.26 | 0.24 | 0.26 |
| 354 | 304 | 272 | 257 | 239 | 247 | 339 | 413 | 440 | 418 | 285 | 212 | 335 |
| 139 | 124 | 114 | 112 | 107 | 114 | 162 | 205 | 226 | 222 | 110 | 67 | 153 |
| 0.00 | 0.00 | 0.00 | 0.00 | 0.00 | 0.00 | 0.00 | 0.00 | 0.00 | 0.00 | 0.00 | 0.00 | 0.00 |
| ... | ... | ... | ... | ... | ... | ... | ... | ... | ... | ... | ... | ... |
| ... | ... | ... | ... | ... | ... | ... | ... | ... | ... | ... | ... | ... |
| ... | ... | ... | ... | ... | ... | ... | ... | ... | ... | ... | ... | ... |
| 261 | 260 | 269 | 271 | 273 | 272 | 268 | 269 | 269 | 266 | 285 | 307 | 269 |
| 103 | 106 | 113 | 118 | 122 | 126 | 128 | 133 | 138 | 141 | 110 | 97 | 123 |
| 0.00 | 0.00 | 0.00 | 0.00 | 0.00 | 0.00 | 0.00 | 0.00 | 0.00 | 0.00 | 0.00 | 0.00 | 0.00 |
| 259 | 283 | 311 | 323 | 337 | 345 | 347 | 359 | 370 | 381 | 282 | 203 | 337 |
| 102 | 115 | 131 | 140 | 151 | 160 | 166 | 178 | 190 | 203 | 109 | 64 | 154 |
| 0.00 | 0.00 | 0.00 | 0.00 | 0.00 | 0.00 | 0.00 | 0.00 | 0.00 | 0.00 | 0.00 | 0.00 | 0.00 |
| 325 | 323 | 334 | 336 | 339 | 337 | 333 | 334 | 334 | 330 | 354 | 381 | 335 |
| 128 | 132 | 141 | 146 | 152 | 156 | 160 | 166 | 171 | 176 | 136 | 120 | 153 |
| 0.00 | 0.00 | 0.00 | 0.00 | 0.00 | 0.00 | 0.00 | 0.00 | 0.00 | 0.00 | 0.00 | 0.00 | 0.00 |
| 354 | 304 | 272 | 257 | 239 | 247 | 339 | 413 | 440 | 418 | 285 | 212 | 335 |
| 139 | 124 | 114 | 112 | 107 | 114 | 162 | 205 | 226 | 222 | 110 | 67 | 153 |
| 0.00 | 0.00 | 0.00 | 0.00 | 0.00 | 0.00 | 0.00 | 0.00 | 0.00 | 0.00 | 0.00 | 0.00 | 0.00 |

**Table A.1** Total and per capita gross domestic product of individual countries or areas, expressed in United States dollars, and their individual shares of gross world product, based on alternative conversion rates, 1970−1989 [*cont.*]

| Country or area | 1970 (1) | 1971 (2) | 1972 (3) | 1973 (4) | 1974 (5) | 1975 (6) | 1976 (7) | 1977 (8) | 1978 (9) | 1979 (10) |
|---|---|---|---|---|---|---|---|---|---|---|
| **Congo** | | | | | | | | | | |
| **1. MER** | | | | | | | | | | |
| 1a. Per capita GDP | 217 | 240 | 283 | 362 | 412 | 530 | 507 | 503 | 558 | 736 |
| 1b. GDP | 274 | 311 | 377 | 496 | 580 | 767 | 755 | 769 | 879 | 1 194 |
| 1c. % of GWP | 0.01 | 0.01 | 0.01 | 0.01 | 0.01 | 0.01 | 0.01 | 0.01 | 0.01 | 0.01 |
| **2. PPPs** | | | | | | | | | | |
| 2a. Per capita GDP | 342 | 383 | 400 | 468 | 562 | 578 | 592 | 568 | 559 | 687 |
| 2b. GDP | 432 | 496 | 533 | 642 | 791 | 837 | 881 | 869 | 881 | 1 114 |
| 2c. % of GWP | ... | ... | ... | ... | ... | ... | ... | ... | ... | ... |
| **3. Absolute 1970−1989 PARE** | | | | | | | | | | |
| 3a. Per capita GDP | 690 | 691 | 673 | 731 | 741 | 726 | 689 | 634 | 603 | 652 |
| 3b. GDP | 872 | 897 | 897 | 1 002 | 1 043 | 1 051 | 1 025 | 971 | 950 | 1 057 |
| 3c. % of GWP | 0.01 | 0.01 | 0.01 | 0.01 | 0.01 | 0.01 | 0.01 | 0.01 | 0.01 | 0.01 |
| **4. Relative 1970−1989 PARE** | | | | | | | | | | |
| 4a. Per capita GDP | 337 | 354 | 361 | 418 | 462 | 497 | 501 | 493 | 503 | 592 |
| 4b. GDP | 425 | 460 | 481 | 573 | 650 | 720 | 746 | 754 | 792 | 960 |
| 4c. % of GWP | 0.01 | 0.01 | 0.01 | 0.01 | 0.01 | 0.01 | 0.01 | 0.01 | 0.01 | 0.01 |
| **5. Absolute 1980−1989 PARE** | | | | | | | | | | |
| 5a. Per capita GDP | 822 | 824 | 801 | 871 | 882 | 865 | 820 | 755 | 718 | 776 |
| 5b. GDP | 1 039 | 1 068 | 1 068 | 1 194 | 1 242 | 1 252 | 1 221 | 1 157 | 1 132 | 1 259 |
| 5c. % of GWP | 0.01 | 0.01 | 0.01 | 0.01 | 0.01 | 0.01 | 0.01 | 0.01 | 0.01 | 0.01 |
| **6. WA** | | | | | | | | | | |
| 6a. Per capita GDP | 217 | 240 | 283 | 362 | 412 | 530 | 507 | 503 | 558 | 736 |
| 6b. GDP | 274 | 311 | 377 | 496 | 580 | 767 | 755 | 769 | 879 | 1 194 |
| 6c. % of GWP | 0.01 | 0.01 | 0.01 | 0.01 | 0.01 | 0.01 | 0.01 | 0.01 | 0.01 | 0.01 |
| **Cook Islands** | | | | | | | | | | |
| **1. MER** | | | | | | | | | | |
| 1a. Per capita GDP | 443 | 435 | 461 | 582 | 695 | 667 | 720 | 837 | 973 | 1 062 |
| 1b. GDP | 9 | 9 | 10 | 12 | 14 | 13 | 14 | 16 | 18 | 20 |
| 1c. % of GWP | 0.00 | 0.00 | 0.00 | 0.00 | 0.00 | 0.00 | 0.00 | 0.00 | 0.00 | 0.00 |
| **2. PPPs** | | | | | | | | | | |
| 2a. Per capita GDP | ... | ... | ... | ... | ... | ... | ... | ... | ... | ... |
| 2b. GDP | ... | ... | ... | ... | ... | ... | ... | ... | ... | ... |
| 2c. % of GWP | ... | ... | ... | ... | ... | ... | ... | ... | ... | ... |
| **3. Absolute 1970−1989 PARE** | | | | | | | | | | |
| 3a. Per capita GDP | 1 293 | 1 164 | 1 026 | 1 005 | 1 037 | 996 | 1 089 | 1 079 | 1 050 | 1 045 |
| 3b. GDP | 27 | 24 | 22 | 21 | 21 | 20 | 21 | 21 | 20 | 20 |
| 3c. % of GWP | 0.00 | 0.00 | 0.00 | 0.00 | 0.00 | 0.00 | 0.00 | 0.00 | 0.00 | 0.00 |
| **4. Relative 1970−1989 PARE** | | | | | | | | | | |
| 4a. Per capita GDP | 630 | 596 | 550 | 575 | 647 | 682 | 793 | 839 | 875 | 949 |
| 4b. GDP | 13 | 13 | 12 | 12 | 13 | 14 | 15 | 16 | 17 | 18 |
| 4c. % of GWP | 0.00 | 0.00 | 0.00 | 0.00 | 0.00 | 0.00 | 0.00 | 0.00 | 0.00 | 0.00 |
| **5. Absolute 1980−1989 PARE** | | | | | | | | | | |
| 5a. Per capita GDP | 1 742 | 1 568 | 1 383 | 1 355 | 1 398 | 1 342 | 1 467 | 1 454 | 1 415 | 1 409 |
| 5b. GDP | 37 | 33 | 29 | 28 | 28 | 27 | 28 | 28 | 27 | 27 |
| 5c. % of GWP | 0.00 | 0.00 | 0.00 | 0.00 | 0.00 | 0.00 | 0.00 | 0.00 | 0.00 | 0.00 |
| **6. WA[a]** | | | | | | | | | | |
| 6a. Per capita GDP | 406 | 398 | 394 | 455 | 572 | 634 | 726 | 754 | 811 | 935 |
| 6b. GDP | 9 | 8 | 8 | 10 | 11 | 13 | 14 | 14 | 15 | 18 |
| 6c. % of GWP | 0.00 | 0.00 | 0.00 | 0.00 | 0.00 | 0.00 | 0.00 | 0.00 | 0.00 | 0.00 |

| | | | | | | | | | | Averages | | |
|---|---|---|---|---|---|---|---|---|---|---|---|---|
| 1980 | 1981 | 1982 | 1983 | 1984 | 1985 | 1986 | 1987 | 1988 | 1989 | 1970–89 | 1970–79 | 1980–89 |
| (11) | (12) | (13) | (14) | (15) | (16) | (17) | (18) | (19) | (20) | (21) | (22) | (23) |
| 1 022 | 1 160 | 1 220 | 1 149 | 1 166 | 1 114 | 924 | 1 112 | 1 042 | 1 031 | 831 | 448 | 1 096 |
| 1 706 | 1 994 | 2 161 | 2 097 | 2 194 | 2 161 | 1 849 | 2 296 | 2 220 | 2 268 | 1 367 | 640 | 2 095 |
| 0.01 | 0.02 | 0.02 | 0.02 | 0.02 | 0.02 | 0.01 | 0.01 | 0.01 | 0.01 | 0.01 | 0.01 | 0.01 |
| 943 | 1 138 | 1 337 | 1 408 | 1 516 | 1 388 | 1 278 | 1 289 | 1 208 | 1 221 | 971 | 524 | 1 282 |
| 1 574 | 1 957 | 2 367 | 2 570 | 2 851 | 2 692 | 2 558 | 2 660 | 2 573 | 2 684 | 1 598 | 748 | 2 449 |
| ... | ... | ... | ... | ... | ... | ... | ... | ... | ... | ... | ... | ... |
| 714 | 840 | 1 007 | 1 032 | 1 074 | 1 029 | 929 | 911 | 826 | 802 | 831 | 684 | 920 |
| 1 191 | 1 444 | 1 784 | 1 884 | 2 020 | 1 997 | 1 860 | 1 880 | 1 760 | 1 763 | 1 367 | 976 | 1 758 |
| 0.01 | 0.01 | 0.02 | 0.02 | 0.02 | 0.02 | 0.02 | 0.01 | 0.01 | 0.01 | 0.01 | 0.01 | 0.01 |
| 707 | 911 | 1 164 | 1 233 | 1 329 | 1 308 | 1 204 | 1 214 | 1 138 | 1 150 | 867 | 460 | 1 150 |
| 1 181 | 1 567 | 2 061 | 2 250 | 2 499 | 2 537 | 2 410 | 2 507 | 2 425 | 2 529 | 1 426 | 656 | 2 197 |
| 0.01 | 0.01 | 0.02 | 0.02 | 0.02 | 0.02 | 0.02 | 0.01 | 0.01 | 0.01 | 0.01 | 0.01 | 0.01 |
| 850 | 1 001 | 1 200 | 1 230 | 1 279 | 1 226 | 1 107 | 1 085 | 984 | 955 | 990 | 815 | 1 096 |
| 1 419 | 1 720 | 2 125 | 2 245 | 2 407 | 2 379 | 2 215 | 2 239 | 2 096 | 2 100 | 1 629 | 1 163 | 2 095 |
| 0.01 | 0.01 | 0.02 | 0.02 | 0.02 | 0.02 | 0.01 | 0.01 | 0.01 | 0.01 | 0.01 | 0.01 | 0.01 |
| 1 022 | 1 160 | 1 220 | 1 149 | 1 166 | 1 114 | 924 | 1 112 | 1 042 | 1 031 | 831 | 448 | 1 096 |
| 1 706 | 1 994 | 2 161 | 2 097 | 2 194 | 2 161 | 1 849 | 2 295 | 2 220 | 2 268 | 1 367 | 640 | 2 094 |
| 0.01 | 0.02 | 0.02 | 0.02 | 0.02 | 0.02 | 0.01 | 0.01 | 0.01 | 0.01 | 0.01 | 0.01 | 0.01 |
| 1 114 | 1 217 | 1 202 | 1 241 | 1 264 | 1 268 | 1 637 | 2 073 | 3 025 | 3 155 | 1 175 | 679 | 1 726 |
| 21 | 22 | 22 | 22 | 23 | 23 | 29 | 37 | 54 | 57 | 22 | 14 | 31 |
| 0.00 | 0.00 | 0.00 | 0.00 | 0.00 | 0.00 | 0.00 | 0.00 | 0.00 | 0.00 | 0.00 | 0.00 | 0.00 |
| ... | ... | ... | ... | ... | ... | ... | ... | ... | ... | ... | ... | ... |
| ... | ... | ... | ... | ... | ... | ... | ... | ... | ... | ... | ... | ... |
| ... | ... | ... | ... | ... | ... | ... | ... | ... | ... | ... | ... | ... |
| 1 013 | 1 026 | 1 043 | 1 120 | 1 179 | 1 218 | 1 359 | 1 384 | 1 646 | 1 763 | 1 175 | 1 080 | 1 281 |
| 19 | 18 | 19 | 20 | 21 | 22 | 24 | 25 | 30 | 32 | 22 | 22 | 23 |
| 0.00 | 0.00 | 0.00 | 0.00 | 0.00 | 0.00 | 0.00 | 0.00 | 0.00 | 0.00 | 0.00 | 0.00 | 0.00 |
| 1 004 | 1 114 | 1 204 | 1 337 | 1 459 | 1 547 | 1 762 | 1 845 | 2 269 | 2 528 | 1 136 | 708 | 1 612 |
| 19 | 20 | 22 | 24 | 26 | 28 | 32 | 33 | 41 | 46 | 22 | 14 | 29 |
| 0.00 | 0.00 | 0.00 | 0.00 | 0.00 | 0.00 | 0.00 | 0.00 | 0.00 | 0.00 | 0.00 | 0.00 | 0.00 |
| 1 365 | 1 383 | 1 405 | 1 509 | 1 589 | 1 641 | 1 832 | 1 865 | 2 218 | 2 375 | 1 583 | 1 455 | 1 726 |
| 26 | 25 | 25 | 27 | 29 | 30 | 33 | 34 | 40 | 43 | 30 | 29 | 31 |
| 0.00 | 0.00 | 0.00 | 0.00 | 0.00 | 0.00 | 0.00 | 0.00 | 0.00 | 0.00 | 0.00 | 0.00 | 0.00 |
| 1 022 | 1 125 | 1 194 | 1 285 | 1 309 | 1 307 | 1 497 | 1 688 | 2 418 | 2 987 | 1 069 | 601 | 1 589 |
| 19 | 20 | 21 | 23 | 24 | 24 | 27 | 30 | 44 | 54 | 20 | 12 | 29 |
| 0.00 | 0.00 | 0.00 | 0.00 | 0.00 | 0.00 | 0.00 | 0.00 | 0.00 | 0.00 | 0.00 | 0.00 | 0.00 |

**Table A.1**    Total and per capita gross domestic product of individual countries or areas, expressed in United States dollars, and their individual shares of gross world product, based on alternative conversion rates, 1970–1989 [*cont.*]

| Country or area | 1970 (1) | 1971 (2) | 1972 (3) | 1973 (4) | 1974 (5) | 1975 (6) | 1976 (7) | 1977 (8) | 1978 (9) | 1979 (10) |
|---|---|---|---|---|---|---|---|---|---|---|
| **Costa Rica** | | | | | | | | | | |
| **1.    MER** | | | | | | | | | | |
| 1a.   Per capita GDP | 569 | 605 | 679 | 818 | 869 | 996 | 1 191 | 1 473 | 1 638 | 1 820 |
| 1b.   GDP | 985 | 1 076 | 1 238 | 1 529 | 1 667 | 1 961 | 2 413 | 3 072 | 3 523 | 4 035 |
| 1c.   % of GWP | 0.03 | 0.03 | 0.03 | 0.03 | 0.03 | 0.03 | 0.04 | 0.04 | 0.04 | 0.04 |
| **2.    PPPs** | | | | | | | | | | |
| 2a.   Per capita GDP | 1 196 | 1 264 | 1 351 | 1 472 | 1 601 | 1 783 | 2 004 | 2 363 | 2 555 | 2 789 |
| 2b.   GDP | 2 070 | 2 248 | 2 463 | 2 751 | 3 069 | 3 511 | 4 058 | 4 929 | 5 496 | 6 184 |
| 2c.   % of GWP | ... | ... | ... | ... | ... | ... | ... | ... | ... | ... |
| **3.    Absolute 1970–1989 PARE** | | | | | | | | | | |
| 3a.   Per capita GDP | 1 125 | 1 169 | 1 233 | 1 296 | 1 333 | 1 325 | 1 360 | 1 438 | 1 482 | 1 508 |
| 3b.   GDP | 1 947 | 2 078 | 2 248 | 2 422 | 2 556 | 2 610 | 2 754 | 2 999 | 3 187 | 3 344 |
| 3c.   % of GWP | 0.03 | 0.03 | 0.03 | 0.03 | 0.03 | 0.03 | 0.03 | 0.03 | 0.03 | 0.03 |
| **4.    Relative 1970–1989 PARE** | | | | | | | | | | |
| 4a.   Per capita GDP | 548 | 599 | 661 | 741 | 831 | 908 | 990 | 1 117 | 1 235 | 1 370 |
| 4b.   GDP | 949 | 1 065 | 1 205 | 1 384 | 1 594 | 1 788 | 2 004 | 2 330 | 2 657 | 3 037 |
| 4c.   % of GWP | 0.03 | 0.03 | 0.03 | 0.03 | 0.03 | 0.03 | 0.03 | 0.03 | 0.03 | 0.03 |
| **5.    Absolute 1980–1989 PARE** | | | | | | | | | | |
| 5a.   Per capita GDP | 1 273 | 1 324 | 1 397 | 1 467 | 1 510 | 1 501 | 1 540 | 1 628 | 1 678 | 1 708 |
| 5b.   GDP | 2 204 | 2 353 | 2 546 | 2 742 | 2 894 | 2 955 | 3 118 | 3 396 | 3 609 | 3 787 |
| 5c.   % of GWP | 0.03 | 0.03 | 0.03 | 0.03 | 0.03 | 0.03 | 0.03 | 0.03 | 0.03 | 0.03 |
| **6.    WA** | | | | | | | | | | |
| 6a.   Per capita GDP | 569 | 606 | 679 | 818 | 869 | 996 | 1 191 | 1 473 | 1 638 | 1 820 |
| 6b.   GDP | 985 | 1 077 | 1 238 | 1 529 | 1 667 | 1 961 | 2 413 | 3 072 | 3 523 | 4 035 |
| 6c.   % of GWP | 0.03 | 0.03 | 0.03 | 0.03 | 0.03 | 0.03 | 0.04 | 0.04 | 0.04 | 0.04 |
| **Côte d'Ivoire** | | | | | | | | | | |
| **1.    MER** | | | | | | | | | | |
| 1a.   Per capita GDP | 271 | 276 | 312 | 407 | 473 | 576 | 664 | 858 | 1 041 | 1 159 |
| 1b.   GDP | 1 494 | 1 587 | 1 869 | 2 540 | 3 070 | 3 894 | 4 662 | 6 265 | 7 902 | 9 142 |
| 1c.   % of GWP | 0.05 | 0.05 | 0.05 | 0.05 | 0.06 | 0.06 | 0.07 | 0.08 | 0.09 | 0.09 |
| **2.    PPPs** | | | | | | | | | | |
| 2a.   Per capita GDP | 449 | 470 | 488 | 546 | 611 | 667 | 809 | 950 | 1 030 | 1 066 |
| 2b.   GDP | 2 476 | 2 700 | 2 921 | 3 403 | 3 968 | 4 507 | 5 681 | 6 940 | 7 815 | 8 409 |
| 2c.   % of GWP | ... | ... | ... | ... | ... | ... | ... | ... | ... | ... |
| **3.    Absolute 1970–1989 PARE** | | | | | | | | | | |
| 3a.   Per capita GDP | 708 | 718 | 730 | 754 | 760 | 789 | 849 | 855 | 905 | 887 |
| 3b.   GDP | 3 907 | 4 125 | 4 370 | 4 701 | 4 931 | 5 328 | 5 967 | 6 247 | 6 866 | 6 996 |
| 3c.   % of GWP | 0.05 | 0.06 | 0.06 | 0.06 | 0.06 | 0.06 | 0.07 | 0.07 | 0.07 | 0.07 |
| **4.    Relative 1970–1989 PARE** | | | | | | | | | | |
| 4a.   Per capita GDP | 345 | 368 | 391 | 431 | 474 | 540 | 618 | 665 | 754 | 806 |
| 4b.   GDP | 1 905 | 2 114 | 2 343 | 2 688 | 3 075 | 3 650 | 4 343 | 4 854 | 5 724 | 6 354 |
| 4c.   % of GWP | 0.05 | 0.06 | 0.06 | 0.06 | 0.06 | 0.06 | 0.07 | 0.07 | 0.07 | 0.07 |
| **5.    Absolute 1980–1989 PARE** | | | | | | | | | | |
| 5a.   Per capita GDP | 811 | 822 | 836 | 863 | 869 | 903 | 972 | 979 | 1 036 | 1 015 |
| 5b.   GDP | 4 472 | 4 720 | 5 002 | 5 380 | 5 644 | 6 097 | 6 829 | 7 150 | 7 857 | 8 007 |
| 5c.   % of GWP | 0.05 | 0.05 | 0.05 | 0.05 | 0.05 | 0.06 | 0.06 | 0.06 | 0.07 | 0.06 |
| **6.    WA** | | | | | | | | | | |
| 6a.   Per capita GDP | 271 | 276 | 312 | 407 | 473 | 576 | 664 | 858 | 1 041 | 1 159 |
| 6b.   GDP | 1 494 | 1 587 | 1 869 | 2 540 | 3 070 | 3 894 | 4 662 | 6 265 | 7 901 | 9 142 |
| 6c.   % of GWP | 0.05 | 0.05 | 0.05 | 0.05 | 0.06 | 0.06 | 0.07 | 0.08 | 0.09 | 0.09 |

| | | | | | | | | | | Averages | | |
|---|---|---|---|---|---|---|---|---|---|---|---|---|
| 1980 | 1981 | 1982 | 1983 | 1984 | 1985 | 1986 | 1987 | 1988 | 1989 | 1970–89 | 1970–79 | 1980–89 |
| (11) | (12) | (13) | (14) | (15) | (16) | (17) | (18) | (19) | (20) | (21) | (22) | (23) |
| 2 114 | 1 115 | 1 075 | 1 261 | 1 425 | 1 484 | 1 621 | 1 622 | 1 639 | 1 807 | 1 360 | 1 106 | 1 525 |
| 4 832 | 2 624 | 2 607 | 3 147 | 3 660 | 3 923 | 4 404 | 4 528 | 4 696 | 5 315 | 3 062 | 2 150 | 3 973 |
| 0.04 | 0.02 | 0.02 | 0.03 | 0.03 | 0.03 | 0.03 | 0.03 | 0.02 | 0.03 | 0.03 | 0.04 | 0.03 |
| 2 978 | 2 927 | 2 684 | 2 765 | 3 284 | 3 325 | 3 482 | 3 652 | 3 804 | 4 077 | 2 747 | 1 893 | 3 334 |
| 6 804 | 6 890 | 6 508 | 6 903 | 8 436 | 8 788 | 9 460 | 10 195 | 10 903 | 11 991 | 6 183 | 3 678 | 8 688 |
| ... | ... | ... | ... | ... | ... | ... | ... | ... | ... | ... | ... | ... |
| 1 475 | 1 399 | 1 259 | 1 258 | 1 321 | 1 293 | 1 327 | 1 353 | 1 364 | 1 404 | 1 360 | 1 346 | 1 346 |
| 3 369 | 3 293 | 3 053 | 3 141 | 3 393 | 3 417 | 3 606 | 3 778 | 3 909 | 4 130 | 3 062 | 2 614 | 3 509 |
| 0.03 | 0.03 | 0.03 | 0.03 | 0.03 | 0.03 | 0.03 | 0.03 | 0.03 | 0.03 | 0.03 | 0.03 | 0.03 |
| 1 462 | 1 518 | 1 454 | 1 503 | 1 634 | 1 643 | 1 720 | 1 804 | 1 879 | 2 014 | 1 372 | 927 | 1 679 |
| 3 340 | 3 573 | 3 527 | 3 750 | 4 197 | 4 341 | 4 674 | 5 037 | 5 386 | 5 924 | 3 088 | 1 801 | 4 375 |
| 0.03 | 0.03 | 0.03 | 0.03 | 0.03 | 0.03 | 0.03 | 0.03 | 0.03 | 0.03 | 0.03 | 0.03 | 0.03 |
| 1 670 | 1 584 | 1 426 | 1 425 | 1 495 | 1 464 | 1 503 | 1 532 | 1 544 | 1 590 | 1 540 | 1 524 | 1 525 |
| 3 815 | 3 729 | 3 458 | 3 556 | 3 842 | 3 870 | 4 084 | 4 278 | 4 426 | 4 676 | 3 467 | 2 961 | 3 973 |
| 0.03 | 0.03 | 0.03 | 0.03 | 0.03 | 0.03 | 0.03 | 0.03 | 0.03 | 0.03 | 0.03 | 0.03 | 0.03 |
| 2 114 | 1 115 | 1 075 | 1 261 | 1 425 | 1 484 | 1 621 | 1 622 | 1 638 | 1 807 | 1 360 | 1 107 | 1 525 |
| 4 832 | 2 624 | 2 607 | 3 147 | 3 660 | 3 923 | 4 404 | 4 529 | 4 696 | 5 314 | 3 062 | 2 150 | 3 974 |
| 0.04 | 0.02 | 0.02 | 0.03 | 0.03 | 0.03 | 0.03 | 0.03 | 0.03 | 0.03 | 0.03 | 0.04 | 0.03 |
| 1 242 | 990 | 855 | 743 | 690 | 703 | 908 | 992 | 976 | 849 | 807 | 641 | 895 |
| 10 176 | 8 433 | 7 567 | 6 839 | 6 599 | 6 984 | 9 372 | 10 624 | 10 860 | 9 805 | 6 484 | 4 242 | 8 726 |
| 0.09 | 0.07 | 0.07 | 0.06 | 0.05 | 0.06 | 0.06 | 0.06 | 0.06 | 0.05 | 0.06 | 0.07 | 0.06 |
| 1 090 | 1 168 | 1 191 | 1 205 | 1 164 | 1 190 | 1 210 | 1 180 | 1 153 | 1 141 | 1 016 | 737 | 1 176 |
| 8 931 | 9 947 | 10 547 | 11 084 | 11 131 | 11 819 | 12 479 | 12 644 | 12 831 | 13 182 | 8 171 | 4 882 | 11 460 |
| ... | ... | ... | ... | ... | ... | ... | ... | ... | ... | ... | ... | ... |
| 898 | 887 | 871 | 808 | 762 | 776 | 774 | 734 | 694 | 659 | 807 | 807 | 782 |
| 7 360 | 7 559 | 7 709 | 7 437 | 7 291 | 7 711 | 7 981 | 7 861 | 7 718 | 7 617 | 6 484 | 5 344 | 7 624 |
| 0.07 | 0.07 | 0.07 | 0.07 | 0.06 | 0.06 | 0.07 | 0.06 | 0.06 | 0.06 | 0.06 | 0.06 | 0.06 |
| 890 | 963 | 1 006 | 965 | 943 | 986 | 1 003 | 978 | 956 | 946 | 818 | 559 | 969 |
| 7 296 | 8 202 | 8 905 | 8 881 | 9 018 | 9 796 | 10 344 | 10 480 | 10 635 | 10 926 | 6 577 | 3 705 | 9 448 |
| 0.07 | 0.07 | 0.07 | 0.07 | 0.06 | 0.06 | 0.07 | 0.06 | 0.06 | 0.06 | 0.06 | 0.06 | 0.06 |
| 1 028 | 1 016 | 997 | 925 | 873 | 888 | 885 | 840 | 794 | 755 | 923 | 923 | 895 |
| 8 423 | 8 651 | 8 823 | 8 512 | 8 344 | 8 825 | 9 134 | 8 996 | 8 833 | 8 717 | 7 421 | 6 116 | 8 726 |
| 0.07 | 0.07 | 0.07 | 0.06 | 0.06 | 0.06 | 0.06 | 0.06 | 0.06 | 0.05 | 0.06 | 0.06 | 0.06 |
| 1 242 | 990 | 855 | 743 | 690 | 703 | 908 | 992 | 976 | 849 | 806 | 641 | 895 |
| 10 176 | 8 433 | 7 567 | 6 839 | 6 599 | 6 984 | 9 369 | 10 623 | 10 858 | 9 805 | 6 484 | 4 242 | 8 725 |
| 0.09 | 0.07 | 0.06 | 0.06 | 0.05 | 0.06 | 0.06 | 0.06 | 0.06 | 0.05 | 0.06 | 0.07 | 0.06 |

**Table A.1** Total and per capita gross domestic product of individual countries or areas, expressed in United States dollars, and their individual shares of gross world product, based on alternative conversion rates, 1970−1989 [*cont.*]

| Country or area | 1970 (1) | 1971 (2) | 1972 (3) | 1973 (4) | 1974 (5) | 1975 (6) | 1976 (7) | 1977 (8) | 1978 (9) | 1979 (10) |
|---|---|---|---|---|---|---|---|---|---|---|
| **Cuba** | | | | | | | | | | |
| 1. **MER** | | | | | | | | | | |
| 1a. Per capita GDP | 655 | 705 | 829 | 1 068 | 1 171 | 1 278 | 1 305 | 1 293 | 1 552 | 1 661 |
| 1b. GDP | 5 583 | 6 125 | 7 345 | 9 641 | 10 746 | 11 893 | 12 278 | 12 271 | 14 831 | 15 970 |
| 1c. % of GWP | 0.18 | 0.18 | 0.18 | 0.20 | 0.19 | 0.19 | 0.18 | 0.16 | 0.17 | 0.15 |
| 2. **PPPs** | | | | | | | | | | |
| 2a. Per capita GDP | ... | ... | ... | ... | ... | ... | ... | ... | ... | ... |
| 2b. GDP | ... | ... | ... | ... | ... | ... | ... | ... | ... | ... |
| 2c. % of GWP | ... | ... | ... | ... | ... | ... | ... | ... | ... | ... |
| 3. **Absolute 1970−1989 PARE** | | | | | | | | | | |
| 3a. Per capita GDP | 938 | 1 000 | 1 067 | 1 138 | 1 140 | 1 236 | 1 284 | 1 379 | 1 465 | 1 465 |
| 3b. GDP | 7 996 | 8 691 | 9 448 | 10 269 | 10 461 | 11 498 | 12 079 | 13 084 | 13 996 | 14 086 |
| 3c. % of GWP | 0.11 | 0.12 | 0.12 | 0.12 | 0.12 | 0.13 | 0.13 | 0.14 | 0.14 | 0.14 |
| 4. **Relative 1970−1989 PARE** | | | | | | | | | | |
| 4a. Per capita GDP | 458 | 513 | 572 | 651 | 711 | 846 | 934 | 1 071 | 1 221 | 1 330 |
| 4b. GDP | 3 898 | 4 455 | 5 065 | 5 871 | 6 523 | 7 877 | 8 792 | 10 167 | 11 669 | 12 792 |
| 4c. % of GWP | 0.11 | 0.12 | 0.12 | 0.12 | 0.12 | 0.13 | 0.13 | 0.14 | 0.14 | 0.14 |
| 5. **Absolute 1980−1989 PARE** | | | | | | | | | | |
| 5a. Per capita GDP | 964 | 1 028 | 1 096 | 1 169 | 1 171 | 1 269 | 1 319 | 1 417 | 1 505 | 1 505 |
| 5b. GDP | 8 215 | 8 930 | 9 707 | 10 551 | 10 749 | 11 814 | 12 411 | 13 444 | 14 381 | 14 474 |
| 5c. % of GWP | 0.09 | 0.10 | 0.10 | 0.10 | 0.10 | 0.11 | 0.11 | 0.12 | 0.12 | 0.12 |
| 6. **WA**[a] | | | | | | | | | | |
| 6a. Per capita GDP | 701 | 713 | 773 | 905 | 1 029 | 1 233 | 1 317 | 1 371 | 1 468 | 1 520 |
| 6b. GDP | 5 969 | 6 192 | 6 851 | 8 171 | 9 439 | 11 477 | 12 393 | 13 011 | 14 025 | 14 612 |
| 6c. % of GWP | 0.19 | 0.18 | 0.17 | 0.17 | 0.17 | 0.19 | 0.18 | 0.17 | 0.16 | 0.14 |
| **Cyprus** | | | | | | | | | | |
| 1. **MER** | | | | | | | | | | |
| 1a. Per capita GDP | 891 | 1 047 | 1 271 | 1 553 | 1 382 | 1 156 | 1 333 | 1 689 | 2 194 | 2 851 |
| 1b. GDP | 549 | 646 | 781 | 952 | 843 | 705 | 814 | 1 037 | 1 358 | 1 779 |
| 1c. % of GWP | 0.02 | 0.02 | 0.02 | 0.02 | 0.02 | 0.01 | 0.01 | 0.01 | 0.02 | 0.02 |
| 2. **PPPs** | | | | | | | | | | |
| 2a. Per capita GDP | 1 551 | 1 791 | 2 030 | 2 245 | 1 930 | 1 744 | 2 291 | 2 866 | 3 248 | 3 836 |
| 2b. GDP | 956 | 1 105 | 1 248 | 1 376 | 1 177 | 1 064 | 1 400 | 1 759 | 2 010 | 2 394 |
| 2c. % of GWP | ... | ... | ... | ... | ... | ... | ... | ... | ... | ... |
| 3. **Absolute 1970−1989 PARE** | | | | | | | | | | |
| 3a. Per capita GDP | 2 372 | 2 397 | 2 490 | 2 562 | 2 139 | 1 733 | 2 041 | 2 351 | 2 510 | 2 736 |
| 3b. GDP | 1 461 | 1 479 | 1 531 | 1 571 | 1 305 | 1 057 | 1 247 | 1 443 | 1 554 | 1 707 |
| 3c. % of GWP | 0.02 | 0.02 | 0.02 | 0.02 | 0.02 | 0.01 | 0.01 | 0.02 | 0.02 | 0.02 |
| 4. **Relative 1970−1989 PARE** | | | | | | | | | | |
| 4a. Per capita GDP | 1 156 | 1 229 | 1 335 | 1 465 | 1 334 | 1 187 | 1 485 | 1 827 | 2 093 | 2 485 |
| 4b. GDP | 712 | 758 | 821 | 898 | 814 | 724 | 908 | 1 122 | 1 295 | 1 550 |
| 4c. % of GWP | 0.02 | 0.02 | 0.02 | 0.02 | 0.02 | 0.01 | 0.01 | 0.02 | 0.02 | 0.02 |
| 5. **Absolute 1980−1989 PARE** | | | | | | | | | | |
| 5a. Per capita GDP | 2 867 | 2 898 | 3 010 | 3 097 | 2 586 | 2 094 | 2 467 | 2 842 | 3 035 | 3 307 |
| 5b. GDP | 1 766 | 1 788 | 1 851 | 1 899 | 1 577 | 1 278 | 1 507 | 1 745 | 1 878 | 2 064 |
| 5c. % of GWP | 0.02 | 0.02 | 0.02 | 0.02 | 0.02 | 0.01 | 0.01 | 0.02 | 0.02 | 0.02 |
| 6. **WA** | | | | | | | | | | |
| 6a. Per capita GDP | 1 579 | 1 602 | 1 659 | 1 709 | 1 425 | 1 154 | 1 331 | 1 688 | 2 188 | 2 851 |
| 6b. GDP | 973 | 988 | 1 020 | 1 048 | 869 | 704 | 813 | 1 037 | 1 355 | 1 779 |
| 6c. % of GWP | 0.03 | 0.03 | 0.03 | 0.02 | 0.02 | 0.01 | 0.01 | 0.01 | 0.02 | 0.02 |

| | 1980 (11) | 1981 (12) | 1982 (13) | 1983 (14) | 1984 (15) | 1985 (16) | 1986 (17) | 1987 (18) | 1988 (19) | 1989 (20) | Averages 1970–89 (21) | 1970–79 (22) | 1980–89 (23) |
|---|---|---|---|---|---|---|---|---|---|---|---|---|---|
| | 1 721 | 1 714 | 1 764 | 1 835 | 1 892 | 1 783 | 1 876 | 1 863 | 1 951 | 1 880 | 1 507 | 1 154 | 1 834 |
| | 16 653 | 16 711 | 17 324 | 18 172 | 18 898 | 17 968 | 19 090 | 19 154 | 20 278 | 19 745 | 14 534 | 10 668 | 18 399 |
| | 0.14 | 0.14 | 0.15 | 0.15 | 0.15 | 0.14 | 0.13 | 0.11 | 0.11 | 0.10 | 0.14 | 0.18 | 0.13 |
| | ... | ... | ... | ... | ... | ... | ... | ... | ... | ... | ... | ... | ... |
| | ... | ... | ... | ... | ... | ... | ... | ... | ... | ... | ... | ... | ... |
| | ... | ... | ... | ... | ... | ... | ... | ... | ... | ... | ... | ... | ... |
| | 1 379 | 1 654 | 1 725 | 1 804 | 1 922 | 1 983 | 1 920 | 1 796 | 1 814 | 1 786 | 1 507 | 1 208 | 1 785 |
| | 13 347 | 16 122 | 16 941 | 17 863 | 19 195 | 19 986 | 19 542 | 18 464 | 18 852 | 18 756 | 14 534 | 11 161 | 17 907 |
| | 0.13 | 0.15 | 0.16 | 0.16 | 0.17 | 0.17 | 0.16 | 0.15 | 0.14 | 0.14 | 0.14 | 0.13 | 0.15 |
| | 1 367 | 1 794 | 1 992 | 2 154 | 2 377 | 2 519 | 2 489 | 2 394 | 2 500 | 2 562 | 1 558 | 834 | 2 229 |
| | 13 230 | 17 493 | 19 569 | 21 331 | 23 744 | 25 392 | 25 327 | 24 617 | 25 978 | 26 905 | 15 035 | 7 711 | 22 359 |
| | 0.13 | 0.15 | 0.16 | 0.16 | 0.17 | 0.17 | 0.16 | 0.15 | 0.14 | 0.14 | 0.15 | 0.13 | 0.15 |
| | 1 417 | 1 699 | 1 772 | 1 854 | 1 975 | 2 038 | 1 973 | 1 845 | 1 864 | 1 835 | 1 548 | 1 241 | 1 834 |
| | 13 714 | 16 566 | 17 406 | 18 354 | 19 723 | 20 536 | 20 080 | 18 972 | 19 371 | 19 271 | 14 933 | 11 468 | 18 399 |
| | 0.11 | 0.13 | 0.13 | 0.14 | 0.14 | 0.14 | 0.14 | 0.12 | 0.12 | 0.12 | 0.12 | 0.11 | 0.13 |
| | 1 575 | 1 873 | 1 885 | 1 850 | 1 937 | 1 912 | 1 828 | 1 738 | 1 866 | 1 884 | 1 486 | 1 105 | 1 840 |
| | 15 240 | 18 263 | 18 520 | 18 317 | 19 346 | 19 273 | 18 602 | 17 869 | 19 386 | 19 787 | 14 337 | 10 214 | 18 460 |
| | 0.13 | 0.15 | 0.16 | 0.15 | 0.16 | 0.15 | 0.13 | 0.11 | 0.10 | 0.10 | 0.14 | 0.17 | 0.13 |
| | 3 419 | 3 279 | 3 321 | 3 320 | 3 462 | 3 649 | 4 569 | 5 233 | 5 791 | 6 394 | 3 011 | 1 552 | 4 275 |
| | 2 154 | 2 086 | 2 135 | 2 161 | 2 278 | 2 431 | 3 075 | 3 558 | 3 984 | 4 437 | 1 888 | 946 | 2 830 |
| | 0.02 | 0.02 | 0.02 | 0.02 | 0.02 | 0.02 | 0.02 | 0.02 | 0.02 | 0.02 | 0.02 | 0.02 | 0.02 |
| | 4 370 | 4 946 | 5 702 | 6 050 | 6 793 | 7 012 | 7 349 | 8 006 | 8 869 | 9 760 | 4 816 | 2 375 | 6 935 |
| | 2 753 | 3 146 | 3 666 | 3 938 | 4 470 | 4 670 | 4 946 | 5 444 | 6 102 | 6 773 | 3 020 | 1 449 | 4 591 |
| | ... | ... | ... | ... | ... | ... | ... | ... | ... | ... | ... | ... | ... |
| | 2 870 | 2 930 | 3 080 | 3 204 | 3 450 | 3 568 | 3 666 | 3 883 | 4 162 | 4 399 | 3 011 | 2 353 | 3 536 |
| | 1 808 | 1 863 | 1 981 | 2 086 | 2 270 | 2 377 | 2 467 | 2 640 | 2 863 | 3 053 | 1 888 | 1 435 | 2 341 |
| | 0.02 | 0.02 | 0.02 | 0.02 | 0.02 | 0.02 | 0.02 | 0.02 | 0.02 | 0.02 | 0.02 | 0.02 | 0.02 |
| | 2 845 | 3 179 | 3 558 | 3 827 | 4 267 | 4 534 | 4 752 | 5 176 | 5 735 | 6 311 | 3 115 | 1 574 | 4 451 |
| | 1 792 | 2 022 | 2 288 | 2 491 | 2 808 | 3 019 | 3 198 | 3 520 | 3 945 | 4 380 | 1 953 | 960 | 2 946 |
| | 0.02 | 0.02 | 0.02 | 0.02 | 0.02 | 0.02 | 0.02 | 0.02 | 0.02 | 0.02 | 0.02 | 0.02 | 0.02 |
| | 3 470 | 3 542 | 3 724 | 3 874 | 4 171 | 4 314 | 4 432 | 4 694 | 5 031 | 5 318 | 3 641 | 2 845 | 4 275 |
| | 2 186 | 2 253 | 2 394 | 2 522 | 2 744 | 2 873 | 2 983 | 3 192 | 3 461 | 3 691 | 2 283 | 1 735 | 2 830 |
| | 0.02 | 0.02 | 0.02 | 0.02 | 0.02 | 0.02 | 0.02 | 0.02 | 0.02 | 0.02 | 0.02 | 0.02 | 0.02 |
| | 3 419 | 3 272 | 3 353 | 3 313 | 3 462 | 3 646 | 4 598 | 5 443 | 6 210 | 6 481 | 3 142 | 1 735 | 4 353 |
| | 2 154 | 2 081 | 2 156 | 2 157 | 2 278 | 2 429 | 3 094 | 3 701 | 4 272 | 4 498 | 1 970 | 1 059 | 2 882 |
| | 0.02 | 0.02 | 0.02 | 0.02 | 0.02 | 0.02 | 0.02 | 0.02 | 0.02 | 0.02 | 0.02 | 0.02 | 0.02 |

**Table A.1** Total and per capita gross domestic product of individual countries or areas, expressed in United States dollars, and their individual shares of gross world product, based on alternative conversion rates, 1970–1989 [*cont.*]

| Country or area | 1970 (1) | 1971 (2) | 1972 (3) | 1973 (4) | 1974 (5) | 1975 (6) | 1976 (7) | 1977 (8) | 1978 (9) | 1979 (10) |
|---|---|---|---|---|---|---|---|---|---|---|
| **former Czechoslovakia** | | | | | | | | | | |
| **1. MER** | | | | | | | | | | |
| 1a. Per capita GDP | 1 012 | 1 052 | 1 191 | 1 398 | 1 486 | 1 614 | 1 586 | 2 286 | 2 499 | 2 659 |
| 1b. GDP | 14 500 | 15 150 | 17 255 | 20 390 | 21 842 | 23 898 | 23 658 | 34 343 | 37 816 | 40 497 |
| 1c. % of GWP | 0.45 | 0.43 | 0.43 | 0.42 | 0.39 | 0.38 | 0.35 | 0.45 | 0.42 | 0.39 |
| **2. PPPs** | | | | | | | | | | |
| 2a. Per capita GDP | ... | ... | ... | ... | ... | ... | ... | ... | ... | ... |
| 2b. GDP | ... | ... | ... | ... | ... | ... | ... | ... | ... | ... |
| 2c. % of GWP | ... | ... | ... | ... | ... | ... | ... | ... | ... | ... |
| **3. Absolute 1970–1989 PARE** | | | | | | | | | | |
| 3a. Per capita GDP | 1 671 | 1 747 | 1 828 | 1 902 | 2 002 | 2 114 | 2 177 | 2 255 | 2 331 | 2 385 |
| 3b. GDP | 23 947 | 25 155 | 26 489 | 27 745 | 29 411 | 31 295 | 32 471 | 33 888 | 35 272 | 36 329 |
| 3c. % of GWP | 0.34 | 0.34 | 0.34 | 0.33 | 0.35 | 0.36 | 0.36 | 0.36 | 0.36 | 0.36 |
| **4. Relative 1970–1989 PARE** | | | | | | | | | | |
| 4a. Per capita GDP | 815 | 895 | 980 | 1 087 | 1 248 | 1 448 | 1 585 | 1 752 | 1 943 | 2 166 |
| 4b. GDP | 11 676 | 12 894 | 14 201 | 15 862 | 18 341 | 21 440 | 23 636 | 26 331 | 29 406 | 32 992 |
| 4c. % of GWP | 0.34 | 0.34 | 0.34 | 0.33 | 0.35 | 0.36 | 0.36 | 0.36 | 0.36 | 0.36 |
| **5. Absolute 1980–1989 PARE** | | | | | | | | | | |
| 5a. Per capita GDP | 1 889 | 1 975 | 2 068 | 2 151 | 2 263 | 2 391 | 2 462 | 2 550 | 2 636 | 2 697 |
| 5b. GDP | 27 080 | 28 446 | 29 955 | 31 375 | 33 260 | 35 390 | 36 720 | 38 322 | 39 887 | 41 083 |
| 5c. % of GWP | 0.31 | 0.31 | 0.31 | 0.31 | 0.32 | 0.34 | 0.33 | 0.33 | 0.33 | 0.33 |
| **6. WA** | | | | | | | | | | |
| 6a. Per capita GDP | 1 378 | 1 246 | 1 132 | 1 252 | 1 415 | 1 579 | 1 621 | 1 844 | 2 124 | 2 541 |
| 6b. GDP | 19 749 | 17 951 | 16 395 | 18 268 | 20 798 | 23 373 | 24 180 | 27 710 | 32 143 | 38 696 |
| 6c. % of GWP | 0.62 | 0.51 | 0.41 | 0.38 | 0.37 | 0.38 | 0.36 | 0.37 | 0.36 | 0.38 |
| **Denmark** | | | | | | | | | | |
| **1. MER** | | | | | | | | | | |
| 1a. Per capita GDP | 3 209 | 3 563 | 4 349 | 5 697 | 6 305 | 7 438 | 8 182 | 9 132 | 11 053 | 12 886 |
| 1b. GDP | 15 817 | 17 671 | 21 691 | 28 572 | 31 768 | 37 636 | 41 557 | 46 529 | 56 460 | 65 937 |
| 1c. % of GWP | 0.50 | 0.51 | 0.54 | 0.58 | 0.57 | 0.61 | 0.62 | 0.62 | 0.63 | 0.64 |
| **2. PPPs** | | | | | | | | | | |
| 2a. Per capita GDP | 3 994 | 4 239 | 4 717 | 5 228 | 5 505 | 6 006 | 6 719 | 7 259 | 7 985 | 8 892 |
| 2b. GDP | 19 685 | 21 024 | 23 531 | 26 219 | 27 740 | 30 391 | 34 125 | 36 987 | 40 785 | 45 500 |
| 2c. % of GWP | ... | ... | ... | ... | ... | ... | ... | ... | ... | ... |
| **3. Absolute 1970–1989 PARE** | | | | | | | | | | |
| 3a. Per capita GDP | 9 001 | 9 183 | 9 614 | 9 909 | 9 770 | 9 665 | 10 252 | 10 386 | 10 513 | 10 866 |
| 3b. GDP | 44 367 | 45 550 | 47 953 | 49 695 | 49 231 | 48 906 | 52 072 | 52 917 | 53 698 | 55 602 |
| 3c. % of GWP | 0.62 | 0.62 | 0.61 | 0.60 | 0.58 | 0.57 | 0.58 | 0.56 | 0.55 | 0.55 |
| **4. Relative 1970–1989 PARE** | | | | | | | | | | |
| 4a. Per capita GDP | 4 389 | 4 707 | 5 154 | 5 665 | 6 093 | 6 622 | 7 463 | 8 070 | 8 764 | 9 868 |
| 4b. GDP | 21 632 | 23 348 | 25 708 | 28 411 | 30 700 | 33 506 | 37 904 | 41 117 | 44 768 | 50 494 |
| 4c. % of GWP | 0.62 | 0.62 | 0.61 | 0.60 | 0.58 | 0.57 | 0.58 | 0.56 | 0.55 | 0.55 |
| **5. Absolute 1980–1989 PARE** | | | | | | | | | | |
| 5a. Per capita GDP | 11 016 | 11 239 | 11 765 | 12 127 | 11 957 | 11 828 | 12 547 | 12 710 | 12 865 | 13 298 |
| 5b. GDP | 54 296 | 55 744 | 58 685 | 60 816 | 60 249 | 59 851 | 63 726 | 64 760 | 65 716 | 68 045 |
| 5c. % of GWP | 0.62 | 0.61 | 0.61 | 0.60 | 0.58 | 0.57 | 0.58 | 0.56 | 0.55 | 0.55 |
| **6. WA** | | | | | | | | | | |
| 6a. Per capita GDP | 3 209 | 3 564 | 4 348 | 5 698 | 6 305 | 7 438 | 8 182 | 9 132 | 11 054 | 12 886 |
| 6b. GDP | 15 817 | 17 678 | 21 690 | 28 574 | 31 769 | 37 635 | 41 557 | 46 527 | 56 464 | 65 937 |
| 6c. % of GWP | 0.50 | 0.51 | 0.54 | 0.59 | 0.57 | 0.61 | 0.62 | 0.62 | 0.64 | 0.64 |

| | 1980 (11) | 1981 (12) | 1982 (13) | 1983 (14) | 1984 (15) | 1985 (16) | 1986 (17) | 1987 (18) | 1988 (19) | 1989 (20) | Averages 1970–89 (21) | 1970–79 (22) | 1980–89 (23) |
|---|---|---|---|---|---|---|---|---|---|---|---|---|---|
| | 2 765 | 2 891 | 2 894 | 2 844 | 2 565 | 2 548 | 2 984 | 3 352 | 3 304 | 3 228 | 2 306 | 1 691 | 2 938 |
| | 42 338 | 44 441 | 44 617 | 43 929 | 39 693 | 39 501 | 46 343 | 52 163 | 51 530 | 50 464 | 35 218 | 24 935 | 45 502 |
| | 0.37 | 0.38 | 0.38 | 0.37 | 0.33 | 0.31 | 0.31 | 0.30 | 0.27 | 0.25 | 0.35 | 0.41 | 0.32 |
| | ... | ... | ... | ... | ... | ... | ... | ... | ... | ... | ... | ... | ... |
| | ... | ... | ... | ... | ... | ... | ... | ... | ... | ... | ... | ... | ... |
| | ... | ... | ... | ... | ... | ... | ... | ... | ... | ... | ... | ... | ... |
| | 2 443 | 2 431 | 2 428 | 2 479 | 2 554 | 2 623 | 2 686 | 2 734 | 2 798 | 2 802 | 2 306 | 2 048 | 2 598 |
| | 37 410 | 37 374 | 37 423 | 38 289 | 39 519 | 40 655 | 41 711 | 42 548 | 43 636 | 43 805 | 35 218 | 30 200 | 40 237 |
| | 0.36 | 0.35 | 0.35 | 0.35 | 0.34 | 0.34 | 0.34 | 0.34 | 0.33 | 0.32 | 0.35 | 0.35 | 0.34 |
| | 2 422 | 2 638 | 2 804 | 2 960 | 3 159 | 3 332 | 3 481 | 3 645 | 3 855 | 4 020 | 2 317 | 1 402 | 3 234 |
| | 37 083 | 40 552 | 43 228 | 45 723 | 48 883 | 51 651 | 54 057 | 56 727 | 60 131 | 62 837 | 35 383 | 20 678 | 50 087 |
| | 0.36 | 0.35 | 0.35 | 0.35 | 0.34 | 0.34 | 0.34 | 0.34 | 0.33 | 0.32 | 0.34 | 0.35 | 0.34 |
| | 2 763 | 2 749 | 2 745 | 2 803 | 2 888 | 2 966 | 3 037 | 3 092 | 3 164 | 3 169 | 2 608 | 2 316 | 2 938 |
| | 42 305 | 42 264 | 42 320 | 43 299 | 44 690 | 45 975 | 47 169 | 48 116 | 49 346 | 49 537 | 39 827 | 34 152 | 45 502 |
| | 0.33 | 0.33 | 0.33 | 0.32 | 0.32 | 0.32 | 0.32 | 0.31 | 0.31 | 0.30 | 0.32 | 0.32 | 0.32 |
| | 2 701 | 2 782 | 2 841 | 2 915 | 2 832 | 2 717 | 2 755 | 2 988 | 3 275 | 3 322 | 2 261 | 1 622 | 2 913 |
| | 41 361 | 42 767 | 43 798 | 45 022 | 43 813 | 42 109 | 42 782 | 46 502 | 51 086 | 51 932 | 34 522 | 23 927 | 45 117 |
| | 0.36 | 0.36 | 0.38 | 0.38 | 0.36 | 0.33 | 0.29 | 0.28 | 0.27 | 0.26 | 0.34 | 0.39 | 0.32 |
| | 12 943 | 11 169 | 10 875 | 10 938 | 10 654 | 11 331 | 16 075 | 19 951 | 21 049 | 20 402 | 10 831 | 7 201 | 14 554 |
| | 66 321 | 57 250 | 55 745 | 56 046 | 54 580 | 58 048 | 82 385 | 102 329 | 108 067 | 104 845 | 55 463 | 36 364 | 74 562 |
| | 0.57 | 0.49 | 0.48 | 0.47 | 0.45 | 0.46 | 0.55 | 0.60 | 0.57 | 0.52 | 0.54 | 0.60 | 0.52 |
| | 9 596 | 10 242 | 11 193 | 11 921 | 12 805 | 13 443 | 14 207 | 14 518 | 14 966 | 15 771 | 9 430 | 6 060 | 12 878 |
| | 49 171 | 52 499 | 57 373 | 61 085 | 65 601 | 68 866 | 72 810 | 74 463 | 76 837 | 81 045 | 48 287 | 30 599 | 65 975 |
| | ... | ... | ... | ... | ... | ... | ... | ... | ... | ... | ... | ... | ... |
| | 10 803 | 10 703 | 11 026 | 11 308 | 11 807 | 12 313 | 12 757 | 12 672 | 12 639 | 12 794 | 10 831 | 9 902 | 11 893 |
| | 55 356 | 54 863 | 56 520 | 57 943 | 60 487 | 63 081 | 65 379 | 64 996 | 64 890 | 65 748 | 55 463 | 49 999 | 60 926 |
| | 0.53 | 0.52 | 0.53 | 0.53 | 0.53 | 0.53 | 0.54 | 0.51 | 0.49 | 0.48 | 0.54 | 0.58 | 0.52 |
| | 10 709 | 11 613 | 12 737 | 13 504 | 14 605 | 15 644 | 16 533 | 16 895 | 17 417 | 18 353 | 10 707 | 6 686 | 14 815 |
| | 54 872 | 59 529 | 65 288 | 69 194 | 74 819 | 80 142 | 84 731 | 86 655 | 89 418 | 94 315 | 54 828 | 33 759 | 75 896 |
| | 0.53 | 0.52 | 0.53 | 0.53 | 0.53 | 0.53 | 0.54 | 0.51 | 0.49 | 0.48 | 0.53 | 0.57 | 0.52 |
| | 13 221 | 13 098 | 13 494 | 13 839 | 14 449 | 15 069 | 15 612 | 15 508 | 15 468 | 15 657 | 13 256 | 12 118 | 14 554 |
| | 67 744 | 67 142 | 69 169 | 70 911 | 74 024 | 77 199 | 80 011 | 79 543 | 79 412 | 80 462 | 67 875 | 61 189 | 74 562 |
| | 0.54 | 0.52 | 0.53 | 0.53 | 0.53 | 0.54 | 0.54 | 0.52 | 0.50 | 0.49 | 0.55 | 0.58 | 0.52 |
| | 12 943 | 11 168 | 10 874 | 10 938 | 10 654 | 11 330 | 16 073 | 19 833 | 20 951 | 20 373 | 10 819 | 7 202 | 14 529 |
| | 66 322 | 57 247 | 55 742 | 56 046 | 54 582 | 58 045 | 82 375 | 101 726 | 107 561 | 104 699 | 55 400 | 36 365 | 74 434 |
| | 0.58 | 0.49 | 0.48 | 0.47 | 0.45 | 0.46 | 0.56 | 0.61 | 0.57 | 0.53 | 0.55 | 0.60 | 0.53 |

**Table A.1**  Total and per capita gross domestic product of individual countries or areas, expressed in United States dollars, and their individual shares of gross world product, based on alternative conversion rates, 1970–1989 [cont.]

| Country or area | 1970 (1) | 1971 (2) | 1972 (3) | 1973 (4) | 1974 (5) | 1975 (6) | 1976 (7) | 1977 (8) | 1978 (9) | 1979 (10) |
|---|---|---|---|---|---|---|---|---|---|---|
| **Djibouti** | | | | | | | | | | |
| **1. MER** | | | | | | | | | | |
| 1a. Per capita GDP | 422 | 441 | 490 | 566 | 666 | 697 | 787 | 807 | 847 | 974 |
| 1b. GDP | 71 | 81 | 97 | 121 | 152 | 169 | 202 | 218 | 239 | 285 |
| 1c. % of GWP | 0.00 | 0.00 | 0.00 | 0.00 | 0.00 | 0.00 | 0.00 | 0.00 | 0.00 | 0.00 |
| **2. PPPs** | | | | | | | | | | |
| 2a. Per capita GDP | ... | ... | ... | ... | ... | ... | ... | ... | ... | ... |
| 2b. GDP | ... | ... | ... | ... | ... | ... | ... | ... | ... | ... |
| 2c. % of GWP | ... | ... | ... | ... | ... | ... | ... | ... | ... | ... |
| **3. Absolute 1970–1989 PARE** | | | | | | | | | | |
| 3a. Per capita GDP | 1 437 | 1 410 | 1 347 | 1 308 | 1 180 | 1 237 | 1 271 | 1 066 | 942 | 954 |
| 3b. GDP | 243 | 258 | 267 | 280 | 270 | 301 | 327 | 288 | 266 | 280 |
| 3c. % of GWP | 0.00 | 0.00 | 0.00 | 0.00 | 0.00 | 0.00 | 0.00 | 0.00 | 0.00 | 0.00 |
| **4. Relative 1970–1989 PARE** | | | | | | | | | | |
| 4a. Per capita GDP | 701 | 723 | 722 | 748 | 736 | 847 | 925 | 828 | 785 | 867 |
| 4b. GDP | 118 | 132 | 143 | 160 | 168 | 206 | 238 | 224 | 221 | 254 |
| 4c. % of GWP | 0.00 | 0.00 | 0.00 | 0.00 | 0.00 | 0.00 | 0.00 | 0.00 | 0.00 | 0.00 |
| **5. Absolute 1980–1989 PARE** | | | | | | | | | | |
| 5a. Per capita GDP | 1 970 | 1 932 | 1 846 | 1 793 | 1 617 | 1 695 | 1 742 | 1 461 | 1 291 | 1 308 |
| 5b. GDP | 333 | 354 | 365 | 384 | 370 | 412 | 448 | 395 | 364 | 383 |
| 5c. % of GWP | 0.00 | 0.00 | 0.00 | 0.00 | 0.00 | 0.00 | 0.00 | 0.00 | 0.00 | 0.00 |
| **6. WA[a]** | | | | | | | | | | |
| 6a. Per capita GDP | 372 | 405 | 432 | 475 | 518 | 634 | 739 | 679 | 698 | 839 |
| 6b. GDP | 63 | 74 | 86 | 102 | 119 | 154 | 190 | 183 | 197 | 246 |
| 6c. % of GWP | 0.00 | 0.00 | 0.00 | 0.00 | 0.00 | 0.00 | 0.00 | 0.00 | 0.00 | 0.00 |
| **Dominica** | | | | | | | | | | |
| **1. MER** | | | | | | | | | | |
| 1a. Per capita GDP | 303 | 328 | 378 | 404 | 448 | 472 | 454 | 505 | 619 | 599 |
| 1b. GDP | 21 | 23 | 27 | 29 | 32 | 33 | 33 | 36 | 45 | 44 |
| 1c. % of GWP | 0.00 | 0.00 | 0.00 | 0.00 | 0.00 | 0.00 | 0.00 | 0.00 | 0.00 | 0.00 |
| **2. PPPs** | | | | | | | | | | |
| 2a. Per capita GDP | ... | ... | ... | ... | ... | ... | ... | ... | ... | ... |
| 2b. GDP | ... | ... | ... | ... | ... | ... | ... | ... | ... | ... |
| 2c. % of GWP | ... | ... | ... | ... | ... | ... | ... | ... | ... | ... |
| **3. Absolute 1970–1989 PARE** | | | | | | | | | | |
| 3a. Per capita GDP | 925 | 980 | 997 | 953 | 858 | 780 | 822 | 844 | 930 | 748 |
| 3b. GDP | 66 | 70 | 71 | 68 | 61 | 55 | 59 | 61 | 68 | 55 |
| 3c. % of GWP | 0.00 | 0.00 | 0.00 | 0.00 | 0.00 | 0.00 | 0.00 | 0.00 | 0.00 | 0.00 |
| **4. Relative 1970–1989 PARE** | | | | | | | | | | |
| 4a. Per capita GDP | 451 | 502 | 535 | 545 | 535 | 534 | 598 | 656 | 776 | 679 |
| 4b. GDP | 32 | 36 | 38 | 39 | 38 | 38 | 43 | 47 | 57 | 50 |
| 4c. % of GWP | 0.00 | 0.00 | 0.00 | 0.00 | 0.00 | 0.00 | 0.00 | 0.00 | 0.00 | 0.00 |
| **5. Absolute 1980–1989 PARE** | | | | | | | | | | |
| 5a. Per capita GDP | 1 337 | 1 416 | 1 441 | 1 377 | 1 240 | 1 127 | 1 188 | 1 219 | 1 344 | 1 081 |
| 5b. GDP | 95 | 101 | 102 | 98 | 88 | 80 | 86 | 88 | 98 | 80 |
| 5c. % of GWP | 0.00 | 0.00 | 0.00 | 0.00 | 0.00 | 0.00 | 0.00 | 0.00 | 0.00 | 0.00 |
| **6. WA** | | | | | | | | | | |
| 6a. Per capita GDP | 303 | 327 | 378 | 404 | 448 | 472 | 454 | 505 | 619 | 599 |
| 6b. GDP | 21 | 23 | 27 | 29 | 32 | 34 | 33 | 36 | 45 | 44 |
| 6c. % of GWP | 0.00 | 0.00 | 0.00 | 0.00 | 0.00 | 0.00 | 0.00 | 0.00 | 0.00 | 0.00 |

| 1980 (11) | 1981 (12) | 1982 (13) | 1983 (14) | 1984 (15) | 1985 (16) | 1986 (17) | 1987 (18) | 1988 (19) | 1989 (20) | Averages 1970–89 (21) | 1970–79 (22) | 1980–89 (23) |
|---|---|---|---|---|---|---|---|---|---|---|---|---|
| 1 116 | 1 200 | 1 218 | 1 186 | 1 176 | 1 182 | 1 207 | 1 261 | 1 249 | 1 236 | 981 | 693 | 1 207 |
| 339 | 378 | 396 | 397 | 406 | 420 | 440 | 473 | 482 | 492 | 293 | 164 | 422 |
| 0.00 | 0.00 | 0.00 | 0.00 | 0.00 | 0.00 | 0.00 | 0.00 | 0.00 | 0.00 | 0.00 | 0.00 | 0.00 |
| ... | ... | ... | ... | ... | ... | ... | ... | ... | ... | ... | ... | ... |
| ... | ... | ... | ... | ... | ... | ... | ... | ... | ... | ... | ... | ... |
| ... | ... | ... | ... | ... | ... | ... | ... | ... | ... | ... | ... | ... |
| 963 | 919 | 900 | 874 | 884 | 867 | 858 | 866 | 862 | 829 | 981 | 1 177 | 880 |
| 293 | 289 | 293 | 293 | 305 | 308 | 313 | 325 | 333 | 330 | 293 | 278 | 308 |
| 0.00 | 0.00 | 0.00 | 0.00 | 0.00 | 0.00 | 0.00 | 0.00 | 0.00 | 0.00 | 0.00 | 0.00 | 0.00 |
| 955 | 997 | 1 040 | 1 044 | 1 094 | 1 101 | 1 112 | 1 155 | 1 188 | 1 190 | 954 | 790 | 1 095 |
| 290 | 314 | 338 | 350 | 377 | 391 | 406 | 433 | 458 | 473 | 285 | 186 | 383 |
| 0.00 | 0.00 | 0.00 | 0.00 | 0.00 | 0.00 | 0.00 | 0.00 | 0.00 | 0.00 | 0.00 | 0.00 | 0.00 |
| 1 320 | 1 260 | 1 234 | 1 198 | 1 212 | 1 188 | 1 176 | 1 187 | 1 181 | 1 137 | 1 345 | 1 613 | 1 207 |
| 401 | 397 | 401 | 401 | 418 | 422 | 429 | 445 | 456 | 452 | 402 | 381 | 422 |
| 0.00 | 0.00 | 0.00 | 0.00 | 0.00 | 0.00 | 0.00 | 0.00 | 0.00 | 0.00 | 0.00 | 0.00 | 0.00 |
| 978 | 1 057 | 1 141 | 1 170 | 1 191 | 1 170 | 1 172 | 1 219 | 1 238 | 1 215 | 918 | 598 | 1 162 |
| 297 | 333 | 371 | 392 | 411 | 415 | 428 | 457 | 478 | 483 | 274 | 141 | 407 |
| 0.00 | 0.00 | 0.00 | 0.00 | 0.00 | 0.00 | 0.00 | 0.00 | 0.00 | 0.00 | 0.00 | 0.00 | 0.00 |
| 799 | 871 | 936 | 1 025 | 1 137 | 1 232 | 1 384 | 1 532 | 1 788 | 1 872 | 897 | 456 | 1 262 |
| 59 | 66 | 72 | 80 | 90 | 99 | 112 | 126 | 147 | 154 | 66 | 32 | 100 |
| 0.00 | 0.00 | 0.00 | 0.00 | 0.00 | 0.00 | 0.00 | 0.00 | 0.00 | 0.00 | 0.00 | 0.00 | 0.00 |
| ... | ... | ... | ... | ... | ... | ... | ... | ... | ... | ... | ... | ... |
| ... | ... | ... | ... | ... | ... | ... | ... | ... | ... | ... | ... | ... |
| ... | ... | ... | ... | ... | ... | ... | ... | ... | ... | ... | ... | ... |
| 770 | 798 | 807 | 813 | 846 | 850 | 897 | 946 | 1 021 | 1 005 | 897 | 892 | 874 |
| 57 | 61 | 62 | 63 | 67 | 68 | 73 | 78 | 84 | 82 | 66 | 63 | 69 |
| 0.00 | 0.00 | 0.00 | 0.00 | 0.00 | 0.00 | 0.00 | 0.00 | 0.00 | 0.00 | 0.00 | 0.00 | 0.00 |
| 764 | 866 | 932 | 971 | 1 047 | 1 080 | 1 162 | 1 262 | 1 407 | 1 442 | 870 | 588 | 1 095 |
| 57 | 66 | 72 | 76 | 83 | 86 | 94 | 103 | 115 | 118 | 64 | 42 | 87 |
| 0.00 | 0.00 | 0.00 | 0.00 | 0.00 | 0.00 | 0.00 | 0.00 | 0.00 | 0.00 | 0.00 | 0.00 | 0.00 |
| 1 113 | 1 154 | 1 166 | 1 175 | 1 223 | 1 228 | 1 296 | 1 367 | 1 476 | 1 453 | 1 296 | 1 289 | 1 262 |
| 82 | 88 | 90 | 92 | 97 | 98 | 105 | 112 | 121 | 119 | 96 | 92 | 100 |
| 0.00 | 0.00 | 0.00 | 0.00 | 0.00 | 0.00 | 0.00 | 0.00 | 0.00 | 0.00 | 0.00 | 0.00 | 0.00 |
| 799 | 871 | 936 | 1 025 | 1 137 | 1 232 | 1 384 | 1 532 | 1 788 | 1 872 | 897 | 456 | 1 262 |
| 59 | 66 | 72 | 80 | 90 | 99 | 112 | 126 | 147 | 154 | 66 | 32 | 100 |
| 0.00 | 0.00 | 0.00 | 0.00 | 0.00 | 0.00 | 0.00 | 0.00 | 0.00 | 0.00 | 0.00 | 0.00 | 0.00 |

**Table A.1** Total and per capita gross domestic product of individual countries or areas, expressed in United States dollars, and their individual shares of gross world product, based on alternative conversion rates, 1970–1989 [*cont.*]

| Country or area | 1970 (1) | 1971 (2) | 1972 (3) | 1973 (4) | 1974 (5) | 1975 (6) | 1976 (7) | 1977 (8) | 1978 (9) | 1979 (10) |
|---|---|---|---|---|---|---|---|---|---|---|
| **Dominican Republic** | | | | | | | | | | |
| **1. MER** | | | | | | | | | | |
| 1a. Per capita GDP | 336 | 366 | 425 | 489 | 594 | 713 | 763 | 865 | 872 | 988 |
| 1b. GDP | 1 486 | 1 667 | 1 987 | 2 345 | 2 926 | 3 599 | 3 952 | 4 587 | 4 734 | 5 499 |
| 1c. % of GWP | 0.05 | 0.05 | 0.05 | 0.05 | 0.05 | 0.06 | 0.06 | 0.06 | 0.05 | 0.05 |
| **2. PPPs** | | | | | | | | | | |
| 2a. Per capita GDP | 608 | 678 | 738 | 839 | 1 005 | 1 162 | 1 187 | 1 288 | 1 344 | 1 492 |
| 2b. GDP | 2 689 | 3 085 | 3 451 | 4 024 | 4 946 | 5 865 | 6 143 | 6 831 | 7 297 | 8 298 |
| 2c. % of GWP | ... | ... | ... | ... | ... | ... | ... | ... | ... | ... |
| **3. Absolute 1970–1989 PARE** | | | | | | | | | | |
| 3a. Per capita GDP | 619 | 667 | 717 | 789 | 815 | 836 | 870 | 891 | 889 | 907 |
| 3b. GDP | 2 738 | 3 036 | 3 351 | 3 783 | 4 010 | 4 219 | 4 503 | 4 727 | 4 828 | 5 047 |
| 3c. % of GWP | 0.04 | 0.04 | 0.04 | 0.05 | 0.05 | 0.05 | 0.05 | 0.05 | 0.05 | 0.05 |
| **4. Relative 1970–1989 PARE** | | | | | | | | | | |
| 4a. Per capita GDP | 302 | 342 | 384 | 451 | 508 | 572 | 633 | 693 | 741 | 824 |
| 4b. GDP | 1 335 | 1 556 | 1 797 | 2 163 | 2 501 | 2 890 | 3 278 | 3 673 | 4 025 | 4 583 |
| 4c. % of GWP | 0.04 | 0.04 | 0.04 | 0.05 | 0.05 | 0.05 | 0.05 | 0.05 | 0.05 | 0.05 |
| **5. Absolute 1980–1989 PARE** | | | | | | | | | | |
| 5a. Per capita GDP | 696 | 751 | 807 | 887 | 916 | 940 | 978 | 1 003 | 1 000 | 1 020 |
| 5b. GDP | 3 079 | 3 414 | 3 769 | 4 255 | 4 511 | 4 745 | 5 064 | 5 316 | 5 430 | 5 676 |
| 5c. % of GWP | 0.04 | 0.04 | 0.04 | 0.04 | 0.04 | 0.05 | 0.05 | 0.05 | 0.05 | 0.05 |
| **6. WA** | | | | | | | | | | |
| 6a. Per capita GDP | 336 | 366 | 425 | 489 | 594 | 713 | 763 | 865 | 872 | 988 |
| 6b. GDP | 1 486 | 1 667 | 1 987 | 2 345 | 2 926 | 3 599 | 3 952 | 4 587 | 4 734 | 5 499 |
| 6c. % of GWP | 0.05 | 0.05 | 0.05 | 0.05 | 0.05 | 0.06 | 0.06 | 0.06 | 0.05 | 0.05 |
| **Ecuador** | | | | | | | | | | |
| **1. MER** | | | | | | | | | | |
| 1a. Per capita GDP | 277 | 257 | 291 | 375 | 543 | 613 | 734 | 892 | 997 | 1 185 |
| 1b. GDP | 1 674 | 1 602 | 1 874 | 2 489 | 3 711 | 4 310 | 5 317 | 6 655 | 7 654 | 9 359 |
| 1c. % of GWP | 0.05 | 0.05 | 0.05 | 0.05 | 0.07 | 0.07 | 0.08 | 0.09 | 0.09 | 0.09 |
| **2. PPPs** | | | | | | | | | | |
| 2a. Per capita GDP | 685 | 728 | 762 | 859 | 1 167 | 1 339 | 1 469 | 1 707 | 1 865 | 2 120 |
| 2b. GDP | 4 145 | 4 546 | 4 902 | 5 696 | 7 971 | 9 418 | 10 639 | 12 730 | 14 312 | 16 745 |
| 2c. % of GWP | ... | ... | ... | ... | ... | ... | ... | ... | ... | ... |
| **3. Absolute 1970–1989 PARE** | | | | | | | | | | |
| 3a. Per capita GDP | 663 | 683 | 758 | 922 | 952 | 976 | 1 036 | 1 072 | 1 110 | 1 136 |
| 3b. GDP | 4 010 | 4 262 | 4 876 | 6 111 | 6 505 | 6 868 | 7 502 | 7 992 | 8 518 | 8 970 |
| 3c. % of GWP | 0.06 | 0.06 | 0.06 | 0.07 | 0.08 | 0.08 | 0.08 | 0.08 | 0.09 | 0.09 |
| **4. Relative 1970–1989 PARE** | | | | | | | | | | |
| 4a. Per capita GDP | 323 | 350 | 406 | 527 | 594 | 669 | 754 | 833 | 925 | 1 032 |
| 4b. GDP | 1 955 | 2 184 | 2 614 | 3 494 | 4 056 | 4 705 | 5 461 | 6 210 | 7 102 | 8 146 |
| 4c. % of GWP | 0.06 | 0.06 | 0.06 | 0.07 | 0.08 | 0.08 | 0.08 | 0.08 | 0.09 | 0.09 |
| **5. Absolute 1980–1989 PARE** | | | | | | | | | | |
| 5a. Per capita GDP | 798 | 822 | 913 | 1 110 | 1 147 | 1 176 | 1 247 | 1 290 | 1 337 | 1 368 |
| 5b. GDP | 4 829 | 5 132 | 5 872 | 7 359 | 7 834 | 8 271 | 9 034 | 9 624 | 10 258 | 10 802 |
| 5c. % of GWP | 0.06 | 0.06 | 0.06 | 0.07 | 0.08 | 0.08 | 0.08 | 0.08 | 0.09 | 0.09 |
| **6. WA** | | | | | | | | | | |
| 6a. Per capita GDP | 277 | 257 | 291 | 375 | 543 | 613 | 734 | 892 | 997 | 1 185 |
| 6b. GDP | 1 674 | 1 602 | 1 874 | 2 489 | 3 711 | 4 310 | 5 317 | 6 655 | 7 654 | 9 359 |
| 6c. % of GWP | 0.05 | 0.05 | 0.05 | 0.05 | 0.07 | 0.07 | 0.08 | 0.09 | 0.09 | 0.09 |

| 1980 (11) | 1981 (12) | 1982 (13) | 1983 (14) | 1984 (15) | 1985 (16) | 1986 (17) | 1987 (18) | 1988 (19) | 1989 (20) | Averages 1970–89 (21) | 1970–79 (22) | 1980–89 (23) |
|---|---|---|---|---|---|---|---|---|---|---|---|---|
| 1 164 | 1 245 | 1 332 | 1 409 | 1 649 | 699 | 829 | 765 | 677 | 959 | 889 | 657 | 1 061 |
| 6 631 | 7 267 | 7 964 | 8 623 | 10 335 | 4 488 | 5 442 | 5 141 | 4 648 | 6 729 | 5 002 | 3 278 | 6 727 |
| 0.06 | 0.06 | 0.07 | 0.07 | 0.08 | 0.04 | 0.04 | 0.03 | 0.02 | 0.03 | 0.05 | 0.05 | 0.05 |
| 1 825 | 2 051 | 2 010 | 2 082 | 2 052 | 1 957 | 2 012 | 2 183 | 2 222 | 2 356 | 1 642 | 1 056 | 2 084 |
| 10 395 | 11 968 | 12 014 | 12 745 | 12 864 | 12 555 | 13 212 | 14 662 | 15 259 | 16 536 | 9 242 | 5 263 | 13 221 |
| ... | ... | ... | ... | ... | ... | ... | ... | ... | ... | ... | ... | ... |
| 939 | 954 | 946 | 966 | 946 | 900 | 908 | 957 | 943 | 960 | 889 | 807 | 943 |
| 5 352 | 5 570 | 5 657 | 5 915 | 5 931 | 5 778 | 5 961 | 6 430 | 6 474 | 6 740 | 5 002 | 4 024 | 5 981 |
| 0.05 | 0.05 | 0.05 | 0.05 | 0.05 | 0.05 | 0.05 | 0.05 | 0.05 | 0.05 | 0.05 | 0.05 | 0.05 |
| 931 | 1 036 | 1 093 | 1 154 | 1 170 | 1 144 | 1 177 | 1 276 | 1 299 | 1 377 | 909 | 558 | 1 175 |
| 5 305 | 6 043 | 6 534 | 7 064 | 7 337 | 7 341 | 7 725 | 8 573 | 8 922 | 9 668 | 5 116 | 2 780 | 7 451 |
| 0.05 | 0.05 | 0.05 | 0.05 | 0.05 | 0.05 | 0.05 | 0.05 | 0.05 | 0.05 | 0.05 | 0.05 | 0.05 |
| 1 057 | 1 073 | 1 064 | 1 087 | 1 064 | 1 013 | 1 021 | 1 077 | 1 060 | 1 080 | 999 | 908 | 1 061 |
| 6 019 | 6 265 | 6 363 | 6 653 | 6 671 | 6 499 | 6 704 | 7 232 | 7 282 | 7 581 | 5 626 | 4 526 | 6 727 |
| 0.05 | 0.05 | 0.05 | 0.05 | 0.05 | 0.05 | 0.05 | 0.05 | 0.05 | 0.05 | 0.05 | 0.04 | 0.05 |
| 1 164 | 1 245 | 1 222 | 1 118 | 800 | 700 | 828 | 756 | 675 | 953 | 819 | 657 | 936 |
| 6 631 | 7 267 | 7 307 | 6 844 | 5 017 | 4 489 | 5 433 | 5 081 | 4 638 | 6 687 | 4 609 | 3 278 | 5 939 |
| 0.06 | 0.06 | 0.06 | 0.06 | 0.04 | 0.04 | 0.04 | 0.03 | 0.02 | 0.03 | 0.05 | 0.05 | 0.04 |
| 1 444 | 1 669 | 1 612 | 1 438 | 1 432 | 1 713 | 1 178 | 1 072 | 1 022 | 1 005 | 1 050 | 644 | 1 345 |
| 11 733 | 13 946 | 13 845 | 12 700 | 12 995 | 15 958 | 11 266 | 10 525 | 10 293 | 10 381 | 8 414 | 4 464 | 12 364 |
| 0.10 | 0.12 | 0.12 | 0.11 | 0.11 | 0.13 | 0.08 | 0.06 | 0.05 | 0.05 | 0.08 | 0.07 | 0.09 |
| 2 436 | 2 644 | 2 721 | 2 485 | 2 673 | 2 611 | 2 675 | 2 521 | 2 825 | 2 872 | 2 093 | 1 314 | 2 656 |
| 19 793 | 22 088 | 23 373 | 21 941 | 24 253 | 24 329 | 25 587 | 24 747 | 28 449 | 29 662 | 16 766 | 9 110 | 24 422 |
| ... | ... | ... | ... | ... | ... | ... | ... | ... | ... | ... | ... | ... |
| 1 158 | 1 171 | 1 152 | 1 089 | 1 105 | 1 122 | 1 127 | 1 033 | 1 120 | 1 093 | 1 050 | 946 | 1 117 |
| 9 410 | 9 781 | 9 897 | 9 618 | 10 022 | 10 458 | 10 782 | 10 137 | 11 274 | 11 292 | 8 414 | 6 561 | 10 267 |
| 0.09 | 0.09 | 0.09 | 0.09 | 0.09 | 0.09 | 0.09 | 0.08 | 0.09 | 0.08 | 0.08 | 0.08 | 0.09 |
| 1 148 | 1 270 | 1 331 | 1 301 | 1 367 | 1 426 | 1 461 | 1 377 | 1 543 | 1 569 | 1 084 | 662 | 1 390 |
| 9 328 | 10 613 | 11 433 | 11 486 | 12 397 | 13 286 | 13 973 | 13 514 | 15 536 | 16 199 | 8 685 | 4 593 | 12 777 |
| 0.09 | 0.09 | 0.09 | 0.09 | 0.09 | 0.09 | 0.09 | 0.08 | 0.09 | 0.08 | 0.08 | 0.08 | 0.09 |
| 1 395 | 1 410 | 1 388 | 1 312 | 1 330 | 1 352 | 1 357 | 1 243 | 1 348 | 1 317 | 1 265 | 1 140 | 1 345 |
| 11 332 | 11 779 | 11 919 | 11 583 | 12 069 | 12 594 | 12 984 | 12 207 | 13 577 | 13 598 | 10 133 | 7 901 | 12 364 |
| 0.09 | 0.09 | 0.09 | 0.09 | 0.09 | 0.09 | 0.09 | 0.08 | 0.08 | 0.08 | 0.08 | 0.08 | 0.09 |
| 1 444 | 1 669 | 1 449 | 1 199 | 1 127 | 1 302 | 1 178 | 1 072 | 1 022 | 1 005 | 987 | 644 | 1 235 |
| 11 733 | 13 946 | 12 447 | 10 591 | 10 222 | 12 130 | 11 265 | 10 527 | 10 293 | 10 382 | 7 909 | 4 464 | 11 354 |
| 0.10 | 0.12 | 0.11 | 0.09 | 0.08 | 0.10 | 0.08 | 0.06 | 0.05 | 0.05 | 0.08 | 0.07 | 0.08 |

**Table A.1** Total and per capita gross domestic product of individual countries or areas, expressed in United States dollars, and their individual shares of gross world product, based on alternative conversion rates, 1970−1989 [*cont.*]

| Country or area | 1970 (1) | 1971 (2) | 1972 (3) | 1973 (4) | 1974 (5) | 1975 (6) | 1976 (7) | 1977 (8) | 1978 (9) | 1979 (10) |
|---|---|---|---|---|---|---|---|---|---|---|
| **Egypt** | | | | | | | | | | |
| 1. **MER** | | | | | | | | | | |
| 1a. Per capita GDP | 234 | 245 | 229 | 287 | 319 | 370 | 462 | 553 | 644 | 452 |
| 1b. GDP | 7 723 | 8 258 | 7 855 | 10 028 | 11 360 | 13 418 | 17 147 | 20 997 | 25 032 | 18 015 |
| 1c. % of GWP | 0.24 | 0.24 | 0.20 | 0.20 | 0.20 | 0.22 | 0.26 | 0.28 | 0.28 | 0.17 |
| 2. **PPPs** | | | | | | | | | | |
| 2a. Per capita GDP | 378 | 409 | 407 | 443 | 498 | 573 | 616 | 665 | 715 | 841 |
| 2b. GDP | 12 488 | 13 786 | 13 977 | 15 470 | 17 709 | 20 794 | 22 833 | 25 237 | 27 786 | 33 509 |
| 2c. % of GWP | ... | ... | ... | ... | ... | ... | ... | ... | ... | ... |
| 3. **Absolute 1970−1989 PARE** | | | | | | | | | | |
| 3a. Per capita GDP | 399 | 407 | 419 | 417 | 431 | 480 | 506 | 534 | 575 | 616 |
| 3b. GDP | 13 195 | 13 703 | 14 388 | 14 574 | 15 315 | 17 415 | 18 770 | 20 257 | 22 342 | 24 565 |
| 3c. % of GWP | 0.19 | 0.19 | 0.18 | 0.18 | 0.18 | 0.20 | 0.21 | 0.21 | 0.23 | 0.24 |
| 4. **Relative 1970−1989 PARE** | | | | | | | | | | |
| 4a. Per capita GDP | 195 | 208 | 225 | 239 | 268 | 329 | 368 | 415 | 479 | 560 |
| 4b. GDP | 6 433 | 7 024 | 7 714 | 8 332 | 9 550 | 11 931 | 13 663 | 15 740 | 18 626 | 22 308 |
| 4c. % of GWP | 0.19 | 0.19 | 0.18 | 0.18 | 0.18 | 0.20 | 0.21 | 0.21 | 0.23 | 0.24 |
| 5. **Absolute 1980−1989 PARE** | | | | | | | | | | |
| 5a. Per capita GDP | 430 | 438 | 452 | 449 | 464 | 517 | 545 | 575 | 619 | 664 |
| 5b. GDP | 14 210 | 14 757 | 15 495 | 15 695 | 16 493 | 18 754 | 20 215 | 21 815 | 24 060 | 26 455 |
| 5c. % of GWP | 0.16 | 0.16 | 0.16 | 0.15 | 0.16 | 0.18 | 0.18 | 0.19 | 0.20 | 0.21 |
| 6. **WA** | | | | | | | | | | |
| 6a. Per capita GDP | 255 | 272 | 257 | 287 | 259 | 317 | 359 | 380 | 382 | 452 |
| 6b. GDP | 8 439 | 9 161 | 8 834 | 10 033 | 9 229 | 11 501 | 13 316 | 14 401 | 14 839 | 18 015 |
| 6c. % of GWP | 0.26 | 0.26 | 0.22 | 0.21 | 0.17 | 0.19 | 0.20 | 0.19 | 0.17 | 0.18 |
| **El Salvador** | | | | | | | | | | |
| 1. **MER** | | | | | | | | | | |
| 1a. Per capita GDP | 287 | 293 | 304 | 342 | 395 | 438 | 546 | 670 | 704 | 773 |
| 1b. GDP | 1 028 | 1 082 | 1 153 | 1 333 | 1 578 | 1 791 | 2 282 | 2 867 | 3 077 | 3 443 |
| 1c. % of GWP | 0.03 | 0.03 | 0.03 | 0.03 | 0.03 | 0.03 | 0.03 | 0.04 | 0.03 | 0.03 |
| 2. **PPPs** | | | | | | | | | | |
| 2a. Per capita GDP | 707 | 734 | 772 | 847 | 919 | 1 005 | 1 180 | 1 413 | 1 522 | 1 489 |
| 2b. GDP | 2 536 | 2 713 | 2 933 | 3 301 | 3 666 | 4 104 | 4 933 | 6 044 | 6 653 | 6 634 |
| 2c. % of GWP | ... | ... | ... | ... | ... | ... | ... | ... | ... | ... |
| 3. **Absolute 1970−1989 PARE** | | | | | | | | | | |
| 3a. Per capita GDP | 717 | 730 | 749 | 768 | 797 | 822 | 835 | 865 | 901 | 869 |
| 3b. GDP | 2 573 | 2 698 | 2 846 | 2 990 | 3 182 | 3 359 | 3 491 | 3 702 | 3 941 | 3 873 |
| 3c. % of GWP | 0.04 | 0.04 | 0.04 | 0.04 | 0.04 | 0.04 | 0.04 | 0.04 | 0.04 | 0.04 |
| 4. **Relative 1970−1989 PARE** | | | | | | | | | | |
| 4a. Per capita GDP | 350 | 374 | 402 | 439 | 497 | 563 | 608 | 672 | 751 | 789 |
| 4b. GDP | 1 255 | 1 383 | 1 526 | 1 710 | 1 984 | 2 301 | 2 541 | 2 877 | 3 285 | 3 517 |
| 4c. % of GWP | 0.04 | 0.04 | 0.04 | 0.04 | 0.04 | 0.04 | 0.04 | 0.04 | 0.04 | 0.04 |
| 5. **Absolute 1980−1989 PARE** | | | | | | | | | | |
| 5a. Per capita GDP | 1 003 | 1 021 | 1 048 | 1 074 | 1 115 | 1 150 | 1 168 | 1 210 | 1 261 | 1 216 |
| 5b. GDP | 3 599 | 3 773 | 3 981 | 4 182 | 4 450 | 4 698 | 4 883 | 5 178 | 5 512 | 5 417 |
| 5c. % of GWP | 0.04 | 0.04 | 0.04 | 0.04 | 0.04 | 0.04 | 0.04 | 0.04 | 0.05 | 0.04 |
| 6. **WA** | | | | | | | | | | |
| 6a. Per capita GDP | 287 | 293 | 304 | 342 | 395 | 438 | 546 | 670 | 704 | 773 |
| 6b. GDP | 1 028 | 1 082 | 1 153 | 1 333 | 1 578 | 1 791 | 2 282 | 2 867 | 3 077 | 3 443 |
| 6c. % of GWP | 0.03 | 0.03 | 0.03 | 0.03 | 0.03 | 0.03 | 0.03 | 0.04 | 0.03 | 0.03 |

| 1980 (11) | 1981 (12) | 1982 (13) | 1983 (14) | 1984 (15) | 1985 (16) | 1986 (17) | 1987 (18) | 1988 (19) | 1989 (20) | Averages 1970–89 (21) | 1970–79 (22) | 1980–89 (23) |
|---|---|---|---|---|---|---|---|---|---|---|---|---|
| 541 | 584 | 671 | 833 | 984 | 1 125 | 1 223 | 1 396 | 1 557 | 1 403 | 775 | 389 | 1 057 |
| 22 100 | 24 499 | 28 888 | 36 818 | 44 638 | 52 311 | 58 314 | 68 205 | 77 933 | 71 876 | 31 271 | 13 983 | 48 558 |
| 0.19 | 0.21 | 0.25 | 0.31 | 0.37 | 0.42 | 0.39 | 0.40 | 0.41 | 0.36 | 0.31 | 0.23 | 0.34 |
| 882 | 940 | 1 022 | 1 324 | 1 365 | 1 329 | 1 390 | 1 456 | 1 502 | 1 609 | 991 | 567 | 1 299 |
| 36 064 | 39 437 | 44 003 | 58 487 | 61 902 | 61 826 | 66 284 | 71 165 | 75 172 | 82 424 | 40 018 | 20 359 | 59 677 |
| ... | ... | ... | ... | ... | ... | ... | ... | ... | ... | ... | ... | ... |
| 712 | 773 | 929 | 962 | 982 | 1 035 | 1 061 | 1 080 | 1 078 | 1 109 | 775 | 486 | 982 |
| 29 106 | 32 423 | 40 010 | 42 494 | 44 543 | 48 136 | 50 590 | 52 798 | 53 959 | 56 834 | 31 271 | 17 452 | 45 089 |
| 0.28 | 0.31 | 0.38 | 0.39 | 0.39 | 0.41 | 0.41 | 0.42 | 0.41 | 0.42 | 0.31 | 0.20 | 0.38 |
| 706 | 839 | 1 074 | 1 148 | 1 215 | 1 315 | 1 375 | 1 441 | 1 486 | 1 591 | 855 | 338 | 1 239 |
| 28 852 | 35 180 | 46 217 | 50 745 | 55 098 | 61 155 | 65 564 | 70 392 | 74 355 | 81 529 | 34 520 | 12 132 | 56 909 |
| 0.28 | 0.31 | 0.38 | 0.39 | 0.39 | 0.41 | 0.41 | 0.42 | 0.41 | 0.42 | 0.34 | 0.21 | 0.39 |
| 767 | 833 | 1 001 | 1 036 | 1 058 | 1 115 | 1 143 | 1 164 | 1 161 | 1 195 | 834 | 523 | 1 057 |
| 31 345 | 34 917 | 43 088 | 45 763 | 47 970 | 51 839 | 54 482 | 56 860 | 58 110 | 61 207 | 33 677 | 18 795 | 48 558 |
| 0.25 | 0.27 | 0.33 | 0.34 | 0.34 | 0.36 | 0.37 | 0.37 | 0.36 | 0.37 | 0.27 | 0.18 | 0.34 |
| 526 | 553 | 579 | 679 | 741 | 824 | 801 | 768 | 619 | 652 | 532 | 328 | 678 |
| 21 486 | 23 174 | 24 903 | 30 003 | 33 591 | 38 339 | 38 185 | 37 505 | 30 978 | 33 399 | 21 467 | 11 777 | 31 156 |
| 0.19 | 0.20 | 0.21 | 0.25 | 0.27 | 0.30 | 0.26 | 0.23 | 0.17 | 0.17 | 0.21 | 0.19 | 0.22 |
| 788 | 755 | 775 | 870 | 990 | 1 202 | 842 | 939 | 1 089 | 1 255 | 727 | 486 | 964 |
| 3 567 | 3 459 | 3 586 | 4 061 | 4 663 | 5 732 | 4 075 | 4 628 | 5 473 | 6 446 | 3 266 | 1 963 | 4 569 |
| 0.03 | 0.03 | 0.03 | 0.03 | 0.04 | 0.05 | 0.03 | 0.03 | 0.03 | 0.03 | 0.03 | 0.03 | 0.03 |
| 1 494 | 1 462 | 1 457 | 1 530 | 1 569 | 1 597 | 1 615 | 1 676 | 1 726 | 1 777 | 1 333 | 1 078 | 1 608 |
| 6 763 | 6 697 | 6 741 | 7 137 | 7 392 | 7 616 | 7 818 | 8 259 | 8 674 | 9 125 | 5 987 | 4 352 | 7 622 |
| ... | ... | ... | ... | ... | ... | ... | ... | ... | ... | ... | ... | ... |
| 781 | 708 | 662 | 662 | 670 | 675 | 669 | 675 | 672 | 665 | 727 | 809 | 689 |
| 3 536 | 3 244 | 3 062 | 3 086 | 3 157 | 3 219 | 3 240 | 3 327 | 3 381 | 3 416 | 3 266 | 3 266 | 3 267 |
| 0.03 | 0.03 | 0.03 | 0.03 | 0.03 | 0.03 | 0.03 | 0.03 | 0.03 | 0.03 | 0.03 | 0.04 | 0.03 |
| 775 | 768 | 765 | 790 | 829 | 858 | 867 | 900 | 927 | 954 | 699 | 554 | 853 |
| 3 506 | 3 520 | 3 537 | 3 685 | 3 905 | 4 090 | 4 199 | 4 435 | 4 658 | 4 900 | 3 141 | 2 238 | 4 044 |
| 0.03 | 0.03 | 0.03 | 0.03 | 0.03 | 0.03 | 0.03 | 0.03 | 0.03 | 0.03 | 0.03 | 0.04 | 0.03 |
| 1 093 | 990 | 926 | 925 | 937 | 944 | 936 | 944 | 941 | 930 | 1 017 | 1 131 | 964 |
| 4 946 | 4 537 | 4 283 | 4 316 | 4 415 | 4 503 | 4 531 | 4 653 | 4 728 | 4 778 | 4 568 | 4 567 | 4 569 |
| 0.04 | 0.04 | 0.03 | 0.03 | 0.03 | 0.03 | 0.03 | 0.03 | 0.03 | 0.03 | 0.04 | 0.04 | 0.03 |
| 788 | 755 | 754 | 797 | 878 | 819 | 816 | 939 | 1 089 | 1 121 | 687 | 486 | 888 |
| 3 567 | 3 459 | 3 489 | 3 719 | 4 134 | 3 905 | 3 953 | 4 628 | 5 473 | 5 755 | 3 086 | 1 963 | 4 208 |
| 0.03 | 0.03 | 0.03 | 0.03 | 0.03 | 0.03 | 0.03 | 0.03 | 0.03 | 0.03 | 0.03 | 0.03 | 0.03 |

**Table A.1**   Total and per capita gross domestic product of individual countries or areas,
expressed in United States dollars, and their individual shares of gross world
product, based on alternative conversion rates, 1970−1989 [*cont.*]

| Country or area | 1970 (1) | 1971 (2) | 1972 (3) | 1973 (4) | 1974 (5) | 1975 (6) | 1976 (7) | 1977 (8) | 1978 (9) | 1979 (10) |
|---|---|---|---|---|---|---|---|---|---|---|
| **Equatorial Guinea** | | | | | | | | | | |
| 1.  **MER** | | | | | | | | | | |
| 1a.  Per capita GDP | 170 | 161 | 175 | 202 | 245 | 254 | 193 | 201 | 253 | 268 |
| 1b.  GDP | 50 | 46 | 47 | 51 | 58 | 57 | 42 | 42 | 52 | 56 |
| 1c.  % of GWP | 0.00 | 0.00 | 0.00 | 0.00 | 0.00 | 0.00 | 0.00 | 0.00 | 0.00 | 0.00 |
| 2.  **PPPs** | | | | | | | | | | |
| 2a.  Per capita GDP | ... | ... | ... | ... | ... | ... | ... | ... | ... | ... |
| 2b.  GDP | ... | ... | ... | ... | ... | ... | ... | ... | ... | ... |
| 2c.  % of GWP | ... | ... | ... | ... | ... | ... | ... | ... | ... | ... |
| 3.  **Absolute 1970−1989 PARE** | | | | | | | | | | |
| 3a.  Per capita GDP | 498 | 469 | 460 | 480 | 527 | 399 | 269 | 260 | 251 | 226 |
| 3b.  GDP | 145 | 133 | 124 | 122 | 125 | 90 | 58 | 55 | 52 | 47 |
| 3c.  % of GWP | 0.00 | 0.00 | 0.00 | 0.00 | 0.00 | 0.00 | 0.00 | 0.00 | 0.00 | 0.00 |
| 4.  **Relative 1970−1989 PARE** | | | | | | | | | | |
| 4a.  Per capita GDP | 243 | 240 | 247 | 275 | 328 | 273 | 195 | 202 | 209 | 205 |
| 4b.  GDP | 71 | 68 | 67 | 70 | 78 | 62 | 42 | 42 | 43 | 43 |
| 4c.  % of GWP | 0.00 | 0.00 | 0.00 | 0.00 | 0.00 | 0.00 | 0.00 | 0.00 | 0.00 | 0.00 |
| 5.  **Absolute 1980−1989 PARE** | | | | | | | | | | |
| 5a.  Per capita GDP | 971 | 915 | 898 | 937 | 1 027 | 778 | 524 | 507 | 490 | 441 |
| 5b.  GDP | 284 | 260 | 242 | 238 | 245 | 176 | 113 | 106 | 101 | 93 |
| 5c.  % of GWP | 0.00 | 0.00 | 0.00 | 0.00 | 0.00 | 0.00 | 0.00 | 0.00 | 0.00 | 0.00 |
| 6.  **WA** | | | | | | | | | | |
| 6a.  Per capita GDP | 170 | 161 | 175 | 202 | 245 | 254 | 193 | 201 | 253 | 268 |
| 6b.  GDP | 50 | 46 | 47 | 51 | 58 | 57 | 42 | 42 | 52 | 56 |
| 6c.  % of GWP | 0.00 | 0.00 | 0.00 | 0.00 | 0.00 | 0.00 | 0.00 | 0.00 | 0.00 | 0.00 |
| **Ethiopia** | | | | | | | | | | |
| 1.  **MER** | | | | | | | | | | |
| 1a.  Per capita GDP | 58 | 60 | 64 | 73 | 80 | 78 | 83 | 91 | 95 | 102 |
| 1b.  GDP | 1 784 | 1 892 | 2 062 | 2 385 | 2 682 | 2 669 | 2 900 | 3 298 | 3 510 | 3 858 |
| 1c.  % of GWP | 0.06 | 0.05 | 0.05 | 0.05 | 0.05 | 0.04 | 0.04 | 0.04 | 0.04 | 0.04 |
| 2.  **PPPs** | | | | | | | | | | |
| 2a.  Per capita GDP | 165 | 179 | 172 | 168 | 199 | 200 | 202 | 232 | 245 | 272 |
| 2b.  GDP | 5 043 | 5 603 | 5 498 | 5 511 | 6 683 | 6 875 | 7 099 | 8 370 | 9 065 | 10 301 |
| 2c.  % of GWP | ... | ... | ... | ... | ... | ... | ... | ... | ... | ... |
| 3.  **Absolute 1970−1989 PARE** | | | | | | | | | | |
| 3a.  Per capita GDP | 98 | 100 | 103 | 103 | 102 | 100 | 100 | 98 | 94 | 97 |
| 3b.  GDP | 3 007 | 3 142 | 3 291 | 3 380 | 3 429 | 3 432 | 3 512 | 3 533 | 3 493 | 3 678 |
| 3c.  % of GWP | 0.04 | 0.04 | 0.04 | 0.04 | 0.04 | 0.04 | 0.04 | 0.04 | 0.04 | 0.04 |
| 4.  **Relative 1970−1989 PARE** | | | | | | | | | | |
| 4a.  Per capita GDP | 48 | 51 | 55 | 59 | 64 | 69 | 73 | 76 | 79 | 88 |
| 4b.  GDP | 1 466 | 1 610 | 1 764 | 1 932 | 2 138 | 2 351 | 2 557 | 2 745 | 2 912 | 3 340 |
| 4c.  % of GWP | 0.04 | 0.04 | 0.04 | 0.04 | 0.04 | 0.04 | 0.04 | 0.04 | 0.04 | 0.04 |
| 5.  **Absolute 1980−1989 PARE** | | | | | | | | | | |
| 5a.  Per capita GDP | 114 | 116 | 119 | 120 | 119 | 116 | 116 | 114 | 110 | 113 |
| 5b.  GDP | 3 492 | 3 648 | 3 822 | 3 925 | 3 982 | 3 985 | 4 078 | 4 103 | 4 056 | 4 271 |
| 5c.  % of GWP | 0.04 | 0.04 | 0.04 | 0.04 | 0.04 | 0.04 | 0.04 | 0.04 | 0.03 | 0.03 |
| 6.  **WA** | | | | | | | | | | |
| 6a.  Per capita GDP | 58 | 60 | 64 | 73 | 80 | 78 | 83 | 91 | 95 | 102 |
| 6b.  GDP | 1 784 | 1 889 | 2 062 | 2 385 | 2 682 | 2 669 | 2 900 | 3 298 | 3 510 | 3 858 |
| 6c.  % of GWP | 0.06 | 0.05 | 0.05 | 0.05 | 0.05 | 0.04 | 0.04 | 0.04 | 0.04 | 0.04 |

| | | | | | | | | | | Averages | | |
|---|---|---|---|---|---|---|---|---|---|---|---|---|
| 1980 | 1981 | 1982 | 1983 | 1984 | 1985 | 1986 | 1987 | 1988 | 1989 | 1970–89 | 1970–79 | 1980–89 |
| (11) | (12) | (13) | (14) | (15) | (16) | (17) | (18) | (19) | (20) | (21) | (22) | (23) |
| 259 | 253 | 240 | 251 | 234 | 276 | 335 | 401 | 434 | 390 | 333 | 216 | 304 |
| 56 | 59 | 60 | 69 | 69 | 86 | 109 | 134 | 147 | 135 | 71 | 50 | 92 |
| 0.00 | 0.00 | 0.00 | 0.00 | 0.00 | 0.00 | 0.00 | 0.00 | 0.00 | 0.00 | 0.00 | 0.00 | 0.00 |
| ... | ... | ... | ... | ... | ... | ... | ... | ... | ... | ... | ... | ... |
| ... | ... | ... | ... | ... | ... | ... | ... | ... | ... | ... | ... | ... |
| ... | ... | ... | ... | ... | ... | ... | ... | ... | ... | ... | ... | ... |
| 198 | 190 | 182 | 163 | 154 | 156 | 144 | 151 | 156 | 150 | 333 | 410 | 156 |
| 43 | 44 | 46 | 44 | 45 | 49 | 47 | 50 | 53 | 52 | 71 | 95 | 47 |
| 0.00 | 0.00 | 0.00 | 0.00 | 0.00 | 0.00 | 0.00 | 0.00 | 0.00 | 0.00 | 0.00 | 0.00 | 0.00 |
| 196 | 206 | 211 | 194 | 190 | 198 | 187 | 201 | 215 | 215 | 275 | 253 | 194 |
| 43 | 48 | 53 | 53 | 56 | 62 | 61 | 67 | 73 | 74 | 59 | 59 | 59 |
| 0.00 | 0.00 | 0.00 | 0.00 | 0.00 | 0.00 | 0.00 | 0.00 | 0.00 | 0.00 | 0.00 | 0.00 | 0.00 |
| 386 | 371 | 356 | 317 | 300 | 305 | 282 | 294 | 304 | 292 | 650 | 801 | 304 |
| 84 | 86 | 89 | 87 | 89 | 95 | 91 | 98 | 104 | 101 | 139 | 186 | 92 |
| 0.00 | 0.00 | 0.00 | 0.00 | 0.00 | 0.00 | 0.00 | 0.00 | 0.00 | 0.00 | 0.00 | 0.00 | 0.00 |
| 259 | 253 | 240 | 251 | 234 | 276 | 335 | 401 | 434 | 390 | 333 | 216 | 304 |
| 56 | 59 | 60 | 69 | 69 | 86 | 109 | 134 | 147 | 135 | 71 | 50 | 92 |
| 0.00 | 0.00 | 0.00 | 0.00 | 0.00 | 0.00 | 0.00 | 0.00 | 0.00 | 0.00 | 0.00 | 0.00 | 0.00 |
| 106 | 109 | 110 | 118 | 115 | 111 | 119 | 118 | 120 | 124 | 100 | 80 | 116 |
| 4 106 | 4 301 | 4 429 | 4 846 | 4 831 | 4 778 | 5 233 | 5 331 | 5 603 | 5 948 | 3 822 | 2 704 | 4 941 |
| 0.04 | 0.04 | 0.04 | 0.04 | 0.04 | 0.04 | 0.04 | 0.03 | 0.03 | 0.03 | 0.04 | 0.04 | 0.03 |
| 304 | 324 | 335 | 369 | 367 | 368 | 385 | 417 | 425 | 443 | 302 | 207 | 379 |
| 11 768 | 12 812 | 13 522 | 15 210 | 15 446 | 15 867 | 16 996 | 18 883 | 19 791 | 21 210 | 11 578 | 7 005 | 16 150 |
| ... | ... | ... | ... | ... | ... | ... | ... | ... | ... | ... | ... | ... |
| 100 | 100 | 100 | 103 | 101 | 93 | 96 | 101 | 99 | 100 | 100 | 100 | 100 |
| 3 882 | 3 978 | 4 021 | 4 227 | 4 235 | 4 024 | 4 225 | 4 563 | 4 627 | 4 764 | 3 822 | 3 390 | 4 255 |
| 0.04 | 0.04 | 0.04 | 0.04 | 0.04 | 0.03 | 0.03 | 0.04 | 0.04 | 0.04 | 0.04 | 0.04 | 0.04 |
| 99 | 109 | 115 | 122 | 124 | 119 | 124 | 134 | 137 | 143 | 99 | 67 | 124 |
| 3 848 | 4 317 | 4 645 | 5 048 | 5 239 | 5 112 | 5 476 | 6 084 | 6 376 | 6 834 | 3 790 | 2 282 | 5 298 |
| 0.04 | 0.04 | 0.04 | 0.04 | 0.04 | 0.03 | 0.03 | 0.04 | 0.04 | 0.04 | 0.04 | 0.04 | 0.04 |
| 116 | 117 | 116 | 119 | 117 | 108 | 111 | 117 | 115 | 116 | 116 | 116 | 116 |
| 4 508 | 4 619 | 4 669 | 4 908 | 4 918 | 4 672 | 4 906 | 5 299 | 5 373 | 5 532 | 4 438 | 3 936 | 4 941 |
| 0.04 | 0.04 | 0.04 | 0.04 | 0.04 | 0.03 | 0.03 | 0.03 | 0.03 | 0.03 | 0.04 | 0.04 | 0.03 |
| 106 | 109 | 110 | 118 | 115 | 111 | 119 | 119 | 122 | 126 | 100 | 80 | 117 |
| 4 106 | 4 301 | 4 429 | 4 846 | 4 831 | 4 778 | 5 233 | 5 409 | 5 685 | 6 034 | 3 834 | 2 704 | 4 965 |
| 0.04 | 0.04 | 0.04 | 0.04 | 0.04 | 0.04 | 0.04 | 0.03 | 0.03 | 0.03 | 0.04 | 0.04 | 0.04 |

**Table A.1**     Total and per capita gross domestic product of individual countries or areas, expressed in United States dollars, and their individual shares of gross world product, based on alternative conversion rates, 1970−1989 [*cont.*]

| Country or area | 1970 (1) | 1971 (2) | 1972 (3) | 1973 (4) | 1974 (5) | 1975 (6) | 1976 (7) | 1977 (8) | 1978 (9) | 1979 (10) |
|---|---|---|---|---|---|---|---|---|---|---|
| **Fiji** | | | | | | | | | | |
| 1. **MER** | | | | | | | | | | |
| 1a. Per capita GDP | 423 | 463 | 579 | 768 | 983 | 1 183 | 1 179 | 1 202 | 1 359 | 1 638 |
| 1b. GDP | 220 | 247 | 314 | 426 | 556 | 683 | 693 | 720 | 829 | 1 019 |
| 1c. % of GWP | 0.01 | 0.01 | 0.01 | 0.01 | 0.01 | 0.01 | 0.01 | 0.01 | 0.01 | 0.01 |
| 2. **PPPs** | | | | | | | | | | |
| 2a. Per capita GDP | 1 012 | 1 104 | 1 256 | 1 520 | 1 720 | 1 961 | 2 070 | 2 301 | 2 412 | 2 903 |
| 2b. GDP | 527 | 587 | 682 | 842 | 972 | 1 132 | 1 217 | 1 378 | 1 472 | 1 806 |
| 2c. % of GWP | ... | ... | ... | ... | ... | ... | ... | ... | ... | ... |
| 3. **Absolute 1970−1989 PARE** | | | | | | | | | | |
| 3a. Per capita GDP | 1 109 | 1 156 | 1 221 | 1 333 | 1 343 | 1 345 | 1 343 | 1 387 | 1 388 | 1 527 |
| 3b. GDP | 578 | 615 | 663 | 738 | 759 | 776 | 790 | 831 | 847 | 950 |
| 3c. % of GWP | 0.01 | 0.01 | 0.01 | 0.01 | 0.01 | 0.01 | 0.01 | 0.01 | 0.01 | 0.01 |
| 4. **Relative 1970−1989 PARE** | | | | | | | | | | |
| 4a. Per capita GDP | 541 | 593 | 655 | 762 | 837 | 921 | 977 | 1 077 | 1 157 | 1 387 |
| 4b. GDP | 282 | 315 | 355 | 422 | 473 | 531 | 575 | 645 | 706 | 863 |
| 4c. % of GWP | 0.01 | 0.01 | 0.01 | 0.01 | 0.01 | 0.01 | 0.01 | 0.01 | 0.01 | 0.01 |
| 5. **Absolute 1980−1989 PARE** | | | | | | | | | | |
| 5a. Per capita GDP | 1 312 | 1 369 | 1 446 | 1 578 | 1 590 | 1 592 | 1 590 | 1 641 | 1 644 | 1 808 |
| 5b. GDP | 684 | 728 | 785 | 874 | 898 | 918 | 935 | 983 | 1 003 | 1 125 |
| 5c. % of GWP | 0.01 | 0.01 | 0.01 | 0.01 | 0.01 | 0.01 | 0.01 | 0.01 | 0.01 | 0.01 |
| 6. **WA** | | | | | | | | | | |
| 6a. Per capita GDP | 423 | 464 | 582 | 768 | 989 | 1 182 | 1 180 | 1 202 | 1 359 | 1 638 |
| 6b. GDP | 220 | 247 | 316 | 426 | 559 | 682 | 694 | 720 | 829 | 1 019 |
| 6c. % of GWP | 0.01 | 0.01 | 0.01 | 0.01 | 0.01 | 0.01 | 0.01 | 0.01 | 0.01 | 0.01 |
| **Finland** | | | | | | | | | | |
| 1. **MER** | | | | | | | | | | |
| 1a. Per capita GDP | 2 364 | 2 601 | 3 044 | 4 000 | 5 086 | 6 016 | 6 441 | 6 798 | 7 332 | 8 984 |
| 1b. GDP | 10 891 | 12 023 | 14 140 | 18 677 | 23 862 | 28 348 | 30 446 | 32 214 | 34 825 | 42 793 |
| 1c. % of GWP | 0.34 | 0.34 | 0.35 | 0.38 | 0.43 | 0.46 | 0.45 | 0.43 | 0.39 | 0.42 |
| 2. **PPPs** | | | | | | | | | | |
| 2a. Per capita GDP | 3 075 | 3 279 | 3 701 | 4 296 | 4 925 | 5 459 | 5 620 | 5 904 | 6 361 | 7 531 |
| 2b. GDP | 14 165 | 15 161 | 17 192 | 20 056 | 23 107 | 25 724 | 26 567 | 27 979 | 30 213 | 35 868 |
| 2c. % of GWP | ... | ... | ... | ... | ... | ... | ... | ... | ... | ... |
| 3. **Absolute 1970−1989 PARE** | | | | | | | | | | |
| 3a. Per capita GDP | 7 250 | 7 376 | 7 901 | 8 388 | 8 600 | 8 662 | 8 658 | 8 646 | 8 813 | 9 428 |
| 3b. GDP | 33 402 | 34 099 | 36 702 | 39 163 | 40 349 | 40 815 | 40 924 | 40 971 | 41 864 | 44 906 |
| 3c. % of GWP | 0.47 | 0.46 | 0.47 | 0.47 | 0.48 | 0.47 | 0.45 | 0.43 | 0.43 | 0.44 |
| 4. **Relative 1970−1989 PARE** | | | | | | | | | | |
| 4a. Per capita GDP | 3 535 | 3 781 | 4 236 | 4 795 | 5 363 | 5 934 | 6 302 | 6 718 | 7 348 | 8 562 |
| 4b. GDP | 16 286 | 17 479 | 19 676 | 22 390 | 25 162 | 27 962 | 29 790 | 31 835 | 34 902 | 40 781 |
| 4c. % of GWP | 0.47 | 0.46 | 0.47 | 0.47 | 0.48 | 0.47 | 0.45 | 0.43 | 0.43 | 0.44 |
| 5. **Absolute 1980−1989 PARE** | | | | | | | | | | |
| 5a. Per capita GDP | 9 187 | 9 346 | 10 012 | 10 629 | 10 897 | 10 976 | 10 970 | 10 955 | 11 168 | 11 947 |
| 5b. GDP | 42 324 | 43 208 | 46 505 | 49 625 | 51 127 | 51 717 | 51 856 | 51 915 | 53 046 | 56 901 |
| 5c. % of GWP | 0.49 | 0.48 | 0.49 | 0.49 | 0.49 | 0.49 | 0.47 | 0.45 | 0.44 | 0.46 |
| 6. **WA** | | | | | | | | | | |
| 6a. Per capita GDP | 2 364 | 2 598 | 3 044 | 4 000 | 5 086 | 6 017 | 6 440 | 6 797 | 7 331 | 8 995 |
| 6b. GDP | 10 891 | 12 011 | 14 139 | 18 676 | 23 864 | 28 350 | 30 443 | 32 211 | 34 823 | 42 844 |
| 6c. % of GWP | 0.34 | 0.34 | 0.35 | 0.38 | 0.43 | 0.46 | 0.45 | 0.43 | 0.39 | 0.42 |

| | | | | | | | | | | Averages | | |
|---|---|---|---|---|---|---|---|---|---|---|---|---|
| 1980 (11) | 1981 (12) | 1982 (13) | 1983 (14) | 1984 (15) | 1985 (16) | 1986 (17) | 1987 (18) | 1988 (19) | 1989 (20) | 1970–89 (21) | 1970–79 (22) | 1980–89 (23) |
| 1 900 | 1 913 | 1 809 | 1 670 | 1 719 | 1 631 | 1 813 | 1 660 | 1 487 | 1 550 | 1 397 | 999 | 1 709 |
| 1 204 | 1 238 | 1 194 | 1 124 | 1 179 | 1 141 | 1 293 | 1 205 | 1 099 | 1 165 | 877 | 571 | 1 184 |
| 0.01 | 0.01 | 0.01 | 0.01 | 0.01 | 0.01 | 0.01 | 0.01 | 0.01 | 0.01 | 0.01 | 0.01 | 0.01 |
| 3 073 | 3 294 | 3 098 | 3 291 | 3 705 | 3 452 | 3 701 | 3 511 | 3 538 | 4 173 | 2 778 | 1 859 | 3 502 |
| 1 949 | 2 132 | 2 045 | 2 215 | 2 541 | 2 417 | 2 639 | 2 549 | 2 648 | 3 138 | 1 744 | 1 061 | 2 427 |
| ... | ... | ... | ... | ... | ... | ... | ... | ... | ... | ... | ... | ... |
| 1 473 | 1 537 | 1 472 | 1 402 | 1 490 | 1 402 | 1 474 | 1 359 | 1 342 | 1 501 | 1 397 | 1 321 | 1 444 |
| 934 | 994 | 971 | 944 | 1 022 | 982 | 1 051 | 987 | 992 | 1 129 | 877 | 755 | 1 000 |
| 0.01 | 0.01 | 0.01 | 0.01 | 0.01 | 0.01 | 0.01 | 0.01 | 0.01 | 0.01 | 0.01 | 0.01 | 0.01 |
| 1 460 | 1 667 | 1 700 | 1 675 | 1 842 | 1 781 | 1 910 | 1 812 | 1 849 | 2 153 | 1 401 | 905 | 1 793 |
| 926 | 1 079 | 1 122 | 1 127 | 1 264 | 1 247 | 1 362 | 1 315 | 1 366 | 1 619 | 880 | 517 | 1 243 |
| 0.01 | 0.01 | 0.01 | 0.01 | 0.01 | 0.01 | 0.01 | 0.01 | 0.01 | 0.01 | 0.01 | 0.01 | 0.01 |
| 1 743 | 1 819 | 1 743 | 1 660 | 1 763 | 1 660 | 1 745 | 1 609 | 1 588 | 1 777 | 1 654 | 1 564 | 1 709 |
| 1 105 | 1 177 | 1 150 | 1 117 | 1 210 | 1 162 | 1 244 | 1 168 | 1 174 | 1 336 | 1 039 | 893 | 1 184 |
| 0.01 | 0.01 | 0.01 | 0.01 | 0.01 | 0.01 | 0.01 | 0.01 | 0.01 | 0.01 | 0.01 | 0.01 | 0.01 |
| 1 900 | 1 913 | 1 809 | 1 669 | 1 717 | 1 630 | 1 809 | 1 601 | 1 455 | 1 567 | 1 393 | 1 000 | 1 700 |
| 1 204 | 1 238 | 1 194 | 1 123 | 1 178 | 1 141 | 1 290 | 1 162 | 1 075 | 1 178 | 875 | 571 | 1 178 |
| 0.01 | 0.01 | 0.01 | 0.01 | 0.01 | 0.01 | 0.01 | 0.01 | 0.01 | 0.01 | 0.01 | 0.01 | 0.01 |
| 10 803 | 10 532 | 10 561 | 10 158 | 10 514 | 11 023 | 14 329 | 18 023 | 21 234 | 23 211 | 9 808 | 5 279 | 14 060 |
| 51 637 | 50 573 | 50 978 | 49 308 | 51 307 | 54 047 | 70 526 | 88 999 | 105 128 | 115 219 | 46 797 | 24 822 | 68 772 |
| 0.45 | 0.43 | 0.44 | 0.42 | 0.42 | 0.43 | 0.47 | 0.52 | 0.55 | 0.57 | 0.46 | 0.41 | 0.48 |
| 8 655 | 9 427 | 10 285 | 10 447 | 11 395 | 11 698 | 12 137 | 12 942 | 14 066 | 15 358 | 8 441 | 5 020 | 11 642 |
| 41 372 | 45 268 | 49 648 | 50 708 | 55 606 | 57 357 | 59 738 | 63 905 | 69 640 | 76 238 | 40 276 | 23 603 | 56 948 |
| ... | ... | ... | ... | ... | ... | ... | ... | ... | ... | ... | ... | ... |
| 9 895 | 10 005 | 10 310 | 10 557 | 10 823 | 11 131 | 11 321 | 11 734 | 12 339 | 12 942 | 9 808 | 8 362 | 11 096 |
| 47 298 | 48 045 | 49 765 | 51 244 | 52 816 | 54 575 | 55 721 | 57 943 | 61 092 | 64 246 | 46 797 | 39 320 | 54 275 |
| 0.46 | 0.45 | 0.47 | 0.47 | 0.46 | 0.46 | 0.46 | 0.46 | 0.46 | 0.47 | 0.46 | 0.46 | 0.46 |
| 9 808 | 10 856 | 11 909 | 12 607 | 13 387 | 14 142 | 14 672 | 15 644 | 17 004 | 18 566 | 9 897 | 5 663 | 13 864 |
| 46 884 | 52 131 | 57 486 | 61 195 | 65 331 | 69 336 | 72 214 | 77 252 | 84 184 | 92 161 | 47 222 | 26 626 | 67 817 |
| 0.46 | 0.45 | 0.47 | 0.47 | 0.46 | 0.46 | 0.46 | 0.46 | 0.46 | 0.47 | 0.46 | 0.45 | 0.46 |
| 12 538 | 12 678 | 13 064 | 13 377 | 13 714 | 14 104 | 14 345 | 14 869 | 15 635 | 16 400 | 12 427 | 10 596 | 14 060 |
| 59 932 | 60 879 | 63 059 | 64 932 | 66 924 | 69 154 | 70 605 | 73 421 | 77 411 | 81 408 | 59 297 | 49 823 | 68 772 |
| 0.47 | 0.47 | 0.49 | 0.49 | 0.48 | 0.48 | 0.48 | 0.48 | 0.48 | 0.49 | 0.48 | 0.47 | 0.48 |
| 10 802 | 10 543 | 10 560 | 10 158 | 10 514 | 11 024 | 14 330 | 18 042 | 21 321 | 23 258 | 9 816 | 5 280 | 14 076 |
| 51 636 | 50 629 | 50 974 | 49 308 | 51 307 | 54 048 | 70 533 | 89 089 | 105 560 | 115 454 | 46 839 | 24 825 | 68 854 |
| 0.45 | 0.43 | 0.44 | 0.42 | 0.42 | 0.43 | 0.48 | 0.53 | 0.56 | 0.59 | 0.46 | 0.41 | 0.49 |

**Table A.1**    Total and per capita gross domestic product of individual countries or areas,
expressed in United States dollars, and their individual shares of gross world
product, based on alternative conversion rates, 1970−1989 [*cont.*]

| Country or area | 1970 (1) | 1971 (2) | 1972 (3) | 1973 (4) | 1974 (5) | 1975 (6) | 1976 (7) | 1977 (8) | 1978 (9) | 1979 (10) |
|---|---|---|---|---|---|---|---|---|---|---|
| **France** | | | | | | | | | | |
| **1.    MER** | | | | | | | | | | |
| 1a.    Per capita GDP | 2 814 | 3 119 | 3 793 | 4 873 | 5 173 | 6 499 | 6 715 | 7 334 | 9 050 | 10 868 |
| 1b.    GDP | 142 873 | 159 600 | 195 633 | 253 327 | 270 890 | 342 483 | 355 764 | 390 352 | 483 623 | 583 102 |
| 1c.    % of GWP | 4.48 | 4.56 | 4.86 | 5.16 | 4.88 | 5.51 | 5.30 | 5.16 | 5.38 | 5.66 |
| **2.    PPPs** | | | | | | | | | | |
| 2a.    Per capita GDP | 3 491 | 3 862 | 4 271 | 4 835 | 5 376 | 5 852 | 6 461 | 7 059 | 7 929 | 8 912 |
| 2b.    GDP | 177 240 | 197 638 | 220 297 | 251 366 | 281 532 | 308 420 | 342 292 | 375 700 | 423 720 | 478 172 |
| 2c.    % of GWP | ... | ... | ... | ... | ... | ... | ... | ... | ... | ... |
| **3.    Absolute 1970−1989 PARE** | | | | | | | | | | |
| 3a.    Per capita GDP | 7 357 | 7 649 | 7 924 | 8 290 | 8 486 | 8 409 | 8 719 | 8 959 | 9 222 | 9 483 |
| 3b.    GDP | 373 539 | 391 405 | 408 748 | 430 985 | 444 386 | 443 149 | 461 955 | 476 818 | 492 793 | 508 767 |
| 3c.    % of GWP | 5.26 | 5.29 | 5.24 | 5.19 | 5.24 | 5.15 | 5.10 | 5.05 | 5.01 | 5.00 |
| **4.    Relative 1970−1989 PARE** | | | | | | | | | | |
| 4a.    Per capita GDP | 3 587 | 3 921 | 4 248 | 4 740 | 5 292 | 5 761 | 6 347 | 6 961 | 7 688 | 8 612 |
| 4b.    GDP | 182 126 | 200 627 | 219 129 | 246 397 | 277 118 | 303 604 | 336 268 | 370 497 | 410 844 | 462 031 |
| 4c.    % of GWP | 5.26 | 5.29 | 5.24 | 5.19 | 5.24 | 5.15 | 5.10 | 5.05 | 5.01 | 5.00 |
| **5.    Absolute 1980−1989 PARE** | | | | | | | | | | |
| 5a.    Per capita GDP | 9 002 | 9 359 | 9 696 | 10 143 | 10 383 | 10 289 | 10 668 | 10 962 | 11 283 | 11 603 |
| 5b.    GDP | 457 042 | 478 902 | 500 122 | 527 329 | 543 727 | 542 213 | 565 223 | 583 409 | 602 955 | 622 499 |
| 5c.    % of GWP | 5.25 | 5.28 | 5.23 | 5.19 | 5.24 | 5.16 | 5.11 | 5.06 | 5.03 | 5.02 |
| **6.    WA** | | | | | | | | | | |
| 6a.    Per capita GDP | 2 814 | 3 117 | 3 793 | 4 875 | 5 169 | 6 498 | 6 716 | 7 333 | 9 050 | 10 870 |
| 6b.    GDP | 142 869 | 159 525 | 195 646 | 253 454 | 270 661 | 342 463 | 355 839 | 390 307 | 483 612 | 583 182 |
| 6c.    % of GWP | 4.48 | 4.57 | 4.88 | 5.21 | 4.85 | 5.56 | 5.30 | 5.18 | 5.45 | 5.70 |
| **French Guiana** | | | | | | | | | | |
| **1.    MER** | | | | | | | | | | |
| 1a.    Per capita GDP | 877 | 1 108 | 1 436 | 1 768 | 1 949 | 2 332 | 2 167 | 2 005 | 2 343 | 2 421 |
| 1b.    GDP | 44 | 57 | 76 | 97 | 109 | 135 | 130 | 124 | 150 | 162 |
| 1c.    % of GWP | 0.00 | 0.00 | 0.00 | 0.00 | 0.00 | 0.00 | 0.00 | 0.00 | 0.00 | 0.00 |
| **2.    PPPs** | | | | | | | | | | |
| 2a.    Per capita GDP | ... | ... | ... | ... | ... | ... | ... | ... | ... | ... |
| 2b.    GDP | ... | ... | ... | ... | ... | ... | ... | ... | ... | ... |
| 2c.    % of GWP | ... | ... | ... | ... | ... | ... | ... | ... | ... | ... |
| **3.    Absolute 1970−1989 PARE** | | | | | | | | | | |
| 3a.    Per capita GDP | 2 143 | 2 555 | 2 678 | 2 684 | 2 946 | 2 821 | 2 761 | 2 454 | 2 304 | 2 189 |
| 3b.    GDP | 107 | 130 | 142 | 148 | 165 | 164 | 166 | 152 | 147 | 147 |
| 3c.    % of GWP | 0.00 | 0.00 | 0.00 | 0.00 | 0.00 | 0.00 | 0.00 | 0.00 | 0.00 | 0.00 |
| **4.    Relative 1970−1989 PARE** | | | | | | | | | | |
| 4a.    Per capita GDP | 1 045 | 1 309 | 1 436 | 1 534 | 1 837 | 1 933 | 2 010 | 1 907 | 1 921 | 1 988 |
| 4b.    GDP | 52 | 67 | 76 | 84 | 103 | 112 | 121 | 118 | 123 | 133 |
| 4c.    % of GWP | 0.00 | 0.00 | 0.00 | 0.00 | 0.00 | 0.00 | 0.00 | 0.00 | 0.00 | 0.00 |
| **5.    Absolute 1980−1989 PARE** | | | | | | | | | | |
| 5a.    Per capita GDP | 2 686 | 3 202 | 3 357 | 3 364 | 3 693 | 3 536 | 3 461 | 3 076 | 2 889 | 2 744 |
| 5b.    GDP | 134 | 163 | 178 | 185 | 207 | 205 | 208 | 191 | 185 | 184 |
| 5c.    % of GWP | 0.00 | 0.00 | 0.00 | 0.00 | 0.00 | 0.00 | 0.00 | 0.00 | 0.00 | 0.00 |
| **6.    WA** | | | | | | | | | | |
| 6a.    Per capita GDP | 796 | 1 033 | 1 215 | 1 416 | 1 806 | 1 996 | 2 073 | 1 986 | 1 986 | 2 110 |
| 6b.    GDP | 40 | 53 | 64 | 78 | 101 | 116 | 124 | 123 | 127 | 141 |
| 6c.    % of GWP | 0.00 | 0.00 | 0.00 | 0.00 | 0.00 | 0.00 | 0.00 | 0.00 | 0.00 | 0.00 |

| | | | | | | | | | | Averages | | |
|---|---|---|---|---|---|---|---|---|---|---|---|---|
| 1980 (11) | 1981 (12) | 1982 (13) | 1983 (14) | 1984 (15) | 1985 (16) | 1986 (17) | 1987 (18) | 1988 (19) | 1989 (20) | 1970–89 (21) | 1970–79 (22) | 1980–89 (23) |
| 12 333 | 10 757 | 10 143 | 9 616 | 9 087 | 9 476 | 13 207 | 15 954 | 17 013 | 17 071 | 9 342 | 6 049 | 12 477 |
| 664 529 | 582 300 | 551 738 | 525 718 | 499 131 | 522 819 | 731 500 | 886 806 | 948 788 | 955 175 | 502 308 | 317 765 | 686 850 |
| 5.73 | 4.97 | 4.75 | 4.43 | 4.09 | 4.15 | 4.91 | 5.16 | 4.97 | 4.76 | 4.93 | 5.21 | 4.81 |
| 9 808 | 10 593 | 11 480 | 11 852 | 12 434 | 12 820 | 13 355 | 13 990 | 14 966 | 16 122 | 9 369 | 5 818 | 12 749 |
| 528 447 | 573 412 | 624 491 | 647 915 | 683 009 | 707 288 | 739 669 | 777 594 | 834 654 | 902 038 | 503 745 | 305 638 | 701 852 |
| ... | ... | ... | ... | ... | ... | ... | ... | ... | ... | ... | ... | ... |
| 9 596 | 9 664 | 9 861 | 9 880 | 9 963 | 10 106 | 10 320 | 10 509 | 10 877 | 11 255 | 9 342 | 8 438 | 10 197 |
| 517 031 | 523 112 | 536 429 | 540 155 | 547 255 | 557 550 | 571 589 | 584 113 | 606 609 | 629 761 | 502 308 | 443 255 | 561 361 |
| 4.98 | 4.94 | 5.03 | 4.92 | 4.77 | 4.70 | 4.68 | 4.62 | 4.60 | 4.63 | 4.93 | 5.14 | 4.77 |
| 9 512 | 10 486 | 11 391 | 11 799 | 12 323 | 12 839 | 13 375 | 14 010 | 14 989 | 16 146 | 9 297 | 5 727 | 12 695 |
| 512 513 | 567 603 | 619 648 | 645 042 | 676 929 | 708 347 | 740 777 | 778 759 | 835 904 | 903 389 | 499 878 | 300 864 | 698 891 |
| 4.98 | 4.94 | 5.03 | 4.92 | 4.77 | 4.70 | 4.68 | 4.62 | 4.60 | 4.63 | 4.86 | 5.12 | 4.76 |
| 11 741 | 11 824 | 12 066 | 12 089 | 12 190 | 12 365 | 12 627 | 12 858 | 13 309 | 13 771 | 11 431 | 10 324 | 12 477 |
| 632 612 | 640 052 | 656 345 | 660 905 | 669 591 | 682 188 | 699 366 | 714 689 | 742 214 | 770 542 | 614 596 | 542 342 | 686 850 |
| 5.00 | 4.97 | 5.06 | 4.96 | 4.81 | 4.73 | 4.72 | 4.66 | 4.64 | 4.67 | 4.95 | 5.15 | 4.81 |
| 12 335 | 10 758 | 10 143 | 9 616 | 9 086 | 9 481 | 13 215 | 15 926 | 17 136 | 17 124 | 9 351 | 6 049 | 12 493 |
| 664 597 | 582 342 | 551 729 | 525 698 | 499 126 | 523 097 | 731 913 | 885 226 | 955 646 | 958 148 | 502 754 | 317 756 | 687 752 |
| 5.77 | 4.94 | 4.73 | 4.43 | 4.08 | 4.14 | 4.98 | 5.31 | 5.11 | 4.88 | 4.98 | 5.24 | 4.86 |
| 2 650 | 2 265 | 2 064 | 1 941 | 1 825 | 1 828 | 2 115 | 2 678 | 2 826 | 2 796 | 2 190 | 1 903 | 2 324 |
| 183 | 163 | 155 | 149 | 146 | 152 | 182 | 238 | 260 | 266 | 149 | 108 | 189 |
| 0.00 | 0.00 | 0.00 | 0.00 | 0.00 | 0.00 | 0.00 | 0.00 | 0.00 | 0.00 | 0.00 | 0.00 | 0.00 |
| ... | ... | ... | ... | ... | ... | ... | ... | ... | ... | ... | ... | ... |
| ... | ... | ... | ... | ... | ... | ... | ... | ... | ... | ... | ... | ... |
| ... | ... | ... | ... | ... | ... | ... | ... | ... | ... | ... | ... | ... |
| 2 125 | 2 041 | 1 962 | 1 933 | 1 904 | 1 829 | 1 607 | 1 691 | 1 743 | 1 769 | 2 190 | 2 575 | 1 854 |
| 147 | 147 | 147 | 149 | 152 | 152 | 138 | 150 | 160 | 168 | 149 | 147 | 151 |
| 0.00 | 0.00 | 0.00 | 0.00 | 0.00 | 0.00 | 0.00 | 0.00 | 0.00 | 0.00 | 0.00 | 0.00 | 0.00 |
| 2 107 | 2 215 | 2 267 | 2 308 | 2 355 | 2 324 | 2 082 | 2 254 | 2 402 | 2 538 | 2 107 | 1 736 | 2 301 |
| 145 | 159 | 170 | 178 | 188 | 193 | 179 | 201 | 221 | 241 | 143 | 99 | 188 |
| 0.00 | 0.00 | 0.00 | 0.00 | 0.00 | 0.00 | 0.00 | 0.00 | 0.00 | 0.00 | 0.00 | 0.00 | 0.00 |
| 2 664 | 2 558 | 2 460 | 2 422 | 2 387 | 2 292 | 2 014 | 2 119 | 2 185 | 2 218 | 2 745 | 3 227 | 2 324 |
| 184 | 184 | 184 | 187 | 191 | 190 | 173 | 189 | 201 | 211 | 187 | 184 | 189 |
| 0.00 | 0.00 | 0.00 | 0.00 | 0.00 | 0.00 | 0.00 | 0.00 | 0.00 | 0.00 | 0.00 | 0.00 | 0.00 |
| 2 370 | 2 348 | 2 218 | 2 036 | 1 911 | 1 805 | 1 719 | 2 121 | 2 605 | 2 822 | 2 037 | 1 698 | 2 212 |
| 164 | 169 | 166 | 157 | 153 | 150 | 148 | 189 | . 240 | 268 | 139 | 97 | 180 |
| 0.00 | 0.00 | 0.00 | 0.00 | 0.00 | 0.00 | 0.00 | 0.00 | 0.00 | 0.00 | 0.00 | 0.00 | 0.00 |

**Table A.1**    Total and per capita gross domestic product of individual countries or areas,
expressed in United States dollars, and their individual shares of gross world
product, based on alternative conversion rates, 1970−1989 [*cont.*]

| Country or area | 1970 (1) | 1971 (2) | 1972 (3) | 1973 (4) | 1974 (5) | 1975 (6) | 1976 (7) | 1977 (8) | 1978 (9) | 1979 (10) |
|---|---|---|---|---|---|---|---|---|---|---|
| **French Polynesia** | | | | | | | | | | |
| 1.   **MER** | | | | | | | | | | |
| 1a.   Per capita GDP | 1 933 | 2 190 | 2 294 | 2 913 | 3 634 | 4 344 | 4 810 | 5 065 | 6 269 | 7 626 |
| 1b.   GDP | 213 | 250 | 273 | 361 | 465 | 578 | 654 | 704 | 890 | 1 106 |
| 1c.   % of GWP | 0.01 | 0.01 | 0.01 | 0.01 | 0.01 | 0.01 | 0.01 | 0.01 | 0.01 | 0.01 |
| 2.   **PPPs** | | | | | | | | | | |
| 2a.   Per capita GDP | ... | ... | ... | ... | ... | ... | ... | ... | ... | ... |
| 2b.   GDP | ... | ... | ... | ... | ... | ... | ... | ... | ... | ... |
| 2c.   % of GWP | ... | ... | ... | ... | ... | ... | ... | ... | ... | ... |
| 3.   **Absolute 1970−1989 PARE** | | | | | | | | | | |
| 3a.   Per capita GDP | 6 241 | 6 744 | 6 158 | 6 371 | 7 283 | 6 665 | 7 053 | 7 176 | 7 306 | 7 441 |
| 3b.   GDP | 686 | 769 | 733 | 790 | 932 | 886 | 959 | 998 | 1 037 | 1 079 |
| 3c.   % of GWP | 0.01 | 0.01 | 0.01 | 0.01 | 0.01 | 0.01 | 0.01 | 0.01 | 0.01 | 0.01 |
| 4.   **Relative 1970−1989 PARE** | | | | | | | | | | |
| 4a.   Per capita GDP | 3 043 | 3 457 | 3 301 | 3 642 | 4 541 | 4 566 | 5 134 | 5 576 | 6 091 | 6 758 |
| 4b.   GDP | 335 | 394 | 393 | 452 | 581 | 607 | 698 | 775 | 865 | 980 |
| 4c.   % of GWP | 0.01 | 0.01 | 0.01 | 0.01 | 0.01 | 0.01 | 0.01 | 0.01 | 0.01 | 0.01 |
| 5.   **Absolute 1980−1989 PARE** | | | | | | | | | | |
| 5a.   Per capita GDP | 7 698 | 8 319 | 7 595 | 7 858 | 8 983 | 8 221 | 8 699 | 8 852 | 9 012 | 9 178 |
| 5b.   GDP | 847 | 948 | 904 | 974 | 1 150 | 1 093 | 1 183 | 1 230 | 1 280 | 1 331 |
| 5c.   % of GWP | 0.01 | 0.01 | 0.01 | 0.01 | 0.01 | 0.01 | 0.01 | 0.01 | 0.01 | 0.01 |
| 6.   **WA**[a] | | | | | | | | | | |
| 6a.   Per capita GDP | 2 005 | 2 124 | 2 054 | 2 404 | 3 178 | 3 492 | 4 228 | 4 874 | 5 414 | 6 274 |
| 6b.   GDP | 221 | 242 | 244 | 298 | 407 | 464 | 575 | 677 | 769 | 910 |
| 6c.   % of GWP | 0.01 | 0.01 | 0.01 | 0.01 | 0.01 | 0.01 | 0.01 | 0.01 | 0.01 | 0.01 |
| **Gabon** | | | | | | | | | | |
| 1.   **MER** | | | | | | | | | | |
| 1a.   Per capita GDP | 664 | 706 | 787 | 1 259 | 2 548 | 3 382 | 4 492 | 3 990 | 3 242 | 3 925 |
| 1b.   GDP | 335 | 369 | 430 | 723 | 1 544 | 2 158 | 3 009 | 2 809 | 2 390 | 3 030 |
| 1c.   % of GWP | 0.01 | 0.01 | 0.01 | 0.01 | 0.03 | 0.03 | 0.04 | 0.04 | 0.03 | 0.03 |
| 2.   **PPPs** | | | | | | | | | | |
| 2a.   Per capita GDP | 844 | 899 | 880 | 1 346 | 2 584 | 2 893 | 3 800 | 3 510 | 2 742 | 3 177 |
| 2b.   GDP | 426 | 469 | 481 | 773 | 1 566 | 1 846 | 2 546 | 2 471 | 2 021 | 2 452 |
| 2c.   % of GWP | ... | ... | ... | ... | ... | ... | ... | ... | ... | ... |
| 3.   **Absolute 1970−1989 PARE** | | | | | | | | | | |
| 3a.   Per capita GDP | 2 796 | 2 572 | 2 470 | 3 336 | 4 562 | 4 956 | 6 522 | 5 313 | 3 598 | 3 387 |
| 3b.   GDP | 1 412 | 1 343 | 1 349 | 1 915 | 2 765 | 3 162 | 4 370 | 3 740 | 2 652 | 2 614 |
| 3c.   % of GWP | 0.02 | 0.02 | 0.02 | 0.02 | 0.03 | 0.04 | 0.05 | 0.04 | 0.03 | 0.03 |
| 4.   **Relative 1970−1989 PARE** | | | | | | | | | | |
| 4a.   Per capita GDP | 1 363 | 1 318 | 1 324 | 1 907 | 2 845 | 3 395 | 4 747 | 4 128 | 3 000 | 3 076 |
| 4b.   GDP | 689 | 688 | 723 | 1 095 | 1 724 | 2 166 | 3 181 | 2 906 | 2 211 | 2 374 |
| 4c.   % of GWP | 0.02 | 0.02 | 0.02 | 0.02 | 0.03 | 0.04 | 0.05 | 0.04 | 0.03 | 0.03 |
| 5.   **Absolute 1980−1989 PARE** | | | | | | | | | | |
| 5a.   Per capita GDP | 3 668 | 3 374 | 3 240 | 4 376 | 5 984 | 6 500 | 8 555 | 6 969 | 4 719 | 4 442 |
| 5b.   GDP | 1 852 | 1 761 | 1 769 | 2 512 | 3 626 | 4 147 | 5 732 | 4 906 | 3 478 | 3 430 |
| 5c.   % of GWP | 0.02 | 0.02 | 0.02 | 0.02 | 0.03 | 0.04 | 0.05 | 0.04 | 0.03 | 0.03 |
| 6.   **WA** | | | | | | | | | | |
| 6a.   Per capita GDP | 664 | 706 | 787 | 1 259 | 2 548 | 3 382 | 4 492 | 3 990 | 3 242 | 3 925 |
| 6b.   GDP | 335 | 369 | 430 | 723 | 1 544 | 2 158 | 3 009 | 2 809 | 2 390 | 3 030 |
| 6c.   % of GWP | 0.01 | 0.01 | 0.01 | 0.01 | 0.03 | 0.04 | 0.04 | 0.04 | 0.03 | 0.03 |

|  |  |  |  |  |  |  |  |  |  | Averages | | |
| 1980 (11) | 1981 (12) | 1982 (13) | 1983 (14) | 1984 (15) | 1985 (16) | 1986 (17) | 1987 (18) | 1988 (19) | 1989 (20) | 1970–89 (21) | 1970–79 (22) | 1980–89 (23) |
|---|---|---|---|---|---|---|---|---|---|---|---|---|
| 8 459 | 7 705 | 7 499 | 7 502 | 7 471 | 7 887 | 11 647 | 14 109 | 14 390 | 13 807 | 7 936 | 4 210 | 10 311 |
| 1 260 | 1 179 | 1 185 | 1 230 | 1 270 | 1 388 | 2 120 | 2 653 | 2 792 | 2 761 | 1 167 | 549 | 1 784 |
| 0.01 | 0.01 | 0.01 | 0.01 | 0.01 | 0.01 | 0.01 | 0.02 | 0.01 | 0.01 | 0.01 | 0.01 | 0.01 |
| ... | ... | ... | ... | ... | ... | ... | ... | ... | ... | ... | ... | ... |
| ... | ... | ... | ... | ... | ... | ... | ... | ... | ... | ... | ... | ... |
| ... | ... | ... | ... | ... | ... | ... | ... | ... | ... | ... | ... | ... |
| 7 029 | 7 428 | 7 910 | 8 055 | 8 201 | 8 345 | 8 748 | 9 074 | 9 004 | 8 996 | 7 936 | 6 797 | 8 359 |
| 1 047 | 1 136 | 1 250 | 1 321 | 1 394 | 1 469 | 1 592 | 1 706 | 1 747 | 1 799 | 1 167 | 887 | 1 446 |
| 0.01 | 0.01 | 0.01 | 0.01 | 0.01 | 0.01 | 0.01 | 0.01 | 0.01 | 0.01 | 0.01 | 0.01 | 0.01 |
| 6 968 | 8 059 | 9 137 | 9 619 | 10 144 | 10 602 | 11 338 | 12 098 | 12 408 | 12 905 | 8 262 | 4 659 | 10 525 |
| 1 038 | 1 233 | 1 444 | 1 578 | 1 724 | 1 866 | 2 063 | 2 274 | 2 407 | 2 581 | 1 214 | 608 | 1 821 |
| 0.01 | 0.01 | 0.01 | 0.01 | 0.01 | 0.01 | 0.01 | 0.01 | 0.01 | 0.01 | 0.01 | 0.01 | 0.01 |
| 8 670 | 9 162 | 9 756 | 9 935 | 10 115 | 10 293 | 10 791 | 11 192 | 11 107 | 11 097 | 9 789 | 8 384 | 10 311 |
| 1 292 | 1 402 | 1 542 | 1 629 | 1 720 | 1 812 | 1 964 | 2 104 | 2 155 | 2 219 | 1 439 | 1 094 | 1 784 |
| 0.01 | 0.01 | 0.01 | 0.01 | 0.01 | 0.01 | 0.01 | 0.01 | 0.01 | 0.01 | 0.01 | 0.01 | 0.01 |
| 7 095 | 8 042 | 8 326 | 7 814 | 7 626 | 7 752 | 9 028 | 11 100 | 13 373 | 14 054 | 7 309 | 3 684 | 9 642 |
| 1 057 | 1 230 | 1 316 | 1 281 | 1 296 | 1 364 | 1 643 | 2 087 | 2 594 | 2 811 | 1 074 | 481 | 1 668 |
| 0.01 | 0.01 | 0.01 | 0.01 | 0.01 | 0.01 | 0.01 | 0.01 | 0.01 | 0.01 | 0.01 | 0.01 | 0.01 |
| 5 305 | 4 587 | 4 121 | 3 722 | 3 685 | 3 715 | 3 394 | 3 252 | 2 975 | 2 978 | 3 335 | 2 700 | 3 707 |
| 4 281 | 3 863 | 3 618 | 3 398 | 3 497 | 3 663 | 3 468 | 3 444 | 3 261 | 3 374 | 2 633 | 1 680 | 3 587 |
| 0.04 | 0.03 | 0.03 | 0.03 | 0.03 | 0.03 | 0.02 | 0.02 | 0.02 | 0.02 | 0.03 | 0.03 | 0.03 |
| 4 037 | 4 243 | 4 162 | 3 896 | 3 736 | 3 466 | 2 748 | 2 328 | 2 181 | 2 284 | 2 933 | 2 420 | 3 231 |
| 3 258 | 3 572 | 3 654 | 3 557 | 3 545 | 3 418 | 2 809 | 2 465 | 2 390 | 2 587 | 2 315 | 1 505 | 3 126 |
| ... | ... | ... | ... | ... | ... | ... | ... | ... | ... | ... | ... | ... |
| 3 811 | 3 524 | 3 414 | 3 223 | 3 332 | 3 249 | 2 525 | 2 079 | 1 884 | 1 896 | 3 335 | 4 071 | 2 826 |
| 3 076 | 2 968 | 2 997 | 2 942 | 3 162 | 3 204 | 2 581 | 2 202 | 2 065 | 2 148 | 2 633 | 2 532 | 2 734 |
| 0.03 | 0.03 | 0.03 | 0.03 | 0.03 | 0.03 | 0.02 | 0.02 | 0.02 | 0.02 | 0.03 | 0.03 | 0.02 |
| 3 778 | 3 824 | 3 943 | 3 849 | 4 121 | 4 128 | 3 273 | 2 772 | 2 597 | 2 719 | 3 242 | 2 855 | 3 456 |
| 3 049 | 3 220 | 3 462 | 3 514 | 3 911 | 4 070 | 3 345 | 2 935 | 2 846 | 3 081 | 2 559 | 1 776 | 3 343 |
| 0.03 | 0.03 | 0.03 | 0.03 | 0.03 | 0.03 | 0.02 | 0.02 | 0.02 | 0.02 | 0.02 | 0.03 | 0.02 |
| 5 000 | 4 623 | 4 478 | 4 228 | 4 371 | 4 262 | 3 313 | 2 727 | 2 472 | 2 487 | 4 375 | 5 340 | 3 707 |
| 4 035 | 3 893 | 3 932 | 3 860 | 4 148 | 4 202 | 3 385 | 2 888 | 2 709 | 2 817 | 3 454 | 3 321 | 3 587 |
| 0.03 | 0.03 | 0.03 | 0.03 | 0.03 | 0.03 | 0.02 | 0.02 | 0.02 | 0.02 | 0.03 | 0.03 | 0.03 |
| 5 305 | 4 587 | 4 121 | 3 722 | 3 685 | 3 715 | 3 394 | 3 252 | 2 975 | 2 978 | 3 335 | 2 700 | 3 707 |
| 4 281 | 3 863 | 3 618 | 3 398 | 3 497 | 3 663 | 3 468 | 3 444 | 3 260 | 3 374 | 2 633 | 1 680 | 3 587 |
| 0.04 | 0.03 | 0.03 | 0.03 | 0.03 | 0.03 | 0.02 | 0.02 | 0.02 | 0.02 | 0.03 | 0.03 | 0.03 |

**Table A.1**  Total and per capita gross domestic product of individual countries or areas, expressed in United States dollars, and their individual shares of gross world product, based on alternative conversion rates, 1970−1989 [*cont.*]

| Country or area | 1970 (1) | 1971 (2) | 1972 (3) | 1973 (4) | 1974 (5) | 1975 (6) | 1976 (7) | 1977 (8) | 1978 (9) | 1979 (10) |
|---|---|---|---|---|---|---|---|---|---|---|
| **Gambia** | | | | | | | | | | |
| **1.   MER** | | | | | | | | | | |
| 1a.  Per capita GDP | 116 | 122 | 121 | 211 | 283 | 326 | 326 | 313 | 385 | 420 |
| 1b.  GDP | 54 | 58 | 60 | 108 | 150 | 178 | 185 | 183 | 232 | 261 |
| 1c.  % of GWP | 0.00 | 0.00 | 0.00 | 0.00 | 0.00 | 0.00 | 0.00 | 0.00 | 0.00 | 0.00 |
| **2.   PPPs** | | | | | | | | | | |
| 2a.  Per capita GDP | 288 | 287 | 260 | 388 | 495 | 460 | 527 | 535 | 636 | 659 |
| 2b.  GDP | 134 | 137 | 129 | 199 | 262 | 252 | 298 | 313 | 384 | 410 |
| 2c.  % of GWP | ... | ... | ... | ... | ... | ... | ... | ... | ... | ... |
| **3.   Absolute 1970−1989 PARE** | | | | | | | | | | |
| 3a.  Per capita GDP | 267 | 283 | 244 | 297 | 317 | 337 | 335 | 308 | 324 | 319 |
| 3b.  GDP | 124 | 136 | 121 | 153 | 168 | 185 | 190 | 180 | 195 | 198 |
| 3c.  % of GWP | 0.00 | 0.00 | 0.00 | 0.00 | 0.00 | 0.00 | 0.00 | 0.00 | 0.00 | 0.00 |
| **4.   Relative 1970−1989 PARE** | | | | | | | | | | |
| 4a.  Per capita GDP | 130 | 145 | 131 | 170 | 198 | 231 | 244 | 239 | 270 | 290 |
| 4b.  GDP | 60 | 70 | 65 | 87 | 105 | 127 | 138 | 140 | 163 | 180 |
| 4c.  % of GWP | 0.00 | 0.00 | 0.00 | 0.00 | 0.00 | 0.00 | 0.00 | 0.00 | 0.00 | 0.00 |
| **5.   Absolute 1980−1989 PARE** | | | | | | | | | | |
| 5a.  Per capita GDP | 287 | 304 | 263 | 320 | 341 | 362 | 360 | 331 | 348 | 343 |
| 5b.  GDP | 133 | 146 | 130 | 164 | 181 | 199 | 204 | 193 | 210 | 213 |
| 5c.  % of GWP | 0.00 | 0.00 | 0.00 | 0.00 | 0.00 | 0.00 | 0.00 | 0.00 | 0.00 | 0.00 |
| **6.   WA** | | | | | | | | | | |
| 6a.  Per capita GDP | 116 | 126 | 126 | 213 | 284 | 293 | 311 | 327 | 402 | 442 |
| 6b.  GDP | 54 | 61 | 63 | 109 | 151 | 160 | 176 | 191 | 243 | 275 |
| 6c.  % of GWP | 0.00 | 0.00 | 0.00 | 0.00 | 0.00 | 0.00 | 0.00 | 0.00 | 0.00 | 0.00 |
| **Federal Republic of Germany[b]** | | | | | | | | | | |
| **1.   MER** | | | | | | | | | | |
| 1a.  Per capita GDP | 3 042 | 3 530 | 4 219 | 5 581 | 6 166 | 6 751 | 7 199 | 8 339 | 10 354 | 12 314 |
| 1b.  GDP | 184 508 | 215 060 | 258 307 | 343 161 | 380 440 | 417 439 | 445 481 | 515 857 | 639 781 | 759 574 |
| 1c.  % of GWP | 5.78 | 6.15 | 6.42 | 6.99 | 6.85 | 6.72 | 6.64 | 6.82 | 7.12 | 7.37 |
| **2.   PPPs** | | | | | | | | | | |
| 2a.  Per capita GDP | 3 592 | 3 922 | 4 318 | 4 841 | 5 305 | 5 702 | 6 345 | 6 980 | 7 820 | 8 857 |
| 2b.  GDP | 217 837 | 238 980 | 264 361 | 297 662 | 327 317 | 352 565 | 392 633 | 431 799 | 483 183 | 546 307 |
| 2c.  % of GWP | ... | ... | ... | ... | ... | ... | ... | ... | ... | ... |
| **3.   Absolute 1970−1989 PARE** | | | | | | | | | | |
| 3a.  Per capita GDP | 8 211 | 8 409 | 8 722 | 9 092 | 9 085 | 8 921 | 9 397 | 9 677 | 9 967 | 10 398 |
| 3b.  GDP | 497 975 | 512 385 | 533 969 | 559 004 | 560 520 | 551 610 | 581 462 | 598 628 | 615 820 | 641 378 |
| 3c.  % of GWP | 7.01 | 6.92 | 6.85 | 6.74 | 6.61 | 6.41 | 6.43 | 6.34 | 6.26 | 6.31 |
| **4.   Relative 1970−1989 PARE** | | | | | | | | | | |
| 4a.  Per capita GDP | 4 003 | 4 310 | 4 676 | 5 198 | 5 665 | 6 112 | 6 840 | 7 519 | 8 309 | 9 443 |
| 4b.  GDP | 242 798 | 262 639 | 286 260 | 319 587 | 349 538 | 377 911 | 423 259 | 465 146 | 513 412 | 582 461 |
| 4c.  % of GWP | 7.01 | 6.92 | 6.84 | 6.74 | 6.61 | 6.41 | 6.43 | 6.34 | 6.26 | 6.31 |
| **5.   Absolute 1980−1989 PARE** | | | | | | | | | | |
| 5a.  Per capita GDP | 9 985 | 10 226 | 10 607 | 11 057 | 11 049 | 10 849 | 11 427 | 11 768 | 12 120 | 12 645 |
| 5b.  GDP | 605 593 | 623 116 | 649 365 | 679 810 | 681 654 | 670 818 | 707 122 | 727 997 | 748 905 | 779 986 |
| 5c.  % of GWP | 6.96 | 6.87 | 6.79 | 6.69 | 6.57 | 6.38 | 6.39 | 6.31 | 6.24 | 6.29 |
| **6.   WA** | | | | | | | | | | |
| 6a.  Per capita GDP | 3 042 | 3 529 | 4 220 | 5 582 | 6 167 | 6 751 | 7 199 | 8 338 | 10 356 | 12 315 |
| 6b.  GDP | 184 508 | 215 012 | 258 336 | 343 213 | 380 477 | 417 390 | 445 481 | 515 817 | 639 902 | 759 624 |
| 6c.  % of GWP | 5.78 | 6.16 | 6.45 | 7.06 | 6.82 | 6.77 | 6.64 | 6.84 | 7.21 | 7.43 |

| | | | | | | | | | | Averages | | |
| 1980 (11) | 1981 (12) | 1982 (13) | 1983 (14) | 1984 (15) | 1985 (16) | 1986 (17) | 1987 (18) | 1988 (19) | 1989 (20) | 1970–89 (21) | 1970–79 (22) | 1980–89 (23) |
|---|---|---|---|---|---|---|---|---|---|---|---|---|
| 434 | 398 | 388 | 334 | 301 | 378 | 286 | 304 | 335 | 357 | 320 | 273 | 350 |
| 278 | 263 | 265 | 234 | 218 | 281 | 220 | 241 | 273 | 299 | 202 | 147 | 257 |
| 0.00 | 0.00 | 0.00 | 0.00 | 0.00 | 0.00 | 0.00 | 0.00 | 0.00 | 0.00 | 0.00 | 0.00 | 0.00 |
| 647 | 768 | 894 | 841 | 1 112 | 1 151 | 1 203 | 1 267 | 1 396 | 1 526 | 843 | 467 | 1 106 |
| 414 | 507 | 609 | 590 | 805 | 857 | 924 | 1 002 | 1 137 | 1 277 | 532 | 252 | 812 |
| ... | ... | ... | ... | ... | ... | ... | ... | ... | ... | ... | ... | ... |
| 316 | 293 | 317 | 351 | 316 | 306 | 314 | 322 | 343 | 360 | 320 | 306 | 326 |
| 203 | 194 | 216 | 246 | 229 | 228 | 241 | 254 | 279 | 301 | 202 | 165 | 239 |
| 0.00 | 0.00 | 0.00 | 0.00 | 0.00 | 0.00 | 0.00 | 0.00 | 0.00 | 0.00 | 0.00 | 0.00 | 0.00 |
| 313 | 318 | 366 | 419 | 391 | 389 | 407 | 429 | 472 | 516 | 327 | 210 | 408 |
| 201 | 210 | 249 | 294 | 283 | 290 | 313 | 339 | 385 | 432 | 207 | 113 | 300 |
| 0.00 | 0.00 | 0.00 | 0.00 | 0.00 | 0.00 | 0.00 | 0.00 | 0.00 | 0.00 | 0.00 | 0.00 | 0.00 |
| 340 | 315 | 341 | 378 | 340 | 329 | 338 | 346 | 369 | 387 | 344 | 329 | 350 |
| 218 | 209 | 232 | 265 | 246 | 245 | 259 | 273 | 300 | 324 | 217 | 177 | 257 |
| 0.00 | 0.00 | 0.00 | 0.00 | 0.00 | 0.00 | 0.00 | 0.00 | 0.00 | 0.00 | 0.00 | 0.00 | 0.00 |
| 425 | 363 | 358 | 300 | 263 | 295 | 272 | 320 | 319 | 334 | 306 | 275 | 324 |
| 272 | 240 | 244 | 211 | 190 | 220 | 209 | 253 | 260 | 280 | 193 | 148 | 238 |
| 0.00 | 0.00 | 0.00 | 0.00 | 0.00 | 0.00 | 0.00 | 0.00 | 0.00 | 0.00 | 0.00 | 0.00 | 0.00 |
| 13 213 | 11 098 | 10 741 | 10 725 | 10 102 | 10 189 | 14 582 | 18 243 | 19 162 | 19 202 | 10 192 | 6 735 | 13 763 |
| 813 498 | 681 827 | 658 393 | 656 028 | 616 950 | 621 770 | 890 055 | 1 114 639 | 1 172 533 | 1 176 632 | 628 097 | 415 961 | 840 233 |
| 7.02 | 5.82 | 5.66 | 5.53 | 5.06 | 4.94 | 5.98 | 6.49 | 6.14 | 5.87 | 6.17 | 6.82 | 5.88 |
| 9 779 | 10 514 | 11 090 | 11 661 | 12 412 | 12 741 | 13 299 | 13 918 | 14 894 | 16 097 | 9 159 | 5 752 | 12 673 |
| 602 071 | 645 976 | 679 807 | 713 307 | 758 017 | 777 504 | 811 726 | 850 398 | 911 385 | 986 341 | 564 459 | 355 264 | 773 653 |
| ... | ... | ... | ... | ... | ... | ... | ... | ... | ... | ... | ... | ... |
| 10 560 | 10 599 | 10 555 | 10 736 | 11 056 | 11 284 | 11 547 | 11 746 | 12 162 | 12 626 | 10 192 | 9 152 | 11 317 |
| 650 126 | 651 203 | 647 001 | 656 711 | 675 204 | 688 607 | 704 754 | 717 708 | 744 194 | 773 677 | 628 097 | 565 275 | 690 918 |
| 6.26 | 6.15 | 6.07 | 5.99 | 5.89 | 5.80 | 5.77 | 5.68 | 5.64 | 5.69 | 6.17 | 6.56 | 5.88 |
| 10 467 | 11 501 | 12 192 | 12 821 | 13 675 | 14 336 | 14 964 | 15 661 | 16 759 | 18 112 | 10 078 | 6 190 | 14 084 |
| 644 444 | 706 587 | 747 373 | 784 230 | 835 197 | 874 851 | 913 357 | 956 872 | 1 025 494 | 1 109 835 | 621 063 | 382 301 | 859 824 |
| 6.26 | 6.15 | 6.07 | 5.99 | 5.89 | 5.80 | 5.77 | 5.68 | 5.64 | 5.69 | 6.04 | 6.51 | 5.86 |
| 12 842 | 12 890 | 12 836 | 13 056 | 13 445 | 13 723 | 14 042 | 14 285 | 14 790 | 15 355 | 12 395 | 11 130 | 13 763 |
| 790 625 | 791 934 | 786 824 | 798 632 | 821 123 | 837 422 | 857 058 | 872 812 | 905 021 | 940 876 | 763 835 | 687 437 | 840 233 |
| 6.25 | 6.15 | 6.07 | 5.99 | 5.89 | 5.81 | 5.78 | 5.69 | 5.66 | 5.71 | 6.16 | 6.53 | 5.88 |
| 13 216 | 11 098 | 10 742 | 10 724 | 10 102 | 10 189 | 14 573 | 18 269 | 19 639 | 19 406 | 10 227 | 6 735 | 13 834 |
| 813 646 | 681 827 | 658 504 | 655 961 | 616 963 | 621 776 | 889 449 | 1 116 257 | 1 201 763 | 1 189 124 | 630 251 | 415 976 | 844 527 |
| 7.06 | 5.78 | 5.65 | 5.53 | 5.05 | 4.92 | 6.05 | 6.70 | 6.42 | 6.06 | 6.24 | 6.86 | 5.97 |

**Table A.1**  Total and per capita gross domestic product of individual countries or areas, expressed in United States dollars, and their individual shares of gross world product, based on alternative conversion rates, 1970−1989 [*cont.*]

| Country or area | 1970 (1) | 1971 (2) | 1972 (3) | 1973 (4) | 1974 (5) | 1975 (6) | 1976 (7) | 1977 (8) | 1978 (9) | 1979 (10) |
|---|---|---|---|---|---|---|---|---|---|---|
| **German Democratic Republic (former)**[b] | | | | | | | | | | |
| **1.    MER** | | | | | | | | | | |
| 1a.   Per capita GDP | 2 019 | 2 102 | 2 964 | 3 424 | 3 879 | 4 577 | 4 623 | 5 188 | 6 339 | 7 833 |
| 1b.   GDP | 34 438 | 35 801 | 50 371 | 58 017 | 65 526 | 77 120 | 77 738 | 87 111 | 106 302 | 131 216 |
| 1c.   % of GWP | 1.08 | 1.02 | 1.25 | 1.18 | 1.18 | 1.24 | 1.16 | 1.15 | 1.18 | 1.27 |
| **2.    PPPs** | | | | | | | | | | |
| 2a.   Per capita GDP | ... | ... | ... | ... | ... | ... | ... | ... | ... | ... |
| 2b.   GDP | ... | ... | ... | ... | ... | ... | ... | ... | ... | ... |
| 2c.   % of GWP | ... | ... | ... | ... | ... | ... | ... | ... | ... | ... |
| **3.    Absolute 1970−1989 PARE** | | | | | | | | | | |
| 3a.   Per capita GDP | 3 889 | 4 068 | 3 987 | 4 563 | 4 872 | 5 123 | 5 310 | 5 588 | 5 801 | 6 042 |
| 3b.   GDP | 66 349 | 69 293 | 67 750 | 77 310 | 82 311 | 86 322 | 89 303 | 93 814 | 97 283 | 101 221 |
| 3c.   % of GWP | 0.93 | 0.94 | 0.87 | 0.93 | 0.97 | 1.00 | 0.99 | 0.99 | 0.99 | 1.00 |
| **4.    Relative 1970−1989 PARE** | | | | | | | | | | |
| 4a.   Per capita GDP | 1 896 | 2 085 | 2 137 | 2 609 | 3 038 | 3 510 | 3 865 | 4 342 | 4 837 | 5 487 |
| 4b.   GDP | 32 350 | 35 518 | 36 321 | 44 199 | 51 329 | 59 140 | 65 006 | 72 896 | 81 106 | 91 923 |
| 4c.   % of GWP | 0.93 | 0.94 | 0.87 | 0.93 | 0.97 | 1.00 | 0.99 | 0.99 | 0.99 | 1.00 |
| **5.    Absolute 1980−1989 PARE** | | | | | | | | | | |
| 5a.   Per capita GDP | 4 218 | 4 412 | 4 324 | 4 949 | 5 285 | 5 556 | 5 759 | 6 060 | 6 292 | 6 553 |
| 5b.   GDP | 71 960 | 75 152 | 73 480 | 83 848 | 89 271 | 93 622 | 96 855 | 101 748 | 105 510 | 109 781 |
| 5c.   % of GWP | 0.83 | 0.83 | 0.77 | 0.83 | 0.86 | 0.89 | 0.88 | 0.88 | 0.88 | 0.89 |
| **6.    WA**[a] | | | | | | | | | | |
| 6a.   Per capita GDP | 2 010 | 2 105 | 2 297 | 2 967 | 3 716 | 4 145 | 4 520 | 5 011 | 5 541 | 6 559 |
| 6b.   GDP | 34 296 | 35 861 | 39 033 | 50 277 | 62 773 | 69 840 | 76 019 | 84 137 | 92 920 | 109 883 |
| 6c.   % of GWP | 1.07 | 1.03 | 0.97 | 1.03 | 1.13 | 1.13 | 1.13 | 1.12 | 1.05 | 1.07 |
| **Ghana** | | | | | | | | | | |
| **1.    MER** | | | | | | | | | | |
| 1a.   Per capita GDP | 257 | 277 | 233 | 251 | 271 | 293 | 323 | 353 | 381 | 403 |
| 1b.   GDP | 2 214 | 2 451 | 2 120 | 2 350 | 2 605 | 2 882 | 3 237 | 3 586 | 3 923 | 4 225 |
| 1c.   % of GWP | 0.07 | 0.07 | 0.05 | 0.05 | 0.05 | 0.05 | 0.05 | 0.05 | 0.04 | 0.04 |
| **2.    PPPs** | | | | | | | | | | |
| 2a.   Per capita GDP | 290 | 289 | 289 | 319 | 360 | 340 | 332 | 374 | 512 | 468 |
| 2b.   GDP | 2 494 | 2 555 | 2 627 | 2 984 | 3 464 | 3 341 | 3 328 | 3 794 | 5 274 | 4 904 |
| 2c.   % of GWP | ... | ... | ... | ... | ... | ... | ... | ... | ... | ... |
| **3.    Absolute 1970−1989 PARE** | | | | | | | | | | |
| 3a.   Per capita GDP | 468 | 482 | 457 | 468 | 487 | 417 | 395 | 398 | 426 | 408 |
| 3b.   GDP | 4 033 | 4 258 | 4 152 | 4 382 | 4 682 | 4 100 | 3 955 | 4 045 | 4 388 | 4 278 |
| 3c.   % of GWP | 0.06 | 0.06 | 0.05 | 0.05 | 0.06 | 0.05 | 0.04 | 0.04 | 0.04 | 0.04 |
| **4.    Relative 1970−1989 PARE** | | | | | | | | | | |
| 4a.   Per capita GDP | 228 | 247 | 245 | 268 | 304 | 286 | 288 | 310 | 355 | 371 |
| 4b.   GDP | 1 966 | 2 183 | 2 226 | 2 505 | 2 920 | 2 809 | 2 879 | 3 143 | 3 658 | 3 885 |
| 4c.   % of GWP | 0.06 | 0.06 | 0.05 | 0.05 | 0.06 | 0.05 | 0.04 | 0.04 | 0.04 | 0.04 |
| **5.    Absolute 1980−1989 PARE** | | | | | | | | | | |
| 5a.   Per capita GDP | 605 | 623 | 590 | 605 | 629 | 539 | 511 | 515 | 551 | 527 |
| 5b.   GDP | 5 211 | 5 502 | 5 364 | 5 662 | 6 050 | 5 298 | 5 111 | 5 227 | 5 670 | 5 527 |
| 5c.   % of GWP | 0.06 | 0.06 | 0.06 | 0.06 | 0.06 | 0.05 | 0.05 | 0.05 | 0.05 | 0.04 |
| **6.    WA** | | | | | | | | | | |
| 6a.   Per capita GDP | 257 | 273 | 232 | 321 | 422 | 467 | 567 | 956 | 1 155 | 979 |
| 6b.   GDP | 2 213 | 2 416 | 2 111 | 3 005 | 4 052 | 4 594 | 5 675 | 9 707 | 11 900 | 10 262 |
| 6c.   % of GWP | 0.07 | 0.07 | 0.05 | 0.06 | 0.07 | 0.07 | 0.08 | 0.13 | 0.13 | 0.10 |

| 1980 (11) | 1981 (12) | 1982 (13) | 1983 (14) | 1984 (15) | 1985 (16) | 1986 (17) | 1987 (18) | 1988 (19) | 1989 (20) | Averages 1970–89 (21) | 1970–79 (22) | 1980–89 (23) |
|---|---|---|---|---|---|---|---|---|---|---|---|---|
| 7 501 | 6 756 | 6 312 | 6 566 | 6 232 | 6 371 | 8 867 | 11 150 | 12 133 | 11 200 | 6 271 | 4 289 | 8 258 |
| 125 544 | 113 015 | 105 543 | 109 724 | 103 997 | 106 039 | 147 002 | 183 873 | 198 925 | 182 695 | 105 000 | 72 364 | 137 636 |
| 1.08 | 0.97 | 0.91 | 0.93 | 0.85 | 0.84 | 0.99 | 1.07 | 1.04 | 0.91 | 1.03 | 1.19 | 0.96 |
| ... | ... | ... | ... | ... | ... | ... | ... | ... | ... | ... | ... | ... |
| ... | ... | ... | ... | ... | ... | ... | ... | ... | ... | ... | ... | ... |
| ... | ... | ... | ... | ... | ... | ... | ... | ... | ... | ... | ... | ... |
| 6 314 | 6 580 | 6 770 | 7 083 | 7 440 | 7 834 | 8 175 | 8 491 | 8 804 | 9 028 | 6 271 | 4 925 | 7 614 |
| 105 691 | 110 070 | 113 201 | 118 373 | 124 159 | 130 390 | 135 518 | 140 020 | 144 350 | 147 268 | 105 000 | 83 096 | 126 904 |
| 1.02 | 1.04 | 1.06 | 1.08 | 1.08 | 1.10 | 1.11 | 1.11 | 1.09 | 1.08 | 1.03 | 0.96 | 1.08 |
| 6 259 | 7 140 | 7 820 | 8 458 | 9 203 | 9 952 | 10 594 | 11 320 | 12 132 | 12 951 | 6 443 | 3 377 | 9 528 |
| 104 767 | 119 431 | 130 762 | 141 358 | 153 579 | 165 655 | 175 631 | 186 680 | 198 914 | 211 255 | 107 891 | 56 979 | 158 803 |
| 1.02 | 1.04 | 1.06 | 1.08 | 1.08 | 1.10 | 1.11 | 1.11 | 1.09 | 1.08 | 1.05 | 0.97 | 1.08 |
| 6 848 | 7 136 | 7 342 | 7 682 | 8 069 | 8 496 | 8 866 | 9 209 | 9 548 | 9 792 | 6 801 | 5 342 | 8 258 |
| 114 629 | 119 378 | 122 774 | 128 383 | 134 659 | 141 416 | 146 979 | 151 861 | 156 557 | 159 722 | 113 879 | 90 123 | 137 636 |
| 0.91 | 0.93 | 0.95 | 0.96 | 0.97 | 0.98 | 0.99 | 0.99 | 0.98 | 0.97 | 0.92 | 0.86 | 0.96 |
| 7 492 | 7 630 | 7 032 | 6 799 | 6 672 | 6 710 | 7 331 | 8 744 | 10 964 | 11 811 | 5 973 | 3 882 | 8 073 |
| 125 403 | 127 631 | 117 576 | 113 626 | 111 345 | 111 688 | 121 527 | 144 201 | 179 761 | 192 654 | 100 023 | 65 504 | 134 541 |
| 1.09 | 1.08 | 1.01 | 0.96 | 0.91 | 0.88 | 0.83 | 0.87 | 0.96 | 0.98 | 0.99 | 1.08 | 0.95 |
| 446 | 418 | 480 | 515 | 624 | 494 | 432 | 354 | 370 | 353 | 404 | 304 | 445 |
| 4 788 | 4 629 | 5 510 | 6 135 | 7 730 | 6 346 | 5 733 | 4 854 | 5 229 | 5 137 | 4 284 | 2 959 | 5 609 |
| 0.04 | 0.04 | 0.05 | 0.05 | 0.06 | 0.05 | 0.04 | 0.03 | 0.03 | 0.03 | 0.04 | 0.05 | 0.04 |
| 522 | 600 | 601 | 602 | 599 | 606 | 629 | 657 | 699 | 749 | 539 | 358 | 632 |
| 5 600 | 6 646 | 6 899 | 7 175 | 7 424 | 7 781 | 8 351 | 9 004 | 9 883 | 10 916 | 5 722 | 3 477 | 7 968 |
| ... | ... | ... | ... | ... | ... | ... | ... | ... | ... | ... | ... | ... |
| 400 | 375 | 336 | 309 | 323 | 328 | 333 | 338 | 349 | 359 | 404 | 435 | 344 |
| 4 298 | 4 147 | 3 860 | 3 684 | 4 003 | 4 206 | 4 425 | 4 638 | 4 925 | 5 225 | 4 284 | 4 227 | 4 341 |
| 0.04 | 0.04 | 0.04 | 0.03 | 0.03 | 0.04 | 0.04 | 0.04 | 0.04 | 0.04 | 0.04 | 0.05 | 0.04 |
| 397 | 407 | 389 | 369 | 400 | 416 | 432 | 451 | 480 | 515 | 388 | 290 | 429 |
| 4 260 | 4 500 | 4 459 | 4 399 | 4 951 | 5 344 | 5 735 | 6 183 | 6 787 | 7 496 | 4 114 | 2 817 | 5 411 |
| 0.04 | 0.04 | 0.04 | 0.03 | 0.03 | 0.04 | 0.04 | 0.04 | 0.04 | 0.04 | 0.04 | 0.05 | 0.04 |
| 517 | 484 | 435 | 399 | 418 | 423 | 431 | 437 | 450 | 463 | 522 | 562 | 445 |
| 5 553 | 5 359 | 4 988 | 4 760 | 5 172 | 5 434 | 5 718 | 5 992 | 6 364 | 6 752 | 5 536 | 5 462 | 5 609 |
| 0.04 | 0.04 | 0.04 | 0.04 | 0.04 | 0.04 | 0.04 | 0.04 | 0.04 | 0.04 | 0.04 | 0.05 | 0.04 |
| 1 451 | 2 386 | 2 740 | 1 748 | 607 | 491 | 432 | 354 | 370 | 353 | 872 | 575 | 1 023 |
| 15 583 | 26 409 | 31 437 | 20 842 | 7 518 | 6 310 | 5 733 | 4 853 | 5 228 | 5 137 | 9 249 | 5 594 | 12 905 |
| 0.14 | 0.22 | 0.27 | 0.18 | 0.06 | 0.05 | 0.04 | 0.03 | 0.03 | 0.03 | 0.09 | 0.09 | 0.09 |

**Table A.1**   Total and per capita gross domestic product of individual countries or areas,
expressed in United States dollars, and their individual shares of gross world
product, based on alternative conversion rates, 1970−1989 [*cont.*]

| Country or area | 1970 (1) | 1971 (2) | 1972 (3) | 1973 (4) | 1974 (5) | 1975 (6) | 1976 (7) | 1977 (8) | 1978 (9) | 1979 (10) |
|---|---|---|---|---|---|---|---|---|---|---|
| **Greece** | | | | | | | | | | |
| **1.    MER** | | | | | | | | | | |
| 1a.    Per capita GDP | 1 133 | 1 246 | 1 419 | 1 834 | 2 097 | 2 318 | 2 469 | 2 821 | 3 360 | 4 046 |
| 1b.    GDP | 9 964 | 11 010 | 12 591 | 16 343 | 18 807 | 20 972 | 22 590 | 26 161 | 31 607 | 38 576 |
| 1c.    % of GWP | 0.31 | 0.31 | 0.31 | 0.33 | 0.34 | 0.34 | 0.34 | 0.35 | 0.35 | 0.37 |
| **2.    PPPs** | | | | | | | | | | |
| 2a.    Per capita GDP | 1 482 | 1 646 | 1 889 | 2 261 | 2 222 | 2 618 | 2 916 | 3 193 | 3 574 | 3 986 |
| 2b.    GDP | 13 037 | 14 540 | 16 759 | 20 150 | 19 929 | 23 686 | 26 686 | 29 609 | 33 616 | 38 006 |
| 2c.    % of GWP | ... | ... | ... | ... | ... | ... | ... | ... | ... | ... |
| **3.    Absolute 1970−1989 PARE** | | | | | | | | | | |
| 3a.    Per capita GDP | 2 383 | 2 541 | 2 756 | 2 943 | 2 819 | 2 963 | 3 116 | 3 180 | 3 345 | 3 422 |
| 3b.    GDP | 20 959 | 22 451 | 24 445 | 26 235 | 25 281 | 26 810 | 28 515 | 29 493 | 31 468 | 32 630 |
| 3c.    % of GWP | 0.29 | 0.30 | 0.31 | 0.32 | 0.30 | 0.31 | 0.32 | 0.31 | 0.32 | 0.32 |
| **4.    Relative 1970−1989 PARE** | | | | | | | | | | |
| 4a.    Per capita GDP | 1 162 | 1 303 | 1 477 | 1 683 | 1 758 | 2 030 | 2 269 | 2 471 | 2 789 | 3 108 |
| 4b.    GDP | 10 219 | 11 508 | 13 105 | 14 999 | 15 765 | 18 368 | 20 757 | 22 917 | 26 235 | 29 632 |
| 4c.    % of GWP | 0.29 | 0.30 | 0.31 | 0.32 | 0.30 | 0.31 | 0.32 | 0.31 | 0.32 | 0.32 |
| **5.    Absolute 1980−1989 PARE** | | | | | | | | | | |
| 5a.    Per capita GDP | 2 789 | 2 974 | 3 225 | 3 445 | 3 299 | 3 468 | 3 647 | 3 722 | 3 915 | 4 005 |
| 5b.    GDP | 24 527 | 26 274 | 28 607 | 30 701 | 29 584 | 31 374 | 33 370 | 34 514 | 36 825 | 38 184 |
| 5c.    % of GWP | 0.28 | 0.29 | 0.30 | 0.30 | 0.29 | 0.30 | 0.30 | 0.30 | 0.31 | 0.31 |
| **6.    WA** | | | | | | | | | | |
| 6a.    Per capita GDP | 1 133 | 1 246 | 1 419 | 1 834 | 2 097 | 2 318 | 2 469 | 2 821 | 3 360 | 4 046 |
| 6b.    GDP | 9 964 | 11 010 | 12 591 | 16 343 | 18 807 | 20 972 | 22 590 | 26 161 | 31 607 | 38 576 |
| 6c.    % of GWP | 0.31 | 0.32 | 0.31 | 0.34 | 0.34 | 0.34 | 0.34 | 0.35 | 0.36 | 0.38 |
| **Grenada** | | | | | | | | | | |
| **1.    MER** | | | | | | | | | | |
| 1a.    Per capita GDP | 285 | 288 | 317 | 319 | 330 | 406 | 411 | 465 | 603 | 717 |
| 1b.    GDP | 27 | 27 | 30 | 30 | 31 | 39 | 39 | 43 | 56 | 65 |
| 1c.    % of GWP | 0.00 | 0.00 | 0.00 | 0.00 | 0.00 | 0.00 | 0.00 | 0.00 | 0.00 | 0.00 |
| **2.    PPPs** | | | | | | | | | | |
| 2a.    Per capita GDP | ... | ... | ... | ... | ... | ... | ... | ... | ... | ... |
| 2b.    GDP | ... | ... | ... | ... | ... | ... | ... | ... | ... | ... |
| 2c.    % of GWP | ... | ... | ... | ... | ... | ... | ... | ... | ... | ... |
| **3.    Absolute 1970−1989 PARE** | | | | | | | | | | |
| 3a.    Per capita GDP | 678 | 725 | 805 | 693 | 548 | 608 | 670 | 718 | 784 | 812 |
| 3b.    GDP | 64 | 69 | 76 | 66 | 52 | 58 | 63 | 67 | 72 | 74 |
| 3c.    % of GWP | 0.00 | 0.00 | 0.00 | 0.00 | 0.00 | 0.00 | 0.00 | 0.00 | 0.00 | 0.00 |
| **4.    Relative 1970−1989 PARE** | | | | | | | | | | |
| 4a.    Per capita GDP | 330 | 371 | 431 | 396 | 342 | 417 | 488 | 558 | 654 | 737 |
| 4b.    GDP | 31 | 35 | 41 | 38 | 32 | 40 | 46 | 52 | 60 | 67 |
| 4c.    % of GWP | 0.00 | 0.00 | 0.00 | 0.00 | 0.00 | 0.00 | 0.00 | 0.00 | 0.00 | 0.00 |
| **5.    Absolute 1980−1989 PARE** | | | | | | | | | | |
| 5a.    Per capita GDP | 880 | 941 | 1 045 | 899 | 711 | 789 | 871 | 932 | 1 019 | 1 054 |
| 5b.    GDP | 84 | 89 | 99 | 85 | 68 | 75 | 82 | 87 | 94 | 96 |
| 5c.    % of GWP | 0.00 | 0.00 | 0.00 | 0.00 | 0.00 | 0.00 | 0.00 | 0.00 | 0.00 | 0.00 |
| **6.    WA** | | | | | | | | | | |
| 6a.    Per capita GDP | 285 | 288 | 317 | 319 | 330 | 406 | 411 | 465 | 603 | 717 |
| 6b.    GDP | 27 | 27 | 30 | 30 | 31 | 39 | 39 | 43 | 56 | 65 |
| 6c.    % of GWP | 0.00 | 0.00 | 0.00 | 0.00 | 0.00 | 0.00 | 0.00 | 0.00 | 0.00 | 0.00 |

| | | | | | | | | | | Averages | | |
|---|---|---|---|---|---|---|---|---|---|---|---|---|
| 1980 (11) | 1981 (12) | 1982 (13) | 1983 (14) | 1984 (15) | 1985 (16) | 1986 (17) | 1987 (18) | 1988 (19) | 1989 (20) | 1970–89 (21) | 1970–79 (22) | 1980–89 (23) |
| 4 163 | 3 802 | 3 933 | 3 548 | 3 411 | 3 365 | 3 940 | 4 603 | 5 280 | 5 401 | 3 227 | 2 316 | 4 136 |
| 40 147 | 36 999 | 38 541 | 34 967 | 33 762 | 33 433 | 39 275 | 45 997 | 52 868 | 54 177 | 30 939 | 20 862 | 41 017 |
| 0.35 | 0.32 | 0.33 | 0.29 | 0.28 | 0.27 | 0.26 | 0.27 | 0.28 | 0.27 | 0.30 | 0.34 | 0.29 |
| 4 384 | 4 765 | 5 044 | 5 179 | 5 450 | 5 716 | 5 893 | 6 018 | 6 460 | 6 904 | 4 113 | 2 620 | 5 573 |
| 42 270 | 46 365 | 49 433 | 51 035 | 53 942 | 56 792 | 58 736 | 60 139 | 64 689 | 69 258 | 39 434 | 23 602 | 55 266 |
| ... | ... | ... | ... | ... | ... | ... | ... | ... | ... | ... | ... | ... |
| 3 443 | 3 414 | 3 403 | 3 398 | 3 476 | 3 571 | 3 609 | 3 583 | 3 721 | 3 820 | 3 227 | 2 978 | 3 535 |
| 33 201 | 33 220 | 33 351 | 33 485 | 34 406 | 35 480 | 35 972 | 35 802 | 37 260 | 38 321 | 30 939 | 26 829 | 35 050 |
| 0.32 | 0.31 | 0.31 | 0.31 | 0.30 | 0.30 | 0.29 | 0.28 | 0.28 | 0.28 | 0.30 | 0.31 | 0.30 |
| 3 413 | 3 704 | 3 931 | 4 058 | 4 300 | 4 537 | 4 677 | 4 777 | 5 128 | 5 480 | 3 229 | 2 037 | 4 395 |
| 32 911 | 36 045 | 38 525 | 39 987 | 42 559 | 45 076 | 46 619 | 47 733 | 51 344 | 54 971 | 30 964 | 18 351 | 43 577 |
| 0.32 | 0.31 | 0.31 | 0.31 | 0.30 | 0.30 | 0.29 | 0.28 | 0.28 | 0.28 | 0.30 | 0.31 | 0.30 |
| 4 029 | 3 995 | 3 982 | 3 977 | 4 068 | 4 179 | 4 223 | 4 193 | 4 355 | 4 471 | 3 776 | 3 485 | 4 136 |
| 38 854 | 38 875 | 39 028 | 39 185 | 40 264 | 41 520 | 42 096 | 41 897 | 43 603 | 44 844 | 36 206 | 31 396 | 41 017 |
| 0.31 | 0.30 | 0.30 | 0.29 | 0.29 | 0.29 | 0.28 | 0.27 | 0.27 | 0.27 | 0.29 | 0.30 | 0.29 |
| 4 163 | 3 802 | 3 933 | 3 548 | 3 411 | 3 365 | 3 940 | 4 602 | 5 281 | 5 400 | 3 227 | 2 316 | 4 136 |
| 40 147 | 36 999 | 38 541 | 34 965 | 33 762 | 33 433 | 39 275 | 45 987 | 52 883 | 54 171 | 30 939 | 20 862 | 41 016 |
| 0.35 | 0.31 | 0.33 | 0.29 | 0.28 | 0.26 | 0.27 | 0.28 | 0.28 | 0.28 | 0.31 | 0.34 | 0.29 |
| 831 | 902 | 996 | 1 052 | 1 157 | 1 310 | 1 492 | 1 729 | 1 950 | 2 181 | 872 | 408 | 1 352 |
| 75 | 80 | 89 | 94 | 102 | 115 | 130 | 150 | 168 | 188 | 79 | 39 | 119 |
| 0.00 | 0.00 | 0.00 | 0.00 | 0.00 | 0.00 | 0.00 | 0.00 | 0.00 | 0.00 | 0.00 | 0.00 | 0.00 |
| ... | ... | ... | ... | ... | ... | ... | ... | ... | ... | ... | ... | ... |
| ... | ... | ... | ... | ... | ... | ... | ... | ... | ... | ... | ... | ... |
| ... | ... | ... | ... | ... | ... | ... | ... | ... | ... | ... | ... | ... |
| 822 | 844 | 903 | 928 | 983 | 1 063 | 1 117 | 1 174 | 1 269 | 1 347 | 872 | 696 | 1 041 |
| 74 | 75 | 80 | 83 | 86 | 94 | 97 | 102 | 109 | 116 | 79 | 66 | 92 |
| 0.00 | 0.00 | 0.00 | 0.00 | 0.00 | 0.00 | 0.00 | 0.00 | 0.00 | 0.00 | 0.00 | 0.00 | 0.00 |
| 815 | 915 | 1 043 | 1 109 | 1 216 | 1 351 | 1 448 | 1 566 | 1 748 | 1 933 | 880 | 466 | 1 308 |
| 73 | 81 | 93 | 99 | 107 | 119 | 126 | 136 | 150 | 166 | 80 | 44 | 115 |
| 0.00 | 0.00 | 0.00 | 0.00 | 0.00 | 0.00 | 0.00 | 0.00 | 0.00 | 0.00 | 0.00 | 0.00 | 0.00 |
| 1 068 | 1 095 | 1 173 | 1 205 | 1 276 | 1 380 | 1 451 | 1 525 | 1 647 | 1 749 | 1 132 | 903 | 1 352 |
| 96 | 97 | 104 | 107 | 112 | 121 | 126 | 133 | 142 | 150 | 102 | 86 | 119 |
| 0.00 | 0.00 | 0.00 | 0.00 | 0.00 | 0.00 | 0.00 | 0.00 | 0.00 | 0.00 | 0.00 | 0.00 | 0.00 |
| 831 | 902 | 996 | 1 052 | 1 157 | 1 310 | 1 492 | 1 729 | 1 950 | 2 181 | 872 | 408 | 1 352 |
| 75 | 80 | 89 | 94 | 102 | 115 | 130 | 150 | 168 | 188 | 79 | 39 | 119 |
| 0.00 | 0.00 | 0.00 | 0.00 | 0.00 | 0.00 | 0.00 | 0.00 | 0.00 | 0.00 | 0.00 | 0.00 | 0.00 |

**Table A.1**     Total and per capita gross domestic product of individual countries or areas,
expressed in United States dollars, and their individual shares of gross world
product, based on alternative conversion rates, 1970–1989 [cont.]

| Country or area | 1970 (1) | 1971 (2) | 1972 (3) | 1973 (4) | 1974 (5) | 1975 (6) | 1976 (7) | 1977 (8) | 1978 (9) | 1979 (10) |
|---|---|---|---|---|---|---|---|---|---|---|
| **Guadeloupe** | | | | | | | | | | |
| 1.  **MER** | | | | | | | | | | |
| 1a.  Per capita GDP | 746 | 869 | 1 052 | 1 409 | 1 557 | 2 004 | 2 080 | 2 308 | 3 088 | 3 748 |
| 1b.  GDP | 239 | 281 | 342 | 461 | 511 | 659 | 684 | 759 | 1 013 | 1 226 |
| 1c.  % of GWP | 0.01 | 0.01 | 0.01 | 0.01 | 0.01 | 0.01 | 0.01 | 0.01 | 0.01 | 0.01 |
| 2.  **PPPs** | | | | | | | | | | |
| 2a.  Per capita GDP | ... | ... | ... | ... | ... | ... | ... | ... | ... | ... |
| 2b.  GDP | ... | ... | ... | ... | ... | ... | ... | ... | ... | ... |
| 2c.  % of GWP | ... | ... | ... | ... | ... | ... | ... | ... | ... | ... |
| 3.  **Absolute 1970–1989 PARE** | | | | | | | | | | |
| 3a.  Per capita GDP | 2 155 | 2 340 | 2 404 | 2 659 | 2 738 | 2 684 | 2 861 | 2 986 | 3 173 | 3 498 |
| 3b.  GDP | 692 | 756 | 781 | 870 | 898 | 883 | 941 | 982 | 1 041 | 1 144 |
| 3c.  % of GWP | 0.01 | 0.01 | 0.01 | 0.01 | 0.01 | 0.01 | 0.01 | 0.01 | 0.01 | 0.01 |
| 4.  **Relative 1970–1989 PARE** | | | | | | | | | | |
| 4a.  Per capita GDP | 1 051 | 1 199 | 1 289 | 1 520 | 1 708 | 1 839 | 2 083 | 2 320 | 2 645 | 3 176 |
| 4b.  GDP | 337 | 387 | 419 | 497 | 560 | 605 | 685 | 763 | 868 | 1 039 |
| 4c.  % of GWP | 0.01 | 0.01 | 0.01 | 0.01 | 0.01 | 0.01 | 0.01 | 0.01 | 0.01 | 0.01 |
| 5.  **Absolute 1980–1989 PARE** | | | | | | | | | | |
| 5a.  Per capita GDP | 2 671 | 2 900 | 2 979 | 3 296 | 3 394 | 3 327 | 3 547 | 3 701 | 3 933 | 4 335 |
| 5b.  GDP | 857 | 937 | 968 | 1 078 | 1 113 | 1 095 | 1 167 | 1 218 | 1 290 | 1 418 |
| 5c.  % of GWP | 0.01 | 0.01 | 0.01 | 0.01 | 0.01 | 0.01 | 0.01 | 0.01 | 0.01 | 0.01 |
| 6.  **WA**[a] | | | | | | | | | | |
| 6a.  Per capita GDP | 732 | 821 | 917 | 1 162 | 1 385 | 1 615 | 1 919 | 2 235 | 2 575 | 3 224 |
| 6b.  GDP | 235 | 265 | 298 | 380 | 454 | 531 | 631 | 735 | 845 | 1 054 |
| 6c.  % of GWP | 0.01 | 0.01 | 0.01 | 0.01 | 0.01 | 0.01 | 0.01 | 0.01 | 0.01 | 0.01 |
| **Guatemala** | | | | | | | | | | |
| 1.  **MER** | | | | | | | | | | |
| 1a.  Per capita GDP | 363 | 368 | 379 | 451 | 540 | 605 | 705 | 861 | 928 | 1 026 |
| 1b.  GDP | 1 904 | 1 985 | 2 102 | 2 569 | 3 162 | 3 646 | 4 365 | 5 481 | 6 071 | 6 903 |
| 1c.  % of GWP | 0.06 | 0.06 | 0.05 | 0.05 | 0.06 | 0.06 | 0.07 | 0.07 | 0.07 | 0.07 |
| 2.  **PPPs** | | | | | | | | | | |
| 2a.  Per capita GDP | 874 | 930 | 980 | 1 039 | 1 150 | 1 236 | 1 363 | 1 560 | 1 681 | 1 833 |
| 2b.  GDP | 4 586 | 5 013 | 5 433 | 5 920 | 6 735 | 7 445 | 8 440 | 9 927 | 10 999 | 12 333 |
| 2c.  % of GWP | ... | ... | ... | ... | ... | ... | ... | ... | ... | ... |
| 3.  **Absolute 1970–1989 PARE** | | | | | | | | | | |
| 3a.  Per capita GDP | 789 | 811 | 847 | 879 | 910 | 902 | 943 | 989 | 1 010 | 1 028 |
| 3b.  GDP | 4 141 | 4 373 | 4 693 | 5 011 | 5 331 | 5 435 | 5 836 | 6 292 | 6 607 | 6 918 |
| 3c.  % of GWP | 0.06 | 0.06 | 0.06 | 0.06 | 0.06 | 0.06 | 0.06 | 0.07 | 0.07 | 0.07 |
| 4.  **Relative 1970–1989 PARE** | | | | | | | | | | |
| 4a.  Per capita GDP | 385 | 416 | 454 | 503 | 567 | 618 | 686 | 768 | 842 | 934 |
| 4b.  GDP | 2 019 | 2 241 | 2 516 | 2 865 | 3 324 | 3 723 | 4 248 | 4 889 | 5 508 | 6 282 |
| 4c.  % of GWP | 0.06 | 0.06 | 0.06 | 0.06 | 0.06 | 0.06 | 0.06 | 0.07 | 0.07 | 0.07 |
| 5.  **Absolute 1980–1989 PARE** | | | | | | | | | | |
| 5a.  Per capita GDP | 974 | 1 000 | 1 044 | 1 085 | 1 122 | 1 113 | 1 163 | 1 219 | 1 246 | 1 269 |
| 5b.  GDP | 5 108 | 5 394 | 5 789 | 6 182 | 6 576 | 6 704 | 7 200 | 7 762 | 8 150 | 8 533 |
| 5c.  % of GWP | 0.06 | 0.06 | 0.06 | 0.06 | 0.06 | 0.06 | 0.07 | 0.07 | 0.07 | 0.07 |
| 6.  **WA** | | | | | | | | | | |
| 6a.  Per capita GDP | 363 | 368 | 379 | 451 | 540 | 605 | 705 | 861 | 928 | 1 026 |
| 6b.  GDP | 1 904 | 1 985 | 2 102 | 2 569 | 3 162 | 3 646 | 4 365 | 5 481 | 6 071 | 6 903 |
| 6c.  % of GWP | 0.06 | 0.06 | 0.05 | 0.05 | 0.06 | 0.06 | 0.07 | 0.07 | 0.07 | 0.07 |

| 1980 (11) | 1981 (12) | 1982 (13) | 1983 (14) | 1984 (15) | 1985 (16) | 1986 (17) | 1987 (18) | 1988 (19) | 1989 (20) | Averages 1970−89 (21) | 1970−79 (22) | 1980−89 (23) |
|---|---|---|---|---|---|---|---|---|---|---|---|---|
| 4 241 | 3 631 | 3 487 | 3 351 | 3 119 | 3 216 | 4 542 | 5 802 | 6 096 | 6 073 | 3 170 | 1 880 | 4 372 |
| 1 387 | 1 191 | 1 147 | 1 106 | 1 035 | 1 074 | 1 526 | 1 955 | 2 066 | 2 071 | 1 037 | 617 | 1 456 |
| 0.01 | 0.01 | 0.01 | 0.01 | 0.01 | 0.01 | 0.01 | 0.01 | 0.01 | 0.01 | 0.01 | 0.01 | 0.01 |
| ... | ... | ... | ... | ... | ... | ... | ... | ... | ... | ... | ... | ... |
| ... | ... | ... | ... | ... | ... | ... | ... | ... | ... | ... | ... | ... |
| ... | ... | ... | ... | ... | ... | ... | ... | ... | ... | ... | ... | ... |
| 3 335 | 3 258 | 3 340 | 3 371 | 3 369 | 3 323 | 3 422 | 3 803 | 3 918 | 4 070 | 3 170 | 2 736 | 3 527 |
| 1 090 | 1 069 | 1 099 | 1 112 | 1 118 | 1 110 | 1 150 | 1 282 | 1 328 | 1 388 | 1 037 | 899 | 1 175 |
| 0.01 | 0.01 | 0.01 | 0.01 | 0.01 | 0.01 | 0.01 | 0.01 | 0.01 | 0.01 | 0.01 | 0.01 | 0.01 |
| 3 305 | 3 535 | 3 858 | 4 025 | 4 167 | 4 222 | 4 435 | 5 071 | 5 399 | 5 838 | 3 182 | 1 875 | 4 400 |
| 1 081 | 1 159 | 1 269 | 1 328 | 1 383 | 1 410 | 1 490 | 1 709 | 1 830 | 1 991 | 1 041 | 616 | 1 465 |
| 0.01 | 0.01 | 0.01 | 0.01 | 0.01 | 0.01 | 0.01 | 0.01 | 0.01 | 0.01 | 0.01 | 0.01 | 0.01 |
| 4 133 | 4 038 | 4 139 | 4 178 | 4 176 | 4 119 | 4 242 | 4 714 | 4 856 | 5 045 | 3 930 | 3 391 | 4 372 |
| 1 352 | 1 324 | 1 362 | 1 379 | 1 386 | 1 376 | 1 425 | 1 589 | 1 646 | 1 720 | 1 285 | 1 114 | 1 456 |
| 0.01 | 0.01 | 0.01 | 0.01 | 0.01 | 0.01 | 0.01 | 0.01 | 0.01 | 0.01 | 0.01 | 0.01 | 0.01 |
| 3 642 | 3 735 | 3 793 | 3 535 | 3 320 | 3 196 | 3 581 | 4 672 | 5 728 | 6 203 | 2 946 | 1 653 | 4 155 |
| 1 191 | 1 225 | 1 248 | 1 166 | 1 102 | 1 067 | 1 203 | 1 574 | 1 942 | 2 115 | 963 | 543 | 1 383 |
| 0.01 | 0.01 | 0.01 | 0.01 | 0.01 | 0.01 | 0.01 | 0.01 | 0.01 | 0.01 | 0.01 | 0.01 | 0.01 |
| 1 139 | 1 210 | 1 192 | 1 203 | 1 224 | 1 404 | 1 034 | 840 | 910 | 954 | 917 | 643 | 1 107 |
| 7 879 | 8 608 | 8 717 | 9 050 | 9 470 | 11 180 | 8 470 | 7 084 | 7 901 | 8 527 | 6 254 | 3 819 | 8 689 |
| 0.07 | 0.07 | 0.07 | 0.08 | 0.08 | 0.09 | 0.06 | 0.04 | 0.04 | 0.04 | 0.06 | 0.06 | 0.06 |
| 2 050 | 2 161 | 2 158 | 2 128 | 2 159 | 2 067 | 2 052 | 2 124 | 2 213 | 2 316 | 1 803 | 1 293 | 2 154 |
| 14 177 | 15 371 | 15 789 | 16 015 | 16 711 | 16 465 | 16 820 | 17 916 | 19 211 | 20 692 | 12 300 | 7 683 | 16 917 |
| ... | ... | ... | ... | ... | ... | ... | ... | ... | ... | ... | ... | ... |
| 1 038 | 1 016 | 953 | 903 | 881 | 852 | 829 | 834 | 840 | 845 | 917 | 920 | 897 |
| 7 177 | 7 225 | 6 969 | 6 791 | 6 823 | 6 783 | 6 792 | 7 033 | 7 296 | 7 549 | 6 254 | 5 464 | 7 044 |
| 0.07 | 0.07 | 0.07 | 0.06 | 0.06 | 0.06 | 0.06 | 0.06 | 0.06 | 0.06 | 0.06 | 0.06 | 0.06 |
| 1 029 | 1 102 | 1 100 | 1 078 | 1 090 | 1 082 | 1 074 | 1 112 | 1 158 | 1 212 | 915 | 633 | 1 111 |
| 7 114 | 7 839 | 8 050 | 8 109 | 8 439 | 8 617 | 8 802 | 9 376 | 10 054 | 10 829 | 6 242 | 3 762 | 8 723 |
| 0.07 | 0.07 | 0.07 | 0.06 | 0.06 | 0.06 | 0.06 | 0.06 | 0.06 | 0.06 | 0.06 | 0.06 | 0.06 |
| 1 280 | 1 253 | 1 175 | 1 113 | 1 087 | 1 051 | 1 022 | 1 029 | 1 037 | 1 042 | 1 131 | 1 134 | 1 107 |
| 8 853 | 8 912 | 8 596 | 8 377 | 8 416 | 8 367 | 8 378 | 8 675 | 9 000 | 9 312 | 7 714 | 6 740 | 8 689 |
| 0.07 | 0.07 | 0.07 | 0.06 | 0.06 | 0.06 | 0.06 | 0.06 | 0.06 | 0.06 | 0.06 | 0.06 | 0.06 |
| 1 139 | 1 210 | 1 192 | 1 203 | 1 224 | 1 221 | 882 | 840 | 903 | 949 | 896 | 643 | 1 071 |
| 7 879 | 8 608 | 8 717 | 9 050 | 9 470 | 9 722 | 7 232 | 7 084 | 7 841 | 8 479 | 6 113 | 3 819 | 8 408 |
| 0.07 | 0.07 | 0.07 | 0.08 | 0.08 | 0.08 | 0.05 | 0.04 | 0.04 | 0.04 | 0.06 | 0.06 | 0.06 |

**Table A.1**   Total and per capita gross domestic product of individual countries or areas, expressed in United States dollars, and their individual shares of gross world product, based on alternative conversion rates, 1970−1989 [cont.]

| Country or area | 1970 (1) | 1971 (2) | 1972 (3) | 1973 (4) | 1974 (5) | 1975 (6) | 1976 (7) | 1977 (8) | 1978 (9) | 1979 (10) |
|---|---|---|---|---|---|---|---|---|---|---|
| **Guinea** | | | | | | | | | | |
| **1. MER** | | | | | | | | | | |
| 1a. Per capita GDP | 180 | 185 | 205 | 246 | 271 | 296 | 313 | 304 | 346 | 367 |
| 1b. GDP | 702 | 733 | 822 | 996 | 1 110 | 1 228 | 1 315 | 1 293 | 1 495 | 1 610 |
| 1c. % of GWP | 0.02 | 0.02 | 0.02 | 0.02 | 0.02 | 0.02 | 0.02 | 0.02 | 0.02 | 0.02 |
| **2. PPPs** | | | | | | | | | | |
| 2a. Per capita GDP | 258 | 278 | 283 | 282 | 323 | 360 | 414 | 430 | 479 | 506 |
| 2b. GDP | 1 008 | 1 101 | 1 134 | 1 146 | 1 325 | 1 492 | 1 741 | 1 832 | 2 068 | 2 218 |
| 2c. % of GWP | ... | ... | ... | ... | ... | ... | ... | ... | ... | ... |
| **3. Absolute 1970−1989 PARE** | | | | | | | | | | |
| 3a. Per capita GDP | 318 | 327 | 324 | 323 | 336 | 342 | 368 | 353 | 367 | 362 |
| 3b. GDP | 1 239 | 1 294 | 1 299 | 1 312 | 1 379 | 1 419 | 1 546 | 1 502 | 1 586 | 1 586 |
| 3c. % of GWP | 0.02 | 0.02 | 0.02 | 0.02 | 0.02 | 0.02 | 0.02 | 0.02 | 0.02 | 0.02 |
| **4. Relative 1970−1989 PARE** | | | | | | | | | | |
| 4a. Per capita GDP | 155 | 167 | 174 | 185 | 210 | 234 | 268 | 274 | 306 | 328 |
| 4b. GDP | 604 | 663 | 696 | 750 | 860 | 972 | 1 126 | 1 167 | 1 322 | 1 440 |
| 4c. % of GWP | 0.02 | 0.02 | 0.02 | 0.02 | 0.02 | 0.02 | 0.02 | 0.02 | 0.02 | 0.02 |
| **5. Absolute 1980−1989 PARE** | | | | | | | | | | |
| 5a. Per capita GDP | 372 | 382 | 379 | 378 | 393 | 400 | 431 | 413 | 430 | 423 |
| 5b. GDP | 1 451 | 1 515 | 1 521 | 1 535 | 1 614 | 1 661 | 1 810 | 1 758 | 1 856 | 1 856 |
| 5c. % of GWP | 0.02 | 0.02 | 0.02 | 0.02 | 0.02 | 0.02 | 0.02 | 0.02 | 0.02 | 0.01 |
| **6. WA[a]** | | | | | | | | | | |
| 6a. Per capita GDP | 518 | 272 | 190 | 208 | 244 | 276 | 309 | 303 | 324 | 338 |
| 6b. GDP | 2 020 | 1 076 | 762 | 844 | 999 | 1 146 | 1 298 | 1 290 | 1 400 | 1 484 |
| 6c. % of GWP | 0.06 | 0.03 | 0.02 | 0.02 | 0.02 | 0.02 | 0.02 | 0.02 | 0.02 | 0.01 |
| **Guinea−Bissau** | | | | | | | | | | |
| **1. MER** | | | | | | | | | | |
| 1a. Per capita GDP | 178 | 173 | 196 | 233 | 246 | 262 | 234 | 216 | 246 | 284 |
| 1b. GDP | 94 | 93 | 109 | 134 | 147 | 164 | 155 | 150 | 180 | 218 |
| 1c. % of GWP | 0.00 | 0.00 | 0.00 | 0.00 | 0.00 | 0.00 | 0.00 | 0.00 | 0.00 | 0.00 |
| **2. PPPs** | | | | | | | | | | |
| 2a. Per capita GDP | ... | ... | ... | ... | ... | ... | ... | ... | ... | ... |
| 2b. GDP | ... | ... | ... | ... | ... | ... | ... | ... | ... | ... |
| 2c. % of GWP | ... | ... | ... | ... | ... | ... | ... | ... | ... | ... |
| **3. Absolute 1970−1989 PARE** | | | | | | | | | | |
| 3a. Per capita GDP | 98 | 92 | 95 | 92 | 93 | 344 | 330 | 298 | 296 | 289 |
| 3b. GDP | 51 | 49 | 52 | 53 | 55 | 216 | 218 | 208 | 217 | 222 |
| 3c. % of GWP | 0.00 | 0.00 | 0.00 | 0.00 | 0.00 | 0.00 | 0.00 | 0.00 | 0.00 | 0.00 |
| **4. Relative 1970−1989 PARE** | | | | | | | | | | |
| 4a. Per capita GDP | 48 | 47 | 51 | 53 | 58 | 235 | 240 | 232 | 247 | 263 |
| 4b. GDP | 25 | 25 | 28 | 30 | 35 | 148 | 159 | 161 | 181 | 202 |
| 4c. % of GWP | 0.00 | 0.00 | 0.00 | 0.00 | 0.00 | 0.00 | 0.00 | 0.00 | 0.00 | 0.00 |
| **5. Absolute 1980−1989 PARE** | | | | | | | | | | |
| 5a. Per capita GDP | 94 | 88 | 91 | 89 | 89 | 329 | 316 | 286 | 284 | 277 |
| 5b. GDP | 49 | 47 | 50 | 51 | 53 | 207 | 209 | 199 | 208 | 213 |
| 5c. % of GWP | 0.00 | 0.00 | 0.00 | 0.00 | 0.00 | 0.00 | 0.00 | 0.00 | 0.00 | 0.00 |
| **6. WA** | | | | | | | | | | |
| 6a. Per capita GDP | 178 | 173 | 196 | 233 | 246 | 262 | 234 | 216 | 246 | 284 |
| 6b. GDP | 94 | 93 | 109 | 134 | 147 | 164 | 155 | 150 | 180 | 218 |
| 6c. % of GWP | 0.00 | 0.00 | 0.00 | 0.00 | 0.00 | 0.00 | 0.00 | 0.00 | 0.00 | 0.00 |

| 1980 (11) | 1981 (12) | 1982 (13) | 1983 (14) | 1984 (15) | 1985 (16) | 1986 (17) | 1987 (18) | 1988 (19) | 1989 (20) | Averages 1970–89 (21) | 1970–79 (22) | 1980–89 (23) |
|---|---|---|---|---|---|---|---|---|---|---|---|---|
| 425 | 389 | 375 | 360 | 348 | 364 | 368 | 389 | 437 | 480 | 349 | 274 | 398 |
| 1 897 | 1 769 | 1 742 | 1 710 | 1 694 | 1 815 | 1 887 | 2 048 | 2 368 | 2 682 | 1 546 | 1 130 | 1 961 |
| 0.02 | 0.02 | 0.01 | 0.01 | 0.01 | 0.01 | 0.01 | 0.01 | 0.01 | 0.01 | 0.02 | 0.02 | 0.01 |
| 586 | 564 | 552 | 522 | 525 | 547 | 569 | 600 | 610 | 642 | 492 | 365 | 578 |
| 2 615 | 2 564 | 2 561 | 2 476 | 2 552 | 2 726 | 2 917 | 3 162 | 3 310 | 3 588 | 2 177 | 1 507 | 2 847 |
| ... | ... | ... | ... | ... | ... | ... | ... | ... | ... | ... | ... | ... |
| 375 | 359 | 357 | 332 | 316 | 320 | 327 | 335 | 329 | 333 | 349 | 343 | 340 |
| 1 675 | 1 632 | 1 658 | 1 575 | 1 536 | 1 596 | 1 674 | 1 763 | 1 786 | 1 860 | 1 546 | 1 416 | 1 675 |
| 0.02 | 0.02 | 0.02 | 0.01 | 0.01 | 0.01 | 0.01 | 0.01 | 0.01 | 0.01 | 0.02 | 0.02 | 0.01 |
| 372 | 390 | 413 | 396 | 391 | 406 | 423 | 446 | 454 | 477 | 344 | 233 | 422 |
| 1 660 | 1 771 | 1 915 | 1 881 | 1 900 | 2 027 | 2 169 | 2 351 | 2 461 | 2 667 | 1 520 | 960 | 2 080 |
| 0.02 | 0.02 | 0.02 | 0.01 | 0.01 | 0.01 | 0.01 | 0.01 | 0.01 | 0.01 | 0.01 | 0.02 | 0.01 |
| 439 | 420 | 418 | 388 | 370 | 374 | 382 | 392 | 385 | 390 | 409 | 402 | 398 |
| 1 960 | 1 911 | 1 941 | 1 843 | 1 798 | 1 868 | 1 959 | 2 064 | 2 091 | 2 177 | 1 809 | 1 658 | 1 961 |
| 0.02 | 0.01 | 0.01 | 0.01 | 0.01 | 0.01 | 0.01 | 0.01 | 0.01 | 0.01 | 0.01 | 0.02 | 0.01 |
| 385 | 386 | 389 | 356 | 341 | 355 | 367 | 382 | 395 | 432 | 352 | 299 | 383 |
| 1 716 | 1 755 | 1 804 | 1 690 | 1 658 | 1 768 | 1 879 | 2 014 | 2 142 | 2 416 | 1 558 | 1 232 | 1 884 |
| 0.01 | 0.01 | 0.02 | 0.01 | 0.01 | 0.01 | 0.01 | 0.01 | 0.01 | 0.01 | 0.02 | 0.02 | 0.01 |
| 286 | 285 | 291 | 467 | 307 | 284 | 259 | 182 | 167 | 179 | 242 | 235 | 269 |
| 227 | 234 | 243 | 396 | 264 | 248 | 230 | 165 | 155 | 169 | 189 | 144 | 233 |
| 0.00 | 0.00 | 0.00 | 0.00 | 0.00 | 0.00 | 0.00 | 0.00 | 0.00 | 0.00 | 0.00 | 0.00 | 0.00 |
| ... | ... | ... | ... | ... | ... | ... | ... | ... | ... | ... | ... | ... |
| ... | ... | ... | ... | ... | ... | ... | ... | ... | ... | ... | ... | ... |
| ... | ... | ... | ... | ... | ... | ... | ... | ... | ... | ... | ... | ... |
| 268 | 268 | 264 | 265 | 281 | 270 | 277 | 287 | 301 | 309 | 242 | 219 | 281 |
| 213 | 219 | 220 | 225 | 242 | 236 | 246 | 260 | 278 | 292 | 189 | 134 | 243 |
| 0.00 | 0.00 | 0.00 | 0.00 | 0.00 | 0.00 | 0.00 | 0.00 | 0.00 | 0.00 | 0.00 | 0.00 | 0.00 |
| 265 | 291 | 305 | 317 | 348 | 344 | 359 | 382 | 414 | 443 | 258 | 162 | 351 |
| 211 | 238 | 254 | 268 | 299 | 300 | 319 | 347 | 383 | 419 | 202 | 99 | 304 |
| 0.00 | 0.00 | 0.00 | 0.00 | 0.00 | 0.00 | 0.00 | 0.00 | 0.00 | 0.00 | 0.00 | 0.00 | 0.00 |
| 256 | 257 | 253 | 254 | 270 | 259 | 265 | 275 | 288 | 296 | 232 | 210 | 269 |
| 204 | 210 | 211 | 215 | 232 | 226 | 236 | 249 | 267 | 280 | 181 | 129 | 233 |
| 0.00 | 0.00 | 0.00 | 0.00 | 0.00 | 0.00 | 0.00 | 0.00 | 0.00 | 0.00 | 0.00 | 0.00 | 0.00 |
| 286 | 285 | 291 | 467 | 307 | 284 | 259 | 182 | 167 | 179 | 242 | 235 | 269 |
| 227 | 234 | 243 | 396 | 264 | 248 | 230 | 165 | 155 | 169 | 189 | 144 | 233 |
| 0.00 | 0.00 | 0.00 | 0.00 | 0.00 | 0.00 | 0.00 | 0.00 | 0.00 | 0.00 | 0.00 | 0.00 | 0.00 |

**Table A.1** Total and per capita gross domestic product of individual countries or areas,
expressed in United States dollars, and their individual shares of gross world
product, based on alternative conversion rates, 1970–1989 [*cont.*]

| Country or area | 1970 (1) | 1971 (2) | 1972 (3) | 1973 (4) | 1974 (5) | 1975 (6) | 1976 (7) | 1977 (8) | 1978 (9) | 1979 (10) |
|---|---|---|---|---|---|---|---|---|---|---|
| **Guyana** | | | | | | | | | | |
| **1. MER** | | | | | | | | | | |
| 1a. Per capita GDP | 377 | 398 | 397 | 420 | 587 | 686 | 603 | 594 | 665 | 690 |
| 1b. GDP | 268 | 285 | 287 | 306 | 429 | 503 | 446 | 441 | 497 | 520 |
| 1c. % of GWP | 0.01 | 0.01 | 0.01 | 0.01 | 0.01 | 0.01 | 0.01 | 0.01 | 0.01 | 0.01 |
| **2. PPPs** | | | | | | | | | | |
| 2a. Per capita GDP | 787 | 801 | 836 | 963 | 1 137 | 1 545 | 1 602 | 1 504 | 1 405 | 1 540 |
| 2b. GDP | 559 | 575 | 604 | 700 | 831 | 1 134 | 1 184 | 1 117 | 1 051 | 1 161 |
| 2c. % of GWP | ... | ... | ... | ... | ... | ... | ... | ... | ... | ... |
| **3. Absolute 1970–1989 PARE** | | | | | | | | | | |
| 3a. Per capita GDP | 556 | 567 | 551 | 557 | 593 | 652 | 666 | 643 | 622 | 607 |
| 3b. GDP | 395 | 406 | 398 | 405 | 433 | 478 | 492 | 478 | 465 | 458 |
| 3c. % of GWP | 0.01 | 0.01 | 0.01 | 0.00 | 0.01 | 0.01 | 0.01 | 0.01 | 0.00 | 0.00 |
| **4. Relative 1970–1989 PARE** | | | | | | | | | | |
| 4a. Per capita GDP | 271 | 290 | 295 | 319 | 370 | 447 | 485 | 500 | 518 | 551 |
| 4b. GDP | 193 | 208 | 213 | 232 | 270 | 328 | 358 | 371 | 388 | 416 |
| 4c. % of GWP | 0.01 | 0.01 | 0.01 | 0.00 | 0.01 | 0.01 | 0.01 | 0.01 | 0.00 | 0.00 |
| **5. Absolute 1980–1989 PARE** | | | | | | | | | | |
| 5a. Per capita GDP | 616 | 627 | 609 | 616 | 656 | 721 | 737 | 712 | 688 | 671 |
| 5b. GDP | 437 | 449 | 441 | 448 | 479 | 529 | 545 | 529 | 515 | 506 |
| 5c. % of GWP | 0.01 | 0.00 | 0.00 | 0.00 | 0.00 | 0.01 | 0.00 | 0.00 | 0.00 | 0.00 |
| **6. WA** | | | | | | | | | | |
| 6a. Per capita GDP | 377 | 397 | 397 | 421 | 587 | 687 | 603 | 594 | 665 | 690 |
| 6b. GDP | 268 | 285 | 287 | 306 | 429 | 504 | 446 | 441 | 497 | 520 |
| 6c. % of GWP | 0.01 | 0.01 | 0.01 | 0.01 | 0.01 | 0.01 | 0.01 | 0.01 | 0.01 | 0.01 |
| **Haiti** | | | | | | | | | | |
| **1. MER** | | | | | | | | | | |
| 1a. Per capita GDP | 73 | 79 | 79 | 98 | 116 | 138 | 175 | 192 | 195 | 212 |
| 1b. GDP | 331 | 363 | 372 | 467 | 565 | 681 | 879 | 979 | 1 012 | 1 120 |
| 1c. % of GWP | 0.01 | 0.01 | 0.01 | 0.01 | 0.01 | 0.01 | 0.01 | 0.01 | 0.01 | 0.01 |
| **2. PPPs** | | | | | | | | | | |
| 2a. Per capita GDP | 228 | 247 | 241 | 253 | 279 | 340 | 416 | 447 | 501 | 548 |
| 2b. GDP | 1 034 | 1 141 | 1 131 | 1 207 | 1 356 | 1 680 | 2 087 | 2 281 | 2 602 | 2 894 |
| 2c. % of GWP | ... | ... | ... | ... | ... | ... | ... | ... | ... | ... |
| **3. Absolute 1970–1989 PARE** | | | | | | | | | | |
| 3a. Per capita GDP | 206 | 216 | 214 | 220 | 229 | 228 | 243 | 240 | 248 | 262 |
| 3b. GDP | 935 | 995 | 1 005 | 1 053 | 1 114 | 1 126 | 1 221 | 1 227 | 1 287 | 1 385 |
| 3c. % of GWP | 0.01 | 0.01 | 0.01 | 0.01 | 0.01 | 0.01 | 0.01 | 0.01 | 0.01 | 0.01 |
| **4. Relative 1970–1989 PARE** | | | | | | | | | | |
| 4a. Per capita GDP | 100 | 111 | 115 | 126 | 143 | 156 | 177 | 187 | 207 | 238 |
| 4b. GDP | 456 | 510 | 539 | 602 | 694 | 772 | 889 | 953 | 1 073 | 1 257 |
| 4c. % of GWP | 0.01 | 0.01 | 0.01 | 0.01 | 0.01 | 0.01 | 0.01 | 0.01 | 0.01 | 0.01 |
| **5. Absolute 1980–1989 PARE** | | | | | | | | | | |
| 5a. Per capita GDP | 272 | 285 | 283 | 291 | 303 | 301 | 321 | 318 | 328 | 347 |
| 5b. GDP | 1 235 | 1 315 | 1 328 | 1 391 | 1 471 | 1 488 | 1 613 | 1 621 | 1 700 | 1 829 |
| 5c. % of GWP | 0.01 | 0.01 | 0.01 | 0.01 | 0.01 | 0.01 | 0.01 | 0.01 | 0.01 | 0.01 |
| **6. WA** | | | | | | | | | | |
| 6a. Per capita GDP | 73 | 79 | 79 | 98 | 116 | 138 | 175 | 192 | 195 | 212 |
| 6b. GDP | 331 | 363 | 372 | 467 | 565 | 681 | 879 | 979 | 1 012 | 1 120 |
| 6c. % of GWP | 0.01 | 0.01 | 0.01 | 0.01 | 0.01 | 0.01 | 0.01 | 0.01 | 0.01 | 0.01 |

| | | | | | | | | | | Averages | | |
| 1980 (11) | 1981 (12) | 1982 (13) | 1983 (14) | 1984 (15) | 1985 (16) | 1986 (17) | 1987 (18) | 1988 (19) | 1989 (20) | 1970–89 (21) | 1970–79 (22) | 1980–89 (23) |
|---|---|---|---|---|---|---|---|---|---|---|---|---|
| 778 | 741 | 624 | 622 | 564 | 584 | 655 | 435 | 453 | 239 | 557 | 544 | 564 |
| 591 | 568 | 482 | 485 | 444 | 462 | 520 | 345 | 360 | 190 | 421 | 398 | 445 |
| 0.01 | 0.00 | 0.00 | 0.00 | 0.00 | 0.00 | 0.00 | 0.00 | 0.00 | 0.00 | 0.00 | 0.01 | 0.00 |
| 1 692 | 1 969 | 2 034 | 1 957 | 1 514 | 1 611 | 1 646 | 1 697 | 1 696 | 1 704 | 1 494 | 1 217 | 1 739 |
| 1 286 | 1 508 | 1 572 | 1 527 | 1 190 | 1 274 | 1 305 | 1 347 | 1 347 | 1 353 | 1 131 | 892 | 1 371 |
| ... | ... | ... | ... | ... | ... | ... | ... | ... | ... | ... | ... | ... |
| 612 | 606 | 537 | 482 | 489 | 491 | 492 | 493 | 477 | 460 | 557 | 602 | 510 |
| 465 | 464 | 415 | 376 | 384 | 388 | 390 | 391 | 378 | 365 | 421 | 441 | 402 |
| 0.00 | 0.00 | 0.00 | 0.00 | 0.00 | 0.00 | 0.00 | 0.00 | 0.00 | 0.00 | 0.00 | 0.01 | 0.00 |
| 607 | 657 | 621 | 576 | 605 | 624 | 637 | 657 | 657 | 660 | 523 | 406 | 626 |
| 461 | 503 | 480 | 449 | 476 | 493 | 505 | 522 | 521 | 524 | 396 | 298 | 494 |
| 0.00 | 0.00 | 0.00 | 0.00 | 0.00 | 0.00 | 0.00 | 0.00 | 0.00 | 0.00 | 0.00 | 0.01 | 0.00 |
| 677 | 670 | 595 | 534 | 541 | 543 | 544 | 545 | 527 | 509 | 616 | 666 | 564 |
| 515 | 513 | 460 | 416 | 425 | 430 | 431 | 433 | 419 | 404 | 466 | 488 | 445 |
| 0.00 | 0.00 | 0.00 | 0.00 | 0.00 | 0.00 | 0.00 | 0.00 | 0.00 | 0.00 | 0.00 | 0.01 | 0.00 |
| 778 | 741 | 624 | 622 | 564 | 584 | 655 | 437 | 453 | 240 | 557 | 544 | 564 |
| 591 | 568 | 482 | 485 | 444 | 462 | 519 | 347 | 360 | 190 | 422 | 398 | 445 |
| 0.01 | 0.00 | 0.00 | 0.00 | 0.00 | 0.00 | 0.00 | 0.00 | 0.00 | 0.00 | 0.00 | 0.01 | 0.00 |
| 267 | 271 | 267 | 287 | 314 | 341 | 372 | 324 | 311 | 439 | 240 | 138 | 323 |
| 1 437 | 1 479 | 1 485 | 1 630 | 1 816 | 2 009 | 2 235 | 1 986 | 1 946 | 2 800 | 1 280 | 677 | 1 882 |
| 0.01 | 0.01 | 0.01 | 0.01 | 0.01 | 0.02 | 0.02 | 0.01 | 0.01 | 0.01 | 0.01 | 0.01 | 0.01 |
| 672 | 686 | 645 | 672 | 703 | 745 | 752 | 757 | 765 | 784 | 559 | 356 | 722 |
| 3 610 | 3 751 | 3 592 | 3 807 | 4 064 | 4 385 | 4 518 | 4 636 | 4 781 | 5 000 | 2 978 | 1 741 | 4 215 |
| ... | ... | ... | ... | ... | ... | ... | ... | ... | ... | ... | ... | ... |
| 277 | 264 | 250 | 248 | 244 | 240 | 237 | 232 | 227 | 224 | 240 | 232 | 244 |
| 1 486 | 1 444 | 1 394 | 1 405 | 1 409 | 1 413 | 1 426 | 1 423 | 1 420 | 1 426 | 1 280 | 1 135 | 1 425 |
| 0.01 | 0.01 | 0.01 | 0.01 | 0.01 | 0.01 | 0.01 | 0.01 | 0.01 | 0.01 | 0.01 | 0.01 | 0.01 |
| 274 | 287 | 289 | 296 | 302 | 305 | 308 | 310 | 313 | 321 | 238 | 158 | 302 |
| 1 473 | 1 566 | 1 611 | 1 678 | 1 743 | 1 795 | 1 849 | 1 897 | 1 957 | 2 046 | 1 268 | 774 | 1 761 |
| 0.01 | 0.01 | 0.01 | 0.01 | 0.01 | 0.01 | 0.01 | 0.01 | 0.01 | 0.01 | 0.01 | 0.01 | 0.01 |
| 366 | 349 | 331 | 327 | 322 | 317 | 314 | 307 | 300 | 295 | 318 | 306 | 323 |
| 1 964 | 1 908 | 1 842 | 1 856 | 1 862 | 1 866 | 1 885 | 1 880 | 1 876 | 1 885 | 1 691 | 1 499 | 1 882 |
| 0.02 | 0.01 | 0.01 | 0.01 | 0.01 | 0.01 | 0.01 | 0.01 | 0.01 | 0.01 | 0.01 | 0.01 | 0.01 |
| 267 | 271 | 267 | 287 | 314 | 341 | 372 | 324 | 311 | 439 | 240 | 138 | 323 |
| 1 437 | 1 479 | 1 485 | 1 630 | 1 816 | 2 009 | 2 235 | 1 986 | 1 946 | 2 800 | 1 280 | 677 | 1 882 |
| 0.01 | 0.01 | 0.01 | 0.01 | 0.01 | 0.02 | 0.02 | 0.01 | 0.01 | 0.01 | 0.01 | 0.01 | 0.01 |

**Table A.1**  Total and per capita gross domestic product of individual countries or areas,
expressed in United States dollars, and their individual shares of gross world
product, based on alternative conversion rates, 1970−1989 [*cont.*]

| Country or area | 1970 (1) | 1971 (2) | 1972 (3) | 1973 (4) | 1974 (5) | 1975 (6) | 1976 (7) | 1977 (8) | 1978 (9) | 1979 (10) |
|---|---|---|---|---|---|---|---|---|---|---|
| **Honduras** | | | | | | | | | | |
| **1. MER** | | | | | | | | | | |
| 1a. Per capita GDP | 263 | 270 | 288 | 316 | 347 | 365 | 423 | 506 | 556 | 626 |
| 1b. GDP | 691 | 731 | 803 | 913 | 1 035 | 1 124 | 1 348 | 1 670 | 1 899 | 2 213 |
| 1c. % of GWP | 0.02 | 0.02 | 0.02 | 0.02 | 0.02 | 0.02 | 0.02 | 0.02 | 0.02 | 0.02 |
| **2. PPPs** | | | | | | | | | | |
| 2a. Per capita GDP | 434 | 447 | 478 | 520 | 554 | 599 | 691 | 807 | 900 | 983 |
| 2b. GDP | 1 139 | 1 209 | 1 335 | 1 499 | 1 650 | 1 846 | 2 201 | 2 661 | 3 072 | 3 473 |
| 2c. % of GWP | ... | ... | ... | ... | ... | ... | ... | ... | ... | ... |
| **3. Absolute 1970−1989 PARE** | | | | | | | | | | |
| 3a. Per capita GDP | 584 | 590 | 605 | 631 | 604 | 596 | 637 | 680 | 711 | 730 |
| 3b. GDP | 1 535 | 1 596 | 1 688 | 1 821 | 1 799 | 1 837 | 2 030 | 2 241 | 2 426 | 2 579 |
| 3c. % of GWP | 0.02 | 0.02 | 0.02 | 0.02 | 0.02 | 0.02 | 0.02 | 0.02 | 0.02 | 0.03 |
| **4. Relative 1970−1989 PARE** | | | | | | | | | | |
| 4a. Per capita GDP | 285 | 302 | 324 | 361 | 376 | 408 | 464 | 528 | 593 | 663 |
| 4b. GDP | 748 | 818 | 905 | 1 041 | 1 122 | 1 258 | 1 478 | 1 741 | 2 022 | 2 342 |
| 4c. % of GWP | 0.02 | 0.02 | 0.02 | 0.02 | 0.02 | 0.02 | 0.02 | 0.02 | 0.02 | 0.03 |
| **5. Absolute 1980−1989 PARE** | | | | | | | | | | |
| 5a. Per capita GDP | 733 | 740 | 758 | 792 | 757 | 748 | 799 | 852 | 891 | 915 |
| 5b. GDP | 1 925 | 2 002 | 2 117 | 2 284 | 2 256 | 2 304 | 2 546 | 2 810 | 3 042 | 3 235 |
| 5c. % of GWP | 0.02 | 0.02 | 0.02 | 0.02 | 0.02 | 0.02 | 0.02 | 0.02 | 0.03 | 0.03 |
| **6. WA** | | | | | | | | | | |
| 6a. Per capita GDP | 263 | 270 | 288 | 316 | 347 | 365 | 423 | 506 | 556 | 626 |
| 6b. GDP | 691 | 731 | 803 | 913 | 1 035 | 1 124 | 1 348 | 1 670 | 1 899 | 2 213 |
| 6c. % of GWP | 0.02 | 0.02 | 0.02 | 0.02 | 0.02 | 0.02 | 0.02 | 0.02 | 0.02 | 0.02 |
| **Hong Kong** | | | | | | | | | | |
| **1. MER** | | | | | | | | | | |
| 1a. Per capita GDP | 916 | 1 050 | 1 317 | 1 816 | 2 069 | 2 140 | 2 679 | 3 177 | 3 620 | 4 351 |
| 1b. GDP | 3 610 | 4 210 | 5 387 | 7 592 | 8 862 | 9 406 | 12 110 | 14 786 | 17 343 | 21 409 |
| 1c. % of GWP | 0.11 | 0.12 | 0.13 | 0.15 | 0.16 | 0.15 | 0.18 | 0.20 | 0.19 | 0.21 |
| **2. PPPs** | | | | | | | | | | |
| 2a. Per capita GDP | ... | ... | ... | ... | ... | ... | ... | ... | ... | ... |
| 2b. GDP | ... | ... | ... | ... | ... | ... | ... | ... | ... | ... |
| 2c. % of GWP | ... | ... | ... | ... | ... | ... | ... | ... | ... | ... |
| **3. Absolute 1970−1989 PARE** | | | | | | | | | | |
| 3a. Per capita GDP | 2 543 | 2 683 | 2 920 | 3 219 | 3 211 | 3 135 | 3 570 | 3 901 | 4 149 | 4 511 |
| 3b. GDP | 10 026 | 10 758 | 11 941 | 13 458 | 13 754 | 13 781 | 16 138 | 18 155 | 19 879 | 22 198 |
| 3c. % of GWP | 0.14 | 0.15 | 0.15 | 0.16 | 0.16 | 0.16 | 0.18 | 0.19 | 0.20 | 0.22 |
| **4. Relative 1970−1989 PARE** | | | | | | | | | | |
| 4a. Per capita GDP | 1 240 | 1 375 | 1 566 | 1 840 | 2 002 | 2 148 | 2 599 | 3 031 | 3 459 | 4 097 |
| 4b. GDP | 4 888 | 5 514 | 6 402 | 7 694 | 8 577 | 9 442 | 11 747 | 14 107 | 16 573 | 20 159 |
| 4c. % of GWP | 0.14 | 0.15 | 0.15 | 0.16 | 0.16 | 0.16 | 0.18 | 0.19 | 0.20 | 0.22 |
| **5. Absolute 1980−1989 PARE** | | | | | | | | | | |
| 5a. Per capita GDP | 2 882 | 3 041 | 3 309 | 3 647 | 3 638 | 3 552 | 4 046 | 4 421 | 4 702 | 5 112 |
| 5b. GDP | 11 361 | 12 191 | 13 532 | 15 250 | 15 586 | 15 617 | 18 287 | 20 573 | 22 526 | 25 154 |
| 5c. % of GWP | 0.13 | 0.13 | 0.14 | 0.15 | 0.15 | 0.15 | 0.17 | 0.18 | 0.19 | 0.20 |
| **6. WA** | | | | | | | | | | |
| 6a. Per capita GDP | 916 | 1 051 | 1 317 | 1 817 | 2 068 | 2 142 | 2 677 | 3 176 | 3 617 | 4 348 |
| 6b. GDP | 3 610 | 4 212 | 5 386 | 7 598 | 8 860 | 9 415 | 12 098 | 14 780 | 17 329 | 21 398 |
| 6c. % of GWP | 0.11 | 0.12 | 0.13 | 0.16 | 0.16 | 0.15 | 0.18 | 0.20 | 0.20 | 0.21 |

| | | | | | | | | | | Averages | | |
|---|---|---|---|---|---|---|---|---|---|---|---|---|
| 1980 (11) | 1981 (12) | 1982 (13) | 1983 (14) | 1984 (15) | 1985 (16) | 1986 (17) | 1987 (18) | 1988 (19) | 1989 (20) | 1970–89 (21) | 1970–79 (22) | 1980–89 (23) |
| 695 | 731 | 731 | 738 | 763 | 799 | 838 | 868 | 923 | 980 | 661 | 410 | 816 |
| 2 544 | 2 777 | 2 881 | 3 018 | 3 231 | 3 504 | 3 798 | 4 064 | 4 457 | 4 885 | 2 379 | 1 243 | 3 516 |
| 0.02 | 0.02 | 0.02 | 0.03 | 0.03 | 0.03 | 0.03 | 0.02 | 0.02 | 0.02 | 0.02 | 0.02 | 0.02 |
| 1 107 | 1 146 | 1 098 | 1 091 | 1 061 | 1 104 | 1 120 | 1 173 | 1 231 | 1 268 | 965 | 663 | 1 145 |
| 4 055 | 4 353 | 4 326 | 4 458 | 4 493 | 4 838 | 5 074 | 5 490 | 5 944 | 6 317 | 3 472 | 2 008 | 4 935 |
| ... | ... | ... | ... | ... | ... | ... | ... | ... | ... | ... | ... | ... |
| 713 | 698 | 660 | 635 | 630 | 630 | 626 | 638 | 647 | 641 | 661 | 645 | 651 |
| 2 612 | 2 653 | 2 601 | 2 594 | 2 667 | 2 761 | 2 838 | 2 985 | 3 127 | 3 193 | 2 379 | 1 955 | 2 803 |
| 0.03 | 0.03 | 0.02 | 0.02 | 0.02 | 0.02 | 0.02 | 0.02 | 0.02 | 0.02 | 0.02 | 0.02 | 0.02 |
| 707 | 758 | 763 | 758 | 779 | 800 | 812 | 850 | 892 | 919 | 673 | 445 | 811 |
| 2 589 | 2 878 | 3 004 | 3 098 | 3 298 | 3 508 | 3 679 | 3 980 | 4 309 | 4 580 | 2 420 | 1 348 | 3 492 |
| 0.03 | 0.03 | 0.02 | 0.02 | 0.02 | 0.02 | 0.02 | 0.02 | 0.02 | 0.02 | 0.02 | 0.02 | 0.02 |
| 894 | 876 | 828 | 796 | 790 | 790 | 786 | 800 | 812 | 804 | 829 | 809 | 816 |
| 3 276 | 3 327 | 3 262 | 3 254 | 3 344 | 3 463 | 3 560 | 3 744 | 3 922 | 4 005 | 2 984 | 2 452 | 3 516 |
| 0.03 | 0.03 | 0.03 | 0.02 | 0.02 | 0.02 | 0.02 | 0.02 | 0.02 | 0.02 | 0.02 | 0.02 | 0.02 |
| 695 | 731 | 731 | 738 | 763 | 799 | 838 | 868 | 792 | 660 | 630 | 410 | 764 |
| 2 544 | 2 777 | 2 881 | 3 018 | 3 231 | 3 504 | 3 798 | 4 064 | 3 825 | 3 290 | 2 268 | 1 243 | 3 293 |
| 0.02 | 0.02 | 0.02 | 0.03 | 0.03 | 0.03 | 0.03 | 0.02 | 0.02 | 0.02 | 0.02 | 0.02 | 0.02 |
| 5 463 | 5 742 | 5 873 | 5 382 | 5 913 | 6 144 | 6 964 | 8 423 | 9 757 | 10 877 | 4 928 | 2 413 | 7 126 |
| 27 526 | 29 512 | 30 697 | 28 550 | 31 807 | 33 530 | 38 566 | 47 343 | 55 651 | 62 891 | 24 539 | 10 472 | 38 607 |
| 0.24 | 0.25 | 0.26 | 0.24 | 0.26 | 0.27 | 0.26 | 0.28 | 0.29 | 0.31 | 0.24 | 0.17 | 0.27 |
| ... | ... | ... | ... | ... | ... | ... | ... | ... | ... | ... | ... | ... |
| ... | ... | ... | ... | ... | ... | ... | ... | ... | ... | ... | ... | ... |
| ... | ... | ... | ... | ... | ... | ... | ... | ... | ... | ... | ... | ... |
| 4 884 | 5 239 | 5 307 | 5 569 | 6 013 | 5 920 | 6 528 | 7 328 | 7 792 | 7 860 | 4 928 | 3 458 | 6 288 |
| 24 611 | 26 928 | 27 740 | 29 543 | 32 343 | 32 307 | 36 149 | 41 189 | 44 443 | 45 447 | 24 539 | 15 009 | 34 070 |
| 0.24 | 0.25 | 0.26 | 0.27 | 0.28 | 0.27 | 0.30 | 0.33 | 0.34 | 0.33 | 0.24 | 0.17 | 0.29 |
| 4 841 | 5 684 | 6 130 | 6 650 | 7 438 | 7 521 | 8 460 | 9 770 | 10 737 | 11 275 | 5 374 | 2 422 | 7 940 |
| 24 396 | 29 218 | 32 044 | 35 279 | 40 007 | 41 045 | 46 850 | 54 915 | 61 242 | 65 193 | 26 765 | 10 510 | 43 019 |
| 0.24 | 0.25 | 0.26 | 0.27 | 0.28 | 0.27 | 0.30 | 0.33 | 0.34 | 0.33 | 0.26 | 0.18 | 0.29 |
| 5 535 | 5 937 | 6 014 | 6 310 | 6 814 | 6 709 | 7 397 | 8 304 | 8 829 | 8 907 | 5 584 | 3 919 | 7 126 |
| 27 888 | 30 514 | 31 435 | 33 477 | 36 650 | 36 609 | 40 964 | 46 675 | 50 362 | 51 499 | 27 808 | 17 008 | 38 607 |
| 0.22 | 0.24 | 0.24 | 0.25 | 0.26 | 0.25 | 0.28 | 0.30 | 0.31 | 0.31 | 0.22 | 0.16 | 0.27 |
| 5 467 | 5 742 | 5 873 | 5 385 | 5 915 | 6 144 | 6 961 | 8 424 | 9 749 | 10 877 | 4 927 | 2 412 | 7 126 |
| 27 548 | 29 516 | 30 697 | 28 569 | 31 815 | 33 526 | 38 550 | 47 354 | 55 609 | 62 892 | 24 538 | 10 469 | 38 608 |
| 0.24 | 0.25 | 0.26 | 0.24 | 0.26 | 0.27 | 0.26 | 0.28 | 0.30 | 0.32 | 0.24 | 0.17 | 0.27 |

**Table A.1**    Total and per capita gross domestic product of individual countries or areas,
expressed in United States dollars, and their individual shares of gross world
product, based on alternative conversion rates, 1970−1989 [*cont.*]

| Country or area | 1970 (1) | 1971 (2) | 1972 (3) | 1973 (4) | 1974 (5) | 1975 (6) | 1976 (7) | 1977 (8) | 1978 (9) | 1979 (10) |
|---|---|---|---|---|---|---|---|---|---|---|
| **Hungary** | | | | | | | | | | |
| **1.   MER** | | | | | | | | | | |
| 1a.   Per capita GDP | 1 075 | 1 162 | 1 362 | 1 630 | 1 723 | 2 191 | 1 203 | 1 338 | 1 558 | 1 793 |
| 1b.   GDP | 11 113 | 12 057 | 14 187 | 17 040 | 18 074 | 23 074 | 12 720 | 14 208 | 16 610 | 19 176 |
| 1c.   % of GWP | 0.35 | 0.34 | 0.35 | 0.35 | 0.33 | 0.37 | 0.19 | 0.19 | 0.18 | 0.19 |
| **2.   PPPs** | | | | | | | | | | |
| 2a.   Per capita GDP | ... | ... | ... | ... | ... | ... | ... | ... | ... | ... |
| 2b.   GDP | ... | ... | ... | ... | ... | ... | ... | ... | ... | ... |
| 2c.   % of GWP | ... | ... | ... | ... | ... | ... | ... | ... | ... | ... |
| **3.   Absolute 1970−1989 PARE** | | | | | | | | | | |
| 3a.   Per capita GDP | 1 257 | 1 331 | 1 409 | 1 491 | 1 579 | 1 671 | 1 722 | 1 831 | 1 907 | 1 931 |
| 3b.   GDP | 12 994 | 13 807 | 14 671 | 15 589 | 16 565 | 17 602 | 18 212 | 19 440 | 20 332 | 20 642 |
| 3c.   % of GWP | 0.18 | 0.19 | 0.19 | 0.19 | 0.20 | 0.20 | 0.20 | 0.21 | 0.21 | 0.20 |
| **4.   Relative 1970−1989 PARE** | | | | | | | | | | |
| 4a.   Per capita GDP | 613 | 682 | 755 | 853 | 985 | 1 145 | 1 254 | 1 422 | 1 590 | 1 753 |
| 4b.   GDP | 6 336 | 7 077 | 7 865 | 8 913 | 10 330 | 12 059 | 13 257 | 15 105 | 16 951 | 18 746 |
| 4c.   % of GWP | 0.18 | 0.19 | 0.19 | 0.19 | 0.20 | 0.20 | 0.20 | 0.21 | 0.21 | 0.20 |
| **5.   Absolute 1980−1989 PARE** | | | | | | | | | | |
| 5a.   Per capita GDP | 1 322 | 1 399 | 1 481 | 1 568 | 1 660 | 1 757 | 1 811 | 1 925 | 2 006 | 2 030 |
| 5b.   GDP | 13 663 | 14 518 | 15 427 | 16 392 | 17 418 | 18 508 | 19 150 | 20 441 | 21 380 | 21 706 |
| 5c.   % of GWP | 0.16 | 0.16 | 0.16 | 0.16 | 0.17 | 0.18 | 0.17 | 0.18 | 0.18 | 0.18 |
| **6.   WA** | | | | | | | | | | |
| 6a.   Per capita GDP | 537 | 583 | 681 | 840 | 917 | 1 042 | 1 203 | 1 338 | 1 558 | 1 794 |
| 6b.   GDP | 5 557 | 6 047 | 7 094 | 8 784 | 9 626 | 10 978 | 12 721 | 14 207 | 16 609 | 19 177 |
| 6c.   % of GWP | 0.17 | 0.17 | 0.18 | 0.18 | 0.17 | 0.18 | 0.19 | 0.19 | 0.19 | 0.19 |
| **Iceland** | | | | | | | | | | |
| **1.   MER** | | | | | | | | | | |
| 1a.   Per capita GDP | 2 430 | 3 060 | 3 780 | 5 064 | 6 566 | 6 034 | 7 116 | 9 341 | 10 618 | 12 015 |
| 1b.   GDP | 498 | 633 | 794 | 1 079 | 1 418 | 1 321 | 1 573 | 2 083 | 2 389 | 2 727 |
| 1c.   % of GWP | 0.02 | 0.02 | 0.02 | 0.02 | 0.03 | 0.02 | 0.02 | 0.03 | 0.03 | 0.03 |
| **2.   PPPs** | | | | | | | | | | |
| 2a.   Per capita GDP | 3 067 | 3 675 | 4 077 | 4 719 | 5 142 | 5 428 | 6 174 | 7 198 | 8 281 | 9 081 |
| 2b.   GDP | 629 | 761 | 856 | 1 005 | 1 111 | 1 189 | 1 364 | 1 605 | 1 863 | 2 061 |
| 2c.   % of GWP | ... | ... | ... | ... | ... | ... | ... | ... | ... | ... |
| **3.   Absolute 1970−1989 PARE** | | | | | | | | | | |
| 3a.   Per capita GDP | 7 417 | 8 306 | 8 661 | 9 032 | 9 469 | 9 425 | 9 908 | 10 694 | 11 337 | 11 851 |
| 3b.   GDP | 1 520 | 1 719 | 1 819 | 1 924 | 2 045 | 2 064 | 2 190 | 2 385 | 2 551 | 2 690 |
| 3c.   % of GWP | 0.02 | 0.02 | 0.02 | 0.02 | 0.02 | 0.02 | 0.02 | 0.03 | 0.03 | 0.03 |
| **4.   Relative 1970−1989 PARE** | | | | | | | | | | |
| 4a.   Per capita GDP | 3 616 | 4 257 | 4 643 | 5 164 | 5 905 | 6 457 | 7 212 | 8 310 | 9 452 | 10 762 |
| 4b.   GDP | 741 | 881 | 975 | 1 100 | 1 275 | 1 414 | 1 594 | 1 853 | 2 127 | 2 443 |
| 4c.   % of GWP | 0.02 | 0.02 | 0.02 | 0.02 | 0.02 | 0.02 | 0.02 | 0.03 | 0.03 | 0.03 |
| **5.   Absolute 1980−1989 PARE** | | | | | | | | | | |
| 5a.   Per capita GDP | 8 901 | 9 968 | 10 394 | 10 840 | 11 365 | 11 312 | 11 891 | 12 835 | 13 607 | 14 223 |
| 5b.   GDP | 1 825 | 2 063 | 2 183 | 2 309 | 2 455 | 2 477 | 2 628 | 2 862 | 3 061 | 3 229 |
| 5c.   % of GWP | 0.02 | 0.02 | 0.02 | 0.02 | 0.02 | 0.02 | 0.02 | 0.02 | 0.03 | 0.03 |
| **6.   WA** | | | | | | | | | | |
| 6a.   Per capita GDP | 2 430 | 3 057 | 3 756 | 5 062 | 6 569 | 6 034 | 7 117 | 9 342 | 10 618 | 12 015 |
| 6b.   GDP | 498 | 633 | 789 | 1 078 | 1 419 | 1 321 | 1 573 | 2 083 | 2 389 | 2 727 |
| 6c.   % of GWP | 0.02 | 0.02 | 0.02 | 0.02 | 0.03 | 0.02 | 0.02 | 0.03 | 0.03 | 0.03 |

| | | | | | | | | | | Averages | | |
|---|---|---|---|---|---|---|---|---|---|---|---|---|
| 1980 (11) | 1981 (12) | 1982 (13) | 1983 (14) | 1984 (15) | 1985 (16) | 1986 (17) | 1987 (18) | 1988 (19) | 1989 (20) | 1970–89 (21) | 1970–79 (22) | 1980–89 (23) |
| 2 069 | 2 121 | 2 161 | 1 965 | 1 909 | 1 937 | 2 235 | 2 460 | 2 641 | 2 731 | 1 845 | 1 506 | 2 221 |
| 22 165 | 22 731 | 23 147 | 21 007 | 20 368 | 20 624 | 23 757 | 26 093 | 27 967 | 28 866 | 19 749 | 15 826 | 23 672 |
| 0.19 | 0.19 | 0.20 | 0.18 | 0.17 | 0.16 | 0.16 | 0.15 | 0.15 | 0.14 | 0.19 | 0.26 | 0.17 |
| ... | ... | ... | ... | ... | ... | ... | ... | ... | ... | ... | ... | ... |
| ... | ... | ... | ... | ... | ... | ... | ... | ... | ... | ... | ... | ... |
| ... | ... | ... | ... | ... | ... | ... | ... | ... | ... | ... | ... | ... |
| 1 928 | 1 983 | 2 040 | 2 058 | 2 117 | 2 116 | 2 153 | 2 245 | 2 247 | 2 247 | 1 845 | 1 616 | 2 112 |
| 20 655 | 21 247 | 21 851 | 22 009 | 22 594 | 22 537 | 22 883 | 23 810 | 23 794 | 23 749 | 19 749 | 16 986 | 22 513 |
| 0.20 | 0.20 | 0.20 | 0.20 | 0.20 | 0.19 | 0.19 | 0.19 | 0.18 | 0.17 | 0.19 | 0.20 | 0.19 |
| 1 911 | 2 151 | 2 357 | 2 458 | 2 619 | 2 689 | 2 790 | 2 993 | 3 097 | 3 223 | 1 853 | 1 110 | 2 626 |
| 20 475 | 23 054 | 25 241 | 26 283 | 27 948 | 28 632 | 29 656 | 31 744 | 32 788 | 34 067 | 19 826 | 11 664 | 27 989 |
| 0.20 | 0.20 | 0.20 | 0.20 | 0.20 | 0.19 | 0.19 | 0.19 | 0.18 | 0.17 | 0.19 | 0.20 | 0.19 |
| 2 028 | 2 085 | 2 146 | 2 164 | 2 226 | 2 225 | 2 264 | 2 360 | 2 363 | 2 363 | 1 940 | 1 699 | 2 221 |
| 21 719 | 22 342 | 22 977 | 23 143 | 23 758 | 23 698 | 24 061 | 25 036 | 25 020 | 24 972 | 20 766 | 17 860 | 23 672 |
| 0.17 | 0.17 | 0.18 | 0.17 | 0.17 | 0.16 | 0.16 | 0.16 | 0.16 | 0.15 | 0.17 | 0.17 | 0.17 |
| 2 069 | 2 121 | 2 161 | 1 965 | 1 909 | 1 937 | 2 235 | 2 461 | 2 641 | 2 733 | 1 624 | 1 054 | 2 221 |
| 22 164 | 22 729 | 23 146 | 21 006 | 20 367 | 20 624 | 23 756 | 26 109 | 27 959 | 28 883 | 17 377 | 11 080 | 23 674 |
| 0.19 | 0.19 | 0.20 | 0.18 | 0.17 | 0.16 | 0.16 | 0.16 | 0.15 | 0.15 | 0.17 | 0.18 | 0.17 |
| 14 104 | 14 583 | 13 193 | 11 182 | 11 552 | 11 856 | 15 750 | 21 770 | 23 782 | 20 613 | 11 586 | 6 674 | 15 933 |
| 3 230 | 3 369 | 3 087 | 2 650 | 2 761 | 2 869 | 3 859 | 5 377 | 5 922 | 5 194 | 2 642 | 1 452 | 3 832 |
| 0.03 | 0.03 | 0.03 | 0.02 | 0.02 | 0.02 | 0.03 | 0.03 | 0.03 | 0.03 | 0.03 | 0.02 | 0.03 |
| 10 350 | 11 519 | 12 111 | 12 538 | 13 239 | 13 573 | 14 691 | 16 290 | 16 573 | 16 568 | 10 012 | 5 721 | 13 809 |
| 2 370 | 2 661 | 2 834 | 2 971 | 3 164 | 3 285 | 3 599 | 4 024 | 4 127 | 4 175 | 2 283 | 1 244 | 3 321 |
| ... | ... | ... | ... | ... | ... | ... | ... | ... | ... | ... | ... | ... |
| 12 417 | 12 815 | 12 898 | 12 240 | 12 596 | 12 858 | 13 643 | 14 705 | 14 475 | 13 901 | 11 586 | 9 612 | 13 275 |
| 2 844 | 2 960 | 3 018 | 2 901 | 3 010 | 3 112 | 3 343 | 3 632 | 3 604 | 3 503 | 2 642 | 2 091 | 3 193 |
| 0.03 | 0.03 | 0.03 | 0.03 | 0.03 | 0.03 | 0.03 | 0.03 | 0.03 | 0.03 | 0.03 | 0.02 | 0.03 |
| 12 309 | 13 905 | 14 899 | 14 617 | 15 581 | 16 335 | 17 682 | 19 605 | 19 946 | 19 940 | 11 892 | 6 622 | 16 559 |
| 2 819 | 3 212 | 3 486 | 3 464 | 3 724 | 3 953 | 4 332 | 4 842 | 4 967 | 5 025 | 2 711 | 1 440 | 3 982 |
| 0.03 | 0.03 | 0.03 | 0.03 | 0.03 | 0.03 | 0.03 | 0.03 | 0.03 | 0.03 | 0.03 | 0.02 | 0.03 |
| 14 903 | 15 380 | 15 480 | 14 691 | 15 118 | 15 432 | 16 374 | 17 649 | 17 373 | 16 683 | 13 906 | 11 537 | 15 933 |
| 3 413 | 3 553 | 3 622 | 3 482 | 3 613 | 3 734 | 4 012 | 4 359 | 4 326 | 4 204 | 3 171 | 2 509 | 3 832 |
| 0.03 | 0.03 | 0.03 | 0.03 | 0.03 | 0.03 | 0.03 | 0.03 | 0.03 | 0.03 | 0.03 | 0.02 | 0.03 |
| 14 105 | 14 583 | 13 193 | 11 182 | 11 553 | 11 856 | 15 749 | 21 783 | 23 775 | 20 598 | 11 585 | 6 672 | 15 932 |
| 3 230 | 3 369 | 3 087 | 2 650 | 2 761 | 2 869 | 3 858 | 5 380 | 5 920 | 5 191 | 2 641 | 1 451 | 3 832 |
| 0.03 | 0.03 | 0.03 | 0.02 | 0.02 | 0.02 | 0.03 | 0.03 | 0.03 | 0.03 | 0.03 | 0.02 | 0.03 |

**Table A.1** Total and per capita gross domestic product of individual countries or areas, expressed in United States dollars, and their individual shares of gross world product, based on alternative conversion rates, 1970–1989 [*cont.*]

| Country or area | 1970 (1) | 1971 (2) | 1972 (3) | 1973 (4) | 1974 (5) | 1975 (6) | 1976 (7) | 1977 (8) | 1978 (9) | 1979 (10) |
|---|---|---|---|---|---|---|---|---|---|---|
| **India** | | | | | | | | | | |
| **1. MER** | | | | | | | | | | |
| 1a. Per capita GDP | 104 | 109 | 116 | 135 | 149 | 151 | 149 | 170 | 193 | 209 |
| 1b. GDP | 57 551 | 61 676 | 67 165 | 80 092 | 90 391 | 94 032 | 94 747 | 109 929 | 127 170 | 140 729 |
| 1c. % of GWP | 1.80 | 1.76 | 1.67 | 1.63 | 1.63 | 1.51 | 1.41 | 1.45 | 1.42 | 1.37 |
| **2. PPPs** | | | | | | | | | | |
| 2a. Per capita GDP | 308 | 326 | 329 | 345 | 365 | 430 | 445 | 507 | 561 | 568 |
| 2b. GDP | 171 180 | 185 300 | 191 003 | 205 024 | 221 820 | 267 208 | 282 320 | 328 418 | 370 614 | 382 982 |
| 2c. % of GWP | ... | ... | ... | ... | ... | ... | ... | ... | ... | ... |
| **3. Absolute 1970–1989 PARE** | | | | | | | | | | |
| 3a. Per capita GDP | 197 | 196 | 191 | 192 | 190 | 203 | 202 | 213 | 220 | 204 |
| 3b. GDP | 109 543 | 111 532 | 110 844 | 114 119 | 115 479 | 126 092 | 128 332 | 137 567 | 145 184 | 137 868 |
| 3c. % of GWP | 1.54 | 1.51 | 1.42 | 1.38 | 1.36 | 1.47 | 1.42 | 1.46 | 1.48 | 1.36 |
| **4. Relative 1970–1989 PARE** | | | | | | | | | | |
| 4a. Per capita GDP | 96 | 101 | 102 | 110 | 119 | 139 | 147 | 165 | 183 | 186 |
| 4b. GDP | 53 410 | 57 169 | 59 423 | 65 243 | 72 012 | 86 386 | 93 416 | 106 892 | 121 040 | 125 204 |
| 4c. % of GWP | 1.54 | 1.51 | 1.42 | 1.38 | 1.36 | 1.47 | 1.42 | 1.46 | 1.48 | 1.36 |
| **5. Absolute 1980–1989 PARE** | | | | | | | | | | |
| 5a. Per capita GDP | 230 | 229 | 222 | 224 | 222 | 237 | 236 | 248 | 256 | 238 |
| 5b. GDP | 127 651 | 129 970 | 129 168 | 132 984 | 134 569 | 146 936 | 149 547 | 160 308 | 169 184 | 160 659 |
| 5c. % of GWP | 1.47 | 1.43 | 1.35 | 1.31 | 1.30 | 1.40 | 1.35 | 1.39 | 1.41 | 1.30 |
| **6. WA** | | | | | | | | | | |
| 6a. Per capita GDP | 104 | 109 | 114 | 134 | 151 | 147 | 150 | 173 | 192 | 210 |
| 6b. GDP | 57 551 | 62 140 | 66 189 | 79 588 | 91 819 | 91 022 | 94 969 | 112 189 | 126 968 | 141 600 |
| 6c. % of GWP | 1.80 | 1.78 | 1.65 | 1.64 | 1.65 | 1.48 | 1.42 | 1.49 | 1.43 | 1.38 |
| **Indonesia** | | | | | | | | | | |
| **1. MER** | | | | | | | | | | |
| 1a. Per capita GDP | 79 | 81 | 93 | 134 | 207 | 239 | 286 | 345 | 379 | 378 |
| 1b. GDP | 9 513 | 9 988 | 11 723 | 17 346 | 27 504 | 32 473 | 39 727 | 48 887 | 54 849 | 55 918 |
| 1c. % of GWP | 0.30 | 0.29 | 0.29 | 0.35 | 0.50 | 0.52 | 0.59 | 0.65 | 0.61 | 0.54 |
| **2. PPPs** | | | | | | | | | | |
| 2a. Per capita GDP | 259 | 283 | 309 | 360 | 447 | 501 | 555 | 633 | 723 | 900 |
| 2b. GDP | 31 191 | 34 850 | 39 030 | 46 624 | 59 220 | 67 973 | 76 971 | 89 681 | 104 707 | 133 041 |
| 2c. % of GWP | ... | ... | ... | ... | ... | ... | ... | ... | ... | ... |
| **3. Absolute 1970–1989 PARE** | | | | | | | | | | |
| 3a. Per capita GDP | 234 | 245 | 261 | 284 | 298 | 306 | 320 | 341 | 359 | 372 |
| 3b. GDP | 28 179 | 30 151 | 32 992 | 36 724 | 39 528 | 41 495 | 44 353 | 48 299 | 52 021 | 55 034 |
| 3c. % of GWP | 0.40 | 0.41 | 0.42 | 0.44 | 0.47 | 0.48 | 0.49 | 0.51 | 0.53 | 0.54 |
| **4. Relative 1970–1989 PARE** | | | | | | | | | | |
| 4a. Per capita GDP | 114 | 125 | 140 | 162 | 186 | 210 | 233 | 265 | 300 | 338 |
| 4b. GDP | 13 739 | 15 455 | 17 687 | 20 995 | 24 649 | 28 428 | 32 285 | 37 529 | 43 370 | 49 979 |
| 4c. % of GWP | 0.40 | 0.41 | 0.42 | 0.44 | 0.47 | 0.48 | 0.49 | 0.51 | 0.53 | 0.54 |
| **5. Absolute 1980–1989 PARE** | | | | | | | | | | |
| 5a. Per capita GDP | 265 | 277 | 296 | 321 | 338 | 347 | 362 | 386 | 407 | 422 |
| 5b. GDP | 31 927 | 34 162 | 37 381 | 41 609 | 44 786 | 47 015 | 50 252 | 54 724 | 58 941 | 62 355 |
| 5c. % of GWP | 0.37 | 0.38 | 0.39 | 0.41 | 0.43 | 0.45 | 0.45 | 0.47 | 0.49 | 0.50 |
| **6. WA** | | | | | | | | | | |
| 6a. Per capita GDP | 79 | 81 | 93 | 134 | 207 | 239 | 286 | 345 | 379 | 378 |
| 6b. GDP | 9 513 | 9 988 | 11 723 | 17 346 | 27 504 | 32 473 | 39 727 | 48 887 | 54 849 | 55 918 |
| 6c. % of GWP | 0.30 | 0.29 | 0.29 | 0.36 | 0.49 | 0.53 | 0.59 | 0.65 | 0.62 | 0.55 |

| | | | | | | | | | | Averages | | |
|---|---|---|---|---|---|---|---|---|---|---|---|---|
| 1980 (11) | 1981 (12) | 1982 (13) | 1983 (14) | 1984 (15) | 1985 (16) | 1986 (17) | 1987 (18) | 1988 (19) | 1989 (20) | 1970–89 (21) | 1970–79 (22) | 1980–89 (23) |
| 251 | 262 | 261 | 278 | 270 | 276 | 296 | 319 | 344 | 326 | 230 | 150 | 290 |
| 172 723 | 184 109 | 187 725 | 204 829 | 203 009 | 212 307 | 232 642 | 255 810 | 281 409 | 272 407 | 156 523 | 92 348 | 220 697 |
| 1.49 | 1.57 | 1.61 | 1.73 | 1.66 | 1.69 | 1.56 | 1.49 | 1.47 | 1.36 | 1.54 | 1.52 | 1.55 |
| 653 | 748 | 765 | 811 | 949 | 1 025 | 1 072 | 1 129 | 1 254 | 1 340 | 743 | 424 | 988 |
| 449 679 | 526 929 | 550 966 | 597 344 | 713 980 | 788 092 | 842 339 | 905 909 | 1 026 549 | 1 119 940 | 506 380 | 260 587 | 752 173 |
| ... | ... | ... | ... | ... | ... | ... | ... | ... | ... | ... | ... | ... |
| 213 | 222 | 225 | 236 | 240 | 249 | 256 | 262 | 281 | 289 | 230 | 201 | 249 |
| 146 773 | 156 282 | 162 034 | 173 986 | 180 502 | 191 750 | 200 911 | 210 039 | 230 279 | 241 333 | 156 523 | 123 656 | 189 389 |
| 1.41 | 1.48 | 1.52 | 1.59 | 1.57 | 1.62 | 1.65 | 1.66 | 1.75 | 1.77 | 1.54 | 1.44 | 1.61 |
| 211 | 241 | 260 | 282 | 297 | 317 | 331 | 349 | 388 | 414 | 236 | 137 | 313 |
| 145 491 | 169 574 | 187 171 | 207 770 | 223 273 | 243 612 | 260 380 | 280 031 | 317 323 | 346 191 | 161 051 | 84 020 | 238 082 |
| 1.41 | 1.48 | 1.52 | 1.59 | 1.57 | 1.62 | 1.65 | 1.66 | 1.75 | 1.77 | 1.57 | 1.43 | 1.62 |
| 248 | 259 | 262 | 275 | 279 | 291 | 298 | 305 | 328 | 337 | 268 | 235 | 290 |
| 171 036 | 182 118 | 188 820 | 202 747 | 210 341 | 223 449 | 234 124 | 244 761 | 268 346 | 281 228 | 182 397 | 144 098 | 220 697 |
| 1.35 | 1.41 | 1.46 | 1.52 | 1.51 | 1.55 | 1.58 | 1.60 | 1.68 | 1.71 | 1.47 | 1.37 | 1.55 |
| 250 | 254 | 256 | 272 | 258 | 279 | 292 | 320 | 330 | 317 | 227 | 150 | 285 |
| 172 066 | 178 542 | 184 450 | 200 598 | 194 060 | 214 598 | 229 421 | 256 441 | 270 193 | 264 838 | 154 462 | 92 403 | 216 521 |
| 1.49 | 1.51 | 1.58 | 1.69 | 1.59 | 1.70 | 1.56 | 1.54 | 1.44 | 1.35 | 1.53 | 1.52 | 1.53 |
| 517 | 597 | 600 | 531 | 534 | 522 | 469 | 436 | 475 | 520 | 391 | 230 | 519 |
| 78 013 | 92 008 | 94 457 | 85 369 | 87 612 | 87 339 | 80 061 | 75 932 | 84 250 | 93 966 | 58 347 | 30 793 | 85 901 |
| 0.67 | 0.79 | 0.81 | 0.72 | 0.72 | 0.69 | 0.54 | 0.44 | 0.44 | 0.47 | 0.57 | 0.51 | 0.60 |
| 1 110 | 1 308 | 1 363 | 1 524 | 1 628 | 1 633 | 1 729 | 1 830 | 1 962 | 2 152 | 1 139 | 509 | 1 642 |
| 167 548 | 201 552 | 214 551 | 244 937 | 266 959 | 273 271 | 295 140 | 318 576 | 348 147 | 389 204 | 170 159 | 68 329 | 271 988 |
| ... | ... | ... | ... | ... | ... | ... | ... | ... | ... | ... | ... | ... |
| 396 | 415 | 406 | 432 | 453 | 455 | 472 | 486 | 504 | 531 | 391 | 305 | 458 |
| 59 708 | 64 030 | 63 858 | 69 462 | 74 307 | 76 137 | 80 610 | 84 581 | 89 429 | 96 038 | 58 347 | 40 878 | 75 816 |
| 0.57 | 0.60 | 0.60 | 0.63 | 0.65 | 0.64 | 0.66 | 0.67 | 0.68 | 0.71 | 0.57 | 0.47 | 0.64 |
| 392 | 451 | 469 | 516 | 560 | 578 | 612 | 648 | 695 | 762 | 414 | 212 | 575 |
| 59 186 | 69 476 | 73 765 | 82 950 | 91 915 | 96 729 | 104 470 | 112 766 | 123 233 | 137 766 | 61 819 | 28 412 | 95 225 |
| 0.57 | 0.60 | 0.60 | 0.63 | 0.65 | 0.64 | 0.66 | 0.67 | 0.68 | 0.71 | 0.60 | 0.48 | 0.65 |
| 448 | 471 | 460 | 490 | 513 | 516 | 535 | 551 | 571 | 602 | 442 | 345 | 519 |
| 67 650 | 72 547 | 72 352 | 78 702 | 84 191 | 86 264 | 91 332 | 95 831 | 101 325 | 108 813 | 66 108 | 46 315 | 85 901 |
| 0.53 | 0.56 | 0.56 | 0.59 | 0.60 | 0.60 | 0.62 | 0.63 | 0.63 | 0.66 | 0.53 | 0.44 | 0.60 |
| 517 | 597 | 600 | 531 | 534 | 522 | 469 | 436 | 475 | 520 | 391 | 230 | 519 |
| 78 013 | 92 009 | 94 457 | 85 369 | 87 612 | 87 339 | 80 061 | 75 930 | 84 250 | 93 968 | 58 347 | 30 793 | 85 901 |
| 0.68 | 0.78 | 0.81 | 0.72 | 0.72 | 0.69 | 0.54 | 0.46 | 0.45 | 0.48 | 0.58 | 0.51 | 0.61 |

**Table A.1**  Total and per capita gross domestic product of individual countries or areas, expressed in United States dollars, and their individual shares of gross world product, based on alternative conversion rates, 1970−1989 [*cont.*]

| Country or area | 1970 (1) | 1971 (2) | 1972 (3) | 1973 (4) | 1974 (5) | 1975 (6) | 1976 (7) | 1977 (8) | 1978 (9) | 1979 (10) |
|---|---|---|---|---|---|---|---|---|---|---|
| **Iran (Islamic Republic of)** | | | | | | | | | | |
| **1.   MER** | | | | | | | | | | |
| 1a.   Per capita GDP | 388 | 473 | 570 | 886 | 1 531 | 1 687 | 2 110 | 2 424 | 2 158 | 2 395 |
| 1b.   GDP | 11 034 | 13 860 | 17 285 | 27 745 | 49 507 | 56 260 | 72 472 | 85 635 | 78 462 | 89 894 |
| 1c.   % of GWP | 0.35 | 0.40 | 0.43 | 0.57 | 0.89 | 0.91 | 1.08 | 1.13 | 0.87 | 0.87 |
| **2.   PPPs** | | | | | | | | | | |
| 2a.   Per capita GDP | 862 | 1 046 | 1 228 | 1 564 | 2 399 | 2 809 | 3 395 | 3 607 | 3 174 | 3 254 |
| 2b.   GDP | 24 497 | 30 670 | 37 203 | 48 977 | 77 547 | 93 655 | 116 593 | 127 414 | 115 433 | 122 144 |
| 2c.   % of GWP | ... | ... | ... | ... | ... | ... | ... | ... | ... | ... |
| **3.   Absolute 1970−1989 PARE** | | | | | | | | | | |
| 3a.   Per capita GDP | 3 106 | 3 382 | 3 807 | 4 001 | 4 218 | 4 203 | 4 829 | 4 826 | 4 018 | 3 556 |
| 3b.   GDP | 88 290 | 99 216 | 115 349 | 125 251 | 136 349 | 140 166 | 165 830 | 170 490 | 146 114 | 133 480 |
| 3c.   % of GWP | 1.24 | 1.34 | 1.48 | 1.51 | 1.61 | 1.63 | 1.83 | 1.81 | 1.49 | 1.31 |
| **4.   Relative 1970−1989 PARE** | | | | | | | | | | |
| 4a.   Per capita GDP | 1 514 | 1 734 | 2 041 | 2 287 | 2 630 | 2 880 | 3 515 | 3 750 | 3 350 | 3 229 |
| 4b.   GDP | 43 047 | 50 856 | 61 838 | 71 607 | 85 027 | 96 028 | 120 711 | 132 474 | 121 816 | 121 219 |
| 4c.   % of GWP | 1.24 | 1.34 | 1.48 | 1.51 | 1.61 | 1.63 | 1.83 | 1.81 | 1.49 | 1.31 |
| **5.   Absolute 1980−1989 PARE** | | | | | | | | | | |
| 5a.   Per capita GDP | 4 921 | 5 359 | 6 032 | 6 339 | 6 683 | 6 660 | 7 652 | 7 647 | 6 367 | 5 634 |
| 5b.   GDP | 139 893 | 157 205 | 182 767 | 198 456 | 216 041 | 222 089 | 262 754 | 270 137 | 231 514 | 211 496 |
| 5c.   % of GWP | 1.61 | 1.73 | 1.91 | 1.95 | 2.08 | 2.11 | 2.38 | 2.34 | 1.93 | 1.71 |
| **6.   WA** | | | | | | | | | | |
| 6a.   Per capita GDP | 388 | 473 | 570 | 886 | 1 531 | 1 674 | 2 101 | 2 426 | 2 158 | 2 395 |
| 6b.   GDP | 11 034 | 13 860 | 17 285 | 27 745 | 49 507 | 55 825 | 72 151 | 85 681 | 78 462 | 89 894 |
| 6c.   % of GWP | 0.35 | 0.40 | 0.43 | 0.57 | 0.89 | 0.91 | 1.08 | 1.14 | 0.88 | 0.88 |
| **Iraq** | | | | | | | | | | |
| **1.   MER** | | | | | | | | | | |
| 1a.   Per capita GDP | 376 | 427 | 439 | 525 | 1 075 | 1 237 | 1 565 | 1 697 | 1 954 | 2 965 |
| 1b.   GDP | 3 521 | 4 126 | 4 371 | 5 403 | 11 437 | 13 635 | 17 886 | 20 140 | 24 083 | 37 970 |
| 1c.   % of GWP | 0.11 | 0.12 | 0.11 | 0.11 | 0.21 | 0.22 | 0.27 | 0.27 | 0.27 | 0.37 |
| **2.   PPPs** | | | | | | | | | | |
| 2a.   Per capita GDP | 838 | 964 | 1 007 | 1 097 | 1 906 | 2 256 | 2 467 | 2 799 | 3 077 | 5 124 |
| 2b.   GDP | 7 837 | 9 308 | 10 040 | 11 297 | 20 288 | 24 859 | 28 195 | 33 217 | 37 930 | 65 602 |
| 2c.   % of GWP | ... | ... | ... | ... | ... | ... | ... | ... | ... | ... |
| **3.   Absolute 1970−1989 PARE** | | | | | | | | | | |
| 3a.   Per capita GDP | 1 998 | 2 070 | 1 930 | 2 223 | 2 324 | 2 567 | 2 986 | 2 929 | 3 333 | 3 978 |
| 3b.   GDP | 18 694 | 19 991 | 19 245 | 22 887 | 24 731 | 28 284 | 34 123 | 34 752 | 41 089 | 50 936 |
| 3c.   % of GWP | 0.26 | 0.27 | 0.25 | 0.28 | 0.29 | 0.33 | 0.38 | 0.37 | 0.42 | 0.50 |
| **4.   Relative 1970−1989 PARE** | | | | | | | | | | |
| 4a.   Per capita GDP | 974 | 1 061 | 1 035 | 1 271 | 1 449 | 1 758 | 2 173 | 2 276 | 2 779 | 3 613 |
| 4b.   GDP | 9 115 | 10 247 | 10 317 | 13 085 | 15 422 | 19 378 | 24 839 | 27 003 | 34 256 | 46 257 |
| 4c.   % of GWP | 0.26 | 0.27 | 0.25 | 0.28 | 0.29 | 0.33 | 0.38 | 0.37 | 0.42 | 0.50 |
| **5.   Absolute 1980−1989 PARE** | | | | | | | | | | |
| 5a.   Per capita GDP | 2 860 | 2 963 | 2 763 | 3 182 | 3 326 | 3 674 | 4 274 | 4 192 | 4 771 | 5 694 |
| 5b.   GDP | 26 757 | 28 614 | 27 546 | 32 759 | 35 398 | 40 485 | 48 842 | 49 743 | 58 812 | 72 907 |
| 5c.   % of GWP | 0.31 | 0.32 | 0.29 | 0.32 | 0.34 | 0.39 | 0.44 | 0.43 | 0.49 | 0.59 |
| **6.   WA**[a] | | | | | | | | | | |
| 6a.   Per capita GDP | 391 | 405 | 398 | 495 | 645 | 909 | 1 458 | 1 539 | 1 873 | 2 500 |
| 6b.   GDP | 3 662 | 3 914 | 3 966 | 5 092 | 6 869 | 10 015 | 16 660 | 18 266 | 23 086 | 32 014 |
| 6c.   % of GWP | 0.11 | 0.11 | 0.10 | 0.10 | 0.12 | 0.16 | 0.25 | 0.24 | 0.26 | 0.31 |

| | | | | | | | | | | Averages | | |
|---|---|---|---|---|---|---|---|---|---|---|---|---|
| 1980 (11) | 1981 (12) | 1982 (13) | 1983 (14) | 1984 (15) | 1985 (16) | 1986 (17) | 1987 (18) | 1988 (19) | 1989 (20) | 1970–89 (21) | 1970–79 (22) | 1980–89 (23) |
| 2 521 | 2 625 | 3 047 | 3 612 | 3 637 | 3 818 | 4 676 | 5 868 | 7 571 | 8 537 | 3 559 | 1 529 | 4 744 |
| 98 081 | 106 257 | 128 661 | 159 215 | 166 940 | 181 828 | 230 136 | 297 488 | 394 265 | 455 703 | 136 036 | 50 216 | 221 857 |
| 0.85 | 0.91 | 1.11 | 1.34 | 1.37 | 1.44 | 1.55 | 1.73 | 2.06 | 2.27 | 1.34 | 0.82 | 1.55 |
| 3 228 | 3 330 | 4 335 | 5 447 | 5 695 | 6 239 | 5 640 | 5 570 | 5 548 | 5 579 | 4 164 | 2 418 | 5 108 |
| 125 588 | 134 793 | 183 069 | 240 107 | 261 415 | 297 105 | 277 575 | 282 373 | 288 932 | 297 775 | 159 143 | 79 413 | 238 873 |
| ... | ... | ... | ... | ... | ... | ... | ... | ... | ... | ... | ... | ... |
| 2 948 | 2 876 | 3 176 | 3 440 | 3 311 | 3 334 | 2 955 | 2 837 | 2 734 | 2 641 | 3 559 | 4 022 | 2 994 |
| 114 679 | 116 410 | 134 128 | 151 638 | 151 998 | 158 787 | 145 427 | 143 809 | 142 370 | 140 948 | 136 036 | 132 053 | 140 020 |
| 1.10 | 1.10 | 1.26 | 1.38 | 1.33 | 1.34 | 1.19 | 1.14 | 1.08 | 1.04 | 1.34 | 1.53 | 1.19 |
| 2 922 | 3 121 | 3 669 | 4 108 | 4 096 | 4 236 | 3 830 | 3 782 | 3 767 | 3 788 | 3 465 | 2 755 | 3 730 |
| 113 677 | 126 311 | 154 936 | 181 082 | 188 015 | 201 734 | 188 473 | 191 731 | 196 185 | 202 189 | 132 448 | 90 462 | 174 433 |
| 1.10 | 1.10 | 1.26 | 1.38 | 1.33 | 1.34 | 1.19 | 1.14 | 1.08 | 1.04 | 1.29 | 1.54 | 1.19 |
| 4 671 | 4 557 | 5 033 | 5 451 | 5 247 | 5 283 | 4 682 | 4 495 | 4 332 | 4 184 | 5 640 | 6 372 | 4 744 |
| 181 707 | 184 449 | 212 523 | 240 266 | 240 838 | 251 594 | 230 426 | 227 862 | 225 581 | 223 328 | 215 546 | 209 235 | 221 857 |
| 1.44 | 1.43 | 1.64 | 1.80 | 1.73 | 1.75 | 1.55 | 1.49 | 1.41 | 1.35 | 1.74 | 1.99 | 1.55 |
| 2 488 | 2 569 | 3 016 | 3 576 | 3 563 | 3 963 | 4 811 | 2 895 | 2 922 | 2 720 | 2 643 | 1 527 | 3 248 |
| 96 766 | 104 001 | 127 366 | 157 627 | 163 539 | 188 707 | 236 780 | 146 784 | 152 194 | 145 180 | 101 019 | 50 144 | 151 894 |
| 0.84 | 0.88 | 1.09 | 1.33 | 1.34 | 1.49 | 1.61 | 0.88 | 0.81 | 0.74 | 1.00 | 0.83 | 1.07 |
| 3 969 | 2 662 | 3 063 | 2 863 | 3 101 | 3 108 | 2 913 | 3 499 | 3 277 | 3 652 | 2 481 | 1 316 | 3 232 |
| 52 749 | 36 708 | 43 783 | 42 415 | 47 584 | 49 419 | 47 968 | 59 669 | 57 854 | 66 764 | 32 374 | 14 257 | 50 491 |
| 0.46 | 0.31 | 0.38 | 0.36 | 0.39 | 0.39 | 0.32 | 0.35 | 0.30 | 0.33 | 0.32 | 0.23 | 0.35 |
| 6 272 | 5 096 | 2 225 | 2 986 | 2 961 | 2 839 | 2 571 | 2 497 | 2 710 | 2 476 | 2 862 | 2 295 | 3 189 |
| 83 362 | 70 263 | 31 801 | 44 229 | 45 449 | 45 131 | 42 342 | 42 586 | 47 854 | 45 263 | 37 343 | 24 857 | 49 828 |
| ... | ... | ... | ... | ... | ... | ... | ... | ... | ... | ... | ... | ... |
| 3 802 | 2 998 | 2 857 | 2 555 | 2 269 | 1 978 | 1 757 | 1 659 | 1 742 | 1 529 | 2 481 | 2 721 | 2 258 |
| 50 541 | 41 336 | 40 834 | 37 854 | 34 825 | 31 456 | 28 931 | 28 285 | 30 752 | 27 941 | 32 374 | 29 473 | 35 276 |
| 0.49 | 0.39 | 0.38 | 0.35 | 0.30 | 0.27 | 0.24 | 0.22 | 0.23 | 0.21 | 0.32 | 0.34 | 0.30 |
| 3 769 | 3 253 | 3 300 | 3 052 | 2 807 | 2 514 | 2 277 | 2 211 | 2 400 | 2 193 | 2 445 | 1 938 | 2 740 |
| 50 099 | 44 852 | 47 169 | 45 205 | 43 077 | 39 964 | 37 494 | 37 711 | 42 375 | 40 081 | 31 897 | 20 992 | 42 803 |
| 0.49 | 0.39 | 0.38 | 0.35 | 0.30 | 0.27 | 0.24 | 0.22 | 0.23 | 0.21 | 0.31 | 0.36 | 0.29 |
| 5 442 | 4 291 | 4 089 | 3 658 | 3 248 | 2 832 | 2 515 | 2 374 | 2 493 | 2 188 | 3 551 | 3 895 | 3 232 |
| 72 341 | 59 167 | 58 448 | 54 182 | 49 846 | 45 025 | 41 410 | 40 486 | 44 016 | 39 993 | 46 339 | 42 186 | 50 491 |
| 0.57 | 0.46 | 0.45 | 0.41 | 0.36 | 0.31 | 0.28 | 0.26 | 0.28 | 0.24 | 0.37 | 0.40 | 0.35 |
| 2 848 | 2 625 | 2 841 | 2 598 | 2 662 | 2 625 | 2 673 | 2 904 | 3 248 | 3 220 | 2 181 | 1 141 | 2 851 |
| 37 851 | 36 200 | 40 606 | 38 480 | 40 859 | 41 740 | 44 024 | 49 516 | 57 347 | 58 861 | 28 451 | 12 355 | 44 548 |
| 0.33 | 0.31 | 0.35 | 0.32 | 0.33 | 0.33 | 0.30 | 0.30 | 0.31 | 0.30 | 0.28 | 0.20 | 0.32 |

**Table A.1**    Total and per capita gross domestic product of individual countries or areas,
expressed in United States dollars, and their individual shares of gross world
product, based on alternative conversion rates, 1970–1989 [*cont.*]

| Country or area | 1970 (1) | 1971 (2) | 1972 (3) | 1973 (4) | 1974 (5) | 1975 (6) | 1976 (7) | 1977 (8) | 1978 (9) | 1979 (10) |
|---|---|---|---|---|---|---|---|---|---|---|
| **Ireland** | | | | | | | | | | |
| **1.    MER** | | | | | | | | | | |
| 1a.    Per capita GDP | 1 315 | 1 516 | 1 846 | 2 150 | 2 231 | 2 652 | 2 576 | 3 040 | 3 906 | 4 825 |
| 1b.    GDP | 3 885 | 4 531 | 5 594 | 6 620 | 6 980 | 8 427 | 8 309 | 9 954 | 12 969 | 16 223 |
| 1c.    % of GWP | 0.12 | 0.13 | 0.14 | 0.13 | 0.13 | 0.14 | 0.12 | 0.13 | 0.14 | 0.16 |
| **2.    PPPs** | | | | | | | | | | |
| 2a.    Per capita GDP | 1 970 | 2 127 | 2 368 | 2 680 | 2 835 | 3 097 | 3 385 | 3 884 | 4 471 | 4 837 |
| 2b.    GDP | 5 819 | 6 358 | 7 176 | 8 250 | 8 872 | 9 842 | 10 919 | 12 717 | 14 845 | 16 262 |
| 2c.    % of GWP | ... | ... | ... | ... | ... | ... | ... | ... | ... | ... |
| **3.    Absolute 1970–1989 PARE** | | | | | | | | | | |
| 3a.    Per capita GDP | 3 514 | 3 593 | 3 774 | 3 890 | 3 991 | 4 152 | 4 147 | 4 422 | 4 674 | 4 757 |
| 3b.    GDP | 10 380 | 10 741 | 11 438 | 11 978 | 12 488 | 13 194 | 13 378 | 14 477 | 15 517 | 15 994 |
| 3c.    % of GWP | 0.15 | 0.15 | 0.15 | 0.14 | 0.15 | 0.15 | 0.15 | 0.15 | 0.16 | 0.16 |
| **4.    Relative 1970–1989 PARE** | | | | | | | | | | |
| 4a.    Per capita GDP | 1 713 | 1 842 | 2 023 | 2 224 | 2 489 | 2 844 | 3 019 | 3 436 | 3 897 | 4 320 |
| 4b.    GDP | 5 061 | 5 505 | 6 132 | 6 848 | 7 787 | 9 040 | 9 738 | 11 249 | 12 937 | 14 525 |
| 4c.    % of GWP | 0.15 | 0.15 | 0.15 | 0.14 | 0.15 | 0.15 | 0.15 | 0.15 | 0.16 | 0.16 |
| **5.    Absolute 1980–1989 PARE** | | | | | | | | | | |
| 5a.    Per capita GDP | 4 393 | 4 492 | 4 717 | 4 863 | 4 989 | 5 190 | 5 184 | 5 528 | 5 843 | 5 947 |
| 5b.    GDP | 12 977 | 13 427 | 14 299 | 14 974 | 15 612 | 16 495 | 16 725 | 18 098 | 19 399 | 19 995 |
| 5c.    % of GWP | 0.15 | 0.15 | 0.15 | 0.15 | 0.15 | 0.16 | 0.15 | 0.16 | 0.16 | 0.16 |
| **6.    WA** | | | | | | | | | | |
| 6a.    Per capita GDP | 1 316 | 1 509 | 1 844 | 2 149 | 2 232 | 2 640 | 2 592 | 3 039 | 3 903 | 4 820 |
| 6b.    GDP | 3 888 | 4 510 | 5 588 | 6 617 | 6 984 | 8 389 | 8 361 | 9 949 | 12 956 | 16 203 |
| 6c.    % of GWP | 0.12 | 0.13 | 0.14 | 0.14 | 0.13 | 0.14 | 0.12 | 0.13 | 0.15 | 0.16 |
| **Israel** | | | | | | | | | | |
| **1.    MER** | | | | | | | | | | |
| 1a.    Per capita GDP | 1 921 | 2 231 | 2 559 | 3 211 | 4 165 | 3 979 | 4 088 | 4 349 | 4 179 | 5 294 |
| 1b.    GDP | 5 714 | 6 842 | 8 095 | 10 476 | 14 000 | 13 750 | 14 500 | 15 810 | 15 543 | 20 118 |
| 1c.    % of GWP | 0.18 | 0.20 | 0.20 | 0.21 | 0.25 | 0.22 | 0.22 | 0.21 | 0.17 | 0.20 |
| **2.    PPPs** | | | | | | | | | | |
| 2a.    Per capita GDP | 2 481 | 2 883 | 3 300 | 3 776 | 4 106 | 4 649 | 4 861 | 4 964 | 5 519 | 6 058 |
| 2b.    GDP | 7 382 | 8 841 | 10 443 | 12 322 | 13 801 | 16 067 | 17 241 | 18 044 | 20 527 | 23 022 |
| 2c.    % of GWP | ... | ... | ... | ... | ... | ... | ... | ... | ... | ... |
| **3.    Absolute 1970–1989 PARE** | | | | | | | | | | |
| 3a.    Per capita GDP | 4 547 | 4 891 | 5 333 | 5 450 | 5 629 | 5 646 | 5 511 | 5 426 | 5 544 | 5 746 |
| 3b.    GDP | 13 528 | 15 000 | 16 872 | 17 784 | 18 918 | 19 512 | 19 546 | 19 724 | 20 618 | 21 834 |
| 3c.    % of GWP | 0.19 | 0.20 | 0.22 | 0.21 | 0.22 | 0.23 | 0.22 | 0.21 | 0.21 | 0.21 |
| **4.    Relative 1970–1989 PARE** | | | | | | | | | | |
| 4a.    Per capita GDP | 2 217 | 2 507 | 2 859 | 3 116 | 3 510 | 3 868 | 4 011 | 4 216 | 4 622 | 5 218 |
| 4b.    GDP | 6 596 | 7 689 | 9 045 | 10 167 | 11 797 | 13 368 | 14 228 | 15 326 | 17 189 | 19 828 |
| 4c.    % of GWP | 0.19 | 0.20 | 0.22 | 0.21 | 0.22 | 0.23 | 0.22 | 0.21 | 0.21 | 0.21 |
| **5.    Absolute 1980–1989 PARE** | | | | | | | | | | |
| 5a.    Per capita GDP | 5 571 | 5 992 | 6 534 | 6 678 | 6 896 | 6 917 | 6 752 | 6 648 | 6 792 | 7 040 |
| 5b.    GDP | 16 575 | 18 378 | 20 672 | 21 789 | 23 178 | 23 906 | 23 948 | 24 166 | 25 261 | 26 751 |
| 5c.    % of GWP | 0.19 | 0.20 | 0.22 | 0.21 | 0.22 | 0.23 | 0.22 | 0.21 | 0.21 | 0.22 |
| **6.    WA** | | | | | | | | | | |
| 6a.    Per capita GDP | 1 921 | 2 236 | 2 571 | 3 215 | 4 211 | 4 019 | 4 126 | 4 372 | 4 195 | 5 293 |
| 6b.    GDP | 5 714 | 6 857 | 8 134 | 10 489 | 14 152 | 13 889 | 14 636 | 15 892 | 15 600 | 20 113 |
| 6c.    % of GWP | 0.18 | 0.20 | 0.20 | 0.22 | 0.25 | 0.23 | 0.22 | 0.21 | 0.18 | 0.20 |

| | | | | | | | | | | Averages | | |
|---|---|---|---|---|---|---|---|---|---|---|---|---|
| 1980 (11) | 1981 (12) | 1982 (13) | 1983 (14) | 1984 (15) | 1985 (16) | 1986 (17) | 1987 (18) | 1988 (19) | 1989 (20) | 1970–89 (21) | 1970–79 (22) | 1980–89 (23) |
| 5 662 | 5 341 | 5 491 | 5 279 | 5 062 | 5 241 | 7 065 | 7 916 | 8 406 | 9 273 | 4 640 | 2 648 | 6 511 |
| 19 261 | 18 351 | 19 036 | 18 451 | 17 833 | 18 622 | 25 320 | 28 630 | 30 689 | 34 170 | 15 693 | 8 349 | 23 036 |
| 0.17 | 0.16 | 0.16 | 0.16 | 0.15 | 0.15 | 0.17 | 0.17 | 0.16 | 0.17 | 0.15 | 0.14 | 0.16 |
| 5 203 | 5 886 | 6 380 | 6 455 | 6 987 | 7 128 | 7 182 | 7 641 | 8 127 | 8 875 | 5 165 | 3 205 | 7 018 |
| 17 700 | 20 223 | 22 119 | 22 559 | 24 615 | 25 326 | 25 740 | 27 638 | 29 670 | 32 705 | 17 468 | 10 106 | 24 829 |
| ... | ... | ... | ... | ... | ... | ... | ... | ... | ... | ... | ... | ... |
| 4 846 | 4 958 | 5 026 | 4 973 | 5 149 | 5 233 | 5 169 | 5 346 | 5 501 | 5 771 | 4 640 | 4 109 | 5 208 |
| 16 487 | 17 035 | 17 424 | 17 381 | 18 138 | 18 594 | 18 525 | 19 336 | 20 083 | 21 266 | 15 693 | 12 959 | 18 427 |
| 0.16 | 0.16 | 0.16 | 0.16 | 0.16 | 0.16 | 0.15 | 0.15 | 0.15 | 0.16 | 0.15 | 0.15 | 0.16 |
| 4 804 | 5 379 | 5 805 | 5 939 | 6 369 | 6 649 | 6 699 | 7 127 | 7 580 | 8 278 | 4 710 | 2 817 | 6 493 |
| 16 343 | 18 484 | 20 127 | 20 757 | 22 436 | 23 623 | 24 009 | 25 779 | 27 674 | 30 505 | 15 928 | 8 882 | 22 974 |
| 0.16 | 0.16 | 0.16 | 0.16 | 0.16 | 0.16 | 0.15 | 0.15 | 0.15 | 0.16 | 0.15 | 0.15 | 0.16 |
| 6 058 | 6 198 | 6 283 | 6 217 | 6 436 | 6 542 | 6 462 | 6 683 | 6 877 | 7 214 | 5 801 | 5 137 | 6 511 |
| 20 611 | 21 296 | 21 782 | 21 729 | 22 676 | 23 245 | 23 159 | 24 172 | 25 107 | 26 585 | 19 618 | 16 200 | 23 036 |
| 0.16 | 0.17 | 0.17 | 0.16 | 0.16 | 0.16 | 0.16 | 0.16 | 0.16 | 0.16 | 0.16 | 0.15 | 0.16 |
| 5 654 | 5 321 | 5 478 | 5 255 | 5 048 | 5 266 | 7 035 | 8 234 | 8 963 | 9 200 | 4 678 | 2 646 | 6 585 |
| 19 235 | 18 283 | 18 994 | 18 367 | 17 784 | 18 708 | 25 213 | 29 783 | 32 724 | 33 902 | 15 822 | 8 345 | 23 299 |
| 0.17 | 0.16 | 0.16 | 0.15 | 0.15 | 0.15 | 0.17 | 0.18 | 0.17 | 0.17 | 0.16 | 0.14 | 0.16 |
| 5 893 | 6 131 | 6 512 | 7 118 | 6 589 | 6 064 | 7 445 | 8 722 | 10 323 | 10 256 | 5 770 | 3 663 | 7 579 |
| 22 852 | 24 234 | 26 205 | 29 141 | 27 432 | 25 671 | 32 058 | 38 195 | 45 968 | 46 428 | 22 152 | 12 485 | 31 818 |
| 0.20 | 0.21 | 0.23 | 0.25 | 0.22 | 0.20 | 0.22 | 0.22 | 0.24 | 0.23 | 0.22 | 0.20 | 0.22 |
| 6 512 | 7 496 | 8 222 | 8 773 | 8 902 | 8 961 | 9 375 | 10 098 | 10 430 | 10 724 | 6 853 | 4 333 | 9 015 |
| 25 253 | 29 631 | 33 084 | 35 918 | 37 059 | 37 930 | 40 370 | 44 221 | 46 445 | 48 545 | 26 307 | 14 769 | 37 846 |
| ... | ... | ... | ... | ... | ... | ... | ... | ... | ... | ... | ... | ... |
| 5 766 | 5 948 | 5 949 | 6 052 | 6 006 | 6 110 | 6 267 | 6 562 | 6 557 | 6 476 | 5 770 | 5 379 | 6 186 |
| 22 362 | 23 513 | 23 938 | 24 779 | 25 002 | 25 865 | 26 986 | 28 735 | 29 199 | 29 318 | 22 152 | 18 334 | 25 970 |
| 0.22 | 0.22 | 0.22 | 0.23 | 0.22 | 0.22 | 0.22 | 0.23 | 0.22 | 0.22 | 0.22 | 0.21 | 0.22 |
| 5 716 | 6 454 | 6 872 | 7 228 | 7 429 | 7 763 | 8 122 | 8 749 | 9 036 | 9 290 | 5 855 | 3 674 | 7 725 |
| 22 166 | 25 513 | 27 652 | 29 590 | 30 927 | 32 860 | 34 974 | 38 310 | 40 236 | 42 056 | 22 476 | 12 523 | 32 428 |
| 0.22 | 0.22 | 0.22 | 0.23 | 0.22 | 0.22 | 0.22 | 0.23 | 0.22 | 0.22 | 0.22 | 0.21 | 0.22 |
| 7 065 | 7 288 | 7 289 | 7 415 | 7 358 | 7 486 | 7 679 | 8 040 | 8 034 | 7 935 | 7 070 | 6 590 | 7 579 |
| 27 398 | 28 808 | 29 329 | 30 359 | 30 633 | 31 690 | 33 064 | 35 206 | 35 775 | 35 921 | 27 140 | 22 462 | 31 818 |
| 0.22 | 0.22 | 0.23 | 0.23 | 0.22 | 0.22 | 0.22 | 0.23 | 0.22 | 0.22 | 0.22 | 0.21 | 0.22 |
| 5 888 | 6 130 | 6 513 | 7 117 | 6 589 | 6 064 | 7 456 | 8 752 | 10 330 | 10 168 | 5 776 | 3 681 | 7 574 |
| 22 832 | 24 233 | 26 208 | 29 138 | 27 431 | 25 670 | 32 104 | 38 323 | 45 999 | 46 030 | 22 172 | 12 548 | 31 797 |
| 0.20 | 0.21 | 0.22 | 0.25 | 0.22 | 0.20 | 0.22 | 0.23 | 0.25 | 0.23 | 0.22 | 0.21 | 0.22 |

**Table A.1**    Total and per capita gross domestic product of individual countries or areas,
expressed in United States dollars, and their individual shares of gross world
product, based on alternative conversion rates, 1970–1989 [*cont.*]

| Country or area | 1970 (1) | 1971 (2) | 1972 (3) | 1973 (4) | 1974 (5) | 1975 (6) | 1976 (7) | 1977 (8) | 1978 (9) | 1979 (10) |
|---|---|---|---|---|---|---|---|---|---|---|
| **Italy** | | | | | | | | | | |
| **1.   MER** | | | | | | | | | | |
| 1a.   Per capita GDP | 1 997 | 2 174 | 2 510 | 3 025 | 3 406 | 3 830 | 3 773 | 4 347 | 5 327 | 6 628 |
| 1b.   GDP | 107 485 | 117 746 | 136 844 | 165 931 | 187 886 | 212 349 | 210 096 | 242 974 | 298 749 | 372 908 |
| 1c.   % of GWP | 3.37 | 3.36 | 3.40 | 3.38 | 3.38 | 3.42 | 3.13 | 3.21 | 3.32 | 3.62 |
| **2.   PPPs** | | | | | | | | | | |
| 2a.   Per capita GDP | 2 710 | 2 905 | 3 144 | 3 586 | 4 098 | 4 368 | 4 937 | 5 438 | 6 135 | 7 136 |
| 2b.   GDP | 145 877 | 157 363 | 171 392 | 196 687 | 226 065 | 242 171 | 274 937 | 303 983 | 344 084 | 401 512 |
| 2c.   % of GWP | ... | ... | ... | ... | ... | ... | ... | ... | ... | ... |
| **3.   Absolute 1970–1989 PARE** | | | | | | | | | | |
| 3a.   Per capita GDP | 5 171 | 5 220 | 5 327 | 5 671 | 5 945 | 5 758 | 6 110 | 6 292 | 6 502 | 6 870 |
| 3b.   GDP | 278 301 | 282 767 | 290 400 | 311 045 | 327 930 | 319 234 | 340 237 | 351 720 | 364 670 | 386 504 |
| 3c.   % of GWP | 3.92 | 3.82 | 3.72 | 3.75 | 3.87 | 3.71 | 3.76 | 3.73 | 3.71 | 3.80 |
| **4.   Relative 1970–1989 PARE** | | | | | | | | | | |
| 4a.   Per capita GDP | 2 521 | 2 676 | 2 856 | 3 242 | 3 707 | 3 945 | 4 447 | 4 889 | 5 421 | 6 239 |
| 4b.   GDP | 135 691 | 144 941 | 155 683 | 177 827 | 204 496 | 218 709 | 247 666 | 273 294 | 304 027 | 350 999 |
| 4c.   % of GWP | 3.92 | 3.82 | 3.72 | 3.75 | 3.87 | 3.71 | 3.76 | 3.73 | 3.71 | 3.80 |
| **5.   Absolute 1980–1989 PARE** | | | | | | | | | | |
| 5a.   Per capita GDP | 6 590 | 6 653 | 6 789 | 7 228 | 7 577 | 7 338 | 7 786 | 8 019 | 8 286 | 8 755 |
| 5b.   GDP | 354 669 | 360 361 | 370 089 | 396 398 | 417 917 | 406 834 | 433 601 | 448 236 | 464 739 | 492 563 |
| 5c.   % of GWP | 4.08 | 3.98 | 3.87 | 3.90 | 4.03 | 3.87 | 3.92 | 3.89 | 3.87 | 3.97 |
| **6.   WA** | | | | | | | | | | |
| 6a.   Per capita GDP | 1 997 | 2 174 | 2 510 | 3 025 | 3 406 | 3 830 | 3 773 | 4 347 | 5 327 | 6 628 |
| 6b.   GDP | 107 485 | 117 745 | 136 844 | 165 933 | 187 885 | 212 349 | 210 094 | 242 975 | 298 748 | 372 907 |
| 6c.   % of GWP | 3.37 | 3.38 | 3.42 | 3.41 | 3.37 | 3.45 | 3.13 | 3.22 | 3.36 | 3.65 |
| **Jamaica** | | | | | | | | | | |
| **1.   MER** | | | | | | | | | | |
| 1a.   Per capita GDP | 751 | 811 | 965 | 969 | 1 196 | 1 421 | 1 454 | 1 576 | 1 273 | 1 158 |
| 1b.   GDP | 1 405 | 1 537 | 1 858 | 1 896 | 2 375 | 2 861 | 2 963 | 3 246 | 2 651 | 2 439 |
| 1c.   % of GWP | 0.04 | 0.04 | 0.05 | 0.04 | 0.04 | 0.05 | 0.04 | 0.04 | 0.03 | 0.02 |
| **2.   PPPs** | | | | | | | | | | |
| 2a.   Per capita GDP | 1 257 | 1 326 | 1 455 | 1 442 | 1 493 | 1 727 | 1 633 | 1 609 | 1 781 | 1 904 |
| 2b.   GDP | 2 350 | 2 513 | 2 803 | 2 821 | 2 966 | 3 477 | 3 328 | 3 315 | 3 709 | 4 011 |
| 2c.   % of GWP | ... | ... | ... | ... | ... | ... | ... | ... | ... | ... |
| **3.   Absolute 1970–1989 PARE** | | | | | | | | | | |
| 3a.   Per capita GDP | 1 395 | 1 417 | 1 523 | 1 518 | 1 437 | 1 414 | 1 306 | 1 262 | 1 255 | 1 218 |
| 3b.   GDP | 2 608 | 2 687 | 2 933 | 2 970 | 2 855 | 2 846 | 2 662 | 2 599 | 2 613 | 2 565 |
| 3c.   % of GWP | 0.04 | 0.04 | 0.04 | 0.04 | 0.03 | 0.03 | 0.03 | 0.03 | 0.03 | 0.03 |
| **4.   Relative 1970–1989 PARE** | | | | | | | | | | |
| 4a.   Per capita GDP | 680 | 726 | 816 | 868 | 896 | 969 | 951 | 980 | 1 046 | 1 106 |
| 4b.   GDP | 1 272 | 1 377 | 1 572 | 1 698 | 1 780 | 1 950 | 1 938 | 2 019 | 2 178 | 2 329 |
| 4c.   % of GWP | 0.04 | 0.04 | 0.04 | 0.04 | 0.03 | 0.03 | 0.03 | 0.03 | 0.03 | 0.03 |
| **5.   Absolute 1980–1989 PARE** | | | | | | | | | | |
| 5a.   Per capita GDP | 1 619 | 1 645 | 1 768 | 1 763 | 1 669 | 1 642 | 1 517 | 1 465 | 1 457 | 1 414 |
| 5b.   GDP | 3 028 | 3 120 | 3 405 | 3 449 | 3 315 | 3 304 | 3 091 | 3 017 | 3 034 | 2 978 |
| 5c.   % of GWP | 0.03 | 0.03 | 0.04 | 0.03 | 0.03 | 0.03 | 0.03 | 0.03 | 0.03 | 0.02 |
| **6.   WA** | | | | | | | | | | |
| 6a.   Per capita GDP | 748 | 818 | 925 | 970 | 1 196 | 1 421 | 1 455 | 1 578 | 1 239 | 1 156 |
| 6b.   GDP | 1 399 | 1 552 | 1 782 | 1 898 | 2 375 | 2 861 | 2 966 | 3 250 | 2 579 | 2 435 |
| 6c.   % of GWP | 0.04 | 0.04 | 0.04 | 0.04 | 0.04 | 0.05 | 0.04 | 0.04 | 0.03 | 0.02 |

|  |  |  |  |  |  |  |  |  |  | Averages | | |
| 1980 (11) | 1981 (12) | 1982 (13) | 1983 (14) | 1984 (15) | 1985 (16) | 1986 (17) | 1987 (18) | 1988 (19) | 1989 (20) | 1970–89 (21) | 1970–79 (22) | 1980–89 (23) |
|---|---|---|---|---|---|---|---|---|---|---|---|---|
| 8 021 | 7 211 | 7 098 | 7 325 | 7 254 | 7 449 | 10 516 | 13 223 | 14 509 | 15 166 | 6 766 | 3 712 | 9 759 |
| 452 646 | 408 204 | 403 046 | 417 053 | 413 911 | 425 649 | 601 231 | 755 865 | 828 872 | 865 826 | 381 264 | 205 297 | 557 230 |
| 3.91 | 3.49 | 3.47 | 3.52 | 3.39 | 3.38 | 4.04 | 4.40 | 4.34 | 4.32 | 3.74 | 3.37 | 3.90 |
| 8 196 | 8 887 | 9 495 | 9 868 | 10 569 | 10 959 | 11 458 | 12 141 | 13 049 | 14 023 | 7 680 | 4 456 | 10 842 |
| 462 546 | 503 068 | 539 149 | 561 848 | 603 091 | 626 244 | 655 072 | 693 988 | 745 474 | 800 587 | 432 757 | 246 407 | 619 107 |
| ... | ... | ... | ... | ... | ... | ... | ... | ... | ... | ... | ... | ... |
| 7 139 | 7 185 | 7 187 | 7 247 | 7 450 | 7 635 | 7 825 | 8 059 | 8 381 | 8 652 | 6 766 | 5 882 | 7 657 |
| 402 879 | 406 742 | 408 066 | 412 658 | 425 091 | 436 258 | 447 351 | 460 689 | 478 793 | 493 937 | 381 264 | 325 281 | 437 246 |
| 3.88 | 3.84 | 3.83 | 3.76 | 3.71 | 3.68 | 3.66 | 3.65 | 3.63 | 3.63 | 3.74 | 3.77 | 3.72 |
| 7 077 | 7 796 | 8 302 | 8 655 | 9 215 | 9 700 | 10 141 | 10 745 | 11 549 | 12 411 | 6 798 | 4 002 | 9 539 |
| 399 358 | 441 335 | 471 371 | 492 787 | 525 818 | 554 250 | 579 764 | 614 206 | 659 773 | 708 551 | 383 027 | 221 333 | 544 721 |
| 3.88 | 3.84 | 3.83 | 3.76 | 3.71 | 3.68 | 3.66 | 3.65 | 3.63 | 3.63 | 3.73 | 3.77 | 3.71 |
| 9 098 | 9 157 | 9 159 | 9 236 | 9 494 | 9 730 | 9 972 | 10 271 | 10 681 | 11 026 | 8 623 | 7 496 | 9 759 |
| 513 432 | 518 355 | 520 042 | 525 895 | 541 740 | 555 971 | 570 108 | 587 106 | 610 178 | 629 478 | 485 886 | 414 541 | 557 230 |
| 4.06 | 4.02 | 4.01 | 3.94 | 3.89 | 3.86 | 3.85 | 3.83 | 3.82 | 3.82 | 3.92 | 3.93 | 3.90 |
| 8 021 | 7 211 | 7 098 | 7 325 | 7 254 | 7 449 | 10 516 | 13 223 | 14 509 | 15 166 | 6 766 | 3 712 | 9 759 |
| 452 648 | 408 204 | 403 046 | 417 053 | 413 911 | 425 649 | 601 231 | 755 883 | 828 853 | 865 832 | 381 264 | 205 296 | 557 231 |
| 3.93 | 3.46 | 3.46 | 3.52 | 3.39 | 3.37 | 4.09 | 4.54 | 4.43 | 4.41 | 3.77 | 3.38 | 3.94 |
| 1 250 | 1 372 | 1 492 | 1 613 | 1 038 | 875 | 1 038 | 1 226 | 1 420 | 1 612 | 1 246 | 1 162 | 1 290 |
| 2 667 | 2 971 | 3 284 | 3 612 | 2 365 | 2 023 | 2 432 | 2 909 | 3 409 | 3 915 | 2 641 | 2 323 | 2 959 |
| 0.02 | 0.03 | 0.03 | 0.03 | 0.02 | 0.02 | 0.02 | 0.02 | 0.02 | 0.02 | 0.03 | 0.04 | 0.02 |
| 1 896 | 1 987 | 2 164 | 2 264 | 2 248 | 2 213 | 2 265 | 2 444 | 2 534 | 2 726 | 1 970 | 1 565 | 2 276 |
| 4 046 | 4 305 | 4 764 | 5 070 | 5 118 | 5 115 | 5 306 | 5 799 | 6 082 | 6 620 | 4 176 | 3 129 | 5 222 |
| ... | ... | ... | ... | ... | ... | ... | ... | ... | ... | ... | ... | ... |
| 1 133 | 1 145 | 1 140 | 1 146 | 1 118 | 1 050 | 1 054 | 1 105 | 1 109 | 1 146 | 1 246 | 1 367 | 1 111 |
| 2 418 | 2 480 | 2 510 | 2 568 | 2 546 | 2 427 | 2 469 | 2 622 | 2 661 | 2 782 | 2 641 | 2 734 | 2 548 |
| 0.02 | 0.02 | 0.02 | 0.02 | 0.02 | 0.02 | 0.02 | 0.02 | 0.02 | 0.02 | 0.03 | 0.03 | 0.02 |
| 1 123 | 1 242 | 1 317 | 1 369 | 1 383 | 1 334 | 1 365 | 1 473 | 1 528 | 1 644 | 1 173 | 906 | 1 379 |
| 2 397 | 2 690 | 2 900 | 3 066 | 3 149 | 3 084 | 3 199 | 3 496 | 3 667 | 3 991 | 2 488 | 1 811 | 3 164 |
| 0.02 | 0.02 | 0.02 | 0.02 | 0.02 | 0.02 | 0.02 | 0.02 | 0.02 | 0.02 | 0.02 | 0.03 | 0.02 |
| 1 316 | 1 329 | 1 324 | 1 331 | 1 298 | 1 219 | 1 223 | 1 283 | 1 287 | 1 330 | 1 446 | 1 587 | 1 290 |
| 2 807 | 2 879 | 2 915 | 2 981 | 2 956 | 2 819 | 2 866 | 3 045 | 3 089 | 3 230 | 3 066 | 3 174 | 2 959 |
| 0.02 | 0.02 | 0.02 | 0.02 | 0.02 | 0.02 | 0.02 | 0.02 | 0.02 | 0.02 | 0.02 | 0.03 | 0.02 |
| 1 250 | 1 266 | 1 335 | 1 449 | 1 038 | 875 | 1 039 | 1 229 | 1 423 | 1 600 | 1 220 | 1 155 | 1 248 |
| 2 667 | 2 742 | 2 939 | 3 246 | 2 365 | 2 023 | 2 433 | 2 916 | 3 416 | 3 884 | 2 586 | 2 310 | 2 863 |
| 0.02 | 0.02 | 0.03 | 0.03 | 0.02 | 0.02 | 0.02 | 0.02 | 0.02 | 0.02 | 0.03 | 0.04 | 0.02 |

**Table A.1**   Total and per capita gross domestic product of individual countries or areas, expressed in United States dollars, and their individual shares of gross world product, based on alternative conversion rates, 1970–1989 [*cont.*]

| Country or area | 1970 (1) | 1971 (2) | 1972 (3) | 1973 (4) | 1974 (5) | 1975 (6) | 1976 (7) | 1977 (8) | 1978 (9) | 1979 (10) |
|---|---|---|---|---|---|---|---|---|---|---|
| **Japan** | | | | | | | | | | |
| **1.   MER** | | | | | | | | | | |
| 1a.  Per capita GDP | 1 953 | 2 186 | 2 844 | 3 809 | 4 172 | 4 481 | 4 981 | 6 070 | 8 453 | 8 725 |
| 1b.  GDP | 203 736 | 231 017 | 304 763 | 414 049 | 459 614 | 499 774 | 561 703 | 691 304 | 971 322 | 1 010 979 |
| 1c.  % of GWP | 6.39 | 6.60 | 7.58 | 8.44 | 8.28 | 8.05 | 8.37 | 9.14 | 10.81 | 9.81 |
| **2.   PPPs** | | | | | | | | | | |
| 2a.  Per capita GDP | 2 763 | 3 029 | 3 483 | 4 055 | 4 335 | 4 750 | 5 173 | 5 751 | 6 553 | 7 388 |
| 2b.  GDP | 288 275 | 320 183 | 373 269 | 440 736 | 477 554 | 529 754 | 583 325 | 654 908 | 752 990 | 856 052 |
| 2c.  % of GWP | ... | ... | ... | ... | ... | ... | ... | ... | ... | ... |
| **3.   Absolute 1970–1989 PARE** | | | | | | | | | | |
| 3a.  Per capita GDP | 6 892 | 7 095 | 7 584 | 8 067 | 7 863 | 7 968 | 8 258 | 8 609 | 8 967 | 9 354 |
| 3b.  GDP | 719 052 | 749 924 | 812 782 | 876 796 | 866 126 | 888 644 | 931 154 | 980 399 | 1 030 417 | 1 083 879 |
| 3c.  % of GWP | 10.12 | 10.13 | 10.42 | 10.57 | 10.22 | 10.33 | 10.29 | 10.39 | 10.48 | 10.66 |
| **4.   Relative 1970–1989 PARE** | | | | | | | | | | |
| 4a.  Per capita GDP | 3 360 | 3 637 | 4 066 | 4 612 | 4 903 | 5 459 | 6 011 | 6 689 | 7 476 | 8 495 |
| 4b.  GDP | 350 588 | 384 397 | 435 731 | 501 271 | 540 113 | 608 815 | 677 808 | 761 789 | 859 062 | 984 314 |
| 4c.  % of GWP | 10.12 | 10.13 | 10.42 | 10.57 | 10.22 | 10.33 | 10.29 | 10.39 | 10.48 | 10.66 |
| **5.   Absolute 1980–1989 PARE** | | | | | | | | | | |
| 5a.  Per capita GDP | 8 726 | 8 982 | 9 601 | 10 213 | 9 955 | 10 088 | 10 455 | 10 900 | 11 353 | 11 843 |
| 5b.  GDP | 910 374 | 949 461 | 1 029 044 | 1 110 090 | 1 096 581 | 1 125 091 | 1 178 911 | 1 241 259 | 1 304 587 | 1 372 273 |
| 5c.  % of GWP | 10.46 | 10.47 | 10.77 | 10.92 | 10.57 | 10.71 | 10.66 | 10.77 | 10.87 | 11.07 |
| **6.   WA** | | | | | | | | | | |
| 6a.  Per capita GDP | 1 953 | 2 185 | 2 844 | 3 809 | 4 172 | 4 481 | 4 981 | 6 070 | 8 453 | 8 725 |
| 6b.  GDP | 203 736 | 231 015 | 304 761 | 414 046 | 459 611 | 499 779 | 561 699 | 691 304 | 971 313 | 1 010 979 |
| 6c.  % of GWP | 6.38 | 6.62 | 7.61 | 8.51 | 8.24 | 8.11 | 8.37 | 9.17 | 10.94 | 9.88 |
| **Jordan** | | | | | | | | | | |
| **1.   MER** | | | | | | | | | | |
| 1a.  Per capita GDP | 258 | 268 | 291 | 327 | 368 | 470 | 592 | 713 | 920 | 1 091 |
| 1b.  GDP | 593 | 634 | 705 | 811 | 936 | 1 223 | 1 574 | 1 939 | 2 559 | 3 106 |
| 1c.  % of GWP | 0.02 | 0.02 | 0.02 | 0.02 | 0.02 | 0.02 | 0.02 | 0.03 | 0.03 | 0.03 |
| **2.   PPPs** | | | | | | | | | | |
| 2a.  Per capita GDP | 966 | 958 | 981 | 896 | 1 087 | 1 239 | 1 472 | 1 565 | 1 775 | 2 040 |
| 2b.  GDP | 2 222 | 2 263 | 2 378 | 2 224 | 2 764 | 3 222 | 3 913 | 4 255 | 4 937 | 5 811 |
| 2c.  % of GWP | ... | ... | ... | ... | ... | ... | ... | ... | ... | ... |
| **3.   Absolute 1970–1989 PARE** | | | | | | | | | | |
| 3a.  Per capita GDP | 752 | 742 | 751 | 693 | 642 | 707 | 838 | 872 | 979 | 1 027 |
| 3b.  GDP | 1 729 | 1 753 | 1 820 | 1 722 | 1 633 | 1 839 | 2 228 | 2 372 | 2 724 | 2 926 |
| 3c.  % of GWP | 0.02 | 0.02 | 0.02 | 0.02 | 0.02 | 0.02 | 0.02 | 0.03 | 0.03 | 0.03 |
| **4.   Relative 1970–1989 PARE** | | | | | | | | | | |
| 4a.  Per capita GDP | 366 | 380 | 403 | 396 | 401 | 484 | 610 | 678 | 817 | 933 |
| 4b.  GDP | 843 | 899 | 976 | 984 | 1 018 | 1 260 | 1 622 | 1 843 | 2 271 | 2 657 |
| 4c.  % of GWP | 0.02 | 0.02 | 0.02 | 0.02 | 0.02 | 0.02 | 0.02 | 0.03 | 0.03 | 0.03 |
| **5.   Absolute 1980–1989 PARE** | | | | | | | | | | |
| 5a.  Per capita GDP | 873 | 862 | 872 | 806 | 747 | 821 | 974 | 1 013 | 1 138 | 1 194 |
| 5b.  GDP | 2 009 | 2 037 | 2 115 | 2 000 | 1 898 | 2 136 | 2 589 | 2 755 | 3 165 | 3 400 |
| 5c.  % of GWP | 0.02 | 0.02 | 0.02 | 0.02 | 0.02 | 0.02 | 0.02 | 0.02 | 0.03 | 0.03 |
| **6.   WA** | | | | | | | | | | |
| 6a.  Per capita GDP | 258 | 268 | 291 | 325 | 367 | 469 | 592 | 713 | 921 | 1 089 |
| 6b.  GDP | 593 | 633 | 705 | 807 | 933 | 1 220 | 1 574 | 1 937 | 2 562 | 3 103 |
| 6c.  % of GWP | 0.02 | 0.02 | 0.02 | 0.02 | 0.02 | 0.02 | 0.02 | 0.03 | 0.03 | 0.03 |

| | | | | | | | | | | Averages | | |
|---|---|---|---|---|---|---|---|---|---|---|---|---|
| 1980 (11) | 1981 (12) | 1982 (13) | 1983 (14) | 1984 (15) | 1985 (16) | 1986 (17) | 1987 (18) | 1988 (19) | 1989 (20) | 1970–89 (21) | 1970–79 (22) | 1980–89 (23) |
| 9 068 | 9 914 | 9 129 | 9 883 | 10 440 | 10 973 | 16 125 | 19 467 | 23 265 | 23 046 | 9 642 | 4 825 | 14 180 |
| 1 059 262 | 1 166 972 | 1 082 496 | 1 179 976 | 1 254 408 | 1 325 996 | 1 958 373 | 2 374 979 | 2 850 008 | 2 834 232 | 1 121 748 | 534 826 | 1 708 670 |
| 9.14 | 9.97 | 9.31 | 9.95 | 10.28 | 10.53 | 13.15 | 13.82 | 14.92 | 14.13 | 11.01 | 8.78 | 11.97 |
| 8 262 | 9 201 | 9 918 | 10 388 | 10 987 | 11 363 | 11 817 | 12 635 | 13 748 | 14 955 | 8 138 | 4 761 | 11 335 |
| 965 063 | 1 083 037 | 1 176 113 | 1 240 278 | 1 320 152 | 1 373 093 | 1 435 150 | 1 541 438 | 1 684 193 | 1 839 159 | 946 736 | 527 705 | 1 365 767 |
| ... | ... | ... | ... | ... | ... | ... | ... | ... | ... | ... | ... | ... |
| 9 691 | 9 988 | 10 197 | 10 446 | 10 901 | 11 350 | 11 571 | 12 026 | 12 661 | 13 229 | 9 642 | 8 065 | 11 200 |
| 1 132 044 | 1 175 737 | 1 209 109 | 1 247 217 | 1 309 764 | 1 371 514 | 1 405 259 | 1 467 178 | 1 550 984 | 1 626 984 | 1 121 748 | 893 917 | 1 349 579 |
| 10.90 | 11.10 | 11.34 | 11.37 | 11.42 | 11.56 | 11.51 | 11.61 | 11.76 | 11.96 | 11.01 | 10.37 | 11.48 |
| 9 607 | 10 838 | 11 778 | 12 474 | 13 484 | 14 420 | 14 996 | 16 034 | 17 447 | 18 978 | 9 884 | 5 507 | 14 021 |
| 1 122 150 | 1 275 732 | 1 396 685 | 1 489 400 | 1 620 118 | 1 742 459 | 1 821 208 | 1 956 090 | 2 137 247 | 2 333 900 | 1 149 944 | 610 389 | 1 689 499 |
| 10.90 | 11.10 | 11.34 | 11.37 | 11.42 | 11.56 | 11.51 | 11.61 | 11.76 | 11.96 | 11.19 | 10.40 | 11.51 |
| 12 270 | 12 646 | 12 910 | 13 225 | 13 801 | 14 370 | 14 649 | 15 226 | 16 030 | 16 749 | 12 207 | 10 211 | 14 180 |
| 1 433 253 | 1 488 572 | 1 530 825 | 1 579 073 | 1 658 262 | 1 736 441 | 1 779 165 | 1 857 559 | 1 963 664 | 2 059 885 | 1 420 219 | 1 131 767 | 1 708 670 |
| 11.33 | 11.55 | 11.81 | 11.84 | 11.90 | 12.05 | 12.01 | 12.12 | 12.28 | 12.49 | 11.45 | 10.74 | 11.97 |
| 9 068 | 9 914 | 9 129 | 9 883 | 10 440 | 10 974 | 16 125 | 19 462 | 23 256 | 23 052 | 9 641 | 4 825 | 14 180 |
| 1 059 257 | 1 166 993 | 1 082 509 | 1 179 966 | 1 254 397 | 1 326 018 | 1 958 373 | 2 374 372 | 2 848 852 | 2 834 971 | 1 121 697 | 5 34 824 | 1 708 571 |
| 9.20 | 9.90 | 9.29 | 9.95 | 10.26 | 10.49 | 13.32 | 14.25 | 15.22 | 14.45 | 11.10 | 8.82 | 12.08 |
| 1 373 | 1 425 | 1 472 | 1 490 | 1 435 | 1 401 | 1 644 | 1 426 | 1 458 | 1 098 | 1 073 | 548 | 1 426 |
| 4 012 | 4 285 | 4 559 | 4 761 | 4 736 | 4 772 | 5 785 | 5 183 | 5 474 | 4 261 | 3 095 | 1 408 | 4 783 |
| 0.03 | 0.04 | 0.04 | 0.04 | 0.04 | 0.04 | 0.04 | 0.03 | 0.03 | 0.02 | 0.03 | 0.02 | 0.03 |
| 2 257 | 2 569 | 2 827 | 2 950 | 3 548 | 3 486 | 3 487 | 3 583 | 3 508 | 3 395 | 2 456 | 1 322 | 3 212 |
| 6 596 | 7 724 | 8 760 | 9 427 | 11 709 | 11 878 | 12 271 | 13 021 | 13 170 | 13 171 | 7 086 | 3 399 | 10 773 |
| ... | ... | ... | ... | ... | ... | ... | ... | ... | ... | ... | ... | ... |
| 1 169 | 1 233 | 1 303 | 1 274 | 1 279 | 1 259 | 1 234 | 1 233 | 1 168 | 1 086 | 1 073 | 807 | 1 227 |
| 3 417 | 3 707 | 4 036 | 4 070 | 4 222 | 4 289 | 4 344 | 4 481 | 4 384 | 4 212 | 3 095 | 2 074 | 4 116 |
| 0.03 | 0.04 | 0.04 | 0.04 | 0.04 | 0.04 | 0.04 | 0.04 | 0.03 | 0.03 | 0.03 | 0.02 | 0.04 |
| 1 159 | 1 337 | 1 505 | 1 521 | 1 583 | 1 599 | 1 600 | 1 644 | 1 609 | 1 558 | 1 138 | 559 | 1 529 |
| 3 387 | 4 022 | 4 662 | 4 861 | 5 223 | 5 449 | 5 630 | 5 974 | 6 042 | 6 042 | 3 283 | 1 437 | 5 129 |
| 0.03 | 0.04 | 0.04 | 0.04 | 0.04 | 0.04 | 0.04 | 0.04 | 0.03 | 0.03 | 0.03 | 0.02 | 0.03 |
| 1 358 | 1 432 | 1 514 | 1 480 | 1 487 | 1 463 | 1 434 | 1 433 | 1 357 | 1 262 | 1 246 | 937 | 1 426 |
| 3 970 | 4 307 | 4 690 | 4 729 | 4 906 | 4 984 | 5 047 | 5 206 | 5 094 | 4 894 | 3 597 | 2 410 | 4 783 |
| 0.03 | 0.03 | 0.04 | 0.04 | 0.04 | 0.03 | 0.03 | 0.03 | 0.03 | 0.03 | 0.03 | 0.02 | 0.03 |
| 1 373 | 1 423 | 1 470 | 1 489 | 1 433 | 1 398 | 1 644 | 1 686 | 1 558 | 1 147 | 1 098 | 547 | 1 470 |
| 4 013 | 4 280 | 4 553 | 4 760 | 4 730 | 4 764 | 5 785 | 6 125 | 5 850 | 4 450 | 3 169 | 1 407 | 4 931 |
| 0.03 | 0.04 | 0.04 | 0.04 | 0.04 | 0.04 | 0.04 | 0.04 | 0.03 | 0.02 | 0.03 | 0.02 | 0.03 |

**Table A.1**     Total and per capita gross domestic product of individual countries or areas, expressed in United States dollars, and their individual shares of gross world product, based on alternative conversion rates, 1970−1989 [*cont.*]

| Country or area | 1970 (1) | 1971 (2) | 1972 (3) | 1973 (4) | 1974 (5) | 1975 (6) | 1976 (7) | 1977 (8) | 1978 (9) | 1979 (10) |
|---|---|---|---|---|---|---|---|---|---|---|
| **Kenya** | | | | | | | | | | |
| **1.   MER** | | | | | | | | | | |
| 1a.  Per capita GDP | 148 | 158 | 171 | 195 | 224 | 237 | 243 | 302 | 345 | 380 |
| 1b.  GDP | 1 697 | 1 882 | 2 109 | 2 494 | 2 965 | 3 253 | 3 468 | 4 479 | 5 310 | 6 081 |
| 1c.  % of GWP | 0.05 | 0.05 | 0.05 | 0.05 | 0.05 | 0.05 | 0.05 | 0.06 | 0.06 | 0.06 |
| **2.   PPPs** | | | | | | | | | | |
| 2a.  Per capita GDP | 296 | 328 | 343 | 352 | 396 | 418 | 448 | 526 | 575 | 616 |
| 2b.  GDP | 3 407 | 3 907 | 4 233 | 4 497 | 5 238 | 5 738 | 6 390 | 7 801 | 8 851 | 9 861 |
| 2c.  % of GWP | ... | ... | ... | ... | ... | ... | ... | ... | ... | ... |
| **3.   Absolute 1970−1989 PARE** | | | | | | | | | | |
| 3a.  Per capita GDP | 282 | 289 | 294 | 298 | 302 | 290 | 290 | 305 | 320 | 319 |
| 3b.  GDP | 3 237 | 3 443 | 3 621 | 3 808 | 3 997 | 3 981 | 4 141 | 4 521 | 4 928 | 5 113 |
| 3c.  % of GWP | 0.05 | 0.05 | 0.05 | 0.05 | 0.05 | 0.05 | 0.05 | 0.05 | 0.05 | 0.05 |
| **4.   Relative 1970−1989 PARE** | | | | | | | | | | |
| 4a.  Per capita GDP | 137 | 148 | 157 | 170 | 188 | 198 | 211 | 237 | 267 | 290 |
| 4b.  GDP | 1 578 | 1 765 | 1 941 | 2 177 | 2 492 | 2 727 | 3 014 | 3 513 | 4 109 | 4 644 |
| 4c.  % of GWP | 0.05 | 0.05 | 0.05 | 0.05 | 0.05 | 0.05 | 0.05 | 0.05 | 0.05 | 0.05 |
| **5.   Absolute 1980−1989 PARE** | | | | | | | | | | |
| 5a.  Per capita GDP | 313 | 321 | 326 | 331 | 335 | 322 | 322 | 339 | 355 | 355 |
| 5b.  GDP | 3 595 | 3 824 | 4 021 | 4 229 | 4 438 | 4 421 | 4 598 | 5 020 | 5 473 | 5 678 |
| 5c.  % of GWP | 0.04 | 0.04 | 0.04 | 0.04 | 0.04 | 0.04 | 0.04 | 0.04 | 0.05 | 0.05 |
| **6.   WA** | | | | | | | | | | |
| 6a.  Per capita GDP | 148 | 158 | 171 | 195 | 224 | 237 | 243 | 302 | 344 | 380 |
| 6b.  GDP | 1 696 | 1 881 | 2 108 | 2 493 | 2 963 | 3 252 | 3 465 | 4 481 | 5 304 | 6 084 |
| 6c.  % of GWP | 0.05 | 0.05 | 0.05 | 0.05 | 0.05 | 0.05 | 0.05 | 0.06 | 0.06 | 0.06 |
| **Kiribati** | | | | | | | | | | |
| **1.   MER** | | | | | | | | | | |
| 1a.  Per capita GDP | 308 | 321 | 389 | 652 | 1 156 | 1 097 | 806 | 743 | 837 | 784 |
| 1b.  GDP | 15 | 16 | 20 | 34 | 61 | 59 | 44 | 42 | 49 | 46 |
| 1c.  % of GWP | 0.00 | 0.00 | 0.00 | 0.00 | 0.00 | 0.00 | 0.00 | 0.00 | 0.00 | 0.00 |
| **2.   PPPs** | | | | | | | | | | |
| 2a.  Per capita GDP | ... | ... | ... | ... | ... | ... | ... | ... | ... | ... |
| 2b.  GDP | ... | ... | ... | ... | ... | ... | ... | ... | ... | ... |
| 2c.  % of GWP | ... | ... | ... | ... | ... | ... | ... | ... | ... | ... |
| **3.   Absolute 1970−1989 PARE** | | | | | | | | | | |
| 3a.  Per capita GDP | 634 | 608 | 667 | 808 | 1 151 | 1 191 | 856 | 802 | 782 | 697 |
| 3b.  GDP | 32 | 31 | 35 | 42 | 61 | 64 | 47 | 45 | 45 | 41 |
| 3c.  % of GWP | 0.00 | 0.00 | 0.00 | 0.00 | 0.00 | 0.00 | 0.00 | 0.00 | 0.00 | 0.00 |
| **4.   Relative 1970−1989 PARE** | | | | | | | | | | |
| 4a.  Per capita GDP | 309 | 312 | 358 | 462 | 718 | 816 | 623 | 623 | 652 | 633 |
| 4b.  GDP | 15 | 16 | 19 | 24 | 38 | 44 | 34 | 35 | 38 | 37 |
| 4c.  % of GWP | 0.00 | 0.00 | 0.00 | 0.00 | 0.00 | 0.00 | 0.00 | 0.00 | 0.00 | 0.00 |
| **5.   Absolute 1980−1989 PARE** | | | | | | | | | | |
| 5a.  Per capita GDP | 806 | 773 | 848 | 1 028 | 1 463 | 1 514 | 1 089 | 1 020 | 995 | 886 |
| 5b.  GDP | 40 | 39 | 44 | 53 | 78 | 82 | 60 | 57 | 58 | 52 |
| 5c.  % of GWP | 0.00 | 0.00 | 0.00 | 0.00 | 0.00 | 0.00 | 0.00 | 0.00 | 0.00 | 0.00 |
| **6.   WA[a]** | | | | | | | | | | |
| 6a.  Per capita GDP | 238 | 278 | 353 | 500 | 874 | 1 076 | 817 | 746 | 763 | 720 |
| 6b.  GDP | 12 | 14 | 18 | 26 | 46 | 58 | 45 | 42 | 44 | 43 |
| 6c.  % of GWP | 0.00 | 0.00 | 0.00 | 0.00 | 0.00 | 0.00 | 0.00 | 0.00 | 0.00 | 0.00 |

|  |  |  |  |  |  |  |  |  |  | Averages | | |
| 1980 (11) | 1981 (12) | 1982 (13) | 1983 (14) | 1984 (15) | 1985 (16) | 1986 (17) | 1987 (18) | 1988 (19) | 1989 (20) | 1970–89 (21) | 1970–79 (22) | 1980–89 (23) |
|---|---|---|---|---|---|---|---|---|---|---|---|---|
| 426 | 387 | 361 | 319 | 318 | 302 | 346 | 380 | 379 | 368 | 321 | 250 | 359 |
| 7 088 | 6 689 | 6 490 | 5 948 | 6 160 | 6 075 | 7 213 | 8 201 | 8 482 | 8 521 | 5 230 | 3 374 | 7 087 |
| 0.06 | 0.06 | 0.06 | 0.05 | 0.05 | 0.05 | 0.05 | 0.05 | 0.04 | 0.04 | 0.05 | 0.06 | 0.05 |
| 662 | 697 | 759 | 750 | 788 | 763 | 804 | 844 | 894 | 911 | 666 | 444 | 797 |
| 11 003 | 12 050 | 13 624 | 13 990 | 15 265 | 15 340 | 16 747 | 18 231 | 19 985 | 21 117 | 10 864 | 5 992 | 15 735 |
| ... | ... | ... | ... | ... | ... | ... | ... | ... | ... | ... | ... | ... |
| 325 | 324 | 326 | 317 | 309 | 310 | 320 | 327 | 335 | 328 | 321 | 302 | 323 |
| 5 399 | 5 602 | 5 856 | 5 906 | 5 991 | 6 235 | 6 673 | 7 061 | 7 489 | 7 602 | 5 230 | 4 079 | 6 381 |
| 0.05 | 0.05 | 0.05 | 0.05 | 0.05 | 0.05 | 0.05 | 0.06 | 0.06 | 0.06 | 0.05 | 0.05 | 0.05 |
| 322 | 352 | 377 | 378 | 383 | 394 | 415 | 436 | 461 | 470 | 330 | 207 | 405 |
| 5 352 | 6 078 | 6 765 | 7 053 | 7 411 | 7 922 | 8 648 | 9 414 | 10 320 | 10 905 | 5 391 | 2 796 | 7 987 |
| 0.05 | 0.05 | 0.05 | 0.05 | 0.05 | 0.05 | 0.05 | 0.06 | 0.06 | 0.06 | 0.05 | 0.05 | 0.05 |
| 361 | 360 | 362 | 352 | 343 | 345 | 356 | 363 | 372 | 364 | 356 | 336 | 359 |
| 5 996 | 6 221 | 6 503 | 6 559 | 6 653 | 6 924 | 7 410 | 7 842 | 8 317 | 8 442 | 5 808 | 4 530 | 7 087 |
| 0.05 | 0.05 | 0.05 | 0.05 | 0.05 | 0.05 | 0.05 | 0.05 | 0.05 | 0.05 | 0.05 | 0.04 | 0.05 |
| 426 | 387 | 361 | 319 | 318 | 302 | 346 | 369 | 385 | 357 | 319 | 250 | 357 |
| 7 087 | 6 683 | 6 489 | 5 952 | 6 162 | 6 078 | 7 202 | 7 975 | 8 603 | 8 284 | 5 212 | 3 373 | 7 052 |
| 0.06 | 0.06 | 0.06 | 0.05 | 0.05 | 0.05 | 0.05 | 0.05 | 0.05 | 0.04 | 0.05 | 0.06 | 0.05 |
| 426 | 440 | 432 | 390 | 421 | 338 | 338 | 374 | 496 | 534 | 546 | 724 | 420 |
| 26 | 26 | 26 | 24 | 26 | 21 | 21 | 24 | 32 | 35 | 32 | 39 | 26 |
| 0.00 | 0.00 | 0.00 | 0.00 | 0.00 | 0.00 | 0.00 | 0.00 | 0.00 | 0.00 | 0.00 | 0.00 | 0.00 |
| ... | ... | ... | ... | ... | ... | ... | ... | ... | ... | ... | ... | ... |
| ... | ... | ... | ... | ... | ... | ... | ... | ... | ... | ... | ... | ... |
| ... | ... | ... | ... | ... | ... | ... | ... | ... | ... | ... | ... | ... |
| 371 | 333 | 339 | 330 | 337 | 301 | 299 | 291 | 346 | 355 | 546 | 829 | 331 |
| 22 | 20 | 21 | 20 | 21 | 19 | 19 | 19 | 23 | 23 | 32 | 44 | 21 |
| 0.00 | 0.00 | 0.00 | 0.00 | 0.00 | 0.00 | 0.00 | 0.00 | 0.00 | 0.00 | 0.00 | 0.00 | 0.00 |
| 368 | 361 | 392 | 394 | 417 | 382 | 388 | 388 | 477 | 509 | 467 | 562 | 409 |
| 22 | 22 | 24 | 24 | 26 | 24 | 24 | 25 | 31 | 34 | 28 | 30 | 26 |
| 0.00 | 0.00 | 0.00 | 0.00 | 0.00 | 0.00 | 0.00 | 0.00 | 0.00 | 0.00 | 0.00 | 0.00 | 0.00 |
| 472 | 423 | 431 | 419 | 429 | 382 | 380 | 370 | 440 | 451 | 694 | 1 053 | 420 |
| 28 | 25 | 26 | 26 | 27 | 24 | 24 | 24 | 29 | 30 | 41 | 56 | 26 |
| 0.00 | 0.00 | 0.00 | 0.00 | 0.00 | 0.00 | 0.00 | 0.00 | 0.00 | 0.00 | 0.00 | 0.00 | 0.00 |
| 413 | 397 | 422 | 415 | 416 | 356 | 348 | 342 | 440 | 498 | 506 | 651 | 406 |
| 25 | 24 | 26 | 26 | 26 | 22 | 22 | 22 | 29 | 33 | 30 | 35 | 25 |
| 0.00 | 0.00 | 0.00 | 0.00 | 0.00 | 0.00 | 0.00 | 0.00 | 0.00 | 0.00 | 0.00 | 0.00 | 0.00 |

**Table A.1** Total and per capita gross domestic product of individual countries or areas, expressed in United States dollars, and their individual shares of gross world product, based on alternative conversion rates, 1970–1989 [*cont.*]

| Country or area | 1970 (1) | 1971 (2) | 1972 (3) | 1973 (4) | 1974 (5) | 1975 (6) | 1976 (7) | 1977 (8) | 1978 (9) | 1979 (10) |
|---|---|---|---|---|---|---|---|---|---|---|
| **Korea, Democratic People's Republic of** | | | | | | | | | | |
| **1. MER** | | | | | | | | | | |
| 1a. Per capita GDP | 277 | 294 | 336 | 383 | 423 | 471 | 526 | 588 | 622 | 659 |
| 1b. GDP | 4 050 | 4 428 | 5 181 | 6 062 | 6 848 | 7 807 | 8 900 | 10 146 | 10 955 | 11 813 |
| 1c. % of GWP | 0.13 | 0.13 | 0.13 | 0.12 | 0.12 | 0.13 | 0.13 | 0.13 | 0.12 | 0.11 |
| **2. PPPs** | | | | | | | | | | |
| 2a. Per capita GDP | ... | ... | ... | ... | ... | ... | ... | ... | ... | ... |
| 2b. GDP | ... | ... | ... | ... | ... | ... | ... | ... | ... | ... |
| 2c. % of GWP | ... | ... | ... | ... | ... | ... | ... | ... | ... | ... |
| **3. Absolute 1970–1989 PARE** | | | | | | | | | | |
| 3a. Per capita GDP | 263 | 286 | 317 | 346 | 374 | 408 | 447 | 492 | 542 | 591 |
| 3b. GDP | 3 842 | 4 308 | 4 890 | 5 472 | 6 054 | 6 753 | 7 568 | 8 499 | 9 547 | 10 595 |
| 3c. % of GWP | 0.05 | 0.06 | 0.06 | 0.07 | 0.07 | 0.08 | 0.08 | 0.09 | 0.10 | 0.10 |
| **4. Relative 1970–1989 PARE** | | | | | | | | | | |
| 4a. Per capita GDP | 128 | 147 | 170 | 198 | 233 | 279 | 326 | 383 | 452 | 536 |
| 4b. GDP | 1 873 | 2 208 | 2 622 | 3 128 | 3 775 | 4 626 | 5 509 | 6 604 | 7 959 | 9 622 |
| 4c. % of GWP | 0.05 | 0.06 | 0.06 | 0.07 | 0.07 | 0.08 | 0.08 | 0.09 | 0.10 | 0.10 |
| **5. Absolute 1980–1989 PARE** | | | | | | | | | | |
| 5a. Per capita GDP | 250 | 272 | 301 | 329 | 355 | 387 | 425 | 468 | 515 | 561 |
| 5b. GDP | 3 651 | 4 094 | 4 648 | 5 200 | 5 753 | 6 417 | 7 193 | 8 077 | 9 073 | 10 069 |
| 5c. % of GWP | 0.04 | 0.05 | 0.05 | 0.05 | 0.06 | 0.06 | 0.07 | 0.07 | 0.08 | 0.08 |
| **6. WA[a]** | | | | | | | | | | |
| 6a. Per capita GDP | 283 | 302 | 332 | 368 | 411 | 461 | 516 | 578 | 636 | 680 |
| 6b. GDP | 4 140 | 4 535 | 5 120 | 5 822 | 6 651 | 7 639 | 8 735 | 9 987 | 11 190 | 12 196 |
| 6c. % of GWP | 0.13 | 0.13 | 0.13 | 0.12 | 0.12 | 0.12 | 0.13 | 0.13 | 0.13 | 0.12 |
| **Korea, Republic of** | | | | | | | | | | |
| **1. MER** | | | | | | | | | | |
| 1a. Per capita GDP | 279 | 302 | 322 | 400 | 547 | 603 | 812 | 1 024 | 1 358 | 1 722 |
| 1b. GDP | 8 913 | 9 855 | 10 714 | 13 608 | 18 962 | 21 286 | 29 134 | 37 343 | 50 263 | 64 717 |
| 1c. % of GWP | 0.28 | 0.28 | 0.27 | 0.28 | 0.34 | 0.34 | 0.43 | 0.49 | 0.56 | 0.63 |
| **2. PPPs** | | | | | | | | | | |
| 2a. Per capita GDP | ... | ... | ... | ... | ... | ... | ... | ... | ... | ... |
| 2b. GDP | ... | ... | ... | ... | ... | ... | ... | ... | ... | ... |
| 2c. % of GWP | ... | ... | ... | ... | ... | ... | ... | ... | ... | ... |
| **3. Absolute 1970–1989 PARE** | | | | | | | | | | |
| 3a. Per capita GDP | 881 | 942 | 972 | 1 082 | 1 149 | 1 208 | 1 341 | 1 453 | 1 570 | 1 664 |
| 3b. GDP | 28 117 | 30 722 | 32 367 | 36 751 | 39 793 | 42 630 | 48 125 | 52 974 | 58 118 | 62 529 |
| 3c. % of GWP | 0.40 | 0.42 | 0.41 | 0.44 | 0.47 | 0.50 | 0.53 | 0.56 | 0.59 | 0.61 |
| **4. Relative 1970–1989 PARE** | | | | | | | | | | |
| 4a. Per capita GDP | 429 | 483 | 521 | 618 | 716 | 828 | 976 | 1 129 | 1 309 | 1 511 |
| 4b. GDP | 13 709 | 15 748 | 17 352 | 21 011 | 24 815 | 29 206 | 35 032 | 41 162 | 48 453 | 56 785 |
| 4c. % of GWP | 0.40 | 0.41 | 0.41 | 0.44 | 0.47 | 0.50 | 0.53 | 0.56 | 0.59 | 0.61 |
| **5. Absolute 1980–1989 PARE** | | | | | | | | | | |
| 5a. Per capita GDP | 1 039 | 1 111 | 1 146 | 1 275 | 1 355 | 1 425 | 1 581 | 1 713 | 1 851 | 1 963 |
| 5b. GDP | 33 156 | 36 229 | 38 169 | 43 338 | 46 926 | 50 271 | 56 752 | 62 469 | 68 535 | 73 737 |
| 5c. % of GWP | 0.38 | 0.40 | 0.40 | 0.43 | 0.45 | 0.48 | 0.51 | 0.54 | 0.57 | 0.59 |
| **6. WA** | | | | | | | | | | |
| 6a. Per capita GDP | 279 | 302 | 322 | 400 | 547 | 603 | 812 | 1 024 | 1 358 | 1 722 |
| 6b. GDP | 8 913 | 9 855 | 10 714 | 13 608 | 18 962 | 21 286 | 29 134 | 37 343 | 50 263 | 64 717 |
| 6c. % of GWP | 0.28 | 0.28 | 0.27 | 0.28 | 0.34 | 0.35 | 0.43 | 0.50 | 0.57 | 0.63 |

| | 1980 (11) | 1981 (12) | 1982 (13) | 1983 (14) | 1984 (15) | 1985 (16) | 1986 (17) | 1987 (18) | 1988 (19) | 1989 (20) | Averages 1970–89 (21) | 1970–79 (22) | 1980–89 (23) |
|---|---|---|---|---|---|---|---|---|---|---|---|---|---|
| | 697 | 698 | 720 | 770 | 813 | 840 | 860 | 942 | 978 | 1 017 | 668 | 465 | 841 |
| | 12 730 | 12 977 | 13 600 | 14 800 | 15 900 | 16 700 | 17 400 | 19 400 | 20 506 | 21 736 | 12 097 | 7 619 | 16 575 |
| | 0.11 | 0.11 | 0.12 | 0.12 | 0.13 | 0.13 | 0.12 | 0.11 | 0.11 | 0.11 | 0.12 | 0.13 | 0.12 |
| | ... | ... | ... | ... | ... | ... | ... | ... | ... | ... | ... | ... | ... |
| | ... | ... | ... | ... | ... | ... | ... | ... | ... | ... | ... | ... | ... |
| | ... | ... | ... | ... | ... | ... | ... | ... | ... | ... | ... | ... | ... |
| | 638 | 689 | 745 | 806 | 870 | 937 | 955 | 1 000 | 1 038 | 1 079 | 668 | 412 | 884 |
| | 11 643 | 12 807 | 14 088 | 15 484 | 16 999 | 18 629 | 19 327 | 20 608 | 21 772 | 23 053 | 12 097 | 6 753 | 17 441 |
| | 0.11 | 0.12 | 0.13 | 0.14 | 0.15 | 0.16 | 0.16 | 0.16 | 0.17 | 0.17 | 0.12 | 0.08 | 0.15 |
| | 632 | 748 | 861 | 962 | 1 076 | 1 190 | 1 238 | 1 334 | 1 430 | 1 548 | 742 | 293 | 1 118 |
| | 11 541 | 13 896 | 16 273 | 18 491 | 21 027 | 23 667 | 25 048 | 27 475 | 30 002 | 33 069 | 13 421 | 4 793 | 22 049 |
| | 0.11 | 0.12 | 0.13 | 0.14 | 0.15 | 0.16 | 0.16 | 0.16 | 0.17 | 0.17 | 0.13 | 0.08 | 0.15 |
| | 606 | 655 | 708 | 766 | 826 | 890 | 908 | 951 | 986 | 1 025 | 635 | 392 | 841 |
| | 11 065 | 12 171 | 13 388 | 14 715 | 16 155 | 17 704 | 18 368 | 19 585 | 20 691 | 21 908 | 11 496 | 6 417 | 16 575 |
| | 0.09 | 0.09 | 0.10 | 0.11 | 0.12 | 0.12 | 0.12 | 0.13 | 0.13 | 0.13 | 0.09 | 0.06 | 0.12 |
| | 713 | 739 | 761 | 787 | 828 | 870 | 869 | 913 | 963 | 1 016 | 674 | 464 | 852 |
| | 13 019 | 13 730 | 14 388 | 15 136 | 16 183 | 17 298 | 17 595 | 18 800 | 20 192 | 21 716 | 12 204 | 7 602 | 16 806 |
| | 0.11 | 0.12 | 0.12 | 0.13 | 0.13 | 0.14 | 0.12 | 0.11 | 0.11 | 0.11 | 0.12 | 0.13 | 0.12 |
| | 1 643 | 1 802 | 1 898 | 2 068 | 2 235 | 2 277 | 2 581 | 3 190 | 4 184 | 5 029 | 1 804 | 757 | 2 714 |
| | 62 626 | 69 721 | 74 469 | 82 285 | 90 132 | 92 925 | 106 463 | 132 915 | 175 941 | 213 346 | 68 281 | 26 479 | 110 082 |
| | 0.54 | 0.60 | 0.64 | 0.69 | 0.74 | 0.74 | 0.71 | 0.77 | 0.92 | 1.06 | 0.67 | 0.43 | 0.77 |
| | ... | ... | ... | ... | ... | ... | ... | ... | ... | ... | ... | ... | ... |
| | ... | ... | ... | ... | ... | ... | ... | ... | ... | ... | ... | ... | ... |
| | ... | ... | ... | ... | ... | ... | ... | ... | ... | ... | ... | ... | ... |
| | 1 605 | 1 688 | 1 785 | 1 968 | 2 125 | 2 245 | 2 491 | 2 761 | 3 048 | 3 192 | 1 804 | 1 236 | 2 301 |
| | 61 177 | 65 287 | 70 052 | 78 302 | 85 673 | 91 611 | 102 774 | 115 045 | 128 179 | 135 393 | 68 281 | 43 212 | 93 349 |
| | 0.59 | 0.62 | 0.66 | 0.71 | 0.75 | 0.77 | 0.84 | 0.91 | 0.97 | 1.00 | 0.67 | 0.50 | 0.79 |
| | 1 591 | 1 831 | 2 062 | 2 350 | 2 628 | 2 852 | 3 229 | 3 681 | 4 201 | 4 578 | 1 967 | 867 | 2 923 |
| | 60 642 | 70 839 | 80 920 | 93 506 | 105 974 | 116 389 | 133 195 | 153 381 | 176 630 | 194 221 | 74 448 | 30 327 | 118 570 |
| | 0.59 | 0.62 | 0.66 | 0.71 | 0.75 | 0.77 | 0.84 | 0.91 | 0.97 | 1.00 | 0.72 | 0.52 | 0.81 |
| | 1 892 | 1 990 | 2 105 | 2 320 | 2 506 | 2 647 | 2 938 | 3 256 | 3 595 | 3 764 | 2 127 | 1 458 | 2 714 |
| | 72 143 | 76 989 | 82 609 | 92 337 | 101 030 | 108 033 | 121 196 | 135 667 | 151 156 | 159 663 | 80 520 | 50 958 | 110 082 |
| | 0.57 | 0.60 | 0.64 | 0.69 | 0.73 | 0.75 | 0.82 | 0.89 | 0.95 | 0.97 | 0.65 | 0.48 | 0.77 |
| | 1 643 | 1 802 | 1 898 | 2 068 | 2 235 | 2 277 | 2 581 | 3 190 | 4 184 | 5 030 | 1 804 | 757 | 2 714 |
| | 62 626 | 69 721 | 74 469 | 82 285 | 90 132 | 92 925 | 106 462 | 132 920 | 175 949 | 213 360 | 68 282 | 26 479 | 110 085 |
| | 0.54 | 0.59 | 0.64 | 0.69 | 0.74 | 0.73 | 0.72 | 0.80 | 0.94 | 1.09 | 0.68 | 0.44 | 0.78 |

**Table A.1** Total and per capita gross domestic product of individual countries or areas, expressed in United States dollars, and their individual shares of gross world product, based on alternative conversion rates, 1970–1989 [*cont.*]

| Country or area | 1970 (1) | 1971 (2) | 1972 (3) | 1973 (4) | 1974 (5) | 1975 (6) | 1976 (7) | 1977 (8) | 1978 (9) | 1979 (10) |
|---|---|---|---|---|---|---|---|---|---|---|
| **Kuwait** | | | | | | | | | | |
| **1. MER** | | | | | | | | | | |
| 1a. Per capita GDP | 3 858 | 4 823 | 5 279 | 5 977 | 13 724 | 11 934 | 12 232 | 12 309 | 12 452 | 19 064 |
| 1b. GDP | 2 874 | 3 839 | 4 460 | 5 343 | 13 010 | 12 017 | 13 137 | 14 118 | 15 229 | 24 783 |
| 1c. % of GWP | 0.09 | 0.11 | 0.11 | 0.11 | 0.23 | 0.19 | 0.20 | 0.19 | 0.17 | 0.24 |
| **2. PPPs** | | | | | | | | | | |
| 2a. Per capita GDP | 4 189 | 5 275 | 5 669 | 6 488 | 13 864 | 12 030 | 12 383 | 12 329 | 12 379 | 18 557 |
| 2b. GDP | 3 120 | 4 199 | 4 790 | 5 800 | 13 143 | 12 114 | 13 299 | 14 141 | 15 139 | 24 124 |
| 2c. % of GWP | ... | ... | ... | ... | ... | ... | ... | ... | ... | ... |
| **3. Absolute 1970–1989 PARE** | | | | | | | | | | |
| 3a. Per capita GDP | 27 598 | 27 649 | 27 062 | 23 898 | 19 609 | 16 194 | 16 187 | 14 574 | 14 673 | 15 723 |
| 3b. GDP | 20 561 | 22 009 | 22 867 | 21 365 | 18 589 | 16 308 | 17 385 | 16 716 | 17 945 | 20 440 |
| 3c. % of GWP | 0.29 | 0.30 | 0.29 | 0.26 | 0.22 | 0.19 | 0.19 | 0.18 | 0.18 | 0.20 |
| **4. Relative 1970–1989 PARE** | | | | | | | | | | |
| 4a. Per capita GDP | 13 456 | 14 172 | 14 508 | 13 663 | 12 228 | 11 095 | 11 783 | 11 324 | 12 233 | 14 279 |
| 4b. GDP | 10 025 | 11 281 | 12 259 | 12 214 | 11 592 | 11 172 | 12 655 | 12 989 | 14 961 | 18 562 |
| 4c. % of GWP | 0.29 | 0.30 | 0.29 | 0.26 | 0.22 | 0.19 | 0.19 | 0.18 | 0.18 | 0.20 |
| **5. Absolute 1980–1989 PARE** | | | | | | | | | | |
| 5a. Per capita GDP | 45 227 | 45 311 | 44 348 | 39 164 | 32 135 | 26 539 | 26 527 | 23 883 | 24 046 | 25 766 |
| 5b. GDP | 33 694 | 36 067 | 37 474 | 35 012 | 30 464 | 26 724 | 28 490 | 27 394 | 29 409 | 33 496 |
| 5c. % of GWP | 0.39 | 0.40 | 0.39 | 0.34 | 0.29 | 0.25 | 0.26 | 0.24 | 0.25 | 0.27 |
| **6. WA** | | | | | | | | | | |
| 6a. Per capita GDP | 3 856 | 4 876 | 5 263 | 6 046 | 13 717 | 11 932 | 12 216 | 12 328 | 12 676 | 19 038 |
| 6b. GDP | 2 873 | 3 881 | 4 447 | 5 405 | 13 004 | 12 016 | 13 120 | 14 140 | 15 502 | 24 750 |
| 6c. % of GWP | 0.09 | 0.11 | 0.11 | 0.11 | 0.23 | 0.19 | 0.20 | 0.19 | 0.17 | 0.24 |
| **Lao People's Democratic Republic** | | | | | | | | | | |
| **1. MER** | | | | | | | | | | |
| 1a. Per capita GDP | 62 | 52 | 68 | 86 | 84 | 99 | 98 | 99 | 111 | 121 |
| 1b. GDP | 167 | 145 | 193 | 249 | 250 | 300 | 300 | 306 | 348 | 383 |
| 1c. % of GWP | 0.01 | 0.00 | 0.00 | 0.01 | 0.00 | 0.00 | 0.00 | 0.00 | 0.00 | 0.00 |
| **2. PPPs** | | | | | | | | | | |
| 2a. Per capita GDP | ... | ... | ... | ... | ... | ... | ... | ... | ... | ... |
| 2b. GDP | ... | ... | ... | ... | ... | ... | ... | ... | ... | ... |
| 2c. % of GWP | ... | ... | ... | ... | ... | ... | ... | ... | ... | ... |
| **3. Absolute 1970–1989 PARE** | | | | | | | | | | |
| 3a. Per capita GDP | 182 | 184 | 187 | 181 | 180 | 178 | 165 | 161 | 150 | 157 |
| 3b. GDP | 493 | 512 | 532 | 526 | 535 | 538 | 507 | 500 | 469 | 497 |
| 3c. % of GWP | 0.01 | 0.01 | 0.01 | 0.01 | 0.01 | 0.01 | 0.01 | 0.01 | 0.00 | 0.00 |
| **4. Relative 1970–1989 PARE** | | | | | | | | | | |
| 4a. Per capita GDP | 89 | 95 | 100 | 103 | 112 | 122 | 120 | 125 | 125 | 143 |
| 4b. GDP | 240 | 263 | 285 | 301 | 334 | 368 | 369 | 389 | 391 | 452 |
| 4c. % of GWP | 0.01 | 0.01 | 0.01 | 0.01 | 0.01 | 0.01 | 0.01 | 0.01 | 0.00 | 0.00 |
| **5. Absolute 1980–1989 PARE** | | | | | | | | | | |
| 5a. Per capita GDP | 246 | 250 | 254 | 245 | 244 | 241 | 224 | 219 | 203 | 213 |
| 5b. GDP | 668 | 694 | 721 | 713 | 725 | 728 | 687 | 677 | 636 | 674 |
| 5c. % of GWP | 0.01 | 0.01 | 0.01 | 0.01 | 0.01 | 0.01 | 0.01 | 0.01 | 0.01 | 0.01 |
| **6. WA[a]** | | | | | | | | | | |
| 6a. Per capita GDP | 38 | 50 | 61 | 65 | 77 | 88 | 88 | 95 | 96 | 110 |
| 6b. GDP | 103 | 140 | 173 | 188 | 229 | 267 | 271 | 293 | 301 | 349 |
| 6c. % of GWP | 0.00 | 0.00 | 0.00 | 0.00 | 0.00 | 0.00 | 0.00 | 0.00 | 0.00 | 0.00 |

| | | | | | | | | | | Averages | | |
| 1980 (11) | 1981 (12) | 1982 (13) | 1983 (14) | 1984 (15) | 1985 (16) | 1986 (17) | 1987 (18) | 1988 (19) | 1989 (20) | 1970–89 (21) | 1970–79 (22) | 1980–89 (23) |
|---|---|---|---|---|---|---|---|---|---|---|---|---|
| 20 889 | 17 424 | 14 214 | 13 172 | 13 123 | 12 451 | 9 926 | 11 088 | 9 728 | 11 430 | 12 256 | 11 132 | 12 979 |
| 28 722 | 25 229 | 21 576 | 20 904 | 21 706 | 21 429 | 17 728 | 20 513 | 18 620 | 22 597 | 16 392 | 10 881 | 21 902 |
| 0.25 | 0.22 | 0.19 | 0.18 | 0.18 | 0.17 | 0.12 | 0.12 | 0.10 | 0.11 | 0.16 | 0.18 | 0.15 |
| | | | | | | | | | | | | |
| 20 204 | 17 158 | 13 904 | 12 723 | 13 674 | 13 971 | 14 805 | 14 205 | 12 691 | 15 019 | 13 352 | 11 240 | 14 654 |
| 27 780 | 24 844 | 21 106 | 20 191 | 22 618 | 24 045 | 26 442 | 26 279 | 24 290 | 29 692 | 17 858 | 10 987 | 24 729 |
| ... | ... | ... | ... | ... | ... | ... | ... | ... | ... | ... | ... | ... |
| | | | | | | | | | | | | |
| 11 980 | 9 223 | 7 764 | 8 016 | 8 094 | 7 446 | 7 735 | 7 214 | 6 236 | 7 089 | 12 256 | 19 865 | 7 920 |
| 16 472 | 13 355 | 11 786 | 12 721 | 13 388 | 12 815 | 13 815 | 13 347 | 11 936 | 14 015 | 16 392 | 19 418 | 13 365 |
| 0.16 | 0.13 | 0.11 | 0.12 | 0.12 | 0.11 | 0.11 | 0.11 | 0.09 | 0.10 | 0.16 | 0.23 | 0.11 |
| | | | | | | | | | | | | |
| 11 875 | 10 007 | 8 968 | 9 573 | 10 012 | 9 460 | 10 025 | 9 618 | 8 593 | 10 169 | 10 932 | 13 065 | 9 761 |
| 16 328 | 14 491 | 13 614 | 15 192 | 16 561 | 16 281 | 17 905 | 17 794 | 16 447 | 20 105 | 14 621 | 12 771 | 16 472 |
| 0.16 | 0.13 | 0.11 | 0.12 | 0.12 | 0.11 | 0.11 | 0.11 | 0.09 | 0.10 | 0.14 | 0.22 | 0.11 |
| | | | | | | | | | | | | |
| 19 632 | 15 114 | 12 724 | 13 136 | 13 265 | 12 203 | 12 677 | 11 823 | 10 220 | 11 618 | 20 084 | 32 555 | 12 979 |
| 26 994 | 21 886 | 19 314 | 20 848 | 21 940 | 21 001 | 22 640 | 21 872 | 19 560 | 22 968 | 26 862 | 31 822 | 21 902 |
| 0.21 | 0.17 | 0.15 | 0.16 | 0.16 | 0.15 | 0.15 | 0.14 | 0.12 | 0.14 | 0.22 | 0.30 | 0.15 |
| | | | | | | | | | | | | |
| 20 866 | 17 437 | 14 218 | 13 150 | 13 121 | 12 461 | 9 906 | 11 937 | 10 459 | 11 672 | 12 394 | 11 165 | 13 180 |
| 28 691 | 25 249 | 21 583 | 20 870 | 21 702 | 21 446 | 17 691 | 22 084 | 20 019 | 23 075 | 16 577 | 10 914 | 22 241 |
| 0.25 | 0.21 | 0.19 | 0.18 | 0.18 | 0.17 | 0.12 | 0.13 | 0.11 | 0.12 | 0.16 | 0.18 | 0.16 |
| | | | | | | | | | | | | |
| 144 | 111 | 108 | 168 | 290 | 332 | 294 | 389 | 313 | 417 | 190 | 88 | 266 |
| 462 | 363 | 360 | 575 | 1 016 | 1 193 | 1 088 | 1 477 | 1 223 | 1 676 | 604 | 264 | 943 |
| 0.00 | 0.00 | 0.00 | 0.00 | 0.01 | 0.01 | 0.01 | 0.01 | 0.01 | 0.01 | 0.01 | 0.00 | 0.01 |
| | | | | | | | | | | | | |
| ... | ... | ... | ... | ... | ... | ... | ... | ... | ... | ... | ... | ... |
| ... | ... | ... | ... | ... | ... | ... | ... | ... | ... | ... | ... | ... |
| ... | ... | ... | ... | ... | ... | ... | ... | ... | ... | ... | ... | ... |
| | | | | | | | | | | | | |
| 158 | 174 | 177 | 173 | 188 | 201 | 205 | 213 | 218 | 226 | 190 | 170 | 196 |
| 506 | 569 | 591 | 591 | 659 | 724 | 757 | 808 | 851 | 907 | 604 | 511 | 696 |
| 0.00 | 0.01 | 0.01 | 0.01 | 0.01 | 0.01 | 0.01 | 0.01 | 0.01 | 0.01 | 0.01 | 0.01 | 0.01 |
| | | | | | | | | | | | | |
| 156 | 189 | 205 | 207 | 233 | 256 | 266 | 284 | 300 | 324 | 191 | 113 | 247 |
| 501 | 617 | 683 | 706 | 815 | 919 | 981 | 1 078 | 1 173 | 1 300 | 608 | 339 | 877 |
| 0.00 | 0.01 | 0.01 | 0.01 | 0.01 | 0.01 | 0.01 | 0.01 | 0.01 | 0.01 | 0.01 | 0.01 | 0.01 |
| | | | | | | | | | | | | |
| 214 | 236 | 240 | 235 | 255 | 273 | 278 | 289 | 295 | 306 | 257 | 231 | 266 |
| 685 | 770 | 801 | 801 | 892 | 980 | 1 025 | 1 095 | 1 153 | 1 228 | 818 | 692 | 943 |
| 0.01 | 0.01 | 0.01 | 0.01 | 0.01 | 0.01 | 0.01 | 0.01 | 0.01 | 0.01 | 0.01 | 0.01 | 0.01 |
| | | | | | | | | | | | | |
| 126 | 132 | 124 | 123 | 170 | 264 | 315 | 345 | 337 | 379 | 170 | 77 | 240 |
| 406 | 431 | 412 | 419 | 595 | 951 | 1 164 | 1 311 | 1 317 | 1 524 | 542 | 231 | 853 |
| 0.00 | 0.00 | 0.00 | 0.00 | 0.00 | 0.01 | 0.01 | 0.01 | 0.01 | 0.01 | 0.01 | 0.00 | 0.01 |

**Table A.1**  Total and per capita gross domestic product of individual countries or areas, expressed in United States dollars, and their individual shares of gross world product, based on alternative conversion rates, 1970−1989 [*cont.*]

| Country or area | 1970 (1) | 1971 (2) | 1972 (3) | 1973 (4) | 1974 (5) | 1975 (6) | 1976 (7) | 1977 (8) | 1978 (9) | 1979 (10) |
|---|---|---|---|---|---|---|---|---|---|---|
| **Lebanon** | | | | | | | | | | |
| **1.  MER** | | | | | | | | | | |
| 1a.  Per capita GDP | 603 | 658 | 798 | 1 014 | 1 277 | 1 173 | 515 | 969 | 1 091 | 1 277 |
| 1b.  GDP | 1 489 | 1 673 | 2 086 | 2 721 | 3 495 | 3 247 | 1 428 | 2 672 | 2 973 | 3 438 |
| 1c.  % of GWP | 0.05 | 0.05 | 0.05 | 0.06 | 0.06 | 0.05 | 0.02 | 0.04 | 0.03 | 0.03 |
| **2.  PPPs** | | | | | | | | | | |
| 2a.  Per capita GDP | ... | ... | ... | ... | ... | ... | ... | ... | ... | ... |
| 2b.  GDP | ... | ... | ... | ... | ... | ... | ... | ... | ... | ... |
| 2c.  % of GWP | ... | ... | ... | ... | ... | ... | ... | ... | ... | ... |
| **3.  Absolute 1970−1989 PARE** | | | | | | | | | | |
| 3a.  Per capita GDP | 1 309 | 1 390 | 1 515 | 1 546 | 1 566 | 1 251 | 537 | 990 | 971 | 1 075 |
| 3b.  GDP | 3 234 | 3 532 | 3 961 | 4 148 | 4 287 | 3 462 | 1 489 | 2 730 | 2 646 | 2 895 |
| 3c.  % of GWP | 0.05 | 0.05 | 0.05 | 0.05 | 0.05 | 0.04 | 0.02 | 0.03 | 0.03 | 0.03 |
| **4.  Relative 1970−1989 PARE** | | | | | | | | | | |
| 4a.  Per capita GDP | 638 | 713 | 812 | 884 | 977 | 857 | 391 | 770 | 810 | 976 |
| 4b.  GDP | 1 577 | 1 811 | 2 124 | 2 372 | 2 673 | 2 372 | 1 084 | 2 121 | 2 206 | 2 629 |
| 4c.  % of GWP | 0.05 | 0.05 | 0.05 | 0.05 | 0.05 | 0.04 | 0.02 | 0.03 | 0.03 | 0.03 |
| **5.  Absolute 1980−1989 PARE** | | | | | | | | | | |
| 5a.  Per capita GDP | 1 869 | 1 984 | 2 162 | 2 206 | 2 236 | 1 785 | 767 | 1 414 | 1 386 | 1 535 |
| 5b.  GDP | 4 616 | 5 042 | 5 655 | 5 921 | 6 119 | 4 942 | 2 126 | 3 896 | 3 777 | 4 133 |
| 5c.  % of GWP | 0.05 | 0.06 | 0.06 | 0.06 | 0.06 | 0.05 | 0.02 | 0.03 | 0.03 | 0.03 |
| **6.  WA[a]** | | | | | | | | | | |
| 6a.  Per capita GDP | 549 | 624 | 735 | 838 | 1 011 | 983 | 483 | 949 | 986 | 1 171 |
| 6b.  GDP | 1 356 | 1 586 | 1 922 | 2 248 | 2 766 | 2 721 | 1 339 | 2 615 | 2 687 | 3 154 |
| 6c.  % of GWP | 0.04 | 0.05 | 0.05 | 0.05 | 0.05 | 0.04 | 0.02 | 0.03 | 0.03 | 0.03 |
| **Lesotho** | | | | | | | | | | |
| **1.  MER** | | | | | | | | | | |
| 1a.  Per capita GDP | 66 | 62 | 72 | 107 | 119 | 121 | 117 | 150 | 201 | 214 |
| 1b.  GDP | 71 | 67 | 80 | 122 | 138 | 144 | 142 | 186 | 257 | 279 |
| 1c.  % of GWP | 0.00 | 0.00 | 0.00 | 0.00 | 0.00 | 0.00 | 0.00 | 0.00 | 0.00 | 0.00 |
| **2.  PPPs** | | | | | | | | | | |
| 2a.  Per capita GDP | 198 | 197 | 248 | 295 | 333 | 397 | 440 | 494 | 594 | 565 |
| 2b.  GDP | 211 | 214 | 276 | 336 | 387 | 472 | 535 | 615 | 757 | 737 |
| 2c.  % of GWP | ... | ... | ... | ... | ... | ... | ... | ... | ... | ... |
| **3.  Absolute 1970−1989 PARE** | | | | | | | | | | |
| 3a.  Per capita GDP | 123 | 109 | 127 | 157 | 163 | 146 | 167 | 191 | 224 | 195 |
| 3b.  GDP | 131 | 119 | 142 | 179 | 189 | 174 | 202 | 238 | 285 | 254 |
| 3c.  % of GWP | 0.00 | 0.00 | 0.00 | 0.00 | 0.00 | 0.00 | 0.00 | 0.00 | 0.00 | 0.00 |
| **4.  Relative 1970−1989 PARE** | | | | | | | | | | |
| 4a.  Per capita GDP | 60 | 56 | 68 | 90 | 102 | 100 | 121 | 149 | 187 | 177 |
| 4b.  GDP | 64 | 61 | 76 | 102 | 118 | 119 | 147 | 185 | 238 | 231 |
| 4c.  % of GWP | 0.00 | 0.00 | 0.00 | 0.00 | 0.00 | 0.00 | 0.00 | 0.00 | 0.00 | 0.00 |
| **5.  Absolute 1980−1989 PARE** | | | | | | | | | | |
| 5a.  Per capita GDP | 140 | 125 | 145 | 179 | 186 | 167 | 190 | 218 | 255 | 222 |
| 5b.  GDP | 150 | 136 | 161 | 204 | 216 | 198 | 231 | 272 | 325 | 290 |
| 5c.  % of GWP | 0.00 | 0.00 | 0.00 | 0.00 | 0.00 | 0.00 | 0.00 | 0.00 | 0.00 | 0.00 |
| **6.  WA** | | | | | | | | | | |
| 6a.  Per capita GDP | 66 | 62 | 72 | 107 | 119 | 121 | 117 | 150 | 201 | 214 |
| 6b.  GDP | 71 | 68 | 80 | 121 | 138 | 144 | 142 | 186 | 257 | 279 |
| 6c.  % of GWP | 0.00 | 0.00 | 0.00 | 0.00 | 0.00 | 0.00 | 0.00 | 0.00 | 0.00 | 0.00 |

| | | | | | | | | | | Averages | | |
|---|---|---|---|---|---|---|---|---|---|---|---|---|
| 1980 | 1981 | 1982 | 1983 | 1984 | 1985 | 1986 | 1987 | 1988 | 1989 | 1970–89 | 1970–79 | 1980–89 |
| (11) | (12) | (13) | (14) | (15) | (16) | (17) | (18) | (19) | (20) | (21) | (22) | (23) |
| 1 526 | 1 465 | 1 000 | 1 145 | 947 | 572 | 592 | 701 | 567 | 467 | 916 | 916 | 897 |
| 4 075 | 3 894 | 2 656 | 3 046 | 2 524 | 1 525 | 1 579 | 1 866 | 1 511 | 1 250 | 2 457 | 2 522 | 2 393 |
| 0.04 | 0.03 | 0.02 | 0.03 | 0.02 | 0.01 | 0.01 | 0.01 | 0.01 | 0.01 | 0.02 | 0.04 | 0.02 |
| ... | ... | ... | ... | ... | ... | ... | ... | ... | ... | ... | ... | ... |
| ... | ... | ... | ... | ... | ... | ... | ... | ... | ... | ... | ... | ... |
| ... | ... | ... | ... | ... | ... | ... | ... | ... | ... | ... | ... | ... |
| 1 122 | 1 167 | 848 | 670 | 584 | 485 | 534 | 446 | 263 | 175 | 916 | 1 177 | 629 |
| 2 995 | 3 102 | 2 253 | 1 783 | 1 556 | 1 294 | 1 424 | 1 187 | 700 | 469 | 2 457 | 3 239 | 1 676 |
| 0.03 | 0.03 | 0.02 | 0.02 | 0.01 | 0.01 | 0.01 | 0.01 | 0.01 | 0.00 | 0.02 | 0.04 | 0.01 |
| 1 112 | 1 266 | 980 | 800 | 722 | 616 | 692 | 594 | 362 | 251 | 758 | 762 | 739 |
| 2 969 | 3 366 | 2 602 | 2 129 | 1 924 | 1 644 | 1 845 | 1 582 | 965 | 672 | 2 033 | 2 097 | 1 970 |
| 0.03 | 0.03 | 0.02 | 0.02 | 0.01 | 0.01 | 0.01 | 0.01 | 0.01 | 0.00 | 0.02 | 0.04 | 0.01 |
| 1 601 | 1 666 | 1 211 | 956 | 833 | 692 | 762 | 636 | 375 | 250 | 1 308 | 1 679 | 897 |
| 4 275 | 4 428 | 3 216 | 2 544 | 2 221 | 1 848 | 2 032 | 1 694 | 999 | 669 | 3 508 | 4 623 | 2 393 |
| 0.03 | 0.03 | 0.02 | 0.02 | 0.02 | 0.01 | 0.01 | 0.01 | 0.01 | 0.00 | 0.03 | 0.04 | 0.02 |
| 1 364 | 1 475 | 1 069 | 901 | 854 | 710 | 677 | 560 | 394 | 356 | 833 | 814 | 835 |
| 3 642 | 3 921 | 2 840 | 2 398 | 2 277 | 1 894 | 1 805 | 1 492 | 1 050 | 954 | 2 233 | 2 240 | 2 227 |
| 0.03 | 0.03 | 0.02 | 0.02 | 0.02 | 0.01 | 0.01 | 0.01 | 0.01 | 0.00 | 0.02 | 0.04 | 0.02 |
| 275 | 271 | 241 | 242 | 205 | 159 | 171 | 223 | 252 | 245 | 187 | 127 | 228 |
| 368 | 373 | 341 | 352 | 307 | 244 | 271 | 363 | 422 | 423 | 247 | 149 | 346 |
| 0.00 | 0.00 | 0.00 | 0.00 | 0.00 | 0.00 | 0.00 | 0.00 | 0.00 | 0.00 | 0.00 | 0.00 | 0.00 |
| 617 | 714 | 813 | 780 | 933 | 1 331 | 1 329 | 1 423 | 1 600 | 1 653 | 832 | 387 | 1 152 |
| 827 | 982 | 1 150 | 1 135 | 1 395 | 2 048 | 2 104 | 2 319 | 2 681 | 2 849 | 1 101 | 454 | 1 749 |
| ... | ... | ... | ... | ... | ... | ... | ... | ... | ... | ... | ... | ... |
| 206 | 202 | 204 | 182 | 192 | 193 | 189 | 197 | 214 | 212 | 187 | 163 | 200 |
| 275 | 278 | 289 | 265 | 288 | 297 | 299 | 321 | 359 | 366 | 247 | 191 | 304 |
| 0.00 | 0.00 | 0.00 | 0.00 | 0.00 | 0.00 | 0.00 | 0.00 | 0.00 | 0.00 | 0.00 | 0.00 | 0.00 |
| 204 | 220 | 236 | 218 | 238 | 245 | 245 | 262 | 295 | 305 | 194 | 114 | 250 |
| 273 | 302 | 333 | 317 | 356 | 377 | 388 | 427 | 494 | 525 | 257 | 134 | 379 |
| 0.00 | 0.00 | 0.00 | 0.00 | 0.00 | 0.00 | 0.00 | 0.00 | 0.00 | 0.00 | 0.00 | 0.00 | 0.00 |
| 234 | 231 | 233 | 208 | 219 | 220 | 216 | 224 | 244 | 242 | 213 | 186 | 228 |
| 314 | 318 | 329 | 303 | 328 | 339 | 341 | 366 | 409 | 418 | 282 | 218 | 346 |
| 0.00 | 0.00 | 0.00 | 0.00 | 0.00 | 0.00 | 0.00 | 0.00 | 0.00 | 0.00 | 0.00 | 0.00 | 0.00 |
| 274 | 272 | 242 | 242 | 206 | 159 | 171 | 219 | 255 | 243 | 187 | 127 | 228 |
| 368 | 374 | 342 | 351 | 308 | 244 | 271 | 356 | 427 | 419 | 247 | 149 | 346 |
| 0.00 | 0.00 | 0.00 | 0.00 | 0.00 | 0.00 | 0.00 | 0.00 | 0.00 | 0.00 | 0.00 | 0.00 | 0.00 |

**Table A.1**     Total and per capita gross domestic product of individual countries or areas,
expressed in United States dollars, and their individual shares of gross world
product, based on alternative conversion rates, 1970–1989 [*cont.*]

| Country or area | 1970 (1) | 1971 (2) | 1972 (3) | 1973 (4) | 1974 (5) | 1975 (6) | 1976 (7) | 1977 (8) | 1978 (9) | 1979 (10) |
|---|---|---|---|---|---|---|---|---|---|---|
| **Liberia** | | | | | | | | | | |
| **1.  MER** | | | | | | | | | | |
| 1a.  Per capita GDP | 224 | 229 | 241 | 273 | 325 | 379 | 381 | 413 | 439 | 490 |
| 1b.  GDP | 310 | 327 | 355 | 415 | 507 | 610 | 632 | 706 | 774 | 891 |
| 1c.  % of GWP | 0.01 | 0.01 | 0.01 | 0.01 | 0.01 | 0.01 | 0.01 | 0.01 | 0.01 | 0.01 |
| **2.  PPPs** | | | | | | | | | | |
| 2a.  Per capita GDP | 364 | 394 | 399 | 417 | 467 | 498 | 561 | 581 | 621 | 679 |
| 2b.  GDP | 505 | 563 | 587 | 632 | 730 | 803 | 930 | 994 | 1 096 | 1 236 |
| 2c.  % of GWP | ... | ... | ... | ... | ... | ... | ... | ... | ... | ... |
| **3.  Absolute 1970–1989 PARE** | | | | | | | | | | |
| 3a.  Per capita GDP | 507 | 517 | 520 | 524 | 526 | 491 | 499 | 488 | 501 | 509 |
| 3b.  GDP | 703 | 739 | 765 | 795 | 822 | 790 | 828 | 836 | 884 | 926 |
| 3c.  % of GWP | 0.01 | 0.01 | 0.01 | 0.01 | 0.01 | 0.01 | 0.01 | 0.01 | 0.01 | 0.01 |
| **4.  Relative 1970–1989 PARE** | | | | | | | | | | |
| 4a.  Per capita GDP | 247 | 265 | 279 | 300 | 328 | 336 | 363 | 380 | 418 | 462 |
| 4b.  GDP | 343 | 379 | 410 | 454 | 512 | 541 | 603 | 649 | 737 | 841 |
| 4c.  % of GWP | 0.01 | 0.01 | 0.01 | 0.01 | 0.01 | 0.01 | 0.01 | 0.01 | 0.01 | 0.01 |
| **5.  Absolute 1980–1989 PARE** | | | | | | | | | | |
| 5a.  Per capita GDP | 665 | 678 | 682 | 687 | 690 | 643 | 654 | 640 | 657 | 667 |
| 5b.  GDP | 922 | 968 | 1 003 | 1 042 | 1 077 | 1 036 | 1 085 | 1 096 | 1 159 | 1 214 |
| 5c.  % of GWP | 0.01 | 0.01 | 0.01 | 0.01 | 0.01 | 0.01 | 0.01 | 0.01 | 0.01 | 0.01 |
| **6.  WA** | | | | | | | | | | |
| 6a.  Per capita GDP | 224 | 229 | 241 | 273 | 325 | 379 | 381 | 413 | 439 | 490 |
| 6b.  GDP | 310 | 327 | 355 | 415 | 507 | 610 | 632 | 706 | 774 | 891 |
| 6c.  % of GWP | 0.01 | 0.01 | 0.01 | 0.01 | 0.01 | 0.01 | 0.01 | 0.01 | 0.01 | 0.01 |
| **Libyan Arab Jamahiriya** | | | | | | | | | | |
| **1.  MER** | | | | | | | | | | |
| 1a.  Per capita GDP | 1 874 | 2 183 | 2 534 | 3 331 | 5 594 | 5 219 | 6 491 | 7 300 | 6 897 | 9 106 |
| 1b.  GDP | 3 724 | 4 519 | 5 467 | 7 487 | 13 119 | 12 770 | 16 578 | 19 470 | 19 215 | 26 508 |
| 1c.  % of GWP | 0.12 | 0.13 | 0.14 | 0.15 | 0.24 | 0.21 | 0.25 | 0.26 | 0.21 | 0.26 |
| **2.  PPPs** | | | | | | | | | | |
| 2a.  Per capita GDP | ... | ... | ... | ... | ... | ... | ... | ... | ... | ... |
| 2b.  GDP | ... | ... | ... | ... | ... | ... | ... | ... | ... | ... |
| 2c.  % of GWP | ... | ... | ... | ... | ... | ... | ... | ... | ... | ... |
| **3.  Absolute 1970–1989 PARE** | | | | | | | | | | |
| 3a.  Per capita GDP | 6 038 | 6 084 | 6 094 | 6 438 | 6 799 | 7 083 | 8 339 | 8 693 | 8 596 | 8 964 |
| 3b.  GDP | 11 998 | 12 595 | 13 145 | 14 472 | 15 944 | 17 332 | 21 298 | 23 183 | 23 949 | 26 095 |
| 3c.  % of GWP | 0.17 | 0.17 | 0.17 | 0.17 | 0.19 | 0.20 | 0.24 | 0.25 | 0.24 | 0.26 |
| **4.  Relative 1970–1989 PARE** | | | | | | | | | | |
| 4a.  Per capita GDP | 2 944 | 3 119 | 3 267 | 3 681 | 4 240 | 4 853 | 6 070 | 6 754 | 7 167 | 8 141 |
| 4b.  GDP | 5 850 | 6 456 | 7 047 | 8 274 | 9 943 | 11 874 | 15 503 | 18 014 | 19 967 | 23 698 |
| 4c.  % of GWP | 0.17 | 0.17 | 0.17 | 0.17 | 0.19 | 0.20 | 0.24 | 0.25 | 0.24 | 0.26 |
| **5.  Absolute 1980–1989 PARE** | | | | | | | | | | |
| 5a.  Per capita GDP | 7 452 | 7 508 | 7 520 | 7 944 | 8 390 | 8 741 | 10 290 | 10 727 | 10 608 | 11 062 |
| 5b.  GDP | 14 806 | 15 542 | 16 222 | 17 859 | 19 675 | 21 388 | 26 282 | 28 609 | 29 554 | 32 201 |
| 5c.  % of GWP | 0.17 | 0.17 | 0.17 | 0.18 | 0.19 | 0.20 | 0.24 | 0.25 | 0.25 | 0.26 |
| **6.  WA** | | | | | | | | | | |
| 6a.  Per capita GDP | 1 873 | 2 206 | 2 535 | 3 330 | 5 593 | 5 218 | 6 490 | 7 299 | 6 896 | 9 105 |
| 6b.  GDP | 3 722 | 4 565 | 5 467 | 7 487 | 13 117 | 12 768 | 16 575 | 19 466 | 19 212 | 26 504 |
| 6c.  % of GWP | 0.12 | 0.13 | 0.14 | 0.15 | 0.24 | 0.21 | 0.25 | 0.26 | 0.22 | 0.26 |

| 1980 (11) | 1981 (12) | 1982 (13) | 1983 (14) | 1984 (15) | 1985 (16) | 1986 (17) | 1987 (18) | 1988 (19) | 1989 (20) | Averages 1970–89 (21) | 1970–79 (22) | 1980–89 (23) |
|---|---|---|---|---|---|---|---|---|---|---|---|---|
| 488 | 544 | 547 | 526 | 503 | 481 | 456 | 464 | 478 | 497 | 442 | 348 | 499 |
| 917 | 1 054 | 1 093 | 1 086 | 1 073 | 1 057 | 1 035 | 1 087 | 1 156 | 1 239 | 816 | 553 | 1 080 |
| 0.01 | 0.01 | 0.01 | 0.01 | 0.01 | 0.01 | 0.01 | 0.01 | 0.01 | 0.01 | 0.01 | 0.01 | 0.01 |
| 678 | 775 | 780 | 774 | 827 | 797 | 774 | 790 | 810 | 837 | 681 | 509 | 790 |
| 1 273 | 1 501 | 1 559 | 1 597 | 1 763 | 1 752 | 1 758 | 1 850 | 1 958 | 2 087 | 1 259 | 808 | 1 710 |
| ... | ... | ... | ... | ... | ... | ... | ... | ... | ... | ... | ... | ... |
| 462 | 431 | 425 | 397 | 382 | 363 | 346 | 343 | 340 | 338 | 442 | 510 | 380 |
| 868 | 834 | 849 | 819 | 815 | 798 | 785 | 803 | 822 | 842 | 816 | 809 | 824 |
| 0.01 | 0.01 | 0.01 | 0.01 | 0.01 | 0.01 | 0.01 | 0.01 | 0.01 | 0.01 | 0.01 | 0.01 | 0.01 |
| 458 | 467 | 490 | 474 | 473 | 461 | 448 | 457 | 469 | 484 | 423 | 345 | 470 |
| 860 | 905 | 980 | 979 | 1 008 | 1 014 | 1 017 | 1 071 | 1 133 | 1 208 | 782 | 547 | 1 017 |
| 0.01 | 0.01 | 0.01 | 0.01 | 0.01 | 0.01 | 0.01 | 0.01 | 0.01 | 0.01 | 0.01 | 0.01 | 0.01 |
| 606 | 564 | 557 | 520 | 501 | 476 | 453 | 449 | 446 | 443 | 579 | 668 | 499 |
| 1 138 | 1 093 | 1 113 | 1 074 | 1 068 | 1 046 | 1 029 | 1 053 | 1 078 | 1 104 | 1 070 | 1 060 | 1 080 |
| 0.01 | 0.01 | 0.01 | 0.01 | 0.01 | 0.01 | 0.01 | 0.01 | 0.01 | 0.01 | 0.01 | 0.01 | 0.01 |
| 488 | 544 | 547 | 526 | 503 | 481 | 456 | 464 | 478 | 497 | 442 | 348 | 499 |
| 917 | 1 054 | 1 093 | 1 086 | 1 073 | 1 057 | 1 035 | 1 087 | 1 156 | 1 239 | 816 | 553 | 1 080 |
| 0.01 | 0.01 | 0.01 | 0.01 | 0.01 | 0.01 | 0.01 | 0.01 | 0.01 | 0.01 | 0.01 | 0.01 | 0.01 |
| 11 737 | 9 825 | 9 226 | 8 543 | 7 448 | 7 386 | 5 373 | 5 691 | 4 859 | 5 080 | 6 694 | 5 378 | 7 270 |
| 35 727 | 31 284 | 30 730 | 29 747 | 27 072 | 27 963 | 21 142 | 23 237 | 20 564 | 22 278 | 19 930 | 12 886 | 26 974 |
| 0.31 | 0.27 | 0.26 | 0.25 | 0.22 | 0.22 | 0.14 | 0.14 | 0.11 | 0.11 | 0.20 | 0.21 | 0.19 |
| ... | ... | ... | ... | ... | ... | ... | ... | ... | ... | ... | ... | ... |
| ... | ... | ... | ... | ... | ... | ... | ... | ... | ... | ... | ... | ... |
| ... | ... | ... | ... | ... | ... | ... | ... | ... | ... | ... | ... | ... |
| 8 631 | 6 668 | 6 553 | 6 114 | 5 561 | 5 784 | 5 509 | 5 112 | 5 046 | 5 006 | 6 694 | 7 513 | 5 891 |
| 26 274 | 21 232 | 21 827 | 21 288 | 20 214 | 21 898 | 21 680 | 20 874 | 21 353 | 21 951 | 19 930 | 18 001 | 21 859 |
| 0.25 | 0.20 | 0.20 | 0.19 | 0.18 | 0.18 | 0.18 | 0.17 | 0.16 | 0.16 | 0.20 | 0.21 | 0.19 |
| 8 556 | 7 235 | 7 569 | 7 301 | 6 879 | 7 348 | 7 140 | 6 816 | 6 953 | 7 181 | 6 650 | 5 285 | 7 260 |
| 26 044 | 23 037 | 25 214 | 25 421 | 25 004 | 27 820 | 28 097 | 27 830 | 29 424 | 31 488 | 19 800 | 12 662 | 26 938 |
| 0.25 | 0.20 | 0.20 | 0.19 | 0.18 | 0.18 | 0.18 | 0.17 | 0.16 | 0.16 | 0.19 | 0.22 | 0.18 |
| 10 651 | 8 229 | 8 086 | 7 544 | 6 862 | 7 137 | 6 799 | 6 309 | 6 226 | 6 177 | 8 260 | 9 271 | 7 270 |
| 32 422 | 26 200 | 26 936 | 26 270 | 24 945 | 27 022 | 26 753 | 25 759 | 26 350 | 27 088 | 24 594 | 22 214 | 26 974 |
| 0.26 | 0.20 | 0.21 | 0.20 | 0.18 | 0.19 | 0.18 | 0.17 | 0.16 | 0.16 | 0.20 | 0.21 | 0.19 |
| 11 735 | 9 824 | 9 224 | 8 542 | 7 446 | 7 385 | 5 458 | 5 796 | 5 093 | 5 094 | 6 724 | 5 379 | 7 318 |
| 35 721 | 31 278 | 30 725 | 29 742 | 27 067 | 27 958 | 21 476 | 23 665 | 21 554 | 22 337 | 20 020 | 12 888 | 27 152 |
| 0.31 | 0.27 | 0.26 | 0.25 | 0.22 | 0.22 | 0.15 | 0.14 | 0.12 | 0.11 | 0.20 | 0.21 | 0.19 |

**Table A.1**     Total and per capita gross domestic product of individual countries or areas,
                  expressed in United States dollars, and their individual shares of gross world
                  product, based on alternative conversion rates, 1970–1989 [*cont.*]

| Country or area | 1970 (1) | 1971 (2) | 1972 (3) | 1973 (4) | 1974 (5) | 1975 (6) | 1976 (7) | 1977 (8) | 1978 (9) | 1979 (10) |
|---|---|---|---|---|---|---|---|---|---|---|
| **Luxembourg** | | | | | | | | | | |
| **1.    MER** | | | | | | | | | | |
| 1a.   Per capita GDP | 3 238 | 3 334 | 4 115 | 5 567 | 6 697 | 6 497 | 7 082 | 7 818 | 9 762 | 11 414 |
| 1b.   GDP | 1 101 | 1 147 | 1 436 | 1 971 | 2 404 | 2 358 | 2 585 | 2 861 | 3 563 | 4 166 |
| 1c.   % of GWP | 0.03 | 0.03 | 0.04 | 0.04 | 0.04 | 0.04 | 0.04 | 0.04 | 0.04 | 0.04 |
| **2.    PPPs** | | | | | | | | | | |
| 2a.   Per capita GDP | 4 072 | 4 138 | 4 630 | 5 606 | 6 714 | 6 049 | 6 586 | 6 949 | 7 701 | 8 673 |
| 2b.   GDP | 1 385 | 1 423 | 1 616 | 1 985 | 2 410 | 2 196 | 2 404 | 2 543 | 2 811 | 3 166 |
| 2c.   % of GWP | ... | ... | ... | ... | ... | ... | ... | ... | ... | ... |
| **3.    Absolute 1970–1989 PARE** | | | | | | | | | | |
| 3a.   Per capita GDP | 7 915 | 8 032 | 8 439 | 9 012 | 9 260 | 8 556 | 8 725 | 8 838 | 9 223 | 9 440 |
| 3b.   GDP | 2 691 | 2 763 | 2 945 | 3 190 | 3 324 | 3 106 | 3 185 | 3 235 | 3 367 | 3 445 |
| 3c.   % of GWP | 0.04 | 0.04 | 0.04 | 0.04 | 0.04 | 0.04 | 0.04 | 0.03 | 0.03 | 0.03 |
| **4.    Relative 1970–1989 PARE** | | | | | | | | | | |
| 4a.   Per capita GDP | 3 859 | 4 117 | 4 524 | 5 152 | 5 775 | 5 862 | 6 351 | 6 867 | 7 690 | 8 573 |
| 4b.   GDP | 1 312 | 1 416 | 1 579 | 1 824 | 2 073 | 2 128 | 2 318 | 2 513 | 2 807 | 3 129 |
| 4c.   % of GWP | 0.04 | 0.04 | 0.04 | 0.04 | 0.04 | 0.04 | 0.04 | 0.03 | 0.03 | 0.03 |
| **5.    Absolute 1980–1989 PARE** | | | | | | | | | | |
| 5a.   Per capita GDP | 9 456 | 9 595 | 10 082 | 10 766 | 11 063 | 10 222 | 10 424 | 10 558 | 11 019 | 11 277 |
| 5b.   GDP | 3 215 | 3 301 | 3 519 | 3 811 | 3 972 | 3 711 | 3 805 | 3 864 | 4 022 | 4 116 |
| 5c.   % of GWP | 0.04 | 0.04 | 0.04 | 0.04 | 0.04 | 0.04 | 0.03 | 0.03 | 0.03 | 0.03 |
| **6.    WA** | | | | | | | | | | |
| 6a.   Per capita GDP | 3 238 | 3 334 | 4 115 | 5 567 | 6 697 | 6 497 | 7 083 | 7 818 | 9 762 | 11 414 |
| 6b.   GDP | 1 101 | 1 147 | 1 436 | 1 971 | 2 404 | 2 358 | 2 585 | 2 861 | 3 563 | 4 166 |
| 6c.   % of GWP | 0.03 | 0.03 | 0.04 | 0.04 | 0.04 | 0.04 | 0.04 | 0.04 | 0.04 | 0.04 |
| **Madagascar** | | | | | | | | | | |
| **1.    MER** | | | | | | | | | | |
| 1a.   Per capita GDP | 133 | 141 | 157 | 189 | 209 | 243 | 226 | 237 | 261 | 328 |
| 1b.   GDP | 898 | 971 | 1 108 | 1 367 | 1 549 | 1 844 | 1 762 | 1 905 | 2 156 | 2 798 |
| 1c.   % of GWP | 0.03 | 0.03 | 0.03 | 0.03 | 0.03 | 0.03 | 0.03 | 0.03 | 0.02 | 0.03 |
| **2.    PPPs** | | | | | | | | | | |
| 2a.   Per capita GDP | 386 | 415 | 426 | 412 | 419 | 432 | 439 | 478 | 490 | 551 |
| 2b.   GDP | 2 605 | 2 863 | 3 005 | 2 978 | 3 103 | 3 283 | 3 424 | 3 837 | 4 055 | 4 698 |
| 2c.   % of GWP | ... | ... | ... | ... | ... | ... | ... | ... | ... | ... |
| **3.    Absolute 1970–1989 PARE** | | | | | | | | | | |
| 3a.   Per capita GDP | 290 | 295 | 285 | 272 | 269 | 266 | 250 | 249 | 236 | 251 |
| 3b.   GDP | 1 955 | 2 038 | 2 012 | 1 968 | 1 992 | 2 017 | 1 955 | 2 002 | 1 949 | 2 140 |
| 3c.   % of GWP | 0.03 | 0.03 | 0.03 | 0.02 | 0.02 | 0.02 | 0.02 | 0.02 | 0.02 | 0.02 |
| **4.    Relative 1970–1989 PARE** | | | | | | | | | | |
| 4a.   Per capita GDP | 141 | 151 | 153 | 156 | 168 | 182 | 182 | 194 | 196 | 228 |
| 4b.   GDP | 953 | 1 044 | 1 078 | 1 125 | 1 242 | 1 382 | 1 423 | 1 555 | 1 625 | 1 944 |
| 4c.   % of GWP | 0.03 | 0.03 | 0.03 | 0.02 | 0.02 | 0.02 | 0.02 | 0.02 | 0.02 | 0.02 |
| **5.    Absolute 1980–1989 PARE** | | | | | | | | | | |
| 5a.   Per capita GDP | 342 | 348 | 336 | 321 | 317 | 313 | 295 | 294 | 278 | 296 |
| 5b.   GDP | 2 303 | 2 401 | 2 370 | 2 319 | 2 347 | 2 377 | 2 304 | 2 358 | 2 296 | 2 522 |
| 5c.   % of GWP | 0.03 | 0.03 | 0.02 | 0.02 | 0.02 | 0.02 | 0.02 | 0.02 | 0.02 | 0.02 |
| **6.    WA** | | | | | | | | | | |
| 6a.   Per capita GDP | 133 | 141 | 157 | 189 | 209 | 243 | 226 | 237 | 261 | 328 |
| 6b.   GDP | 898 | 971 | 1 108 | 1 367 | 1 549 | 1 844 | 1 762 | 1 905 | 2 156 | 2 798 |
| 6c.   % of GWP | 0.03 | 0.03 | 0.03 | 0.03 | 0.03 | 0.03 | 0.03 | 0.03 | 0.02 | 0.03 |

| 1980 (11) | 1981 (12) | 1982 (13) | 1983 (14) | 1984 (15) | 1985 (16) | 1986 (17) | 1987 (18) | 1988 (19) | 1989 (20) | Averages 1970–89 (21) | 1970–79 (22) | 1980–89 (23) |
|---|---|---|---|---|---|---|---|---|---|---|---|---|
| 12 454 | 10 455 | 9 521 | 9 334 | 9 157 | 9 419 | 13 586 | 16 749 | 18 168 | 18 866 | 9 670 | 6 535 | 12 824 |
| 4 546 | 3 816 | 3 475 | 3 416 | 3 352 | 3 457 | 5 000 | 6 180 | 6 740 | 7 018 | 3 530 | 2 359 | 4 700 |
| 0.04 | 0.03 | 0.03 | 0.03 | 0.03 | 0.03 | 0.03 | 0.04 | 0.04 | 0.03 | 0.03 | 0.04 | 0.03 |
| 9 972 | 10 195 | 11 059 | 12 080 | 11 520 | 12 031 | 12 760 | 13 541 | 14 688 | 16 174 | 9 253 | 6 077 | 12 444 |
| 3 640 | 3 721 | 4 036 | 4 421 | 4 216 | 4 415 | 4 696 | 4 997 | 5 449 | 6 017 | 3 377 | 2 194 | 4 561 |
| ... | ... | ... | ... | ... | ... | ... | ... | ... | ... | ... | ... | ... |
| 9 519 | 9 467 | 9 574 | 9 833 | 10 441 | 10 717 | 11 142 | 11 494 | 12 063 | 12 760 | 9 670 | 8 657 | 10 734 |
| 3 474 | 3 455 | 3 494 | 3 599 | 3 822 | 3 933 | 4 100 | 4 241 | 4 475 | 4 747 | 3 530 | 3 125 | 3 934 |
| 0.03 | 0.03 | 0.03 | 0.03 | 0.03 | 0.03 | 0.03 | 0.03 | 0.03 | 0.03 | 0.03 | 0.04 | 0.03 |
| 9 436 | 10 272 | 11 059 | 11 742 | 12 915 | 13 615 | 14 440 | 15 324 | 16 623 | 18 304 | 9 629 | 5 845 | 13 423 |
| 3 444 | 3 749 | 4 037 | 4 298 | 4 727 | 4 997 | 5 314 | 5 655 | 6 167 | 6 809 | 3 515 | 2 110 | 4 920 |
| 0.03 | 0.03 | 0.03 | 0.03 | 0.03 | 0.03 | 0.03 | 0.03 | 0.03 | 0.03 | 0.03 | 0.04 | 0.03 |
| 11 372 | 11 309 | 11 437 | 11 747 | 12 474 | 12 803 | 13 311 | 13 732 | 14 411 | 15 244 | 11 553 | 10 342 | 12 824 |
| 4 151 | 4 128 | 4 175 | 4 299 | 4 565 | 4 699 | 4 898 | 5 067 | 5 347 | 5 671 | 4 217 | 3 733 | 4 700 |
| 0.03 | 0.03 | 0.03 | 0.03 | 0.03 | 0.03 | 0.03 | 0.03 | 0.03 | 0.03 | 0.03 | 0.04 | 0.03 |
| 12 454 | 10 455 | 9 521 | 9 334 | 9 157 | 9 419 | 13 585 | 16 733 | 18 183 | 18 864 | 9 670 | 6 536 | 12 824 |
| 4 546 | 3 816 | 3 475 | 3 416 | 3 352 | 3 457 | 4 999 | 6 175 | 6 746 | 7 017 | 3 530 | 2 359 | 4 700 |
| 0.04 | 0.03 | 0.03 | 0.03 | 0.03 | 0.03 | 0.03 | 0.04 | 0.04 | 0.04 | 0.03 | 0.04 | 0.03 |
| 372 | 321 | 305 | 295 | 239 | 229 | 253 | 167 | 139 | 139 | 235 | 218 | 241 |
| 3 265 | 2 904 | 2 848 | 2 837 | 2 374 | 2 345 | 2 672 | 1 824 | 1 563 | 1 622 | 2 031 | 1 636 | 2 425 |
| 0.03 | 0.02 | 0.02 | 0.02 | 0.02 | 0.02 | 0.02 | 0.01 | 0.01 | 0.01 | 0.02 | 0.03 | 0.02 |
| 584 | 572 | 603 | 623 | 627 | 627 | 625 | 636 | 649 | 686 | 562 | 451 | 629 |
| 5 133 | 5 183 | 5 630 | 5 991 | 6 227 | 6 419 | 6 599 | 6 937 | 7 303 | 7 975 | 4 862 | 3 385 | 6 340 |
| ... | ... | ... | ... | ... | ... | ... | ... | ... | ... | ... | ... | ... |
| 246 | 218 | 207 | 203 | 201 | 199 | 194 | 193 | 190 | 193 | 235 | 267 | 204 |
| 2 158 | 1 971 | 1 935 | 1 951 | 1 994 | 2 039 | 2 055 | 2 100 | 2 139 | 2 244 | 2 031 | 2 003 | 2 058 |
| 0.02 | 0.02 | 0.02 | 0.02 | 0.02 | 0.02 | 0.02 | 0.02 | 0.02 | 0.02 | 0.02 | 0.02 | 0.02 |
| 243 | 236 | 239 | 242 | 249 | 253 | 252 | 257 | 262 | 277 | 225 | 178 | 253 |
| 2 139 | 2 139 | 2 235 | 2 329 | 2 466 | 2 590 | 2 663 | 2 800 | 2 947 | 3 218 | 1 945 | 1 337 | 2 553 |
| 0.02 | 0.02 | 0.02 | 0.02 | 0.02 | 0.02 | 0.02 | 0.02 | 0.02 | 0.02 | 0.02 | 0.02 | 0.02 |
| 289 | 256 | 244 | 239 | 237 | 235 | 229 | 227 | 224 | 227 | 276 | 315 | 241 |
| 2 542 | 2 322 | 2 280 | 2 298 | 2 349 | 2 402 | 2 421 | 2 474 | 2 520 | 2 644 | 2 392 | 2 360 | 2 425 |
| 0.02 | 0.02 | 0.02 | 0.02 | 0.02 | 0.02 | 0.02 | 0.02 | 0.02 | 0.02 | 0.02 | 0.02 | 0.02 |
| 372 | 321 | 305 | 295 | 239 | 229 | 253 | 167 | 139 | 139 | 235 | 218 | 241 |
| 3 265 | 2 904 | 2 848 | 2 837 | 2 374 | 2 345 | 2 672 | 1 824 | 1 563 | 1 622 | 2 031 | 1 636 | 2 425 |
| 0.03 | 0.02 | 0.02 | 0.02 | 0.02 | 0.02 | 0.02 | 0.01 | 0.01 | 0.01 | 0.02 | 0.03 | 0.02 |

**Table A.1**   Total and per capita gross domestic product of individual countries or areas, expressed in United States dollars, and their individual shares of gross world product, based on alternative conversion rates, 1970–1989 [*cont.*]

| Country or area | 1970 (1) | 1971 (2) | 1972 (3) | 1973 (4) | 1974 (5) | 1975 (6) | 1976 (7) | 1977 (8) | 1978 (9) | 1979 (10) |
|---|---|---|---|---|---|---|---|---|---|---|
| **Malawi** | | | | | | | | | | |
| **1. MER** | | | | | | | | | | |
| 1a. Per capita GDP | 71 | 87 | 96 | 90 | 108 | 117 | 124 | 144 | 164 | 170 |
| 1b. GDP | 321 | 405 | 460 | 444 | 549 | 613 | 670 | 806 | 949 | 1 018 |
| 1c. % of GWP | 0.01 | 0.01 | 0.01 | 0.01 | 0.01 | 0.01 | 0.01 | 0.01 | 0.01 | 0.01 |
| **2. PPPs** | | | | | | | | | | |
| 2a. Per capita GDP | 156 | 187 | 205 | 198 | 242 | 269 | 289 | 315 | 346 | 362 |
| 2b. GDP | 707 | 867 | 980 | 975 | 1 232 | 1 410 | 1 563 | 1 764 | 2 002 | 2 167 |
| 2c. % of GWP | ... | ... | ... | ... | ... | ... | ... | ... | ... | ... |
| **3. Absolute 1970–1989 PARE** | | | | | | | | | | |
| 3a. Per capita GDP | 110 | 122 | 130 | 136 | 141 | 145 | 152 | 157 | 167 | 171 |
| 3b. GDP | 495 | 567 | 624 | 671 | 718 | 761 | 825 | 880 | 968 | 1 023 |
| 3c. % of GWP | 0.01 | 0.01 | 0.01 | 0.01 | 0.01 | 0.01 | 0.01 | 0.01 | 0.01 | 0.01 |
| **4. Relative 1970–1989 PARE** | | | | | | | | | | |
| 4a. Per capita GDP | 53 | 63 | 70 | 78 | 88 | 99 | 111 | 122 | 140 | 155 |
| 4b. GDP | 242 | 290 | 335 | 384 | 447 | 521 | 600 | 684 | 807 | 929 |
| 4c. % of GWP | 0.01 | 0.01 | 0.01 | 0.01 | 0.01 | 0.01 | 0.01 | 0.01 | 0.01 | 0.01 |
| **5. Absolute 1980–1989 PARE** | | | | | | | | | | |
| 5a. Per capita GDP | 122 | 136 | 145 | 152 | 157 | 162 | 170 | 175 | 187 | 191 |
| 5b. GDP | 552 | 632 | 696 | 748 | 800 | 848 | 920 | 981 | 1 079 | 1 140 |
| 5c. % of GWP | 0.01 | 0.01 | 0.01 | 0.01 | 0.01 | 0.01 | 0.01 | 0.01 | 0.01 | 0.01 |
| **6. WA** | | | | | | | | | | |
| 6a. Per capita GDP | 71 | 87 | 96 | 90 | 108 | 117 | 124 | 144 | 164 | 170 |
| 6b. GDP | 321 | 403 | 461 | 444 | 549 | 613 | 670 | 806 | 949 | 1 018 |
| 6c. % of GWP | 0.01 | 0.01 | 0.01 | 0.01 | 0.01 | 0.01 | 0.01 | 0.01 | 0.01 | 0.01 |
| **Malaysia** | | | | | | | | | | |
| **1. MER** | | | | | | | | | | |
| 1a. Per capita GDP | 319 | 382 | 442 | 656 | 793 | 762 | 881 | 1 024 | 1 246 | 1 579 |
| 1b. GDP | 3 459 | 4 248 | 5 043 | 7 664 | 9 496 | 9 344 | 11 048 | 13 141 | 16 358 | 21 218 |
| 1c. % of GWP | 0.11 | 0.12 | 0.13 | 0.16 | 0.17 | 0.15 | 0.16 | 0.17 | 0.18 | 0.21 |
| **2. PPPs** | | | | | | | | | | |
| 2a. Per capita GDP | 706 | 877 | 953 | 1 170 | 1 422 | 1 433 | 1 690 | 1 953 | 2 301 | 2 777 |
| 2b. GDP | 7 658 | 9 758 | 10 875 | 13 680 | 17 029 | 17 571 | 21 198 | 25 064 | 30 202 | 37 315 |
| 2c. % of GWP | ... | ... | ... | ... | ... | ... | ... | ... | ... | ... |
| **3. Absolute 1970–1989 PARE** | | | | | | | | | | |
| 3a. Per capita GDP | 776 | 930 | 992 | 1 082 | 1 144 | 1 126 | 1 228 | 1 294 | 1 348 | 1 441 |
| 3b. GDP | 8 418 | 10 349 | 11 320 | 12 645 | 13 697 | 13 806 | 15 403 | 16 597 | 17 701 | 19 356 |
| 3c. % of GWP | 0.12 | 0.14 | 0.15 | 0.15 | 0.16 | 0.16 | 0.17 | 0.18 | 0.18 | 0.19 |
| **4. Relative 1970–1989 PARE** | | | | | | | | | | |
| 4a. Per capita GDP | 378 | 477 | 532 | 618 | 713 | 772 | 894 | 1 005 | 1 124 | 1 308 |
| 4b. GDP | 4 104 | 5 304 | 6 069 | 7 229 | 8 541 | 9 459 | 11 212 | 12 896 | 14 758 | 17 578 |
| 4c. % of GWP | 0.12 | 0.14 | 0.15 | 0.15 | 0.16 | 0.16 | 0.17 | 0.18 | 0.18 | 0.19 |
| **5. Absolute 1980–1989 PARE** | | | | | | | | | | |
| 5a. Per capita GDP | 888 | 1 064 | 1 135 | 1 238 | 1 309 | 1 289 | 1 405 | 1 480 | 1 543 | 1 648 |
| 5b. GDP | 9 632 | 11 841 | 12 953 | 14 468 | 15 672 | 15 797 | 17 624 | 18 991 | 20 254 | 22 148 |
| 5c. % of GWP | 0.11 | 0.13 | 0.14 | 0.14 | 0.15 | 0.15 | 0.16 | 0.16 | 0.17 | 0.18 |
| **6. WA** | | | | | | | | | | |
| 6a. Per capita GDP | 319 | 381 | 442 | 656 | 793 | 761 | 881 | 1 024 | 1 246 | 1 579 |
| 6b. GDP | 3 459 | 4 244 | 5 043 | 7 663 | 9 496 | 9 329 | 11 050 | 13 140 | 16 358 | 21 213 |
| 6c. % of GWP | 0.11 | 0.12 | 0.13 | 0.16 | 0.17 | 0.15 | 0.16 | 0.17 | 0.18 | 0.21 |

| | | | | | | | | | | Averages | | |
|---|---|---|---|---|---|---|---|---|---|---|---|---|
| 1980 (11) | 1981 (12) | 1982 (13) | 1983 (14) | 1984 (15) | 1985 (16) | 1986 (17) | 1987 (18) | 1988 (19) | 1989 (20) | 1970–89 (21) | 1970–79 (22) | 1980–89 (23) |
| 201 | 194 | 177 | 178 | 168 | 153 | 155 | 157 | 165 | 192 | 155 | 121 | 174 |
| 1 245 | 1 241 | 1 169 | 1 219 | 1 195 | 1 122 | 1 176 | 1 233 | 1 348 | 1 620 | 940 | 624 | 1 257 |
| 0.01 | 0.01 | 0.01 | 0.01 | 0.01 | 0.01 | 0.01 | 0.01 | 0.01 | 0.01 | 0.01 | 0.01 | 0.01 |
| 413 | 416 | 397 | 431 | 457 | 420 | 415 | 422 | 432 | 456 | 367 | 265 | 429 |
| 2 554 | 2 663 | 2 626 | 2 955 | 3 242 | 3 081 | 3 155 | 3 324 | 3 525 | 3 851 | 2 232 | 1 367 | 3 098 |
| ... | ... | ... | ... | ... | ... | ... | ... | ... | ... | ... | ... | ... |
| 169 | 155 | 151 | 152 | 154 | 160 | 155 | 154 | 152 | 154 | 155 | 146 | 156 |
| 1 043 | 991 | 1 000 | 1 043 | 1 090 | 1 176 | 1 180 | 1 209 | 1 240 | 1 301 | 940 | 753 | 1 127 |
| 0.01 | 0.01 | 0.01 | 0.01 | 0.01 | 0.01 | 0.01 | 0.01 | 0.01 | 0.01 | 0.01 | 0.01 | 0.01 |
| 167 | 168 | 175 | 182 | 190 | 203 | 201 | 205 | 210 | 221 | 159 | 101 | 195 |
| 1 034 | 1 075 | 1 155 | 1 245 | 1 348 | 1 493 | 1 530 | 1 612 | 1 709 | 1 867 | 965 | 524 | 1 407 |
| 0.01 | 0.01 | 0.01 | 0.01 | 0.01 | 0.01 | 0.01 | 0.01 | 0.01 | 0.01 | 0.01 | 0.01 | 0.01 |
| 188 | 173 | 168 | 170 | 171 | 179 | 173 | 171 | 170 | 172 | 172 | 163 | 174 |
| 1 163 | 1 104 | 1 115 | 1 162 | 1 215 | 1 311 | 1 316 | 1 348 | 1 382 | 1 451 | 1 048 | 840 | 1 257 |
| 0.01 | 0.01 | 0.01 | 0.01 | 0.01 | 0.01 | 0.01 | 0.01 | 0.01 | 0.01 | 0.01 | 0.01 | 0.01 |
| 201 | 195 | 177 | 178 | 168 | 153 | 155 | 156 | 168 | 195 | 155 | 121 | 175 |
| 1 245 | 1 247 | 1 170 | 1 220 | 1 194 | 1 122 | 1 175 | 1 228 | 1 369 | 1 644 | 942 | 623 | 1 261 |
| 0.01 | 0.01 | 0.01 | 0.01 | 0.01 | 0.01 | 0.01 | 0.01 | 0.01 | 0.01 | 0.01 | 0.01 | 0.01 |
| 1 779 | 1 772 | 1 848 | 2 027 | 2 224 | 1 990 | 1 723 | 1 925 | 2 056 | 2 156 | 1 488 | 834 | 1 963 |
| 24 487 | 25 006 | 26 752 | 30 134 | 33 938 | 31 200 | 27 750 | 31 850 | 34 947 | 37 606 | 20 234 | 10 102 | 30 367 |
| 0.21 | 0.21 | 0.23 | 0.25 | 0.28 | 0.25 | 0.19 | 0.19 | 0.18 | 0.19 | 0.20 | 0.17 | 0.21 |
| 3 225 | 3 594 | 3 616 | 3 881 | 4 503 | 4 132 | 4 150 | 4 380 | 4 801 | 5 298 | 3 097 | 1 571 | 4 214 |
| 44 389 | 50 721 | 52 361 | 57 684 | 68 728 | 64 782 | 66 844 | 72 472 | 81 594 | 92 416 | 42 117 | 19 035 | 65 199 |
| ... | ... | ... | ... | ... | ... | ... | ... | ... | ... | ... | ... | ... |
| 1 511 | 1 576 | 1 628 | 1 684 | 1 768 | 1 701 | 1 675 | 1 719 | 1 823 | 1 932 | 1 488 | 1 150 | 1 715 |
| 20 797 | 22 241 | 23 570 | 25 035 | 26 978 | 26 675 | 26 982 | 28 437 | 30 976 | 33 703 | 20 234 | 13 929 | 26 539 |
| 0.20 | 0.21 | 0.22 | 0.23 | 0.24 | 0.22 | 0.22 | 0.23 | 0.23 | 0.25 | 0.20 | 0.16 | 0.23 |
| 1 498 | 1 710 | 1 880 | 2 011 | 2 186 | 2 162 | 2 171 | 2 291 | 2 512 | 2 771 | 1 582 | 802 | 2 153 |
| 20 615 | 24 133 | 27 226 | 29 896 | 33 371 | 33 890 | 34 969 | 37 913 | 42 685 | 48 347 | 21 510 | 9 715 | 33 305 |
| 0.20 | 0.21 | 0.22 | 0.23 | 0.24 | 0.22 | 0.22 | 0.23 | 0.23 | 0.25 | 0.21 | 0.17 | 0.23 |
| 1 729 | 1 803 | 1 863 | 1 927 | 2 022 | 1 947 | 1 917 | 1 966 | 2 086 | 2 211 | 1 702 | 1 315 | 1 963 |
| 23 796 | 25 448 | 26 969 | 28 645 | 30 869 | 30 522 | 30 874 | 32 538 | 35 443 | 38 563 | 23 152 | 15 938 | 30 367 |
| 0.19 | 0.20 | 0.21 | 0.21 | 0.22 | 0.21 | 0.21 | 0.21 | 0.22 | 0.23 | 0.19 | 0.15 | 0.21 |
| 1 779 | 1 772 | 1 851 | 2 027 | 2 224 | 1 990 | 1 722 | 1 910 | 2 042 | 2 149 | 1 486 | 834 | 1 959 |
| 24 488 | 25 004 | 26 805 | 30 131 | 33 943 | 31 200 | 27 734 | 31 602 | 34 696 | 37 483 | 20 204 | 10 100 | 30 309 |
| 0.21 | 0.21 | 0.23 | 0.25 | 0.28 | 0.25 | 0.19 | 0.19 | 0.19 | 0.19 | 0.20 | 0.17 | 0.21 |

**Table A.1** Total and per capita gross domestic product of individual countries or areas, expressed in United States dollars, and their individual shares of gross world product, based on alternative conversion rates, 1970–1989 [*cont.*]

| Country or area | 1970 (1) | 1971 (2) | 1972 (3) | 1973 (4) | 1974 (5) | 1975 (6) | 1976 (7) | 1977 (8) | 1978 (9) | 1979 (10) |
|---|---|---|---|---|---|---|---|---|---|---|
| **Maldives** | | | | | | | | | | |
| 1. **MER** | | | | | | | | | | |
| 1a. Per capita GDP | 136 | 142 | 167 | 214 | 261 | 198 | 133 | 142 | 161 | 246 |
| 1b. GDP | 16 | 17 | 20 | 27 | 34 | 26 | 18 | 20 | 24 | 37 |
| 1c. % of GWP | 0.00 | 0.00 | 0.00 | 0.00 | 0.00 | 0.00 | 0.00 | 0.00 | 0.00 | 0.00 |
| 2. **PPPs** | | | | | | | | | | |
| 2a. Per capita GDP | ... | ... | ... | ... | ... | ... | ... | ... | ... | ... |
| 2b. GDP | ... | ... | ... | ... | ... | ... | ... | ... | ... | ... |
| 2c. % of GWP | ... | ... | ... | ... | ... | ... | ... | ... | ... | ... |
| 3. **Absolute 1970–1989 PARE** | | | | | | | | | | |
| 3a. Per capita GDP | 123 | 135 | 149 | 164 | 183 | 201 | 224 | 240 | 268 | 287 |
| 3b. GDP | 14 | 16 | 18 | 21 | 24 | 27 | 31 | 34 | 39 | 43 |
| 3c. % of GWP | 0.00 | 0.00 | 0.00 | 0.00 | 0.00 | 0.00 | 0.00 | 0.00 | 0.00 | 0.00 |
| 4. **Relative 1970–1989 PARE** | | | | | | | | | | |
| 4a. Per capita GDP | 60 | 69 | 80 | 94 | 114 | 138 | 163 | 187 | 223 | 260 |
| 4b. GDP | 7 | 8 | 10 | 12 | 15 | 18 | 22 | 27 | 33 | 39 |
| 4c. % of GWP | 0.00 | 0.00 | 0.00 | 0.00 | 0.00 | 0.00 | 0.00 | 0.00 | 0.00 | 0.00 |
| 5. **Absolute 1980–1989 PARE** | | | | | | | | | | |
| 5a. Per capita GDP | 128 | 139 | 155 | 170 | 189 | 208 | 232 | 249 | 278 | 297 |
| 5b. GDP | 15 | 17 | 19 | 21 | 24 | 28 | 32 | 35 | 41 | 45 |
| 5c. % of GWP | 0.00 | 0.00 | 0.00 | 0.00 | 0.00 | 0.00 | 0.00 | 0.00 | 0.00 | 0.00 |
| 6. **WA**[a] | | | | | | | | | | |
| 6a. Per capita GDP | 182 | 145 | 163 | 189 | 232 | 243 | 198 | 164 | 160 | 190 |
| 6b. GDP | 21 | 17 | 20 | 24 | 30 | 32 | 27 | 23 | 23 | 29 |
| 6c. % of GWP | 0.00 | 0.00 | 0.00 | 0.00 | 0.00 | 0.00 | 0.00 | 0.00 | 0.00 | 0.00 |
| **Mali** | | | | | | | | | | |
| 1. **MER** | | | | | | | | | | |
| 1a. Per capita GDP | 63 | 68 | 82 | 93 | 86 | 130 | 144 | 158 | 180 | 230 |
| 1b. GDP | 346 | 380 | 470 | 545 | 521 | 803 | 908 | 1 015 | 1 182 | 1 543 |
| 1c. % of GWP | 0.01 | 0.01 | 0.01 | 0.01 | 0.01 | 0.01 | 0.01 | 0.01 | 0.01 | 0.01 |
| 2. **PPPs** | | | | | | | | | | |
| 2a. Per capita GDP | 100 | 107 | 120 | 123 | 127 | 161 | 192 | 191 | 181 | 199 |
| 2b. GDP | 548 | 602 | 689 | 725 | 766 | 993 | 1 209 | 1 225 | 1 188 | 1 333 |
| 2c. % of GWP | ... | ... | ... | ... | ... | ... | ... | ... | ... | ... |
| 3. **Absolute 1970–1989 PARE** | | | | | | | | | | |
| 3a. Per capita GDP | 153 | 154 | 157 | 145 | 149 | 153 | 161 | 166 | 170 | 171 |
| 3b. GDP | 837 | 865 | 903 | 856 | 901 | 944 | 1 016 | 1 070 | 1 116 | 1 149 |
| 3c. % of GWP | 0.01 | 0.01 | 0.01 | 0.01 | 0.01 | 0.01 | 0.01 | 0.01 | 0.01 | 0.01 |
| 4. **Relative 1970–1989 PARE** | | | | | | | | | | |
| 4a. Per capita GDP | 74 | 79 | 84 | 83 | 93 | 105 | 117 | 129 | 142 | 156 |
| 4b. GDP | 408 | 443 | 484 | 489 | 562 | 647 | 739 | 832 | 931 | 1 044 |
| 4c. % of GWP | 0.01 | 0.01 | 0.01 | 0.01 | 0.01 | 0.01 | 0.01 | 0.01 | 0.01 | 0.01 |
| 5. **Absolute 1980–1989 PARE** | | | | | | | | | | |
| 5a. Per capita GDP | 175 | 177 | 180 | 167 | 171 | 176 | 185 | 191 | 195 | 197 |
| 5b. GDP | 960 | 993 | 1 037 | 982 | 1 034 | 1 083 | 1 166 | 1 228 | 1 281 | 1 319 |
| 5c. % of GWP | 0.01 | 0.01 | 0.01 | 0.01 | 0.01 | 0.01 | 0.01 | 0.01 | 0.01 | 0.01 |
| 6. **WA** | | | | | | | | | | |
| 6a. Per capita GDP | 63 | 68 | 82 | 93 | 86 | 130 | 144 | 158 | 180 | 230 |
| 6b. GDP | 346 | 380 | 470 | 545 | 521 | 803 | 908 | 1 015 | 1 182 | 1 543 |
| 6c. % of GWP | 0.01 | 0.01 | 0.01 | 0.01 | 0.01 | 0.01 | 0.01 | 0.01 | 0.01 | 0.02 |

| | | | | | | | | | | Averages | | |
|---|---|---|---|---|---|---|---|---|---|---|---|---|
| 1980 | 1981 | 1982 | 1983 | 1984 | 1985 | 1986 | 1987 | 1988 | 1989 | 1970–89 | 1970–79 | 1980–89 |
| (11) | (12) | (13) | (14) | (15) | (16) | (17) | (18) | (19) | (20) | (21) | (22) | (23) |
| 302 | 309 | 363 | 384 | 428 | 456 | 487 | 406 | 559 | 618 | 338 | 182 | 441 |
| 47 | 50 | 60 | 66 | 76 | 84 | 92 | 80 | 113 | 129 | 52 | 24 | 80 |
| 0.00 | 0.00 | 0.00 | 0.00 | 0.00 | 0.00 | 0.00 | 0.00 | 0.00 | 0.00 | 0.00 | 0.00 | 0.00 |
| ... | ... | ... | ... | ... | ... | ... | ... | ... | ... | ... | ... | ... |
| ... | ... | ... | ... | ... | ... | ... | ... | ... | ... | ... | ... | ... |
| ... | ... | ... | ... | ... | ... | ... | ... | ... | ... | ... | ... | ... |
| 329 | 356 | 368 | 369 | 402 | 443 | 439 | 469 | 495 | 518 | 338 | 203 | 425 |
| 51 | 57 | 61 | 63 | 72 | 82 | 83 | 92 | 100 | 108 | 52 | 27 | 77 |
| 0.00 | 0.00 | 0.00 | 0.00 | 0.00 | 0.00 | 0.00 | 0.00 | 0.00 | 0.00 | 0.00 | 0.00 | 0.00 |
| 326 | 386 | 425 | 440 | 498 | 563 | 569 | 625 | 682 | 744 | 380 | 145 | 539 |
| 51 | 62 | 71 | 76 | 89 | 104 | 108 | 123 | 138 | 155 | 58 | 19 | 98 |
| 0.00 | 0.00 | 0.00 | 0.00 | 0.00 | 0.00 | 0.00 | 0.00 | 0.00 | 0.00 | 0.00 | 0.00 | 0.00 |
| 341 | 369 | 381 | 382 | 417 | 459 | 455 | 486 | 513 | 537 | 350 | 211 | 441 |
| 53 | 59 | 63 | 66 | 74 | 84 | 86 | 95 | 104 | 112 | 54 | 28 | 80 |
| 0.00 | 0.00 | 0.00 | 0.00 | 0.00 | 0.00 | 0.00 | 0.00 | 0.00 | 0.00 | 0.00 | 0.00 | 0.00 |
| 252 | 314 | 339 | 354 | 414 | 463 | 468 | 465 | 505 | 540 | 328 | 188 | 420 |
| 39 | 51 | 56 | 61 | 74 | 85 | 89 | 91 | 102 | 113 | 50 | 25 | 76 |
| 0.00 | 0.00 | 0.00 | 0.00 | 0.00 | 0.00 | 0.00 | 0.00 | 0.00 | 0.00 | 0.00 | 0.00 | 0.00 |
| 243 | 199 | 170 | 145 | 138 | 134 | 192 | 225 | 237 | 236 | 168 | 126 | 194 |
| 1 670 | 1 399 | 1 228 | 1 079 | 1 061 | 1 057 | 1 568 | 1 894 | 2 056 | 2 107 | 1 142 | 771 | 1 512 |
| 0.01 | 0.01 | 0.01 | 0.01 | 0.01 | 0.01 | 0.01 | 0.01 | 0.01 | 0.01 | 0.01 | 0.01 | 0.01 |
| 204 | 214 | 195 | 176 | 263 | 260 | 290 | 295 | 309 | 343 | 218 | 152 | 260 |
| 1 399 | 1 507 | 1 414 | 1 309 | 2 023 | 2 059 | 2 366 | 2 483 | 2 681 | 3 067 | 1 479 | 928 | 2 031 |
| ... | ... | ... | ... | ... | ... | ... | ... | ... | ... | ... | ... | ... |
| 174 | 170 | 175 | 163 | 159 | 154 | 169 | 167 | 169 | 180 | 168 | 158 | 169 |
| 1 195 | 1 196 | 1 267 | 1 212 | 1 223 | 1 222 | 1 377 | 1 404 | 1 467 | 1 612 | 1 142 | 966 | 1 318 |
| 0.01 | 0.01 | 0.01 | 0.01 | 0.01 | 0.01 | 0.01 | 0.01 | 0.01 | 0.01 | 0.01 | 0.01 | 0.01 |
| 173 | 184 | 202 | 194 | 197 | 196 | 219 | 223 | 233 | 259 | 170 | 108 | 211 |
| 1 185 | 1 298 | 1 464 | 1 447 | 1 513 | 1 552 | 1 784 | 1 872 | 2 022 | 2 313 | 1 151 | 658 | 1 645 |
| 0.01 | 0.01 | 0.01 | 0.01 | 0.01 | 0.01 | 0.01 | 0.01 | 0.01 | 0.01 | 0.01 | 0.01 | 0.01 |
| 200 | 195 | 201 | 186 | 183 | 177 | 194 | 192 | 194 | 207 | 193 | 182 | 194 |
| 1 371 | 1 373 | 1 454 | 1 391 | 1 404 | 1 402 | 1 580 | 1 611 | 1 684 | 1 850 | 1 310 | 1 108 | 1 512 |
| 0.01 | 0.01 | 0.01 | 0.01 | 0.01 | 0.01 | 0.01 | 0.01 | 0.01 | 0.01 | 0.01 | 0.01 | 0.01 |
| 243 | 199 | 170 | 145 | 138 | 134 | 192 | 225 | 237 | 236 | 168 | 126 | 194 |
| 1 670 | 1 399 | 1 228 | 1 079 | 1 061 | 1 057 | 1 568 | 1 894 | 2 055 | 2 107 | 1 142 | 771 | 1 512 |
| 0.01 | 0.01 | 0.01 | 0.01 | 0.01 | 0.01 | 0.01 | 0.01 | 0.01 | 0.01 | 0.01 | 0.01 | 0.01 |

**Table A.1**    Total and per capita gross domestic product of individual countries or areas,
expressed in United States dollars, and their individual shares of gross world
product, based on alternative conversion rates, 1970−1989 [*cont.*]

| Country or area | 1970 (1) | 1971 (2) | 1972 (3) | 1973 (4) | 1974 (5) | 1975 (6) | 1976 (7) | 1977 (8) | 1978 (9) | 1979 (10) |
|---|---|---|---|---|---|---|---|---|---|---|
| **Malta** | | | | | | | | | | |
| **1.  MER** | | | | | | | | | | |
| 1a.  Per capita GDP | 698 | 737 | 821 | 973 | 1 052 | 1 323 | 1 414 | 1 652 | 2 017 | 2 521 |
| 1b.  GDP | 227 | 240 | 267 | 315 | 342 | 434 | 474 | 568 | 712 | 910 |
| 1c.  % of GWP | 0.01 | 0.01 | 0.01 | 0.01 | 0.01 | 0.01 | 0.01 | 0.01 | 0.01 | 0.01 |
| **2.  PPPs** | | | | | | | | | | |
| 2a.  Per capita GDP | 1 335 | 1 402 | 1 492 | 1 636 | 1 847 | 2 306 | 2 779 | 3 140 | 3 542 | 4 034 |
| 2b.  GDP | 435 | 457 | 485 | 530 | 600 | 756 | 931 | 1 080 | 1 250 | 1 456 |
| 2c.  % of GWP | ... | ... | ... | ... | ... | ... | ... | ... | ... | ... |
| **3.  Absolute 1970−1989 PARE** | | | | | | | | | | |
| 3a.  Per capita GDP | 1 532 | 1 569 | 1 666 | 1 429 | 1 567 | 1 856 | 2 127 | 2 324 | 2 517 | 2 720 |
| 3b.  GDP | 499 | 512 | 541 | 463 | 509 | 609 | 713 | 799 | 889 | 982 |
| 3c.  % of GWP | 0.01 | 0.01 | 0.01 | 0.01 | 0.01 | 0.01 | 0.01 | 0.01 | 0.01 | 0.01 |
| **4.  Relative 1970−1989 PARE** | | | | | | | | | | |
| 4a.  Per capita GDP | 747 | 804 | 893 | 817 | 977 | 1 272 | 1 548 | 1 806 | 2 099 | 2 470 |
| 4b.  GDP | 243 | 262 | 290 | 265 | 318 | 417 | 519 | 621 | 741 | 892 |
| 4c.  % of GWP | 0.01 | 0.01 | 0.01 | 0.01 | 0.01 | 0.01 | 0.01 | 0.01 | 0.01 | 0.01 |
| **5.  Absolute 1980−1989 PARE** | | | | | | | | | | |
| 5a.  Per capita GDP | 1 794 | 1 838 | 1 951 | 1 673 | 1 836 | 2 175 | 2 491 | 2 722 | 2 949 | 3 186 |
| 5b.  GDP | 585 | 599 | 634 | 542 | 597 | 713 | 835 | 936 | 1 041 | 1 150 |
| 5c.  % of GWP | 0.01 | 0.01 | 0.01 | 0.01 | 0.01 | 0.01 | 0.01 | 0.01 | 0.01 | 0.01 |
| **6.  WA** | | | | | | | | | | |
| 6a.  Per capita GDP | 698 | 739 | 824 | 968 | 1 050 | 1 313 | 1 430 | 1 651 | 2 041 | 2 517 |
| 6b.  GDP | 228 | 241 | 268 | 314 | 341 | 431 | 479 | 568 | 720 | 909 |
| 6c.  % of GWP | 0.01 | 0.01 | 0.01 | 0.01 | 0.01 | 0.01 | 0.01 | 0.01 | 0.01 | 0.01 |
| **Martinique** | | | | | | | | | | |
| **1.  MER** | | | | | | | | | | |
| 1a.  Per capita GDP | 884 | 1 013 | 1 253 | 1 631 | 1 648 | 2 381 | 2 377 | 2 728 | 3 368 | 3 980 |
| 1b.  GDP | 288 | 331 | 411 | 537 | 542 | 783 | 782 | 895 | 1 101 | 1 302 |
| 1c.  % of GWP | 0.01 | 0.01 | 0.01 | 0.01 | 0.01 | 0.01 | 0.01 | 0.01 | 0.01 | 0.01 |
| **2.  PPPs** | | | | | | | | | | |
| 2a.  Per capita GDP | ... | ... | ... | ... | ... | ... | ... | ... | ... | ... |
| 2b.  GDP | ... | ... | ... | ... | ... | ... | ... | ... | ... | ... |
| 2c.  % of GWP | ... | ... | ... | ... | ... | ... | ... | ... | ... | ... |
| **3.  Absolute 1970−1989 PARE** | | | | | | | | | | |
| 3a.  Per capita GDP | 2 451 | 2 614 | 2 796 | 2 983 | 2 741 | 3 074 | 3 077 | 3 300 | 3 446 | 3 550 |
| 3b.  GDP | 799 | 855 | 917 | 982 | 902 | 1 011 | 1 012 | 1 082 | 1 127 | 1 161 |
| 3c.  % of GWP | 0.01 | 0.01 | 0.01 | 0.01 | 0.01 | 0.01 | 0.01 | 0.01 | 0.01 | 0.01 |
| **4.  Relative 1970−1989 PARE** | | | | | | | | | | |
| 4a.  Per capita GDP | 1 195 | 1 340 | 1 499 | 1 706 | 1 710 | 2 106 | 2 240 | 2 564 | 2 873 | 3 224 |
| 4b.  GDP | 390 | 438 | 492 | 561 | 562 | 693 | 737 | 841 | 939 | 1 054 |
| 4c.  % of GWP | 0.01 | 0.01 | 0.01 | 0.01 | 0.01 | 0.01 | 0.01 | 0.01 | 0.01 | 0.01 |
| **5.  Absolute 1980−1989 PARE** | | | | | | | | | | |
| 5a.  Per capita GDP | 2 923 | 3 118 | 3 335 | 3 559 | 3 270 | 3 667 | 3 671 | 3 936 | 4 110 | 4 234 |
| 5b.  GDP | 953 | 1 020 | 1 094 | 1 171 | 1 076 | 1 206 | 1 208 | 1 291 | 1 344 | 1 385 |
| 5c.  % of GWP | 0.01 | 0.01 | 0.01 | 0.01 | 0.01 | 0.01 | 0.01 | 0.01 | 0.01 | 0.01 |
| **6.  WA[a]** | | | | | | | | | | |
| 6a.  Per capita GDP | 887 | 971 | 1 106 | 1 348 | 1 437 | 1 928 | 2 173 | 2 608 | 2 931 | 3 409 |
| 6b.  GDP | 289 | 318 | 363 | 443 | 473 | 634 | 715 | 856 | 958 | 1 115 |
| 6c.  % of GWP | 0.01 | 0.01 | 0.01 | 0.01 | 0.01 | 0.01 | 0.01 | 0.01 | 0.01 | 0.01 |

| | | | | | | | | | | Averages | | |
|---|---|---|---|---|---|---|---|---|---|---|---|---|
| 1980 (11) | 1981 (12) | 1982 (13) | 1983 (14) | 1984 (15) | 1985 (16) | 1986 (17) | 1987 (18) | 1988 (19) | 1989 (20) | 1970–89 (21) | 1970–79 (22) | 1980–89 (23) |
| 3 068 | 3 106 | 3 113 | 2 992 | 2 880 | 2 948 | 3 815 | 5 306 | 5 809 | 6 364 | 2 526 | 1 375 | 3 997 |
| 1 120 | 1 131 | 1 121 | 1 059 | 1 002 | 1 017 | 1 312 | 1 831 | 2 022 | 2 234 | 917 | 449 | 1 385 |
| 0.01 | 0.01 | 0.01 | 0.01 | 0.01 | 0.01 | 0.01 | 0.01 | 0.01 | 0.01 | 0.01 | 0.01 | 0.01 |
| 4 617 | 5 323 | 5 978 | 6 104 | 6 558 | 6 996 | 7 435 | 7 940 | 8 820 | 9 848 | 4 468 | 2 445 | 7 058 |
| 1 685 | 1 937 | 2 152 | 2 161 | 2 282 | 2 414 | 2 558 | 2 739 | 3 070 | 3 457 | 1 622 | 798 | 2 445 |
| ... | ... | ... | ... | ... | ... | ... | ... | ... | ... | ... | ... | ... |
| 2 879 | 2 983 | 3 085 | 3 118 | 3 202 | 3 313 | 3 452 | 3 583 | 3 851 | 4 131 | 2 526 | 1 996 | 3 412 |
| 1 051 | 1 086 | 1 111 | 1 104 | 1 114 | 1 143 | 1 187 | 1 236 | 1 340 | 1 450 | 917 | 652 | 1 182 |
| 0.01 | 0.01 | 0.01 | 0.01 | 0.01 | 0.01 | 0.01 | 0.01 | 0.01 | 0.01 | 0.01 | 0.01 | 0.01 |
| 2 854 | 3 237 | 3 564 | 3 724 | 3 960 | 4 209 | 4 473 | 4 777 | 5 307 | 5 925 | 2 663 | 1 399 | 4 261 |
| 1 042 | 1 178 | 1 283 | 1 318 | 1 378 | 1 452 | 1 539 | 1 648 | 1 847 | 2 080 | 967 | 457 | 1 476 |
| 0.01 | 0.01 | 0.01 | 0.01 | 0.01 | 0.01 | 0.01 | 0.01 | 0.01 | 0.01 | 0.01 | 0.01 | 0.01 |
| 3 373 | 3 494 | 3 614 | 3 652 | 3 750 | 3 881 | 4 043 | 4 197 | 4 511 | 4 839 | 2 959 | 2 338 | 3 997 |
| 1 231 | 1 272 | 1 301 | 1 293 | 1 305 | 1 339 | 1 391 | 1 448 | 1 570 | 1 698 | 1 074 | 763 | 1 385 |
| 0.01 | 0.01 | 0.01 | 0.01 | 0.01 | 0.01 | 0.01 | 0.01 | 0.01 | 0.01 | 0.01 | 0.01 | 0.01 |
| 3 109 | 3 101 | 3 112 | 2 989 | 2 874 | 2 941 | 3 786 | 4 607 | 5 267 | 5 479 | 2 425 | 1 378 | 3 782 |
| 1 135 | 1 129 | 1 120 | 1 058 | 1 000 | 1 015 | 1 302 | 1 590 | 1 833 | 1 923 | 880 | 450 | 1 310 |
| 0.01 | 0.01 | 0.01 | 0.01 | 0.01 | 0.01 | 0.01 | 0.01 | 0.01 | 0.01 | 0.01 | 0.01 | 0.01 |
| 4 415 | 4 077 | 4 117 | 4 034 | 3 810 | 4 216 | 5 985 | 7 349 | 7 693 | 7 704 | 3 786 | 2 119 | 5 366 |
| 1 444 | 1 333 | 1 350 | 1 327 | 1 261 | 1 400 | 1 999 | 2 469 | 2 593 | 2 612 | 1 238 | 697 | 1 779 |
| 0.01 | 0.01 | 0.01 | 0.01 | 0.01 | 0.01 | 0.01 | 0.01 | 0.01 | 0.01 | 0.01 | 0.01 | 0.01 |
| ... | ... | ... | ... | ... | ... | ... | ... | ... | ... | ... | ... | ... |
| ... | ... | ... | ... | ... | ... | ... | ... | ... | ... | ... | ... | ... |
| ... | ... | ... | ... | ... | ... | ... | ... | ... | ... | ... | ... | ... |
| 3 649 | 3 810 | 4 115 | 4 134 | 4 294 | 4 474 | 4 647 | 4 958 | 5 243 | 5 521 | 3 786 | 2 993 | 4 498 |
| 1 193 | 1 246 | 1 350 | 1 360 | 1 421 | 1 485 | 1 552 | 1 666 | 1 767 | 1 872 | 1 238 | 985 | 1 491 |
| 0.01 | 0.01 | 0.01 | 0.01 | 0.01 | 0.01 | 0.01 | 0.01 | 0.01 | 0.01 | 0.01 | 0.01 | 0.01 |
| 3 617 | 4 134 | 4 754 | 4 937 | 5 312 | 5 684 | 6 022 | 6 610 | 7 225 | 7 920 | 3 887 | 2 039 | 5 646 |
| 1 183 | 1 352 | 1 559 | 1 624 | 1 758 | 1 887 | 2 011 | 2 221 | 2 435 | 2 685 | 1 271 | 671 | 1 872 |
| 0.01 | 0.01 | 0.01 | 0.01 | 0.01 | 0.01 | 0.01 | 0.01 | 0.01 | 0.01 | 0.01 | 0.01 | 0.01 |
| 4 353 | 4 545 | 4 909 | 4 931 | 5 122 | 5 336 | 5 542 | 5 914 | 6 254 | 6 585 | 4 516 | 3 570 | 5 366 |
| 1 423 | 1 486 | 1 610 | 1 622 | 1 695 | 1 772 | 1 851 | 1 987 | 2 108 | 2 232 | 1 477 | 1 175 | 1 779 |
| 0.01 | 0.01 | 0.01 | 0.01 | 0.01 | 0.01 | 0.01 | 0.01 | 0.01 | 0.01 | 0.01 | 0.01 | 0.01 |
| 3 994 | 4 308 | 4 472 | 4 191 | 4 088 | 4 177 | 4 702 | 5 921 | 7 376 | 7 990 | 3 550 | 1 873 | 5 145 |
| 1 306 | 1 409 | 1 467 | 1 379 | 1 353 | 1 387 | 1 570 | 1 989 | 2 486 | 2 709 | 1 161 | 616 | 1 705 |
| 0.01 | 0.01 | 0.01 | 0.01 | 0.01 | 0.01 | 0.01 | 0.01 | 0.01 | 0.01 | 0.01 | 0.01 | 0.01 |

**Table A.1**   Total and per capita gross domestic product of individual countries or areas,
expressed in United States dollars, and their individual shares of gross world
product, based on alternative conversion rates, 1970−1989 [*cont.*]

| Country or area | 1970 (1) | 1971 (2) | 1972 (3) | 1973 (4) | 1974 (5) | 1975 (6) | 1976 (7) | 1977 (8) | 1978 (9) | 1979 (10) |
|---|---|---|---|---|---|---|---|---|---|---|
| **Mauritania** | | | | | | | | | | |
| 1.   **MER** | | | | | | | | | | |
| 1a.   Per capita GDP | 167 | 175 | 199 | 222 | 274 | 348 | 381 | 381 | 366 | 444 |
| 1b.   GDP | 204 | 219 | 255 | 290 | 368 | 478 | 535 | 548 | 540 | 672 |
| 1c.   % of GWP | 0.01 | 0.01 | 0.01 | 0.01 | 0.01 | 0.01 | 0.01 | 0.01 | 0.01 | 0.01 |
| 2.   **PPPs** | | | | | | | | | | |
| 2a.   Per capita GDP | 297 | 301 | 308 | 325 | 419 | 494 | 513 | 506 | 487 | 577 |
| 2b.   GDP | 363 | 376 | 394 | 425 | 561 | 678 | 721 | 729 | 718 | 874 |
| 2c.   % of GWP | ... | ... | ... | ... | ... | ... | ... | ... | ... | ... |
| 3.   **Absolute 1970−1989 PARE** | | | | | | | | | | |
| 3a.   Per capita GDP | 424 | 415 | 421 | 383 | 412 | 438 | 447 | 422 | 388 | 391 |
| 3b.   GDP | 518 | 519 | 538 | 501 | 552 | 600 | 628 | 607 | 573 | 591 |
| 3c.   % of GWP | 0.01 | 0.01 | 0.01 | 0.01 | 0.01 | 0.01 | 0.01 | 0.01 | 0.01 | 0.01 |
| 4.   **Relative 1970−1989 PARE** | | | | | | | | | | |
| 4a.   Per capita GDP | 207 | 213 | 225 | 219 | 257 | 300 | 325 | 328 | 324 | 355 |
| 4b.   GDP | 252 | 266 | 288 | 286 | 344 | 411 | 457 | 472 | 478 | 537 |
| 4c.   % of GWP | 0.01 | 0.01 | 0.01 | 0.01 | 0.01 | 0.01 | 0.01 | 0.01 | 0.01 | 0.01 |
| 5.   **Absolute 1980−1989 PARE** | | | | | | | | | | |
| 5a.   Per capita GDP | 522 | 511 | 518 | 471 | 507 | 539 | 551 | 519 | 478 | 481 |
| 5b.   GDP | 637 | 639 | 662 | 617 | 679 | 739 | 773 | 748 | 706 | 728 |
| 5c.   % of GWP | 0.01 | 0.01 | 0.01 | 0.01 | 0.01 | 0.01 | 0.01 | 0.01 | 0.01 | 0.01 |
| 6.   **WA** | | | | | | | | | | |
| 6a.   Per capita GDP | 167 | 175 | 199 | 222 | 274 | 348 | 381 | 381 | 366 | 444 |
| 6b.   GDP | 204 | 219 | 255 | 290 | 368 | 478 | 535 | 548 | 540 | 672 |
| 6c.   % of GWP | 0.01 | 0.01 | 0.01 | 0.01 | 0.01 | 0.01 | 0.01 | 0.01 | 0.01 | 0.01 |
| **Mauritius** | | | | | | | | | | |
| 1.   **MER** | | | | | | | | | | |
| 1a.   Per capita GDP | 271 | 300 | 371 | 457 | 749 | 741 | 776 | 892 | 1 083 | 1 271 |
| 1b.   GDP | 224 | 252 | 316 | 396 | 658 | 661 | 704 | 824 | 1 015 | 1 211 |
| 1c.   % of GWP | 0.01 | 0.01 | 0.01 | 0.01 | 0.01 | 0.01 | 0.01 | 0.01 | 0.01 | 0.01 |
| 2.   **PPPs** | | | | | | | | | | |
| 2a.   Per capita GDP | 616 | 693 | 799 | 899 | 1 067 | 1 190 | 1 230 | 1 362 | 1 496 | 1 687 |
| 2b.   GDP | 509 | 582 | 682 | 778 | 938 | 1 063 | 1 115 | 1 257 | 1 404 | 1 608 |
| 2c.   % of GWP | ... | ... | ... | ... | ... | ... | ... | ... | ... | ... |
| 3.   **Absolute 1970−1989 PARE** | | | | | | | | | | |
| 3a.   Per capita GDP | 84 | 91 | 98 | 919 | 974 | 958 | 1 096 | 1 147 | 1 172 | 1 194 |
| 3b.   GDP | 69 | 76 | 83 | 796 | 856 | 855 | 994 | 1 059 | 1 099 | 1 138 |
| 3c.   % of GWP | 0.00 | 0.00 | 0.00 | 0.01 | 0.01 | 0.01 | 0.01 | 0.01 | 0.01 | 0.01 |
| 4.   **Relative 1970−1989 PARE** | | | | | | | | | | |
| 4a.   Per capita GDP | 310 | 353 | 399 | 525 | 608 | 656 | 798 | 891 | 977 | 1 084 |
| 4b.   GDP | 257 | 297 | 341 | 455 | 534 | 586 | 723 | 823 | 917 | 1 033 |
| 4c.   % of GWP | 0.01 | 0.01 | 0.01 | 0.01 | 0.01 | 0.01 | 0.01 | 0.01 | 0.01 | 0.01 |
| 5.   **Absolute 1980−1989 PARE** | | | | | | | | | | |
| 5a.   Per capita GDP | 88 | 96 | 103 | 972 | 1 030 | 1 013 | 1 159 | 1 213 | 1 240 | 1 263 |
| 5b.   GDP | 73 | 80 | 88 | 841 | 906 | 905 | 1 051 | 1 120 | 1 163 | 1 204 |
| 5c.   % of GWP | 0.00 | 0.00 | 0.00 | 0.01 | 0.01 | 0.01 | 0.01 | 0.01 | 0.01 | 0.01 |
| 6.   **WA** | | | | | | | | | | |
| 6a.   Per capita GDP | 271 | 300 | 371 | 457 | 749 | 741 | 776 | 892 | 1 083 | 1 271 |
| 6b.   GDP | 224 | 252 | 316 | 396 | 658 | 661 | 704 | 824 | 1 015 | 1 211 |
| 6c.   % of GWP | 0.01 | 0.01 | 0.01 | 0.01 | 0.01 | 0.01 | 0.01 | 0.01 | 0.01 | 0.01 |

| | | | | | | | | | | Averages | | |
|---|---|---|---|---|---|---|---|---|---|---|---|---|
| 1980 (11) | 1981 (12) | 1982 (13) | 1983 (14) | 1984 (15) | 1985 (16) | 1986 (17) | 1987 (18) | 1988 (19) | 1989 (20) | 1970−89 (21) | 1970−79 (22) | 1980−89 (23) |

| 535 | 563 | 505 | 500 | 405 | 377 | 409 | 437 | 460 | 454 | 398 | 303 | 464 |
|---|---|---|---|---|---|---|---|---|---|---|---|---|
| 829 | 895 | 824 | 838 | 697 | 667 | 743 | 815 | 881 | 894 | 610 | 411 | 808 |
| 0.01 | 0.01 | 0.01 | 0.01 | 0.01 | 0.01 | 0.00 | 0.00 | 0.00 | 0.00 | 0.01 | 0.01 | 0.01 |
| 681 | 679 | 620 | 660 | 635 | 617 | 637 | 646 | 671 | 704 | 565 | 431 | 658 |
| 1 056 | 1 081 | 1 013 | 1 106 | 1 093 | 1 091 | 1 157 | 1 204 | 1 286 | 1 387 | 866 | 584 | 1 147 |
| ... | ... | ... | ... | ... | ... | ... | ... | ... | ... | ... | ... | ... |
| 396 | 395 | 377 | 384 | 365 | 367 | 371 | 365 | 367 | 370 | 398 | 415 | 377 |
| 615 | 628 | 615 | 644 | 628 | 648 | 673 | 681 | 704 | 729 | 610 | 563 | 657 |
| 0.01 | 0.01 | 0.01 | 0.01 | 0.01 | 0.01 | 0.01 | 0.01 | 0.01 | 0.01 | 0.01 | 0.01 | 0.01 |
| 393 | 428 | 435 | 459 | 452 | 466 | 481 | 487 | 506 | 531 | 390 | 280 | 468 |
| 609 | 682 | 710 | 769 | 777 | 823 | 873 | 908 | 970 | 1 046 | 598 | 379 | 817 |
| 0.01 | 0.01 | 0.01 | 0.01 | 0.01 | 0.01 | 0.01 | 0.01 | 0.01 | 0.01 | 0.01 | 0.01 | 0.01 |
| 488 | 486 | 464 | 473 | 450 | 451 | 457 | 450 | 452 | 456 | 490 | 511 | 464 |
| 757 | 773 | 757 | 793 | 773 | 797 | 829 | 839 | 867 | 898 | 751 | 693 | 808 |
| 0.01 | 0.01 | 0.01 | 0.01 | 0.01 | 0.01 | 0.01 | 0.01 | 0.01 | 0.01 | 0.01 | 0.01 | 0.01 |
| 535 | 563 | 505 | 500 | 405 | 377 | 409 | 437 | 460 | 454 | 398 | 303 | 464 |
| 829 | 895 | 824 | 838 | 697 | 667 | 743 | 815 | 881 | 894 | 610 | 411 | 808 |
| 0.01 | 0.01 | 0.01 | 0.01 | 0.01 | 0.01 | 0.01 | 0.00 | 0.00 | 0.00 | 0.01 | 0.01 | 0.01 |
| | | | | | | | | | | | | |
| 1 170 | 1 167 | 1 089 | 1 090 | 1 030 | 1 054 | 1 417 | 1 749 | 1 963 | 1 933 | 1 055 | 707 | 1 378 |
| 1 132 | 1 142 | 1 078 | 1 090 | 1 041 | 1 076 | 1 463 | 1 828 | 2 075 | 2 068 | 1 013 | 626 | 1 399 |
| 0.01 | 0.01 | 0.01 | 0.01 | 0.01 | 0.01 | 0.01 | 0.01 | 0.01 | 0.01 | 0.01 | 0.01 | 0.01 |
| 1 469 | 1 742 | 1 817 | 1 889 | 2 055 | 2 159 | 2 391 | 2 676 | 2 920 | 3 114 | 1 704 | 1 122 | 2 243 |
| 1 420 | 1 706 | 1 799 | 1 889 | 2 076 | 2 204 | 2 468 | 2 797 | 3 086 | 3 332 | 1 636 | 994 | 2 278 |
| ... | ... | ... | ... | ... | ... | ... | ... | ... | ... | ... | ... | ... |
| 1 058 | 1 107 | 1 155 | 1 148 | 1 191 | 1 259 | 1 367 | 1 487 | 1 570 | 1 608 | 1 055 | 793 | 1 303 |
| 1 024 | 1 084 | 1 143 | 1 148 | 1 202 | 1 285 | 1 410 | 1 554 | 1 659 | 1 721 | 1 013 | 703 | 1 323 |
| 0.01 | 0.01 | 0.01 | 0.01 | 0.01 | 0.01 | 0.01 | 0.01 | 0.01 | 0.01 | 0.01 | 0.01 | 0.01 |
| 1 049 | 1 201 | 1 334 | 1 371 | 1 473 | 1 599 | 1 771 | 1 982 | 2 163 | 2 307 | 1 178 | 673 | 1 640 |
| 1 015 | 1 176 | 1 321 | 1 371 | 1 487 | 1 633 | 1 828 | 2 071 | 2 286 | 2 468 | 1 131 | 597 | 1 666 |
| 0.01 | 0.01 | 0.01 | 0.01 | 0.01 | 0.01 | 0.01 | 0.01 | 0.01 | 0.01 | 0.01 | 0.01 | 0.01 |
| 1 120 | 1 171 | 1 221 | 1 214 | 1 259 | 1 331 | 1 446 | 1 573 | 1 660 | 1 701 | 1 116 | 839 | 1 378 |
| 1 083 | 1 146 | 1 209 | 1 214 | 1 272 | 1 359 | 1 492 | 1 643 | 1 755 | 1 820 | 1 071 | 743 | 1 399 |
| 0.01 | 0.01 | 0.01 | 0.01 | 0.01 | 0.01 | 0.01 | 0.01 | 0.01 | 0.01 | 0.01 | 0.01 | 0.01 |
| 1 170 | 1 167 | 1 089 | 1 090 | 1 030 | 1 054 | 1 418 | 1 752 | 1 957 | 1 939 | 1 055 | 707 | 1 378 |
| 1 132 | 1 142 | 1 078 | 1 090 | 1 041 | 1 076 | 1 463 | 1 831 | 2 069 | 2 075 | 1 013 | 626 | 1 400 |
| 0.01 | 0.01 | 0.01 | 0.01 | 0.01 | 0.01 | 0.01 | 0.01 | 0.01 | 0.01 | 0.01 | 0.01 | 0.01 |

**Table A.1** Total and per capita gross domestic product of individual countries or areas, expressed in United States dollars, and their individual shares of gross world product, based on alternative conversion rates, 1970–1989 [*cont.*]

| Country or area | 1970 (1) | 1971 (2) | 1972 (3) | 1973 (4) | 1974 (5) | 1975 (6) | 1976 (7) | 1977 (8) | 1978 (9) | 1979 (10) |
|---|---|---|---|---|---|---|---|---|---|---|
| **Mexico** | | | | | | | | | | |
| **1. MER** | | | | | | | | | | |
| 1a. Per capita GDP | 704 | 751 | 837 | 992 | 1 251 | 1 486 | 1 459 | 1 310 | 1 601 | 2 046 |
| 1b. GDP | 37 152 | 40 976 | 47 224 | 57 776 | 75 232 | 91 984 | 92 895 | 85 633 | 107 313 | 140 601 |
| 1c. % of GWP | 1.16 | 1.17 | 1.17 | 1.18 | 1.35 | 1.48 | 1.38 | 1.13 | 1.19 | 1.36 |
| **2. PPPs** | | | | | | | | | | |
| 2a. Per capita GDP | 1 538 | 1 629 | 1 763 | 1 934 | 2 208 | 2 471 | 2 631 | 2 781 | 3 158 | 3 713 |
| 2b. GDP | 81 153 | 88 854 | 99 406 | 112 690 | 132 755 | 152 975 | 167 530 | 181 773 | 211 705 | 255 127 |
| 2c. % of GWP | ... | ... | ... | ... | ... | ... | ... | ... | ... | ... |
| **3. Absolute 1970–1989 PARE** | | | | | | | | | | |
| 3a. Per capita GDP | 1 438 | 1 449 | 1 521 | 1 596 | 1 641 | 1 683 | 1 706 | 1 719 | 1 814 | 1 932 |
| 3b. GDP | 75 885 | 79 050 | 85 760 | 92 972 | 98 653 | 104 186 | 108 603 | 112 344 | 121 612 | 132 745 |
| 3c. % of GWP | 1.07 | 1.07 | 1.10 | 1.12 | 1.16 | 1.21 | 1.20 | 1.19 | 1.24 | 1.31 |
| **4. Relative 1970–1989 PARE** | | | | | | | | | | |
| 4a. Per capita GDP | 701 | 743 | 815 | 912 | 1 023 | 1 153 | 1 242 | 1 336 | 1 513 | 1 755 |
| 4b. GDP | 36 999 | 40 519 | 45 976 | 53 153 | 61 520 | 71 379 | 79 054 | 87 293 | 101 388 | 120 551 |
| 4c. % of GWP | 1.07 | 1.07 | 1.10 | 1.12 | 1.16 | 1.21 | 1.20 | 1.19 | 1.24 | 1.31 |
| **5. Absolute 1980–1989 PARE** | | | | | | | | | | |
| 5a. Per capita GDP | 1 657 | 1 670 | 1 752 | 1 839 | 1 891 | 1 939 | 1 966 | 1 980 | 2 090 | 2 226 |
| 5b. GDP | 87 439 | 91 086 | 98 818 | 107 128 | 113 674 | 120 049 | 125 138 | 129 449 | 140 128 | 152 956 |
| 5c. % of GWP | 1.00 | 1.00 | 1.03 | 1.05 | 1.10 | 1.14 | 1.13 | 1.12 | 1.17 | 1.23 |
| **6. WA** | | | | | | | | | | |
| 6a. Per capita GDP | 704 | 751 | 837 | 992 | 1 251 | 1 486 | 1 459 | 1 310 | 1 601 | 2 046 |
| 6b. GDP | 37 152 | 40 976 | 47 224 | 57 776 | 75 232 | 91 984 | 92 896 | 85 634 | 107 312 | 140 601 |
| 6c. % of GWP | 1.16 | 1.17 | 1.18 | 1.19 | 1.35 | 1.49 | 1.38 | 1.14 | 1.21 | 1.37 |
| **Mongolia** | | | | | | | | | | |
| **1. MER** | | | | | | | | | | |
| 1a. Per capita GDP | 416 | 426 | 466 | 555 | 585 | 641 | 636 | 633 | 726 | 801 |
| 1b. GDP | 523 | 550 | 619 | 760 | 823 | 928 | 947 | 970 | 1 143 | 1 296 |
| 1c. % of GWP | 0.02 | 0.02 | 0.02 | 0.02 | 0.01 | 0.01 | 0.01 | 0.01 | 0.01 | 0.01 |
| **2. PPPs** | | | | | | | | | | |
| 2a. Per capita GDP | ... | ... | ... | ... | ... | ... | ... | ... | ... | ... |
| 2b. GDP | ... | ... | ... | ... | ... | ... | ... | ... | ... | ... |
| 2c. % of GWP | ... | ... | ... | ... | ... | ... | ... | ... | ... | ... |
| **3. Absolute 1970–1989 PARE** | | | | | | | | | | |
| 3a. Per capita GDP | 534 | 550 | 554 | 598 | 614 | 639 | 657 | 648 | 686 | 725 |
| 3b. GDP | 670 | 711 | 737 | 818 | 865 | 925 | 979 | 992 | 1 080 | 1 173 |
| 3c. % of GWP | 0.01 | 0.01 | 0.01 | 0.01 | 0.01 | 0.01 | 0.01 | 0.01 | 0.01 | 0.01 |
| **4. Relative 1970–1989 PARE** | | | | | | | | | | |
| 4a. Per capita GDP | 260 | 282 | 297 | 342 | 383 | 438 | 478 | 504 | 572 | 659 |
| 4b. GDP | 327 | 364 | 395 | 468 | 539 | 634 | 712 | 771 | 900 | 1 066 |
| 4c. % of GWP | 0.01 | 0.01 | 0.01 | 0.01 | 0.01 | 0.01 | 0.01 | 0.01 | 0.01 | 0.01 |
| **5. Absolute 1980–1989 PARE** | | | | | | | | | | |
| 5a. Per capita GDP | 547 | 563 | 568 | 612 | 629 | 654 | 673 | 664 | 702 | 743 |
| 5b. GDP | 687 | 728 | 755 | 838 | 886 | 947 | 1 002 | 1 016 | 1 106 | 1 202 |
| 5c. % of GWP | 0.01 | 0.01 | 0.01 | 0.01 | 0.01 | 0.01 | 0.01 | 0.01 | 0.01 | 0.01 |
| **6. WA[a]** | | | | | | | | | | |
| 6a. Per capita GDP | 823 | 568 | 442 | 504 | 555 | 614 | 640 | 637 | 685 | 757 |
| 6b. GDP | 1 033 | 734 | 587 | 689 | 782 | 888 | 953 | 975 | 1 079 | 1 225 |
| 6c. % of GWP | 0.03 | 0.02 | 0.01 | 0.01 | 0.01 | 0.01 | 0.01 | 0.01 | 0.01 | 0.01 |

| | | | | | | | | | | Averages | | |
|---|---|---|---|---|---|---|---|---|---|---|---|---|
| 1980 (11) | 1981 (12) | 1982 (13) | 1983 (14) | 1984 (15) | 1985 (16) | 1986 (17) | 1987 (18) | 1988 (19) | 1989 (20) | 1970–89 (21) | 1970–79 (22) | 1980–89 (23) |
| 2 766 | 3 464 | 2 350 | 1 966 | 2 264 | 2 324 | 1 601 | 1 693 | 2 035 | 2 396 | 1 837 | 1 273 | 2 267 |
| 194 767 | 250 004 | 173 720 | 148 878 | 175 604 | 184 498 | 130 008 | 140 546 | 172 766 | 207 815 | 127 770 | 77 679 | 177 861 |
| 1.68 | 2.14 | 1.49 | 1.26 | 1.44 | 1.46 | 0.87 | 0.82 | 0.90 | 1.04 | 1.25 | 1.27 | 1.25 |
| 4 463 | 5 110 | 5 123 | 4 686 | 4 758 | 4 902 | 4 705 | 4 815 | 4 935 | 5 186 | 3 816 | 2 432 | 4 875 |
| 314 293 | 368 717 | 378 795 | 354 932 | 368 993 | 389 072 | 382 048 | 399 830 | 418 915 | 449 842 | 265 470 | 148 397 | 382 544 |
| ... | ... | ... | ... | ... | ... | ... | ... | ... | ... | ... | ... | ... |
| 2 042 | 2 167 | 2 102 | 1 966 | 1 989 | 1 994 | 1 876 | 1 866 | 1 851 | 1 868 | 1 837 | 1 658 | 1 967 |
| 143 795 | 156 408 | 155 427 | 148 903 | 154 278 | 158 267 | 152 348 | 154 986 | 157 109 | 162 063 | 127 770 | 101 181 | 154 358 |
| 1.38 | 1.48 | 1.46 | 1.36 | 1.35 | 1.33 | 1.25 | 1.23 | 1.19 | 1.19 | 1.25 | 1.17 | 1.31 |
| 2 024 | 2 352 | 2 428 | 2 348 | 2 461 | 2 533 | 2 431 | 2 488 | 2 550 | 2 680 | 1 878 | 1 144 | 2 440 |
| 142 538 | 169 710 | 179 539 | 177 817 | 190 835 | 201 073 | 197 442 | 206 632 | 216 495 | 232 478 | 130 620 | 69 783 | 191 456 |
| 1.38 | 1.48 | 1.46 | 1.36 | 1.35 | 1.33 | 1.25 | 1.23 | 1.19 | 1.19 | 1.27 | 1.19 | 1.30 |
| 2 353 | 2 497 | 2 422 | 2 265 | 2 292 | 2 297 | 2 162 | 2 151 | 2 133 | 2 153 | 2 116 | 1 911 | 2 267 |
| 165 688 | 180 222 | 179 092 | 171 575 | 177 768 | 182 365 | 175 544 | 178 584 | 181 030 | 186 738 | 147 224 | 116 587 | 177 861 |
| 1.31 | 1.40 | 1.38 | 1.29 | 1.28 | 1.27 | 1.18 | 1.17 | 1.13 | 1.13 | 1.19 | 1.11 | 1.25 |
| 2 766 | 3 464 | 2 349 | 1 966 | 2 264 | 2 324 | 1 601 | 1 693 | 2 035 | 2 396 | 1 837 | 1 273 | 2 267 |
| 194 767 | 249 957 | 173 715 | 148 873 | 175 606 | 184 496 | 130 007 | 140 548 | 172 766 | 207 818 | 127 767 | 77 679 | 177 855 |
| 1.69 | 2.12 | 1.49 | 1.26 | 1.44 | 1.46 | 0.88 | 0.84 | 0.92 | 1.06 | 1.26 | 1.28 | 1.26 |
| 821 | 784 | 823 | 840 | 792 | 745 | 886 | 1 003 | 1 032 | 1 002 | 767 | 599 | 881 |
| 1 366 | 1 341 | 1 446 | 1 518 | 1 471 | 1 423 | 1 739 | 2 024 | 2 141 | 2 136 | 1 258 | 856 | 1 660 |
| 0.01 | 0.01 | 0.01 | 0.01 | 0.01 | 0.01 | 0.01 | 0.01 | 0.01 | 0.01 | 0.01 | 0.01 | 0.01 |
| ... | ... | ... | ... | ... | ... | ... | ... | ... | ... | ... | ... | ... |
| ... | ... | ... | ... | ... | ... | ... | ... | ... | ... | ... | ... | ... |
| ... | ... | ... | ... | ... | ... | ... | ... | ... | ... | ... | ... | ... |
| 729 | 769 | 812 | 839 | 852 | 874 | 895 | 904 | 928 | 931 | 767 | 627 | 861 |
| 1 214 | 1 314 | 1 428 | 1 515 | 1 582 | 1 669 | 1 757 | 1 824 | 1 924 | 1 985 | 1 258 | 895 | 1 621 |
| 0.01 | 0.01 | 0.01 | 0.01 | 0.01 | 0.01 | 0.01 | 0.01 | 0.01 | 0.01 | 0.01 | 0.01 | 0.01 |
| 723 | 834 | 938 | 1 002 | 1 054 | 1 110 | 1 160 | 1 205 | 1 278 | 1 336 | 809 | 433 | 1 081 |
| 1 203 | 1 426 | 1 650 | 1 810 | 1 957 | 2 121 | 2 277 | 2 432 | 2 652 | 2 847 | 1 328 | 618 | 2 037 |
| 0.01 | 0.01 | 0.01 | 0.01 | 0.01 | 0.01 | 0.01 | 0.01 | 0.01 | 0.01 | 0.01 | 0.01 | 0.01 |
| 747 | 787 | 832 | 859 | 872 | 895 | 917 | 926 | 950 | 954 | 785 | 642 | 881 |
| 1 243 | 1 346 | 1 463 | 1 552 | 1 621 | 1 710 | 1 799 | 1 868 | 1 971 | 2 033 | 1 289 | 917 | 1 660 |
| 0.01 | 0.01 | 0.01 | 0.01 | 0.01 | 0.01 | 0.01 | 0.01 | 0.01 | 0.01 | 0.01 | 0.01 | 0.01 |
| 799 | 831 | 853 | 848 | 835 | 808 | 824 | 879 | 990 | 1 024 | 775 | 627 | 876 |
| 1 329 | 1 421 | 1 500 | 1 533 | 1 551 | 1 542 | 1 617 | 1 774 | 2 054 | 2 182 | 1 273 | 895 | 1 650 |
| 0.01 | 0.01 | 0.01 | 0.01 | 0.01 | 0.01 | 0.01 | 0.01 | 0.01 | 0.01 | 0.01 | 0.01 | 0.01 |

**Table A.1** Total and per capita gross domestic product of individual countries or areas, expressed in United States dollars, and their individual shares of gross world product, based on alternative conversion rates, 1970–1989 [*cont.*]

| Country or area | 1970 (1) | 1971 (2) | 1972 (3) | 1973 (4) | 1974 (5) | 1975 (6) | 1976 (7) | 1977 (8) | 1978 (9) | 1979 (10) |
|---|---|---|---|---|---|---|---|---|---|---|
| **Montserrat** | | | | | | | | | | |
| **1. MER** | | | | | | | | | | |
| 1a. Per capita GDP | 550 | 645 | 750 | 821 | 909 | 975 | 854 | 941 | 1 086 | 1 333 |
| 1b. GDP | 7 | 8 | 9 | 10 | 11 | 12 | 10 | 11 | 13 | 16 |
| 1c. % of GWP | 0.00 | 0.00 | 0.00 | 0.00 | 0.00 | 0.00 | 0.00 | 0.00 | 0.00 | 0.00 |
| **2. PPPs** | | | | | | | | | | |
| 2a. Per capita GDP | ... | ... | ... | ... | ... | ... | ... | ... | ... | ... |
| 2b. GDP | ... | ... | ... | ... | ... | ... | ... | ... | ... | ... |
| 2c. % of GWP | ... | ... | ... | ... | ... | ... | ... | ... | ... | ... |
| **3. Absolute 1970–1989 PARE** | | | | | | | | | | |
| 3a. Per capita GDP | 1 276 | 1 326 | 1 380 | 1 440 | 1 495 | 1 560 | 1 540 | 1 520 | 1 615 | 1 804 |
| 3b. GDP | 15 | 16 | 17 | 17 | 18 | 19 | 18 | 18 | 19 | 22 |
| 3c. % of GWP | 0.00 | 0.00 | 0.00 | 0.00 | 0.00 | 0.00 | 0.00 | 0.00 | 0.00 | 0.00 |
| **4. Relative 1970–1989 PARE** | | | | | | | | | | |
| 4a. Per capita GDP | 622 | 679 | 740 | 823 | 932 | 1 069 | 1 121 | 1 181 | 1 346 | 1 638 |
| 4b. GDP | 7 | 8 | 9 | 10 | 11 | 13 | 13 | 14 | 16 | 20 |
| 4c. % of GWP | 0.00 | 0.00 | 0.00 | 0.00 | 0.00 | 0.00 | 0.00 | 0.00 | 0.00 | 0.00 |
| **5. Absolute 1980–1989 PARE** | | | | | | | | | | |
| 5a. Per capita GDP | 1 603 | 1 665 | 1 734 | 1 809 | 1 878 | 1 960 | 1 935 | 1 910 | 2 029 | 2 266 |
| 5b. GDP | 19 | 20 | 21 | 22 | 23 | 24 | 23 | 23 | 24 | 27 |
| 5c. % of GWP | 0.00 | 0.00 | 0.00 | 0.00 | 0.00 | 0.00 | 0.00 | 0.00 | 0.00 | 0.00 |
| **6. WA[a]** | | | | | | | | | | |
| 6a. Per capita GDP | 506 | 574 | 666 | 765 | 856 | 936 | 915 | 909 | 988 | 1 215 |
| 6b. GDP | 6 | 7 | 8 | 9 | 10 | 11 | 11 | 11 | 12 | 15 |
| 6c. % of GWP | 0.00 | 0.00 | 0.00 | 0.00 | 0.00 | 0.00 | 0.00 | 0.00 | 0.00 | 0.00 |
| **Morocco** | | | | | | | | | | |
| **1. MER** | | | | | | | | | | |
| 1a. Per capita GDP | 258 | 272 | 315 | 379 | 451 | 513 | 544 | 611 | 710 | 840 |
| 1b. GDP | 3 957 | 4 276 | 5 076 | 6 251 | 7 623 | 8 880 | 9 627 | 11 058 | 13 131 | 15 908 |
| 1c. % of GWP | 0.12 | 0.12 | 0.13 | 0.13 | 0.14 | 0.14 | 0.14 | 0.15 | 0.15 | 0.15 |
| **2. PPPs** | | | | | | | | | | |
| 2a. Per capita GDP | 493 | 514 | 543 | 568 | 639 | 702 | 805 | 882 | 962 | 1 067 |
| 2b. GDP | 7 555 | 8 076 | 8 743 | 9 375 | 10 807 | 12 152 | 14 254 | 15 964 | 17 795 | 20 203 |
| 2c. % of GWP | ... | ... | ... | ... | ... | ... | ... | ... | ... | ... |
| **3. Absolute 1970–1989 PARE** | | | | | | | | | | |
| 3a. Per capita GDP | 486 | 501 | 499 | 506 | 523 | 558 | 610 | 650 | 688 | 704 |
| 3b. GDP | 7 444 | 7 877 | 8 043 | 8 350 | 8 835 | 9 651 | 10 793 | 11 763 | 12 728 | 13 327 |
| 3c. % of GWP | 0.10 | 0.11 | 0.10 | 0.10 | 0.10 | 0.11 | 0.12 | 0.12 | 0.13 | 0.13 |
| **4. Relative 1970–1989 PARE** | | | | | | | | | | |
| 4a. Per capita GDP | 237 | 257 | 268 | 289 | 326 | 382 | 444 | 505 | 573 | 639 |
| 4b. GDP | 3 629 | 4 038 | 4 312 | 4 774 | 5 509 | 6 612 | 7 857 | 9 140 | 10 612 | 12 103 |
| 4c. % of GWP | 0.10 | 0.11 | 0.10 | 0.10 | 0.10 | 0.11 | 0.12 | 0.12 | 0.13 | 0.13 |
| **5. Absolute 1980–1989 PARE** | | | | | | | | | | |
| 5a. Per capita GDP | 527 | 543 | 541 | 548 | 566 | 604 | 660 | 704 | 745 | 763 |
| 5b. GDP | 8 064 | 8 533 | 8 712 | 9 046 | 9 571 | 10 454 | 11 692 | 12 742 | 13 788 | 14 437 |
| 5c. % of GWP | 0.09 | 0.09 | 0.09 | 0.09 | 0.09 | 0.10 | 0.11 | 0.11 | 0.11 | 0.12 |
| **6. WA[a]** | | | | | | | | | | |
| 6a. Per capita GDP | 258 | 269 | 315 | 378 | 454 | 519 | 541 | 611 | 715 | 840 |
| 6b. GDP | 3 956 | 4 234 | 5 075 | 6 241 | 7 675 | 8 985 | 9 585 | 11 050 | 13 236 | 15 911 |
| 6c. % of GWP | 0.12 | 0.12 | 0.13 | 0.13 | 0.14 | 0.15 | 0.14 | 0.15 | 0.15 | 0.16 |

| | | | | | | | | | | Averages | | |
|---|---|---|---|---|---|---|---|---|---|---|---|---|
| 1980 (11) | 1981 (12) | 1982 (13) | 1983 (14) | 1984 (15) | 1985 (16) | 1986 (17) | 1987 (18) | 1988 (19) | 1989 (20) | 1970–89 (21) | 1970–79 (22) | 1980–89 (23) |
| 2 019 | 2 262 | 2 500 | 2 670 | 2 889 | 2 654 | 3 022 | 3 234 | 3 621 | 4 066 | 1 936 | 887 | 2 985 |
| 24 | 27 | 30 | 32 | 35 | 32 | 36 | 42 | 47 | 53 | 23 | 11 | 36 |
| 0.00 | 0.00 | 0.00 | 0.00 | 0.00 | 0.00 | 0.00 | 0.00 | 0.00 | 0.00 | 0.00 | 0.00 | 0.00 |
| ... | ... | ... | ... | ... | ... | ... | ... | ... | ... | ... | ... | ... |
| ... | ... | ... | ... | ... | ... | ... | ... | ... | ... | ... | ... | ... |
| ... | ... | ... | ... | ... | ... | ... | ... | ... | ... | ... | ... | ... |
| 1 988 | 2 048 | 2 133 | 2 073 | 2 108 | 2 208 | 2 322 | 2 392 | 2 774 | 3 027 | 1 936 | 1 496 | 2 376 |
| 24 | 25 | 26 | 25 | 25 | 26 | 28 | 31 | 36 | 39 | 23 | 18 | 29 |
| 0.00 | 0.00 | 0.00 | 0.00 | 0.00 | 0.00 | 0.00 | 0.00 | 0.00 | 0.00 | 0.00 | 0.00 | 0.00 |
| 1 971 | 2 222 | 2 464 | 2 476 | 2 608 | 2 805 | 3 010 | 3 189 | 3 822 | 4 342 | 2 000 | 1 015 | 2 985 |
| 24 | 27 | 30 | 30 | 31 | 34 | 36 | 41 | 50 | 56 | 24 | 12 | 36 |
| 0.00 | 0.00 | 0.00 | 0.00 | 0.00 | 0.00 | 0.00 | 0.00 | 0.00 | 0.00 | 0.00 | 0.00 | 0.00 |
| 2 498 | 2 573 | 2 680 | 2 605 | 2 648 | 2 774 | 2 918 | 3 005 | 3 485 | 3 803 | 2 432 | 1 879 | 2 985 |
| 30 | 31 | 32 | 31 | 32 | 33 | 35 | 39 | 45 | 49 | 29 | 23 | 36 |
| 0.00 | 0.00 | 0.00 | 0.00 | 0.00 | 0.00 | 0.00 | 0.00 | 0.00 | 0.00 | 0.00 | 0.00 | 0.00 |
| 1 560 | 1 894 | 2 332 | 2 453 | 2 680 | 2 833 | 2 990 | 3 067 | 3 659 | 4 035 | 1 837 | 833 | 2 840 |
| 19 | 23 | 28 | 29 | 32 | 34 | 36 | 40 | 48 | 52 | 22 | 10 | 34 |
| 0.00 | 0.00 | 0.00 | 0.00 | 0.00 | 0.00 | 0.00 | 0.00 | 0.00 | 0.00 | 0.00 | 0.00 | 0.00 |
| 980 | 765 | 760 | 668 | 595 | 582 | 752 | 812 | 924 | 915 | 666 | 501 | 779 |
| 18 997 | 15 198 | 15 483 | 13 963 | 12 766 | 12 823 | 17 003 | 18 852 | 22 011 | 22 354 | 12 762 | 8 579 | 16 945 |
| 0.16 | 0.13 | 0.13 | 0.12 | 0.10 | 0.10 | 0.11 | 0.11 | 0.12 | 0.11 | 0.13 | 0.14 | 0.12 |
| 1 257 | 1 322 | 1 460 | 1 486 | 1 622 | 1 696 | 1 753 | 1 792 | 1 930 | 2 016 | 1 266 | 730 | 1 656 |
| 24 363 | 26 268 | 29 748 | 31 071 | 34 798 | 37 351 | 39 628 | 41 584 | 45 956 | 49 255 | 24 247 | 12 493 | 36 002 |
| ... | ... | ... | ... | ... | ... | ... | ... | ... | ... | ... | ... | ... |
| 713 | 686 | 710 | 705 | 698 | 713 | 722 | 718 | 748 | 750 | 666 | 578 | 719 |
| 13 828 | 13 633 | 14 456 | 14 734 | 14 977 | 15 694 | 16 323 | 16 650 | 17 803 | 18 329 | 12 762 | 9 881 | 15 643 |
| 0.13 | 0.13 | 0.14 | 0.13 | 0.13 | 0.13 | 0.13 | 0.13 | 0.13 | 0.13 | 0.13 | 0.11 | 0.13 |
| 707 | 745 | 820 | 842 | 863 | 905 | 936 | 957 | 1 030 | 1 076 | 689 | 401 | 899 |
| 13 707 | 14 792 | 16 699 | 17 595 | 18 526 | 19 939 | 21 154 | 22 198 | 24 532 | 26 293 | 13 201 | 6 859 | 19 544 |
| 0.13 | 0.13 | 0.14 | 0.13 | 0.13 | 0.13 | 0.13 | 0.13 | 0.13 | 0.13 | 0.13 | 0.12 | 0.13 |
| 773 | 743 | 769 | 763 | 756 | 772 | 782 | 777 | 810 | 813 | 722 | 626 | 779 |
| 14 979 | 14 768 | 15 660 | 15 961 | 16 224 | 17 001 | 17 682 | 18 036 | 19 285 | 19 855 | 13 825 | 10 704 | 16 945 |
| 0.12 | 0.11 | 0.12 | 0.12 | 0.12 | 0.12 | 0.12 | 0.12 | 0.12 | 0.12 | 0.11 | 0.10 | 0.12 |
| 971 | 769 | 757 | 667 | 594 | 584 | 752 | 816 | 923 | 916 | 666 | 502 | 779 |
| 18 821 | 15 279 | 15 424 | 13 941 | 12 751 | 12 870 | 16 995 | 18 944 | 21 986 | 22 386 | 12 767 | 8 595 | 16 940 |
| 0.16 | 0.13 | 0.13 | 0.12 | 0.10 | 0.10 | 0.12 | 0.11 | 0.12 | 0.11 | 0.13 | 0.14 | 0.12 |

**Table A.1** Total and per capita gross domestic product of individual countries or areas, expressed in United States dollars, and their individual shares of gross world product, based on alternative conversion rates, 1970–1989 [*cont.*]

| Country or area | 1970 (1) | 1971 (2) | 1972 (3) | 1973 (4) | 1974 (5) | 1975 (6) | 1976 (7) | 1977 (8) | 1978 (9) | 1979 (10) |
|---|---|---|---|---|---|---|---|---|---|---|
| **Mozambique** | | | | | | | | | | |
| **1. MER** | | | | | | | | | | |
| 1a. Per capita GDP | 114 | 135 | 149 | 179 | 183 | 162 | 136 | 145 | 155 | 175 |
| 1b. GDP | 1 072 | 1 299 | 1 464 | 1 792 | 1 877 | 1 703 | 1 468 | 1 605 | 1 767 | 2 061 |
| 1c. % of GWP | 0.03 | 0.04 | 0.04 | 0.04 | 0.03 | 0.03 | 0.02 | 0.02 | 0.02 | 0.02 |
| **2. PPPs** | | | | | | | | | | |
| 2a. Per capita GDP | 273 | 296 | 309 | 341 | 305 | 282 | 274 | 289 | 300 | 330 |
| 2b. GDP | 2 568 | 2 845 | 3 032 | 3 413 | 3 123 | 2 958 | 2 959 | 3 213 | 3 426 | 3 886 |
| 2c. % of GWP | ... | ... | ... | ... | ... | ... | ... | ... | ... | ... |
| **3. Absolute 1970–1989 PARE** | | | | | | | | | | |
| 3a. Per capita GDP | 237 | 248 | 251 | 259 | 226 | 192 | 178 | 174 | 170 | 168 |
| 3b. GDP | 2 228 | 2 381 | 2 459 | 2 597 | 2 316 | 2 013 | 1 917 | 1 933 | 1 948 | 1 974 |
| 3c. % of GWP | 0.03 | 0.03 | 0.03 | 0.03 | 0.03 | 0.02 | 0.02 | 0.02 | 0.02 | 0.02 |
| **4. Relative 1970–1989 PARE** | | | | | | | | | | |
| 4a. Per capita GDP | 116 | 127 | 134 | 148 | 141 | 131 | 129 | 135 | 142 | 152 |
| 4b. GDP | 1 086 | 1 221 | 1 318 | 1 484 | 1 445 | 1 379 | 1 395 | 1 502 | 1 624 | 1 793 |
| 4c. % of GWP | 0.03 | 0.03 | 0.03 | 0.03 | 0.03 | 0.02 | 0.02 | 0.02 | 0.02 | 0.02 |
| **5. Absolute 1980–1989 PARE** | | | | | | | | | | |
| 5a. Per capita GDP | 311 | 326 | 329 | 340 | 297 | 252 | 233 | 229 | 224 | 220 |
| 5b. GDP | 2 925 | 3 126 | 3 228 | 3 408 | 3 040 | 2 642 | 2 516 | 2 537 | 2 557 | 2 591 |
| 5c. % of GWP | 0.03 | 0.03 | 0.03 | 0.03 | 0.03 | 0.03 | 0.02 | 0.02 | 0.02 | 0.02 |
| **6. WA** | | | | | | | | | | |
| 6a. Per capita GDP | 108 | 130 | 150 | 179 | 184 | 173 | 141 | 141 | 154 | 176 |
| 6b. GDP | 1 016 | 1 250 | 1 475 | 1 795 | 1 885 | 1 816 | 1 525 | 1 566 | 1 761 | 2 070 |
| 6c. % of GWP | 0.03 | 0.04 | 0.04 | 0.04 | 0.03 | 0.03 | 0.02 | 0.02 | 0.02 | 0.02 |
| **Myanmar** | | | | | | | | | | |
| **1. MER** | | | | | | | | | | |
| 1a. Per capita GDP | 105 | 103 | 91 | 108 | 134 | 121 | 130 | 131 | 142 | 160 |
| 1b. GDP | 2 836 | 2 866 | 2 598 | 3 133 | 3 981 | 3 682 | 4 053 | 4 159 | 4 619 | 5 310 |
| 1c. % of GWP | 0.09 | 0.08 | 0.06 | 0.06 | 0.07 | 0.06 | 0.06 | 0.05 | 0.05 | 0.05 |
| **2. PPPs** | | | | | | | | | | |
| 2a. Per capita GDP | 202 | 212 | 220 | 222 | 242 | 271 | 297 | 328 | 363 | 410 |
| 2b. GDP | 5 487 | 5 890 | 6 247 | 6 465 | 7 198 | 8 257 | 9 247 | 10 434 | 11 783 | 13 584 |
| 2c. % of GWP | ... | ... | ... | ... | ... | ... | ... | ... | ... | ... |
| **3. Absolute 1970–1989 PARE** | | | | | | | | | | |
| 3a. Per capita GDP | 151 | 153 | 153 | 148 | 149 | 151 | 157 | 163 | 170 | 175 |
| 3b. GDP | 4 083 | 4 252 | 4 355 | 4 313 | 4 425 | 4 609 | 4 889 | 5 180 | 5 518 | 5 805 |
| 3c. % of GWP | 0.06 | 0.06 | 0.06 | 0.05 | 0.05 | 0.05 | 0.05 | 0.05 | 0.06 | 0.06 |
| **4. Relative 1970–1989 PARE** | | | | | | | | | | |
| 4a. Per capita GDP | 73 | 79 | 82 | 85 | 93 | 104 | 114 | 127 | 142 | 159 |
| 4b. GDP | 1 991 | 2 179 | 2 335 | 2 466 | 2 759 | 3 158 | 3 559 | 4 025 | 4 600 | 5 271 |
| 4c. % of GWP | 0.06 | 0.06 | 0.06 | 0.05 | 0.05 | 0.05 | 0.05 | 0.05 | 0.06 | 0.06 |
| **5. Absolute 1980–1989 PARE** | | | | | | | | | | |
| 5a. Per capita GDP | 172 | 175 | 175 | 169 | 169 | 172 | 179 | 186 | 194 | 200 |
| 5b. GDP | 4 652 | 4 844 | 4 962 | 4 914 | 5 042 | 5 251 | 5 570 | 5 902 | 6 287 | 6 613 |
| 5c. % of GWP | 0.05 | 0.05 | 0.05 | 0.05 | 0.05 | 0.05 | 0.05 | 0.05 | 0.05 | 0.05 |
| **6. WA[a]** | | | | | | | | | | |
| 6a. Per capita GDP | 104 | 106 | 100 | 98 | 107 | 121 | 132 | 132 | 140 | 149 |
| 6b. GDP | 2 831 | 2 930 | 2 841 | 2 852 | 3 188 | 3 697 | 4 109 | 4 196 | 4 540 | 4 928 |
| 6c. % of GWP | 0.09 | 0.08 | 0.07 | 0.06 | 0.06 | 0.06 | 0.06 | 0.06 | 0.05 | 0.05 |

| 1980 (11) | 1981 (12) | 1982 (13) | 1983 (14) | 1984 (15) | 1985 (16) | 1986 (17) | 1987 (18) | 1988 (19) | 1989 (20) | Averages 1970–89 (21) | 1970–79 (22) | 1980–89 (23) |
|---|---|---|---|---|---|---|---|---|---|---|---|---|
| 199 | 187 | 191 | 174 | 192 | 265 | 294 | 101 | 85 | 84 | 167 | 155 | 176 |
| 2 407 | 2 320 | 2 436 | 2 265 | 2 568 | 3 639 | 4 134 | 1 465 | 1 256 | 1 275 | 1 994 | 1 611 | 2 377 |
| 0.02 | 0.02 | 0.02 | 0.02 | 0.02 | 0.03 | 0.03 | 0.01 | 0.01 | 0.01 | 0.02 | 0.03 | 0.02 |
| 354 | 354 | 366 | 374 | 454 | 624 | 630 | 662 | 696 | 726 | 436 | 303 | 537 |
| 4 280 | 4 395 | 4 660 | 4 882 | 6 073 | 8 555 | 8 868 | 9 557 | 10 327 | 11 062 | 5 204 | 3 142 | 7 266 |
| ... | ... | ... | ... | ... | ... | ... | ... | ... | ... | ... | ... | ... |
| 167 | 165 | 155 | 131 | 132 | 117 | 116 | 119 | 121 | 121 | 167 | 210 | 134 |
| 2 023 | 2 049 | 1 971 | 1 712 | 1 764 | 1 608 | 1 634 | 1 712 | 1 790 | 1 842 | 1 994 | 2 177 | 1 811 |
| 0.02 | 0.02 | 0.02 | 0.02 | 0.02 | 0.01 | 0.01 | 0.01 | 0.01 | 0.01 | 0.02 | 0.03 | 0.02 |
| 166 | 179 | 179 | 157 | 163 | 149 | 151 | 158 | 166 | 173 | 153 | 137 | 165 |
| 2 006 | 2 224 | 2 277 | 2 044 | 2 182 | 2 043 | 2 118 | 2 283 | 2 466 | 2 642 | 1 827 | 1 425 | 2 228 |
| 0.02 | 0.02 | 0.02 | 0.02 | 0.02 | 0.01 | 0.01 | 0.01 | 0.01 | 0.01 | 0.02 | 0.02 | 0.02 |
| 220 | 217 | 203 | 172 | 173 | 154 | 152 | 156 | 158 | 159 | 219 | 275 | 176 |
| 2 656 | 2 690 | 2 588 | 2 247 | 2 315 | 2 111 | 2 145 | 2 247 | 2 349 | 2 417 | 2 617 | 2 857 | 2 377 |
| 0.02 | 0.02 | 0.02 | 0.02 | 0.02 | 0.01 | 0.01 | 0.01 | 0.01 | 0.01 | 0.02 | 0.03 | 0.02 |
| 199 | 187 | 191 | 174 | 192 | 248 | 294 | 101 | 85 | 84 | 166 | 156 | 174 |
| 2 407 | 2 320 | 2 436 | 2 265 | 2 568 | 3 404 | 4 131 | 1 465 | 1 256 | 1 275 | 1 984 | 1 616 | 2 353 |
| 0.02 | 0.02 | 0.02 | 0.02 | 0.02 | 0.03 | 0.03 | 0.01 | 0.01 | 0.01 | 0.02 | 0.03 | 0.02 |
| 173 | 171 | 170 | 172 | 174 | 176 | 209 | 262 | 294 | 401 | 180 | 124 | 224 |
| 5 851 | 5 889 | 6 008 | 6 200 | 6 391 | 6 606 | 8 016 | 10 253 | 11 748 | 16 378 | 6 029 | 3 724 | 8 334 |
| 0.05 | 0.05 | 0.05 | 0.05 | 0.05 | 0.05 | 0.05 | 0.06 | 0.06 | 0.08 | 0.06 | 0.06 | 0.06 |
| 478 | 539 | 609 | 638 | 665 | 671 | 676 | 654 | 586 | 642 | 470 | 281 | 619 |
| 16 152 | 18 625 | 21 474 | 22 964 | 24 454 | 25 173 | 25 926 | 25 603 | 23 436 | 26 192 | 15 730 | 8 459 | 23 000 |
| ... | ... | ... | ... | ... | ... | ... | ... | ... | ... | ... | ... | ... |
| 185 | 193 | 200 | 204 | 211 | 213 | 211 | 198 | 172 | 181 | 180 | 158 | 197 |
| 6 265 | 6 664 | 7 037 | 7 346 | 7 755 | 8 003 | 8 080 | 7 756 | 6 869 | 7 375 | 6 029 | 4 743 | 7 315 |
| 0.06 | 0.06 | 0.07 | 0.07 | 0.07 | 0.07 | 0.07 | 0.06 | 0.05 | 0.05 | 0.06 | 0.06 | 0.06 |
| 184 | 209 | 231 | 244 | 261 | 271 | 273 | 264 | 237 | 259 | 184 | 107 | 245 |
| 6 211 | 7 230 | 8 129 | 8 773 | 9 593 | 10 168 | 10 472 | 10 341 | 9 466 | 10 579 | 6 165 | 3 234 | 9 096 |
| 0.06 | 0.06 | 0.07 | 0.07 | 0.07 | 0.07 | 0.07 | 0.06 | 0.05 | 0.05 | 0.06 | 0.06 | 0.06 |
| 211 | 220 | 227 | 232 | 240 | 243 | 240 | 226 | 196 | 206 | 205 | 179 | 224 |
| 7 138 | 7 592 | 8 018 | 8 370 | 8 836 | 9 118 | 9 206 | 8 837 | 7 826 | 8 402 | 6 869 | 5 404 | 8 334 |
| 0.06 | 0.06 | 0.06 | 0.06 | 0.06 | 0.06 | 0.06 | 0.06 | 0.05 | 0.05 | 0.06 | 0.05 | 0.06 |
| 165 | 176 | 177 | 175 | 177 | 177 | 184 | 200 | 220 | 303 | 164 | 120 | 198 |
| 5 596 | 6 066 | 6 258 | 6 319 | 6 518 | 6 651 | 7 061 | 7 819 | 8 773 | 12 350 | 5 476 | 3 611 | 7 341 |
| 0.05 | 0.05 | 0.05 | 0.05 | 0.05 | 0.05 | 0.05 | 0.05 | 0.05 | 0.06 | 0.05 | 0.06 | 0.05 |

**Table A.1**    Total and per capita gross domestic product of individual countries or areas,
expressed in United States dollars, and their individual shares of gross world
product, based on alternative conversion rates, 1970−1989 [*cont.*]

| Country or area | 1970 (1) | 1971 (2) | 1972 (3) | 1973 (4) | 1974 (5) | 1975 (6) | 1976 (7) | 1977 (8) | 1978 (9) | 1979 (10) |
|---|---|---|---|---|---|---|---|---|---|---|
| **Namibia** | | | | | | | | | | |
| **1. MER** | | | | | | | | | | |
| 1a. Per capita GDP | 495 | 499 | 536 | 761 | 806 | 826 | 810 | 983 | 1 154 | 1 301 |
| 1b. GDP | 503 | 519 | 570 | 828 | 898 | 943 | 949 | 1 182 | 1 425 | 1 652 |
| 1c. % of GWP | 0.02 | 0.01 | 0.01 | 0.02 | 0.02 | 0.02 | 0.01 | 0.02 | 0.02 | 0.02 |
| **2. PPPs** | | | | | | | | | | |
| 2a. Per capita GDP | ... | ... | ... | ... | ... | ... | ... | ... | ... | ... |
| 2b. GDP | ... | ... | ... | ... | ... | ... | ... | ... | ... | ... |
| 2c. % of GWP | ... | ... | ... | ... | ... | ... | ... | ... | ... | ... |
| **3. Absolute 1970−1989 PARE** | | | | | | | | | | |
| 3a. Per capita GDP | 1 137 | 1 099 | 1 077 | 1 051 | 1 063 | 1 121 | 1 107 | 1 172 | 1 136 | 1 103 |
| 3b. GDP | 1 155 | 1 142 | 1 145 | 1 143 | 1 184 | 1 281 | 1 296 | 1 409 | 1 403 | 1 401 |
| 3c. % of GWP | 0.02 | 0.02 | 0.01 | 0.01 | 0.01 | 0.01 | 0.01 | 0.01 | 0.01 | 0.01 |
| **4. Relative 1970−1989 PARE** | | | | | | | | | | |
| 4a. Per capita GDP | 554 | 563 | 577 | 601 | 663 | 768 | 806 | 911 | 947 | 1 002 |
| 4b. GDP | 563 | 585 | 614 | 653 | 738 | 877 | 943 | 1 095 | 1 169 | 1 272 |
| 4c. % of GWP | 0.02 | 0.02 | 0.01 | 0.01 | 0.01 | 0.01 | 0.01 | 0.01 | 0.01 | 0.01 |
| **5. Absolute 1980−1989 PARE** | | | | | | | | | | |
| 5a. Per capita GDP | 1 393 | 1 347 | 1 320 | 1 288 | 1 302 | 1 374 | 1 356 | 1 436 | 1 392 | 1 352 |
| 5b. GDP | 1 415 | 1 399 | 1 403 | 1 401 | 1 451 | 1 570 | 1 588 | 1 726 | 1 719 | 1 717 |
| 5c. % of GWP | 0.02 | 0.02 | 0.01 | 0.01 | 0.01 | 0.01 | 0.01 | 0.01 | 0.01 | 0.01 |
| **6. WA** | | | | | | | | | | |
| 6a. Per capita GDP | 495 | 498 | 538 | 759 | 805 | 818 | 811 | 984 | 1 155 | 1 301 |
| 6b. GDP | 503 | 517 | 572 | 826 | 897 | 934 | 949 | 1 183 | 1 426 | 1 652 |
| 6c. % of GWP | 0.02 | 0.01 | 0.01 | 0.02 | 0.02 | 0.02 | 0.01 | 0.02 | 0.02 | 0.02 |
| **Nepal** | | | | | | | | | | |
| **1. MER** | | | | | | | | | | |
| 1a. Per capita GDP | 75 | 75 | 85 | 77 | 96 | 116 | 104 | 101 | 116 | 128 |
| 1b. GDP | 866 | 883 | 1 024 | 947 | 1 213 | 1 506 | 1 392 | 1 382 | 1 629 | 1 851 |
| 1c. % of GWP | 0.03 | 0.03 | 0.03 | 0.02 | 0.02 | 0.02 | 0.02 | 0.02 | 0.02 | 0.02 |
| **2. PPPs** | | | | | | | | | | |
| 2a. Per capita GDP | 234 | 236 | 239 | 234 | 265 | 320 | 331 | 374 | 413 | 444 |
| 2b. GDP | 2 691 | 2 773 | 2 883 | 2 887 | 3 359 | 4 162 | 4 419 | 5 131 | 5 814 | 6 428 |
| 2c. % of GWP | ... | ... | ... | ... | ... | ... | ... | ... | ... | ... |
| **3. Absolute 1970−1989 PARE** | | | | | | | | | | |
| 3a. Per capita GDP | 123 | 119 | 120 | 116 | 121 | 119 | 121 | 122 | 124 | 123 |
| 3b. GDP | 1 417 | 1 400 | 1 444 | 1 437 | 1 528 | 1 550 | 1 618 | 1 667 | 1 741 | 1 782 |
| 3c. % of GWP | 0.02 | 0.02 | 0.02 | 0.02 | 0.02 | 0.02 | 0.02 | 0.02 | 0.02 | 0.02 |
| **4. Relative 1970−1989 PARE** | | | | | | | | | | |
| 4a. Per capita GDP | 60 | 61 | 64 | 67 | 75 | 82 | 88 | 94 | 103 | 112 |
| 4b. GDP | 691 | 718 | 774 | 821 | 953 | 1 062 | 1 178 | 1 295 | 1 451 | 1 618 |
| 4c. % of GWP | 0.02 | 0.02 | 0.02 | 0.02 | 0.02 | 0.02 | 0.02 | 0.02 | 0.02 | 0.02 |
| **5. Absolute 1980−1989 PARE** | | | | | | | | | | |
| 5a. Per capita GDP | 140 | 135 | 136 | 132 | 137 | 135 | 137 | 138 | 140 | 140 |
| 5b. GDP | 1 606 | 1 587 | 1 636 | 1 628 | 1 731 | 1 757 | 1 834 | 1 889 | 1 972 | 2 019 |
| 5c. % of GWP | 0.02 | 0.02 | 0.02 | 0.02 | 0.02 | 0.02 | 0.02 | 0.02 | 0.02 | 0.02 |
| **6. WA** | | | | | | | | | | |
| 6a. Per capita GDP | 75 | 75 | 85 | 78 | 96 | 121 | 109 | 101 | 113 | 128 |
| 6b. GDP | 866 | 883 | 1 024 | 969 | 1 213 | 1 569 | 1 453 | 1 382 | 1 596 | 1 851 |
| 6c. % of GWP | 0.03 | 0.03 | 0.03 | 0.02 | 0.02 | 0.03 | 0.02 | 0.02 | 0.02 | 0.02 |

| | | | | | | | | | | Averages | | |
|---|---|---|---|---|---|---|---|---|---|---|---|---|
| 1980 (11) | 1981 (12) | 1982 (13) | 1983 (14) | 1984 (15) | 1985 (16) | 1986 (17) | 1987 (18) | 1988 (19) | 1989 (20) | 1970–89 (21) | 1970–79 (22) | 1980–89 (23) |
| 1 536 | 1 376 | 1 197 | 1 183 | 998 | 824 | 896 | 1 042 | 1 114 | 1 100 | 1 018 | 839 | 1 122 |
| 2 007 | 1 850 | 1 658 | 1 690 | 1 469 | 1 251 | 1 404 | 1 686 | 1 862 | 1 898 | 1 312 | 947 | 1 678 |
| 0.02 | 0.02 | 0.01 | 0.01 | 0.01 | 0.01 | 0.01 | 0.01 | 0.01 | 0.01 | 0.01 | 0.02 | 0.01 |
| ... | ... | ... | ... | ... | ... | ... | ... | ... | ... | ... | ... | ... |
| ... | ... | ... | ... | ... | ... | ... | ... | ... | ... | ... | ... | ... |
| ... | ... | ... | ... | ... | ... | ... | ... | ... | ... | ... | ... | ... |
| 1 074 | 1 037 | 988 | 928 | 889 | 861 | 862 | 858 | 849 | 824 | 1 018 | 1 113 | 915 |
| 1 403 | 1 395 | 1 368 | 1 325 | 1 309 | 1 309 | 1 350 | 1 388 | 1 419 | 1 422 | 1 312 | 1 256 | 1 369 |
| 0.01 | 0.01 | 0.01 | 0.01 | 0.01 | 0.01 | 0.01 | 0.01 | 0.01 | 0.01 | 0.01 | 0.01 | 0.01 |
| 1 064 | 1 125 | 1 141 | 1 108 | 1 100 | 1 094 | 1 117 | 1 144 | 1 171 | 1 182 | 988 | 754 | 1 133 |
| 1 391 | 1 513 | 1 581 | 1 582 | 1 619 | 1 662 | 1 750 | 1 851 | 1 956 | 2 040 | 1 273 | 851 | 1 695 |
| 0.01 | 0.01 | 0.01 | 0.01 | 0.01 | 0.01 | 0.01 | 0.01 | 0.01 | 0.01 | 0.01 | 0.01 | 0.01 |
| 1 316 | 1 271 | 1 211 | 1 137 | 1 089 | 1 056 | 1 056 | 1 052 | 1 041 | 1 010 | 1 248 | 1 364 | 1 122 |
| 1 720 | 1 709 | 1 677 | 1 623 | 1 604 | 1 604 | 1 655 | 1 701 | 1 740 | 1 743 | 1 608 | 1 539 | 1 678 |
| 0.01 | 0.01 | 0.01 | 0.01 | 0.01 | 0.01 | 0.01 | 0.01 | 0.01 | 0.01 | 0.01 | 0.01 | 0.01 |
| 1 534 | 1 364 | 1 193 | 1 181 | 973 | 810 | 890 | 1 024 | 1 127 | 1 090 | 1 013 | 839 | 1 114 |
| 2 005 | 1 834 | 1 652 | 1 687 | 1 432 | 1 230 | 1 394 | 1 657 | 1 884 | 1 882 | 1 306 | 946 | 1 666 |
| 0.02 | 0.02 | 0.01 | 0.01 | 0.01 | 0.01 | 0.01 | 0.01 | 0.01 | 0.01 | 0.01 | 0.02 | 0.01 |
| 131 | 145 | 149 | 144 | 145 | 144 | 137 | 153 | 164 | 152 | 127 | 99 | 147 |
| 1 946 | 2 214 | 2 340 | 2 321 | 2 393 | 2 434 | 2 375 | 2 720 | 2 983 | 2 846 | 1 863 | 1 269 | 2 457 |
| 0.02 | 0.02 | 0.02 | 0.02 | 0.02 | 0.02 | 0.02 | 0.02 | 0.02 | 0.01 | 0.02 | 0.02 | 0.02 |
| 483 | 510 | 559 | 560 | 608 | 648 | 673 | 692 | 766 | 790 | 501 | 316 | 637 |
| 7 172 | 7 785 | 8 757 | 9 003 | 10 021 | 10 954 | 11 668 | 12 307 | 13 960 | 14 754 | 7 346 | 4 055 | 10 638 |
| ... | ... | ... | ... | ... | ... | ... | ... | ... | ... | ... | ... | ... |
| 117 | 124 | 125 | 118 | 126 | 131 | 133 | 133 | 142 | 141 | 127 | 121 | 130 |
| 1 740 | 1 886 | 1 957 | 1 899 | 2 082 | 2 210 | 2 308 | 2 367 | 2 597 | 2 637 | 1 863 | 1 558 | 2 168 |
| 0.02 | 0.02 | 0.02 | 0.02 | 0.02 | 0.02 | 0.02 | 0.02 | 0.02 | 0.02 | 0.02 | 0.02 | 0.02 |
| 116 | 134 | 144 | 141 | 156 | 166 | 172 | 177 | 196 | 202 | 129 | 82 | 163 |
| 1 725 | 2 046 | 2 260 | 2 267 | 2 576 | 2 808 | 2 991 | 3 155 | 3 579 | 3 783 | 1 888 | 1 056 | 2 719 |
| 0.02 | 0.02 | 0.02 | 0.02 | 0.02 | 0.02 | 0.02 | 0.02 | 0.02 | 0.02 | 0.02 | 0.02 | 0.02 |
| 133 | 140 | 142 | 134 | 143 | 148 | 151 | 151 | 161 | 160 | 144 | 138 | 147 |
| 1 972 | 2 137 | 2 218 | 2 152 | 2 360 | 2 505 | 2 616 | 2 682 | 2 943 | 2 988 | 2 112 | 1 766 | 2 457 |
| 0.02 | 0.02 | 0.02 | 0.02 | 0.02 | 0.02 | 0.02 | 0.02 | 0.02 | 0.02 | 0.02 | 0.02 | 0.02 |
| 131 | 149 | 153 | 152 | 157 | 148 | 147 | 154 | 173 | 164 | 131 | 100 | 154 |
| 1 946 | 2 276 | 2 395 | 2 447 | 2 581 | 2 499 | 2 547 | 2 746 | 3 152 | 3 057 | 1 923 | 1 281 | 2 565 |
| 0.02 | 0.02 | 0.02 | 0.02 | 0.02 | 0.02 | 0.02 | 0.02 | 0.02 | 0.02 | 0.02 | 0.02 | 0.02 |

**Table A.1**  Total and per capita gross domestic product of individual countries or areas, expressed in United States dollars, and their individual shares of gross world product, based on alternative conversion rates, 1970−1989 [*cont.*]

| Country or area | 1970 (1) | 1971 (2) | 1972 (3) | 1973 (4) | 1974 (5) | 1975 (6) | 1976 (7) | 1977 (8) | 1978 (9) | 1979 (10) |
|---|---|---|---|---|---|---|---|---|---|---|
| **Netherlands** | | | | | | | | | | |
| **1. MER** | | | | | | | | | | |
| 1a. Per capita GDP | 2 568 | 2 967 | 3 614 | 4 691 | 5 489 | 6 370 | 6 923 | 8 078 | 9 825 | 11 202 |
| 1b. GDP | 33 475 | 39 064 | 48 056 | 62 961 | 74 323 | 86 975 | 95 284 | 112 033 | 137 250 | 157 507 |
| 1c. % of GWP | 1.05 | 1.12 | 1.19 | 1.28 | 1.34 | 1.40 | 1.42 | 1.48 | 1.53 | 1.53 |
| **2. PPPs** | | | | | | | | | | |
| 2a. Per capita GDP | 3 528 | 3 809 | 4 144 | 4 651 | 5 215 | 5 617 | 6 207 | 6 777 | 7 442 | 8 195 |
| 2b. GDP | 45 976 | 50 156 | 55 102 | 62 427 | 70 607 | 76 691 | 85 431 | 93 995 | 103 951 | 115 228 |
| 2c. % of GWP | ... | ... | ... | ... | ... | ... | ... | ... | ... | ... |
| **3. Absolute 1970−1989 PARE** | | | | | | | | | | |
| 3a. Per capita GDP | 7 548 | 7 786 | 7 965 | 8 262 | 8 514 | 8 435 | 8 796 | 8 932 | 9 086 | 9 240 |
| 3b. GDP | 98 369 | 102 521 | 105 915 | 110 881 | 115 278 | 115 173 | 121 069 | 123 875 | 126 918 | 129 926 |
| 3c. % of GWP | 1.38 | 1.38 | 1.36 | 1.34 | 1.36 | 1.34 | 1.34 | 1.31 | 1.29 | 1.28 |
| **4. Relative 1970−1989 PARE** | | | | | | | | | | |
| 4a. Per capita GDP | 3 680 | 3 991 | 4 270 | 4 723 | 5 309 | 5 779 | 6 403 | 6 940 | 7 575 | 8 391 |
| 4b. GDP | 47 962 | 52 550 | 56 781 | 63 391 | 71 887 | 78 906 | 88 129 | 96 253 | 105 812 | 117 991 |
| 4c. % of GWP | 1.38 | 1.38 | 1.36 | 1.34 | 1.36 | 1.34 | 1.34 | 1.31 | 1.29 | 1.28 |
| **5. Absolute 1980−1989 PARE** | | | | | | | | | | |
| 5a. Per capita GDP | 9 216 | 9 507 | 9 726 | 10 088 | 10 396 | 10 300 | 10 740 | 10 906 | 11 094 | 11 283 |
| 5b. GDP | 120 113 | 125 183 | 129 327 | 135 390 | 140 760 | 140 631 | 147 830 | 151 256 | 154 972 | 158 646 |
| 5c. % of GWP | 1.38 | 1.38 | 1.35 | 1.33 | 1.36 | 1.34 | 1.34 | 1.31 | 1.29 | 1.28 |
| **6. WA** | | | | | | | | | | |
| 6a. Per capita GDP | 2 568 | 2 961 | 3 615 | 4 692 | 5 488 | 6 370 | 6 923 | 8 077 | 9 827 | 11 202 |
| 6b. GDP | 33 475 | 38 982 | 48 064 | 62 972 | 74 312 | 86 975 | 95 286 | 112 022 | 137 277 | 157 508 |
| 6c. % of GWP | 1.05 | 1.12 | 1.20 | 1.29 | 1.33 | 1.41 | 1.42 | 1.49 | 1.55 | 1.54 |
| **Netherlands Antilles and Aruba** | | | | | | | | | | |
| **1. MER** | | | | | | | | | | |
| 1a. Per capita GDP | 1 691 | 1 812 | 2 006 | 2 223 | 2 508 | 2 723 | 2 855 | 3 219 | 3 774 | 4 492 |
| 1b. GDP | 274 | 297 | 331 | 369 | 419 | 458 | 485 | 550 | 649 | 782 |
| 1c. % of GWP | 0.01 | 0.01 | 0.01 | 0.01 | 0.01 | 0.01 | 0.01 | 0.01 | 0.01 | 0.01 |
| **2. PPPs** | | | | | | | | | | |
| 2a. Per capita GDP | ... | ... | ... | ... | ... | ... | ... | ... | ... | ... |
| 2b. GDP | ... | ... | ... | ... | ... | ... | ... | ... | ... | ... |
| 2c. % of GWP | ... | ... | ... | ... | ... | ... | ... | ... | ... | ... |
| **3. Absolute 1970−1989 PARE** | | | | | | | | | | |
| 3a. Per capita GDP | 3 907 | 3 970 | 4 043 | 4 317 | 4 237 | 4 042 | 4 111 | 4 287 | 4 593 | 4 720 |
| 3b. GDP | 633 | 651 | 667 | 717 | 708 | 679 | 699 | 733 | 790 | 821 |
| 3c. % of GWP | 0.01 | 0.01 | 0.01 | 0.01 | 0.01 | 0.01 | 0.01 | 0.01 | 0.01 | 0.01 |
| **4. Relative 1970−1989 PARE** | | | | | | | | | | |
| 4a. Per capita GDP | 1 905 | 2 035 | 2 168 | 2 468 | 2 642 | 2 769 | 2 993 | 3 331 | 3 829 | 4 286 |
| 4b. GDP | 309 | 334 | 358 | 410 | 441 | 465 | 509 | 570 | 659 | 746 |
| 4c. % of GWP | 0.01 | 0.01 | 0.01 | 0.01 | 0.01 | 0.01 | 0.01 | 0.01 | 0.01 | 0.01 |
| **5. Absolute 1980−1989 PARE** | | | | | | | | | | |
| 5a. Per capita GDP | 5 036 | 5 117 | 5 212 | 5 565 | 5 461 | 5 211 | 5 299 | 5 526 | 5 920 | 6 084 |
| 5b. GDP | 816 | 839 | 860 | 924 | 912 | 875 | 901 | 945 | 1 018 | 1 059 |
| 5c. % of GWP | 0.01 | 0.01 | 0.01 | 0.01 | 0.01 | 0.01 | 0.01 | 0.01 | 0.01 | 0.01 |
| **6. WA[a]** | | | | | | | | | | |
| 6a. Per capita GDP | 1 579 | 1 708 | 1 861 | 2 107 | 2 251 | 2 371 | 2 673 | 3 022 | 3 454 | 3 934 |
| 6b. GDP | 256 | 280 | 307 | 350 | 376 | 398 | 454 | 517 | 594 | 684 |
| 6c. % of GWP | 0.01 | 0.01 | 0.01 | 0.01 | 0.01 | 0.01 | 0.01 | 0.01 | 0.01 | 0.01 |

| | | | | | | | | | | Averages | | |
|---|---|---|---|---|---|---|---|---|---|---|---|---|
| 1980 | 1981 | 1982 | 1983 | 1984 | 1985 | 1986 | 1987 | 1988 | 1989 | 1970–89 | 1970–79 | 1980–89 |
| (11) | (12) | (13) | (14) | (15) | (16) | (17) | (18) | (19) | (20) | (21) | (22) | (23) |
| 11 976 | 9 947 | 9 672 | 9 306 | 8 655 | 8 693 | 12 009 | 14 673 | 15 228 | 15 208 | 8 937 | 6 229 | 11 585 |
| 169 386 | 141 423 | 138 150 | 133 504 | 124 727 | 125 920 | 174 943 | 215 085 | 224 710 | 225 895 | 126 034 | 84 693 | 167 374 |
| 1.46 | 1.21 | 1.19 | 1.13 | 1.02 | 1.00 | 1.17 | 1.25 | 1.18 | 1.13 | 1.24 | 1.39 | 1.17 |
| 9 040 | 9 443 | 10 048 | 10 255 | 10 854 | 11 151 | 11 540 | 11 895 | 12 547 | 13 498 | 8 362 | 5 586 | 11 066 |
| 127 868 | 134 266 | 143 517 | 147 112 | 156 418 | 161 519 | 168 116 | 174 374 | 185 148 | 200 499 | 117 920 | 75 956 | 159 884 |
| ... | ... | ... | ... | ... | ... | ... | ... | ... | ... | ... | ... | ... |
| 9 265 | 9 152 | 8 982 | 9 068 | 9 313 | 9 509 | 9 647 | 9 667 | 9 865 | 10 195 | 8 937 | 8 457 | 9 487 |
| 131 047 | 130 125 | 128 292 | 130 094 | 134 203 | 137 741 | 140 543 | 141 702 | 145 571 | 151 431 | 126 034 | 114 992 | 137 075 |
| 1.26 | 1.23 | 1.20 | 1.19 | 1.17 | 1.16 | 1.15 | 1.12 | 1.10 | 1.11 | 1.24 | 1.33 | 1.17 |
| 9 184 | 9 930 | 10 376 | 10 829 | 11 519 | 12 081 | 12 503 | 12 888 | 13 594 | 14 624 | 8 808 | 5 734 | 11 798 |
| 129 902 | 141 192 | 148 194 | 155 355 | 166 003 | 174 995 | 182 143 | 188 922 | 200 595 | 217 228 | 124 210 | 77 966 | 170 453 |
| 1.26 | 1.23 | 1.20 | 1.19 | 1.17 | 1.16 | 1.15 | 1.12 | 1.10 | 1.11 | 1.21 | 1.33 | 1.16 |
| 11 313 | 11 175 | 10 968 | 11 073 | 11 371 | 11 611 | 11 780 | 11 803 | 12 046 | 12 448 | 10 912 | 10 327 | 11 585 |
| 160 014 | 158 888 | 156 650 | 158 850 | 163 868 | 168 187 | 171 609 | 173 025 | 177 748 | 184 904 | 153 893 | 140 411 | 167 374 |
| 1.27 | 1.23 | 1.21 | 1.19 | 1.18 | 1.17 | 1.16 | 1.13 | 1.11 | 1.12 | 1.24 | 1.33 | 1.17 |
| 11 975 | 9 946 | 9 672 | 9 306 | 8 656 | 8 692 | 12 009 | 14 486 | 15 409 | 15 059 | 8 929 | 6 228 | 11 569 |
| 169 376 | 141 412 | 138 139 | 133 498 | 124 740 | 125 905 | 174 941 | 212 356 | 227 373 | 223 686 | 125 915 | 84 687 | 167 143 |
| 1.47 | 1.20 | 1.19 | 1.13 | 1.02 | 1.00 | 1.19 | 1.27 | 1.21 | 1.14 | 1.25 | 1.40 | 1.18 |
| 4 948 | 5 665 | 5 990 | 5 927 | 5 953 | 6 000 | 5 877 | 6 470 | 7 049 | 7 200 | 4 496 | 2 755 | 6 120 |
| 866 | 997 | 1 066 | 1 061 | 1 072 | 1 092 | 1 076 | 1 190 | 1 311 | 1 346 | 785 | 461 | 1 108 |
| 0.01 | 0.01 | 0.01 | 0.01 | 0.01 | 0.01 | 0.01 | 0.01 | 0.01 | 0.01 | 0.01 | 0.01 | 0.01 |
| ... | ... | ... | ... | ... | ... | ... | ... | ... | ... | ... | ... | ... |
| ... | ... | ... | ... | ... | ... | ... | ... | ... | ... | ... | ... | ... |
| ... | ... | ... | ... | ... | ... | ... | ... | ... | ... | ... | ... | ... |
| 4 884 | 4 936 | 4 906 | 4 811 | 4 643 | 4 497 | 4 348 | 4 613 | 4 901 | 4 949 | 4 496 | 4 237 | 4 748 |
| 855 | 869 | 873 | 861 | 836 | 818 | 796 | 849 | 912 | 926 | 785 | 710 | 859 |
| 0.01 | 0.01 | 0.01 | 0.01 | 0.01 | 0.01 | 0.01 | 0.01 | 0.01 | 0.01 | 0.01 | 0.01 | 0.01 |
| 4 841 | 5 355 | 5 667 | 5 746 | 5 743 | 5 713 | 5 635 | 6 151 | 6 753 | 7 100 | 4 426 | 2 865 | 5 882 |
| 847 | 943 | 1 009 | 1 028 | 1 034 | 1 040 | 1 031 | 1 132 | 1 256 | 1 328 | 772 | 480 | 1 065 |
| 0.01 | 0.01 | 0.01 | 0.01 | 0.01 | 0.01 | 0.01 | 0.01 | 0.01 | 0.01 | 0.01 | 0.01 | 0.01 |
| 6 295 | 6 362 | 6 323 | 6 202 | 5 985 | 5 796 | 5 605 | 5 947 | 6 317 | 6 380 | 5 795 | 5 462 | 6 120 |
| 1 102 | 1 120 | 1 126 | 1 110 | 1 077 | 1 055 | 1 026 | 1 094 | 1 175 | 1 193 | 1 011 | 915 | 1 108 |
| 0.01 | 0.01 | 0.01 | 0.01 | 0.01 | 0.01 | 0.01 | 0.01 | 0.01 | 0.01 | 0.01 | 0.01 | 0.01 |
| 4 501 | 5 090 | 5 497 | 5 769 | 5 778 | 5 762 | 5 749 | 6 284 | 6 844 | 7 085 | 4 243 | 2 517 | 5 851 |
| 788 | 896 | 978 | 1 033 | 1 040 | 1 049 | 1 052 | 1 156 | 1 273 | 1 325 | 740 | 422 | 1 059 |
| 0.01 | 0.01 | 0.01 | 0.01 | 0.01 | 0.01 | 0.01 | 0.01 | 0.01 | 0.01 | 0.01 | 0.01 | 0.01 |

**Table A.1** Total and per capita gross domestic product of individual countries or areas, expressed in United States dollars, and their individual shares of gross world product, based on alternative conversion rates, 1970–1989 [*cont.*]

| Country or area | 1970 (1) | 1971 (2) | 1972 (3) | 1973 (4) | 1974 (5) | 1975 (6) | 1976 (7) | 1977 (8) | 1978 (9) | 1979 (10) |
|---|---|---|---|---|---|---|---|---|---|---|
| **New Caledonia** | | | | | | | | | | |
| **1. MER** | | | | | | | | | | |
| 1a. Per capita GDP | 3 408 | 3 785 | 4 207 | 4 325 | 4 918 | 6 095 | 5 869 | 6 115 | 6 131 | 7 589 |
| 1b. GDP | 378 | 439 | 509 | 545 | 644 | 817 | 798 | 838 | 846 | 1 047 |
| 1c. % of GWP | 0.01 | 0.01 | 0.01 | 0.01 | 0.01 | 0.01 | 0.01 | 0.01 | 0.01 | 0.01 |
| **2. PPPs** | | | | | | | | | | |
| 2a. Per capita GDP | ... | ... | ... | ... | ... | ... | ... | ... | ... | ... |
| 2b. GDP | ... | ... | ... | ... | ... | ... | ... | ... | ... | ... |
| 2c. % of GWP | ... | ... | ... | ... | ... | ... | ... | ... | ... | ... |
| **3. Absolute 1970–1989 PARE** | | | | | | | | | | |
| 3a. Per capita GDP | 7 328 | 7 503 | 7 437 | 6 342 | 6 874 | 7 157 | 7 215 | 7 298 | 7 957 | 6 873 |
| 3b. GDP | 813 | 870 | 900 | 799 | 901 | 959 | 981 | 1 000 | 1 098 | 948 |
| 3c. % of GWP | 0.01 | 0.01 | 0.01 | 0.01 | 0.01 | 0.01 | 0.01 | 0.01 | 0.01 | 0.01 |
| **4. Relative 1970–1989 PARE** | | | | | | | | | | |
| 4a. Per capita GDP | 3 573 | 3 846 | 3 987 | 3 626 | 4 287 | 4 904 | 5 252 | 5 671 | 6 634 | 6 241 |
| 4b. GDP | 397 | 446 | 482 | 457 | 562 | 657 | 714 | 777 | 915 | 861 |
| 4c. % of GWP | 0.01 | 0.01 | 0.01 | 0.01 | 0.01 | 0.01 | 0.01 | 0.01 | 0.01 | 0.01 |
| **5. Absolute 1980–1989 PARE** | | | | | | | | | | |
| 5a. Per capita GDP | 9 071 | 9 287 | 9 206 | 7 851 | 8 509 | 8 860 | 8 931 | 9 034 | 9 850 | 8 507 |
| 5b. GDP | 1 007 | 1 077 | 1 114 | 989 | 1 115 | 1 187 | 1 215 | 1 238 | 1 359 | 1 174 |
| 5c. % of GWP | 0.01 | 0.01 | 0.01 | 0.01 | 0.01 | 0.01 | 0.01 | 0.01 | 0.01 | 0.01 |
| **6. WA[a]** | | | | | | | | | | |
| 6a. Per capita GDP | 2 591 | 3 210 | 3 781 | 3 647 | 4 452 | 5 317 | 5 694 | 6 086 | 6 416 | 6 069 |
| 6b. GDP | 288 | 372 | 458 | 460 | 583 | 712 | 774 | 834 | 885 | 838 |
| 6c. % of GWP | 0.01 | 0.01 | 0.01 | 0.01 | 0.01 | 0.01 | 0.01 | 0.01 | 0.01 | 0.01 |
| **New Zealand** | | | | | | | | | | |
| **1. MER** | | | | | | | | | | |
| 1a. Per capita GDP | 2 233 | 2 629 | 3 097 | 4 026 | 4 476 | 4 433 | 4 363 | 4 645 | 5 626 | 6 479 |
| 1b. GDP | 6 297 | 7 554 | 9 086 | 12 053 | 13 633 | 13 670 | 13 542 | 14 447 | 17 487 | 20 130 |
| 1c. % of GWP | 0.20 | 0.22 | 0.23 | 0.25 | 0.25 | 0.22 | 0.20 | 0.19 | 0.19 | 0.20 |
| **2. PPPs** | | | | | | | | | | |
| 2a. Per capita GDP | 3 173 | 3 460 | 3 818 | 4 432 | 4 740 | 5 013 | 5 434 | 5 546 | 5 985 | 6 433 |
| 2b. GDP | 8 947 | 9 940 | 11 202 | 13 268 | 14 437 | 15 461 | 16 867 | 17 248 | 18 601 | 19 988 |
| 2c. % of GWP | ... | ... | ... | ... | ... | ... | ... | ... | ... | ... |
| **3. Absolute 1970–1989 PARE** | | | | | | | | | | |
| 3a. Per capita GDP | 6 122 | 6 103 | 6 223 | 6 323 | 6 730 | 6 555 | 6 704 | 6 349 | 6 241 | 6 214 |
| 3b. GDP | 17 265 | 17 535 | 18 257 | 18 931 | 20 499 | 20 216 | 20 808 | 19 747 | 19 397 | 19 306 |
| 3c. % of GWP | 0.24 | 0.24 | 0.23 | 0.23 | 0.24 | 0.24 | 0.23 | 0.21 | 0.20 | 0.19 |
| **4. Relative 1970–1989 PARE** | | | | | | | | | | |
| 4a. Per capita GDP | 2 985 | 3 129 | 3 336 | 3 615 | 4 197 | 4 491 | 4 880 | 4 934 | 5 203 | 5 643 |
| 4b. GDP | 8 418 | 8 988 | 9 787 | 10 823 | 12 783 | 13 850 | 15 146 | 15 344 | 16 171 | 17 533 |
| 4c. % of GWP | 0.24 | 0.24 | 0.23 | 0.23 | 0.24 | 0.24 | 0.23 | 0.21 | 0.20 | 0.19 |
| **5. Absolute 1980–1989 PARE** | | | | | | | | | | |
| 5a. Per capita GDP | 7 914 | 7 889 | 8 043 | 8 173 | 8 699 | 8 473 | 8 665 | 8 207 | 8 067 | 8 032 |
| 5b. GDP | 22 317 | 22 666 | 23 599 | 24 470 | 26 496 | 26 132 | 26 896 | 25 525 | 25 072 | 24 955 |
| 5c. % of GWP | 0.26 | 0.25 | 0.25 | 0.24 | 0.26 | 0.25 | 0.24 | 0.22 | 0.21 | 0.20 |
| **6. WA** | | | | | | | | | | |
| 6a. Per capita GDP | 2 233 | 2 661 | 3 150 | 4 111 | 4 406 | 4 120 | 4 267 | 4 724 | 5 668 | 6 347 |
| 6b. GDP | 6 298 | 7 645 | 9 243 | 12 308 | 13 422 | 12 706 | 13 246 | 14 693 | 17 617 | 19 720 |
| 6c. % of GWP | 0.20 | 0.22 | 0.23 | 0.25 | 0.24 | 0.21 | 0.20 | 0.19 | 0.20 | 0.19 |

| | 1980 (11) | 1981 (12) | 1982 (13) | 1983 (14) | 1984 (15) | 1985 (16) | 1986 (17) | 1987 (18) | 1988 (19) | 1989 (20) | Averages 1970–89 (21) | 1970–79 (22) | 1980–89 (23) |
|---|---|---|---|---|---|---|---|---|---|---|---|---|---|
| | 8 446 | 6 912 | 6 282 | 5 604 | 5 307 | 5 587 | 7 701 | 9 375 | 12 796 | 13 534 | 6 977 | 5 178 | 8 274 |
| | 1 182 | 975 | 905 | 824 | 796 | 855 | 1 201 | 1 491 | 2 073 | 2 233 | 970 | 686 | 1 253 |
| | 0.01 | 0.01 | 0.01 | 0.01 | 0.01 | 0.01 | 0.01 | 0.01 | 0.01 | 0.01 | 0.01 | 0.01 | 0.01 |
| | ... | ... | ... | ... | ... | ... | ... | ... | ... | ... | ... | ... | ... |
| | ... | ... | ... | ... | ... | ... | ... | ... | ... | ... | ... | ... | ... |
| | ... | ... | ... | ... | ... | ... | ... | ... | ... | ... | ... | ... | ... |
| | 6 748 | 6 228 | 6 242 | 5 990 | 5 975 | 6 122 | 5 945 | 6 164 | 8 144 | 8 872 | 6 977 | 6 996 | 6 684 |
| | 945 | 878 | 899 | 881 | 896 | 937 | 927 | 980 | 1 319 | 1 464 | 970 | 927 | 1 013 |
| | 0.01 | 0.01 | 0.01 | 0.01 | 0.01 | 0.01 | 0.01 | 0.01 | 0.01 | 0.01 | 0.01 | 0.01 | 0.01 |
| | 6 689 | 6 758 | 7 211 | 7 153 | 7 391 | 7 778 | 7 704 | 8 218 | 11 223 | 12 727 | 6 825 | 4 731 | 8 386 |
| | 936 | 953 | 1 038 | 1 051 | 1 109 | 1 190 | 1 202 | 1 307 | 1 818 | 2 100 | 949 | 627 | 1 270 |
| | 0.01 | 0.01 | 0.01 | 0.01 | 0.01 | 0.01 | 0.01 | 0.01 | 0.01 | 0.01 | 0.01 | 0.01 | 0.01 |
| | 8 353 | 7 710 | 7 727 | 7 415 | 7 397 | 7 579 | 7 359 | 7 630 | 10 081 | 10 982 | 8 636 | 8 660 | 8 274 |
| | 1 169 | 1 087 | 1 113 | 1 090 | 1 110 | 1 160 | 1 148 | 1 213 | 1 633 | 1 812 | 1 200 | 1 147 | 1 253 |
| | 0.01 | 0.01 | 0.01 | 0.01 | 0.01 | 0.01 | 0.01 | 0.01 | 0.01 | 0.01 | 0.01 | 0.01 | 0.01 |
| | 6 742 | 7 171 | 6 952 | 6 064 | 5 622 | 5 582 | 5 957 | 7 323 | 11 827 | 13 653 | 6 479 | 4 682 | 7 793 |
| | 944 | 1 011 | 1 001 | 891 | 843 | 854 | 929 | 1 164 | 1 916 | 2 253 | 901 | 620 | 1 181 |
| | 0.01 | 0.01 | 0.01 | 0.01 | 0.01 | 0.01 | 0.01 | 0.01 | 0.01 | 0.01 | 0.01 | 0.01 | 0.01 |
| | 7 178 | 7 715 | 7 411 | 7 219 | 6 975 | 6 863 | 8 546 | 10 528 | 12 755 | 11 915 | 6 606 | 4 173 | 8 755 |
| | 22 344 | 24 147 | 23 380 | 22 993 | 22 439 | 22 293 | 28 005 | 34 807 | 42 537 | 40 069 | 20 546 | 12 790 | 28 301 |
| | 0.19 | 0.21 | 0.20 | 0.19 | 0.18 | 0.18 | 0.19 | 0.20 | 0.22 | 0.20 | 0.20 | 0.21 | 0.20 |
| | 7 002 | 7 985 | 8 454 | 8 850 | 9 465 | 9 569 | 10 007 | 10 053 | 10 405 | 10 848 | 7 176 | 4 762 | 9 293 |
| | 21 799 | 24 994 | 26 672 | 28 188 | 30 451 | 31 079 | 32 793 | 33 234 | 34 699 | 36 483 | 22 318 | 14 596 | 30 039 |
| | ... | ... | ... | ... | ... | ... | ... | ... | ... | ... | ... | ... | ... |
| | 6 307 | 6 479 | 6 560 | 6 815 | 6 981 | 6 863 | 7 036 | 6 871 | 6 880 | 6 891 | 6 606 | 6 263 | 6 773 |
| | 19 633 | 20 278 | 20 696 | 21 704 | 22 458 | 22 291 | 23 057 | 22 715 | 22 945 | 23 175 | 20 546 | 19 196 | 21 895 |
| | 0.19 | 0.19 | 0.19 | 0.20 | 0.20 | 0.19 | 0.19 | 0.18 | 0.17 | 0.17 | 0.20 | 0.22 | 0.19 |
| | 6 252 | 7 030 | 7 577 | 8 138 | 8 635 | 8 719 | 9 119 | 9 160 | 9 481 | 9 885 | 6 451 | 4 204 | 8 427 |
| | 19 462 | 22 003 | 23 907 | 25 919 | 27 780 | 28 320 | 29 882 | 30 284 | 31 619 | 33 244 | 20 063 | 12 884 | 27 242 |
| | 0.19 | 0.19 | 0.19 | 0.20 | 0.20 | 0.19 | 0.19 | 0.18 | 0.17 | 0.17 | 0.20 | 0.22 | 0.19 |
| | 8 152 | 8 374 | 8 479 | 8 808 | 9 024 | 8 871 | 9 095 | 8 881 | 8 893 | 8 907 | 8 539 | 8 095 | 8 755 |
| | 25 378 | 26 211 | 26 751 | 28 055 | 29 029 | 28 813 | 29 803 | 29 360 | 29 659 | 29 956 | 26 557 | 24 813 | 28 301 |
| | 0.20 | 0.20 | 0.21 | 0.21 | 0.21 | 0.20 | 0.20 | 0.19 | 0.19 | 0.18 | 0.21 | 0.24 | 0.20 |
| | 7 113 | 7 380 | 7 178 | 7 093 | 6 253 | 7 042 | 8 615 | 11 079 | 12 323 | 12 113 | 6 544 | 4 140 | 8 667 |
| | 22 144 | 23 100 | 22 647 | 22 591 | 20 116 | 22 874 | 28 232 | 36 627 | 41 099 | 40 736 | 20 353 | 12 690 | 28 016 |
| | 0.19 | 0.20 | 0.19 | 0.19 | 0.16 | 0.18 | 0.19 | 0.22 | 0.22 | 0.21 | 0.20 | 0.21 | 0.20 |

**Table A.1**　　Total and per capita gross domestic product of individual countries or areas, expressed in United States dollars, and their individual shares of gross world product, based on alternative conversion rates, 1970—1989 [*cont.*]

| Country or area | 1970 (1) | 1971 (2) | 1972 (3) | 1973 (4) | 1974 (5) | 1975 (6) | 1976 (7) | 1977 (8) | 1978 (9) | 1979 (10) |
|---|---|---|---|---|---|---|---|---|---|---|
| **Nicaragua** | | | | | | | | | | |
| **1.　MER** | | | | | | | | | | |
| 1a.　Per capita GDP | 378 | 390 | 402 | 483 | 542 | 449 | 507 | 598 | 556 | 397 |
| 1b.　GDP | 777 | 827 | 881 | 1 094 | 1 267 | 1 081 | 1 256 | 1 522 | 1 455 | 1 067 |
| 1c.　% of GWP | 0.02 | 0.02 | 0.02 | 0.02 | 0.02 | 0.02 | 0.02 | 0.02 | 0.02 | 0.01 |
| **2.　PPPs** | | | | | | | | | | |
| 2a.　Per capita GDP | 1 030 | 1 085 | 1 093 | 1 212 | 1 458 | 1 483 | 1 702 | 2 063 | 1 907 | 1 350 |
| 2b.　GDP | 2 114 | 2 301 | 2 396 | 2 744 | 3 407 | 3 574 | 4 217 | 5 254 | 4 989 | 3 632 |
| 2c.　% of GWP | ... | ... | ... | ... | ... | ... | ... | ... | ... | ... |
| **3.　Absolute 1970—1989 PARE** | | | | | | | | | | |
| 3a.　Per capita GDP | 1 249 | 1 249 | 1 235 | 1 272 | 1 408 | 1 364 | 1 395 | 1 471 | 1 320 | 943 |
| 3b.　GDP | 2 564 | 2 649 | 2 708 | 2 882 | 3 291 | 3 286 | 3 457 | 3 746 | 3 453 | 2 538 |
| 3c.　% of GWP | 0.04 | 0.04 | 0.03 | 0.03 | 0.04 | 0.04 | 0.04 | 0.04 | 0.04 | 0.02 |
| **4.　Relative 1970—1989 PARE** | | | | | | | | | | |
| 4a.　Per capita GDP | 609 | 640 | 662 | 727 | 878 | 934 | 1 015 | 1 143 | 1 100 | 857 |
| 4b.　GDP | 1 250 | 1 358 | 1 452 | 1 647 | 2 052 | 2 251 | 2 516 | 2 911 | 2 878 | 2 305 |
| 4c.　% of GWP | 0.04 | 0.04 | 0.03 | 0.03 | 0.04 | 0.04 | 0.04 | 0.04 | 0.04 | 0.02 |
| **5.　Absolute 1980—1989 PARE** | | | | | | | | | | |
| 5a.　Per capita GDP | 2 149 | 2 148 | 2 125 | 2 188 | 2 422 | 2 346 | 2 400 | 2 530 | 2 270 | 1 623 |
| 5b.　GDP | 4 411 | 4 557 | 4 658 | 4 957 | 5 660 | 5 652 | 5 946 | 6 444 | 5 939 | 4 366 |
| 5c.　% of GWP | 0.05 | 0.05 | 0.05 | 0.05 | 0.05 | 0.05 | 0.05 | 0.06 | 0.05 | 0.04 |
| **6.　WA** | | | | | | | | | | |
| 6a.　Per capita GDP | 378 | 390 | 402 | 483 | 650 | 658 | 743 | 876 | 815 | 583 |
| 6b.　GDP | 777 | 827 | 881 | 1 094 | 1 518 | 1 584 | 1 841 | 2 231 | 2 133 | 1 568 |
| 6c.　% of GWP | 0.02 | 0.02 | 0.02 | 0.02 | 0.03 | 0.03 | 0.03 | 0.03 | 0.02 | 0.02 |
| **Niger** | | | | | | | | | | |
| **1.　MER** | | | | | | | | | | |
| 1a.　Per capita GDP | 96 | 101 | 123 | 128 | 143 | 176 | 202 | 232 | 304 | 386 |
| 1b.　GDP | 400 | 430 | 539 | 576 | 661 | 841 | 995 | 1 176 | 1 592 | 2 084 |
| 1c.　% of GWP | 0.01 | 0.01 | 0.01 | 0.01 | 0.01 | 0.01 | 0.01 | 0.02 | 0.02 | 0.02 |
| **2.　PPPs** | | | | | | | | | | |
| 2a.　Per capita GDP | 204 | 210 | 219 | 185 | 241 | 262 | 286 | 282 | 324 | 380 |
| 2b.　GDP | 851 | 896 | 962 | 834 | 1 118 | 1 252 | 1 407 | 1 428 | 1 696 | 2 055 |
| 2c.　% of GWP | ... | ... | ... | ... | ... | ... | ... | ... | ... | ... |
| **3.　Absolute 1970—1989 PARE** | | | | | | | | | | |
| 3a.　Per capita GDP | 262 | 258 | 260 | 217 | 245 | 232 | 265 | 260 | 283 | 301 |
| 3b.　GDP | 1 092 | 1 101 | 1 139 | 979 | 1 135 | 1 107 | 1 303 | 1 320 | 1 480 | 1 629 |
| 3c.　% of GWP | 0.02 | 0.01 | 0.01 | 0.01 | 0.01 | 0.01 | 0.01 | 0.01 | 0.02 | 0.02 |
| **4.　Relative 1970—1989 PARE** | | | | | | | | | | |
| 4a.　Per capita GDP | 128 | 132 | 139 | 124 | 153 | 159 | 193 | 202 | 236 | 274 |
| 4b.　GDP | 533 | 565 | 611 | 560 | 708 | 758 | 948 | 1 026 | 1 234 | 1 479 |
| 4c.　% of GWP | 0.02 | 0.01 | 0.01 | 0.01 | 0.01 | 0.01 | 0.01 | 0.01 | 0.02 | 0.02 |
| **5.　Absolute 1980—1989 PARE** | | | | | | | | | | |
| 5a.　Per capita GDP | 309 | 304 | 306 | 256 | 289 | 273 | 312 | 307 | 333 | 355 |
| 5b.　GDP | 1 287 | 1 298 | 1 342 | 1 154 | 1 338 | 1 304 | 1 535 | 1 556 | 1 744 | 1 920 |
| 5c.　% of GWP | 0.01 | 0.01 | 0.01 | 0.01 | 0.01 | 0.01 | 0.01 | 0.01 | 0.01 | 0.02 |
| **6.　WA** | | | | | | | | | | |
| 6a.　Per capita GDP | 96 | 100 | 123 | 128 | 143 | 176 | 203 | 232 | 304 | 386 |
| 6b.　GDP | 400 | 428 | 539 | 575 | 661 | 841 | 996 | 1 176 | 1 592 | 2 084 |
| 6c.　% of GWP | 0.01 | 0.01 | 0.01 | 0.01 | 0.01 | 0.01 | 0.01 | 0.02 | 0.02 | 0.02 |

| | | | | | | | | | | Averages | | |
|---|---|---|---|---|---|---|---|---|---|---|---|---|
| 1980 (11) | 1981 (12) | 1982 (13) | 1983 (14) | 1984 (15) | 1985 (16) | 1986 (17) | 1987 (18) | 1988 (19) | 1989 (20) | 1970–89 (21) | 1970–79 (22) | 1980–89 (23) |
| 537 | 582 | 653 | 733 | 968 | 904 | 1 320 | 7 503 | 338 | 239 | 1 051 | 473 | 1 436 |
| 1 489 | 1 666 | 1 929 | 2 239 | 3 063 | 2 959 | 4 469 | 26 275 | 1 226 | 897 | 2 872 | 1 123 | 4 621 |
| 0.01 | 0.01 | 0.02 | 0.02 | 0.03 | 0.02 | 0.03 | 0.15 | 0.01 | 0.00 | 0.03 | 0.02 | 0.03 |
| 2 026 | 2 161 | 2 172 | 2 169 | 2 296 | 2 426 | 2 368 | 2 338 | 2 081 | 2 035 | 1 941 | 1 459 | 2 219 |
| 5 617 | 6 180 | 6 417 | 6 629 | 7 263 | 7 940 | 8 017 | 8 189 | 7 539 | 7 622 | 5 302 | 3 463 | 7 141 |
| ... | ... | ... | ... | ... | ... | ... | ... | ... | ... | ... | ... | ... |
| 958 | 978 | 939 | 950 | 903 | 837 | 801 | 769 | 662 | 622 | 1 051 | 1 288 | 835 |
| 2 655 | 2 798 | 2 775 | 2 903 | 2 858 | 2 741 | 2 713 | 2 694 | 2 399 | 2 330 | 2 872 | 3 057 | 2 687 |
| 0.03 | 0.03 | 0.03 | 0.03 | 0.02 | 0.02 | 0.02 | 0.02 | 0.02 | 0.02 | 0.03 | 0.04 | 0.02 |
| 950 | 1 061 | 1 085 | 1 134 | 1 118 | 1 064 | 1 038 | 1 026 | 913 | 893 | 984 | 869 | 1 029 |
| 2 632 | 3 036 | 3 205 | 3 467 | 3 535 | 3 482 | 3 516 | 3 592 | 3 306 | 3 343 | 2 687 | 2 062 | 3 311 |
| 0.03 | 0.03 | 0.03 | 0.03 | 0.02 | 0.02 | 0.02 | 0.02 | 0.02 | 0.02 | 0.03 | 0.04 | 0.02 |
| 1 648 | 1 683 | 1 615 | 1 633 | 1 554 | 1 440 | 1 378 | 1 323 | 1 139 | 1 070 | 1 809 | 2 216 | 1 436 |
| 4 568 | 4 813 | 4 773 | 4 994 | 4 915 | 4 715 | 4 666 | 4 634 | 4 127 | 4 008 | 4 940 | 5 259 | 4 621 |
| 0.04 | 0.04 | 0.04 | 0.04 | 0.04 | 0.03 | 0.03 | 0.03 | 0.03 | 0.02 | 0.04 | 0.05 | 0.03 |
| 786 | 852 | 820 | 816 | 949 | 881 | 809 | 818 | 843 | 792 | 770 | 609 | 858 |
| 2 178 | 2 436 | 2 423 | 2 494 | 3 002 | 2 885 | 2 741 | 3 428 | 3 053 | 2 964 | 2 103 | 1 445 | 2 760 |
| 0.02 | 0.02 | 0.02 | 0.02 | 0.02 | 0.02 | 0.02 | 0.02 | 0.02 | 0.02 | 0.02 | 0.02 | 0.02 |
| 454 | 383 | 338 | 292 | 228 | 218 | 272 | 307 | 314 | 266 | 264 | 198 | 304 |
| 2 538 | 2 213 | 2 018 | 1 803 | 1 461 | 1 440 | 1 858 | 2 163 | 2 279 | 1 994 | 1 453 | 929 | 1 977 |
| 0.02 | 0.02 | 0.02 | 0.02 | 0.01 | 0.01 | 0.01 | 0.01 | 0.01 | 0.01 | 0.01 | 0.02 | 0.01 |
| 443 | 445 | 461 | 456 | 435 | 461 | 479 | 457 | 490 | 477 | 387 | 266 | 462 |
| 2 474 | 2 573 | 2 758 | 2 817 | 2 784 | 3 046 | 3 265 | 3 215 | 3 555 | 3 571 | 2 128 | 1 250 | 3 006 |
| ... | ... | ... | ... | ... | ... | ... | ... | ... | ... | ... | ... | ... |
| 306 | 280 | 264 | 273 | 246 | 252 | 256 | 238 | 247 | 231 | 264 | 261 | 258 |
| 1 709 | 1 617 | 1 575 | 1 689 | 1 575 | 1 665 | 1 750 | 1 675 | 1 792 | 1 729 | 1 453 | 1 229 | 1 677 |
| 0.02 | 0.02 | 0.01 | 0.02 | 0.01 | 0.01 | 0.01 | 0.01 | 0.01 | 0.01 | 0.01 | 0.01 | 0.01 |
| 303 | 304 | 304 | 326 | 305 | 320 | 332 | 317 | 340 | 331 | 266 | 179 | 320 |
| 1 694 | 1 755 | 1 819 | 2 017 | 1 948 | 2 115 | 2 268 | 2 233 | 2 469 | 2 480 | 1 461 | 842 | 2 080 |
| 0.02 | 0.02 | 0.01 | 0.02 | 0.01 | 0.01 | 0.01 | 0.01 | 0.01 | 0.01 | 0.01 | 0.01 | 0.01 |
| 360 | 330 | 311 | 322 | 290 | 297 | 302 | 280 | 291 | 272 | 312 | 308 | 304 |
| 2 014 | 1 906 | 1 856 | 1 990 | 1 856 | 1 962 | 2 062 | 1 973 | 2 111 | 2 037 | 1 712 | 1 448 | 1 977 |
| 0.02 | 0.01 | 0.01 | 0.01 | 0.01 | 0.01 | 0.01 | 0.01 | 0.01 | 0.01 | 0.01 | 0.01 | 0.01 |
| 454 | 383 | 338 | 292 | 228 | 218 | 272 | 307 | 314 | 266 | 264 | 198 | 304 |
| 2 538 | 2 213 | 2 018 | 1 803 | 1 461 | 1 440 | 1 858 | 2 162 | 2 279 | 1 994 | 1 453 | 929 | 1 977 |
| 0.02 | 0.02 | 0.02 | 0.02 | 0.01 | 0.01 | 0.01 | 0.01 | 0.01 | 0.01 | 0.01 | 0.02 | 0.01 |

**Table A.1**   Total and per capita gross domestic product of individual countries or areas, expressed in United States dollars, and their individual shares of gross world product, based on alternative conversion rates, 1970—1989 [*cont.*]

| Country or area | 1970 (1) | 1971 (2) | 1972 (3) | 1973 (4) | 1974 (5) | 1975 (6) | 1976 (7) | 1977 (8) | 1978 (9) | 1979 (10) |
|---|---|---|---|---|---|---|---|---|---|---|
| **Nigeria** | | | | | | | | | | |
| **1.  MER** | | | | | | | | | | |
| 1a.  Per capita GDP | 175 | 215 | 245 | 277 | 466 | 534 | 641 | 710 | 751 | 898 |
| 1b.  GDP | 9 908 | 12 548 | 14 735 | 17 244 | 29 906 | 35 413 | 43 974 | 50 404 | 55 142 | 68 131 |
| 1c.  % of GWP | 0.31 | 0.36 | 0.37 | 0.35 | 0.54 | 0.57 | 0.66 | 0.67 | 0.61 | 0.66 |
| **2.  PPPs** | | | | | | | | | | |
| 2a.  Per capita GDP | 356 | 412 | 414 | 448 | 592 | 625 | 693 | 727 | 690 | 814 |
| 2b.  GDP | 20 158 | 24 047 | 24 953 | 27 882 | 38 015 | 41 462 | 47 513 | 51 601 | 50 616 | 61 780 |
| 2c.  % of GWP | ... | ... | ... | ... | ... | ... | ... | ... | ... | ... |
| **3.  Absolute 1970—1989 PARE** | | | | | | | | | | |
| 3a.  Per capita GDP | 564 | 608 | 625 | 642 | 698 | 657 | 702 | 731 | 663 | 631 |
| 3b.  GDP | 31 936 | 35 501 | 37 632 | 39 941 | 44 841 | 43 613 | 48 182 | 51 846 | 48 656 | 47 902 |
| 3c.  % of GWP | 0.45 | 0.48 | 0.48 | 0.48 | 0.53 | 0.51 | 0.53 | 0.55 | 0.49 | 0.47 |
| **4.  Relative 1970—1989 PARE** | | | | | | | | | | |
| 4a.  Per capita GDP | 275 | 312 | 335 | 367 | 436 | 450 | 511 | 568 | 553 | 573 |
| 4b.  GDP | 15 571 | 18 197 | 20 175 | 22 834 | 27 963 | 29 880 | 35 073 | 40 285 | 40 565 | 43 502 |
| 4c.  % of GWP | 0.45 | 0.48 | 0.48 | 0.48 | 0.53 | 0.51 | 0.53 | 0.55 | 0.49 | 0.47 |
| **5.  Absolute 1980—1989 PARE** | | | | | | | | | | |
| 5a.  Per capita GDP | 680 | 733 | 753 | 774 | 842 | 792 | 847 | 881 | 799 | 761 |
| 5b.  GDP | 38 488 | 42 785 | 45 354 | 48 136 | 54 042 | 52 562 | 58 069 | 62 484 | 58 640 | 57 731 |
| 5c.  % of GWP | 0.44 | 0.47 | 0.47 | 0.47 | 0.52 | 0.50 | 0.53 | 0.54 | 0.49 | 0.47 |
| **6.  WA** | | | | | | | | | | |
| 6a.  Per capita GDP | 175 | 215 | 245 | 277 | 465 | 533 | 641 | 711 | 751 | 896 |
| 6b.  GDP | 9 903 | 12 532 | 14 737 | 17 220 | 29 845 | 35 384 | 44 002 | 50 427 | 55 116 | 68 018 |
| 6c.  % of GWP | 0.31 | 0.36 | 0.37 | 0.35 | 0.53 | 0.57 | 0.66 | 0.67 | 0.62 | 0.66 |
| **Norway** | | | | | | | | | | |
| **1.  MER** | | | | | | | | | | |
| 1a.  Per capita GDP | 2 884 | 3 238 | 3 796 | 4 896 | 5 875 | 7 098 | 7 768 | 8 896 | 10 014 | 11 574 |
| 1b.  GDP | 11 183 | 12 650 | 14 937 | 19 399 | 23 417 | 28 449 | 31 283 | 35 976 | 40 649 | 47 131 |
| 1c.  % of GWP | 0.35 | 0.36 | 0.37 | 0.40 | 0.42 | 0.46 | 0.47 | 0.48 | 0.45 | 0.46 |
| **2.  PPPs** | | | | | | | | | | |
| 2a.  Per capita GDP | 3 441 | 3 768 | 4 092 | 4 595 | 5 306 | 5 860 | 6 398 | 6 859 | 7 785 | 9 216 |
| 2b.  GDP | 13 346 | 14 720 | 16 103 | 18 205 | 21 152 | 23 486 | 25 765 | 27 738 | 31 599 | 37 529 |
| 2c.  % of GWP | ... | ... | ... | ... | ... | ... | ... | ... | ... | ... |
| **3.  Absolute 1970—1989 PARE** | | | | | | | | | | |
| 3a.  Per capita GDP | 2 629 | 2 729 | 2 849 | 2 946 | 3 081 | 10 908 | 11 596 | 11 960 | 12 457 | 13 046 |
| 3b.  GDP | 10 194 | 10 661 | 11 212 | 11 673 | 12 279 | 43 718 | 46 696 | 48 368 | 50 564 | 53 125 |
| 3c.  % of GWP | 0.14 | 0.14 | 0.14 | 0.14 | 0.14 | 0.51 | 0.52 | 0.51 | 0.51 | 0.52 |
| **4.  Relative 1970—1989 PARE** | | | | | | | | | | |
| 4a.  Per capita GDP | 1 282 | 1 399 | 1 527 | 1 684 | 1 921 | 7 473 | 8 441 | 9 294 | 10 386 | 11 848 |
| 4b.  GDP | 4 970 | 5 465 | 6 011 | 6 673 | 7 657 | 29 952 | 33 991 | 37 583 | 42 155 | 48 245 |
| 4c.  % of GWP | 0.14 | 0.14 | 0.14 | 0.14 | 0.14 | 0.51 | 0.52 | 0.51 | 0.51 | 0.52 |
| **5.  Absolute 1980—1989 PARE** | | | | | | | | | | |
| 5a.  Per capita GDP | 2 766 | 2 871 | 2 998 | 3 100 | 3 241 | 11 477 | 12 201 | 12 585 | 13 108 | 13 728 |
| 5b.  GDP | 10 726 | 11 218 | 11 797 | 12 282 | 12 920 | 46 001 | 49 134 | 50 893 | 53 204 | 55 899 |
| 5c.  % of GWP | 0.12 | 0.12 | 0.12 | 0.12 | 0.12 | 0.44 | 0.44 | 0.44 | 0.44 | 0.45 |
| **6.  WA** | | | | | | | | | | |
| 6a.  Per capita GDP | 2 884 | 3 239 | 3 796 | 4 896 | 5 875 | 7 098 | 7 769 | 8 897 | 10 014 | 11 574 |
| 6b.  GDP | 11 183 | 12 654 | 14 936 | 19 399 | 23 418 | 28 449 | 31 285 | 35 979 | 40 647 | 47 130 |
| 6c.  % of GWP | 0.35 | 0.36 | 0.37 | 0.40 | 0.42 | 0.46 | 0.47 | 0.48 | 0.46 | 0.46 |

| | | | | | | | | | | Averages | | |
| 1980 | 1981 | 1982 | 1983 | 1984 | 1985 | 1986 | 1987 | 1988 | 1989 | 1970–89 | 1970–79 | 1980–89 |
| (11) | (12) | (13) | (14) | (15) | (16) | (17) | (18) | (19) | (20) | (21) | (22) | (23) |
|---|---|---|---|---|---|---|---|---|---|---|---|---|
| 1 125 | 978 | 910 | 780 | 790 | 738 | 358 | 216 | 230 | 157 | 571 | 517 | 601 |
| 88 222 | 79 222 | 76 063 | 67 291 | 70 381 | 67 891 | 34 037 | 21 251 | 23 396 | 16 441 | 44 080 | 33 740 | 54 420 |
| 0.76 | 0.68 | 0.65 | 0.57 | 0.58 | 0.54 | 0.23 | 0.12 | 0.12 | 0.08 | 0.43 | 0.55 | 0.38 |
| | | | | | | | | | | | | |
| 922 | 868 | 859 | 778 | 697 | 680 | 687 | 655 | 685 | 718 | 693 | 594 | 752 |
| 72 342 | 70 314 | 71 818 | 67 144 | 62 125 | 62 590 | 65 311 | 64 350 | 69 617 | 75 361 | 53 450 | 38 803 | 68 097 |
| ... | ... | ... | ... | ... | ... | ... | ... | ... | ... | ... | ... | ... |
| | | | | | | | | | | | | |
| 632 | 598 | 569 | 515 | 453 | 472 | 467 | 433 | 438 | 441 | 571 | 659 | 499 |
| 49 574 | 48 427 | 47 620 | 44 432 | 40 331 | 43 412 | 44 408 | 42 532 | 44 518 | 46 293 | 44 080 | 43 005 | 45 155 |
| 0.48 | 0.46 | 0.45 | 0.41 | 0.35 | 0.37 | 0.36 | 0.34 | 0.34 | 0.34 | 0.43 | 0.50 | 0.38 |
| | | | | | | | | | | | | |
| 627 | 649 | 658 | 615 | 560 | 599 | 605 | 577 | 604 | 632 | 551 | 450 | 615 |
| 49 141 | 52 545 | 55 007 | 53 060 | 49 888 | 55 154 | 57 552 | 56 704 | 61 346 | 66 407 | 42 542 | 29 404 | 55 680 |
| 0.48 | 0.46 | 0.45 | 0.41 | 0.35 | 0.37 | 0.36 | 0.34 | 0.34 | 0.34 | 0.41 | 0.50 | 0.38 |
| | | | | | | | | | | | | |
| 762 | 721 | 686 | 620 | 546 | 569 | 563 | 522 | 528 | 531 | 688 | 794 | 601 |
| 59 745 | 58 363 | 57 390 | 53 549 | 48 607 | 52 320 | 53 519 | 51 258 | 53 653 | 55 792 | 53 124 | 51 829 | 54 420 |
| 0.47 | 0.45 | 0.44 | 0.40 | 0.35 | 0.36 | 0.36 | 0.33 | 0.34 | 0.34 | 0.43 | 0.49 | 0.38 |
| | | | | | | | | | | | | |
| 1 125 | 972 | 909 | 778 | 787 | 736 | 367 | 215 | 228 | 157 | 571 | 517 | 601 |
| 88 254 | 78 748 | 76 006 | 67 161 | 70 149 | 67 757 | 34 919 | 21 166 | 23 205 | 16 520 | 44 053 | 33 718 | 54 389 |
| 0.77 | 0.67 | 0.65 | 0.57 | 0.57 | 0.54 | 0.24 | 0.13 | 0.12 | 0.08 | 0.44 | 0.56 | 0.38 |
| | | | | | | | | | | | | |
| 14 125 | 13 923 | 13 644 | 13 357 | 13 392 | 14 010 | 16 679 | 20 063 | 21 409 | 21 651 | 11 506 | 6 632 | 16 245 |
| 57 713 | 57 086 | 56 131 | 55 126 | 55 441 | 58 183 | 69 468 | 83 803 | 89 681 | 90 954 | 46 933 | 26 507 | 67 359 |
| 0.50 | 0.49 | 0.48 | 0.46 | 0.45 | 0.46 | 0.47 | 0.49 | 0.47 | 0.45 | 0.46 | 0.43 | 0.47 |
| | | | | | | | | | | | | |
| 11 108 | 12 329 | 12 972 | 13 469 | 15 173 | 15 596 | 16 527 | 17 290 | 19 116 | 20 085 | 10 635 | 5 745 | 15 386 |
| 45 387 | 50 550 | 53 367 | 55 585 | 62 816 | 64 770 | 68 834 | 72 222 | 80 078 | 84 377 | 43 381 | 22 964 | 63 799 |
| ... | ... | ... | ... | ... | ... | ... | ... | ... | ... | ... | ... | ... |
| | | | | | | | | | | | | |
| 13 549 | 13 621 | 13 620 | 14 206 | 14 975 | 15 715 | 16 325 | 16 603 | 17 760 | 17 925 | 11 506 | 7 468 | 15 439 |
| 55 360 | 55 846 | 56 032 | 58 629 | 61 996 | 65 266 | 67 995 | 69 349 | 74 395 | 75 301 | 46 933 | 29 849 | 64 017 |
| 0.53 | 0.53 | 0.53 | 0.53 | 0.54 | 0.55 | 0.56 | 0.55 | 0.56 | 0.55 | 0.46 | 0.35 | 0.54 |
| | | | | | | | | | | | | |
| 13 430 | 14 779 | 15 733 | 16 965 | 18 523 | 19 966 | 21 157 | 22 135 | 24 472 | 25 713 | 12 548 | 5 572 | 19 316 |
| 54 876 | 60 595 | 64 724 | 70 013 | 76 686 | 82 918 | 88 121 | 92 458 | 102 515 | 108 019 | 51 181 | 22 270 | 80 093 |
| 0.53 | 0.53 | 0.53 | 0.53 | 0.54 | 0.55 | 0.56 | 0.55 | 0.56 | 0.55 | 0.50 | 0.38 | 0.55 |
| | | | | | | | | | | | | |
| 14 256 | 14 332 | 14 331 | 14 948 | 15 757 | 16 536 | 17 177 | 17 469 | 18 687 | 18 860 | 12 107 | 7 858 | 16 245 |
| 58 250 | 58 761 | 58 957 | 61 689 | 65 232 | 68 673 | 71 544 | 72 969 | 78 278 | 79 232 | 49 383 | 31 407 | 67 359 |
| 0.46 | 0.46 | 0.45 | 0.46 | 0.47 | 0.48 | 0.48 | 0.48 | 0.49 | 0.48 | 0.40 | 0.30 | 0.47 |
| | | | | | | | | | | | | |
| 14 124 | 13 925 | 13 644 | 13 357 | 13 393 | 14 009 | 16 680 | 19 951 | 21 353 | 21 636 | 11 497 | 6 632 | 16 226 |
| 57 711 | 57 091 | 56 131 | 55 123 | 55 445 | 58 181 | 69 471 | 83 337 | 89 447 | 90 895 | 46 896 | 26 508 | 67 283 |
| 0.50 | 0.48 | 0.48 | 0.47 | 0.45 | 0.46 | 0.47 | 0.50 | 0.48 | 0.46 | 0.46 | 0.44 | 0.48 |

**Table A.1**  Total and per capita gross domestic product of individual countries or areas, expressed in United States dollars, and their individual shares of gross world product, based on alternative conversion rates, 1970–1989 [*cont.*]

| Country or area | 1970 (1) | 1971 (2) | 1972 (3) | 1973 (4) | 1974 (5) | 1975 (6) | 1976 (7) | 1977 (8) | 1978 (9) | 1979 (10) |
|---|---|---|---|---|---|---|---|---|---|---|
| **Oman** | | | | | | | | | | |
| **1.** **MER** | | | | | | | | | | |
| 1a. Per capita GDP | 418 | 473 | 567 | 729 | 2 357 | 2 885 | 3 150 | 3 209 | 3 047 | 3 942 |
| 1b. GDP | 274 | 319 | 392 | 519 | 1 737 | 2 213 | 2 527 | 2 705 | 2 705 | 3 685 |
| 1c. % of GWP | 0.01 | 0.01 | 0.01 | 0.01 | 0.03 | 0.04 | 0.04 | 0.04 | 0.03 | 0.04 |
| **2.** **PPPs** | | | | | | | | | | |
| 2a. Per capita GDP | 618 | 954 | 1 346 | 1 276 | 3 589 | 5 005 | 5 528 | 5 781 | 5 387 | 6 098 |
| 2b. GDP | 405 | 642 | 930 | 909 | 2 645 | 3 839 | 4 434 | 4 874 | 4 783 | 5 702 |
| 2c. % of GWP | ... | ... | ... | ... | ... | ... | ... | ... | ... | ... |
| **3.** **Absolute 1970–1989 PARE** | | | | | | | | | | |
| 3a. Per capita GDP | 4 906 | 5 889 | 5 857 | 5 863 | 4 920 | 4 644 | 4 384 | 3 814 | 3 363 | 3 331 |
| 3b. GDP | 3 214 | 3 963 | 4 047 | 4 175 | 3 626 | 3 562 | 3 516 | 3 215 | 2 986 | 3 114 |
| 3c. % of GWP | 0.05 | 0.05 | 0.05 | 0.05 | 0.04 | 0.04 | 0.04 | 0.03 | 0.03 | 0.03 |
| **4.** **Relative 1970–1989 PARE** | | | | | | | | | | |
| 4a. Per capita GDP | 2 392 | 3 019 | 3 140 | 3 352 | 3 068 | 3 182 | 3 191 | 2 964 | 2 804 | 3 025 |
| 4b. GDP | 1 567 | 2 031 | 2 170 | 2 387 | 2 261 | 2 440 | 2 559 | 2 498 | 2 490 | 2 828 |
| 4c. % of GWP | 0.05 | 0.05 | 0.05 | 0.05 | 0.04 | 0.04 | 0.04 | 0.03 | 0.03 | 0.03 |
| **5.** **Absolute 1980–1989 PARE** | | | | | | | | | | |
| 5a. Per capita GDP | 6 406 | 7 689 | 7 648 | 7 656 | 6 424 | 6 064 | 5 724 | 4 980 | 4 391 | 4 349 |
| 5b. GDP | 4 196 | 5 175 | 5 285 | 5 451 | 4 734 | 4 651 | 4 591 | 4 198 | 3 900 | 4 066 |
| 5c. % of GWP | 0.05 | 0.06 | 0.06 | 0.05 | 0.05 | 0.04 | 0.04 | 0.04 | 0.03 | 0.03 |
| **6.** **WA** | | | | | | | | | | |
| 6a. Per capita GDP | 418 | 478 | 568 | 725 | 2 388 | 2 923 | 3 192 | 3 252 | 3 087 | 3 994 |
| 6b. GDP | 274 | 322 | 392 | 517 | 1 760 | 2 242 | 2 560 | 2 741 | 2 741 | 3 735 |
| 6c. % of GWP | 0.01 | 0.01 | 0.01 | 0.01 | 0.03 | 0.04 | 0.04 | 0.04 | 0.03 | 0.04 |
| **Pakistan** | | | | | | | | | | |
| **1.** **MER** | | | | | | | | | | |
| 1a. Per capita GDP | 162 | 170 | 109 | 124 | 154 | 176 | 198 | 227 | 245 | 286 |
| 1b. GDP | 10 666 | 11 469 | 7 539 | 8 815 | 11 231 | 13 168 | 15 126 | 17 812 | 19 688 | 23 654 |
| 1c. % of GWP | 0.33 | 0.33 | 0.19 | 0.18 | 0.20 | 0.21 | 0.23 | 0.24 | 0.22 | 0.23 |
| **2.** **PPPs** | | | | | | | | | | |
| 2a. Per capita GDP | 386 | 401 | 429 | 466 | 489 | 547 | 601 | 685 | 729 | 841 |
| 2b. GDP | 25 341 | 27 027 | 29 706 | 33 096 | 35 653 | 40 869 | 46 004 | 53 714 | 58 649 | 69 551 |
| 2c. % of GWP | ... | ... | ... | ... | ... | ... | ... | ... | ... | ... |
| **3.** **Absolute 1970–1989 PARE** | | | | | | | | | | |
| 3a. Per capita GDP | 216 | 214 | 222 | 228 | 229 | 234 | 237 | 250 | 255 | 270 |
| 3b. GDP | 14 216 | 14 423 | 15 368 | 16 186 | 16 709 | 17 479 | 18 143 | 19 595 | 20 536 | 22 323 |
| 3c. % of GWP | 0.20 | 0.19 | 0.20 | 0.20 | 0.20 | 0.20 | 0.20 | 0.21 | 0.21 | 0.22 |
| **4.** **Relative 1970–1989 PARE** | | | | | | | | | | |
| 4a. Per capita GDP | 105 | 110 | 119 | 130 | 143 | 160 | 172 | 194 | 213 | 245 |
| 4b. GDP | 6 932 | 7 393 | 8 239 | 9 254 | 10 420 | 11 975 | 13 206 | 15 225 | 17 121 | 20 272 |
| 4c. % of GWP | 0.20 | 0.19 | 0.20 | 0.20 | 0.20 | 0.20 | 0.20 | 0.21 | 0.21 | 0.22 |
| **5.** **Absolute 1980–1989 PARE** | | | | | | | | | | |
| 5a. Per capita GDP | 241 | 238 | 247 | 253 | 255 | 260 | 264 | 278 | 284 | 301 |
| 5b. GDP | 15 826 | 16 056 | 17 108 | 18 018 | 18 600 | 19 457 | 20 196 | 21 813 | 22 861 | 24 850 |
| 5c. % of GWP | 0.18 | 0.18 | 0.18 | 0.18 | 0.18 | 0.19 | 0.18 | 0.19 | 0.19 | 0.20 |
| **6.** **WA** | | | | | | | | | | |
| 6a. Per capita GDP | 162 | 170 | 168 | 117 | 154 | 176 | 198 | 227 | 245 | 286 |
| 6b. GDP | 10 666 | 11 481 | 11 623 | 8 333 | 11 231 | 13 168 | 15 126 | 17 812 | 19 688 | 23 654 |
| 6c. % of GWP | 0.33 | 0.33 | 0.29 | 0.17 | 0.20 | 0.21 | 0.23 | 0.24 | 0.22 | 0.23 |

| | | | | | | | | | | Averages | | |
| 1980 (11) | 1981 (12) | 1982 (13) | 1983 (14) | 1984 (15) | 1985 (16) | 1986 (17) | 1987 (18) | 1988 (19) | 1989 (20) | 1970–89 (21) | 1970–79 (22) | 1980–89 (23) |
|---|---|---|---|---|---|---|---|---|---|---|---|---|
| 5 992 | 6 875 | 6 876 | 6 873 | 7 309 | 7 939 | 5 695 | 5 875 | 5 507 | 5 871 | 4 972 | 2 271 | 6 437 |
| 5 896 | 7 116 | 7 467 | 7 828 | 8 705 | 9 868 | 7 369 | 7 902 | 7 682 | 8 502 | 4 771 | 1 708 | 7 834 |
| 0.05 | 0.06 | 0.06 | 0.07 | 0.07 | 0.08 | 0.05 | 0.05 | 0.04 | 0.04 | 0.05 | 0.03 | 0.05 |
| | | | | | | | | | | | | |
| 6 629 | 7 699 | 8 283 | 8 528 | 9 049 | 9 733 | 10 306 | 9 843 | 10 371 | 11 230 | 7 428 | 3 878 | 9 316 |
| 6 523 | 7 969 | 8 995 | 9 713 | 10 777 | 12 098 | 13 336 | 13 239 | 14 468 | 16 261 | 7 127 | 2 916 | 11 338 |
| ... | ... | ... | ... | ... | ... | ... | ... | ... | ... | ... | ... | ... |
| | | | | | | | | | | | | |
| 3 549 | 3 949 | 4 199 | 4 642 | 5 181 | 5 406 | 5 611 | 5 210 | 5 311 | 5 524 | 4 972 | 4 710 | 4 930 |
| 3 492 | 4 087 | 4 560 | 5 287 | 6 171 | 6 719 | 7 261 | 7 007 | 7 409 | 7 999 | 4 771 | 3 542 | 5 999 |
| 0.03 | 0.04 | 0.04 | 0.05 | 0.05 | 0.06 | 0.06 | 0.06 | 0.06 | 0.06 | 0.05 | 0.04 | 0.05 |
| | | | | | | | | | | | | |
| 3 518 | 4 285 | 4 850 | 5 544 | 6 409 | 6 868 | 7 272 | 6 946 | 7 318 | 7 924 | 5 175 | 3 089 | 6 252 |
| 3 462 | 4 435 | 5 267 | 6 314 | 7 633 | 8 537 | 9 410 | 9 342 | 10 209 | 11 474 | 4 966 | 2 323 | 7 608 |
| 0.03 | 0.04 | 0.04 | 0.05 | 0.05 | 0.06 | 0.06 | 0.06 | 0.06 | 0.06 | 0.05 | 0.04 | 0.05 |
| | | | | | | | | | | | | |
| 4 634 | 5 157 | 5 482 | 6 061 | 6 765 | 7 058 | 7 327 | 6 803 | 6 935 | 7 213 | 6 492 | 6 150 | 6 437 |
| 4 560 | 5 337 | 5 954 | 6 904 | 8 058 | 8 774 | 9 481 | 9 149 | 9 674 | 10 444 | 6 229 | 4 625 | 7 834 |
| 0.04 | 0.04 | 0.05 | 0.05 | 0.06 | 0.06 | 0.06 | 0.06 | 0.06 | 0.06 | 0.05 | 0.04 | 0.05 |
| | | | | | | | | | | | | |
| 6 071 | 6 967 | 6 968 | 6 964 | 7 406 | 8 045 | 5 666 | 5 806 | 5 443 | 5 803 | 4 999 | 2 298 | 6 462 |
| 5 974 | 7 210 | 7 567 | 7 933 | 8 821 | 10 000 | 7 331 | 7 809 | 7 592 | 8 402 | 4 796 | 1 728 | 7 864 |
| 0.05 | 0.06 | 0.06 | 0.07 | 0.07 | 0.08 | 0.05 | 0.05 | 0.04 | 0.04 | 0.05 | 0.03 | 0.06 |
| | | | | | | | | | | | | |
| 333 | 375 | 339 | 339 | 342 | 317 | 325 | 354 | 378 | 361 | 293 | 189 | 348 |
| 28 418 | 33 137 | 31 118 | 32 373 | 34 002 | 32 699 | 34 814 | 39 294 | 43 411 | 42 888 | 24 566 | 13 917 | 35 216 |
| 0.25 | 0.28 | 0.27 | 0.27 | 0.28 | 0.26 | 0.23 | 0.23 | 0.23 | 0.21 | 0.24 | 0.23 | 0.25 |
| | | | | | | | | | | | | |
| 949 | 1 050 | 1 132 | 1 195 | 1 239 | 1 268 | 1 327 | 1 418 | 1 486 | 1 570 | 1 026 | 568 | 1 286 |
| 80 987 | 92 742 | 103 935 | 114 159 | 123 142 | 130 929 | 142 178 | 157 416 | 170 811 | 186 556 | 86 123 | 41 961 | 130 286 |
| ... | ... | ... | ... | ... | ... | ... | ... | ... | ... | ... | ... | ... |
| | | | | | | | | | | | | |
| 277 | 285 | 293 | 296 | 306 | 311 | 319 | 331 | 336 | 341 | 293 | 237 | 312 |
| 23 637 | 25 183 | 26 890 | 28 252 | 30 397 | 32 069 | 34 138 | 36 741 | 38 572 | 40 469 | 24 566 | 17 498 | 31 635 |
| 0.23 | 0.24 | 0.25 | 0.26 | 0.27 | 0.27 | 0.28 | 0.29 | 0.29 | 0.30 | 0.24 | 0.20 | 0.27 |
| | | | | | | | | | | | | |
| 275 | 309 | 338 | 353 | 378 | 395 | 413 | 441 | 463 | 489 | 309 | 163 | 393 |
| 23 431 | 27 324 | 31 061 | 33 737 | 37 599 | 40 742 | 44 243 | 48 984 | 53 153 | 58 052 | 25 918 | 12 004 | 39 833 |
| 0.23 | 0.24 | 0.25 | 0.26 | 0.27 | 0.27 | 0.28 | 0.29 | 0.29 | 0.30 | 0.25 | 0.20 | 0.27 |
| | | | | | | | | | | | | |
| 308 | 317 | 326 | 329 | 341 | 346 | 355 | 368 | 374 | 379 | 326 | 264 | 348 |
| 26 313 | 28 033 | 29 933 | 31 450 | 33 837 | 35 699 | 38 002 | 40 900 | 42 939 | 45 049 | 27 347 | 19 478 | 35 216 |
| 0.21 | 0.22 | 0.23 | 0.24 | 0.24 | 0.25 | 0.26 | 0.27 | 0.27 | 0.27 | 0.22 | 0.18 | 0.25 |
| | | | | | | | | | | | | |
| 333 | 375 | 381 | 350 | 357 | 333 | 335 | 359 | 387 | 386 | 303 | 193 | 361 |
| 28 418 | 33 137 | 34 944 | 33 436 | 35 440 | 34 356 | 35 932 | 39 832 | 44 512 | 45 884 | 25 434 | 14 278 | 36 589 |
| 0.25 | 0.28 | 0.30 | 0.28 | 0.29 | 0.27 | 0.24 | 0.24 | 0.24 | 0.23 | 0.25 | 0.24 | 0.26 |

**Table A.1** Total and per capita gross domestic product of individual countries or areas, expressed in United States dollars, and their individual shares of gross world product, based on alternative conversion rates, 1970−1989 [*cont.*]

| Country or area | 1970 (1) | 1971 (2) | 1972 (3) | 1973 (4) | 1974 (5) | 1975 (6) | 1976 (7) | 1977 (8) | 1978 (9) | 1979 (10) |
|---|---|---|---|---|---|---|---|---|---|---|
| **Panama** | | | | | | | | | | |
| **1. MER** | | | | | | | | | | |
| 1a. Per capita GDP | 667 | 731 | 782 | 870 | 970 | 1 053 | 1 093 | 1 130 | 1 309 | 1 462 |
| 1b. GDP | 1 021 | 1 152 | 1 265 | 1 447 | 1 654 | 1 841 | 1 956 | 2 070 | 2 453 | 2 800 |
| 1c. % of GWP | 0.03 | 0.03 | 0.03 | 0.03 | 0.03 | 0.03 | 0.03 | 0.03 | 0.03 | 0.03 |
| **2. PPPs** | | | | | | | | | | |
| 2a. Per capita GDP | 1 006 | 1 150 | 1 265 | 1 388 | 1 515 | 1 648 | 1 708 | 1 730 | 2 021 | 2 226 |
| 2b. GDP | 1 541 | 1 812 | 2 047 | 2 306 | 2 583 | 2 880 | 3 058 | 3 170 | 3 785 | 4 263 |
| 2c. % of GWP | ... | ... | ... | ... | ... | ... | ... | ... | ... | ... |
| **3. Absolute 1970−1989 PARE** | | | | | | | | | | |
| 3a. Per capita GDP | 1 317 | 1 404 | 1 429 | 1 466 | 1 464 | 1 453 | 1 442 | 1 425 | 1 530 | 1 564 |
| 3b. GDP | 2 017 | 2 211 | 2 312 | 2 437 | 2 496 | 2 540 | 2 582 | 2 610 | 2 866 | 2 995 |
| 3c. % of GWP | 0.03 | 0.03 | 0.03 | 0.03 | 0.03 | 0.03 | 0.03 | 0.03 | 0.03 | 0.03 |
| **4. Relative 1970−1989 PARE** | | | | | | | | | | |
| 4a. Per capita GDP | 642 | 720 | 766 | 838 | 913 | 995 | 1 050 | 1 107 | 1 276 | 1 420 |
| 4b. GDP | 984 | 1 133 | 1 240 | 1 393 | 1 557 | 1 740 | 1 879 | 2 028 | 2 389 | 2 720 |
| 4c. % of GWP | 0.03 | 0.03 | 0.03 | 0.03 | 0.03 | 0.03 | 0.03 | 0.03 | 0.03 | 0.03 |
| **5. Absolute 1980−1989 PARE** | | | | | | | | | | |
| 5a. Per capita GDP | 1 575 | 1 680 | 1 710 | 1 754 | 1 752 | 1 738 | 1 726 | 1 705 | 1 831 | 1 871 |
| 5b. GDP | 2 414 | 2 646 | 2 767 | 2 915 | 2 987 | 3 039 | 3 089 | 3 123 | 3 429 | 3 584 |
| 5c. % of GWP | 0.03 | 0.03 | 0.03 | 0.03 | 0.03 | 0.03 | 0.03 | 0.03 | 0.03 | 0.03 |
| **6. WA** | | | | | | | | | | |
| 6a. Per capita GDP | 667 | 731 | 782 | 870 | 970 | 1 053 | 1 093 | 1 130 | 1 309 | 1 462 |
| 6b. GDP | 1 021 | 1 152 | 1 265 | 1 447 | 1 654 | 1 841 | 1 956 | 2 070 | 2 453 | 2 800 |
| 6c. % of GWP | 0.03 | 0.03 | 0.03 | 0.03 | 0.03 | 0.03 | 0.03 | 0.03 | 0.03 | 0.03 |
| **Papua New Guinea** | | | | | | | | | | |
| **1. MER** | | | | | | | | | | |
| 1a. Per capita GDP | 317 | 328 | 411 | 631 | 604 | 567 | 624 | 622 | 738 | 827 |
| 1b. GDP | 769 | 815 | 1 043 | 1 642 | 1 608 | 1 546 | 1 745 | 1 784 | 2 170 | 2 492 |
| 1c. % of GWP | 0.02 | 0.02 | 0.03 | 0.03 | 0.03 | 0.02 | 0.03 | 0.02 | 0.02 | 0.02 |
| **2. PPPs** | | | | | | | | | | |
| 2a. Per capita GDP | 963 | 992 | 982 | 1 101 | 1 114 | 1 158 | 1 226 | 1 292 | 1 401 | 1 581 |
| 2b. GDP | 2 332 | 2 461 | 2 494 | 2 865 | 2 968 | 3 160 | 3 430 | 3 706 | 4 119 | 4 765 |
| 2c. % of GWP | ... | ... | ... | ... | ... | ... | ... | ... | ... | ... |
| **3. Absolute 1970−1989 PARE** | | | | | | | | | | |
| 3a. Per capita GDP | 781 | 782 | 830 | 839 | 826 | 794 | 741 | 689 | 730 | 725 |
| 3b. GDP | 1 893 | 1 940 | 2 108 | 2 182 | 2 201 | 2 166 | 2 072 | 1 977 | 2 147 | 2 185 |
| 3c. % of GWP | 0.03 | 0.03 | 0.03 | 0.03 | 0.03 | 0.03 | 0.02 | 0.02 | 0.02 | 0.02 |
| **4. Relative 1970−1989 PARE** | | | | | | | | | | |
| 4a. Per capita GDP | 381 | 401 | 445 | 480 | 515 | 544 | 539 | 536 | 609 | 659 |
| 4b. GDP | 923 | 994 | 1 130 | 1 248 | 1 373 | 1 484 | 1 509 | 1 536 | 1 790 | 1 985 |
| 4c. % of GWP | 0.03 | 0.03 | 0.03 | 0.03 | 0.03 | 0.03 | 0.02 | 0.02 | 0.02 | 0.02 |
| **5. Absolute 1980−1989 PARE** | | | | | | | | | | |
| 5a. Per capita GDP | 960 | 961 | 1 020 | 1 031 | 1 016 | 975 | 911 | 847 | 897 | 891 |
| 5b. GDP | 2 327 | 2 384 | 2 592 | 2 682 | 2 706 | 2 662 | 2 547 | 2 430 | 2 638 | 2 686 |
| 5c. % of GWP | 0.03 | 0.03 | 0.03 | 0.03 | 0.03 | 0.03 | 0.02 | 0.02 | 0.02 | 0.02 |
| **6. WA** | | | | | | | | | | |
| 6a. Per capita GDP | 317 | 326 | 411 | 627 | 600 | 566 | 623 | 622 | 737 | 828 |
| 6b. GDP | 769 | 808 | 1 043 | 1 632 | 1 599 | 1 545 | 1 743 | 1 784 | 2 167 | 2 493 |
| 6c. % of GWP | 0.02 | 0.02 | 0.03 | 0.03 | 0.03 | 0.03 | 0.03 | 0.02 | 0.02 | 0.02 |

| | | | | | | | | | | Averages | | |
|---|---|---|---|---|---|---|---|---|---|---|---|---|
| 1980 | 1981 | 1982 | 1983 | 1984 | 1985 | 1986 | 1987 | 1988 | 1989 | 1970–89 | 1970–79 | 1980–89 |
| (11) | (12) | (13) | (14) | (15) | (16) | (17) | (18) | (19) | (20) | (21) | (22) | (23) |
| 1 818 | 1 939 | 2 093 | 2 094 | 2 138 | 2 247 | 2 309 | 2 334 | 1 960 | 1 919 | 1 621 | 1 023 | 2 090 |
| 3 559 | 3 878 | 4 279 | 4 374 | 4 566 | 4 901 | 5 145 | 5 310 | 4 551 | 4 549 | 3 138 | 1 766 | 4 511 |
| 0.03 | 0.03 | 0.04 | 0.04 | 0.04 | 0.04 | 0.03 | 0.03 | 0.02 | 0.02 | 0.03 | 0.03 | 0.03 |
| 2 635 | 2 994 | 3 229 | 3 321 | 3 389 | 3 559 | 3 674 | 3 786 | 3 220 | 3 257 | 2 560 | 1 590 | 3 321 |
| 5 157 | 5 988 | 6 599 | 6 937 | 7 236 | 7 762 | 8 185 | 8 614 | 7 477 | 7 719 | 4 956 | 2 744 | 7 168 |
| ... | ... | ... | ... | ... | ... | ... | ... | ... | ... | ... | ... | ... |
| 1 762 | 1 796 | 1 854 | 1 821 | 1 774 | 1 819 | 1 841 | 1 844 | 1 517 | 1 474 | 1 621 | 1 452 | 1 747 |
| 3 448 | 3 593 | 3 790 | 3 804 | 3 788 | 3 967 | 4 101 | 4 195 | 3 523 | 3 494 | 3 138 | 2 507 | 3 770 |
| 0.03 | 0.03 | 0.04 | 0.03 | 0.03 | 0.03 | 0.03 | 0.03 | 0.03 | 0.03 | 0.03 | 0.03 | 0.03 |
| 1 747 | 1 949 | 2 142 | 2 174 | 2 195 | 2 311 | 2 385 | 2 459 | 2 091 | 2 115 | 1 648 | 988 | 2 166 |
| 3 418 | 3 898 | 4 378 | 4 542 | 4 685 | 5 040 | 5 315 | 5 593 | 4 855 | 5 012 | 3 190 | 1 706 | 4 674 |
| 0.03 | 0.03 | 0.04 | 0.03 | 0.03 | 0.03 | 0.03 | 0.03 | 0.03 | 0.03 | 0.03 | 0.03 | 0.03 |
| 2 108 | 2 149 | 2 218 | 2 179 | 2 123 | 2 176 | 2 202 | 2 206 | 1 816 | 1 764 | 1 940 | 1 737 | 2 090 |
| 4 126 | 4 299 | 4 534 | 4 551 | 4 532 | 4 747 | 4 906 | 5 019 | 4 216 | 4 181 | 3 755 | 2 999 | 4 511 |
| 0.03 | 0.03 | 0.03 | 0.03 | 0.03 | 0.03 | 0.03 | 0.03 | 0.03 | 0.03 | 0.03 | 0.03 | 0.03 |
| 1 818 | 1 939 | 2 093 | 2 094 | 2 138 | 2 247 | 2 309 | 2 334 | 1 960 | 1 919 | 1 621 | 1 023 | 2 090 |
| 3 559 | 3 878 | 4 279 | 4 374 | 4 566 | 4 901 | 5 145 | 5 310 | 4 551 | 4 549 | 3 138 | 1 766 | 4 511 |
| 0.03 | 0.03 | 0.04 | 0.04 | 0.04 | 0.04 | 0.03 | 0.03 | 0.02 | 0.02 | 0.03 | 0.03 | 0.03 |
| 898 | 861 | 797 | 778 | 754 | 694 | 743 | 869 | 942 | 884 | 718 | 579 | 824 |
| 2 771 | 2 720 | 2 576 | 2 573 | 2 553 | 2 403 | 2 631 | 3 146 | 3 490 | 3 349 | 2 191 | 1 561 | 2 821 |
| 0.02 | 0.02 | 0.02 | 0.02 | 0.02 | 0.02 | 0.02 | 0.02 | 0.02 | 0.02 | 0.02 | 0.03 | 0.02 |
| 1 623 | 1 632 | 1 677 | 1 778 | 1 736 | 1 783 | 1 850 | 1 928 | 2 006 | 2 011 | 1 547 | 1 198 | 1 814 |
| 5 009 | 5 158 | 5 423 | 5 883 | 5 874 | 6 172 | 6 549 | 6 981 | 7 428 | 7 619 | 4 720 | 3 230 | 6 209 |
| ... | ... | ... | ... | ... | ... | ... | ... | ... | ... | ... | ... | ... |
| 692 | 674 | 664 | 671 | 650 | 658 | 669 | 678 | 683 | 657 | 718 | 774 | 671 |
| 2 135 | 2 129 | 2 147 | 2 221 | 2 199 | 2 278 | 2 370 | 2 455 | 2 528 | 2 490 | 2 191 | 2 087 | 2 295 |
| 0.02 | 0.02 | 0.02 | 0.02 | 0.02 | 0.02 | 0.02 | 0.02 | 0.02 | 0.02 | 0.02 | 0.02 | 0.02 |
| 686 | 731 | 767 | 802 | 804 | 836 | 868 | 904 | 941 | 943 | 697 | 518 | 835 |
| 2 117 | 2 310 | 2 480 | 2 652 | 2 720 | 2 894 | 3 071 | 3 273 | 3 483 | 3 573 | 2 127 | 1 397 | 2 857 |
| 0.02 | 0.02 | 0.02 | 0.02 | 0.02 | 0.02 | 0.02 | 0.02 | 0.02 | 0.02 | 0.02 | 0.02 | 0.02 |
| 850 | 828 | 816 | 825 | 799 | 809 | 823 | 833 | 839 | 808 | 883 | 951 | 824 |
| 2 624 | 2 617 | 2 639 | 2 730 | 2 703 | 2 800 | 2 912 | 3 018 | 3 107 | 3 061 | 2 693 | 2 565 | 2 821 |
| 0.02 | 0.02 | 0.02 | 0.02 | 0.02 | 0.02 | 0.02 | 0.02 | 0.02 | 0.02 | 0.02 | 0.02 | 0.02 |
| 896 | 859 | 796 | 776 | 751 | 694 | 743 | 861 | 978 | 926 | 722 | 578 | 831 |
| 2 767 | 2 716 | 2 575 | 2 566 | 2 540 | 2 402 | 2 630 | 3 118 | 3 623 | 3 509 | 2 201 | 1 558 | 2 845 |
| 0.02 | 0.02 | 0.02 | 0.02 | 0.02 | 0.02 | 0.02 | 0.02 | 0.02 | 0.02 | 0.02 | 0.03 | 0.02 |

**Table A.1**    Total and per capita gross domestic product of individual countries or areas, expressed in United States dollars, and their individual shares of gross world product, based on alternative conversion rates, 1970−1989 [*cont.*]

| Country or area | 1970 (1) | 1971 (2) | 1972 (3) | 1973 (4) | 1974 (5) | 1975 (6) | 1976 (7) | 1977 (8) | 1978 (9) | 1979 (10) |
|---|---|---|---|---|---|---|---|---|---|---|
| **Paraguay** | | | | | | | | | | |
| 1.  **MER** | | | | | | | | | | |
| 1a.  Per capita GDP | 253 | 275 | 311 | 392 | 511 | 564 | 615 | 733 | 869 | 1 122 |
| 1b.  GDP | 595 | 665 | 769 | 996 | 1 333 | 1 511 | 1 699 | 2 092 | 2 560 | 3 417 |
| 1c.  % of GWP | 0.02 | 0.02 | 0.02 | 0.02 | 0.02 | 0.02 | 0.03 | 0.03 | 0.03 | 0.03 |
| 2.  **PPPs** | | | | | | | | | | |
| 2a.  Per capita GDP | 608 | 665 | 696 | 753 | 862 | 933 | 1 052 | 1 233 | 1 401 | 1 573 |
| 2b.  GDP | 1 431 | 1 604 | 1 723 | 1 913 | 2 248 | 2 502 | 2 909 | 3 518 | 4 129 | 4 791 |
| 2c.  % of GWP | ... | ... | ... | ... | ... | ... | ... | ... | ... | ... |
| 3.  **Absolute 1970−1989 PARE** | | | | | | | | | | |
| 3a.  Per capita GDP | 720 | 741 | 771 | 808 | 854 | 890 | 926 | 995 | 1 073 | 1 156 |
| 3b.  GDP | 1 692 | 1 789 | 1 909 | 2 052 | 2 226 | 2 387 | 2 560 | 2 840 | 3 162 | 3 521 |
| 3c.  % of GWP | 0.02 | 0.02 | 0.02 | 0.02 | 0.03 | 0.03 | 0.03 | 0.03 | 0.03 | 0.03 |
| 4.  **Relative 1970−1989 PARE** | | | | | | | | | | |
| 4a.  Per capita GDP | 351 | 380 | 413 | 462 | 533 | 610 | 674 | 773 | 894 | 1 050 |
| 4b.  GDP | 825 | 917 | 1 023 | 1 173 | 1 388 | 1 635 | 1 863 | 2 206 | 2 636 | 3 198 |
| 4c.  % of GWP | 0.02 | 0.02 | 0.02 | 0.02 | 0.03 | 0.03 | 0.03 | 0.03 | 0.03 | 0.03 |
| 5.  **Absolute 1980−1989 PARE** | | | | | | | | | | |
| 5a.  Per capita GDP | 858 | 884 | 920 | 964 | 1 018 | 1 061 | 1 105 | 1 187 | 1 280 | 1 379 |
| 5b.  GDP | 2 018 | 2 134 | 2 276 | 2 447 | 2 655 | 2 846 | 3 053 | 3 387 | 3 771 | 4 199 |
| 5c.  % of GWP | 0.02 | 0.02 | 0.02 | 0.02 | 0.03 | 0.03 | 0.03 | 0.03 | 0.03 | 0.03 |
| 6.  **WA** | | | | | | | | | | |
| 6a.  Per capita GDP | 253 | 275 | 311 | 392 | 511 | 564 | 615 | 733 | 869 | 1 122 |
| 6b.  GDP | 595 | 665 | 769 | 996 | 1 333 | 1 511 | 1 699 | 2 092 | 2 560 | 3 417 |
| 6c.  % of GWP | 0.02 | 0.02 | 0.02 | 0.02 | 0.02 | 0.02 | 0.03 | 0.03 | 0.03 | 0.03 |
| **Peru** | | | | | | | | | | |
| 1.  **MER** | | | | | | | | | | |
| 1a.  Per capita GDP | 515 | 558 | 604 | 702 | 861 | 1 067 | 911 | 906 | 703 | 915 |
| 1b.  GDP | 6 800 | 7 575 | 8 425 | 10 075 | 12 700 | 16 175 | 14 200 | 14 500 | 11 556 | 15 432 |
| 1c.  % of GWP | 0.21 | 0.22 | 0.21 | 0.21 | 0.23 | 0.26 | 0.21 | 0.19 | 0.13 | 0.15 |
| 2.  **PPPs** | | | | | | | | | | |
| 2a.  Per capita GDP | 1 090 | 1 176 | 1 206 | 1 342 | 1 537 | 1 655 | 1 748 | 1 807 | 1 798 | 2 027 |
| 2b.  GDP | 14 374 | 15 955 | 16 833 | 19 254 | 22 668 | 25 099 | 27 227 | 28 928 | 29 544 | 34 187 |
| 2c.  % of GWP | ... | ... | ... | ... | ... | ... | ... | ... | ... | ... |
| 3.  **Absolute 1970−1989 PARE** | | | | | | | | | | |
| 3a.  Per capita GDP | 1 118 | 1 133 | 1 133 | 1 161 | 1 233 | 1 241 | 1 231 | 1 203 | 1 175 | 1 212 |
| 3b.  GDP | 14 751 | 15 366 | 15 805 | 16 654 | 18 194 | 18 815 | 19 184 | 19 260 | 19 319 | 20 437 |
| 3c.  % of GWP | 0.21 | 0.21 | 0.20 | 0.20 | 0.21 | 0.22 | 0.21 | 0.20 | 0.20 | 0.20 |
| 4.  **Relative 1970−1989 PARE** | | | | | | | | | | |
| 4a.  Per capita GDP | 545 | 581 | 607 | 664 | 769 | 850 | 896 | 935 | 980 | 1 100 |
| 4b.  GDP | 7 192 | 7 876 | 8 473 | 9 521 | 11 346 | 12 890 | 13 964 | 14 965 | 16 106 | 18 560 |
| 4c.  % of GWP | 0.21 | 0.21 | 0.20 | 0.20 | 0.21 | 0.22 | 0.21 | 0.20 | 0.20 | 0.20 |
| 5.  **Absolute 1980−1989 PARE** | | | | | | | | | | |
| 5a.  Per capita GDP | 1 428 | 1 446 | 1 447 | 1 483 | 1 575 | 1 585 | 1 573 | 1 537 | 1 501 | 1 548 |
| 5b.  GDP | 18 841 | 19 626 | 20 187 | 21 272 | 23 239 | 24 031 | 24 503 | 24 600 | 24 675 | 26 103 |
| 5c.  % of GWP | 0.22 | 0.22 | 0.21 | 0.21 | 0.22 | 0.23 | 0.22 | 0.21 | 0.21 | 0.21 |
| 6.  **WA** | | | | | | | | | | |
| 6a.  Per capita GDP | 529 | 573 | 619 | 720 | 883 | 1 041 | 977 | 863 | 721 | 895 |
| 6b.  GDP | 6 974 | 7 769 | 8 641 | 10 333 | 13 026 | 15 780 | 15 214 | 13 810 | 11 853 | 15 089 |
| 6c.  % of GWP | 0.22 | 0.22 | 0.22 | 0.21 | 0.23 | 0.26 | 0.23 | 0.18 | 0.13 | 0.15 |

| | | | | | | | | | | Averages | | |
|---|---|---|---|---|---|---|---|---|---|---|---|---|
| 1980 (11) | 1981 (12) | 1982 (13) | 1983 (14) | 1984 (15) | 1985 (16) | 1986 (17) | 1987 (18) | 1988 (19) | 1989 (20) | 1970–89 (21) | 1970–79 (22) | 1980–89 (23) |
| 1 413 | 1 730 | 1 741 | 1 872 | 1 487 | 1 230 | 1 420 | 1 155 | 1 494 | 1 049 | 1 102 | 591 | 1 447 |
| 4 448 | 5 625 | 5 850 | 6 493 | 5 326 | 4 545 | 5 407 | 4 534 | 6 035 | 4 363 | 3 413 | 1 564 | 5 262 |
| 0.04 | 0.05 | 0.05 | 0.05 | 0.04 | 0.04 | 0.04 | 0.03 | 0.03 | 0.02 | 0.03 | 0.03 | 0.04 |
| 1 875 | 2 123 | 2 107 | 2 045 | 2 275 | 2 343 | 2 319 | 2 415 | 2 578 | 2 759 | 1 788 | 1 012 | 2 308 |
| 5 902 | 6 903 | 7 077 | 7 093 | 8 147 | 8 654 | 8 829 | 9 476 | 10 416 | 11 472 | 5 537 | 2 677 | 8 397 |
| ... | ... | ... | ... | ... | ... | ... | ... | ... | ... | ... | ... | ... |
| 1 247 | 1 312 | 1 257 | 1 181 | 1 179 | 1 189 | 1 153 | 1 167 | 1 206 | 1 240 | 1 102 | 913 | 1 213 |
| 3 924 | 4 266 | 4 224 | 4 097 | 4 223 | 4 391 | 4 391 | 4 581 | 4 872 | 5 155 | 3 413 | 2 414 | 4 412 |
| 0.04 | 0.04 | 0.04 | 0.04 | 0.04 | 0.04 | 0.04 | 0.04 | 0.04 | 0.04 | 0.03 | 0.03 | 0.04 |
| 1 236 | 1 423 | 1 453 | 1 410 | 1 459 | 1 510 | 1 494 | 1 556 | 1 662 | 1 778 | 1 160 | 638 | 1 512 |
| 3 890 | 4 629 | 4 879 | 4 893 | 5 224 | 5 578 | 5 691 | 6 108 | 6 714 | 7 395 | 3 593 | 1 687 | 5 500 |
| 0.04 | 0.04 | 0.04 | 0.04 | 0.04 | 0.04 | 0.04 | 0.04 | 0.04 | 0.04 | 0.03 | 0.03 | 0.04 |
| 1 487 | 1 564 | 1 500 | 1 409 | 1 406 | 1 418 | 1 375 | 1 392 | 1 438 | 1 479 | 1 315 | 1 089 | 1 447 |
| 4 680 | 5 088 | 5 038 | 4 886 | 5 037 | 5 237 | 5 237 | 5 464 | 5 811 | 6 148 | 4 071 | 2 879 | 5 262 |
| 0.04 | 0.04 | 0.04 | 0.04 | 0.04 | 0.04 | 0.04 | 0.04 | 0.04 | 0.04 | 0.03 | 0.03 | 0.04 |
| 1 413 | 1 730 | 1 613 | 1 615 | 1 227 | 856 | 931 | 951 | 978 | 990 | 963 | 591 | 1 209 |
| 4 448 | 5 625 | 5 419 | 5 604 | 4 392 | 3 163 | 3 544 | 3 733 | 3 951 | 4 115 | 2 982 | 1 564 | 4 399 |
| 0.04 | 0.05 | 0.05 | 0.05 | 0.04 | 0.03 | 0.02 | 0.02 | 0.02 | 0.02 | 0.03 | 0.03 | 0.03 |
| 1 157 | 1 394 | 1 374 | 1 046 | 1 075 | 913 | 1 323 | 2 171 | 1 805 | 2 046 | 1 158 | 785 | 1 448 |
| 20 017 | 24 707 | 24 943 | 19 433 | 20 419 | 17 720 | 26 257 | 43 988 | 37 345 | 43 190 | 19 773 | 11 744 | 27 802 |
| 0.17 | 0.21 | 0.21 | 0.16 | 0.17 | 0.14 | 0.18 | 0.26 | 0.20 | 0.22 | 0.19 | 0.19 | 0.19 |
| 2 442 | 2 698 | 2 765 | 2 432 | 2 616 | 2 680 | 2 922 | 3 193 | 2 978 | 2 696 | 2 232 | 1 565 | 2 751 |
| 42 242 | 47 810 | 50 176 | 45 176 | 49 690 | 52 037 | 57 969 | 64 692 | 61 589 | 56 914 | 38 118 | 23 407 | 52 829 |
| ... | ... | ... | ... | ... | ... | ... | ... | ... | ... | ... | ... | ... |
| 1 235 | 1 258 | 1 231 | 1 051 | 1 077 | 1 078 | 1 152 | 1 224 | 1 104 | 960 | 1 158 | 1 189 | 1 133 |
| 21 357 | 22 299 | 22 340 | 19 524 | 20 461 | 20 929 | 22 856 | 24 794 | 22 838 | 20 273 | 19 773 | 17 779 | 21 767 |
| 0.21 | 0.21 | 0.21 | 0.18 | 0.18 | 0.18 | 0.19 | 0.20 | 0.17 | 0.15 | 0.19 | 0.21 | 0.19 |
| 1 224 | 1 365 | 1 422 | 1 255 | 1 332 | 1 369 | 1 493 | 1 632 | 1 522 | 1 377 | 1 143 | 808 | 1 404 |
| 21 170 | 24 196 | 25 806 | 23 315 | 25 309 | 26 590 | 29 621 | 33 056 | 31 471 | 29 082 | 19 525 | 12 090 | 26 961 |
| 0.21 | 0.21 | 0.21 | 0.18 | 0.18 | 0.18 | 0.19 | 0.20 | 0.17 | 0.15 | 0.19 | 0.21 | 0.18 |
| 1 577 | 1 607 | 1 572 | 1 343 | 1 376 | 1 377 | 1 471 | 1 563 | 1 410 | 1 226 | 1 479 | 1 518 | 1 448 |
| 27 278 | 28 482 | 28 534 | 24 936 | 26 133 | 26 732 | 29 192 | 31 668 | 29 170 | 25 894 | 25 255 | 22 708 | 27 802 |
| 0.22 | 0.22 | 0.22 | 0.19 | 0.19 | 0.19 | 0.20 | 0.21 | 0.18 | 0.16 | 0.20 | 0.22 | 0.19 |
| 1 161 | 1 387 | 1 378 | 1 047 | 1 076 | 855 | 1 198 | 1 352 | 922 | 1 356 | 1 006 | 792 | 1 172 |
| 20 087 | 24 590 | 25 014 | 19 444 | 20 437 | 16 608 | 23 771 | 27 390 | 19 070 | 28 627 | 17 176 | 11 849 | 22 504 |
| 0.17 | 0.21 | 0.21 | 0.16 | 0.17 | 0.13 | 0.16 | 0.16 | 0.10 | 0.15 | 0.17 | 0.20 | 0.16 |

**Table A.1**    Total and per capita gross domestic product of individual countries or areas,
expressed in United States dollars, and their individual shares of gross world
product, based on alternative conversion rates, 1970−1989 [*cont.*]

| Country or area | 1970 (1) | 1971 (2) | 1972 (3) | 1973 (4) | 1974 (5) | 1975 (6) | 1976 (7) | 1977 (8) | 1978 (9) | 1979 (10) |
|---|---|---|---|---|---|---|---|---|---|---|
| **Philippines** | | | | | | | | | | |
| **1. MER** | | | | | | | | | | |
| 1a. Per capita GDP | 182 | 202 | 213 | 264 | 353 | 372 | 417 | 466 | 526 | 626 |
| 1b. GDP | 6 846 | 7 781 | 8 426 | 10 705 | 14 657 | 15 825 | 18 182 | 20 833 | 24 120 | 29 485 |
| 1c. % of GWP | 0.21 | 0.22 | 0.21 | 0.22 | 0.26 | 0.25 | 0.27 | 0.28 | 0.27 | 0.29 |
| **2. PPPs** | | | | | | | | | | |
| 2a. Per capita GDP | 549 | 597 | 636 | 708 | 811 | 915 | 1 008 | 1 082 | 1 216 | 1 350 |
| 2b. GDP | 20 615 | 23 012 | 25 172 | 28 715 | 33 697 | 38 967 | 44 003 | 48 389 | 55 803 | 63 565 |
| 2c. % of GWP | ... | ... | ... | ... | ... | ... | ... | ... | ... | ... |
| **3. Absolute 1970−1989 PARE** | | | | | | | | | | |
| 3a. Per capita GDP | 427 | 439 | 450 | 477 | 489 | 508 | 535 | 554 | 569 | 590 |
| 3b. GDP | 16 022 | 16 938 | 17 824 | 19 336 | 20 302 | 21 604 | 23 335 | 24 770 | 26 133 | 27 767 |
| 3c. % of GWP | 0.23 | 0.23 | 0.23 | 0.23 | 0.24 | 0.25 | 0.26 | 0.26 | 0.27 | 0.27 |
| **4. Relative 1970−1989 PARE** | | | | | | | | | | |
| 4a. Per capita GDP | 208 | 225 | 241 | 273 | 305 | 348 | 389 | 430 | 475 | 536 |
| 4b. GDP | 7 812 | 8 682 | 9 556 | 11 054 | 12 660 | 14 801 | 16 986 | 19 247 | 21 787 | 25 217 |
| 4c. % of GWP | 0.23 | 0.23 | 0.23 | 0.23 | 0.24 | 0.25 | 0.26 | 0.26 | 0.27 | 0.27 |
| **5. Absolute 1980−1989 PARE** | | | | | | | | | | |
| 5a. Per capita GDP | 507 | 521 | 535 | 566 | 580 | 603 | 635 | 657 | 676 | 700 |
| 5b. GDP | 19 024 | 20 112 | 21 164 | 22 958 | 24 106 | 25 652 | 27 707 | 29 411 | 31 029 | 32 970 |
| 5c. % of GWP | 0.22 | 0.22 | 0.22 | 0.23 | 0.23 | 0.24 | 0.25 | 0.26 | 0.26 | 0.27 |
| **6. WA** | | | | | | | | | | |
| 6a. Per capita GDP | 187 | 202 | 214 | 264 | 353 | 372 | 417 | 466 | 526 | 626 |
| 6b. GDP | 7 032 | 7 795 | 8 459 | 10 704 | 14 657 | 15 825 | 18 181 | 20 833 | 24 121 | 29 487 |
| 6c. % of GWP | 0.22 | 0.22 | 0.21 | 0.22 | 0.26 | 0.26 | 0.27 | 0.28 | 0.27 | 0.29 |
| **Poland** | | | | | | | | | | |
| **1. MER** | | | | | | | | | | |
| 1a. Per capita GDP | 1 245 | 1 413 | 1 124 | 1 247 | 1 402 | 1 550 | 1 823 | 1 958 | 2 127 | 1 773 |
| 1b. GDP | 40 508 | 46 326 | 37 169 | 41 617 | 47 265 | 52 726 | 62 590 | 67 822 | 74 325 | 62 505 |
| 1c. % of GWP | 1.27 | 1.32 | 0.92 | 0.85 | 0.85 | 0.85 | 0.93 | 0.90 | 0.83 | 0.61 |
| **2. PPPs** | | | | | | | | | | |
| 2a. Per capita GDP | ... | ... | ... | ... | ... | ... | ... | ... | ... | ... |
| 2b. GDP | ... | ... | ... | ... | ... | ... | ... | ... | ... | ... |
| 2c. % of GWP | ... | ... | ... | ... | ... | ... | ... | ... | ... | ... |
| **3. Absolute 1970−1989 PARE** | | | | | | | | | | |
| 3a. Per capita GDP | 1 203 | 1 289 | 1 414 | 1 552 | 1 698 | 1 833 | 1 940 | 2 020 | 2 062 | 1 997 |
| 3b. GDP | 39 113 | 42 262 | 46 750 | 51 807 | 57 219 | 62 350 | 66 620 | 69 956 | 72 054 | 70 407 |
| 3c. % of GWP | 0.55 | 0.57 | 0.60 | 0.62 | 0.68 | 0.72 | 0.74 | 0.74 | 0.73 | 0.69 |
| **4. Relative 1970−1989 PARE** | | | | | | | | | | |
| 4a. Per capita GDP | 586 | 661 | 758 | 887 | 1 059 | 1 256 | 1 413 | 1 569 | 1 719 | 1 814 |
| 4b. GDP | 19 070 | 21 663 | 25 063 | 29 618 | 35 682 | 42 716 | 48 494 | 54 357 | 60 072 | 63 939 |
| 4c. % of GWP | 0.55 | 0.57 | 0.60 | 0.62 | 0.68 | 0.72 | 0.74 | 0.74 | 0.73 | 0.69 |
| **5. Absolute 1980−1989 PARE** | | | | | | | | | | |
| 5a. Per capita GDP | 1 288 | 1 381 | 1 514 | 1 662 | 1 819 | 1 963 | 2 079 | 2 164 | 2 209 | 2 140 |
| 5b. GDP | 41 902 | 45 275 | 50 083 | 55 500 | 61 298 | 66 795 | 71 370 | 74 943 | 77 191 | 75 426 |
| 5c. % of GWP | 0.48 | 0.50 | 0.52 | 0.55 | 0.59 | 0.64 | 0.65 | 0.65 | 0.64 | 0.61 |
| **6. WA** | | | | | | | | | | |
| 6a. Per capita GDP | 1 870 | 1 361 | 1 352 | 1 363 | 1 372 | 1 511 | 1 684 | 1 848 | 2 018 | 1 916 |
| 6b. GDP | 60 826 | 44 621 | 44 728 | 45 512 | 46 229 | 51 416 | 57 805 | 64 016 | 70 519 | 67 540 |
| 6c. % of GWP | 1.91 | 1.28 | 1.12 | 0.94 | 0.83 | 0.83 | 0.86 | 0.85 | 0.79 | 0.66 |

| 1980 (11) | 1981 (12) | 1982 (13) | 1983 (14) | 1984 (15) | 1985 (16) | 1986 (17) | 1987 (18) | 1988 (19) | 1989 (20) | Averages 1970–89 (21) | 1970–79 (22) | 1980–89 (23) |
|---|---|---|---|---|---|---|---|---|---|---|---|---|
| 729 | 779 | 783 | 661 | 603 | 597 | 544 | 593 | 658 | 729 | 544 | 373 | 666 |
| 35 235 | 38 640 | 39 883 | 34 563 | 32 365 | 32 928 | 30 763 | 34 387 | 39 140 | 44 424 | 25 959 | 15 686 | 36 233 |
| 0.30 | 0.33 | 0.34 | 0.29 | 0.27 | 0.26 | 0.21 | 0.20 | 0.20 | 0.22 | 0.25 | 0.26 | 0.25 |
| 1 543 | 1 693 | 1 803 | 1 848 | 1 807 | 1 697 | 1 712 | 1 796 | 1 926 | 2 066 | 1 427 | 908 | 1 799 |
| 74 549 | 83 982 | 91 832 | 96 662 | 97 018 | 93 558 | 96 792 | 104 150 | 114 508 | 125 893 | 68 044 | 38 194 | 97 894 |
| ... | ... | ... | ... | ... | ... | ... | ... | ... | ... | ... | ... | ... |
| 605 | 612 | 614 | 603 | 552 | 515 | 509 | 519 | 539 | 555 | 544 | 509 | 561 |
| 29 221 | 30 370 | 31 252 | 31 542 | 29 650 | 28 381 | 28 783 | 30 106 | 32 025 | 33 822 | 25 959 | 21 403 | 30 515 |
| 0.28 | 0.29 | 0.29 | 0.29 | 0.26 | 0.24 | 0.24 | 0.24 | 0.24 | 0.25 | 0.25 | 0.25 | 0.26 |
| 599 | 664 | 709 | 720 | 683 | 654 | 660 | 692 | 742 | 796 | 552 | 351 | 696 |
| 28 966 | 32 953 | 36 100 | 37 667 | 36 676 | 36 056 | 37 303 | 40 139 | 44 131 | 48 518 | 26 316 | 14 780 | 37 851 |
| 0.28 | 0.29 | 0.29 | 0.29 | 0.26 | 0.24 | 0.24 | 0.24 | 0.24 | 0.25 | 0.26 | 0.25 | 0.26 |
| 718 | 727 | 729 | 716 | 656 | 611 | 604 | 616 | 640 | 659 | 646 | 604 | 666 |
| 34 696 | 36 060 | 37 107 | 37 452 | 35 206 | 33 698 | 34 176 | 35 747 | 38 026 | 40 159 | 30 823 | 25 413 | 36 233 |
| 0.27 | 0.28 | 0.29 | 0.28 | 0.25 | 0.23 | 0.23 | 0.23 | 0.24 | 0.24 | 0.25 | 0.24 | 0.25 |
| 729 | 779 | 783 | 661 | 603 | 597 | 544 | 594 | 658 | 728 | 544 | 374 | 666 |
| 35 233 | 38 642 | 39 883 | 34 564 | 32 366 | 32 927 | 30 763 | 34 441 | 39 150 | 44 349 | 25 971 | 15 709 | 36 232 |
| 0.31 | 0.33 | 0.34 | 0.29 | 0.26 | 0.26 | 0.21 | 0.21 | 0.21 | 0.23 | 0.26 | 0.26 | 0.26 |
| 1 594 | 1 496 | 1 804 | 2 067 | 2 053 | 1 894 | 1 971 | 1 693 | 1 812 | 2 152 | 1 721 | 1 573 | 1 853 |
| 56 707 | 53 717 | 65 386 | 75 590 | 75 760 | 70 476 | 73 890 | 63 900 | 68 825 | 82 212 | 60 966 | 53 285 | 68 646 |
| 0.49 | 0.46 | 0.56 | 0.64 | 0.62 | 0.56 | 0.50 | 0.37 | 0.36 | 0.41 | 0.60 | 0.87 | 0.48 |
| ... | ... | ... | ... | ... | ... | ... | ... | ... | ... | ... | ... | ... |
| ... | ... | ... | ... | ... | ... | ... | ... | ... | ... | ... | ... | ... |
| ... | ... | ... | ... | ... | ... | ... | ... | ... | ... | ... | ... | ... |
| 1 860 | 1 622 | 1 518 | 1 595 | 1 670 | 1 712 | 1 783 | 1 805 | 1 881 | 1 866 | 1 721 | 1 708 | 1 729 |
| 66 182 | 58 244 | 55 035 | 58 338 | 61 613 | 63 688 | 66 826 | 68 128 | 71 435 | 71 292 | 60 966 | 57 854 | 64 078 |
| 0.64 | 0.55 | 0.52 | 0.53 | 0.54 | 0.54 | 0.55 | 0.54 | 0.54 | 0.52 | 0.60 | 0.67 | 0.54 |
| 1 844 | 1 760 | 1 754 | 1 905 | 2 065 | 2 175 | 2 310 | 2 406 | 2 591 | 2 676 | 1 691 | 1 183 | 2 152 |
| 65 603 | 63 197 | 63 573 | 69 665 | 76 212 | 80 913 | 86 606 | 90 830 | 98 437 | 102 269 | 59 899 | 40 067 | 79 731 |
| 0.64 | 0.55 | 0.52 | 0.53 | 0.54 | 0.54 | 0.55 | 0.54 | 0.54 | 0.52 | 0.58 | 0.68 | 0.54 |
| 1 993 | 1 738 | 1 627 | 1 709 | 1 789 | 1 834 | 1 910 | 1 934 | 2 015 | 1 999 | 1 844 | 1 830 | 1 853 |
| 70 900 | 62 396 | 58 958 | 62 497 | 66 005 | 68 228 | 71 590 | 72 985 | 76 528 | 76 375 | 65 312 | 61 978 | 68 646 |
| 0.56 | 0.48 | 0.45 | 0.47 | 0.47 | 0.47 | 0.48 | 0.48 | 0.48 | 0.46 | 0.53 | 0.59 | 0.48 |
| 1 710 | 1 441 | 1 473 | 1 774 | 2 064 | 2 064 | 2 040 | 1 884 | 1 875 | 1 865 | 1 732 | 1 634 | 1 819 |
| 60 849 | 51 730 | 53 379 | 64 874 | 76 168 | 76 772 | 76 479 | 71 109 | 71 234 | 71 265 | 61 354 | 55 321 | 67 386 |
| 0.53 | 0.44 | 0.46 | 0.55 | 0.62 | 0.61 | 0.52 | 0.43 | 0.38 | 0.36 | 0.61 | 0.91 | 0.48 |

**Table A.1**    Total and per capita gross domestic product of individual countries or areas,
expressed in United States dollars, and their individual shares of gross world
product, based on alternative conversion rates, 1970–1989 [*cont.*]

| Country or area | 1970 (1) | 1971 (2) | 1972 (3) | 1973 (4) | 1974 (5) | 1975 (6) | 1976 (7) | 1977 (8) | 1978 (9) | 1979 (10) |
|---|---|---|---|---|---|---|---|---|---|---|
| **Portugal** | | | | | | | | | | |
| **1.    MER** | | | | | | | | | | |
| 1a.    Per capita GDP | 684 | 782 | 953 | 1 270 | 1 478 | 1 623 | 1 687 | 1 753 | 1 890 | 2 108 |
| 1b.    GDP | 6 184 | 7 057 | 8 583 | 11 438 | 13 353 | 14 762 | 15 513 | 16 350 | 17 917 | 20 303 |
| 1c.    % of GWP | 0.19 | 0.20 | 0.21 | 0.23 | 0.24 | 0.24 | 0.23 | 0.22 | 0.20 | 0.20 |
| **2.    PPPs** | | | | | | | | | | |
| 2a.    Per capita GDP | 1 331 | 1 531 | 1 679 | 2 020 | 2 256 | 2 264 | 2 522 | 2 813 | 3 036 | 3 420 |
| 2b.    GDP | 12 038 | 13 816 | 15 122 | 18 191 | 20 379 | 20 587 | 23 187 | 26 235 | 28 785 | 32 944 |
| 2c.    % of GWP | ... | ... | ... | ... | ... | ... | ... | ... | ... | ... |
| **3.    Absolute 1970–1989 PARE** | | | | | | | | | | |
| 3a.    Per capita GDP | 1 545 | 1 651 | 1 787 | 1 987 | 2 004 | 1 904 | 2 013 | 2 096 | 2 120 | 2 204 |
| 3b.    GDP | 13 974 | 14 901 | 16 095 | 17 898 | 18 103 | 17 316 | 18 510 | 19 547 | 20 098 | 21 231 |
| 3c.    % of GWP | 0.20 | 0.20 | 0.21 | 0.22 | 0.21 | 0.20 | 0.20 | 0.21 | 0.20 | 0.21 |
| **4.    Relative 1970–1989 PARE** | | | | | | | | | | |
| 4a.    Per capita GDP | 753 | 846 | 958 | 1 136 | 1 250 | 1 304 | 1 466 | 1 628 | 1 767 | 2 002 |
| 4b.    GDP | 6 813 | 7 638 | 8 629 | 10 232 | 11 289 | 11 863 | 13 474 | 15 189 | 16 756 | 19 281 |
| 4c.    % of GWP | 0.20 | 0.20 | 0.21 | 0.22 | 0.21 | 0.20 | 0.20 | 0.21 | 0.20 | 0.21 |
| **5.    Absolute 1980–1989 PARE** | | | | | | | | | | |
| 5a.    Per capita GDP | 1 842 | 1 969 | 2 130 | 2 369 | 2 389 | 2 270 | 2 400 | 2 498 | 2 527 | 2 628 |
| 5b.    GDP | 16 659 | 17 764 | 19 188 | 21 337 | 21 581 | 20 643 | 22 067 | 23 303 | 23 960 | 25 311 |
| 5c.    % of GWP | 0.19 | 0.20 | 0.20 | 0.21 | 0.21 | 0.20 | 0.20 | 0.20 | 0.20 | 0.20 |
| **6.    WA** | | | | | | | | | | |
| 6a.    Per capita GDP | 684 | 779 | 951 | 1 278 | 1 478 | 1 623 | 1 687 | 1 753 | 1 890 | 2 108 |
| 6b.    GDP | 6 184 | 7 032 | 8 570 | 11 512 | 13 353 | 14 762 | 15 510 | 16 350 | 17 918 | 20 303 |
| 6c.    % of GWP | 0.19 | 0.20 | 0.21 | 0.24 | 0.24 | 0.24 | 0.23 | 0.22 | 0.20 | 0.20 |
| **Puerto Rico** | | | | | | | | | | |
| **1.    MER** | | | | | | | | | | |
| 1a.    Per capita GDP | 2 077 | 2 291 | 2 486 | 2 671 | 2 791 | 2 996 | 3 254 | 3 607 | 4 062 | 4 544 |
| 1b.    GDP | 5 647 | 6 329 | 7 002 | 7 685 | 8 198 | 8 969 | 9 911 | 11 165 | 12 750 | 14 436 |
| 1c.    % of GWP | 0.18 | 0.18 | 0.17 | 0.16 | 0.15 | 0.14 | 0.15 | 0.15 | 0.14 | 0.14 |
| **2.    PPPs** | | | | | | | | | | |
| 2a.    Per capita GDP | ... | ... | ... | ... | ... | ... | ... | ... | ... | ... |
| 2b.    GDP | ... | ... | ... | ... | ... | ... | ... | ... | ... | ... |
| 2c.    % of GWP | ... | ... | ... | ... | ... | ... | ... | ... | ... | ... |
| **3.    Absolute 1970–1989 PARE** | | | | | | | | | | |
| 3a.    Per capita GDP | 4 026 | 4 255 | 4 422 | 4 332 | 4 136 | 4 271 | 4 473 | 4 693 | 4 910 | 4 925 |
| 3b.    GDP | 10 947 | 11 756 | 12 456 | 12 463 | 12 147 | 12 788 | 13 624 | 14 524 | 15 412 | 15 647 |
| 3c.    % of GWP | 0.15 | 0.16 | 0.16 | 0.15 | 0.14 | 0.15 | 0.15 | 0.15 | 0.16 | 0.15 |
| **4.    Relative 1970–1989 PARE** | | | | | | | | | | |
| 4a.    Per capita GDP | 1 963 | 2 181 | 2 371 | 2 477 | 2 579 | 2 926 | 3 256 | 3 646 | 4 093 | 4 473 |
| 4b.    GDP | 5 338 | 6 026 | 6 678 | 7 125 | 7 575 | 8 761 | 9 917 | 11 286 | 12 849 | 14 209 |
| 4c.    % of GWP | 0.15 | 0.16 | 0.16 | 0.15 | 0.14 | 0.15 | 0.15 | 0.15 | 0.16 | 0.15 |
| **5.    Absolute 1980–1989 PARE** | | | | | | | | | | |
| 5a.    Per capita GDP | 4 911 | 5 189 | 5 393 | 5 283 | 5 044 | 5 209 | 5 455 | 5 724 | 5 988 | 6 007 |
| 5b.    GDP | 13 352 | 14 338 | 15 192 | 15 201 | 14 815 | 15 596 | 16 616 | 17 714 | 18 797 | 19 083 |
| 5c.    % of GWP | 0.15 | 0.16 | 0.16 | 0.15 | 0.14 | 0.15 | 0.15 | 0.15 | 0.16 | 0.15 |
| **6.    WA[a]** | | | | | | | | | | |
| 6a.    Per capita GDP | 1 904 | 2 162 | 2 379 | 2 472 | 2 541 | 2 829 | 3 134 | 3 433 | 3 792 | 4 112 |
| 6b.    GDP | 5 178 | 5 973 | 6 703 | 7 111 | 7 464 | 8 470 | 9 545 | 10 624 | 11 903 | 13 062 |
| 6c.    % of GWP | 0.16 | 0.17 | 0.17 | 0.15 | 0.13 | 0.14 | 0.14 | 0.14 | 0.13 | 0.13 |

| | | | | | | | | | | Averages | | |
|---|---|---|---|---|---|---|---|---|---|---|---|---|
| 1980 (11) | 1981 (12) | 1982 (13) | 1983 (14) | 1984 (15) | 1985 (16) | 1986 (17) | 1987 (18) | 1988 (19) | 1989 (20) | 1970–89 (21) | 1970–79 (22) | 1980–89 (23) |
| 2 569 | 2 469 | 2 335 | 2 068 | 1 903 | 2 036 | 2 898 | 3 591 | 4 068 | 4 413 | 2 156 | 1 450 | 2 830 |
| 25 090 | 24 390 | 23 284 | 20 777 | 19 234 | 20 682 | 29 551 | 36 726 | 41 686 | 45 297 | 20 909 | 13 146 | 28 672 |
| 0.22 | 0.21 | 0.20 | 0.18 | 0.16 | 0.16 | 0.20 | 0.21 | 0.22 | 0.23 | 0.21 | 0.22 | 0.20 |
| 3 863 | 4 202 | 4 501 | 4 524 | 4 513 | 4 646 | 4 917 | 5 309 | 5 691 | 6 231 | 3 610 | 2 331 | 4 827 |
| 37 729 | 41 508 | 44 878 | 45 440 | 45 612 | 47 197 | 50 139 | 54 289 | 58 312 | 63 959 | 35 017 | 21 128 | 48 906 |
| ... | ... | ... | ... | ... | ... | ... | ... | ... | ... | ... | ... | ... |
| 2 274 | 2 284 | 2 311 | 2 290 | 2 234 | 2 285 | 2 370 | 2 488 | 2 580 | 2 713 | 2 156 | 1 960 | 2 374 |
| 22 206 | 22 565 | 23 047 | 23 007 | 22 574 | 23 208 | 24 169 | 25 438 | 26 436 | 27 854 | 20 909 | 17 767 | 24 050 |
| 0.21 | 0.21 | 0.22 | 0.21 | 0.20 | 0.20 | 0.20 | 0.20 | 0.20 | 0.20 | 0.21 | 0.21 | 0.20 |
| 2 254 | 2 479 | 2 670 | 2 735 | 2 763 | 2 903 | 3 072 | 3 317 | 3 555 | 3 892 | 2 169 | 1 337 | 2 957 |
| 22 012 | 24 484 | 26 622 | 27 474 | 27 923 | 29 485 | 31 323 | 33 915 | 36 429 | 39 956 | 21 039 | 12 116 | 29 962 |
| 0.21 | 0.21 | 0.22 | 0.21 | 0.20 | 0.20 | 0.20 | 0.20 | 0.20 | 0.20 | 0.20 | 0.21 | 0.20 |
| 2 710 | 2 723 | 2 756 | 2 730 | 2 663 | 2 724 | 2 826 | 2 966 | 3 076 | 3 235 | 2 570 | 2 337 | 2 830 |
| 26 472 | 26 901 | 27 475 | 27 428 | 26 912 | 27 667 | 28 813 | 30 326 | 31 516 | 33 206 | 24 926 | 21 181 | 28 672 |
| 0.21 | 0.21 | 0.21 | 0.21 | 0.19 | 0.19 | 0.19 | 0.20 | 0.20 | 0.20 | 0.20 | 0.20 | 0.20 |
| 2 569 | 2 469 | 2 335 | 2 068 | 1 903 | 2 036 | 2 898 | 3 592 | 4 070 | 4 414 | 2 156 | 1 451 | 2 830 |
| 25 090 | 24 390 | 23 283 | 20 777 | 19 234 | 20 681 | 29 551 | 36 731 | 41 699 | 45 309 | 20 912 | 13 149 | 28 675 |
| 0.22 | 0.21 | 0.20 | 0.18 | 0.16 | 0.16 | 0.20 | 0.22 | 0.22 | 0.23 | 0.21 | 0.22 | 0.20 |
| 4 975 | 5 195 | 5 332 | 5 896 | 6 218 | 6 704 | 7 252 | 7 874 | 8 295 | 8 799 | 4 893 | 3 105 | 6 731 |
| 15 956 | 16 764 | 17 277 | 19 163 | 20 289 | 22 009 | 24 026 | 26 386 | 28 161 | 30 260 | 15 619 | 9 209 | 22 029 |
| 0.14 | 0.14 | 0.15 | 0.16 | 0.17 | 0.17 | 0.16 | 0.15 | 0.15 | 0.15 | 0.15 | 0.15 | 0.15 |
| ... | ... | ... | ... | ... | ... | ... | ... | ... | ... | ... | ... | ... |
| ... | ... | ... | ... | ... | ... | ... | ... | ... | ... | ... | ... | ... |
| ... | ... | ... | ... | ... | ... | ... | ... | ... | ... | ... | ... | ... |
| 4 931 | 4 751 | 4 754 | 5 086 | 5 171 | 5 518 | 5 762 | 6 101 | 6 223 | 6 365 | 4 893 | 4 443 | 5 518 |
| 15 814 | 15 332 | 15 404 | 16 531 | 16 871 | 18 117 | 19 090 | 20 445 | 21 128 | 21 888 | 15 619 | 13 176 | 18 062 |
| 0.15 | 0.14 | 0.14 | 0.15 | 0.15 | 0.15 | 0.16 | 0.16 | 0.16 | 0.16 | 0.15 | 0.15 | 0.15 |
| 4 888 | 5 155 | 5 492 | 6 074 | 6 396 | 7 011 | 7 468 | 8 134 | 8 576 | 9 130 | 4 950 | 3 027 | 6 912 |
| 15 676 | 16 636 | 17 793 | 19 741 | 20 869 | 23 017 | 24 740 | 27 258 | 29 114 | 31 399 | 15 800 | 8 976 | 22 624 |
| 0.15 | 0.14 | 0.14 | 0.15 | 0.15 | 0.15 | 0.16 | 0.16 | 0.16 | 0.16 | 0.15 | 0.15 | 0.15 |
| 6 014 | 5 795 | 5 798 | 6 204 | 6 306 | 6 730 | 7 028 | 7 441 | 7 590 | 7 763 | 5 968 | 5 419 | 6 731 |
| 19 287 | 18 699 | 18 787 | 20 162 | 20 577 | 22 096 | 23 283 | 24 935 | 25 769 | 26 696 | 19 050 | 16 070 | 22 029 |
| 0.15 | 0.15 | 0.14 | 0.15 | 0.15 | 0.15 | 0.16 | 0.16 | 0.16 | 0.16 | 0.15 | 0.15 | 0.15 |
| 4 505 | 4 768 | 5 099 | 5 718 | 5 999 | 6 576 | 7 058 | 7 650 | 8 049 | 8 492 | 4 663 | 2 901 | 6 466 |
| 14 448 | 15 386 | 16 520 | 18 582 | 19 574 | 21 590 | 23 382 | 25 636 | 27 325 | 29 205 | 14 884 | 8 603 | 21 165 |
| 0.13 | 0.13 | 0.14 | 0.16 | 0.16 | 0.17 | 0.16 | 0.15 | 0.15 | 0.15 | 0.15 | 0.14 | 0.15 |

**Table A.1**    Total and per capita gross domestic product of individual countries or areas,
expressed in United States dollars, and their individual shares of gross world
product, based on alternative conversion rates, 1970−1989 [*cont.*]

| Country or area | 1970 (1) | 1971 (2) | 1972 (3) | 1973 (4) | 1974 (5) | 1975 (6) | 1976 (7) | 1977 (8) | 1978 (9) | 1979 (10) |
|---|---|---|---|---|---|---|---|---|---|---|
| **Qatar** | | | | | | | | | | |
| **1.    MER** | | | | | | | | | | |
| 1a.   Per capita GDP | 2 694 | 3 153 | 3 780 | 5 406 | 15 010 | 14 357 | 17 527 | 17 997 | 19 086 | 25 961 |
| 1b.   GDP | 302 | 388 | 510 | 795 | 2 402 | 2 469 | 3 207 | 3 509 | 3 932 | 5 633 |
| 1c.   % of GWP | 0.01 | 0.01 | 0.01 | 0.02 | 0.04 | 0.04 | 0.05 | 0.05 | 0.04 | 0.05 |
| **2.    PPPs** | | | | | | | | | | |
| 2a.   Per capita GDP | ... | ... | ... | ... | ... | ... | ... | ... | ... | ... |
| 2b.   GDP | ... | ... | ... | ... | ... | ... | ... | ... | ... | ... |
| 2c.   % of GWP | ... | ... | ... | ... | ... | ... | ... | ... | ... | ... |
| **3.    Absolute 1970−1989 PARE** | | | | | | | | | | |
| 3a.   Per capita GDP | 30 988 | 33 455 | 34 379 | 37 220 | 31 104 | 24 452 | 26 131 | 21 870 | 22 661 | 22 392 |
| 3b.   GDP | 3 471 | 4 115 | 4 641 | 5 471 | 4 977 | 4 206 | 4 782 | 4 265 | 4 668 | 4 859 |
| 3c.   % of GWP | 0.05 | 0.06 | 0.06 | 0.07 | 0.06 | 0.05 | 0.05 | 0.05 | 0.05 | 0.05 |
| **4.    Relative 1970−1989 PARE** | | | | | | | | | | |
| 4a.   Per capita GDP | 15 109 | 17 149 | 18 431 | 21 279 | 19 396 | 16 752 | 19 022 | 16 994 | 18 893 | 20 335 |
| 4b.   GDP | 1 692 | 2 109 | 2 488 | 3 128 | 3 103 | 2 881 | 3 481 | 3 314 | 3 892 | 4 413 |
| 4c.   % of GWP | 0.05 | 0.06 | 0.06 | 0.07 | 0.06 | 0.05 | 0.05 | 0.05 | 0.05 | 0.05 |
| **5.    Absolute 1980−1989 PARE** | | | | | | | | | | |
| 5a.   Per capita GDP | 46 550 | 50 257 | 51 645 | 55 913 | 46 724 | 36 732 | 39 255 | 32 853 | 34 042 | 33 637 |
| 5b.   GDP | 5 214 | 6 182 | 6 972 | 8 219 | 7 476 | 6 318 | 7 184 | 6 406 | 7 013 | 7 299 |
| 5c.   % of GWP | 0.06 | 0.07 | 0.07 | 0.08 | 0.07 | 0.06 | 0.06 | 0.06 | 0.06 | 0.06 |
| **6.    WA[a]** | | | | | | | | | | |
| 6a.   Per capita GDP | 1 627 | 2 510 | 3 305 | 4 199 | 5 169 | 6 881 | 14 886 | 14 880 | 17 461 | 20 574 |
| 6b.   GDP | 182 | 309 | 446 | 617 | 827 | 1 184 | 2 724 | 2 902 | 3 597 | 4 465 |
| 6c.   % of GWP | 0.01 | 0.01 | 0.01 | 0.01 | 0.01 | 0.02 | 0.04 | 0.04 | 0.04 | 0.04 |
| **Reunion** | | | | | | | | | | |
| **1.    MER** | | | | | | | | | | |
| 1a.   Per capita GDP | 820 | 938 | 1 169 | 1 447 | 1 649 | 2 184 | 2 220 | 2 421 | 2 930 | 3 491 |
| 1b.   GDP | 363 | 423 | 539 | 680 | 788 | 1 059 | 1 088 | 1 198 | 1 462 | 1 756 |
| 1c.   % of GWP | 0.01 | 0.01 | 0.01 | 0.01 | 0.01 | 0.02 | 0.02 | 0.02 | 0.02 | 0.02 |
| **2.    PPPs** | | | | | | | | | | |
| 2a.   Per capita GDP | ... | ... | ... | ... | ... | ... | ... | ... | ... | ... |
| 2b.   GDP | ... | ... | ... | ... | ... | ... | ... | ... | ... | ... |
| 2c.   % of GWP | ... | ... | ... | ... | ... | ... | ... | ... | ... | ... |
| **3.    Absolute 1970−1989 PARE** | | | | | | | | | | |
| 3a.   Per capita GDP | 2 181 | 2 249 | 2 391 | 2 469 | 2 531 | 2 540 | 2 769 | 2 901 | 3 097 | 3 250 |
| 3b.   GDP | 964 | 1 014 | 1 102 | 1 160 | 1 210 | 1 232 | 1 357 | 1 436 | 1 545 | 1 635 |
| 3c.   % of GWP | 0.01 | 0.01 | 0.01 | 0.01 | 0.01 | 0.01 | 0.01 | 0.02 | 0.02 | 0.02 |
| **4.    Relative 1970−1989 PARE** | | | | | | | | | | |
| 4a.   Per capita GDP | 1 064 | 1 153 | 1 282 | 1 412 | 1 578 | 1 740 | 2 015 | 2 254 | 2 582 | 2 951 |
| 4b.   GDP | 470 | 520 | 591 | 663 | 754 | 844 | 987 | 1 116 | 1 288 | 1 484 |
| 4c.   % of GWP | 0.01 | 0.01 | 0.01 | 0.01 | 0.01 | 0.01 | 0.01 | 0.02 | 0.02 | 0.02 |
| **5.    Absolute 1980−1989 PARE** | | | | | | | | | | |
| 5a.   Per capita GDP | 2 530 | 2 609 | 2 773 | 2 864 | 2 936 | 2 946 | 3 211 | 3 364 | 3 592 | 3 769 |
| 5b.   GDP | 1 118 | 1 177 | 1 279 | 1 346 | 1 403 | 1 429 | 1 573 | 1 665 | 1 792 | 1 896 |
| 5c.   % of GWP | 0.01 | 0.01 | 0.01 | 0.01 | 0.01 | 0.01 | 0.01 | 0.01 | 0.01 | 0.02 |
| **6.    WA[a]** | | | | | | | | | | |
| 6a.   Per capita GDP | 818 | 875 | 1 010 | 1 205 | 1 436 | 1 730 | 2 105 | 2 412 | 2 653 | 3 060 |
| 6b.   GDP | 362 | 395 | 466 | 566 | 687 | 839 | 1 032 | 1 194 | 1 324 | 1 539 |
| 6c.   % of GWP | 0.01 | 0.01 | 0.01 | 0.01 | 0.01 | 0.01 | 0.02 | 0.02 | 0.01 | 0.02 |

| | 1980 (11) | 1981 (12) | 1982 (13) | 1983 (14) | 1984 (15) | 1985 (16) | 1986 (17) | 1987 (18) | 1988 (19) | 1989 (20) | Averages 1970–89 (21) | 1970–79 (22) | 1980–89 (23) |
|---|---|---|---|---|---|---|---|---|---|---|---|---|---|
| | 34 078 | 35 689 | 29 616 | 23 929 | 24 106 | 20 580 | 16 144 | 16 841 | 16 967 | 19 069 | 20 106 | 13 944 | 22 851 |
| | 7 838 | 8 673 | 7 611 | 6 485 | 6 870 | 6 153 | 5 053 | 5 507 | 5 786 | 6 750 | 4 494 | 2 315 | 6 673 |
| | 0.07 | 0.07 | 0.07 | 0.05 | 0.06 | 0.05 | 0.03 | 0.03 | 0.03 | 0.03 | 0.04 | 0.04 | 0.05 |
| | ... | ... | ... | ... | ... | ... | ... | ... | ... | ... | ... | ... | ... |
| | ... | ... | ... | ... | ... | ... | ... | ... | ... | ... | ... | ... | ... |
| | ... | ... | ... | ... | ... | ... | ... | ... | ... | ... | ... | ... | ... |
| | 22 626 | 20 068 | 17 077 | 15 085 | 15 377 | 14 083 | 14 151 | 12 636 | 12 125 | 12 916 | 20 106 | 27 382 | 15 212 |
| | 5 204 | 4 876 | 4 389 | 4 088 | 4 382 | 4 211 | 4 429 | 4 132 | 4 135 | 4 572 | 4 494 | 4 545 | 4 442 |
| | 0.05 | 0.05 | 0.04 | 0.04 | 0.04 | 0.04 | 0.04 | 0.03 | 0.03 | 0.03 | 0.04 | 0.05 | 0.04 |
| | 22 429 | 21 774 | 19 726 | 18 015 | 19 020 | 17 892 | 18 340 | 16 847 | 16 708 | 18 528 | 19 056 | 18 375 | 18 725 |
| | 5 159 | 5 291 | 5 070 | 4 882 | 5 421 | 5 350 | 5 740 | 5 509 | 5 698 | 6 559 | 4 259 | 3 050 | 5 468 |
| | 0.05 | 0.05 | 0.04 | 0.04 | 0.04 | 0.04 | 0.04 | 0.03 | 0.03 | 0.03 | 0.04 | 0.05 | 0.04 |
| | 33 989 | 30 145 | 25 653 | 22 661 | 23 099 | 21 156 | 21 258 | 18 982 | 18 214 | 19 402 | 30 203 | 41 134 | 22 851 |
| | 7 818 | 7 325 | 6 593 | 6 141 | 6 583 | 6 326 | 6 654 | 6 207 | 6 211 | 6 868 | 6 750 | 6 828 | 6 673 |
| | 0.06 | 0.06 | 0.05 | 0.05 | 0.05 | 0.04 | 0.04 | 0.04 | 0.04 | 0.04 | 0.05 | 0.06 | 0.05 |
| | 25 012 | 28 822 | 28 416 | 25 578 | 25 004 | 21 638 | 19 308 | 16 402 | 15 535 | 18 087 | 18 109 | 10 393 | 21 813 |
| | 5 753 | 7 004 | 7 303 | 6 932 | 7 126 | 6 470 | 6 043 | 5 363 | 5 297 | 6 403 | 4 047 | 1 725 | 6 369 |
| | 0.05 | 0.06 | 0.06 | 0.06 | 0.06 | 0.05 | 0.04 | 0.03 | 0.03 | 0.03 | 0.04 | 0.03 | 0.05 |
| | 3 928 | 3 618 | 3 581 | 3 386 | 3 125 | 3 324 | 4 684 | 5 986 | 6 187 | 5 674 | 3 291 | 1 943 | 4 414 |
| | 1 999 | 1 864 | 1 869 | 1 794 | 1 681 | 1 818 | 2 609 | 3 394 | 3 576 | 3 342 | 1 665 | 936 | 2 395 |
| | 0.02 | 0.02 | 0.02 | 0.02 | 0.01 | 0.01 | 0.02 | 0.02 | 0.02 | 0.02 | 0.02 | 0.02 | 0.02 |
| | ... | ... | ... | ... | ... | ... | ... | ... | ... | ... | ... | ... | ... |
| | ... | ... | ... | ... | ... | ... | ... | ... | ... | ... | ... | ... | ... |
| | ... | ... | ... | ... | ... | ... | ... | ... | ... | ... | ... | ... | ... |
| | 3 346 | 3 504 | 3 617 | 3 738 | 3 757 | 3 824 | 3 936 | 4 044 | 4 127 | 3 881 | 3 291 | 2 628 | 3 806 |
| | 1 703 | 1 805 | 1 888 | 1 981 | 2 021 | 2 092 | 2 192 | 2 293 | 2 385 | 2 286 | 1 665 | 1 266 | 2 065 |
| | 0.02 | 0.02 | 0.02 | 0.02 | 0.02 | 0.02 | 0.02 | 0.02 | 0.02 | 0.02 | 0.02 | 0.01 | 0.02 |
| | 3 317 | 3 802 | 4 178 | 4 464 | 4 647 | 4 859 | 5 101 | 5 392 | 5 687 | 5 567 | 3 413 | 1 811 | 4 759 |
| | 1 688 | 1 958 | 2 181 | 2 366 | 2 500 | 2 658 | 2 841 | 3 057 | 3 287 | 3 279 | 1 727 | 872 | 2 582 |
| | 0.02 | 0.02 | 0.02 | 0.02 | 0.02 | 0.02 | 0.02 | 0.02 | 0.02 | 0.02 | 0.02 | 0.01 | 0.02 |
| | 3 881 | 4 064 | 4 195 | 4 336 | 4 358 | 4 435 | 4 565 | 4 691 | 4 786 | 4 501 | 3 817 | 3 048 | 4 414 |
| | 1 975 | 2 093 | 2 190 | 2 298 | 2 344 | 2 426 | 2 543 | 2 660 | 2 767 | 2 651 | 1 931 | 1 468 | 2 395 |
| | 0.02 | 0.02 | 0.02 | 0.02 | 0.02 | 0.02 | 0.02 | 0.02 | 0.02 | 0.02 | 0.02 | 0.01 | 0.02 |
| | 3 535 | 3 821 | 3 834 | 3 638 | 3 399 | 3 319 | 3 698 | 4 550 | 5 671 | 5 745 | 3 068 | 1 745 | 4 174 |
| | 1 799 | 1 968 | 2 001 | 1 928 | 1 828 | 1 815 | 2 060 | 2 580 | 3 278 | 3 384 | 1 552 | 840 | 2 264 |
| | 0.02 | 0.02 | 0.02 | 0.02 | 0.01 | 0.01 | 0.01 | 0.02 | 0.02 | 0.02 | 0.02 | 0.01 | 0.02 |

**Table A.1**    Total and per capita gross domestic product of individual countries or areas,
expressed in United States dollars, and their individual shares of gross world
product, based on alternative conversion rates, 1970–1989 [*cont.*]

| Country or area | 1970 (1) | 1971 (2) | 1972 (3) | 1973 (4) | 1974 (5) | 1975 (6) | 1976 (7) | 1977 (8) | 1978 (9) | 1979 (10) |
|---|---|---|---|---|---|---|---|---|---|---|
| **Romania** | | | | | | | | | | |
| **1.  MER** | | | | | | | | | | |
| 1a.  Per capita GDP | 606 | 678 | 742 | 812 | 904 | 988 | 1 100 | 1 178 | 1 369 | 1 500 |
| 1b.  GDP | 12 275 | 13 872 | 15 348 | 16 945 | 19 030 | 20 994 | 23 596 | 25 503 | 29 911 | 33 072 |
| 1c.  % of GWP | 0.38 | 0.40 | 0.38 | 0.35 | 0.34 | 0.34 | 0.35 | 0.34 | 0.33 | 0.32 |
| **2.  PPPs** | | | | | | | | | | |
| 2a.  Per capita GDP | ... | ... | ... | ... | ... | ... | ... | ... | ... | ... |
| 2b.  GDP | ... | ... | ... | ... | ... | ... | ... | ... | ... | ... |
| 2c.  % of GWP | ... | ... | ... | ... | ... | ... | ... | ... | ... | ... |
| **3.  Absolute 1970–1989 PARE** | | | | | | | | | | |
| 3a.  Per capita GDP | 777 | 868 | 951 | 1 041 | 1 158 | 1 266 | 1 394 | 1 497 | 1 591 | 1 677 |
| 3b.  GDP | 15 731 | 17 780 | 19 664 | 21 713 | 24 385 | 26 907 | 29 894 | 32 408 | 34 772 | 36 971 |
| 3c.  % of GWP | 0.22 | 0.24 | 0.25 | 0.26 | 0.29 | 0.31 | 0.33 | 0.34 | 0.35 | 0.36 |
| **4.  Relative 1970–1989 PARE** | | | | | | | | | | |
| 4a.  Per capita GDP | 379 | 445 | 510 | 595 | 722 | 868 | 1 015 | 1 163 | 1 326 | 1 523 |
| 4b.  GDP | 7 670 | 9 114 | 10 542 | 12 413 | 15 206 | 18 434 | 21 760 | 25 182 | 28 990 | 33 575 |
| 4c.  % of GWP | 0.22 | 0.24 | 0.25 | 0.26 | 0.29 | 0.31 | 0.33 | 0.34 | 0.35 | 0.36 |
| **5.  Absolute 1980–1989 PARE** | | | | | | | | | | |
| 5a.  Per capita GDP | 867 | 969 | 1 061 | 1 161 | 1 293 | 1 413 | 1 555 | 1 670 | 1 775 | 1 872 |
| 5b.  GDP | 17 554 | 19 840 | 21 943 | 24 229 | 27 211 | 30 025 | 33 358 | 36 163 | 38 802 | 41 255 |
| 5c.  % of GWP | 0.20 | 0.22 | 0.23 | 0.24 | 0.26 | 0.29 | 0.30 | 0.31 | 0.32 | 0.33 |
| **6.  WA** | | | | | | | | | | |
| 6a.  Per capita GDP | 640 | 698 | 742 | 812 | 904 | 988 | 1 092 | 1 176 | 1 290 | 1 417 |
| 6b.  GDP | 12 953 | 14 281 | 15 344 | 16 944 | 19 031 | 20 996 | 23 416 | 25 456 | 28 192 | 31 233 |
| 6c.  % of GWP | 0.41 | 0.41 | 0.38 | 0.35 | 0.34 | 0.34 | 0.35 | 0.34 | 0.32 | 0.31 |
| **Rwanda** | | | | | | | | | | |
| **1.  MER** | | | | | | | | | | |
| 1a.  Per capita GDP | 58 | 67 | 73 | 88 | 112 | 130 | 147 | 165 | 181 | 207 |
| 1b.  GDP | 216 | 259 | 292 | 362 | 475 | 568 | 666 | 772 | 873 | 1 036 |
| 1c.  % of GWP | 0.01 | 0.01 | 0.01 | 0.01 | 0.01 | 0.01 | 0.01 | 0.01 | 0.01 | 0.01 |
| **2.  PPPs** | | | | | | | | | | |
| 2a.  Per capita GDP | 150 | 190 | 194 | 199 | 332 | 249 | 271 | 292 | 305 | 349 |
| 2b.  GDP | 559 | 731 | 771 | 818 | 1 410 | 1 092 | 1 229 | 1 368 | 1 475 | 1 744 |
| 2c.  % of GWP | ... | ... | ... | ... | ... | ... | ... | ... | ... | ... |
| **3.  Absolute 1970–1989 PARE** | | | | | | | | | | |
| 3a.  Per capita GDP | 152 | 156 | 154 | 153 | 188 | 199 | 208 | 212 | 226 | 239 |
| 3b.  GDP | 568 | 601 | 613 | 629 | 796 | 872 | 944 | 993 | 1 091 | 1 193 |
| 3c.  % of GWP | 0.01 | 0.01 | 0.01 | 0.01 | 0.01 | 0.01 | 0.01 | 0.01 | 0.01 | 0.01 |
| **4.  Relative 1970–1989 PARE** | | | | | | | | | | |
| 4a.  Per capita GDP | 74 | 80 | 83 | 88 | 117 | 136 | 152 | 165 | 188 | 217 |
| 4b.  GDP | 277 | 308 | 329 | 360 | 497 | 598 | 687 | 772 | 909 | 1 083 |
| 4c.  % of GWP | 0.01 | 0.01 | 0.01 | 0.01 | 0.01 | 0.01 | 0.01 | 0.01 | 0.01 | 0.01 |
| **5.  Absolute 1980–1989 PARE** | | | | | | | | | | |
| 5a.  Per capita GDP | 182 | 186 | 184 | 182 | 224 | 237 | 248 | 253 | 269 | 285 |
| 5b.  GDP | 677 | 716 | 731 | 750 | 949 | 1 040 | 1 125 | 1 184 | 1 300 | 1 422 |
| 5c.  % of GWP | 0.01 | 0.01 | 0.01 | 0.01 | 0.01 | 0.01 | 0.01 | 0.01 | 0.01 | 0.01 |
| **6.  WA** | | | | | | | | | | |
| 6a.  Per capita GDP | 58 | 67 | 73 | 88 | 112 | 130 | 147 | 165 | 181 | 207 |
| 6b.  GDP | 216 | 259 | 292 | 361 | 475 | 568 | 666 | 772 | 873 | 1 036 |
| 6c.  % of GWP | 0.01 | 0.01 | 0.01 | 0.01 | 0.01 | 0.01 | 0.01 | 0.01 | 0.01 | 0.01 |

| | | | | | | | | | | Averages | | |
| 1980 (11) | 1981 (12) | 1982 (13) | 1983 (14) | 1984 (15) | 1985 (16) | 1986 (17) | 1987 (18) | 1988 (19) | 1989 (20) | 1970–89 (21) | 1970–79 (22) | 1980–89 (23) |
|---|---|---|---|---|---|---|---|---|---|---|---|---|
| 1 544 | 1 862 | 2 161 | 1 985 | 1 695 | 2 098 | 2 274 | 2 524 | 2 600 | 2 312 | 1 557 | 996 | 2 110 |
| 34 272 | 41 580 | 48 493 | 44 746 | 38 351 | 47 687 | 51 916 | 57 884 | 59 930 | 53 557 | 34 448 | 21 054 | 47 842 |
| 0.30 | 0.36 | 0.42 | 0.38 | 0.31 | 0.38 | 0.35 | 0.34 | 0.31 | 0.27 | 0.34 | 0.35 | 0.34 |
| ... | ... | ... | ... | ... | ... | ... | ... | ... | ... | ... | ... | ... |
| ... | ... | ... | ... | ... | ... | ... | ... | ... | ... | ... | ... | ... |
| ... | ... | ... | ... | ... | ... | ... | ... | ... | ... | ... | ... | ... |
| 1 736 | 1 719 | 1 781 | 1 878 | 1 995 | 1 966 | 2 012 | 2 024 | 1 973 | 1 807 | 1 557 | 1 230 | 1 891 |
| 38 547 | 38 390 | 39 966 | 42 323 | 45 152 | 44 687 | 45 940 | 46 413 | 45 467 | 41 850 | 34 448 | 26 023 | 42 874 |
| 0.37 | 0.36 | 0.37 | 0.39 | 0.39 | 0.38 | 0.38 | 0.37 | 0.34 | 0.31 | 0.34 | 0.30 | 0.36 |
| 1 721 | 1 865 | 2 057 | 2 242 | 2 468 | 2 498 | 2 608 | 2 698 | 2 718 | 2 592 | 1 619 | 865 | 2 352 |
| 38 211 | 41 655 | 46 166 | 50 541 | 55 851 | 56 773 | 59 538 | 61 879 | 62 654 | 60 033 | 35 809 | 18 289 | 53 330 |
| 0.37 | 0.36 | 0.37 | 0.39 | 0.39 | 0.38 | 0.38 | 0.37 | 0.34 | 0.31 | 0.35 | 0.31 | 0.36 |
| 1 937 | 1 918 | 1 987 | 2 095 | 2 226 | 2 194 | 2 246 | 2 258 | 2 201 | 2 016 | 1 738 | 1 373 | 2 110 |
| 43 014 | 42 838 | 44 597 | 47 227 | 50 384 | 49 865 | 51 264 | 51 791 | 50 736 | 46 699 | 38 440 | 29 038 | 47 842 |
| 0.34 | 0.33 | 0.34 | 0.35 | 0.36 | 0.35 | 0.35 | 0.34 | 0.32 | 0.28 | 0.31 | 0.28 | 0.34 |
| 1 530 | 1 629 | 1 860 | 2 092 | 2 031 | 1 928 | 2 013 | 2 314 | 2 420 | 2 315 | 1 504 | 983 | 2 017 |
| 33 961 | 36 378 | 41 745 | 47 143 | 45 959 | 43 807 | 45 950 | 53 067 | 55 779 | 53 610 | 33 262 | 20 785 | 45 740 |
| 0.29 | 0.31 | 0.36 | 0.40 | 0.38 | 0.35 | 0.31 | 0.32 | 0.30 | 0.27 | 0.33 | 0.34 | 0.32 |
| 225 | 248 | 256 | 264 | 269 | 281 | 308 | 329 | 345 | 310 | 225 | 128 | 288 |
| 1 163 | 1 321 | 1 411 | 1 507 | 1 588 | 1 715 | 1 944 | 2 151 | 2 329 | 2 168 | 1 141 | 552 | 1 730 |
| 0.01 | 0.01 | 0.01 | 0.01 | 0.01 | 0.01 | 0.01 | 0.01 | 0.01 | 0.01 | 0.01 | 0.01 | 0.01 |
| 377 | 424 | 416 | 420 | 476 | 468 | 487 | 481 | 496 | 475 | 380 | 259 | 457 |
| 1 949 | 2 261 | 2 293 | 2 395 | 2 806 | 2 858 | 3 075 | 3 139 | 3 350 | 3 325 | 1 932 | 1 120 | 2 745 |
| ... | ... | ... | ... | ... | ... | ... | ... | ... | ... | ... | ... | ... |
| 245 | 256 | 250 | 257 | 238 | 240 | 245 | 235 | 234 | 216 | 225 | 192 | 242 |
| 1 265 | 1 367 | 1 382 | 1 465 | 1 403 | 1 464 | 1 545 | 1 533 | 1 583 | 1 509 | 1 141 | 830 | 1 451 |
| 0.01 | 0.01 | 0.01 | 0.01 | 0.01 | 0.01 | 0.01 | 0.01 | 0.01 | 0.01 | 0.01 | 0.01 | 0.01 |
| 243 | 278 | 289 | 307 | 294 | 305 | 317 | 313 | 323 | 309 | 235 | 135 | 301 |
| 1 254 | 1 484 | 1 597 | 1 749 | 1 735 | 1 861 | 2 002 | 2 043 | 2 181 | 2 164 | 1 194 | 582 | 1 807 |
| 0.01 | 0.01 | 0.01 | 0.01 | 0.01 | 0.01 | 0.01 | 0.01 | 0.01 | 0.01 | 0.01 | 0.01 | 0.01 |
| 292 | 305 | 299 | 306 | 283 | 286 | 292 | 280 | 279 | 257 | 268 | 229 | 288 |
| 1 507 | 1 629 | 1 647 | 1 746 | 1 672 | 1 745 | 1 841 | 1 826 | 1 886 | 1 798 | 1 360 | 989 | 1 730 |
| 0.01 | 0.01 | 0.01 | 0.01 | 0.01 | 0.01 | 0.01 | 0.01 | 0.01 | 0.01 | 0.01 | 0.01 | 0.01 |
| 225 | 248 | 256 | 264 | 269 | 281 | 308 | 329 | 344 | 310 | 225 | 128 | 288 |
| 1 163 | 1 321 | 1 411 | 1 507 | 1 588 | 1 715 | 1 944 | 2 152 | 2 327 | 2 169 | 1 141 | 552 | 1 730 |
| 0.01 | 0.01 | 0.01 | 0.01 | 0.01 | 0.01 | 0.01 | 0.01 | 0.01 | 0.01 | 0.01 | 0.01 | 0.01 |

**Table A.1**     Total and per capita gross domestic product of individual countries or areas, expressed in United States dollars, and their individual shares of gross world product, based on alternative conversion rates, 1970−1989 [cont.]

| Country or area | 1970 (1) | 1971 (2) | 1972 (3) | 1973 (4) | 1974 (5) | 1975 (6) | 1976 (7) | 1977 (8) | 1978 (9) | 1979 (10) |
|---|---|---|---|---|---|---|---|---|---|---|
| **Saint Kitts−Nevis** | | | | | | | | | | |
| **1.   MER** | | | | | | | | | | |
| 1a.   Per capita GDP | 338 | 403 | 470 | 506 | 657 | 696 | 628 | 650 | 760 | 884 |
| 1b.   GDP | 16 | 19 | 22 | 23 | 30 | 32 | 29 | 30 | 34 | 40 |
| 1c.   % of GWP | 0.00 | 0.00 | 0.00 | 0.00 | 0.00 | 0.00 | 0.00 | 0.00 | 0.00 | 0.00 |
| **2.   PPPs** | | | | | | | | | | |
| 2a.   Per capita GDP | ... | ... | ... | ... | ... | ... | ... | ... | ... | ... |
| 2b.   GDP | ... | ... | ... | ... | ... | ... | ... | ... | ... | ... |
| 2c.   % of GWP | ... | ... | ... | ... | ... | ... | ... | ... | ... | ... |
| **3.   Absolute 1970−1989 PARE** | | | | | | | | | | |
| 3a.   Per capita GDP | 771 | 752 | 839 | 893 | 891 | 922 | 936 | 938 | 1 030 | 1 128 |
| 3b.   GDP | 36 | 35 | 39 | 41 | 41 | 42 | 43 | 43 | 46 | 51 |
| 3c.   % of GWP | 0.00 | 0.00 | 0.00 | 0.00 | 0.00 | 0.00 | 0.00 | 0.00 | 0.00 | 0.00 |
| **4.   Relative 1970−1989 PARE** | | | | | | | | | | |
| 4a.   Per capita GDP | 376 | 385 | 450 | 510 | 556 | 631 | 681 | 729 | 859 | 1 024 |
| 4b.   GDP | 18 | 18 | 21 | 23 | 26 | 29 | 31 | 34 | 39 | 46 |
| 4c.   % of GWP | 0.00 | 0.00 | 0.00 | 0.00 | 0.00 | 0.00 | 0.00 | 0.00 | 0.00 | 0.00 |
| **5.   Absolute 1980−1989 PARE** | | | | | | | | | | |
| 5a.   Per capita GDP | 962 | 938 | 1 047 | 1 114 | 1 112 | 1 150 | 1 168 | 1 170 | 1 285 | 1 407 |
| 5b.   GDP | 45 | 44 | 49 | 51 | 51 | 53 | 54 | 54 | 58 | 63 |
| 5c.   % of GWP | 0.00 | 0.00 | 0.00 | 0.00 | 0.00 | 0.00 | 0.00 | 0.00 | 0.00 | 0.00 |
| **6.   WA** | | | | | | | | | | |
| 6a.   Per capita GDP | 338 | 401 | 470 | 506 | 657 | 696 | 628 | 650 | 760 | 884 |
| 6b.   GDP | 16 | 19 | 22 | 23 | 30 | 32 | 29 | 30 | 34 | 40 |
| 6c.   % of GWP | 0.00 | 0.00 | 0.00 | 0.00 | 0.00 | 0.00 | 0.00 | 0.00 | 0.00 | 0.00 |
| **Saint Lucia** | | | | | | | | | | |
| **1.   MER** | | | | | | | | | | |
| 1a.   Per capita GDP | 385 | 400 | 427 | 480 | 501 | 526 | 531 | 584 | 690 | 826 |
| 1b.   GDP | 39 | 42 | 45 | 52 | 55 | 59 | 61 | 68 | 82 | 101 |
| 1c.   % of GWP | 0.00 | 0.00 | 0.00 | 0.00 | 0.00 | 0.00 | 0.00 | 0.00 | 0.00 | 0.00 |
| **2.   PPPs** | | | | | | | | | | |
| 2a.   Per capita GDP | ... | ... | ... | ... | ... | ... | ... | ... | ... | ... |
| 2b.   GDP | ... | ... | ... | ... | ... | ... | ... | ... | ... | ... |
| 2c.   % of GWP | ... | ... | ... | ... | ... | ... | ... | ... | ... | ... |
| **3.   Absolute 1970−1989 PARE** | | | | | | | | | | |
| 3a.   Per capita GDP | 685 | 766 | 795 | 787 | 793 | 780 | 726 | 829 | 907 | 936 |
| 3b.   GDP | 70 | 80 | 84 | 85 | 87 | 88 | 83 | 97 | 108 | 114 |
| 3c.   % of GWP | 0.00 | 0.00 | 0.00 | 0.00 | 0.00 | 0.00 | 0.00 | 0.00 | 0.00 | 0.00 |
| **4.   Relative 1970−1989 PARE** | | | | | | | | | | |
| 4a.   Per capita GDP | 334 | 393 | 426 | 450 | 494 | 535 | 528 | 644 | 756 | 850 |
| 4b.   GDP | 34 | 41 | 45 | 49 | 54 | 60 | 61 | 75 | 90 | 104 |
| 4c.   % of GWP | 0.00 | 0.00 | 0.00 | 0.00 | 0.00 | 0.00 | 0.00 | 0.00 | 0.00 | 0.00 |
| **5.   Absolute 1980−1989 PARE** | | | | | | | | | | |
| 5a.   Per capita GDP | 833 | 931 | 966 | 957 | 964 | 949 | 883 | 1 008 | 1 103 | 1 138 |
| 5b.   GDP | 85 | 97 | 102 | 103 | 106 | 107 | 102 | 118 | 131 | 139 |
| 5c.   % of GWP | 0.00 | 0.00 | 0.00 | 0.00 | 0.00 | 0.00 | 0.00 | 0.00 | 0.00 | 0.00 |
| **6.   WA** | | | | | | | | | | |
| 6a.   Per capita GDP | 385 | 398 | 427 | 480 | 501 | 526 | 531 | 584 | 690 | 826 |
| 6b.   GDP | 39 | 41 | 45 | 52 | 55 | 59 | 61 | 68 | 82 | 101 |
| 6c.   % of GWP | 0.00 | 0.00 | 0.00 | 0.00 | 0.00 | 0.00 | 0.00 | 0.00 | 0.00 | 0.00 |

| | | | | | | | | | | Averages | | |
|---|---|---|---|---|---|---|---|---|---|---|---|---|
| 1980 (11) | 1981 (12) | 1982 (13) | 1983 (14) | 1984 (15) | 1985 (16) | 1986 (17) | 1987 (18) | 1988 (19) | 1989 (20) | 1970–89 (21) | 1970–79 (22) | 1980–89 (23) |
| 1 064 | 1 230 | 1 301 | 1 268 | 1 376 | 1 500 | 1 860 | 2 092 | 2 176 | 2 361 | 1 110 | 598 | 1 608 |
| 48 | 55 | 59 | 57 | 62 | 67 | 84 | 92 | 96 | 104 | 50 | 28 | 72 |
| 0.00 | 0.00 | 0.00 | 0.00 | 0.00 | 0.00 | 0.00 | 0.00 | 0.00 | 0.00 | 0.00 | 0.00 | 0.00 |
| ... | ... | ... | ... | ... | ... | ... | ... | ... | ... | ... | ... | ... |
| ... | ... | ... | ... | ... | ... | ... | ... | ... | ... | ... | ... | ... |
| ... | ... | ... | ... | ... | ... | ... | ... | ... | ... | ... | ... | ... |
| 1 183 | 1 227 | 1 213 | 1 214 | 1 268 | 1 258 | 1 309 | 1 389 | 1 437 | 1 487 | 1 110 | 910 | 1 289 |
| 53 | 55 | 55 | 55 | 57 | 57 | 59 | 61 | 63 | 65 | 50 | 42 | 58 |
| 0.00 | 0.00 | 0.00 | 0.00 | 0.00 | 0.00 | 0.00 | 0.00 | 0.00 | 0.00 | 0.00 | 0.00 | 0.00 |
| 1 172 | 1 331 | 1 401 | 1 450 | 1 568 | 1 598 | 1 697 | 1 852 | 1 980 | 2 133 | 1 119 | 619 | 1 605 |
| 53 | 60 | 63 | 65 | 71 | 72 | 76 | 82 | 87 | 94 | 50 | 28 | 72 |
| 0.00 | 0.00 | 0.00 | 0.00 | 0.00 | 0.00 | 0.00 | 0.00 | 0.00 | 0.00 | 0.00 | 0.00 | 0.00 |
| 1 476 | 1 531 | 1 513 | 1 515 | 1 582 | 1 569 | 1 633 | 1 734 | 1 793 | 1 855 | 1 385 | 1 136 | 1 608 |
| 66 | 69 | 68 | 68 | 71 | 71 | 73 | 76 | 79 | 82 | 62 | 52 | 72 |
| 0.00 | 0.00 | 0.00 | 0.00 | 0.00 | 0.00 | 0.00 | 0.00 | 0.00 | 0.00 | 0.00 | 0.00 | 0.00 |
| 1 064 | 1 230 | 1 301 | 1 268 | 1 376 | 1 500 | 1 860 | 2 092 | 2 176 | 2 361 | 1 110 | 598 | 1 608 |
| 48 | 55 | 59 | 57 | 62 | 67 | 84 | 92 | 96 | 104 | 50 | 28 | 72 |
| 0.00 | 0.00 | 0.00 | 0.00 | 0.00 | 0.00 | 0.00 | 0.00 | 0.00 | 0.00 | 0.00 | 0.00 | 0.00 |
| 912 | 994 | 1 044 | 1 066 | 1 120 | 1 219 | 1 331 | 1 378 | 1 417 | 1 477 | 914 | 542 | 1 204 |
| 113 | 126 | 135 | 141 | 151 | 168 | 186 | 197 | 207 | 219 | 112 | 60 | 164 |
| 0.00 | 0.00 | 0.00 | 0.00 | 0.00 | 0.00 | 0.00 | 0.00 | 0.00 | 0.00 | 0.00 | 0.00 | 0.00 |
| ... | ... | ... | ... | ... | ... | ... | ... | ... | ... | ... | ... | ... |
| ... | ... | ... | ... | ... | ... | ... | ... | ... | ... | ... | ... | ... |
| ... | ... | ... | ... | ... | ... | ... | ... | ... | ... | ... | ... | ... |
| 924 | 908 | 924 | 919 | 961 | 1 001 | 1 047 | 1 046 | 1 063 | 1 092 | 914 | 804 | 990 |
| 115 | 115 | 119 | 121 | 130 | 138 | 147 | 150 | 155 | 162 | 112 | 90 | 135 |
| 0.00 | 0.00 | 0.00 | 0.00 | 0.00 | 0.00 | 0.00 | 0.00 | 0.00 | 0.00 | 0.00 | 0.00 | 0.00 |
| 916 | 985 | 1 067 | 1 097 | 1 189 | 1 271 | 1 357 | 1 394 | 1 465 | 1 567 | 937 | 550 | 1 240 |
| 114 | 125 | 138 | 145 | 161 | 175 | 190 | 199 | 214 | 232 | 115 | 61 | 169 |
| 0.00 | 0.00 | 0.00 | 0.00 | 0.00 | 0.00 | 0.00 | 0.00 | 0.00 | 0.00 | 0.00 | 0.00 | 0.00 |
| 1 123 | 1 104 | 1 123 | 1 117 | 1 169 | 1 217 | 1 273 | 1 272 | 1 293 | 1 328 | 1 111 | 978 | 1 204 |
| 139 | 140 | 145 | 147 | 158 | 168 | 178 | 182 | 189 | 197 | 137 | 109 | 164 |
| 0.00 | 0.00 | 0.00 | 0.00 | 0.00 | 0.00 | 0.00 | 0.00 | 0.00 | 0.00 | 0.00 | 0.00 | 0.00 |
| 912 | 994 | 1 044 | 1 066 | 1 120 | 1 219 | 1 331 | 1 378 | 1 417 | 1 477 | 914 | 542 | 1 204 |
| 113 | 126 | 135 | 141 | 151 | 168 | 186 | 197 | 207 | 219 | 112 | 60 | 164 |
| 0.00 | 0.00 | 0.00 | 0.00 | 0.00 | 0.00 | 0.00 | 0.00 | 0.00 | 0.00 | 0.00 | 0.00 | 0.00 |

**Table A.1**  Total and per capita gross domestic product of individual countries or areas, expressed in United States dollars, and their individual shares of gross world product, based on alternative conversion rates, 1970−1989 [*cont.*]

| Country or area | 1970 (1) | 1971 (2) | 1972 (3) | 1973 (4) | 1974 (5) | 1975 (6) | 1976 (7) | 1977 (8) | 1978 (9) | 1979 (10) |
|---|---|---|---|---|---|---|---|---|---|---|
| **Saint Vincent−Grenadines** | | | | | | | | | | |
| **1.  MER** | | | | | | | | | | |
| 1a.  Per capita GDP | 196 | 212 | 287 | 311 | 336 | 335 | 321 | 359 | 448 | 516 |
| 1b.  GDP | 18 | 20 | 28 | 30 | 33 | 33 | 32 | 36 | 45 | 53 |
| 1c.  % of GWP | 0.00 | 0.00 | 0.00 | 0.00 | 0.00 | 0.00 | 0.00 | 0.00 | 0.00 | 0.00 |
| **2.  PPPs** | | | | | | | | | | |
| 2a.  Per capita GDP | ... | ... | ... | ... | ... | ... | ... | ... | ... | ... |
| 2b.  GDP | ... | ... | ... | ... | ... | ... | ... | ... | ... | ... |
| 2c.  % of GWP | ... | ... | ... | ... | ... | ... | ... | ... | ... | ... |
| **3.  Absolute 1970−1989 PARE** | | | | | | | | | | |
| 3a.  Per capita GDP | 529 | 539 | 671 | 591 | 533 | 493 | 515 | 536 | 581 | 600 |
| 3b.  GDP | 50 | 51 | 64 | 57 | 52 | 48 | 51 | 54 | 59 | 61 |
| 3c.  % of GWP | 0.00 | 0.00 | 0.00 | 0.00 | 0.00 | 0.00 | 0.00 | 0.00 | 0.00 | 0.00 |
| **4.  Relative 1970−1989 PARE** | | | | | | | | | | |
| 4a.  Per capita GDP | 258 | 276 | 360 | 338 | 332 | 337 | 375 | 416 | 484 | 545 |
| 4b.  GDP | 24 | 26 | 35 | 33 | 33 | 33 | 37 | 42 | 49 | 56 |
| 4c.  % of GWP | 0.00 | 0.00 | 0.00 | 0.00 | 0.00 | 0.00 | 0.00 | 0.00 | 0.00 | 0.00 |
| **5.  Absolute 1980−1989 PARE** | | | | | | | | | | |
| 5a.  Per capita GDP | 664 | 676 | 842 | 741 | 669 | 618 | 645 | 672 | 729 | 753 |
| 5b.  GDP | 62 | 64 | 81 | 72 | 66 | 61 | 64 | 67 | 74 | 77 |
| 5c.  % of GWP | 0.00 | 0.00 | 0.00 | 0.00 | 0.00 | 0.00 | 0.00 | 0.00 | 0.00 | 0.00 |
| **6.  WA** | | | | | | | | | | |
| 6a.  Per capita GDP | 196 | 208 | 276 | 305 | 345 | 364 | 279 | 323 | 403 | 464 |
| 6b.  GDP | 18 | 20 | 27 | 30 | 34 | 36 | 28 | 32 | 41 | 47 |
| 6c.  % of GWP | 0.00 | 0.00 | 0.00 | 0.00 | 0.00 | 0.00 | 0.00 | 0.00 | 0.00 | 0.00 |
| **Samoa** | | | | | | | | | | |
| **1.  MER** | | | | | | | | | | |
| 1a.  Per capita GDP | 297 | 329 | 385 | 481 | 630 | 658 | 565 | 567 | 649 | 635 |
| 1b.  GDP | 43 | 48 | 57 | 71 | 94 | 98 | 85 | 86 | 99 | 98 |
| 1c.  % of GWP | 0.00 | 0.00 | 0.00 | 0.00 | 0.00 | 0.00 | 0.00 | 0.00 | 0.00 | 0.00 |
| **2.  PPPs** | | | | | | | | | | |
| 2a.  Per capita GDP | ... | ... | ... | ... | ... | ... | ... | ... | ... | ... |
| 2b.  GDP | ... | ... | ... | ... | ... | ... | ... | ... | ... | ... |
| 2c.  % of GWP | ... | ... | ... | ... | ... | ... | ... | ... | ... | ... |
| **3.  Absolute 1970−1989 PARE** | | | | | | | | | | |
| 3a.  Per capita GDP | 512 | 518 | 534 | 544 | 559 | 572 | 588 | 599 | 614 | 629 |
| 3b.  GDP | 74 | 76 | 79 | 80 | 83 | 85 | 88 | 91 | 94 | 97 |
| 3c.  % of GWP | 0.00 | 0.00 | 0.00 | 0.00 | 0.00 | 0.00 | 0.00 | 0.00 | 0.00 | 0.00 |
| **4.  Relative 1970−1989 PARE** | | | | | | | | | | |
| 4a.  Per capita GDP | 249 | 265 | 286 | 311 | 349 | 392 | 428 | 466 | 512 | 572 |
| 4b.  GDP | 36 | 39 | 42 | 46 | 52 | 58 | 64 | 71 | 78 | 88 |
| 4c.  % of GWP | 0.00 | 0.00 | 0.00 | 0.00 | 0.00 | 0.00 | 0.00 | 0.00 | 0.00 | 0.00 |
| **5.  Absolute 1980−1989 PARE** | | | | | | | | | | |
| 5a.  Per capita GDP | 548 | 555 | 573 | 583 | 600 | 614 | 630 | 643 | 659 | 675 |
| 5b.  GDP | 79 | 81 | 84 | 86 | 89 | 91 | 95 | 98 | 101 | 104 |
| 5c.  % of GWP | 0.00 | 0.00 | 0.00 | 0.00 | 0.00 | 0.00 | 0.00 | 0.00 | 0.00 | 0.00 |
| **6.  WA** | | | | | | | | | | |
| 6a.  Per capita GDP | 297 | 328 | 385 | 479 | 631 | 657 | 567 | 567 | 649 | 630 |
| 6b.  GDP | 43 | 48 | 57 | 71 | 94 | 98 | 85 | 86 | 99 | 97 |
| 6c.  % of GWP | 0.00 | 0.00 | 0.00 | 0.00 | 0.00 | 0.00 | 0.00 | 0.00 | 0.00 | 0.00 |

| | | | | | | | | | | Averages | | |
|---|---|---|---|---|---|---|---|---|---|---|---|---|
| 1980 (11) | 1981 (12) | 1982 (13) | 1983 (14) | 1984 (15) | 1985 (16) | 1986 (17) | 1987 (18) | 1988 (19) | 1989 (20) | 1970–89 (21) | 1970–79 (22) | 1980–89 (23) |
| 572 | 689 | 791 | 877 | 934 | 1 019 | 1 137 | 1 176 | 1 277 | 1 388 | 690 | 334 | 992 |
| 59 | 72 | 84 | 94 | 102 | 112 | 126 | 132 | 146 | 160 | 71 | 33 | 109 |
| 0.00 | 0.00 | 0.00 | 0.00 | 0.00 | 0.00 | 0.00 | 0.00 | 0.00 | 0.00 | 0.00 | 0.00 | 0.00 |
| ... | ... | ... | ... | ... | ... | ... | ... | ... | ... | ... | ... | ... |
| ... | ... | ... | ... | ... | ... | ... | ... | ... | ... | ... | ... | ... |
| ... | ... | ... | ... | ... | ... | ... | ... | ... | ... | ... | ... | ... |
| 620 | 651 | 696 | 734 | 760 | 808 | 851 | 869 | 928 | 975 | 690 | 559 | 791 |
| 64 | 68 | 74 | 79 | 83 | 89 | 94 | 97 | 106 | 112 | 71 | 55 | 87 |
| 0.00 | 0.00 | 0.00 | 0.00 | 0.00 | 0.00 | 0.00 | 0.00 | 0.00 | 0.00 | 0.00 | 0.00 | 0.00 |
| 615 | 707 | 804 | 877 | 940 | 1 026 | 1 102 | 1 158 | 1 279 | 1 398 | 711 | 374 | 996 |
| 63 | 74 | 85 | 94 | 103 | 113 | 122 | 130 | 146 | 161 | 73 | 37 | 109 |
| 0.00 | 0.00 | 0.00 | 0.00 | 0.00 | 0.00 | 0.00 | 0.00 | 0.00 | 0.00 | 0.00 | 0.00 | 0.00 |
| 778 | 817 | 873 | 921 | 953 | 1 013 | 1 067 | 1 089 | 1 164 | 1 222 | 865 | 701 | 992 |
| 80 | 86 | 93 | 99 | 104 | 111 | 118 | 122 | 133 | 141 | 89 | 69 | 109 |
| 0.00 | 0.00 | 0.00 | 0.00 | 0.00 | 0.00 | 0.00 | 0.00 | 0.00 | 0.00 | 0.00 | 0.00 | 0.00 |
| 515 | 620 | 712 | 789 | 841 | 917 | 1 023 | 1 059 | 1 150 | 1 249 | 629 | 318 | 893 |
| 53 | 65 | 75 | 84 | 92 | 101 | 114 | 119 | 131 | 144 | 64 | 31 | 98 |
| 0.00 | 0.00 | 0.00 | 0.00 | 0.00 | 0.00 | 0.00 | 0.00 | 0.00 | 0.00 | 0.00 | 0.00 | 0.00 |
| 718 | 670 | 685 | 627 | 612 | 523 | 549 | 610 | 674 | 639 | 580 | 523 | 630 |
| 112 | 105 | 108 | 100 | 99 | 85 | 90 | 101 | 113 | 107 | 90 | 78 | 102 |
| 0.00 | 0.00 | 0.00 | 0.00 | 0.00 | 0.00 | 0.00 | 0.00 | 0.00 | 0.00 | 0.00 | 0.00 | 0.00 |
| ... | ... | ... | ... | ... | ... | ... | ... | ... | ... | ... | ... | ... |
| ... | ... | ... | ... | ... | ... | ... | ... | ... | ... | ... | ... | ... |
| ... | ... | ... | ... | ... | ... | ... | ... | ... | ... | ... | ... | ... |
| 640 | 580 | 570 | 563 | 566 | 595 | 595 | 597 | 584 | 588 | 580 | 569 | 587 |
| 100 | 91 | 90 | 90 | 91 | 97 | 98 | 98 | 98 | 99 | 90 | 85 | 95 |
| 0.00 | 0.00 | 0.00 | 0.00 | 0.00 | 0.00 | 0.00 | 0.00 | 0.00 | 0.00 | 0.00 | 0.00 | 0.00 |
| 634 | 630 | 659 | 673 | 700 | 755 | 771 | 796 | 805 | 844 | 566 | 386 | 728 |
| 99 | 99 | 104 | 108 | 113 | 123 | 126 | 131 | 134 | 142 | 88 | 57 | 118 |
| 0.00 | 0.00 | 0.00 | 0.00 | 0.00 | 0.00 | 0.00 | 0.00 | 0.00 | 0.00 | 0.00 | 0.00 | 0.00 |
| 686 | 622 | 612 | 604 | 607 | 637 | 637 | 640 | 626 | 631 | 622 | 609 | 630 |
| 107 | 98 | 97 | 97 | 98 | 104 | 105 | 106 | 105 | 106 | 96 | 91 | 102 |
| 0.00 | 0.00 | 0.00 | 0.00 | 0.00 | 0.00 | 0.00 | 0.00 | 0.00 | 0.00 | 0.00 | 0.00 | 0.00 |
| 718 | 671 | 684 | 623 | 604 | 522 | 548 | 603 | 680 | 648 | 580 | 522 | 629 |
| 112 | 105 | 108 | 100 | 97 | 85 | 90 | 100 | 114 | 109 | 90 | 78 | 102 |
| 0.00 | 0.00 | 0.00 | 0.00 | 0.00 | 0.00 | 0.00 | 0.00 | 0.00 | 0.00 | 0.00 | 0.00 | 0.00 |

**Table A.1**    Total and per capita gross domestic product of individual countries or areas, expressed in United States dollars, and their individual shares of gross world product, based on alternative conversion rates, 1970−1989 [*cont.*]

| Country or area | 1970 (1) | 1971 (2) | 1972 (3) | 1973 (4) | 1974 (5) | 1975 (6) | 1976 (7) | 1977 (8) | 1978 (9) | 1979 (10) |
|---|---|---|---|---|---|---|---|---|---|---|
| **Sao Tome−Principe** | | | | | | | | | | |
| **1.  MER** | | | | | | | | | | |
| 1a.  Per capita GDP | 208 | 201 | 216 | 287 | 329 | 291 | 272 | 412 | 419 | 459 |
| 1b.  GDP | 15 | 15 | 16 | 22 | 26 | 24 | 23 | 35 | 37 | 42 |
| 1c.  % of GWP | 0.00 | 0.00 | 0.00 | 0.00 | 0.00 | 0.00 | 0.00 | 0.00 | 0.00 | 0.00 |
| **2.  PPPs** | | | | | | | | | | |
| 2a.  Per capita GDP | ... | ... | ... | ... | ... | ... | ... | ... | ... | ... |
| 2b.  GDP | ... | ... | ... | ... | ... | ... | ... | ... | ... | ... |
| 2c.  % of GWP | ... | ... | ... | ... | ... | ... | ... | ... | ... | ... |
| **3.  Absolute 1970−1989 PARE** | | | | | | | | | | |
| 3a.  Per capita GDP | 578 | 592 | 610 | 554 | 464 | 411 | 401 | 416 | 408 | 406 |
| 3b.  GDP | 42 | 44 | 46 | 43 | 37 | 33 | 34 | 36 | 36 | 37 |
| 3c.  % of GWP | 0.00 | 0.00 | 0.00 | 0.00 | 0.00 | 0.00 | 0.00 | 0.00 | 0.00 | 0.00 |
| **4.  Relative 1970−1989 PARE** | | | | | | | | | | |
| 4a.  Per capita GDP | 282 | 303 | 327 | 317 | 289 | 281 | 292 | 323 | 340 | 369 |
| 4b.  GDP | 21 | 23 | 25 | 25 | 23 | 23 | 25 | 28 | 30 | 34 |
| 4c.  % of GWP | 0.00 | 0.00 | 0.00 | 0.00 | 0.00 | 0.00 | 0.00 | 0.00 | 0.00 | 0.00 |
| **5.  Absolute 1980−1989 PARE** | | | | | | | | | | |
| 5a.  Per capita GDP | 824 | 844 | 870 | 791 | 662 | 586 | 572 | 594 | 581 | 579 |
| 5b.  GDP | 60 | 63 | 66 | 62 | 52 | 47 | 48 | 51 | 52 | 53 |
| 5c.  % of GWP | 0.00 | 0.00 | 0.00 | 0.00 | 0.00 | 0.00 | 0.00 | 0.00 | 0.00 | 0.00 |
| **6.  WA** | | | | | | | | | | |
| 6a.  Per capita GDP | 208 | 201 | 216 | 287 | 329 | 291 | 272 | 412 | 419 | 459 |
| 6b.  GDP | 15 | 15 | 16 | 22 | 26 | 24 | 23 | 35 | 37 | 42 |
| 6c.  % of GWP | 0.00 | 0.00 | 0.00 | 0.00 | 0.00 | 0.00 | 0.00 | 0.00 | 0.00 | 0.00 |
| **Saudi Arabia** | | | | | | | | | | |
| **1.  MER** | | | | | | | | | | |
| 1a.  Per capita GDP | 673 | 855 | 1 086 | 1 668 | 4 057 | 5 472 | 6 101 | 7 223 | 7 810 | 8 313 |
| 1b.  GDP | 3 867 | 5 127 | 6 809 | 10 957 | 27 976 | 39 682 | 46 608 | 58 172 | 66 294 | 74 245 |
| 1c.  % of GWP | 0.12 | 0.15 | 0.17 | 0.22 | 0.50 | 0.64 | 0.69 | 0.77 | 0.74 | 0.72 |
| **2.  PPPs** | | | | | | | | | | |
| 2a.  Per capita GDP | 978 | 1 206 | 1 424 | 1 947 | 4 410 | 5 459 | 5 738 | 6 512 | 6 485 | 7 350 |
| 2b.  GDP | 5 621 | 7 230 | 8 926 | 12 793 | 30 412 | 39 591 | 43 833 | 52 450 | 55 048 | 65 646 |
| 2c.  % of GWP | ... | ... | ... | ... | ... | ... | ... | ... | ... | ... |
| **3.  Absolute 1970−1989 PARE** | | | | | | | | | | |
| 3a.  Per capita GDP | 6 135 | 6 725 | 7 419 | 8 478 | 9 294 | 8 860 | 9 137 | 9 976 | 10 029 | 9 958 |
| 3b.  GDP | 35 244 | 40 322 | 46 511 | 55 691 | 64 091 | 64 255 | 69 801 | 80 347 | 85 128 | 88 934 |
| 3c.  % of GWP | 0.50 | 0.54 | 0.60 | 0.67 | 0.76 | 0.75 | 0.77 | 0.85 | 0.87 | 0.87 |
| **4.  Relative 1970−1989 PARE** | | | | | | | | | | |
| 4a.  Per capita GDP | 2 991 | 3 447 | 3 977 | 4 847 | 5 796 | 6 070 | 6 651 | 7 752 | 8 361 | 9 043 |
| 4b.  GDP | 17 184 | 20 668 | 24 935 | 31 839 | 39 967 | 44 021 | 50 809 | 62 431 | 70 971 | 80 765 |
| 4c.  % of GWP | 0.50 | 0.54 | 0.60 | 0.67 | 0.76 | 0.75 | 0.77 | 0.85 | 0.87 | 0.87 |
| **5.  Absolute 1980−1989 PARE** | | | | | | | | | | |
| 5a.  Per capita GDP | 8 424 | 9 234 | 10 188 | 11 642 | 12 762 | 12 167 | 12 547 | 13 699 | 13 772 | 13 674 |
| 5b.  GDP | 48 396 | 55 369 | 63 869 | 76 474 | 88 009 | 88 234 | 95 850 | 110 332 | 116 897 | 122 124 |
| 5c.  % of GWP | 0.56 | 0.61 | 0.67 | 0.75 | 0.85 | 0.84 | 0.87 | 0.96 | 0.97 | 0.98 |
| **6.  WA** | | | | | | | | | | |
| 6a.  Per capita GDP | 673 | 852 | 1 088 | 1 665 | 4 057 | 5 472 | 6 101 | 7 223 | 7 811 | 8 314 |
| 6b.  GDP | 3 867 | 5 109 | 6 818 | 10 940 | 27 976 | 39 686 | 46 608 | 58 171 | 66 303 | 74 249 |
| 6c.  % of GWP | 0.12 | 0.15 | 0.17 | 0.22 | 0.50 | 0.64 | 0.69 | 0.77 | 0.75 | 0.73 |

| | 1980 (11) | 1981 (12) | 1982 (13) | 1983 (14) | 1984 (15) | 1985 (16) | 1986 (17) | 1987 (18) | 1988 (19) | 1989 (20) | Averages 1970–89 (21) | 1970–79 (22) | 1980–89 (23) |
|---|---|---|---|---|---|---|---|---|---|---|---|---|---|
| | 497 | 379 | 378 | 353 | 347 | 346 | 584 | 490 | 422 | 382 | 377 | 321 | 419 |
| | 47 | 37 | 38 | 36 | 36 | 37 | 64 | 55 | 49 | 45 | 35 | 26 | 44 |
| | 0.00 | 0.00 | 0.00 | 0.00 | 0.00 | 0.00 | 0.00 | 0.00 | 0.00 | 0.00 | 0.00 | 0.00 | 0.00 |
| | ... | ... | ... | ... | ... | ... | ... | ... | ... | ... | ... | ... | ... |
| | ... | ... | ... | ... | ... | ... | ... | ... | ... | ... | ... | ... | ... |
| | ... | ... | ... | ... | ... | ... | ... | ... | ... | ... | ... | ... | ... |
| | 408 | 342 | 349 | 294 | 273 | 255 | 258 | 262 | 261 | 263 | 377 | 486 | 294 |
| | 38 | 33 | 35 | 30 | 29 | 27 | 28 | 30 | 30 | 31 | 35 | 39 | 31 |
| | 0.00 | 0.00 | 0.00 | 0.00 | 0.00 | 0.00 | 0.00 | 0.00 | 0.00 | 0.00 | 0.00 | 0.00 | 0.00 |
| | 404 | 371 | 403 | 351 | 338 | 324 | 334 | 349 | 359 | 377 | 343 | 319 | 361 |
| | 38 | 36 | 40 | 36 | 36 | 35 | 37 | 39 | 42 | 44 | 32 | 26 | 38 |
| | 0.00 | 0.00 | 0.00 | 0.00 | 0.00 | 0.00 | 0.00 | 0.00 | 0.00 | 0.00 | 0.00 | 0.00 | 0.00 |
| | 581 | 487 | 498 | 419 | 390 | 364 | 368 | 374 | 372 | 375 | 537 | 694 | 419 |
| | 55 | 47 | 50 | 43 | 41 | 39 | 40 | 42 | 43 | 44 | 50 | 56 | 44 |
| | 0.00 | 0.00 | 0.00 | 0.00 | 0.00 | 0.00 | 0.00 | 0.00 | 0.00 | 0.00 | 0.00 | 0.00 | 0.00 |
| | 497 | 379 | 378 | 353 | 347 | 346 | 584 | 490 | 421 | 382 | 377 | 320 | 419 |
| | 47 | 37 | 38 | 36 | 36 | 37 | 64 | 55 | 49 | 45 | 35 | 26 | 44 |
| | 0.00 | 0.00 | 0.00 | 0.00 | 0.00 | 0.00 | 0.00 | 0.00 | 0.00 | 0.00 | 0.00 | 0.00 | 0.00 |
| | 12 372 | 14 792 | 15 979 | 12 409 | 9 529 | 8 366 | 7 022 | 5 831 | 5 695 | 5 606 | 7 698 | 4 803 | 9 408 |
| | 115 962 | 145 120 | 163 740 | 132 597 | 106 096 | 97 017 | 84 780 | 73 268 | 74 446 | 76 208 | 70 449 | 33 974 | 106 924 |
| | 1.00 | 1.24 | 1.41 | 1.12 | 0.87 | 0.77 | 0.57 | 0.43 | 0.39 | 0.38 | 0.69 | 0.56 | 0.75 |
| | 10 931 | 13 624 | 15 108 | 10 921 | 8 766 | 8 136 | 7 487 | 7 741 | 7 734 | 7 836 | 7 738 | 4 546 | 9 634 |
| | 102 458 | 133 665 | 154 807 | 116 703 | 97 596 | 94 345 | 90 394 | 97 269 | 101 101 | 106 530 | 70 821 | 32 155 | 109 487 |
| | ... | ... | ... | ... | ... | ... | ... | ... | ... | ... | ... | ... | ... |
| | 10 309 | 10 425 | 9 715 | 7 359 | 6 721 | 5 739 | 5 177 | 5 203 | 5 029 | 4 895 | 7 698 | 8 910 | 6 851 |
| | 96 623 | 102 283 | 99 553 | 78 641 | 74 834 | 66 544 | 62 502 | 65 377 | 65 745 | 66 547 | 70 449 | 63 032 | 77 865 |
| | 0.93 | 0.97 | 0.93 | 0.72 | 0.65 | 0.56 | 0.51 | 0.52 | 0.50 | 0.49 | 0.69 | 0.73 | 0.66 |
| | 10 219 | 11 312 | 11 223 | 8 788 | 8 314 | 7 291 | 6 709 | 6 937 | 6 931 | 7 022 | 7 597 | 6 271 | 8 333 |
| | 95 779 | 110 982 | 114 998 | 93 911 | 92 566 | 84 542 | 81 002 | 87 163 | 90 596 | 95 461 | 69 530 | 44 359 | 94 700 |
| | 0.93 | 0.97 | 0.93 | 0.72 | 0.65 | 0.56 | 0.51 | 0.52 | 0.50 | 0.49 | 0.68 | 0.76 | 0.64 |
| | 14 156 | 14 316 | 13 341 | 10 106 | 9 230 | 7 880 | 7 109 | 7 145 | 6 906 | 6 722 | 10 570 | 12 236 | 9 408 |
| | 132 682 | 140 455 | 136 706 | 107 989 | 102 762 | 91 378 | 85 827 | 89 775 | 90 280 | 91 381 | 96 740 | 86 555 | 106 924 |
| | 1.05 | 1.09 | 1.05 | 0.81 | 0.74 | 0.63 | 0.58 | 0.59 | 0.56 | 0.55 | 0.78 | 0.82 | 0.75 |
| | 12 373 | 14 794 | 15 974 | 12 409 | 9 530 | 8 366 | 7 022 | 5 761 | 5 627 | 5 538 | 7 683 | 4 802 | 9 384 |
| | 115 971 | 145 141 | 163 684 | 132 607 | 106 102 | 97 014 | 84 773 | 72 387 | 73 552 | 75 293 | 70 312 | 33 973 | 106 652 |
| | 1.01 | 1.23 | 1.40 | 1.12 | 0.87 | 0.77 | 0.58 | 0.43 | 0.39 | 0.38 | 0.70 | 0.56 | 0.75 |

**Table A.1**     Total and per capita gross domestic product of individual countries or areas,
expressed in United States dollars, and their individual shares of gross world
product, based on alternative conversion rates, 1970–1989 [*cont.*]

| Country or area | 1970 (1) | 1971 (2) | 1972 (3) | 1973 (4) | 1974 (5) | 1975 (6) | 1976 (7) | 1977 (8) | 1978 (9) | 1979 (10) |
|---|---|---|---|---|---|---|---|---|---|---|
| **Senegal** | | | | | | | | | | |
| 1.   **MER** | | | | | | | | | | |
| 1a.  Per capita GDP | 208 | 210 | 246 | 275 | 302 | 395 | 389 | 387 | 419 | 508 |
| 1b.  GDP | 865 | 897 | 1 085 | 1 249 | 1 409 | 1 896 | 1 922 | 1 968 | 2 192 | 2 736 |
| 1c.  % of GWP | 0.03 | 0.03 | 0.03 | 0.03 | 0.03 | 0.03 | 0.03 | 0.03 | 0.02 | 0.03 |
| 2.   **PPPs** | | | | | | | | | | |
| 2a.  Per capita GDP | 415 | 428 | 436 | 424 | 477 | 543 | 601 | 629 | 629 | 726 |
| 2b.  GDP | 1 724 | 1 832 | 1 920 | 1 923 | 2 229 | 2 612 | 2 972 | 3 201 | 3 294 | 3 909 |
| 2c.  % of GWP | ... | ... | ... | ... | ... | ... | ... | ... | ... | ... |
| 3.   **Absolute 1970–1989 PARE** | | | | | | | | | | |
| 3a.  Per capita GDP | 485 | 471 | 487 | 446 | 452 | 472 | 499 | 472 | 431 | 459 |
| 3b.  GDP | 2 018 | 2 015 | 2 144 | 2 024 | 2 109 | 2 268 | 2 470 | 2 404 | 2 254 | 2 471 |
| 3c.  % of GWP | 0.03 | 0.03 | 0.03 | 0.02 | 0.02 | 0.03 | 0.03 | 0.03 | 0.02 | 0.02 |
| 4.   **Relative 1970–1989 PARE** | | | | | | | | | | |
| 4a.  Per capita GDP | 237 | 241 | 261 | 255 | 282 | 323 | 364 | 367 | 359 | 417 |
| 4b.  GDP | 984 | 1 033 | 1 149 | 1 157 | 1 315 | 1 554 | 1 798 | 1 868 | 1 879 | 2 244 |
| 4c.  % of GWP | 0.03 | 0.03 | 0.03 | 0.02 | 0.02 | 0.03 | 0.03 | 0.03 | 0.02 | 0.02 |
| 5.   **Absolute 1980–1989 PARE** | | | | | | | | | | |
| 5a.  Per capita GDP | 589 | 572 | 591 | 542 | 548 | 573 | 606 | 573 | 523 | 557 |
| 5b.  GDP | 2 449 | 2 446 | 2 602 | 2 457 | 2 560 | 2 753 | 2 999 | 2 918 | 2 736 | 2 999 |
| 5c.  % of GWP | 0.03 | 0.03 | 0.03 | 0.02 | 0.02 | 0.03 | 0.03 | 0.03 | 0.02 | 0.02 |
| 6.   **WA** | | | | | | | | | | |
| 6a.  Per capita GDP | 208 | 208 | 246 | 275 | 301 | 395 | 389 | 387 | 419 | 508 |
| 6b.  GDP | 865 | 892 | 1 084 | 1 248 | 1 408 | 1 896 | 1 922 | 1 968 | 2 192 | 2 736 |
| 6c.  % of GWP | 0.03 | 0.03 | 0.03 | 0.03 | 0.03 | 0.03 | 0.03 | 0.03 | 0.02 | 0.03 |
| **Seychelles** | | | | | | | | | | |
| 1.   **MER** | | | | | | | | | | |
| 1a.  Per capita GDP | 380 | 445 | 598 | 670 | 711 | 763 | 808 | 1 040 | 1 358 | 2 021 |
| 1b.  GDP | 21 | 24 | 33 | 39 | 42 | 46 | 49 | 65 | 86 | 127 |
| 1c.  % of GWP | 0.00 | 0.00 | 0.00 | 0.00 | 0.00 | 0.00 | 0.00 | 0.00 | 0.00 | 0.00 |
| 2.   **PPPs** | | | | | | | | | | |
| 2a.  Per capita GDP | ... | ... | ... | ... | ... | ... | ... | ... | ... | ... |
| 2b.  GDP | ... | ... | ... | ... | ... | ... | ... | ... | ... | ... |
| 2c.  % of GWP | ... | ... | ... | ... | ... | ... | ... | ... | ... | ... |
| 3.   **Absolute 1970–1989 PARE** | | | | | | | | | | |
| 3a.  Per capita GDP | 307 | 312 | 350 | 354 | 338 | 335 | 2 163 | 2 291 | 2 412 | 2 809 |
| 3b.  GDP | 17 | 17 | 20 | 21 | 20 | 20 | 132 | 142 | 152 | 177 |
| 3c.  % of GWP | 0.00 | 0.00 | 0.00 | 0.00 | 0.00 | 0.00 | 0.00 | 0.00 | 0.00 | 0.00 |
| 4.   **Relative 1970–1989 PARE** | | | | | | | | | | |
| 4a.  Per capita GDP | 150 | 160 | 187 | 202 | 211 | 229 | 1 575 | 1 780 | 2 011 | 2 551 |
| 4b.  GDP | 8 | 9 | 10 | 12 | 12 | 14 | 96 | 110 | 127 | 161 |
| 4c.  % of GWP | 0.00 | 0.00 | 0.00 | 0.00 | 0.00 | 0.00 | 0.00 | 0.00 | 0.00 | 0.00 |
| 5.   **Absolute 1980–1989 PARE** | | | | | | | | | | |
| 5a.  Per capita GDP | 339 | 345 | 386 | 391 | 373 | 370 | 2 391 | 2 532 | 2 666 | 3 105 |
| 5b.  GDP | 18 | 19 | 22 | 23 | 22 | 22 | 146 | 157 | 168 | 196 |
| 5c.  % of GWP | 0.00 | 0.00 | 0.00 | 0.00 | 0.00 | 0.00 | 0.00 | 0.00 | 0.00 | 0.00 |
| 6.   **WA** | | | | | | | | | | |
| 6a.  Per capita GDP | 380 | 445 | 598 | 669 | 711 | 763 | 808 | 1 040 | 1 358 | 2 021 |
| 6b.  GDP | 21 | 24 | 33 | 39 | 42 | 46 | 49 | 65 | 86 | 127 |
| 6c.  % of GWP | 0.00 | 0.00 | 0.00 | 0.00 | 0.00 | 0.00 | 0.00 | 0.00 | 0.00 | 0.00 |

| 1980 (11) | 1981 (12) | 1982 (13) | 1983 (14) | 1984 (15) | 1985 (16) | 1986 (17) | 1987 (18) | 1988 (19) | 1989 (20) | Averages 1970–89 (21) | 1970–79 (22) | 1980–89 (23) |
|---|---|---|---|---|---|---|---|---|---|---|---|---|
| 536 | 433 | 438 | 403 | 375 | 402 | 576 | 679 | 755 | 690 | 458 | 342 | 538 |
| 2 970 | 2 465 | 2 569 | 2 427 | 2 324 | 2 564 | 3 774 | 4 574 | 5 230 | 4 915 | 2 502 | 1 622 | 3 381 |
| 0.03 | 0.02 | 0.02 | 0.02 | 0.02 | 0.02 | 0.03 | 0.03 | 0.03 | 0.02 | 0.02 | 0.03 | 0.02 |
| 747 | 807 | 934 | 973 | 966 | 1 000 | 1 038 | 1 071 | 1 129 | 1 125 | 805 | 541 | 991 |
| 4 139 | 4 597 | 5 473 | 5 867 | 5 991 | 6 377 | 6 805 | 7 221 | 7 826 | 8 015 | 4 396 | 2 562 | 6 231 |
| ... | ... | ... | ... | ... | ... | ... | ... | ... | ... | ... | ... | ... |
| 431 | 416 | 466 | 465 | 431 | 435 | 442 | 444 | 453 | 433 | 458 | 468 | 443 |
| 2 389 | 2 371 | 2 731 | 2 801 | 2 672 | 2 773 | 2 901 | 2 992 | 3 138 | 3 087 | 2 502 | 2 218 | 2 786 |
| 0.02 | 0.02 | 0.03 | 0.03 | 0.02 | 0.02 | 0.02 | 0.02 | 0.02 | 0.02 | 0.02 | 0.03 | 0.02 |
| 428 | 452 | 538 | 555 | 533 | 553 | 573 | 592 | 624 | 621 | 455 | 316 | 553 |
| 2 369 | 2 573 | 3 155 | 3 345 | 3 305 | 3 523 | 3 760 | 3 990 | 4 323 | 4 428 | 2 488 | 1 498 | 3 477 |
| 0.02 | 0.02 | 0.03 | 0.03 | 0.02 | 0.02 | 0.02 | 0.02 | 0.02 | 0.02 | 0.02 | 0.03 | 0.02 |
| 524 | 505 | 566 | 564 | 523 | 528 | 537 | 539 | 549 | 526 | 556 | 568 | 538 |
| 2 900 | 2 878 | 3 316 | 3 401 | 3 243 | 3 366 | 3 521 | 3 632 | 3 809 | 3 747 | 3 037 | 2 692 | 3 381 |
| 0.02 | 0.02 | 0.03 | 0.03 | 0.02 | 0.02 | 0.02 | 0.02 | 0.02 | 0.02 | 0.02 | 0.03 | 0.02 |
| 536 | 433 | 438 | 403 | 375 | 402 | 576 | 679 | 755 | 690 | 458 | 342 | 538 |
| 2 970 | 2 465 | 2 569 | 2 427 | 2 324 | 2 564 | 3 774 | 4 574 | 5 231 | 4 915 | 2 501 | 1 621 | 3 381 |
| 0.03 | 0.02 | 0.02 | 0.02 | 0.02 | 0.02 | 0.03 | 0.03 | 0.03 | 0.03 | 0.02 | 0.03 | 0.02 |
| 2 302 | 2 404 | 2 273 | 2 249 | 2 327 | 2 559 | 3 102 | 3 693 | 4 150 | 4 239 | 1 950 | 894 | 2 970 |
| 147 | 154 | 148 | 146 | 151 | 169 | 208 | 247 | 282 | 293 | 124 | 53 | 195 |
| 0.00 | 0.00 | 0.00 | 0.00 | 0.00 | 0.00 | 0.00 | 0.00 | 0.00 | 0.00 | 0.00 | 0.00 | 0.00 |
| ... | ... | ... | ... | ... | ... | ... | ... | ... | ... | ... | ... | ... |
| ... | ... | ... | ... | ... | ... | ... | ... | ... | ... | ... | ... | ... |
| ... | ... | ... | ... | ... | ... | ... | ... | ... | ... | ... | ... | ... |
| 2 695 | 2 513 | 2 389 | 2 310 | 2 536 | 2 765 | 2 728 | 2 817 | 2 877 | 2 999 | 1 950 | 1 205 | 2 687 |
| 172 | 161 | 155 | 150 | 165 | 182 | 183 | 189 | 196 | 207 | 124 | 72 | 176 |
| 0.00 | 0.00 | 0.00 | 0.00 | 0.00 | 0.00 | 0.00 | 0.00 | 0.00 | 0.00 | 0.00 | 0.00 | 0.00 |
| 2 672 | 2 727 | 2 760 | 2 758 | 3 137 | 3 513 | 3 535 | 3 756 | 3 964 | 4 303 | 2 168 | 940 | 3 351 |
| 171 | 175 | 179 | 179 | 204 | 232 | 237 | 252 | 270 | 297 | 138 | 56 | 219 |
| 0.00 | 0.00 | 0.00 | 0.00 | 0.00 | 0.00 | 0.00 | 0.00 | 0.00 | 0.00 | 0.00 | 0.00 | 0.00 |
| 2 979 | 2 777 | 2 640 | 2 553 | 2 803 | 3 056 | 3 015 | 3 113 | 3 179 | 3 315 | 2 156 | 1 331 | 2 970 |
| 191 | 178 | 172 | 166 | 182 | 202 | 202 | 209 | 216 | 229 | 137 | 79 | 195 |
| 0.00 | 0.00 | 0.00 | 0.00 | 0.00 | 0.00 | 0.00 | 0.00 | 0.00 | 0.00 | 0.00 | 0.00 | 0.00 |
| 2 302 | 2 405 | 2 273 | 2 249 | 2 327 | 2 559 | 3 102 | 3 693 | 4 163 | 4 205 | 1 949 | 894 | 2 968 |
| 147 | 154 | 148 | 146 | 151 | 169 | 208 | 247 | 283 | 290 | 124 | 53 | 194 |
| 0.00 | 0.00 | 0.00 | 0.00 | 0.00 | 0.00 | 0.00 | 0.00 | 0.00 | 0.00 | 0.00 | 0.00 | 0.00 |

**Table A.1** Total and per capita gross domestic product of individual countries or areas, expressed in United States dollars, and their individual shares of gross world product, based on alternative conversion rates, 1970−1989 [*cont.*]

| Country or area | 1970 (1) | 1971 (2) | 1972 (3) | 1973 (4) | 1974 (5) | 1975 (6) | 1976 (7) | 1977 (8) | 1978 (9) | 1979 (10) |
|---|---|---|---|---|---|---|---|---|---|---|
| **Sierra Leone** | | | | | | | | | | |
| 1. **MER** | | | | | | | | | | |
| 1a. Per capita GDP | 156 | 157 | 161 | 171 | 195 | 217 | 185 | 212 | 260 | 305 |
| 1b. GDP | 415 | 426 | 445 | 482 | 559 | 636 | 554 | 649 | 813 | 974 |
| 1c. % of GWP | 0.01 | 0.01 | 0.01 | 0.01 | 0.01 | 0.01 | 0.01 | 0.01 | 0.01 | 0.01 |
| 2. **PPPs** | | | | | | | | | | |
| 2a. Per capita GDP | 294 | 295 | 293 | 288 | 299 | 344 | 328 | 362 | 400 | 433 |
| 2b. GDP | 781 | 799 | 808 | 810 | 860 | 1 007 | 983 | 1 106 | 1 249 | 1 381 |
| 2c. % of GWP | ... | ... | ... | ... | ... | ... | ... | ... | ... | ... |
| 3. **Absolute 1970−1989 PARE** | | | | | | | | | | |
| 3a. Per capita GDP | 252 | 255 | 247 | 250 | 255 | 257 | 244 | 243 | 238 | 250 |
| 3b. GDP | 670 | 690 | 683 | 704 | 732 | 754 | 731 | 742 | 744 | 799 |
| 3c. % of GWP | 0.01 | 0.01 | 0.01 | 0.01 | 0.01 | 0.01 | 0.01 | 0.01 | 0.01 | 0.01 |
| 4. **Relative 1970−1989 PARE** | | | | | | | | | | |
| 4a. Per capita GDP | 123 | 131 | 133 | 143 | 159 | 176 | 178 | 189 | 199 | 227 |
| 4b. GDP | 327 | 354 | 366 | 402 | 457 | 517 | 532 | 576 | 620 | 726 |
| 4c. % of GWP | 0.01 | 0.01 | 0.01 | 0.01 | 0.01 | 0.01 | 0.01 | 0.01 | 0.01 | 0.01 |
| 5. **Absolute 1980−1989 PARE** | | | | | | | | | | |
| 5a. Per capita GDP | 290 | 293 | 284 | 287 | 293 | 296 | 281 | 279 | 274 | 288 |
| 5b. GDP | 770 | 793 | 785 | 809 | 841 | 867 | 840 | 852 | 855 | 919 |
| 5c. % of GWP | 0.01 | 0.01 | 0.01 | 0.01 | 0.01 | 0.01 | 0.01 | 0.01 | 0.01 | 0.01 |
| 6. **WA** | | | | | | | | | | |
| 6a. Per capita GDP | 156 | 155 | 162 | 170 | 198 | 229 | 204 | 208 | 248 | 308 |
| 6b. GDP | 415 | 418 | 446 | 479 | 569 | 672 | 609 | 637 | 776 | 982 |
| 6c. % of GWP | 0.01 | 0.01 | 0.01 | 0.01 | 0.01 | 0.01 | 0.01 | 0.01 | 0.01 | 0.01 |
| **Singapore** | | | | | | | | | | |
| 1. **MER** | | | | | | | | | | |
| 1a. Per capita GDP | 914 | 1 069 | 1 356 | 1 915 | 2 322 | 2 505 | 2 582 | 2 825 | 3 327 | 3 955 |
| 1b. GDP | 1 896 | 2 260 | 2 917 | 4 197 | 5 174 | 5 670 | 5 929 | 6 576 | 7 841 | 9 436 |
| 1c. % of GWP | 0.06 | 0.06 | 0.07 | 0.09 | 0.09 | 0.09 | 0.09 | 0.09 | 0.09 | 0.09 |
| 2. **PPPs** | | | | | | | | | | |
| 2a. Per capita GDP | 1 556 | 1 833 | 2 104 | 2 353 | 2 750 | 3 039 | 3 384 | 3 751 | 4 326 | 5 008 |
| 2b. GDP | 3 228 | 3 873 | 4 529 | 5 155 | 6 127 | 6 878 | 7 770 | 8 732 | 10 197 | 11 950 |
| 2c. % of GWP | ... | ... | ... | ... | ... | ... | ... | ... | ... | ... |
| 3. **Absolute 1970−1989 PARE** | | | | | | | | | | |
| 3a. Per capita GDP | 2 387 | 2 638 | 2 936 | 3 208 | 3 368 | 3 447 | 3 642 | 3 870 | 4 151 | 4 482 |
| 3b. GDP | 4 953 | 5 574 | 6 317 | 7 028 | 7 503 | 7 801 | 8 361 | 9 010 | 9 784 | 10 695 |
| 3c. % of GWP | 0.07 | 0.08 | 0.08 | 0.08 | 0.09 | 0.09 | 0.09 | 0.10 | 0.10 | 0.11 |
| 4. **Relative 1970−1989 PARE** | | | | | | | | | | |
| 4a. Per capita GDP | 1 164 | 1 352 | 1 574 | 1 834 | 2 100 | 2 362 | 2 651 | 3 007 | 3 461 | 4 071 |
| 4b. GDP | 2 415 | 2 857 | 3 387 | 4 018 | 4 679 | 5 344 | 6 086 | 7 001 | 8 157 | 9 712 |
| 4c. % of GWP | 0.07 | 0.08 | 0.08 | 0.08 | 0.09 | 0.09 | 0.09 | 0.10 | 0.10 | 0.11 |
| 5. **Absolute 1980−1989 PARE** | | | | | | | | | | |
| 5a. Per capita GDP | 2 762 | 3 052 | 3 397 | 3 712 | 3 897 | 3 988 | 4 214 | 4 478 | 4 803 | 5 186 |
| 5b. GDP | 5 731 | 6 449 | 7 310 | 8 132 | 8 682 | 9 026 | 9 674 | 10 425 | 11 321 | 12 375 |
| 5c. % of GWP | 0.07 | 0.07 | 0.08 | 0.08 | 0.08 | 0.09 | 0.09 | 0.09 | 0.09 | 0.10 |
| 6. **WA** | | | | | | | | | | |
| 6a. Per capita GDP | 914 | 1 061 | 1 354 | 1 905 | 2 323 | 2 505 | 2 583 | 2 824 | 3 327 | 3 955 |
| 6b. GDP | 1 896 | 2 242 | 2 914 | 4 174 | 5 175 | 5 669 | 5 930 | 6 575 | 7 841 | 9 438 |
| 6c. % of GWP | 0.06 | 0.06 | 0.07 | 0.09 | 0.09 | 0.09 | 0.09 | 0.09 | 0.09 | 0.09 |

|  |  |  |  |  |  |  |  |  |  | Averages | | |
|---|---|---|---|---|---|---|---|---|---|---|---|---|
| 1980 | 1981 | 1982 | 1983 | 1984 | 1985 | 1986 | 1987 | 1988 | 1989 | 1970–89 | 1970–79 | 1980–89 |
| (11) | (12) | (13) | (14) | (15) | (16) | (17) | (18) | (19) | (20) | (21) | (22) | (23) |
| 337 | 334 | 380 | 320 | 304 | 274 | 236 | 164 | 243 | 200 | 247 | 205 | 276 |
| 1 100 | 1 116 | 1 296 | 1 118 | 1 087 | 1 005 | 886 | 630 | 957 | 809 | 798 | 595 | 1 001 |
| 0.01 | 0.01 | 0.01 | 0.01 | 0.01 | 0.01 | 0.01 | 0.00 | 0.01 | 0.00 | 0.01 | 0.01 | 0.01 |
| 462 | 451 | 445 | 360 | 422 | 527 | 506 | 529 | 530 | 524 | 421 | 337 | 480 |
| 1 509 | 1 506 | 1 520 | 1 259 | 1 510 | 1 930 | 1 899 | 2 036 | 2 090 | 2 122 | 1 358 | 979 | 1 738 |
| ... | ... | ... | ... | ... | ... | ... | ... | ... | ... | ... | ... | ... |
| 252 | 258 | 256 | 249 | 232 | 246 | 231 | 235 | 228 | 217 | 247 | 250 | 240 |
| 823 | 862 | 876 | 869 | 830 | 900 | 868 | 905 | 899 | 877 | 798 | 725 | 871 |
| 0.01 | 0.01 | 0.01 | 0.01 | 0.01 | 0.01 | 0.01 | 0.01 | 0.01 | 0.01 | 0.01 | 0.01 | 0.01 |
| 250 | 280 | 296 | 297 | 287 | 312 | 300 | 314 | 314 | 311 | 243 | 168 | 298 |
| 816 | 935 | 1 012 | 1 037 | 1 026 | 1 144 | 1 125 | 1 207 | 1 238 | 1 257 | 784 | 488 | 1 080 |
| 0.01 | 0.01 | 0.01 | 0.01 | 0.01 | 0.01 | 0.01 | 0.01 | 0.01 | 0.01 | 0.01 | 0.01 | 0.01 |
| 290 | 297 | 295 | 286 | 266 | 282 | 266 | 270 | 262 | 249 | 284 | 287 | 276 |
| 946 | 990 | 1 006 | 998 | 953 | 1 034 | 997 | 1 040 | 1 033 | 1 007 | 917 | 833 | 1 001 |
| 0.01 | 0.01 | 0.01 | 0.01 | 0.01 | 0.01 | 0.01 | 0.01 | 0.01 | 0.01 | 0.01 | 0.01 | 0.01 |
| 337 | 356 | 391 | 425 | 304 | 356 | 379 | 142 | 298 | 251 | 274 | 207 | 322 |
| 1 101 | 1 188 | 1 335 | 1 486 | 1 087 | 1 306 | 1 423 | 545 | 1 174 | 1 016 | 883 | 600 | 1 166 |
| 0.01 | 0.01 | 0.01 | 0.01 | 0.01 | 0.01 | 0.01 | 0.00 | 0.01 | 0.01 | 0.01 | 0.01 | 0.01 |
| 4 853 | 5 684 | 6 178 | 6 956 | 7 427 | 6 914 | 6 855 | 7 735 | 9 290 | 10 277 | 4 937 | 2 311 | 7 278 |
| 11 719 | 13 885 | 15 266 | 17 384 | 18 775 | 17 693 | 17 755 | 20 290 | 24 683 | 27 655 | 11 850 | 5 190 | 18 511 |
| 0.10 | 0.12 | 0.13 | 0.15 | 0.15 | 0.14 | 0.12 | 0.12 | 0.13 | 0.14 | 0.12 | 0.09 | 0.13 |
| 6 007 | 6 911 | 8 234 | 8 728 | 8 729 | 9 065 | 9 305 | 10 345 | 11 732 | 13 173 | 6 355 | 3 048 | 9 305 |
| 14 507 | 16 884 | 20 347 | 21 810 | 22 068 | 23 197 | 24 100 | 27 135 | 31 172 | 35 448 | 15 255 | 6 844 | 23 667 |
| ... | ... | ... | ... | ... | ... | ... | ... | ... | ... | ... | ... | ... |
| 4 858 | 5 264 | 5 561 | 5 949 | 6 369 | 6 189 | 6 228 | 6 730 | 7 385 | 7 965 | 4 937 | 3 430 | 6 290 |
| 11 732 | 12 859 | 13 741 | 14 866 | 16 102 | 15 837 | 16 130 | 17 654 | 19 622 | 21 434 | 11 850 | 7 703 | 15 998 |
| 0.11 | 0.12 | 0.13 | 0.14 | 0.14 | 0.13 | 0.13 | 0.14 | 0.15 | 0.16 | 0.12 | 0.09 | 0.14 |
| 4 815 | 5 711 | 6 424 | 7 104 | 7 878 | 7 863 | 8 071 | 8 973 | 10 176 | 11 426 | 5 314 | 2 390 | 7 921 |
| 11 629 | 13 953 | 15 873 | 17 753 | 19 917 | 20 121 | 20 904 | 23 537 | 27 038 | 30 747 | 12 756 | 5 366 | 20 147 |
| 0.11 | 0.12 | 0.13 | 0.14 | 0.14 | 0.13 | 0.13 | 0.14 | 0.15 | 0.16 | 0.12 | 0.09 | 0.14 |
| 5 621 | 6 090 | 6 435 | 6 883 | 7 370 | 7 161 | 7 206 | 7 788 | 8 545 | 9 216 | 5 712 | 3 969 | 7 278 |
| 13 574 | 14 879 | 15 900 | 17 202 | 18 631 | 18 325 | 18 663 | 20 427 | 22 704 | 24 801 | 13 712 | 8 913 | 18 511 |
| 0.11 | 0.12 | 0.12 | 0.13 | 0.13 | 0.13 | 0.13 | 0.13 | 0.14 | 0.15 | 0.11 | 0.08 | 0.13 |
| 4 852 | 5 684 | 6 178 | 6 956 | 7 427 | 6 913 | 6 854 | 7 714 | 9 232 | 10 539 | 4 946 | 2 309 | 7 297 |
| 11 718 | 13 887 | 15 266 | 17 384 | 18 775 | 17 691 | 17 752 | 20 233 | 24 530 | 28 360 | 11 872 | 5 185 | 18 560 |
| 0.10 | 0.12 | 0.13 | 0.15 | 0.15 | 0.14 | 0.12 | 0.12 | 0.13 | 0.14 | 0.12 | 0.09 | 0.13 |

**Table A.1** Total and per capita gross domestic product of individual countries or areas, expressed in United States dollars, and their individual shares of gross world product, based on alternative conversion rates, 1970−1989 [*cont.*]

| Country or area | 1970 (1) | 1971 (2) | 1972 (3) | 1973 (4) | 1974 (5) | 1975 (6) | 1976 (7) | 1977 (8) | 1978 (9) | 1979 (10) |
|---|---|---|---|---|---|---|---|---|---|---|
| **Solomon Islands** | | | | | | | | | | |
| 1. **MER** | | | | | | | | | | |
| 1a. Per capita GDP | 195 | 203 | 214 | 278 | 389 | 345 | 370 | 396 | 463 | 597 |
| 1b. GDP | 32 | 35 | 38 | 51 | 73 | 67 | 74 | 81 | 98 | 130 |
| 1c. % of GWP | 0.00 | 0.00 | 0.00 | 0.00 | 0.00 | 0.00 | 0.00 | 0.00 | 0.00 | 0.00 |
| 2. **PPPs** | | | | | | | | | | |
| 2a. Per capita GDP | ... | ... | ... | ... | ... | ... | ... | ... | ... | ... |
| 2b. GDP | ... | ... | ... | ... | ... | ... | ... | ... | ... | ... |
| 2c. % of GWP | ... | ... | ... | ... | ... | ... | ... | ... | ... | ... |
| 3. **Absolute 1970−1989 PARE** | | | | | | | | | | |
| 3a. Per capita GDP | 320 | 335 | 377 | 397 | 463 | 409 | 451 | 490 | 522 | 617 |
| 3b. GDP | 52 | 57 | 66 | 72 | 87 | 79 | 90 | 101 | 111 | 135 |
| 3c. % of GWP | 0.00 | 0.00 | 0.00 | 0.00 | 0.00 | 0.00 | 0.00 | 0.00 | 0.00 | 0.00 |
| 4. **Relative 1970−1989 PARE** | | | | | | | | | | |
| 4a. Per capita GDP | 156 | 172 | 202 | 227 | 289 | 281 | 329 | 380 | 435 | 561 |
| 4b. GDP | 26 | 29 | 36 | 41 | 54 | 54 | 66 | 78 | 92 | 122 |
| 4c. % of GWP | 0.00 | 0.00 | 0.00 | 0.00 | 0.00 | 0.00 | 0.00 | 0.00 | 0.00 | 0.00 |
| 5. **Absolute 1980−1989 PARE** | | | | | | | | | | |
| 5a. Per capita GDP | 358 | 375 | 422 | 445 | 518 | 458 | 505 | 548 | 584 | 691 |
| 5b. GDP | 59 | 64 | 74 | 81 | 97 | 89 | 101 | 113 | 124 | 151 |
| 5c. % of GWP | 0.00 | 0.00 | 0.00 | 0.00 | 0.00 | 0.00 | 0.00 | 0.00 | 0.00 | 0.00 |
| 6. **WA** | | | | | | | | | | |
| 6a. Per capita GDP | 195 | 204 | 214 | 278 | 388 | 346 | 370 | 396 | 463 | 597 |
| 6b. GDP | 32 | 35 | 38 | 51 | 73 | 67 | 74 | 82 | 98 | 130 |
| 6c. % of GWP | 0.00 | 0.00 | 0.00 | 0.00 | 0.00 | 0.00 | 0.00 | 0.00 | 0.00 | 0.00 |
| **Somalia** | | | | | | | | | | |
| 1. **MER** | | | | | | | | | | |
| 1a. Per capita GDP | 93 | 93 | 117 | 124 | 143 | 182 | 200 | 238 | 268 | 280 |
| 1b. GDP | 341 | 347 | 448 | 484 | 573 | 757 | 871 | 1 093 | 1 299 | 1 427 |
| 1c. % of GWP | 0.01 | 0.01 | 0.01 | 0.01 | 0.01 | 0.01 | 0.01 | 0.01 | 0.01 | 0.01 |
| 2. **PPPs** | | | | | | | | | | |
| 2a. Per capita GDP | 293 | 309 | 387 | 378 | 412 | 455 | 501 | 521 | 584 | 655 |
| 2b. GDP | 1 075 | 1 157 | 1 477 | 1 471 | 1 650 | 1 893 | 2 179 | 2 389 | 2 827 | 3 340 |
| 2c. % of GWP | ... | ... | ... | ... | ... | ... | ... | ... | ... | ... |
| 3. **Absolute 1970−1989 PARE** | | | | | | | | | | |
| 3a. Per capita GDP | 304 | 303 | 341 | 293 | 287 | 318 | 298 | 321 | 326 | 271 |
| 3b. GDP | 1 115 | 1 132 | 1 301 | 1 143 | 1 151 | 1 321 | 1 296 | 1 473 | 1 580 | 1 384 |
| 3c. % of GWP | 0.02 | 0.02 | 0.02 | 0.01 | 0.01 | 0.02 | 0.01 | 0.02 | 0.02 | 0.01 |
| 4. **Relative 1970−1989 PARE** | | | | | | | | | | |
| 4a. Per capita GDP | 148 | 155 | 183 | 168 | 179 | 218 | 217 | 250 | 272 | 246 |
| 4b. GDP | 544 | 580 | 697 | 653 | 718 | 905 | 943 | 1 145 | 1 318 | 1 257 |
| 4c. % of GWP | 0.02 | 0.02 | 0.02 | 0.01 | 0.01 | 0.02 | 0.01 | 0.02 | 0.02 | 0.01 |
| 5. **Absolute 1980−1989 PARE** | | | | | | | | | | |
| 5a. Per capita GDP | 395 | 394 | 444 | 382 | 374 | 413 | 388 | 418 | 424 | 353 |
| 5b. GDP | 1 450 | 1 473 | 1 692 | 1 487 | 1 498 | 1 718 | 1 686 | 1 916 | 2 056 | 1 801 |
| 5c. % of GWP | 0.02 | 0.02 | 0.02 | 0.01 | 0.01 | 0.02 | 0.02 | 0.02 | 0.02 | 0.01 |
| 6. **WA** | | | | | | | | | | |
| 6a. Per capita GDP | 93 | 93 | 117 | 124 | 143 | 182 | 200 | 238 | 268 | 280 |
| 6b. GDP | 341 | 347 | 448 | 484 | 573 | 757 | 871 | 1 093 | 1 299 | 1 427 |
| 6c. % of GWP | 0.01 | 0.01 | 0.01 | 0.01 | 0.01 | 0.01 | 0.01 | 0.01 | 0.01 | 0.01 |

| | | | | | | | | | | Averages | | |
|---|---|---|---|---|---|---|---|---|---|---|---|---|
| 1980 | 1981 | 1982 | 1983 | 1984 | 1985 | 1986 | 1987 | 1988 | 1989 | 1970–89 | 1970–79 | 1980–89 |
| (11) | (12) | (13) | (14) | (15) | (16) | (17) | (18) | (19) | (20) | (21) | (22) | (23) |
| 637 | 691 | 672 | 602 | 661 | 584 | 510 | 505 | 585 | 608 | 515 | 355 | 603 |
| 144 | 162 | 163 | 152 | 173 | 159 | 144 | 147 | 176 | 189 | 114 | 68 | 161 |
| 0.00 | 0.00 | 0.00 | 0.00 | 0.00 | 0.00 | 0.00 | 0.00 | 0.00 | 0.00 | 0.00 | 0.00 | 0.00 |
| ... | ... | ... | ... | ... | ... | ... | ... | ... | ... | ... | ... | ... |
| ... | ... | ... | ... | ... | ... | ... | ... | ... | ... | ... | ... | ... |
| ... | ... | ... | ... | ... | ... | ... | ... | ... | ... | ... | ... | ... |
| 558 | 575 | 548 | 546 | 568 | 564 | 532 | 489 | 510 | 506 | 515 | 445 | 538 |
| 126 | 135 | 133 | 138 | 149 | 153 | 150 | 142 | 153 | 157 | 114 | 85 | 144 |
| 0.00 | 0.00 | 0.00 | 0.00 | 0.00 | 0.00 | 0.00 | 0.00 | 0.00 | 0.00 | 0.00 | 0.00 | 0.00 |
| 553 | 624 | 632 | 653 | 703 | 717 | 690 | 653 | 702 | 725 | 538 | 314 | 670 |
| 125 | 146 | 154 | 165 | 184 | 195 | 195 | 190 | 211 | 226 | 119 | 60 | 179 |
| 0.00 | 0.00 | 0.00 | 0.00 | 0.00 | 0.00 | 0.00 | 0.00 | 0.00 | 0.00 | 0.00 | 0.00 | 0.00 |
| 625 | 644 | 613 | 612 | 636 | 632 | 596 | 548 | 570 | 566 | 577 | 499 | 603 |
| 141 | 151 | 149 | 155 | 167 | 172 | 168 | 159 | 172 | 176 | 128 | 95 | 161 |
| 0.00 | 0.00 | 0.00 | 0.00 | 0.00 | 0.00 | 0.00 | 0.00 | 0.00 | 0.00 | 0.00 | 0.00 | 0.00 |
| 637 | 690 | 672 | 602 | 661 | 585 | 510 | 504 | 589 | 610 | 516 | 355 | 603 |
| 144 | 162 | 163 | 152 | 173 | 159 | 144 | 147 | 177 | 190 | 115 | 68 | 161 |
| 0.00 | 0.00 | 0.00 | 0.00 | 0.00 | 0.00 | 0.00 | 0.00 | 0.00 | 0.00 | 0.00 | 0.00 | 0.00 |
| 515 | 629 | 469 | 373 | 505 | 347 | 250 | 236 | 238 | 173 | 291 | 187 | 362 |
| 2 755 | 3 504 | 2 708 | 2 225 | 3 110 | 2 211 | 1 650 | 1 612 | 1 680 | 1 264 | 1 518 | 764 | 2 272 |
| 0.02 | 0.03 | 0.02 | 0.02 | 0.03 | 0.02 | 0.01 | 0.01 | 0.01 | 0.01 | 0.01 | 0.01 | 0.02 |
| 729 | 704 | 860 | 787 | 622 | 608 | 608 | 652 | 655 | 680 | 600 | 477 | 690 |
| 3 895 | 3 921 | 4 963 | 4 694 | 3 834 | 3 876 | 4 006 | 4 450 | 4 625 | 4 955 | 3 134 | 1 946 | 4 322 |
| ... | ... | ... | ... | ... | ... | ... | ... | ... | ... | ... | ... | ... |
| 253 | 292 | 295 | 255 | 270 | 282 | 276 | 288 | 280 | 279 | 291 | 316 | 279 |
| 1 353 | 1 625 | 1 701 | 1 521 | 1 665 | 1 797 | 1 821 | 1 966 | 1 977 | 2 035 | 1 518 | 1 290 | 1 746 |
| 0.01 | 0.02 | 0.02 | 0.01 | 0.01 | 0.02 | 0.01 | 0.02 | 0.01 | 0.01 | 0.01 | 0.01 | 0.01 |
| 251 | 317 | 340 | 304 | 334 | 358 | 358 | 384 | 386 | 401 | 293 | 215 | 349 |
| 1 341 | 1 763 | 1 965 | 1 816 | 2 060 | 2 283 | 2 360 | 2 621 | 2 725 | 2 919 | 1 531 | 876 | 2 185 |
| 0.01 | 0.02 | 0.02 | 0.01 | 0.01 | 0.02 | 0.01 | 0.02 | 0.01 | 0.01 | 0.01 | 0.01 | 0.01 |
| 329 | 380 | 383 | 332 | 352 | 367 | 359 | 375 | 364 | 363 | 378 | 411 | 362 |
| 1 761 | 2 114 | 2 213 | 1 979 | 2 166 | 2 338 | 2 369 | 2 558 | 2 572 | 2 647 | 1 975 | 1 678 | 2 272 |
| 0.01 | 0.02 | 0.02 | 0.01 | 0.02 | 0.02 | 0.02 | 0.02 | 0.02 | 0.02 | 0.02 | 0.02 | 0.02 |
| 515 | 629 | 469 | 373 | 505 | 347 | 250 | 236 | 238 | 173 | 291 | 187 | 363 |
| 2 755 | 3 504 | 2 708 | 2 225 | 3 110 | 2 211 | 1 650 | 1 613 | 1 681 | 1 264 | 1 518 | 764 | 2 272 |
| 0.02 | 0.03 | 0.02 | 0.02 | 0.03 | 0.02 | 0.01 | 0.01 | 0.01 | 0.01 | 0.02 | 0.01 | 0.02 |

**Table A.1**    Total and per capita gross domestic product of individual countries or areas, expressed in United States dollars, and their individual shares of gross world product, based on alternative conversion rates, 1970–1989 [*cont.*]

| Country or area | 1970 (1) | 1971 (2) | 1972 (3) | 1973 (4) | 1974 (5) | 1975 (6) | 1976 (7) | 1977 (8) | 1978 (9) | 1979 (10) |
|---|---|---|---|---|---|---|---|---|---|---|
| **South Africa** | | | | | | | | | | |
| **1. MER** | | | | | | | | | | |
| 1a. Per capita GDP | 768 | 828 | 844 | 1 137 | 1 391 | 1 414 | 1 308 | 1 422 | 1 593 | 1 913 |
| 1b. GDP | 17 247 | 19 060 | 19 901 | 27 459 | 34 383 | 35 780 | 33 857 | 37 627 | 43 091 | 52 910 |
| 1c. % of GWP | 0.54 | 0.54 | 0.49 | 0.56 | 0.62 | 0.58 | 0.50 | 0.50 | 0.48 | 0.51 |
| **2. PPPs** | | | | | | | | | | |
| 2a. Per capita GDP | 1 655 | 1 790 | 1 853 | 2 087 | 2 509 | 2 699 | 2 771 | 2 787 | 2 989 | 3 370 |
| 2b. GDP | 37 162 | 41 202 | 43 677 | 50 384 | 62 030 | 68 283 | 71 716 | 73 750 | 80 877 | 93 200 |
| 2c. % of GWP | ... | ... | ... | ... | ... | ... | ... | ... | ... | ... |
| **3. Absolute 1970–1989 PARE** | | | | | | | | | | |
| 3a. Per capita GDP | 1 817 | 1 866 | 1 857 | 1 885 | 1 972 | 1 970 | 1 955 | 1 912 | 1 924 | 1 943 |
| 3b. GDP | 40 799 | 42 940 | 43 785 | 45 511 | 48 760 | 49 855 | 50 588 | 50 604 | 52 056 | 53 746 |
| 3c. % of GWP | 0.57 | 0.58 | 0.56 | 0.55 | 0.58 | 0.58 | 0.56 | 0.54 | 0.53 | 0.53 |
| **4. Relative 1970–1989 PARE** | | | | | | | | | | |
| 4a. Per capita GDP | 886 | 956 | 996 | 1 078 | 1 230 | 1 350 | 1 423 | 1 486 | 1 604 | 1 765 |
| 4b. GDP | 19 892 | 22 010 | 23 473 | 26 019 | 30 407 | 34 156 | 36 824 | 39 321 | 43 399 | 48 809 |
| 4c. % of GWP | 0.57 | 0.58 | 0.56 | 0.55 | 0.58 | 0.58 | 0.56 | 0.54 | 0.53 | 0.53 |
| **5. Absolute 1980–1989 PARE** | | | | | | | | | | |
| 5a. Per capita GDP | 2 285 | 2 347 | 2 336 | 2 371 | 2 481 | 2 479 | 2 459 | 2 405 | 2 420 | 2 445 |
| 5b. GDP | 51 325 | 54 018 | 55 081 | 57 252 | 61 340 | 62 717 | 63 640 | 63 660 | 65 486 | 67 612 |
| 5c. % of GWP | 0.59 | 0.60 | 0.58 | 0.56 | 0.59 | 0.60 | 0.58 | 0.55 | 0.55 | 0.55 |
| **6. WA** | | | | | | | | | | |
| 6a. Per capita GDP | 768 | 826 | 848 | 1 134 | 1 390 | 1 400 | 1 309 | 1 422 | 1 593 | 1 913 |
| 6b. GDP | 17 240 | 19 001 | 19 985 | 27 382 | 34 359 | 35 417 | 33 874 | 37 646 | 43 113 | 52 908 |
| 6c. % of GWP | 0.54 | 0.54 | 0.50 | 0.56 | 0.62 | 0.57 | 0.50 | 0.50 | 0.49 | 0.52 |
| **Spain** | | | | | | | | | | |
| **1. MER** | | | | | | | | | | |
| 1a. Per capita GDP | 1 110 | 1 252 | 1 568 | 2 064 | 2 526 | 2 947 | 3 009 | 3 324 | 3 985 | 5 269 |
| 1b. GDP | 37 489 | 42 750 | 54 076 | 71 926 | 88 951 | 104 919 | 108 331 | 121 047 | 146 743 | 196 018 |
| 1c. % of GWP | 1.18 | 1.22 | 1.34 | 1.47 | 1.60 | 1.69 | 1.61 | 1.60 | 1.63 | 1.90 |
| **2. PPPs** | | | | | | | | | | |
| 2a. Per capita GDP | 2 303 | 2 496 | 2 774 | 3 103 | 3 507 | 3 818 | 4 106 | 4 414 | 4 780 | 5 192 |
| 2b. GDP | 77 794 | 85 181 | 95 677 | 108 106 | 123 491 | 135 895 | 147 818 | 160 748 | 176 003 | 193 153 |
| 2c. % of GWP | ... | ... | ... | ... | ... | ... | ... | ... | ... | ... |
| **3. Absolute 1970–1989 PARE** | | | | | | | | | | |
| 3a. Per capita GDP | 3 464 | 3 585 | 3 833 | 4 086 | 4 257 | 4 234 | 4 324 | 4 403 | 4 417 | 4 365 |
| 3b. GDP | 117 001 | 122 360 | 132 189 | 142 349 | 149 912 | 150 717 | 155 650 | 160 320 | 162 642 | 162 417 |
| 3c. % of GWP | 1.65 | 1.65 | 1.69 | 1.72 | 1.77 | 1.75 | 1.72 | 1.70 | 1.65 | 1.60 |
| **4. Relative 1970–1989 PARE** | | | | | | | | | | |
| 4a. Per capita GDP | 1 689 | 1 838 | 2 055 | 2 336 | 2 655 | 2 901 | 3 147 | 3 421 | 3 682 | 3 964 |
| 4b. GDP | 57 046 | 62 720 | 70 866 | 81 382 | 93 485 | 103 257 | 113 301 | 124 572 | 135 596 | 147 497 |
| 4c. % of GWP | 1.65 | 1.65 | 1.69 | 1.72 | 1.77 | 1.75 | 1.72 | 1.70 | 1.65 | 1.60 |
| **5. Absolute 1980–1989 PARE** | | | | | | | | | | |
| 5a. Per capita GDP | 4 394 | 4 548 | 4 863 | 5 183 | 5 401 | 5 372 | 5 486 | 5 586 | 5 604 | 5 538 |
| 5b. GDP | 148 440 | 155 239 | 167 708 | 180 598 | 190 194 | 191 215 | 197 473 | 203 399 | 206 345 | 206 058 |
| 5c. % of GWP | 1.71 | 1.71 | 1.75 | 1.78 | 1.83 | 1.82 | 1.79 | 1.76 | 1.72 | 1.66 |
| **6. WA** | | | | | | | | | | |
| 6a. Per capita GDP | 1 110 | 1 249 | 1 568 | 2 064 | 2 526 | 2 947 | 3 009 | 3 324 | 3 985 | 5 269 |
| 6b. GDP | 37 489 | 42 635 | 54 077 | 71 926 | 88 952 | 104 919 | 108 332 | 121 048 | 146 743 | 196 018 |
| 6c. % of GWP | 1.17 | 1.22 | 1.35 | 1.48 | 1.59 | 1.70 | 1.61 | 1.61 | 1.65 | 1.92 |

| | 1980 (11) | 1981 (12) | 1982 (13) | 1983 (14) | 1984 (15) | 1985 (16) | 1986 (17) | 1987 (18) | 1988 (19) | 1989 (20) | Averages 1970–89 (21) | 1970–79 (22) | 1980–89 (23) |
|---|---|---|---|---|---|---|---|---|---|---|---|---|---|
| | 2 743 | 2 827 | 2 519 | 2 723 | 2 415 | 1 780 | 1 941 | 2 492 | 2 552 | 2 592 | 1 946 | 1 285 | 2 457 |
| | 77 542 | 81 701 | 74 428 | 82 246 | 74 563 | 56 196 | 62 642 | 82 262 | 86 135 | 89 435 | 54 423 | 32 131 | 76 715 |
| | 0.67 | 0.70 | 0.64 | 0.69 | 0.61 | 0.45 | 0.42 | 0.48 | 0.45 | 0.45 | 0.53 | 0.53 | 0.54 |
| | 4 177 | 4 792 | 4 910 | 4 796 | 5 039 | 4 862 | 4 852 | 4 984 | 5 244 | 5 451 | 3 869 | 2 488 | 4 938 |
| | 118 097 | 138 477 | 145 042 | 144 849 | 155 598 | 153 500 | 156 612 | 164 497 | 176 988 | 188 113 | 108 203 | 62 228 | 154 177 |
| | ... | ... | ... | ... | ... | ... | ... | ... | ... | ... | ... | ... | ... |
| | 2 008 | 2 068 | 2 015 | 1 935 | 1 990 | 1 923 | 1 881 | 1 878 | 1 912 | 1 909 | 1 946 | 1 914 | 1 953 |
| | 56 777 | 59 761 | 59 533 | 58 433 | 61 455 | 60 711 | 60 722 | 61 997 | 64 538 | 65 893 | 54 423 | 47 864 | 60 982 |
| | 0.55 | 0.56 | 0.56 | 0.53 | 0.54 | 0.51 | 0.50 | 0.49 | 0.49 | 0.48 | 0.53 | 0.56 | 0.52 |
| | 1 991 | 2 244 | 2 328 | 2 310 | 2 462 | 2 443 | 2 438 | 2 504 | 2 635 | 2 739 | 1 935 | 1 297 | 2 427 |
| | 56 281 | 64 844 | 68 769 | 69 780 | 76 017 | 77 131 | 78 695 | 82 657 | 88 933 | 94 523 | 54 097 | 32 431 | 75 763 |
| | 0.55 | 0.56 | 0.56 | 0.53 | 0.54 | 0.51 | 0.50 | 0.49 | 0.49 | 0.48 | 0.53 | 0.55 | 0.52 |
| | 2 526 | 2 601 | 2 535 | 2 434 | 2 504 | 2 419 | 2 366 | 2 363 | 2 406 | 2 402 | 2 448 | 2 407 | 2 457 |
| | 71 425 | 75 179 | 74 892 | 73 509 | 77 310 | 76 374 | 76 387 | 77 992 | 81 188 | 82 893 | 68 464 | 60 213 | 76 715 |
| | 0.56 | 0.58 | 0.58 | 0.55 | 0.55 | 0.53 | 0.52 | 0.51 | 0.51 | 0.50 | 0.55 | 0.57 | 0.54 |
| | 2 740 | 2 803 | 2 510 | 2 718 | 2 354 | 1 750 | 1 927 | 2 448 | 2 582 | 2 569 | 1 935 | 1 283 | 2 439 |
| | 77 459 | 80 996 | 74 166 | 82 090 | 72 678 | 55 246 | 62 203 | 80 806 | 87 140 | 88 662 | 54 119 | 32 092 | 76 145 |
| | 0.67 | 0.69 | 0.64 | 0.69 | 0.59 | 0.44 | 0.42 | 0.48 | 0.47 | 0.45 | 0.54 | 0.53 | 0.54 |
| | 5 650 | 4 865 | 4 678 | 4 050 | 4 063 | 4 249 | 5 889 | 7 443 | 8 728 | 9 601 | 4 354 | 2 746 | 5 923 |
| | 212 115 | 184 043 | 178 111 | 155 021 | 156 204 | 164 013 | 228 115 | 289 186 | 340 069 | 375 102 | 162 711 | 97 225 | 228 198 |
| | 1.83 | 1.57 | 1.53 | 1.31 | 1.28 | 1.30 | 1.53 | 1.68 | 1.78 | 1.87 | 1.60 | 1.60 | 1.60 |
| | 6 115 | 6 423 | 6 796 | 6 555 | 7 421 | 7 706 | 8 089 | 8 757 | 9 473 | 10 354 | 5 747 | 3 683 | 7 767 |
| | 229 564 | 242 993 | 258 737 | 250 892 | 285 303 | 297 449 | 313 370 | 340 246 | 369 082 | 404 542 | 214 802 | 130 387 | 299 218 |
| | ... | ... | ... | ... | ... | ... | ... | ... | ... | ... | ... | ... | ... |
| | 4 380 | 4 336 | 4 361 | 4 416 | 4 475 | 4 560 | 4 693 | 4 938 | 5 169 | 5 427 | 4 354 | 4 111 | 4 669 |
| | 164 427 | 164 019 | 166 015 | 169 012 | 172 054 | 176 035 | 181 804 | 191 883 | 201 384 | 212 039 | 162 711 | 145 556 | 179 867 |
| | 1.58 | 1.55 | 1.56 | 1.54 | 1.50 | 1.48 | 1.49 | 1.52 | 1.53 | 1.56 | 1.60 | 1.69 | 1.53 |
| | 4 342 | 4 705 | 5 037 | 5 273 | 5 535 | 5 794 | 6 082 | 6 584 | 7 122 | 7 785 | 4 326 | 2 795 | 5 825 |
| | 162 990 | 177 968 | 191 769 | 201 831 | 212 822 | 223 647 | 235 617 | 255 825 | 277 506 | 304 168 | 161 693 | 98 972 | 224 414 |
| | 1.58 | 1.55 | 1.56 | 1.54 | 1.50 | 1.48 | 1.49 | 1.52 | 1.53 | 1.56 | 1.57 | 1.69 | 1.53 |
| | 5 557 | 5 501 | 5 532 | 5 602 | 5 677 | 5 786 | 5 954 | 6 265 | 6 557 | 6 885 | 5 523 | 5 216 | 5 923 |
| | 208 609 | 208 091 | 210 623 | 214 427 | 218 285 | 223 336 | 230 655 | 243 443 | 255 497 | 269 014 | 206 432 | 184 667 | 228 198 |
| | 1.65 | 1.62 | 1.62 | 1.61 | 1.57 | 1.55 | 1.56 | 1.59 | 1.60 | 1.63 | 1.66 | 1.75 | 1.60 |
| | 5 650 | 4 865 | 4 678 | 4 050 | 4 063 | 4 249 | 5 889 | 7 444 | 8 729 | 9 602 | 4 354 | 2 746 | 5 924 |
| | 212 116 | 184 019 | 178 113 | 155 021 | 156 203 | 164 009 | 228 118 | 289 238 | 340 107 | 375 172 | 162 713 | 97 214 | 228 212 |
| | 1.84 | 1.56 | 1.53 | 1.31 | 1.28 | 1.30 | 1.55 | 1.74 | 1.82 | 1.91 | 1.61 | 1.60 | 1.61 |

**Table A.1**    Total and per capita gross domestic product of individual countries or areas,
expressed in United States dollars, and their individual shares of gross world
product, based on alternative conversion rates, 1970−1989 [*cont.*]

| Country or area | 1970 (1) | 1971 (2) | 1972 (3) | 1973 (4) | 1974 (5) | 1975 (6) | 1976 (7) | 1977 (8) | 1978 (9) | 1979 (10) |
|---|---|---|---|---|---|---|---|---|---|---|
| **Sri Lanka** | | | | | | | | | | |
| 1.    **MER** | | | | | | | | | | |
| 1a.   Per capita GDP | 190 | 191 | 210 | 225 | 275 | 284 | 266 | 296 | 199 | 242 |
| 1b.   GDP | 2 379 | 2 435 | 2 720 | 2 960 | 3 684 | 3 859 | 3 682 | 4 160 | 2 854 | 3 527 |
| 1c.   % of GWP | 0.07 | 0.07 | 0.07 | 0.06 | 0.07 | 0.06 | 0.05 | 0.05 | 0.03 | 0.03 |
| 2.    **PPPs** | | | | | | | | | | |
| 2a.   Per capita GDP | 533 | 541 | 570 | 578 | 640 | 657 | 749 | 825 | 1 020 | 1 073 |
| 2b.   GDP | 6 675 | 6 903 | 7 394 | 7 614 | 8 563 | 8 938 | 10 359 | 11 605 | 14 606 | 15 622 |
| 2c.   % of GWP | ... | ... | ... | ... | ... | ... | ... | ... | ... | ... |
| 3.    **Absolute 1970−1989 PARE** | | | | | | | | | | |
| 3a.   Per capita GDP | 232 | 228 | 232 | 236 | 242 | 249 | 256 | 261 | 275 | 287 |
| 3b.   GDP | 2 898 | 2 913 | 3 005 | 3 111 | 3 234 | 3 386 | 3 536 | 3 671 | 3 943 | 4 183 |
| 3c.   % of GWP | 0.04 | 0.04 | 0.04 | 0.04 | 0.04 | 0.04 | 0.04 | 0.04 | 0.04 | 0.04 |
| 4.    **Relative 1970−1989 PARE** | | | | | | | | | | |
| 4a.   Per capita GDP | 113 | 117 | 124 | 135 | 151 | 171 | 186 | 203 | 230 | 261 |
| 4b.   GDP | 1 413 | 1 493 | 1 611 | 1 779 | 2 017 | 2 320 | 2 574 | 2 852 | 3 287 | 3 798 |
| 4c.   % of GWP | 0.04 | 0.04 | 0.04 | 0.04 | 0.04 | 0.04 | 0.04 | 0.04 | 0.04 | 0.04 |
| 5.    **Absolute 1980−1989 PARE** | | | | | | | | | | |
| 5a.   Per capita GDP | 238 | 235 | 239 | 243 | 249 | 256 | 263 | 269 | 284 | 296 |
| 5b.   GDP | 2 984 | 2 999 | 3 094 | 3 203 | 3 330 | 3 486 | 3 641 | 3 780 | 4 060 | 4 307 |
| 5c.   % of GWP | 0.03 | 0.03 | 0.03 | 0.03 | 0.03 | 0.03 | 0.03 | 0.03 | 0.03 | 0.03 |
| 6.    **WA** | | | | | | | | | | |
| 6a.   Per capita GDP | 190 | 191 | 210 | 225 | 275 | 284 | 266 | 296 | 199 | 242 |
| 6b.   GDP | 2 379 | 2 435 | 2 720 | 2 960 | 3 684 | 3 859 | 3 682 | 4 160 | 2 855 | 3 527 |
| 6c.   % of GWP | 0.07 | 0.07 | 0.07 | 0.06 | 0.07 | 0.06 | 0.05 | 0.06 | 0.03 | 0.03 |
| **Sudan** | | | | | | | | | | |
| 1.    **MER** | | | | | | | | | | |
| 1a.   Per capita GDP | 145 | 154 | 163 | 171 | 230 | 271 | 322 | 395 | 437 | 423 |
| 1b.   GDP | 2 016 | 2 187 | 2 392 | 2 577 | 3 581 | 4 341 | 5 310 | 6 723 | 7 667 | 7 656 |
| 1c.   % of GWP | 0.06 | 0.06 | 0.06 | 0.05 | 0.06 | 0.07 | 0.08 | 0.09 | 0.09 | 0.07 |
| 2.    **PPPs** | | | | | | | | | | |
| 2a.   Per capita GDP | 322 | 352 | 309 | 240 | 334 | 377 | 467 | 575 | 618 | 607 |
| 2b.   GDP | 4 458 | 5 009 | 4 519 | 3 616 | 5 191 | 6 031 | 7 711 | 9 779 | 10 843 | 10 989 |
| 2c.   % of GWP | ... | ... | ... | ... | ... | ... | ... | ... | ... | ... |
| 3.    **Absolute 1970−1989 PARE** | | | | | | | | | | |
| 3a.   Per capita GDP | 335 | 353 | 370 | 348 | 334 | 341 | 345 | 341 | 356 | 364 |
| 3b.   GDP | 4 637 | 5 027 | 5 423 | 5 252 | 5 192 | 5 456 | 5 694 | 5 807 | 6 249 | 6 593 |
| 3c.   % of GWP | 0.07 | 0.07 | 0.07 | 0.06 | 0.06 | 0.06 | 0.06 | 0.06 | 0.06 | 0.06 |
| 4.    **Relative 1970−1989 PARE** | | | | | | | | | | |
| 4a.   Per capita GDP | 163 | 181 | 199 | 199 | 208 | 233 | 251 | 265 | 297 | 331 |
| 4b.   GDP | 2 261 | 2 577 | 2 907 | 3 002 | 3 238 | 3 738 | 4 145 | 4 512 | 5 210 | 5 987 |
| 4c.   % of GWP | 0.07 | 0.07 | 0.07 | 0.06 | 0.06 | 0.06 | 0.06 | 0.06 | 0.06 | 0.06 |
| 5.    **Absolute 1980−1989 PARE** | | | | | | | | | | |
| 5a.   Per capita GDP | 392 | 414 | 434 | 408 | 391 | 399 | 404 | 400 | 417 | 426 |
| 5b.   GDP | 5 432 | 5 888 | 6 352 | 6 151 | 6 081 | 6 391 | 6 669 | 6 801 | 7 319 | 7 722 |
| 5c.   % of GWP | 0.06 | 0.06 | 0.07 | 0.06 | 0.06 | 0.06 | 0.06 | 0.06 | 0.06 | 0.06 |
| 6.    **WA** | | | | | | | | | | |
| 6a.   Per capita GDP | 167 | 177 | 185 | 174 | 167 | 170 | 172 | 171 | 178 | 182 |
| 6b.   GDP | 2 319 | 2 514 | 2 712 | 2 626 | 2 596 | 2 728 | 2 847 | 2 903 | 3 125 | 3 296 |
| 6c.   % of GWP | 0.07 | 0.07 | 0.07 | 0.05 | 0.05 | 0.04 | 0.04 | 0.04 | 0.04 | 0.03 |

| 1980 (11) | 1981 (12) | 1982 (13) | 1983 (14) | 1984 (15) | 1985 (16) | 1986 (17) | 1987 (18) | 1988 (19) | 1989 (20) | Averages 1970–89 (21) | 1970–79 (22) | 1980–89 (23) |
|---|---|---|---|---|---|---|---|---|---|---|---|---|
| 279 | 291 | 305 | 325 | 365 | 360 | 377 | 388 | 410 | 406 | 301 | 239 | 352 |
| 4 133 | 4 392 | 4 686 | 5 066 | 5 792 | 5 808 | 6 154 | 6 423 | 6 880 | 6 895 | 4 424 | 3 226 | 5 623 |
| 0.04 | 0.04 | 0.04 | 0.04 | 0.05 | 0.05 | 0.04 | 0.04 | 0.04 | 0.03 | 0.04 | 0.05 | 0.04 |
| 1 192 | 1 334 | 1 489 | 1 556 | 1 744 | 1 892 | 1 984 | 2 046 | 2 146 | 2 249 | 1 300 | 728 | 1 774 |
| 17 669 | 20 119 | 22 848 | 24 286 | 27 675 | 30 488 | 32 430 | 33 903 | 36 015 | 38 232 | 19 097 | 9 828 | 28 366 |
| ... | ... | ... | ... | ... | ... | ... | ... | ... | ... | ... | ... | ... |
| 298 | 309 | 320 | 329 | 340 | 352 | 362 | 363 | 368 | 371 | 301 | 251 | 342 |
| 4 421 | 4 666 | 4 908 | 5 141 | 5 401 | 5 672 | 5 914 | 6 010 | 6 177 | 6 299 | 4 424 | 3 388 | 5 461 |
| 0.04 | 0.04 | 0.05 | 0.05 | 0.05 | 0.05 | 0.05 | 0.05 | 0.05 | 0.05 | 0.04 | 0.04 | 0.05 |
| 296 | 336 | 370 | 393 | 421 | 447 | 469 | 484 | 507 | 532 | 311 | 172 | 428 |
| 4 382 | 5 063 | 5 669 | 6 140 | 6 681 | 7 206 | 7 665 | 8 013 | 8 512 | 9 036 | 4 576 | 2 314 | 6 837 |
| 0.04 | 0.04 | 0.05 | 0.05 | 0.05 | 0.05 | 0.05 | 0.05 | 0.05 | 0.05 | 0.04 | 0.04 | 0.05 |
| 307 | 319 | 329 | 339 | 351 | 362 | 373 | 373 | 379 | 382 | 310 | 259 | 352 |
| 4 552 | 4 804 | 5 054 | 5 294 | 5 561 | 5 840 | 6 090 | 6 188 | 6 360 | 6 486 | 4 556 | 3 488 | 5 623 |
| 0.04 | 0.04 | 0.04 | 0.04 | 0.04 | 0.04 | 0.04 | 0.04 | 0.04 | 0.04 | 0.04 | 0.03 | 0.04 |
| 279 | 291 | 305 | 325 | 365 | 361 | 377 | 387 | 410 | 405 | 301 | 239 | 352 |
| 4 133 | 4 392 | 4 686 | 5 066 | 5 792 | 5 808 | 6 155 | 6 413 | 6 878 | 6 886 | 4 423 | 3 226 | 5 621 |
| 0.04 | 0.04 | 0.04 | 0.04 | 0.05 | 0.05 | 0.04 | 0.04 | 0.04 | 0.04 | 0.04 | 0.05 | 0.04 |
| 418 | 493 | 360 | 344 | 412 | 283 | 285 | 322 | 264 | 320 | 323 | 282 | 346 |
| 7 807 | 9 506 | 7 165 | 7 066 | 8 715 | 6 183 | 6 406 | 7 445 | 6 275 | 7 844 | 5 943 | 4 445 | 7 441 |
| 0.07 | 0.08 | 0.06 | 0.06 | 0.07 | 0.05 | 0.04 | 0.04 | 0.03 | 0.04 | 0.06 | 0.07 | 0.05 |
| 637 | 692 | 831 | 891 | 737 | 612 | 536 | 591 | 623 | 640 | 580 | 432 | 676 |
| 11 893 | 13 350 | 16 539 | 18 282 | 15 610 | 13 355 | 12 055 | 13 667 | 14 818 | 15 686 | 10 670 | 6 815 | 14 525 |
| ... | ... | ... | ... | ... | ... | ... | ... | ... | ... | ... | ... | ... |
| 341 | 331 | 337 | 329 | 305 | 287 | 247 | 264 | 270 | 266 | 323 | 351 | 296 |
| 6 368 | 6 381 | 6 701 | 6 746 | 6 459 | 6 271 | 5 550 | 6 116 | 6 416 | 6 524 | 5 943 | 5 533 | 6 353 |
| 0.06 | 0.06 | 0.06 | 0.06 | 0.06 | 0.05 | 0.05 | 0.05 | 0.05 | 0.05 | 0.06 | 0.06 | 0.05 |
| 338 | 359 | 389 | 392 | 377 | 365 | 320 | 352 | 371 | 382 | 316 | 238 | 365 |
| 6 312 | 6 924 | 7 740 | 8 056 | 7 989 | 7 968 | 7 192 | 8 154 | 8 841 | 9 359 | 5 806 | 3 758 | 7 854 |
| 0.06 | 0.06 | 0.06 | 0.06 | 0.06 | 0.05 | 0.05 | 0.05 | 0.05 | 0.05 | 0.06 | 0.06 | 0.05 |
| 399 | 388 | 394 | 385 | 357 | 337 | 289 | 310 | 316 | 312 | 378 | 411 | 346 |
| 7 459 | 7 474 | 7 849 | 7 901 | 7 565 | 7 346 | 6 500 | 7 163 | 7 515 | 7 641 | 6 961 | 6 481 | 7 441 |
| 0.06 | 0.06 | 0.06 | 0.06 | 0.05 | 0.05 | 0.04 | 0.05 | 0.05 | 0.05 | 0.06 | 0.06 | 0.05 |
| 209 | 264 | 338 | 447 | 535 | 648 | 356 | 483 | 297 | 240 | 299 | 175 | 384 |
| 3 903 | 5 086 | 6 721 | 9 186 | 11 329 | 14 147 | 8 008 | 11 168 | 7 059 | 5 883 | 5 508 | 2 767 | 8 249 |
| 0.03 | 0.04 | 0.06 | 0.08 | 0.09 | 0.11 | 0.05 | 0.07 | 0.04 | 0.03 | 0.05 | 0.05 | 0.06 |

**Table A.1** Total and per capita gross domestic product of individual countries or areas, expressed in United States dollars, and their individual shares of gross world product, based on alternative conversion rates, 1970−1989 [*cont.*]

| Country or area | 1970 (1) | 1971 (2) | 1972 (3) | 1973 (4) | 1974 (5) | 1975 (6) | 1976 (7) | 1977 (8) | 1978 (9) | 1979 (10) |
|---|---|---|---|---|---|---|---|---|---|---|
| **Suriname** | | | | | | | | | | |
| 1.    MER | | | | | | | | | | |
| 1a.   Per capita GDP | 756 | 824 | 927 | 1 023 | 1 245 | 1 429 | 1 570 | 2 013 | 2 328 | 2 491 |
| 1b.   GDP | 282 | 309 | 347 | 380 | 459 | 521 | 567 | 719 | 824 | 877 |
| 1c.   % of GWP | 0.01 | 0.01 | 0.01 | 0.01 | 0.01 | 0.01 | 0.01 | 0.01 | 0.01 | 0.01 |
| 2.    PPPs | | | | | | | | | | |
| 2a.   Per capita GDP | 1 251 | 1 422 | 1 509 | 1 563 | 1 783 | 1 966 | 2 104 | 2 628 | 3 242 | 3 335 |
| 2b.   GDP | 467 | 533 | 565 | 581 | 658 | 717 | 760 | 938 | 1 148 | 1 174 |
| 2c.   % of GWP | ... | ... | ... | ... | ... | ... | ... | ... | ... | ... |
| 3.    Absolute 1970−1989 PARE | | | | | | | | | | |
| 3a.   Per capita GDP | 1 440 | 1 493 | 1 548 | 1 621 | 1 813 | 2 128 | 2 346 | 2 617 | 2 783 | 2 634 |
| 3b.   GDP | 537 | 560 | 579 | 603 | 669 | 777 | 847 | 934 | 985 | 927 |
| 3c.   % of GWP | 0.01 | 0.01 | 0.01 | 0.01 | 0.01 | 0.01 | 0.01 | 0.01 | 0.01 | 0.01 |
| 4.    Relative 1970−1989 PARE | | | | | | | | | | |
| 4a.   Per capita GDP | 702 | 765 | 830 | 926 | 1 131 | 1 458 | 1 707 | 2 033 | 2 320 | 2 392 |
| 4b.   GDP | 262 | 287 | 310 | 345 | 417 | 532 | 616 | 726 | 821 | 842 |
| 4c.   % of GWP | 0.01 | 0.01 | 0.01 | 0.01 | 0.01 | 0.01 | 0.01 | 0.01 | 0.01 | 0.01 |
| 5.    Absolute 1980−1989 PARE | | | | | | | | | | |
| 5a.   Per capita GDP | 1 801 | 1 868 | 1 936 | 2 027 | 2 268 | 2 661 | 2 934 | 3 273 | 3 481 | 3 294 |
| 5b.   GDP | 672 | 700 | 724 | 754 | 837 | 971 | 1 059 | 1 168 | 1 232 | 1 160 |
| 5c.   % of GWP | 0.01 | 0.01 | 0.01 | 0.01 | 0.01 | 0.01 | 0.01 | 0.01 | 0.01 | 0.01 |
| 6.    WA | | | | | | | | | | |
| 6a.   Per capita GDP | 756 | 825 | 927 | 1 023 | 1 245 | 1 429 | 1 570 | 2 013 | 2 328 | 2 491 |
| 6b.   GDP | 282 | 309 | 347 | 380 | 459 | 521 | 567 | 719 | 824 | 877 |
| 6c.   % of GWP | 0.01 | 0.01 | 0.01 | 0.01 | 0.01 | 0.01 | 0.01 | 0.01 | 0.01 | 0.01 |
| **Swaziland** | | | | | | | | | | |
| 1.    MER | | | | | | | | | | |
| 1a.   Per capita GDP | 256 | 320 | 317 | 424 | 503 | 605 | 544 | 592 | 641 | 753 |
| 1b.   GDP | 108 | 138 | 141 | 193 | 235 | 291 | 270 | 303 | 339 | 411 |
| 1c.   % of GWP | 0.00 | 0.00 | 0.00 | 0.00 | 0.00 | 0.00 | 0.00 | 0.00 | 0.00 | 0.00 |
| 2.    PPPs | | | | | | | | | | |
| 2a.   Per capita GDP | 418 | 508 | 600 | 536 | 611 | 857 | 903 | 893 | 904 | 973 |
| 2b.   GDP | 175 | 219 | 266 | 244 | 286 | 413 | 449 | 457 | 478 | 531 |
| 2c.   % of GWP | ... | ... | ... | ... | ... | ... | ... | ... | ... | ... |
| 3.    Absolute 1970−1989 PARE | | | | | | | | | | |
| 3a.   Per capita GDP | 381 | 388 | 455 | 395 | 587 | 686 | 713 | 714 | 714 | 715 |
| 3b.   GDP | 160 | 167 | 202 | 180 | 275 | 330 | 354 | 366 | 378 | 390 |
| 3c.   % of GWP | 0.00 | 0.00 | 0.00 | 0.00 | 0.00 | 0.00 | 0.00 | 0.00 | 0.00 | 0.00 |
| 4.    Relative 1970−1989 PARE | | | | | | | | | | |
| 4a.   Per capita GDP | 186 | 199 | 244 | 226 | 366 | 470 | 519 | 555 | 595 | 649 |
| 4b.   GDP | 78 | 86 | 108 | 103 | 171 | 226 | 258 | 284 | 315 | 354 |
| 4c.   % of GWP | 0.00 | 0.00 | 0.00 | 0.00 | 0.00 | 0.00 | 0.00 | 0.00 | 0.00 | 0.00 |
| 5.    Absolute 1980−1989 PARE | | | | | | | | | | |
| 5a.   Per capita GDP | 411 | 417 | 490 | 425 | 632 | 738 | 767 | 769 | 769 | 769 |
| 5b.   GDP | 172 | 180 | 217 | 194 | 296 | 356 | 381 | 394 | 407 | 420 |
| 5c.   % of GWP | 0.00 | 0.00 | 0.00 | 0.00 | 0.00 | 0.00 | 0.00 | 0.00 | 0.00 | 0.00 |
| 6.    WA | | | | | | | | | | |
| 6a.   Per capita GDP | 256 | 319 | 319 | 424 | 503 | 598 | 544 | 592 | 642 | 753 |
| 6b.   GDP | 108 | 137 | 141 | 193 | 235 | 288 | 271 | 303 | 339 | 411 |
| 6c.   % of GWP | 0.00 | 0.00 | 0.00 | 0.00 | 0.00 | 0.00 | 0.00 | 0.00 | 0.00 | 0.00 |

| | | | | | | | | | | Averages | | |
|---|---|---|---|---|---|---|---|---|---|---|---|---|
| 1980 (11) | 1981 (12) | 1982 (13) | 1983 (14) | 1984 (15) | 1985 (16) | 1986 (17) | 1987 (18) | 1988 (19) | 1989 (20) | 1970−89 (21) | 1970−79 (22) | 1980−89 (23) |
| 2 523 | 2 793 | 2 841 | 2 690 | 2 582 | 2 555 | 2 583 | 2 749 | 3 176 | 3 361 | 2 258 | 1 440 | 2 805 |
| 891 | 992 | 1 025 | 990 | 968 | 978 | 1 010 | 1 097 | 1 290 | 1 392 | 796 | 529 | 1 063 |
| 0.01 | 0.01 | 0.01 | 0.01 | 0.01 | 0.01 | 0.01 | 0.01 | 0.01 | 0.01 | 0.01 | 0.01 | 0.01 |
| 3 377 | 3 594 | 3 441 | 3 355 | 3 415 | 3 208 | 3 230 | 3 056 | 3 324 | 3 619 | 2 883 | 2 055 | 3 373 |
| 1 192 | 1 276 | 1 242 | 1 235 | 1 281 | 1 229 | 1 263 | 1 219 | 1 350 | 1 498 | 1 016 | 754 | 1 278 |
| ... | ... | ... | ... | ... | ... | ... | ... | ... | ... | ... | ... | ... |
| 2 401 | 2 557 | 2 409 | 2 270 | 2 186 | 2 184 | 2 155 | 1 982 | 2 086 | 2 182 | 2 258 | 2 021 | 2 243 |
| 848 | 908 | 870 | 836 | 820 | 836 | 843 | 791 | 847 | 903 | 796 | 742 | 850 |
| 0.01 | 0.01 | 0.01 | 0.01 | 0.01 | 0.01 | 0.01 | 0.01 | 0.01 | 0.01 | 0.01 | 0.01 | 0.01 |
| 2 380 | 2 775 | 2 783 | 2 711 | 2 704 | 2 774 | 2 793 | 2 643 | 2 875 | 3 129 | 2 223 | 1 406 | 2 774 |
| 840 | 985 | 1 005 | 998 | 1 014 | 1 063 | 1 092 | 1 054 | 1 167 | 1 296 | 784 | 516 | 1 051 |
| 0.01 | 0.01 | 0.01 | 0.01 | 0.01 | 0.01 | 0.01 | 0.01 | 0.01 | 0.01 | 0.01 | 0.01 | 0.01 |
| 3 003 | 3 198 | 3 013 | 2 840 | 2 734 | 2 731 | 2 696 | 2 479 | 2 609 | 2 729 | 2 824 | 2 528 | 2 805 |
| 1 060 | 1 135 | 1 088 | 1 045 | 1 025 | 1 046 | 1 054 | 989 | 1 059 | 1 130 | 996 | 928 | 1 063 |
| 0.01 | 0.01 | 0.01 | 0.01 | 0.01 | 0.01 | 0.01 | 0.01 | 0.01 | 0.01 | 0.01 | 0.01 | 0.01 |
| 2 523 | 2 793 | 2 841 | 2 690 | 2 582 | 2 555 | 2 583 | 2 772 | 3 203 | 3 201 | 2 251 | 1 440 | 2 793 |
| 891 | 992 | 1 025 | 990 | 968 | 978 | 1 010 | 1 106 | 1 300 | 1 325 | 794 | 529 | 1 059 |
| 0.01 | 0.01 | 0.01 | 0.01 | 0.01 | 0.01 | 0.01 | 0.01 | 0.01 | 0.01 | 0.01 | 0.01 | 0.01 |
| 964 | 989 | 841 | 839 | 716 | 513 | 613 | 852 | 861 | 845 | 693 | 511 | 803 |
| 543 | 576 | 505 | 521 | 461 | 340 | 421 | 606 | 634 | 644 | 384 | 243 | 525 |
| 0.00 | 0.00 | 0.00 | 0.00 | 0.00 | 0.00 | 0.00 | 0.00 | 0.00 | 0.00 | 0.00 | 0.00 | 0.00 |
| 1 100 | 1 324 | 1 529 | 1 495 | 1 532 | 1 970 | 2 114 | 2 151 | 2 322 | 2 431 | 1 406 | 741 | 1 848 |
| 620 | 771 | 919 | 928 | 985 | 1 308 | 1 452 | 1 530 | 1 709 | 1 852 | 780 | 352 | 1 207 |
| ... | ... | ... | ... | ... | ... | ... | ... | ... | ... | ... | ... | ... |
| 716 | 752 | 747 | 721 | 719 | 713 | 750 | 742 | 774 | 779 | 693 | 590 | 746 |
| 403 | 437 | 449 | 448 | 462 | 473 | 515 | 527 | 570 | 593 | 384 | 280 | 488 |
| 0.00 | 0.00 | 0.00 | 0.00 | 0.00 | 0.00 | 0.00 | 0.00 | 0.00 | 0.00 | 0.00 | 0.00 | 0.00 |
| 710 | 816 | 863 | 861 | 889 | 905 | 971 | 989 | 1 067 | 1 117 | 730 | 418 | 935 |
| 399 | 475 | 519 | 535 | 572 | 601 | 667 | 703 | 785 | 851 | 405 | 198 | 611 |
| 0.00 | 0.00 | 0.00 | 0.00 | 0.00 | 0.00 | 0.00 | 0.00 | 0.00 | 0.00 | 0.00 | 0.00 | 0.00 |
| 770 | 809 | 804 | 776 | 774 | 767 | 807 | 798 | 834 | 838 | 745 | 635 | 803 |
| 434 | 471 | 483 | 482 | 498 | 509 | 554 | 568 | 613 | 639 | 413 | 302 | 525 |
| 0.00 | 0.00 | 0.00 | 0.00 | 0.00 | 0.00 | 0.00 | 0.00 | 0.00 | 0.00 | 0.00 | 0.00 | 0.00 |
| 963 | 989 | 841 | 839 | 716 | 511 | 613 | 838 | 876 | 840 | 692 | 511 | 803 |
| 542 | 576 | 505 | 521 | 461 | 339 | 421 | 596 | 645 | 640 | 384 | 243 | 525 |
| 0.00 | 0.00 | 0.00 | 0.00 | 0.00 | 0.00 | 0.00 | 0.00 | 0.00 | 0.00 | 0.00 | 0.00 | 0.00 |

**Table A.1**    Total and per capita gross domestic product of individual countries or areas, expressed in United States dollars, and their individual shares of gross world product, based on alternative conversion rates, 1970—1989 [*cont.*]

| Country or area | 1970 (1) | 1971 (2) | 1972 (3) | 1973 (4) | 1974 (5) | 1975 (6) | 1976 (7) | 1977 (8) | 1978 (9) | 1979 (10) |
|---|---|---|---|---|---|---|---|---|---|---|
| **Sweden** | | | | | | | | | | |
| **1.   MER** | | | | | | | | | | |
| 1a.   Per capita GDP | 4 164 | 4 536 | 5 302 | 6 413 | 7 106 | 8 895 | 9 559 | 10 072 | 11 100 | 13 080 |
| 1b.   GDP | 33 493 | 36 675 | 43 045 | 52 234 | 58 046 | 72 879 | 78 568 | 83 052 | 91 819 | 108 487 |
| 1c.   % of GWP | 1.05 | 1.05 | 1.07 | 1.06 | 1.05 | 1.17 | 1.17 | 1.10 | 1.02 | 1.05 |
| **2.   PPPs** | | | | | | | | | | |
| 2a.   Per capita GDP | 3 817 | 4 046 | 4 371 | 4 871 | 5 387 | 6 214 | 6 540 | 6 686 | 7 268 | 8 119 |
| 2b.   GDP | 30 700 | 32 718 | 35 487 | 39 674 | 44 007 | 50 911 | 53 754 | 55 136 | 60 118 | 67 335 |
| 2c.   % of GWP | ... | ... | ... | ... | ... | ... | ... | ... | ... | ... |
| **3.   Absolute 1970—1989 PARE** | | | | | | | | | | |
| 3a.   Per capita GDP | 10 065 | 10 106 | 10 296 | 10 669 | 10 978 | 11 225 | 11 308 | 11 091 | 11 250 | 11 651 |
| 3b.   GDP | 80 950 | 81 714 | 83 585 | 86 901 | 89 680 | 91 970 | 92 943 | 91 459 | 93 061 | 96 635 |
| 3c.   % of GWP | 1.14 | 1.10 | 1.07 | 1.05 | 1.06 | 1.07 | 1.03 | 0.97 | 0.95 | 0.95 |
| **4.   Relative 1970—1989 PARE** | | | | | | | | | | |
| 4a.   Per capita GDP | 4 907 | 5 180 | 5 520 | 6 100 | 6 846 | 7 691 | 8 232 | 8 618 | 9 379 | 10 581 |
| 4b.   GDP | 39 469 | 41 885 | 44 810 | 49 682 | 55 924 | 63 009 | 67 655 | 71 066 | 77 586 | 87 758 |
| 4c.   % of GWP | 1.14 | 1.10 | 1.07 | 1.05 | 1.06 | 1.07 | 1.03 | 0.97 | 0.95 | 0.95 |
| **5.   Absolute 1980—1989 PARE** | | | | | | | | | | |
| 5a.   Per capita GDP | 12 241 | 12 291 | 12 522 | 12 976 | 13 352 | 13 652 | 13 753 | 13 489 | 13 683 | 14 170 |
| 5b.   GDP | 98 451 | 99 381 | 101 656 | 105 690 | 109 070 | 111 854 | 113 038 | 111 233 | 113 182 | 117 528 |
| 5c.   % of GWP | 1.13 | 1.10 | 1.06 | 1.04 | 1.05 | 1.06 | 1.02 | 0.96 | 0.94 | 0.95 |
| **6.   WA** | | | | | | | | | | |
| 6a.   Per capita GDP | 4 164 | 4 528 | 5 302 | 6 413 | 7 105 | 8 895 | 9 560 | 10 073 | 11 101 | 13 080 |
| 6b.   GDP | 33 492 | 36 612 | 43 042 | 52 231 | 58 041 | 72 875 | 78 570 | 83 059 | 91 829 | 108 485 |
| 6c.   % of GWP | 1.05 | 1.05 | 1.07 | 1.07 | 1.04 | 1.18 | 1.17 | 1.10 | 1.03 | 1.06 |
| **Switzerland** | | | | | | | | | | |
| **1.   MER** | | | | | | | | | | |
| 1a.   Per capita GDP | 3 351 | 4 016 | 4 873 | 6 514 | 7 486 | 8 566 | 8 955 | 9 576 | 13 418 | 15 094 |
| 1b.   GDP | 20 733 | 25 029 | 30 560 | 41 067 | 47 365 | 54 303 | 56 784 | 60 645 | 84 829 | 95 337 |
| 1c.   % of GWP | 0.65 | 0.72 | 0.76 | 0.84 | 0.85 | 0.87 | 0.85 | 0.80 | 0.94 | 0.93 |
| **2.   PPPs** | | | | | | | | | | |
| 2a.   Per capita GDP | ... | ... | ... | ... | ... | ... | ... | ... | ... | ... |
| 2b.   GDP | ... | ... | ... | ... | ... | ... | ... | ... | ... | ... |
| 2c.   % of GWP | ... | ... | ... | ... | ... | ... | ... | ... | ... | ... |
| **3.   Absolute 1970—1989 PARE** | | | | | | | | | | |
| 3a.   Per capita GDP | 12 474 | 12 886 | 13 216 | 13 550 | 13 697 | 12 676 | 12 494 | 12 814 | 12 889 | 13 222 |
| 3b.   GDP | 77 176 | 80 321 | 82 892 | 85 420 | 86 663 | 80 351 | 79 223 | 81 151 | 81 483 | 83 513 |
| 3c.   % of GWP | 1.09 | 1.09 | 1.06 | 1.03 | 1.02 | 0.93 | 0.88 | 0.86 | 0.83 | 0.82 |
| **4.   Relative 1970—1989 PARE** | | | | | | | | | | |
| 4a.   Per capita GDP | 6 082 | 6 605 | 7 085 | 7 747 | 8 542 | 8 684 | 9 095 | 9 957 | 10 745 | 12 008 |
| 4b.   GDP | 37 629 | 41 171 | 44 438 | 48 835 | 54 043 | 55 049 | 57 668 | 63 056 | 67 933 | 75 842 |
| 4c.   % of GWP | 1.09 | 1.08 | 1.06 | 1.03 | 1.02 | 0.93 | 0.88 | 0.86 | 0.83 | 0.82 |
| **5.   Absolute 1980—1989 PARE** | | | | | | | | | | |
| 5a.   Per capita GDP | 16 490 | 17 036 | 17 472 | 17 913 | 18 108 | 16 757 | 16 517 | 16 940 | 17 039 | 17 480 |
| 5b.   GDP | 102 027 | 106 185 | 109 583 | 112 925 | 114 568 | 106 224 | 104 733 | 107 282 | 107 721 | 110 405 |
| 5c.   % of GWP | 1.17 | 1.17 | 1.15 | 1.11 | 1.10 | 1.01 | 0.95 | 0.93 | 0.90 | 0.89 |
| **6.   WA** | | | | | | | | | | |
| 6a.   Per capita GDP | 3 351 | 3 997 | 4 872 | 6 519 | 7 486 | 8 566 | 8 956 | 9 578 | 13 418 | 15 097 |
| 6b.   GDP | 20 733 | 24 915 | 30 558 | 41 095 | 47 361 | 54 297 | 56 792 | 60 657 | 84 828 | 95 353 |
| 6c.   % of GWP | 0.65 | 0.71 | 0.76 | 0.84 | 0.85 | 0.88 | 0.85 | 0.80 | 0.96 | 0.93 |

|  |  |  |  |  |  |  |  |  |  | Averages | | |
| 1980 (11) | 1981 (12) | 1982 (13) | 1983 (14) | 1984 (15) | 1985 (16) | 1986 (17) | 1987 (18) | 1988 (19) | 1989 (20) | 1970–89 (21) | 1970–79 (22) | 1980–89 (23) |
|---|---|---|---|---|---|---|---|---|---|---|---|---|
| 15 026 | 13 738 | 12 108 | 11 109 | 11 512 | 12 050 | 15 866 | 19 303 | 21 653 | 22 703 | 11 776 | 8 047 | 15 542 |
| 124 883 | 114 342 | 100 857 | 92 585 | 96 022 | 100 626 | 132 732 | 161 833 | 181 994 | 191 298 | 97 774 | 65 830 | 129 717 |
| 1.08 | 0.98 | 0.87 | 0.78 | 0.79 | 0.80 | 0.89 | 0.94 | 0.95 | 0.95 | 0.96 | 1.08 | 0.91 |
|  |  |  |  |  |  |  |  |  |  |  |  |  |
| 8 916 | 9 810 | 10 429 | 11 052 | 11 827 | 12 198 | 12 697 | 13 405 | 14 139 | 14 995 | 8 846 | 5 743 | 11 970 |
| 74 097 | 81 649 | 86 870 | 92 106 | 98 646 | 101 869 | 106 221 | 112 386 | 118 840 | 126 346 | 73 444 | 46 984 | 99 903 |
| ... | ... | ... | ... | ... | ... | ... | ... | ... | ... | ... | ... | ... |
| 11 821 | 11 808 | 11 929 | 12 140 | 12 612 | 12 877 | 13 139 | 13 484 | 13 761 | 14 019 | 11 776 | 10 865 | 12 779 |
| 98 248 | 98 280 | 99 372 | 101 172 | 105 200 | 107 537 | 109 922 | 113 054 | 115 663 | 118 125 | 97 774 | 88 890 | 106 657 |
| 0.95 | 0.93 | 0.93 | 0.92 | 0.92 | 0.91 | 0.90 | 0.89 | 0.88 | 0.87 | 0.96 | 1.03 | 0.91 |
|  |  |  |  |  |  |  |  |  |  |  |  |  |
| 11 718 | 12 813 | 13 780 | 14 497 | 15 601 | 16 360 | 17 028 | 17 978 | 18 963 | 20 110 | 11 606 | 7 320 | 15 917 |
| 97 389 | 106 638 | 114 788 | 120 817 | 130 128 | 136 622 | 142 459 | 150 727 | 159 383 | 169 450 | 96 362 | 59 884 | 132 840 |
| 0.95 | 0.93 | 0.93 | 0.92 | 0.92 | 0.91 | 0.90 | 0.89 | 0.88 | 0.87 | 0.94 | 1.02 | 0.90 |
|  |  |  |  |  |  |  |  |  |  |  |  |  |
| 14 377 | 14 361 | 14 509 | 14 764 | 15 339 | 15 661 | 15 980 | 16 400 | 16 736 | 17 050 | 14 323 | 13 215 | 15 542 |
| 119 489 | 119 529 | 120 856 | 123 046 | 127 945 | 130 787 | 133 688 | 137 496 | 140 670 | 143 664 | 118 913 | 108 108 | 129 717 |
| 0.94 | 0.93 | 0.93 | 0.92 | 0.92 | 0.91 | 0.90 | 0.90 | 0.88 | 0.87 | 0.96 | 1.03 | 0.91 |
|  |  |  |  |  |  |  |  |  |  |  |  |  |
| 15 028 | 13 737 | 12 108 | 11 109 | 11 512 | 12 050 | 15 867 | 19 179 | 21 557 | 22 538 | 11 757 | 8 046 | 15 504 |
| 124 896 | 114 332 | 100 863 | 92 584 | 96 025 | 100 627 | 132 740 | 160 801 | 181 187 | 189 906 | 97 610 | 65 824 | 129 396 |
| 1.08 | 0.97 | 0.87 | 0.78 | 0.79 | 0.80 | 0.90 | 0.97 | 0.97 | 0.97 | 0.97 | 1.09 | 0.92 |
|  |  |  |  |  |  |  |  |  |  |  |  |  |
| 16 081 | 14 845 | 15 170 | 15 178 | 14 098 | 14 337 | 20 801 | 25 986 | 27 269 | 27 497 | 13 886 | 8 158 | 19 183 |
| 101 629 | 94 071 | 96 542 | 97 125 | 90 736 | 92 776 | 135 270 | 169 790 | 178 940 | 181 125 | 87 733 | 51 665 | 123 800 |
| 0.88 | 0.80 | 0.83 | 0.82 | 0.74 | 0.74 | 0.91 | 0.99 | 0.94 | 0.90 | 0.86 | 0.85 | 0.87 |
|  |  |  |  |  |  |  |  |  |  |  |  |  |
| ... | ... | ... | ... | ... | ... | ... | ... | ... | ... | ... | ... | ... |
| ... | ... | ... | ... | ... | ... | ... | ... | ... | ... | ... | ... | ... |
| ... | ... | ... | ... | ... | ... | ... | ... | ... | ... | ... | ... | ... |
| 13 822 | 13 983 | 13 795 | 13 858 | 14 022 | 14 463 | 14 804 | 15 033 | 15 403 | 15 882 | 13 886 | 12 920 | 14 511 |
| 87 357 | 88 613 | 87 793 | 88 675 | 90 244 | 93 590 | 96 273 | 98 227 | 101 076 | 104 615 | 87 733 | 81 819 | 93 646 |
| 0.84 | 0.84 | 0.82 | 0.81 | 0.79 | 0.79 | 0.79 | 0.78 | 0.77 | 0.77 | 0.86 | 0.95 | 0.80 |
|  |  |  |  |  |  |  |  |  |  |  |  |  |
| 13 701 | 15 173 | 15 935 | 16 548 | 17 344 | 18 375 | 19 186 | 20 043 | 21 226 | 22 783 | 13 543 | 8 616 | 18 062 |
| 86 593 | 96 150 | 101 412 | 105 893 | 111 628 | 118 903 | 124 769 | 130 959 | 139 282 | 150 069 | 85 566 | 54 566 | 116 566 |
| 0.84 | 0.84 | 0.82 | 0.81 | 0.79 | 0.79 | 0.79 | 0.78 | 0.77 | 0.77 | 0.83 | 0.93 | 0.79 |
|  |  |  |  |  |  |  |  |  |  |  |  |  |
| 18 273 | 18 486 | 18 237 | 18 320 | 18 537 | 19 120 | 19 571 | 19 874 | 20 363 | 20 996 | 18 358 | 17 080 | 19 183 |
| 115 485 | 117 147 | 116 062 | 117 228 | 119 303 | 123 727 | 127 273 | 129 856 | 133 622 | 138 301 | 115 983 | 108 165 | 123 800 |
| 0.91 | 0.91 | 0.90 | 0.88 | 0.86 | 0.86 | 0.86 | 0.85 | 0.84 | 0.84 | 0.93 | 1.03 | 0.87 |
|  |  |  |  |  |  |  |  |  |  |  |  |  |
| 16 083 | 14 843 | 15 168 | 15 177 | 14 100 | 14 336 | 20 802 | 26 139 | 27 953 | 26 894 | 13 898 | 8 157 | 19 207 |
| 101 646 | 94 059 | 96 529 | 97 118 | 90 749 | 92 771 | 135 276 | 170 793 | 183 428 | 177 148 | 87 805 | 51 659 | 123 952 |
| 0.88 | 0.80 | 0.83 | 0.82 | 0.74 | 0.73 | 0.92 | 1.03 | 0.98 | 0.90 | 0.87 | 0.85 | 0.88 |

**Table A.1**    Total and per capita gross domestic product of individual countries or areas,
expressed in United States dollars, and their individual shares of gross world
product, based on alternative conversion rates, 1970–1989 [*cont.*]

| Country or area | 1970 (1) | 1971 (2) | 1972 (3) | 1973 (4) | 1974 (5) | 1975 (6) | 1976 (7) | 1977 (8) | 1978 (9) | 1979 (10) |
|---|---|---|---|---|---|---|---|---|---|---|
| **Syrian Arab Republic** | | | | | | | | | | |
| **1. MER** | | | | | | | | | | |
| 1a. Per capita GDP | 286 | 325 | 363 | 375 | 594 | 752 | 841 | 873 | 1 012 | 1 177 |
| 1b. GDP | 1 793 | 2 106 | 2 431 | 2 603 | 4 273 | 5 598 | 6 468 | 6 946 | 8 330 | 10 013 |
| 1c. % of GWP | 0.06 | 0.06 | 0.06 | 0.05 | 0.08 | 0.09 | 0.10 | 0.09 | 0.09 | 0.10 |
| **2. PPPs** | | | | | | | | | | |
| 2a. Per capita GDP | 691 | 806 | 892 | 931 | 1 418 | 1 827 | 1 958 | 1 971 | 2 250 | 2 607 |
| 2b. GDP | 4 327 | 5 217 | 5 980 | 6 460 | 10 191 | 13 593 | 15 064 | 15 684 | 18 512 | 22 183 |
| 2c. % of GWP | ... | ... | ... | ... | ... | ... | ... | ... | ... | ... |
| **3. Absolute 1970–1989 PARE** | | | | | | | | | | |
| 3a. Per capita GDP | 871 | 925 | 1 117 | 986 | 1 183 | 1 366 | 1 465 | 1 399 | 1 471 | 1 474 |
| 3b. GDP | 5 449 | 5 989 | 7 488 | 6 848 | 8 500 | 10 160 | 11 273 | 11 130 | 12 101 | 12 541 |
| 3c. % of GWP | 0.08 | 0.08 | 0.10 | 0.08 | 0.10 | 0.12 | 0.12 | 0.12 | 0.12 | 0.12 |
| **4. Relative 1970–1989 PARE** | | | | | | | | | | |
| 4a. Per capita GDP | 424 | 474 | 599 | 564 | 737 | 936 | 1 066 | 1 087 | 1 226 | 1 338 |
| 4b. GDP | 2 657 | 3 070 | 4 014 | 3 915 | 5 301 | 6 961 | 8 206 | 8 648 | 10 089 | 11 389 |
| 4c. % of GWP | 0.08 | 0.08 | 0.10 | 0.08 | 0.10 | 0.12 | 0.12 | 0.12 | 0.12 | 0.12 |
| **5. Absolute 1980–1989 PARE** | | | | | | | | | | |
| 5a. Per capita GDP | 1 095 | 1 164 | 1 405 | 1 241 | 1 488 | 1 719 | 1 844 | 1 760 | 1 851 | 1 855 |
| 5b. GDP | 6 856 | 7 536 | 9 422 | 8 617 | 10 696 | 12 785 | 14 186 | 14 005 | 15 227 | 15 781 |
| 5c. % of GWP | 0.08 | 0.08 | 0.10 | 0.08 | 0.10 | 0.12 | 0.13 | 0.12 | 0.13 | 0.13 |
| **6. WA** | | | | | | | | | | |
| 6a. Per capita GDP | 344 | 401 | 459 | 471 | 723 | 923 | 1 000 | 976 | 1 138 | 1 177 |
| 6b. GDP | 2 155 | 2 600 | 3 079 | 3 267 | 5 194 | 6 865 | 7 692 | 7 768 | 9 363 | 10 013 |
| 6c. % of GWP | 0.07 | 0.07 | 0.08 | 0.07 | 0.09 | 0.11 | 0.11 | 0.10 | 0.11 | 0.10 |
| **Thailand** | | | | | | | | | | |
| **1. MER** | | | | | | | | | | |
| 1a. Per capita GDP | 198 | 199 | 214 | 275 | 341 | 360 | 400 | 454 | 538 | 599 |
| 1b. GDP | 7 086 | 7 331 | 8 127 | 10 772 | 13 703 | 14 884 | 16 986 | 19 781 | 24 008 | 27 370 |
| 1c. % of GWP | 0.22 | 0.21 | 0.20 | 0.22 | 0.25 | 0.24 | 0.25 | 0.26 | 0.27 | 0.27 |
| **2. PPPs** | | | | | | | | | | |
| 2a. Per capita GDP | 606 | 632 | 669 | 758 | 844 | 929 | 1 041 | 1 205 | 1 367 | 1 510 |
| 2b. GDP | 21 676 | 23 297 | 25 386 | 29 643 | 33 953 | 38 430 | 44 189 | 52 469 | 60 990 | 68 969 |
| 2c. % of GWP | ... | ... | ... | ... | ... | ... | ... | ... | ... | ... |
| **3. Absolute 1970–1989 PARE** | | | | | | | | | | |
| 3a. Per capita GDP | 419 | 427 | 431 | 460 | 466 | 476 | 507 | 543 | 585 | 602 |
| 3b. GDP | 14 984 | 15 728 | 16 368 | 17 982 | 18 765 | 19 674 | 21 519 | 23 649 | 26 118 | 27 506 |
| 3c. % of GWP | 0.21 | 0.21 | 0.21 | 0.22 | 0.22 | 0.23 | 0.24 | 0.25 | 0.27 | 0.27 |
| **4. Relative 1970–1989 PARE** | | | | | | | | | | |
| 4a. Per capita GDP | 204 | 219 | 231 | 263 | 291 | 326 | 369 | 422 | 488 | 547 |
| 4b. GDP | 7 306 | 8 062 | 8 775 | 10 281 | 11 702 | 13 479 | 15 664 | 18 376 | 21 775 | 24 979 |
| 4c. % of GWP | 0.21 | 0.21 | 0.21 | 0.22 | 0.22 | 0.23 | 0.24 | 0.25 | 0.27 | 0.27 |
| **5. Absolute 1980–1989 PARE** | | | | | | | | | | |
| 5a. Per capita GDP | 476 | 484 | 489 | 522 | 529 | 540 | 575 | 616 | 664 | 683 |
| 5b. GDP | 17 001 | 17 845 | 18 572 | 20 403 | 21 291 | 22 323 | 24 416 | 26 832 | 29 633 | 31 208 |
| 5c. % of GWP | 0.20 | 0.20 | 0.19 | 0.20 | 0.21 | 0.21 | 0.22 | 0.23 | 0.25 | 0.25 |
| **6. WA** | | | | | | | | | | |
| 6a. Per capita GDP | 198 | 200 | 215 | 275 | 341 | 360 | 400 | 454 | 538 | 599 |
| 6b. GDP | 7 086 | 7 376 | 8 177 | 10 772 | 13 703 | 14 884 | 16 986 | 19 781 | 24 008 | 27 370 |
| 6c. % of GWP | 0.22 | 0.21 | 0.20 | 0.22 | 0.25 | 0.24 | 0.25 | 0.26 | 0.27 | 0.27 |

| | | | | | | | | | | Averages | | |
|---|---|---|---|---|---|---|---|---|---|---|---|---|
| 1980 (11) | 1981 (12) | 1982 (13) | 1983 (14) | 1984 (15) | 1985 (16) | 1986 (17) | 1987 (18) | 1988 (19) | 1989 (20) | 1970–89 (21) | 1970–79 (22) | 1980–89 (23) |
| 1 484 | 1 841 | 1 860 | 1 915 | 1 901 | 2 027 | 2 349 | 2 918 | 1 416 | 1 502 | 1 443 | 691 | 1 939 |
| 13 062 | 16 758 | 17 526 | 18 673 | 19 195 | 21 204 | 25 461 | 32 781 | 16 493 | 18 145 | 12 493 | 5 056 | 19 930 |
| 0.11 | 0.14 | 0.15 | 0.16 | 0.16 | 0.17 | 0.17 | 0.19 | 0.09 | 0.09 | 0.12 | 0.08 | 0.14 |
| 3 005 | 3 761 | 3 682 | 3 522 | 3 746 | 3 851 | 3 603 | 3 653 | 4 080 | 3 953 | 2 891 | 1 603 | 3 729 |
| 26 448 | 34 236 | 34 690 | 34 344 | 37 816 | 40 281 | 39 058 | 41 041 | 47 536 | 47 764 | 25 021 | 11 721 | 38 321 |
| ... | ... | ... | ... | ... | ... | ... | ... | ... | ... | ... | ... | ... |
| 1 596 | 1 689 | 1 667 | 1 634 | 1 514 | 1 550 | 1 422 | 1 401 | 1 514 | 1 409 | 1 443 | 1 251 | 1 541 |
| 14 043 | 15 379 | 15 705 | 15 929 | 15 281 | 16 215 | 15 413 | 15 743 | 17 643 | 17 029 | 12 493 | 9 148 | 15 838 |
| 0.14 | 0.15 | 0.15 | 0.15 | 0.13 | 0.14 | 0.13 | 0.12 | 0.13 | 0.13 | 0.12 | 0.11 | 0.13 |
| 1 582 | 1 833 | 1 926 | 1 951 | 1 872 | 1 970 | 1 843 | 1 868 | 2 087 | 2 022 | 1 509 | 878 | 1 917 |
| 13 921 | 16 687 | 18 141 | 19 023 | 18 902 | 20 601 | 19 976 | 20 990 | 24 312 | 24 428 | 13 061 | 6 425 | 19 698 |
| 0.14 | 0.15 | 0.15 | 0.15 | 0.13 | 0.14 | 0.13 | 0.12 | 0.13 | 0.13 | 0.13 | 0.11 | 0.13 |
| 2 008 | 2 126 | 2 098 | 2 056 | 1 905 | 1 951 | 1 789 | 1 763 | 1 905 | 1 773 | 1 816 | 1 574 | 1 939 |
| 17 672 | 19 352 | 19 762 | 20 045 | 19 229 | 20 405 | 19 395 | 19 811 | 22 201 | 21 429 | 15 721 | 11 511 | 19 930 |
| 0.14 | 0.15 | 0.15 | 0.15 | 0.14 | 0.14 | 0.13 | 0.13 | 0.14 | 0.13 | 0.13 | 0.11 | 0.14 |
| 1 484 | 1 712 | 1 738 | 1 816 | 1 744 | 1 624 | 1 227 | 1 013 | 901 | 884 | 1 162 | 793 | 1 393 |
| 13 062 | 15 587 | 16 378 | 17 703 | 17 603 | 16 985 | 13 301 | 11 379 | 10 503 | 10 679 | 10 059 | 5 800 | 14 318 |
| 0.11 | 0.13 | 0.14 | 0.15 | 0.14 | 0.13 | 0.09 | 0.07 | 0.06 | 0.05 | 0.10 | 0.10 | 0.10 |
| 688 | 730 | 731 | 796 | 812 | 724 | 794 | 915 | 1 101 | 1 269 | 639 | 368 | 861 |
| 32 160 | 34 839 | 35 652 | 39 568 | 41 178 | 37 350 | 41 651 | 48 761 | 59 564 | 69 681 | 29 523 | 15 005 | 44 040 |
| 0.28 | 0.30 | 0.31 | 0.33 | 0.34 | 0.30 | 0.28 | 0.28 | 0.31 | 0.35 | 0.29 | 0.25 | 0.31 |
| 1 619 | 1 801 | 1 859 | 1 977 | 2 262 | 2 246 | 2 363 | 2 620 | 3 020 | 3 476 | 1 730 | 978 | 2 345 |
| 75 657 | 86 002 | 90 653 | 98 352 | 114 639 | 115 887 | 124 028 | 139 671 | 163 442 | 190 911 | 79 912 | 39 900 | 119 924 |
| ... | ... | ... | ... | ... | ... | ... | ... | ... | ... | ... | ... | ... |
| 617 | 642 | 654 | 688 | 723 | 735 | 758 | 817 | 911 | 1 008 | 639 | 496 | 759 |
| 28 822 | 30 647 | 31 893 | 34 205 | 36 643 | 37 930 | 39 795 | 43 562 | 49 321 | 55 340 | 29 523 | 20 229 | 38 816 |
| 0.28 | 0.29 | 0.30 | 0.31 | 0.32 | 0.32 | 0.33 | 0.34 | 0.37 | 0.41 | 0.29 | 0.23 | 0.33 |
| 612 | 696 | 756 | 821 | 894 | 934 | 983 | 1 089 | 1 256 | 1 446 | 682 | 344 | 958 |
| 28 570 | 33 254 | 36 840 | 40 847 | 45 325 | 48 189 | 51 574 | 58 079 | 67 964 | 79 386 | 31 521 | 14 040 | 49 003 |
| 0.28 | 0.29 | 0.30 | 0.31 | 0.32 | 0.32 | 0.33 | 0.34 | 0.37 | 0.41 | 0.31 | 0.24 | 0.33 |
| 700 | 728 | 742 | 780 | 820 | 834 | 860 | 927 | 1 034 | 1 143 | 725 | 563 | 861 |
| 32 701 | 34 772 | 36 185 | 38 809 | 41 575 | 43 036 | 45 151 | 49 426 | 55 959 | 62 789 | 33 496 | 22 952 | 44 040 |
| 0.26 | 0.27 | 0.28 | 0.29 | 0.30 | 0.30 | 0.30 | 0.32 | 0.35 | 0.38 | 0.27 | 0.22 | 0.31 |
| 688 | 730 | 731 | 796 | 812 | 724 | 794 | 914 | 1 101 | 1 269 | 639 | 368 | 861 |
| 32 160 | 34 839 | 35 652 | 39 568 | 41 178 | 37 351 | 41 651 | 48 718 | 59 579 | 69 676 | 29 526 | 15 014 | 44 037 |
| 0.28 | 0.30 | 0.31 | 0.33 | 0.34 | 0.30 | 0.28 | 0.29 | 0.32 | 0.36 | 0.29 | 0.25 | 0.31 |

**Table A.1**  Total and per capita gross domestic product of individual countries or areas, expressed in United States dollars, and their individual shares of gross world product, based on alternative conversion rates, 1970—1989 [cont.]

| Country or area | 1970 (1) | 1971 (2) | 1972 (3) | 1973 (4) | 1974 (5) | 1975 (6) | 1976 (7) | 1977 (8) | 1978 (9) | 1979 (10) |
|---|---|---|---|---|---|---|---|---|---|---|
| **Togo** | | | | | | | | | | |
| **1. MER** | | | | | | | | | | |
| 1a. Per capita GDP | 130 | 143 | 162 | 186 | 243 | 262 | 243 | 285 | 344 | 400 |
| 1b. GDP | 263 | 298 | 347 | 406 | 543 | 599 | 570 | 687 | 851 | 1 017 |
| 1c. % of GWP | 0.01 | 0.01 | 0.01 | 0.01 | 0.01 | 0.01 | 0.01 | 0.01 | 0.01 | 0.01 |
| **2. PPPs** | | | | | | | | | | |
| 2a. Per capita GDP | 351 | 373 | 397 | 378 | 464 | 461 | 429 | 467 | 522 | 577 |
| 2b. GDP | 709 | 778 | 849 | 825 | 1 036 | 1 053 | 1 005 | 1 125 | 1 292 | 1 466 |
| 2c. % of GWP | ... | ... | ... | ... | ... | ... | ... | ... | ... | ... |
| **3. Absolute 1970—1989 PARE** | | | | | | | | | | |
| 3a. Per capita GDP | 323 | 335 | 338 | 317 | 324 | 314 | 305 | 314 | 336 | 346 |
| 3b. GDP | 652 | 699 | 723 | 693 | 723 | 718 | 715 | 755 | 831 | 880 |
| 3c. % of GWP | 0.01 | 0.01 | 0.01 | 0.01 | 0.01 | 0.01 | 0.01 | 0.01 | 0.01 | 0.01 |
| **4. Relative 1970—1989 PARE** | | | | | | | | | | |
| 4a. Per capita GDP | 157 | 172 | 181 | 181 | 202 | 215 | 222 | 244 | 280 | 314 |
| 4b. GDP | 318 | 358 | 388 | 396 | 451 | 492 | 520 | 586 | 693 | 800 |
| 4c. % of GWP | 0.01 | 0.01 | 0.01 | 0.01 | 0.01 | 0.01 | 0.01 | 0.01 | 0.01 | 0.01 |
| **5. Absolute 1980—1989 PARE** | | | | | | | | | | |
| 5a. Per capita GDP | 394 | 410 | 413 | 387 | 395 | 384 | 372 | 383 | 410 | 423 |
| 5b. GDP | 796 | 854 | 883 | 846 | 882 | 877 | 873 | 921 | 1 014 | 1 075 |
| 5c. % of GWP | 0.01 | 0.01 | 0.01 | 0.01 | 0.01 | 0.01 | 0.01 | 0.01 | 0.01 | 0.01 |
| **6. WA** | | | | | | | | | | |
| 6a. Per capita GDP | 130 | 142 | 162 | 186 | 243 | 262 | 243 | 285 | 344 | 400 |
| 6b. GDP | 263 | 296 | 347 | 406 | 543 | 599 | 570 | 687 | 851 | 1 017 |
| 6c. % of GWP | 0.01 | 0.01 | 0.01 | 0.01 | 0.01 | 0.01 | 0.01 | 0.01 | 0.01 | 0.01 |
| **Tonga** | | | | | | | | | | |
| **1. MER** | | | | | | | | | | |
| 1a. Per capita GDP | 154 | 164 | 202 | 302 | 404 | 369 | 335 | 371 | 442 | 464 |
| 1b. GDP | 13 | 14 | 17 | 26 | 35 | 33 | 30 | 34 | 42 | 45 |
| 1c. % of GWP | 0.00 | 0.00 | 0.00 | 0.00 | 0.00 | 0.00 | 0.00 | 0.00 | 0.00 | 0.00 |
| **2. PPPs** | | | | | | | | | | |
| 2a. Per capita GDP | ... | ... | ... | ... | ... | ... | ... | ... | ... | ... |
| 2b. GDP | ... | ... | ... | ... | ... | ... | ... | ... | ... | ... |
| 2c. % of GWP | ... | ... | ... | ... | ... | ... | ... | ... | ... | ... |
| **3. Absolute 1970—1989 PARE** | | | | | | | | | | |
| 3a. Per capita GDP | 415 | 414 | 424 | 396 | 440 | 465 | 458 | 469 | 468 | 467 |
| 3b. GDP | 35 | 36 | 36 | 34 | 38 | 41 | 41 | 43 | 44 | 45 |
| 3c. % of GWP | 0.00 | 0.00 | 0.00 | 0.00 | 0.00 | 0.00 | 0.00 | 0.00 | 0.00 | 0.00 |
| **4. Relative 1970—1989 PARE** | | | | | | | | | | |
| 4a. Per capita GDP | 202 | 212 | 227 | 226 | 274 | 318 | 333 | 365 | 390 | 424 |
| 4b. GDP | 17 | 18 | 20 | 20 | 24 | 28 | 30 | 34 | 37 | 41 |
| 4c. % of GWP | 0.00 | 0.00 | 0.00 | 0.00 | 0.00 | 0.00 | 0.00 | 0.00 | 0.00 | 0.00 |
| **5. Absolute 1980—1989 PARE** | | | | | | | | | | |
| 5a. Per capita GDP | 476 | 474 | 485 | 454 | 504 | 532 | 525 | 538 | 537 | 535 |
| 5b. GDP | 40 | 41 | 42 | 39 | 44 | 47 | 47 | 49 | 50 | 51 |
| 5c. % of GWP | 0.00 | 0.00 | 0.00 | 0.00 | 0.00 | 0.00 | 0.00 | 0.00 | 0.00 | 0.00 |
| **6. WA[a]** | | | | | | | | | | |
| 6a. Per capita GDP | 144 | 154 | 174 | 202 | 300 | 375 | 366 | 359 | 380 | 416 |
| 6b. GDP | 12 | 13 | 15 | 18 | 26 | 33 | 33 | 33 | 36 | 40 |
| 6c. % of GWP | 0.00 | 0.00 | 0.00 | 0.00 | 0.00 | 0.00 | 0.00 | 0.00 | 0.00 | 0.00 |

| | | | | | | | | | | Averages | | |
| 1980 (11) | 1981 (12) | 1982 (13) | 1983 (14) | 1984 (15) | 1985 (16) | 1986 (17) | 1987 (18) | 1988 (19) | 1989 (20) | 1970–89 (21) | 1970–79 (22) | 1980–89 (23) |
|---|---|---|---|---|---|---|---|---|---|---|---|---|
| 432 | 353 | 296 | 259 | 237 | 244 | 336 | 385 | 397 | 381 | 302 | 247 | 335 |
| 1 131 | 949 | 821 | 738 | 698 | 740 | 1 050 | 1 238 | 1 319 | 1 304 | 778 | 558 | 999 |
| 0.01 | 0.01 | 0.01 | 0.01 | 0.01 | 0.01 | 0.01 | 0.01 | 0.01 | 0.01 | 0.01 | 0.01 | 0.01 |
| 616 | 610 | 610 | 581 | 627 | 663 | 683 | 724 | 751 | 786 | 586 | 449 | 674 |
| 1 611 | 1 642 | 1 689 | 1 658 | 1 843 | 2 009 | 2 131 | 2 331 | 2 493 | 2 691 | 1 512 | 1 014 | 2 010 |
| ... | ... | ... | ... | ... | ... | ... | ... | ... | ... | ... | ... | ... |
| 321 | 293 | 274 | 252 | 262 | 259 | 262 | 270 | 271 | 272 | 302 | 327 | 274 |
| 840 | 788 | 760 | 720 | 770 | 785 | 817 | 868 | 898 | 932 | 778 | 739 | 818 |
| 0.01 | 0.01 | 0.01 | 0.01 | 0.01 | 0.01 | 0.01 | 0.01 | 0.01 | 0.01 | 0.01 | 0.01 | 0.01 |
| 318 | 318 | 317 | 301 | 324 | 329 | 339 | 360 | 373 | 390 | 294 | 221 | 341 |
| 833 | 856 | 878 | 859 | 952 | 998 | 1 059 | 1 158 | 1 238 | 1 337 | 758 | 500 | 1 017 |
| 0.01 | 0.01 | 0.01 | 0.01 | 0.01 | 0.01 | 0.01 | 0.01 | 0.01 | 0.01 | 0.01 | 0.01 | 0.01 |
| 392 | 358 | 335 | 308 | 320 | 317 | 320 | 330 | 331 | 332 | 368 | 399 | 335 |
| 1 026 | 963 | 928 | 879 | 940 | 959 | 997 | 1 060 | 1 097 | 1 138 | 950 | 902 | 999 |
| 0.01 | 0.01 | 0.01 | 0.01 | 0.01 | 0.01 | 0.01 | 0.01 | 0.01 | 0.01 | 0.01 | 0.01 | 0.01 |
| 432 | 353 | 296 | 259 | 237 | 244 | 336 | 385 | 397 | 381 | 302 | 247 | 335 |
| 1 130 | 949 | 821 | 738 | 698 | 740 | 1 050 | 1 237 | 1 319 | 1 304 | 778 | 558 | 999 |
| 0.01 | 0.01 | 0.01 | 0.01 | 0.01 | 0.01 | 0.01 | 0.01 | 0.01 | 0.01 | 0.01 | 0.01 | 0.01 |
| 615 | 638 | 666 | 676 | 870 | 752 | 852 | 993 | 1 218 | 1 299 | 575 | 330 | 857 |
| 60 | 63 | 65 | 66 | 84 | 72 | 82 | 95 | 116 | 123 | 56 | 29 | 83 |
| 0.00 | 0.00 | 0.00 | 0.00 | 0.00 | 0.00 | 0.00 | 0.00 | 0.00 | 0.00 | 0.00 | 0.00 | 0.00 |
| ... | ... | ... | ... | ... | ... | ... | ... | ... | ... | ... | ... | ... |
| ... | ... | ... | ... | ... | ... | ... | ... | ... | ... | ... | ... | ... |
| ... | ... | ... | ... | ... | ... | ... | ... | ... | ... | ... | ... | ... |
| 530 | 604 | 693 | 741 | 760 | 809 | 790 | 824 | 854 | 875 | 575 | 450 | 747 |
| 52 | 59 | 68 | 72 | 74 | 78 | 76 | 79 | 81 | 83 | 56 | 39 | 72 |
| 0.00 | 0.00 | 0.00 | 0.00 | 0.00 | 0.00 | 0.00 | 0.00 | 0.00 | 0.00 | 0.00 | 0.00 | 0.00 |
| 525 | 655 | 801 | 885 | 940 | 1 027 | 1 024 | 1 099 | 1 176 | 1 254 | 604 | 306 | 937 |
| 51 | 64 | 78 | 86 | 91 | 99 | 98 | 105 | 112 | 119 | 59 | 27 | 90 |
| 0.00 | 0.00 | 0.00 | 0.00 | 0.00 | 0.00 | 0.00 | 0.00 | 0.00 | 0.00 | 0.00 | 0.00 | 0.00 |
| 607 | 692 | 794 | 849 | 870 | 927 | 905 | 944 | 978 | 1 002 | 659 | 516 | 857 |
| 59 | 68 | 78 | 82 | 84 | 89 | 87 | 91 | 93 | 95 | 64 | 45 | 83 |
| 0.00 | 0.00 | 0.00 | 0.00 | 0.00 | 0.00 | 0.00 | 0.00 | 0.00 | 0.00 | 0.00 | 0.00 | 0.00 |
| 532 | 630 | 712 | 711 | 762 | 812 | 837 | 878 | 1 040 | 1 190 | 536 | 296 | 809 |
| 52 | 62 | 70 | 69 | 74 | 78 | 80 | 84 | 99 | 113 | 52 | 26 | 78 |
| 0.00 | 0.00 | 0.00 | 0.00 | 0.00 | 0.00 | 0.00 | 0.00 | 0.00 | 0.00 | 0.00 | 0.00 | 0.00 |

**Table A.1**     Total and per capita gross domestic product of individual countries or areas,
expressed in United States dollars, and their individual shares of gross world
product, based on alternative conversion rates, 1970−1989 [cont.]

| Country or area | 1970 (1) | 1971 (2) | 1972 (3) | 1973 (4) | 1974 (5) | 1975 (6) | 1976 (7) | 1977 (8) | 1978 (9) | 1979 (10) |
|---|---|---|---|---|---|---|---|---|---|---|
| **Trinidad and Tobago** | | | | | | | | | | |
| **1. MER** | | | | | | | | | | |
| 1a. Per capita GDP | 847 | 919 | 1 096 | 1 314 | 2 036 | 2 413 | 2 442 | 3 030 | 3 393 | 4 318 |
| 1b. GDP | 822 | 902 | 1 084 | 1 309 | 2 042 | 2 442 | 2 498 | 3 139 | 3 563 | 4 603 |
| 1c. % of GWP | 0.03 | 0.03 | 0.03 | 0.03 | 0.04 | 0.04 | 0.04 | 0.04 | 0.04 | 0.04 |
| **2. PPPs** | | | | | | | | | | |
| 2a. Per capita GDP | 1 306 | 1 277 | 1 550 | 1 844 | 2 762 | 3 126 | 3 373 | 4 250 | 4 916 | 5 882 |
| 2b. GDP | 1 268 | 1 253 | 1 533 | 1 837 | 2 770 | 3 163 | 3 450 | 4 403 | 5 162 | 6 270 |
| 2c. % of GWP | ... | ... | ... | ... | ... | ... | ... | ... | ... | ... |
| **3. Absolute 1970−1989 PARE** | | | | | | | | | | |
| 3a. Per capita GDP | 3 197 | 3 197 | 3 355 | 3 386 | 3 490 | 3 510 | 3 695 | 3 981 | 4 322 | 4 411 |
| 3b. GDP | 3 104 | 3 136 | 3 318 | 3 373 | 3 501 | 3 552 | 3 780 | 4 124 | 4 538 | 4 702 |
| 3c. % of GWP | 0.04 | 0.04 | 0.04 | 0.04 | 0.04 | 0.04 | 0.04 | 0.04 | 0.05 | 0.05 |
| **4. Relative 1970−1989 PARE** | | | | | | | | | | |
| 4a. Per capita GDP | 1 559 | 1 639 | 1 798 | 1 936 | 2 177 | 2 405 | 2 690 | 3 093 | 3 603 | 4 006 |
| 4b. GDP | 1 514 | 1 608 | 1 779 | 1 928 | 2 183 | 2 433 | 2 752 | 3 204 | 3 783 | 4 270 |
| 4c. % of GWP | 0.04 | 0.04 | 0.04 | 0.04 | 0.04 | 0.04 | 0.04 | 0.04 | 0.05 | 0.05 |
| **5. Absolute 1980−1989 PARE** | | | | | | | | | | |
| 5a. Per capita GDP | 4 191 | 4 191 | 4 398 | 4 439 | 4 576 | 4 601 | 4 844 | 5 218 | 5 665 | 5 782 |
| 5b. GDP | 4 070 | 4 112 | 4 349 | 4 421 | 4 589 | 4 656 | 4 956 | 5 406 | 5 948 | 6 164 |
| 5c. % of GWP | 0.05 | 0.05 | 0.05 | 0.04 | 0.04 | 0.04 | 0.04 | 0.05 | 0.05 | 0.05 |
| **6. WA** | | | | | | | | | | |
| 6a. Per capita GDP | 847 | 914 | 1 096 | 1 314 | 2 036 | 2 414 | 2 444 | 3 030 | 3 393 | 4 318 |
| 6b. GDP | 822 | 897 | 1 084 | 1 309 | 2 042 | 2 443 | 2 501 | 3 139 | 3 562 | 4 602 |
| 6c. % of GWP | 0.03 | 0.03 | 0.03 | 0.03 | 0.04 | 0.04 | 0.04 | 0.04 | 0.04 | 0.04 |
| **Tunisia** | | | | | | | | | | |
| **1. MER** | | | | | | | | | | |
| 1a. Per capita GDP | 281 | 326 | 422 | 508 | 644 | 772 | 784 | 867 | 987 | 1 155 |
| 1b. GDP | 1 439 | 1 701 | 2 238 | 2 741 | 3 542 | 4 332 | 4 506 | 5 109 | 5 971 | 7 179 |
| 1c. % of GWP | 0.05 | 0.05 | 0.06 | 0.06 | 0.06 | 0.07 | 0.07 | 0.07 | 0.07 | 0.07 |
| **2. PPPs** | | | | | | | | | | |
| 2a. Per capita GDP | 515 | 583 | 680 | 725 | 925 | 998 | 1 103 | 1 229 | 1 375 | 1 575 |
| 2b. GDP | 2 639 | 3 045 | 3 611 | 3 915 | 5 082 | 5 600 | 6 336 | 7 239 | 8 320 | 9 793 |
| 2c. % of GWP | ... | ... | ... | ... | ... | ... | ... | ... | ... | ... |
| **3. Absolute 1970−1989 PARE** | | | | | | | | | | |
| 3a. Per capita GDP | 650 | 702 | 813 | 795 | 843 | 885 | 933 | 940 | 975 | 1 011 |
| 3b. GDP | 3 333 | 3 666 | 4 316 | 4 288 | 4 634 | 4 965 | 5 357 | 5 539 | 5 896 | 6 283 |
| 3c. % of GWP | 0.05 | 0.05 | 0.06 | 0.05 | 0.05 | 0.06 | 0.06 | 0.06 | 0.06 | 0.06 |
| **4. Relative 1970−1989 PARE** | | | | | | | | | | |
| 4a. Per capita GDP | 317 | 360 | 436 | 454 | 526 | 606 | 679 | 731 | 813 | 918 |
| 4b. GDP | 1 625 | 1 879 | 2 314 | 2 452 | 2 889 | 3 401 | 3 899 | 4 304 | 4 916 | 5 706 |
| 4c. % of GWP | 0.05 | 0.05 | 0.06 | 0.05 | 0.05 | 0.06 | 0.06 | 0.06 | 0.06 | 0.06 |
| **5. Absolute 1980−1989 PARE** | | | | | | | | | | |
| 5a. Per capita GDP | 728 | 787 | 911 | 890 | 944 | 991 | 1 045 | 1 053 | 1 092 | 1 133 |
| 5b. GDP | 3 734 | 4 107 | 4 836 | 4 805 | 5 191 | 5 562 | 6 002 | 6 206 | 6 606 | 7 040 |
| 5c. % of GWP | 0.04 | 0.05 | 0.05 | 0.05 | 0.05 | 0.05 | 0.05 | 0.05 | 0.06 | 0.06 |
| **6. WA** | | | | | | | | | | |
| 6a. Per capita GDP | 281 | 323 | 422 | 506 | 645 | 771 | 785 | 867 | 987 | 1 157 |
| 6b. GDP | 1 439 | 1 685 | 2 238 | 2 731 | 3 546 | 4 329 | 4 508 | 5 110 | 5 968 | 7 189 |
| 6c. % of GWP | 0.05 | 0.05 | 0.06 | 0.06 | 0.06 | 0.07 | 0.07 | 0.07 | 0.07 | 0.07 |

| | | | | | | | | | | Averages | | |
|---|---|---|---|---|---|---|---|---|---|---|---|---|
| 1980 (11) | 1981 (12) | 1982 (13) | 1983 (14) | 1984 (15) | 1985 (16) | 1986 (17) | 1987 (18) | 1988 (19) | 1989 (20) | 1970–89 (21) | 1970–79 (22) | 1980–89 (23) |

| | | | | | | | | | | | | |
|---|---|---|---|---|---|---|---|---|---|---|---|---|
| 5 761 | 6 227 | 7 140 | 6 854 | 6 696 | 6 167 | 4 025 | 3 956 | 3 653 | 3 172 | 3 933 | 2 224 | 5 313 |
| 6 233 | 6 849 | 7 990 | 7 800 | 7 754 | 7 271 | 4 826 | 4 827 | 4 533 | 4 003 | 4 224 | 2 240 | 6 209 |
| 0.05 | 0.06 | 0.07 | 0.07 | 0.06 | 0.06 | 0.03 | 0.03 | 0.02 | 0.02 | 0.04 | 0.04 | 0.04 |
| 6 823 | 7 294 | 7 525 | 6 659 | 8 921 | 7 600 | 7 440 | 7 055 | 6 918 | 6 896 | 5 429 | 3 088 | 7 318 |
| 7 383 | 8 023 | 8 420 | 7 578 | 10 331 | 8 960 | 8 921 | 8 607 | 8 585 | 8 703 | 5 831 | 3 111 | 8 551 |
| ... | ... | ... | ... | ... | ... | ... | ... | ... | ... | ... | ... | ... |
| 4 796 | 4 934 | 5 046 | 4 505 | 4 151 | 3 873 | 3 717 | 3 426 | 3 251 | 3 113 | 3 933 | 3 685 | 4 053 |
| 5 189 | 5 427 | 5 646 | 5 127 | 4 807 | 4 566 | 4 457 | 4 180 | 4 034 | 3 928 | 4 224 | 3 713 | 4 736 |
| 0.05 | 0.05 | 0.05 | 0.05 | 0.04 | 0.04 | 0.04 | 0.03 | 0.03 | 0.03 | 0.04 | 0.04 | 0.04 |
| 4 754 | 5 353 | 5 828 | 5 380 | 5 135 | 4 921 | 4 817 | 4 568 | 4 479 | 4 465 | 3 884 | 2 526 | 4 961 |
| 5 144 | 5 889 | 6 522 | 6 122 | 5 946 | 5 802 | 5 776 | 5 573 | 5 559 | 5 635 | 4 171 | 2 545 | 5 797 |
| 0.05 | 0.05 | 0.05 | 0.05 | 0.04 | 0.04 | 0.04 | 0.03 | 0.03 | 0.03 | 0.04 | 0.04 | 0.04 |
| 6 287 | 6 467 | 6 614 | 5 906 | 5 442 | 5 077 | 4 873 | 4 492 | 4 261 | 4 080 | 5 156 | 4 831 | 5 313 |
| 6 802 | 7 114 | 7 401 | 6 721 | 6 301 | 5 986 | 5 842 | 5 480 | 5 288 | 5 149 | 5 538 | 4 867 | 6 209 |
| 0.05 | 0.06 | 0.06 | 0.05 | 0.05 | 0.04 | 0.04 | 0.04 | 0.03 | 0.03 | 0.04 | 0.05 | 0.04 |
| 5 763 | 6 227 | 7 140 | 6 854 | 6 696 | 6 167 | 4 025 | 3 956 | 3 611 | 3 209 | 3 933 | 2 223 | 5 313 |
| 6 236 | 6 849 | 7 990 | 7 800 | 7 754 | 7 271 | 4 826 | 4 827 | 4 482 | 4 050 | 4 224 | 2 240 | 6 208 |
| 0.05 | 0.06 | 0.07 | 0.07 | 0.06 | 0.06 | 0.03 | 0.03 | 0.02 | 0.02 | 0.04 | 0.04 | 0.04 |
| 1 369 | 1 285 | 1 208 | 1 173 | 1 134 | 1 140 | 1 185 | 1 304 | 1 224 | 1 319 | 1 011 | 698 | 1 235 |
| 8 742 | 8 425 | 8 129 | 8 096 | 8 031 | 8 275 | 8 821 | 9 949 | 9 561 | 10 552 | 6 367 | 3 876 | 8 858 |
| 0.08 | 0.07 | 0.07 | 0.07 | 0.07 | 0.07 | 0.06 | 0.06 | 0.05 | 0.05 | 0.06 | 0.06 | 0.06 |
| 1 851 | 2 128 | 2 296 | 2 426 | 2 545 | 2 599 | 2 545 | 2 703 | 2 768 | 2 901 | 1 864 | 1 001 | 2 500 |
| 11 817 | 13 951 | 15 449 | 16 745 | 18 019 | 18 873 | 18 948 | 20 620 | 21 623 | 23 203 | 11 741 | 5 558 | 17 925 |
| ... | ... | ... | ... | ... | ... | ... | ... | ... | ... | ... | ... | ... |
| 1 057 | 1 086 | 1 053 | 1 075 | 1 108 | 1 141 | 1 096 | 1 131 | 1 120 | 1 128 | 1 011 | 869 | 1 103 |
| 6 749 | 7 121 | 7 087 | 7 419 | 7 844 | 8 286 | 8 155 | 8 627 | 8 753 | 9 022 | 6 367 | 4 828 | 7 906 |
| 0.06 | 0.07 | 0.07 | 0.07 | 0.07 | 0.07 | 0.07 | 0.07 | 0.07 | 0.07 | 0.06 | 0.06 | 0.07 |
| 1 048 | 1 179 | 1 217 | 1 283 | 1 370 | 1 450 | 1 420 | 1 508 | 1 544 | 1 618 | 1 049 | 601 | 1 377 |
| 6 690 | 7 727 | 8 187 | 8 859 | 9 703 | 10 527 | 10 569 | 11 502 | 12 061 | 12 942 | 6 608 | 3 339 | 9 877 |
| 0.06 | 0.07 | 0.07 | 0.07 | 0.07 | 0.07 | 0.07 | 0.07 | 0.07 | 0.07 | 0.06 | 0.06 | 0.07 |
| 1 184 | 1 217 | 1 180 | 1 204 | 1 241 | 1 279 | 1 227 | 1 267 | 1 255 | 1 264 | 1 132 | 974 | 1 235 |
| 7 561 | 7 979 | 7 940 | 8 312 | 8 788 | 9 284 | 9 137 | 9 666 | 9 806 | 10 108 | 7 134 | 5 409 | 8 858 |
| 0.06 | 0.06 | 0.06 | 0.06 | 0.06 | 0.06 | 0.06 | 0.06 | 0.06 | 0.06 | 0.06 | 0.05 | 0.06 |
| 1 370 | 1 286 | 1 209 | 1 173 | 1 134 | 1 140 | 1 185 | 1 259 | 1 284 | 1 251 | 1 007 | 698 | 1 230 |
| 8 743 | 8 429 | 8 134 | 8 099 | 8 033 | 8 280 | 8 821 | 9 605 | 10 031 | 10 004 | 6 346 | 3 874 | 8 818 |
| 0.08 | 0.07 | 0.07 | 0.07 | 0.07 | 0.07 | 0.06 | 0.06 | 0.05 | 0.05 | 0.06 | 0.06 | 0.06 |

**Table A.1** Total and per capita gross domestic product of individual countries or areas, expressed in United States dollars, and their individual shares of gross world product, based on alternative conversion rates, 1970–1989 [*cont.*]

| Country or area | 1970 (1) | 1971 (2) | 1972 (3) | 1973 (4) | 1974 (5) | 1975 (6) | 1976 (7) | 1977 (8) | 1978 (9) | 1979 (10) |
|---|---|---|---|---|---|---|---|---|---|---|
| **Turkey** | | | | | | | | | | |
| **1. MER** | | | | | | | | | | |
| 1a. Per capita GDP | 362 | 347 | 441 | 547 | 752 | 898 | 1 011 | 1 149 | 1 233 | 1 596 |
| 1b. GDP | 12 797 | 12 591 | 16 403 | 20 883 | 29 418 | 35 951 | 41 357 | 47 939 | 52 500 | 69 373 |
| 1c. % of GWP | 0.40 | 0.36 | 0.41 | 0.43 | 0.53 | 0.58 | 0.62 | 0.63 | 0.58 | 0.67 |
| **2. PPPs** | | | | | | | | | | |
| 2a. Per capita GDP | 910 | 1 023 | 1 112 | 1 174 | 1 386 | 1 634 | 1 895 | 2 039 | 2 066 | 2 161 |
| 2b. GDP | 32 134 | 37 063 | 41 379 | 44 785 | 54 198 | 65 393 | 77 500 | 85 080 | 87 933 | 93 896 |
| 2c. % of GWP | ... | ... | ... | ... | ... | ... | ... | ... | ... | ... |
| **3. Absolute 1970–1989 PARE** | | | | | | | | | | |
| 3a. Per capita GDP | 769 | 817 | 848 | 863 | 914 | 973 | 1 035 | 1 058 | 1 067 | 1 036 |
| 3b. GDP | 27 146 | 29 607 | 31 553 | 32 947 | 35 752 | 38 933 | 42 325 | 44 149 | 45 406 | 45 006 |
| 3c. % of GWP | 0.38 | 0.40 | 0.40 | 0.40 | 0.42 | 0.45 | 0.47 | 0.47 | 0.46 | 0.44 |
| **4. Relative 1970–1989 PARE** | | | | | | | | | | |
| 4a. Per capita GDP | 375 | 419 | 455 | 494 | 570 | 666 | 753 | 822 | 889 | 940 |
| 4b. GDP | 13 236 | 15 176 | 16 915 | 18 836 | 22 295 | 26 673 | 30 809 | 34 305 | 37 855 | 40 872 |
| 4c. % of GWP | 0.38 | 0.40 | 0.40 | 0.40 | 0.42 | 0.45 | 0.47 | 0.47 | 0.46 | 0.44 |
| **5. Absolute 1980–1989 PARE** | | | | | | | | | | |
| 5a. Per capita GDP | 814 | 866 | 899 | 915 | 969 | 1 031 | 1 097 | 1 121 | 1 130 | 1 097 |
| 5b. GDP | 28 762 | 31 369 | 33 431 | 34 908 | 37 880 | 41 250 | 44 844 | 46 777 | 48 108 | 47 684 |
| 5c. % of GWP | 0.33 | 0.35 | 0.35 | 0.34 | 0.37 | 0.39 | 0.41 | 0.41 | 0.40 | 0.38 |
| **6. WA** | | | | | | | | | | |
| 6a. Per capita GDP | 358 | 346 | 441 | 547 | 752 | 898 | 1 011 | 1 149 | 1 233 | 1 596 |
| 6b. GDP | 12 652 | 12 543 | 16 403 | 20 883 | 29 417 | 35 950 | 41 356 | 47 939 | 52 499 | 69 372 |
| 6c. % of GWP | 0.40 | 0.36 | 0.41 | 0.43 | 0.53 | 0.58 | 0.62 | 0.64 | 0.59 | 0.68 |
| **Uganda** | | | | | | | | | | |
| **1. MER** | | | | | | | | | | |
| 1a. Per capita GDP | 242 | 258 | 273 | 306 | 369 | 505 | 504 | 898 | 1 151 | 1 422 |
| 1b. GDP | 2 371 | 2 601 | 2 833 | 3 250 | 4 021 | 5 647 | 5 809 | 10 666 | 14 120 | 18 036 |
| 1c. % of GWP | 0.07 | 0.07 | 0.07 | 0.07 | 0.07 | 0.09 | 0.09 | 0.14 | 0.16 | 0.18 |
| **2. PPPs** | | | | | | | | | | |
| 2a. Per capita GDP | 338 | 363 | 372 | 372 | 391 | 416 | 449 | 472 | 488 | 396 |
| 2b. GDP | 3 317 | 3 667 | 3 853 | 3 955 | 4 259 | 4 647 | 5 168 | 5 606 | 5 982 | 5 026 |
| 2c. % of GWP | ... | ... | ... | ... | ... | ... | ... | ... | ... | ... |
| **3. Absolute 1970–1989 PARE** | | | | | | | | | | |
| 3a. Per capita GDP | 676 | 676 | 663 | 643 | 628 | 599 | 586 | 577 | 533 | 455 |
| 3b. GDP | 6 633 | 6 829 | 6 870 | 6 828 | 6 840 | 6 701 | 6 749 | 6 856 | 6 541 | 5 766 |
| 3c. % of GWP | 0.09 | 0.09 | 0.09 | 0.08 | 0.08 | 0.08 | 0.07 | 0.07 | 0.07 | 0.06 |
| **4. Relative 1970–1989 PARE** | | | | | | | | | | |
| 4a. Per capita GDP | 330 | 347 | 355 | 368 | 392 | 411 | 427 | 449 | 445 | 413 |
| 4b. GDP | 3 234 | 3 500 | 3 683 | 3 904 | 4 265 | 4 591 | 4 913 | 5 327 | 5 453 | 5 236 |
| 4c. % of GWP | 0.09 | 0.09 | 0.09 | 0.08 | 0.08 | 0.08 | 0.07 | 0.07 | 0.07 | 0.06 |
| **5. Absolute 1980–1989 PARE** | | | | | | | | | | |
| 5a. Per capita GDP | 646 | 646 | 633 | 614 | 600 | 572 | 560 | 551 | 509 | 434 |
| 5b. GDP | 6 336 | 6 524 | 6 563 | 6 523 | 6 534 | 6 402 | 6 448 | 6 550 | 6 249 | 5 508 |
| 5c. % of GWP | 0.07 | 0.07 | 0.07 | 0.06 | 0.06 | 0.06 | 0.06 | 0.06 | 0.05 | 0.04 |
| **6. WA** | | | | | | | | | | |
| 6a. Per capita GDP | 197 | 197 | 193 | 187 | 183 | 174 | 171 | 168 | 155 | 132 |
| 6b. GDP | 1 930 | 1 987 | 1 999 | 1 987 | 1 990 | 1 950 | 1 964 | 1 995 | 1 903 | 1 678 |
| 6c. % of GWP | 0.06 | 0.06 | 0.05 | 0.04 | 0.04 | 0.03 | 0.03 | 0.03 | 0.02 | 0.02 |

|  |  |  |  |  |  |  |  |  |  | Averages | | |
| 1980 (11) | 1981 (12) | 1982 (13) | 1983 (14) | 1984 (15) | 1985 (16) | 1986 (17) | 1987 (18) | 1988 (19) | 1989 (20) | 1970−89 (21) | 1970−79 (22) | 1980−89 (23) |
|---|---|---|---|---|---|---|---|---|---|---|---|---|
| 1 281 | 1 267 | 1 136 | 1 067 | 1 010 | 1 048 | 1 131 | 1 293 | 1 321 | 1 461 | 1 067 | 857 | 1 203 |
| 56 919 | 57 666 | 53 032 | 51 148 | 49 668 | 52 783 | 58 246 | 68 011 | 70 889 | 80 016 | 46 879 | 33 921 | 59 838 |
| 0.49 | 0.49 | 0.46 | 0.43 | 0.41 | 0.42 | 0.39 | 0.40 | 0.37 | 0.40 | 0.46 | 0.56 | 0.42 |
| 2 317 | 2 539 | 2 735 | 2 927 | 3 047 | 3 137 | 3 389 | 3 666 | 3 857 | 3 973 | 2 509 | 1 565 | 3 188 |
| 102 965 | 115 563 | 127 717 | 140 277 | 149 782 | 157 939 | 174 506 | 192 797 | 207 037 | 217 563 | 110 275 | 61 936 | 158 615 |
| ... | ... | ... | ... | ... | ... | ... | ... | ... | ... | ... | ... | ... |
| 1 005 | 1 024 | 1 048 | 1 059 | 1 092 | 1 120 | 1 187 | 1 248 | 1 270 | 1 257 | 1 067 | 942 | 1 135 |
| 44 670 | 46 616 | 48 944 | 50 756 | 53 668 | 56 408 | 61 097 | 65 616 | 68 173 | 68 817 | 46 879 | 37 282 | 56 477 |
| 0.43 | 0.44 | 0.46 | 0.46 | 0.47 | 0.48 | 0.50 | 0.52 | 0.52 | 0.51 | 0.46 | 0.43 | 0.48 |
| 996 | 1 111 | 1 211 | 1 265 | 1 351 | 1 423 | 1 538 | 1 663 | 1 750 | 1 803 | 1 099 | 649 | 1 426 |
| 44 280 | 50 581 | 56 537 | 60 612 | 66 385 | 71 664 | 79 181 | 87 481 | 93 942 | 98 718 | 48 318 | 25 697 | 70 938 |
| 0.43 | 0.44 | 0.46 | 0.46 | 0.47 | 0.48 | 0.50 | 0.52 | 0.52 | 0.51 | 0.47 | 0.44 | 0.48 |
| 1 065 | 1 085 | 1 110 | 1 122 | 1 157 | 1 187 | 1 257 | 1 322 | 1 346 | 1 332 | 1 130 | 998 | 1 203 |
| 47 329 | 49 391 | 51 857 | 53 777 | 56 862 | 59 765 | 64 733 | 69 521 | 72 230 | 72 913 | 49 670 | 39 501 | 59 838 |
| 0.37 | 0.38 | 0.40 | 0.40 | 0.41 | 0.41 | 0.44 | 0.45 | 0.45 | 0.44 | 0.40 | 0.37 | 0.42 |
| 1 281 | 1 267 | 1 136 | 1 067 | 1 010 | 1 048 | 1 131 | 1 293 | 1 321 | 1 461 | 1 066 | 857 | 1 203 |
| 56 919 | 57 666 | 53 031 | 51 149 | 49 668 | 52 783 | 58 246 | 68 010 | 70 887 | 80 017 | 46 870 | 33 902 | 59 838 |
| 0.49 | 0.49 | 0.46 | 0.43 | 0.41 | 0.42 | 0.40 | 0.41 | 0.38 | 0.41 | 0.46 | 0.56 | 0.42 |
| 1 765 | 364 | 265 | 241 | 160 | 214 | 233 | 252 | 279 | 257 | 496 | 629 | 381 |
| 23 159 | 4 940 | 3 723 | 3 513 | 2 408 | 3 344 | 3 780 | 4 247 | 4 871 | 4 646 | 6 399 | 6 936 | 5 863 |
| 0.20 | 0.04 | 0.03 | 0.03 | 0.02 | 0.03 | 0.03 | 0.02 | 0.03 | 0.02 | 0.06 | 0.11 | 0.04 |
| 434 | 630 | 808 | 1 058 | 1 257 | 1 333 | 1 309 | 1 326 | 1 417 | 1 515 | 860 | 412 | 1 148 |
| 5 696 | 8 553 | 11 356 | 15 403 | 18 979 | 20 859 | 21 235 | 22 304 | 24 720 | 27 422 | 11 100 | 4 548 | 17 653 |
| ... | ... | ... | ... | ... | ... | ... | ... | ... | ... | ... | ... | ... |
| 425 | 426 | 446 | 451 | 412 | 375 | 361 | 356 | 368 | 378 | 496 | 604 | 399 |
| 5 570 | 5 787 | 6 267 | 6 568 | 6 213 | 5 872 | 5 860 | 5 983 | 6 416 | 6 837 | 6 399 | 6 661 | 6 137 |
| 0.05 | 0.05 | 0.06 | 0.06 | 0.05 | 0.05 | 0.05 | 0.05 | 0.05 | 0.05 | 0.06 | 0.08 | 0.05 |
| 421 | 462 | 515 | 539 | 509 | 477 | 468 | 474 | 507 | 542 | 466 | 400 | 496 |
| 5 521 | 6 279 | 7 240 | 7 844 | 7 686 | 7 460 | 7 595 | 7 977 | 8 841 | 9 807 | 6 018 | 4 411 | 7 625 |
| 0.05 | 0.05 | 0.06 | 0.06 | 0.05 | 0.05 | 0.05 | 0.05 | 0.05 | 0.05 | 0.06 | 0.08 | 0.05 |
| 406 | 407 | 426 | 431 | 393 | 358 | 345 | 340 | 351 | 361 | 474 | 577 | 381 |
| 5 321 | 5 528 | 5 987 | 6 275 | 5 936 | 5 609 | 5 598 | 5 716 | 6 129 | 6 531 | 6 113 | 6 363 | 5 863 |
| 0.04 | 0.04 | 0.05 | 0.05 | 0.04 | 0.04 | 0.04 | 0.04 | 0.04 | 0.04 | 0.05 | 0.06 | 0.04 |
| 124 | 182 | 124 | 124 | 144 | 131 | 204 | 212 | 233 | 173 | 176 | 176 | 169 |
| 1 621 | 2 470 | 1 750 | 1 803 | 2 168 | 2 043 | 3 308 | 3 567 | 4 071 | 3 131 | 2 266 | 1 938 | 2 593 |
| 0.01 | 0.02 | 0.02 | 0.02 | 0.02 | 0.02 | 0.02 | 0.02 | 0.02 | 0.02 | 0.02 | 0.03 | 0.02 |

**Table A.1**  Total and per capita gross domestic product of individual countries or areas, expressed in United States dollars, and their individual shares of gross world product, based on alternative conversion rates, 1970–1989 [*cont.*]

| Country or area | 1970 (1) | 1971 (2) | 1972 (3) | 1973 (4) | 1974 (5) | 1975 (6) | 1976 (7) | 1977 (8) | 1978 (9) | 1979 (10) |
|---|---|---|---|---|---|---|---|---|---|---|
| **former USSR** | | | | | | | | | | |
| **1. MER** | | | | | | | | | | |
| 1a. Per capita GDP | 1 659 | 1 737 | 1 954 | 2 328 | 2 331 | 2 569 | 2 573 | 2 756 | 3 129 | 3 351 |
| 1b. GDP | 402 711 | 425 711 | 483 451 | 581 527 | 587 850 | 653 762 | 660 434 | 713 491 | 816 798 | 882 287 |
| 1c. % of GWP | 12.62 | 12.17 | 12.02 | 11.85 | 10.58 | 10.53 | 9.84 | 9.43 | 9.09 | 8.56 |
| **2. PPPs** | | | | | | | | | | |
| 2a. Per capita GDP | ... | ... | ... | ... | ... | ... | ... | ... | ... | ... |
| 2b. GDP | ... | ... | ... | ... | ... | ... | ... | ... | ... | ... |
| 2c. % of GWP | ... | ... | ... | ... | ... | ... | ... | ... | ... | ... |
| **3. Absolute 1970–1989 PARE** | | | | | | | | | | |
| 3a. Per capita GDP | 2 224 | 2 312 | 2 397 | 2 587 | 2 703 | 2 784 | 2 932 | 3 044 | 3 153 | 3 228 |
| 3b. GDP | 539 968 | 566 593 | 593 218 | 646 276 | 681 712 | 708 337 | 752 584 | 788 020 | 823 264 | 849 889 |
| 3c. % of GWP | 7.60 | 7.65 | 7.60 | 7.79 | 8.04 | 8.24 | 8.32 | 8.35 | 8.37 | 8.36 |
| **4. Relative 1970–1989 PARE** | | | | | | | | | | |
| 4a. Per capita GDP | 1 084 | 1 185 | 1 285 | 1 479 | 1 686 | 1 907 | 2 134 | 2 365 | 2 629 | 2 932 |
| 4b. GDP | 263 272 | 290 425 | 318 023 | 369 481 | 425 113 | 485 286 | 547 823 | 612 307 | 686 358 | 771 819 |
| 4c. % of GWP | 7.60 | 7.65 | 7.60 | 7.79 | 8.04 | 8.24 | 8.32 | 8.35 | 8.37 | 8.36 |
| **5. Absolute 1980–1989 PARE** | | | | | | | | | | |
| 5a. Per capita GDP | 2 386 | 2 480 | 2 572 | 2 775 | 2 900 | 2 986 | 3 145 | 3 265 | 3 383 | 3 463 |
| 5b. GDP | 579 208 | 607 768 | 636 328 | 693 242 | 731 253 | 759 813 | 807 276 | 845 287 | 883 093 | 911 652 |
| 5c. % of GWP | 6.66 | 6.70 | 6.66 | 6.82 | 7.05 | 7.23 | 7.30 | 7.33 | 7.36 | 7.35 |
| **6. WA[a]** | | | | | | | | | | |
| 6a. Per capita GDP | 1 592 | 1 699 | 1 845 | 2 115 | 2 318 | 2 489 | 2 600 | 2 744 | 2 909 | 3 149 |
| 6b. GDP | 386 563 | 416 349 | 456 460 | 528 388 | 584 648 | 633 482 | 667 445 | 710 469 | 759 492 | 828 984 |
| 6c. % of GWP | 12.11 | 11.94 | 11.40 | 10.86 | 10.48 | 10.28 | 9.95 | 9.42 | 8.55 | 8.10 |
| **United Arab Emirates** | | | | | | | | | | |
| **1. MER** | | | | | | | | | | |
| 1a. Per capita GDP | 2 976 | 4 247 | 4 822 | 7 941 | 18 454 | 19 727 | 21 589 | 23 113 | 19 278 | 22 804 |
| 1b. GDP | 664 | 1 104 | 1 471 | 2 851 | 7 861 | 9 962 | 12 910 | 16 249 | 15 673 | 20 957 |
| 1c. % of GWP | 0.02 | 0.03 | 0.04 | 0.06 | 0.14 | 0.16 | 0.19 | 0.21 | 0.17 | 0.20 |
| **2. PPPs** | | | | | | | | | | |
| 2a. Per capita GDP | 4 637 | 5 931 | 6 857 | 9 342 | 18 269 | 17 679 | 19 152 | 19 519 | 16 576 | 19 775 |
| 2b. GDP | 1 034 | 1 542 | 2 091 | 3 354 | 7 783 | 8 928 | 11 453 | 13 722 | 13 476 | 18 173 |
| 2c. % of GWP | ... | ... | ... | ... | ... | ... | ... | ... | ... | ... |
| **3. Absolute 1970–1989 PARE** | | | | | | | | | | |
| 3a. Per capita GDP | 6 587 | 6 539 | 6 453 | 10 022 | 24 557 | 27 436 | 26 655 | 26 628 | 22 485 | 24 842 |
| 3b. GDP | 1 469 | 1 700 | 1 968 | 3 598 | 10 461 | 13 855 | 15 939 | 18 719 | 18 280 | 22 830 |
| 3c. % of GWP | 0.02 | 0.02 | 0.03 | 0.04 | 0.12 | 0.16 | 0.18 | 0.20 | 0.19 | 0.22 |
| **4. Relative 1970–1989 PARE** | | | | | | | | | | |
| 4a. Per capita GDP | 3 212 | 3 352 | 3 459 | 5 730 | 15 313 | 18 797 | 19 402 | 20 690 | 18 746 | 22 560 |
| 4b. GDP | 716 | 871 | 1 055 | 2 057 | 6 524 | 9 492 | 11 603 | 14 545 | 15 240 | 20 733 |
| 4c. % of GWP | 0.02 | 0.02 | 0.03 | 0.04 | 0.12 | 0.16 | 0.18 | 0.20 | 0.19 | 0.22 |
| **5. Absolute 1980–1989 PARE** | | | | | | | | | | |
| 5a. Per capita GDP | 7 085 | 7 034 | 6 941 | 10 780 | 26 414 | 29 511 | 28 670 | 28 641 | 24 185 | 26 720 |
| 5b. GDP | 1 580 | 1 829 | 2 117 | 3 870 | 11 252 | 14 903 | 17 145 | 20 135 | 19 663 | 24 556 |
| 5c. % of GWP | 0.02 | 0.02 | 0.02 | 0.04 | 0.11 | 0.14 | 0.16 | 0.17 | 0.16 | 0.20 |
| **6. WA** | | | | | | | | | | |
| 6a. Per capita GDP | 2 976 | 4 247 | 4 822 | 7 940 | 18 453 | 19 725 | 21 588 | 23 112 | 19 277 | 22 806 |
| 6b. GDP | 664 | 1 104 | 1 471 | 2 851 | 7 861 | 9 961 | 12 910 | 16 248 | 15 672 | 20 959 |
| 6c. % of GWP | 0.02 | 0.03 | 0.04 | 0.06 | 0.14 | 0.16 | 0.19 | 0.22 | 0.18 | 0.20 |

|  |  |  |  |  |  |  |  |  |  | Averages | | |
|---|---|---|---|---|---|---|---|---|---|---|---|---|
| 1980 (11) | 1981 (12) | 1982 (13) | 1983 (14) | 1984 (15) | 1985 (16) | 1986 (17) | 1987 (18) | 1988 (19) | 1989 (20) | 1970–89 (21) | 1970–79 (22) | 1980–89 (23) |
| 3 464 | 3 349 | 3 515 | 3 605 | 3 382 | 3 294 | 4 024 | 4 591 | 5 072 | 5 205 | 3 245 | 2 451 | 3 962 |
| 919 864 | 897 153 | 950 205 | 983 320 | 930 627 | 914 118 | 1 126 234 | 1 295 133 | 1 442 175 | 1 491 069 | 857 896 | 620 802 | 1 094 990 |
| 7.94 | 7.66 | 8.17 | 8.29 | 7.63 | 7.26 | 7.56 | 7.54 | 7.55 | 7.44 | 8.42 | 10.19 | 7.67 |
| ... | ... | ... | ... | ... | ... | ... | ... | ... | ... | ... | ... | ... |
| ... | ... | ... | ... | ... | ... | ... | ... | ... | ... | ... | ... | ... |
| ... | ... | ... | ... | ... | ... | ... | ... | ... | ... | ... | ... | ... |
| 3 334 | 3 404 | 3 505 | 3 636 | 3 700 | 3 732 | 3 796 | 3 829 | 3 955 | 4 018 | 3 245 | 2 743 | 3 694 |
| 885 325 | 911 950 | 947 386 | 991 633 | 1 018 067 | 1 035 880 | 1 062 314 | 1 080 128 | 1 124 375 | 1 151 000 | 857 896 | 694 986 | 1 020 806 |
| 8.52 | 8.61 | 8.89 | 9.04 | 8.88 | 8.73 | 8.70 | 8.55 | 8.52 | 8.46 | 8.42 | 8.07 | 8.68 |
| 3 305 | 3 694 | 4 049 | 4 342 | 4 577 | 4 742 | 4 920 | 5 105 | 5 449 | 5 763 | 3 311 | 1 883 | 4 609 |
| 877 588 | 989 511 | 1 094 359 | 1 184 187 | 1 259 302 | 1 316 049 | 1 376 753 | 1 440 062 | 1 549 381 | 1 651 103 | 875 410 | 476 991 | 1 273 829 |
| 8.52 | 8.61 | 8.89 | 9.04 | 8.88 | 8.73 | 8.70 | 8.55 | 8.52 | 8.46 | 8.52 | 8.12 | 8.68 |
| 3 576 | 3 652 | 3 760 | 3 900 | 3 969 | 4 004 | 4 072 | 4 107 | 4 242 | 4 310 | 3 480 | 2 943 | 3 962 |
| 949 664 | 978 223 | 1 016 235 | 1 063 697 | 1 092 051 | 1 111 160 | 1 139 514 | 1 158 622 | 1 206 085 | 1 234 645 | 920 241 | 745 492 | 1 094 990 |
| 7.51 | 7.59 | 7.84 | 7.98 | 7.84 | 7.71 | 7.69 | 7.56 | 7.54 | 7.49 | 7.42 | 7.08 | 7.67 |
| 3 409 | 3 471 | 3 533 | 3 609 | 3 581 | 3 461 | 3 592 | 3 947 | 4 640 | 5 053 | 3 135 | 2 358 | 3 838 |
| 905 349 | 929 857 | 955 033 | 984 420 | 985 402 | 960 448 | 1 005 216 | 1 113 367 | 1 319 238 | 1 447 460 | 828 904 | 597 228 | 1 060 579 |
| 7.86 | 7.88 | 8.19 | 8.30 | 8.06 | 7.60 | 6.84 | 6.68 | 7.05 | 7.38 | 8.20 | 9.85 | 7.50 |
| 29 162 | 29 989 | 26 133 | 22 680 | 21 439 | 20 060 | 15 437 | 16 240 | 15 643 | 17 497 | 18 690 | 19 270 | 20 571 |
| 29 629 | 32 988 | 30 627 | 28 033 | 27 743 | 27 081 | 21 674 | 23 612 | 23 496 | 27 068 | 18 083 | 8 970 | 27 195 |
| 0.26 | 0.28 | 0.26 | 0.24 | 0.23 | 0.22 | 0.15 | 0.14 | 0.12 | 0.13 | 0.18 | 0.15 | 0.19 |
| 25 629 | 25 397 | 22 681 | 19 726 | 20 422 | 18 514 | 14 275 | 14 786 | 14 795 | 16 624 | 16 920 | 17 520 | 18 596 |
| 26 039 | 27 937 | 26 582 | 24 381 | 26 427 | 24 994 | 20 042 | 21 499 | 22 222 | 25 717 | 16 370 | 8 156 | 24 584 |
| ... | ... | ... | ... | ... | ... | ... | ... | ... | ... | ... | ... | ... |
| 28 407 | 26 983 | 23 236 | 20 925 | 20 851 | 19 508 | 14 745 | 14 847 | 14 373 | 15 513 | 18 690 | 23 377 | 19 125 |
| 28 861 | 29 682 | 27 233 | 25 864 | 26 981 | 26 336 | 20 702 | 21 587 | 21 588 | 23 999 | 18 083 | 10 882 | 25 283 |
| 0.28 | 0.28 | 0.26 | 0.24 | 0.24 | 0.22 | 0.17 | 0.17 | 0.16 | 0.18 | 0.18 | 0.13 | 0.22 |
| 28 159 | 29 278 | 26 841 | 24 989 | 25 791 | 24 785 | 19 110 | 19 794 | 19 805 | 22 254 | 20 290 | 17 795 | 23 432 |
| 28 609 | 32 206 | 31 458 | 30 886 | 33 374 | 33 459 | 26 830 | 28 781 | 29 748 | 34 427 | 19 631 | 8 284 | 30 978 |
| 0.28 | 0.28 | 0.26 | 0.24 | 0.24 | 0.22 | 0.17 | 0.17 | 0.16 | 0.18 | 0.19 | 0.14 | 0.21 |
| 30 555 | 29 024 | 24 993 | 22 508 | 22 427 | 20 983 | 15 860 | 15 969 | 15 459 | 16 687 | 20 103 | 25 145 | 20 571 |
| 31 044 | 31 926 | 29 292 | 27 819 | 29 021 | 28 328 | 22 268 | 23 219 | 23 220 | 25 814 | 19 450 | 11 705 | 27 195 |
| 0.25 | 0.25 | 0.23 | 0.21 | 0.21 | 0.20 | 0.15 | 0.15 | 0.15 | 0.16 | 0.16 | 0.11 | 0.19 |
| 29 159 | 29 989 | 26 133 | 22 680 | 21 439 | 20 060 | 15 437 | 16 368 | 15 767 | 17 635 | 18 720 | 19 269 | 20 615 |
| 29 625 | 32 988 | 30 627 | 28 033 | 27 743 | 27 081 | 21 674 | 23 799 | 23 681 | 27 282 | 18 112 | 8 970 | 27 253 |
| 0.26 | 0.28 | 0.26 | 0.24 | 0.23 | 0.21 | 0.15 | 0.14 | 0.13 | 0.14 | 0.18 | 0.15 | 0.19 |

**Table A.1**    Total and per capita gross domestic product of individual countries or areas,
expressed in United States dollars, and their individual shares of gross world
product, based on alternative conversion rates, 1970−1989 [*cont.*]

| Country or area | 1970 (1) | 1971 (2) | 1972 (3) | 1973 (4) | 1974 (5) | 1975 (6) | 1976 (7) | 1977 (8) | 1978 (9) | 1979 (10) |
|---|---|---|---|---|---|---|---|---|---|---|
| **United Kingdom** | | | | | | | | | | |
| 1.    MER | | | | | | | | | | |
| 1a.    Per capita GDP | 2 218 | 2 514 | 2 870 | 3 225 | 3 467 | 4 154 | 3 988 | 4 492 | 5 699 | 7 419 |
| 1b.    GDP | 123 758 | 140 758 | 161 115 | 181 392 | 195 341 | 234 367 | 225 137 | 253 705 | 321 958 | 419 185 |
| 1c.    % of GWP | 3.88 | 4.02 | 4.01 | 3.70 | 3.52 | 3.77 | 3.36 | 3.35 | 3.58 | 4.07 |
| 2.    PPPs | | | | | | | | | | |
| 2a.    Per capita GDP | 3 097 | 3 350 | 3 667 | 4 097 | 4 310 | 4 774 | 5 190 | 5 697 | 6 462 | 7 358 |
| 2b.    GDP | 172 822 | 187 564 | 205 845 | 230 456 | 242 871 | 269 325 | 293 033 | 321 757 | 365 073 | 415 775 |
| 2c.    % of GWP | ... | ... | ... | ... | ... | ... | ... | ... | ... | ... |
| 3.    Absolute 1970−1989 PARE | | | | | | | | | | |
| 3a.    Per capita GDP | 5 859 | 5 956 | 6 147 | 6 575 | 6 451 | 6 392 | 6 564 | 6 714 | 6 956 | 7 150 |
| 3b.    GDP | 326 959 | 333 433 | 345 029 | 369 833 | 363 486 | 360 636 | 370 584 | 379 203 | 392 956 | 404 007 |
| 3c.    % of GWP | 4.60 | 4.50 | 4.42 | 4.46 | 4.29 | 4.19 | 4.10 | 4.02 | 4.00 | 3.97 |
| 4.    Relative 1970−1989 PARE | | | | | | | | | | |
| 4a.    Per capita GDP | 2 857 | 3 053 | 3 295 | 3 759 | 4 023 | 4 379 | 4 778 | 5 217 | 5 799 | 6 493 |
| 4b.    GDP | 159 415 | 170 911 | 184 970 | 211 437 | 226 668 | 247 074 | 269 756 | 294 648 | 327 609 | 366 895 |
| 4c.    % of GWP | 4.60 | 4.50 | 4.42 | 4.46 | 4.29 | 4.19 | 4.10 | 4.02 | 4.00 | 3.97 |
| 5.    Absolute 1980−1989 PARE | | | | | | | | | | |
| 5a.    Per capita GDP | 7 723 | 7 852 | 8 103 | 8 667 | 8 504 | 8 427 | 8 653 | 8 850 | 9 169 | 9 425 |
| 5b.    GDP | 431 013 | 439 548 | 454 835 | 487 533 | 479 165 | 475 408 | 488 522 | 499 884 | 518 015 | 532 581 |
| 5c.    % of GWP | 4.95 | 4.85 | 4.76 | 4.80 | 4.62 | 4.52 | 4.42 | 4.34 | 4.32 | 4.30 |
| 6.    WA | | | | | | | | | | |
| 6a.    Per capita GDP | 2 219 | 2 503 | 2 868 | 3 223 | 3 469 | 4 136 | 3 970 | 4 490 | 5 693 | 7 400 |
| 6b.    GDP | 123 857 | 140 100 | 160 958 | 181 316 | 195 453 | 233 308 | 224 122 | 253 585 | 321 646 | 418 136 |
| 6c.    % of GWP | 3.88 | 4.02 | 4.02 | 3.73 | 3.50 | 3.79 | 3.34 | 3.36 | 3.62 | 4.09 |
| **United Republic of Tanzania** | | | | | | | | | | |
| 1.    MER | | | | | | | | | | |
| 1a.    Per capita GDP | 99 | 103 | 113 | 131 | 152 | 169 | 177 | 205 | 237 | 243 |
| 1b.    GDP | 1 339 | 1 433 | 1 631 | 1 947 | 2 338 | 2 692 | 2 915 | 3 483 | 4 171 | 4 416 |
| 1c.    % of GWP | 0.04 | 0.04 | 0.04 | 0.04 | 0.04 | 0.04 | 0.04 | 0.05 | 0.05 | 0.04 |
| 2.    PPPs | | | | | | | | | | |
| 2a.    Per capita GDP | 183 | 196 | 200 | 225 | 262 | 295 | 312 | 313 | 333 | 353 |
| 2b.    GDP | 2 470 | 2 736 | 2 885 | 3 356 | 4 033 | 4 698 | 5 128 | 5 312 | 5 854 | 6 424 |
| 2c.    % of GWP | ... | ... | ... | ... | ... | ... | ... | ... | ... | ... |
| 3.    Absolute 1970−1989 PARE | | | | | | | | | | |
| 3a.    Per capita GDP | 224 | 226 | 233 | 233 | 231 | 237 | 243 | 236 | 233 | 232 |
| 3b.    GDP | 3 023 | 3 150 | 3 362 | 3 464 | 3 551 | 3 761 | 4 001 | 4 017 | 4 102 | 4 222 |
| 3c.    % of GWP | 0.04 | 0.04 | 0.04 | 0.04 | 0.04 | 0.04 | 0.04 | 0.04 | 0.04 | 0.04 |
| 4.    Relative 1970−1989 PARE | | | | | | | | | | |
| 4a.    Per capita GDP | 109 | 116 | 125 | 133 | 144 | 162 | 177 | 184 | 195 | 211 |
| 4b.    GDP | 1 474 | 1 614 | 1 802 | 1 981 | 2 214 | 2 576 | 2 912 | 3 121 | 3 420 | 3 834 |
| 4c.    % of GWP | 0.04 | 0.04 | 0.04 | 0.04 | 0.04 | 0.04 | 0.04 | 0.04 | 0.04 | 0.04 |
| 5.    Absolute 1980−1989 PARE | | | | | | | | | | |
| 5a.    Per capita GDP | 281 | 283 | 292 | 292 | 289 | 297 | 305 | 296 | 293 | 291 |
| 5b.    GDP | 3 791 | 3 949 | 4 215 | 4 343 | 4 452 | 4 715 | 5 016 | 5 036 | 5 143 | 5 293 |
| 5c.    % of GWP | 0.04 | 0.04 | 0.04 | 0.04 | 0.04 | 0.04 | 0.05 | 0.04 | 0.04 | 0.04 |
| 6.    WA | | | | | | | | | | |
| 6a.    Per capita GDP | 101 | 105 | 116 | 131 | 155 | 178 | 186 | 212 | 229 | 249 |
| 6b.    GDP | 1 367 | 1 462 | 1 665 | 1 952 | 2 383 | 2 833 | 3 052 | 3 609 | 4 021 | 4 535 |
| 6c.    % of GWP | 0.04 | 0.04 | 0.04 | 0.04 | 0.04 | 0.05 | 0.05 | 0.05 | 0.05 | 0.04 |

| | | | | | | | | | | Averages | | |
|---|---|---|---|---|---|---|---|---|---|---|---|---|
| 1980 | 1981 | 1982 | 1983 | 1984 | 1985 | 1986 | 1987 | 1988 | 1989 | 1970–89 | 1970–79 | 1980–89 |
| (11) | (12) | (13) | (14) | (15) | (16) | (17) | (18) | (19) | (20) | (21) | (22) | (23) |
| 9 493 | 9 097 | 8 590 | 8 103 | 7 622 | 8 085 | 9 774 | 12 172 | 13 485 | 14 752 | 7 088 | 4 003 | 10 138 |
| 536 588 | 514 481 | 486 175 | 459 325 | 432 393 | 459 348 | 556 323 | 694 268 | 770 940 | 845 350 | 400 595 | 225 672 | 575 519 |
| 4.63 | 4.39 | 4.18 | 3.87 | 3.55 | 3.65 | 3.74 | 4.04 | 4.04 | 4.22 | 3.93 | 3.70 | 4.03 |
| 8 110 | 8 784 | 9 478 | 10 027 | 10 677 | 11 127 | 11 723 | 12 605 | 13 535 | 14 538 | 7 959 | 4 797 | 11 081 |
| 458 387 | 496 795 | 536 440 | 568 401 | 605 677 | 632 188 | 667 288 | 718 948 | 773 803 | 833 078 | 449 776 | 270 452 | 629 100 |
| ... | ... | ... | ... | ... | ... | ... | ... | ... | ... | ... | ... | ... |
| 6 988 | 6 894 | 7 007 | 7 245 | 7 394 | 7 653 | 7 905 | 8 262 | 8 583 | 8 856 | 7 088 | 6 467 | 7 690 |
| 394 968 | 389 899 | 396 615 | 410 698 | 419 414 | 434 833 | 449 933 | 471 227 | 490 706 | 507 488 | 400 595 | 364 612 | 436 578 |
| 3.80 | 3.68 | 3.72 | 3.74 | 3.66 | 3.66 | 3.68 | 3.73 | 3.72 | 3.73 | 3.93 | 4.23 | 3.71 |
| 6 927 | 7 481 | 8 095 | 8 652 | 9 145 | 9 723 | 10 245 | 11 015 | 11 828 | 12 704 | 6 998 | 4 362 | 9 600 |
| 391 516 | 423 060 | 458 144 | 490 447 | 518 796 | 552 439 | 583 112 | 628 256 | 676 190 | 727 989 | 395 467 | 245 938 | 544 995 |
| 3.80 | 3.68 | 3.72 | 3.74 | 3.66 | 3.66 | 3.68 | 3.73 | 3.72 | 3.73 | 3.85 | 4.19 | 3.71 |
| 9 211 | 9 088 | 9 238 | 9 551 | 9 747 | 10 089 | 10 421 | 10 891 | 11 315 | 11 674 | 9 344 | 8 525 | 10 138 |
| 520 666 | 513 984 | 522 838 | 541 403 | 552 893 | 573 218 | 593 125 | 621 195 | 646 873 | 668 996 | 528 085 | 480 650 | 575 519 |
| 4.12 | 3.99 | 4.03 | 4.06 | 3.97 | 3.98 | 4.00 | 4.05 | 4.05 | 4.06 | 4.26 | 4.56 | 4.03 |
| 9 487 | 9 012 | 8 568 | 8 094 | 7 584 | 7 999 | 9 771 | 11 935 | 14 393 | 14 482 | 7 092 | 3 995 | 10 153 |
| 536 221 | 509 683 | 484 946 | 458 820 | 430 204 | 454 487 | 556 162 | 680 738 | 822 819 | 829 896 | 400 823 | 225 248 | 576 397 |
| 4.66 | 4.32 | 4.16 | 3.87 | 3.52 | 3.59 | 3.78 | 4.09 | 4.40 | 4.23 | 3.97 | 3.71 | 4.08 |
| 272 | 303 | 309 | 300 | 265 | 303 | 207 | 141 | 130 | 107 | 208 | 169 | 228 |
| 5 138 | 5 927 | 6 272 | 6 328 | 5 813 | 6 904 | 4 883 | 3 448 | 3 300 | 2 818 | 3 860 | 2 636 | 5 083 |
| 0.04 | 0.05 | 0.05 | 0.05 | 0.05 | 0.05 | 0.03 | 0.02 | 0.02 | 0.01 | 0.04 | 0.04 | 0.04 |
| 364 | 399 | 457 | 492 | 505 | 604 | 613 | 632 | 655 | 686 | 450 | 274 | 554 |
| 6 859 | 7 804 | 9 288 | 10 387 | 11 058 | 13 741 | 14 475 | 15 472 | 16 628 | 18 067 | 8 334 | 4 290 | 12 378 |
| ... | ... | ... | ... | ... | ... | ... | ... | ... | ... | ... | ... | ... |
| 203 | 195 | 189 | 178 | 177 | 175 | 174 | 174 | 175 | 176 | 208 | 234 | 182 |
| 3 837 | 3 818 | 3 840 | 3 749 | 3 876 | 3 978 | 4 107 | 4 268 | 4 438 | 4 632 | 3 860 | 3 665 | 4 054 |
| 0.04 | 0.04 | 0.04 | 0.03 | 0.03 | 0.03 | 0.03 | 0.03 | 0.03 | 0.03 | 0.04 | 0.04 | 0.03 |
| 202 | 212 | 218 | 212 | 219 | 222 | 226 | 232 | 241 | 252 | 203 | 160 | 226 |
| 3 803 | 4 142 | 4 436 | 4 477 | 4 794 | 5 054 | 5 323 | 5 690 | 6 115 | 6 645 | 3 771 | 2 495 | 5 048 |
| 0.04 | 0.04 | 0.04 | 0.03 | 0.03 | 0.03 | 0.03 | 0.03 | 0.03 | 0.03 | 0.04 | 0.04 | 0.03 |
| 255 | 245 | 237 | 223 | 222 | 219 | 218 | 219 | 219 | 221 | 261 | 294 | 228 |
| 4 811 | 4 786 | 4 815 | 4 700 | 4 859 | 4 987 | 5 150 | 5 351 | 5 564 | 5 807 | 4 839 | 4 595 | 5 083 |
| 0.04 | 0.04 | 0.04 | 0.04 | 0.03 | 0.03 | 0.03 | 0.03 | 0.03 | 0.04 | 0.04 | 0.04 | 0.04 |
| 279 | 314 | 318 | 304 | 270 | 312 | 205 | 142 | 130 | 107 | 212 | 172 | 232 |
| 5 265 | 6 138 | 6 470 | 6 410 | 5 926 | 7 095 | 4 838 | 3 464 | 3 310 | 2 826 | 3 931 | 2 688 | 5 174 |
| 0.05 | 0.05 | 0.06 | 0.05 | 0.05 | 0.06 | 0.03 | 0.02 | 0.02 | 0.01 | 0.04 | 0.04 | 0.04 |

**Table A.1**    Total and per capita gross domestic product of individual countries or areas,
expressed in United States dollars, and their individual shares of gross world
product, based on alternative conversion rates, 1970−1989 [*cont.*]

| Country or area | 1970 (1) | 1971 (2) | 1972 (3) | 1973 (4) | 1974 (5) | 1975 (6) | 1976 (7) | 1977 (8) | 1978 (9) | 1979 (10) |
|---|---|---|---|---|---|---|---|---|---|---|
| **United States** | | | | | | | | | | |
| **1. MER** | | | | | | | | | | |
| 1a. Per capita GDP | 4 922 | 5 288 | 5 751 | 6 359 | 6 815 | 7 334 | 8 085 | 8 918 | 9 951 | 10 936 |
| 1b. GDP | 1 009 220 | 1 095 420 | 1 203 650 | 1 344 960 | 1 456 410 | 1 583 920 | 1 764 810 | 1 967 490 | 2 218 910 | 2 464 810 |
| 1c. % of GWP | 31.63 | 31.31 | 29.93 | 27.41 | 26.22 | 25.50 | 26.31 | 26.01 | 24.70 | 23.92 |
| **2. PPPs** | | | | | | | | | | |
| 2a. Per capita GDP | 4 922 | 5 288 | 5 751 | 6 359 | 6 815 | 7 334 | 8 085 | 8 918 | 9 951 | 10 936 |
| 2b. GDP | 1 009 220 | 1 095 420 | 1 203 650 | 1 344 960 | 1 456 410 | 1 583 920 | 1 764 810 | 1 967 490 | 2 218 910 | 2 464 810 |
| 2c. % of GWP | ... | ... | ... | ... | ... | ... | ... | ... | ... | ... |
| **3. Absolute 1970−1989 PARE** | | | | | | | | | | |
| 3a. Per capita GDP | 10 095 | 10 316 | 10 727 | 11 123 | 10 928 | 10 705 | 11 107 | 11 477 | 11 935 | 12 043 |
| 3b. GDP | 2 069 900 | 2 137 067 | 2 245 202 | 2 352 530 | 2 335 501 | 2 311 935 | 2 424 448 | 2 532 099 | 2 661 510 | 2 714 130 |
| 3c. % of GWP | 29.13 | 28.87 | 28.78 | 28.35 | 27.55 | 26.88 | 26.79 | 26.83 | 27.07 | 26.69 |
| **4. Relative 1970−1989 PARE** | | | | | | | | | | |
| 4a. Per capita GDP | 4 922 | 5 288 | 5 751 | 6 359 | 6 815 | 7 334 | 8 085 | 8 918 | 9 951 | 10 936 |
| 4b. GDP | 1 009 220 | 1 095 420 | 1 203 650 | 1 344 960 | 1 456 410 | 1 583 920 | 1 764 810 | 1 967 490 | 2 218 910 | 2 464 810 |
| 4c. % of GWP | 29.13 | 28.87 | 28.78 | 28.35 | 27.55 | 26.88 | 26.79 | 26.83 | 27.07 | 26.69 |
| **5. Absolute 1980−1989 PARE** | | | | | | | | | | |
| 5a. Per capita GDP | 12 613 | 12 890 | 13 403 | 13 899 | 13 655 | 13 376 | 13 879 | 14 341 | 14 914 | 15 047 |
| 5b. GDP | 2 586 381 | 2 670 307 | 2 805 424 | 2 939 532 | 2 918 254 | 2 888 808 | 3 029 396 | 3 163 907 | 3 325 609 | 3 391 359 |
| 5c. % of GWP | 29.72 | 29.46 | 29.35 | 28.93 | 28.13 | 27.50 | 27.39 | 27.44 | 27.72 | 27.35 |
| **6. WA** | | | | | | | | | | |
| 6a. Per capita GDP | 4 922 | 5 288 | 5 751 | 6 359 | 6 815 | 7 334 | 8 085 | 8 918 | 9 951 | 10 936 |
| 6b. GDP | 1 009 220 | 1 095 420 | 1 203 650 | 1 344 960 | 1 456 410 | 1 583 920 | 1 764 810 | 1 967 490 | 2 218 910 | 2 464 810 |
| 6c. % of GWP | 31.62 | 31.41 | 30.05 | 27.65 | 26.10 | 25.70 | 26.30 | 26.09 | 24.98 | 24.10 |
| **US Virgin Islands** | | | | | | | | | | |
| **1. MER** | | | | | | | | | | |
| 1a. Per capita GDP | 4 656 | 5 010 | 5 438 | 5 708 | 5 927 | 6 159 | 6 124 | 6 425 | 6 810 | 7 085 |
| 1b. GDP | 298 | 351 | 419 | 479 | 539 | 585 | 600 | 630 | 667 | 694 |
| 1c. % of GWP | 0.01 | 0.01 | 0.01 | 0.01 | 0.01 | 0.01 | 0.01 | 0.01 | 0.01 | 0.01 |
| **2. PPPs** | | | | | | | | | | |
| 2a. Per capita GDP | ... | ... | ... | ... | ... | ... | ... | ... | ... | ... |
| 2b. GDP | ... | ... | ... | ... | ... | ... | ... | ... | ... | ... |
| 2c. % of GWP | ... | ... | ... | ... | ... | ... | ... | ... | ... | ... |
| **3. Absolute 1970−1989 PARE** | | | | | | | | | | |
| 3a. Per capita GDP | 9 112 | 9 329 | 9 725 | 9 657 | 9 139 | 8 681 | 8 195 | 8 130 | 8 030 | 7 702 |
| 3b. GDP | 583 | 653 | 749 | 811 | 832 | 825 | 803 | 797 | 787 | 755 |
| 3c. % of GWP | 0.01 | 0.01 | 0.01 | 0.01 | 0.01 | 0.01 | 0.01 | 0.01 | 0.01 | 0.01 |
| **4. Relative 1970−1989 PARE** | | | | | | | | | | |
| 4a. Per capita GDP | 4 443 | 4 782 | 5 214 | 5 521 | 5 699 | 5 947 | 5 965 | 6 317 | 6 695 | 6 994 |
| 4b. GDP | 284 | 335 | 401 | 464 | 519 | 565 | 585 | 619 | 656 | 685 |
| 4c. % of GWP | 0.01 | 0.01 | 0.01 | 0.01 | 0.01 | 0.01 | 0.01 | 0.01 | 0.01 | 0.01 |
| **5. Absolute 1980−1989 PARE** | | | | | | | | | | |
| 5a. Per capita GDP | 11 784 | 12 064 | 12 576 | 12 488 | 11 818 | 11 226 | 10 597 | 10 513 | 10 384 | 9 960 |
| 5b. GDP | 754 | 845 | 968 | 1 049 | 1 075 | 1 066 | 1 039 | 1 030 | 1 018 | 976 |
| 5c. % of GWP | 0.01 | 0.01 | 0.01 | 0.01 | 0.01 | 0.01 | 0.01 | 0.01 | 0.01 | 0.01 |
| **6. WA** | | | | | | | | | | |
| 6a. Per capita GDP | 4 124 | 4 650 | 5 203 | 5 423 | 5 459 | 5 609 | 5 731 | 6 078 | 6 369 | 6 543 |
| 6b. GDP | 264 | 326 | 401 | 456 | 497 | 533 | 562 | 596 | 624 | 641 |
| 6c. % of GWP | 0.01 | 0.01 | 0.01 | 0.01 | 0.01 | 0.01 | 0.01 | 0.01 | 0.01 | 0.01 |

|  |  |  |  |  |  |  |  |  | | Averages | | |
| 1980 | 1981 | 1982 | 1983 | 1984 | 1985 | 1986 | 1987 | 1988 | 1989 | 1970–89 | 1970–79 | 1980–89 |
| (11) | (12) | (13) | (14) | (15) | (16) | (17) | (18) | (19) | (20) | (21) | (22) | (23) |
|---|---|---|---|---|---|---|---|---|---|---|---|---|
| 11 804 | 13 077 | 13 426 | 14 281 | 15 701 | 16 581 | 17 299 | 18 292 | 19 596 | 20 749 | 12 037 | 7 498 | 16 136 |
| 2 688 470 | 3 009 470 | 3 121 400 | 3 353 470 | 3 722 340 | 3 967 470 | 4 176 096 | 4 452 878 | 4 809 081 | 5 132 001 | 2 727 114 | 1 610 960 | 3 843 268 |
| 23.20 | 25.70 | 26.85 | 28.29 | 30.52 | 31.50 | 28.05 | 25.91 | 25.17 | 25.59 | 26.77 | 26.43 | 26.91 |
| 11 804 | 13 077 | 13 426 | 14 281 | 15 701 | 16 581 | 17 299 | 18 292 | 19 596 | 20 749 | 12 037 | 7 498 | 16 136 |
| 2 688 470 | 3 009 470 | 3 121 400 | 3 353 470 | 3 722 340 | 3 967 470 | 4 176 096 | 4 452 878 | 4 809 081 | 5 132 001 | 2 727 114 | 1 610 960 | 3 843 268 |
| ... | ... | ... | ... | ... | ... | ... | ... | ... | ... | ... | ... | ... |
| 11 908 | 12 052 | 11 623 | 11 959 | 12 693 | 13 051 | 13 348 | 13 720 | 14 221 | 14 465 | 12 037 | 11 071 | 12 914 |
| 2 712 172 | 2 773 580 | 2 702 195 | 2 808 183 | 3 009 279 | 3 122 851 | 3 222 309 | 3 339 910 | 3 489 914 | 3 577 566 | 2 727 114 | 2 378 432 | 3 075 796 |
| 26.11 | 26.20 | 25.34 | 25.60 | 26.24 | 26.32 | 26.38 | 26.43 | 26.46 | 26.30 | 26.77 | 27.60 | 26.16 |
| 11 804 | 13 077 | 13 426 | 14 281 | 15 701 | 16 581 | 17 299 | 18 292 | 19 596 | 20 749 | 12 037 | 7 498 | 16 136 |
| 2 688 470 | 3 009 470 | 3 121 400 | 3 353 470 | 3 722 340 | 3 967 470 | 4 176 096 | 4 452 878 | 4 809 081 | 5 132 001 | 2 727 114 | 1 610 960 | 3 843 268 |
| 26.11 | 26.20 | 25.34 | 25.60 | 26.24 | 26.32 | 26.38 | 26.43 | 26.46 | 26.30 | 26.54 | 27.44 | 26.18 |
| 14 879 | 15 060 | 14 523 | 14 943 | 15 860 | 16 307 | 16 679 | 17 143 | 17 769 | 18 074 | 15 040 | 13 833 | 16 136 |
| 3 388 913 | 3 465 642 | 3 376 447 | 3 508 878 | 3 760 154 | 3 902 064 | 4 026 336 | 4 173 285 | 4 360 716 | 4 470 240 | 3 407 583 | 2 971 898 | 3 843 268 |
| 26.79 | 26.90 | 26.04 | 26.31 | 26.99 | 27.08 | 27.17 | 27.23 | 27.27 | 27.11 | 27.46 | 28.21 | 26.91 |
| 11 804 | 13 077 | 13 426 | 14 281 | 15 701 | 16 581 | 17 299 | 18 292 | 19 596 | 20 749 | 12 037 | 7 498 | 16 136 |
| 2 688 470 | 3 009 470 | 3 121 400 | 3 353 470 | 3 722 340 | 3 967 470 | 4 176 096 | 4 452 878 | 4 809 081 | 5 132 001 | 2 727 114 | 1 610 960 | 3 843 268 |
| 23.34 | 25.52 | 26.78 | 28.29 | 30.45 | 31.38 | 28.40 | 26.72 | 25.69 | 26.15 | 26.99 | 26.56 | 27.18 |
| 7 968 | 8 677 | 8 699 | 8 821 | 9 424 | 9 537 | 9 982 | 10 423 | 11 053 | 11 670 | 7 931 | 5 659 | 9 655 |
| 781 | 859 | 879 | 909 | 990 | 1 030 | 1 088 | 1 157 | 1 249 | 1 342 | 777 | 526 | 1 028 |
| 0.01 | 0.01 | 0.01 | 0.01 | 0.01 | 0.01 | 0.01 | 0.01 | 0.01 | 0.01 | 0.01 | 0.01 | 0.01 |
| ... | ... | ... | ... | ... | ... | ... | ... | ... | ... | ... | ... | ... |
| ... | ... | ... | ... | ... | ... | ... | ... | ... | ... | ... | ... | ... |
| ... | ... | ... | ... | ... | ... | ... | ... | ... | ... | ... | ... | ... |
| 7 946 | 7 892 | 7 462 | 7 287 | 7 505 | 7 339 | 7 301 | 7 213 | 7 433 | 7 566 | 7 931 | 8 166 | 7 466 |
| 779 | 781 | 754 | 751 | 788 | 793 | 796 | 801 | 840 | 870 | 777 | 759 | 795 |
| 0.01 | 0.01 | 0.01 | 0.01 | 0.01 | 0.01 | 0.01 | 0.01 | 0.01 | 0.01 | 0.01 | 0.01 | 0.01 |
| 7 876 | 8 564 | 8 619 | 8 702 | 9 284 | 9 324 | 9 462 | 9 617 | 10 242 | 10 854 | 7 646 | 5 498 | 9 270 |
| 772 | 848 | 871 | 896 | 975 | 1 007 | 1 031 | 1 067 | 1 157 | 1 248 | 749 | 511 | 987 |
| 0.01 | 0.01 | 0.01 | 0.01 | 0.01 | 0.01 | 0.01 | 0.01 | 0.01 | 0.01 | 0.01 | 0.01 | 0.01 |
| 10 275 | 10 206 | 9 650 | 9 424 | 9 706 | 9 491 | 9 442 | 9 328 | 9 612 | 9 785 | 10 257 | 10 560 | 9 655 |
| 1 007 | 1 010 | 975 | 971 | 1 019 | 1 025 | 1 029 | 1 035 | 1 086 | 1 125 | 1 005 | 982 | 1 028 |
| 0.01 | 0.01 | 0.01 | 0.01 | 0.01 | 0.01 | 0.01 | 0.01 | 0.01 | 0.01 | 0.01 | 0.01 | 0.01 |
| 7 304 | 7 909 | 8 097 | 8 430 | 9 078 | 9 204 | 9 534 | 9 867 | 10 639 | 11 277 | 7 481 | 5 266 | 9 170 |
| 716 | 783 | 818 | 868 | 953 | 994 | 1 039 | 1 095 | 1 202 | 1 297 | 733 | 490 | 977 |
| 0.01 | 0.01 | 0.01 | 0.01 | 0.01 | 0.01 | 0.01 | 0.01 | 0.01 | 0.01 | 0.01 | 0.01 | 0.01 |

**Table A.1** Total and per capita gross domestic product of individual countries or areas, expressed in United States dollars, and their individual shares of gross world product, based on alternative conversion rates, 1970–1989 [*cont.*]

| Country or area | 1970 (1) | 1971 (2) | 1972 (3) | 1973 (4) | 1974 (5) | 1975 (6) | 1976 (7) | 1977 (8) | 1978 (9) | 1979 (10) |
|---|---|---|---|---|---|---|---|---|---|---|
| **Uruguay** | | | | | | | | | | |
| **1. MER** | | | | | | | | | | |
| 1a. Per capita GDP | 856 | 1 005 | 821 | 1 048 | 1 346 | 1 281 | 1 334 | 1 491 | 1 775 | 2 532 |
| 1b. GDP | 2 404 | 2 831 | 2 317 | 2 957 | 3 801 | 3 623 | 3 788 | 4 257 | 5 104 | 7 330 |
| 1c. % of GWP | 0.08 | 0.08 | 0.06 | 0.06 | 0.07 | 0.06 | 0.06 | 0.06 | 0.06 | 0.07 |
| **2. PPPs** | | | | | | | | | | |
| 2a. Per capita GDP | 1 863 | 1 966 | 1 979 | 2 086 | 2 232 | 2 551 | 2 766 | 2 932 | 3 310 | 3 897 |
| 2b. GDP | 5 232 | 5 538 | 5 583 | 5 884 | 6 301 | 7 216 | 7 855 | 8 373 | 9 516 | 11 281 |
| 2c. % of GWP | ... | ... | ... | ... | ... | ... | ... | ... | ... | ... |
| **3. Absolute 1970–1989 PARE** | | | | | | | | | | |
| 3a. Per capita GDP | 1 752 | 1 749 | 1 719 | 1 725 | 1 778 | 1 879 | 1 946 | 1 958 | 2 047 | 2 158 |
| 3b. GDP | 4 920 | 4 926 | 4 850 | 4 868 | 5 020 | 5 315 | 5 527 | 5 592 | 5 886 | 6 249 |
| 3c. % of GWP | 0.07 | 0.07 | 0.06 | 0.06 | 0.06 | 0.06 | 0.06 | 0.06 | 0.06 | 0.06 |
| **4. Relative 1970–1989 PARE** | | | | | | | | | | |
| 4a. Per capita GDP | 854 | 896 | 922 | 986 | 1 109 | 1 287 | 1 417 | 1 521 | 1 707 | 1 960 |
| 4b. GDP | 2 399 | 2 525 | 2 600 | 2 783 | 3 131 | 3 641 | 4 023 | 4 345 | 4 907 | 5 675 |
| 4c. % of GWP | 0.07 | 0.07 | 0.06 | 0.06 | 0.06 | 0.06 | 0.06 | 0.06 | 0.06 | 0.06 |
| **5. Absolute 1980–1989 PARE** | | | | | | | | | | |
| 5a. Per capita GDP | 2 166 | 2 162 | 2 126 | 2 133 | 2 199 | 2 323 | 2 406 | 2 421 | 2 531 | 2 669 |
| 5b. GDP | 6 084 | 6 091 | 5 997 | 6 019 | 6 208 | 6 572 | 6 834 | 6 914 | 7 278 | 7 726 |
| 5c. % of GWP | 0.07 | 0.07 | 0.06 | 0.06 | 0.06 | 0.06 | 0.06 | 0.06 | 0.06 | 0.06 |
| **6. WA** | | | | | | | | | | |
| 6a. Per capita GDP | 856 | 1 005 | 821 | 1 049 | 1 346 | 1 281 | 1 334 | 1 491 | 1 775 | 2 532 |
| 6b. GDP | 2 404 | 2 831 | 2 317 | 2 958 | 3 800 | 3 623 | 3 789 | 4 257 | 5 104 | 7 331 |
| 6c. % of GWP | 0.08 | 0.08 | 0.06 | 0.06 | 0.07 | 0.06 | 0.06 | 0.06 | 0.06 | 0.07 |
| **Vanuatu** | | | | | | | | | | |
| **1. MER** | | | | | | | | | | |
| 1a. Per capita GDP | 467 | 493 | 567 | 669 | 646 | 757 | 702 | 707 | 831 | 1 055 |
| 1b. GDP | 39 | 42 | 50 | 61 | 61 | 73 | 71 | 74 | 91 | 119 |
| 1c. % of GWP | 0.00 | 0.00 | 0.00 | 0.00 | 0.00 | 0.00 | 0.00 | 0.00 | 0.00 | 0.00 |
| **2. PPPs** | | | | | | | | | | |
| 2a. Per capita GDP | ... | ... | ... | ... | ... | ... | ... | ... | ... | ... |
| 2b. GDP | ... | ... | ... | ... | ... | ... | ... | ... | ... | ... |
| 2c. % of GWP | ... | ... | ... | ... | ... | ... | ... | ... | ... | ... |
| **3. Absolute 1970–1989 PARE** | | | | | | | | | | |
| 3a. Per capita GDP | 557 | 558 | 561 | 634 | 826 | 763 | 748 | 712 | 807 | 808 |
| 3b. GDP | 47 | 48 | 49 | 58 | 78 | 74 | 75 | 75 | 88 | 91 |
| 3c. % of GWP | 0.00 | 0.00 | 0.00 | 0.00 | 0.00 | 0.00 | 0.00 | 0.00 | 0.00 | 0.00 |
| **4. Relative 1970–1989 PARE** | | | | | | | | | | |
| 4a. Per capita GDP | 271 | 286 | 301 | 362 | 515 | 523 | 544 | 553 | 672 | 734 |
| 4b. GDP | 23 | 25 | 26 | 33 | 48 | 51 | 55 | 58 | 73 | 83 |
| 4c. % of GWP | 0.00 | 0.00 | 0.00 | 0.00 | 0.00 | 0.00 | 0.00 | 0.00 | 0.00 | 0.00 |
| **5. Absolute 1980–1989 PARE** | | | | | | | | | | |
| 5a. Per capita GDP | 557 | 559 | 561 | 635 | 827 | 764 | 748 | 713 | 807 | 809 |
| 5b. GDP | 47 | 48 | 49 | 58 | 78 | 74 | 76 | 75 | 88 | 91 |
| 5c. % of GWP | 0.00 | 0.00 | 0.00 | 0.00 | 0.00 | 0.00 | 0.00 | 0.00 | 0.00 | 0.00 |
| **6. WA** | | | | | | | | | | |
| 6a. Per capita GDP | 414 | 440 | 567 | 669 | 645 | 757 | 702 | 707 | 831 | 1 055 |
| 6b. GDP | 35 | 38 | 50 | 61 | 61 | 73 | 71 | 74 | 91 | 119 |
| 6c. % of GWP | 0.00 | 0.00 | 0.00 | 0.00 | 0.00 | 0.00 | 0.00 | 0.00 | 0.00 | 0.00 |

| | 1980 (11) | 1981 (12) | 1982 (13) | 1983 (14) | 1984 (15) | 1985 (16) | 1986 (17) | 1987 (18) | 1988 (19) | 1989 (20) | Averages 1970–89 (21) | 1970–79 (22) | 1980–89 (23) |
|---|---|---|---|---|---|---|---|---|---|---|---|---|---|
| | 3 477 | 3 859 | 3 133 | 1 802 | 1 754 | 1 730 | 2 132 | 2 542 | 2 596 | 2 736 | 1 988 | 1 359 | 2 569 |
| | 10 133 | 11 317 | 9 253 | 5 356 | 5 245 | 5 207 | 6 455 | 7 736 | 7 945 | 8 419 | 5 774 | 3 841 | 7 707 |
| | 0.09 | 0.10 | 0.08 | 0.05 | 0.04 | 0.04 | 0.04 | 0.05 | 0.04 | 0.04 | 0.06 | 0.06 | 0.05 |
| | 4 491 | 4 879 | 4 662 | 4 356 | 4 294 | 4 340 | 4 731 | 5 125 | 5 296 | 5 565 | 3 719 | 2 575 | 4 776 |
| | 13 086 | 14 311 | 13 768 | 12 947 | 12 840 | 13 058 | 14 319 | 15 601 | 16 205 | 17 123 | 10 802 | 7 278 | 14 326 |
| | ... | ... | ... | ... | ... | ... | ... | ... | ... | ... | ... | ... | ... |
| | 2 273 | 2 301 | 2 071 | 1 937 | 1 898 | 1 891 | 2 021 | 2 128 | 2 128 | 2 148 | 1 988 | 1 881 | 2 078 |
| | 6 624 | 6 749 | 6 116 | 5 758 | 5 674 | 5 691 | 6 118 | 6 479 | 6 511 | 6 609 | 5 774 | 5 315 | 6 233 |
| | 0.06 | 0.06 | 0.06 | 0.05 | 0.05 | 0.05 | 0.05 | 0.05 | 0.05 | 0.05 | 0.06 | 0.06 | 0.05 |
| | 2 253 | 2 497 | 2 392 | 2 313 | 2 347 | 2 403 | 2 619 | 2 838 | 2 932 | 3 081 | 1 947 | 1 275 | 2 570 |
| | 6 566 | 7 324 | 7 064 | 6 876 | 7 018 | 7 230 | 7 928 | 8 638 | 8 972 | 9 480 | 5 656 | 3 603 | 7 710 |
| | 0.06 | 0.06 | 0.06 | 0.05 | 0.05 | 0.05 | 0.05 | 0.05 | 0.05 | 0.05 | 0.06 | 0.06 | 0.05 |
| | 2 811 | 2 845 | 2 561 | 2 395 | 2 346 | 2 338 | 2 499 | 2 632 | 2 631 | 2 656 | 2 458 | 2 326 | 2 569 |
| | 8 190 | 8 346 | 7 562 | 7 119 | 7 015 | 7 036 | 7 564 | 8 011 | 8 051 | 8 172 | 7 139 | 6 572 | 7 707 |
| | 0.06 | 0.06 | 0.06 | 0.05 | 0.05 | 0.05 | 0.05 | 0.05 | 0.05 | 0.05 | 0.06 | 0.06 | 0.05 |
| | 3 477 | 3 859 | 3 133 | 1 802 | 1 754 | 1 730 | 2 132 | 2 542 | 2 596 | 2 736 | 1 988 | 1 359 | 2 569 |
| | 10 133 | 11 317 | 9 253 | 5 356 | 5 245 | 5 207 | 6 455 | 7 738 | 7 944 | 8 418 | 5 774 | 3 841 | 7 707 |
| | 0.09 | 0.10 | 0.08 | 0.05 | 0.04 | 0.04 | 0.04 | 0.05 | 0.04 | 0.04 | 0.06 | 0.06 | 0.05 |
| | 961 | 809 | 785 | 792 | 935 | 863 | 812 | 826 | 864 | 784 | 788 | 714 | 844 |
| | 113 | 99 | 98 | 102 | 124 | 118 | 115 | 120 | 130 | 121 | 91 | 68 | 114 |
| | 0.00 | 0.00 | 0.00 | 0.00 | 0.00 | 0.00 | 0.00 | 0.00 | 0.00 | 0.00 | 0.00 | 0.00 | 0.00 |
| | ... | ... | ... | ... | ... | ... | ... | ... | ... | ... | ... | ... | ... |
| | ... | ... | ... | ... | ... | ... | ... | ... | ... | ... | ... | ... | ... |
| | ... | ... | ... | ... | ... | ... | ... | ... | ... | ... | ... | ... | ... |
| | 685 | 690 | 745 | 876 | 908 | 891 | 849 | 831 | 931 | 938 | 788 | 715 | 843 |
| | 81 | 84 | 93 | 113 | 121 | 122 | 120 | 120 | 140 | 144 | 91 | 68 | 114 |
| | 0.00 | 0.00 | 0.00 | 0.00 | 0.00 | 0.00 | 0.00 | 0.00 | 0.00 | 0.00 | 0.00 | 0.00 | 0.00 |
| | 679 | 749 | 861 | 1 046 | 1 123 | 1 132 | 1 100 | 1 108 | 1 282 | 1 346 | 827 | 498 | 1 062 |
| | 80 | 91 | 108 | 135 | 149 | 155 | 155 | 161 | 192 | 207 | 95 | 48 | 143 |
| | 0.00 | 0.00 | 0.00 | 0.00 | 0.00 | 0.00 | 0.00 | 0.00 | 0.00 | 0.00 | 0.00 | 0.00 | 0.00 |
| | 686 | 691 | 746 | 877 | 909 | 892 | 850 | 832 | 932 | 939 | 789 | 716 | 844 |
| | 81 | 84 | 93 | 113 | 121 | 122 | 120 | 121 | 140 | 145 | 91 | 68 | 114 |
| | 0.00 | 0.00 | 0.00 | 0.00 | 0.00 | 0.00 | 0.00 | 0.00 | 0.00 | 0.00 | 0.00 | 0.00 | 0.00 |
| | 961 | 809 | 785 | 792 | 935 | 863 | 805 | 825 | 864 | 784 | 784 | 704 | 843 |
| | 113 | 99 | 98 | 102 | 124 | 118 | 113 | 120 | 130 | 121 | 91 | 67 | 114 |
| | 0.00 | 0.00 | 0.00 | 0.00 | 0.00 | 0.00 | 0.00 | 0.00 | 0.00 | 0.00 | 0.00 | 0.00 | 0.00 |

**Table A.1** Total and per capita gross domestic product of individual countries or areas, expressed in United States dollars, and their individual shares of gross world product, based on alternative conversion rates, 1970−1989 [*cont.*]

| Country or area | 1970 (1) | 1971 (2) | 1972 (3) | 1973 (4) | 1974 (5) | 1975 (6) | 1976 (7) | 1977 (8) | 1978 (9) | 1979 (10) |
|---|---|---|---|---|---|---|---|---|---|---|
| **Venezuela** | | | | | | | | | | |
| **1. MER** | | | | | | | | | | |
| 1a. Per capita GDP | 1 285 | 1 362 | 1 448 | 1 700 | 2 525 | 2 564 | 2 827 | 3 143 | 3 297 | 3 918 |
| 1b. GDP | 13 622 | 14 958 | 16 470 | 20 049 | 30 862 | 32 474 | 37 107 | 42 736 | 46 401 | 57 017 |
| 1c. % of GWP | 0.43 | 0.43 | 0.41 | 0.41 | 0.56 | 0.52 | 0.55 | 0.56 | 0.52 | 0.55 |
| **2. PPPs** | | | | | | | | | | |
| 2a. Per capita GDP | 1 855 | 1 976 | 2 113 | 2 315 | 3 304 | 3 428 | 3 718 | 3 992 | 4 234 | 4 809 |
| 2b. GDP | 19 668 | 21 704 | 24 043 | 27 303 | 40 383 | 43 415 | 48 793 | 54 275 | 59 588 | 69 985 |
| 2c. % of GWP | ... | ... | ... | ... | ... | ... | ... | ... | ... | ... |
| **3. Absolute 1970−1989 PARE** | | | | | | | | | | |
| 3a. Per capita GDP | 3 087 | 3 073 | 3 062 | 3 139 | 3 213 | 3 288 | 3 452 | 3 556 | 3 509 | 3 439 |
| 3b. GDP | 32 737 | 33 742 | 34 841 | 37 021 | 39 266 | 41 648 | 45 301 | 48 346 | 49 380 | 50 040 |
| 3c. % of GWP | 0.46 | 0.46 | 0.45 | 0.45 | 0.46 | 0.48 | 0.50 | 0.51 | 0.50 | 0.49 |
| **4. Relative 1970−1989 PARE** | | | | | | | | | | |
| 4a. Per capita GDP | 1 505 | 1 575 | 1 642 | 1 795 | 2 003 | 2 253 | 2 513 | 2 763 | 2 925 | 3 123 |
| 4b. GDP | 15 962 | 17 296 | 18 678 | 21 165 | 24 486 | 28 533 | 32 976 | 37 566 | 41 168 | 45 443 |
| 4c. % of GWP | 0.46 | 0.46 | 0.45 | 0.45 | 0.46 | 0.48 | 0.50 | 0.51 | 0.50 | 0.49 |
| **5. Absolute 1980−1989 PARE** | | | | | | | | | | |
| 5a. Per capita GDP | 3 720 | 3 703 | 3 691 | 3 784 | 3 872 | 3 963 | 4 160 | 4 286 | 4 229 | 4 144 |
| 5b. GDP | 39 455 | 40 666 | 41 991 | 44 618 | 47 323 | 50 194 | 54 597 | 58 267 | 59 513 | 60 308 |
| 5c. % of GWP | 0.45 | 0.45 | 0.44 | 0.44 | 0.46 | 0.48 | 0.49 | 0.51 | 0.50 | 0.49 |
| **6. WA** | | | | | | | | | | |
| 6a. Per capita GDP | 1 299 | 1 362 | 1 448 | 1 700 | 2 525 | 2 564 | 2 828 | 3 144 | 3 297 | 3 919 |
| 6b. GDP | 13 775 | 14 959 | 16 470 | 20 052 | 30 865 | 32 474 | 37 108 | 42 741 | 46 406 | 57 023 |
| 6c. % of GWP | 0.43 | 0.43 | 0.41 | 0.41 | 0.55 | 0.53 | 0.55 | 0.57 | 0.52 | 0.56 |
| **Viet Nam** | | | | | | | | | | |
| **1. MER** | | | | | | | | | | |
| 1a. Per capita GDP | 127 | 125 | 112 | 110 | 112 | 115 | 119 | 119 | 119 | 116 |
| 1b. GDP | 5 410 | 5 470 | 5 000 | 5 020 | 5 270 | 5 520 | 5 870 | 5 990 | 6 110 | 6 090 |
| 1c. % of GWP | 0.17 | 0.16 | 0.12 | 0.10 | 0.09 | 0.09 | 0.09 | 0.08 | 0.07 | 0.06 |
| **2. PPPs** | | | | | | | | | | |
| 2a. Per capita GDP | ... | ... | ... | ... | ... | ... | ... | ... | ... | ... |
| 2b. GDP | ... | ... | ... | ... | ... | ... | ... | ... | ... | ... |
| 2c. % of GWP | ... | ... | ... | ... | ... | ... | ... | ... | ... | ... |
| **3. Absolute 1970−1989 PARE** | | | | | | | | | | |
| 3a. Per capita GDP | 142 | 124 | 110 | 108 | 112 | 114 | 119 | 118 | 119 | 114 |
| 3b. GDP | 6 062 | 5 428 | 4 908 | 4 966 | 5 255 | 5 485 | 5 832 | 5 948 | 6 121 | 6 005 |
| 3c. % of GWP | 0.09 | 0.07 | 0.06 | 0.06 | 0.06 | 0.06 | 0.06 | 0.06 | 0.06 | 0.06 |
| **4. Relative 1970−1989 PARE** | | | | | | | | | | |
| 4a. Per capita GDP | 69 | 64 | 59 | 62 | 70 | 78 | 86 | 92 | 99 | 104 |
| 4b. GDP | 2 956 | 2 782 | 2 631 | 2 839 | 3 277 | 3 758 | 4 245 | 4 622 | 5 103 | 5 453 |
| 4c. % of GWP | 0.09 | 0.07 | 0.06 | 0.06 | 0.06 | 0.06 | 0.06 | 0.06 | 0.06 | 0.06 |
| **5. Absolute 1980−1989 PARE** | | | | | | | | | | |
| 5a. Per capita GDP | 142 | 125 | 110 | 109 | 112 | 115 | 119 | 119 | 120 | 115 |
| 5b. GDP | 6 083 | 5 447 | 4 925 | 4 983 | 5 273 | 5 504 | 5 852 | 5 968 | 6 142 | 6 026 |
| 5c. % of GWP | 0.07 | 0.06 | 0.05 | 0.05 | 0.05 | 0.05 | 0.05 | 0.05 | 0.05 | 0.05 |
| **6. WA[a]** | | | | | | | | | | |
| 6a. Per capita GDP | 70 | 93 | 106 | 110 | 113 | 115 | 119 | 119 | 120 | 115 |
| 6b. GDP | 3 004 | 4 061 | 4 758 | 5 028 | 5 311 | 5 522 | 5 863 | 5 987 | 6 145 | 6 044 |
| 6c. % of GWP | 0.09 | 0.12 | 0.12 | 0.10 | 0.10 | 0.09 | 0.09 | 0.08 | 0.07 | 0.06 |

| | | | | | | | | | | Averages | | |
| 1980 (11) | 1981 (12) | 1982 (13) | 1983 (14) | 1984 (15) | 1985 (16) | 1986 (17) | 1987 (18) | 1988 (19) | 1989 (20) | 1970–89 (21) | 1970–79 (22) | 1980–89 (23) |
|---|---|---|---|---|---|---|---|---|---|---|---|---|
| 4 644 | 1 500 | 5 014 | 4 857 | 3 462 | 3 577 | 3 434 | 2 716 | 3 317 | 2 352 | 3 052 | 2 505 | 3 459 |
| 69 769 | 23 176 | 79 943 | 79 637 | 58 348 | 61 949 | 61 087 | 49 615 | 62 216 | 45 258 | 45 135 | 31 170 | 59 100 |
| 0.60 | 0.20 | 0.69 | 0.67 | 0.48 | 0.49 | 0.41 | 0.29 | 0.33 | 0.23 | 0.44 | 0.51 | 0.41 |
| | | | | | | | | | | | | |
| 5 421 | 5 615 | 5 379 | 5 255 | 5 085 | 5 305 | 5 628 | 5 809 | 6 189 | 5 770 | 4 599 | 3 288 | 5 567 |
| 81 449 | 86 746 | 85 757 | 86 159 | 85 692 | 91 872 | 100 123 | 106 126 | 116 075 | 111 047 | 68 010 | 40 916 | 95 105 |
| ... | ... | ... | ... | ... | ... | ... | ... | ... | ... | ... | ... | ... |
| 3 264 | 3 165 | 3 088 | 2 834 | 2 720 | 2 681 | 2 788 | 2 797 | 2 883 | 2 582 | 3 052 | 3 313 | 2 870 |
| 49 045 | 48 896 | 49 230 | 46 465 | 45 836 | 46 425 | 49 597 | 51 103 | 54 078 | 49 698 | 45 135 | 41 232 | 49 037 |
| 0.47 | 0.46 | 0.46 | 0.42 | 0.40 | 0.39 | 0.41 | 0.40 | 0.41 | 0.37 | 0.44 | 0.48 | 0.42 |
| | | | | | | | | | | | | |
| 3 236 | 3 434 | 3 567 | 3 384 | 3 364 | 3 406 | 3 613 | 3 729 | 3 973 | 3 704 | 3 013 | 2 276 | 3 558 |
| 48 616 | 53 055 | 56 867 | 55 487 | 56 697 | 58 981 | 64 278 | 68 132 | 74 519 | 71 291 | 44 560 | 28 327 | 60 792 |
| 0.47 | 0.46 | 0.46 | 0.42 | 0.40 | 0.39 | 0.41 | 0.40 | 0.41 | 0.37 | 0.43 | 0.48 | 0.41 |
| | | | | | | | | | | | | |
| 3 934 | 3 815 | 3 721 | 3 415 | 3 278 | 3 231 | 3 360 | 3 371 | 3 475 | 3 112 | 3 678 | 3 993 | 3 459 |
| 59 109 | 58 930 | 59 332 | 56 000 | 55 241 | 55 951 | 59 775 | 61 590 | 65 175 | 59 896 | 54 396 | 49 693 | 59 100 |
| 0.47 | 0.46 | 0.46 | 0.42 | 0.40 | 0.39 | 0.40 | 0.40 | 0.41 | 0.36 | 0.44 | 0.47 | 0.41 |
| | | | | | | | | | | | | |
| 4 644 | 5 068 | 5 015 | 4 857 | 3 462 | 3 577 | 3 434 | 2 716 | 3 317 | 2 353 | 3 239 | 2 506 | 3 782 |
| 69 777 | 78 289 | 79 952 | 79 646 | 58 352 | 61 949 | 61 087 | 49 615 | 62 216 | 45 283 | 47 902 | 31 187 | 64 617 |
| 0.61 | 0.66 | 0.69 | 0.67 | 0.48 | 0.49 | 0.42 | 0.30 | 0.33 | 0.23 | 0.47 | 0.51 | 0.46 |
| | | | | | | | | | | | | |
| 107 | 108 | 115 | 120 | 128 | 132 | 133 | 134 | 139 | 139 | 123 | 117 | 126 |
| 5 770 | 5 910 | 6 450 | 6 900 | 7 520 | 7 890 | 8 150 | 8 360 | 8 850 | 9 060 | 6 531 | 5 575 | 7 486 |
| 0.05 | 0.05 | 0.06 | 0.06 | 0.06 | 0.06 | 0.05 | 0.05 | 0.05 | 0.05 | 0.06 | 0.09 | 0.05 |
| | | | | | | | | | | | | |
| ... | ... | ... | ... | ... | ... | ... | ... | ... | ... | ... | ... | ... |
| ... | ... | ... | ... | ... | ... | ... | ... | ... | ... | ... | ... | ... |
| ... | ... | ... | ... | ... | ... | ... | ... | ... | ... | ... | ... | ... |
| 106 | 108 | 115 | 120 | 127 | 132 | 133 | 133 | 137 | 138 | 123 | 118 | 126 |
| 5 716 | 5 948 | 6 467 | 6 871 | 7 449 | 7 910 | 8 142 | 8 315 | 8 776 | 9 008 | 6 531 | 5 601 | 7 460 |
| 0.06 | 0.06 | 0.06 | 0.06 | 0.06 | 0.07 | 0.07 | 0.07 | 0.07 | 0.07 | 0.06 | 0.06 | 0.06 |
| | | | | | | | | | | | | |
| 106 | 118 | 133 | 143 | 157 | 168 | 172 | 177 | 189 | 198 | 124 | 79 | 158 |
| 5 666 | 6 454 | 7 470 | 8 205 | 9 213 | 10 050 | 10 551 | 11 085 | 12 094 | 12 921 | 6 569 | 3 767 | 9 371 |
| 0.06 | 0.06 | 0.06 | 0.06 | 0.06 | 0.07 | 0.07 | 0.07 | 0.07 | 0.07 | 0.06 | 0.06 | 0.06 |
| | | | | | | | | | | | | |
| 107 | 109 | 116 | 120 | 128 | 133 | 133 | 133 | 138 | 139 | 123 | 118 | 126 |
| 5 736 | 5 968 | 6 489 | 6 895 | 7 474 | 7 938 | 8 170 | 8 343 | 8 807 | 9 039 | 6 553 | 5 620 | 7 486 |
| 0.05 | 0.05 | 0.05 | 0.05 | 0.05 | 0.06 | 0.06 | 0.05 | 0.06 | 0.05 | 0.05 | 0.05 | 0.05 |
| | | | | | | | | | | | | |
| 107 | 109 | 115 | 120 | 128 | 133 | 133 | 133 | 138 | 139 | 119 | 109 | 126 |
| 5 758 | 5 981 | 6 468 | 6 860 | 7 476 | 7 940 | 8 163 | 8 325 | 8 820 | 9 067 | 6 329 | 5 172 | 7 486 |
| 0.05 | 0.05 | 0.06 | 0.06 | 0.06 | 0.06 | 0.06 | 0.05 | 0.05 | 0.05 | 0.06 | 0.09 | 0.05 |

**Table A.1** Total and per capita gross domestic product of individual countries or areas, expressed in United States dollars, and their individual shares of gross world product, based on alternative conversion rates, 1970–1989 [*cont.*]

| Country or area | 1970 (1) | 1971 (2) | 1972 (3) | 1973 (4) | 1974 (5) | 1975 (6) | 1976 (7) | 1977 (8) | 1978 (9) | 1979 (10) |
|---|---|---|---|---|---|---|---|---|---|---|
| **Yemen[c]** | | | | | | | | | | |
| **1.   MER** | | | | | | | | | | |
| 1a.   Per capita GDP | 81 | 96 | 137 | 172 | 223 | 285 | 364 | 449 | 536 | 593 |
| 1b.   GDP | 394 | 473 | 685 | 875 | 1 161 | 1 520 | 2 001 | 2 555 | 3 165 | 3 636 |
| 1c.   % of GWP | 0.01 | 0.01 | 0.02 | 0.02 | 0.02 | 0.02 | 0.03 | 0.03 | 0.04 | 0.04 |
| **2.   PPPs** | | | | | | | | | | |
| 2a.   Per capita GDP | 442 | 497 | 585 | 641 | 738 | 880 | 989 | 1 059 | 1 166 | 1 280 |
| 2b.   GDP | 2 135 | 2 442 | 2 920 | 3 260 | 3 840 | 4 699 | 5 443 | 6 026 | 6 884 | 7 847 |
| 2c.   % of GWP | ... | ... | ... | ... | ... | ... | ... | ... | ... | ... |
| **3.   Absolute 1970–1989 PARE** | | | | | | | | | | |
| 3a.   Per capita GDP | 288 | 304 | 341 | 354 | 385 | 419 | 436 | 470 | 483 | 489 |
| 3b.   GDP | 1 394 | 1 495 | 1 703 | 1 798 | 2 004 | 2 237 | 2 397 | 2 675 | 2 849 | 2 994 |
| 3c.   % of GWP | 0.02 | 0.02 | 0.02 | 0.02 | 0.02 | 0.03 | 0.03 | 0.03 | 0.03 | 0.03 |
| **4.   Relative 1970–1989 PARE** | | | | | | | | | | |
| 4a.   Per capita GDP | 141 | 156 | 183 | 202 | 240 | 287 | 317 | 365 | 402 | 444 |
| 4b.   GDP | 680 | 766 | 913 | 1 028 | 1 250 | 1 532 | 1 745 | 2 078 | 2 375 | 2 719 |
| 4c.   % of GWP | 0.02 | 0.02 | 0.02 | 0.02 | 0.02 | 0.03 | 0.03 | 0.03 | 0.03 | 0.03 |
| **5.   Absolute 1980–1989 PARE** | | | | | | | | | | |
| 5a.   Per capita GDP | 323 | 341 | 382 | 396 | 431 | 469 | 488 | 526 | 540 | 547 |
| 5b.   GDP | 1 561 | 1 673 | 1 906 | 2 013 | 2 243 | 2 504 | 2 683 | 2 994 | 3 189 | 3 351 |
| 5c.   % of GWP | 0.02 | 0.02 | 0.02 | 0.02 | 0.02 | 0.02 | 0.02 | 0.03 | 0.03 | 0.03 |
| **6.   WA[a]** | | | | | | | | | | |
| 6a.   Per capita GDP | 77 | 89 | 111 | 138 | 184 | 239 | 297 | 379 | 460 | 529 |
| 6b.   GDP | 373 | 438 | 556 | 700 | 959 | 1 277 | 1 636 | 2 159 | 2 718 | 3 242 |
| 6c.   % of GWP | 0.01 | 0.01 | 0.01 | 0.01 | 0.02 | 0.02 | 0.02 | 0.03 | 0.03 | 0.03 |
| **Democratic Yemen (former)[c]** | | | | | | | | | | |
| **1.   MER** | | | | | | | | | | |
| 1a.   Per capita GDP | 137 | 121 | 136 | 152 | 162 | 158 | 184 | 225 | 262 | 297 |
| 1b.   GDP | 206 | 184 | 212 | 241 | 263 | 262 | 312 | 389 | 464 | 539 |
| 1c.   % of GWP | 0.01 | 0.01 | 0.01 | 0.00 | 0.00 | 0.00 | 0.00 | 0.01 | 0.01 | 0.01 |
| **2.   PPPs** | | | | | | | | | | |
| 2a.   Per capita GDP | ... | ... | ... | ... | ... | ... | ... | ... | ... | ... |
| 2b.   GDP | ... | ... | ... | ... | ... | ... | ... | ... | ... | ... |
| 2c.   % of GWP | ... | ... | ... | ... | ... | ... | ... | ... | ... | ... |
| **3.   Absolute 1970–1989 PARE** | | | | | | | | | | |
| 3a.   Per capita GDP | 343 | 296 | 286 | 237 | 226 | 207 | 256 | 298 | 337 | 336 |
| 3b.   GDP | 514 | 452 | 446 | 376 | 367 | 342 | 433 | 516 | 597 | 611 |
| 3c.   % of GWP | 0.01 | 0.01 | 0.01 | 0.00 | 0.00 | 0.00 | 0.00 | 0.01 | 0.01 | 0.01 |
| **4.   Relative 1970–1989 PARE** | | | | | | | | | | |
| 4a.   Per capita GDP | 167 | 152 | 153 | 135 | 141 | 142 | 186 | 232 | 281 | 305 |
| 4b.   GDP | 250 | 232 | 239 | 215 | 229 | 234 | 315 | 401 | 498 | 554 |
| 4c.   % of GWP | 0.01 | 0.01 | 0.01 | 0.00 | 0.00 | 0.00 | 0.00 | 0.01 | 0.01 | 0.01 |
| **5.   Absolute 1980–1989 PARE** | | | | | | | | | | |
| 5a.   Per capita GDP | 406 | 350 | 339 | 281 | 268 | 245 | 303 | 353 | 399 | 398 |
| 5b.   GDP | 608 | 535 | 528 | 445 | 434 | 405 | 512 | 611 | 707 | 723 |
| 5c.   % of GWP | 0.01 | 0.01 | 0.01 | 0.00 | 0.00 | 0.00 | 0.00 | 0.01 | 0.01 | 0.01 |
| **6.   WA[a]** | | | | | | | | | | |
| 6a.   Per capita GDP | 141 | 120 | 122 | 116 | 134 | 145 | 188 | 223 | 253 | 269 |
| 6b.   GDP | 212 | 184 | 190 | 185 | 218 | 241 | 318 | 385 | 448 | 489 |
| 6c.   % of GWP | 0.01 | 0.01 | 0.00 | 0.00 | 0.00 | 0.00 | 0.00 | 0.01 | 0.01 | 0.00 |

| | | | | | | | | | | Averages | | |
|---|---|---|---|---|---|---|---|---|---|---|---|---|
| 1980 (11) | 1981 (12) | 1982 (13) | 1983 (14) | 1984 (15) | 1985 (16) | 1986 (17) | 1987 (18) | 1988 (19) | 1989 (20) | 1970–89 (21) | 1970–79 (22) | 1980–89 (23) |
| 620 | 631 | 722 | 751 | 648 | 549 | 493 | 515 | 644 | 761 | 514 | 313 | 637 |
| 3 942 | 4 160 | 4 934 | 5 319 | 4 757 | 4 181 | 3 903 | 4 229 | 5 491 | 6 744 | 3 206 | 1 646 | 4 766 |
| 0.03 | 0.04 | 0.04 | 0.04 | 0.04 | 0.03 | 0.03 | 0.02 | 0.03 | 0.03 | 0.03 | 0.03 | 0.03 |
| 1 452 | 1 532 | 1 613 | 1 580 | 1 527 | 1 513 | 1 573 | 1 709 | 1 937 | 2 025 | 1 367 | 864 | 1 673 |
| 9 233 | 10 098 | 11 025 | 11 189 | 11 219 | 11 529 | 12 446 | 14 034 | 16 521 | 17 938 | 8 536 | 4 550 | 12 523 |
| ... | ... | ... | ... | ... | ... | ... | ... | ... | ... | ... | ... | ... |
| 499 | 498 | 528 | 527 | 520 | 553 | 564 | 596 | 653 | 656 | 514 | 409 | 569 |
| 3 175 | 3 281 | 3 608 | 3 734 | 3 824 | 4 218 | 4 463 | 4 893 | 5 573 | 5 812 | 3 206 | 2 155 | 4 258 |
| 0.03 | 0.03 | 0.03 | 0.03 | 0.03 | 0.04 | 0.04 | 0.04 | 0.04 | 0.04 | 0.03 | 0.03 | 0.04 |
| 495 | 540 | 610 | 629 | 644 | 703 | 731 | 794 | 900 | 941 | 551 | 286 | 718 |
| 3 147 | 3 560 | 4 167 | 4 459 | 4 730 | 5 358 | 5 785 | 6 523 | 7 679 | 8 337 | 3 442 | 1 509 | 5 375 |
| 0.03 | 0.03 | 0.03 | 0.03 | 0.03 | 0.04 | 0.04 | 0.04 | 0.04 | 0.04 | 0.03 | 0.03 | 0.04 |
| 559 | 557 | 591 | 590 | 583 | 619 | 632 | 667 | 731 | 735 | 575 | 458 | 637 |
| 3 554 | 3 672 | 4 038 | 4 179 | 4 280 | 4 721 | 4 996 | 5 476 | 6 238 | 6 506 | 3 589 | 2 412 | 4 766 |
| 0.03 | 0.03 | 0.03 | 0.03 | 0.03 | 0.03 | 0.03 | 0.04 | 0.04 | 0.04 | 0.03 | 0.02 | 0.03 |
| 592 | 618 | 681 | 712 | 698 | 660 | 573 | 540 | 591 | 649 | 493 | 267 | 634 |
| 3 766 | 4 071 | 4 655 | 5 042 | 5 128 | 5 032 | 4 530 | 4 435 | 5 043 | 5 748 | 3 075 | 1 406 | 4 745 |
| 0.03 | 0.03 | 0.04 | 0.04 | 0.04 | 0.04 | 0.03 | 0.03 | 0.03 | 0.03 | 0.03 | 0.02 | 0.03 |
| 359 | 398 | 473 | 504 | 522 | 501 | 409 | 514 | 531 | 551 | 360 | 188 | 483 |
| 668 | 760 | 928 | 1 017 | 1 084 | 1 071 | 900 | 1 165 | 1 242 | 1 330 | 662 | 307 | 1 017 |
| 0.01 | 0.01 | 0.01 | 0.01 | 0.01 | 0.01 | 0.01 | 0.01 | 0.01 | 0.01 | 0.01 | 0.01 | 0.01 |
| ... | ... | ... | ... | ... | ... | ... | ... | ... | ... | ... | ... | ... |
| ... | ... | ... | ... | ... | ... | ... | ... | ... | ... | ... | ... | ... |
| ... | ... | ... | ... | ... | ... | ... | ... | ... | ... | ... | ... | ... |
| 376 | 396 | 445 | 451 | 464 | 437 | 372 | 373 | 377 | 373 | 360 | 284 | 408 |
| 701 | 756 | 873 | 910 | 963 | 935 | 819 | 845 | 883 | 901 | 662 | 465 | 859 |
| 0.01 | 0.01 | 0.01 | 0.01 | 0.01 | 0.01 | 0.01 | 0.01 | 0.01 | 0.01 | 0.01 | 0.01 | 0.01 |
| 373 | 429 | 514 | 538 | 574 | 556 | 482 | 497 | 520 | 535 | 377 | 193 | 507 |
| 695 | 820 | 1 009 | 1 087 | 1 192 | 1 188 | 1 061 | 1 127 | 1 217 | 1 292 | 693 | 317 | 1 069 |
| 0.01 | 0.01 | 0.01 | 0.01 | 0.01 | 0.01 | 0.01 | 0.01 | 0.01 | 0.01 | 0.01 | 0.01 | 0.01 |
| 446 | 468 | 527 | 534 | 549 | 518 | 440 | 441 | 447 | 442 | 426 | 336 | 483 |
| 830 | 895 | 1 034 | 1 077 | 1 141 | 1 107 | 969 | 1 001 | 1 046 | 1 067 | 784 | 551 | 1 017 |
| 0.01 | 0.01 | 0.01 | 0.01 | 0.01 | 0.01 | 0.01 | 0.01 | 0.01 | 0.01 | 0.01 | 0.01 | 0.01 |
| 325 | 374 | 447 | 478 | 511 | 494 | 418 | 446 | 483 | 530 | 340 | 175 | 457 |
| 606 | 714 | 878 | 964 | 1 061 | 1 056 | 919 | 1 011 | 1 129 | 1 278 | 624 | 287 | 962 |
| 0.01 | 0.01 | 0.01 | 0.01 | 0.01 | 0.01 | 0.01 | 0.01 | 0.01 | 0.01 | 0.01 | 0.00 | 0.01 |

**Table A.1**   Total and per capita gross domestic product of individual countries or areas,
expressed in United States dollars, and their individual shares of gross world
product, based on alternative conversion rates, 1970−1989 [*cont.*]

| Country or area | 1970 (1) | 1971 (2) | 1972 (3) | 1973 (4) | 1974 (5) | 1975 (6) | 1976 (7) | 1977 (8) | 1978 (9) | 1979 (10) |
|---|---|---|---|---|---|---|---|---|---|---|
| **Yugoslavia[d]** | | | | | | | | | | |
| **1.   MER** | | | | | | | | | | |
| 1a.   Per capita GDP | 714 | 769 | 794 | 1 024 | 1 404 | 1 559 | 1 743 | 2 101 | 2 477 | 3 083 |
| 1b.   GDP | 14 552 | 15 818 | 16 482 | 21 469 | 29 705 | 33 280 | 37 562 | 45 672 | 54 338 | 68 197 |
| 1c.   % of GWP | 0.46 | 0.45 | 0.41 | 0.44 | 0.53 | 0.54 | 0.56 | 0.60 | 0.60 | 0.66 |
| **2.   PPPs** | | | | | | | | | | |
| 2a.   Per capita GDP | ... | ... | ... | ... | ... | ... | ... | ... | ... | ... |
| 2b.   GDP | ... | ... | ... | ... | ... | ... | ... | ... | ... | ... |
| 2c.   % of GWP | ... | ... | ... | ... | ... | ... | ... | ... | ... | ... |
| **3.   Absolute 1970−1989 PARE** | | | | | | | | | | |
| 3a.   Per capita GDP | 1 491 | 1 612 | 1 627 | 1 656 | 1 884 | 1 873 | 1 953 | 2 101 | 2 271 | 2 361 |
| 3b.   GDP | 30 367 | 33 150 | 33 778 | 34 705 | 39 851 | 40 001 | 42 095 | 45 686 | 49 814 | 52 238 |
| 3c.   % of GWP | 0.43 | 0.45 | 0.43 | 0.42 | 0.47 | 0.47 | 0.47 | 0.48 | 0.51 | 0.51 |
| **4.   Relative 1970−1989 PARE** | | | | | | | | | | |
| 4a.   Per capita GDP | 727 | 826 | 872 | 947 | 1 175 | 1 283 | 1 422 | 1 633 | 1 893 | 2 144 |
| 4b.   GDP | 14 806 | 16 992 | 18 108 | 19 841 | 24 851 | 27 405 | 30 642 | 35 499 | 41 530 | 47 439 |
| 4c.   % of GWP | 0.43 | 0.45 | 0.43 | 0.42 | 0.47 | 0.47 | 0.47 | 0.48 | 0.51 | 0.51 |
| **5.   Absolute 1980−1989 PARE** | | | | | | | | | | |
| 5a.   Per capita GDP | 1 666 | 1 802 | 1 819 | 1 851 | 2 106 | 2 094 | 2 184 | 2 349 | 2 539 | 2 639 |
| 5b.   GDP | 33 945 | 37 056 | 37 758 | 38 795 | 44 547 | 44 714 | 47 055 | 51 069 | 55 684 | 58 393 |
| 5c.   % of GWP | 0.39 | 0.41 | 0.40 | 0.38 | 0.43 | 0.43 | 0.43 | 0.44 | 0.46 | 0.47 |
| **6.   WA** | | | | | | | | | | |
| 6a.   Per capita GDP | 714 | 769 | 794 | 1 024 | 1 404 | 1 559 | 1 743 | 2 101 | 2 477 | 3 083 |
| 6b.   GDP | 14 552 | 15 818 | 16 482 | 21 469 | 29 707 | 33 280 | 37 562 | 45 672 | 54 338 | 68 197 |
| 6c.   % of GWP | 0.46 | 0.45 | 0.41 | 0.44 | 0.53 | 0.54 | 0.56 | 0.61 | 0.61 | 0.67 |
| **Zaire** | | | | | | | | | | |
| **1.   MER** | | | | | | | | | | |
| 1a.   Per capita GDP | 95 | 103 | 111 | 137 | 163 | 169 | 155 | 192 | 265 | 252 |
| 1b.   GDP | 1 876 | 2 098 | 2 314 | 2 950 | 3 598 | 3 838 | 3 620 | 4 616 | 6 556 | 6 423 |
| 1c.   % of GWP | 0.06 | 0.06 | 0.06 | 0.06 | 0.06 | 0.06 | 0.05 | 0.06 | 0.07 | 0.06 |
| **2.   PPPs** | | | | | | | | | | |
| 2a.   Per capita GDP | 177 | 193 | 193 | 226 | 228 | 211 | 207 | 175 | 188 | 211 |
| 2b.   GDP | 3 506 | 3 919 | 4 031 | 4 850 | 5 037 | 4 790 | 4 843 | 4 206 | 4 658 | 5 381 |
| 2c.   % of GWP | ... | ... | ... | ... | ... | ... | ... | ... | ... | ... |
| **3.   Absolute 1970−1989 PARE** | | | | | | | | | | |
| 3a.   Per capita GDP | 186 | 195 | 191 | 201 | 207 | 181 | 164 | 159 | 146 | 142 |
| 3b.   GDP | 3 683 | 3 971 | 3 993 | 4 315 | 4 577 | 4 121 | 3 846 | 3 818 | 3 614 | 3 624 |
| 3c.   % of GWP | 0.05 | 0.05 | 0.05 | 0.05 | 0.05 | 0.05 | 0.04 | 0.04 | 0.04 | 0.04 |
| **4.   Relative 1970−1989 PARE** | | | | | | | | | | |
| 4a.   Per capita GDP | 91 | 100 | 102 | 115 | 129 | 124 | 120 | 123 | 122 | 129 |
| 4b.   GDP | 1 796 | 2 035 | 2 141 | 2 467 | 2 854 | 2 824 | 2 800 | 2 967 | 3 013 | 3 291 |
| 4c.   % of GWP | 0.05 | 0.05 | 0.05 | 0.05 | 0.05 | 0.05 | 0.04 | 0.04 | 0.04 | 0.04 |
| **5.   Absolute 1980−1989 PARE** | | | | | | | | | | |
| 5a.   Per capita GDP | 194 | 204 | 199 | 209 | 216 | 189 | 171 | 165 | 152 | 148 |
| 5b.   GDP | 3 837 | 4 137 | 4 161 | 4 496 | 4 768 | 4 294 | 4 007 | 3 978 | 3 765 | 3 775 |
| 5c.   % of GWP | 0.04 | 0.05 | 0.04 | 0.04 | 0.05 | 0.04 | 0.04 | 0.03 | 0.03 | 0.03 |
| **6.   WA** | | | | | | | | | | |
| 6a.   Per capita GDP | 95 | 103 | 111 | 137 | 163 | 169 | 154 | 192 | 265 | 252 |
| 6b.   GDP | 1 876 | 2 098 | 2 314 | 2 950 | 3 598 | 3 838 | 3 610 | 4 617 | 6 557 | 6 424 |
| 6c.   % of GWP | 0.06 | 0.06 | 0.06 | 0.06 | 0.06 | 0.06 | 0.05 | 0.06 | 0.07 | 0.06 |

| 1980 (11) | 1981 (12) | 1982 (13) | 1983 (14) | 1984 (15) | 1985 (16) | 1986 (17) | 1987 (18) | 1988 (19) | 1989 (20) | Averages 1970–89 (21) | 1970–79 (22) | 1980–89 (23) |
|---|---|---|---|---|---|---|---|---|---|---|---|---|
| 3 136 | 3 066 | 2 774 | 2 022 | 1 895 | 1 913 | 2 652 | 3 033 | 2 665 | 3 456 | 2 138 | 1 586 | 2 659 |
| 69 958 | 68 930 | 62 827 | 46 133 | 43 538 | 44 237 | 61 705 | 71 018 | 62 764 | 81 848 | 47 502 | 33 708 | 61 296 |
| 0.60 | 0.59 | 0.54 | 0.39 | 0.36 | 0.35 | 0.41 | 0.41 | 0.33 | 0.41 | 0.47 | 0.55 | 0.43 |
| ... | ... | ... | ... | ... | ... | ... | ... | ... | ... | ... | ... | ... |
| ... | ... | ... | ... | ... | ... | ... | ... | ... | ... | ... | ... | ... |
| ... | ... | ... | ... | ... | ... | ... | ... | ... | ... | ... | ... | ... |
| 2 389 | 2 384 | 2 364 | 2 315 | 2 333 | 2 340 | 2 422 | 2 452 | 2 395 | 2 417 | 2 138 | 1 890 | 2 379 |
| 53 285 | 53 584 | 53 554 | 52 806 | 53 584 | 54 123 | 56 367 | 57 414 | 56 396 | 57 234 | 47 502 | 40 169 | 54 835 |
| 0.51 | 0.51 | 0.50 | 0.48 | 0.47 | 0.46 | 0.46 | 0.45 | 0.43 | 0.42 | 0.47 | 0.47 | 0.47 |
| 2 368 | 2 586 | 2 731 | 2 764 | 2 885 | 2 973 | 3 139 | 3 269 | 3 300 | 3 467 | 2 155 | 1 304 | 2 952 |
| 52 819 | 58 141 | 61 862 | 63 060 | 66 281 | 68 761 | 73 051 | 76 546 | 77 714 | 82 102 | 47 873 | 27 711 | 68 034 |
| 0.51 | 0.51 | 0.50 | 0.48 | 0.47 | 0.46 | 0.46 | 0.45 | 0.43 | 0.42 | 0.47 | 0.47 | 0.46 |
| 2 670 | 2 664 | 2 643 | 2 587 | 2 607 | 2 616 | 2 708 | 2 741 | 2 677 | 2 702 | 2 390 | 2 113 | 2 659 |
| 59 563 | 59 898 | 59 864 | 59 028 | 59 898 | 60 500 | 63 008 | 64 179 | 63 042 | 63 978 | 53 099 | 44 902 | 61 296 |
| 0.47 | 0.46 | 0.46 | 0.44 | 0.43 | 0.42 | 0.43 | 0.42 | 0.39 | 0.39 | 0.43 | 0.43 | 0.43 |
| 3 136 | 3 066 | 2 774 | 2 022 | 1 895 | 1 913 | 2 652 | 3 033 | 2 665 | 3 456 | 2 138 | 1 586 | 2 659 |
| 69 958 | 68 930 | 62 827 | 46 133 | 43 538 | 44 237 | 61 706 | 71 018 | 62 764 | 81 837 | 47 501 | 33 708 | 61 295 |
| 0.61 | 0.58 | 0.54 | 0.39 | 0.36 | 0.35 | 0.42 | 0.43 | 0.34 | 0.42 | 0.47 | 0.56 | 0.43 |
| 234 | 201 | 195 | 160 | 94 | 97 | 111 | 118 | 104 | 102 | 154 | 169 | 139 |
| 6 137 | 5 424 | 5 410 | 4 588 | 2 760 | 2 953 | 3 475 | 3 826 | 3 486 | 3 512 | 3 973 | 3 789 | 4 157 |
| 0.05 | 0.05 | 0.05 | 0.04 | 0.02 | 0.02 | 0.02 | 0.02 | 0.02 | 0.02 | 0.04 | 0.06 | 0.03 |
| 247 | 244 | 232 | 262 | 207 | 229 | 233 | 237 | 243 | 244 | 226 | 202 | 239 |
| 6 476 | 6 578 | 6 459 | 7 503 | 6 116 | 6 964 | 7 317 | 7 678 | 8 095 | 8 404 | 5 841 | 4 522 | 7 159 |
| ... | ... | ... | ... | ... | ... | ... | ... | ... | ... | ... | ... | ... |
| 141 | 142 | 134 | 132 | 132 | 132 | 132 | 130 | 129 | 124 | 154 | 177 | 133 |
| 3 709 | 3 829 | 3 736 | 3 793 | 3 908 | 4 008 | 4 128 | 4 211 | 4 295 | 4 283 | 3 973 | 3 956 | 3 990 |
| 0.04 | 0.04 | 0.04 | 0.03 | 0.03 | 0.03 | 0.03 | 0.03 | 0.03 | 0.03 | 0.04 | 0.05 | 0.03 |
| 140 | 154 | 155 | 158 | 164 | 168 | 171 | 174 | 177 | 178 | 147 | 117 | 166 |
| 3 677 | 4 154 | 4 316 | 4 529 | 4 834 | 5 092 | 5 350 | 5 614 | 5 918 | 6 145 | 3 791 | 2 619 | 4 963 |
| 0.04 | 0.04 | 0.04 | 0.03 | 0.03 | 0.03 | 0.03 | 0.03 | 0.03 | 0.03 | 0.04 | 0.04 | 0.03 |
| 147 | 148 | 140 | 138 | 138 | 137 | 137 | 136 | 134 | 130 | 160 | 184 | 139 |
| 3 865 | 3 989 | 3 893 | 3 951 | 4 071 | 4 176 | 4 301 | 4 387 | 4 475 | 4 463 | 4 139 | 4 122 | 4 157 |
| 0.03 | 0.03 | 0.03 | 0.03 | 0.03 | 0.03 | 0.03 | 0.03 | 0.03 | 0.03 | 0.03 | 0.04 | 0.03 |
| 234 | 201 | 195 | 160 | 94 | 97 | 111 | 118 | 104 | 102 | 154 | 169 | 139 |
| 6 137 | 5 425 | 5 411 | 4 588 | 2 760 | 2 953 | 3 475 | 3 826 | 3 486 | 3 511 | 3 973 | 3 788 | 4 157 |
| 0.05 | 0.05 | 0.05 | 0.04 | 0.02 | 0.02 | 0.02 | 0.02 | 0.02 | 0.02 | 0.04 | 0.06 | 0.03 |

**Table A.1**     Total and per capita gross domestic product of individual countries or areas,
expressed in United States dollars, and their individual shares of gross world
product, based on alternative conversion rates, 1970–1989 [*cont.*]

| Country or area | 1970 (1) | 1971 (2) | 1972 (3) | 1973 (4) | 1974 (5) | 1975 (6) | 1976 (7) | 1977 (8) | 1978 (9) | 1979 (10) |
|---|---|---|---|---|---|---|---|---|---|---|
| **Zambia** | | | | | | | | | | |
| **1. MER** | | | | | | | | | | |
| 1a. Per capita GDP | 427 | 386 | 426 | 535 | 627 | 509 | 526 | 487 | 527 | 607 |
| 1b. GDP | 1 790 | 1 665 | 1 888 | 2 440 | 2 943 | 2 463 | 2 626 | 2 514 | 2 813 | 3 355 |
| 1c. % of GWP | 0.06 | 0.05 | 0.05 | 0.05 | 0.05 | 0.04 | 0.04 | 0.03 | 0.03 | 0.03 |
| **2. PPPs** | | | | | | | | | | |
| 2a. Per capita GDP | 566 | 526 | 588 | 679 | 767 | 684 | 699 | 626 | 645 | 663 |
| 2b. GDP | 2 371 | 2 266 | 2 606 | 3 096 | 3 600 | 3 312 | 3 495 | 3 233 | 3 441 | 3 665 |
| 2c. % of GWP | ... | ... | ... | ... | ... | ... | ... | ... | ... | ... |
| **3. Absolute 1970–1989 PARE** | | | | | | | | | | |
| 3a. Per capita GDP | 585 | 569 | 603 | 581 | 602 | 570 | 576 | 531 | 517 | 483 |
| 3b. GDP | 2 453 | 2 451 | 2 676 | 2 651 | 2 829 | 2 760 | 2 879 | 2 741 | 2 757 | 2 673 |
| 3c. % of GWP | 0.03 | 0.03 | 0.03 | 0.03 | 0.03 | 0.03 | 0.03 | 0.03 | 0.03 | 0.03 |
| **4. Relative 1970–1989 PARE** | | | | | | | | | | |
| 4a. Per capita GDP | 285 | 291 | 324 | 332 | 376 | 391 | 420 | 413 | 431 | 439 |
| 4b. GDP | 1 196 | 1 256 | 1 434 | 1 515 | 1 764 | 1 891 | 2 096 | 2 130 | 2 299 | 2 428 |
| 4c. % of GWP | 0.03 | 0.03 | 0.03 | 0.03 | 0.03 | 0.03 | 0.03 | 0.03 | 0.03 | 0.03 |
| **5. Absolute 1980–1989 PARE** | | | | | | | | | | |
| 5a. Per capita GDP | 634 | 615 | 653 | 629 | 652 | 617 | 624 | 575 | 559 | 523 |
| 5b. GDP | 2 655 | 2 653 | 2 896 | 2 869 | 3 062 | 2 987 | 3 116 | 2 967 | 2 984 | 2 893 |
| 5c. % of GWP | 0.03 | 0.03 | 0.03 | 0.03 | 0.03 | 0.03 | 0.03 | 0.03 | 0.02 | 0.02 |
| **6. WA** | | | | | | | | | | |
| 6a. Per capita GDP | 427 | 386 | 426 | 535 | 626 | 508 | 519 | 487 | 527 | 606 |
| 6b. GDP | 1 789 | 1 665 | 1 887 | 2 439 | 2 941 | 2 461 | 2 594 | 2 515 | 2 811 | 3 354 |
| 6c. % of GWP | 0.06 | 0.05 | 0.05 | 0.05 | 0.05 | 0.04 | 0.04 | 0.03 | 0.03 | 0.03 |
| **Zimbabwe** | | | | | | | | | | |
| **1. MER** | | | | | | | | | | |
| 1a. Per capita GDP | 287 | 322 | 383 | 460 | 536 | 573 | 547 | 537 | 519 | 600 |
| 1b. GDP | 1 511 | 1 747 | 2 147 | 2 659 | 3 198 | 3 518 | 3 460 | 3 500 | 3 484 | 4 150 |
| 1c. % of GWP | 0.05 | 0.05 | 0.05 | 0.05 | 0.06 | 0.06 | 0.05 | 0.05 | 0.04 | 0.04 |
| **2. PPPs** | | | | | | | | | | |
| 2a. Per capita GDP | 457 | 529 | 576 | 612 | 704 | 736 | 723 | 693 | 699 | 731 |
| 2b. GDP | 2 403 | 2 873 | 3 228 | 3 538 | 4 199 | 4 522 | 4 576 | 4 521 | 4 695 | 5 060 |
| 2c. % of GWP | ... | ... | ... | ... | ... | ... | ... | ... | ... | ... |
| **3. Absolute 1970–1989 PARE** | | | | | | | | | | |
| 3a. Per capita GDP | 595 | 628 | 659 | 658 | 654 | 640 | 617 | 561 | 533 | 537 |
| 3b. GDP | 3 130 | 3 409 | 3 692 | 3 804 | 3 899 | 3 935 | 3 904 | 3 660 | 3 581 | 3 717 |
| 3c. % of GWP | 0.04 | 0.05 | 0.05 | 0.05 | 0.05 | 0.05 | 0.04 | 0.04 | 0.04 | 0.04 |
| **4. Relative 1970–1989 PARE** | | | | | | | | | | |
| 4a. Per capita GDP | 290 | 322 | 353 | 376 | 408 | 439 | 449 | 436 | 445 | 488 |
| 4b. GDP | 1 526 | 1 748 | 1 979 | 2 174 | 2 431 | 2 696 | 2 842 | 2 844 | 2 986 | 3 376 |
| 4c. % of GWP | 0.04 | 0.05 | 0.05 | 0.05 | 0.05 | 0.05 | 0.04 | 0.04 | 0.04 | 0.04 |
| **5. Absolute 1980–1989 PARE** | | | | | | | | | | |
| 5a. Per capita GDP | 683 | 721 | 757 | 756 | 751 | 736 | 708 | 645 | 612 | 617 |
| 5b. GDP | 3 595 | 3 916 | 4 241 | 4 368 | 4 478 | 4 519 | 4 484 | 4 204 | 4 113 | 4 270 |
| 5c. % of GWP | 0.04 | 0.04 | 0.04 | 0.04 | 0.04 | 0.04 | 0.04 | 0.04 | 0.03 | 0.03 |
| **6. WA** | | | | | | | | | | |
| 6a. Per capita GDP | 287 | 322 | 383 | 459 | 536 | 570 | 547 | 537 | 519 | 600 |
| 6b. GDP | 1 511 | 1 747 | 2 147 | 2 653 | 3 193 | 3 505 | 3 462 | 3 499 | 3 483 | 4 151 |
| 6c. % of GWP | 0.05 | 0.05 | 0.05 | 0.05 | 0.06 | 0.06 | 0.05 | 0.05 | 0.04 | 0.04 |

Note:  PPPs for 1986–1989 have been estimated by the Statistical Division, United Nations Secretariat.
Three dots (...) indicate that data are not available.

a   Estimated by the Statistical Division, United Nations Secretariat, using the *World Bank Atlas* methodology.
b   Through accession of the German Democratic Republic to the Federal Republic of Germany with effect from 3 October 1990, the two German States have united to form one sovereign State. As from the date of unification, the Federal Republic of Germany acts in the United Nations under the designation of "Germany". All data shown which pertain to Germany prior to 3 October 1990 are indicated separately for the Federal Republic of Germany and the former German Democratic Republic based on their respective territories at the time indicated.

| 1980 (11) | 1981 (12) | 1982 (13) | 1983 (14) | 1984 (15) | 1985 (16) | 1986 (17) | 1987 (18) | 1988 (19) | 1989 (20) | Averages 1970-89 (21) | 1970-79 (22) | 1980-89 (23) |
|---|---|---|---|---|---|---|---|---|---|---|---|---|
| 677 | 673 | 624 | 517 | 408 | 374 | 244 | 294 | 431 | 416 | 495 | 514 | 455 |
| 3 883 | 4 015 | 3 874 | 3 342 | 2 749 | 2 619 | 1 776 | 2 222 | 3 381 | 3 383 | 2 787 | 2 450 | 3 124 |
| 0.03 | 0.03 | 0.03 | 0.03 | 0.02 | 0.02 | 0.01 | 0.01 | 0.02 | 0.02 | 0.03 | 0.04 | 0.02 |
| 725 | 783 | 694 | 751 | 738 | 751 | 743 | 756 | 800 | 804 | 739 | 652 | 759 |
| 4 161 | 4 670 | 4 310 | 4 859 | 4 970 | 5 265 | 5 410 | 5 714 | 6 277 | 6 542 | 4 163 | 3 108 | 5 218 |
| ... | ... | ... | ... | ... | ... | ... | ... | ... | ... | ... | ... | ... |
| 480 | 490 | 458 | 431 | 412 | 403 | 390 | 386 | 395 | 381 | 495 | 563 | 420 |
| 2 754 | 2 924 | 2 842 | 2 786 | 2 776 | 2 822 | 2 842 | 2 918 | 3 101 | 3 105 | 2 787 | 2 687 | 2 887 |
| 0.03 | 0.03 | 0.03 | 0.03 | 0.02 | 0.02 | 0.02 | 0.02 | 0.02 | 0.02 | 0.03 | 0.03 | 0.02 |
| 476 | 532 | 529 | 514 | 510 | 512 | 506 | 515 | 545 | 547 | 478 | 378 | 521 |
| 2 730 | 3 173 | 3 283 | 3 327 | 3 434 | 3 585 | 3 683 | 3 890 | 4 273 | 4 454 | 2 692 | 1 801 | 3 583 |
| 0.03 | 0.03 | 0.03 | 0.03 | 0.02 | 0.02 | 0.02 | 0.02 | 0.02 | 0.02 | 0.03 | 0.03 | 0.02 |
| 519 | 530 | 495 | 466 | 446 | 436 | 422 | 418 | 428 | 413 | 535 | 610 | 455 |
| 2 981 | 3 165 | 3 076 | 3 015 | 3 004 | 3 054 | 3 076 | 3 158 | 3 356 | 3 361 | 3 016 | 2 908 | 3 124 |
| 0.02 | 0.02 | 0.02 | 0.02 | 0.02 | 0.02 | 0.02 | 0.02 | 0.02 | 0.02 | 0.02 | 0.03 | 0.02 |
| 677 | 672 | 623 | 513 | 404 | 321 | 229 | 275 | 428 | 388 | 486 | 513 | 441 |
| 3 884 | 4 008 | 3 871 | 3 321 | 2 720 | 2 252 | 1 664 | 2 078 | 3 354 | 3 159 | 2 738 | 2 445 | 3 031 |
| 0.03 | 0.03 | 0.03 | 0.03 | 0.02 | 0.02 | 0.01 | 0.01 | 0.02 | 0.02 | 0.03 | 0.04 | 0.02 |
| 751 | 878 | 907 | 800 | 640 | 546 | 588 | 618 | 649 | 631 | 614 | 485 | 697 |
| 5 351 | 6 443 | 6 865 | 6 237 | 5 148 | 4 527 | 5 031 | 5 455 | 5 911 | 5 931 | 4 314 | 2 937 | 5 690 |
| 0.05 | 0.06 | 0.06 | 0.05 | 0.04 | 0.04 | 0.03 | 0.03 | 0.03 | 0.03 | 0.04 | 0.05 | 0.04 |
| 888 | 1 094 | 1 184 | 1 193 | 1 085 | 1 090 | 1 106 | 1 091 | 1 150 | 1 224 | 933 | 655 | 1 120 |
| 6 325 | 8 034 | 8 959 | 9 305 | 8 721 | 9 037 | 9 462 | 9 634 | 10 475 | 11 515 | 6 554 | 3 962 | 9 147 |
| ... | ... | ... | ... | ... | ... | ... | ... | ... | ... | ... | ... | ... |
| 577 | 630 | 627 | 618 | 588 | 610 | 607 | 582 | 593 | 607 | 614 | 607 | 607 |
| 4 111 | 4 625 | 4 747 | 4 822 | 4 730 | 5 059 | 5 193 | 5 139 | 5 407 | 5 709 | 4 314 | 3 673 | 4 954 |
| 0.04 | 0.04 | 0.04 | 0.04 | 0.04 | 0.04 | 0.04 | 0.04 | 0.04 | 0.04 | 0.04 | 0.04 | 0.04 |
| 572 | 684 | 725 | 739 | 728 | 775 | 787 | 776 | 818 | 871 | 615 | 406 | 757 |
| 4 075 | 5 019 | 5 484 | 5 759 | 5 851 | 6 427 | 6 730 | 6 852 | 7 450 | 8 189 | 4 322 | 2 460 | 6 184 |
| 0.04 | 0.04 | 0.04 | 0.04 | 0.04 | 0.04 | 0.04 | 0.04 | 0.04 | 0.04 | 0.04 | 0.04 | 0.04 |
| 662 | 724 | 721 | 710 | 676 | 701 | 697 | 669 | 681 | 697 | 706 | 697 | 697 |
| 4 721 | 5 312 | 5 452 | 5 539 | 5 433 | 5 810 | 5 964 | 5 902 | 6 210 | 6 557 | 4 954 | 4 219 | 5 690 |
| 0.04 | 0.04 | 0.04 | 0.04 | 0.04 | 0.04 | 0.04 | 0.04 | 0.04 | 0.04 | 0.04 | 0.04 | 0.04 |
| 751 | 875 | 905 | 798 | 633 | 545 | 587 | 632 | 647 | 625 | 614 | 485 | 696 |
| 5 355 | 6 423 | 6 846 | 6 225 | 5 093 | 4 522 | 5 026 | 5 581 | 5 893 | 5 878 | 4 309 | 2 935 | 5 684 |
| 0.05 | 0.05 | 0.06 | 0.05 | 0.04 | 0.04 | 0.03 | 0.03 | 0.03 | 0.03 | 0.04 | 0.05 | 0.04 |

c   On 22 May 1990, the Yemen Arab Republic and the People's Democratic Republic of Yemen merged to form a single sovereign state, the "Republic of Yemen". Data prior to that date are indicated separately for Yemen (excluding former Democratic Yemen), and former Democratic Yemen.

d   Unless otherwise indicated, data privided for Yugoslavia are prior to 1 January 1992 and refer to the Socialist Federal Republic of Yugoslavia which was composed of six republics.

**Table A.2**  Conversion rates for individual countries or areas, expressed as the number of local currency units per United States dollar, 1970–1989

| Country or area | 1970 (1) | 1971 (2) | 1972 (3) | 1973 (4) | 1974 (5) | 1975 (6) | 1976 (7) | 1977 (8) | 1978 (9) | 1979 (10) |
|---|---|---|---|---|---|---|---|---|---|---|
| **Afghanistan:** Afghanis | | | | | | | | | | |
| 1. MER | 45.000 | 45.000 | 45.000 | 45.000 | 45.000 | 45.000 | 45.000 | 45.000 | 45.000 | 43.730 |
| 2. PPPs | 17.874 | 18.810 | 16.348 | 15.705 | 16.623 | 16.051 | 15.781 | 16.110 | 16.133 | 16.979 |
| 3. Absolute 1970–1989 PARE | 19.178 | 20.832 | 26.256 | 24.469 | 27.996 | 29.669 | 30.166 | 33.243 | 36.044 | 44.836 |
| 4. Relative 1970–1989 PARE | 39.334 | 40.641 | 48.976 | 42.800 | 44.894 | 43.305 | 41.441 | 42.782 | 43.234 | 49.371 |
| 5. Absolute 1980–1989 PARE | 14.697 | 15.965 | 20.122 | 18.752 | 21.455 | 22.737 | 23.118 | 25.476 | 27.623 | 34.361 |
| 6. WA [a] | 49.471 | 49.156 | 54.442 | 46.598 | 48.156 | 49.084 | 46.414 | 48.337 | 49.187 | 53.467 |
| **Albania:** New leks | | | | | | | | | | |
| 1. MER | 5.000 | 5.000 | 5.000 | 5.000 | 5.000 | 5.000 | 5.000 | 5.000 | 5.000 | 5.000 |
| 2. PPPs | ... | ... | ... | ... | ... | ... | ... | ... | ... | ... |
| 3. Absolute 1970–1989 PARE | 3.519 | 4.050 | 4.162 | 4.199 | 4.802 | 5.101 | 5.041 | 5.032 | 4.990 | 5.006 |
| 4. Relative 1970–1989 PARE | 7.217 | 7.901 | 7.764 | 7.345 | 7.701 | 7.445 | 6.925 | 6.475 | 5.986 | 5.512 |
| 5. Absolute 1980–1989 PARE | 3.374 | 3.883 | 3.991 | 4.026 | 4.604 | 4.890 | 4.833 | 4.824 | 4.784 | 4.799 |
| 6. WA [a] | 5.403 | 5.654 | 5.351 | 5.076 | 5.495 | 5.461 | 5.063 | 4.974 | 4.970 | 4.997 |
| **Algeria:** Algerian dinars | | | | | | | | | | |
| 1. MER | 4.937 | 4.913 | 4.484 | 3.959 | 4.181 | 3.949 | 4.164 | 4.147 | 3.966 | 3.853 |
| 2. PPPs | 3.674 | 3.585 | 3.722 | 3.710 | 3.692 | 3.811 | 3.952 | 4.113 | 4.508 | 4.309 |
| 3. Absolute 1970–1989 PARE | 1.333 | 1.526 | 1.523 | 1.661 | 2.426 | 2.540 | 2.878 | 3.098 | 3.379 | 3.855 |
| 4. Relative 1970–1989 PARE | 2.735 | 2.977 | 2.841 | 2.905 | 3.890 | 3.708 | 3.953 | 3.987 | 4.053 | 4.245 |
| 5. Absolute 1980–1989 PARE | 1.100 | 1.259 | 1.257 | 1.370 | 2.002 | 2.096 | 2.375 | 2.557 | 2.788 | 3.181 |
| 6. WA | 4.937 | 4.913 | 4.484 | 3.959 | 4.181 | 3.949 | 4.164 | 4.147 | 3.966 | 3.853 |
| **Angola:** Angolan kwanza | | | | | | | | | | |
| 1. MER | 28.750 | 28.211 | 27.011 | 24.673 | 25.408 | 25.408 | 25.553 | 30.223 | 29.918 | 29.918 |
| 2. PPPs | 15.713 | 15.566 | 16.633 | 17.618 | 19.954 | 21.074 | 25.998 | 30.453 | 32.050 | 33.900 |
| 3. Absolute 1970–1989 PARE | 6.233 | 6.474 | 6.983 | 8.360 | 11.317 | 14.167 | 18.274 | 22.940 | 25.816 | 29.662 |
| 4. Relative 1970–1989 PARE | 12.784 | 12.629 | 13.025 | 14.622 | 18.147 | 20.679 | 25.104 | 29.524 | 30.965 | 32.662 |
| 5. Absolute 1980–1989 PARE | 3.965 | 4.118 | 4.442 | 5.318 | 7.199 | 9.012 | 11.625 | 14.593 | 16.423 | 18.869 |
| 6. WA [a] | 33.959 | 31.015 | 29.883 | 31.146 | 34.194 | 33.010 | 33.118 | 34.481 | 33.343 | 34.457 |
| **Anguilla:** East Caribbean dollars | | | | | | | | | | |
| 1. MER | 2.000 | 1.964 | 1.922 | 1.959 | 2.053 | 2.170 | 2.615 | 2.700 | 2.700 | 2.700 |
| 2. PPPs | ... | ... | ... | ... | ... | ... | ... | ... | ... | ... |
| 3. Absolute 1970–1989 PARE | 1.410 | 1.458 | 1.526 | 1.564 | 1.666 | 1.705 | 1.766 | 1.850 | 1.921 | 1.985 |
| 4. Relative 1970–1989 PARE | 2.892 | 2.844 | 2.846 | 2.736 | 2.672 | 2.488 | 2.427 | 2.381 | 2.304 | 2.186 |
| 5. Absolute 1980–1989 PARE | 1.293 | 1.336 | 1.398 | 1.434 | 1.527 | 1.563 | 1.619 | 1.696 | 1.761 | 1.820 |
| 6. WA [a] | 2.079 | 2.061 | 2.047 | 2.012 | 2.080 | 2.135 | 2.347 | 2.598 | 2.783 | 2.796 |
| **Antigua and Barbuda:** East Caribbean dollars | | | | | | | | | | |
| 1. MER | 2.000 | 1.964 | 1.922 | 1.959 | 2.053 | 2.170 | 2.615 | 2.700 | 2.700 | 2.700 |
| 2. PPPs | ... | ... | ... | ... | ... | ... | ... | ... | ... | ... |
| 3. Absolute 1970–1989 PARE | 1.018 | 1.092 | 1.170 | 1.312 | 1.418 | 1.621 | 1.783 | 1.954 | 2.135 | 2.375 |
| 4. Relative 1970–1989 PARE | 2.088 | 2.131 | 2.183 | 2.295 | 2.273 | 2.366 | 2.450 | 2.515 | 2.560 | 2.615 |
| 5. Absolute 1980–1989 PARE | 0.846 | 0.908 | 0.972 | 1.091 | 1.178 | 1.347 | 1.482 | 1.624 | 1.774 | 1.974 |
| 6. WA | 2.000 | 1.972 | 1.922 | 1.959 | 2.053 | 2.170 | 2.615 | 2.700 | 2.700 | 2.700 |
| **Argentina:** Australes per thousand US dollars | | | | | | | | | | |
| 1. MER | 0.000400 | 0.000500 | 0.000800 | 0.000900 | 0.000900 | 0.004000 | 0.010000 | 0.040 | 0.080 | 0.130 |
| 2. PPPs | 0.000188 | 0.000241 | 0.000374 | 0.000589 | 0.000693 | 0.001866 | 0.009518 | 0.023 | 0.057 | 0.132 |
| 3. Absolute 1970–1989 PARE | 0.000157 | 0.000219 | 0.000346 | 0.000556 | 0.000738 | 0.002168 | 0.011506 | 0.030 | 0.077 | 0.196 |
| 4. Relative 1970–1989 PARE | 0.000322 | 0.000427 | 0.000645 | 0.000972 | 0.001184 | 0.003164 | 0.015806 | 0.038 | 0.092 | 0.216 |
| 5. Absolute 1980–1989 PARE | 0.000126 | 0.000176 | 0.000278 | 0.000447 | 0.000594 | 0.001744 | 0.009259 | 0.024 | 0.062 | 0.158 |
| 6. WA | 0.000379 | 0.000452 | 0.000500 | 0.000500 | 0.000500 | 0.003658 | 0.013998 | 0.041 | 0.080 | 0.132 |

|  |  |  |  |  |  |  |  |  |  | Averages | | |
| 1980 (11) | 1981 (12) | 1982 (13) | 1983 (14) | 1984 (15) | 1985 (16) | 1986 (17) | 1987 (18) | 1988 (19) | 1989 (20) | 1970–89 (21) | 1970–79 (22) | 1980–89 (23) |
|---|---|---|---|---|---|---|---|---|---|---|---|---|
| 44.130 | 49.480 | 50.600 | 50.600 | 50.600 | 50.600 | 50.600 | 50.600 | 50.600 | 50.600 | 48.369 | 44.786 | 50.031 |
| 15.630 | 17.032 | 17.792 | 17.450 | 18.758 | 21.075 | 20.862 | 24.364 | 31.901 | 44.400 | 20.479 | 16.480 | 22.776 |
| 45.236 | 47.409 | 49.527 | 48.569 | 52.211 | 58.665 | 59.237 | 71.170 | 96.314 | 139.549 | 48.369 | 29.789 | 65.284 |
| 45.635 | 43.693 | 42.875 | 40.672 | 42.210 | 46.176 | 45.708 | 53.382 | 69.894 | 97.281 | 49.886 | 43.954 | 52.849 |
| 34.667 | 36.332 | 37.956 | 37.222 | 40.013 | 44.959 | 45.397 | 54.543 | 73.812 | 106.946 | 37.068 | 22.829 | 50.031 |
| 48.242 | 47.323 | 50.202 | 50.304 | 52.779 | 56.191 | 53.034 | 57.593 | 67.116 | 74.376 | 54.603 | 49.458 | 57.069 |
|  |  |  |  |  |  |  |  |  |  |  |  |  |
| 7.000 | 7.000 | 7.000 | 7.000 | 7.000 | 7.000 | 7.000 | 7.000 | 6.670 | 6.130 | 6.183 | 5.000 | 6.860 |
| ... | ... | ... | ... | ... | ... | ... | ... | ... | ... | ... | ... | ... |
| 7.085 | 7.088 | 7.086 | 7.144 | 7.336 | 7.462 | 7.233 | 7.393 | 7.068 | 6.687 | 6.183 | 4.664 | 7.155 |
| 7.147 | 6.533 | 6.134 | 5.982 | 5.931 | 5.874 | 5.581 | 5.545 | 5.129 | 4.662 | 6.004 | 6.772 | 5.733 |
| 6.793 | 6.796 | 6.794 | 6.849 | 7.034 | 7.155 | 6.935 | 7.088 | 6.776 | 6.411 | 5.928 | 4.471 | 6.860 |
| 7.058 | 7.028 | 6.999 | 7.037 | 7.145 | 7.144 | 6.895 | 7.030 | 6.734 | 6.258 | 6.299 | 5.189 | 6.915 |
|  |  |  |  |  |  |  |  |  |  |  |  |  |
| 3.838 | 4.316 | 4.592 | 4.789 | 4.983 | 5.028 | 4.700 | 4.800 | 5.900 | 7.600 | 4.849 | 4.095 | 5.074 |
| 4.334 | 4.561 | 4.789 | 5.325 | 4.879 | 5.176 | 4.911 | 5.326 | 5.214 | 5.689 | 4.829 | 4.027 | 5.072 |
| 4.542 | 5.221 | 5.319 | 5.694 | 5.995 | 6.303 | 6.100 | 6.805 | 6.886 | 7.822 | 4.849 | 2.581 | 6.148 |
| 4.582 | 4.811 | 4.604 | 4.769 | 4.847 | 4.961 | 4.707 | 5.104 | 4.997 | 5.453 | 4.632 | 3.725 | 4.920 |
| 3.748 | 4.309 | 4.390 | 4.700 | 4.948 | 5.202 | 5.034 | 5.616 | 5.683 | 6.455 | 4.002 | 2.130 | 5.074 |
| 3.838 | 4.316 | 4.592 | 4.789 | 4.983 | 5.028 | 4.702 | 4.850 | 5.915 | 7.609 | 4.855 | 4.095 | 5.082 |
|  |  |  |  |  |  |  |  |  |  |  |  |  |
| 29.918 | 29.918 | 29.918 | 29.918 | 29.918 | 29.918 | 29.918 | 29.900 | 29.900 | 29.900 | 29.358 | 27.690 | 29.911 |
| 35.842 | 35.819 | 36.288 | 36.454 | 42.946 | 55.491 | 56.407 | 59.158 | 59.441 | 62.644 | 38.238 | 23.174 | 47.763 |
| 37.434 | 40.406 | 42.158 | 43.573 | 46.722 | 45.500 | 47.180 | 50.903 | 52.864 | 57.996 | 29.358 | 13.198 | 47.019 |
| 37.764 | 37.239 | 36.496 | 36.488 | 37.772 | 35.814 | 36.405 | 38.180 | 38.363 | 40.430 | 31.594 | 20.747 | 37.629 |
| 23.813 | 25.704 | 26.819 | 27.719 | 29.722 | 28.945 | 30.014 | 32.382 | 33.629 | 36.894 | 18.676 | 8.396 | 29.911 |
| 37.019 | 34.322 | 31.609 | 31.034 | 31.718 | 30.098 | 30.384 | 31.883 | 31.491 | 32.257 | 32.180 | 33.137 | 31.898 |
|  |  |  |  |  |  |  |  |  |  |  |  |  |
| 2.700 | 2.700 | 2.700 | 2.700 | 2.700 | 2.700 | 2.700 | 2.700 | 2.700 | 2.700 | 2.634 | 2.354 | 2.700 |
| ... | ... | ... | ... | ... | ... | ... | ... | ... | ... | ... | ... | ... |
| 2.074 | 2.134 | 2.222 | 2.313 | 2.409 | 2.804 | 3.114 | 3.334 | 3.496 | 3.799 | 2.634 | 1.740 | 2.946 |
| 2.093 | 1.967 | 1.923 | 1.937 | 1.947 | 2.207 | 2.403 | 2.501 | 2.537 | 2.648 | 2.336 | 2.462 | 2.312 |
| 1.901 | 1.956 | 2.036 | 2.120 | 2.208 | 2.570 | 2.854 | 3.056 | 3.204 | 3.482 | 2.414 | 1.595 | 2.700 |
| 2.812 | 2.793 | 2.801 | 2.812 | 2.813 | 3.039 | 3.063 | 2.933 | 2.854 | 2.904 | 2.793 | 2.366 | 2.901 |
|  |  |  |  |  |  |  |  |  |  |  |  |  |
| 2.700 | 2.700 | 2.700 | 2.700 | 2.700 | 2.700 | 2.700 | 2.700 | 2.700 | 2.700 | 2.595 | 2.313 | 2.700 |
| ... | ... | ... | ... | ... | ... | ... | ... | ... | ... | ... | ... | ... |
| 2.298 | 2.464 | 2.689 | 2.827 | 2.981 | 3.187 | 3.323 | 3.584 | 4.005 | 4.034 | 2.595 | 1.590 | 3.249 |
| 2.319 | 2.271 | 2.328 | 2.367 | 2.410 | 2.508 | 2.564 | 2.688 | 2.906 | 2.812 | 2.527 | 2.384 | 2.577 |
| 1.910 | 2.048 | 2.235 | 2.349 | 2.477 | 2.648 | 2.762 | 2.978 | 3.328 | 3.352 | 2.157 | 1.321 | 2.700 |
| 2.700 | 2.700 | 2.700 | 2.700 | 2.700 | 2.700 | 2.700 | 2.700 | 2.700 | 2.700 | 2.596 | 2.314 | 2.700 |
|  |  |  |  |  |  |  |  |  |  |  |  |  |
| 0.180 | 0.440 | 2.590 | 10.530 | 67.650 | 602 | 940 | 2100 | 8800 | 423000 | 19928 | 0.047 | 31171 |
| 0.231 | 0.444 | 1.286 | 5.822 | 39.521 | 312 | 544 | 1206 | 5435 | 178070 | 13068 | 0.031 | 20397 |
| 0.384 | 0.795 | 2.255 | 10.122 | 76.266 | 598 | 1063 | 2423 | 11292 | 385145 | 19928 | 0.035 | 38734 |
| 0.388 | 0.733 | 1.952 | 8.476 | 61.656 | 471 | 820 | 1818 | 8195 | 268488 | 20676 | 0.052 | 31339 |
| 0.309 | 0.640 | 1.814 | 8.145 | 61.373 | 481 | 855 | 1950 | 9087 | 309937 | 16037 | 0.028 | 31171 |
| 0.184 | 0.440 | 2.592 | 10.530 | 67.649 | 602 | 943 | 2144 | 8753 | 423340 | 18578 | 0.039 | 31222 |

**Table A.2**  Conversion rates for individual countries or areas, expressed as the number of
local currency units per United States dollar, 1970–1989 [*cont.*]

| Country or area | 1970 (1) | 1971 (2) | 1972 (3) | 1973 (4) | 1974 (5) | 1975 (6) | 1976 (7) | 1977 (8) | 1978 (9) | 1979 (10) |
|---|---|---|---|---|---|---|---|---|---|---|
| **Australia:** Australian dollars | | | | | | | | | | |
| 1.  MER | 0.893 | 0.880 | 0.839 | 0.704 | 0.695 | 0.763 | 0.816 | 0.902 | 0.874 | 0.895 |
| 2.  PPPs | 0.766 | 0.781 | 0.790 | 0.829 | 0.902 | 0.956 | 1.017 | 1.054 | 1.061 | 1.066 |
| 3.  Absolute 1970–1989 PARE | 0.338 | 0.359 | 0.393 | 0.452 | 0.535 | 0.617 | 0.686 | 0.738 | 0.800 | 0.888 |
| 4.  Relative 1970–1989 PARE | 0.694 | 0.701 | 0.733 | 0.790 | 0.858 | 0.901 | 0.942 | 0.950 | 0.960 | 0.977 |
| 5.  Absolute 1980–1989 PARE | 0.280 | 0.297 | 0.325 | 0.374 | 0.443 | 0.511 | 0.568 | 0.611 | 0.662 | 0.734 |
| 6.  WA | 0.893 | 0.893 | 0.856 | 0.781 | 0.679 | 0.732 | 0.793 | 0.872 | 0.887 | 0.880 |
| **Austria:** Austrian schillings | | | | | | | | | | |
| 1.  MER | 26.000 | 24.914 | 23.115 | 19.580 | 18.693 | 17.417 | 17.940 | 16.527 | 14.522 | 13.368 |
| 2.  PPPs | 17.771 | 17.714 | 18.083 | 18.017 | 18.123 | 17.640 | 17.736 | 17.510 | 17.268 | 16.505 |
| 3.  Absolute 1970–1989 PARE | 8.314 | 8.830 | 9.501 | 10.265 | 11.241 | 11.966 | 12.640 | 13.283 | 14.044 | 14.622 |
| 4.  Relative 1970–1989 PARE | 17.051 | 17.226 | 17.722 | 17.956 | 18.026 | 17.467 | 17.364 | 17.094 | 16.845 | 16.101 |
| 5.  Absolute 1980–1989 PARE | 6.590 | 6.999 | 7.531 | 8.137 | 8.910 | 9.485 | 10.019 | 10.528 | 11.132 | 11.590 |
| 6.  WA | 26.000 | 24.960 | 23.115 | 19.580 | 18.692 | 17.417 | 17.940 | 16.527 | 14.522 | 13.368 |
| **Bahamas:** Bahamian dollars | | | | | | | | | | |
| 1.  MER | 1.000 | 1.000 | 1.000 | 1.000 | 1.000 | 1.000 | 1.000 | 1.000 | 1.000 | 1.000 |
| 2.  PPPs | ... | ... | ... | ... | ... | ... | ... | ... | ... | ... |
| 3.  Absolute 1970–1989 PARE | 0.381 | 0.399 | 0.421 | 0.451 | 0.586 | 0.841 | 0.861 | 0.856 | 0.926 | 1.053 |
| 4.  Relative 1970–1989 PARE | 0.782 | 0.779 | 0.786 | 0.789 | 0.939 | 1.227 | 1.183 | 1.102 | 1.111 | 1.159 |
| 5.  Absolute 1980–1989 PARE | 0.300 | 0.314 | 0.331 | 0.354 | 0.460 | 0.661 | 0.677 | 0.673 | 0.728 | 0.827 |
| 6.  WA | 1.002 | 1.000 | 1.000 | 1.000 | 1.000 | 1.000 | 1.000 | 1.000 | 1.000 | 1.000 |
| **Bahrain:** Bahraini dinars | | | | | | | | | | |
| 1.  MER | 0.476 | 0.475 | 0.439 | 0.399 | 0.395 | 0.396 | 0.396 | 0.396 | 0.387 | 0.381 |
| 2.  PPPs | 0.285 | 0.290 | 0.302 | 0.328 | 0.404 | 0.393 | 0.416 | 0.459 | 0.432 | 0.426 |
| 3.  Absolute 1970–1989 PARE | 0.065 | 0.065 | 0.068 | 0.074 | 0.152 | 0.254 | 0.266 | 0.301 | 0.322 | 0.365 |
| 4.  Relative 1970–1989 PARE | 0.133 | 0.127 | 0.128 | 0.130 | 0.243 | 0.370 | 0.365 | 0.387 | 0.387 | 0.402 |
| 5.  Absolute 1980–1989 PARE | 0.046 | 0.047 | 0.049 | 0.053 | 0.109 | 0.182 | 0.190 | 0.215 | 0.231 | 0.261 |
| 6.  WA | 0.476 | 0.475 | 0.439 | 0.400 | 0.395 | 0.396 | 0.396 | 0.396 | 0.387 | 0.382 |
| **Bangladesh:** Bangladesh taka | | | | | | | | | | |
| 1.  MER | 7.279 | 7.761 | 7.595 | 7.742 | 8.113 | 12.019 | 15.347 | 15.380 | 15.016 | 15.552 |
| 2.  PPPs | 2.076 | 2.017 | 3.173 | 4.117 | 6.601 | 4.554 | 4.068 | 4.402 | 4.652 | 4.939 |
| 3.  Absolute 1970–1989 PARE | 3.349 | 3.471 | 5.313 | 7.376 | 12.312 | 9.691 | 9.670 | 12.332 | 14.160 | 16.006 |
| 4.  Relative 1970–1989 PARE | 6.868 | 6.771 | 9.910 | 12.901 | 19.743 | 14.145 | 13.284 | 15.870 | 16.985 | 17.625 |
| 5.  Absolute 1980–1989 PARE | 3.040 | 3.150 | 4.823 | 6.695 | 11.176 | 8.797 | 8.777 | 11.194 | 12.854 | 14.529 |
| 6.  WA | 4.762 | 4.762 | 6.030 | 7.781 | 7.966 | 8.876 | 14.852 | 15.467 | 15.122 | 15.223 |
| **Barbados:** Barbados dollars | | | | | | | | | | |
| 1.  MER | 2.000 | 1.964 | 1.921 | 1.959 | 2.053 | 2.020 | 2.004 | 2.007 | 2.011 | 2.011 |
| 2.  PPPs | 1.012 | 1.075 | 1.031 | 1.176 | 1.333 | 1.259 | 1.294 | 1.274 | 1.376 | 1.441 |
| 3.  Absolute 1970–1989 PARE | 0.444 | 0.655 | 0.686 | 0.829 | 1.063 | 1.254 | 1.290 | 1.413 | 1.407 | 1.584 |
| 4.  Relative 1970–1989 PARE | 0.911 | 1.278 | 1.280 | 1.449 | 1.705 | 1.830 | 1.773 | 1.818 | 1.688 | 1.744 |
| 5.  Absolute 1980–1989 PARE | 0.331 | 0.488 | 0.511 | 0.617 | 0.792 | 0.934 | 0.961 | 1.052 | 1.048 | 1.180 |
| 6.  WA | 2.000 | 1.975 | 1.921 | 1.959 | 2.053 | 2.020 | 2.004 | 2.007 | 2.011 | 2.011 |
| **Belgium:** Belgian francs | | | | | | | | | | |
| 1.  MER | 50.000 | 48.594 | 44.015 | 38.977 | 38.952 | 36.779 | 38.610 | 35.843 | 31.492 | 29.319 |
| 2.  PPPs | 38.535 | 38.672 | 38.860 | 38.711 | 39.778 | 41.268 | 42.062 | 42.282 | 41.060 | 39.065 |
| 3.  Absolute 1970–1989 PARE | 19.590 | 20.681 | 21.953 | 23.540 | 26.510 | 29.745 | 32.034 | 34.439 | 35.964 | 37.588 |
| 4.  Relative 1970–1989 PARE | 40.178 | 40.346 | 40.949 | 41.174 | 42.512 | 43.416 | 44.007 | 44.322 | 43.137 | 41.390 |
| 5.  Absolute 1980–1989 PARE | 16.687 | 17.616 | 18.700 | 20.052 | 22.582 | 25.337 | 27.288 | 29.336 | 30.635 | 32.018 |
| 6.  WA | 50.000 | 48.870 | 44.015 | 38.977 | 38.952 | 36.779 | 38.605 | 35.843 | 31.492 | 29.319 |

| | | | | | | | | | | Averages | | |
|---|---|---|---|---|---|---|---|---|---|---|---|---|
| 1980 (11) | 1981 (12) | 1982 (13) | 1983 (14) | 1984 (15) | 1985 (16) | 1986 (17) | 1987 (18) | 1988 (19) | 1989 (20) | 1970–89 (21) | 1970–79 (22) | 1980–89 (23) |
| 0.878 | 0.870 | 0.990 | 1.108 | 1.137 | 1.427 | 1.500 | 1.400 | 1.300 | 1.300 | 1.089 | 0.826 | 1.206 |
| 1.067 | 1.085 | 1.143 | 1.209 | 1.261 | 1.330 | 1.400 | 1.470 | 1.556 | 1.582 | 1.225 | 0.954 | 1.341 |
| 0.979 | 1.079 | 1.192 | 1.275 | 1.347 | 1.438 | 1.543 | 1.667 | 1.824 | 1.931 | 1.089 | 0.596 | 1.458 |
| 0.987 | 0.995 | 1.032 | 1.068 | 1.089 | 1.132 | 1.191 | 1.251 | 1.324 | 1.346 | 1.083 | 0.879 | 1.166 |
| 0.810 | 0.893 | 0.986 | 1.056 | 1.115 | 1.190 | 1.277 | 1.380 | 1.510 | 1.598 | 0.901 | 0.493 | 1.206 |
| 0.898 | 0.861 | 0.906 | 1.069 | 1.104 | 1.304 | 1.430 | 1.511 | 1.280 | 1.265 | 1.070 | 0.822 | 1.178 |
| 12.938 | 15.927 | 17.059 | 17.963 | 20.009 | 20.690 | 15.270 | 12.600 | 12.300 | 13.200 | 15.800 | 17.425 | 15.116 |
| 16.035 | 15.881 | 15.819 | 15.912 | 15.735 | 16.043 | 16.328 | 16.206 | 16.017 | 15.826 | 16.459 | 17.532 | 15.984 |
| 15.385 | 16.380 | 17.397 | 18.076 | 18.954 | 19.537 | 20.284 | 20.711 | 21.157 | 21.761 | 15.800 | 11.674 | 19.071 |
| 15.521 | 15.096 | 15.061 | 15.136 | 15.324 | 15.378 | 15.652 | 15.534 | 15.353 | 15.170 | 15.888 | 17.184 | 15.327 |
| 12.195 | 12.983 | 13.789 | 14.327 | 15.024 | 15.486 | 16.078 | 16.416 | 16.770 | 17.248 | 12.524 | 9.253 | 15.116 |
| 12.938 | 15.927 | 17.059 | 17.963 | 20.009 | 20.690 | 15.267 | 12.642 | 12.348 | 13.231 | 15.815 | 17.426 | 15.136 |
| 1.000 | 1.000 | 1.000 | 1.000 | 1.000 | 1.000 | 1.000 | 1.000 | 1.000 | 1.000 | 1.000 | 1.000 | 1.000 |
| ... | ... | ... | ... | ... | ... | ... | ... | ... | ... | ... | ... | ... |
| 1.122 | 1.078 | 1.075 | 1.145 | 1.203 | 1.226 | 1.329 | 1.399 | 1.451 | 1.530 | 1.000 | 0.661 | 1.272 |
| 1.132 | 0.993 | 0.931 | 0.959 | 0.973 | 0.965 | 1.025 | 1.049 | 1.053 | 1.067 | 1.012 | 1.002 | 1.017 |
| 0.882 | 0.847 | 0.845 | 0.900 | 0.946 | 0.964 | 1.044 | 1.100 | 1.140 | 1.203 | 0.786 | 0.520 | 1.000 |
| 1.000 | 1.000 | 1.000 | 1.000 | 1.000 | 1.000 | 1.000 | 1.000 | 1.000 | 1.000 | 1.000 | 1.000 | 1.000 |
| 0.377 | 0.376 | 0.376 | 0.376 | 0.376 | 0.376 | 0.380 | 0.400 | 0.400 | 0.400 | 0.386 | 0.396 | 0.383 |
| 0.429 | 0.433 | 0.470 | 0.478 | 0.456 | 0.441 | 0.349 | 0.347 | 0.333 | 0.323 | 0.401 | 0.406 | 0.400 |
| 0.464 | 0.551 | 0.627 | 0.604 | 0.603 | 0.591 | 0.476 | 0.487 | 0.484 | 0.488 | 0.386 | 0.205 | 0.535 |
| 0.468 | 0.508 | 0.543 | 0.506 | 0.487 | 0.465 | 0.367 | 0.365 | 0.351 | 0.340 | 0.390 | 0.300 | 0.431 |
| 0.332 | 0.395 | 0.449 | 0.433 | 0.432 | 0.423 | 0.341 | 0.349 | 0.346 | 0.350 | 0.277 | 0.147 | 0.383 |
| 0.377 | 0.376 | 0.376 | 0.376 | 0.376 | 0.376 | 0.376 | 0.376 | 0.376 | 0.376 | 0.381 | 0.396 | 0.376 |
| 15.454 | 17.987 | 22.118 | 24.620 | 25.354 | 27.995 | 30.410 | 30.900 | 31.700 | 32.300 | 21.564 | 11.728 | 26.667 |
| 4.883 | 5.040 | 4.935 | 5.063 | 5.808 | 5.756 | 6.309 | 6.537 | 6.828 | 7.015 | 5.594 | 4.320 | 5.998 |
| 17.559 | 19.459 | 20.841 | 24.107 | 27.604 | 29.482 | 32.959 | 35.134 | 37.927 | 40.568 | 21.564 | 9.957 | 29.378 |
| 17.714 | 17.934 | 18.042 | 20.187 | 22.316 | 23.205 | 25.431 | 26.353 | 27.524 | 28.280 | 21.066 | 14.514 | 23.485 |
| 15.939 | 17.664 | 18.918 | 21.883 | 25.057 | 26.762 | 29.918 | 31.893 | 34.428 | 36.825 | 19.574 | 9.039 | 26.667 |
| 15.478 | 16.345 | 20.040 | 23.758 | 24.949 | 26.000 | 29.886 | 30.635 | 31.246 | 32.143 | 20.357 | 10.579 | 25.799 |
| 2.011 | 2.011 | 2.011 | 2.011 | 2.011 | 2.011 | 2.010 | 2.000 | 2.000 | 2.000 | 2.006 | 2.002 | 2.007 |
| 1.560 | 1.555 | 1.632 | 1.660 | 1.610 | 1.514 | 1.478 | 1.481 | 1.473 | 1.507 | 1.463 | 1.270 | 1.535 |
| 1.963 | 2.219 | 2.423 | 2.572 | 2.738 | 2.846 | 2.834 | 2.922 | 3.002 | 3.198 | 2.006 | 1.094 | 2.695 |
| 1.981 | 2.045 | 2.097 | 2.154 | 2.213 | 2.240 | 2.187 | 2.192 | 2.179 | 2.229 | 2.001 | 1.610 | 2.162 |
| 1.462 | 1.653 | 1.804 | 1.915 | 2.039 | 2.119 | 2.111 | 2.176 | 2.236 | 2.382 | 1.494 | 0.815 | 2.007 |
| 2.011 | 2.011 | 2.011 | 2.011 | 2.011 | 2.011 | 2.011 | 2.011 | 2.011 | 2.011 | 2.009 | 2.003 | 2.011 |
| 29.243 | 37.131 | 45.691 | 51.132 | 57.784 | 59.378 | 44.670 | 37.300 | 36.800 | 39.400 | 40.155 | 36.551 | 42.120 |
| 37.702 | 37.339 | 37.611 | 39.561 | 39.732 | 41.167 | 41.842 | 41.613 | 40.962 | 41.154 | 40.121 | 40.255 | 40.058 |
| 38.978 | 40.808 | 43.733 | 46.150 | 48.543 | 51.509 | 53.406 | 54.640 | 55.590 | 58.142 | 40.155 | 28.744 | 49.447 |
| 39.321 | 37.610 | 37.859 | 38.646 | 39.244 | 40.544 | 41.208 | 40.983 | 40.342 | 40.531 | 40.573 | 42.402 | 39.761 |
| 33.202 | 34.762 | 37.253 | 39.312 | 41.351 | 43.877 | 45.493 | 46.544 | 47.354 | 49.527 | 34.205 | 24.485 | 42.120 |
| 29.242 | 37.129 | 45.691 | 51.132 | 57.784 | 59.378 | 44.672 | 37.334 | 36.768 | 39.404 | 40.158 | 36.560 | 42.121 |

**Table A.2**   Conversion rates for individual countries or areas, expressed as the number of
local currency units per United States dollar, 1970–1989 [*cont.*]

| Country or area | 1970 (1) | 1971 (2) | 1972 (3) | 1973 (4) | 1974 (5) | 1975 (6) | 1976 (7) | 1977 (8) | 1978 (9) | 1979 (10) |
|---|---|---|---|---|---|---|---|---|---|---|
| **Belize:** Belize dollars | | | | | | | | | | |
| 1.  MER | 1.667 | 1.644 | 1.602 | 1.633 | 1.711 | 1.808 | 2.226 | 2.000 | 2.000 | 2.000 |
| 2.  PPPs | ... | ... | ... | ... | ... | ... | ... | ... | ... | ... |
| 3.  Absolute 1970–1989 PARE | 0.774 | 0.811 | 0.849 | 0.931 | 1.191 | 1.448 | 1.415 | 1.569 | 1.661 | 1.869 |
| 4.  Relative 1970–1989 PARE | 1.588 | 1.582 | 1.584 | 1.628 | 1.910 | 2.114 | 1.944 | 2.019 | 1.992 | 2.058 |
| 5.  Absolute 1980–1989 PARE | 0.633 | 0.663 | 0.694 | 0.761 | 0.974 | 1.185 | 1.157 | 1.283 | 1.359 | 1.529 |
| 6.  WA | 1.667 | 1.644 | 1.602 | 1.633 | 1.711 | 1.808 | 2.226 | 2.000 | 2.000 | 2.000 |
| **Benin:** CFA francs | | | | | | | | | | |
| 1.  MER | 277.710 | 277.130 | 252.480 | 222.890 | 240.700 | 214.310 | 238.950 | 245.680 | 225.650 | 212.720 |
| 2.  PPPs | 81.181 | 80.266 | 79.696 | 78.913 | 83.310 | 85.123 | 96.007 | 109.932 | 117.343 | 122.190 |
| 3.  Absolute 1970–1989 PARE | 93.146 | 96.949 | 93.022 | 99.651 | 109.530 | 124.789 | 144.434 | 182.938 | 206.770 | 232.141 |
| 4.  Relative 1970–1989 PARE | 191.042 | 189.139 | 173.516 | 174.304 | 175.642 | 182.146 | 198.420 | 235.436 | 248.014 | 255.623 |
| 5.  Absolute 1980–1989 PARE | 68.243 | 71.029 | 68.152 | 73.009 | 80.246 | 91.426 | 105.818 | 134.028 | 151.489 | 170.076 |
| 6.  WA | 277.710 | 277.132 | 252.484 | 222.888 | 240.704 | 214.312 | 238.950 | 245.679 | 225.655 | 212.721 |
| **Bermuda:** Dollars | | | | | | | | | | |
| 1.  MER | 1.000 | 1.000 | 1.000 | 1.000 | 1.000 | 1.000 | 1.000 | 1.000 | 1.000 | 1.000 |
| 2.  PPPs | ... | ... | ... | ... | ... | ... | ... | ... | ... | ... |
| 3.  Absolute 1970–1989 PARE | 0.350 | 0.383 | 0.420 | 0.474 | 0.545 | 0.569 | 0.622 | 0.653 | 0.694 | 0.762 |
| 4.  Relative 1970–1989 PARE | 0.718 | 0.747 | 0.784 | 0.830 | 0.875 | 0.831 | 0.855 | 0.840 | 0.833 | 0.839 |
| 5.  Absolute 1980–1989 PARE | 0.258 | 0.283 | 0.310 | 0.350 | 0.402 | 0.420 | 0.459 | 0.481 | 0.512 | 0.562 |
| 6.  WA [a] | 1.099 | 1.097 | 1.099 | 1.123 | 1.149 | 1.081 | 1.078 | 1.065 | 1.060 | 1.089 |
| **Bhutan:** Ngultrum | | | | | | | | | | |
| 1.  MER | 7.500 | 7.508 | 7.595 | 7.474 | 8.102 | 8.376 | 8.960 | 8.739 | 8.193 | 8.126 |
| 2.  PPPs | ... | ... | ... | ... | ... | ... | ... | ... | ... | ... |
| 3.  Absolute 1970–1989 PARE | 4.956 | 5.382 | 6.461 | 6.159 | 7.241 | 9.696 | 10.715 | 9.590 | 10.201 | 8.846 |
| 4.  Relative 1970–1989 PARE | 10.165 | 10.499 | 12.052 | 10.772 | 11.611 | 14.153 | 14.721 | 12.342 | 12.236 | 9.741 |
| 5.  Absolute 1980–1989 PARE | 4.953 | 5.378 | 6.457 | 6.155 | 7.236 | 9.690 | 10.709 | 9.584 | 10.195 | 8.840 |
| 6.  WA | 7.500 | 7.501 | 7.594 | 7.742 | 8.102 | 8.376 | 8.960 | 8.739 | 8.193 | 8.126 |
| **Bolivia:** Bolivian pesos | | | | | | | | | | |
| 1.  MER | 11.880 | 11.880 | 13.233 | 20.000 | 20.000 | 20.000 | 20.000 | 20.000 | 20.000 | 20.393 |
| 2.  PPPs | 4.712 | 4.703 | 5.485 | 7.366 | 10.426 | 10.236 | 10.738 | 10.852 | 11.774 | 12.626 |
| 3.  Absolute 1970–1989 PARE | 4.262 | 4.733 | 5.323 | 7.699 | 12.369 | 13.135 | 14.349 | 15.866 | 17.939 | 21.498 |
| 4.  Relative 1970–1989 PARE | 8.741 | 9.233 | 9.929 | 13.466 | 19.835 | 19.172 | 19.712 | 20.419 | 21.517 | 23.673 |
| 5.  Absolute 1980–1989 PARE | 3.225 | 3.581 | 4.028 | 5.826 | 9.360 | 9.939 | 10.858 | 12.006 | 13.575 | 16.268 |
| 6.  WA | 11.880 | 11.880 | 13.295 | 20.010 | 20.010 | 20.010 | 20.010 | 20.010 | 20.010 | 20.403 |
| **Botswana:** Botswana pula | | | | | | | | | | |
| 1.  MER | 0.714 | 0.713 | 0.772 | 0.693 | 0.679 | 0.740 | 0.870 | 0.842 | 0.828 | 0.815 |
| 2.  PPPs | 0.275 | 0.307 | 0.369 | 0.413 | 0.427 | 0.450 | 0.478 | 0.476 | 0.526 | 0.556 |
| 3.  Absolute 1970–1989 PARE | 0.251 | 0.308 | 0.314 | 0.420 | 0.483 | 0.552 | 0.616 | 0.693 | 0.667 | 0.854 |
| 4.  Relative 1970–1989 PARE | 0.514 | 0.601 | 0.586 | 0.734 | 0.775 | 0.806 | 0.846 | 0.891 | 0.800 | 0.940 |
| 5.  Absolute 1980–1989 PARE | 0.228 | 0.281 | 0.286 | 0.382 | 0.440 | 0.503 | 0.561 | 0.631 | 0.607 | 0.777 |
| 6.  WA | 0.716 | 0.715 | 0.733 | 0.756 | 0.671 | 0.684 | 0.834 | 0.863 | 0.824 | 0.828 |
| **Brazil:** New cruzados | | | | | | | | | | |
| 1.  MER | 0.000004 | 0.000005 | 0.000006 | 0.000006 | 0.000007 | 0.000008 | 0.000011 | 0.000014 | 0.000018 | 0.000030 |
| 2.  PPPs | 0.000002 | 0.000003 | 0.000003 | 0.000003 | 0.000004 | 0.000005 | 0.000007 | 0.000010 | 0.000013 | 0.000018 |
| 3.  Absolute 1970–1989 PARE | 0.000002 | 0.000002 | 0.000002 | 0.000004 | 0.000005 | 0.000006 | 0.000009 | 0.000013 | 0.000018 | 0.000028 |
| 4.  Relative 1970–1989 PARE | 0.000004 | 0.000004 | 0.000005 | 0.000006 | 0.000007 | 0.000009 | 0.000012 | 0.000017 | 0.000022 | 0.000031 |
| 5.  Absolute 1980–1989 PARE | 0.000002 | 0.000002 | 0.000002 | 0.000003 | 0.000004 | 0.000005 | 0.000008 | 0.000011 | 0.000016 | 0.000024 |
| 6.  WA | 0.000005 | 0.000005 | 0.000006 | 0.000006 | 0.000007 | 0.000008 | 0.000011 | 0.000014 | 0.000018 | 0.000027 |

| 1980 (11) | 1981 (12) | 1982 (13) | 1983 (14) | 1984 (15) | 1985 (16) | 1986 (17) | 1987 (18) | 1988 (19) | 1989 (20) | Averages 1970–89 (21) | 1970–79 (22) | 1980–89 (23) |
|---|---|---|---|---|---|---|---|---|---|---|---|---|
| 2.000 | 2.000 | 2.000 | 2.000 | 2.000 | 2.000 | 2.000 | 2.000 | 2.000 | 2.000 | 1.963 | 1.873 | 2.000 |
| ... | ... | ... | ... | ... | ... | ... | ... | ... | ... | ... | ... | ... |
| 2.171 | 2.241 | 2.157 | 2.248 | 2.349 | 2.317 | 2.440 | 2.570 | 2.746 | 2.947 | 1.963 | 1.295 | 2.445 |
| 2.190 | 2.065 | 1.867 | 1.882 | 1.899 | 1.824 | 1.883 | 1.927 | 1.993 | 2.054 | 1.940 | 1.898 | 1.957 |
| 1.776 | 1.833 | 1.764 | 1.839 | 1.921 | 1.895 | 1.995 | 2.102 | 2.246 | 2.410 | 1.606 | 1.059 | 2.000 |
| 2.000 | 2.000 | 2.000 | 2.000 | 2.000 | 2.000 | 2.000 | 2.000 | 2.000 | 2.000 | 1.963 | 1.873 | 2.000 |
| 211.280 | 271.730 | 328.600 | 381.060 | 436.960 | 449.260 | 346.300 | 300.500 | 297.800 | 319.000 | 303.817 | 234.183 | 330.472 |
| 127.513 | 133.420 | 141.178 | 147.405 | 159.185 | 162.812 | 161.697 | 157.362 | 147.177 | 146.333 | 133.592 | 95.781 | 149.612 |
| 267.443 | 314.879 | 413.101 | 443.543 | 469.907 | 516.576 | 523.349 | 523.953 | 506.494 | 524.238 | 303.817 | 137.880 | 451.069 |
| 269.801 | 290.197 | 357.621 | 371.421 | 379.890 | 406.604 | 403.820 | 392.994 | 367.559 | 365.451 | 313.220 | 206.540 | 364.255 |
| 195.940 | 230.693 | 302.655 | 324.958 | 344.273 | 378.465 | 383.427 | 383.869 | 371.078 | 384.078 | 222.589 | 101.017 | 330.472 |
| 211.279 | 271.730 | 328.605 | 381.065 | 436.955 | 449.261 | 346.305 | 300.535 | 297.847 | 319.007 | 303.826 | 234.185 | 330.485 |
| 1.000 | 1.000 | 1.000 | 1.000 | 1.000 | 1.000 | 1.000 | 1.000 | 1.000 | 1.000 | 1.000 | 1.000 | 1.000 |
| ... | ... | ... | ... | ... | ... | ... | ... | ... | ... | ... | ... | ... |
| 0.896 | 1.008 | 1.118 | 1.233 | 1.342 | 1.405 | 1.487 | 1.559 | 1.661 | 1.749 | 1.000 | 0.561 | 1.356 |
| 0.904 | 0.929 | 0.968 | 1.033 | 1.085 | 1.106 | 1.147 | 1.169 | 1.205 | 1.219 | 1.009 | 0.824 | 1.092 |
| 0.661 | 0.743 | 0.825 | 0.910 | 0.990 | 1.036 | 1.097 | 1.150 | 1.225 | 1.290 | 0.738 | 0.414 | 1.000 |
| 1.155 | 1.149 | 1.119 | 1.109 | 1.096 | 1.062 | 1.056 | 1.053 | 1.061 | 1.059 | 1.084 | 1.089 | 1.082 |
| 7.863 | 8.659 | 9.455 | 10.499 | 11.363 | 12.369 | 12.611 | 13.000 | 13.900 | 16.200 | 10.982 | 8.188 | 12.180 |
| ... | ... | ... | ... | ... | ... | ... | ... | ... | ... | ... | ... | ... |
| 7.749 | 8.235 | 9.140 | 9.954 | 10.954 | 11.997 | 12.756 | 13.941 | 14.742 | 16.284 | 10.982 | 8.176 | 12.187 |
| 7.817 | 7.589 | 7.913 | 8.335 | 8.855 | 9.443 | 9.843 | 10.456 | 10.698 | 11.351 | 10.056 | 11.871 | 9.632 |
| 7.744 | 8.229 | 9.135 | 9.947 | 10.947 | 11.990 | 12.748 | 13.932 | 14.732 | 16.273 | 10.975 | 8.171 | 12.180 |
| 7.863 | 8.659 | 9.455 | 10.099 | 11.363 | 12.369 | 12.611 | 12.962 | 13.917 | 16.225 | 10.966 | 8.209 | 12.140 |
| 24.510 | 24.510 | 64.100 | 231.600 | 3135.900 | 441900.000 | 920000.000 | 055000.000 | 350000.000 | 692000.000 | 527587.312 | 18.952 | 773058.626 |
| 15.113 | 19.110 | 48.609 | 212.759 | 2531.416 | 270398.610 | 887222.896 | 004640.685 | 143560.469 | 244538.588 | 309998.570 | 9.767 | 485913.422 |
| 29.789 | 37.196 | 100.865 | 372.261 | 5004.672 | 579781.200 | 940589.000 | 260548.000 | 659522.000 | 013039.000 | 527587.348 | 12.445 | 021579.732 |
| 30.052 | 34.280 | 87.319 | 311.730 | 4045.965 | 456353.899 | 497373.832 | 695538.589 | 929995.341 | 100417.917 | 545246.066 | 18.195 | 828399.713 |
| 22.543 | 28.147 | 76.328 | 281.701 | 3787.178 | 438737.000 | 468499.000 | 710622.000 | 012537.000 | 280052.000 | 399240.435 | 9.417 | 773058.615 |
| 24.520 | 24.520 | 64.072 | 231.630 | 3135.910 | 440028.995 | 921959.996 | 054850.101 | 350239.992 | 691679.955 | 527597.008 | 18.964 | 772834.512 |
| 0.777 | 0.840 | 1.030 | 1.096 | 1.300 | 1.900 | 1.880 | 1.700 | 1.800 | 2.000 | 1.415 | 0.788 | 1.555 |
| 0.578 | 0.519 | 0.535 | 0.594 | 0.650 | 0.638 | 0.739 | 0.815 | 0.929 | 1.153 | 0.735 | 0.462 | 0.787 |
| 1.019 | 1.043 | 1.072 | 1.145 | 1.184 | 1.396 | 1.650 | 1.871 | 2.204 | 2.849 | 1.415 | 0.563 | 1.708 |
| 1.028 | 0.962 | 0.928 | 0.959 | 0.957 | 1.099 | 1.273 | 1.404 | 1.599 | 1.986 | 1.254 | 0.803 | 1.340 |
| 0.928 | 0.950 | 0.976 | 1.043 | 1.078 | 1.272 | 1.502 | 1.704 | 2.007 | 2.595 | 1.288 | 0.513 | 1.555 |
| 0.795 | 0.779 | 0.921 | 1.088 | 1.144 | 1.609 | 1.912 | 1.821 | 1.688 | 1.993 | 1.373 | 0.784 | 1.501 |
| 0.000050 | 0.000090 | 0.000180 | 0.000580 | 0.001850 | 0.006200 | 0.013660 | 0.039200 | 0.262400 | 2.834000 | 0.368333 | 0.000014 | 0.516896 |
| 0.000032 | 0.000059 | 0.000111 | 0.000260 | 0.000811 | 0.002700 | 0.006428 | 0.019485 | 0.145674 | 2.018245 | 0.209067 | 0.000009 | 0.282978 |
| 0.000053 | 0.000114 | 0.000230 | 0.000552 | 0.001728 | 0.005726 | 0.013904 | 0.043360 | 0.335042 | 4.832195 | 0.368333 | 0.000010 | 0.600772 |
| 0.000053 | 0.000105 | 0.000200 | 0.000462 | 0.001397 | 0.004507 | 0.010729 | 0.032522 | 0.243138 | 3.368569 | 0.355886 | 0.000015 | 0.481154 |
| 0.000046 | 0.000098 | 0.000198 | 0.000475 | 0.001487 | 0.004926 | 0.011963 | 0.037306 | 0.288266 | 4.157552 | 0.316908 | 0.000009 | 0.516896 |
| 0.000053 | 0.000093 | 0.000180 | 0.000577 | 0.001848 | 0.006200 | 0.013656 | 0.039228 | 0.262383 | 2.833920 | 0.368606 | 0.000014 | 0.520497 |

**Table A.2**    Conversion rates for individual countries or areas, expressed as the number of
local currency units per United States dollar, 1970−1989 [*cont.*]

| Country or area | 1970 (1) | 1971 (2) | 1972 (3) | 1973 (4) | 1974 (5) | 1975 (6) | 1976 (7) | 1977 (8) | 1978 (9) | 1979 (10) |
|---|---|---|---|---|---|---|---|---|---|---|
| **British Virgin Islands:** Dollars | | | | | | | | | | |
| 1.  MER | 1.000 | 1.000 | 1.000 | 1.000 | 1.000 | 1.000 | 1.000 | 1.000 | 1.000 | 1.000 |
| 2.  PPPs | ... | ... | ... | ... | ... | ... | ... | ... | ... | ... |
| 3.  Absolute 1970−1989 PARE | 0.469 | 0.450 | 0.469 | 0.503 | 0.549 | 0.577 | 0.631 | 0.641 | 0.691 | 0.817 |
| 4.  Relative 1970−1989 PARE | 0.963 | 0.878 | 0.876 | 0.881 | 0.880 | 0.842 | 0.867 | 0.824 | 0.829 | 0.899 |
| 5.  Absolute 1980−1989 PARE | 0.378 | 0.362 | 0.378 | 0.405 | 0.442 | 0.464 | 0.507 | 0.515 | 0.556 | 0.657 |
| 6.  WA [a] | 1.282 | 1.011 | 1.014 | 1.063 | 1.086 | 1.066 | 1.081 | 1.042 | 1.058 | 1.152 |
| **Brunei Darussalam:** Brunei dollars | | | | | | | | | | |
| 1.  MER | 3.061 | 3.020 | 2.805 | 2.443 | 2.407 | 2.402 | 2.542 | 2.461 | 2.316 | 2.188 |
| 2.  PPPs | ... | ... | ... | ... | ... | ... | ... | ... | ... | ... |
| 3.  Absolute 1970−1989 PARE | 0.419 | 0.427 | 0.502 | 0.595 | 1.476 | 1.557 | 1.645 | 1.782 | 1.743 | 1.965 |
| 4.  Relative 1970−1989 PARE | 0.859 | 0.833 | 0.936 | 1.040 | 2.366 | 2.273 | 2.259 | 2.294 | 2.091 | 2.163 |
| 5.  Absolute 1980−1989 PARE | 0.309 | 0.314 | 0.370 | 0.438 | 1.087 | 1.147 | 1.211 | 1.313 | 1.284 | 1.447 |
| 6.  WA [a] | 4.274 | 3.455 | 3.341 | 3.323 | 5.572 | 3.780 | 2.587 | 2.655 | 2.473 | 2.503 |
| **Bulgaria:** Bulgarian leva | | | | | | | | | | |
| 1.  MER | 2.000 | 1.940 | 1.850 | 1.680 | 1.580 | 1.200 | 1.200 | 1.200 | 1.340 | 1.300 |
| 2.  PPPs | ... | ... | ... | ... | ... | ... | ... | ... | ... | ... |
| 3.  Absolute 1970−1989 PARE | 1.318 | 1.314 | 1.220 | 1.221 | 1.223 | 1.227 | 1.220 | 1.172 | 1.174 | 1.190 |
| 4.  Relative 1970−1989 PARE | 2.703 | 2.563 | 2.276 | 2.136 | 1.962 | 1.791 | 1.676 | 1.508 | 1.408 | 1.310 |
| 5.  Absolute 1980−1989 PARE | 1.211 | 1.207 | 1.121 | 1.122 | 1.124 | 1.128 | 1.121 | 1.077 | 1.079 | 1.093 |
| 6.  WA [a] | 2.099 | 2.015 | 1.835 | 1.778 | 1.706 | 1.491 | 1.323 | 1.166 | 1.232 | 1.292 |
| **Burkina Faso:** CFA francs | | | | | | | | | | |
| 1.  MER | 277.710 | 275.520 | 252.210 | 222.700 | 240.500 | 214.320 | 238.980 | 245.670 | 225.660 | 212.720 |
| 2.  PPPs | 136.772 | 96.497 | 104.844 | 103.422 | 105.243 | 101.588 | 103.287 | 110.822 | 126.223 | 123.888 |
| 3.  Absolute 1970−1989 PARE | 122.128 | 124.747 | 119.077 | 128.527 | 144.892 | 149.893 | 161.855 | 187.796 | 199.045 | 250.184 |
| 4.  Relative 1970−1989 PARE | 250.484 | 243.370 | 222.117 | 224.813 | 232.349 | 218.789 | 222.353 | 241.687 | 238.748 | 275.490 |
| 5.  Absolute 1980−1989 PARE | 99.373 | 101.504 | 96.890 | 104.580 | 117.895 | 121.965 | 131.698 | 152.805 | 161.958 | 203.569 |
| 6.  WA | 277.710 | 277.132 | 252.484 | 222.888 | 240.704 | 214.312 | 238.950 | 245.679 | 225.655 | 212.721 |
| **Burundi:** Burundi francs | | | | | | | | | | |
| 1.  MER | 87.500 | 87.500 | 87.500 | 79.480 | 78.750 | 78.750 | 86.250 | 90.000 | 90.000 | 90.000 |
| 2.  PPPs | 37.954 | 36.499 | 36.648 | 37.990 | 39.687 | 43.570 | 43.685 | 44.498 | 47.621 | 56.063 |
| 3.  Absolute 1970−1989 PARE | 38.560 | 38.424 | 39.871 | 42.300 | 47.447 | 56.818 | 62.138 | 70.628 | 76.073 | 96.716 |
| 4.  Relative 1970−1989 PARE | 79.085 | 74.961 | 74.372 | 73.988 | 76.086 | 82.934 | 85.363 | 90.896 | 91.247 | 106.499 |
| 5.  Absolute 1980−1989 PARE | 31.562 | 31.451 | 32.635 | 34.623 | 38.836 | 46.507 | 50.861 | 57.810 | 62.267 | 79.164 |
| 6.  WA | 87.500 | 87.500 | 87.500 | 80.026 | 78.750 | 78.750 | 86.250 | 90.000 | 90.000 | 90.000 |
| **Cambodia:** Riels | | | | | | | | | | |
| 1.  MER | 4.000 | 4.000 | 4.000 | 4.000 | 4.000 | 4.000 | 4.000 | 4.000 | 4.000 | 4.000 |
| 2.  PPPs | ... | ... | ... | ... | ... | ... | ... | ... | ... | ... |
| 3.  Absolute 1970−1989 PARE | 2.597 | 3.693 | 2.037 | 3.423 | 3.083 | 3.147 | 3.110 | 3.593 | 3.537 | 4.019 |
| 4.  Relative 1970−1989 PARE | 5.327 | 7.205 | 3.799 | 5.987 | 4.944 | 4.594 | 4.273 | 4.624 | 4.243 | 4.426 |
| 5.  Absolute 1980−1989 PARE | 1.917 | 2.726 | 1.503 | 2.526 | 2.276 | 2.323 | 2.295 | 2.652 | 2.611 | 2.967 |
| 6.  WA [a] | 4.393 | 5.306 | 3.114 | 4.810 | 4.553 | 3.920 | 3.996 | 4.396 | 4.162 | 4.340 |
| **Cameroon:** CFA francs | | | | | | | | | | |
| 1.  MER | 277.710 | 275.520 | 252.210 | 222.700 | 240.500 | 214.320 | 238.980 | 245.670 | 225.660 | 212.720 |
| 2.  PPPs | 146.209 | 142.713 | 153.087 | 163.704 | 172.076 | 177.583 | 203.897 | 205.061 | 219.751 | 218.235 |
| 3.  Absolute 1970−1989 PARE | 90.230 | 87.605 | 93.011 | 103.164 | 121.472 | 136.074 | 151.231 | 171.987 | 201.058 | 215.798 |
| 4.  Relative 1970−1989 PARE | 185.060 | 170.909 | 173.495 | 180.448 | 194.793 | 198.618 | 207.758 | 221.342 | 241.162 | 237.626 |
| 5.  Absolute 1980−1989 PARE | 74.128 | 71.972 | 76.413 | 84.754 | 99.795 | 111.792 | 124.244 | 141.296 | 165.179 | 177.288 |
| 6.  WA | 274.330 | 277.710 | 265.390 | 240.960 | 230.050 | 222.418 | 225.085 | 247.780 | 238.585 | 216.645 |

| 1980 (11) | 1981 (12) | 1982 (13) | 1983 (14) | 1984 (15) | 1985 (16) | 1986 (17) | 1987 (18) | 1988 (19) | 1989 (20) | Averages 1970−89 (21) | 1970−79 (22) | 1980−89 (23) |
|---|---|---|---|---|---|---|---|---|---|---|---|---|
| 1.000 | 1.000 | 1.000 | 1.000 | 1.000 | 1.000 | 1.000 | 1.000 | 1.000 | 1.000 | 1.000 | 1.000 | 1.000 |
| ... | ... | ... | ... | ... | ... | ... | ... | ... | ... | ... | ... | ... |
| 0.845 | 0.918 | 1.057 | 1.125 | 1.168 | 1.216 | 1.261 | 1.457 | 1.507 | 1.607 | 1.000 | 0.591 | 1.243 |
| 0.853 | 0.846 | 0.915 | 0.942 | 0.944 | 0.957 | 0.973 | 1.093 | 1.093 | 1.120 | 0.963 | 0.869 | 0.993 |
| 0.680 | 0.739 | 0.850 | 0.905 | 0.940 | 0.978 | 1.014 | 1.172 | 1.212 | 1.292 | 0.804 | 0.476 | 1.000 |
| 1.086 | 1.070 | 1.134 | 1.097 | 1.048 | 1.041 | 1.039 | 1.118 | 1.076 | 1.056 | 1.076 | 1.085 | 1.074 |
| 2.177 | 2.304 | 2.335 | 2.321 | 2.344 | 2.483 | 2.581 | 2.500 | 2.600 | 2.700 | 2.396 | 2.394 | 2.397 |
| ... | ... | ... | ... | ... | ... | ... | ... | ... | ... | ... | ... | ... |
| 3.656 | 3.986 | 3.793 | 3.360 | 3.317 | 3.273 | 2.686 | 2.732 | 2.718 | 2.786 | 2.396 | 1.355 | 3.254 |
| 3.689 | 3.674 | 3.284 | 2.814 | 2.682 | 2.576 | 2.073 | 2.049 | 1.973 | 1.942 | 2.416 | 1.927 | 2.647 |
| 2.693 | 2.936 | 2.794 | 2.475 | 2.443 | 2.410 | 1.978 | 2.012 | 2.002 | 2.052 | 1.765 | 0.998 | 2.397 |
| 3.702 | 3.039 | 2.262 | 2.110 | 2.226 | 2.352 | 2.172 | 2.399 | 2.566 | 2.638 | 2.600 | 2.884 | 2.515 |
| 1.290 | 1.390 | 1.460 | 1.460 | 0.990 | 1.010 | 1.090 | 1.270 | 1.470 | 1.820 | 1.336 | 1.431 | 1.291 |
| ... | ... | ... | ... | ... | ... | ... | ... | ... | ... | ... | ... | ... |
| 1.321 | 1.357 | 1.358 | 1.355 | 1.376 | 1.391 | 1.395 | 1.409 | 1.444 | 1.588 | 1.336 | 1.220 | 1.405 |
| 1.333 | 1.251 | 1.176 | 1.135 | 1.112 | 1.095 | 1.076 | 1.057 | 1.048 | 1.107 | 1.282 | 1.760 | 1.124 |
| 1.214 | 1.247 | 1.248 | 1.245 | 1.264 | 1.278 | 1.282 | 1.295 | 1.327 | 1.459 | 1.227 | 1.121 | 1.291 |
| 1.414 | 1.399 | 1.393 | 1.435 | 1.317 | 1.170 | 1.035 | 1.131 | 1.300 | 1.623 | 1.357 | 1.483 | 1.299 |
| 211.280 | 271.730 | 328.610 | 381.060 | 436.960 | 449.260 | 346.300 | 300.500 | 297.800 | 319.000 | 297.589 | 233.577 | 325.297 |
| 122.237 | 122.577 | 125.106 | 126.820 | 130.170 | 133.565 | 135.085 | 138.149 | 137.935 | 137.084 | 126.620 | 111.931 | 132.004 |
| 273.502 | 304.872 | 333.407 | 371.041 | 388.604 | 423.319 | 436.741 | 459.480 | 474.171 | 490.568 | 297.589 | 163.291 | 399.787 |
| 275.913 | 280.975 | 288.631 | 310.708 | 314.162 | 333.200 | 336.993 | 344.636 | 344.102 | 341.980 | 296.970 | 239.219 | 321.062 |
| 222.542 | 248.067 | 271.286 | 301.907 | 316.198 | 344.445 | 355.366 | 373.868 | 385.822 | 399.164 | 242.141 | 132.866 | 325.297 |
| 211.279 | 271.730 | 328.605 | 381.065 | 436.955 | 449.261 | 346.305 | 300.535 | 297.847 | 319.007 | 297.642 | 233.693 | 325.311 |
| 90.000 | 90.000 | 90.000 | 92.950 | 119.710 | 120.690 | 114.170 | 123.600 | 140.400 | 158.700 | 106.789 | 86.357 | 114.728 |
| 58.436 | 57.140 | 57.965 | 61.311 | 62.213 | 65.390 | 61.523 | 58.573 | 59.207 | 64.058 | 56.004 | 44.045 | 60.834 |
| 118.189 | 111.260 | 117.631 | 124.752 | 146.187 | 153.598 | 147.419 | 144.384 | 150.846 | 169.896 | 106.789 | 58.864 | 140.166 |
| 119.231 | 102.539 | 101.833 | 104.467 | 118.183 | 120.899 | 113.749 | 108.296 | 109.468 | 118.436 | 104.992 | 86.479 | 112.005 |
| 96.740 | 91.069 | 96.283 | 102.112 | 119.656 | 125.723 | 120.665 | 118.181 | 123.470 | 139.063 | 87.409 | 48.181 | 114.728 |
| 90.000 | 90.000 | 90.000 | 92.948 | 119.709 | 120.691 | 114.171 | 123.564 | 140.395 | 158.667 | 106.799 | 86.400 | 114.722 |
| 4.000 | 4.000 | 4.000 | 7.000 | 7.000 | 7.000 | 7.000 | 39.000 | 138.000 | 187.000 | 29.714 | 4.000 | 54.720 |
| ... | ... | ... | ... | ... | ... | ... | ... | ... | ... | ... | ... | ... |
| 4.273 | 4.287 | 4.295 | 9.357 | 9.984 | 9.886 | 9.949 | 56.551 | 219.273 | 337.152 | 29.714 | 3.151 | 74.138 |
| 4.310 | 3.951 | 3.718 | 7.835 | 8.072 | 7.781 | 7.677 | 42.416 | 159.125 | 235.032 | 34.540 | 4.934 | 60.234 |
| 3.154 | 3.164 | 3.170 | 6.906 | 7.369 | 7.297 | 7.343 | 41.740 | 161.843 | 248.848 | 21.932 | 2.326 | 54.720 |
| 4.361 | 4.093 | 4.009 | 8.149 | 7.923 | 7.109 | 7.007 | 39.610 | 147.834 | 210.567 | 31.816 | 4.306 | 58.284 |
| 211.280 | 271.730 | 328.610 | 381.060 | 436.960 | 449.260 | 346.300 | 300.500 | 297.800 | 319.000 | 310.556 | 232.638 | 332.576 |
| 223.377 | 227.137 | 241.283 | 270.307 | 284.985 | 305.856 | 301.189 | 298.392 | 292.929 | 282.511 | 258.431 | 188.077 | 279.068 |
| 248.452 | 284.593 | 320.009 | 360.878 | 409.808 | 455.469 | 457.532 | 466.307 | 473.139 | 475.021 | 310.556 | 142.598 | 404.816 |
| 250.642 | 262.286 | 277.031 | 302.198 | 331.304 | 358.506 | 353.036 | 349.757 | 343.353 | 331.142 | 296.720 | 208.725 | 323.698 |
| 204.115 | 233.807 | 262.903 | 296.479 | 336.678 | 374.190 | 375.885 | 383.094 | 388.707 | 390.253 | 255.137 | 117.151 | 332.576 |
| 209.210 | 235.267 | 296.683 | 354.655 | 409.517 | 471.130 | 386.600 | 318.663 | 291.712 | 315.360 | 309.500 | 236.235 | 329.716 |

**Table A.2** Conversion rates for individual countries or areas, expressed as the number of local currency units per United States dollar, 1970−1989 [*cont.*]

| Country or area | 1970 (1) | 1971 (2) | 1972 (3) | 1973 (4) | 1974 (5) | 1975 (6) | 1976 (7) | 1977 (8) | 1978 (9) | 1979 (10) |
|---|---|---|---|---|---|---|---|---|---|---|
| **Canada:** Canadian dollars | | | | | | | | | | |
| 1. MER | 1.044 | 1.010 | 0.991 | 1.000 | 0.978 | 1.017 | 0.986 | 1.064 | 1.141 | 1.171 |
| 2. PPPs | 0.995 | 0.978 | 0.976 | 0.990 | 1.013 | 1.040 | 1.074 | 1.101 | 1.111 | 1.108 |
| 3. Absolute 1970−1989 PARE | 0.512 | 0.528 | 0.558 | 0.608 | 0.695 | 0.764 | 0.830 | 0.882 | 0.936 | 1.031 |
| 4. Relative 1970−1989 PARE | 1.050 | 1.031 | 1.041 | 1.063 | 1.115 | 1.115 | 1.141 | 1.136 | 1.122 | 1.135 |
| 5. Absolute 1980−1989 PARE | 0.427 | 0.440 | 0.465 | 0.506 | 0.579 | 0.636 | 0.692 | 0.735 | 0.779 | 0.859 |
| 6. WA | 1.048 | 1.010 | 0.990 | 1.000 | 0.978 | 1.017 | 0.986 | 1.063 | 1.141 | 1.171 |
| **Cape Verde:** Cape Verde escudos | | | | | | | | | | |
| 1. MER | 28.750 | 28.312 | 27.053 | 24.515 | 25.408 | 25.543 | 30.229 | 34.047 | 35.501 | 37.433 |
| 2. PPPs | ... | ... | ... | ... | ... | ... | ... | ... | ... | ... |
| 3. Absolute 1970−1989 PARE | 9.509 | 11.075 | 12.123 | 14.199 | 19.673 | 23.853 | 25.609 | 27.926 | 39.239 | 43.872 |
| 4. Relative 1970−1989 PARE | 19.503 | 21.607 | 22.613 | 24.835 | 31.547 | 34.816 | 35.181 | 35.940 | 47.066 | 48.310 |
| 5. Absolute 1980−1989 PARE | 8.057 | 9.384 | 10.272 | 12.030 | 16.669 | 20.210 | 21.698 | 23.661 | 33.247 | 37.173 |
| 6. WA | 28.750 | 28.312 | 27.053 | 24.515 | 25.408 | 25.543 | 30.229 | 34.046 | 35.501 | 37.433 |
| **Central African Republic:** CFA francs | | | | | | | | | | |
| 1. MER | 277.710 | 275.520 | 252.210 | 222.700 | 240.500 | 214.320 | 238.980 | 245.670 | 225.660 | 212.720 |
| 2. PPPs | 113.882 | 113.169 | 116.416 | 117.389 | 115.743 | 121.302 | 125.231 | 138.724 | 137.000 | 142.699 |
| 3. Absolute 1970−1989 PARE | 87.912 | 96.137 | 103.468 | 101.657 | 132.125 | 145.262 | 184.644 | 197.255 | 211.364 | 241.239 |
| 4. Relative 1970−1989 PARE | 180.307 | 187.556 | 193.002 | 177.812 | 211.875 | 212.029 | 253.659 | 253.861 | 253.524 | 265.641 |
| 5. Absolute 1980−1989 PARE | 67.195 | 73.482 | 79.085 | 77.700 | 100.988 | 111.030 | 141.131 | 150.770 | 161.554 | 184.389 |
| 6. WA | 277.710 | 277.132 | 252.484 | 222.888 | 240.704 | 214.312 | 238.950 | 245.679 | 225.655 | 212.721 |
| **Chad:** CFA francs | | | | | | | | | | |
| 1. MER | 277.710 | 275.520 | 252.210 | 222.700 | 240.500 | 214.320 | 238.980 | 245.670 | 225.660 | 212.720 |
| 2. PPPs | 107.090 | 107.242 | 106.694 | 105.683 | 109.066 | 114.901 | 114.152 | 115.370 | 121.507 | 130.936 |
| 3. Absolute 1970−1989 PARE | 129.202 | 137.890 | 140.799 | 145.121 | 160.615 | 176.219 | 187.311 | 210.554 | 235.261 | 267.704 |
| 4. Relative 1970−1989 PARE | 264.991 | 269.010 | 262.637 | 253.837 | 257.563 | 257.214 | 257.322 | 270.977 | 282.188 | 294.783 |
| 5. Absolute 1980−1989 PARE | 99.149 | 105.816 | 108.049 | 111.365 | 123.256 | 135.230 | 143.742 | 161.579 | 180.539 | 205.435 |
| 6. WA | 277.710 | 277.132 | 252.484 | 222.888 | 240.704 | 214.312 | 238.950 | 245.679 | 225.655 | 212.721 |
| **Chile:** Chilean pesos | | | | | | | | | | |
| 1. MER | 0.012 | 0.016 | 0.025 | 0.360 | 1.870 | 8.500 | 17.420 | 27.960 | 33.950 | 39.000 |
| 2. PPPs | 0.006 | 0.007 | 0.012 | 0.059 | 0.364 | 1.702 | 5.413 | 10.390 | 14.597 | 19.434 |
| 3. Absolute 1970−1989 PARE | 0.007 | 0.009 | 0.016 | 0.086 | 0.680 | 3.008 | 10.549 | 21.475 | 33.617 | 49.177 |
| 4. Relative 1970−1989 PARE | 0.015 | 0.017 | 0.031 | 0.150 | 1.090 | 4.391 | 14.492 | 27.637 | 40.323 | 54.151 |
| 5. Absolute 1980−1989 PARE | 0.006 | 0.007 | 0.013 | 0.068 | 0.537 | 2.378 | 8.339 | 16.975 | 26.573 | 38.872 |
| 6. WA | 0.012 | 0.012 | 0.019 | 0.111 | 0.832 | 4.911 | 13.054 | 21.529 | 31.656 | 37.246 |
| **China:** Yuan renminbi | | | | | | | | | | |
| 1. MER | 2.460 | 2.460 | 2.250 | 1.990 | 1.961 | 1.860 | 1.941 | 1.858 | 1.684 | 1.555 |
| 2. PPPs | ... | ... | ... | ... | ... | ... | ... | ... | ... | ... |
| 3. Absolute 1970−1989 PARE | 1.923 | 1.938 | 1.938 | 1.941 | 1.943 | 1.913 | 1.905 | 1.925 | 2.002 | 2.085 |
| 4. Relative 1970−1989 PARE | 3.945 | 3.780 | 3.614 | 3.395 | 3.117 | 2.792 | 2.617 | 2.478 | 2.401 | 2.296 |
| 5. Absolute 1980−1989 PARE | 1.943 | 1.958 | 1.958 | 1.961 | 1.964 | 1.933 | 1.925 | 1.945 | 2.022 | 2.107 |
| 6. WA | 2.462 | 2.462 | 2.245 | 1.989 | 1.961 | 1.860 | 1.941 | 1.858 | 1.684 | 1.555 |
| **Colombia:** Colombian pesos | | | | | | | | | | |
| 1. MER | 18.440 | 19.330 | 21.870 | 23.640 | 26.064 | 30.929 | 34.694 | 36.775 | 39.095 | 42.556 |
| 2. PPPs | 7.371 | 7.546 | 8.315 | 9.409 | 10.580 | 12.081 | 14.008 | 16.618 | 18.289 | 21.076 |
| 3. Absolute 1970−1989 PARE | 8.355 | 9.258 | 10.459 | 12.568 | 15.757 | 19.351 | 24.277 | 31.355 | 36.716 | 45.543 |
| 4. Relative 1970−1989 PARE | 17.136 | 18.062 | 19.510 | 21.983 | 25.268 | 28.245 | 33.351 | 40.352 | 44.040 | 50.150 |
| 5. Absolute 1980−1989 PARE | 6.967 | 7.719 | 8.721 | 10.479 | 13.138 | 16.135 | 20.242 | 26.144 | 30.614 | 37.974 |
| 6. WA | 18.443 | 19.932 | 21.866 | 23.637 | 26.064 | 30.929 | 34.694 | 36.775 | 39.095 | 42.550 |

**Table A.2**　Conversion rates for individual countries or areas, expressed as the number of
local currency units per United States dollar, 1970−1989 [*cont.*]

| Country or area | 1970 (1) | 1971 (2) | 1972 (3) | 1973 (4) | 1974 (5) | 1975 (6) | 1976 (7) | 1977 (8) | 1978 (9) | 1979 (10) |
|---|---|---|---|---|---|---|---|---|---|---|
| **Comoros:** CFA francs | | | | | | | | | | |
| 1.　MER | 277.710 | 277.130 | 252.480 | 222.890 | 240.700 | 214.310 | 238.950 | 245.680 | 225.650 | 212.720 |
| 2.　PPPs | ... | ... | ... | ... | ... | ... | ... | ... | ... | ... |
| 3.　Absolute 1970−1989 PARE | 100.401 | 107.161 | 111.450 | 124.123 | 168.483 | 170.682 | 181.787 | 194.061 | 224.477 | 257.951 |
| 4.　Relative 1970−1989 PARE | 205.921 | 209.062 | 207.891 | 217.110 | 270.179 | 249.132 | 249.734 | 249.750 | 269.253 | 284.043 |
| 5.　Absolute 1980−1989 PARE | 80.825 | 86.267 | 89.720 | 99.922 | 135.633 | 137.403 | 146.343 | 156.224 | 180.710 | 207.656 |
| 6.　WA | 277.710 | 277.132 | 252.484 | 222.888 | 240.704 | 214.312 | 238.950 | 245.679 | 225.655 | 212.721 |
| **Congo:** CFA francs | | | | | | | | | | |
| 1.　MER | 277.710 | 277.130 | 252.480 | 222.890 | 240.700 | 214.310 | 238.950 | 245.680 | 225.650 | 212.720 |
| 2.　PPPs | 176.148 | 173.874 | 178.572 | 172.352 | 176.394 | 196.452 | 204.656 | 217.503 | 225.182 | 228.002 |
| 3.　Absolute 1970−1989 PARE | 87.192 | 96.244 | 106.144 | 110.384 | 133.858 | 156.470 | 175.849 | 194.661 | 208.706 | 240.338 |
| 4.　Relative 1970−1989 PARE | 178.830 | 187.764 | 197.994 | 193.077 | 214.655 | 228.387 | 241.576 | 250.522 | 250.336 | 264.649 |
| 5.　Absolute 1980−1989 PARE | 73.196 | 80.796 | 89.106 | 92.665 | 112.372 | 131.354 | 147.623 | 163.415 | 175.206 | 201.760 |
| 6.　WA | 277.710 | 277.132 | 252.484 | 222.888 | 240.704 | 214.312 | 238.950 | 245.679 | 225.655 | 212.721 |
| **Cook Islands:** New Zealand dollars | | | | | | | | | | |
| 1.　MER | 0.893 | 0.877 | 0.837 | 0.734 | 0.714 | 0.823 | 1.004 | 1.030 | 0.964 | 0.978 |
| 2.　PPPs | ... | ... | ... | ... | ... | ... | ... | ... | ... | ... |
| 3.　Absolute 1970−1989 PARE | 0.306 | 0.328 | 0.376 | 0.425 | 0.478 | 0.551 | 0.664 | 0.798 | 0.893 | 0.993 |
| 4.　Relative 1970−1989 PARE | 0.627 | 0.640 | 0.702 | 0.743 | 0.767 | 0.805 | 0.912 | 1.027 | 1.071 | 1.094 |
| 5.　Absolute 1980−1989 PARE | 0.227 | 0.244 | 0.279 | 0.315 | 0.355 | 0.409 | 0.493 | 0.592 | 0.663 | 0.737 |
| 6.　WA [a] | 0.974 | 0.960 | 0.981 | 0.938 | 0.868 | 0.866 | 0.995 | 1.143 | 1.156 | 1.111 |
| **Costa Rica:** Costa Rican colones | | | | | | | | | | |
| 1.　MER | 6.625 | 6.635 | 6.635 | 6.647 | 7.930 | 8.570 | 8.570 | 8.570 | 8.570 | 8.570 |
| 2.　PPPs | 3.153 | 3.175 | 3.336 | 3.694 | 4.306 | 4.786 | 5.096 | 5.342 | 5.493 | 5.593 |
| 3.　Absolute 1970−1989 PARE | 3.352 | 3.434 | 3.654 | 4.196 | 5.171 | 6.439 | 7.508 | 8.780 | 9.475 | 10.341 |
| 4.　Relative 1970−1989 PARE | 6.875 | 6.700 | 6.816 | 7.340 | 8.291 | 9.399 | 10.315 | 11.300 | 11.365 | 11.387 |
| 5.　Absolute 1980−1989 PARE | 2.960 | 3.033 | 3.227 | 3.706 | 4.566 | 5.686 | 6.631 | 7.754 | 8.367 | 9.132 |
| 6.　WA | 6.625 | 6.626 | 6.635 | 6.647 | 7.930 | 8.570 | 8.570 | 8.570 | 8.570 | 8.570 |
| **Côte d'Ivoire:** CFA francs | | | | | | | | | | |
| 1.　MER | 277.710 | 277.130 | 252.480 | 222.890 | 240.700 | 214.310 | 238.950 | 245.680 | 225.650 | 212.720 |
| 2.　PPPs | 167.566 | 162.907 | 161.541 | 166.366 | 186.246 | 185.147 | 196.080 | 221.789 | 228.158 | 231.255 |
| 3.　Absolute 1970−1989 PARE | 106.180 | 106.621 | 107.962 | 120.437 | 149.866 | 156.641 | 186.692 | 246.391 | 259.697 | 277.962 |
| 4.　Relative 1970−1989 PARE | 217.773 | 208.007 | 201.385 | 210.662 | 240.325 | 228.638 | 256.473 | 317.097 | 311.498 | 306.078 |
| 5.　Absolute 1980−1989 PARE | 92.778 | 93.163 | 94.335 | 105.236 | 130.950 | 136.870 | 163.128 | 215.292 | 226.919 | 242.878 |
| 6.　WA | 277.710 | 277.132 | 252.484 | 222.888 | 240.704 | 214.312 | 238.950 | 245.679 | 225.655 | 212.721 |
| **Cuba:** Cuban pesos | | | | | | | | | | |
| 1.　MER | 1.000 | 1.000 | 0.953 | 0.829 | 0.820 | 0.820 | 0.821 | 0.830 | 0.770 | 0.730 |
| 2.　PPPs | ... | ... | ... | ... | ... | ... | ... | ... | ... | ... |
| 3.　Absolute 1970−1989 PARE | 0.698 | 0.705 | 0.741 | 0.778 | 0.842 | 0.848 | 0.835 | 0.778 | 0.816 | 0.828 |
| 4.　Relative 1970−1989 PARE | 1.432 | 1.375 | 1.382 | 1.361 | 1.351 | 1.238 | 1.146 | 1.002 | 0.979 | 0.911 |
| 5.　Absolute 1980−1989 PARE | 0.680 | 0.686 | 0.721 | 0.757 | 0.820 | 0.825 | 0.812 | 0.758 | 0.794 | 0.805 |
| 6.　WA [a] | 0.935 | 0.989 | 1.022 | 0.978 | 0.934 | 0.850 | 0.813 | 0.783 | 0.814 | 0.798 |
| **Cyprus:** Cyprus pounds | | | | | | | | | | |
| 1.　MER | 0.417 | 0.409 | 0.384 | 0.350 | 0.365 | 0.368 | 0.410 | 0.408 | 0.373 | 0.354 |
| 2.　PPPs | 0.239 | 0.239 | 0.240 | 0.242 | 0.261 | 0.244 | 0.239 | 0.240 | 0.252 | 0.263 |
| 3.　Absolute 1970−1989 PARE | 0.157 | 0.179 | 0.196 | 0.212 | 0.236 | 0.246 | 0.268 | 0.293 | 0.326 | 0.369 |
| 4.　Relative 1970−1989 PARE | 0.321 | 0.348 | 0.365 | 0.371 | 0.378 | 0.358 | 0.368 | 0.377 | 0.391 | 0.406 |
| 5.　Absolute 1980−1989 PARE | 0.130 | 0.148 | 0.162 | 0.175 | 0.195 | 0.203 | 0.222 | 0.242 | 0.270 | 0.305 |
| 6.　WA | 0.235 | 0.267 | 0.294 | 0.318 | 0.354 | 0.369 | 0.410 | 0.408 | 0.374 | 0.354 |

| | | | | | | | | | | Averages | | |
|---|---|---|---|---|---|---|---|---|---|---|---|---|
| 1980 | 1981 | 1982 | 1983 | 1984 | 1985 | 1986 | 1987 | 1988 | 1989 | 1970–89 | 1970–79 | 1980–89 |
| (11) | (12) | (13) | (14) | (15) | (16) | (17) | (18) | (19) | (20) | (21) | (22) | (23) |
| 211.280 | 271.730 | 328.600 | 381.060 | 436.950 | 449.260 | 346.300 | 300.500 | 297.800 | 319.000 | 298.039 | 234.308 | 325.981 |
| ... | ... | ... | ... | ... | ... | ... | ... | ... | ... | ... | ... | ... |
| 285.900 | 317.267 | 332.300 | 361.574 | 383.530 | 408.927 | 438.175 | 461.154 | 488.171 | 501.867 | 298.039 | 162.183 | 404.934 |
| 288.421 | 292.399 | 287.672 | 302.780 | 310.060 | 321.872 | 338.099 | 345.891 | 354.262 | 349.856 | 300.960 | 245.790 | 323.869 |
| 230.156 | 255.408 | 267.509 | 291.076 | 308.751 | 329.196 | 352.741 | 371.240 | 392.989 | 404.015 | 239.929 | 130.562 | 325.981 |
| 211.279 | 271.730 | 328.605 | 381.065 | 436.955 | 449.261 | 346.305 | 300.535 | 297.847 | 319.007 | 298.050 | 234.310 | 325.996 |
| | | | | | | | | | | | | |
| 211.280 | 271.730 | 328.600 | 381.060 | 436.960 | 449.260 | 346.300 | 300.500 | 297.800 | 319.000 | 312.619 | 233.312 | 336.862 |
| 228.985 | 276.845 | 299.931 | 311.026 | 336.241 | 360.576 | 250.395 | 259.339 | 256.954 | 269.549 | 267.492 | 199.815 | 288.155 |
| 302.560 | 375.169 | 397.949 | 424.163 | 474.437 | 486.149 | 344.381 | 366.931 | 375.762 | 410.343 | 312.619 | 152.982 | 401.272 |
| 305.228 | 345.762 | 344.504 | 355.192 | 383.553 | 382.655 | 265.727 | 275.219 | 272.687 | 286.054 | 299.699 | 227.661 | 321.219 |
| 253.995 | 314.949 | 334.072 | 356.078 | 398.283 | 408.115 | 289.103 | 308.033 | 315.446 | 344.477 | 262.439 | 128.426 | 336.862 |
| 211.279 | 271.730 | 328.605 | 381.065 | 436.955 | 449.261 | 346.305 | 300.535 | 297.847 | 319.007 | 312.627 | 233.314 | 336.873 |
| | | | | | | | | | | | | |
| 1.027 | 1.149 | 1.330 | 1.495 | 1.729 | 2.006 | 1.909 | 1.700 | 1.500 | 1.700 | 1.375 | 0.898 | 1.584 |
| ... | ... | ... | ... | ... | ... | ... | ... | ... | ... | ... | ... | ... |
| 1.130 | 1.362 | 1.533 | 1.656 | 1.854 | 2.088 | 2.299 | 2.546 | 2.757 | 3.043 | 1.375 | 0.565 | 2.135 |
| 1.139 | 1.256 | 1.327 | 1.387 | 1.499 | 1.644 | 1.774 | 1.910 | 2.000 | 2.121 | 1.422 | 0.861 | 1.695 |
| 0.838 | 1.011 | 1.137 | 1.229 | 1.376 | 1.550 | 1.706 | 1.890 | 2.046 | 2.258 | 1.021 | 0.419 | 1.584 |
| 1.119 | 1.243 | 1.339 | 1.443 | 1.671 | 1.946 | 2.087 | 2.087 | 1.877 | 1.796 | 1.512 | 1.015 | 1.721 |
| | | | | | | | | | | | | |
| 8.570 | 21.763 | 37.407 | 41.094 | 44.533 | 50.453 | 55.990 | 62.800 | 75.800 | 81.500 | 35.604 | 8.086 | 50.492 |
| 6.086 | 8.287 | 14.983 | 18.734 | 19.323 | 22.522 | 26.065 | 27.889 | 32.648 | 36.122 | 17.630 | 4.727 | 23.093 |
| 12.289 | 17.339 | 31.934 | 41.175 | 48.047 | 57.918 | 68.377 | 75.262 | 91.065 | 104.885 | 35.604 | 6.650 | 57.176 |
| 12.397 | 15.980 | 27.645 | 34.479 | 38.843 | 45.588 | 52.760 | 56.451 | 66.085 | 73.116 | 35.298 | 9.650 | 45.858 |
| 10.852 | 15.312 | 28.201 | 36.361 | 42.430 | 51.147 | 60.384 | 66.464 | 80.419 | 92.623 | 31.441 | 5.872 | 50.492 |
| 8.570 | 21.763 | 37.407 | 41.094 | 44.533 | 50.453 | 55.986 | 62.776 | 75.805 | 81.504 | 35.602 | 8.086 | 50.490 |
| | | | | | | | | | | | | |
| 211.280 | 271.730 | 328.600 | 381.060 | 436.960 | 449.260 | 346.200 | 300.500 | 297.800 | 319.000 | 294.572 | 232.107 | 324.943 |
| 240.717 | 230.371 | 235.755 | 235.115 | 259.030 | 265.468 | 259.987 | 252.492 | 252.048 | 237.278 | 233.764 | 201.701 | 247.423 |
| 292.096 | 303.146 | 322.536 | 350.388 | 395.485 | 406.904 | 406.511 | 406.137 | 419.033 | 410.653 | 294.572 | 184.271 | 371.881 |
| 294.671 | 279.384 | 279.219 | 293.414 | 319.725 | 320.280 | 313.667 | 304.625 | 304.089 | 286.270 | 290.424 | 265.778 | 300.088 |
| 255.228 | 264.884 | 281.826 | 306.163 | 345.568 | 355.546 | 355.202 | 354.875 | 366.144 | 358.822 | 257.392 | 161.013 | 324.943 |
| 211.279 | 271.730 | 328.605 | 381.065 | 436.955 | 449.261 | 346.305 | 300.535 | 297.847 | 319.007 | 294.587 | 232.109 | 324.966 |
| | | | | | | | | | | | | |
| 0.720 | 0.830 | 0.850 | 0.860 | 0.880 | 0.920 | 0.830 | 0.786 | 0.758 | 0.780 | 0.824 | 0.831 | 0.821 |
| ... | ... | ... | ... | ... | ... | ... | ... | ... | ... | ... | ... | ... |
| 0.898 | 0.860 | 0.869 | 0.875 | 0.866 | 0.827 | 0.811 | 0.815 | 0.815 | 0.821 | 0.824 | 0.794 | 0.844 |
| 0.906 | 0.793 | 0.752 | 0.733 | 0.700 | 0.651 | 0.626 | 0.612 | 0.592 | 0.572 | 0.797 | 1.149 | 0.676 |
| 0.874 | 0.837 | 0.846 | 0.851 | 0.843 | 0.805 | 0.789 | 0.794 | 0.794 | 0.799 | 0.802 | 0.773 | 0.821 |
| 0.787 | 0.759 | 0.795 | 0.853 | 0.860 | 0.858 | 0.852 | 0.843 | 0.793 | 0.778 | 0.836 | 0.868 | 0.818 |
| | | | | | | | | | | | | |
| 0.353 | 0.420 | 0.480 | 0.526 | 0.587 | 0.609 | 0.520 | 0.500 | 0.500 | 0.500 | 0.471 | 0.379 | 0.502 |
| 0.276 | 0.278 | 0.280 | 0.289 | 0.299 | 0.317 | 0.323 | 0.327 | 0.326 | 0.328 | 0.295 | 0.248 | 0.309 |
| 0.421 | 0.470 | 0.517 | 0.545 | 0.589 | 0.623 | 0.648 | 0.674 | 0.696 | 0.727 | 0.471 | 0.250 | 0.607 |
| 0.424 | 0.433 | 0.448 | 0.456 | 0.476 | 0.490 | 0.500 | 0.505 | 0.505 | 0.507 | 0.455 | 0.374 | 0.482 |
| 0.348 | 0.389 | 0.428 | 0.451 | 0.487 | 0.515 | 0.536 | 0.557 | 0.576 | 0.601 | 0.390 | 0.207 | 0.502 |
| 0.353 | 0.421 | 0.475 | 0.527 | 0.587 | 0.609 | 0.517 | 0.481 | 0.466 | 0.493 | 0.451 | 0.339 | 0.493 |

**Table A.2**    Conversion rates for individual countries or areas, expressed as the number of
local currency units per United States dollar, 1970−1989 [*cont.*]

| Country or area | 1970 (1) | 1971 (2) | 1972 (3) | 1973 (4) | 1974 (5) | 1975 (6) | 1976 (7) | 1977 (8) | 1978 (9) | 1979 (10) |
|---|---|---|---|---|---|---|---|---|---|---|
| **Czechoslovakia (former):** Czechoslovak koruny | | | | | | | | | | |
| 1.   MER | 27.000 | 27.000 | 24.780 | 21.920 | 21.980 | 20.930 | 21.660 | 15.030 | 14.400 | 14.110 |
| 2.   PPPs | ... | ... | ... | ... | ... | ... | ... | ... | ... | ... |
| 3.   Absolute 1970−1989 PARE | 16.349 | 16.261 | 16.142 | 16.110 | 16.323 | 15.983 | 15.781 | 15.232 | 15.439 | 15.729 |
| 4.   Relative 1970−1989 PARE | 33.531 | 31.724 | 30.111 | 28.178 | 26.176 | 23.330 | 21.680 | 19.603 | 18.518 | 17.320 |
| 5.   Absolute 1980−1989 PARE | 14.457 | 14.379 | 14.274 | 14.245 | 14.434 | 14.134 | 13.955 | 13.470 | 13.652 | 13.909 |
| 6.   WA | 19.824 | 22.786 | 26.081 | 24.466 | 23.083 | 21.400 | 21.192 | 18.628 | 16.941 | 14.767 |
| **Denmark:** Danish kroner | | | | | | | | | | |
| 1.   MER | 7.500 | 7.420 | 6.949 | 6.050 | 6.095 | 5.746 | 6.045 | 6.003 | 5.515 | 5.261 |
| 2.   PPPs | 6.026 | 6.237 | 6.406 | 6.593 | 6.980 | 7.116 | 7.362 | 7.552 | 7.635 | 7.624 |
| 3.   Absolute 1970−1989 PARE | 2.674 | 2.879 | 3.143 | 3.478 | 3.933 | 4.422 | 4.824 | 5.278 | 5.799 | 6.239 |
| 4.   Relative 1970−1989 PARE | 5.484 | 5.616 | 5.863 | 6.084 | 6.307 | 6.454 | 6.628 | 6.793 | 6.955 | 6.870 |
| 5.   Absolute 1980−1989 PARE | 2.185 | 2.352 | 2.568 | 2.842 | 3.214 | 3.613 | 3.942 | 4.313 | 4.738 | 5.098 |
| 6.   WA | 7.500 | 7.417 | 6.949 | 6.049 | 6.095 | 5.746 | 6.045 | 6.003 | 5.515 | 5.261 |
| **Djibouti:** Djibouti francs | | | | | | | | | | |
| 1.   MER | 214.392 | 213.779 | 197.466 | 179.942 | 177.721 | 177.721 | 177.721 | 177.721 | 177.721 | 177.721 |
| 2.   PPPs | ... | ... | ... | ... | ... | ... | ... | ... | ... | ... |
| 3.   Absolute 1970−1989 PARE | 62.998 | 66.835 | 71.816 | 77.867 | 100.328 | 100.137 | 109.993 | 134.428 | 159.723 | 181.355 |
| 4.   Relative 1970−1989 PARE | 129.208 | 130.390 | 133.961 | 136.201 | 160.886 | 146.163 | 151.106 | 173.004 | 191.583 | 199.699 |
| 5.   Absolute 1980−1989 PARE | 45.964 | 48.764 | 52.398 | 56.813 | 73.201 | 73.061 | 80.252 | 98.080 | 116.536 | 132.319 |
| 6.   WA [a] | 243.502 | 232.761 | 223.860 | 214.371 | 228.477 | 195.503 | 189.259 | 211.167 | 215.652 | 206.424 |
| **Dominica:** East Caribbean dollars | | | | | | | | | | |
| 1.   MER | 2.000 | 1.970 | 1.922 | 1.959 | 2.053 | 2.170 | 2.615 | 2.700 | 2.700 | 2.700 |
| 2.   PPPs | ... | ... | ... | ... | ... | ... | ... | ... | ... | ... |
| 3.   Absolute 1970−1989 PARE | 0.654 | 0.659 | 0.729 | 0.830 | 1.071 | 1.313 | 1.443 | 1.617 | 1.796 | 2.161 |
| 4.   Relative 1970−1989 PARE | 1.341 | 1.285 | 1.360 | 1.452 | 1.718 | 1.917 | 1.982 | 2.082 | 2.154 | 2.379 |
| 5.   Absolute 1980−1989 PARE | 0.452 | 0.456 | 0.504 | 0.574 | 0.741 | 0.909 | 0.999 | 1.119 | 1.243 | 1.495 |
| 6.   WA | 2.000 | 1.972 | 1.922 | 1.959 | 2.053 | 2.170 | 2.615 | 2.700 | 2.700 | 2.700 |
| **Dominican Republic:** Dominican pesos | | | | | | | | | | |
| 1.   MER | 1.000 | 1.000 | 1.000 | 1.000 | 1.000 | 1.000 | 1.000 | 1.000 | 1.000 | 1.000 |
| 2.   PPPs | 0.552 | 0.540 | 0.576 | 0.583 | 0.592 | 0.614 | 0.643 | 0.672 | 0.649 | 0.663 |
| 3.   Absolute 1970−1989 PARE | 0.543 | 0.549 | 0.593 | 0.620 | 0.730 | 0.853 | 0.878 | 0.970 | 0.981 | 1.090 |
| 4.   Relative 1970−1989 PARE | 1.113 | 1.071 | 1.106 | 1.084 | 1.170 | 1.245 | 1.206 | 1.249 | 1.176 | 1.200 |
| 5.   Absolute 1980−1989 PARE | 0.482 | 0.488 | 0.527 | 0.551 | 0.649 | 0.759 | 0.780 | 0.863 | 0.872 | 0.969 |
| 6.   WA | 1.000 | 1.000 | 1.000 | 1.000 | 1.000 | 1.000 | 1.000 | 1.000 | 1.000 | 1.000 |
| **Ecuador:** Ecuadoran sucres | | | | | | | | | | |
| 1.   MER | 20.917 | 25.000 | 25.000 | 25.000 | 25.000 | 25.000 | 25.000 | 25.000 | 25.000 | 25.000 |
| 2.   PPPs | 8.449 | 8.810 | 9.560 | 10.925 | 11.638 | 11.440 | 12.493 | 13.070 | 13.370 | 13.973 |
| 3.   Absolute 1970−1989 PARE | 8.732 | 9.398 | 9.610 | 10.183 | 14.260 | 15.687 | 17.718 | 20.819 | 22.462 | 26.082 |
| 4.   Relative 1970−1989 PARE | 17.910 | 18.334 | 17.926 | 17.811 | 22.868 | 22.898 | 24.341 | 26.793 | 26.943 | 28.721 |
| 5.   Absolute 1980−1989 PARE | 7.251 | 7.804 | 7.980 | 8.456 | 11.842 | 13.027 | 14.713 | 17.288 | 18.653 | 21.659 |
| 6.   WA | 20.917 | 25.000 | 25.000 | 25.000 | 25.000 | 25.000 | 25.000 | 25.000 | 25.000 | 25.000 |
| **Egypt:** Egyptian pounds | | | | | | | | | | |
| 1.   MER | 0.435 | 0.435 | 0.435 | 0.396 | 0.391 | 0.391 | 0.391 | 0.391 | 0.391 | 0.700 |
| 2.   PPPs | 0.269 | 0.261 | 0.244 | 0.257 | 0.251 | 0.252 | 0.294 | 0.325 | 0.352 | 0.376 |
| 3.   Absolute 1970−1989 PARE | 0.255 | 0.262 | 0.237 | 0.272 | 0.290 | 0.301 | 0.357 | 0.405 | 0.438 | 0.513 |
| 4.   Relative 1970−1989 PARE | 0.522 | 0.511 | 0.443 | 0.477 | 0.465 | 0.440 | 0.491 | 0.522 | 0.525 | 0.565 |
| 5.   Absolute 1980−1989 PARE | 0.236 | 0.243 | 0.221 | 0.253 | 0.269 | 0.280 | 0.332 | 0.376 | 0.407 | 0.477 |
| 6.   WA | 0.398 | 0.392 | 0.387 | 0.396 | 0.481 | 0.456 | 0.503 | 0.570 | 0.660 | 0.700 |

| 1980 (11) | 1981 (12) | 1982 (13) | 1983 (14) | 1984 (15) | 1985 (16) | 1986 (17) | 1987 (18) | 1988 (19) | 1989 (20) | Averages 1970–89 (21) | 1970–79 (22) | 1980–89 (23) |
|---|---|---|---|---|---|---|---|---|---|---|---|---|
| 14.270 | 13.270 | 13.710 | 14.160 | 16.610 | 17.140 | 14.990 | 13.690 | 14.360 | 15.050 | 16.287 | 19.250 | 14.664 |
| ... | ... | ... | ... | ... | ... | ... | ... | ... | ... | ... | ... | ... |
| 16.150 | 15.779 | 16.346 | 16.246 | 16.683 | 16.653 | 16.655 | 16.784 | 16.958 | 17.338 | 16.287 | 15.894 | 16.582 |
| 16.292 | 14.542 | 14.150 | 13.604 | 13.487 | 13.108 | 12.851 | 12.589 | 12.306 | 12.087 | 16.212 | 23.213 | 13.321 |
| 14.281 | 13.953 | 14.454 | 14.366 | 14.753 | 14.726 | 14.728 | 14.842 | 14.995 | 15.332 | 14.403 | 14.055 | 14.664 |
| 14.607 | 13.789 | 13.966 | 13.816 | 15.048 | 16.079 | 16.238 | 15.357 | 14.485 | 14.625 | 16.616 | 20.061 | 14.789 |
| | | | | | | | | | | | | |
| 5.636 | 7.123 | 8.332 | 9.145 | 10.357 | 10.596 | 8.090 | 6.800 | 6.700 | 7.300 | 7.178 | 5.973 | 7.766 |
| 7.602 | 7.768 | 8.096 | 8.391 | 8.617 | 8.931 | 9.154 | 9.345 | 9.423 | 9.444 | 8.245 | 7.098 | 8.777 |
| 6.752 | 7.433 | 8.218 | 8.846 | 9.346 | 9.751 | 10.194 | 10.706 | 11.158 | 11.641 | 7.178 | 4.344 | 9.504 |
| 6.812 | 6.850 | 7.114 | 7.407 | 7.555 | 7.675 | 7.866 | 8.030 | 8.097 | 8.115 | 7.262 | 6.434 | 7.630 |
| 5.518 | 6.074 | 6.715 | 7.228 | 7.637 | 7.967 | 8.330 | 8.748 | 9.118 | 9.512 | 5.866 | 3.550 | 7.766 |
| 5.636 | 7.123 | 8.332 | 9.145 | 10.357 | 10.596 | 8.091 | 6.840 | 6.732 | 7.310 | 7.187 | 5.973 | 7.780 |
| | | | | | | | | | | | | |
| 177.721 | 177.721 | 177.721 | 177.721 | 177.721 | 177.721 | 177.720 | 177.700 | 177.700 | 177.700 | 179.031 | 182.433 | 177.714 |
| ... | ... | ... | ... | ... | ... | ... | ... | ... | ... | ... | ... | ... |
| 205.951 | 232.114 | 240.529 | 241.251 | 236.332 | 242.381 | 249.848 | 258.746 | 257.391 | 264.745 | 179.031 | 107.440 | 243.573 |
| 207.767 | 213.920 | 208.226 | 202.023 | 191.060 | 190.781 | 192.785 | 194.074 | 186.787 | 184.556 | 184.157 | 160.042 | 195.894 |
| 150.264 | 169.353 | 175.493 | 176.020 | 172.431 | 176.844 | 182.292 | 188.784 | 187.795 | 193.161 | 130.623 | 78.390 | 177.714 |
| 202.901 | 201.827 | 189.815 | 180.231 | 175.479 | 179.515 | 182.934 | 183.823 | 179.185 | 180.766 | 191.498 | 211.339 | 184.606 |
| | | | | | | | | | | | | |
| 2.700 | 2.700 | 2.700 | 2.700 | 2.700 | 2.700 | 2.700 | 2.700 | 2.700 | 2.700 | 2.613 | 2.344 | 2.700 |
| ... | ... | ... | ... | ... | ... | ... | ... | ... | ... | ... | ... | ... |
| 2.799 | 2.947 | 3.132 | 3.403 | 3.628 | 3.914 | 4.165 | 4.373 | 4.728 | 5.028 | 2.613 | 1.200 | 3.902 |
| 2.824 | 2.716 | 2.712 | 2.850 | 2.933 | 3.081 | 3.214 | 3.280 | 3.431 | 3.505 | 2.695 | 1.820 | 3.114 |
| 1.937 | 2.039 | 2.168 | 2.355 | 2.510 | 2.709 | 2.882 | 3.026 | 3.272 | 3.479 | 1.808 | 0.830 | 2.700 |
| 2.700 | 2.700 | 2.700 | 2.700 | 2.700 | 2.700 | 2.700 | 2.700 | 2.700 | 2.700 | 2.613 | 2.344 | 2.700 |
| | | | | | | | | | | | | |
| 1.000 | 1.000 | 1.000 | 1.000 | 1.000 | 3.113 | 2.900 | 3.800 | 6.100 | 6.300 | 1.935 | 1.000 | 2.391 |
| 0.638 | 0.607 | 0.663 | 0.677 | 0.803 | 1.113 | 1.194 | 1.332 | 1.858 | 2.564 | 1.048 | 0.623 | 1.217 |
| 1.239 | 1.305 | 1.408 | 1.458 | 1.742 | 2.418 | 2.647 | 3.038 | 4.379 | 6.290 | 1.935 | 0.815 | 2.690 |
| 1.250 | 1.202 | 1.219 | 1.221 | 1.409 | 1.903 | 2.043 | 2.279 | 3.178 | 4.385 | 1.893 | 1.179 | 2.159 |
| 1.102 | 1.160 | 1.252 | 1.296 | 1.549 | 2.150 | 2.354 | 2.701 | 3.894 | 5.592 | 1.721 | 0.724 | 2.391 |
| 1.000 | 1.000 | 1.090 | 1.260 | 2.060 | 3.113 | 2.904 | 3.845 | 6.113 | 6.340 | 2.101 | 1.000 | 2.708 |
| | | | | | | | | | | | | |
| 25.000 | 25.000 | 30.026 | 44.115 | 62.536 | 69.556 | 122.780 | 170.500 | 301.600 | 526.400 | 97.432 | 24.847 | 123.641 |
| 14.820 | 15.785 | 17.786 | 25.535 | 33.507 | 45.622 | 54.060 | 72.514 | 109.119 | 184.228 | 48.897 | 12.176 | 62.596 |
| 31.172 | 35.646 | 42.002 | 58.251 | 81.081 | 106.136 | 128.295 | 177.033 | 275.344 | 483.931 | 97.432 | 16.906 | 148.894 |
| 31.447 | 32.852 | 36.361 | 48.779 | 65.549 | 83.541 | 98.993 | 132.784 | 199.815 | 337.353 | 94.399 | 24.152 | 119.651 |
| 25.885 | 29.600 | 34.879 | 48.371 | 67.329 | 88.135 | 106.536 | 147.007 | 228.645 | 401.855 | 80.907 | 14.039 | 123.641 |
| 25.000 | 25.000 | 33.400 | 52.900 | 79.500 | 91.500 | 122.790 | 170.462 | 301.611 | 526.348 | 103.657 | 24.847 | 134.646 |
| | | | | | | | | | | | | |
| 0.700 | 0.700 | 0.700 | 0.700 | 0.700 | 0.700 | 0.700 | 0.700 | 0.700 | 0.900 | 0.665 | 0.439 | 0.730 |
| 0.429 | 0.435 | 0.460 | 0.441 | 0.505 | 0.592 | 0.616 | 0.671 | 0.726 | 0.785 | 0.519 | 0.301 | 0.594 |
| 0.532 | 0.529 | 0.505 | 0.606 | 0.701 | 0.761 | 0.807 | 0.904 | 1.011 | 1.138 | 0.665 | 0.351 | 0.786 |
| 0.536 | 0.487 | 0.438 | 0.508 | 0.567 | 0.599 | 0.623 | 0.678 | 0.734 | 0.793 | 0.602 | 0.506 | 0.623 |
| 0.494 | 0.491 | 0.469 | 0.563 | 0.651 | 0.706 | 0.749 | 0.840 | 0.939 | 1.057 | 0.617 | 0.326 | 0.730 |
| 0.720 | 0.740 | 0.812 | 0.859 | 0.930 | 0.955 | 1.069 | 1.273 | 1.761 | 1.937 | 0.968 | 0.521 | 1.137 |

**Table A.2**   Conversion rates for individual countries or areas, expressed as the number of
local currency units per United States dollar, 1970−1989 [*cont.*]

| Country or area | 1970 (1) | 1971 (2) | 1972 (3) | 1973 (4) | 1974 (5) | 1975 (6) | 1976 (7) | 1977 (8) | 1978 (9) | 1979 (10) |
|---|---|---|---|---|---|---|---|---|---|---|
| **El Salvador:** Salvadoran colones | | | | | | | | | | |
| 1.  MER | 2.500 | 2.500 | 2.500 | 2.500 | 2.500 | 2.500 | 2.500 | 2.500 | 2.500 | 2.500 |
| 2.  PPPs | 1.014 | 0.997 | 0.983 | 1.010 | 1.076 | 1.091 | 1.157 | 1.186 | 1.156 | 1.298 |
| 3.  Absolute 1970−1989 PARE | 0.999 | 1.002 | 1.013 | 1.114 | 1.240 | 1.333 | 1.634 | 1.936 | 1.952 | 2.222 |
| 4.  Relative 1970−1989 PARE | 2.049 | 1.955 | 1.889 | 1.949 | 1.988 | 1.946 | 2.245 | 2.491 | 2.341 | 2.447 |
| 5.  Absolute 1980−1989 PARE | 0.714 | 0.717 | 0.724 | 0.797 | 0.886 | 0.953 | 1.169 | 1.384 | 1.396 | 1.589 |
| 6.  WA | 2.500 | 2.500 | 2.500 | 2.500 | 2.500 | 2.500 | 2.500 | 2.500 | 2.500 | 2.500 |
| **Equatorial Guinea:** CFA francs | | | | | | | | | | |
| 1.  MER | 277.710 | 275.520 | 252.210 | 222.700 | 240.500 | 214.320 | 238.980 | 245.670 | 225.660 | 212.720 |
| 2.  PPPs | ... | ... | ... | ... | ... | ... | ... | ... | ... | ... |
| 3.  Absolute 1970−1989 PARE | 94.804 | 94.765 | 95.641 | 93.483 | 111.877 | 136.510 | 171.679 | 189.800 | 227.010 | 252.775 |
| 4.  Relative 1970−1989 PARE | 194.442 | 184.878 | 178.402 | 163.516 | 179.406 | 199.254 | 235.848 | 244.266 | 272.291 | 278.343 |
| 5.  Absolute 1980−1989 PARE | 48.591 | 48.571 | 49.020 | 47.914 | 57.341 | 69.966 | 87.992 | 97.279 | 116.351 | 129.556 |
| 6.  WA | 70.000 | 69.469 | 64.271 | 58.260 | 57.687 | 57.407 | 66.903 | 75.962 | 76.668 | 68.341 |
| **Ethiopia:** Ethopian birr | | | | | | | | | | |
| 1.  MER | 2.500 | 2.490 | 2.300 | 2.099 | 2.070 | 2.070 | 2.070 | 2.070 | 2.070 | 2.070 |
| 2.  PPPs | 0.885 | 0.841 | 0.863 | 0.908 | 0.831 | 0.804 | 0.846 | 0.816 | 0.802 | 0.775 |
| 3.  Absolute 1970−1989 PARE | 1.483 | 1.499 | 1.441 | 1.481 | 1.619 | 1.610 | 1.709 | 1.932 | 2.080 | 2.171 |
| 4.  Relative 1970−1989 PARE | 3.043 | 2.925 | 2.688 | 2.590 | 2.596 | 2.349 | 2.348 | 2.487 | 2.495 | 2.391 |
| 5.  Absolute 1980−1989 PARE | 1.278 | 1.291 | 1.241 | 1.275 | 1.394 | 1.386 | 1.472 | 1.664 | 1.791 | 1.870 |
| 6.  WA | 2.500 | 2.493 | 2.300 | 2.099 | 2.070 | 2.070 | 2.070 | 2.070 | 2.070 | 2.070 |
| **Fiji:** Fiji dollars | | | | | | | | | | |
| 1.  MER | 0.871 | 0.860 | 0.830 | 0.794 | 0.810 | 0.823 | 0.900 | 0.917 | 0.847 | 0.836 |
| 2.  PPPs | 0.364 | 0.361 | 0.383 | 0.401 | 0.463 | 0.497 | 0.513 | 0.479 | 0.477 | 0.472 |
| 3.  Absolute 1970−1989 PARE | 0.332 | 0.345 | 0.394 | 0.458 | 0.593 | 0.724 | 0.790 | 0.795 | 0.829 | 0.897 |
| 4.  Relative 1970−1989 PARE | 0.682 | 0.672 | 0.734 | 0.801 | 0.951 | 1.057 | 1.086 | 1.023 | 0.994 | 0.987 |
| 5.  Absolute 1980−1989 PARE | 0.281 | 0.291 | 0.333 | 0.387 | 0.501 | 0.612 | 0.668 | 0.671 | 0.700 | 0.758 |
| 6.  WA | 0.871 | 0.859 | 0.825 | 0.794 | 0.806 | 0.824 | 0.899 | 0.917 | 0.847 | 0.836 |
| **Finland:** Finnish markaa | | | | | | | | | | |
| 1.  MER | 4.200 | 4.180 | 4.146 | 3.821 | 3.774 | 3.679 | 3.864 | 4.029 | 4.117 | 3.900 |
| 2.  PPPs | 3.229 | 3.315 | 3.410 | 3.558 | 3.897 | 4.054 | 4.428 | 4.639 | 4.746 | 4.653 |
| 3.  Absolute 1970−1989 PARE | 1.369 | 1.474 | 1.597 | 1.822 | 2.232 | 2.555 | 2.875 | 3.168 | 3.425 | 3.716 |
| 4.  Relative 1970−1989 PARE | 2.809 | 2.875 | 2.980 | 3.187 | 3.579 | 3.730 | 3.949 | 4.077 | 4.108 | 4.092 |
| 5.  Absolute 1980−1989 PARE | 1.081 | 1.163 | 1.261 | 1.438 | 1.761 | 2.017 | 2.269 | 2.500 | 2.703 | 2.933 |
| 6.  WA | 4.200 | 4.184 | 4.146 | 3.821 | 3.774 | 3.679 | 3.864 | 4.029 | 4.117 | 3.895 |
| **France:** French francs | | | | | | | | | | |
| 1.  MER | 5.554 | 5.540 | 5.050 | 4.460 | 4.810 | 4.286 | 4.780 | 4.913 | 4.513 | 4.255 |
| 2.  PPPs | 4.477 | 4.474 | 4.485 | 4.495 | 4.628 | 4.759 | 4.968 | 5.105 | 5.151 | 5.189 |
| 3.  Absolute 1970−1989 PARE | 2.124 | 2.259 | 2.417 | 2.622 | 2.932 | 3.312 | 3.681 | 4.022 | 4.429 | 4.877 |
| 4.  Relative 1970−1989 PARE | 4.357 | 4.407 | 4.509 | 4.585 | 4.702 | 4.835 | 5.057 | 5.176 | 5.312 | 5.370 |
| 5.  Absolute 1980−1989 PARE | 1.736 | 1.846 | 1.975 | 2.143 | 2.396 | 2.707 | 3.009 | 3.287 | 3.620 | 3.986 |
| 6.  WA | 5.554 | 5.543 | 5.050 | 4.458 | 4.814 | 4.286 | 4.779 | 4.914 | 4.513 | 4.254 |
| **French Guiana:** Francs | | | | | | | | | | |
| 1.  MER | 5.554 | 5.543 | 5.044 | 4.454 | 4.810 | 4.286 | 4.780 | 4.913 | 4.513 | 4.255 |
| 2.  PPPs | ... | ... | ... | ... | ... | ... | ... | ... | ... | ... |
| 3.  Absolute 1970−1989 PARE | 2.273 | 2.405 | 2.705 | 2.934 | 3.182 | 3.543 | 3.752 | 4.014 | 4.589 | 4.706 |
| 4.  Relative 1970−1989 PARE | 4.661 | 4.691 | 5.045 | 5.132 | 5.102 | 5.171 | 5.155 | 5.166 | 5.504 | 5.182 |
| 5.  Absolute 1980−1989 PARE | 1.813 | 1.918 | 2.158 | 2.341 | 2.538 | 2.826 | 2.993 | 3.202 | 3.661 | 3.754 |
| 6.  WA | 6.118 | 5.946 | 5.963 | 5.563 | 5.191 | 5.007 | 4.997 | 4.961 | 5.325 | 4.881 |

| | | | | | | | | | | Averages | | |
|---|---|---|---|---|---|---|---|---|---|---|---|---|
| 1980 (11) | 1981 (12) | 1982 (13) | 1983 (14) | 1984 (15) | 1985 (16) | 1986 (17) | 1987 (18) | 1988 (19) | 1989 (20) | 1970–89 (21) | 1970–79 (22) | 1980–89 (23) |
| 2.500 | 2.500 | 2.500 | 2.500 | 2.500 | 2.500 | 4.850 | 5.000 | 5.000 | 5.000 | 3.280 | 2.500 | 3.615 |
| 1.319 | 1.291 | 1.330 | 1.423 | 1.577 | 1.882 | 2.528 | 2.802 | 3.155 | 3.532 | 1.789 | 1.128 | 2.167 |
| 2.521 | 2.666 | 2.928 | 3.290 | 3.693 | 4.452 | 6.100 | 6.956 | 8.095 | 9.435 | 3.280 | 1.503 | 5.056 |
| 2.544 | 2.457 | 2.535 | 2.755 | 2.985 | 3.504 | 4.707 | 5.217 | 5.875 | 6.577 | 3.411 | 2.193 | 4.085 |
| 1.803 | 1.906 | 2.093 | 2.352 | 2.640 | 3.183 | 4.362 | 4.973 | 5.788 | 6.746 | 2.345 | 1.075 | 3.615 |
| 2.500 | 2.500 | 2.570 | 2.730 | 2.820 | 3.670 | 5.000 | 5.000 | 5.000 | 5.600 | 3.472 | 2.500 | 3.925 |
| | | | | | | | | | | | | |
| 211.280 | 271.730 | 328.610 | 381.060 | 436.960 | 449.260 | 346.300 | 300.500 | 297.800 | 319.000 | 299.872 | 239.305 | 332.781 |
| ... | ... | ... | ... | ... | ... | ... | ... | ... | ... | ... | ... | ... |
| 276.386 | 361.222 | 432.527 | 588.724 | 662.688 | 795.096 | 804.692 | 797.913 | 827.568 | 831.881 | 299.872 | 126.141 | 649.282 |
| 278.823 | 332.909 | 374.439 | 492.995 | 535.741 | 625.831 | 620.907 | 598.480 | 600.560 | 579.912 | 363.517 | 204.826 | 521.340 |
| 141.658 | 185.140 | 221.687 | 301.743 | 339.652 | 407.517 | 412.435 | 408.961 | 424.160 | 426.370 | 153.696 | 64.652 | 332.781 |
| 110.630 | 184.630 | 219.720 | 286.860 | 321.520 | 449.260 | 346.300 | 300.530 | 297.850 | 319.010 | 146.874 | 65.598 | 284.702 |
| | | | | | | | | | | | | |
| 2.070 | 2.070 | 2.070 | 2.070 | 2.070 | 2.070 | 2.070 | 2.100 | 2.100 | 2.100 | 2.104 | 2.148 | 2.080 |
| 0.722 | 0.695 | 0.678 | 0.660 | 0.647 | 0.623 | 0.637 | 0.593 | 0.595 | 0.589 | 0.695 | 0.829 | 0.636 |
| 2.189 | 2.238 | 2.280 | 2.373 | 2.361 | 2.458 | 2.564 | 2.453 | 2.543 | 2.622 | 2.104 | 1.713 | 2.416 |
| 2.208 | 2.062 | 1.974 | 1.987 | 1.909 | 1.935 | 1.978 | 1.840 | 1.845 | 1.828 | 2.122 | 2.545 | 1.940 |
| 1.885 | 1.927 | 1.963 | 2.044 | 2.034 | 2.117 | 2.208 | 2.113 | 2.190 | 2.258 | 1.812 | 1.475 | 2.080 |
| 2.070 | 2.070 | 2.070 | 2.070 | 2.070 | 2.070 | 2.070 | 2.070 | 2.070 | 2.070 | 2.098 | 2.148 | 2.070 |
| | | | | | | | | | | | | |
| 0.817 | 0.853 | 0.932 | 1.016 | 1.081 | 1.153 | 1.130 | 1.200 | 1.400 | 1.500 | 1.022 | 0.850 | 1.104 |
| 0.505 | 0.495 | 0.544 | 0.516 | 0.502 | 0.545 | 0.554 | 0.567 | 0.581 | 0.557 | 0.514 | 0.457 | 0.539 |
| 1.054 | 1.062 | 1.146 | 1.210 | 1.248 | 1.341 | 1.390 | 1.466 | 1.551 | 1.549 | 1.022 | 0.643 | 1.307 |
| 1.063 | 0.979 | 0.992 | 1.013 | 1.009 | 1.055 | 1.073 | 1.099 | 1.126 | 1.080 | 1.019 | 0.939 | 1.052 |
| 0.890 | 0.897 | 0.968 | 1.022 | 1.054 | 1.133 | 1.175 | 1.238 | 1.310 | 1.308 | 0.863 | 0.543 | 1.104 |
| 0.817 | 0.853 | 0.932 | 1.017 | 1.083 | 1.154 | 1.133 | 1.244 | 1.430 | 1.483 | 1.025 | 0.850 | 1.110 |
| | | | | | | | | | | | | |
| 3.730 | 4.320 | 4.820 | 5.570 | 6.010 | 6.198 | 5.070 | 4.400 | 4.200 | 4.300 | 4.529 | 3.940 | 4.742 |
| 4.655 | 4.826 | 4.949 | 5.416 | 5.545 | 5.840 | 5.986 | 6.128 | 6.340 | 6.499 | 5.262 | 4.144 | 5.726 |
| 4.072 | 4.547 | 4.937 | 5.360 | 5.838 | 6.138 | 6.417 | 6.758 | 7.227 | 7.712 | 4.529 | 2.487 | 6.008 |
| 4.108 | 4.191 | 4.274 | 4.488 | 4.720 | 4.831 | 4.951 | 5.069 | 5.245 | 5.376 | 4.488 | 3.673 | 4.808 |
| 3.214 | 3.589 | 3.897 | 4.230 | 4.608 | 4.844 | 5.064 | 5.334 | 5.704 | 6.086 | 3.574 | 1.963 | 4.742 |
| 3.730 | 4.315 | 4.820 | 5.570 | 6.010 | 6.198 | 5.070 | 4.396 | 4.183 | 4.291 | 4.525 | 3.940 | 4.736 |
| | | | | | | | | | | | | |
| 4.226 | 5.435 | 6.572 | 7.621 | 8.739 | 8.990 | 6.930 | 6.000 | 6.000 | 6.400 | 5.944 | 4.673 | 6.532 |
| 5.314 | 5.519 | 5.806 | 6.184 | 6.386 | 6.645 | 6.853 | 6.843 | 6.820 | 6.777 | 5.927 | 4.858 | 6.392 |
| 5.432 | 6.050 | 6.760 | 7.417 | 7.971 | 8.430 | 8.869 | 9.109 | 9.384 | 9.707 | 5.944 | 3.350 | 7.992 |
| 5.479 | 5.576 | 5.852 | 6.211 | 6.444 | 6.635 | 6.843 | 6.832 | 6.810 | 6.767 | 5.973 | 4.935 | 6.419 |
| 4.439 | 4.945 | 5.525 | 6.062 | 6.514 | 6.890 | 7.248 | 7.445 | 7.670 | 7.934 | 4.858 | 2.738 | 6.532 |
| 4.226 | 5.435 | 6.572 | 7.621 | 8.739 | 8.985 | 6.926 | 6.011 | 5.957 | 6.380 | 5.938 | 4.673 | 6.523 |
| | | | | | | | | | | | | |
| 4.226 | 5.435 | 6.572 | 7.622 | 8.739 | 8.985 | 6.926 | 6.000 | 6.000 | 6.400 | 5.870 | 4.682 | 6.550 |
| ... | ... | ... | ... | ... | ... | ... | ... | ... | ... | ... | ... | ... |
| 5.268 | 6.032 | 6.913 | 7.654 | 8.377 | 8.979 | 9.120 | 9.503 | 9.727 | 10.114 | 5.870 | 3.460 | 8.210 |
| 5.315 | 5.559 | 5.985 | 6.410 | 6.772 | 7.067 | 7.037 | 7.128 | 7.059 | 7.051 | 6.102 | 5.132 | 6.614 |
| 4.203 | 4.812 | 5.515 | 6.106 | 6.683 | 7.163 | 7.276 | 7.581 | 7.760 | 8.069 | 4.683 | 2.760 | 6.550 |
| 4.724 | 5.243 | 6.115 | 7.265 | 8.348 | 9.098 | 8.522 | 7.575 | 6.509 | 6.342 | 6.310 | 5.248 | 6.881 |

**Table A.2**  Conversion rates for individual countries or areas, expressed as the number of
local currency units per United States dollar, 1970–1989 [*cont.*]

| Country or area | 1970 (1) | 1971 (2) | 1972 (3) | 1973 (4) | 1974 (5) | 1975 (6) | 1976 (7) | 1977 (8) | 1978 (9) | 1979 (10) |
|---|---|---|---|---|---|---|---|---|---|---|
| **French Polynesia:** CFP francs | | | | | | | | | | |
| 1.  MER | 100.985 | 100.182 | 91.709 | 80.982 | 87.454 | 77.927 | 86.909 | 89.327 | 82.055 | 77.353 |
| 2.  PPPs | ... | ... | ... | ... | ... | ... | ... | ... | ... | ... |
| 3.  Absolute 1970–1989 PARE | 31.273 | 32.533 | 34.165 | 37.027 | 43.637 | 50.786 | 59.277 | 63.050 | 70.412 | 79.273 |
| 4.  Relative 1970–1989 PARE | 64.140 | 63.470 | 63.728 | 64.766 | 69.977 | 74.129 | 81.433 | 81.143 | 84.457 | 87.291 |
| 5.  Absolute 1980–1989 PARE | 25.353 | 26.376 | 27.698 | 30.019 | 35.378 | 41.174 | 48.057 | 51.116 | 57.085 | 64.268 |
| 6.  WA [a] | 97.316 | 103.311 | 102.413 | 98.132 | 100.010 | 96.928 | 98.887 | 92.837 | 95.016 | 94.015 |
| **Gabon:** CFA francs | | | | | | | | | | |
| 1.  MER | 277.710 | 277.130 | 252.480 | 222.890 | 240.700 | 214.310 | 238.950 | 245.680 | 225.650 | 212.720 |
| 2.  PPPs | 218.409 | 217.809 | 225.630 | 208.394 | 237.368 | 250.540 | 282.431 | 279.266 | 266.866 | 262.849 |
| 3.  Absolute 1970–1989 PARE | 65.927 | 76.115 | 80.414 | 84.111 | 134.445 | 146.264 | 164.568 | 184.529 | 203.349 | 246.548 |
| 4.  Relative 1970–1989 PARE | 135.215 | 148.493 | 149.998 | 147.122 | 215.595 | 213.490 | 226.080 | 237.483 | 243.910 | 271.487 |
| 5.  Absolute 1980–1989 PARE | 50.260 | 58.026 | 61.304 | 64.122 | 102.494 | 111.504 | 125.459 | 140.676 | 155.023 | 187.957 |
| 6.  WA | 277.710 | 277.132 | 252.484 | 222.888 | 240.704 | 214.312 | 238.950 | 245.679 | 225.655 | 212.721 |
| **Gambia:** Gambian dalasis | | | | | | | | | | |
| 1.  MER | 2.083 | 2.046 | 1.998 | 1.700 | 1.710 | 1.810 | 2.230 | 2.291 | 2.090 | 1.890 |
| 2.  PPPs | 0.838 | 0.871 | 0.930 | 0.923 | 0.979 | 1.280 | 1.382 | 1.339 | 1.264 | 1.204 |
| 3.  Absolute 1970–1989 PARE | 0.905 | 0.882 | 0.991 | 1.205 | 1.526 | 1.749 | 2.172 | 2.329 | 2.481 | 2.486 |
| 4.  Relative 1970–1989 PARE | 1.856 | 1.721 | 1.848 | 2.108 | 2.447 | 2.552 | 2.984 | 2.997 | 2.976 | 2.737 |
| 5.  Absolute 1980–1989 PARE | 0.841 | 0.820 | 0.921 | 1.121 | 1.419 | 1.626 | 2.020 | 2.166 | 2.308 | 2.312 |
| 6.  WA | 2.083 | 1.974 | 1.919 | 1.680 | 1.703 | 2.013 | 2.337 | 2.192 | 1.999 | 1.793 |
| **Germany** [b] | | | | | | | | | | |
| **Federal Republic of Germany:** Deutsche marks | | | | | | | | | | |
| 1.  MER | 3.660 | 3.490 | 3.189 | 2.673 | 2.588 | 2.460 | 2.518 | 2.322 | 2.009 | 1.833 |
| 2.  PPPs | 3.100 | 3.141 | 3.116 | 3.082 | 3.008 | 2.913 | 2.857 | 2.774 | 2.660 | 2.549 |
| 3.  Absolute 1970–1989 PARE | 1.356 | 1.465 | 1.543 | 1.641 | 1.757 | 1.862 | 1.929 | 2.001 | 2.087 | 2.171 |
| 4.  Relative 1970–1989 PARE | 2.781 | 2.858 | 2.878 | 2.870 | 2.817 | 2.717 | 2.650 | 2.575 | 2.503 | 2.390 |
| 5.  Absolute 1980–1989 PARE | 1.115 | 1.205 | 1.269 | 1.349 | 1.444 | 1.531 | 1.586 | 1.645 | 1.716 | 1.785 |
| 6.  WA | 3.660 | 3.491 | 3.189 | 2.673 | 2.588 | 2.460 | 2.518 | 2.322 | 2.009 | 1.833 |
| **German Democratic Republic (former):** Marks der DDR | | | | | | | | | | |
| 1.  MER | 4.200 | 4.200 | 3.150 | 2.880 | 2.720 | 2.420 | 2.520 | 2.350 | 2.050 | 1.740 |
| 2.  PPPs | ... | ... | ... | ... | ... | ... | ... | ... | ... | ... |
| 3.  Absolute 1970–1989 PARE | 2.180 | 2.170 | 2.342 | 2.161 | 2.165 | 2.162 | 2.194 | 2.182 | 2.240 | 2.256 |
| 4.  Relative 1970–1989 PARE | 4.471 | 4.233 | 4.369 | 3.780 | 3.472 | 3.156 | 3.014 | 2.808 | 2.687 | 2.484 |
| 5.  Absolute 1980–1989 PARE | 2.010 | 2.001 | 2.159 | 1.993 | 1.997 | 1.993 | 2.023 | 2.012 | 2.065 | 2.080 |
| 6.  WA [a] | 4.217 | 4.193 | 4.065 | 3.323 | 2.839 | 2.672 | 2.577 | 2.433 | 2.345 | 2.078 |
| **Ghana:** Ghanaian cedis | | | | | | | | | | |
| 1.  MER | 1.020 | 1.020 | 1.328 | 1.490 | 1.789 | 1.833 | 2.016 | 3.113 | 5.350 | 6.680 |
| 2.  PPPs | 0.906 | 0.979 | 1.072 | 1.173 | 1.345 | 1.581 | 1.961 | 2.942 | 3.979 | 5.755 |
| 3.  Absolute 1970–1989 PARE | 0.560 | 0.587 | 0.678 | 0.799 | 0.995 | 1.289 | 1.650 | 2.760 | 4.782 | 6.597 |
| 4.  Relative 1970–1989 PARE | 1.149 | 1.146 | 1.265 | 1.398 | 1.596 | 1.881 | 2.267 | 3.552 | 5.736 | 7.264 |
| 5.  Absolute 1980–1989 PARE | 0.433 | 0.454 | 0.525 | 0.618 | 0.770 | 0.997 | 1.277 | 2.136 | 3.701 | 5.106 |
| 6.  WA | 1.020 | 1.035 | 1.333 | 1.165 | 1.150 | 1.150 | 1.150 | 1.150 | 1.764 | 2.750 |
| **Greece:** Greek drachmas | | | | | | | | | | |
| 1.  MER | 30.000 | 30.000 | 30.000 | 29.625 | 30.000 | 32.050 | 36.518 | 36.838 | 36.745 | 37.038 |
| 2.  PPPs | 22.929 | 22.716 | 22.539 | 24.027 | 28.311 | 28.377 | 30.913 | 32.548 | 34.548 | 37.593 |
| 3.  Absolute 1970–1989 PARE | 14.262 | 14.712 | 15.452 | 18.454 | 22.318 | 25.071 | 28.929 | 32.676 | 36.907 | 43.787 |
| 4.  Relative 1970–1989 PARE | 29.251 | 28.701 | 28.823 | 32.279 | 35.789 | 36.594 | 39.742 | 42.054 | 44.268 | 48.216 |
| 5.  Absolute 1980–1989 PARE | 12.187 | 12.572 | 13.204 | 15.770 | 19.071 | 21.424 | 24.721 | 27.923 | 31.538 | 37.417 |
| 6.  WA | 30.000 | 30.000 | 30.000 | 29.625 | 30.000 | 32.051 | 36.518 | 36.838 | 36.745 | 37.038 |

| | | | | | | | | | | Averages | | |
|---|---|---|---|---|---|---|---|---|---|---|---|---|
| 1980 (11) | 1981 (12) | 1982 (13) | 1983 (14) | 1984 (15) | 1985 (16) | 1986 (17) | 1987 (18) | 1988 (19) | 1989 (20) | 1970–89 (21) | 1970–79 (22) | 1980–89 (23) |
| 76.829 | 98.811 | 119.493 | 138.569 | 158.893 | 163.367 | 125.929 | 109.100 | 108.300 | 116.000 | 111.341 | 84.607 | 119.574 |
| ... | ... | ... | ... | ... | ... | ... | ... | ... | ... | ... | ... | ... |
| 92.455 | 102.498 | 113.283 | 129.061 | 144.756 | 154.398 | 167.656 | 169.641 | 173.070 | 178.032 | 111.341 | 52.402 | 147.490 |
| 93.270 | 94.464 | 98.069 | 108.075 | 117.026 | 121.529 | 129.364 | 127.240 | 125.595 | 124.108 | 106.952 | 76.447 | 117.137 |
| 74.956 | 83.097 | 91.842 | 104.633 | 117.357 | 125.174 | 135.923 | 137.532 | 140.312 | 144.335 | 90.267 | 42.484 | 119.574 |
| 91.596 | 94.667 | 107.613 | 133.041 | 155.668 | 166.205 | 162.451 | 138.672 | 116.534 | 113.968 | 120.892 | 96.682 | 127.870 |
| | | | | | | | | | | | | |
| 211.280 | 271.730 | 328.600 | 381.060 | 436.960 | 449.260 | 346.300 | 300.500 | 297.800 | 319.000 | 299.771 | 231.714 | 331.641 |
| 277.639 | 293.819 | 325.332 | 364.087 | 430.974 | 481.517 | 427.598 | 419.867 | 406.289 | 416.014 | 340.926 | 258.588 | 380.575 |
| 294.070 | 353.691 | 396.670 | 440.105 | 483.244 | 513.747 | 465.387 | 470.103 | 470.173 | 501.167 | 299.771 | 153.709 | 435.024 |
| 296.663 | 325.968 | 343.397 | 368.543 | 390.672 | 404.377 | 359.096 | 352.604 | 341.201 | 349.368 | 308.409 | 219.187 | 355.796 |
| 224.185 | 269.637 | 302.402 | 335.515 | 368.402 | 391.656 | 354.789 | 358.384 | 358.438 | 382.066 | 228.531 | 117.181 | 331.641 |
| 211.279 | 271.730 | 328.605 | 381.065 | 436.955 | 449.261 | 346.305 | 300.535 | 297.847 | 319.007 | 299.778 | 231.715 | 331.651 |
| | | | | | | | | | | | | |
| 1.719 | 1.990 | 2.290 | 2.637 | 3.583 | 3.890 | 6.940 | 7.100 | 6.700 | 7.600 | 3.554 | 1.990 | 4.447 |
| 1.153 | 1.032 | 0.994 | 1.047 | 0.971 | 1.277 | 1.651 | 1.704 | 1.608 | 1.780 | 1.349 | 1.161 | 1.408 |
| 2.357 | 2.700 | 2.805 | 2.507 | 3.418 | 4.796 | 6.325 | 6.714 | 6.550 | 7.548 | 3.554 | 1.773 | 4.782 |
| 2.378 | 2.488 | 2.428 | 2.099 | 2.763 | 3.775 | 4.880 | 5.036 | 4.754 | 5.262 | 3.477 | 2.578 | 3.817 |
| 2.192 | 2.511 | 2.609 | 2.331 | 3.179 | 4.460 | 5.883 | 6.245 | 6.092 | 7.020 | 3.305 | 1.649 | 4.447 |
| 1.754 | 2.179 | 2.482 | 2.935 | 4.107 | 4.987 | 7.305 | 6.749 | 7.034 | 8.131 | 3.720 | 1.972 | 4.808 |
| | | | | | | | | | | | | |
| 1.818 | 2.260 | 2.427 | 2.553 | 2.846 | 2.944 | 2.170 | 1.800 | 1.800 | 1.900 | 2.256 | 2.446 | 2.162 |
| 2.456 | 2.385 | 2.351 | 2.348 | 2.316 | 2.354 | 2.379 | 2.359 | 2.316 | 2.267 | 2.510 | 2.864 | 2.348 |
| 2.275 | 2.366 | 2.470 | 2.550 | 2.600 | 2.658 | 2.741 | 2.795 | 2.836 | 2.890 | 2.256 | 1.800 | 2.629 |
| 2.295 | 2.181 | 2.138 | 2.136 | 2.102 | 2.092 | 2.115 | 2.097 | 2.058 | 2.014 | 2.281 | 2.662 | 2.112 |
| 1.871 | 1.946 | 2.031 | 2.097 | 2.138 | 2.186 | 2.254 | 2.299 | 2.332 | 2.376 | 1.855 | 1.480 | 2.162 |
| 1.818 | 2.260 | 2.427 | 2.553 | 2.846 | 2.944 | 2.171 | 1.797 | 1.756 | 1.880 | 2.248 | 2.446 | 2.151 |
| | | | | | | | | | | | | |
| 1.950 | 2.240 | 2.500 | 2.520 | 2.820 | 2.940 | 2.190 | 1.810 | 1.740 | 1.870 | 2.294 | 2.532 | 2.169 |
| ... | ... | ... | ... | ... | ... | ... | ... | ... | ... | ... | ... | ... |
| 2.316 | 2.300 | 2.331 | 2.336 | 2.362 | 2.391 | 2.376 | 2.377 | 2.398 | 2.320 | 2.294 | 2.205 | 2.353 |
| 2.337 | 2.120 | 2.018 | 1.956 | 1.910 | 1.882 | 1.833 | 1.783 | 1.740 | 1.617 | 2.233 | 3.216 | 1.880 |
| 2.136 | 2.121 | 2.149 | 2.154 | 2.178 | 2.205 | 2.190 | 2.192 | 2.211 | 2.139 | 2.116 | 2.033 | 2.169 |
| 1.952 | 1.983 | 2.244 | 2.433 | 2.634 | 2.791 | 2.649 | 2.308 | 1.925 | 1.773 | 2.409 | 2.797 | 2.219 |
| | | | | | | | | | | | | |
| 8.950 | 15.690 | 15.690 | 30.000 | 35.000 | 54.054 | 89.200 | 153.700 | 202.300 | 270.000 | 55.900 | 2.971 | 83.825 |
| 7.652 | 10.928 | 12.532 | 25.650 | 36.446 | 44.086 | 61.232 | 82.855 | 107.041 | 127.066 | 41.852 | 2.529 | 59.010 |
| 9.972 | 17.511 | 22.395 | 49.956 | 67.596 | 81.562 | 115.559 | 160.860 | 214.793 | 265.430 | 55.900 | 2.080 | 108.309 |
| 10.060 | 16.139 | 19.387 | 41.833 | 54.647 | 64.199 | 89.166 | 120.654 | 155.873 | 185.034 | 58.207 | 3.120 | 86.887 |
| 7.717 | 13.553 | 17.332 | 38.663 | 52.315 | 63.125 | 89.436 | 124.497 | 166.237 | 205.428 | 43.263 | 1.610 | 83.825 |
| 2.750 | 2.750 | 2.750 | 8.830 | 35.986 | 54.365 | 89.204 | 153.733 | 202.346 | 270.000 | 25.892 | 1.572 | 36.434 |
| | | | | | | | | | | | | |
| 42.617 | 55.408 | 66.803 | 88.060 | 112.720 | 138.120 | 139.980 | 135.400 | 141.900 | 162.400 | 85.604 | 34.063 | 111.819 |
| 40.476 | 44.216 | 52.084 | 60.334 | 70.551 | 81.311 | 93.600 | 103.561 | 115.970 | 127.038 | 67.164 | 30.109 | 82.989 |
| 51.532 | 61.712 | 77.199 | 91.958 | 110.610 | 130.152 | 152.833 | 173.956 | 201.340 | 229.599 | 85.604 | 26.487 | 130.855 |
| 51.986 | 56.875 | 66.831 | 77.005 | 89.421 | 102.444 | 117.927 | 130.477 | 146.111 | 160.056 | 85.537 | 38.725 | 105.249 |
| 44.035 | 52.735 | 65.969 | 78.580 | 94.519 | 111.218 | 130.600 | 148.650 | 172.051 | 196.198 | 73.151 | 22.634 | 111.819 |
| 42.617 | 55.408 | 66.803 | 88.064 | 112.720 | 138.120 | 139.980 | 135.430 | 141.860 | 162.420 | 85.605 | 34.063 | 111.820 |

**Table A.2**   Conversion rates for individual countries or areas, expressed as the number of
local currency units per United States dollar, 1970−1989 [*cont.*]

| Country or area | 1970 (1) | 1971 (2) | 1972 (3) | 1973 (4) | 1974 (5) | 1975 (6) | 1976 (7) | 1977 (8) | 1978 (9) | 1979 (10) |
|---|---|---|---|---|---|---|---|---|---|---|
| **Grenada:** East Caribbean dollars | | | | | | | | | | |
| 1.  MER | 2.000 | 1.970 | 1.922 | 1.959 | 2.053 | 2.170 | 2.615 | 2.700 | 2.700 | 2.700 |
| 2.  PPPs | ... | ... | ... | ... | ... | ... | ... | ... | ... | ... |
| 3.  Absolute 1970−1989 PARE | 0.842 | 0.784 | 0.758 | 0.903 | 1.237 | 1.449 | 1.603 | 1.750 | 2.077 | 2.386 |
| 4.  Relative 1970−1989 PARE | 1.727 | 1.529 | 1.414 | 1.579 | 1.984 | 2.115 | 2.202 | 2.252 | 2.491 | 2.628 |
| 5.  Absolute 1980−1989 PARE | 0.649 | 0.603 | 0.584 | 0.695 | 0.953 | 1.116 | 1.234 | 1.348 | 1.600 | 1.838 |
| 6.  WA | 2.000 | 1.975 | 1.921 | 1.959 | 2.053 | 2.170 | 2.615 | 2.700 | 2.700 | 2.700 |
| **Guadeloupe:** French francs | | | | | | | | | | |
| 1.  MER | 5.554 | 5.510 | 5.044 | 4.454 | 4.810 | 4.286 | 4.780 | 4.913 | 4.513 | 4.255 |
| 2.  PPPs | ... | ... | ... | ... | ... | ... | ... | ... | ... | ... |
| 3.  Absolute 1970−1989 PARE | 1.923 | 2.045 | 2.209 | 2.359 | 2.735 | 3.200 | 3.475 | 3.797 | 4.392 | 4.559 |
| 4.  Relative 1970−1989 PARE | 3.943 | 3.990 | 4.120 | 4.126 | 4.386 | 4.670 | 4.774 | 4.887 | 5.268 | 5.021 |
| 5.  Absolute 1980−1989 PARE | 1.551 | 1.650 | 1.782 | 1.903 | 2.207 | 2.582 | 2.804 | 3.063 | 3.544 | 3.678 |
| 6.  WA [a] | 5.658 | 5.830 | 5.791 | 5.399 | 5.407 | 5.318 | 5.182 | 5.074 | 5.413 | 4.946 |
| **Guatemala:** Guatemalan quetzales | | | | | | | | | | |
| 1.  MER | 1.000 | 1.000 | 1.000 | 1.000 | 1.000 | 1.000 | 1.000 | 1.000 | 1.000 | 1.000 |
| 2.  PPPs | 0.415 | 0.396 | 0.387 | 0.434 | 0.469 | 0.490 | 0.517 | 0.552 | 0.552 | 0.560 |
| 3.  Absolute 1970−1989 PARE | 0.460 | 0.454 | 0.448 | 0.513 | 0.593 | 0.671 | 0.748 | 0.871 | 0.919 | 0.998 |
| 4.  Relative 1970−1989 PARE | 0.943 | 0.886 | 0.835 | 0.897 | 0.951 | 0.979 | 1.028 | 1.121 | 1.102 | 1.099 |
| 5.  Absolute 1980−1989 PARE | 0.373 | 0.368 | 0.363 | 0.416 | 0.481 | 0.544 | 0.606 | 0.706 | 0.745 | 0.809 |
| 6.  WA | 1.000 | 1.000 | 1.000 | 1.000 | 1.000 | 1.000 | 1.000 | 1.000 | 1.000 | 1.000 |
| **Guinea:** Francs | | | | | | | | | | |
| 1.  MER | 24.685 | 24.610 | 22.736 | 20.720 | 20.560 | 20.673 | 21.381 | 21.143 | 19.717 | 19.106 |
| 2.  PPPs | 17.183 | 16.376 | 16.483 | 18.017 | 17.222 | 17.009 | 16.148 | 14.920 | 14.257 | 13.871 |
| 3.  Absolute 1970−1989 PARE | 13.980 | 13.936 | 14.386 | 15.737 | 16.555 | 17.888 | 18.178 | 18.201 | 18.592 | 19.402 |
| 4.  Relative 1970−1989 PARE | 28.673 | 27.187 | 26.835 | 27.527 | 26.547 | 26.110 | 24.972 | 23.424 | 22.301 | 21.364 |
| 5.  Absolute 1980−1989 PARE | 11.943 | 11.905 | 12.290 | 13.444 | 14.143 | 15.282 | 15.529 | 15.549 | 15.883 | 16.575 |
| 6.  WA [a] | 8.578 | 16.754 | 24.515 | 24.461 | 22.840 | 22.147 | 21.655 | 21.195 | 21.061 | 20.740 |
| **Guinea−Bissau:** Guinea−Bissau pesos | | | | | | | | | | |
| 1.  MER | 28.750 | 28.312 | 27.053 | 24.515 | 25.408 | 25.543 | 30.229 | 33.644 | 35.039 | 34.057 |
| 2.  PPPs | ... | ... | ... | ... | ... | ... | ... | ... | ... | ... |
| 3.  Absolute 1970−1989 PARE | 52.401 | 53.353 | 56.004 | 61.848 | 67.363 | 19.452 | 21.473 | 24.301 | 29.067 | 33.410 |
| 4.  Relative 1970−1989 PARE | 107.473 | 104.086 | 104.465 | 108.181 | 108.023 | 28.393 | 29.499 | 31.275 | 34.865 | 36.789 |
| 5.  Absolute 1980−1989 PARE | 54.672 | 55.665 | 58.431 | 64.528 | 70.282 | 20.295 | 22.403 | 25.354 | 30.327 | 34.858 |
| 6.  WA | 28.750 | 28.312 | 27.053 | 24.515 | 25.408 | 25.543 | 30.229 | 33.644 | 35.039 | 34.057 |
| **Guyana:** Guyana dollars | | | | | | | | | | |
| 1.  MER | 2.000 | 1.978 | 2.087 | 2.110 | 2.227 | 2.360 | 2.550 | 2.550 | 2.550 | 2.550 |
| 2.  PPPs | 0.959 | 0.982 | 0.992 | 0.921 | 1.149 | 1.048 | 0.960 | 1.007 | 1.206 | 1.142 |
| 3.  Absolute 1970−1989 PARE | 1.356 | 1.389 | 1.505 | 1.592 | 2.203 | 2.483 | 2.307 | 2.353 | 2.725 | 2.897 |
| 4.  Relative 1970−1989 PARE | 2.781 | 2.709 | 2.808 | 2.785 | 3.533 | 3.624 | 3.169 | 3.029 | 3.269 | 3.191 |
| 5.  Absolute 1980−1989 PARE | 1.225 | 1.255 | 1.360 | 1.439 | 1.991 | 2.244 | 2.085 | 2.127 | 2.463 | 2.619 |
| 6.  WA | 2.000 | 1.981 | 2.087 | 2.106 | 2.227 | 2.355 | 2.550 | 2.550 | 2.550 | 2.550 |
| **Haiti:** Haitian gourdes | | | | | | | | | | |
| 1.  MER | 5.000 | 5.000 | 5.000 | 5.000 | 5.000 | 5.000 | 5.000 | 5.000 | 5.000 | 5.000 |
| 2.  PPPs | 1.601 | 1.590 | 1.644 | 1.934 | 2.085 | 2.029 | 2.106 | 2.147 | 1.945 | 1.935 |
| 3.  Absolute 1970−1989 PARE | 1.772 | 1.823 | 1.851 | 2.217 | 2.539 | 3.025 | 3.599 | 3.991 | 3.932 | 4.045 |
| 4.  Relative 1970−1989 PARE | 3.634 | 3.556 | 3.452 | 3.878 | 4.071 | 4.416 | 4.944 | 5.136 | 4.717 | 4.454 |
| 5.  Absolute 1980−1989 PARE | 1.341 | 1.379 | 1.401 | 1.678 | 1.921 | 2.290 | 2.724 | 3.021 | 2.976 | 3.061 |
| 6.  WA | 5.000 | 5.000 | 5.000 | 5.000 | 5.000 | 5.000 | 5.000 | 5.000 | 5.000 | 5.000 |

| | | | | | | | | | | Averages | | |
|---|---|---|---|---|---|---|---|---|---|---|---|---|
| 1980 | 1981 | 1982 | 1983 | 1984 | 1985 | 1986 | 1987 | 1988 | 1989 | 1970−89 | 1970−79 | 1980−89 |
| (11) | (12) | (13) | (14) | (15) | (16) | (17) | (18) | (19) | (20) | (21) | (22) | (23) |
| 2.700 | 2.700 | 2.700 | 2.700 | 2.700 | 2.700 | 2.700 | 2.700 | 2.700 | 2.700 | 2.618 | 2.367 | 2.700 |
| ... | ... | ... | ... | ... | ... | ... | ... | ... | ... | ... | ... | ... |
| 2.729 | 2.886 | 2.978 | 3.061 | 3.179 | 3.326 | 3.604 | 3.975 | 4.151 | 4.371 | 2.618 | 1.388 | 3.506 |
| 2.753 | 2.660 | 2.578 | 2.563 | 2.570 | 2.618 | 2.781 | 2.981 | 3.012 | 3.047 | 2.593 | 2.075 | 2.792 |
| 2.102 | 2.223 | 2.294 | 2.357 | 2.448 | 2.562 | 2.776 | 3.061 | 3.197 | 3.367 | 2.017 | 1.069 | 2.700 |
| 2.700 | 2.700 | 2.700 | 2.700 | 2.700 | 2.700 | 2.700 | 2.700 | 2.700 | 2.700 | 2.618 | 2.368 | 2.700 |
| | | | | | | | | | | | | |
| 4.226 | 5.435 | 6.572 | 7.621 | 8.739 | 8.985 | 6.926 | 6.000 | 6.000 | 6.400 | 5.965 | 4.652 | 6.522 |
| ... | ... | ... | ... | ... | ... | ... | ... | ... | ... | ... | ... | ... |
| 5.374 | 6.058 | 6.863 | 7.576 | 8.091 | 8.694 | 9.192 | 9.153 | 9.335 | 9.550 | 5.965 | 3.196 | 8.084 |
| 5.422 | 5.583 | 5.941 | 6.344 | 6.541 | 6.843 | 7.093 | 6.865 | 6.775 | 6.658 | 5.942 | 4.662 | 6.481 |
| 4.336 | 4.888 | 5.537 | 6.112 | 6.528 | 7.014 | 7.416 | 7.384 | 7.532 | 7.705 | 4.812 | 2.578 | 6.522 |
| 4.921 | 5.284 | 6.042 | 7.224 | 8.209 | 9.040 | 8.785 | 7.452 | 6.385 | 6.266 | 6.420 | 5.290 | 6.863 |
| | | | | | | | | | | | | |
| 1.000 | 1.000 | 1.000 | 1.000 | 1.000 | 1.000 | 1.870 | 2.500 | 2.600 | 2.800 | 1.368 | 1.000 | 1.529 |
| 0.556 | 0.560 | 0.552 | 0.565 | 0.567 | 0.679 | 0.942 | 0.989 | 1.069 | 1.154 | 0.695 | 0.497 | 0.785 |
| 1.098 | 1.191 | 1.251 | 1.333 | 1.388 | 1.648 | 2.332 | 2.518 | 2.816 | 3.163 | 1.368 | 0.699 | 1.886 |
| 1.108 | 1.098 | 1.083 | 1.116 | 1.122 | 1.297 | 1.799 | 1.889 | 2.043 | 2.205 | 1.370 | 1.015 | 1.523 |
| 0.890 | 0.966 | 1.014 | 1.080 | 1.125 | 1.336 | 1.890 | 2.042 | 2.283 | 2.564 | 1.109 | 0.567 | 1.529 |
| 1.000 | 1.000 | 1.000 | 1.000 | 1.000 | 1.150 | 2.190 | 2.500 | 2.620 | 2.816 | 1.399 | 1.000 | 1.580 |
| | | | | | | | | | | | | |
| 18.966 | 20.950 | 22.370 | 23.092 | 24.090 | 24.330 | 333.450 | 428.400 | 474.400 | 591.600 | 151.759 | 21.107 | 227.068 |
| 13.757 | 14.453 | 15.217 | 15.941 | 15.989 | 16.199 | 215.762 | 277.484 | 339.356 | 442.225 | 107.764 | 15.837 | 156.408 |
| 21.478 | 22.699 | 23.509 | 25.069 | 26.570 | 27.678 | 376.071 | 497.550 | 628.918 | 853.168 | 151.759 | 16.848 | 265.796 |
| 21.668 | 20.920 | 20.352 | 20.993 | 21.480 | 21.786 | 290.180 | 373.190 | 456.401 | 594.752 | 154.316 | 24.852 | 214.064 |
| 18.349 | 19.391 | 20.084 | 21.416 | 22.698 | 23.645 | 321.275 | 425.053 | 537.281 | 728.856 | 129.647 | 14.393 | 227.068 |
| 20.965 | 21.115 | 21.609 | 23.361 | 24.615 | 24.973 | 335.003 | 435.643 | 524.517 | 656.583 | 150.569 | 19.368 | 236.353 |
| | | | | | | | | | | | | |
| 33.811 | 37.339 | 39.866 | 42.099 | 105.287 | 159.620 | 203.951 | 559.300 | 1111.100 | 1811.400 | 204.387 | 29.748 | 312.548 |
| ... | ... | ... | ... | ... | ... | ... | ... | ... | ... | ... | ... | ... |
| 36.105 | 39.798 | 43.923 | 74.197 | 114.802 | 167.500 | 190.751 | 355.090 | 618.102 | 1050.788 | 204.387 | 31.987 | 299.564 |
| 36.424 | 36.679 | 38.024 | 62.132 | 92.810 | 131.841 | 147.185 | 266.337 | 448.552 | 732.514 | 191.259 | 43.199 | 239.686 |
| 37.670 | 41.523 | 45.827 | 77.413 | 119.777 | 174.760 | 199.019 | 370.480 | 644.892 | 1096.331 | 213.246 | 33.373 | 312.548 |
| 33.811 | 37.339 | 39.866 | 42.099 | 105.287 | 159.620 | 203.951 | 559.331 | 1111.060 | 1811.420 | 204.387 | 29.748 | 312.548 |
| | | | | | | | | | | | | |
| 2.550 | 2.813 | 3.000 | 3.000 | 3.832 | 4.252 | 4.270 | 9.800 | 10.000 | 27.200 | 3.961 | 2.346 | 5.406 |
| 1.173 | 1.059 | 0.920 | 0.953 | 1.429 | 1.541 | 1.700 | 2.510 | 2.673 | 3.819 | 1.475 | 1.048 | 1.754 |
| 3.242 | 3.443 | 3.480 | 3.867 | 4.422 | 5.057 | 5.690 | 8.643 | 9.513 | 14.148 | 3.961 | 2.118 | 5.982 |
| 3.271 | 3.173 | 3.013 | 3.238 | 3.575 | 3.980 | 4.391 | 6.482 | 6.903 | 9.863 | 4.219 | 3.138 | 4.871 |
| 2.930 | 3.111 | 3.145 | 3.495 | 3.996 | 4.570 | 5.143 | 7.811 | 8.597 | 12.787 | 3.579 | 1.915 | 5.406 |
| 2.550 | 2.813 | 3.000 | 3.000 | 3.832 | 4.252 | 4.272 | 9.756 | 10.000 | 27.159 | 3.959 | 2.345 | 5.404 |
| | | | | | | | | | | | | |
| 5.000 | 5.000 | 5.000 | 5.000 | 5.000 | 5.000 | 5.000 | 5.000 | 5.000 | 5.000 | 5.000 | 5.000 | 5.000 |
| 1.990 | 1.972 | 2.067 | 2.140 | 2.235 | 2.291 | 2.474 | 2.141 | 2.035 | 2.800 | 2.149 | 1.944 | 2.233 |
| 4.833 | 5.124 | 5.325 | 5.800 | 6.446 | 7.112 | 7.835 | 6.977 | 6.852 | 9.814 | 5.000 | 2.983 | 6.606 |
| 4.876 | 4.722 | 4.610 | 4.857 | 5.211 | 5.598 | 6.046 | 5.233 | 4.973 | 6.842 | 5.046 | 4.371 | 5.343 |
| 3.658 | 3.878 | 4.031 | 4.390 | 4.879 | 5.383 | 5.930 | 5.280 | 5.186 | 7.428 | 3.784 | 2.258 | 5.000 |
| 5.000 | 5.000 | 5.000 | 5.000 | 5.000 | 5.000 | 5.000 | 5.000 | 5.000 | 5.000 | 5.000 | 5.000 | 5.000 |

**Table A.2** Conversion rates for individual countries or areas, expressed as the number of local currency units per United States dollar, 1970−1989 [*cont.*]

| Country or area | 1970 (1) | 1971 (2) | 1972 (3) | 1973 (4) | 1974 (5) | 1975 (6) | 1976 (7) | 1977 (8) | 1978 (9) | 1979 (10) |
|---|---|---|---|---|---|---|---|---|---|---|
| **Honduras:** Honduran lempiras | | | | | | | | | | |
| 1. MER | 2.000 | 2.000 | 2.000 | 2.000 | 2.000 | 2.000 | 2.000 | 2.000 | 2.000 | 2.000 |
| 2. PPPs | 1.213 | 1.209 | 1.203 | 1.217 | 1.254 | 1.218 | 1.225 | 1.255 | 1.236 | 1.274 |
| 3. Absolute 1970−1989 PARE | 0.900 | 0.916 | 0.951 | 1.002 | 1.150 | 1.224 | 1.328 | 1.490 | 1.566 | 1.716 |
| 4. Relative 1970−1989 PARE | 1.847 | 1.787 | 1.775 | 1.753 | 1.845 | 1.786 | 1.825 | 1.918 | 1.878 | 1.889 |
| 5. Absolute 1980−1989 PARE | 0.718 | 0.730 | 0.759 | 0.799 | 0.917 | 0.976 | 1.059 | 1.188 | 1.248 | 1.368 |
| 6. WA | 2.000 | 2.000 | 2.000 | 2.000 | 2.000 | 2.000 | 2.000 | 2.000 | 2.000 | 2.000 |
| **Hong Kong:** Hong Kong dollars | | | | | | | | | | |
| 1. MER | 6.061 | 5.980 | 5.640 | 5.150 | 5.030 | 4.940 | 4.900 | 4.660 | 4.680 | 5.000 |
| 2. PPPs | ... | ... | ... | ... | ... | ... | ... | ... | ... | ... |
| 3. Absolute 1970−1989 PARE | 2.182 | 2.340 | 2.544 | 2.905 | 3.241 | 3.372 | 3.677 | 3.795 | 4.083 | 4.822 |
| 4. Relative 1970−1989 PARE | 4.476 | 4.566 | 4.746 | 5.082 | 5.197 | 4.921 | 5.051 | 4.884 | 4.897 | 5.310 |
| 5. Absolute 1980−1989 PARE | 1.926 | 2.065 | 2.245 | 2.564 | 2.860 | 2.975 | 3.245 | 3.349 | 3.603 | 4.256 |
| 6. WA | 6.061 | 5.977 | 5.641 | 5.147 | 5.032 | 4.935 | 4.905 | 4.662 | 4.684 | 5.003 |
| **Hungary:** Hungarian forint | | | | | | | | | | |
| 1. MER | 30.000 | 30.000 | 27.630 | 25.240 | 24.900 | 20.920 | 41.580 | 40.960 | 37.910 | 35.580 |
| 2. PPPs | ... | ... | ... | ... | ... | ... | ... | ... | ... | ... |
| 3. Absolute 1970−1989 PARE | 25.658 | 26.198 | 26.719 | 27.589 | 27.169 | 27.424 | 29.040 | 29.935 | 30.969 | 33.052 |
| 4. Relative 1970−1989 PARE | 52.624 | 51.110 | 49.839 | 48.257 | 43.567 | 40.029 | 39.895 | 38.526 | 37.147 | 36.395 |
| 5. Absolute 1980−1989 PARE | 24.401 | 24.915 | 25.410 | 26.238 | 25.838 | 26.081 | 27.618 | 28.469 | 29.452 | 31.433 |
| 6. WA | 60.000 | 59.822 | 55.260 | 48.966 | 46.752 | 43.971 | 41.575 | 40.961 | 37.911 | 35.578 |
| **Iceland:** Icelandic kroner | | | | | | | | | | |
| 1. MER | 0.880 | 0.879 | 0.877 | 0.901 | 1.000 | 1.537 | 1.822 | 1.989 | 2.711 | 3.526 |
| 2. PPPs | 0.697 | 0.732 | 0.813 | 0.967 | 1.277 | 1.708 | 2.100 | 2.581 | 3.476 | 4.666 |
| 3. Absolute 1970−1989 PARE | 0.288 | 0.324 | 0.383 | 0.505 | 0.693 | 0.984 | 1.309 | 1.737 | 2.539 | 3.575 |
| 4. Relative 1970−1989 PARE | 0.591 | 0.632 | 0.714 | 0.884 | 1.112 | 1.436 | 1.798 | 2.236 | 3.046 | 3.937 |
| 5. Absolute 1980−1989 PARE | 0.240 | 0.270 | 0.319 | 0.421 | 0.578 | 0.820 | 1.090 | 1.447 | 2.116 | 2.979 |
| 6. WA | 0.880 | 0.880 | 0.883 | 0.901 | 1.000 | 1.537 | 1.822 | 1.989 | 2.711 | 3.526 |
| **India:** Indian rupees | | | | | | | | | | |
| 1. MER | 7.500 | 7.500 | 7.594 | 7.742 | 8.102 | 8.376 | 8.960 | 8.739 | 8.193 | 8.126 |
| 2. PPPs | 2.522 | 2.496 | 2.670 | 3.024 | 3.302 | 2.948 | 3.007 | 2.925 | 2.811 | 2.986 |
| 3. Absolute 1970−1989 PARE | 3.940 | 4.147 | 4.602 | 5.434 | 6.342 | 6.246 | 6.615 | 6.983 | 7.176 | 8.295 |
| 4. Relative 1970−1989 PARE | 8.081 | 8.091 | 8.583 | 9.504 | 10.170 | 9.117 | 9.088 | 8.987 | 8.608 | 9.134 |
| 5. Absolute 1980−1989 PARE | 3.381 | 3.559 | 3.949 | 4.663 | 5.442 | 5.360 | 5.677 | 5.993 | 6.158 | 7.118 |
| 6. WA | 7.500 | 7.444 | 7.706 | 7.791 | 7.976 | 8.653 | 8.939 | 8.563 | 8.206 | 8.076 |
| **Indonesia:** Indonesian rupiahs | | | | | | | | | | |
| 1. MER | 362.830 | 391.880 | 415.000 | 415.000 | 415.000 | 415.000 | 415.000 | 415.000 | 442.050 | 623.060 |
| 2. PPPs | 110.657 | 112.313 | 124.648 | 154.399 | 192.739 | 198.257 | 214.191 | 226.224 | 231.559 | 261.875 |
| 3. Absolute 1970−1989 PARE | 122.486 | 129.817 | 147.457 | 196.023 | 288.762 | 324.766 | 371.716 | 420.052 | 466.078 | 633.063 |
| 4. Relative 1970−1989 PARE | 251.218 | 253.261 | 275.055 | 342.872 | 463.059 | 474.037 | 510.654 | 540.594 | 559.046 | 697.098 |
| 5. Absolute 1980−1989 PARE | 108.106 | 114.576 | 130.145 | 173.009 | 254.861 | 286.637 | 328.076 | 370.737 | 411.360 | 558.740 |
| 6. WA | 362.833 | 391.875 | 415.000 | 415.000 | 415.000 | 415.000 | 415.000 | 415.000 | 442.045 | 623.055 |
| **Iran (Islamic Republic of):** Iranian rials | | | | | | | | | | |
| 1. MER | 75.750 | 75.750 | 75.750 | 68.880 | 67.625 | 67.639 | 70.222 | 70.617 | 70.475 | 70.475 |
| 2. PPPs | 34.119 | 34.232 | 35.194 | 39.021 | 43.173 | 40.632 | 43.649 | 47.462 | 47.903 | 51.867 |
| 3. Absolute 1970−1989 PARE | 9.467 | 10.582 | 11.351 | 15.258 | 24.554 | 27.149 | 30.689 | 35.470 | 37.844 | 47.462 |
| 4. Relative 1970−1989 PARE | 19.416 | 20.645 | 21.173 | 26.689 | 39.375 | 39.628 | 42.160 | 45.649 | 45.393 | 52.263 |
| 5. Absolute 1980−1989 PARE | 5.975 | 6.679 | 7.164 | 9.630 | 15.497 | 17.135 | 19.369 | 22.386 | 23.884 | 29.955 |
| 6. WA | 75.750 | 75.750 | 75.750 | 68.882 | 67.625 | 68.166 | 70.535 | 70.579 | 70.475 | 70.475 |

| | | | | | | | | | | Averages | | |
|---|---|---|---|---|---|---|---|---|---|---|---|---|
| 1980 | 1981 | 1982 | 1983 | 1984 | 1985 | 1986 | 1987 | 1988 | 1989 | 1970–89 | 1970–79 | 1980–89 |
| (11) | (12) | (13) | (14) | (15) | (16) | (17) | (18) | (19) | (20) | (21) | (22) | (23) |
| 2.000 | 2.000 | 2.000 | 2.000 | 2.000 | 2.000 | 2.000 | 2.000 | 2.000 | 2.000 | 2.000 | 2.000 | 2.000 |
| 1.255 | 1.276 | 1.332 | 1.354 | 1.438 | 1.448 | 1.497 | 1.481 | 1.500 | 1.547 | 1.371 | 1.237 | 1.425 |
| 1.948 | 2.093 | 2.215 | 2.326 | 2.423 | 2.538 | 2.676 | 2.723 | 2.850 | 3.060 | 2.000 | 1.271 | 2.508 |
| 1.965 | 1.929 | 1.918 | 1.948 | 1.959 | 1.998 | 2.065 | 2.042 | 2.068 | 2.133 | 1.966 | 1.844 | 2.013 |
| 1.553 | 1.669 | 1.766 | 1.855 | 1.932 | 2.024 | 2.134 | 2.171 | 2.273 | 2.440 | 1.595 | 1.013 | 2.000 |
| 2.000 | 2.000 | 2.000 | 2.000 | 2.000 | 2.000 | 2.000 | 2.000 | 2.330 | 2.970 | 2.098 | 2.000 | 2.135 |
| | | | | | | | | | | | | |
| 4.980 | 5.590 | 6.070 | 7.270 | 7.820 | 7.790 | 7.800 | 7.800 | 7.800 | 7.800 | 6.774 | 5.004 | 7.254 |
| ... | ... | ... | ... | ... | ... | ... | ... | ... | ... | ... | ... | ... |
| 5.570 | 6.126 | 6.717 | 7.026 | 7.690 | 8.085 | 8.321 | 8.965 | 9.767 | 10.794 | 6.774 | 3.492 | 8.220 |
| 5.619 | 5.646 | 5.815 | 5.883 | 6.217 | 6.364 | 6.421 | 6.724 | 7.088 | 7.525 | 6.211 | 4.986 | 6.510 |
| 4.915 | 5.406 | 5.927 | 6.200 | 6.786 | 7.135 | 7.344 | 7.912 | 8.619 | 9.525 | 5.978 | 3.081 | 7.254 |
| 4.976 | 5.589 | 6.070 | 7.265 | 7.818 | 7.791 | 7.803 | 7.798 | 7.806 | 7.800 | 6.774 | 5.006 | 7.254 |
| | | | | | | | | | | | | |
| 32.530 | 34.310 | 36.630 | 42.670 | 48.040 | 50.120 | 45.830 | 47.000 | 50.400 | 59.100 | 39.396 | 30.790 | 45.149 |
| ... | ... | ... | ... | ... | ... | ... | ... | ... | ... | ... | ... | ... |
| 34.908 | 36.706 | 38.802 | 40.727 | 43.306 | 45.865 | 47.582 | 51.507 | 59.238 | 71.836 | 39.396 | 28.688 | 47.475 |
| 35.216 | 33.829 | 33.591 | 34.105 | 35.010 | 36.101 | 36.714 | 38.633 | 42.988 | 50.077 | 39.243 | 41.776 | 38.187 |
| 33.198 | 34.908 | 36.902 | 38.732 | 41.185 | 43.619 | 45.251 | 48.984 | 56.336 | 68.317 | 37.466 | 27.282 | 45.149 |
| 32.532 | 34.314 | 36.631 | 42.671 | 48.042 | 50.119 | 45.832 | 46.971 | 50.413 | 59.066 | 44.774 | 43.978 | 45.146 |
| | | | | | | | | | | | | |
| 4.798 | 7.224 | 12.352 | 24.843 | 31.694 | 41.508 | 41.100 | 38.700 | 43.000 | 57.000 | 24.549 | 2.013 | 33.086 |
| 6.538 | 9.146 | 13.455 | 22.157 | 27.656 | 36.257 | 44.062 | 51.720 | 61.705 | 70.914 | 28.410 | 2.348 | 38.176 |
| 5.450 | 8.221 | 12.634 | 22.695 | 29.068 | 38.273 | 47.447 | 57.294 | 70.649 | 84.523 | 24.549 | 1.397 | 39.710 |
| 5.498 | 7.577 | 10.937 | 19.005 | 23.499 | 30.125 | 36.611 | 42.973 | 51.270 | 58.921 | 23.918 | 2.028 | 31.835 |
| 4.541 | 6.850 | 10.527 | 18.910 | 24.219 | 31.889 | 39.533 | 47.737 | 58.865 | 70.424 | 20.454 | 1.164 | 33.086 |
| 4.798 | 7.224 | 12.351 | 24.843 | 31.694 | 41.508 | 41.104 | 38.677 | 43.014 | 57.042 | 24.553 | 2.013 | 33.089 |
| | | | | | | | | | | | | |
| 7.863 | 8.659 | 9.460 | 10.099 | 11.363 | 12.369 | 12.610 | 13.000 | 13.900 | 16.200 | 10.814 | 8.164 | 11.923 |
| 3.020 | 3.025 | 3.223 | 3.463 | 3.231 | 3.332 | 3.483 | 3.671 | 3.810 | 3.940 | 3.343 | 2.893 | 3.498 |
| 9.253 | 10.201 | 10.960 | 11.889 | 12.780 | 13.695 | 14.602 | 15.833 | 16.986 | 18.286 | 10.814 | 6.097 | 13.894 |
| 9.335 | 9.401 | 9.488 | 9.956 | 10.332 | 10.780 | 11.267 | 11.876 | 12.327 | 12.747 | 10.510 | 8.973 | 11.052 |
| 7.941 | 8.754 | 9.405 | 10.203 | 10.967 | 11.752 | 12.530 | 13.587 | 14.577 | 15.692 | 9.280 | 5.232 | 11.923 |
| 7.893 | 8.929 | 9.628 | 10.312 | 11.887 | 12.237 | 12.787 | 12.968 | 14.477 | 16.663 | 10.958 | 8.159 | 12.153 |
| | | | | | | | | | | | | |
| 626.990 | 631.760 | 661.420 | 909.260 | 1025.940 | 1110.580 | 1282.560 | 1643.800 | 1685.700 | 1770.100 | 951.254 | 455.239 | 1129.059 |
| 291.938 | 288.398 | 291.193 | 316.909 | 336.700 | 354.948 | 347.912 | 391.796 | 407.932 | 427.358 | 326.181 | 205.155 | 356.585 |
| 819.216 | 907.809 | 978.353 | 1117.489 | 1209.643 | 1273.983 | 1273.824 | 1475.717 | 1588.078 | 1731.919 | 951.254 | 342.927 | 1279.245 |
| 826.439 | 836.652 | 846.959 | 935.781 | 977.921 | 1002.770 | 982.893 | 1106.871 | 1152.456 | 1207.337 | 897.830 | 493.388 | 1018.501 |
| 723.039 | 801.230 | 863.492 | 986.294 | 1067.629 | 1124.415 | 1124.274 | 1302.465 | 1401.635 | 1528.588 | 839.575 | 302.667 | 1129.059 |
| 626.994 | 631.757 | 661.421 | 909.265 | 1025.940 | 1110.580 | 1282.560 | 1643.850 | 1685.700 | 1770.060 | 951.253 | 455.238 | 1129.060 |
| | | | | | | | | | | | | |
| 70.615 | 78.328 | 83.602 | 86.358 | 90.030 | 91.052 | 78.760 | 71.500 | 68.700 | 72.000 | 75.676 | 70.219 | 76.911 |
| 55.149 | 61.746 | 58.755 | 57.264 | 57.493 | 55.724 | 65.300 | 75.327 | 93.745 | 110.186 | 64.688 | 44.402 | 71.432 |
| 60.394 | 71.496 | 80.194 | 90.673 | 98.880 | 104.264 | 124.636 | 147.907 | 190.251 | 232.786 | 75.676 | 26.702 | 121.863 |
| 60.927 | 65.892 | 69.424 | 75.930 | 79.938 | 82.068 | 96.170 | 110.939 | 138.064 | 162.277 | 77.726 | 38.978 | 97.821 |
| 38.116 | 45.123 | 50.612 | 57.226 | 62.406 | 65.804 | 78.661 | 93.348 | 120.072 | 146.917 | 47.761 | 16.852 | 76.911 |
| 71.575 | 80.027 | 84.452 | 87.228 | 91.902 | 87.733 | 76.550 | 144.910 | 177.970 | 226.000 | 101.908 | 70.319 | 112.336 |

**Table A.2** Conversion rates for individual countries or areas, expressed as the number of local currency units per United States dollar, 1970–1989 [*cont.*]

| Country or area | 1970 (1) | 1971 (2) | 1972 (3) | 1973 (4) | 1974 (5) | 1975 (6) | 1976 (7) | 1977 (8) | 1978 (9) | 1979 (10) |
|---|---|---|---|---|---|---|---|---|---|---|
| **Iraq:** Iraqi dinars | | | | | | | | | | |
| 1. MER | 0.357 | 0.353 | 0.333 | 0.302 | 0.300 | 0.300 | 0.300 | 0.300 | 0.300 | 0.300 |
| 2. PPPs | 0.160 | 0.156 | 0.145 | 0.144 | 0.169 | 0.165 | 0.190 | 0.182 | 0.190 | 0.174 |
| 3. Absolute 1970–1989 PARE | 0.067 | 0.073 | 0.076 | 0.071 | 0.139 | 0.145 | 0.157 | 0.174 | 0.176 | 0.224 |
| 4. Relative 1970–1989 PARE | 0.138 | 0.142 | 0.141 | 0.125 | 0.222 | 0.211 | 0.216 | 0.224 | 0.211 | 0.246 |
| 5. Absolute 1980–1989 PARE | 0.047 | 0.051 | 0.053 | 0.050 | 0.097 | 0.101 | 0.110 | 0.121 | 0.123 | 0.156 |
| 6. WA [a] | 0.343 | 0.372 | 0.367 | 0.320 | 0.499 | 0.408 | 0.322 | 0.331 | 0.313 | 0.356 |
| **Ireland:** Irish pounds | | | | | | | | | | |
| 1. MER | 0.417 | 0.409 | 0.400 | 0.408 | 0.428 | 0.450 | 0.560 | 0.573 | 0.521 | 0.488 |
| 2. PPPs | 0.278 | 0.291 | 0.312 | 0.327 | 0.337 | 0.385 | 0.426 | 0.448 | 0.455 | 0.487 |
| 3. Absolute 1970–1989 PARE | 0.156 | 0.173 | 0.196 | 0.226 | 0.239 | 0.287 | 0.348 | 0.394 | 0.435 | 0.495 |
| 4. Relative 1970–1989 PARE | 0.320 | 0.337 | 0.365 | 0.394 | 0.384 | 0.419 | 0.478 | 0.507 | 0.522 | 0.545 |
| 5. Absolute 1980–1989 PARE | 0.125 | 0.138 | 0.156 | 0.180 | 0.191 | 0.230 | 0.278 | 0.315 | 0.348 | 0.396 |
| 6. WA | 0.417 | 0.411 | 0.400 | 0.408 | 0.428 | 0.452 | 0.557 | 0.573 | 0.522 | 0.489 |
| **Israel:** New sheqels | | | | | | | | | | |
| 1. MER | 0.000 | 0.000 | 0.000 | 0.000 | 0.000 | 0.001 | 0.001 | 0.001 | 0.002 | 0.003 |
| 2. PPPs | 0.000 | 0.000 | 0.000 | 0.000 | 0.000 | 0.001 | 0.001 | 0.001 | 0.001 | 0.002 |
| 3. Absolute 1970–1989 PARE | 0.000 | 0.000 | 0.000 | 0.000 | 0.000 | 0.000 | 0.001 | 0.001 | 0.001 | 0.002 |
| 4. Relative 1970–1989 PARE | 0.000 | 0.000 | 0.000 | 0.000 | 0.001 | 0.001 | 0.001 | 0.001 | 0.002 | 0.003 |
| 5. Absolute 1980–1989 PARE | 0.000 | 0.000 | 0.000 | 0.000 | 0.000 | 0.000 | 0.000 | 0.001 | 0.001 | 0.002 |
| 6. WA | 0.000 | 0.000 | 0.000 | 0.000 | 0.000 | 0.001 | 0.001 | 0.001 | 0.002 | 0.003 |
| **Italy:** Italian lire | | | | | | | | | | |
| 1. MER | 625.000 | 619.930 | 583.220 | 583.000 | 650.340 | 652.850 | 832.330 | 882.390 | 848.660 | 830.860 |
| 2. PPPs | 460.511 | 463.856 | 465.656 | 491.836 | 540.508 | 572.454 | 636.033 | 705.296 | 736.843 | 771.667 |
| 3. Absolute 1970–1989 PARE | 241.387 | 258.142 | 274.828 | 311.010 | 372.610 | 434.265 | 513.963 | 609.569 | 695.247 | 801.633 |
| 4. Relative 1970–1989 PARE | 495.081 | 503.611 | 512.643 | 544.001 | 597.517 | 633.865 | 706.068 | 784.497 | 833.926 | 882.720 |
| 5. Absolute 1980–1989 PARE | 189.411 | 202.558 | 215.651 | 244.043 | 292.379 | 340.758 | 403.295 | 478.316 | 545.545 | 629.024 |
| 6. WA | 625.000 | 619.934 | 583.217 | 582.996 | 650.343 | 652.849 | 832.335 | 882.388 | 848.663 | 830.862 |
| **Jamaica:** Jamaican dollars | | | | | | | | | | |
| 1. MER | 0.830 | 0.830 | 0.770 | 0.910 | 0.909 | 0.909 | 0.910 | 0.910 | 1.410 | 1.760 |
| 2. PPPs | 0.496 | 0.508 | 0.510 | 0.612 | 0.728 | 0.748 | 0.810 | 0.891 | 1.008 | 1.070 |
| 3. Absolute 1970–1989 PARE | 0.447 | 0.475 | 0.488 | 0.581 | 0.756 | 0.914 | 1.013 | 1.137 | 1.430 | 1.674 |
| 4. Relative 1970–1989 PARE | 0.917 | 0.926 | 0.910 | 1.016 | 1.213 | 1.334 | 1.391 | 1.463 | 1.716 | 1.843 |
| 5. Absolute 1980–1989 PARE | 0.385 | 0.409 | 0.420 | 0.500 | 0.651 | 0.787 | 0.872 | 0.979 | 1.232 | 1.442 |
| 6. WA | 0.833 | 0.822 | 0.803 | 0.909 | 0.909 | 0.909 | 0.909 | 0.909 | 1.449 | 1.763 |
| **Japan:** Japanese yen | | | | | | | | | | |
| 1. MER | 360.000 | 349.330 | 303.170 | 271.700 | 292.080 | 296.790 | 296.550 | 268.510 | 210.440 | 219.140 |
| 2. PPPs | 254.428 | 252.046 | 247.529 | 255.248 | 281.108 | 279.994 | 285.558 | 283.432 | 271.458 | 258.800 |
| 3. Absolute 1970–1989 PARE | 102.002 | 107.612 | 113.678 | 128.305 | 154.994 | 166.915 | 178.889 | 189.333 | 198.371 | 204.401 |
| 4. Relative 1970–1989 PARE | 209.206 | 209.942 | 212.046 | 224.423 | 248.548 | 243.634 | 245.753 | 243.666 | 237.940 | 225.077 |
| 5. Absolute 1980–1989 PARE | 80.566 | 84.997 | 89.787 | 101.340 | 122.421 | 131.836 | 141.294 | 149.543 | 156.682 | 161.445 |
| 6. WA | 360.000 | 349.333 | 303.172 | 271.702 | 292.082 | 296.787 | 296.552 | 268.510 | 210.442 | 219.140 |
| **Jordan:** Jordanian dinars | | | | | | | | | | |
| 1. MER | 0.357 | 0.357 | 0.357 | 0.327 | 0.321 | 0.319 | 0.332 | 0.329 | 0.306 | 0.300 |
| 2. PPPs | 0.095 | 0.100 | 0.106 | 0.119 | 0.109 | 0.121 | 0.134 | 0.150 | 0.159 | 0.160 |
| 3. Absolute 1970–1989 PARE | 0.123 | 0.129 | 0.138 | 0.154 | 0.184 | 0.212 | 0.235 | 0.269 | 0.287 | 0.319 |
| 4. Relative 1970–1989 PARE | 0.251 | 0.252 | 0.258 | 0.269 | 0.295 | 0.310 | 0.322 | 0.346 | 0.345 | 0.351 |
| 5. Absolute 1980–1989 PARE | 0.105 | 0.111 | 0.119 | 0.133 | 0.158 | 0.183 | 0.202 | 0.232 | 0.247 | 0.274 |
| 6. WA | 0.357 | 0.357 | 0.357 | 0.329 | 0.322 | 0.320 | 0.332 | 0.329 | 0.306 | 0.300 |

| | | | | | | | | | | Averages | | |
|---|---|---|---|---|---|---|---|---|---|---|---|---|
| 1980 (11) | 1981 (12) | 1982 (13) | 1983 (14) | 1984 (15) | 1985 (16) | 1986 (17) | 1987 (18) | 1988 (19) | 1989 (20) | 1970–89 (21) | 1970–79 (22) | 1980–89 (23) |
| 0.300 | 0.300 | 0.298 | 0.311 | 0.311 | 0.311 | 0.310 | 0.300 | 0.300 | 0.300 | 0.304 | 0.304 | 0.304 |
| 0.190 | 0.157 | 0.410 | 0.298 | 0.326 | 0.341 | 0.351 | 0.420 | 0.363 | 0.443 | 0.263 | 0.174 | 0.308 |
| 0.313 | 0.266 | 0.320 | 0.348 | 0.425 | 0.489 | 0.514 | 0.633 | 0.564 | 0.717 | 0.304 | 0.147 | 0.435 |
| 0.316 | 0.246 | 0.277 | 0.292 | 0.344 | 0.385 | 0.397 | 0.475 | 0.410 | 0.500 | 0.308 | 0.206 | 0.358 |
| 0.219 | 0.186 | 0.223 | 0.243 | 0.297 | 0.341 | 0.359 | 0.442 | 0.394 | 0.501 | 0.212 | 0.103 | 0.304 |
| 0.418 | 0.304 | 0.321 | 0.343 | 0.362 | 0.368 | 0.338 | 0.362 | 0.303 | 0.340 | 0.346 | 0.351 | 0.344 |
| 0.486 | 0.619 | 0.703 | 0.801 | 0.920 | 0.950 | 0.740 | 0.700 | 0.700 | 0.700 | 0.661 | 0.482 | 0.726 |
| 0.529 | 0.562 | 0.605 | 0.655 | 0.667 | 0.699 | 0.728 | 0.725 | 0.724 | 0.731 | 0.594 | 0.398 | 0.673 |
| 0.568 | 0.667 | 0.768 | 0.850 | 0.905 | 0.951 | 1.011 | 1.037 | 1.070 | 1.125 | 0.661 | 0.310 | 0.907 |
| 0.573 | 0.615 | 0.665 | 0.712 | 0.731 | 0.749 | 0.780 | 0.777 | 0.776 | 0.784 | 0.651 | 0.453 | 0.728 |
| 0.454 | 0.533 | 0.614 | 0.680 | 0.724 | 0.761 | 0.809 | 0.829 | 0.856 | 0.900 | 0.529 | 0.248 | 0.726 |
| 0.487 | 0.621 | 0.705 | 0.805 | 0.923 | 0.946 | 0.743 | 0.673 | 0.656 | 0.706 | 0.655 | 0.482 | 0.717 |
| 0.005 | 0.011 | 0.024 | 0.056 | 0.293 | 1.179 | 1.490 | 1.600 | 1.600 | 1.900 | 0.704 | 0.001 | 0.979 |
| 0.005 | 0.009 | 0.019 | 0.046 | 0.217 | 0.798 | 1.183 | 1.382 | 1.584 | 1.817 | 0.593 | 0.001 | 0.823 |
| 0.005 | 0.012 | 0.027 | 0.066 | 0.322 | 1.170 | 1.770 | 2.127 | 2.519 | 3.009 | 0.704 | 0.001 | 1.200 |
| 0.005 | 0.011 | 0.023 | 0.055 | 0.260 | 0.921 | 1.366 | 1.595 | 1.828 | 2.097 | 0.694 | 0.001 | 0.961 |
| 0.004 | 0.010 | 0.022 | 0.054 | 0.263 | 0.955 | 1.445 | 1.736 | 2.056 | 2.456 | 0.574 | 0.001 | 0.979 |
| 0.005 | 0.011 | 0.024 | 0.056 | 0.293 | 1.179 | 1.488 | 1.595 | 1.599 | 1.916 | 0.703 | 0.001 | 0.980 |
| 856.450 | 1136.760 | 1352.510 | 1518.850 | 1756.960 | 1909.440 | 1490.810 | 1296.100 | 1301.600 | 1372.100 | 1212.190 | 745.350 | 1384.185 |
| 838.120 | 922.400 | 1011.082 | 1127.425 | 1205.829 | 1297.819 | 1368.278 | 1411.664 | 1447.213 | 1483.912 | 1067.952 | 620.996 | 1245.843 |
| 962.247 | 1140.847 | 1335.873 | 1535.027 | 1710.750 | 1863.006 | 2003.621 | 2126.546 | 2253.293 | 2405.163 | 1212.190 | 470.418 | 1764.017 |
| 970.731 | 1051.424 | 1156.465 | 1285.426 | 1383.034 | 1466.398 | 1546.010 | 1595.030 | 1635.198 | 1676.662 | 1206.608 | 691.346 | 1415.971 |
| 755.054 | 895.197 | 1048.230 | 1204.501 | 1342.388 | 1461.859 | 1572.196 | 1668.653 | 1768.108 | 1887.278 | 951.178 | 369.126 | 1384.184 |
| 856.447 | 1136.760 | 1352.510 | 1518.850 | 1756.960 | 1909.440 | 1490.810 | 1296.070 | 1301.630 | 1372.090 | 1212.189 | 745.351 | 1384.183 |
| 1.781 | 1.781 | 1.781 | 1.932 | 3.943 | 5.559 | 5.480 | 5.500 | 5.500 | 5.700 | 2.610 | 1.035 | 3.847 |
| 1.174 | 1.229 | 1.228 | 1.376 | 1.822 | 2.198 | 2.512 | 2.760 | 3.083 | 3.371 | 1.651 | 0.768 | 2.180 |
| 1.965 | 2.134 | 2.330 | 2.718 | 3.662 | 4.632 | 5.399 | 6.102 | 7.046 | 8.021 | 2.610 | 0.879 | 4.467 |
| 1.982 | 1.967 | 2.017 | 2.276 | 2.961 | 3.646 | 4.166 | 4.577 | 5.113 | 5.591 | 2.771 | 1.327 | 3.598 |
| 1.692 | 1.838 | 2.007 | 2.341 | 3.154 | 3.989 | 4.650 | 5.256 | 6.068 | 6.908 | 2.248 | 0.757 | 3.847 |
| 1.781 | 1.930 | 1.990 | 2.150 | 3.943 | 5.559 | 5.478 | 5.487 | 5.489 | 5.745 | 2.665 | 1.041 | 3.976 |
| 226.740 | 220.540 | 249.080 | 237.510 | 237.520 | 238.540 | 168.520 | 144.600 | 128.100 | 138.000 | 201.070 | 265.443 | 180.920 |
| 248.872 | 237.632 | 229.254 | 225.962 | 225.692 | 230.358 | 229.959 | 222.793 | 216.772 | 212.665 | 238.239 | 269.025 | 226.344 |
| 212.162 | 218.896 | 222.997 | 224.705 | 227.481 | 230.623 | 234.850 | 234.070 | 235.390 | 240.398 | 201.070 | 158.813 | 229.059 |
| 214.033 | 201.738 | 193.049 | 188.167 | 183.904 | 181.527 | 181.212 | 175.566 | 170.821 | 167.584 | 196.139 | 232.582 | 182.973 |
| 167.575 | 172.893 | 176.133 | 177.481 | 179.674 | 182.156 | 185.494 | 184.878 | 185.921 | 189.877 | 158.813 | 125.437 | 180.920 |
| 226.741 | 220.536 | 249.077 | 237.512 | 237.522 | 238.536 | 168.520 | 144.637 | 128.152 | 137.964 | 201.079 | 265.443 | 180.931 |
| 0.298 | 0.330 | 0.352 | 0.363 | 0.384 | 0.394 | 0.350 | 0.400 | 0.400 | 0.600 | 0.372 | 0.321 | 0.387 |
| 0.181 | 0.183 | 0.183 | 0.183 | 0.155 | 0.158 | 0.165 | 0.159 | 0.166 | 0.194 | 0.162 | 0.133 | 0.172 |
| 0.350 | 0.382 | 0.398 | 0.425 | 0.431 | 0.438 | 0.466 | 0.463 | 0.499 | 0.607 | 0.372 | 0.218 | 0.449 |
| 0.353 | 0.352 | 0.344 | 0.356 | 0.348 | 0.345 | 0.360 | 0.347 | 0.362 | 0.423 | 0.350 | 0.315 | 0.360 |
| 0.301 | 0.328 | 0.342 | 0.365 | 0.371 | 0.377 | 0.401 | 0.398 | 0.430 | 0.522 | 0.320 | 0.188 | 0.387 |
| 0.298 | 0.330 | 0.352 | 0.363 | 0.384 | 0.395 | 0.350 | 0.338 | 0.374 | 0.575 | 0.363 | 0.321 | 0.375 |

**Table A.2** Conversion rates for individual countries or areas, expressed as the number of local currency units per United States dollar, 1970−1989 [*cont.*]

| Country or area | 1970 (1) | 1971 (2) | 1972 (3) | 1973 (4) | 1974 (5) | 1975 (6) | 1976 (7) | 1977 (8) | 1978 (9) | 1979 (10) |
|---|---|---|---|---|---|---|---|---|---|---|
| **Kenya:** Kenyan pounds | | | | | | | | | | |
| 1. MER | 0.357 | 0.357 | 0.357 | 0.350 | 0.357 | 0.367 | 0.418 | 0.414 | 0.386 | 0.374 |
| 2. PPPs | 0.178 | 0.172 | 0.178 | 0.194 | 0.202 | 0.208 | 0.227 | 0.238 | 0.232 | 0.231 |
| 3. Absolute 1970−1989 PARE | 0.187 | 0.195 | 0.208 | 0.229 | 0.265 | 0.300 | 0.350 | 0.410 | 0.416 | 0.445 |
| 4. Relative 1970−1989 PARE | 0.384 | 0.381 | 0.388 | 0.401 | 0.425 | 0.438 | 0.481 | 0.528 | 0.499 | 0.490 |
| 5. Absolute 1980−1989 PARE | 0.168 | 0.176 | 0.187 | 0.206 | 0.238 | 0.270 | 0.315 | 0.369 | 0.375 | 0.400 |
| 6. WA | 0.357 | 0.357 | 0.357 | 0.350 | 0.357 | 0.367 | 0.418 | 0.414 | 0.386 | 0.374 |
| **Kiribati:** Australian dollars | | | | | | | | | | |
| 1. MER | 0.893 | 0.880 | 0.839 | 0.704 | 0.640 | 0.763 | 0.816 | 0.902 | 0.874 | 0.895 |
| 2. PPPs | ... | ... | ... | ... | ... | ... | ... | ... | ... | ... |
| 3. Absolute 1970−1989 PARE | 0.434 | 0.464 | 0.490 | 0.568 | 0.643 | 0.703 | 0.768 | 0.836 | 0.936 | 1.006 |
| 4. Relative 1970−1989 PARE | 0.890 | 0.906 | 0.913 | 0.994 | 1.031 | 1.026 | 1.055 | 1.076 | 1.122 | 1.108 |
| 5. Absolute 1980−1989 PARE | 0.341 | 0.365 | 0.385 | 0.447 | 0.506 | 0.553 | 0.604 | 0.658 | 0.736 | 0.791 |
| 6. WA [a] | 1.156 | 1.017 | 0.925 | 0.918 | 0.846 | 0.778 | 0.804 | 0.899 | 0.959 | 0.973 |
| **Korea, Dem. People's Rep. of:** Won | | | | | | | | | | |
| 1. MER | 1.200 | 1.100 | 1.100 | 1.100 | 0.960 | 0.960 | 0.960 | 0.960 | 0.930 | 0.860 |
| 2. PPPs | ... | ... | ... | ... | ... | ... | ... | ... | ... | ... |
| 3. Absolute 1970−1989 PARE | 1.265 | 1.131 | 1.165 | 1.219 | 1.086 | 1.110 | 1.129 | 1.146 | 1.067 | 0.959 |
| 4. Relative 1970−1989 PARE | 2.594 | 2.206 | 2.174 | 2.131 | 1.741 | 1.620 | 1.551 | 1.475 | 1.280 | 1.056 |
| 5. Absolute 1980−1989 PARE | 1.331 | 1.190 | 1.226 | 1.282 | 1.143 | 1.168 | 1.188 | 1.206 | 1.123 | 1.009 |
| 6. WA [a] | 1.174 | 1.074 | 1.113 | 1.145 | 0.988 | 0.981 | 0.978 | 0.975 | 0.911 | 0.833 |
| **Korea, Republic of:** Korean won | | | | | | | | | | |
| 1. MER | 310.560 | 347.150 | 392.890 | 398.320 | 404.470 | 484.000 | 484.000 | 484.000 | 484.000 | 484.000 |
| 2. PPPs | ... | ... | ... | ... | ... | ... | ... | ... | ... | ... |
| 3. Absolute 1970−1989 PARE | 98.444 | 111.355 | 130.058 | 147.489 | 192.733 | 241.666 | 293.005 | 341.190 | 418.584 | 500.940 |
| 4. Relative 1970−1989 PARE | 201.907 | 217.244 | 242.601 | 257.979 | 309.067 | 352.743 | 402.523 | 439.101 | 502.078 | 551.610 |
| 5. Absolute 1980−1989 PARE | 83.480 | 94.429 | 110.289 | 125.070 | 163.437 | 204.932 | 248.467 | 289.328 | 354.957 | 424.794 |
| 6. WA | 310.556 | 347.147 | 392.894 | 398.322 | 404.472 | 484.000 | 484.000 | 484.000 | 484.000 | 484.000 |
| **Kuwait:** Kuwaiti dinars | | | | | | | | | | |
| 1. MER | 0.357 | 0.360 | 0.328 | 0.300 | 0.293 | 0.290 | 0.292 | 0.287 | 0.280 | 0.276 |
| 2. PPPs | 0.329 | 0.329 | 0.305 | 0.276 | 0.290 | 0.288 | 0.288 | 0.287 | 0.282 | 0.284 |
| 3. Absolute 1970−1989 PARE | 0.050 | 0.063 | 0.064 | 0.075 | 0.205 | 0.214 | 0.221 | 0.242 | 0.238 | 0.335 |
| 4. Relative 1970−1989 PARE | 0.102 | 0.123 | 0.119 | 0.131 | 0.329 | 0.312 | 0.303 | 0.312 | 0.285 | 0.368 |
| 5. Absolute 1980−1989 PARE | 0.030 | 0.038 | 0.039 | 0.046 | 0.125 | 0.130 | 0.135 | 0.148 | 0.145 | 0.204 |
| 6. WA | 0.357 | 0.356 | 0.329 | 0.297 | 0.293 | 0.290 | 0.292 | 0.287 | 0.275 | 0.276 |
| **Lao People's Dem Rep. :** Kip | | | | | | | | | | |
| 1. MER | 0.120 | 0.120 | 0.247 | 0.300 | 0.300 | 0.360 | 1.626 | 2.520 | 4.199 | 5.714 |
| 2. PPPs | ... | ... | ... | ... | ... | ... | ... | ... | ... | ... |
| 3. Absolute 1970−1989 PARE | 0.041 | 0.034 | 0.090 | 0.142 | 0.140 | 0.201 | 0.962 | 1.542 | 3.113 | 4.400 |
| 4. Relative 1970−1989 PARE | 0.083 | 0.066 | 0.167 | 0.248 | 0.225 | 0.293 | 1.322 | 1.985 | 3.734 | 4.845 |
| 5. Absolute 1980−1989 PARE | 0.030 | 0.025 | 0.066 | 0.105 | 0.103 | 0.148 | 0.710 | 1.138 | 2.298 | 3.248 |
| 6. WA [a] | 0.195 | 0.125 | 0.276 | 0.398 | 0.328 | 0.405 | 1.803 | 2.630 | 4.850 | 6.279 |
| **Lebanon:** Lebanese pounds | | | | | | | | | | |
| 1. MER | 3.269 | 3.228 | 3.051 | 2.610 | 2.328 | 2.310 | 2.870 | 3.069 | 2.960 | 3.243 |
| 2. PPPs | ... | ... | ... | ... | ... | ... | ... | ... | ... | ... |
| 3. Absolute 1970−1989 PARE | 1.505 | 1.529 | 1.607 | 1.712 | 1.898 | 2.166 | 2.752 | 3.004 | 3.325 | 3.851 |
| 4. Relative 1970−1989 PARE | 3.086 | 2.982 | 2.997 | 2.995 | 3.044 | 3.162 | 3.781 | 3.866 | 3.988 | 4.241 |
| 5. Absolute 1980−1989 PARE | 1.054 | 1.071 | 1.126 | 1.200 | 1.330 | 1.518 | 1.928 | 2.104 | 2.329 | 2.698 |
| 6. WA [a] | 3.588 | 3.404 | 3.312 | 3.159 | 2.942 | 2.756 | 3.060 | 3.135 | 3.275 | 3.535 |

| | | | | | | | | | | Averages | | |
|---|---|---|---|---|---|---|---|---|---|---|---|---|
| 1980 (11) | 1981 (12) | 1982 (13) | 1983 (14) | 1984 (15) | 1985 (16) | 1986 (17) | 1987 (18) | 1988 (19) | 1989 (20) | 1970–89 (21) | 1970–79 (22) | 1980–89 (23) |
| 0.371 | 0.452 | 0.546 | 0.666 | 0.721 | 0.822 | 0.810 | 0.800 | 0.900 | 1.000 | 0.611 | 0.379 | 0.722 |
| 0.239 | 0.251 | 0.260 | 0.283 | 0.291 | 0.326 | 0.349 | 0.360 | 0.382 | 0.404 | 0.294 | 0.213 | 0.325 |
| 0.487 | 0.540 | 0.605 | 0.671 | 0.741 | 0.801 | 0.876 | 0.929 | 1.019 | 1.121 | 0.611 | 0.313 | 0.802 |
| 0.491 | 0.497 | 0.524 | 0.562 | 0.599 | 0.630 | 0.676 | 0.697 | 0.740 | 0.781 | 0.593 | 0.457 | 0.640 |
| 0.439 | 0.486 | 0.545 | 0.604 | 0.668 | 0.721 | 0.788 | 0.837 | 0.918 | 1.009 | 0.550 | 0.282 | 0.722 |
| 0.371 | 0.452 | 0.546 | 0.666 | 0.721 | 0.822 | 0.811 | 0.823 | 0.887 | 1.029 | 0.613 | 0.379 | 0.725 |
| | | | | | | | | | | | | |
| 0.878 | 0.870 | 0.990 | 1.108 | 1.137 | 1.427 | 1.500 | 1.400 | 1.300 | 1.300 | 0.958 | 0.803 | 1.186 |
| ... | ... | ... | ... | ... | ... | ... | ... | ... | ... | ... | ... | ... |
| 1.008 | 1.150 | 1.262 | 1.311 | 1.419 | 1.604 | 1.695 | 1.802 | 1.862 | 1.957 | 0.958 | 0.702 | 1.508 |
| 1.017 | 1.060 | 1.093 | 1.098 | 1.147 | 1.263 | 1.308 | 1.351 | 1.351 | 1.364 | 1.119 | 1.035 | 1.218 |
| 0.793 | 0.905 | 0.993 | 1.031 | 1.116 | 1.262 | 1.333 | 1.417 | 1.465 | 1.539 | 0.754 | 0.552 | 1.186 |
| 0.905 | 0.965 | 1.015 | 1.042 | 1.150 | 1.356 | 1.455 | 1.532 | 1.465 | 1.396 | 1.034 | 0.893 | 1.229 |
| | | | | | | | | | | | | |
| 1.880 | 1.870 | 2.110 | 2.200 | 2.370 | 2.520 | 2.260 | 2.180 | 2.160 | 2.170 | 1.807 | 0.982 | 2.186 |
| ... | ... | ... | ... | ... | ... | ... | ... | ... | ... | ... | ... | ... |
| 2.056 | 1.895 | 2.037 | 2.103 | 2.217 | 2.259 | 2.035 | 2.052 | 2.034 | 2.046 | 1.807 | 1.108 | 2.077 |
| 2.074 | 1.746 | 1.763 | 1.761 | 1.792 | 1.778 | 1.570 | 1.539 | 1.476 | 1.426 | 1.628 | 1.561 | 1.643 |
| 2.163 | 1.994 | 2.143 | 2.213 | 2.333 | 2.377 | 2.141 | 2.159 | 2.141 | 2.153 | 1.901 | 1.166 | 2.186 |
| 1.838 | 1.767 | 1.994 | 2.151 | 2.329 | 2.433 | 2.235 | 2.250 | 2.194 | 2.172 | 1.791 | 0.984 | 2.156 |
| | | | | | | | | | | | | |
| 607.430 | 681.030 | 731.080 | 775.750 | 805.980 | 870.020 | 881.450 | 822.600 | 731.500 | 671.500 | 698.619 | 459.284 | 756.189 |
| ... | ... | ... | ... | ... | ... | ... | ... | ... | ... | ... | ... | ... |
| 621.819 | 727.285 | 777.176 | 815.218 | 847.924 | 882.499 | 913.085 | 950.378 | 1004.070 | 1058.119 | 698.619 | 281.437 | 891.737 |
| 627.302 | 670.278 | 672.801 | 682.660 | 685.494 | 694.627 | 704.544 | 712.837 | 728.646 | 737.625 | 640.743 | 401.014 | 702.060 |
| 527.300 | 616.734 | 659.041 | 691.301 | 719.036 | 748.355 | 774.292 | 805.916 | 851.446 | 897.280 | 592.425 | 238.657 | 756.189 |
| 607.432 | 681.028 | 731.084 | 775.748 | 805.976 | 870.020 | 881.454 | 822.567 | 731.468 | 671.456 | 698.605 | 459.284 | 756.170 |
| | | | | | | | | | | | | |
| 0.270 | 0.279 | 0.288 | 0.291 | 0.296 | 0.301 | 0.290 | 0.300 | 0.300 | 0.300 | 0.291 | 0.292 | 0.290 |
| 0.279 | 0.283 | 0.294 | 0.301 | 0.284 | 0.268 | 0.194 | 0.234 | 0.230 | 0.228 | 0.267 | 0.289 | 0.257 |
| 0.471 | 0.527 | 0.527 | 0.478 | 0.480 | 0.503 | 0.372 | 0.461 | 0.468 | 0.484 | 0.291 | 0.164 | 0.476 |
| 0.475 | 0.486 | 0.456 | 0.400 | 0.388 | 0.396 | 0.287 | 0.346 | 0.340 | 0.337 | 0.326 | 0.249 | 0.386 |
| 0.287 | 0.322 | 0.322 | 0.292 | 0.293 | 0.307 | 0.227 | 0.281 | 0.286 | 0.295 | 0.178 | 0.100 | 0.290 |
| 0.270 | 0.279 | 0.288 | 0.291 | 0.296 | 0.301 | 0.291 | 0.279 | 0.279 | 0.294 | 0.288 | 0.291 | 0.286 |
| | | | | | | | | | | | | |
| 10.217 | 20.000 | 85.000 | 35.000 | 35.000 | 45.000 | 95.000 | 175.117 | 392.012 | 583.015 | 163.637 | 1.988 | 208.899 |
| ... | ... | ... | ... | ... | ... | ... | ... | ... | ... | ... | ... | ... |
| 9.331 | 12.765 | 51.748 | 34.042 | 53.965 | 74.187 | 136.549 | 320.056 | 562.988 | 1077.817 | 163.637 | 1.028 | 283.005 |
| 9.414 | 11.765 | 44.798 | 28.506 | 43.628 | 58.393 | 105.362 | 240.060 | 408.556 | 751.356 | 162.392 | 1.548 | 224.579 |
| 6.888 | 9.423 | 38.198 | 25.128 | 39.834 | 54.761 | 100.793 | 236.249 | 415.568 | 795.589 | 120.788 | 0.758 | 208.899 |
| 11.640 | 16.852 | 74.245 | 48.084 | 59.709 | 56.463 | 88.796 | 197.309 | 363.911 | 641.076 | 182.230 | 2.271 | 231.018 |
| | | | | | | | | | | | | |
| 3.436 | 4.314 | 4.744 | 4.528 | 6.511 | 16.417 | 38.370 | 224.600 | 409.200 | 496.700 | 38.438 | 2.840 | 75.963 |
| ... | ... | ... | ... | ... | ... | ... | ... | ... | ... | ... | ... | ... |
| 4.674 | 5.415 | 5.592 | 7.736 | 10.564 | 19.346 | 42.561 | 353.235 | 883.212 | 1324.880 | 38.438 | 2.211 | 108.429 |
| 4.715 | 4.991 | 4.841 | 6.478 | 8.540 | 15.228 | 32.840 | 264.946 | 640.940 | 923.586 | 46.452 | 3.415 | 92.262 |
| 3.275 | 3.794 | 3.918 | 5.420 | 7.401 | 13.553 | 29.817 | 247.469 | 618.759 | 928.183 | 26.929 | 1.549 | 75.963 |
| 3.844 | 4.285 | 4.437 | 5.751 | 7.218 | 13.221 | 33.573 | 280.935 | 589.006 | 650.979 | 42.294 | 3.198 | 81.608 |

**Table A.2** Conversion rates for individual countries or areas, expressed as the number of
local currency units per United States dollar, 1970–1989 [*cont.*]

| Country or area | 1970 (1) | 1971 (2) | 1972 (3) | 1973 (4) | 1974 (5) | 1975 (6) | 1976 (7) | 1977 (8) | 1978 (9) | 1979 (10) |
|---|---|---|---|---|---|---|---|---|---|---|
| **Lesotho:** Lesotho maloti | | | | | | | | | | |
| 1.  MER | 0.714 | 0.720 | 0.772 | 0.692 | 0.679 | 0.740 | 0.870 | 0.870 | 0.870 | 0.842 |
| 2.  PPPs | 0.239 | 0.226 | 0.224 | 0.251 | 0.243 | 0.226 | 0.231 | 0.263 | 0.295 | 0.319 |
| 3.  Absolute 1970–1989 PARE | 0.384 | 0.407 | 0.436 | 0.472 | 0.497 | 0.613 | 0.611 | 0.680 | 0.783 | 0.926 |
| 4.  Relative 1970–1989 PARE | 0.788 | 0.795 | 0.812 | 0.825 | 0.797 | 0.895 | 0.839 | 0.875 | 0.939 | 1.019 |
| 5.  Absolute 1980–1989 PARE | 0.337 | 0.357 | 0.382 | 0.414 | 0.436 | 0.537 | 0.535 | 0.596 | 0.686 | 0.811 |
| 6.  WA | 0.714 | 0.715 | 0.769 | 0.694 | 0.679 | 0.740 | 0.870 | 0.870 | 0.870 | 0.842 |
| **Liberia:** Liberian dollars | | | | | | | | | | |
| 1.  MER | 1.000 | 1.000 | 1.000 | 1.000 | 1.000 | 1.000 | 1.000 | 1.000 | 1.000 | 1.000 |
| 2.  PPPs | 0.614 | 0.581 | 0.604 | 0.656 | 0.695 | 0.760 | 0.679 | 0.711 | 0.706 | 0.721 |
| 3.  Absolute 1970–1989 PARE | 0.441 | 0.443 | 0.463 | 0.522 | 0.617 | 0.772 | 0.679 | 0.711 | 0.706 | 0.721 |
| 4.  Relative 1970–1989 PARE | 0.905 | 0.864 | 0.864 | 0.912 | 0.990 | 1.126 | 1.048 | 1.088 | 1.050 | 1.060 |
| 5.  Absolute 1980–1989 PARE | 0.337 | 0.338 | 0.353 | 0.398 | 0.471 | 0.589 | 0.582 | 0.645 | 0.668 | 0.734 |
| 6.  WA | 1.000 | 1.000 | 1.000 | 1.000 | 1.000 | 1.000 | 1.000 | 1.000 | 1.000 | 1.000 |
| **Libyan Arab Jamahiriya:** Libyan dinars | | | | | | | | | | |
| 1.  MER | 0.357 | 0.360 | 0.329 | 0.300 | 0.296 | 0.296 | 0.296 | 0.296 | 0.296 | 0.296 |
| 2.  PPPs | ... | ... | ... | ... | ... | ... | ... | ... | ... | ... |
| 3.  Absolute 1970–1989 PARE | 0.111 | 0.129 | 0.137 | 0.155 | 0.244 | 0.218 | 0.230 | 0.249 | 0.237 | 0.301 |
| 4.  Relative 1970–1989 PARE | 0.227 | 0.252 | 0.255 | 0.271 | 0.391 | 0.318 | 0.317 | 0.320 | 0.285 | 0.331 |
| 5.  Absolute 1980–1989 PARE | 0.090 | 0.105 | 0.111 | 0.126 | 0.197 | 0.177 | 0.187 | 0.201 | 0.192 | 0.244 |
| 6.  WA | 0.357 | 0.356 | 0.329 | 0.300 | 0.296 | 0.296 | 0.296 | 0.296 | 0.296 | 0.296 |
| **Luxembourg:** Luxembourg francs | | | | | | | | | | |
| 1.  MER | 50.000 | 48.870 | 44.015 | 38.977 | 38.952 | 36.779 | 38.610 | 35.843 | 31.492 | 29.319 |
| 2.  PPPs | 39.755 | 39.375 | 39.116 | 38.707 | 38.852 | 39.505 | 41.519 | 40.325 | 39.924 | 38.584 |
| 3.  Absolute 1970–1989 PARE | 20.453 | 20.286 | 21.461 | 24.079 | 28.168 | 27.927 | 31.339 | 31.706 | 33.333 | 35.451 |
| 4.  Relative 1970–1989 PARE | 41.949 | 39.577 | 40.031 | 42.118 | 45.171 | 40.763 | 43.052 | 40.805 | 39.981 | 39.037 |
| 5.  Absolute 1980–1989 PARE | 17.120 | 16.981 | 17.964 | 20.156 | 23.578 | 23.377 | 26.232 | 26.540 | 27.901 | 29.674 |
| 6.  WA | 50.000 | 48.870 | 44.015 | 38.977 | 38.952 | 36.779 | 38.605 | 35.843 | 31.492 | 29.319 |
| **Madagascar:** Malagasi francs | | | | | | | | | | |
| 1.  MER | 277.710 | 277.130 | 252.480 | 222.890 | 240.700 | 214.310 | 238.950 | 245.680 | 225.650 | 212.720 |
| 2.  PPPs | 95.750 | 93.985 | 93.063 | 102.327 | 120.131 | 120.381 | 122.989 | 121.984 | 119.992 | 126.661 |
| 3.  Absolute 1970–1989 PARE | 127.600 | 132.067 | 139.033 | 154.838 | 187.134 | 195.912 | 215.361 | 233.868 | 249.660 | 278.049 |
| 4.  Relative 1970–1989 PARE | 261.707 | 257.650 | 259.342 | 270.834 | 300.088 | 285.958 | 295.857 | 300.980 | 299.459 | 306.174 |
| 5.  Absolute 1980–1989 PARE | 108.297 | 112.088 | 118.001 | 131.415 | 158.825 | 166.275 | 182.782 | 198.489 | 211.892 | 235.986 |
| 6.  WA | 277.710 | 277.132 | 252.484 | 222.888 | 240.704 | 214.312 | 238.950 | 245.679 | 225.655 | 212.721 |
| **Malawi:** Malawi kwacha | | | | | | | | | | |
| 1.  MER | 0.833 | 0.828 | 0.802 | 0.819 | 0.841 | 0.864 | 0.913 | 0.903 | 0.844 | 0.817 |
| 2.  PPPs | 0.378 | 0.386 | 0.377 | 0.373 | 0.374 | 0.376 | 0.392 | 0.413 | 0.400 | 0.384 |
| 3.  Absolute 1970–1989 PARE | 0.539 | 0.591 | 0.592 | 0.543 | 0.643 | 0.696 | 0.742 | 0.827 | 0.827 | 0.813 |
| 4.  Relative 1970–1989 PARE | 1.106 | 1.153 | 1.104 | 0.949 | 1.031 | 1.017 | 1.019 | 1.065 | 0.992 | 0.896 |
| 5.  Absolute 1980–1989 PARE | 0.484 | 0.530 | 0.531 | 0.487 | 0.577 | 0.625 | 0.666 | 0.742 | 0.742 | 0.730 |
| 6.  WA | 0.833 | 0.831 | 0.802 | 0.819 | 0.841 | 0.864 | 0.913 | 0.903 | 0.844 | 0.817 |
| **Malaysia:** Malaysian ringgit | | | | | | | | | | |
| 1.  MER | 3.061 | 3.050 | 2.820 | 2.443 | 2.407 | 2.390 | 2.542 | 2.461 | 2.316 | 2.188 |
| 2.  PPPs | 1.383 | 1.328 | 1.308 | 1.369 | 1.342 | 1.271 | 1.325 | 1.290 | 1.254 | 1.244 |
| 3.  Absolute 1970–1989 PARE | 1.258 | 1.252 | 1.256 | 1.481 | 1.669 | 1.618 | 1.823 | 1.949 | 2.140 | 2.398 |
| 4.  Relative 1970–1989 PARE | 2.580 | 2.442 | 2.343 | 2.590 | 2.676 | 2.361 | 2.505 | 2.508 | 2.567 | 2.641 |
| 5.  Absolute 1980–1989 PARE | 1.099 | 1.094 | 1.098 | 1.294 | 1.459 | 1.414 | 1.594 | 1.703 | 1.871 | 2.096 |
| 6.  WA | 3.061 | 3.052 | 2.820 | 2.443 | 2.407 | 2.394 | 2.542 | 2.461 | 2.316 | 2.188 |

| | | | | | | | | | | Averages | | |
| 1980 (11) | 1981 (12) | 1982 (13) | 1983 (14) | 1984 (15) | 1985 (16) | 1986 (17) | 1987 (18) | 1988 (19) | 1989 (20) | 1970–89 (21) | 1970–79 (22) | 1980–89 (23) |
|---|---|---|---|---|---|---|---|---|---|---|---|---|
| 0.778 | 0.880 | 1.090 | 1.112 | 1.480 | 2.230 | 2.290 | 2.000 | 2.300 | 2.600 | 1.410 | 0.800 | 1.672 |
| 0.346 | 0.334 | 0.323 | 0.345 | 0.326 | 0.266 | 0.294 | 0.313 | 0.362 | 0.386 | 0.317 | 0.262 | 0.331 |
| 1.040 | 1.180 | 1.288 | 1.476 | 1.579 | 1.834 | 2.071 | 2.264 | 2.706 | 3.004 | 1.410 | 0.622 | 1.907 |
| 1.049 | 1.087 | 1.115 | 1.236 | 1.277 | 1.443 | 1.598 | 1.698 | 1.963 | 2.094 | 1.360 | 0.887 | 1.527 |
| 0.911 | 1.034 | 1.129 | 1.294 | 1.385 | 1.608 | 1.815 | 1.985 | 2.372 | 2.634 | 1.237 | 0.545 | 1.672 |
| 0.779 | 0.878 | 1.086 | 1.114 | 1.475 | 2.229 | 2.285 | 2.036 | 2.273 | 2.623 | 1.411 | 0.800 | 1.673 |
| | | | | | | | | | | | | |
| 1.000 | 1.000 | 1.000 | 1.000 | 1.000 | 1.000 | 1.000 | 1.000 | 1.000 | 1.000 | 1.000 | 1.000 | 1.000 |
| 0.720 | 0.702 | 0.701 | 0.680 | 0.609 | 0.603 | 0.589 | 0.588 | 0.590 | 0.593 | 0.648 | 0.684 | 0.631 |
| 1.056 | 1.264 | 1.288 | 1.325 | 1.317 | 1.324 | 1.318 | 1.354 | 1.405 | 1.471 | 1.000 | 0.683 | 1.311 |
| 1.066 | 1.165 | 1.115 | 1.109 | 1.065 | 1.042 | 1.017 | 1.015 | 1.020 | 1.025 | 1.043 | 1.010 | 1.061 |
| 0.806 | 0.964 | 0.983 | 1.011 | 1.005 | 1.010 | 1.006 | 1.033 | 1.072 | 1.122 | 0.763 | 0.521 | 1.000 |
| 1.000 | 1.000 | 1.000 | 1.000 | 1.000 | 1.000 | 1.000 | 1.000 | 1.000 | 1.000 | 1.000 | 1.000 | 1.000 |
| | | | | | | | | | | | | |
| 0.296 | 0.296 | 0.296 | 0.296 | 0.296 | 0.296 | 0.320 | 0.300 | 0.300 | 0.300 | 0.300 | 0.302 | 0.299 |
| ... | ... | ... | ... | ... | ... | ... | ... | ... | ... | ... | ... | ... |
| 0.403 | 0.436 | 0.417 | 0.414 | 0.396 | 0.378 | 0.312 | 0.334 | 0.289 | 0.304 | 0.300 | 0.216 | 0.369 |
| 0.406 | 0.402 | 0.361 | 0.346 | 0.320 | 0.298 | 0.241 | 0.250 | 0.210 | 0.212 | 0.302 | 0.307 | 0.299 |
| 0.326 | 0.353 | 0.338 | 0.335 | 0.321 | 0.306 | 0.253 | 0.271 | 0.234 | 0.247 | 0.243 | 0.175 | 0.299 |
| 0.296 | 0.296 | 0.296 | 0.296 | 0.296 | 0.296 | 0.315 | 0.295 | 0.286 | 0.299 | 0.298 | 0.302 | 0.297 |
| | | | | | | | | | | | | |
| 29.243 | 37.131 | 45.691 | 51.132 | 57.784 | 59.378 | 44.670 | 37.300 | 36.800 | 39.400 | 40.424 | 36.800 | 42.243 |
| 36.520 | 38.078 | 39.338 | 39.509 | 45.933 | 46.487 | 47.563 | 46.135 | 45.517 | 45.957 | 42.247 | 39.576 | 43.531 |
| 38.259 | 41.007 | 45.440 | 48.540 | 50.678 | 52.187 | 54.468 | 54.352 | 55.424 | 58.253 | 40.424 | 27.782 | 50.467 |
| 38.596 | 37.792 | 39.337 | 40.647 | 40.970 | 41.077 | 42.028 | 40.767 | 40.221 | 40.609 | 40.595 | 41.149 | 40.357 |
| 32.025 | 34.325 | 38.036 | 40.630 | 42.420 | 43.684 | 45.593 | 45.495 | 46.393 | 48.761 | 33.837 | 23.255 | 42.243 |
| 29.242 | 37.129 | 45.691 | 51.132 | 57.784 | 59.378 | 44.672 | 37.334 | 36.768 | 39.404 | 40.424 | 36.800 | 42.244 |
| | | | | | | | | | | | | |
| 211.280 | 271.730 | 349.740 | 430.450 | 576.640 | 662.480 | 676.340 | 1069.200 | 1407.100 | 1603.400 | 468.273 | 234.851 | 625.714 |
| 134.390 | 152.224 | 176.926 | 203.834 | 219.858 | 242.004 | 273.827 | 281.083 | 301.243 | 326.016 | 195.551 | 113.488 | 239.371 |
| 319.720 | 400.305 | 514.795 | 626.006 | 686.712 | 761.848 | 879.352 | 928.590 | 1028.601 | 1158.834 | 468.273 | 191.828 | 737.242 |
| 322.538 | 368.928 | 445.657 | 524.215 | 555.164 | 599.661 | 678.515 | 696.495 | 746.448 | 807.834 | 488.882 | 287.292 | 594.486 |
| 271.353 | 339.748 | 436.918 | 531.305 | 582.828 | 646.597 | 746.326 | 788.115 | 872.997 | 983.528 | 397.434 | 162.808 | 625.714 |
| 211.279 | 271.730 | 349.736 | 430.449 | 576.642 | 662.477 | 676.341 | 1069.210 | 1407.110 | 1603.440 | 468.274 | 234.853 | 625.715 |
| | | | | | | | | | | | | |
| 0.812 | 0.900 | 1.056 | 1.175 | 1.413 | 1.719 | 1.860 | 2.200 | 2.600 | 2.800 | 1.417 | 0.850 | 1.699 |
| 0.396 | 0.419 | 0.470 | 0.485 | 0.521 | 0.626 | 0.693 | 0.816 | 0.995 | 1.178 | 0.597 | 0.388 | 0.689 |
| 0.969 | 1.127 | 1.234 | 1.374 | 1.549 | 1.641 | 1.853 | 2.243 | 2.827 | 3.485 | 1.417 | 0.704 | 1.894 |
| 0.978 | 1.039 | 1.069 | 1.151 | 1.252 | 1.292 | 1.430 | 1.683 | 2.051 | 2.429 | 1.380 | 1.012 | 1.518 |
| 0.869 | 1.011 | 1.107 | 1.233 | 1.389 | 1.472 | 1.662 | 2.012 | 2.536 | 3.126 | 1.271 | 0.631 | 1.699 |
| 0.812 | 0.895 | 1.056 | 1.175 | 1.413 | 1.719 | 1.861 | 2.209 | 2.561 | 2.760 | 1.414 | 0.850 | 1.693 |
| | | | | | | | | | | | | |
| 2.177 | 2.304 | 2.340 | 2.321 | 2.344 | 2.483 | 2.580 | 2.500 | 2.600 | 2.700 | 2.448 | 2.439 | 2.450 |
| 1.201 | 1.136 | 1.196 | 1.212 | 1.157 | 1.196 | 1.071 | 1.099 | 1.114 | 1.099 | 1.176 | 1.295 | 1.141 |
| 2.563 | 2.590 | 2.656 | 2.794 | 2.949 | 2.904 | 2.653 | 2.800 | 2.933 | 3.013 | 2.448 | 1.769 | 2.804 |
| 2.586 | 2.387 | 2.299 | 2.339 | 2.384 | 2.286 | 2.047 | 2.100 | 2.129 | 2.100 | 2.302 | 2.536 | 2.234 |
| 2.240 | 2.264 | 2.321 | 2.442 | 2.577 | 2.538 | 2.319 | 2.447 | 2.564 | 2.633 | 2.139 | 1.546 | 2.450 |
| 2.177 | 2.304 | 2.335 | 2.321 | 2.344 | 2.483 | 2.581 | 2.520 | 2.619 | 2.709 | 2.451 | 2.440 | 2.455 |

**Table A.2**    Conversion rates for individual countries or areas, expressed as the number of
local currency units per United States dollar, 1970—1989 [*cont.*]

| Country or area | 1970 (1) | 1971 (2) | 1972 (3) | 1973 (4) | 1974 (5) | 1975 (6) | 1976 (7) | 1977 (8) | 1978 (9) | 1979 (10) |
|---|---|---|---|---|---|---|---|---|---|---|
| **Maldives:** Maldivian rufiyaa | | | | | | | | | | |
| 1. MER | 4.750 | 4.734 | 4.375 | 3.986 | 3.930 | 5.765 | 8.365 | 8.767 | 8.969 | 7.489 |
| 2. PPPs | ... | ... | ... | ... | ... | ... | ... | ... | ... | ... |
| 3. Absolute 1970—1989 PARE | 5.236 | 4.993 | 4.889 | 5.196 | 5.619 | 5.681 | 4.976 | 5.182 | 5.392 | 6.436 |
| 4. Relative 1970—1989 PARE | 10.740 | 9.740 | 9.120 | 9.088 | 9.011 | 8.291 | 6.835 | 6.669 | 6.468 | 7.087 |
| 5. Absolute 1980—1989 PARE | 5.055 | 4.820 | 4.720 | 5.016 | 5.425 | 5.484 | 4.804 | 5.003 | 5.206 | 6.213 |
| 6. WA [a] | 3.540 | 4.624 | 4.482 | 4.520 | 4.423 | 4.699 | 5.632 | 7.579 | 9.052 | 9.694 |
| **Mali:** CFA francs | | | | | | | | | | |
| 1. MER | 277.710 | 277.130 | 252.480 | 222.890 | 240.700 | 214.310 | 238.950 | 245.680 | 225.660 | 212.720 |
| 2. PPPs | 175.487 | 174.679 | 172.300 | 167.599 | 163.729 | 173.341 | 179.547 | 203.672 | 224.494 | 246.301 |
| 3. Absolute 1970—1989 PARE | 114.967 | 121.603 | 131.303 | 141.976 | 139.220 | 182.363 | 213.681 | 233.117 | 239.029 | 285.626 |
| 4. Relative 1970—1989 PARE | 235.796 | 237.237 | 244.923 | 248.337 | 223.253 | 266.182 | 293.550 | 300.015 | 286.707 | 314.517 |
| 5. Absolute 1980—1989 PARE | 100.194 | 105.978 | 114.431 | 123.733 | 121.331 | 158.930 | 186.225 | 203.164 | 208.315 | 248.925 |
| 6. WA | 277.710 | 277.132 | 252.484 | 222.888 | 240.704 | 214.312 | 238.950 | 245.679 | 225.655 | 212.721 |
| **Malta:** Maltese liri | | | | | | | | | | |
| 1. MER | 0.417 | 0.407 | 0.383 | 0.367 | 0.385 | 0.382 | 0.430 | 0.422 | 0.390 | 0.358 |
| 2. PPPs | 0.218 | 0.214 | 0.211 | 0.218 | 0.219 | 0.219 | 0.219 | 0.222 | 0.222 | 0.224 |
| 3. Absolute 1970—1989 PARE | 0.190 | 0.191 | 0.189 | 0.250 | 0.258 | 0.272 | 0.286 | 0.300 | 0.312 | 0.332 |
| 4. Relative 1970—1989 PARE | 0.390 | 0.373 | 0.352 | 0.437 | 0.414 | 0.397 | 0.393 | 0.386 | 0.375 | 0.365 |
| 5. Absolute 1980—1989 PARE | 0.162 | 0.163 | 0.161 | 0.213 | 0.221 | 0.232 | 0.244 | 0.256 | 0.267 | 0.283 |
| 6. WA | 0.417 | 0.406 | 0.382 | 0.369 | 0.385 | 0.385 | 0.425 | 0.422 | 0.385 | 0.358 |
| **Martinique:** French francs | | | | | | | | | | |
| 1. MER | 5.554 | 5.510 | 5.044 | 4.454 | 4.810 | 4.286 | 4.780 | 4.913 | 4.513 | 4.255 |
| 2. PPPs | ... | ... | ... | ... | ... | ... | ... | ... | ... | ... |
| 3. Absolute 1970—1989 PARE | 2.003 | 2.136 | 2.261 | 2.435 | 2.892 | 3.320 | 3.692 | 4.062 | 4.412 | 4.771 |
| 4. Relative 1970—1989 PARE | 4.108 | 4.167 | 4.218 | 4.259 | 4.638 | 4.846 | 5.072 | 5.228 | 5.292 | 5.253 |
| 5. Absolute 1980—1989 PARE | 1.679 | 1.790 | 1.896 | 2.041 | 2.425 | 2.783 | 3.095 | 3.406 | 3.699 | 4.000 |
| 6. WA [a] | 5.535 | 5.748 | 5.716 | 5.389 | 5.517 | 5.294 | 5.229 | 5.139 | 5.187 | 4.968 |
| **Mauritania:** Mauritanian ouguiyas | | | | | | | | | | |
| 1. MER | 55.542 | 55.426 | 50.500 | 44.580 | 45.333 | 43.104 | 45.022 | 45.590 | 46.163 | 45.893 |
| 2. PPPs | 31.177 | 32.203 | 32.683 | 30.384 | 29.679 | 30.369 | 33.441 | 34.263 | 34.679 | 35.315 |
| 3. Absolute 1970—1989 PARE | 21.889 | 23.374 | 23.953 | 25.797 | 30.198 | 34.298 | 38.374 | 41.159 | 43.464 | 52.163 |
| 4. Relative 1970—1989 PARE | 44.895 | 45.600 | 44.680 | 45.123 | 48.426 | 50.062 | 52.717 | 52.971 | 52.134 | 57.439 |
| 5. Absolute 1980—1989 PARE | 17.777 | 18.983 | 19.453 | 20.951 | 24.525 | 27.855 | 31.165 | 33.427 | 35.299 | 42.363 |
| 6. WA | 55.542 | 55.426 | 50.497 | 44.578 | 45.333 | 43.104 | 45.022 | 45.587 | 46.163 | 45.893 |
| **Mauritius:** Mauritius rupees | | | | | | | | | | |
| 1. MER | 5.556 | 5.479 | 5.339 | 5.442 | 5.703 | 6.027 | 6.682 | 6.607 | 6.163 | 6.308 |
| 2. PPPs | 2.445 | 2.375 | 2.475 | 2.769 | 4.001 | 3.751 | 4.217 | 4.329 | 4.458 | 4.752 |
| 3. Absolute 1970—1989 PARE | 18.028 | 18.182 | 20.225 | 2.709 | 4.382 | 4.661 | 4.734 | 5.140 | 5.692 | 6.713 |
| 4. Relative 1970—1989 PARE | 36.975 | 35.472 | 37.726 | 4.739 | 7.028 | 6.803 | 6.503 | 6.615 | 6.828 | 7.392 |
| 5. Absolute 1980—1989 PARE | 17.044 | 17.191 | 19.121 | 2.562 | 4.143 | 4.407 | 4.475 | 4.859 | 5.382 | 6.347 |
| 6. WA | 5.556 | 5.479 | 5.338 | 5.442 | 5.703 | 6.027 | 6.681 | 6.607 | 6.163 | 6.308 |
| **Mexico:** Mexican pesos | | | | | | | | | | |
| 1. MER | 12.500 | 12.500 | 12.500 | 12.500 | 12.500 | 12.500 | 15.426 | 22.573 | 22.767 | 22.805 |
| 2. PPPs | 5.723 | 5.765 | 5.938 | 6.409 | 7.084 | 7.516 | 8.554 | 10.634 | 11.541 | 12.568 |
| 3. Absolute 1970—1989 PARE | 6.120 | 6.479 | 6.883 | 7.768 | 9.532 | 11.036 | 13.195 | 17.206 | 20.090 | 24.155 |
| 4. Relative 1970—1989 PARE | 12.552 | 12.641 | 12.839 | 13.587 | 15.286 | 16.108 | 18.127 | 22.144 | 24.098 | 26.598 |
| 5. Absolute 1980—1989 PARE | 5.311 | 5.623 | 5.974 | 6.741 | 8.273 | 9.578 | 11.451 | 14.933 | 17.436 | 20.963 |
| 6. WA | 12.500 | 12.500 | 12.500 | 12.500 | 12.500 | 12.500 | 15.426 | 22.573 | 22.767 | 22.805 |

| 1980 (11) | 1981 (12) | 1982 (13) | 1983 (14) | 1984 (15) | 1985 (16) | 1986 (17) | 1987 (18) | 1988 (19) | 1989 (20) | Averages 1970-89 (21) | 1970-79 (22) | 1980-89 (23) |
|---|---|---|---|---|---|---|---|---|---|---|---|---|
| 7.550 | 7.550 | 7.173 | 7.050 | 7.050 | 7.098 | 7.150 | 9.200 | 8.800 | 9.000 | 7.493 | 6.083 | 7.915 |
| ... | ... | ... | ... | ... | ... | ... | ... | ... | ... | ... | ... | ... |
| 6.926 | 6.558 | 7.077 | 7.346 | 7.499 | 7.310 | 7.927 | 7.977 | 9.933 | 10.728 | 7.493 | 5.454 | 8.198 |
| 6.988 | 6.044 | 6.127 | 6.151 | 6.062 | 5.754 | 6.117 | 5.983 | 7.208 | 7.478 | 6.661 | 7.633 | 6.472 |
| 6.687 | 6.331 | 6.833 | 7.092 | 7.239 | 7.057 | 7.653 | 7.701 | 9.589 | 10.357 | 7.234 | 5.265 | 7.915 |
| 9.044 | 7.443 | 7.678 | 7.651 | 7.282 | 6.995 | 7.433 | 8.047 | 9.738 | 10.292 | 7.708 | 5.895 | 8.296 |
| | | | | | | | | | | | | |
| 211.280 | 271.730 | 328.610 | 381.060 | 436.960 | 449.260 | 346.300 | 300.500 | 297.800 | 319.000 | 292.701 | 233.413 | 322.951 |
| 252.244 | 252.267 | 285.527 | 314.238 | 229.142 | 230.740 | 229.432 | 229.248 | 228.311 | 219.111 | 225.904 | 194.080 | 240.443 |
| 295.307 | 317.847 | 318.495 | 339.400 | 378.883 | 388.726 | 394.290 | 405.294 | 417.188 | 416.794 | 292.701 | 186.457 | 370.565 |
| 297.911 | 292.933 | 275.721 | 284.213 | 306.303 | 305.971 | 304.238 | 303.993 | 302.750 | 290.551 | 290.212 | 273.712 | 296.810 |
| 257.363 | 277.006 | 277.571 | 295.790 | 330.199 | 338.777 | 343.627 | 353.216 | 363.583 | 363.239 | 255.091 | 162.499 | 322.951 |
| 211.279 | 271.730 | 328.605 | 381.065 | 436.955 | 449.261 | 346.305 | 300.535 | 297.847 | 319.007 | 292.708 | 233.413 | 322.963 |
| | | | | | | | | | | | | |
| 0.350 | 0.386 | 0.412 | 0.432 | 0.460 | 0.468 | 0.390 | 0.300 | 0.300 | 0.300 | 0.370 | 0.391 | 0.363 |
| 0.233 | 0.225 | 0.215 | 0.212 | 0.202 | 0.197 | 0.200 | 0.200 | 0.198 | 0.194 | 0.209 | 0.220 | 0.205 |
| 0.373 | 0.402 | 0.416 | 0.415 | 0.414 | 0.416 | 0.431 | 0.444 | 0.452 | 0.462 | 0.370 | 0.269 | 0.425 |
| 0.376 | 0.370 | 0.360 | 0.347 | 0.335 | 0.328 | 0.333 | 0.333 | 0.328 | 0.322 | 0.351 | 0.384 | 0.340 |
| 0.318 | 0.343 | 0.355 | 0.354 | 0.353 | 0.356 | 0.368 | 0.379 | 0.386 | 0.395 | 0.316 | 0.230 | 0.363 |
| 0.345 | 0.387 | 0.412 | 0.432 | 0.461 | 0.469 | 0.393 | 0.345 | 0.331 | 0.348 | 0.385 | 0.390 | 0.383 |
| | | | | | | | | | | | | |
| 4.226 | 5.435 | 6.572 | 7.621 | 8.739 | 8.985 | 6.926 | 6.000 | 6.000 | 6.400 | 6.032 | 4.661 | 6.570 |
| ... | ... | ... | ... | ... | ... | ... | ... | ... | ... | ... | ... | ... |
| 5.113 | 5.815 | 6.574 | 7.436 | 7.753 | 8.468 | 8.921 | 8.893 | 8.803 | 8.931 | 6.032 | 3.300 | 7.837 |
| 5.158 | 5.359 | 5.691 | 6.227 | 6.268 | 6.665 | 6.884 | 6.670 | 6.389 | 6.226 | 5.875 | 4.845 | 6.244 |
| 4.287 | 4.875 | 5.511 | 6.234 | 6.499 | 7.099 | 7.479 | 7.456 | 7.380 | 7.488 | 5.057 | 2.767 | 6.570 |
| 4.672 | 5.143 | 6.050 | 7.335 | 8.145 | 9.069 | 8.816 | 7.447 | 6.258 | 6.171 | 6.433 | 5.273 | 6.852 |
| | | | | | | | | | | | | |
| 45.914 | 48.296 | 51.769 | 54.812 | 63.803 | 77.085 | 74.370 | 73.900 | 75.300 | 83.100 | 58.504 | 46.580 | 64.564 |
| 36.058 | 40.013 | 42.120 | 41.531 | 40.732 | 47.145 | 47.767 | 50.041 | 51.586 | 53.562 | 41.201 | 32.764 | 45.497 |
| 61.930 | 68.835 | 69.400 | 71.343 | 70.846 | 79.389 | 82.053 | 88.429 | 94.219 | 101.839 | 58.504 | 34.009 | 79.498 |
| 62.476 | 63.439 | 60.079 | 59.742 | 57.275 | 62.488 | 63.313 | 66.326 | 68.374 | 70.993 | 59.643 | 50.463 | 63.906 |
| 50.295 | 55.903 | 56.362 | 57.940 | 57.537 | 64.475 | 66.638 | 71.816 | 76.519 | 82.708 | 47.513 | 27.620 | 64.564 |
| 45.914 | 48.296 | 51.769 | 54.812 | 63.803 | 77.085 | 74.375 | 73.878 | 75.261 | 83.051 | 58.498 | 46.579 | 64.554 |
| | | | | | | | | | | | | |
| 7.684 | 8.937 | 10.873 | 11.706 | 13.800 | 15.442 | 13.470 | 12.900 | 13.400 | 15.300 | 10.632 | 6.109 | 12.656 |
| 6.123 | 5.985 | 6.519 | 6.755 | 6.918 | 7.539 | 7.983 | 8.430 | 9.009 | 9.497 | 6.583 | 3.850 | 7.775 |
| 8.497 | 9.420 | 10.255 | 11.121 | 11.942 | 12.930 | 13.968 | 15.174 | 16.759 | 18.393 | 10.632 | 5.445 | 13.386 |
| 8.572 | 8.682 | 8.878 | 9.312 | 9.654 | 10.178 | 10.778 | 11.381 | 12.162 | 12.822 | 9.520 | 6.413 | 10.633 |
| 8.034 | 8.906 | 9.696 | 10.514 | 11.290 | 12.225 | 13.206 | 14.346 | 15.845 | 17.389 | 10.052 | 5.148 | 12.656 |
| 7.684 | 8.937 | 10.873 | 11.706 | 13.800 | 15.442 | 13.466 | 12.878 | 13.438 | 15.250 | 10.630 | 6.109 | 12.652 |
| | | | | | | | | | | | | |
| 22.951 | 24.510 | 56.400 | 120.090 | 167.830 | 256.870 | 611.770 | 1378.200 | 2273.100 | 2461.500 | 511.084 | 17.244 | 726.763 |
| 14.223 | 16.619 | 25.866 | 50.372 | 79.870 | 121.808 | 208.181 | 484.459 | 937.458 | 1137.149 | 245.983 | 9.026 | 337.903 |
| 31.087 | 39.177 | 63.038 | 120.070 | 191.029 | 299.443 | 522.061 | 1249.797 | 2499.634 | 3156.410 | 511.084 | 13.239 | 837.419 |
| 31.361 | 36.106 | 54.572 | 100.546 | 154.435 | 235.696 | 402.826 | 937.418 | 1813.966 | 2200.363 | 499.933 | 19.195 | 675.156 |
| 26.979 | 34.000 | 54.708 | 104.204 | 165.787 | 259.875 | 453.076 | 1084.651 | 2169.335 | 2739.326 | 443.550 | 11.489 | 726.763 |
| 22.951 | 24.515 | 56.402 | 120.094 | 167.828 | 256.872 | 611.773 | 1378.180 | 2273.100 | 2461.470 | 511.095 | 17.244 | 726.785 |

**Table A.2** Conversion rates for individual countries or areas, expressed as the number of
local currency units per United States dollar, 1970−1989 [*cont.*]

| Country or area | 1970 (1) | 1971 (2) | 1972 (3) | 1973 (4) | 1974 (5) | 1975 (6) | 1976 (7) | 1977 (8) | 1978 (9) | 1979 (10) |
|---|---|---|---|---|---|---|---|---|---|---|
| **Mongolia:** Mongolian tugriks | | | | | | | | | | |
| 1.  MER | 4.000 | 4.000 | 3.730 | 3.330 | 3.340 | 3.200 | 3.370 | 3.290 | 3.080 | 2.970 |
| 2.  PPPs | ... | ... | ... | ... | ... | ... | ... | ... | ... | ... |
| 3.  Absolute 1970−1989 PARE | 3.118 | 3.096 | 3.133 | 3.093 | 3.179 | 3.210 | 3.259 | 3.215 | 3.261 | 3.281 |
| 4.  Relative 1970−1989 PARE | 6.394 | 6.040 | 5.843 | 5.411 | 5.098 | 4.686 | 4.477 | 4.138 | 3.911 | 3.613 |
| 5.  Absolute 1980−1989 PARE | 3.044 | 3.023 | 3.059 | 3.020 | 3.104 | 3.135 | 3.182 | 3.139 | 3.184 | 3.204 |
| 6.  WA [a] | 2.023 | 2.996 | 3.932 | 3.670 | 3.516 | 3.343 | 3.348 | 3.273 | 3.263 | 3.142 |
| **Montserrat:** East Caribbean dollars | | | | | | | | | | |
| 1.  MER | 2.000 | 1.964 | 1.922 | 1.959 | 2.053 | 2.170 | 2.615 | 2.700 | 2.700 | 2.700 |
| 2.  PPPs | ... | ... | ... | ... | ... | ... | ... | ... | ... | ... |
| 3.  Absolute 1970−1989 PARE | 0.862 | 0.956 | 1.044 | 1.117 | 1.249 | 1.357 | 1.450 | 1.672 | 1.817 | 1.996 |
| 4.  Relative 1970−1989 PARE | 1.768 | 1.864 | 1.948 | 1.953 | 2.002 | 1.981 | 1.992 | 2.152 | 2.179 | 2.197 |
| 5.  Absolute 1980−1989 PARE | 0.686 | 0.761 | 0.831 | 0.889 | 0.994 | 1.080 | 1.154 | 1.331 | 1.446 | 1.588 |
| 6.  WA [a] | 2.175 | 2.205 | 2.164 | 2.103 | 2.180 | 2.261 | 2.440 | 2.796 | 2.970 | 2.963 |
| **Morocco:** Moroccan dirhams | | | | | | | | | | |
| 1.  MER | 5.060 | 5.000 | 4.600 | 4.100 | 4.400 | 4.100 | 4.400 | 4.500 | 4.200 | 3.900 |
| 2.  PPPs | 2.650 | 2.647 | 2.671 | 2.734 | 3.103 | 2.996 | 2.972 | 3.117 | 3.099 | 3.071 |
| 3.  Absolute 1970−1989 PARE | 2.689 | 2.714 | 2.903 | 3.069 | 3.796 | 3.773 | 3.925 | 4.230 | 4.333 | 4.655 |
| 4.  Relative 1970−1989 PARE | 5.516 | 5.295 | 5.415 | 5.369 | 6.088 | 5.507 | 5.392 | 5.444 | 5.197 | 5.126 |
| 5.  Absolute 1980−1989 PARE | 2.483 | 2.505 | 2.680 | 2.833 | 3.505 | 3.483 | 3.623 | 3.905 | 4.000 | 4.297 |
| 6.  WA | 5.061 | 5.050 | 4.601 | 4.107 | 4.370 | 4.052 | 4.419 | 4.503 | 4.167 | 3.899 |
| **Mozambique:** Mozambique meticais | | | | | | | | | | |
| 1.  MER | 27.250 | 27.250 | 27.250 | 24.560 | 25.520 | 27.240 | 31.410 | 32.220 | 32.880 | 32.710 |
| 2.  PPPs | 11.369 | 12.441 | 13.159 | 12.891 | 15.340 | 15.686 | 15.582 | 16.093 | 16.960 | 17.343 |
| 3.  Absolute 1970−1989 PARE | 13.105 | 14.866 | 16.226 | 16.946 | 20.679 | 23.051 | 24.049 | 26.753 | 29.824 | 34.144 |
| 4.  Relative 1970−1989 PARE | 26.878 | 29.002 | 30.266 | 29.640 | 33.160 | 33.646 | 33.038 | 34.430 | 35.773 | 37.597 |
| 5.  Absolute 1980−1989 PARE | 9.984 | 11.326 | 12.362 | 12.910 | 15.754 | 17.562 | 18.322 | 20.382 | 22.722 | 26.013 |
| 6.  WA | 28.750 | 28.312 | 27.053 | 24.515 | 25.408 | 25.553 | 30.229 | 33.022 | 32.996 | 32.558 |
| **Myanmar:** Myanmarese kyats | | | | | | | | | | |
| 1.  MER | 4.762 | 4.793 | 5.457 | 4.930 | 4.860 | 6.376 | 6.767 | 7.121 | 6.885 | 6.654 |
| 2.  PPPs | 2.461 | 2.332 | 2.269 | 2.389 | 2.688 | 2.843 | 2.966 | 2.839 | 2.699 | 2.601 |
| 3.  Absolute 1970−1989 PARE | 3.307 | 3.231 | 3.256 | 3.581 | 4.372 | 5.094 | 5.610 | 5.717 | 5.763 | 6.087 |
| 4.  Relative 1970−1989 PARE | 6.784 | 6.304 | 6.073 | 6.264 | 7.012 | 7.435 | 7.707 | 7.358 | 6.912 | 6.703 |
| 5.  Absolute 1980−1989 PARE | 2.903 | 2.836 | 2.857 | 3.143 | 3.838 | 4.471 | 4.924 | 5.018 | 5.058 | 5.343 |
| 6.  WA [a] | 4.769 | 4.688 | 4.991 | 5.415 | 6.069 | 6.350 | 6.675 | 7.058 | 7.005 | 7.169 |
| **Namibia:** Rand | | | | | | | | | | |
| 1.  MER | 0.714 | 0.713 | 0.772 | 0.692 | 0.679 | 0.732 | 0.870 | 0.870 | 0.870 | 0.842 |
| 2.  PPPs | ... | ... | ... | ... | ... | ... | ... | ... | ... | ... |
| 3.  Absolute 1970−1989 PARE | 0.311 | 0.324 | 0.384 | 0.502 | 0.515 | 0.539 | 0.637 | 0.730 | 0.884 | 0.993 |
| 4.  Relative 1970−1989 PARE | 0.638 | 0.632 | 0.717 | 0.877 | 0.826 | 0.787 | 0.875 | 0.940 | 1.060 | 1.093 |
| 5.  Absolute 1980−1989 PARE | 0.254 | 0.264 | 0.314 | 0.409 | 0.420 | 0.440 | 0.520 | 0.596 | 0.721 | 0.810 |
| 6.  WA | 0.714 | 0.715 | 0.769 | 0.694 | 0.679 | 0.740 | 0.870 | 0.870 | 0.870 | 0.842 |
| **Nepal:** Nepalese rupees | | | | | | | | | | |
| 1.  MER | 10.125 | 10.125 | 10.125 | 10.524 | 10.560 | 11.003 | 12.500 | 12.500 | 12.111 | 12.000 |
| 2.  PPPs | 3.258 | 3.223 | 3.596 | 3.453 | 3.813 | 3.981 | 3.936 | 3.368 | 3.394 | 3.456 |
| 3.  Absolute 1970−1989 PARE | 6.188 | 6.384 | 7.182 | 6.938 | 8.383 | 10.690 | 10.748 | 10.365 | 11.337 | 12.468 |
| 4.  Relative 1970−1989 PARE | 12.691 | 12.454 | 13.397 | 12.136 | 13.443 | 15.604 | 14.766 | 13.340 | 13.598 | 13.729 |
| 5.  Absolute 1980−1989 PARE | 5.460 | 5.633 | 6.338 | 6.122 | 7.397 | 9.433 | 9.484 | 9.146 | 10.004 | 11.002 |
| 6.  WA | 10.125 | 10.125 | 10.125 | 10.283 | 10.560 | 10.560 | 11.973 | 12.500 | 12.361 | 12.000 |

| | | | | | | | | | | Averages | | |
|---|---|---|---|---|---|---|---|---|---|---|---|---|
| 1980 (11) | 1981 (12) | 1982 (13) | 1983 (14) | 1984 (15) | 1985 (16) | 1986 (17) | 1987 (18) | 1988 (19) | 1989 (20) | 1970−89 (21) | 1970−79 (22) | 1980−89 (23) |
| 2.900 | 3.200 | 3.270 | 3.260 | 3.480 | 3.760 | 3.220 | 2.910 | 2.900 | 3.000 | 3.223 | 3.342 | 3.162 |
| ... | ... | ... | ... | ... | ... | ... | ... | ... | ... | ... | ... | ... |
| 3.263 | 3.264 | 3.312 | 3.266 | 3.235 | 3.205 | 3.188 | 3.229 | 3.226 | 3.228 | 3.223 | 3.195 | 3.238 |
| 3.292 | 3.008 | 2.867 | 2.735 | 2.616 | 2.522 | 2.460 | 2.422 | 2.341 | 2.250 | 3.055 | 4.631 | 2.577 |
| 3.186 | 3.187 | 3.234 | 3.189 | 3.159 | 3.129 | 3.112 | 3.153 | 3.150 | 3.152 | 3.147 | 3.120 | 3.162 |
| 2.979 | 3.018 | 3.154 | 3.229 | 3.301 | 3.468 | 3.463 | 3.320 | 3.022 | 2.937 | 3.187 | 3.197 | 3.181 |
| 2.700 | 2.700 | 2.700 | 2.700 | 2.700 | 2.700 | 2.700 | 2.700 | 2.700 | 2.700 | 2.617 | 2.336 | 2.700 |
| ... | ... | ... | ... | ... | ... | ... | ... | ... | ... | ... | ... | ... |
| 2.741 | 2.982 | 3.165 | 3.477 | 3.700 | 3.246 | 3.513 | 3.650 | 3.525 | 3.626 | 2.617 | 1.385 | 3.392 |
| 2.765 | 2.749 | 2.740 | 2.912 | 2.991 | 2.555 | 2.711 | 2.738 | 2.558 | 2.528 | 2.532 | 2.040 | 2.699 |
| 2.182 | 2.374 | 2.519 | 2.768 | 2.945 | 2.584 | 2.796 | 2.905 | 2.806 | 2.887 | 2.083 | 1.102 | 2.700 |
| 3.494 | 3.224 | 2.894 | 2.938 | 2.910 | 2.530 | 2.728 | 2.847 | 2.672 | 2.720 | 2.758 | 2.486 | 2.837 |
| 3.900 | 5.200 | 6.000 | 7.100 | 8.800 | 10.100 | 9.100 | 8.400 | 8.200 | 8.500 | 6.426 | 4.309 | 7.498 |
| 3.041 | 3.009 | 3.123 | 3.191 | 3.228 | 3.467 | 3.905 | 3.808 | 3.927 | 3.858 | 3.382 | 2.959 | 3.529 |
| 5.358 | 5.797 | 6.426 | 6.729 | 7.501 | 8.252 | 9.479 | 9.511 | 10.138 | 10.367 | 6.426 | 3.741 | 8.123 |
| 5.405 | 5.343 | 5.563 | 5.634 | 6.064 | 6.495 | 7.314 | 7.134 | 7.357 | 7.227 | 6.213 | 5.389 | 6.501 |
| 4.946 | 5.352 | 5.932 | 6.211 | 6.924 | 7.618 | 8.751 | 8.780 | 9.359 | 9.570 | 5.932 | 3.453 | 7.498 |
| 3.937 | 5.172 | 6.023 | 7.111 | 8.811 | 10.063 | 9.104 | 8.359 | 8.209 | 8.488 | 6.424 | 4.301 | 7.501 |
| 32.400 | 35.350 | 37.770 | 40.180 | 42.440 | 40.400 | 40.400 | 290.700 | 524.600 | 744.900 | 81.940 | 28.938 | 117.861 |
| 18.224 | 18.659 | 19.743 | 18.638 | 17.949 | 17.182 | 18.831 | 44.573 | 63.812 | 85.877 | 31.389 | 14.833 | 38.549 |
| 38.551 | 40.015 | 46.667 | 53.154 | 61.795 | 91.403 | 102.191 | 248.830 | 368.190 | 515.824 | 81.940 | 21.414 | 154.701 |
| 38.891 | 36.879 | 40.400 | 44.511 | 49.957 | 71.945 | 78.851 | 186.636 | 267.193 | 359.586 | 89.432 | 32.715 | 125.692 |
| 29.371 | 30.486 | 35.554 | 40.496 | 47.079 | 69.637 | 77.855 | 189.574 | 280.511 | 392.987 | 62.427 | 16.315 | 117.861 |
| 32.400 | 35.349 | 37.770 | 40.183 | 42.443 | 43.181 | 40.429 | 290.731 | 524.645 | 744.918 | 82.324 | 28.846 | 119.053 |
| 6.599 | 7.281 | 7.791 | 8.036 | 8.386 | 8.475 | 7.330 | 6.700 | 6.400 | 6.700 | 6.833 | 6.012 | 7.200 |
| 2.390 | 2.302 | 2.180 | 2.170 | 2.192 | 2.224 | 2.266 | 2.683 | 3.208 | 4.190 | 2.619 | 2.646 | 2.609 |
| 6.162 | 6.435 | 6.652 | 6.782 | 6.911 | 6.996 | 7.272 | 8.857 | 10.946 | 14.880 | 6.833 | 4.720 | 8.203 |
| 6.217 | 5.930 | 5.759 | 5.679 | 5.587 | 5.507 | 5.611 | 6.643 | 7.943 | 10.373 | 6.682 | 6.922 | 6.597 |
| 5.409 | 5.648 | 5.839 | 5.953 | 6.066 | 6.140 | 6.383 | 7.774 | 9.607 | 13.060 | 5.998 | 4.143 | 7.200 |
| 6.899 | 7.069 | 7.480 | 7.885 | 8.223 | 8.418 | 8.321 | 8.786 | 8.571 | 8.885 | 7.523 | 6.199 | 8.174 |
| 0.778 | 0.870 | 1.082 | 1.112 | 1.438 | 2.191 | 2.269 | 2.000 | 2.300 | 2.600 | 1.334 | 0.795 | 1.638 |
| ... | ... | ... | ... | ... | ... | ... | ... | ... | ... | ... | ... | ... |
| 1.113 | 1.154 | 1.311 | 1.418 | 1.614 | 2.095 | 2.359 | 2.430 | 3.017 | 3.470 | 1.334 | 0.599 | 2.007 |
| 1.122 | 1.064 | 1.135 | 1.188 | 1.305 | 1.649 | 1.820 | 1.822 | 2.190 | 2.419 | 1.375 | 0.884 | 1.621 |
| 0.908 | 0.942 | 1.070 | 1.157 | 1.317 | 1.709 | 1.925 | 1.982 | 2.462 | 2.832 | 1.088 | 0.489 | 1.638 |
| 0.779 | 0.878 | 1.086 | 1.114 | 1.475 | 2.229 | 2.285 | 2.036 | 2.273 | 2.623 | 1.340 | 0.796 | 1.650 |
| 12.000 | 12.336 | 13.244 | 14.545 | 16.459 | 18.246 | 21.230 | 21.800 | 23.300 | 27.200 | 16.098 | 11.348 | 18.552 |
| 3.256 | 3.507 | 3.539 | 3.750 | 3.931 | 4.055 | 4.322 | 4.818 | 4.979 | 5.247 | 4.083 | 3.552 | 4.285 |
| 13.417 | 14.482 | 15.835 | 17.782 | 18.915 | 20.095 | 21.848 | 25.056 | 26.765 | 29.359 | 16.098 | 9.244 | 21.024 |
| 13.535 | 13.347 | 13.709 | 14.890 | 15.292 | 15.817 | 16.858 | 18.794 | 19.423 | 20.466 | 15.891 | 13.639 | 16.765 |
| 11.839 | 12.779 | 13.973 | 15.691 | 16.691 | 17.732 | 19.279 | 22.110 | 23.617 | 25.906 | 14.205 | 8.157 | 18.552 |
| 12.000 | 12.000 | 12.936 | 13.796 | 15.259 | 17.777 | 19.800 | 21.596 | 22.055 | 25.323 | 15.601 | 11.247 | 17.776 |

**Table A.2**   Conversion rates for individual countries or areas, expressed as the number of
local currency units per United States dollar, 1970–1989 [*cont.*]

| Country or area | 1970 (1) | 1971 (2) | 1972 (3) | 1973 (4) | 1974 (5) | 1975 (6) | 1976 (7) | 1977 (8) | 1978 (9) | 1979 (10) |
|---|---|---|---|---|---|---|---|---|---|---|
| **Netherlands:** Netherlands guilders | | | | | | | | | | |
| 1. MER | 3.620 | 3.495 | 3.210 | 2.796 | 2.688 | 2.529 | 2.644 | 2.454 | 2.164 | 2.006 |
| 2. PPPs | 2.636 | 2.722 | 2.800 | 2.820 | 2.829 | 2.868 | 2.949 | 2.925 | 2.857 | 2.742 |
| 3. Absolute 1970–1989 PARE | 1.232 | 1.332 | 1.456 | 1.588 | 1.733 | 1.910 | 2.081 | 2.219 | 2.340 | 2.432 |
| 4. Relative 1970–1989 PARE | 2.527 | 2.598 | 2.717 | 2.777 | 2.779 | 2.788 | 2.859 | 2.856 | 2.807 | 2.678 |
| 5. Absolute 1980–1989 PARE | 1.009 | 1.091 | 1.193 | 1.300 | 1.419 | 1.564 | 1.704 | 1.818 | 1.917 | 1.992 |
| 6. WA | 3.620 | 3.502 | 3.210 | 2.796 | 2.688 | 2.529 | 2.644 | 2.454 | 2.164 | 2.006 |
| **Netherlands Antilles:** Netherlands Antillian guilders | | | | | | | | | | |
| 1. MER | 1.886 | 1.870 | 1.800 | 1.800 | 1.800 | 1.800 | 1.800 | 1.800 | 1.800 | 1.800 |
| 2. PPPs | ... | ... | ... | ... | ... | ... | ... | ... | ... | ... |
| 3. Absolute 1970–1989 PARE | 0.816 | 0.853 | 0.893 | 0.927 | 1.066 | 1.213 | 1.250 | 1.352 | 1.479 | 1.713 |
| 4. Relative 1970–1989 PARE | 1.674 | 1.665 | 1.666 | 1.621 | 1.709 | 1.770 | 1.717 | 1.739 | 1.774 | 1.886 |
| 5. Absolute 1980–1989 PARE | 0.633 | 0.662 | 0.693 | 0.719 | 0.827 | 0.941 | 0.970 | 1.049 | 1.147 | 1.329 |
| 6. WA [a] | 2.019 | 1.984 | 1.940 | 1.900 | 2.006 | 2.068 | 1.922 | 1.917 | 1.966 | 2.055 |
| **New Caledonia:** CFP francs | | | | | | | | | | |
| 1. MER | 100.985 | 100.182 | 91.709 | 80.982 | 87.454 | 77.927 | 86.909 | 89.327 | 82.055 | 77.353 |
| 2. PPPs | ... | ... | ... | ... | ... | ... | ... | ... | ... | ... |
| 3. Absolute 1970–1989 PARE | 46.967 | 50.537 | 51.881 | 55.221 | 62.567 | 66.358 | 70.694 | 74.844 | 63.220 | 85.411 |
| 4. Relative 1970–1989 PARE | 96.329 | 98.593 | 96.774 | 96.589 | 100.332 | 96.858 | 97.118 | 96.321 | 75.830 | 94.050 |
| 5. Absolute 1980–1989 PARE | 37.942 | 40.826 | 41.912 | 44.610 | 50.545 | 53.607 | 57.110 | 60.462 | 51.072 | 68.999 |
| 6. WA [a] | 132.825 | 118.105 | 102.035 | 96.021 | 96.603 | 89.332 | 89.581 | 89.743 | 78.410 | 96.716 |
| **New Zealand:** New Zealand dollars | | | | | | | | | | |
| 1. MER | 0.893 | 0.877 | 0.837 | 0.734 | 0.714 | 0.823 | 1.004 | 1.030 | 0.964 | 0.978 |
| 2. PPPs | 0.628 | 0.667 | 0.679 | 0.667 | 0.674 | 0.728 | 0.806 | 0.863 | 0.906 | 0.985 |
| 3. Absolute 1970–1989 PARE | 0.326 | 0.378 | 0.417 | 0.467 | 0.475 | 0.557 | 0.653 | 0.754 | 0.869 | 1.020 |
| 4. Relative 1970–1989 PARE | 0.668 | 0.737 | 0.777 | 0.817 | 0.761 | 0.812 | 0.898 | 0.970 | 1.042 | 1.123 |
| 5. Absolute 1980–1989 PARE | 0.252 | 0.292 | 0.322 | 0.362 | 0.367 | 0.431 | 0.506 | 0.583 | 0.672 | 0.789 |
| 6. WA | 0.893 | 0.867 | 0.823 | 0.719 | 0.725 | 0.885 | 1.027 | 1.013 | 0.957 | 0.998 |
| **Nicaragua:** Nicaraguan cordobas | | | | | | | | | | |
| 1. MER | 7.000 | 7.000 | 7.000 | 7.000 | 8.400 | 10.300 | 10.300 | 10.300 | 10.300 | 13.600 |
| 2. PPPs | 2.572 | 2.514 | 2.573 | 2.790 | 3.125 | 3.115 | 3.068 | 2.984 | 3.004 | 3.996 |
| 3. Absolute 1970–1989 PARE | 2.120 | 2.184 | 2.277 | 2.657 | 3.235 | 3.388 | 3.742 | 4.185 | 4.341 | 5.718 |
| 4. Relative 1970–1989 PARE | 4.348 | 4.261 | 4.247 | 4.647 | 5.188 | 4.946 | 5.141 | 5.386 | 5.207 | 6.296 |
| 5. Absolute 1980–1989 PARE | 1.232 | 1.270 | 1.324 | 1.544 | 1.881 | 1.970 | 2.175 | 2.433 | 2.524 | 3.324 |
| 6. WA | 7.000 | 7.000 | 7.000 | 7.000 | 7.013 | 7.026 | 7.026 | 7.026 | 7.026 | 9.255 |
| **Niger:** CFA francs | | | | | | | | | | |
| 1. MER | 277.710 | 275.520 | 252.210 | 222.700 | 240.500 | 214.320 | 238.980 | 245.670 | 225.660 | 212.720 |
| 2. PPPs | 130.467 | 132.203 | 141.342 | 153.629 | 142.233 | 144.017 | 169.113 | 202.268 | 211.736 | 215.639 |
| 3. Absolute 1970–1989 PARE | 101.631 | 107.601 | 119.418 | 130.902 | 140.071 | 162.910 | 182.610 | 218.780 | 242.674 | 272.077 |
| 4. Relative 1970–1989 PARE | 208.445 | 209.920 | 222.753 | 228.966 | 224.618 | 237.789 | 250.865 | 281.563 | 291.079 | 299.598 |
| 5. Absolute 1980–1989 PARE | 86.247 | 91.313 | 101.341 | 111.087 | 118.868 | 138.250 | 154.968 | 185.663 | 205.940 | 230.893 |
| 6. WA | 277.710 | 277.132 | 252.484 | 222.888 | 240.704 | 214.312 | 238.950 | 245.679 | 225.655 | 212.721 |
| **Nigeria:** Nigerian naira | | | | | | | | | | |
| 1. MER | 0.714 | 0.712 | 0.658 | 0.657 | 0.629 | 0.615 | 0.627 | 0.645 | 0.635 | 0.603 |
| 2. PPPs | 0.351 | 0.372 | 0.389 | 0.406 | 0.495 | 0.525 | 0.580 | 0.630 | 0.692 | 0.665 |
| 3. Absolute 1970–1989 PARE | 0.222 | 0.252 | 0.258 | 0.284 | 0.420 | 0.499 | 0.572 | 0.627 | 0.720 | 0.858 |
| 4. Relative 1970–1989 PARE | 0.454 | 0.491 | 0.481 | 0.496 | 0.673 | 0.729 | 0.786 | 0.807 | 0.863 | 0.944 |
| 5. Absolute 1980–1989 PARE | 0.184 | 0.209 | 0.214 | 0.235 | 0.348 | 0.414 | 0.475 | 0.520 | 0.597 | 0.712 |
| 6. WA | 0.714 | 0.713 | 0.658 | 0.658 | 0.630 | 0.615 | 0.627 | 0.645 | 0.635 | 0.604 |

| | | | | | | | | | | Averages | | |
|---|---|---|---|---|---|---|---|---|---|---|---|---|
| 1980 | 1981 | 1982 | 1983 | 1984 | 1985 | 1986 | 1987 | 1988 | 1989 | 1970−89 | 1970−79 | 1980−89 |
| (11) | (12) | (13) | (14) | (15) | (16) | (17) | (18) | (19) | (20) | (21) | (22) | (23) |
| 1.988 | 2.495 | 2.670 | 2.854 | 3.209 | 3.321 | 2.450 | 2.000 | 2.000 | 2.100 | 2.455 | 2.536 | 2.414 |
| 2.633 | 2.628 | 2.570 | 2.590 | 2.559 | 2.589 | 2.549 | 2.467 | 2.427 | 2.366 | 2.624 | 2.827 | 2.527 |
| 2.570 | 2.712 | 2.875 | 2.929 | 2.982 | 3.036 | 3.050 | 3.036 | 3.087 | 3.133 | 2.455 | 1.868 | 2.948 |
| 2.592 | 2.499 | 2.489 | 2.453 | 2.411 | 2.390 | 2.353 | 2.277 | 2.240 | 2.184 | 2.491 | 2.755 | 2.370 |
| 2.104 | 2.221 | 2.355 | 2.399 | 2.443 | 2.486 | 2.498 | 2.486 | 2.528 | 2.566 | 2.011 | 1.529 | 2.414 |
| 1.988 | 2.495 | 2.670 | 2.854 | 3.209 | 3.321 | 2.450 | 2.026 | 1.977 | 2.121 | 2.457 | 2.536 | 2.417 |
| | | | | | | | | | | | | |
| 1.800 | 1.800 | 1.800 | 1.800 | 1.800 | 1.800 | 1.800 | 1.800 | 1.800 | 1.800 | 1.803 | 1.810 | 1.800 |
| ... | ... | ... | ... | ... | ... | ... | ... | ... | ... | ... | ... | ... |
| 1.824 | 2.066 | 2.198 | 2.217 | 2.308 | 2.402 | 2.433 | 2.524 | 2.589 | 2.619 | 1.803 | 1.176 | 2.320 |
| 1.840 | 1.904 | 1.903 | 1.857 | 1.866 | 1.890 | 1.877 | 1.893 | 1.879 | 1.825 | 1.831 | 1.740 | 1.873 |
| 1.415 | 1.603 | 1.705 | 1.720 | 1.791 | 1.863 | 1.887 | 1.958 | 2.009 | 2.031 | 1.399 | 0.913 | 1.800 |
| 1.978 | 2.003 | 1.961 | 1.849 | 1.855 | 1.874 | 1.840 | 1.853 | 1.854 | 1.829 | 1.911 | 1.980 | 1.883 |
| | | | | | | | | | | | | |
| 76.829 | 98.811 | 119.493 | 138.569 | 158.893 | 163.367 | 125.929 | 109.100 | 108.300 | 116.000 | 106.240 | 85.640 | 117.516 |
| ... | ... | ... | ... | ... | ... | ... | ... | ... | ... | ... | ... | ... |
| 96.167 | 109.664 | 120.250 | 129.652 | 141.120 | 149.084 | 163.132 | 165.939 | 170.155 | 176.960 | 106.240 | 63.389 | 145.467 |
| 97.015 | 101.068 | 104.101 | 108.570 | 114.086 | 117.346 | 125.874 | 124.463 | 123.481 | 123.361 | 108.608 | 93.740 | 115.944 |
| 77.688 | 88.592 | 97.144 | 104.740 | 114.004 | 120.437 | 131.786 | 134.053 | 137.460 | 142.957 | 85.826 | 51.209 | 117.516 |
| 96.247 | 95.247 | 107.971 | 128.075 | 149.983 | 163.522 | 162.789 | 139.677 | 117.174 | 114.993 | 114.408 | 94.716 | 124.755 |
| | | | | | | | | | | | | |
| 1.027 | 1.149 | 1.330 | 1.495 | 1.729 | 2.006 | 1.909 | 1.700 | 1.500 | 1.700 | 1.360 | 0.897 | 1.570 |
| 1.053 | 1.110 | 1.166 | 1.219 | 1.274 | 1.439 | 1.630 | 1.780 | 1.839 | 1.867 | 1.252 | 0.786 | 1.479 |
| 1.169 | 1.368 | 1.503 | 1.584 | 1.728 | 2.006 | 2.319 | 2.605 | 2.781 | 2.939 | 1.360 | 0.598 | 2.029 |
| 1.179 | 1.261 | 1.301 | 1.326 | 1.397 | 1.579 | 1.789 | 1.954 | 2.018 | 2.049 | 1.393 | 0.890 | 1.631 |
| 0.904 | 1.059 | 1.162 | 1.225 | 1.336 | 1.552 | 1.794 | 2.015 | 2.151 | 2.274 | 1.052 | 0.462 | 1.570 |
| 1.036 | 1.201 | 1.373 | 1.522 | 1.929 | 1.955 | 1.894 | 1.616 | 1.553 | 1.672 | 1.373 | 0.904 | 1.586 |
| | | | | | | | | | | | | |
| 14.700 | 14.700 | 14.700 | 14.700 | 14.700 | 39.000 | 97.500 | 102.600 | 270.000 | 15655.000 | 311.161 | 9.348 | 384.480 |
| 3.897 | 3.962 | 4.418 | 4.966 | 6.200 | 14.535 | 54.354 | 329.190 | 43.905 | 1841.754 | 168.544 | 3.030 | 248.801 |
| 8.244 | 8.751 | 10.217 | 11.340 | 15.758 | 42.106 | 160.623 | 1000.745 | 137.953 | 6024.235 | 311.161 | 3.432 | 661.358 |
| 8.317 | 8.065 | 8.845 | 9.496 | 12.739 | 33.142 | 123.938 | 750.615 | 100.111 | 4199.551 | 332.614 | 5.089 | 536.581 |
| 4.793 | 5.087 | 5.940 | 6.593 | 9.161 | 24.478 | 93.378 | 581.782 | 80.199 | 3502.185 | 180.893 | 1.995 | 384.480 |
| 10.050 | 10.050 | 11.700 | 13.200 | 15.000 | 40.000 | 159.000 | 786.500 | 108.429 | 4735.049 | 424.954 | 7.260 | 643.665 |
| | | | | | | | | | | | | |
| 211.280 | 271.730 | 328.610 | 381.060 | 436.960 | 449.260 | 346.300 | 300.500 | 297.800 | 319.000 | 293.989 | 232.649 | 322.828 |
| 216.750 | 233.767 | 240.399 | 243.913 | 229.317 | 212.455 | 197.022 | 202.126 | 190.904 | 178.089 | 200.743 | 172.969 | 212.293 |
| 313.770 | 371.904 | 420.945 | 406.867 | 405.297 | 388.698 | 367.705 | 388.071 | 378.830 | 367.891 | 293.989 | 175.988 | 380.411 |
| 316.536 | 342.753 | 364.412 | 340.709 | 327.658 | 305.949 | 283.724 | 291.075 | 274.914 | 256.460 | 292.398 | 256.753 | 306.831 |
| 266.274 | 315.608 | 357.226 | 345.279 | 343.947 | 329.860 | 312.045 | 329.328 | 321.486 | 312.203 | 249.487 | 149.349 | 322.827 |
| 211.279 | 271.730 | 328.605 | 381.065 | 436.955 | 449.261 | 346.305 | 300.535 | 297.847 | 319.007 | 294.035 | 232.749 | 322.838 |
| | | | | | | | | | | | | |
| 0.547 | 0.614 | 0.673 | 0.723 | 0.764 | 0.892 | 1.800 | 4.000 | 4.500 | 7.400 | 1.019 | 0.634 | 1.257 |
| 0.667 | 0.692 | 0.713 | 0.725 | 0.866 | 0.968 | 0.938 | 1.321 | 1.512 | 1.614 | 0.840 | 0.551 | 1.005 |
| 0.973 | 1.004 | 1.075 | 1.095 | 1.333 | 1.395 | 1.380 | 1.999 | 2.365 | 2.628 | 1.019 | 0.497 | 1.515 |
| 0.982 | 0.926 | 0.931 | 0.917 | 1.078 | 1.098 | 1.065 | 1.499 | 1.716 | 1.832 | 1.056 | 0.727 | 1.229 |
| 0.808 | 0.833 | 0.892 | 0.909 | 1.106 | 1.157 | 1.145 | 1.658 | 1.962 | 2.181 | 0.845 | 0.413 | 1.257 |
| 0.547 | 0.618 | 0.673 | 0.724 | 0.767 | 0.894 | 1.755 | 4.016 | 4.537 | 7.365 | 1.019 | 0.634 | 1.258 |

**Table A.2**   Conversion rates for individual countries or areas, expressed as the number of
local currency units per United States dollar, 1970–1989 [*cont.*]

| Country or area | 1970 (1) | 1971 (2) | 1972 (3) | 1973 (4) | 1974 (5) | 1975 (6) | 1976 (7) | 1977 (8) | 1978 (9) | 1979 (10) |
|---|---|---|---|---|---|---|---|---|---|---|
| **Norway:** Norwegian kroner | | | | | | | | | | |
| 1. MER | 7.143 | 7.044 | 6.588 | 5.766 | 5.540 | 5.227 | 5.457 | 5.324 | 5.242 | 5.064 |
| 2. PPPs | 5.985 | 6.054 | 6.111 | 6.144 | 6.133 | 6.332 | 6.626 | 6.905 | 6.743 | 6.360 |
| 3. Absolute 1970–1989 PARE | 7.836 | 8.358 | 8.777 | 9.582 | 10.565 | 3.401 | 3.656 | 3.960 | 4.214 | 4.493 |
| 4. Relative 1970–1989 PARE | 16.071 | 16.306 | 16.371 | 16.761 | 16.942 | 4.965 | 5.022 | 5.096 | 5.055 | 4.947 |
| 5. Absolute 1980–1989 PARE | 7.447 | 7.943 | 8.341 | 9.107 | 10.041 | 3.233 | 3.474 | 3.763 | 4.005 | 4.270 |
| 6. WA | 7.143 | 7.042 | 6.588 | 5.766 | 5.540 | 5.227 | 5.457 | 5.324 | 5.242 | 5.064 |
| **Oman:** Omani rials | | | | | | | | | | |
| 1. MER | 0.417 | 0.420 | 0.384 | 0.349 | 0.350 | 0.350 | 0.350 | 0.350 | 0.350 | 0.350 |
| 2. PPPs | 0.282 | 0.208 | 0.162 | 0.199 | 0.230 | 0.202 | 0.199 | 0.194 | 0.198 | 0.226 |
| 3. Absolute 1970–1989 PARE | 0.036 | 0.034 | 0.037 | 0.043 | 0.168 | 0.217 | 0.252 | 0.294 | 0.317 | 0.414 |
| 4. Relative 1970–1989 PARE | 0.073 | 0.066 | 0.069 | 0.076 | 0.269 | 0.317 | 0.346 | 0.379 | 0.380 | 0.456 |
| 5. Absolute 1980–1989 PARE | 0.027 | 0.026 | 0.028 | 0.033 | 0.128 | 0.166 | 0.193 | 0.226 | 0.243 | 0.317 |
| 6. WA | 0.417 | 0.416 | 0.384 | 0.351 | 0.345 | 0.345 | 0.345 | 0.345 | 0.345 | 0.345 |
| **Pakistan:** Pakistan rupees | | | | | | | | | | |
| 1. MER | 4.762 | 4.767 | 8.952 | 9.994 | 9.900 | 9.900 | 9.900 | 9.900 | 9.900 | 9.900 |
| 2. PPPs | 2.004 | 2.023 | 2.272 | 2.662 | 3.119 | 3.190 | 3.255 | 3.283 | 3.323 | 3.367 |
| 3. Absolute 1970–1989 PARE | 3.573 | 3.791 | 4.392 | 5.443 | 6.654 | 7.459 | 8.254 | 8.999 | 9.491 | 10.491 |
| 4. Relative 1970–1989 PARE | 7.328 | 7.395 | 8.192 | 9.521 | 10.671 | 10.887 | 11.339 | 11.582 | 11.385 | 11.552 |
| 5. Absolute 1980–1989 PARE | 3.209 | 3.405 | 3.945 | 4.890 | 5.978 | 6.700 | 7.415 | 8.084 | 8.526 | 9.424 |
| 6. WA | 4.762 | 4.762 | 5.807 | 10.573 | 9.900 | 9.900 | 9.900 | 9.900 | 9.900 | 9.900 |
| **Panama:** Panamanian balboas | | | | | | | | | | |
| 1. MER | 1.000 | 1.000 | 1.000 | 1.000 | 1.000 | 1.000 | 1.000 | 1.000 | 1.000 | 1.000 |
| 2. PPPs | 0.663 | 0.636 | 0.618 | 0.627 | 0.640 | 0.639 | 0.640 | 0.653 | 0.648 | 0.657 |
| 3. Absolute 1970–1989 PARE | 0.506 | 0.521 | 0.547 | 0.594 | 0.663 | 0.725 | 0.758 | 0.793 | 0.856 | 0.935 |
| 4. Relative 1970–1989 PARE | 1.038 | 1.016 | 1.020 | 1.038 | 1.063 | 1.058 | 1.041 | 1.021 | 1.026 | 1.029 |
| 5. Absolute 1980–1989 PARE | 0.423 | 0.435 | 0.457 | 0.496 | 0.554 | 0.606 | 0.633 | 0.663 | 0.715 | 0.781 |
| 6. WA | 1.000 | 1.000 | 1.000 | 1.000 | 1.000 | 1.000 | 1.000 | 1.000 | 1.000 | 1.000 |
| **Papua New Guinea:** Papua New Guinea kina | | | | | | | | | | |
| 1. MER | 0.893 | 0.875 | 0.835 | 0.700 | 0.693 | 0.763 | 0.792 | 0.791 | 0.708 | 0.712 |
| 2. PPPs | 0.294 | 0.290 | 0.349 | 0.401 | 0.375 | 0.373 | 0.403 | 0.381 | 0.373 | 0.372 |
| 3. Absolute 1970–1989 PARE | 0.363 | 0.367 | 0.413 | 0.527 | 0.506 | 0.545 | 0.667 | 0.714 | 0.716 | 0.812 |
| 4. Relative 1970–1989 PARE | 0.744 | 0.717 | 0.771 | 0.921 | 0.812 | 0.795 | 0.916 | 0.919 | 0.858 | 0.894 |
| 5. Absolute 1980–1989 PARE | 0.295 | 0.299 | 0.336 | 0.428 | 0.412 | 0.443 | 0.542 | 0.581 | 0.582 | 0.661 |
| 6. WA | 0.893 | 0.882 | 0.835 | 0.704 | 0.697 | 0.764 | 0.793 | 0.791 | 0.709 | 0.712 |
| **Paraguay:** Paraguayan guaranies | | | | | | | | | | |
| 1. MER | 126.000 | 126.000 | 126.000 | 126.000 | 126.000 | 126.000 | 126.000 | 126.000 | 126.000 | 126.000 |
| 2. PPPs | 52.354 | 52.195 | 56.249 | 65.585 | 74.750 | 76.107 | 73.588 | 74.924 | 78.124 | 89.855 |
| 3. Absolute 1970–1989 PARE | 44.269 | 46.809 | 50.766 | 61.132 | 75.469 | 79.795 | 83.630 | 92.835 | 102.010 | 122.271 |
| 4. Relative 1970–1989 PARE | 90.794 | 91.320 | 94.695 | 106.929 | 121.023 | 116.471 | 114.889 | 119.475 | 122.357 | 134.639 |
| 5. Absolute 1980–1989 PARE | 37.118 | 39.248 | 42.566 | 51.257 | 63.278 | 66.905 | 70.121 | 77.839 | 85.532 | 102.521 |
| 6. WA | 126.000 | 126.000 | 126.000 | 126.000 | 126.000 | 126.000 | 126.000 | 126.000 | 126.000 | 126.000 |
| **Peru:** Peruvian intis | | | | | | | | | | |
| 1. MER | 0.040 | 0.040 | 0.040 | 0.040 | 0.040 | 0.040 | 0.060 | 0.080 | 0.160 | 0.220 |
| 2. PPPs | 0.019 | 0.019 | 0.020 | 0.021 | 0.022 | 0.026 | 0.031 | 0.040 | 0.063 | 0.099 |
| 3. Absolute 1970–1989 PARE | 0.018 | 0.020 | 0.021 | 0.024 | 0.028 | 0.034 | 0.044 | 0.060 | 0.096 | 0.166 |
| 4. Relative 1970–1989 PARE | 0.038 | 0.038 | 0.040 | 0.042 | 0.045 | 0.050 | 0.061 | 0.078 | 0.115 | 0.183 |
| 5. Absolute 1980–1989 PARE | 0.014 | 0.015 | 0.017 | 0.019 | 0.022 | 0.027 | 0.035 | 0.047 | 0.075 | 0.130 |
| 6. WA | 0.039 | 0.039 | 0.039 | 0.039 | 0.039 | 0.041 | 0.056 | 0.084 | 0.156 | 0.225 |

| 1980 (11) | 1981 (12) | 1982 (13) | 1983 (14) | 1984 (15) | 1985 (16) | 1986 (17) | 1987 (18) | 1988 (19) | 1989 (20) | Averages 1970–89 (21) | 1970–79 (22) | 1980–89 (23) |
|---|---|---|---|---|---|---|---|---|---|---|---|---|
| 4.939 | 5.740 | 6.454 | 7.296 | 8.162 | 8.597 | 7.395 | 6.700 | 6.500 | 6.900 | 6.485 | 5.552 | 6.852 |
| 6.280 | 6.482 | 6.788 | 7.236 | 7.204 | 7.723 | 7.463 | 7.774 | 7.279 | 7.438 | 7.016 | 6.409 | 7.235 |
| 5.149 | 5.868 | 6.465 | 6.860 | 7.299 | 7.664 | 7.555 | 8.096 | 7.836 | 8.334 | 6.485 | 4.930 | 7.210 |
| 5.194 | 5.408 | 5.597 | 5.745 | 5.901 | 6.032 | 5.830 | 6.073 | 5.686 | 5.810 | 5.947 | 6.608 | 5.763 |
| 4.893 | 5.576 | 6.145 | 6.520 | 6.937 | 7.284 | 7.180 | 7.695 | 7.447 | 7.921 | 6.163 | 4.686 | 6.852 |
| 4.939 | 5.740 | 6.454 | 7.296 | 8.161 | 8.597 | 7.395 | 6.737 | 6.517 | 6.905 | 6.490 | 5.552 | 6.860 |
| | | | | | | | | | | | | |
| 0.350 | 0.350 | 0.350 | 0.350 | 0.350 | 0.350 | 0.380 | 0.380 | 0.380 | 0.380 | 0.360 | 0.353 | 0.362 |
| 0.316 | 0.313 | 0.291 | 0.282 | 0.283 | 0.285 | 0.210 | 0.227 | 0.202 | 0.199 | 0.241 | 0.207 | 0.250 |
| 0.591 | 0.609 | 0.573 | 0.518 | 0.494 | 0.514 | 0.386 | 0.429 | 0.394 | 0.404 | 0.360 | 0.170 | 0.473 |
| 0.596 | 0.562 | 0.496 | 0.434 | 0.399 | 0.405 | 0.298 | 0.321 | 0.286 | 0.282 | 0.346 | 0.260 | 0.373 |
| 0.452 | 0.467 | 0.439 | 0.397 | 0.378 | 0.394 | 0.295 | 0.328 | 0.302 | 0.309 | 0.276 | 0.130 | 0.362 |
| 0.345 | 0.345 | 0.345 | 0.345 | 0.345 | 0.345 | 0.382 | 0.384 | 0.384 | 0.384 | 0.359 | 0.349 | 0.361 |
| | | | | | | | | | | | | |
| 9.900 | 9.900 | 11.847 | 13.117 | 14.046 | 15.928 | 16.648 | 17.400 | 18.000 | 20.500 | 13.398 | 9.038 | 15.121 |
| 3.474 | 3.537 | 3.547 | 3.720 | 3.878 | 3.978 | 4.076 | 4.343 | 4.575 | 4.713 | 3.822 | 2.998 | 4.087 |
| 11.902 | 13.027 | 13.710 | 15.031 | 15.712 | 16.241 | 16.978 | 18.609 | 20.258 | 21.726 | 13.398 | 7.188 | 16.833 |
| 12.007 | 12.006 | 11.869 | 12.586 | 12.702 | 12.784 | 13.100 | 13.958 | 14.701 | 15.145 | 12.699 | 10.478 | 13.369 |
| 10.692 | 11.702 | 12.316 | 13.502 | 14.114 | 14.590 | 15.251 | 16.717 | 18.198 | 19.517 | 12.036 | 6.457 | 15.121 |
| 9.900 | 9.900 | 10.550 | 12.700 | 13.476 | 15.160 | 16.130 | 17.165 | 17.555 | 19.162 | 12.941 | 8.809 | 14.554 |
| | | | | | | | | | | | | |
| 1.000 | 1.000 | 1.000 | 1.000 | 1.000 | 1.000 | 1.000 | 1.000 | 1.000 | 1.000 | 1.000 | 1.000 | 1.000 |
| 0.690 | 0.648 | 0.648 | 0.631 | 0.631 | 0.631 | 0.629 | 0.616 | 0.609 | 0.589 | 0.633 | 0.643 | 0.629 |
| 1.032 | 1.079 | 1.129 | 1.150 | 1.205 | 1.235 | 1.255 | 1.266 | 1.292 | 1.302 | 1.000 | 0.704 | 1.196 |
| 1.041 | 0.995 | 0.977 | 0.963 | 0.974 | 0.972 | 0.968 | 0.949 | 0.937 | 0.908 | 0.984 | 1.035 | 0.965 |
| 0.863 | 0.902 | 0.944 | 0.961 | 1.007 | 1.033 | 1.049 | 1.058 | 1.080 | 1.088 | 0.836 | 0.589 | 1.000 |
| 1.000 | 1.000 | 1.000 | 1.000 | 1.000 | 1.000 | 1.000 | 1.000 | 1.000 | 1.000 | 1.000 | 1.000 | 1.000 |
| | | | | | | | | | | | | |
| 0.670 | 0.672 | 0.738 | 0.834 | 0.894 | 1.000 | 0.971 | 0.900 | 0.900 | 0.900 | 0.816 | 0.757 | 0.849 |
| 0.371 | 0.354 | 0.351 | 0.365 | 0.389 | 0.389 | 0.390 | 0.406 | 0.423 | 0.396 | 0.379 | 0.366 | 0.386 |
| 0.870 | 0.858 | 0.886 | 0.966 | 1.038 | 1.055 | 1.078 | 1.153 | 1.243 | 1.210 | 0.816 | 0.566 | 1.044 |
| 0.877 | 0.791 | 0.767 | 0.809 | 0.839 | 0.830 | 0.832 | 0.865 | 0.902 | 0.844 | 0.841 | 0.846 | 0.838 |
| 0.707 | 0.698 | 0.721 | 0.786 | 0.844 | 0.858 | 0.877 | 0.938 | 1.011 | 0.985 | 0.664 | 0.461 | 0.849 |
| 0.671 | 0.673 | 0.738 | 0.836 | 0.899 | 1.000 | 0.971 | 0.908 | 0.867 | 0.859 | 0.813 | 0.758 | 0.842 |
| | | | | | | | | | | | | |
| 126.000 | 126.000 | 126.000 | 126.000 | 201.000 | 306.670 | 339.170 | 550.000 | 550.000 | 1056.200 | 285.870 | 126.000 | 333.373 |
| 94.959 | 102.665 | 104.143 | 115.340 | 131.394 | 161.064 | 207.704 | 263.158 | 318.641 | 401.699 | 176.216 | 73.603 | 208.927 |
| 142.835 | 166.133 | 174.495 | 199.680 | 253.475 | 317.463 | 417.619 | 544.322 | 681.211 | 893.989 | 285.870 | 81.625 | 397.598 |
| 144.095 | 153.111 | 151.060 | 167.211 | 204.919 | 249.880 | 322.238 | 408.272 | 494.350 | 623.208 | 271.536 | 116.820 | 318.978 |
| 119.763 | 139.297 | 146.308 | 167.425 | 212.530 | 266.182 | 350.159 | 456.396 | 571.173 | 749.580 | 239.693 | 68.440 | 333.373 |
| 126.000 | 126.000 | 136.000 | 146.000 | 243.700 | 440.700 | 517.400 | 668.000 | 840.000 | 1120.000 | 327.245 | 126.000 | 398.771 |
| | | | | | | | | | | | | |
| 0.290 | 0.420 | 0.700 | 1.630 | 3.470 | 10.970 | 14.000 | 16.800 | 128.800 | 2666.000 | 306.992 | 0.083 | 436.634 |
| 0.137 | 0.217 | 0.348 | 0.701 | 1.426 | 3.736 | 6.341 | 11.423 | 78.098 | 2023.149 | 159.244 | 0.042 | 229.781 |
| 0.272 | 0.465 | 0.782 | 1.622 | 3.463 | 9.288 | 16.083 | 29.806 | 210.613 | 5679.665 | 306.992 | 0.055 | 557.688 |
| 0.274 | 0.429 | 0.677 | 1.359 | 2.800 | 7.311 | 12.410 | 22.356 | 152.840 | 3959.348 | 310.881 | 0.080 | 450.243 |
| 0.213 | 0.364 | 0.612 | 1.270 | 2.711 | 7.272 | 12.592 | 23.336 | 164.897 | 4446.815 | 240.355 | 0.043 | 436.634 |
| 0.289 | 0.422 | 0.698 | 1.629 | 3.467 | 11.704 | 15.464 | 26.981 | 252.230 | 4022.200 | 353.398 | 0.082 | 539.429 |

**Table A.2**   Conversion rates for individual countries or areas, expressed as the number of
local currency units per United States dollar, 1970—1989 [*cont.*]

| Country or area | 1970 (1) | 1971 (2) | 1972 (3) | 1973 (4) | 1974 (5) | 1975 (6) | 1976 (7) | 1977 (8) | 1978 (9) | 1979 (10) |
|---|---|---|---|---|---|---|---|---|---|---|
| **Philippines:** Philippine pesos | | | | | | | | | | |
| 1.   MER | 6.065 | 6.443 | 6.701 | 6.756 | 6.788 | 7.248 | 7.440 | 7.403 | 7.366 | 7.378 |
| 2.   PPPs | 2.014 | 2.179 | 2.243 | 2.519 | 2.953 | 2.943 | 3.074 | 3.187 | 3.184 | 3.422 |
| 3.   Absolute 1970—1989 PARE | 2.591 | 2.960 | 3.168 | 3.740 | 4.901 | 5.309 | 5.797 | 6.226 | 6.799 | 7.834 |
| 4.   Relative 1970—1989 PARE | 5.315 | 5.774 | 5.909 | 6.542 | 7.859 | 7.749 | 7.964 | 8.013 | 8.155 | 8.627 |
| 5.   Absolute 1980—1989 PARE | 2.182 | 2.493 | 2.668 | 3.150 | 4.127 | 4.471 | 4.882 | 5.244 | 5.726 | 6.598 |
| 6.   WA | 5.904 | 6.432 | 6.675 | 6.756 | 6.788 | 7.248 | 7.440 | 7.403 | 7.366 | 7.378 |
| **Poland:** Polish zlotych | | | | | | | | | | |
| 1.   MER | 24.000 | 23.950 | 33.200 | 33.200 | 33.200 | 33.200 | 33.200 | 33.200 | 33.200 | 40.160 |
| 2.   PPPs | ... | ... | ... | ... | ... | ... | ... | ... | ... | ... |
| 3.   Absolute 1970—1989 PARE | 24.856 | 26.253 | 26.396 | 26.670 | 27.424 | 28.075 | 31.192 | 32.187 | 34.247 | 35.653 |
| 4.   Relative 1970—1989 PARE | 50.980 | 51.217 | 49.237 | 46.650 | 43.978 | 40.980 | 42.850 | 41.424 | 41.078 | 39.259 |
| 5.   Absolute 1980—1989 PARE | 23.202 | 24.506 | 24.639 | 24.895 | 25.599 | 26.207 | 29.116 | 30.045 | 31.968 | 33.280 |
| 6.   WA | 15.983 | 24.865 | 27.589 | 30.359 | 33.944 | 34.046 | 35.949 | 35.174 | 34.992 | 37.166 |
| **Portugal:** Portuguese escudos | | | | | | | | | | |
| 1.   MER | 28.750 | 28.211 | 27.011 | 24.673 | 25.408 | 25.553 | 30.223 | 38.277 | 43.940 | 48.924 |
| 2.   PPPs | 14.769 | 14.411 | 15.331 | 15.514 | 16.648 | 18.322 | 20.220 | 23.855 | 27.350 | 30.152 |
| 3.   Absolute 1970—1989 PARE | 12.723 | 13.361 | 14.404 | 15.768 | 18.742 | 21.784 | 25.329 | 32.016 | 39.171 | 46.785 |
| 4.   Relative 1970—1989 PARE | 26.095 | 26.067 | 26.868 | 27.580 | 30.055 | 31.797 | 34.797 | 41.204 | 46.985 | 51.518 |
| 5.   Absolute 1980—1989 PARE | 10.672 | 11.208 | 12.082 | 13.226 | 15.721 | 18.273 | 21.247 | 26.856 | 32.858 | 39.244 |
| 6.   WA | 28.750 | 28.312 | 27.053 | 24.515 | 25.408 | 25.553 | 30.229 | 38.277 | 43.937 | 48.923 |
| **Puerto Rico:** United States dollars | | | | | | | | | | |
| 1.   MER | 1.000 | 1.000 | 1.000 | 1.000 | 1.000 | 1.000 | 1.000 | 1.000 | 1.000 | 1.000 |
| 2.   PPPs | ... | ... | ... | ... | ... | ... | ... | ... | ... | ... |
| 3.   Absolute 1970—1989 PARE | 0.516 | 0.538 | 0.562 | 0.617 | 0.675 | 0.701 | 0.727 | 0.769 | 0.827 | 0.923 |
| 4.   Relative 1970—1989 PARE | 1.058 | 1.050 | 1.049 | 1.079 | 1.082 | 1.024 | 0.999 | 0.989 | 0.992 | 1.016 |
| 5.   Absolute 1980—1989 PARE | 0.423 | 0.441 | 0.461 | 0.506 | 0.553 | 0.575 | 0.596 | 0.630 | 0.678 | 0.756 |
| 6.   WA [a] | 1.090 | 1.060 | 1.045 | 1.081 | 1.098 | 1.059 | 1.038 | 1.051 | 1.071 | 1.105 |
| **Qatar:** Qatari riyals | | | | | | | | | | |
| 1.   MER | 4.762 | 4.747 | 4.386 | 3.993 | 3.947 | 3.931 | 3.962 | 3.959 | 3.877 | 3.773 |
| 2.   PPPs | ... | ... | ... | ... | ... | ... | ... | ... | ... | ... |
| 3.   Absolute 1970—1989 PARE | 0.414 | 0.447 | 0.482 | 0.580 | 1.905 | 2.308 | 2.657 | 3.258 | 3.265 | 4.374 |
| 4.   Relative 1970—1989 PARE | 0.849 | 0.873 | 0.899 | 1.014 | 3.054 | 3.369 | 3.651 | 4.193 | 3.917 | 4.817 |
| 5.   Absolute 1980—1989 PARE | 0.276 | 0.298 | 0.321 | 0.386 | 1.268 | 1.536 | 1.769 | 2.169 | 2.174 | 2.912 |
| 6.   WA [a] | 7.888 | 5.963 | 5.016 | 5.140 | 11.462 | 8.202 | 4.665 | 4.788 | 4.238 | 4.761 |
| **Reunion:** French francs | | | | | | | | | | |
| 1.   MER | 5.554 | 5.510 | 5.044 | 4.454 | 4.810 | 4.286 | 4.780 | 4.913 | 4.513 | 4.255 |
| 2.   PPPs | ... | ... | ... | ... | ... | ... | ... | ... | ... | ... |
| 3.   Absolute 1970—1989 PARE | 2.088 | 2.298 | 2.467 | 2.610 | 3.133 | 3.685 | 3.832 | 4.100 | 4.269 | 4.571 |
| 4.   Relative 1970—1989 PARE | 4.283 | 4.483 | 4.601 | 4.566 | 5.025 | 5.379 | 5.265 | 5.277 | 5.120 | 5.034 |
| 5.   Absolute 1980—1989 PARE | 1.800 | 1.981 | 2.127 | 2.251 | 2.702 | 3.177 | 3.304 | 3.535 | 3.681 | 3.942 |
| 6.   WA [a] | 5.569 | 5.904 | 5.840 | 5.350 | 5.521 | 5.410 | 5.040 | 4.932 | 4.984 | 4.855 |
| **Romania:** Romanian lei | | | | | | | | | | |
| 1.   MER | 20.000 | 20.000 | 20.000 | 20.000 | 20.000 | 20.000 | 20.000 | 20.000 | 18.355 | 18.000 |
| 2.   PPPs | ... | ... | ... | ... | ... | ... | ... | ... | ... | ... |
| 3.   Absolute 1970—1989 PARE | 15.606 | 15.603 | 15.610 | 15.608 | 15.608 | 15.605 | 15.787 | 15.739 | 15.789 | 16.102 |
| 4.   Relative 1970—1989 PARE | 32.008 | 30.441 | 29.118 | 27.300 | 25.028 | 22.778 | 21.687 | 20.255 | 18.938 | 17.730 |
| 5.   Absolute 1980—1989 PARE | 13.985 | 13.983 | 13.989 | 13.987 | 13.987 | 13.985 | 14.147 | 14.104 | 14.149 | 14.430 |
| 6.   WA | 18.953 | 19.426 | 20.005 | 20.001 | 19.999 | 19.998 | 20.154 | 20.037 | 19.474 | 19.060 |

| | | | | | | | | | | Averages | | |
|---|---|---|---|---|---|---|---|---|---|---|---|---|
| 1980 (11) | 1981 (12) | 1982 (13) | 1983 (14) | 1984 (15) | 1985 (16) | 1986 (17) | 1987 (18) | 1988 (19) | 1989 (20) | 1970−89 (21) | 1970−79 (22) | 1980−89 (23) |
| 7.511 | 7.900 | 8.540 | 11.113 | 16.699 | 18.607 | 20.386 | 20.600 | 21.100 | 21.700 | 12.890 | 7.136 | 15.381 |
| 3.550 | 3.635 | 3.709 | 3.974 | 5.571 | 6.549 | 6.479 | 6.801 | 7.212 | 7.657 | 4.918 | 2.931 | 5.693 |
| 9.057 | 10.051 | 10.899 | 12.177 | 18.228 | 21.588 | 21.788 | 23.529 | 25.787 | 28.502 | 12.890 | 5.230 | 18.263 |
| 9.137 | 9.263 | 9.435 | 10.197 | 14.736 | 16.992 | 16.812 | 17.648 | 18.714 | 19.869 | 12.716 | 7.573 | 14.724 |
| 7.628 | 8.465 | 9.179 | 10.256 | 15.352 | 18.182 | 18.350 | 19.816 | 21.718 | 24.004 | 10.856 | 4.405 | 15.381 |
| 7.511 | 7.900 | 8.540 | 11.113 | 16.699 | 18.607 | 20.386 | 20.568 | 21.095 | 21.737 | 12.885 | 7.125 | 15.382 |
| | | | | | | | | | | | | |
| 44.280 | 51.250 | 84.820 | 91.600 | 113.200 | 147.100 | 175.300 | 265.100 | 430.500 | 1439.200 | 190.141 | 32.513 | 312.498 |
| ... | ... | ... | ... | ... | ... | ... | ... | ... | ... | ... | ... | ... |
| 37.941 | 47.267 | 100.773 | 118.689 | 139.192 | 162.779 | 193.832 | 248.650 | 414.770 | 1659.628 | 190.141 | 29.946 | 334.777 |
| 38.275 | 43.562 | 87.239 | 99.389 | 112.528 | 128.126 | 149.562 | 186.502 | 300.996 | 1156.942 | 193.528 | 43.239 | 269.054 |
| 35.416 | 44.121 | 94.066 | 110.790 | 129.929 | 151.946 | 180.933 | 232.103 | 387.168 | 1549.182 | 177.488 | 27.953 | 312.498 |
| 41.266 | 53.219 | 103.898 | 106.730 | 112.594 | 135.037 | 169.366 | 238.226 | 415.942 | 1660.268 | 188.940 | 31.316 | 318.343 |
| | | | | | | | | | | | | |
| 50.062 | 61.546 | 79.473 | 110.780 | 146.390 | 170.390 | 149.587 | 140.900 | 144.000 | 157.500 | 96.762 | 34.099 | 125.494 |
| 33.292 | 36.164 | 41.232 | 50.653 | 61.733 | 74.665 | 88.163 | 95.319 | 102.943 | 111.544 | 57.777 | 21.216 | 73.572 |
| 56.565 | 66.525 | 80.290 | 100.045 | 124.732 | 151.842 | 182.895 | 203.421 | 227.068 | 256.128 | 96.762 | 25.230 | 149.607 |
| 57.063 | 61.311 | 69.507 | 83.777 | 100.838 | 119.517 | 141.123 | 152.578 | 164.781 | 178.549 | 96.162 | 36.997 | 120.088 |
| 47.448 | 55.803 | 67.349 | 83.920 | 104.628 | 127.368 | 153.416 | 170.634 | 190.469 | 214.846 | 81.166 | 21.163 | 125.494 |
| 50.062 | 61.546 | 79.473 | 110.780 | 146.390 | 170.395 | 149.587 | 140.882 | 143.954 | 157.458 | 96.748 | 34.090 | 125.481 |
| | | | | | | | | | | | | |
| 1.000 | 1.000 | 1.000 | 1.000 | 1.000 | 1.000 | 1.000 | 1.000 | 1.000 | 1.000 | 1.000 | 1.000 | 1.000 |
| ... | ... | ... | ... | ... | ... | ... | ... | ... | ... | ... | ... | ... |
| 1.009 | 1.093 | 1.122 | 1.159 | 1.203 | 1.215 | 1.259 | 1.291 | 1.333 | 1.382 | 1.000 | 0.699 | 1.220 |
| 1.018 | 1.008 | 0.971 | 0.971 | 0.972 | 0.956 | 0.971 | 0.968 | 0.967 | 0.964 | 0.989 | 1.026 | 0.974 |
| 0.827 | 0.897 | 0.920 | 0.950 | 0.986 | 0.996 | 1.032 | 1.058 | 1.093 | 1.133 | 0.820 | 0.573 | 1.000 |
| 1.104 | 1.090 | 1.046 | 1.031 | 1.037 | 1.019 | 1.028 | 1.029 | 1.031 | 1.036 | 1.049 | 1.070 | 1.041 |
| | | | | | | | | | | | | |
| 3.657 | 3.640 | 3.640 | 3.640 | 3.640 | 3.640 | 3.640 | 3.600 | 3.600 | 3.600 | 3.708 | 3.930 | 3.631 |
| ... | ... | ... | ... | ... | ... | ... | ... | ... | ... | ... | ... | ... |
| 5.508 | 6.474 | 6.313 | 5.774 | 5.706 | 5.319 | 4.153 | 4.798 | 5.038 | 5.315 | 3.708 | 2.001 | 5.455 |
| 5.556 | 5.966 | 5.465 | 4.835 | 4.613 | 4.187 | 3.204 | 3.599 | 3.656 | 3.705 | 3.913 | 2.983 | 4.431 |
| 3.667 | 4.309 | 4.202 | 3.844 | 3.799 | 3.541 | 2.764 | 3.194 | 3.354 | 3.538 | 2.469 | 1.332 | 3.631 |
| 4.982 | 4.507 | 3.794 | 3.405 | 3.509 | 3.462 | 3.044 | 3.696 | 3.932 | 3.795 | 4.117 | 5.273 | 3.804 |
| | | | | | | | | | | | | |
| 4.226 | 5.435 | 6.572 | 7.621 | 8.739 | 8.985 | 6.926 | 6.000 | 6.000 | 6.400 | 6.018 | 4.658 | 6.550 |
| ... | ... | ... | ... | ... | ... | ... | ... | ... | ... | ... | ... | ... |
| 4.960 | 5.612 | 6.507 | 6.902 | 7.268 | 7.809 | 8.242 | 8.880 | 8.995 | 9.357 | 6.018 | 3.443 | 7.596 |
| 5.004 | 5.172 | 5.634 | 5.780 | 5.876 | 6.147 | 6.360 | 6.660 | 6.528 | 6.523 | 5.803 | 4.998 | 6.075 |
| 4.277 | 4.839 | 5.611 | 5.951 | 6.267 | 6.733 | 7.106 | 7.656 | 7.756 | 8.068 | 5.189 | 2.969 | 6.550 |
| 4.696 | 5.147 | 6.139 | 7.092 | 8.035 | 8.999 | 8.773 | 7.893 | 6.546 | 6.321 | 6.456 | 5.187 | 6.927 |
| | | | | | | | | | | | | |
| 18.000 | 15.000 | 15.000 | 17.179 | 21.280 | 17.141 | 16.153 | 14.600 | 14.300 | 14.900 | 17.134 | 19.452 | 16.113 |
| ... | ... | ... | ... | ... | ... | ... | ... | ... | ... | ... | ... | ... |
| 16.004 | 16.246 | 18.200 | 18.163 | 18.074 | 18.292 | 18.254 | 18.208 | 18.849 | 19.068 | 17.134 | 15.738 | 17.981 |
| 16.145 | 14.973 | 15.756 | 15.210 | 14.612 | 14.398 | 14.085 | 13.657 | 13.678 | 13.293 | 16.482 | 22.394 | 14.455 |
| 14.342 | 14.559 | 16.310 | 16.277 | 16.198 | 16.392 | 16.359 | 16.317 | 16.891 | 17.088 | 15.354 | 14.104 | 16.113 |
| 18.165 | 17.145 | 17.425 | 16.306 | 17.757 | 18.659 | 18.250 | 15.925 | 15.364 | 14.885 | 17.745 | 19.705 | 16.854 |

**Table A.2** Conversion rates for individual countries or areas, expressed as the number of local currency units per United States dollar, 1970–1989 [*cont.*]

| Country or area | 1970 (1) | 1971 (2) | 1972 (3) | 1973 (4) | 1974 (5) | 1975 (6) | 1976 (7) | 1977 (8) | 1978 (9) | 1979 (10) |
|---|---|---|---|---|---|---|---|---|---|---|
| **Rwanda:** Rwanda francs | | | | | | | | | | |
| 1. MER | 100.000 | 99.710 | 92.110 | 83.920 | 92.840 | 92.840 | 92.840 | 92.840 | 92.840 | 92.840 |
| 2. PPPs | 38.560 | 35.335 | 34.822 | 37.150 | 31.308 | 48.314 | 50.348 | 52.374 | 54.943 | 55.148 |
| 3. Absolute 1970–1989 PARE | 37.940 | 43.011 | 43.817 | 48.281 | 55.420 | 60.483 | 65.514 | 72.119 | 74.306 | 80.610 |
| 4. Relative 1970–1989 PARE | 77.814 | 83.910 | 81.734 | 84.450 | 88.871 | 88.282 | 90.002 | 92.815 | 89.128 | 88.764 |
| 5. Absolute 1980–1989 PARE | 31.837 | 36.092 | 36.769 | 40.515 | 46.505 | 50.753 | 54.976 | 60.518 | 62.353 | 67.643 |
| 6. WA | 100.000 | 99.743 | 92.106 | 84.046 | 92.840 | 92.840 | 92.840 | 92.840 | 92.840 | 92.840 |
| **Saint Kitts–Nevis:** East Caribbean dollars | | | | | | | | | | |
| 1. MER | 2.000 | 1.964 | 1.922 | 1.959 | 2.053 | 2.170 | 2.615 | 2.700 | 2.700 | 2.700 |
| 2. PPPs | ... | ... | ... | ... | ... | ... | ... | ... | ... | ... |
| 3. Absolute 1970–1989 PARE | 0.875 | 1.052 | 1.077 | 1.109 | 1.515 | 1.639 | 1.754 | 1.871 | 1.992 | 2.116 |
| 4. Relative 1970–1989 PARE | 1.795 | 2.053 | 2.008 | 1.940 | 2.429 | 2.392 | 2.409 | 2.408 | 2.389 | 2.330 |
| 5. Absolute 1980–1989 PARE | 0.702 | 0.843 | 0.863 | 0.889 | 1.214 | 1.314 | 1.406 | 1.500 | 1.597 | 1.696 |
| 6. WA | 2.000 | 1.972 | 1.922 | 1.959 | 2.053 | 2.170 | 2.615 | 2.700 | 2.700 | 2.700 |
| **Saint Lucia:** East Caribbean dollars | | | | | | | | | | |
| 1. MER | 2.000 | 1.964 | 1.922 | 1.959 | 2.053 | 2.170 | 2.615 | 2.700 | 2.700 | 2.700 |
| 2. PPPs | ... | ... | ... | ... | ... | ... | ... | ... | ... | ... |
| 3. Absolute 1970–1989 PARE | 1.124 | 1.026 | 1.032 | 1.195 | 1.297 | 1.463 | 1.913 | 1.902 | 2.054 | 2.383 |
| 4. Relative 1970–1989 PARE | 2.305 | 2.001 | 1.925 | 2.091 | 2.080 | 2.135 | 2.628 | 2.448 | 2.464 | 2.624 |
| 5. Absolute 1980–1989 PARE | 0.924 | 0.843 | 0.849 | 0.983 | 1.067 | 1.203 | 1.573 | 1.564 | 1.689 | 1.959 |
| 6. WA | 2.000 | 1.975 | 1.921 | 1.959 | 2.053 | 2.170 | 2.615 | 2.700 | 2.700 | 2.700 |
| **Saint Vincent–Grenadines:** East Caribbean dollars | | | | | | | | | | |
| 1. MER | 2.000 | 1.964 | 1.922 | 1.959 | 2.053 | 2.170 | 2.615 | 2.700 | 2.700 | 2.700 |
| 2. PPPs | ... | ... | ... | ... | ... | ... | ... | ... | ... | ... |
| 3. Absolute 1970–1989 PARE | 0.742 | 0.773 | 0.822 | 1.031 | 1.294 | 1.477 | 1.629 | 1.811 | 2.082 | 2.319 |
| 4. Relative 1970–1989 PARE | 1.521 | 1.508 | 1.534 | 1.804 | 2.075 | 2.156 | 2.238 | 2.331 | 2.498 | 2.554 |
| 5. Absolute 1980–1989 PARE | 0.591 | 0.616 | 0.656 | 0.822 | 1.032 | 1.178 | 1.299 | 1.444 | 1.660 | 1.849 |
| 6. WA | 2.000 | 2.000 | 2.000 | 2.000 | 2.000 | 2.000 | 3.000 | 3.000 | 3.000 | 3.000 |
| **Samoa:** Samoan tala | | | | | | | | | | |
| 1. MER | 0.721 | 0.717 | 0.675 | 0.612 | 0.607 | 0.631 | 0.797 | 0.787 | 0.736 | 0.819 |
| 2. PPPs | ... | ... | ... | ... | ... | ... | ... | ... | ... | ... |
| 3. Absolute 1970–1989 PARE | 0.418 | 0.455 | 0.487 | 0.542 | 0.684 | 0.726 | 0.766 | 0.744 | 0.778 | 0.826 |
| 4. Relative 1970–1989 PARE | 0.858 | 0.888 | 0.908 | 0.948 | 1.097 | 1.059 | 1.053 | 0.958 | 0.933 | 0.910 |
| 5. Absolute 1980–1989 PARE | 0.390 | 0.424 | 0.454 | 0.506 | 0.638 | 0.677 | 0.715 | 0.694 | 0.725 | 0.771 |
| 6. WA | 0.721 | 0.719 | 0.675 | 0.615 | 0.607 | 0.633 | 0.795 | 0.786 | 0.736 | 0.826 |
| **Sao Tome–Principe:** Sao Tome and Principe dobras | | | | | | | | | | |
| 1. MER | 28.750 | 28.313 | 27.053 | 24.515 | 25.408 | 25.543 | 30.229 | 37.558 | 36.155 | 35.020 |
| 2. PPPs | ... | ... | ... | ... | ... | ... | ... | ... | ... | ... |
| 3. Absolute 1970–1989 PARE | 10.336 | 9.593 | 9.602 | 12.689 | 18.022 | 18.088 | 20.483 | 37.163 | 37.172 | 39.637 |
| 4. Relative 1970–1989 PARE | 21.200 | 18.715 | 17.912 | 22.194 | 28.900 | 26.401 | 28.139 | 47.827 | 44.587 | 43.647 |
| 5. Absolute 1980–1989 PARE | 7.247 | 6.726 | 6.733 | 8.897 | 12.636 | 12.682 | 14.361 | 26.056 | 26.063 | 27.791 |
| 6. WA | 28.750 | 28.312 | 27.053 | 24.515 | 25.408 | 25.543 | 30.229 | 37.558 | 36.155 | 35.025 |
| **Saudi Arabia:** Saudi Arabia riyals | | | | | | | | | | |
| 1. MER | 4.500 | 4.471 | 4.150 | 3.701 | 3.550 | 3.518 | 3.530 | 3.525 | 3.400 | 3.361 |
| 2. PPPs | 3.096 | 3.170 | 3.166 | 3.170 | 3.266 | 3.526 | 3.753 | 3.910 | 4.095 | 3.801 |
| 3. Absolute 1970–1989 PARE | 0.494 | 0.568 | 0.608 | 0.728 | 1.550 | 2.173 | 2.357 | 2.552 | 2.648 | 2.806 |
| 4. Relative 1970–1989 PARE | 1.013 | 1.109 | 1.133 | 1.274 | 2.485 | 3.171 | 3.238 | 3.284 | 3.176 | 3.090 |
| 5. Absolute 1980–1989 PARE | 0.360 | 0.414 | 0.442 | 0.530 | 1.128 | 1.582 | 1.717 | 1.859 | 1.928 | 2.043 |
| 6. WA | 4.500 | 4.487 | 4.145 | 3.707 | 3.550 | 3.518 | 3.530 | 3.525 | 3.400 | 3.361 |

| 1980 (11) | 1981 (12) | 1982 (13) | 1983 (14) | 1984 (15) | 1985 (16) | 1986 (17) | 1987 (18) | 1988 (19) | 1989 (20) | Averages 1970−89 (21) | 1970−79 (22) | 1980−89 (23) |
|---|---|---|---|---|---|---|---|---|---|---|---|---|
| 92.840 | 92.840 | 92.840 | 94.340 | 100.170 | 101.260 | 87.640 | 79.700 | 76.400 | 80.000 | 89.497 | 92.819 | 88.438 |
| 55.416 | 54.230 | 57.112 | 59.368 | 56.696 | 60.776 | 55.397 | 54.617 | 53.106 | 52.175 | 52.836 | 45.750 | 55.726 |
| 85.384 | 89.694 | 94.748 | 97.070 | 113.433 | 118.609 | 110.283 | 111.856 | 112.411 | 114.970 | 89.497 | 61.708 | 105.391 |
| 86.136 | 82.664 | 82.023 | 81.286 | 91.703 | 93.359 | 85.095 | 83.898 | 81.576 | 80.147 | 85.479 | 88.022 | 84.660 |
| 71.649 | 75.266 | 79.507 | 81.456 | 95.186 | 99.529 | 92.543 | 93.862 | 94.328 | 96.476 | 75.101 | 51.781 | 88.438 |
| 92.840 | 92.840 | 92.840 | 94.342 | 100.172 | 101.262 | 87.640 | 79.673 | 76.445 | 79.977 | 89.500 | 92.829 | 88.438 |
|  |  |  |  |  |  |  |  |  |  |  |  |  |
| 2.700 | 2.700 | 2.700 | 2.700 | 2.700 | 2.700 | 2.700 | 2.700 | 2.700 | 2.700 | 2.601 | 2.342 | 2.700 |
| ... | ... | ... | ... | ... | ... | ... | ... | ... | ... | ... | ... | ... |
| 2.428 | 2.707 | 2.896 | 2.820 | 2.930 | 3.219 | 3.836 | 4.066 | 4.088 | 4.288 | 2.601 | 1.539 | 3.369 |
| 2.450 | 2.495 | 2.507 | 2.361 | 2.369 | 2.534 | 2.960 | 3.050 | 2.967 | 2.989 | 2.580 | 2.264 | 2.705 |
| 1.946 | 2.169 | 2.322 | 2.260 | 2.349 | 2.581 | 3.075 | 3.259 | 3.277 | 3.437 | 2.085 | 1.233 | 2.700 |
| 2.700 | 2.700 | 2.700 | 2.700 | 2.700 | 2.700 | 2.700 | 2.700 | 2.700 | 2.700 | 2.602 | 2.343 | 2.700 |
|  |  |  |  |  |  |  |  |  |  |  |  |  |
| 2.700 | 2.700 | 2.700 | 2.700 | 2.700 | 2.700 | 2.700 | 2.700 | 2.700 | 2.700 | 2.609 | 2.363 | 2.700 |
| ... | ... | ... | ... | ... | ... | ... | ... | ... | ... | ... | ... | ... |
| 2.666 | 2.957 | 3.051 | 3.134 | 3.146 | 3.289 | 3.434 | 3.557 | 3.597 | 3.652 | 2.609 | 1.593 | 3.283 |
| 2.689 | 2.725 | 2.641 | 2.625 | 2.543 | 2.589 | 2.649 | 2.668 | 2.611 | 2.546 | 2.544 | 2.330 | 2.622 |
| 2.192 | 2.432 | 2.509 | 2.577 | 2.587 | 2.704 | 2.824 | 2.925 | 2.958 | 3.003 | 2.146 | 1.310 | 2.700 |
| 2.700 | 2.700 | 2.700 | 2.700 | 2.700 | 2.700 | 2.700 | 2.700 | 2.700 | 2.700 | 2.609 | 2.363 | 2.700 |
|  |  |  |  |  |  |  |  |  |  |  |  |  |
| 2.700 | 2.700 | 2.700 | 2.700 | 2.700 | 2.700 | 2.700 | 2.700 | 2.700 | 2.700 | 2.620 | 2.355 | 2.700 |
| ... | ... | ... | ... | ... | ... | ... | ... | ... | ... | ... | ... | ... |
| 2.489 | 2.854 | 3.066 | 3.226 | 3.319 | 3.405 | 3.609 | 3.657 | 3.715 | 3.846 | 2.620 | 1.409 | 3.386 |
| 2.511 | 2.630 | 2.654 | 2.701 | 2.683 | 2.680 | 2.785 | 2.743 | 2.696 | 2.681 | 2.541 | 2.104 | 2.688 |
| 1.985 | 2.276 | 2.445 | 2.572 | 2.646 | 2.716 | 2.878 | 2.916 | 2.963 | 3.067 | 2.089 | 1.124 | 2.700 |
| 3.000 | 3.000 | 3.000 | 3.000 | 3.000 | 3.000 | 3.000 | 3.000 | 3.000 | 3.000 | 2.873 | 2.475 | 3.000 |
|  |  |  |  |  |  |  |  |  |  |  |  |  |
| 0.919 | 1.036 | 1.205 | 1.539 | 1.838 | 2.244 | 2.235 | 2.100 | 2.100 | 2.300 | 1.289 | 0.712 | 1.730 |
| ... | ... | ... | ... | ... | ... | ... | ... | ... | ... | ... | ... | ... |
| 1.032 | 1.195 | 1.447 | 1.713 | 1.989 | 1.973 | 2.062 | 2.145 | 2.424 | 2.499 | 1.289 | 0.655 | 1.855 |
| 1.041 | 1.102 | 1.252 | 1.434 | 1.608 | 1.553 | 1.591 | 1.609 | 1.759 | 1.742 | 1.322 | 0.965 | 1.497 |
| 0.962 | 1.115 | 1.350 | 1.598 | 1.855 | 1.840 | 1.924 | 2.001 | 2.262 | 2.332 | 1.203 | 0.611 | 1.730 |
| 0.919 | 1.034 | 1.207 | 1.549 | 1.862 | 2.245 | 2.236 | 2.122 | 2.080 | 2.270 | 1.291 | 0.713 | 1.731 |
|  |  |  |  |  |  |  |  |  |  |  |  |  |
| 34.771 | 38.400 | 40.999 | 42.335 | 44.159 | 44.604 | 38.589 | 54.200 | 86.300 | 124.700 | 46.611 | 31.071 | 55.580 |
| ... | ... | ... | ... | ... | ... | ... | ... | ... | ... | ... | ... | ... |
| 42.418 | 42.539 | 44.396 | 50.868 | 56.035 | 60.529 | 87.292 | 101.432 | 139.550 | 181.447 | 46.611 | 20.470 | 79.270 |
| 42.792 | 39.205 | 38.433 | 42.597 | 45.301 | 47.643 | 67.355 | 76.080 | 101.271 | 126.488 | 51.224 | 31.239 | 64.546 |
| 29.741 | 29.826 | 31.128 | 35.666 | 39.289 | 42.440 | 61.204 | 71.118 | 97.845 | 127.220 | 32.681 | 14.353 | 55.580 |
| 34.771 | 38.400 | 40.999 | 42.335 | 44.159 | 44.604 | 38.589 | 54.211 | 86.343 | 124.672 | 46.614 | 31.072 | 55.583 |
|  |  |  |  |  |  |  |  |  |  |  |  |  |
| 3.327 | 3.383 | 3.427 | 3.455 | 3.524 | 3.622 | 3.703 | 3.700 | 3.700 | 3.700 | 3.518 | 3.510 | 3.520 |
| 3.765 | 3.673 | 3.625 | 3.926 | 3.831 | 3.725 | 3.473 | 2.787 | 2.725 | 2.647 | 3.499 | 3.709 | 3.438 |
| 3.993 | 4.800 | 5.637 | 5.826 | 4.996 | 5.281 | 5.023 | 4.147 | 4.190 | 4.237 | 3.518 | 1.892 | 4.834 |
| 4.028 | 4.424 | 4.880 | 4.878 | 4.039 | 4.156 | 3.876 | 3.110 | 3.040 | 2.954 | 3.564 | 2.688 | 3.974 |
| 2.908 | 3.495 | 4.105 | 4.242 | 3.638 | 3.846 | 3.658 | 3.020 | 3.051 | 3.086 | 2.562 | 1.378 | 3.520 |
| 3.327 | 3.383 | 3.428 | 3.455 | 3.524 | 3.622 | 3.703 | 3.745 | 3.745 | 3.745 | 3.524 | 3.510 | 3.529 |

**Table A.2**  Conversion rates for individual countries or areas, expressed as the number of local currency units per United States dollar, 1970−1989 [*cont.*]

| Country or area | 1970 (1) | 1971 (2) | 1972 (3) | 1973 (4) | 1974 (5) | 1975 (6) | 1976 (7) | 1977 (8) | 1978 (9) | 1979 (10) |
|---|---|---|---|---|---|---|---|---|---|---|
| **Senegal:** CFA francs | | | | | | | | | | |
| 1. MER | 277.710 | 275.520 | 252.210 | 222.700 | 240.500 | 214.320 | 238.980 | 245.670 | 225.660 | 212.720 |
| 2. PPPs | 139.267 | 134.957 | 142.499 | 144.654 | 151.975 | 155.611 | 154.541 | 151.071 | 150.181 | 148.874 |
| 3. Absolute 1970−1989 PARE | 119.002 | 122.672 | 127.620 | 137.445 | 160.639 | 179.178 | 185.918 | 201.178 | 219.503 | 235.497 |
| 4. Relative 1970−1989 PARE | 244.072 | 239.322 | 238.052 | 240.412 | 257.601 | 261.533 | 255.409 | 258.910 | 263.287 | 259.318 |
| 5. Absolute 1980−1989 PARE | 98.034 | 101.057 | 105.133 | 113.228 | 132.335 | 147.607 | 153.159 | 165.731 | 180.827 | 194.003 |
| 6. WA | 277.710 | 277.132 | 252.484 | 222.888 | 240.704 | 214.312 | 238.950 | 245.679 | 225.655 | 212.721 |
| **Seychelles:** Seychelles rupees | | | | | | | | | | |
| 1. MER | 5.556 | 5.479 | 5.339 | 5.442 | 5.703 | 6.027 | 7.419 | 7.643 | 6.953 | 6.333 |
| 2. PPPs | ... | ... | ... | ... | ... | ... | ... | ... | ... | ... |
| 3. Absolute 1970−1989 PARE | 6.875 | 7.795 | 9.135 | 10.296 | 12.004 | 13.728 | 2.771 | 3.471 | 3.915 | 4.555 |
| 4. Relative 1970−1989 PARE | 14.101 | 15.208 | 17.041 | 18.009 | 19.249 | 20.038 | 3.806 | 4.467 | 4.696 | 5.016 |
| 5. Absolute 1980−1989 PARE | 6.221 | 7.053 | 8.266 | 9.316 | 10.861 | 12.422 | 2.507 | 3.141 | 3.543 | 4.121 |
| 6. WA | 5.556 | 5.479 | 5.339 | 5.442 | 5.703 | 6.027 | 7.419 | 7.643 | 6.952 | 6.333 |
| **Sierra Leone:** Sierra Leone leones | | | | | | | | | | |
| 1. MER | 0.833 | 0.818 | 0.799 | 0.816 | 0.855 | 0.900 | 1.107 | 1.146 | 1.046 | 1.057 |
| 2. PPPs | 0.442 | 0.436 | 0.440 | 0.485 | 0.556 | 0.569 | 0.624 | 0.673 | 0.680 | 0.745 |
| 3. Absolute 1970−1989 PARE | 0.515 | 0.505 | 0.521 | 0.559 | 0.653 | 0.759 | 0.839 | 1.003 | 1.142 | 1.287 |
| 4. Relative 1970−1989 PARE | 1.057 | 0.985 | 0.972 | 0.977 | 1.046 | 1.108 | 1.153 | 1.291 | 1.370 | 1.418 |
| 5. Absolute 1980−1989 PARE | 0.448 | 0.440 | 0.453 | 0.486 | 0.568 | 0.661 | 0.730 | 0.873 | 0.994 | 1.120 |
| 6. WA | 0.833 | 0.833 | 0.798 | 0.820 | 0.840 | 0.852 | 1.007 | 1.169 | 1.096 | 1.048 |
| **Singapore:** Singapore dollars | | | | | | | | | | |
| 1. MER | 3.061 | 3.027 | 2.809 | 2.444 | 2.437 | 2.371 | 2.471 | 2.439 | 2.274 | 2.175 |
| 2. PPPs | 1.798 | 1.766 | 1.810 | 1.990 | 2.058 | 1.954 | 1.886 | 1.837 | 1.749 | 1.717 |
| 3. Absolute 1970−1989 PARE | 1.172 | 1.227 | 1.297 | 1.459 | 1.681 | 1.723 | 1.752 | 1.780 | 1.822 | 1.919 |
| 4. Relative 1970−1989 PARE | 2.404 | 2.394 | 2.420 | 2.553 | 2.695 | 2.515 | 2.407 | 2.291 | 2.186 | 2.113 |
| 5. Absolute 1980−1989 PARE | 1.013 | 1.061 | 1.121 | 1.261 | 1.452 | 1.489 | 1.514 | 1.539 | 1.575 | 1.658 |
| 6. WA | 3.061 | 3.051 | 2.813 | 2.457 | 2.437 | 2.371 | 2.471 | 2.439 | 2.274 | 2.175 |
| **Solomon Islands:** Solomon Islands dollars | | | | | | | | | | |
| 1. MER | 0.893 | 0.882 | 0.839 | 0.704 | 0.696 | 0.764 | 0.818 | 0.902 | 0.874 | 0.866 |
| 2. PPPs | ... | ... | ... | ... | ... | ... | ... | ... | ... | ... |
| 3. Absolute 1970−1989 PARE | 0.545 | 0.535 | 0.477 | 0.492 | 0.585 | 0.644 | 0.671 | 0.729 | 0.776 | 0.837 |
| 4. Relative 1970−1989 PARE | 1.118 | 1.044 | 0.889 | 0.861 | 0.938 | 0.941 | 0.922 | 0.938 | 0.931 | 0.922 |
| 5. Absolute 1980−1989 PARE | 0.487 | 0.478 | 0.426 | 0.440 | 0.523 | 0.576 | 0.600 | 0.651 | 0.693 | 0.748 |
| 6. WA | 0.893 | 0.881 | 0.837 | 0.704 | 0.698 | 0.763 | 0.818 | 0.902 | 0.874 | 0.866 |
| **Somalia:** Somali shillings | | | | | | | | | | |
| 1. MER | 7.143 | 7.128 | 6.979 | 6.282 | 6.295 | 6.295 | 6.295 | 6.295 | 6.295 | 6.295 |
| 2. PPPs | 2.265 | 2.139 | 2.116 | 2.065 | 2.184 | 2.518 | 2.517 | 2.879 | 2.891 | 2.690 |
| 3. Absolute 1970−1989 PARE | 2.185 | 2.185 | 2.403 | 2.659 | 3.130 | 3.609 | 4.232 | 4.671 | 5.173 | 6.490 |
| 4. Relative 1970−1989 PARE | 4.481 | 4.263 | 4.483 | 4.651 | 5.020 | 5.267 | 5.814 | 6.011 | 6.205 | 7.147 |
| 5. Absolute 1980−1989 PARE | 1.679 | 1.679 | 1.847 | 2.044 | 2.406 | 2.774 | 3.253 | 3.590 | 3.976 | 4.988 |
| 6. WA | 7.143 | 7.129 | 6.980 | 6.281 | 6.295 | 6.295 | 6.295 | 6.295 | 6.295 | 6.295 |
| **South Africa:** South African rand | | | | | | | | | | |
| 1. MER | 0.714 | 0.713 | 0.772 | 0.692 | 0.679 | 0.732 | 0.870 | 0.870 | 0.870 | 0.842 |
| 2. PPPs | 0.331 | 0.330 | 0.352 | 0.377 | 0.376 | 0.384 | 0.411 | 0.444 | 0.464 | 0.478 |
| 3. Absolute 1970−1989 PARE | 0.302 | 0.316 | 0.351 | 0.418 | 0.479 | 0.525 | 0.582 | 0.647 | 0.720 | 0.829 |
| 4. Relative 1970−1989 PARE | 0.619 | 0.617 | 0.655 | 0.730 | 0.768 | 0.767 | 0.800 | 0.833 | 0.864 | 0.913 |
| 5. Absolute 1980−1989 PARE | 0.240 | 0.252 | 0.279 | 0.332 | 0.381 | 0.418 | 0.463 | 0.514 | 0.572 | 0.659 |
| 6. WA | 0.714 | 0.715 | 0.769 | 0.694 | 0.679 | 0.740 | 0.870 | 0.870 | 0.870 | 0.842 |

|  |  |  |  |  |  |  |  |  |  | Averages | | |
| 1980 (11) | 1981 (12) | 1982 (13) | 1983 (14) | 1984 (15) | 1985 (16) | 1986 (17) | 1987 (18) | 1988 (19) | 1989 (20) | 1970−89 (21) | 1970−79 (22) | 1980−89 (23) |
|---|---|---|---|---|---|---|---|---|---|---|---|---|
| 211.280 | 271.730 | 328.610 | 381.060 | 436.960 | 449.260 | 346.300 | 300.500 | 297.900 | 319.000 | 296.715 | 234.528 | 326.544 |
| 151.615 | 145.700 | 154.279 | 157.631 | 169.497 | 180.647 | 192.068 | 190.358 | 199.104 | 195.638 | 168.840 | 148.494 | 177.204 |
| 262.615 | 282.493 | 309.108 | 330.145 | 380.086 | 415.410 | 450.548 | 459.368 | 496.603 | 507.967 | 296.715 | 171.521 | 396.386 |
| 264.931 | 260.350 | 267.594 | 276.462 | 307.276 | 326.975 | 347.646 | 344.552 | 360.381 | 354.108 | 298.391 | 253.903 | 317.559 |
| 216.343 | 232.718 | 254.644 | 271.974 | 313.116 | 342.215 | 371.162 | 378.428 | 409.102 | 418.464 | 244.435 | 141.299 | 326.544 |
| 211.279 | 271.730 | 328.605 | 381.065 | 436.955 | 449.261 | 346.305 | 300.535 | 297.847 | 319.007 | 296.763 | 234.649 | 326.541 |
|  |  |  |  |  |  |  |  |  |  |  |  |  |
| 6.392 | 6.315 | 6.553 | 6.768 | 7.059 | 7.134 | 6.177 | 5.600 | 5.400 | 5.600 | 6.213 | 6.419 | 6.156 |
| ... | ... | ... | ... | ... | ... | ... | ... | ... | ... | ... | ... | ... |
| 5.461 | 6.043 | 6.235 | 6.589 | 6.478 | 6.603 | 7.025 | 7.341 | 7.790 | 7.915 | 6.213 | 4.761 | 6.804 |
| 5.509 | 5.569 | 5.398 | 5.518 | 5.237 | 5.197 | 5.420 | 5.506 | 5.653 | 5.517 | 5.588 | 6.104 | 5.456 |
| 4.941 | 5.467 | 5.642 | 5.962 | 5.861 | 5.974 | 6.356 | 6.642 | 7.049 | 7.161 | 5.621 | 4.308 | 6.156 |
| 6.392 | 6.315 | 6.553 | 6.768 | 7.059 | 7.134 | 6.177 | 5.600 | 5.384 | 5.646 | 6.216 | 6.419 | 6.161 |
|  |  |  |  |  |  |  |  |  |  |  |  |  |
| 1.050 | 1.158 | 1.238 | 1.678 | 2.510 | 4.730 | 8.396 | 30.800 | 31.300 | 58.100 | 7.704 | 0.963 | 11.715 |
| 0.766 | 0.858 | 1.055 | 1.490 | 1.807 | 2.462 | 3.919 | 9.529 | 14.339 | 22.143 | 4.525 | 0.586 | 6.744 |
| 1.403 | 1.500 | 1.832 | 2.160 | 3.290 | 5.279 | 8.573 | 21.441 | 33.347 | 53.608 | 7.704 | 0.790 | 13.461 |
| 1.416 | 1.382 | 1.586 | 1.809 | 2.660 | 4.155 | 6.615 | 16.082 | 24.200 | 37.371 | 7.843 | 1.175 | 10.856 |
| 1.221 | 1.305 | 1.594 | 1.880 | 2.864 | 4.594 | 7.461 | 18.660 | 29.023 | 46.656 | 6.705 | 0.688 | 11.715 |
| 1.050 | 1.088 | 1.202 | 1.263 | 2.510 | 3.639 | 5.228 | 35.581 | 25.517 | 46.261 | 6.960 | 0.955 | 10.051 |
|  |  |  |  |  |  |  |  |  |  |  |  |  |
| 2.141 | 2.113 | 2.140 | 2.113 | 2.133 | 2.200 | 2.177 | 2.100 | 2.000 | 2.000 | 2.173 | 2.432 | 2.100 |
| 1.730 | 1.738 | 1.606 | 1.684 | 1.815 | 1.678 | 1.604 | 1.570 | 1.584 | 1.560 | 1.688 | 1.844 | 1.643 |
| 2.139 | 2.282 | 2.377 | 2.471 | 2.487 | 2.458 | 2.396 | 2.414 | 2.516 | 2.580 | 2.173 | 1.638 | 2.430 |
| 2.158 | 2.103 | 2.058 | 2.069 | 2.011 | 1.934 | 1.849 | 1.810 | 1.826 | 1.799 | 2.018 | 2.352 | 1.930 |
| 1.848 | 1.972 | 2.055 | 2.135 | 2.150 | 2.124 | 2.071 | 2.086 | 2.174 | 2.230 | 1.878 | 1.416 | 2.100 |
| 2.141 | 2.113 | 2.140 | 2.113 | 2.133 | 2.200 | 2.177 | 2.106 | 2.012 | 1.950 | 2.169 | 2.434 | 2.095 |
|  |  |  |  |  |  |  |  |  |  |  |  |  |
| 0.830 | 0.870 | 0.971 | 1.149 | 1.274 | 1.481 | 1.740 | 2.000 | 2.100 | 2.300 | 1.293 | 0.826 | 1.491 |
| ... | ... | ... | ... | ... | ... | ... | ... | ... | ... | ... | ... | ... |
| 0.947 | 1.045 | 1.191 | 1.266 | 1.483 | 1.533 | 1.668 | 2.064 | 2.409 | 2.768 | 1.293 | 0.659 | 1.669 |
| 0.955 | 0.963 | 1.031 | 1.060 | 1.199 | 1.207 | 1.287 | 1.548 | 1.748 | 1.930 | 1.239 | 0.937 | 1.340 |
| 0.846 | 0.933 | 1.064 | 1.131 | 1.325 | 1.369 | 1.490 | 1.844 | 2.152 | 2.473 | 1.155 | 0.589 | 1.491 |
| 0.830 | 0.870 | 0.971 | 1.149 | 1.274 | 1.480 | 1.742 | 2.003 | 2.083 | 2.293 | 1.292 | 0.826 | 1.489 |
|  |  |  |  |  |  |  |  |  |  |  |  |  |
| 6.295 | 6.295 | 10.750 | 15.788 | 20.019 | 39.487 | 72.000 | 105.200 | 170.500 | 490.700 | 49.314 | 6.410 | 63.742 |
| 4.452 | 5.625 | 5.865 | 7.484 | 16.237 | 22.519 | 29.647 | 38.113 | 61.942 | 125.135 | 23.884 | 2.516 | 33.504 |
| 12.814 | 13.573 | 17.116 | 23.100 | 37.386 | 48.570 | 65.229 | 86.264 | 144.905 | 304.738 | 49.314 | 3.797 | 82.932 |
| 12.927 | 12.509 | 14.818 | 19.344 | 30.225 | 38.230 | 50.331 | 64.703 | 105.156 | 212.436 | 48.903 | 5.590 | 66.265 |
| 9.849 | 10.433 | 13.156 | 17.755 | 28.735 | 37.331 | 50.135 | 66.303 | 111.374 | 234.223 | 37.903 | 2.919 | 63.742 |
| 6.295 | 6.295 | 10.750 | 15.788 | 20.018 | 39.487 | 72.000 | 105.177 | 170.453 | 490.675 | 49.313 | 6.410 | 63.739 |
|  |  |  |  |  |  |  |  |  |  |  |  |  |
| 0.778 | 0.870 | 1.082 | 1.112 | 1.438 | 2.191 | 2.269 | 2.000 | 2.300 | 2.600 | 1.401 | 0.791 | 1.657 |
| 0.511 | 0.513 | 0.555 | 0.631 | 0.689 | 0.802 | 0.908 | 1.000 | 1.119 | 1.236 | 0.705 | 0.408 | 0.824 |
| 1.063 | 1.189 | 1.353 | 1.565 | 1.745 | 2.028 | 2.341 | 2.654 | 3.070 | 3.529 | 1.401 | 0.531 | 2.084 |
| 1.072 | 1.096 | 1.171 | 1.311 | 1.410 | 1.596 | 1.806 | 1.990 | 2.228 | 2.460 | 1.410 | 0.783 | 1.678 |
| 0.845 | 0.945 | 1.075 | 1.244 | 1.387 | 1.612 | 1.861 | 2.109 | 2.440 | 2.805 | 1.114 | 0.422 | 1.657 |
| 0.779 | 0.878 | 1.086 | 1.114 | 1.475 | 2.229 | 2.285 | 2.036 | 2.273 | 2.623 | 1.409 | 0.792 | 1.669 |

| 1980 | 1981 | 1982 | 1983 | 1984 | 1985 | 1986 | 1987 | 1988 | 1989 | Averages | | |
|------|------|------|------|------|------|------|------|------|------|----------|---|---|
| | | | | | | | | | | 1970–89 | 1970–79 | 1980–89 |
| (11) | (12) | (13) | (14) | (15) | (16) | (17) | (18) | (19) | (20) | (21) | (22) | (23) |
| 1.169 | 1.199 | 1.234 | 1.232 | 1.295 | 1.366 | 1.390 | 1.300 | 1.200 | 1.200 | 1.196 | 1.052 | 1.258 |
| 1.112 | 1.148 | 1.199 | 1.229 | 1.231 | 1.265 | 1.269 | 1.293 | 1.311 | 1.320 | 1.191 | 1.054 | 1.248 |
| 1.140 | 1.262 | 1.372 | 1.438 | 1.483 | 1.522 | 1.559 | 1.634 | 1.712 | 1.795 | 1.196 | 0.758 | 1.510 |
| 1.150 | 1.163 | 1.188 | 1.204 | 1.199 | 1.198 | 1.203 | 1.225 | 1.242 | 1.251 | 1.180 | 1.107 | 1.208 |
| 0.949 | 1.052 | 1.143 | 1.198 | 1.236 | 1.268 | 1.298 | 1.361 | 1.426 | 1.495 | 0.996 | 0.631 | 1.258 |
| 1.169 | 1.199 | 1.234 | 1.232 | 1.295 | 1.365 | 1.390 | 1.326 | 1.231 | 1.184 | 1.199 | 1.053 | 1.262 |
| | | | | | | | | | | | | |
| 40.175 | 48.695 | 56.293 | 71.686 | 84.878 | 91.632 | 80.140 | 72.500 | 72.100 | 78.000 | 58.716 | 30.806 | 70.771 |
| ... | ... | ... | ... | ... | ... | ... | ... | ... | ... | ... | ... | ... |
| 49.168 | 53.888 | 63.255 | 69.950 | 76.079 | 78.884 | 92.844 | 99.255 | 103.281 | 113.854 | 58.716 | 22.759 | 83.525 |
| 49.601 | 49.665 | 54.760 | 58.576 | 61.505 | 62.091 | 71.639 | 74.447 | 74.950 | 79.368 | 57.732 | 34.140 | 66.352 |
| 41.660 | 45.660 | 53.596 | 59.269 | 64.461 | 66.838 | 78.667 | 84.098 | 87.510 | 96.468 | 49.750 | 19.283 | 70.771 |
| 40.175 | 48.695 | 58.293 | 71.686 | 84.878 | 91.632 | 80.145 | 72.466 | 72.067 | 77.978 | 58.821 | 30.806 | 70.952 |
| | | | | | | | | | | | | |
| 211.280 | 271.730 | 328.610 | 381.060 | 436.960 | 449.260 | 346.300 | 300.500 | 297.800 | 319.000 | 299.131 | 233.839 | 328.232 |
| 151.375 | 153.719 | 163.191 | 174.758 | 196.763 | 202.616 | 205.706 | 193.664 | 190.116 | 186.274 | 166.002 | 127.402 | 183.672 |
| 279.709 | 320.793 | 388.765 | 425.110 | 433.902 | 472.603 | 489.453 | 474.040 | 480.979 | 490.582 | 299.131 | 152.963 | 429.432 |
| 282.175 | 295.648 | 336.554 | 355.985 | 350.782 | 371.993 | 377.666 | 355.557 | 349.043 | 341.990 | 306.534 | 227.038 | 344.879 |
| 213.792 | 245.195 | 297.149 | 324.928 | 331.648 | 361.229 | 374.108 | 362.328 | 367.631 | 374.971 | 228.637 | 116.916 | 328.232 |
| 211.279 | 271.730 | 328.605 | 381.065 | 436.955 | 449.261 | 346.305 | 300.535 | 297.847 | 319.007 | 299.182 | 233.947 | 328.245 |
| | | | | | | | | | | | | |
| 211.280 | 271.730 | 328.610 | 381.060 | 436.960 | 449.260 | 346.300 | 300.500 | 297.800 | 319.000 | 285.969 | 235.123 | 324.749 |
| 134.353 | 136.712 | 146.720 | 155.757 | 153.635 | 139.450 | 104.918 | 92.759 | 105.484 | 103.647 | 119.380 | 114.654 | 122.161 |
| 298.090 | 336.929 | 374.110 | 442.511 | 473.167 | 567.643 | 435.658 | 396.236 | 465.723 | 476.376 | 285.969 | 180.175 | 423.183 |
| 300.718 | 310.519 | 323.867 | 370.557 | 382.526 | 446.799 | 336.157 | 297.199 | 337.972 | 332.086 | 311.913 | 268.528 | 342.468 |
| 228.754 | 258.559 | 287.092 | 339.582 | 363.107 | 435.608 | 334.323 | 304.071 | 357.395 | 365.570 | 219.452 | 138.266 | 324.749 |
| 211.279 | 271.730 | 328.605 | 381.065 | 436.955 | 449.261 | 346.305 | 300.535 | 297.847 | 319.007 | 286.044 | 235.254 | 324.761 |
| | | | | | | | | | | | | |
| 39.000 | 39.000 | 50.910 | 78.840 | 98.660 | 161.080 | 193.020 | 219.500 | 245.000 | 267.200 | 99.051 | 19.228 | 131.155 |
| 22.673 | 23.888 | 27.745 | 34.571 | 39.127 | 52.850 | 61.773 | 72.775 | 85.313 | 93.352 | 39.768 | 7.044 | 54.771 |
| 63.534 | 71.281 | 80.752 | 102.241 | 116.864 | 155.234 | 185.088 | 224.317 | 271.794 | 309.598 | 99.051 | 12.641 | 165.924 |
| 64.094 | 65.694 | 69.907 | 85.617 | 94.477 | 122.186 | 142.815 | 168.250 | 197.239 | 215.824 | 99.559 | 18.884 | 133.081 |
| 50.220 | 56.344 | 63.831 | 80.817 | 92.375 | 122.704 | 146.303 | 177.311 | 214.840 | 244.722 | 78.295 | 9.992 | 131.155 |
| 39.000 | 39.000 | 50.909 | 78.842 | 98.656 | 161.080 | 193.020 | 219.540 | 245.050 | 267.160 | 90.685 | 14.548 | 131.157 |
| | | | | | | | | | | | | |
| 1.498 | 1.705 | 1.893 | 1.976 | 2.320 | 2.937 | 3.453 | 3.700 | 3.700 | 3.800 | 2.495 | 1.915 | 2.776 |
| ... | ... | ... | ... | ... | ... | ... | ... | ... | ... | ... | ... | ... |
| 2.190 | 2.231 | 2.237 | 2.274 | 2.399 | 2.610 | 2.746 | 2.901 | 3.228 | 3.508 | 2.495 | 1.957 | 2.748 |
| 2.209 | 2.056 | 1.936 | 1.904 | 1.939 | 2.054 | 2.119 | 2.176 | 2.343 | 2.445 | 2.301 | 2.850 | 2.162 |
| 2.213 | 2.254 | 2.260 | 2.297 | 2.424 | 2.637 | 2.774 | 2.931 | 3.262 | 3.544 | 2.521 | 1.977 | 2.776 |
| 1.498 | 1.705 | 1.893 | 1.976 | 2.320 | 2.937 | 3.453 | 3.722 | 3.722 | 3.765 | 2.495 | 1.915 | 2.776 |
| | | | | | | | | | | | | |
| 47.280 | 54.490 | 64.090 | 78.850 | 100.820 | 142.310 | 194.260 | 242.600 | 299.200 | 382.600 | 126.103 | 32.914 | 162.773 |
| 23.895 | 27.082 | 31.019 | 35.938 | 43.009 | 53.210 | 67.377 | 80.806 | 99.370 | 119.741 | 50.858 | 14.165 | 64.061 |
| 58.120 | 71.352 | 89.023 | 107.186 | 130.960 | 163.548 | 211.253 | 260.637 | 331.277 | 415.557 | 126.103 | 23.141 | 195.217 |
| 58.633 | 65.759 | 77.067 | 89.757 | 105.873 | 128.731 | 163.004 | 195.492 | 240.405 | 289.689 | 123.207 | 33.695 | 156.230 |
| 48.461 | 59.493 | 74.228 | 89.372 | 109.195 | 136.367 | 176.143 | 217.320 | 276.220 | 346.493 | 105.145 | 19.295 | 162.773 |
| 47.280 | 54.490 | 64.085 | 78.854 | 100.820 | 142.310 | 194.260 | 242.610 | 299.170 | 382.570 | 126.160 | 32.968 | 162.770 |

**Table A.2**   Conversion rates for individual countries or areas, expressed as the number of
local currency units per United States dollar, 1970−1989 [*cont.*]

| Country or area | 1970 (1) | 1971 (2) | 1972 (3) | 1973 (4) | 1974 (5) | 1975 (6) | 1976 (7) | 1977 (8) | 1978 (9) | 1979 (10) |
|---|---|---|---|---|---|---|---|---|---|---|
| **Spain:** Spanish pesetas | | | | | | | | | | |
| 1.  MER | 70.000 | 69.282 | 64.273 | 58.260 | 57.687 | 57.407 | 66.903 | 75.962 | 76.668 | 67.125 |
| 2.  PPPs | 33.733 | 34.771 | 36.327 | 38.762 | 41.552 | 44.322 | 49.031 | 57.201 | 63.922 | 68.121 |
| 3.  Absolute 1970−1989 PARE | 22.429 | 24.206 | 26.293 | 29.438 | 34.229 | 39.963 | 46.564 | 57.354 | 69.173 | 81.012 |
| 4.  Relative 1970−1989 PARE | 46.001 | 47.223 | 49.045 | 51.490 | 54.889 | 58.331 | 63.969 | 73.813 | 82.971 | 89.207 |
| 5.  Absolute 1980−1989 PARE | 17.679 | 19.079 | 20.724 | 23.203 | 26.979 | 31.499 | 36.702 | 45.207 | 54.523 | 63.854 |
| 6.  WA | 70.000 | 69.469 | 64.271 | 58.260 | 57.686 | 57.407 | 66.903 | 75.962 | 76.668 | 67.125 |
| **Sri Lanka:** Sri Lanka rupees | | | | | | | | | | |
| 1.  MER | 5.952 | 5.935 | 5.970 | 6.403 | 6.651 | 7.007 | 8.412 | 8.873 | 15.611 | 15.572 |
| 2.  PPPs | 2.122 | 2.094 | 2.196 | 2.489 | 2.861 | 3.025 | 2.990 | 3.181 | 3.051 | 3.515 |
| 3.  Absolute 1970−1989 PARE | 4.887 | 4.961 | 5.404 | 6.091 | 7.576 | 7.987 | 8.759 | 10.055 | 11.301 | 13.130 |
| 4.  Relative 1970−1989 PARE | 10.023 | 9.679 | 10.080 | 10.654 | 12.148 | 11.658 | 12.033 | 12.940 | 13.555 | 14.459 |
| 5.  Absolute 1980−1989 PARE | 4.746 | 4.819 | 5.248 | 5.916 | 7.358 | 7.757 | 8.507 | 9.765 | 10.976 | 12.752 |
| 6.  WA | 5.952 | 5.935 | 5.970 | 6.403 | 6.651 | 7.007 | 8.412 | 8.873 | 15.611 | 15.572 |
| **Sudan:** Sudanese pounds | | | | | | | | | | |
| 1.  MER | 0.348 | 0.348 | 0.348 | 0.348 | 0.348 | 0.348 | 0.348 | 0.348 | 0.376 | 0.425 |
| 2.  PPPs | 0.157 | 0.152 | 0.184 | 0.248 | 0.240 | 0.250 | 0.240 | 0.239 | 0.266 | 0.296 |
| 3.  Absolute 1970−1989 PARE | 0.151 | 0.151 | 0.153 | 0.171 | 0.240 | 0.277 | 0.325 | 0.403 | 0.461 | 0.494 |
| 4.  Relative 1970−1989 PARE | 0.310 | 0.295 | 0.286 | 0.299 | 0.385 | 0.404 | 0.446 | 0.519 | 0.553 | 0.543 |
| 5.  Absolute 1980−1989 PARE | 0.129 | 0.129 | 0.131 | 0.146 | 0.205 | 0.236 | 0.277 | 0.344 | 0.394 | 0.421 |
| 6.  WA | 0.303 | 0.303 | 0.307 | 0.342 | 0.480 | 0.554 | 0.649 | 0.806 | 0.923 | 0.987 |
| **Suriname:** Suriname guilders | | | | | | | | | | |
| 1.  MER | 1.886 | 1.884 | 1.785 | 1.785 | 1.785 | 1.785 | 1.785 | 1.785 | 1.785 | 1.785 |
| 2.  PPPs | 1.140 | 1.093 | 1.097 | 1.168 | 1.246 | 1.297 | 1.331 | 1.367 | 1.282 | 1.333 |
| 3.  Absolute 1970−1989 PARE | 0.990 | 1.040 | 1.069 | 1.126 | 1.225 | 1.199 | 1.195 | 1.373 | 1.493 | 1.688 |
| 4.  Relative 1970−1989 PARE | 2.031 | 2.029 | 1.995 | 1.970 | 1.965 | 1.749 | 1.641 | 1.767 | 1.791 | 1.859 |
| 5.  Absolute 1980−1989 PARE | 0.792 | 0.832 | 0.855 | 0.900 | 0.980 | 0.958 | 0.955 | 1.098 | 1.194 | 1.350 |
| 6.  WA | 1.886 | 1.884 | 1.785 | 1.785 | 1.785 | 1.785 | 1.785 | 1.785 | 1.785 | 1.785 |
| **Swaziland:** Swaziland emalangeni | | | | | | | | | | |
| 1.  MER | 0.714 | 0.713 | 0.772 | 0.693 | 0.679 | 0.732 | 0.870 | 0.870 | 0.870 | 0.842 |
| 2.  PPPs | 0.438 | 0.449 | 0.408 | 0.549 | 0.559 | 0.516 | 0.524 | 0.576 | 0.617 | 0.652 |
| 3.  Absolute 1970−1989 PARE | 0.479 | 0.588 | 0.538 | 0.744 | 0.582 | 0.646 | 0.664 | 0.720 | 0.781 | 0.887 |
| 4.  Relative 1970−1989 PARE | 0.983 | 1.148 | 1.003 | 1.302 | 0.933 | 0.942 | 0.913 | 0.927 | 0.937 | 0.977 |
| 5.  Absolute 1980−1989 PARE | 0.445 | 0.547 | 0.500 | 0.691 | 0.540 | 0.600 | 0.617 | 0.669 | 0.726 | 0.824 |
| 6.  WA | 0.714 | 0.715 | 0.769 | 0.694 | 0.679 | 0.739 | 0.870 | 0.870 | 0.870 | 0.842 |
| **Sweden:** Swedish kroner | | | | | | | | | | |
| 1.  MER | 5.173 | 5.108 | 4.762 | 4.367 | 4.439 | 4.152 | 4.356 | 4.482 | 4.519 | 4.287 |
| 2.  PPPs | 5.644 | 5.726 | 5.776 | 5.750 | 5.855 | 5.944 | 6.367 | 6.751 | 6.902 | 6.907 |
| 3.  Absolute 1970−1989 PARE | 2.140 | 2.293 | 2.452 | 2.625 | 2.873 | 3.290 | 3.682 | 4.070 | 4.459 | 4.813 |
| 4.  Relative 1970−1989 PARE | 4.390 | 4.473 | 4.575 | 4.591 | 4.607 | 4.802 | 5.059 | 5.238 | 5.348 | 5.300 |
| 5.  Absolute 1980−1989 PARE | 1.760 | 1.885 | 2.016 | 2.158 | 2.362 | 2.705 | 3.028 | 3.346 | 3.666 | 3.957 |
| 6.  WA | 5.173 | 5.117 | 4.762 | 4.367 | 4.439 | 4.152 | 4.356 | 4.482 | 4.518 | 4.287 |
| **Switzerland:** Swiss francs | | | | | | | | | | |
| 1.  MER | 4.373 | 4.115 | 3.819 | 3.167 | 2.979 | 2.581 | 2.500 | 2.404 | 1.788 | 1.663 |
| 2.  PPPs | ... | ... | ... | ... | ... | ... | ... | ... | ... | ... |
| 3.  Absolute 1970−1989 PARE | 1.175 | 1.282 | 1.408 | 1.523 | 1.628 | 1.744 | 1.792 | 1.797 | 1.861 | 1.898 |
| 4.  Relative 1970−1989 PARE | 2.409 | 2.502 | 2.626 | 2.663 | 2.611 | 2.546 | 2.462 | 2.312 | 2.233 | 2.090 |
| 5.  Absolute 1980−1989 PARE | 0.889 | 0.970 | 1.065 | 1.152 | 1.232 | 1.319 | 1.355 | 1.359 | 1.408 | 1.436 |
| 6.  WA | 4.373 | 4.134 | 3.819 | 3.165 | 2.979 | 2.581 | 2.500 | 2.404 | 1.788 | 1.663 |

| | | | | | | | | | | Averages | | |
|---|---|---|---|---|---|---|---|---|---|---|---|---|
| 1980 (11) | 1981 (12) | 1982 (13) | 1983 (14) | 1984 (15) | 1985 (16) | 1986 (17) | 1987 (18) | 1988 (19) | 1989 (20) | 1970–89 (21) | 1970–79 (22) | 1980–89 (23) |
| 71.702 | 92.310 | 109.860 | 143.430 | 160.760 | 170.040 | 140.050 | 123.500 | 116.500 | 118.400 | 105.693 | 67.120 | 122.127 |
| 66.252 | 69.916 | 75.626 | 88.623 | 88.016 | 93.760 | 101.948 | 104.967 | 107.342 | 109.784 | 80.062 | 50.049 | 93.140 |
| 92.497 | 103.580 | 117.865 | 131.557 | 145.951 | 158.427 | 175.725 | 186.126 | 196.729 | 209.453 | 105.693 | 44.833 | 154.943 |
| 93.313 | 95.461 | 102.036 | 110.165 | 117.992 | 124.700 | 135.591 | 139.605 | 142.764 | 146.012 | 106.359 | 65.935 | 124.186 |
| 72.907 | 81.642 | 92.902 | 103.694 | 115.039 | 124.874 | 138.508 | 146.706 | 155.063 | 165.092 | 83.308 | 35.338 | 122.127 |
| 71.702 | 92.322 | 109.859 | 143.430 | 160.761 | 170.044 | 140.048 | 123.478 | 116.487 | 118.378 | 105.692 | 67.128 | 122.120 |
| 16.534 | 19.246 | 20.812 | 23.529 | 25.438 | 27.163 | 28.020 | 29.400 | 31.800 | 36.000 | 20.180 | 8.763 | 26.729 |
| 3.868 | 4.201 | 4.269 | 4.908 | 5.324 | 5.175 | 5.317 | 5.569 | 6.075 | 6.493 | 4.675 | 2.877 | 5.298 |
| 15.458 | 18.115 | 19.871 | 23.185 | 27.281 | 27.815 | 29.156 | 31.417 | 35.416 | 39.406 | 20.180 | 8.345 | 27.522 |
| 15.595 | 16.695 | 17.202 | 19.415 | 22.055 | 21.893 | 22.497 | 23.564 | 25.701 | 27.471 | 19.513 | 12.215 | 21.984 |
| 15.013 | 17.594 | 19.299 | 22.518 | 26.495 | 27.014 | 28.317 | 30.512 | 34.396 | 38.272 | 19.598 | 8.104 | 26.729 |
| 16.534 | 19.246 | 20.812 | 23.529 | 25.438 | 27.163 | 28.017 | 29.445 | 31.807 | 36.047 | 20.184 | 8.763 | 26.739 |
| 0.500 | 0.535 | 0.938 | 1.300 | 1.300 | 2.288 | 2.500 | 3.000 | 4.500 | 4.500 | 1.418 | 0.366 | 2.046 |
| 0.328 | 0.381 | 0.406 | 0.502 | 0.726 | 1.059 | 1.329 | 1.634 | 1.906 | 2.250 | 0.790 | 0.239 | 1.048 |
| 0.613 | 0.797 | 1.003 | 1.362 | 1.754 | 2.256 | 2.886 | 3.652 | 4.401 | 5.410 | 1.418 | 0.294 | 2.397 |
| 0.618 | 0.735 | 0.868 | 1.140 | 1.418 | 1.776 | 2.227 | 2.739 | 3.194 | 3.771 | 1.451 | 0.433 | 1.939 |
| 0.523 | 0.680 | 0.856 | 1.163 | 1.498 | 1.926 | 2.464 | 3.118 | 3.758 | 4.619 | 1.211 | 0.251 | 2.046 |
| 1.000 | 1.000 | 1.000 | 1.000 | 1.000 | 1.000 | 2.000 | 2.000 | 4.000 | 6.000 | 1.530 | 0.588 | 1.846 |
| 1.785 | 1.785 | 1.785 | 1.785 | 1.785 | 1.785 | 1.785 | 1.800 | 1.800 | 1.800 | 1.792 | 1.796 | 1.790 |
| 1.334 | 1.387 | 1.474 | 1.431 | 1.349 | 1.421 | 1.427 | 1.619 | 1.720 | 1.672 | 1.404 | 1.259 | 1.489 |
| 1.875 | 1.950 | 2.105 | 2.115 | 2.108 | 2.088 | 2.139 | 2.496 | 2.741 | 2.774 | 1.792 | 1.280 | 2.239 |
| 1.892 | 1.797 | 1.822 | 1.771 | 1.704 | 1.644 | 1.651 | 1.872 | 1.989 | 1.933 | 1.820 | 1.840 | 1.811 |
| 1.499 | 1.559 | 1.683 | 1.691 | 1.686 | 1.670 | 1.710 | 1.996 | 2.191 | 2.217 | 1.433 | 1.023 | 1.790 |
| 1.785 | 1.785 | 1.785 | 1.785 | 1.785 | 1.785 | 1.785 | 1.785 | 1.785 | 1.890 | 1.797 | 1.796 | 1.798 |
| 0.778 | 0.870 | 1.082 | 1.112 | 1.438 | 2.184 | 2.269 | 2.000 | 2.300 | 2.600 | 1.391 | 0.795 | 1.667 |
| 0.681 | 0.650 | 0.595 | 0.624 | 0.672 | 0.568 | 0.658 | 0.792 | 0.853 | 0.904 | 0.685 | 0.549 | 0.725 |
| 1.047 | 1.145 | 1.217 | 1.294 | 1.433 | 1.571 | 1.856 | 2.299 | 2.557 | 2.821 | 1.391 | 0.689 | 1.795 |
| 1.057 | 1.055 | 1.054 | 1.084 | 1.158 | 1.237 | 1.432 | 1.724 | 1.855 | 1.967 | 1.321 | 0.973 | 1.433 |
| 0.973 | 1.064 | 1.131 | 1.203 | 1.331 | 1.460 | 1.725 | 2.136 | 2.376 | 2.621 | 1.293 | 0.640 | 1.667 |
| 0.779 | 0.870 | 1.082 | 1.112 | 1.438 | 2.191 | 2.269 | 2.035 | 2.261 | 2.617 | 1.393 | 0.796 | 1.669 |
| 4.230 | 5.063 | 6.283 | 7.667 | 8.272 | 8.604 | 7.124 | 6.300 | 6.100 | 6.400 | 5.809 | 4.479 | 6.484 |
| 7.129 | 7.090 | 7.295 | 7.707 | 8.052 | 8.499 | 8.902 | 9.072 | 9.342 | 9.690 | 7.733 | 6.275 | 8.419 |
| 5.377 | 5.890 | 6.377 | 7.016 | 7.550 | 8.051 | 8.602 | 9.018 | 9.598 | 10.364 | 5.809 | 3.317 | 7.885 |
| 5.424 | 5.429 | 5.520 | 5.875 | 6.104 | 6.337 | 6.638 | 6.764 | 6.965 | 7.225 | 5.894 | 4.924 | 6.331 |
| 4.421 | 4.843 | 5.243 | 5.769 | 6.208 | 6.620 | 7.073 | 7.415 | 7.892 | 8.522 | 4.776 | 2.727 | 6.484 |
| 4.230 | 5.063 | 6.283 | 7.667 | 8.272 | 8.604 | 7.124 | 6.340 | 6.127 | 6.447 | 5.818 | 4.479 | 6.500 |
| 1.676 | 1.964 | 2.030 | 2.099 | 2.350 | 2.457 | 1.799 | 1.500 | 1.500 | 1.600 | 2.036 | 2.554 | 1.819 |
| ... | ... | ... | ... | ... | ... | ... | ... | ... | ... | ... | ... | ... |
| 1.950 | 2.085 | 2.232 | 2.299 | 2.363 | 2.436 | 2.528 | 2.593 | 2.656 | 2.770 | 2.036 | 1.613 | 2.405 |
| 1.967 | 1.922 | 1.933 | 1.925 | 1.910 | 1.917 | 1.950 | 1.945 | 1.927 | 1.931 | 2.087 | 2.418 | 1.932 |
| 1.475 | 1.577 | 1.689 | 1.739 | 1.787 | 1.842 | 1.912 | 1.961 | 2.009 | 2.095 | 1.540 | 1.220 | 1.819 |
| 1.676 | 1.964 | 2.030 | 2.099 | 2.350 | 2.457 | 1.799 | 1.491 | 1.463 | 1.636 | 2.034 | 2.555 | 1.817 |

**Table A.2** Conversion rates for individual countries or areas, expressed as the number of
local currency units per United States dollar, 1970−1989 [*cont.*]

| Country or area | 1970 (1) | 1971 (2) | 1972 (3) | 1973 (4) | 1974 (5) | 1975 (6) | 1976 (7) | 1977 (8) | 1978 (9) | 1979 (10) |
|---|---|---|---|---|---|---|---|---|---|---|
| **Syrian Arab Republic:** Syrian pounds | | | | | | | | | | |
| 1. MER | 3.820 | 3.820 | 3.820 | 3.821 | 3.733 | 3.700 | 3.852 | 3.925 | 3.925 | 3.925 |
| 2. PPPs | 1.583 | 1.542 | 1.553 | 1.540 | 1.565 | 1.524 | 1.654 | 1.738 | 1.766 | 1.772 |
| 3. Absolute 1970−1989 PARE | 1.257 | 1.343 | 1.240 | 1.452 | 1.877 | 2.039 | 2.210 | 2.450 | 2.702 | 3.134 |
| 4. Relative 1970−1989 PARE | 2.578 | 2.620 | 2.313 | 2.540 | 3.009 | 2.975 | 3.036 | 3.153 | 3.241 | 3.451 |
| 5. Absolute 1980−1989 PARE | 0.999 | 1.067 | 0.986 | 1.154 | 1.491 | 1.620 | 1.756 | 1.947 | 2.147 | 2.491 |
| 6. WA | 3.177 | 3.094 | 3.016 | 3.044 | 3.071 | 3.017 | 3.239 | 3.510 | 3.492 | 3.925 |
| **Thailand:** Thai baht | | | | | | | | | | |
| 1. MER | 20.800 | 20.928 | 20.928 | 20.620 | 20.375 | 20.379 | 20.400 | 20.400 | 20.336 | 20.419 |
| 2. PPPs | 6.800 | 6.585 | 6.700 | 7.493 | 8.223 | 7.893 | 7.842 | 7.691 | 8.005 | 8.103 |
| 3. Absolute 1970−1989 PARE | 9.836 | 9.755 | 10.391 | 12.352 | 14.879 | 15.417 | 16.103 | 17.063 | 18.693 | 20.318 |
| 4. Relative 1970−1989 PARE | 20.174 | 19.030 | 19.382 | 21.605 | 23.860 | 22.503 | 22.122 | 21.960 | 22.422 | 22.373 |
| 5. Absolute 1980−1989 PARE | 8.669 | 8.597 | 9.158 | 10.886 | 13.114 | 13.588 | 14.192 | 15.039 | 16.476 | 17.908 |
| 6. WA | 20.800 | 20.800 | 20.800 | 20.620 | 20.375 | 20.379 | 20.400 | 20.400 | 20.336 | 20.419 |
| **Togo:** CFA francs | | | | | | | | | | |
| 1. MER | 277.710 | 275.520 | 252.210 | 222.700 | 240.500 | 214.320 | 238.980 | 245.670 | 225.660 | 212.720 |
| 2. PPPs | 103.187 | 105.587 | 103.114 | 109.570 | 126.112 | 121.851 | 135.664 | 150.033 | 148.672 | 147.487 |
| 3. Absolute 1970−1989 PARE | 112.175 | 117.506 | 121.033 | 130.382 | 180.751 | 178.633 | 190.682 | 223.695 | 231.248 | 245.610 |
| 4. Relative 1970−1989 PARE | 230.070 | 229.244 | 225.767 | 228.057 | 289.853 | 260.738 | 261.953 | 287.889 | 277.375 | 270.454 |
| 5. Absolute 1980−1989 PARE | 91.870 | 96.236 | 99.124 | 106.781 | 148.033 | 146.298 | 156.165 | 183.203 | 189.389 | 201.151 |
| 6. WA | 277.710 | 277.130 | 252.210 | 222.700 | 240.500 | 214.320 | 238.980 | 245.670 | 225.640 | 212.720 |
| **Tonga:** Tongan pa'anga | | | | | | | | | | |
| 1. MER | 0.893 | 0.880 | 0.839 | 0.704 | 0.695 | 0.763 | 0.816 | 0.902 | 0.874 | 0.895 |
| 2. PPPs | ... | ... | ... | ... | ... | ... | ... | ... | ... | ... |
| 3. Absolute 1970−1989 PARE | 0.331 | 0.349 | 0.399 | 0.537 | 0.639 | 0.607 | 0.597 | 0.713 | 0.825 | 0.890 |
| 4. Relative 1970−1989 PARE | 0.678 | 0.682 | 0.745 | 0.939 | 1.025 | 0.885 | 0.820 | 0.918 | 0.989 | 0.980 |
| 5. Absolute 1980−1989 PARE | 0.288 | 0.305 | 0.349 | 0.468 | 0.558 | 0.529 | 0.521 | 0.622 | 0.720 | 0.777 |
| 6. WA [a] | 0.951 | 0.941 | 0.972 | 1.053 | 0.938 | 0.752 | 0.747 | 0.932 | 1.015 | 0.998 |
| **Trinidad and Tobago:** Trinidad and Tobago dollars | | | | | | | | | | |
| 1. MER | 2.000 | 1.964 | 1.921 | 1.959 | 2.053 | 2.170 | 2.438 | 2.400 | 2.400 | 2.400 |
| 2. PPPs | 1.297 | 1.414 | 1.358 | 1.396 | 1.514 | 1.675 | 1.765 | 1.711 | 1.656 | 1.762 |
| 3. Absolute 1970−1989 PARE | 0.530 | 0.565 | 0.628 | 0.760 | 1.198 | 1.492 | 1.611 | 1.827 | 1.884 | 2.349 |
| 4. Relative 1970−1989 PARE | 1.086 | 1.102 | 1.171 | 1.330 | 1.921 | 2.178 | 2.213 | 2.351 | 2.260 | 2.587 |
| 5. Absolute 1980−1989 PARE | 0.404 | 0.431 | 0.479 | 0.580 | 0.914 | 1.138 | 1.229 | 1.393 | 1.437 | 1.792 |
| 6. WA | 2.000 | 1.975 | 1.921 | 1.959 | 2.053 | 2.170 | 2.436 | 2.400 | 2.400 | 2.400 |
| **Tunisia:** Tunisian dinars | | | | | | | | | | |
| 1. MER | 0.525 | 0.518 | 0.477 | 0.420 | 0.437 | 0.402 | 0.429 | 0.429 | 0.416 | 0.407 |
| 2. PPPs | 0.286 | 0.289 | 0.296 | 0.294 | 0.305 | 0.311 | 0.305 | 0.303 | 0.299 | 0.298 |
| 3. Absolute 1970−1989 PARE | 0.227 | 0.240 | 0.247 | 0.268 | 0.334 | 0.351 | 0.361 | 0.396 | 0.421 | 0.465 |
| 4. Relative 1970−1989 PARE | 0.465 | 0.469 | 0.461 | 0.470 | 0.536 | 0.512 | 0.496 | 0.509 | 0.505 | 0.512 |
| 5. Absolute 1980−1989 PARE | 0.202 | 0.215 | 0.221 | 0.240 | 0.298 | 0.313 | 0.322 | 0.353 | 0.376 | 0.415 |
| 6. WA | 0.525 | 0.523 | 0.477 | 0.422 | 0.437 | 0.402 | 0.429 | 0.429 | 0.416 | 0.406 |
| **Turkey:** Turkish liras | | | | | | | | | | |
| 1. MER | 11.370 | 14.860 | 14.150 | 14.150 | 13.927 | 14.442 | 16.053 | 18.002 | 24.282 | 31.077 |
| 2. PPPs | 4.528 | 5.048 | 5.609 | 6.598 | 7.559 | 7.940 | 8.566 | 10.143 | 14.497 | 22.960 |
| 3. Absolute 1970−1989 PARE | 5.360 | 6.319 | 7.356 | 8.969 | 11.459 | 13.336 | 15.686 | 19.547 | 28.076 | 47.903 |
| 4. Relative 1970−1989 PARE | 10.993 | 12.329 | 13.721 | 15.688 | 18.376 | 19.465 | 21.549 | 25.157 | 33.676 | 52.748 |
| 5. Absolute 1980−1989 PARE | 5.059 | 5.964 | 6.943 | 8.465 | 10.816 | 12.587 | 14.805 | 18.449 | 26.499 | 45.212 |
| 6. WA | 11.500 | 14.917 | 14.150 | 14.150 | 13.927 | 14.442 | 16.053 | 18.002 | 24.282 | 31.077 |

|  |  |  |  |  |  |  |  |  |  | Averages | | |
| 1980 (11) | 1981 (12) | 1982 (13) | 1983 (14) | 1984 (15) | 1985 (16) | 1986 (17) | 1987 (18) | 1988 (19) | 1989 (20) | 1970–89 (21) | 1970–79 (22) | 1980–89 (23) |
|---|---|---|---|---|---|---|---|---|---|---|---|---|
| 3.925 | 3.925 | 3.925 | 3.925 | 3.925 | 3.925 | 3.925 | 3.900 | 11.200 | 11.200 | 4.916 | 3.856 | 5.185 |
| 1.939 | 1.921 | 1.983 | 2.134 | 1.992 | 2.066 | 2.559 | 3.115 | 3.886 | 4.255 | 2.455 | 1.663 | 2.697 |
| 3.651 | 4.277 | 4.380 | 4.601 | 4.930 | 5.132 | 6.484 | 8.121 | 10.470 | 11.934 | 4.916 | 2.131 | 6.525 |
| 3.683 | 3.942 | 3.792 | 3.853 | 3.986 | 4.040 | 5.003 | 6.091 | 7.598 | 8.319 | 4.702 | 3.035 | 5.246 |
| 2.901 | 3.399 | 3.481 | 3.656 | 3.918 | 4.079 | 5.152 | 6.453 | 8.321 | 9.484 | 3.907 | 1.694 | 5.185 |
| 3.925 | 4.220 | 4.200 | 4.140 | 4.280 | 4.900 | 7.513 | 11.235 | 17.588 | 19.030 | 6.106 | 3.362 | 7.218 |
| | | | | | | | | | | | | |
| 20.476 | 21.820 | 23.000 | 23.000 | 23.639 | 27.159 | 26.299 | 25.700 | 25.300 | 25.700 | 23.466 | 20.478 | 24.484 |
| 8.704 | 8.839 | 9.046 | 9.253 | 8.491 | 8.753 | 8.832 | 8.972 | 9.220 | 9.380 | 8.669 | 7.701 | 8.991 |
| 22.848 | 24.805 | 25.711 | 26.606 | 26.565 | 26.744 | 27.525 | 28.767 | 30.555 | 32.360 | 23.466 | 15.189 | 27.780 |
| 23.049 | 22.861 | 22.258 | 22.280 | 21.476 | 21.051 | 21.239 | 21.577 | 22.173 | 22.558 | 21.978 | 21.885 | 22.005 |
| 20.137 | 21.862 | 22.661 | 23.449 | 23.413 | 23.571 | 24.260 | 25.354 | 26.930 | 28.521 | 20.682 | 13.387 | 24.484 |
| 20.476 | 21.820 | 23.000 | 23.000 | 23.639 | 27.159 | 26.299 | 25.723 | 25.294 | 25.702 | 23.464 | 20.465 | 24.486 |
| | | | | | | | | | | | | |
| 211.280 | 271.730 | 328.610 | 381.060 | 436.960 | 449.260 | 346.300 | 300.500 | 297.800 | 319.000 | 291.290 | 233.912 | 323.358 |
| 148.310 | 157.091 | 159.669 | 169.627 | 165.346 | 165.507 | 170.600 | 159.520 | 157.556 | 154.578 | 149.981 | 128.786 | 160.672 |
| 284.205 | 327.222 | 354.866 | 390.891 | 395.868 | 423.378 | 445.174 | 428.223 | 437.150 | 446.473 | 291.290 | 176.686 | 394.828 |
| 286.711 | 301.573 | 307.207 | 327.331 | 320.035 | 333.247 | 343.500 | 321.191 | 317.237 | 311.241 | 298.965 | 261.019 | 317.634 |
| 232.760 | 267.990 | 290.630 | 320.134 | 324.210 | 346.740 | 364.591 | 350.708 | 358.020 | 365.655 | 238.562 | 144.704 | 323.358 |
| 211.300 | 271.730 | 328.620 | 381.070 | 436.960 | 449.260 | 346.300 | 300.540 | 297.847 | 319.007 | 291.332 | 233.982 | 323.376 |
| | | | | | | | | | | | | |
| 0.878 | 0.870 | 0.983 | 1.108 | 1.137 | 1.427 | 1.491 | 1.400 | 1.300 | 1.300 | 1.118 | 0.824 | 1.221 |
| ... | ... | ... | ... | ... | ... | ... | ... | ... | ... | | ... | ... |
| 1.019 | 0.919 | 0.945 | 1.012 | 1.303 | 1.327 | 1.609 | 1.687 | 1.854 | 1.931 | 1.118 | 0.604 | 1.399 |
| 1.028 | 0.847 | 0.818 | 0.847 | 1.053 | 1.044 | 1.241 | 1.266 | 1.346 | 1.346 | 1.064 | 0.890 | 1.116 |
| 0.889 | 0.802 | 0.825 | 0.883 | 1.137 | 1.158 | 1.404 | 1.472 | 1.618 | 1.685 | 0.976 | 0.527 | 1.221 |
| 1.014 | 0.881 | 0.920 | 1.053 | 1.298 | 1.321 | 1.519 | 1.585 | 1.523 | 1.418 | 1.200 | 0.920 | 1.292 |
| | | | | | | | | | | | | |
| 2.401 | 2.400 | 2.400 | 2.400 | 2.400 | 2.450 | 3.600 | 3.600 | 3.800 | 4.300 | 2.671 | 2.266 | 2.817 |
| 2.027 | 2.049 | 2.277 | 2.470 | 1.801 | 1.988 | 1.947 | 2.019 | 2.007 | 1.978 | 1.935 | 1.632 | 2.045 |
| 2.884 | 3.029 | 3.396 | 3.651 | 3.871 | 3.901 | 3.898 | 4.157 | 4.270 | 4.382 | 2.671 | 1.368 | 3.693 |
| 2.910 | 2.792 | 2.940 | 3.058 | 3.130 | 3.071 | 3.008 | 3.118 | 3.099 | 3.055 | 2.705 | 1.995 | 3.017 |
| 2.200 | 2.311 | 2.591 | 2.785 | 2.953 | 2.976 | 2.973 | 3.171 | 3.258 | 3.343 | 2.038 | 1.043 | 2.817 |
| 2.400 | 2.400 | 2.400 | 2.400 | 2.400 | 2.450 | 3.600 | 3.600 | 3.844 | 4.250 | 2.671 | 2.267 | 2.817 |
| | | | | | | | | | | | | |
| 0.405 | 0.494 | 0.591 | 0.679 | 0.777 | 0.835 | 0.794 | 0.800 | 0.900 | 0.900 | 0.635 | 0.430 | 0.725 |
| 0.300 | 0.298 | 0.311 | 0.328 | 0.346 | 0.366 | 0.370 | 0.386 | 0.398 | 0.409 | 0.344 | 0.300 | 0.358 |
| 0.525 | 0.584 | 0.678 | 0.741 | 0.796 | 0.834 | 0.859 | 0.923 | 0.983 | 1.053 | 0.635 | 0.345 | 0.812 |
| 0.529 | 0.539 | 0.587 | 0.621 | 0.643 | 0.656 | 0.663 | 0.692 | 0.713 | 0.734 | 0.612 | 0.499 | 0.650 |
| 0.468 | 0.522 | 0.605 | 0.661 | 0.710 | 0.744 | 0.767 | 0.823 | 0.877 | 0.939 | 0.567 | 0.308 | 0.725 |
| 0.405 | 0.494 | 0.591 | 0.679 | 0.777 | 0.835 | 0.794 | 0.829 | 0.858 | 0.949 | 0.637 | 0.430 | 0.728 |
| | | | | | | | | | | | | |
| 76.038 | 111.220 | 162.550 | 225.460 | 366.680 | 521.980 | 674.510 | 857.200 | 1422.300 | 2121.700 | 481.647 | 19.889 | 743.410 |
| 42.034 | 55.499 | 67.496 | 82.207 | 121.591 | 174.446 | 225.137 | 302.385 | 486.996 | 780.324 | 204.754 | 10.893 | 280.454 |
| 96.887 | 137.583 | 176.128 | 227.200 | 339.346 | 488.441 | 643.043 | 888.494 | 1478.977 | 2466.965 | 481.647 | 18.096 | 787.656 |
| 97.742 | 126.798 | 152.474 | 190.257 | 274.340 | 384.458 | 496.177 | 666.421 | 1073.283 | 1719.745 | 467.311 | 26.255 | 627.083 |
| 91.445 | 129.854 | 166.234 | 214.437 | 320.284 | 461.003 | 606.921 | 838.584 | 1395.897 | 2328.385 | 454.591 | 17.080 | 743.410 |
| 76.038 | 111.219 | 162.553 | 225.457 | 366.678 | 521.983 | 674.512 | 857.214 | 1422.350 | 2121.680 | 481.749 | 19.901 | 743.413 |

**Table A.2**     Conversion rates for individual countries or areas, expressed as the number of local currency units per United States dollar, 1970−1989 [*cont.*]

| Country or area | 1970 (1) | 1971 (2) | 1972 (3) | 1973 (4) | 1974 (5) | 1975 (6) | 1976 (7) | 1977 (8) | 1978 (9) | 1979 (10) |
|---|---|---|---|---|---|---|---|---|---|---|
| **Uganda:** Uganda shillings | | | | | | | | | | |
| 1. MER | 0.070 | 0.070 | 0.070 | 0.070 | 0.070 | 0.070 | 0.080 | 0.080 | 0.080 | 0.070 |
| 2. PPPs | 0.050 | 0.050 | 0.051 | 0.058 | 0.066 | 0.085 | 0.090 | 0.152 | 0.189 | 0.251 |
| 3. Absolute 1970−1989 PARE | 0.025 | 0.027 | 0.029 | 0.033 | 0.041 | 0.059 | 0.069 | 0.124 | 0.173 | 0.219 |
| 4. Relative 1970−1989 PARE | 0.051 | 0.052 | 0.054 | 0.058 | 0.066 | 0.086 | 0.095 | 0.160 | 0.207 | 0.241 |
| 5. Absolute 1980−1989 PARE | 0.026 | 0.028 | 0.030 | 0.035 | 0.043 | 0.062 | 0.072 | 0.130 | 0.181 | 0.229 |
| 6. WA | 0.086 | 0.092 | 0.099 | 0.115 | 0.141 | 0.203 | 0.237 | 0.428 | 0.593 | 0.752 |
| **USSR (former):** USSR roubles | | | | | | | | | | |
| 1. MER | 0.900 | 0.900 | 0.823 | 0.740 | 0.772 | 0.723 | 0.760 | 0.739 | 0.684 | 0.656 |
| 2. PPPs | ... | ... | ... | ... | ... | ... | ... | ... | ... | ... |
| 3. Absolute 1970−1989 PARE | 0.671 | 0.676 | 0.671 | 0.666 | 0.666 | 0.667 | 0.667 | 0.669 | 0.679 | 0.681 |
| 4. Relative 1970−1989 PARE | 1.377 | 1.319 | 1.251 | 1.165 | 1.068 | 0.974 | 0.916 | 0.861 | 0.814 | 0.750 |
| 5. Absolute 1980−1989 PARE | 0.626 | 0.630 | 0.625 | 0.621 | 0.621 | 0.622 | 0.622 | 0.624 | 0.633 | 0.635 |
| 6. WA [a] | 0.938 | 0.920 | 0.872 | 0.814 | 0.776 | 0.746 | 0.752 | 0.742 | 0.736 | 0.698 |
| **United Arab Emirates:** UAE dirhams | | | | | | | | | | |
| 1. MER | 4.762 | 4.748 | 4.386 | 3.996 | 3.959 | 3.961 | 3.953 | 3.903 | 3.871 | 3.816 |
| 2. PPPs | 3.056 | 3.400 | 3.084 | 3.397 | 3.999 | 4.420 | 4.456 | 4.622 | 4.502 | 4.401 |
| 3. Absolute 1970−1989 PARE | 2.151 | 3.084 | 3.277 | 3.166 | 2.975 | 2.848 | 3.202 | 3.388 | 3.319 | 3.503 |
| 4. Relative 1970−1989 PARE | 4.412 | 6.016 | 6.113 | 5.538 | 4.771 | 4.157 | 4.398 | 4.360 | 3.981 | 3.857 |
| 5. Absolute 1980−1989 PARE | 2.000 | 2.867 | 3.047 | 2.944 | 2.766 | 2.648 | 2.977 | 3.150 | 3.086 | 3.257 |
| 6. WA | 4.762 | 4.748 | 4.386 | 3.996 | 3.959 | 3.961 | 3.953 | 3.903 | 3.871 | 3.816 |
| **United Kingdom:** Pounds sterling | | | | | | | | | | |
| 1. MER | 0.417 | 0.409 | 0.400 | 0.408 | 0.428 | 0.450 | 0.554 | 0.573 | 0.521 | 0.471 |
| 2. PPPs | 0.299 | 0.307 | 0.313 | 0.321 | 0.344 | 0.392 | 0.426 | 0.452 | 0.459 | 0.475 |
| 3. Absolute 1970−1989 PARE | 0.158 | 0.173 | 0.187 | 0.200 | 0.230 | 0.292 | 0.337 | 0.383 | 0.427 | 0.489 |
| 4. Relative 1970−1989 PARE | 0.324 | 0.337 | 0.348 | 0.350 | 0.369 | 0.427 | 0.462 | 0.493 | 0.512 | 0.538 |
| 5. Absolute 1980−1989 PARE | 0.120 | 0.131 | 0.142 | 0.152 | 0.174 | 0.222 | 0.255 | 0.291 | 0.324 | 0.371 |
| 6. WA | 0.417 | 0.411 | 0.400 | 0.408 | 0.428 | 0.452 | 0.557 | 0.573 | 0.522 | 0.472 |
| **United Rep. Tanzania:** Tanzanian shillings | | | | | | | | | | |
| 1. MER | 7.143 | 7.143 | 7.143 | 7.021 | 7.135 | 7.367 | 8.377 | 8.289 | 7.712 | 8.217 |
| 2. PPPs | 3.874 | 3.742 | 4.039 | 4.072 | 4.136 | 4.221 | 4.762 | 5.435 | 5.496 | 5.648 |
| 3. Absolute 1970−1989 PARE | 3.165 | 3.250 | 3.466 | 3.945 | 4.698 | 5.273 | 6.103 | 7.187 | 7.841 | 8.594 |
| 4. Relative 1970−1989 PARE | 6.490 | 6.340 | 6.466 | 6.900 | 7.534 | 7.696 | 8.385 | 9.249 | 9.406 | 9.463 |
| 5. Absolute 1980−1989 PARE | 2.524 | 2.592 | 2.765 | 3.147 | 3.747 | 4.205 | 4.868 | 5.732 | 6.254 | 6.854 |
| 6. WA | 7.000 | 7.000 | 7.000 | 7.000 | 7.000 | 7.000 | 8.000 | 8.000 | 8.000 | 8.000 |
| **United States:** United States dollars | | | | | | | | | | |
| 1. MER | 1.000 | 1.000 | 1.000 | 1.000 | 1.000 | 1.000 | 1.000 | 1.000 | 1.000 | 1.000 |
| 2. PPPs | 1.000 | 1.000 | 1.000 | 1.000 | 1.000 | 1.000 | 1.000 | 1.000 | 1.000 | 1.000 |
| 3. Absolute 1970−1989 PARE | 0.488 | 0.513 | 0.536 | 0.572 | 0.624 | 0.685 | 0.728 | 0.777 | 0.834 | 0.908 |
| 4. Relative 1970−1989 PARE | 1.000 | 1.000 | 1.000 | 1.000 | 1.000 | 1.000 | 1.000 | 1.000 | 1.000 | 1.000 |
| 5. Absolute 1980−1989 PARE | 0.390 | 0.410 | 0.429 | 0.458 | 0.499 | 0.548 | 0.583 | 0.622 | 0.667 | 0.727 |
| 6. WA | 1.000 | 1.000 | 1.000 | 1.000 | 1.000 | 1.000 | 1.000 | 1.000 | 1.000 | 1.000 |
| **US Virgin Islands:** US dollars | | | | | | | | | | |
| 1. MER | 1.000 | 1.000 | 1.000 | 1.000 | 1.000 | 1.000 | 1.000 | 1.000 | 1.000 | 1.000 |
| 2. PPPs | ... | ... | ... | ... | ... | ... | ... | ... | ... | ... |
| 3. Absolute 1970−1989 PARE | 0.511 | 0.537 | 0.559 | 0.591 | 0.649 | 0.710 | 0.747 | 0.790 | 0.848 | 0.920 |
| 4. Relative 1970−1989 PARE | 1.048 | 1.048 | 1.043 | 1.034 | 1.040 | 1.036 | 1.027 | 1.017 | 1.017 | 1.013 |
| 5. Absolute 1980−1989 PARE | 0.395 | 0.415 | 0.432 | 0.457 | 0.502 | 0.549 | 0.578 | 0.611 | 0.656 | 0.711 |
| 6. WA | 1.129 | 1.077 | 1.045 | 1.053 | 1.086 | 1.098 | 1.068 | 1.057 | 1.069 | 1.083 |

|  |  |  |  |  |  |  |  |  |  | Averages |  |  |
| 1980 (11) | 1981 (12) | 1982 (13) | 1983 (14) | 1984 (15) | 1985 (16) | 1986 (17) | 1987 (18) | 1988 (19) | 1989 (20) | 1970−89 (21) | 1970−79 (22) | 1980−89 (23) |
|---|---|---|---|---|---|---|---|---|---|---|---|---|
| 0.070 | 0.500 | 0.940 | 1.540 | 3.600 | 6.720 | 14.000 | 42.840 | 106.140 | 223.090 | 14.357 | 0.074 | 31.253 |
| 0.285 | 0.289 | 0.308 | 0.351 | 0.457 | 1.077 | 2.492 | 8.157 | 20.913 | 37.794 | 8.277 | 0.113 | 10.380 |
| 0.291 | 0.427 | 0.558 | 0.824 | 1.395 | 3.827 | 9.031 | 30.409 | 80.579 | 151.592 | 14.357 | 0.077 | 29.856 |
| 0.294 | 0.393 | 0.483 | 0.690 | 1.128 | 3.012 | 6.968 | 22.809 | 58.476 | 105.676 | 15.268 | 0.117 | 24.031 |
| 0.305 | 0.447 | 0.585 | 0.862 | 1.461 | 4.006 | 9.453 | 31.832 | 84.349 | 158.684 | 15.029 | 0.081 | 31.253 |
| 1.000 | 1.000 | 2.000 | 3.000 | 4.000 | 11.000 | 16.000 | 51.000 | 127.000 | 331.000 | 40.550 | 0.266 | 70.662 |
|  |  |  |  |  |  |  |  |  |  |  |  |  |
| 0.660 | 0.720 | 0.730 | 0.738 | 0.814 | 0.850 | 0.709 | 0.637 | 0.607 | 0.627 | 0.717 | 0.752 | 0.698 |
| ... | ... | ... | ... | ... | ... | ... | ... | ... | ... | ... | ... | ... |
| 0.686 | 0.708 | 0.732 | 0.732 | 0.744 | 0.750 | 0.752 | 0.764 | 0.779 | 0.812 | 0.717 | 0.672 | 0.748 |
| 0.692 | 0.653 | 0.634 | 0.613 | 0.602 | 0.590 | 0.580 | 0.573 | 0.565 | 0.566 | 0.703 | 0.978 | 0.600 |
| 0.639 | 0.660 | 0.683 | 0.682 | 0.694 | 0.699 | 0.701 | 0.712 | 0.726 | 0.757 | 0.669 | 0.626 | 0.698 |
| 0.671 | 0.695 | 0.726 | 0.737 | 0.769 | 0.809 | 0.794 | 0.741 | 0.664 | 0.646 | 0.742 | 0.781 | 0.720 |
|  |  |  |  |  |  |  |  |  |  |  |  |  |
| 3.707 | 3.671 | 3.671 | 3.671 | 3.671 | 3.671 | 3.671 | 3.700 | 3.700 | 3.700 | 3.742 | 3.923 | 3.683 |
| 4.218 | 4.335 | 4.230 | 4.221 | 3.854 | 3.978 | 3.970 | 4.064 | 3.912 | 3.894 | 4.134 | 4.315 | 4.074 |
| 3.806 | 4.080 | 4.129 | 3.979 | 3.775 | 3.775 | 3.843 | 4.047 | 4.027 | 4.173 | 3.742 | 3.234 | 3.961 |
| 3.839 | 3.760 | 3.574 | 3.332 | 3.052 | 2.971 | 2.966 | 3.036 | 2.922 | 2.909 | 3.447 | 4.248 | 3.233 |
| 3.538 | 3.793 | 3.838 | 3.699 | 3.509 | 3.509 | 3.573 | 3.763 | 3.744 | 3.880 | 3.479 | 3.007 | 3.683 |
| 3.707 | 3.671 | 3.671 | 3.671 | 3.671 | 3.671 | 3.671 | 3.671 | 3.671 | 3.671 | 3.736 | 3.923 | 3.675 |
|  |  |  |  |  |  |  |  |  |  |  |  |  |
| 0.430 | 0.493 | 0.571 | 0.659 | 0.748 | 0.771 | 0.682 | 0.600 | 0.600 | 0.600 | 0.572 | 0.475 | 0.610 |
| 0.503 | 0.511 | 0.517 | 0.533 | 0.534 | 0.560 | 0.569 | 0.579 | 0.598 | 0.609 | 0.509 | 0.396 | 0.558 |
| 0.584 | 0.651 | 0.700 | 0.737 | 0.771 | 0.814 | 0.843 | 0.884 | 0.943 | 0.999 | 0.572 | 0.294 | 0.804 |
| 0.589 | 0.600 | 0.606 | 0.617 | 0.623 | 0.641 | 0.651 | 0.663 | 0.684 | 0.697 | 0.579 | 0.436 | 0.644 |
| 0.443 | 0.493 | 0.531 | 0.559 | 0.585 | 0.618 | 0.640 | 0.671 | 0.715 | 0.758 | 0.434 | 0.223 | 0.610 |
| 0.430 | 0.498 | 0.572 | 0.660 | 0.752 | 0.779 | 0.682 | 0.612 | 0.562 | 0.611 | 0.571 | 0.476 | 0.609 |
|  |  |  |  |  |  |  |  |  |  |  |  |  |
| 8.197 | 8.284 | 9.283 | 11.143 | 15.292 | 17.472 | 32.698 | 64.300 | 99.300 | 143.400 | 22.618 | 7.714 | 30.349 |
| 6.141 | 6.292 | 6.269 | 6.788 | 8.039 | 8.778 | 11.029 | 14.327 | 19.707 | 22.369 | 10.476 | 4.741 | 12.463 |
| 10.977 | 12.862 | 15.162 | 18.807 | 22.935 | 30.324 | 38.868 | 51.940 | 73.841 | 87.254 | 22.618 | 5.549 | 38.050 |
| 11.074 | 11.854 | 13.126 | 15.749 | 18.542 | 23.869 | 29.991 | 38.958 | 53.586 | 60.825 | 23.148 | 8.151 | 30.560 |
| 8.755 | 10.259 | 12.093 | 15.001 | 18.293 | 24.187 | 31.001 | 41.428 | 58.896 | 69.594 | 18.040 | 4.426 | 30.349 |
| 8.000 | 8.000 | 9.000 | 11.000 | 15.000 | 17.000 | 33.000 | 64.000 | 99.000 | 143.000 | 22.208 | 7.566 | 29.814 |
|  |  |  |  |  |  |  |  |  |  |  |  |  |
| 1.000 | 1.000 | 1.000 | 1.000 | 1.000 | 1.000 | 1.000 | 1.000 | 1.000 | 1.000 | 1.000 | 1.000 | 1.000 |
| 1.000 | 1.000 | 1.000 | 1.000 | 1.000 | 1.000 | 1.000 | 1.000 | 1.000 | 1.000 | 1.000 | 1.000 | 1.000 |
| 0.991 | 1.085 | 1.155 | 1.194 | 1.237 | 1.270 | 1.296 | 1.333 | 1.378 | 1.434 | 1.000 | 0.677 | 1.250 |
| 1.000 | 1.000 | 1.000 | 1.000 | 1.000 | 1.000 | 1.000 | 1.000 | 1.000 | 1.000 | 1.000 | 1.000 | 1.000 |
| 0.793 | 0.868 | 0.924 | 0.956 | 0.990 | 1.017 | 1.037 | 1.067 | 1.103 | 1.148 | 0.800 | 0.542 | 1.000 |
| 1.000 | 1.000 | 1.000 | 1.000 | 1.000 | 1.000 | 1.000 | 1.000 | 1.000 | 1.000 | 1.000 | 1.000 | 1.000 |
|  |  |  |  |  |  |  |  |  |  |  |  |  |
| 1.000 | 1.000 | 1.000 | 1.000 | 1.000 | 1.000 | 1.000 | 1.000 | 1.000 | 1.000 | 1.000 | 1.000 | 1.000 |
| ... | ... | ... | ... | ... | ... | ... | ... | ... | ... | ... | ... | ... |
| 1.003 | 1.099 | 1.166 | 1.210 | 1.256 | 1.299 | 1.367 | 1.445 | 1.487 | 1.542 | 1.000 | 0.693 | 1.293 |
| 1.012 | 1.013 | 1.009 | 1.014 | 1.015 | 1.023 | 1.055 | 1.084 | 1.079 | 1.075 | 1.037 | 1.029 | 1.042 |
| 0.775 | 0.850 | 0.901 | 0.936 | 0.971 | 1.005 | 1.057 | 1.117 | 1.150 | 1.193 | 0.773 | 0.536 | 1.000 |
| 1.091 | 1.097 | 1.074 | 1.046 | 1.038 | 1.036 | 1.047 | 1.056 | 1.039 | 1.035 | 1.060 | 1.075 | 1.053 |

**Table A.2**    Conversion rates for individual countries or areas, expressed as the number of
local currency units per United States dollar, 1970−1989 [*cont.*]

| Country or area | 1970 (1) | 1971 (2) | 1972 (3) | 1973 (4) | 1974 (5) | 1975 (6) | 1976 (7) | 1977 (8) | 1978 (9) | 1979 (10) |
|---|---|---|---|---|---|---|---|---|---|---|
| **Uruguay:** Uruguayan pesos | | | | | | | | | | |
| 1.   MER | 0.250 | 0.255 | 0.536 | 0.866 | 1.196 | 2.254 | 3.336 | 4.678 | 6.060 | 7.861 |
| 2.   PPPs | 0.115 | 0.130 | 0.222 | 0.435 | 0.722 | 1.132 | 1.609 | 2.379 | 3.250 | 5.108 |
| 3.   Absolute 1970−1989 PARE | 0.122 | 0.147 | 0.256 | 0.526 | 0.905 | 1.536 | 2.287 | 3.562 | 5.255 | 9.222 |
| 4.   Relative 1970−1989 PARE | 0.251 | 0.286 | 0.478 | 0.920 | 1.452 | 2.243 | 3.141 | 4.584 | 6.303 | 10.155 |
| 5.   Absolute 1980−1989 PARE | 0.099 | 0.119 | 0.207 | 0.426 | 0.732 | 1.243 | 1.849 | 2.880 | 4.250 | 7.458 |
| 6.   WA | 0.250 | 0.255 | 0.536 | 0.866 | 1.196 | 2.254 | 3.336 | 4.678 | 6.060 | 7.861 |
| **Vanuatu:** Vatu | | | | | | | | | | |
| 1.   MER | 89.340 | 89.080 | 81.520 | 71.980 | 77.730 | 69.280 | 77.250 | 79.410 | 72.940 | 68.760 |
| 2.   PPPs | ... | ... | ... | ... | ... | ... | ... | ... | ... | ... |
| 3.   Absolute 1970−1989 PARE | 75.007 | 78.739 | 82.506 | 75.986 | 60.814 | 68.656 | 72.518 | 78.864 | 75.187 | 89.803 |
| 4.   Relative 1970−1989 PARE | 153.839 | 153.614 | 153.900 | 132.911 | 97.521 | 100.212 | 99.624 | 101.495 | 90.184 | 98.887 |
| 5.   Absolute 1980−1989 PARE | 74.921 | 78.649 | 82.411 | 75.899 | 60.744 | 68.577 | 72.435 | 78.773 | 75.100 | 89.700 |
| 6.   WA | 100.985 | 99.863 | 81.611 | 72.045 | 77.803 | 69.273 | 77.236 | 79.411 | 72.939 | 68.758 |
| **Venezuela:** Venezuelan bolivares | | | | | | | | | | |
| 1.   MER | 4.500 | 4.501 | 4.400 | 4.305 | 4.285 | 4.285 | 4.290 | 4.293 | 4.293 | 4.293 |
| 2.   PPPs | 3.117 | 3.102 | 3.014 | 3.161 | 3.275 | 3.205 | 3.263 | 3.380 | 3.343 | 3.498 |
| 3.   Absolute 1970−1989 PARE | 1.873 | 1.995 | 2.080 | 2.331 | 3.368 | 3.341 | 3.514 | 3.795 | 4.034 | 4.892 |
| 4.   Relative 1970−1989 PARE | 3.840 | 3.893 | 3.880 | 4.078 | 5.401 | 4.877 | 4.828 | 4.884 | 4.839 | 5.386 |
| 5.   Absolute 1980−1989 PARE | 1.554 | 1.656 | 1.726 | 1.934 | 2.794 | 2.772 | 2.916 | 3.149 | 3.347 | 4.059 |
| 6.   WA | 4.450 | 4.501 | 4.400 | 4.305 | 4.285 | 4.285 | 4.290 | 4.293 | 4.293 | 4.293 |
| **Viet Nam:** Dongs | | | | | | | | | | |
| 1.   MER | 0.020 | 0.020 | 0.060 | 0.100 | 0.130 | 0.160 | 0.180 | 0.180 | 0.200 | 0.210 |
| 2.   PPPs | ... | ... | ... | ... | ... | ... | ... | ... | ... | ... |
| 3.   Absolute 1970−1989 PARE | 0.018 | 0.020 | 0.061 | 0.101 | 0.130 | 0.161 | 0.181 | 0.181 | 0.200 | 0.213 |
| 4.   Relative 1970−1989 PARE | 0.037 | 0.039 | 0.114 | 0.177 | 0.209 | 0.235 | 0.249 | 0.233 | 0.239 | 0.235 |
| 5.   Absolute 1980−1989 PARE | 0.018 | 0.020 | 0.061 | 0.101 | 0.130 | 0.160 | 0.181 | 0.181 | 0.199 | 0.212 |
| 6.   WA [a] | 0.036 | 0.027 | 0.063 | 0.100 | 0.129 | 0.160 | 0.180 | 0.180 | 0.199 | 0.212 |
| **Yemen** [c] : Yemeni rials | | | | | | | | | | |
| 1.   MER | 5.500 | 5.433 | 4.690 | 4.617 | 4.575 | 4.563 | 4.563 | 4.563 | 4.563 | 4.563 |
| 2.   PPPs | 1.014 | 1.052 | 1.100 | 1.239 | 1.383 | 1.476 | 1.677 | 1.935 | 2.098 | 2.114 |
| 3.   Absolute 1970−1989 PARE | 1.554 | 1.719 | 1.886 | 2.246 | 2.651 | 3.100 | 3.809 | 4.359 | 5.069 | 5.541 |
| 4.   Relative 1970−1989 PARE | 3.187 | 3.353 | 3.518 | 3.929 | 4.251 | 4.525 | 5.232 | 5.610 | 6.080 | 6.102 |
| 5.   Absolute 1980−1989 PARE | 1.388 | 1.536 | 1.685 | 2.007 | 2.368 | 2.770 | 3.403 | 3.894 | 4.529 | 4.951 |
| 6.   WA [a] | 5.801 | 5.871 | 5.776 | 5.767 | 5.539 | 5.429 | 5.581 | 5.400 | 5.314 | 5.117 |
| **Democratic Yemen (former):** Dinars | | | | | | | | | | |
| 1.   MER | 0.417 | 0.415 | 0.384 | 0.349 | 0.345 | 0.345 | 0.345 | 0.345 | 0.345 | 0.345 |
| 2.   PPPs | ... | ... | ... | ... | ... | ... | ... | ... | ... | ... |
| 3.   Absolute 1970−1989 PARE | 0.167 | 0.169 | 0.183 | 0.223 | 0.247 | 0.264 | 0.249 | 0.260 | 0.268 | 0.304 |
| 4.   Relative 1970−1989 PARE | 0.343 | 0.330 | 0.341 | 0.391 | 0.397 | 0.386 | 0.342 | 0.335 | 0.321 | 0.335 |
| 5.   Absolute 1980−1989 PARE | 0.141 | 0.143 | 0.155 | 0.189 | 0.209 | 0.223 | 0.210 | 0.220 | 0.226 | 0.257 |
| 6.   WA [a] | 0.406 | 0.416 | 0.430 | 0.455 | 0.417 | 0.375 | 0.339 | 0.349 | 0.357 | 0.380 |
| **Yugoslavia** [d] : Yugoslav dinars | | | | | | | | | | |
| 1.   MER | 12.500 | 14.875 | 17.000 | 16.242 | 15.913 | 17.344 | 18.178 | 18.289 | 18.637 | 18.973 |
| 2.   PPPs | ... | ... | ... | ... | ... | ... | ... | ... | ... | ... |
| 3.   Absolute 1970−1989 PARE | 5.990 | 7.098 | 8.295 | 10.047 | 11.862 | 14.430 | 16.220 | 18.284 | 20.329 | 24.769 |
| 4.   Relative 1970−1989 PARE | 12.285 | 13.848 | 15.474 | 17.574 | 19.021 | 21.062 | 22.283 | 23.531 | 24.385 | 27.275 |
| 5.   Absolute 1980−1989 PARE | 5.359 | 6.350 | 7.421 | 8.988 | 10.611 | 12.909 | 14.511 | 16.356 | 18.187 | 22.159 |
| 6.   WA | 12.500 | 14.875 | 17.000 | 16.242 | 15.912 | 17.344 | 18.178 | 18.289 | 18.637 | 18.973 |

| | | | | | | | | | | Averages | | |
| 1980 (11) | 1981 (12) | 1982 (13) | 1983 (14) | 1984 (15) | 1985 (16) | 1986 (17) | 1987 (18) | 1988 (19) | 1989 (20) | 1970−89 (21) | 1970−79 (22) | 1980−89 (23) |
|---|---|---|---|---|---|---|---|---|---|---|---|---|
| 9.099 | 10.820 | 13.909 | 34.540 | 56.122 | 101.431 | 151.993 | 226.700 | 359.400 | 605.500 | 105.451 | 3.617 | 156.211 |
| 7.046 | 8.556 | 9.348 | 14.290 | 22.926 | 40.447 | 68.516 | 112.417 | 176.198 | 297.701 | 56.368 | 1.909 | 84.035 |
| 13.920 | 18.143 | 21.044 | 32.132 | 51.881 | 92.810 | 160.375 | 270.696 | 438.522 | 771.299 | 105.451 | 2.614 | 193.149 |
| 14.043 | 16.720 | 18.218 | 26.907 | 41.942 | 73.052 | 123.746 | 203.037 | 318.232 | 537.680 | 107.646 | 3.857 | 156.149 |
| 11.258 | 14.673 | 17.019 | 25.987 | 41.959 | 75.060 | 129.704 | 218.926 | 354.657 | 623.792 | 85.284 | 2.114 | 156.211 |
| 9.099 | 10.820 | 13.909 | 34.540 | 56.122 | 101.430 | 151.993 | 226.666 | 359.444 | 605.511 | 105.452 | 3.617 | 156.211 |
| | | | | | | | | | | | | |
| 68.290 | 87.830 | 96.210 | 99.370 | 99.230 | 106.030 | 106.080 | 109.800 | 104.400 | 116.000 | 90.841 | 75.886 | 99.785 |
| ... | ... | ... | ... | ... | ... | ... | ... | ... | ... | ... | ... | ... |
| 95.815 | 102.997 | 101.329 | 89.803 | 102.165 | 102.644 | 101.489 | 109.074 | 96.989 | 96.988 | 90.841 | 75.741 | 99.900 |
| 96.660 | 94.924 | 87.721 | 75.201 | 82.594 | 80.793 | 78.310 | 81.811 | 70.384 | 67.611 | 86.658 | 108.843 | 79.306 |
| 95.705 | 102.879 | 101.213 | 89.700 | 102.048 | 102.526 | 101.373 | 108.948 | 96.877 | 96.877 | 90.737 | 75.653 | 99.785 |
| 68.292 | 87.826 | 96.208 | 99.370 | 99.230 | 106.032 | 107.076 | 109.849 | 104.426 | 116.042 | 91.365 | 76.931 | 99.890 |
| | | | | | | | | | | | | |
| 4.293 | 14.500 | 4.293 | 4.298 | 7.018 | 7.500 | 8.083 | 14.500 | 14.500 | 34.700 | 8.005 | 4.316 | 9.951 |
| 3.677 | 3.874 | 4.002 | 3.973 | 4.779 | 5.057 | 4.932 | 6.779 | 7.772 | 14.142 | 5.313 | 3.288 | 6.184 |
| 6.107 | 6.873 | 6.971 | 7.366 | 8.934 | 10.008 | 9.955 | 14.078 | 16.682 | 31.600 | 8.005 | 3.263 | 11.993 |
| 6.161 | 6.334 | 6.035 | 6.169 | 7.222 | 7.877 | 7.682 | 10.559 | 12.106 | 22.029 | 8.109 | 4.750 | 9.674 |
| 5.067 | 5.703 | 5.784 | 6.112 | 7.413 | 8.304 | 8.260 | 11.681 | 13.842 | 26.220 | 6.642 | 2.707 | 9.951 |
| 4.293 | 4.293 | 4.293 | 4.297 | 7.017 | 7.500 | 8.083 | 14.500 | 14.500 | 34.681 | 7.543 | 4.314 | 9.101 |
| | | | | | | | | | | | | |
| 0.210 | 0.580 | 0.940 | 1.000 | 1.030 | 6.700 | 18.000 | 61.960 | 480.000 | 3532.780 | 283.325 | 0.130 | 494.228 |
| ... | ... | ... | ... | ... | ... | ... | ... | ... | ... | ... | ... | ... |
| 0.212 | 0.576 | 0.938 | 1.004 | 1.040 | 6.683 | 18.019 | 62.299 | 484.036 | 3553.321 | 283.325 | 0.129 | 495.945 |
| 0.214 | 0.531 | 0.812 | 0.841 | 0.841 | 5.260 | 13.903 | 46.728 | 351.261 | 2477.054 | 281.673 | 0.192 | 394.812 |
| 0.211 | 0.574 | 0.934 | 1.001 | 1.036 | 6.660 | 17.956 | 62.083 | 482.359 | 3541.014 | 282.344 | 0.129 | 494.228 |
| 0.210 | 0.573 | 0.937 | 1.006 | 1.036 | 6.658 | 17.971 | 62.217 | 481.632 | 3530.245 | 292.346 | 0.140 | 494.243 |
| | | | | | | | | | | | | |
| 4.563 | 4.563 | 4.563 | 4.579 | 5.353 | 7.400 | 9.600 | 10.300 | 9.800 | 9.800 | 6.507 | 4.619 | 7.158 |
| 1.948 | 1.880 | 2.042 | 2.177 | 2.270 | 2.684 | 3.011 | 3.104 | 3.257 | 3.684 | 2.444 | 1.672 | 2.724 |
| 5.666 | 5.786 | 6.240 | 6.523 | 6.660 | 7.335 | 8.395 | 8.903 | 9.656 | 11.372 | 6.507 | 3.530 | 8.013 |
| 5.716 | 5.333 | 5.402 | 5.463 | 5.384 | 5.774 | 6.478 | 6.678 | 7.008 | 7.927 | 6.062 | 5.041 | 6.348 |
| 5.062 | 5.169 | 5.574 | 5.828 | 5.950 | 6.553 | 7.500 | 7.954 | 8.627 | 10.159 | 5.813 | 3.154 | 7.158 |
| 4.776 | 4.663 | 4.836 | 4.831 | 4.966 | 6.148 | 8.272 | 9.821 | 10.671 | 11.499 | 6.783 | 5.410 | 7.190 |
| | | | | | | | | | | | | |
| 0.345 | 0.345 | 0.345 | 0.345 | 0.345 | 0.345 | 0.345 | 0.300 | 0.300 | 0.300 | 0.335 | 0.357 | 0.328 |
| ... | ... | ... | ... | ... | ... | ... | ... | ... | ... | ... | ... | ... |
| 0.329 | 0.347 | 0.367 | 0.386 | 0.388 | 0.395 | 0.379 | 0.414 | 0.422 | 0.443 | 0.335 | 0.236 | 0.389 |
| 0.332 | 0.319 | 0.318 | 0.323 | 0.314 | 0.311 | 0.293 | 0.310 | 0.306 | 0.309 | 0.320 | 0.346 | 0.312 |
| 0.278 | 0.293 | 0.310 | 0.326 | 0.328 | 0.334 | 0.320 | 0.349 | 0.356 | 0.374 | 0.283 | 0.199 | 0.328 |
| 0.380 | 0.367 | 0.365 | 0.364 | 0.352 | 0.350 | 0.338 | 0.346 | 0.330 | 0.312 | 0.355 | 0.382 | 0.347 |
| | | | | | | | | | | | | |
| 24.639 | 34.966 | 50.276 | 92.839 | 152.820 | 270.160 | 379.222 | 737.000 | 2522.600 | 28760.000 | 2762.133 | 17.565 | 4271.419 |
| ... | ... | ... | ... | ... | ... | ... | ... | ... | ... | ... | ... | ... |
| 32.349 | 44.980 | 58.981 | 81.106 | 124.169 | 220.813 | 415.140 | 911.629 | 2807.410 | 41128.400 | 2762.133 | 14.740 | 4774.710 |
| 32.634 | 41.454 | 51.060 | 67.918 | 100.383 | 173.805 | 320.325 | 683.774 | 2037.317 | 28670.996 | 2740.731 | 21.366 | 3848.381 |
| 28.939 | 40.239 | 52.764 | 72.557 | 111.081 | 197.538 | 371.381 | 815.537 | 2511.488 | 36793.150 | 2470.983 | 13.186 | 4271.419 |
| 24.639 | 34.966 | 50.276 | 92.839 | 152.820 | 270.160 | 379.220 | 736.999 | 2522.590 | 28764.000 | 2762.159 | 17.565 | 4271.493 |

**Table A.2**    Conversion rates for individual countries or areas, expressed as the number of
local currency units per United States dollar, 1970–1989 [*cont.*]

| Country or area | 1970 (1) | 1971 (2) | 1972 (3) | 1973 (4) | 1974 (5) | 1975 (6) | 1976 (7) | 1977 (8) | 1978 (9) | 1979 (10) |
|---|---|---|---|---|---|---|---|---|---|---|
| **Zaire:** Zaires | | | | | | | | | | |
| 1. MER | 0.500 | 0.500 | 0.500 | 0.500 | 0.500 | 0.500 | 0.790 | 0.857 | 0.836 | 1.729 |
| 2. PPPs | 0.268 | 0.268 | 0.287 | 0.304 | 0.357 | 0.401 | 0.591 | 0.941 | 1.177 | 2.064 |
| 3. Absolute 1970–1989 PARE | 0.255 | 0.264 | 0.290 | 0.342 | 0.393 | 0.466 | 0.744 | 1.036 | 1.517 | 3.065 |
| 4. Relative 1970–1989 PARE | 0.522 | 0.515 | 0.540 | 0.598 | 0.630 | 0.680 | 1.022 | 1.333 | 1.819 | 3.375 |
| 5. Absolute 1980–1989 PARE | 0.244 | 0.254 | 0.278 | 0.328 | 0.377 | 0.447 | 0.714 | 0.994 | 1.456 | 2.941 |
| 6. WA | 0.500 | 0.500 | 0.500 | 0.500 | 0.500 | 0.500 | 0.792 | 0.857 | 0.836 | 1.729 |
| **Zambia:** Zambian kwacha | | | | | | | | | | |
| 1. MER | 0.714 | 0.714 | 0.714 | 0.652 | 0.643 | 0.643 | 0.713 | 0.790 | 0.800 | 0.793 |
| 2. PPPs | 0.539 | 0.525 | 0.517 | 0.514 | 0.526 | 0.478 | 0.536 | 0.614 | 0.654 | 0.726 |
| 3. Absolute 1970–1989 PARE | 0.521 | 0.485 | 0.504 | 0.600 | 0.669 | 0.574 | 0.650 | 0.725 | 0.816 | 0.995 |
| 4. Relative 1970–1989 PARE | 1.069 | 0.946 | 0.940 | 1.050 | 1.073 | 0.837 | 0.893 | 0.933 | 0.979 | 1.096 |
| 5. Absolute 1980–1989 PARE | 0.481 | 0.448 | 0.466 | 0.555 | 0.618 | 0.530 | 0.601 | 0.670 | 0.754 | 0.920 |
| 6. WA | 0.714 | 0.714 | 0.714 | 0.652 | 0.643 | 0.643 | 0.722 | 0.790 | 0.801 | 0.793 |
| **Zimbabwe:** Zimbabwean dollars | | | | | | | | | | |
| 1. MER | 0.714 | 0.712 | 0.661 | 0.584 | 0.582 | 0.568 | 0.626 | 0.628 | 0.677 | 0.680 |
| 2. PPPs | 0.449 | 0.433 | 0.440 | 0.439 | 0.443 | 0.442 | 0.473 | 0.486 | 0.502 | 0.558 |
| 3. Absolute 1970–1989 PARE | 0.345 | 0.365 | 0.384 | 0.408 | 0.477 | 0.508 | 0.555 | 0.601 | 0.659 | 0.759 |
| 4. Relative 1970–1989 PARE | 0.707 | 0.712 | 0.717 | 0.714 | 0.765 | 0.741 | 0.762 | 0.773 | 0.790 | 0.836 |
| 5. Absolute 1980–1989 PARE | 0.300 | 0.318 | 0.335 | 0.356 | 0.416 | 0.442 | 0.483 | 0.523 | 0.574 | 0.661 |
| 6. WA | 0.714 | 0.712 | 0.661 | 0.585 | 0.583 | 0.570 | 0.626 | 0.628 | 0.677 | 0.680 |

Note:  PPPs for 1986–1989 have been estimated by the Statistical
Division, United Nations Secretariat.
Three dots (...) indicate that data are not available.

a    Estimated by the Statistical Division, United Nations Secretariat,
using the *World Bank Atlas* methodology.

b    Through accession of the German Democratic Republic to the
Federal Republic of Germany with effect from 3 October 1990, the
two German States have united to form one sovereign State. As
from the date of unification, the Federal Republic of Germany
acts in the United Nations under the designation of "Germany".
All data shown which pertain to Germany prior to 3 October 1990
are indicated separately for the Federal Republic of Germany
and the former German Democratic Republic based on their
respective territories at the time indicated.

c    On 22 May 1990, the Yemen Arab Republic and the People's
Democratic Republic of Yemen merged to form a single
sovereign state, the "Republic of Yemen". Data prior to that
date are indicated separately for Yemen (excluding former
Democratic Yemen), and former Democratic Yemen.

d    Unless otherwise indicated, data provided for Yugoslavia are
prior to 1 January 1992 and refer to the Socialist Federal
Republic of Yugoslavia which was composed of six republics.

| | | | | | | | | | | Averages | | |
|---|---|---|---|---|---|---|---|---|---|---|---|---|
| 1980 | 1981 | 1982 | 1983 | 1984 | 1985 | 1986 | 1987 | 1988 | 1989 | 1970−89 | 1970−79 | 1980−89 |
| (11) | (12) | (13) | (14) | (15) | (16) | (17) | (18) | (19) | (20) | (21) | (22) | (23) |
| 2.800 | 4.384 | 5.750 | 12.889 | 36.129 | 49.873 | 59.620 | 112.400 | 187.100 | 381.400 | 38.241 | 0.838 | 72.332 |
| 2.653 | 3.615 | 4.817 | 7.881 | 16.305 | 21.146 | 28.317 | 56.004 | 80.572 | 159.363 | 26.013 | 0.702 | 42.002 |
| 4.632 | 6.211 | 8.326 | 15.592 | 25.520 | 36.745 | 50.193 | 102.124 | 151.856 | 312.669 | 38.241 | 0.802 | 75.362 |
| 4.673 | 5.724 | 7.208 | 13.057 | 20.631 | 28.922 | 38.729 | 76.599 | 110.201 | 217.965 | 40.080 | 1.212 | 60.589 |
| 4.446 | 5.961 | 7.992 | 14.965 | 24.494 | 35.267 | 48.175 | 98.018 | 145.750 | 300.096 | 36.703 | 0.770 | 72.332 |
| 2.800 | 4.384 | 5.750 | 12.889 | 36.129 | 49.873 | 59.625 | 112.403 | 187.070 | 381.445 | 38.244 | 0.838 | 72.331 |
| | | | | | | | | | | | | |
| 0.789 | 0.868 | 0.928 | 1.251 | 1.794 | 2.700 | 7.300 | 8.900 | 8.200 | 12.900 | 2.657 | 0.721 | 4.175 |
| 0.736 | 0.746 | 0.834 | 0.861 | 0.992 | 1.343 | 2.396 | 3.461 | 4.417 | 6.670 | 1.779 | 0.568 | 2.500 |
| 1.112 | 1.192 | 1.265 | 1.501 | 1.776 | 2.506 | 4.561 | 6.778 | 8.940 | 14.053 | 2.657 | 0.657 | 4.518 |
| 1.122 | 1.098 | 1.095 | 1.257 | 1.436 | 1.973 | 3.519 | 5.084 | 6.488 | 9.796 | 2.750 | 0.980 | 3.640 |
| 1.028 | 1.101 | 1.169 | 1.387 | 1.641 | 2.316 | 4.215 | 6.263 | 8.261 | 12.985 | 2.455 | 0.607 | 4.175 |
| 0.789 | 0.870 | 0.929 | 1.259 | 1.813 | 3.140 | 7.788 | 9.519 | 8.266 | 13.814 | 2.704 | 0.722 | 4.303 |
| | | | | | | | | | | | | |
| 0.643 | 0.688 | 0.757 | 1.011 | 1.244 | 1.612 | 1.665 | 1.700 | 1.800 | 2.100 | 1.072 | 0.637 | 1.297 |
| 0.544 | 0.552 | 0.580 | 0.678 | 0.734 | 0.807 | 0.885 | 0.963 | 1.016 | 1.082 | 0.706 | 0.472 | 0.807 |
| 0.837 | 0.958 | 1.095 | 1.308 | 1.354 | 1.442 | 1.613 | 1.804 | 1.968 | 2.182 | 1.072 | 0.509 | 1.490 |
| 0.845 | 0.883 | 0.948 | 1.095 | 1.094 | 1.135 | 1.245 | 1.353 | 1.428 | 1.521 | 1.070 | 0.760 | 1.194 |
| 0.729 | 0.834 | 0.953 | 1.139 | 1.179 | 1.256 | 1.404 | 1.571 | 1.713 | 1.900 | 0.934 | 0.443 | 1.297 |
| 0.643 | 0.690 | 0.759 | 1.013 | 1.258 | 1.614 | 1.667 | 1.662 | 1.806 | 2.119 | 1.073 | 0.637 | 1.299 |

## Table A.3  Country or area rankings based on per capita gross domestic product in 1970

| | Market exchange rate | | PPPs | | Absolute 1970–1989 PARE | |
|---|---|---|---|---|---|---|
| Rank | Country or area | Per capita GDP | Country or area | Per capita GDP | Country or area | Per capita GDP |
| 1 | Bhutan | 44 | Mali | 100 | Bhutan | 67 |
| 2 | Burkina Faso | 54 | Burkina Faso | 109 | Guinea–Bissau | 98 |
| 3 | Rwanda | 58 | Rwanda | 150 | Ethiopia | 98 |
| 4 | Ethiopia | 58 | Malawi | 156 | Malawi | 110 |
| 5 | Lao People's Dem. Republic | 62 | Burundi | 161 | Burkina Faso | 122 |
| 6 | Mali | 63 | Ethiopia | 165 | Lesotho | 123 |
| 7 | Bangladesh | 64 | Zaire | 177 | Maldives | 123 |
| 8 | Lesotho | 66 | United Republic of Tanzania | 183 | Nepal | 123 |
| 9 | Burundi | 70 | Lesotho | 198 | Bangladesh | 138 |
| 10 | Malawi | 71 | Myanmar | 202 | Viet Nam | 142 |
| 11 | Haiti | 73 | Niger | 204 | China | 143 |
| 12 | Nepal | 75 | Bangladesh | 223 | Myanmar | 151 |
| 13 | Indonesia | 79 | Haiti | 228 | Rwanda | 152 |
| 14 | Yemen [a] | 81 | Chad | 231 | Mali | 153 |
| 15 | Chad | 89 | Nepal | 234 | Burundi | 158 |
| 16 | Somalia | 93 | Central African Republic | 236 | Cambodia | 159 |
| 17 | Benin | 93 | Afghanistan | 257 | Lao People's Dem. Republic | 182 |
| 18 | Zaire | 95 | Guinea | 258 | Zaire | 186 |
| 19 | Niger | 96 | Indonesia | 259 | Chad | 192 |
| 20 | Central African Republic | 97 | Mozambique | 273 | India | 197 |
| 21 | United Republic of Tanzania | 99 | Gambia | 288 | Haiti | 206 |
| 22 | Afghanistan | 102 | Ghana | 290 | Pakistan | 216 |
| 23 | Cambodia | 103 | Somalia | 293 | United Republic of Tanzania | 224 |
| 24 | India | 104 | Sierra Leone | 294 | Sri Lanka | 232 |
| 25 | Myanmar | 105 | Angola | 296 | Indonesia | 234 |
| 26 | China | 112 | Kenya | 296 | Mozambique | 237 |
| 27 | Mozambique | 114 | Mauritania | 297 | Afghanistan | 239 |
| 28 | Gambia | 116 | India | 308 | Sierra Leone | 252 |
| 29 | Comoros | 122 | Benin | 319 | Niger | 262 |
| 30 | Viet Nam | 127 | Sudan | 322 | Dem. People's Republic of Korea | 263 |
| 31 | Togo | 130 | Cameroon | 329 | Gambia | 267 |
| 32 | Madagascar | 133 | Uganda | 338 | Benin | 278 |
| 33 | Botswana | 134 | Congo | 342 | Kenya | 282 |
| 34 | Maldives | 136 | Botswana | 349 | Yemen [a] | 288 |
| 35 | Democratic Yemen [a] | 137 | Togo | 351 | Madagascar | 290 |
| 36 | Cape Verde | 145 | Nigeria | 356 | Somalia | 304 |
| 37 | Sudan | 145 | Liberia | 364 | Central African Republic | 306 |
| 38 | Kenya | 148 | Egypt | 378 | Seychelles | 307 |
| 39 | Tonga | 154 | Pakistan | 386 | Guinea | 318 |
| 40 | Sierra Leone | 156 | Madagascar | 386 | Solomon Islands | 320 |
| 41 | Angola | 162 | Senegal | 415 | Togo | 323 |
| 42 | Pakistan | 162 | Swaziland | 418 | Sudan | 335 |
| 43 | Mauritania | 167 | Honduras | 434 | Comoros | 336 |
| 44 | Equatorial Guinea | 170 | Yemen [a] | 442 | Democratic Yemen [a] | 343 |
| 45 | Cameroon | 173 | Côte d'Ivoire | 449 | Swaziland | 381 |
| 46 | Nigeria | 175 | Zimbabwe | 457 | Botswana | 383 |
| 47 | Guinea–Bissau | 178 | Morocco | 493 | Egypt | 399 |
| 48 | Guinea | 180 | Algeria | 505 | Tonga | 415 |
| 49 | Philippines | 182 | Tunisia | 515 | Thailand | 419 |
| 50 | Sri Lanka | 190 | Sri Lanka | 533 | Mauritania | 424 |
| 51 | Solomon Islands | 195 | Philippines | 549 | Philippines | 427 |
| 52 | Saint Vincent and the Grenadines | 196 | Zambia | 566 | Cape Verde | 439 |
| 53 | Thailand | 198 | Bolivia | 589 | Ghana | 468 |
| 54 | Sao Tome–Principe | 208 | Thailand | 606 | Senegal | 485 |
| 55 | Senegal | 208 | Dominican Republic | 608 | Anguilla | 486 |
| 56 | Congo | 217 | Paraguay | 608 | Morocco | 486 |
| 57 | Liberia | 224 | Mauritius | 616 | Equatorial Guinea | 498 |
| 58 | Bolivia | 234 | Oman | 618 | Liberia | 507 |

| Relative 1970–1989 PARE | | Absolute 1980–1989 PARE | | World Bank Atlas method | | |
|---|---|---|---|---|---|---|
| Country or area | Per capita GDP | Country or area | Per capita GDP | Country or area | Per capita GDP | Rank |
| Bhutan | 33 | Bhutan | 67 | Lao People's Dem. Republic | 38 | 1 |
| Guinea–Bissau | 48 | Guinea–Bissau | 94 | Bhutan | 44 | 2 |
| Ethiopia | 48 | Ethiopia | 114 | Burkina Faso | 54 | 3 |
| Malawi | 53 | Malawi | 122 | Rwanda | 58 | 4 |
| Burkina Faso | 60 | Maldives | 128 | Ethiopia | 58 | 5 |
| Lesotho | 60 | Nepal | 140 | Mali | 63 | 6 |
| Maldives | 60 | Lesotho | 140 | Lesotho | 66 | 7 |
| Nepal | 60 | China | 141 | Burundi | 70 | 8 |
| Bangladesh | 67 | Viet Nam | 142 | Viet Nam | 70 | 9 |
| Viet Nam | 69 | Burkina Faso | 150 | Malawi | 71 | 10 |
| China | 70 | Bangladesh | 152 | Haiti | 73 | 11 |
| Myanmar | 73 | Myanmar | 172 | Nepal | 75 | 12 |
| Rwanda | 74 | Mali | 175 | Yemen [a] | 77 | 13 |
| Mali | 74 | Rwanda | 182 | Indonesia | 79 | 14 |
| Burundi | 77 | Burundi | 193 | Chad | 89 | 15 |
| Cambodia | 78 | Zaire | 194 | Afghanistan | 93 | 16 |
| Lao People's Dem. Republic | 89 | Cambodia | 216 | Somalia | 93 | 17 |
| Zaire | 91 | India | 230 | Benin | 93 | 18 |
| Chad | 93 | Sri Lanka | 238 | Cambodia | 94 | 19 |
| India | 96 | Pakistan | 241 | Zaire | 95 | 20 |
| Haiti | 100 | Lao People's Dem. Republic | 246 | Niger | 96 | 21 |
| Pakistan | 105 | Dem. People's Republic of Korea | 250 | Central African Republic | 97 | 22 |
| United Republic of Tanzania | 109 | Chad | 250 | Bangladesh | 97 | 23 |
| Sri Lanka | 113 | Indonesia | 265 | United Republic of Tanzania | 101 | 24 |
| Indonesia | 114 | Haiti | 272 | India | 104 | 25 |
| Mozambique | 116 | United Republic of Tanzania | 281 | Myanmar | 104 | 26 |
| Afghanistan | 117 | Gambia | 287 | Mozambique | 108 | 27 |
| Sierra Leone | 123 | Sierra Leone | 290 | China | 111 | 28 |
| Niger | 128 | Niger | 309 | Gambia | 116 | 29 |
| Dem. People's Republic of Korea | 128 | Mozambique | 311 | Comoros | 122 | 30 |
| Gambia | 130 | Afghanistan | 312 | Togo | 130 | 31 |
| Benin | 135 | Kenya | 313 | Madagascar | 133 | 32 |
| Kenya | 137 | Yemen [a] | 323 | Botswana | 134 | 33 |
| Yemen [a] | 141 | Seychelles | 339 | Angola | 137 | 34 |
| Madagascar | 141 | Madagascar | 342 | Democratic Yemen [a] | 141 | 35 |
| Somalia | 148 | Solomon Islands | 358 | Tonga | 144 | 36 |
| Central African Republic | 149 | Guinea | 372 | Cape Verde | 145 | 37 |
| Seychelles | 150 | Benin | 379 | Kenya | 148 | 38 |
| Guinea | 155 | Sudan | 392 | Sierra Leone | 156 | 39 |
| Solomon Islands | 156 | Togo | 394 | Pakistan | 162 | 40 |
| Togo | 157 | Somalia | 395 | Mauritania | 167 | 41 |
| Sudan | 163 | Central African Republic | 400 | Sudan | 167 | 42 |
| Comoros | 164 | Democratic Yemen [a] | 406 | Nigeria | 175 | 43 |
| Democratic Yemen [a] | 167 | Swaziland | 411 | Cameroon | 175 | 44 |
| Swaziland | 186 | Comoros | 418 | Guinea–Bissau | 178 | 45 |
| Botswana | 187 | Botswana | 420 | Maldives | 182 | 46 |
| Egypt | 195 | Egypt | 430 | Philippines | 187 | 47 |
| Tonga | 202 | Tonga | 476 | Sri Lanka | 190 | 48 |
| Thailand | 204 | Thailand | 476 | Solomon Islands | 195 | 49 |
| Mauritania | 207 | Philippines | 507 | Saint Vincent and the Grenadines | 196 | 50 |
| Philippines | 208 | Cape Verde | 518 | Uganda | 197 | 51 |
| Cape Verde | 214 | Mauritania | 522 | Thailand | 198 | 52 |
| Ghana | 228 | Morocco | 527 | Sao Tome–Principe | 208 | 53 |
| Senegal | 237 | Anguilla | 530 | Senegal | 208 | 54 |
| Anguilla | 237 | Mongolia | 547 | Congo | 217 | 55 |
| Morocco | 237 | Samoa | 548 | Liberia | 224 | 56 |
| Equatorial Guinea | 243 | Vanuatu | 557 | Bolivia | 234 | 57 |
| Liberia | 247 | Senegal | 589 | Kiribati | 238 | 58 |

**Table A.3**    Country or area rankings based on per capita gross domestic product in 1970 [cont.]

| | Market exchange rate | | PPPs | | Absolute 1970–1989 PARE | |
|---|---|---|---|---|---|---|
| Rank | Country or area | Per capita GDP | Country or area | Per capita GDP | Country or area | Per capita GDP |
| 59 | Egypt | 234 | Ecuador | 685 | Samoa | 512 |
| 60 | Uganda | 242 | Syrian Arab Republic | 691 | Saint Vincent and the Grenadines | 529 |
| 61 | Paraguay | 253 | Malaysia | 706 | Cameroon | 534 |
| 62 | Swaziland | 256 | El Salvador | 707 | Mongolia | 534 |
| 63 | Ghana | 257 | Guyana | 787 | Guyana | 556 |
| 64 | Jordan | 258 | Iraq | 838 | Vanuatu | 557 |
| 65 | Morocco | 258 | Colombia | 843 | Nigeria | 564 |
| 66 | Honduras | 263 | Gabon | 844 | Sao Tome – Principe | 578 |
| 67 | Côte d'Ivoire | 271 | Iran (Islamic Republic of) | 862 | Honduras | 584 |
| 68 | Mauritius | 271 | Guatemala | 874 | Zambia | 585 |
| 69 | Ecuador | 277 | Brazil | 902 | Zimbabwe | 595 |
| 70 | Dem. People's Republic of Korea | 277 | Turkey | 910 | Albania | 598 |
| 71 | Republic of Korea | 279 | Papua New Guinea | 963 | Dominican Republic | 619 |
| 72 | Tunisia | 281 | Jordan | 966 | Kiribati | 634 |
| 73 | Grenada | 285 | Saudi Arabia | 978 | Mauritius | 636 |
| 74 | Syrian Arab Republic | 286 | Panama | 1 006 | Tunisia | 650 |
| 75 | El Salvador | 287 | Fiji | 1 012 | Bolivia | 651 |
| 76 | Zimbabwe | 287 | Nicaragua | 1 030 | Ecuador | 663 |
| 77 | Samoa | 297 | Peru | 1 090 | Uganda | 676 |
| 78 | Dominica | 303 | Barbados | 1 094 | Grenada | 678 |
| 79 | Kiribati | 308 | Costa Rica | 1 196 | Saint Lucia | 685 |
| 80 | Papua New Guinea | 317 | Suriname | 1 251 | Congo | 690 |
| 81 | Malaysia | 319 | Jamaica | 1 257 | Côte d'Ivoire | 708 |
| 82 | Dominican Republic | 336 | Trinidad & Tobago | 1 306 | El Salvador | 717 |
| 83 | Colombia | 337 | Portugal | 1 331 | Paraguay | 720 |
| 84 | Saint Kitts – Nevis | 338 | Malta | 1 335 | Colombia | 744 |
| 85 | Anguilla | 343 | Greece | 1 482 | Angola | 746 |
| 86 | Turkey | 362 | Mexico | 1 538 | Jordan | 752 |
| 87 | Guatemala | 363 | Cyprus | 1 551 | Turkey | 769 |
| 88 | Algeria | 376 | Singapore | 1 556 | Saint Kitts – Nevis | 771 |
| 89 | Iraq | 376 | South Africa | 1 655 | Malaysia | 776 |
| 90 | Guyana | 377 | Bahrain | 1 768 | Romania | 777 |
| 91 | Nicaragua | 378 | Chile | 1 777 | Papua New Guinea | 781 |
| 92 | Seychelles | 380 | Venezuela | 1 855 | Guatemala | 789 |
| 93 | Saint Lucia | 385 | Uruguay | 1 863 | Belize | 854 |
| 94 | Iran (Islamic Republic of) | 388 | Ireland | 1 970 | Syrian Arab Republic | 871 |
| 95 | Belize | 397 | Argentina | 1 995 | Republic of Korea | 881 |
| 96 | Mongolia | 416 | Spain | 2 303 | Dominica | 925 |
| 97 | Oman | 418 | Israel | 2 481 | Cuba | 938 |
| 98 | Albania | 421 | Italy | 2 710 | Brazil | 1 030 |
| 99 | Djibouti | 422 | Japan | 2 763 | Fiji | 1 109 |
| 100 | Fiji | 423 | Austria | 2 832 | Peru | 1 118 |
| 101 | Zambia | 427 | Iceland | 3 067 | Costa Rica | 1 125 |
| 102 | Cook Islands | 443 | Finland | 3 075 | Namibia | 1 137 |
| 103 | Vanuatu | 467 | United Kingdom | 3 097 | Bulgaria | 1 171 |
| 104 | Namibia | 495 | New Zealand | 3 173 | Poland | 1 203 |
| 105 | Peru | 515 | Belgium | 3 369 | Nicaragua | 1 249 |
| 106 | Brazil | 522 | Norway | 3 441 | Hungary | 1 257 |
| 107 | Montserrat | 550 | France | 3 491 | Montserrat | 1 276 |
| 108 | Barbados | 553 | Netherlands | 3 528 | Cook Islands | 1 293 |
| 109 | Costa Rica | 569 | Federal Republic of Germany [b] | 3 592 | Lebanon | 1 309 |
| 110 | Lebanon | 603 | Australia | 3 651 | Panama | 1 317 |
| 111 | Romania | 606 | Sweden | 3 817 | Chile | 1 387 |
| 112 | Cuba | 655 | Denmark | 3 994 | Algeria | 1 392 |
| 113 | Gabon | 664 | Luxembourg | 4 072 | Jamaica | 1 395 |
| 114 | Panama | 667 | Canada | 4 168 | Djibouti | 1 437 |
| 115 | Saudi Arabia | 673 | Kuwait | 4 189 | Mexico | 1 438 |
| 116 | Portugal | 684 | United Arab Emirates | 4 637 | Suriname | 1 440 |
| 117 | Malta | 698 | United States of America | 4 922 | Antigua & Barbuda | 1 451 |
| 118 | Mexico | 704 | | | Yugoslavia [c] | 1 491 |

| Relative 1970–1989 PARE | | Absolute 1980–1989 PARE | | World Bank Atlas method | | |
|---|---|---|---|---|---|---|
| Country or area | Per capita GDP | Country or area | Per capita GDP | Country or area | Per capita GDP | Rank |
| Samoa | 249 | Ghana | 605 | Paraguay | 253 | 59 |
| Saint Vincent and the Grenadines | 258 | Guyana | 616 | Egypt | 255 | 60 |
| Cameroon | 260 | Albania | 624 | Swaziland | 256 | 61 |
| Mongolia | 260 | Zambia | 634 | Ghana | 257 | 62 |
| Guyana | 271 | Uganda | 646 | Jordan | 258 | 63 |
| Vanuatu | 271 | Cameroon | 649 | Morocco | 258 | 64 |
| Nigeria | 275 | Saint Vincent and the Grenadines | 664 | Honduras | 263 | 65 |
| Sao Tome–Principe | 282 | Liberia | 665 | Côte d'Ivoire | 271 | 66 |
| Honduras | 285 | Nigeria | 680 | Mauritius | 271 | 67 |
| Zambia | 285 | Zimbabwe | 683 | Ecuador | 277 | 68 |
| Zimbabwe | 290 | Dominican Republic | 696 | Republic of Korea | 279 | 69 |
| Albania | 292 | Mauritius | 728 | Tunisia | 281 | 70 |
| Dominican Republic | 302 | Tunisia | 728 | Dem. People's Republic of Korea | 283 | 71 |
| Kiribati | 309 | Honduras | 733 | Grenada | 285 | 72 |
| Mauritius | 310 | Ecuador | 798 | El Salvador | 287 | 73 |
| Tunisia | 317 | Kiribati | 806 | Zimbabwe | 287 | 74 |
| Bolivia | 317 | Côte d'Ivoire | 811 | Samoa | 297 | 75 |
| Ecuador | 323 | Turkey | 814 | Dominica | 303 | 76 |
| Uganda | 330 | Congo | 822 | Papua New Guinea | 317 | 77 |
| Grenada | 330 | Sao Tome–Principe | 824 | Malaysia | 319 | 78 |
| Saint Lucia | 334 | Saint Lucia | 833 | Anguilla | 329 | 79 |
| Congo | 337 | Paraguay | 858 | Dominican Republic | 336 | 80 |
| Côte d'Ivoire | 345 | Bolivia | 860 | Colombia | 337 | 81 |
| El Salvador | 350 | Romania | 867 | Saint Kitts–Nevis | 338 | 82 |
| Paraguay | 351 | Jordan | 873 | Syrian Arab Republic | 344 | 83 |
| Colombia | 363 | Grenada | 880 | Turkey | 358 | 84 |
| Angola | 364 | Malaysia | 888 | Guatemala | 363 | 85 |
| Jordan | 366 | Colombia | 892 | Djibouti | 372 | 86 |
| Turkey | 375 | Papua New Guinea | 960 | Algeria | 376 | 87 |
| Saint Kitts–Nevis | 376 | Saint Kitts–Nevis | 962 | Guyana | 377 | 88 |
| Malaysia | 378 | Cuba | 964 | Nicaragua | 378 | 89 |
| Romania | 379 | Equatorial Guinea | 971 | Seychelles | 380 | 90 |
| Papua New Guinea | 381 | Guatemala | 974 | Saint Lucia | 385 | 91 |
| Guatemala | 385 | El Salvador | 1 003 | Iran (Islamic Republic of) | 388 | 92 |
| Belize | 416 | Republic of Korea | 1 039 | Albania | 389 | 93 |
| Syrian Arab Republic | 424 | Belize | 1 044 | Iraq | 391 | 94 |
| Republic of Korea | 429 | Syrian Arab Republic | 1 095 | Belize | 397 | 95 |
| Dominica | 451 | Angola | 1 173 | Cook Islands | 406 | 96 |
| Cuba | 458 | Brazil | 1 198 | Vanuatu | 414 | 97 |
| Brazil | 502 | Costa Rica | 1 273 | Oman | 418 | 98 |
| Fiji | 541 | Bulgaria | 1 274 | Fiji | 423 | 99 |
| Peru | 545 | Poland | 1 288 | Zambia | 427 | 100 |
| Costa Rica | 548 | Fiji | 1 312 | Brazil | 454 | 101 |
| Namibia | 554 | Hungary | 1 322 | Namibia | 495 | 102 |
| Bulgaria | 571 | Dominica | 1 337 | Montserrat | 506 | 103 |
| Poland | 586 | Namibia | 1 393 | Guinea | 518 | 104 |
| Nicaragua | 609 | Peru | 1 428 | Peru | 529 | 105 |
| Hungary | 613 | Panama | 1 575 | Hungary | 537 | 106 |
| Montserrat | 622 | Montserrat | 1 603 | Lebanon | 549 | 107 |
| Cook Islands | 630 | Jamaica | 1 619 | Barbados | 553 | 108 |
| Lebanon | 638 | Mexico | 1 657 | Costa Rica | 569 | 109 |
| Panama | 642 | Yugoslavia [c] | 1 666 | Romania | 640 | 110 |
| Chile | 676 | Algeria | 1 686 | Gabon | 664 | 111 |
| Algeria | 678 | Cook Islands | 1 742 | Panama | 667 | 112 |
| Jamaica | 680 | Antigua & Barbuda | 1 747 | Saudi Arabia | 673 | 113 |
| Djibouti | 701 | Chile | 1 755 | Equatorial Guinea | 674 | 114 |
| Mexico | 701 | Malta | 1 794 | Portugal | 684 | 115 |
| Suriname | 702 | Suriname | 1 801 | Malta | 698 | 116 |
| Antigua & Barbuda | 708 | Portugal | 1 842 | Cuba | 701 | 117 |
| Yugoslavia [c] | 727 | Lebanon | 1 869 | Mexico | 704 | 118 |

**Table A.3**    Country or area rankings based on per capita gross domestic product in 1970 [cont.]

| | Market exchange rate | | PPPs | | Absolute 1970–1989 PARE | |
|---|---|---|---|---|---|---|
| Rank | Country or area | Per capita GDP | Country or area | Per capita GDP | Country or area | Per capita GDP |
| 119 | Yugoslavia [c] | 714 | | | Malta | 1 532 |
| 120 | Antigua & Barbuda | 739 | | | Portugal | 1 545 |
| 121 | Guadeloupe | 746 | | | Czechoslovakia | 1 671 |
| 122 | Jamaica | 751 | | | Uruguay | 1 752 |
| 123 | Suriname | 756 | | | South Africa | 1 817 |
| 124 | South Africa | 768 | | | Iraq | 1 998 |
| 125 | Bulgaria | 771 | | | French Guiana | 2 143 |
| 126 | Reunion | 820 | | | Guadeloupe | 2 155 |
| 127 | Trinidad & Tobago | 847 | | | Reunion | 2 181 |
| 128 | Uruguay | 856 | | | Union of Soviet Socialist Rep. | 2 224 |
| 129 | Chile | 859 | | | Cyprus | 2 372 |
| 130 | French Guiana | 877 | | | Greece | 2 383 |
| 131 | Martinique | 884 | | | Singapore | 2 387 |
| 132 | Cyprus | 891 | | | Argentina | 2 391 |
| 133 | Singapore | 914 | | | Martinique | 2 451 |
| 134 | Hong Kong | 916 | | | Barbados | 2 490 |
| 135 | Argentina | 939 | | | Hong Kong | 2 543 |
| 136 | Czechoslovakia | 1 012 | | | Norway | 2 629 |
| 137 | Bahrain | 1 060 | | | Gabon | 2 796 |
| 138 | Hungary | 1 075 | | | Venezuela | 3 087 |
| 139 | Spain | 1 110 | | | Iran (Islamic Republic of) | 3 106 |
| 140 | Greece | 1 133 | | | Trinidad & Tobago | 3 197 |
| 141 | Poland | 1 245 | | | Spain | 3 464 |
| 142 | Venezuela | 1 285 | | | Ireland | 3 514 |
| 143 | Ireland | 1 315 | | | British Virgin Islands | 3 839 |
| 144 | Brunei Darussalam | 1 362 | | | German Democratic Republic [b] | 3 889 |
| 145 | Union of Soviet Socialist Rep. | 1 659 | | | Netherlands Antilles | 3 907 |
| 146 | Netherlands Antilles | 1 691 | | | Puerto Rico | 4 026 |
| 147 | British Virgin Islands | 1 803 | | | Israel | 4 547 |
| 148 | Libyan Arab Jamahiriya | 1 874 | | | Oman | 4 906 |
| 149 | Israel | 1 921 | | | Italy | 5 171 |
| 150 | French Polynesia | 1 933 | | | United Kingdom | 5 859 |
| 151 | Austria | 1 936 | | | Libyan Arab Jamahiriya | 6 038 |
| 152 | Japan | 1 953 | | | Austria | 6 054 |
| 153 | Italy | 1 997 | | | New Zealand | 6 122 |
| 154 | German Democratic Republic [b] | 2 019 | | | Saudi Arabia | 6 135 |
| 155 | Puerto Rico | 2 077 | | | French Polynesia | 6 241 |
| 156 | United Kingdom | 2 218 | | | United Arab Emirates | 6 587 |
| 157 | New Zealand | 2 233 | | | Belgium | 6 628 |
| 158 | Finland | 2 364 | | | Japan | 6 892 |
| 159 | Iceland | 2 430 | | | Finland | 7 250 |
| 160 | Netherlands | 2 568 | | | New Caledonia | 7 328 |
| 161 | Belgium | 2 597 | | | France | 7 357 |
| 162 | Qatar | 2 694 | | | Iceland | 7 417 |
| 163 | France | 2 814 | | | Netherlands | 7 548 |
| 164 | Norway | 2 884 | | | Bahamas | 7 596 |
| 165 | Bahamas | 2 897 | | | Bahrain | 7 799 |
| 166 | United Arab Emirates | 2 976 | | | Luxembourg | 7 915 |
| 167 | Federal Republic of Germany [b] | 3 042 | | | Canada | 8 102 |
| 168 | Australia | 3 133 | | | Federal Republic of Germany [b] | 8 211 |
| 169 | Denmark | 3 209 | | | Australia | 8 265 |
| 170 | Luxembourg | 3 238 | | | Denmark | 9 001 |
| 171 | Switzerland | 3 351 | | | US Virgin Islands | 9 112 |
| 172 | New Caledonia | 3 408 | | | Brunei Darussalam | 9 949 |
| 173 | Bermuda | 3 841 | | | Sweden | 10 065 |
| 174 | Kuwait | 3 858 | | | United States of America | 10 095 |
| 175 | Canada | 3 973 | | | Bermuda | 10 965 |
| 176 | Sweden | 4 164 | | | Switzerland | 12 474 |
| 177 | US Virgin Islands | 4 656 | | | Kuwait | 27 598 |
| 178 | United States of America | 4 922 | | | Qatar | 30 988 |

| Relative 1970–1989 PARE | | Absolute 1980–1989 PARE | | World Bank Atlas method | | |
|---|---|---|---|---|---|---|
| Country or area | Per capita GDP | Country or area | Per capita GDP | Country or area | Per capita GDP | Rank |
| Malta | 747 | Czechoslovakia | 1 889 | Yugoslavia [c] | 714 | 119 |
| Portugal | 753 | Djibouti | 1 970 | Guadeloupe | 732 | 120 |
| Czechoslovakia | 815 | Nicaragua | 2 149 | Bulgaria | 735 | 121 |
| Uruguay | 854 | Uruguay | 2 166 | Antigua & Barbuda | 739 | 122 |
| South Africa | 886 | South Africa | 2 285 | Jamaica | 748 | 123 |
| Iraq | 974 | Union of Soviet Socialist Rep. | 2 386 | Suriname | 756 | 124 |
| French Guiana | 1 045 | Reunion | 2 530 | South Africa | 768 | 125 |
| Guadeloupe | 1 051 | Guadeloupe | 2 671 | French Guiana | 796 | 126 |
| Reunion | 1 064 | French Guiana | 2 686 | Reunion | 818 | 127 |
| Union of Soviet Socialist Rep. | 1 084 | Singapore | 2 762 | Mongolia | 823 | 128 |
| Cyprus | 1 156 | Norway | 2 766 | Trinidad & Tobago | 847 | 129 |
| Greece | 1 162 | Greece | 2 789 | Uruguay | 856 | 130 |
| Singapore | 1 164 | Iraq | 2 860 | Chile | 858 | 131 |
| Argentina | 1 166 | Cyprus | 2 867 | Martinique | 887 | 132 |
| Martinique | 1 195 | Hong Kong | 2 882 | Singapore | 914 | 133 |
| Barbados | 1 214 | Martinique | 2 923 | Hong Kong | 916 | 134 |
| Hong Kong | 1 240 | Argentina | 2 971 | Brunei Darussalam | 975 | 135 |
| Norway | 1 282 | Barbados | 3 343 | Argentina | 991 | 136 |
| Gabon | 1 363 | Gabon | 3 668 | Bahrain | 1 060 | 137 |
| Venezuela | 1 505 | Venezuela | 3 720 | Spain | 1 110 | 138 |
| Iran (Islamic Republic of) | 1 514 | Trinidad & Tobago | 4 191 | Greece | 1 133 | 139 |
| Trinidad & Tobago | 1 559 | German Democratic Republic [b] | 4 218 | Venezuela | 1 299 | 140 |
| Spain | 1 689 | Ireland | 4 393 | Ireland | 1 316 | 141 |
| Ireland | 1 713 | Spain | 4 394 | Czechoslovakia | 1 378 | 142 |
| British Virgin Islands | 1 872 | British Virgin Islands | 4 773 | British Virgin Islands | 1 406 | 143 |
| German Democratic Republic [b] | 1 896 | Puerto Rico | 4 911 | Cyprus | 1 579 | 144 |
| Netherlands Antilles | 1 905 | Iran (Islamic Republic of) | 4 921 | Netherlands Antilles | 1 579 | 145 |
| Puerto Rico | 1 963 | Netherlands Antilles | 5 036 | Union of Soviet Socialist Rep. | 1 592 | 146 |
| Israel | 2 217 | Israel | 5 571 | Qatar | 1 627 | 147 |
| Oman | 2 392 | Oman | 6 406 | Poland | 1 870 | 148 |
| Italy | 2 521 | Italy | 6 590 | Libyan Arab Jamahiriya | 1 873 | 149 |
| United Kingdom | 2 857 | United Arab Emirates | 7 085 | Puerto Rico | 1 904 | 150 |
| Libyan Arab Jamahiriya | 2 944 | Libyan Arab Jamahiriya | 7 452 | Israel | 1 921 | 151 |
| Austria | 2 952 | Austria | 7 638 | Austria | 1 936 | 152 |
| New Zealand | 2 985 | French Polynesia | 7 698 | Japan | 1 953 | 153 |
| Saudi Arabia | 2 991 | United Kingdom | 7 723 | Italy | 1 997 | 154 |
| French Polynesia | 3 043 | Belgium | 7 781 | French Polynesia | 2 005 | 155 |
| United Arab Emirates | 3 212 | New Zealand | 7 914 | German Democratic Republic [b] | 2 010 | 156 |
| Belgium | 3 232 | Saudi Arabia | 8 424 | United Kingdom | 2 219 | 157 |
| Japan | 3 360 | Japan | 8 726 | New Zealand | 2 233 | 158 |
| Finland | 3 535 | Iceland | 8 901 | Finland | 2 364 | 159 |
| New Caledonia | 3 573 | France | 9 002 | Iceland | 2 430 | 160 |
| France | 3 587 | New Caledonia | 9 071 | Netherlands | 2 568 | 161 |
| Iceland | 3 616 | Finland | 9 187 | New Caledonia | 2 591 | 162 |
| Netherlands | 3 680 | Netherlands | 9 216 | Belgium | 2 597 | 163 |
| Bahamas | 3 704 | Luxembourg | 9 456 | France | 2 814 | 164 |
| Bahrain | 3 802 | Bahamas | 9 666 | Norway | 2 884 | 165 |
| Luxembourg | 3 859 | Canada | 9 725 | Bahamas | 2 892 | 166 |
| Canada | 3 950 | Federal Republic of Germany [b] | 9 985 | United Arab Emirates | 2 976 | 167 |
| Federal Republic of Germany [b] | 4 003 | Australia | 9 987 | Federal Republic of Germany [b] | 3 042 | 168 |
| Australia | 4 030 | Bahrain | 10 887 | Australia | 3 133 | 169 |
| Denmark | 4 389 | Denmark | 11 016 | Denmark | 3 209 | 170 |
| US Virgin Islands | 4 443 | US Virgin Islands | 11 784 | Luxembourg | 3 238 | 171 |
| Brunei Darussalam | 4 851 | Sweden | 12 241 | Switzerland | 3 351 | 172 |
| Sweden | 4 907 | United States of America | 12 613 | Bermuda | 3 494 | 173 |
| United States of America | 4 922 | Brunei Darussalam | 13 508 | Kuwait | 3 856 | 174 |
| Bermuda | 5 346 | Bermuda | 14 865 | Canada | 3 960 | 175 |
| Switzerland | 6 082 | Switzerland | 16 490 | US Virgin Islands | 4 124 | 176 |
| Kuwait | 13 456 | Kuwait | 45 227 | Sweden | 4 164 | 177 |
| Qatar | 15 109 | Qatar | 46 550 | United States of America | 4 922 | 178 |

**Table A.3**    Country or area rankings based on per capita gross domestic product in 1970 [cont.]

Note:   Rule divisions within the listings indicate approximate quartile divisions of world population. Where quartile divisions fall within a large country or area, it is shaded.

a    On 22 May 1990 Democratic Yemen and Yemen merged to form a single State. Since that date they have been represented as one Member with the name "Yemen".

b    Through accession of the German Democratic Republic to the Federal Republic of Germany with effect from 3 October 1990, the two German States have united to form one sovereign State.

As from the date of unification, the Federal Republic of Germany acts in the United Nations under the designation Germany.

c    Data provided for Yugoslavia are for periods prior to 1 January 1992 and refer to the Socialist Federal Republic of Yugolavia which was composed of six republics. Data provided for Yugoslavia after that date refer to the Federal Republic of Yugoslavia which is composed of two republics (Serbia and Montenegro).

Table A.4

**Country or area rankings based on per capita
gross domestic product in 1980**

Follows overleaf

## Table A.4  Country or area rankings based on per capita gross domestic product in 1980

| | Market exchange rate | Per capita GDP | PPPs | Per capita GDP | Absolute 1970–1989 PARE | Per capita GDP |
|---|---|---|---|---|---|---|
| Rank | Country or area | | Country or area | | Country or area | |
| 1 | Cambodia | 88 | Mali | 204 | Cambodia | 82 |
| 2 | Ethiopia | 106 | Zaire | 247 | Ethiopia | 100 |
| 3 | Viet Nam | 107 | Ethiopia | 304 | Viet Nam | 106 |
| 4 | Bhutan | 114 | Burkina Faso | 320 | Bhutan | 115 |
| 5 | Nepal | 131 | Chad | 323 | Nepal | 117 |
| 6 | Lao People's Dem. Republic | 144 | Mozambique | 354 | Zaire | 141 |
| 7 | Myanmar | 173 | Burundi | 354 | Burkina Faso | 143 |
| 8 | Bangladesh | 179 | United Republic of Tanzania | 364 | Chad | 146 |
| 9 | Burkina Faso | 185 | Angola | 375 | Bangladesh | 158 |
| 10 | Mozambique | 199 | Rwanda | 377 | Lao People's Dem. Republic | 158 |
| 11 | Malawi | 201 | Malawi | 413 | Mozambique | 167 |
| 12 | Chad | 205 | Uganda | 434 | Malawi | 169 |
| 13 | Rwanda | 225 | Niger | 443 | Mali | 174 |
| 14 | Burundi | 230 | Sierra Leone | 462 | Burundi | 175 |
| 15 | Zaire | 234 | Myanmar | 478 | Myanmar | 185 |
| 16 | Afghanistan | 240 | Central African Republic | 479 | Equatorial Guinea | 198 |
| 17 | Mali | 243 | Nepal | 483 | United Republic of Tanzania | 203 |
| 18 | India | 251 | Ghana | 522 | Lesotho | 206 |
| 19 | Equatorial Guinea | 259 | Benin | 557 | China | 209 |
| 20 | Haiti | 267 | Bangladesh | 567 | India | 213 |
| 21 | United Republic of Tanzania | 272 | Madagascar | 584 | Afghanistan | 234 |
| 22 | Lesotho | 275 | Guinea | 586 | Rwanda | 245 |
| 23 | Sri Lanka | 279 | Togo | 616 | Madagascar | 246 |
| 24 | Guinea – Bissau | 286 | Lesotho | 617 | Sierra Leone | 252 |
| 25 | Maldives | 302 | Sudan | 637 | Somalia | 253 |
| 26 | China | 305 | Gambia | 647 | Central African Republic | 259 |
| 27 | Pakistan | 333 | India | 653 | Comoros | 261 |
| 28 | Benin | 336 | Kenya | 662 | Benin | 266 |
| 29 | Sierra Leone | 337 | Haiti | 672 | Guinea – Bissau | 268 |
| 30 | Central African Republic | 343 | Afghanistan | 677 | Haiti | 277 |
| 31 | Comoros | 354 | Liberia | 678 | Pakistan | 277 |
| 32 | Democratic Yemen [a] | 359 | Mauritania | 681 | Sri Lanka | 298 |
| 33 | Madagascar | 372 | Zambia | 725 | Niger | 306 |
| 34 | Sudan | 418 | Somalia | 729 | Gambia | 316 |
| 35 | Guinea | 425 | Cameroon | 730 | Togo | 321 |
| 36 | Kenya | 426 | Senegal | 747 | Kenya | 325 |
| 37 | Kiribati | 426 | Egypt | 882 | Maldives | 329 |
| 38 | Togo | 432 | Zimbabwe | 888 | Sudan | 341 |
| 39 | Gambia | 434 | Nigeria | 922 | Angola | 359 |
| 40 | Ghana | 446 | Congo | 943 | Kiribati | 371 |
| 41 | Angola | 449 | Pakistan | 949 | Guinea | 375 |
| 42 | Niger | 454 | Côte d'Ivoire | 1 090 | Democratic Yemen [a] | 376 |
| 43 | Liberia | 488 | Swaziland | 1 100 | Indonesia | 396 |
| 44 | Cape Verde | 491 | Honduras | 1 107 | Mauritania | 396 |
| 45 | Sao Tome – Principe | 497 | Indonesia | 1 110 | Ghana | 400 |
| 46 | Somalia | 515 | Sri Lanka | 1 192 | Cape Verde | 401 |
| 47 | Indonesia | 517 | Morocco | 1 257 | Sao Tome – Principe | 408 |
| 48 | Mauritania | 535 | Botswana | 1 361 | Uganda | 425 |
| 49 | Senegal | 536 | Yemen [a] | 1 452 | Senegal | 431 |
| 50 | Nicaragua | 537 | Bolivia | 1 461 | Liberia | 462 |
| 51 | Egypt | 541 | Mauritius | 1 469 | Zambia | 480 |
| 52 | Saint Vincent and the Grenadines | 572 | El Salvador | 1 494 | Yemen [a] | 499 |
| 53 | Tonga | 615 | Philippines | 1 543 | Tonga | 530 |
| 54 | Yemen [a] | 620 | Thailand | 1 619 | Solomon Islands | 558 |
| 55 | Solomon Islands | 637 | Papua New Guinea | 1 623 | Zimbabwe | 577 |
| 56 | Zambia | 677 | Guyana | 1 692 | Philippines | 605 |
| 57 | Thailand | 688 | Dominican Republic | 1 825 | Guyana | 612 |
| 58 | Honduras | 695 | Tunisia | 1 851 | Thailand | 617 |

| Relative 1970–1989 PARE | | Absolute 1980–1989 PARE | | World Bank Atlas method | | |
|---|---|---|---|---|---|---|
| Country or area | Per capita GDP | Country or area | Per capita GDP | Country or area | Per capita GDP | Rank |
| Cambodia | 82 | Viet Nam | 107 | Cambodia | 81 | 1 |
| Ethiopia | 99 | Cambodia | 112 | Ethiopia | 106 | 2 |
| Viet Nam | 106 | Bhutan | 115 | Viet Nam | 107 | 3 |
| Bhutan | 114 | Ethiopia | 116 | Bhutan | 114 | 4 |
| Nepal | 116 | Nepal | 133 | Uganda | 124 | 5 |
| Zaire | 140 | Zaire | 147 | Lao People's Dem. Republic | 126 | 6 |
| Burkina Faso | 142 | Bangladesh | 174 | Nepal | 131 | 7 |
| Chad | 144 | Burkina Faso | 176 | Myanmar | 165 | 8 |
| Bangladesh | 156 | Malawi | 188 | Bangladesh | 179 | 9 |
| Lao People's Dem. Republic | 156 | Chad | 190 | Burkina Faso | 185 | 10 |
| Mozambique | 166 | Mali | 200 | Mozambique | 199 | 11 |
| Malawi | 167 | China | 206 | Malawi | 201 | 12 |
| Mali | 173 | Myanmar | 211 | Chad | 205 | 13 |
| Burundi | 174 | Lao People's Dem. Republic | 214 | Sudan | 209 | 14 |
| Myanmar | 184 | Burundi | 214 | Afghanistan | 219 | 15 |
| Equatorial Guinea | 196 | Mozambique | 220 | Rwanda | 225 | 16 |
| United Republic of Tanzania | 202 | Lesotho | 234 | Burundi | 230 | 17 |
| Lesotho | 204 | India | 248 | Zaire | 234 | 18 |
| China | 207 | United Republic of Tanzania | 255 | Mali | 243 | 19 |
| India | 211 | Guinea–Bissau | 256 | India | 250 | 20 |
| Afghanistan | 232 | Madagascar | 289 | Maldives | 252 | 21 |
| Rwanda | 243 | Sierra Leone | 290 | Equatorial Guinea | 259 | 22 |
| Madagascar | 243 | Rwanda | 292 | Haiti | 267 | 23 |
| Sierra Leone | 250 | Afghanistan | 305 | Lesotho | 274 | 24 |
| Somalia | 251 | Sri Lanka | 307 | Sri Lanka | 279 | 25 |
| Central African Republic | 257 | Pakistan | 308 | United Republic of Tanzania | 279 | 26 |
| Comoros | 259 | Comoros | 325 | Guinea–Bissau | 286 | 27 |
| Benin | 263 | Somalia | 329 | China | 305 | 28 |
| Guinea–Bissau | 265 | Central African Republic | 339 | Democratic Yemen [a] | 325 | 29 |
| Haiti | 274 | Gambia | 340 | Pakistan | 333 | 30 |
| Pakistan | 275 | Maldives | 341 | Benin | 336 | 31 |
| Sri Lanka | 296 | Niger | 360 | Sierra Leone | 337 | 32 |
| Niger | 303 | Kenya | 361 | Central African Republic | 343 | 33 |
| Gambia | 313 | Benin | 362 | Comoros | 354 | 34 |
| Togo | 318 | Haiti | 366 | Angola | 363 | 35 |
| Kenya | 322 | Equatorial Guinea | 386 | Madagascar | 372 | 36 |
| Maldives | 326 | Togo | 392 | Guinea | 385 | 37 |
| Sudan | 338 | Sudan | 399 | Kiribati | 413 | 38 |
| Angola | 356 | Uganda | 406 | Gambia | 425 | 39 |
| Kiribati | 368 | Guinea | 439 | Kenya | 426 | 40 |
| Guinea | 372 | Democratic Yemen [a] | 446 | Togo | 432 | 41 |
| Democratic Yemen [a] | 373 | Indonesia | 448 | Niger | 454 | 42 |
| Indonesia | 392 | Kiribati | 472 | Liberia | 488 | 43 |
| Mauritania | 393 | Cape Verde | 473 | Cape Verde | 491 | 44 |
| Ghana | 397 | Mauritania | 488 | Sao Tome–Principe | 497 | 45 |
| Cape Verde | 397 | Ghana | 517 | Saint Vincent and the Grenadines | 515 | 46 |
| Sao Tome–Principe | 404 | Zambia | 519 | Somalia | 515 | 47 |
| Uganda | 421 | Senegal | 524 | Indonesia | 517 | 48 |
| Senegal | 428 | Yemen [a] | 559 | Egypt | 526 | 49 |
| Liberia | 458 | Angola | 564 | Tonga | 532 | 50 |
| Zambia | 476 | Sao Tome–Principe | 581 | Mauritania | 535 | 51 |
| Yemen [a] | 495 | Dem. People's Republic of Korea | 606 | Senegal | 536 | 52 |
| Tonga | 525 | Liberia | 606 | Yemen [a] | 592 | 53 |
| Solomon Islands | 553 | Tonga | 607 | Solomon Islands | 637 | 54 |
| Zimbabwe | 572 | Solomon Islands | 625 | Zambia | 677 | 55 |
| Philippines | 599 | Zimbabwe | 662 | Thailand | 688 | 56 |
| Guyana | 607 | Guyana | 677 | Honduras | 695 | 57 |
| Thailand | 612 | Vanuatu | 686 | Dem. People's Republic of Korea | 713 | 58 |

**Table A.4**    Country or area rankings based on per capita gross domestic product in 1980 [cont.]

| | Market exchange rate | Per capita GDP | PPPs | Per capita GDP | Absolute 1970–1989 PARE | Per capita GDP |
|---|---|---|---|---|---|---|
| Rank | Country or area | | Country or area | | Country or area | |
| 59 | Dem. People's Republic of Korea | 697 | Paraguay | 1 875 | Saint Vincent and the Grenadines | 620 |
| 60 | Samoa | 718 | Jamaica | 1 896 | Nigeria | 632 |
| 61 | Philippines | 729 | Algeria | 2 001 | Dem. People's Republic of Korea | 638 |
| 62 | Zimbabwe | 751 | Nicaragua | 2 026 | Samoa | 640 |
| 63 | Cameroon | 771 | Guatemala | 2 050 | Cameroon | 656 |
| 64 | Guyana | 778 | Jordan | 2 257 | Vanuatu | 685 |
| 65 | El Salvador | 788 | Turkey | 2 317 | Papua New Guinea | 692 |
| 66 | Dominica | 799 | Ecuador | 2 436 | Egypt | 712 |
| 67 | Mongolia | 821 | Peru | 2 442 | Honduras | 713 |
| 68 | Grenada | 831 | Colombia | 2 456 | Morocco | 713 |
| 69 | Albania | 888 | Panama | 2 635 | Congo | 714 |
| 70 | Papua New Guinea | 898 | Costa Rica | 2 978 | Swaziland | 716 |
| 71 | Bolivia | 901 | Syrian Arab Republic | 3 005 | Mongolia | 729 |
| 72 | Saint Lucia | 912 | Brazil | 3 059 | Bolivia | 741 |
| 73 | Vanuatu | 961 | Fiji | 3 073 | Dominica | 770 |
| 74 | Swaziland | 964 | Malaysia | 3 225 | Botswana | 772 |
| 75 | Morocco | 980 | Iran (Islamic Republic of) | 3 228 | El Salvador | 781 |
| 76 | Botswana | 1 012 | Suriname | 3 377 | Grenada | 822 |
| 77 | Congo | 1 022 | Portugal | 3 863 | Albania | 877 |
| 78 | Anguilla | 1 062 | Gabon | 4 037 | Côte d'Ivoire | 898 |
| 79 | Saint Kitts–Nevis | 1 064 | South Africa | 4 177 | Saint Lucia | 924 |
| 80 | Cook Islands | 1 114 | Chile | 4 255 | Dominican Republic | 939 |
| 81 | Djibouti | 1 116 | Argentina | 4 353 | Nicaragua | 958 |
| 82 | Nigeria | 1 125 | Cyprus | 4 370 | Djibouti | 963 |
| 83 | Guatemala | 1 139 | Greece | 4 384 | Turkey | 1 005 |
| 84 | Peru | 1 157 | Barbados | 4 436 | Colombia | 1 010 |
| 85 | Dominican Republic | 1 164 | Mexico | 4 463 | Cook Islands | 1 013 |
| 86 | Mauritius | 1 170 | Uruguay | 4 491 | Guatemala | 1 038 |
| 87 | Belize | 1 173 | Malta | 4 617 | Tunisia | 1 057 |
| 88 | Colombia | 1 241 | Ireland | 5 203 | Mauritius | 1 058 |
| 89 | Côte d'Ivoire | 1 242 | Venezuela | 5 421 | Namibia | 1 074 |
| 90 | Jamaica | 1 250 | Singapore | 6 007 | Belize | 1 080 |
| 91 | Antigua & Barbuda | 1 253 | Spain | 6 115 | Lebanon | 1 122 |
| 92 | Turkey | 1 281 | Iraq | 6 272 | Jamaica | 1 133 |
| 93 | Tunisia | 1 369 | Israel | 6 512 | Ecuador | 1 158 |
| 94 | Jordan | 1 373 | Oman | 6 629 | Jordan | 1 169 |
| 95 | Paraguay | 1 413 | Trinidad & Tobago | 6 823 | Saint Kitts–Nevis | 1 183 |
| 96 | Ecuador | 1 444 | New Zealand | 7 002 | Peru | 1 235 |
| 97 | Syrian Arab Republic | 1 484 | Bahrain | 7 765 | Paraguay | 1 247 |
| 98 | Lebanon | 1 526 | United Kingdom | 8 110 | Cuba | 1 379 |
| 99 | Namibia | 1 536 | Italy | 8 196 | Anguilla | 1 383 |
| 100 | Romania | 1 544 | Austria | 8 216 | Antigua & Barbuda | 1 473 |
| 101 | Poland | 1 594 | Japan | 8 262 | Fiji | 1 473 |
| 102 | Republic of Korea | 1 643 | Finland | 8 655 | Costa Rica | 1 475 |
| 103 | Cuba | 1 721 | Sweden | 8 916 | Malaysia | 1 511 |
| 104 | Uganda | 1 765 | Australia | 8 920 | Chile | 1 519 |
| 105 | Malaysia | 1 779 | Netherlands | 9 040 | Syrian Arab Republic | 1 596 |
| 106 | Panama | 1 818 | Belgium | 9 291 | Republic of Korea | 1 605 |
| 107 | Fiji | 1 900 | Denmark | 9 596 | Romania | 1 736 |
| 108 | Brazil | 1 979 | Federal Republic of Germany [b] | 9 779 | Panama | 1 762 |
| 109 | Montserrat | 2 019 | France | 9 808 | Poland | 1 860 |
| 110 | Hungary | 2 069 | Luxembourg | 9 972 | Brazil | 1 870 |
| 111 | Costa Rica | 2 114 | Iceland | 10 350 | Algeria | 1 909 |
| 112 | Bulgaria | 2 256 | Saudi Arabia | 10 931 | Hungary | 1 928 |
| 113 | Algeria | 2 259 | Norway | 11 108 | Montserrat | 1 988 |
| 114 | Seychelles | 2 302 | Canada | 11 509 | South Africa | 2 008 |
| 115 | Chile | 2 474 | United States of America | 11 804 | Mexico | 2 042 |
| 116 | Iran (Islamic Republic of) | 2 521 | Kuwait | 20 204 | French Guiana | 2 125 |
| 117 | Suriname | 2 523 | United Arab Emirates | 25 629 | Bulgaria | 2 203 |
| 118 | Portugal | 2 569 | | | Uruguay | 2 273 |

| Relative 1970–1989 PARE | | Absolute 1980–1989 PARE | | World Bank Atlas method | | |
| --- | --- | --- | --- | --- | --- | --- |
| Country or area | Per capita GDP | Country or area | Per capita GDP | Country or area | Per capita GDP | Rank |
| Saint Vincent and the Grenadines | 615 | Samoa | 686 | Samoa | 718 | 59 |
| Nigeria | 627 | Thailand | 700 | Philippines | 729 | 60 |
| Dem. People's Republic of Korea | 632 | Philippines | 718 | Zimbabwe | 751 | 61 |
| Samoa | 634 | Mongolia | 747 | Guyana | 778 | 62 |
| Cameroon | 650 | Nigeria | 762 | Cameroon | 779 | 63 |
| Vanuatu | 679 | Egypt | 767 | Nicaragua | 786 | 64 |
| Papua New Guinea | 686 | Swaziland | 770 | El Salvador | 788 | 65 |
| Egypt | 706 | Morocco | 773 | Dominica | 799 | 66 |
| Honduras | 707 | Saint Vincent–Gren. | 778 | Mongolia | 799 | 67 |
| Morocco | 707 | Cameroon | 798 | Grenada | 831 | 68 |
| Congo | 707 | Botswana | 848 | Albania | 881 | 69 |
| Swaziland | 710 | Congo | 850 | Papua New Guinea | 896 | 70 |
| Mongolia | 723 | Papua New Guinea | 850 | Bolivia | 900 | 71 |
| Bolivia | 735 | Honduras | 894 | Saint Lucia | 912 | 72 |
| Dominica | 764 | Albania | 915 | Vanuatu | 961 | 73 |
| Botswana | 766 | Bolivia | 979 | Swaziland | 963 | 74 |
| El Salvador | 775 | Côte d'Ivoire | 1 028 | Morocco | 971 | 75 |
| Grenada | 815 | Dominican Republic | 1 057 | Djibouti | 978 | 76 |
| Albania | 870 | Turkey | 1 065 | Botswana | 990 | 77 |
| Côte d'Ivoire | 890 | Grenada | 1 068 | Anguilla | 1 020 | 78 |
| Saint Lucia | 916 | El Salvador | 1 093 | Cook Islands | 1 022 | 79 |
| Dominican Republic | 931 | Dominica | 1 113 | Congo | 1 022 | 80 |
| Nicaragua | 950 | Mauritius | 1 120 | Saint Kitts–Nevis | 1 064 | 81 |
| Djibouti | 955 | Saint Lucia | 1 123 | Nigeria | 1 125 | 82 |
| Turkey | 996 | Tunisia | 1 184 | Guatemala | 1 139 | 83 |
| Colombia | 1 001 | Colombia | 1 211 | Peru | 1 161 | 84 |
| Cook Islands | 1 004 | Guatemala | 1 280 | Dominican Republic | 1 164 | 85 |
| Guatemala | 1 029 | Jamaica | 1 316 | Mauritius | 1 170 | 86 |
| Tunisia | 1 048 | Namibia | 1 316 | Belize | 1 173 | 87 |
| Mauritius | 1 049 | Djibouti | 1 320 | Colombia | 1 241 | 88 |
| Namibia | 1 064 | Belize | 1 321 | Côte d'Ivoire | 1 242 | 89 |
| Belize | 1 071 | Jordan | 1 358 | Jamaica | 1 250 | 90 |
| Lebanon | 1 112 | Cook Islands | 1 365 | Antigua & Barbuda | 1 253 | 91 |
| Jamaica | 1 123 | Ecuador | 1 395 | Turkey | 1 281 | 92 |
| Ecuador | 1 148 | Cuba | 1 417 | Lebanon | 1 364 | 93 |
| Jordan | 1 159 | Saint Kitts–Nevis | 1 476 | Tunisia | 1 370 | 94 |
| Saint Kitts–Nevis | 1 172 | Paraguay | 1 487 | Jordan | 1 373 | 95 |
| Peru | 1 224 | Anguilla | 1 508 | Paraguay | 1 413 | 96 |
| Paraguay | 1 236 | Peru | 1 577 | Ecuador | 1 444 | 97 |
| Cuba | 1 367 | Lebanon | 1 601 | Ghana | 1 451 | 98 |
| Anguilla | 1 371 | Nicaragua | 1 648 | Syrian Arab Republic | 1 484 | 99 |
| Antigua & Barbuda | 1 460 | Costa Rica | 1 670 | Romania | 1 530 | 100 |
| Fiji | 1 460 | Malaysia | 1 729 | Namibia | 1 534 | 101 |
| Costa Rica | 1 462 | Fiji | 1 743 | Montserrat | 1 560 | 102 |
| Malaysia | 1 498 | Antigua & Barbuda | 1 772 | Cuba | 1 575 | 103 |
| Chile | 1 505 | Republic of Korea | 1 892 | Republic of Korea | 1 643 | 104 |
| Syrian Arab Republic | 1 582 | Chile | 1 921 | Poland | 1 710 | 105 |
| Republic of Korea | 1 591 | Romania | 1 937 | Malaysia | 1 779 | 106 |
| Romania | 1 721 | Poland | 1 993 | Panama | 1 818 | 107 |
| Panama | 1 747 | Syrian Arab Republic | 2 008 | Brazil | 1 877 | 108 |
| Poland | 1 844 | Hungary | 2 028 | Fiji | 1 900 | 109 |
| Brazil | 1 854 | Panama | 2 108 | Bulgaria | 2 059 | 110 |
| Algeria | 1 893 | Brazil | 2 174 | Hungary | 2 069 | 111 |
| Hungary | 1 911 | Algeria | 2 313 | Costa Rica | 2 114 | 112 |
| Montserrat | 1 971 | Mexico | 2 353 | Algeria | 2 260 | 113 |
| South Africa | 1 991 | Bulgaria | 2 398 | Seychelles | 2 302 | 114 |
| Mexico | 2 024 | Montserrat | 2 498 | French Guiana | 2 370 | 115 |
| French Guiana | 2 107 | South Africa | 2 526 | Chile | 2 474 | 116 |
| Bulgaria | 2 184 | French Guiana | 2 664 | Iran (Islamic Republic of) | 2 488 | 117 |
| Uruguay | 2 253 | Yugoslavia [c] | 2 670 | Suriname | 2 523 | 118 |

**Table A.4**    Country or area rankings based on per capita gross domestic product in 1980 [cont.]

| | Market exchange rate | | | PPPs | | Absolute 1970-1989 PARE | |
|---|---|---|---|---|---|---|---|
| Rank | Country or area | Per capita GDP | | Country or area | Per capita GDP | Country or area | Per capita GDP |
| 119 | French Guiana | 2 650 | | | | Portugal | 2 274 |
| 120 | South Africa | 2 743 | | | | Yugoslavia [c] | 2 389 |
| 121 | Czechoslovakia | 2 765 | | | | Suriname | 2 401 |
| 122 | Mexico | 2 766 | | | | Czechoslovakia | 2 443 |
| 123 | Malta | 3 068 | | | | Argentina | 2 611 |
| 124 | Yugoslavia [c] | 3 136 | | | | Seychelles | 2 695 |
| 125 | Cyprus | 3 419 | | | | Cyprus | 2 870 |
| 126 | Barbados | 3 442 | | | | Malta | 2 879 |
| 127 | Union of Soviet Socialist Rep. | 3 464 | | | | Iran (Islamic Republic of) | 2 948 |
| 128 | Uruguay | 3 477 | | | | Venezuela | 3 264 |
| 129 | Reunion | 3 928 | | | | Union of Soviet Socialist Rep. | 3 334 |
| 130 | Iraq | 3 969 | | | | Guadeloupe | 3 335 |
| 131 | Greece | 4 163 | | | | Reunion | 3 346 |
| 132 | Guadeloupe | 4 241 | | | | Greece | 3 443 |
| 133 | Martinique | 4 415 | | | | Barbados | 3 526 |
| 134 | British Virgin Islands | 4 514 | | | | Oman | 3 549 |
| 135 | Venezuela | 4 644 | | | | Martinique | 3 649 |
| 136 | Singapore | 4 853 | | | | Iraq | 3 802 |
| 137 | Netherlands Antilles | 4 948 | | | | Gabon | 3 811 |
| 138 | Puerto Rico | 4 975 | | | | Spain | 4 380 |
| 139 | Gabon | 5 305 | | | | Trinidad & Tobago | 4 796 |
| 140 | Argentina | 5 454 | | | | Ireland | 4 846 |
| 141 | Hong Kong | 5 463 | | | | Singapore | 4 858 |
| 142 | Spain | 5 650 | | | | Netherlands Antilles | 4 884 |
| 143 | Ireland | 5 662 | | | | Hong Kong | 4 884 |
| 144 | Trinidad & Tobago | 5 761 | | | | Puerto Rico | 4 931 |
| 145 | Israel | 5 893 | | | | British Virgin Islands | 5 342 |
| 146 | Oman | 5 992 | | | | Bahamas | 5 575 |
| 147 | Bahamas | 6 255 | | | | Israel | 5 766 |
| 148 | New Zealand | 7 178 | | | | New Zealand | 6 307 |
| 149 | German Democratic Republic [b] | 7 501 | | | | German Democratic Republic [b] | 6 314 |
| 150 | US Virgin Islands | 7 968 | | | | New Caledonia | 6 748 |
| 151 | Italy | 8 021 | | | | United Kingdom | 6 988 |
| 152 | New Caledonia | 8 446 | | | | French Polynesia | 7 029 |
| 153 | French Polynesia | 8 459 | | | | Italy | 7 139 |
| 154 | Bahrain | 8 827 | | | | Bahrain | 7 175 |
| 155 | Japan | 9 068 | | | | US Virgin Islands | 7 946 |
| 156 | United Kingdom | 9 493 | | | | Austria | 8 563 |
| 157 | Austria | 10 183 | | | | Libyan Arab Jamahiriya | 8 631 |
| 158 | Finland | 10 803 | | | | Belgium | 8 987 |
| 159 | Australia | 10 836 | | | | Netherlands | 9 265 |
| 160 | Canada | 10 949 | | | | Luxembourg | 9 519 |
| 161 | Libyan Arab Jamahiriya | 11 737 | | | | France | 9 596 |
| 162 | United States of America | 11 804 | | | | Japan | 9 691 |
| 163 | Netherlands | 11 976 | | | | Australia | 9 722 |
| 164 | Belgium | 11 979 | | | | Finland | 9 895 |
| 165 | France | 12 333 | | | | Saudi Arabia | 10 309 |
| 166 | Saudi Arabia | 12 372 | | | | Federal Republic of Germany [b] | 10 560 |
| 167 | Luxembourg | 12 454 | | | | Denmark | 10 803 |
| 168 | Denmark | 12 943 | | | | Canada | 11 232 |
| 169 | Federal Republic of Germany [b] | 13 213 | | | | Sweden | 11 821 |
| 170 | Bermuda | 13 678 | | | | United States of America | 11 908 |
| 171 | Iceland | 14 104 | | | | Kuwait | 11 980 |
| 172 | Norway | 14 125 | | | | Iceland | 12 417 |
| 173 | Sweden | 15 026 | | | | Norway | 13 549 |
| 174 | Switzerland | 16 081 | | | | Switzerland | 13 822 |
| 175 | Kuwait | 20 889 | | | | Bermuda | 15 265 |
| 176 | Brunei Darussalam | 26 063 | | | | Brunei Darussalam | 15 518 |
| 177 | United Arab Emirates | 29 162 | | | | Qatar | 22 626 |
| 178 | Qatar | 34 078 | | | | United Arab Emirates | 28 407 |

| Relative 1970–1989 PARE | | Absolute 1980–1989 PARE | | World Bank Atlas method | | |
|---|---|---|---|---|---|---|
| Country or area | Per capita GDP | Country or area | Per capita GDP | Country or area | Per capita GDP | Rank |
| Portugal | 2 254 | Portugal | 2 710 | Portugal | 2 569 | 119 |
| Yugoslavia [c] | 2 368 | Czechoslovakia | 2 763 | Czechoslovakia | 2 701 | 120 |
| Suriname | 2 380 | Uruguay | 2 811 | South Africa | 2 740 | 121 |
| Czechoslovakia | 2 422 | Seychelles | 2 979 | Mexico | 2 766 | 122 |
| Argentina | 2 588 | Suriname | 3 003 | Iraq | 2 848 | 123 |
| Seychelles | 2 672 | Argentina | 3 245 | Malta | 3 109 | 124 |
| Cyprus | 2 845 | Malta | 3 373 | Yugoslavia [c] | 3 136 | 125 |
| Malta | 2 854 | Cyprus | 3 470 | Union of Soviet Socialist Rep. | 3 409 | 126 |
| Iran (Islamic Republic of) | 2 922 | Union of Soviet Socialist Rep. | 3 576 | Cyprus | 3 419 | 127 |
| Venezuela | 3 236 | Reunion | 3 881 | Barbados | 3 442 | 128 |
| Union of Soviet Socialist Rep. | 3 305 | Venezuela | 3 934 | Uruguay | 3 477 | 129 |
| Guadeloupe | 3 305 | Greece | 4 029 | Reunion | 3 535 | 130 |
| Reunion | 3 317 | Guadeloupe | 4 133 | Guadeloupe | 3 642 | 131 |
| Greece | 3 413 | Martinique | 4 353 | Martinique | 3 994 | 132 |
| Barbados | 3 495 | Oman | 4 634 | British Virgin Islands | 4 157 | 133 |
| Oman | 3 518 | Iran (Islamic Republic of) | 4 671 | Greece | 4 163 | 134 |
| Martinique | 3 617 | Barbados | 4 734 | Netherlands Antilles | 4 501 | 135 |
| Iraq | 3 769 | Gabon | 5 000 | Puerto Rico | 4 505 | 136 |
| Gabon | 3 778 | Iraq | 5 442 | Venezuela | 4 644 | 137 |
| Spain | 4 342 | Hong Kong | 5 535 | Singapore | 4 852 | 138 |
| Trinidad & Tobago | 4 754 | Spain | 5 557 | Gabon | 5 305 | 139 |
| Ireland | 4 804 | Singapore | 5 621 | Argentina | 5 462 | 140 |
| Singapore | 4 815 | Puerto Rico | 6 014 | Hong Kong | 5 467 | 141 |
| Netherlands Antilles | 4 841 | Ireland | 6 058 | Spain | 5 650 | 142 |
| Hong Kong | 4 841 | Trinidad & Tobago | 6 287 | Ireland | 5 654 | 143 |
| Puerto Rico | 4 888 | Netherlands Antilles | 6 295 | Trinidad & Tobago | 5 763 | 144 |
| British Virgin Islands | 5 295 | German Democratic Republic [b] | 6 641 | Israel | 5 888 | 145 |
| Bahamas | 5 526 | Israel | 6 848 | Oman | 6 071 | 146 |
| Israel | 5 716 | Bahamas | 7 065 | Bahamas | 6 255 | 147 |
| New Zealand | 6 252 | New Zealand | 7 094 | New Caledonia | 6 742 | 148 |
| German Democratic Republic [b] | 6 259 | New Caledonia | 8 152 | French Polynesia | 7 095 | 149 |
| New Caledonia | 6 689 | French Polynesia | 8 353 | New Zealand | 7 113 | 150 |
| United Kingdom | 6 927 | Italy | 8 670 | US Virgin Islands | 7 304 | 151 |
| French Polynesia | 6 968 | United Kingdom | 9 098 | German Democratic Republic [b] | 7 492 | 152 |
| Italy | 7 077 | Bahrain | 9 211 | Italy | 8 021 | 153 |
| Bahrain | 7 112 | US Virgin Islands | 10 016 | Bahrain | 8 827 | 154 |
| US Virgin Islands | 7 876 | Belgium | 10 275 | Japan | 9 068 | 155 |
| Austria | 8 489 | Libyan Arab Jamahiriya | 10 550 | United Kingdom | 9 487 | 156 |
| Libyan Arab Jamahiriya | 8 556 | Austria | 10 651 | Austria | 10 183 | 157 |
| Belgium | 8 909 | Netherlands | 10 804 | Australia | 10 599 | 158 |
| Netherlands | 9 184 | Luxembourg | 11 313 | Finland | 10 802 | 159 |
| Luxembourg | 9 436 | France | 11 372 | Canada | 10 947 | 160 |
| France | 9 512 | Australia | 11 741 | Libyan Arab Jamahiriya | 11 735 | 161 |
| Japan | 9 607 | Japan | 11 747 | United States of America | 11 804 | 162 |
| Australia | 9 637 | Finland | 12 270 | Bermuda | 11 838 | 163 |
| Finland | 9 808 | Federal Republic of Germany [b] | 12 538 | Netherlands | 11 975 | 164 |
| Saudi Arabia | 10 219 | Denmark | 12 842 | Belgium | 11 979 | 165 |
| Federal Republic of Germany [b] | 10 467 | Canada | 13 221 | France | 12 335 | 166 |
| Denmark | 10 709 | Saudi Arabia | 13 483 | Saudi Arabia | 12 373 | 167 |
| Canada | 11 134 | Norway | 14 156 | Luxembourg | 12 454 | 168 |
| Sweden | 11 718 | Sweden | 14 256 | Denmark | 12 943 | 169 |
| United States of America | 11 804 | United States of America | 14 377 | Federal Republic of Germany [b] | 13 216 | 170 |
| Kuwait | 11 875 | Switzerland | 14 879 | Iceland | 14 105 | 171 |
| Iceland | 12 309 | Kuwait | 14 903 | Norway | 14 124 | 172 |
| Norway | 13 430 | Bermuda | 18 273 | Sweden | 15 028 | 173 |
| Switzerland | 13 701 | Brunei Darussalam | 19 632 | Brunei Darussalam | 15 326 | 174 |
| Bermuda | 15 132 | United Arab Emirates | 20 695 | Switzerland | 16 083 | 175 |
| Brunei Darussalam | 15 383 | Qatar | 21 070 | Kuwait | 20 866 | 176 |
| Qatar | 22 429 | | 30 555 | Qatar | 25 012 | 177 |
| United Arab Emirates | 28 159 | Qatar | 33 989 | United Arab Emirates | 29 159 | 178 |

**Table A.4** Country or area rankings based on per capita gross domestic product in 1980 [cont.]

Note: Rule divisions within the listings indicate approximate quartile divisions of world population. Where quartile divisions fall within a large country or area, it is shaded.

a    On 22 May 1990 Democratic Yemen and Yemen merged to form a single State. Since that date they have been represented as one Member with the name "Yemen".

b    Through accession of the German Democratic Republic to the Federal Republic of Germany with effect from 3 October 1990, the two German States have united to form one sovereign State.

As from the date of unification, the Federal Republic of Germany acts in the United Nations under the designation Germany.

c    Data provided for Yugoslavia are for periods prior to 1 January 1992 and refer to the Socialist Federal Republic of Yugolavia which was composed of six republics. Data provided for Yugoslavia after that date refer to the Federal Republic of Yugoslavia which is composed of two republics (Serbia and Montenegro).

Table A.5

**Country or area rankings based on per capita gross domestic product in 1989**

Follows overleaf

**Table A.5**  Country or area rankings based on per capita gross domestic product in 1989

| | Market exchange rate | | PPPs | | Absolute 1970–1989 PARE | |
|---|---|---|---|---|---|---|
| Rank | Country or area | Per capita GDP | Country or area | Per capita GDP | Country or area | Per capita GDP |
| 1 | Mozambique | 84 | Zaire | 244 | Cambodia | 59 |
| 2 | Zaire | 102 | Angola | 342 | Ethiopia | 100 |
| 3 | Cambodia | 106 | Mali | 343 | Chad | 110 |
| 4 | United Republic of Tanzania | 107 | Ethiopia | 443 | Mozambique | 121 |
| 5 | Ethiopia | 124 | Malawi | 456 | Zaire | 124 |
| 6 | Viet Nam | 139 | Rwanda | 475 | Viet Nam | 138 |
| 7 | Madagascar | 139 | Niger | 477 | Burkina Faso | 140 |
| 8 | Nepal | 152 | Burkina Faso | 503 | Nepal | 141 |
| 9 | Nigeria | 157 | Chad | 508 | Equatorial Guinea | 150 |
| 10 | Chad | 165 | Burundi | 514 | Malawi | 154 |
| 11 | Somalia | 173 | Sierra Leone | 524 | Bangladesh | 172 |
| 12 | Guinea–Bissau | 179 | Central African Republic | 640 | Lebanon | 175 |
| 13 | Malawi | 192 | Sudan | 640 | United Republic of Tanzania | 176 |
| 14 | Bhutan | 196 | Myanmar | 642 | Mali | 180 |
| 15 | Sierra Leone | 200 | Guinea | 642 | Myanmar | 181 |
| 16 | Burundi | 207 | Afghanistan | 670 | Madagascar | 193 |
| 17 | Burkina Faso | 216 | Somalia | 680 | Burundi | 194 |
| 18 | Bangladesh | 217 | Madagascar | 686 | Bhutan | 195 |
| 19 | Mali | 236 | United Republic of Tanzania | 686 | Lesotho | 212 |
| 20 | Guyana | 239 | Mauritania | 704 | Afghanistan | 213 |
| 21 | Nicaragua | 239 | Nigeria | 718 | Rwanda | 216 |
| 22 | Lesotho | 245 | Mozambique | 726 | Benin | 216 |
| 23 | Uganda | 257 | Ghana | 749 | Sierra Leone | 217 |
| 24 | Niger | 266 | Benin | 773 | Haiti | 224 |
| 25 | Rwanda | 310 | Haiti | 784 | Lao's People's Dem. Republic | 226 |
| 26 | Sudan | 320 | Togo | 786 | Niger | 231 |
| 27 | India | 326 | Nepal | 790 | Central African Republic | 243 |
| 28 | Ghana | 353 | Zambia | 804 | Sao Tome–Principe | 263 |
| 29 | Benin | 355 | Liberia | 837 | Comoros | 266 |
| 30 | Gambia | 357 | Kenya | 911 | Sudan | 266 |
| 31 | Pakistan | 361 | Bangladesh | 997 | Togo | 272 |
| 32 | Kenya | 368 | Cameroon | 1 101 | Somalia | 279 |
| 33 | Central African Republic | 374 | Senegal | 1 125 | India | 289 |
| 34 | China | 377 | Côte d'Ivoire | 1 141 | Guinea–Bissau | 309 |
| 35 | Togo | 381 | Congo | 1 221 | Kenya | 328 |
| 36 | Sao Tome–Principe | 382 | Zimbabwe | 1 224 | Guinea | 333 |
| 37 | Equatorial Guinea | 390 | Honduras | 1 268 | Liberia | 338 |
| 38 | Myanmar | 401 | Bolivia | 1 318 | Pakistan | 341 |
| 39 | Sri Lanka | 406 | India | 1 340 | Kiribati | 355 |
| 40 | Zambia | 416 | Uganda | 1 515 | Ghana | 359 |
| 41 | Lao's People's Dem. Republic | 417 | Gambia | 1 526 | Gambia | 360 |
| 42 | Comoros | 418 | Pakistan | 1 570 | Angola | 370 |
| 43 | Haiti | 439 | Egypt | 1 609 | Mauritania | 370 |
| 44 | Mauritania | 454 | Lesotho | 1 653 | Sri Lanka | 371 |
| 45 | Lebanon | 467 | Guyana | 1 704 | Democratic Yemen [a] | 373 |
| 46 | Guinea | 480 | El Salvador | 1 777 | Uganda | 378 |
| 47 | Liberia | 497 | Papua New Guinea | 2 011 | Zambia | 381 |
| 48 | Indonesia | 520 | Morocco | 2 016 | China | 408 |
| 49 | Kiribati | 534 | Yemen [a] | 2 025 | Senegal | 433 |
| 50 | Democratic Yemen [a] | 551 | Nicaragua | 2 035 | Nigeria | 441 |
| 51 | Afghanistan | 588 | Philippines | 2 066 | Guyana | 460 |
| 52 | Solomon Islands | 608 | Indonesia | 2 152 | Solomon Islands | 506 |
| 53 | Bolivia | 609 | Sri Lanka | 2 249 | Maldives | 518 |
| 54 | Maldives | 618 | Gabon | 2 284 | Indonesia | 531 |
| 55 | Zimbabwe | 631 | Guatemala | 2 316 | Bolivia | 544 |
| 56 | Samoa | 639 | Dominican Republic | 2 356 | Philippines | 555 |
| 57 | Senegal | 690 | Swaziland | 2 431 | Cape Verde | 557 |
| 58 | Angola | 717 | Iraq | 2 476 | Samoa | 588 |

| Relative 1970–1989 PARE | | Absolute 1980–1989 PARE | | World Bank Atlas method | | |
|---|---|---|---|---|---|---|
| Country or area | Per capita GDP | Country or area | Per capita GDP | Country or area | Per capita GDP | Rank |
| Cambodia | 84 | Cambodia | 79 | Mozambique | 84 | 1 |
| Ethiopia | 143 | Ethiopia | 116 | Cambodia | 94 | 2 |
| Chad | 158 | Zaire | 130 | Zaire | 102 | 3 |
| Mozambique | 173 | Viet Nam | 139 | United Republic of Tanzania | 107 | 4 |
| Zaire | 178 | Chad | 144 | Ethiopia | 126 | 5 |
| Viet Nam | 198 | Mozambique | 159 | Viet Nam | 139 | 6 |
| Burkina Faso | 201 | Nepal | 160 | Madagascar | 139 | 7 |
| Nepal | 202 | Malawi | 172 | Nigeria | 157 | 8 |
| Equatorial Guinea | 215 | Burkina Faso | 173 | Nepal | 164 | 9 |
| Malawi | 221 | Bangladesh | 190 | Chad | 165 | 10 |
| Bangladesh | 247 | Bhutan | 195 | Uganda | 173 | 11 |
| Lebanon | 251 | Myanmar | 206 | Somalia | 173 | 12 |
| United Republic of Tanzania | 252 | Mali | 207 | Guinea–Bissau | 179 | 13 |
| Mali | 259 | United Republic of Tanzania | 221 | Malawi | 195 | 14 |
| Myanmar | 259 | Madagascar | 227 | Bhutan | 196 | 15 |
| Madagascar | 277 | Burundi | 237 | Burundi | 207 | 16 |
| Burundi | 278 | Lesotho | 242 | Burkina Faso | 216 | 17 |
| Bhutan | 280 | Sierra Leone | 249 | Bangladesh | 218 | 18 |
| Lesotho | 305 | Lebanon | 250 | Mali | 236 | 19 |
| Afghanistan | 306 | Rwanda | 257 | Guyana | 240 | 20 |
| Rwanda | 309 | Niger | 272 | Sudan | 240 | 21 |
| Benin | 310 | Afghanistan | 278 | Lesotho | 243 | 22 |
| Sierra Leone | 311 | Equatorial Guinea | 292 | Sierra Leone | 251 | 23 |
| Haiti | 321 | Benin | 295 | Niger | 266 | 24 |
| Lao's People's Dem. Republic | 324 | Haiti | 295 | Myanmar | 303 | 25 |
| Niger | 331 | Guinea–Bissau | 296 | Rwanda | 310 | 26 |
| Central African Republic | 349 | Lao's People's Dem. Republic | 306 | India | 317 | 27 |
| Sao Tome–Principe | 377 | Sudan | 312 | Gambia | 334 | 28 |
| Comoros | 381 | Central African Republic | 318 | Ghana | 353 | 29 |
| Sudan | 382 | Comoros | 330 | Benin | 355 | 30 |
| Togo | 390 | Togo | 332 | Lebanon | 356 | 31 |
| Somalia | 401 | India | 337 | Kenya | 357 | 32 |
| India | 414 | Uganda | 361 | Central African Republic | 374 | 33 |
| Guinea–Bissau | 443 | Somalia | 363 | Lao's People's Dem. Republic | 379 | 34 |
| Kenya | 470 | Kenya | 364 | China | 381 | 35 |
| Guinea | 477 | Sao Tome–Principe | 375 | Togo | 381 | 36 |
| Liberia | 484 | Pakistan | 379 | Sao Tome–Principe | 382 | 37 |
| Pakistan | 489 | Sri Lanka | 382 | Pakistan | 386 | 38 |
| Kiribati | 509 | Gambia | 387 | Zambia | 388 | 39 |
| Ghana | 515 | Guinea | 390 | Equatorial Guinea | 390 | 40 |
| Gambia | 516 | China | 404 | Afghanistan | 400 | 41 |
| Angola | 530 | Zambia | 413 | Sri Lanka | 405 | 42 |
| Mauritania | 531 | Democratic Yemen [a] | 442 | Comoros | 418 | 43 |
| Sri Lanka | 532 | Liberia | 443 | Guinea | 432 | 44 |
| Democratic Yemen [a] | 535 | Kiribati | 451 | Haiti | 439 | 45 |
| Uganda | 542 | Mauritania | 456 | Mauritania | 454 | 46 |
| Zambia | 547 | Ghana | 463 | Liberia | 497 | 47 |
| China | 586 | Guyana | 509 | Kiribati | 498 | 48 |
| Senegal | 621 | Senegal | 526 | Indonesia | 520 | 49 |
| Nigeria | 632 | Nigeria | 531 | Democratic Yemen [a] | 530 | 50 |
| Guyana | 660 | Maldives | 537 | Maldives | 540 | 51 |
| Solomon Islands | 725 | Solomon Islands | 566 | Bolivia | 609 | 52 |
| Maldives | 744 | Angola | 581 | Solomon Islands | 610 | 53 |
| Indonesia | 762 | Indonesia | 602 | Zimbabwe | 625 | 54 |
| Bolivia | 781 | Samoa | 631 | Samoa | 648 | 55 |
| Philippines | 796 | Cape Verde | 657 | Yem    [a] | 649 | 56 |
| Cape Verde | 799 | Philippines | 659 | Egypt | 652 | 57 |
| Samoa | 844 | Zimbabwe | 697 | Honduras | 660 | 58 |

**Table A.5**    Country or area rankings based on per capita gross domestic product in 1989 [cont.]

| | Market exchange rate | | PPPs | | Absolute 1970–1989 PARE | |
|---|---|---|---|---|---|---|
| Rank | Country or area | Per capita GDP | Country or area | Per capita GDP | Country or area | Per capita GDP |
| 59 | Philippines | 729 | Peru | 2 696 | Zimbabwe | 607 |
| 60 | Yemen [a] | 761 | Algeria | 2 708 | Nicaragua | 622 |
| 61 | Vanuatu | 784 | Jamaica | 2 726 | Honduras | 641 |
| 62 | Cape Verde | 813 | Paraguay | 2 759 | Cameroon | 655 |
| 63 | Swaziland | 845 | Ecuador | 2 872 | Yemen [a] | 656 |
| 64 | Côte d'Ivoire | 849 | Tunisia | 2 901 | Papua New Guinea | 657 |
| 65 | Papua New Guinea | 884 | Mauritius | 3 114 | Côte d'Ivoire | 659 |
| 66 | Morocco | 915 | Panama | 3 257 | El Salvador | 665 |
| 67 | Guatemala | 954 | Jordan | 3 395 | Morocco | 750 |
| 68 | Dominican Republic | 959 | Botswana | 3 438 | Swaziland | 779 |
| 69 | Cameroon | 975 | Thailand | 3 476 | Congo | 802 |
| 70 | Honduras | 980 | Suriname | 3 619 | Namibia | 824 |
| 71 | Mongolia | 1 002 | Colombia | 3 895 | Djibouti | 829 |
| 72 | Ecuador | 1 005 | Syrian Arab Republic | 3 953 | Guatemala | 845 |
| 73 | Dem. People's Republic of Korea | 1 017 | Turkey | 3 973 | Tonga | 875 |
| 74 | Congo | 1 031 | Costa Rica | 4 077 | Mongolia | 931 |
| 75 | Albania | 1 038 | Fiji | 4 173 | Vanuatu | 938 |
| 76 | Paraguay | 1 049 | Argentina | 4 499 | Albania | 951 |
| 77 | Jordan | 1 098 | Brazil | 4 592 | Peru | 960 |
| 78 | Namibia | 1 100 | Mexico | 5 186 | Dominican Republic | 960 |
| 79 | Colombia | 1 219 | Malaysia | 5 298 | Saint Vincent and the Grenadines | 975 |
| 80 | Djibouti | 1 236 | South Africa | 5 451 | Dominica | 1 005 |
| 81 | El Salvador | 1 255 | Uruguay | 5 565 | Thailand | 1 008 |
| 82 | Thailand | 1 269 | Iran (Islamic Republic of) | 5 579 | Dem. People's Republic of Korea | 1 079 |
| 83 | Tonga | 1 299 | Chile | 5 603 | Jordan | 1 086 |
| 84 | Tunisia | 1 319 | Venezuela | 5 770 | Saint Lucia | 1 092 |
| 85 | Saint Vincent and the Grenadines | 1 388 | Portugal | 6 231 | Ecuador | 1 093 |
| 86 | Egypt | 1 403 | Trinidad & Tobago | 6 896 | Egypt | 1 109 |
| 87 | Turkey | 1 461 | Greece | 6 904 | Colombia | 1 122 |
| 88 | Saint Lucia | 1 477 | Saudi Arabia | 7 836 | Tunisia | 1 128 |
| 89 | Syrian Arab Republic | 1 502 | Bahrain | 8 102 | Jamaica | 1 146 |
| 90 | Fiji | 1 550 | Ireland | 8 875 | Belize | 1 153 |
| 91 | Jamaica | 1 612 | Barbados | 8 884 | Paraguay | 1 240 |
| 92 | Belize | 1 699 | Cyprus | 9 760 | Turkey | 1 257 |
| 93 | Costa Rica | 1 807 | Malta | 9 848 | Grenada | 1 347 |
| 94 | Dominica | 1 872 | Spain | 10 354 | Botswana | 1 392 |
| 95 | Cuba | 1 880 | Israel | 10 724 | Costa Rica | 1 404 |
| 96 | Argentina | 1 894 | New Zealand | 10 848 | Syrian Arab Republic | 1 409 |
| 97 | Panama | 1 919 | Oman | 11 230 | Panama | 1 474 |
| 98 | Mauritius | 1 933 | Singapore | 13 173 | Saint Kitts–Nevis | 1 487 |
| 99 | Chile | 1 958 | Netherlands | 13 498 | Fiji | 1 501 |
| 100 | Botswana | 1 982 | Austria | 13 952 | Iraq | 1 529 |
| 101 | Algeria | 2 027 | Australia | 14 002 | Mauritius | 1 608 |
| 102 | Peru | 2 046 | Italy | 14 023 | Chile | 1 689 |
| 103 | Poland | 2 152 | United Kingdom | 14 538 | Cook Islands | 1 763 |
| 104 | Malaysia | 2 156 | Belgium | 14 875 | French Guiana | 1 769 |
| 105 | Grenada | 2 181 | Japan | 14 955 | Cuba | 1 786 |
| 106 | Romania | 2 312 | Sweden | 14 995 | Romania | 1 807 |
| 107 | Venezuela | 2 352 | Kuwait | 15 019 | Poland | 1 866 |
| 108 | Saint Kitts–Nevis | 2 361 | Finland | 15 358 | Mexico | 1 868 |
| 109 | Mexico | 2 396 | Denmark | 15 771 | Gabon | 1 896 |
| 110 | Bulgaria | 2 566 | Federal Republic of Germany [b] | 16 097 | South Africa | 1 909 |
| 111 | South Africa | 2 592 | France | 16 122 | Brazil | 1 918 |
| 112 | Hungary | 2 731 | Luxembourg | 16 174 | Malaysia | 1 932 |
| 113 | Uruguay | 2 736 | Iceland | 16 568 | Algeria | 1 969 |
| 114 | French Guiana | 2 796 | United Arab Emirates | 16 624 | Argentina | 2 080 |
| 115 | Gabon | 2 978 | Canada | 18 596 | Uruguay | 2 148 |
| 116 | Cook Islands | 3 155 | Norway | 20 085 | Suriname | 2 182 |
| 117 | Trinidad & Tobago | 3 172 | United States of America | 20 749 | Hungary | 2 247 |
| 118 | Czechoslovakia | 3 228 | | | Yugoslavia [c] | 2 417 |

| Relative 1970–1989 PARE | | Absolute 1980–1989 PARE | | World Bank Atlas method | | |
|---|---|---|---|---|---|---|
| Country or area | Per capita GDP | Country or area | Per capita GDP | Country or area | Per capita GDP | Rank |
| Zimbabwe | 871 | Bolivia | 719 | Angola | 665 | 59 |
| Nicaragua | 893 | Yemen [a] | 735 | Senegal | 690 | 60 |
| Honduras | 919 | Côte d'Ivoire | 755 | Philippines | 728 | 61 |
| Cameroon | 939 | Cameroon | 797 | Vanuatu | 784 | 62 |
| Yemen [a] | 941 | Honduras | 804 | Nicaragua | 792 | 63 |
| Papua New Guinea | 943 | Papua New Guinea | 808 | Cape Verde | 813 | 64 |
| Côte d'Ivoire | 946 | Morocco | 813 | Swaziland | 840 | 65 |
| El Salvador | 954 | Swaziland | 838 | Côte d'Ivoire | 849 | 66 |
| Morocco | 1 076 | El Salvador | 930 | Syrian Arab Republic | 884 | 67 |
| Swaziland | 1 117 | Vanuatu | 939 | Morocco | 916 | 68 |
| Congo | 1 150 | Mongolia | 954 | Papua New Guinea | 926 | 69 |
| Namibia | 1 182 | Congo | 955 | Guatemala | 949 | 70 |
| Djibouti | 1 190 | Albania | 992 | Dominican Republic | 953 | 71 |
| Guatemala | 1 212 | Tonga | 1 002 | Cameroon | 986 | 72 |
| Tonga | 1 254 | Namibia | 1 010 | Paraguay | 990 | 73 |
| Mongolia | 1 336 | Dem. People's Republic of Korea | 1 025 | Ecuador | 1 005 | 74 |
| Vanuatu | 1 346 | Guatemala | 1 042 | Dem. People's Republic of Korea | 1 016 | 75 |
| Albania | 1 364 | Nicaragua | 1 070 | Albania | 1 016 | 76 |
| Peru | 1 377 | Dominican Republic | 1 080 | Mongolia | 1 024 | 77 |
| Dominican Republic | 1 377 | Djibouti | 1 137 | Congo | 1 031 | 78 |
| Saint Vincent and the Grenadines | 1 398 | Thailand | 1 143 | Namibia | 1 090 | 79 |
| Dominica | 1 442 | Egypt | 1 195 | El Salvador | 1 121 | 80 |
| Thailand | 1 446 | Saint Vincent and the Grenadines | 1 222 | Jordan | 1 147 | 81 |
| Dem. People's Republic of Korea | 1 548 | Peru | 1 226 | Tonga | 1 190 | 82 |
| Jordan | 1 558 | Jordan | 1 262 | Djibouti | 1 215 | 83 |
| Saint Lucia | 1 567 | Tunisia | 1 264 | Colombia | 1 219 | 84 |
| Ecuador | 1 569 | Ecuador | 1 317 | Saint Vincent and the Grenadines | 1 249 | 85 |
| Egypt | 1 591 | Saint Lucia | 1 328 | Tunisia | 1 251 | 86 |
| Colombia | 1 610 | Jamaica | 1 330 | Thailand | 1 269 | 87 |
| Tunisia | 1 618 | Turkey | 1 332 | Peru | 1 356 | 88 |
| Jamaica | 1 644 | Colombia | 1 346 | Turkey | 1 461 | 89 |
| Belize | 1 654 | Belize | 1 410 | Saint Lucia | 1 477 | 90 |
| Paraguay | 1 778 | Dominica | 1 453 | Fiji | 1 567 | 91 |
| Turkey | 1 803 | Paraguay | 1 479 | Jamaica | 1 600 | 92 |
| Grenada | 1 933 | Botswana | 1 528 | Belize | 1 699 | 93 |
| Botswana | 1 996 | Costa Rica | 1 590 | Costa Rica | 1 807 | 94 |
| Costa Rica | 2 014 | Mauritius | 1 701 | Poland | 1 865 | 95 |
| Syrian Arab Republic | 2 022 | Grenada | 1 749 | Dominica | 1 872 | 96 |
| Panama | 2 115 | Panama | 1 764 | Cuba | 1 884 | 97 |
| Saint Kitts–Nevis | 2 133 | Syrian Arab Republic | 1 773 | Argentina | 1 892 | 98 |
| Fiji | 2 153 | Fiji | 1 777 | Panama | 1 919 | 99 |
| Iraq | 2 193 | Cuba | 1 835 | Mauritius | 1 939 | 100 |
| Mauritius | 2 307 | Saint Kitts–Nevis | 1 855 | Chile | 1 958 | 101 |
| Chile | 2 424 | Poland | 1 999 | Botswana | 1 989 | 102 |
| Cook Islands | 2 528 | Romania | 2 016 | Algeria | 2 024 | 103 |
| French Guiana | 2 538 | Chile | 2 137 | Malaysia | 2 149 | 104 |
| Cuba | 2 562 | Mexico | 2 153 | Grenada | 2 181 | 105 |
| Romania | 2 592 | Iraq | 2 188 | Romania | 2 315 | 106 |
| Poland | 2 676 | Malaysia | 2 211 | Venezuela | 2 353 | 107 |
| Mexico | 2 680 | French Guiana | 2 218 | Saint Kitts–Nevis | 2 361 | 108 |
| Gabon | 2 719 | Brazil | 2 229 | Mexico | 2 396 | 109 |
| South Africa | 2 739 | Hungary | 2 363 | South Africa | 2 569 | 110 |
| Brazil | 2 751 | Cook Islands | 2 375 | Iran (Islamic Republic of) | 2 720 | 111 |
| Malaysia | 2 771 | Algeria | 2 386 | Hungary | 2 733 | 112 |
| Algeria | 2 825 | South Africa | 2 402 | Uruguay | 2 736 | 113 |
| Argentina | 2 984 | Gabon | 2 487 | French Guiana | 2 822 | 114 |
| Uruguay | 3 081 | Argentina | 2 585 | Bulgaria | 2 878 | 115 |
| Suriname | 3 129 | Uruguay | 2 656 | Gabon | 2 978 | 116 |
| Hungary | 3 223 | Yugoslavia [c] | 2 702 | Cook Islands | 2 987 | 117 |
| Yugoslavia [c] | 3 467 | Suriname | 2 729 | Suriname | 3 201 | 118 |

**Table A.5**    Country or area rankings based on per capita gross domestic product in 1989 [cont.]

| | Market exchange rate | | | PPPs | | Absolute 1970–1989 PARE | |
|---|---|---|---|---|---|---|---|
| Rank | Country or area | Per capita GDP | | Country or area | Per capita GDP | Country or area | Per capita GDP |
| 119 | Brazil | 3 270 | | | | Antigua & Barbuda | 2 551 |
| 120 | Suriname | 3 361 | | | | Venezuela | 2 582 |
| 121 | Yugoslavia [c] | 3 456 | | | | Iran (Islamic Republic of) | 2 641 |
| 122 | Iraq | 3 652 | | | | Portugal | 2 713 |
| 123 | Antigua & Barbuda | 3 810 | | | | Czechoslovakia | 2 802 |
| 124 | Montserrat | 4 066 | | | | Bulgaria | 2 940 |
| 125 | Seychelles | 4 239 | | | | Seychelles | 2 999 |
| 126 | Anguilla | 4 279 | | | | Montserrat | 3 027 |
| 127 | Portugal | 4 413 | | | | Anguilla | 3 041 |
| 128 | Republic of Korea | 5 029 | | | | Trinidad & Tobago | 3 113 |
| 129 | Libyan Arab Jamahiriya | 5 080 | | | | Republic of Korea | 3 192 |
| 130 | Union of Soviet Socialist Rep. | 5 205 | | | | Greece | 3 820 |
| 131 | Greece | 5 401 | | | | Reunion | 3 881 |
| 132 | Saudi Arabia | 5 606 | | | | Union of Soviet Socialist Rep. | 4 018 |
| 133 | Reunion | 5 674 | | | | Guadeloupe | 4 070 |
| 134 | Oman | 5 871 | | | | Malta | 4 131 |
| 135 | Guadeloupe | 6 073 | | | | Barbados | 4 186 |
| 136 | Malta | 6 364 | | | | Cyprus | 4 399 |
| 137 | Cyprus | 6 394 | | | | Saudi Arabia | 4 895 |
| 138 | Bahrain | 6 549 | | | | Netherlands Antilles | 4 949 |
| 139 | Barbados | 6 694 | | | | Libyan Arab Jamahiriya | 5 006 |
| 140 | Netherlands Antilles | 7 200 | | | | Bahrain | 5 364 |
| 141 | Martinique | 7 704 | | | | Spain | 5 427 |
| 142 | Iran (Islamic Republic of) | 8 537 | | | | Martinique | 5 521 |
| 143 | Puerto Rico | 8 799 | | | | Oman | 5 524 |
| 144 | Brunei Darussalam | 9 101 | | | | Ireland | 5 771 |
| 145 | Ireland | 9 273 | | | | Puerto Rico | 6 365 |
| 146 | Spain | 9 601 | | | | Israel | 6 476 |
| 147 | Israel | 10 256 | | | | New Zealand | 6 891 |
| 148 | Singapore | 10 277 | | | | British Virgin Islands | 6 992 |
| 149 | Bahamas | 10 787 | | | | Bahamas | 7 049 |
| 150 | Hong Kong | 10 877 | | | | Kuwait | 7 089 |
| 151 | German Democratic Republic [b] | 11 200 | | | | US Virgin Islands | 7 566 |
| 152 | British Virgin Islands | 11 235 | | | | Hong Kong | 7 860 |
| 153 | Kuwait | 11 430 | | | | Singapore | 7 965 |
| 154 | US Virgin Islands | 11 670 | | | | Italy | 8 652 |
| 155 | New Zealand | 11 915 | | | | Brunei Darussalam | 8 820 |
| 156 | New Caledonia | 13 534 | | | | United Kingdom | 8 856 |
| 157 | French Polynesia | 13 807 | | | | New Caledonia | 8 872 |
| 158 | United Kingdom | 14 752 | | | | French Polynesia | 8 996 |
| 159 | Italy | 15 166 | | | | German Democratic Republic [b] | 9 028 |
| 160 | Netherlands | 15 208 | | | | Austria | 10 147 |
| 161 | Belgium | 15 537 | | | | Netherlands | 10 195 |
| 162 | Austria | 16 727 | | | | Belgium | 10 529 |
| 163 | Australia | 17 039 | | | | France | 11 255 |
| 164 | France | 17 071 | | | | Australia | 11 474 |
| 165 | United Arab Emirates | 17 497 | | | | Federal Republic of Germany [b] | 12 626 |
| 166 | Luxembourg | 18 866 | | | | Luxembourg | 12 760 |
| 167 | Qatar | 19 069 | | | | Denmark | 12 794 |
| 168 | Federal Republic of Germany [b] | 19 202 | | | | Qatar | 12 916 |
| 169 | Denmark | 20 402 | | | | Finland | 12 942 |
| 170 | Canada | 20 462 | | | | Japan | 13 229 |
| 171 | Iceland | 20 613 | | | | Canada | 13 680 |
| 172 | United States of America | 20 749 | | | | Iceland | 13 901 |
| 173 | Norway | 21 651 | | | | Sweden | 14 019 |
| 174 | Sweden | 22 703 | | | | United States of America | 14 465 |
| 175 | Japan | 23 046 | | | | Bermuda | 15 490 |
| 176 | Finland | 23 211 | | | | United Arab Emirates | 15 513 |
| 177 | Bermuda | 27 098 | | | | Switzerland | 15 882 |
| 178 | Switzerland | 27 497 | | | | Norway | 17 925 |

| Relative 1970–1989 PARE | | Absolute 1980–1989 PARE | | World Bank Atlas method | | |
|---|---|---|---|---|---|---|
| Country or area | Per capita GDP | Country or area | Per capita GDP | Country or area | Per capita GDP | Rank |
| Antigua & Barbuda | 3 659 | Antigua & Barbuda | 3 069 | Trinidad & Tobago | 3 209 | 119 |
| Venezuela | 3 704 | Venezuela | 3 112 | Iraq | 3 220 | 120 |
| Iran (Islamic Republic of) | 3 788 | Czechoslovakia | 3 169 | Brazil | 3 270 | 121 |
| Portugal | 3 892 | Bulgaria | 3 200 | Czechoslovakia | 3 322 | 122 |
| Czechoslovakia | 4 020 | Portugal | 3 235 | Yugoslavia [c] | 3 456 | 123 |
| Bulgaria | 4 218 | Seychelles | 3 315 | Antigua & Barbuda | 3 810 | 124 |
| Seychelles | 4 303 | Anguilla | 3 317 | Anguilla | 3 978 | 125 |
| Montserrat | 4 342 | Republic of Korea | 3 764 | Montserrat | 4 035 | 126 |
| Anguilla | 4 362 | Montserrat | 3 803 | Seychelles | 4 205 | 127 |
| Trinidad & Tobago | 4 465 | Trinidad & Tobago | 4 080 | Portugal | 4 414 | 128 |
| Republic of Korea | 4 578 | Iran (Islamic Republic of) | 4 184 | Republic of Korea | 5 030 | 129 |
| Greece | 5 480 | Union of Soviet Socialist Rep. | 4 310 | Union of Soviet Socialist Rep. | 5 053 | 130 |
| Reunion | 5 567 | Greece | 4 471 | Libyan Arab Jamahiriya | 5 094 | 131 |
| Union of Soviet Socialist Rep. | 5 763 | Reunion | 4 501 | Greece | 5 400 | 132 |
| Guadeloupe | 5 838 | Malta | 4 839 | Malta | 5 479 | 133 |
| Malta | 5 925 | Guadeloupe | 5 045 | Saudi Arabia | 5 538 | 134 |
| Barbados | 6 005 | Cyprus | 5 318 | Reunion | 5 745 | 135 |
| Cyprus | 6 311 | Barbados | 5 621 | Oman | 5 803 | 136 |
| Saudi Arabia | 7 022 | Libyan Arab Jamahiriya | 6 177 | Guadeloupe | 6 203 | 137 |
| Netherlands Antilles | 7 100 | Netherlands Antilles | 6 380 | Cyprus | 6 481 | 138 |
| Libyan Arab Jamahiriya | 7 181 | Martinique | 6 585 | Barbados | 6 656 | 139 |
| Bahrain | 7 694 | Saudi Arabia | 6 722 | Bahrain | 6 967 | 140 |
| Spain | 7 785 | Spain | 6 885 | Netherlands Antilles | 7 085 | 141 |
| Martinique | 7 920 | Oman | 7 213 | Martinique | 7 990 | 142 |
| Oman | 7 924 | Ireland | 7 214 | Puerto Rico | 8 492 | 143 |
| Ireland | 8 278 | Bahrain | 7 487 | Ireland | 9 200 | 144 |
| Puerto Rico | 9 130 | Puerto Rico | 7 763 | Brunei Darussalam | 9 315 | 145 |
| Israel | 9 290 | Israel | 7 935 | Spain | 9 602 | 146 |
| New Zealand | 9 885 | British Virgin Islands | 8 693 | Israel | 10 168 | 147 |
| British Virgin Islands | 10 031 | Hong Kong | 8 907 | Singapore | 10 539 | 148 |
| Bahamas | 10 111 | New Zealand | 8 907 | British Virgin Islands | 10 636 | 149 |
| Kuwait | 10 169 | Bahamas | 8 969 | Bahamas | 10 787 | 150 |
| US Virgin Islands | 10 854 | Singapore | 9 216 | Hong Kong | 10 877 | 151 |
| Hong Kong | 11 275 | US Virgin Islands | 9 785 | US Virgin Islands | 11 277 | 152 |
| Singapore | 11 426 | German Democratic Republic [b] | 9 792 | Kuwait | 11 672 | 153 |
| Italy | 12 411 | New Caledonia | 10 982 | German Democratic Republic [b] | 11 811 | 154 |
| Brunei Darussalam | 12 652 | Italy | 11 026 | New Zealand | 12 113 | 155 |
| United Kingdom | 12 704 | French Polynesia | 11 097 | New Caledonia | 13 653 | 156 |
| New Caledonia | 12 727 | Kuwait | 11 618 | French Polynesia | 14 054 | 157 |
| French Polynesia | 12 905 | United Kingdom | 11 674 | United Kingdom | 14 482 | 158 |
| German Democratic Republic [b] | 12 951 | Brunei Darussalam | 11 976 | Netherlands | 15 059 | 159 |
| Austria | 14 555 | Belgium | 12 360 | Italy | 15 166 | 160 |
| Netherlands | 14 624 | Netherlands | 12 448 | Belgium | 15 535 | 161 |
| Belgium | 15 103 | Austria | 12 801 | Austria | 16 688 | 162 |
| France | 16 146 | France | 13 771 | France | 17 124 | 163 |
| Australia | 16 459 | Australia | 13 864 | Australia | 17 516 | 164 |
| Federal Republic of Germany [b] | 18 112 | Luxembourg | 15 244 | United Arab Emirates | 17 635 | 165 |
| Luxembourg | 18 304 | Federal Republic of Germany [b] | 15 355 | Qatar | 18 087 | 166 |
| Denmark | 18 353 | Denmark | 15 657 | Luxembourg | 18 864 | 167 |
| Qatar | 18 528 | Finland | 16 400 | Federal Republic of Germany [b] | 19 406 | 168 |
| Finland | 18 566 | Canada | 16 422 | Denmark | 20 373 | 169 |
| Japan | 18 978 | Iceland | 16 683 | Iceland | 20 598 | 170 |
| Canada | 19 625 | United Arab Emirates | 16 687 | Canada | 20 739 | 171 |
| Iceland | 19 940 | Japan | 16 749 | United States of America | 20 749 | 172 |
| Sweden | 20 110 | Sweden | 17 050 | Norway | 21 636 | 173 |
| United States of America | 20 749 | United States of America | 18 074 | Sweden | 22 538 | 174 |
| Bermuda | 22 221 | Norway | 18 860 | Japan | 23 052 | 175 |
| United Arab Emirates | 22 254 | Qatar | 19 402 | Finland | 23 258 | 176 |
| Switzerland | 22 783 | Switzerland | 20 996 | Bermuda | 25 600 | 177 |
| Norway | 25 713 | Bermuda | 21 000 | Switzerland | 26 894 | 178 |

**Table A.5**    Country or area rankings based on per capita gross domestic product in 1989 [cont.]

Note:   Rule divisions within the listings indicate approximate quartile divisions of world population.  Where quartile divisions fall within a large country or area, it is shaded.

a       On 22 May 1990 Democratic Yemen and Yemen merged to form a single State.  Since that date they have been represented as one Member with the name "Yemen".

b       Through accession of the German Democratic Republic to the Federal Republic of Germany with effect from 3 October 1990, the two German States have united to form one sovereign State.

As from the date of unification, the Federal Republic of Germany acts in the United Nations under the designation Germany.

c       Data provided for Yugoslavia are for periods prior to 1 January 1992 and refer to the Socialist Federal Republic of Yugolavia which was composed of six republics. Data provided for Yugoslavia after that date refer to the Federal Republic of Yugoslavia which is composed of two republics (Serbia and Montenegro).

Table A.6

**Total and per capita gross regional product expressed in United States dollars using alternative conversion rates, and individual shares of gross world product, 1970–1989**

Follows overleaf

**Table A.6**  Total and per capita gross regional product expressed in United States dollars using alternative conversion rates, and individual shares of gross world product, 1970–1989

| Country or area | 1970 (1) | 1971 (2) | 1972 (3) | 1973 (4) | 1974 (5) | 1975 (6) | 1976 (7) | 1977 (8) | 1978 (9) | 1979 (10) |
|---|---|---|---|---|---|---|---|---|---|---|
| **Africa** | | | | | | | | | | |
| **1. MER** | | | | | | | | | | |
| 1a. Per capita gross regional product | 219 | 238 | 260 | 319 | 415 | 455 | 493 | 562 | 629 | 719 |
| 1b. Gross regional product | 79 294 | 88 367 | 99 029 | 124 897 | 166 814 | 187 887 | 209 547 | 245 632 | 283 304 | 332 999 |
| 1c. % of gross world product | 2.49 | 2.53 | 2.46 | 2.54 | 3.00 | 3.02 | 3.12 | 3.25 | 3.15 | 3.23 |
| **2. PPPs [a]** | | | | | | | | | | |
| 2a. Per capita gross regional product | 399 | 432 | 445 | 479 | 576 | 612 | 655 | 690 | 724 | 813 |
| 2b. Gross regional product | 142 139 | 158 328 | 167 320 | 184 753 | 228 261 | 249 136 | 274 269 | 297 402 | 321 186 | 371 268 |
| 2c. % of gross world product | ... | ... | ... | ... | ... | ... | ... | ... | ... | ... |
| **3. Absolute 1970–1989 PARE** | | | | | | | | | | |
| 3a. Per capita gross regional product | 543 | 552 | 569 | 578 | 600 | 596 | 620 | 628 | 625 | 629 |
| 3b. Gross regional product | 196 447 | 205 053 | 216 778 | 226 190 | 241 302 | 246 410 | 263 298 | 274 745 | 281 445 | 291 684 |
| 3c. % of gross world product | 2.76 | 2.77 | 2.78 | 2.73 | 2.85 | 2.86 | 2.91 | 2.91 | 2.86 | 2.87 |
| **4. Relative 1970–1989 PARE** | | | | | | | | | | |
| 4a. Per capita gross regional product | 265 | 283 | 305 | 330 | 374 | 409 | 451 | 488 | 521 | 572 |
| 4b. Gross regional product | 95 782 | 105 107 | 116 214 | 129 315 | 150 475 | 168 817 | 191 660 | 213 482 | 234 642 | 264 890 |
| 4c. % of gross world product | 2.76 | 2.77 | 2.78 | 2.73 | 2.85 | 2.86 | 2.91 | 2.91 | 2.86 | 2.87 |
| **5. Absolute 1980–1989 PARE** | | | | | | | | | | |
| 5a. Per capita gross regional product | 653 | 664 | 683 | 693 | 720 | 713 | 741 | 750 | 746 | 751 |
| 5b. Gross regional product | 236 177 | 246 447 | 260 490 | 271 270 | 289 397 | 294 650 | 314 715 | 328 146 | 335 871 | 348 102 |
| 5c. % of gross world product | 2.71 | 2.72 | 2.73 | 2.67 | 2.79 | 2.80 | 2.85 | 2.85 | 2.80 | 2.81 |
| **6. WA** | | | | | | | | | | |
| 6a. Per capita gross regional product | 224 | 240 | 261 | 316 | 405 | 440 | 475 | 532 | 586 | 685 |
| 6b. Gross regional product | 81 158 | 89 161 | 99 442 | 123 594 | 162 672 | 181 740 | 201 861 | 232 569 | 263 601 | 317 653 |
| 6c. % of gross world product | 2.54 | 2.56 | 2.48 | 2.54 | 2.92 | 2.95 | 3.01 | 3.08 | 2.97 | 3.11 |
| **Sub–Saharan Africa** | | | | | | | | | | |
| **1. MER** | | | | | | | | | | |
| 1a. Per capita gross regional product | 198 | 217 | 234 | 286 | 368 | 402 | 421 | 476 | 533 | 625 |
| 1b. Gross regional product | 55 270 | 62 050 | 68 814 | 86 553 | 114 300 | 128 553 | 138 589 | 161 238 | 185 856 | 224 454 |
| 1c. % of gross world product | 1.73 | 1.77 | 1.71 | 1.76 | 2.06 | 2.07 | 2.07 | 2.13 | 2.07 | 2.18 |
| **2. PPPs [a]** | | | | | | | | | | |
| 2a. Per capita gross regional product | 392 | 428 | 439 | 477 | 568 | 596 | 628 | 651 | 676 | 751 |
| 2b. Gross regional product | 108 057 | 121 045 | 127 811 | 142 497 | 174 421 | 188 402 | 204 393 | 217 973 | 233 189 | 267 015 |
| 2c. % of gross world product | ... | ... | ... | ... | ... | ... | ... | ... | ... | ... |
| **3. Absolute 1970–1989 PARE** | | | | | | | | | | |
| 3a. Per capita gross regional product | 491 | 506 | 511 | 520 | 542 | 524 | 534 | 532 | 514 | 505 |
| 3b. Gross regional product | 136 711 | 144 878 | 150 302 | 157 181 | 168 476 | 167 352 | 175 645 | 180 034 | 179 252 | 181 557 |
| 3c. % of gross world product | 1.92 | 1.96 | 1.93 | 1.89 | 1.99 | 1.95 | 1.94 | 1.91 | 1.82 | 1.79 |
| **4. Relative 1970–1989 PARE** | | | | | | | | | | |
| 4a. Per capita gross regional product | 239 | 259 | 274 | 297 | 338 | 359 | 389 | 413 | 429 | 459 |
| 4b. Gross regional product | 66 656 | 74 262 | 80 577 | 89 861 | 105 061 | 114 654 | 127 856 | 139 890 | 149 443 | 164 879 |
| 4c. % of gross world product | 1.92 | 1.96 | 1.93 | 1.89 | 1.99 | 1.95 | 1.94 | 1.91 | 1.82 | 1.79 |
| **5. Absolute 1980–1989 PARE** | | | | | | | | | | |
| 5a. Per capita gross regional product | 598 | 617 | 623 | 632 | 659 | 634 | 647 | 643 | 622 | 612 |
| 5b. Gross regional product | 166 752 | 176 647 | 183 234 | 190 968 | 204 631 | 202 729 | 212 666 | 217 849 | 216 947 | 219 942 |
| 5c. % of gross world product | 1.92 | 1.95 | 1.92 | 1.88 | 1.97 | 1.93 | 1.92 | 1.89 | 1.81 | 1.77 |
| **6. WA** | | | | | | | | | | |
| 6a. Per capita gross regional product | 201 | 215 | 231 | 282 | 364 | 394 | 417 | 468 | 518 | 594 |
| 6b. Gross regional product | 56 116 | 61 626 | 67 928 | 85 219 | 113 219 | 125 838 | 137 240 | 158 601 | 180 788 | 213 462 |
| 6c. % of gross world product | 1.76 | 1.77 | 1.70 | 1.75 | 2.03 | 2.04 | 2.05 | 2.10 | 2.04 | 2.09 |

| | 1980 (11) | 1981 (12) | 1982 (13) | 1983 (14) | 1984 (15) | 1985 (16) | 1986 (17) | 1987 (18) | 1988 (19) | 1989 (20) | Averages 1970−89 (21) | 1970−79 (22) | 1980−89 (23) |
|---|---|---|---|---|---|---|---|---|---|---|---|---|---|
| | 890 | 808 | 765 | 752 | 732 | 698 | 663 | 697 | 693 | 653 | 618 | 446 | 733 |
| | 424 774 | 397 145 | 387 212 | 391 713 | 392 677 | 385 718 | 377 458 | 408 768 | 419 160 | 406 817 | 290 460 | 181 777 | 399 144 |
| | 3.67 | 3.39 | 3.33 | 3.30 | 3.22 | 3.06 | 2.53 | 2.38 | 2.19 | 2.03 | 2.85 | 2.98 | 2.80 |
| | 935 | 1 007 | 1 051 | 1 073 | 1 100 | 1 099 | 1 110 | 1 125 | 1 170 | 1 216 | 894 | 596 | 1 099 |
| | 439 496 | 487 410 | 523 697 | 550 550 | 581 134 | 598 192 | 622 509 | 650 034 | 696 327 | 746 030 | 414 472 | 239 406 | 589 538 |
| | ... | ... | ... | ... | ... | ... | ... | ... | ... | ... | ... | ... | ... |
| | 643 | 631 | 639 | 622 | 611 | 618 | 612 | 597 | 598 | 598 | 618 | 599 | 618 |
| | 306 625 | 310 229 | 323 033 | 323 851 | 327 798 | 341 360 | 348 476 | 350 438 | 361 730 | 372 316 | 290 460 | 244 335 | 336 586 |
| | 2.95 | 2.93 | 3.03 | 2.95 | 2.86 | 2.88 | 2.85 | 2.77 | 2.74 | 2.74 | 2.85 | 2.84 | 2.86 |
| | 637 | 685 | 738 | 742 | 756 | 785 | 793 | 796 | 825 | 857 | 623 | 410 | 769 |
| | 303 945 | 336 614 | 373 147 | 386 736 | 405 471 | 433 686 | 451 623 | 467 216 | 498 462 | 534 085 | 293 068 | 167 038 | 419 099 |
| | 2.95 | 2.93 | 3.03 | 2.95 | 2.86 | 2.88 | 2.85 | 2.77 | 2.74 | 2.74 | 4.05 | 2.74 | 5.00 |
| | 766 | 752 | 758 | 737 | 724 | 732 | 725 | 707 | 708 | 707 | 735 | 718 | 733 |
| | 365 637 | 369 376 | 383 635 | 384 005 | 388 761 | 404 606 | 412 699 | 414 618 | 427 911 | 440 192 | 345 835 | 292 526 | 399 144 |
| | 2.89 | 2.87 | 2.96 | 2.88 | 2.79 | 2.81 | 2.78 | 2.71 | 2.68 | 2.67 | 2.79 | 2.78 | 2.80 |
| | 856 | 836 | 805 | 769 | 712 | 682 | 628 | 642 | 619 | 582 | 597 | 430 | 708 |
| | 408 419 | 410 531 | 407 324 | 400 597 | 382 118 | 376 822 | 357 622 | 376 720 | 374 267 | 362 822 | 280 535 | 175 345 | 385 724 |
| | 3.55 | 3.48 | 3.49 | 3.38 | 3.13 | 2.98 | 2.43 | 2.26 | 2.00 | 1.85 | 2.78 | 2.89 | 2.73 |
| | 781 | 692 | 641 | 611 | 574 | 514 | 462 | 475 | 485 | 458 | 495 | 389 | 564 |
| | 289 059 | 263 870 | 251 618 | 247 212 | 239 298 | 221 002 | 204 814 | 216 933 | 228 580 | 222 681 | 180 537 | 122 568 | 238 507 |
| | 2.49 | 2.25 | 2.16 | 2.09 | 1.96 | 1.75 | 1.38 | 1.26 | 1.20 | 1.11 | 1.77 | 2.01 | 1.67 |
| | 868 | 935 | 965 | 955 | 964 | 968 | 975 | 985 | 1 024 | 1 060 | 815 | 573 | 978 |
| | 317 866 | 352 425 | 374 619 | 382 066 | 397 535 | 411 264 | 427 257 | 445 186 | 477 389 | 509 695 | 294 005 | 178 480 | 409 530 |
| | ... | ... | ... | ... | ... | ... | ... | ... | ... | ... | ... | ... | ... |
| | 509 | 506 | 494 | 470 | 457 | 455 | 450 | 438 | 439 | 436 | 495 | 521 | 465 |
| | 188 519 | 192 764 | 193 929 | 190 122 | 190 410 | 195 475 | 199 211 | 200 128 | 206 978 | 211 817 | 180 537 | 164 139 | 196 935 |
| | 1.81 | 1.82 | 1.82 | 1.73 | 1.66 | 1.65 | 1.63 | 1.58 | 1.57 | 1.56 | 1.77 | 1.90 | 1.67 |
| | 505 | 549 | 571 | 561 | 565 | 578 | 583 | 584 | 605 | 625 | 488 | 353 | 578 |
| | 186 871 | 209 159 | 224 014 | 227 040 | 235 528 | 248 344 | 258 177 | 266 818 | 285 215 | 303 851 | 177 908 | 111 314 | 244 502 |
| | 1.81 | 1.82 | 1.82 | 1.73 | 1.66 | 1.65 | 1.63 | 1.58 | 1.57 | 1.56 | 1.73 | 1.90 | 1.67 |
| | 618 | 613 | 598 | 569 | 554 | 551 | 545 | 531 | 532 | 527 | 600 | 632 | 564 |
| | 228 514 | 233 600 | 234 879 | 230 060 | 230 742 | 236 862 | 241 234 | 242 311 | 250 539 | 256 327 | 218 872 | 199 236 | 238 507 |
| | 1.81 | 1.81 | 1.81 | 1.73 | 1.66 | 1.64 | 1.63 | 1.58 | 1.57 | 1.55 | 1.76 | 1.89 | 1.67 |
| | 750 | 742 | 704 | 645 | 569 | 508 | 459 | 465 | 485 | 452 | 496 | 381 | 571 |
| | 277 397 | 282 920 | 276 221 | 260 813 | 237 194 | 218 065 | 203 206 | 212 347 | 228 556 | 219 639 | 180 820 | 120 004 | 241 636 |
| | 2.41 | 2.40 | 2.37 | 2.20 | 1.94 | 1.72 | 1.38 | 1.27 | 1.22 | 1.12 | 1.79 | 1.98 | 1.71 |

**Table A.6** Total and per capita gross regional product expressed in United States dollars using alternative conversion rates, and individual shares of gross world product, 1970−1989 [cont.]

| Country or area | 1970 (1) | 1971 (2) | 1972 (3) | 1973 (4) | 1974 (5) | 1975 (6) | 1976 (7) | 1977 (8) | 1978 (9) | 1979 (10) |
|---|---|---|---|---|---|---|---|---|---|---|
| **Northern Africa** | | | | | | | | | | |
| **1. MER** | | | | | | | | | | |
| 1a. Per capita gross regional product | 289 | 309 | 347 | 430 | 575 | 633 | 738 | 855 | 961 | 1 042 |
| 1b. Gross regional product | 24 025 | 26 316 | 30 215 | 38 343 | 52 514 | 59 335 | 70 958 | 84 394 | 97 448 | 108 544 |
| 1c. % of gross world product | 0.75 | 0.75 | 0.75 | 0.78 | 0.95 | 0.96 | 1.06 | 1.12 | 1.08 | 1.05 |
| **2. PPPs** [a] | | | | | | | | | | |
| 2a. Per capita gross regional product | 420 | 449 | 465 | 486 | 605 | 666 | 747 | 827 | 893 | 1 029 |
| 2b. Gross regional product | 34 083 | 37 283 | 39 508 | 42 255 | 53 839 | 60 735 | 69 876 | 79 428 | 87 997 | 104 253 |
| 2c. % of gross world product | ... | ... | ... | ... | ... | ... | ... | ... | ... | ... |
| **3. Absolute 1970−1989 PARE** | | | | | | | | | | |
| 3a. Per capita gross regional product | 719 | 707 | 763 | 774 | 797 | 844 | 912 | 960 | 1 008 | 1 057 |
| 3b. Gross regional product | 59 737 | 60 176 | 66 475 | 69 010 | 72 825 | 79 058 | 87 653 | 94 711 | 102 193 | 110 127 |
| 3c. % of gross world product | 0.84 | 0.81 | 0.85 | 0.83 | 0.86 | 0.92 | 0.97 | 1.00 | 1.04 | 1.08 |
| **4. Relative 1970−1989 PARE** | | | | | | | | | | |
| 4a. Per capita gross regional product | 351 | 362 | 409 | 442 | 497 | 578 | 664 | 746 | 840 | 960 |
| 4b. Gross regional product | 29 126 | 30 845 | 35 637 | 39 453 | 45 414 | 54 163 | 63 804 | 73 592 | 85 198 | 100 010 |
| 4c. % of gross world product | 0.84 | 0.81 | 0.85 | 0.83 | 0.86 | 0.92 | 0.97 | 1.00 | 1.04 | 1.08 |
| **5. Absolute 1980−1989 PARE** | | | | | | | | | | |
| 5a. Per capita gross regional product | 836 | 820 | 887 | 900 | 928 | 981 | 1 062 | 1 118 | 1 173 | 1 230 |
| 5b. Gross regional product | 69 425 | 69 800 | 77 256 | 80 301 | 84 766 | 91 921 | 102 049 | 110 297 | 118 925 | 128 160 |
| 5c. % of gross world product | 0.80 | 0.77 | 0.81 | 0.79 | 0.82 | 0.87 | 0.92 | 0.96 | 0.99 | 1.03 |
| **6. WA** | | | | | | | | | | |
| 6a. Per capita gross regional product | 301 | 324 | 362 | 430 | 541 | 597 | 672 | 750 | 817 | 1 000 |
| 6b. Gross regional product | 25 041 | 27 535 | 31 513 | 38 375 | 49 453 | 55 901 | 64 622 | 73 968 | 82 812 | 104 191 |
| 6c. % of gross world product | 0.78 | 0.79 | 0.79 | 0.79 | 0.89 | 0.91 | 0.96 | 0.98 | 0.93 | 1.02 |
| **Northern America** | | | | | | | | | | |
| **1. MER** | | | | | | | | | | |
| 1a. Per capita gross regional product | 4 832 | 5 206 | 5 676 | 6 297 | 6 820 | 7 336 | 8 140 | 8 900 | 9 853 | 10 832 |
| 1b. Gross regional product | 1 093 954 | 1 191 014 | 1 312 414 | 1 471 380 | 1 610 762 | 1 751 183 | 1 963 889 | 2 170 580 | 2 428 884 | 2 698 877 |
| 1c. % of gross world product | 34.29 | 34.04 | 32.63 | 29.98 | 29.00 | 28.19 | 29.27 | 28.70 | 27.03 | 26.19 |
| **2. PPPs** [a] | | | | | | | | | | |
| 2a. Per capita gross regional product | 4 851 | 5 219 | 5 683 | 6 302 | 6 798 | 7 321 | 8 072 | 8 872 | 9 876 | 10 886 |
| 2b. Gross regional product | 1 098 092 | 1 194 133 | 1 314 114 | 1 472 631 | 1 605 413 | 1 747 518 | 1 947 535 | 2 163 745 | 2 434 545 | 2 712 238 |
| 2c. % of gross world product | ... | ... | ... | ... | ... | ... | ... | ... | ... | ... |
| **3. Absolute 1970−1989 PARE** | | | | | | | | | | |
| 3a. Per capita gross regional product | 9 907 | 10 139 | 10 545 | 10 957 | 10 808 | 10 619 | 11 029 | 11 387 | 11 836 | 11 960 |
| 3b. Gross regional product | 2 242 669 | 2 319 786 | 2 438 314 | 2 560 534 | 2 552 595 | 2 534 665 | 2 660 878 | 2 776 987 | 2 917 600 | 2 979 938 |
| 3c. % of gross world product | 31.56 | 31.34 | 31.26 | 30.86 | 30.12 | 29.47 | 29.40 | 29.43 | 29.67 | 29.31 |
| **4. Relative 1970−1989 PARE** | | | | | | | | | | |
| 4a. Per capita gross regional product | 4 830 | 5 197 | 5 653 | 6 264 | 6 740 | 7 275 | 8 028 | 8 848 | 9 867 | 10 861 |
| 4b. Gross regional product | 1 093 457 | 1 189 078 | 1 307 177 | 1 463 878 | 1 591 789 | 1 736 514 | 1 936 912 | 2 157 773 | 2 432 413 | 2 706 200 |
| 4c. % of gross world product | 31.56 | 31.34 | 31.26 | 30.86 | 30.12 | 29.47 | 29.40 | 29.43 | 29.67 | 29.31 |
| **5. Absolute 1980−1989 PARE** | | | | | | | | | | |
| 5a. Per capita gross regional product | 12 341 | 12 630 | 13 136 | 13 648 | 13 460 | 13 222 | 13 732 | 14 179 | 14 738 | 14 892 |
| 5b. Gross regional product | 2 793 773 | 2 889 643 | 3 037 235 | 3 189 221 | 3 178 854 | 3 156 174 | 3 313 206 | 3 457 871 | 3 633 018 | 3 710 434 |
| 5c. % of gross world product | 32.10 | 31.87 | 31.78 | 31.38 | 30.65 | 30.04 | 29.96 | 29.99 | 30.28 | 29.93 |
| **6. WA** | | | | | | | | | | |
| 6a. Per capita gross regional product | 4 831 | 5 206 | 5 676 | 6 296 | 6 820 | 7 336 | 8 140 | 8 901 | 9 853 | 10 832 |
| 6b. Gross regional product | 1 093 658 | 1 191 034 | 1 312 531 | 1 471 370 | 1 610 757 | 1 751 156 | 1 963 884 | 2 170 685 | 2 428 944 | 2 698 793 |
| 6c. % of gross world product | 34.27 | 34.15 | 32.77 | 30.25 | 28.87 | 28.42 | 29.27 | 28.79 | 27.35 | 26.38 |

| 1980 (11) | 1981 (12) | 1982 (13) | 1983 (14) | 1984 (15) | 1985 (16) | 1986 (17) | 1987 (18) | 1988 (19) | 1989 (20) | Averages 1970–89 (21) | 1970–79 (22) | 1980–89 (23) |
|---|---|---|---|---|---|---|---|---|---|---|---|---|
| 1 267 | 1 210 | 1 197 | 1 240 | 1 280 | 1 337 | 1 364 | 1 476 | 1 429 | 1346 | 1 040 | 640 | 1 322 |
| 135 715 | 133 274 | 135 594 | 144 501 | 153 379 | 164 715 | 172 644 | 191 835 | 190 581 | 184 136 | 109 923 | 59 209 | 160 637 |
| 1.17 | 1.14 | 1.17 | 1.22 | 1.26 | 1.31 | 1.16 | 1.12 | 1.00 | 0.92 | 1.08 | 0.97 | 1.12 |
| 1 169 | 1 262 | 1 356 | 1 490 | 1 580 | 1 565 | 1 592 | 1 628 | 1 696 | 1784 | 1 173 | 676 | 1 528 |
| 121 631 | 134 985 | 149 078 | 168 484 | 183 599 | 186 927 | 195 252 | 204 848 | 218 938 | 236 335 | 120 467 | 60 926 | 180 008 |
| ... | ... | ... | ... | ... | ... | ... | ... | ... | ... | ... | ... | ... |
| 1 103 | 1 066 | 1 139 | 1 147 | 1 146 | 1 184 | 1 179 | 1 157 | 1 160 | 1 173 | 1 040 | 867 | 1 149 |
| 118 106 | 117 465 | 129 104 | 133 729 | 137 388 | 145 885 | 149 265 | 150 310 | 154 752 | 160 499 | 109 923 | 80 196 | 139 650 |
| 1.14 | 1.11 | 1.21 | 1.22 | 1.20 | 1.23 | 1.22 | 1.19 | 1.17 | 1.18 | 1.08 | 0.93 | 1.19 |
| 1 093 | 1 157 | 1 316 | 1 370 | 1 418 | 1 504 | 1 529 | 1 542 | 1 599 | 1 683 | 1 090 | 602 | 1 437 |
| 117 074 | 127 455 | 149 133 | 159 697 | 169 942 | 185 342 | 193 447 | 200 398 | 213 247 | 230 234 | 115 161 | 55 724 | 174 597 |
| 1.14 | 1.11 | 1.21 | 1.22 | 1.20 | 1.23 | 1.22 | 1.19 | 1.17 | 1.18 | 1.12 | 0.95 | 1.19 |
| 1 280 | 1 233 | 1 313 | 1 321 | 1 318 | 1 362 | 1 355 | 1 326 | 1 330 | 1 344 | 1 202 | 1 008 | 1 322 |
| 137 123 | 135 777 | 148 756 | 153 945 | 158 020 | 167 744 | 171 465 | 172 308 | 177 372 | 183 865 | 126 964 | 93 290 | 160 637 |
| 1.08 | 1.05 | 1.15 | 1.15 | 1.13 | 1.16 | 1.16 | 1.12 | 1.11 | 1.11 | 1.02 | 0.89 | 1.12 |
| 1 223 | 1 159 | 1 157 | 1 199 | 1 209 | 1 289 | 1 220 | 1 265 | 1 093 | 1 046 | 944 | 598 | 1 186 |
| 131 021 | 127 611 | 131 103 | 139 783 | 144 924 | 158 757 | 154 416 | 164 372 | 145 711 | 143 183 | 99 715 | 55 341 | 144 088 |
| 1.14 | 1.08 | 1.12 | 1.18 | 1.19 | 1.26 | 1.05 | 0.99 | 0.78 | 0.73 | 0.99 | 0.91 | 1.02 |
| 11 722 | 12 986 | 13 314 | 14 172 | 15 496 | 16 303 | 16 990 | 18 096 | 19 549 | 20 722 | 11 941 | 7 452 | 15 990 |
| 2 951 712 | 3 304 261 | 3 422 713 | 3 679 955 | 4 063 121 | 4 314 717 | 4 536 834 | 4 873 276 | 5 307 563 | 5 670 246 | 2 990 867 | 1 769 294 | 4 212 440 |
| 25.47 | 28.22 | 29.44 | 31.04 | 33.31 | 34.26 | 30.47 | 28.36 | 27.78 | 28.28 | 29.36 | 29.03 | 29.50 |
| 11 776 | 13 038 | 13 348 | 14 175 | 15 564 | 16 408 | 17 119 | 18 105 | 19 394 | 20 542 | 11 945 | 7 450 | 16 001 |
| 2 965 188 | 3 317 313 | 3 431 520 | 3 680 707 | 4 080 906 | 4 342 579 | 4 571 207 | 4 875 554 | 5 265 444 | 5 621 161 | 2 992 077 | 1 768 997 | 4 215 158 |
| ... | ... | ... | ... | ... | ... | ... | ... | ... | ... | ... | ... | ... |
| 11 844 | 12 001 | 11 566 | 11 891 | 12 611 | 12 977 | 13 272 | 13 645 | 14 142 | 14 389 | 11 941 | 10 944 | 12 843 |
| 2 982 219 | 3 053 590 | 2 973 212 | 3 087 830 | 3 306 771 | 3 434 428 | 3 544 034 | 3 674 468 | 3 839 403 | 3 937 416 | 2 990 867 | 2 598 397 | 3 383 337 |
| 28.71 | 28.84 | 27.89 | 28.15 | 28.84 | 28.94 | 29.02 | 29.08 | 29.11 | 28.94 | 29.36 | 30.15 | 28.77 |
| 11 740 | 13 022 | 13 360 | 14 200 | 15 600 | 16 486 | 17 201 | 18 192 | 19 487 | 20 641 | 11 955 | 7 419 | 16 048 |
| 2 956 157 | 3 313 294 | 3 434 461 | 3 687 419 | 4 090 323 | 4 363 317 | 4 593 051 | 4 898 922 | 5 290 674 | 5 648 204 | 2 994 551 | 1 761 519 | 4 227 582 |
| 28.71 | 28.84 | 27.89 | 28.15 | 28.84 | 28.94 | 29.02 | 29.08 | 29.11 | 28.94 | 29.14 | 30.00 | 28.79 |
| 14 746 | 14 942 | 14 400 | 14 806 | 15 702 | 16 157 | 16 525 | 16 988 | 17 607 | 17 915 | 14 868 | 13 629 | 15 990 |
| 3 713 077 | 3 801 766 | 3 701 775 | 3 844 567 | 4 117 262 | 4 276 080 | 4 412 535 | 4 574 888 | 4 780 242 | 4 902 204 | 3 724 191 | 3 235 943 | 4 212 440 |
| 29.35 | 29.51 | 28.55 | 28.83 | 29.55 | 29.67 | 29.78 | 29.85 | 29.89 | 29.73 | 30.01 | 30.72 | 29.50 |
| 11 722 | 12 986 | 13 314 | 14 171 | 15 496 | 16 303 | 16 991 | 18 066 | 19 504 | 20 748 | 11 938 | 7 452 | 15 985 |
| 2 951 663 | 3 304 283 | 3 422 779 | 3 679 843 | 4 063 102 | 4 314 849 | 4 536 964 | 4 865 036 | 5 295 124 | 5 677 524 | 2 990 199 | 1 769 281 | 4 211 117 |
| 25.63 | 28.02 | 29.37 | 31.04 | 33.23 | 34.13 | 30.85 | 29.20 | 28.29 | 28.93 | 29.60 | 29.17 | 29.78 |

**Table A.6** Total and per capita gross regional product expressed in United States dollars using alternative conversion rates, and individual shares of gross world product, 1970–1989 [cont.]

| Country or area | 1970 (1) | 1971 (2) | 1972 (3) | 1973 (4) | 1974 (5) | 1975 (6) | 1976 (7) | 1977 (8) | 1978 (9) | 1979 (10) |
|---|---|---|---|---|---|---|---|---|---|---|
| **Caribbean and Latin America** | | | | | | | | | | |
| **1. MER** | | | | | | | | | | |
| 1a. Per capita gross regional product | 615 | 610 | 676 | 869 | 1 088 | 1 164 | 1 305 | 1 386 | 1 579 | 1 861 |
| 1b. Gross regional product | 175 579 | 178 703 | 203 290 | 267 723 | 343 483 | 376 567 | 432 148 | 469 918 | 547 440 | 659 870 |
| 1c. % of gross world product | 5.50 | 5.11 | 5.05 | 5.46 | 6.18 | 6.06 | 6.44 | 6.21 | 6.09 | 6.40 |
| **2. PPPs [a]** | | | | | | | | | | |
| 2a. Per capita gross regional product | 1 175 | 1 201 | 1 332 | 1 554 | 1 809 | 1 976 | 2 155 | 2 343 | 2 530 | 2 886 |
| 2b. Gross regional product | 320 338 | 335 993 | 382 285 | 457 420 | 545 935 | 611 046 | 682 630 | 760 116 | 840 440 | 981 147 |
| 2c. % of gross world product | ... | ... | ... | ... | ... | ... | ... | ... | ... | ... |
| **3. Absolute 1970–1989 PARE** | | | | | | | | | | |
| 3a. Per capita gross regional product | 1 302 | 1 350 | 1 410 | 1 488 | 1 543 | 1 563 | 1 617 | 1 658 | 1 693 | 1 757 |
| 3b. Gross regional product | 371 840 | 395 714 | 423 840 | 458 433 | 487 155 | 505 523 | 535 492 | 562 076 | 587 037 | 623 187 |
| 3c. % of gross world product | 5.23 | 5.35 | 5.43 | 5.53 | 5.75 | 5.88 | 5.92 | 5.96 | 5.97 | 6.13 |
| **4. Relative 1970–1989 PARE** | | | | | | | | | | |
| 4a. Per capita gross regional product | 635 | 692 | 756 | 851 | 962 | 1 071 | 1 177 | 1 289 | 1 411 | 1 596 |
| 4b. Gross regional product | 181 298 | 202 835 | 227 220 | 262 090 | 303 788 | 346 337 | 389 797 | 436 744 | 489 415 | 565 941 |
| 4c. % of gross world product | 5.23 | 5.35 | 5.43 | 5.53 | 5.75 | 5.88 | 5.92 | 5.96 | 5.97 | 6.13 |
| **5. Absolute 1980–1989 PARE** | | | | | | | | | | |
| 5a. Per capita gross regional product | 1 559 | 1 616 | 1 686 | 1 776 | 1 841 | 1 864 | 1 927 | 1 977 | 2 016 | 2 090 |
| 5b. Gross regional product | 445 332 | 473 620 | 506 615 | 547 265 | 581 486 | 602 785 | 638 134 | 669 946 | 698 965 | 741 212 |
| 5c. % of gross world product | 5.12 | 5.22 | 5.30 | 5.39 | 5.61 | 5.74 | 5.77 | 5.81 | 5.83 | 5.98 |
| **6. WA** | | | | | | | | | | |
| 6a. Per capita gross regional product | 597 | 618 | 737 | 981 | 1 249 | 1 179 | 1 329 | 1 391 | 1 577 | 1 917 |
| 6b. Gross regional product | 170 496 | 181 156 | 221 417 | 302 238 | 394 540 | 381 316 | 440 206 | 471 601 | 546 861 | 679 807 |
| 6c. % of gross world product | 5.34 | 5.19 | 5.53 | 6.21 | 7.07 | 6.19 | 6.56 | 6.25 | 6.16 | 6.65 |
| **Caribbean** | | | | | | | | | | |
| **1. MER** | | | | | | | | | | |
| 1a. Per capita gross regional product | 700 | 764 | 868 | 1 012 | 1 138 | 1 279 | 1 341 | 1 444 | 1 603 | 1 776 |
| 1b. Gross regional product | 17 408 | 19 360 | 22 434 | 26 652 | 30 512 | 34 857 | 37 100 | 40 483 | 45 540 | 51 109 |
| 1c. % of gross world product | 0.55 | 0.55 | 0.56 | 0.54 | 0.55 | 0.56 | 0.55 | 0.54 | 0.51 | 0.50 |
| **2. PPPs [a]** | | | | | | | | | | |
| 2a. Per capita gross regional product | 632 | 681 | 747 | 812 | 966 | 1 119 | 1 161 | 1 281 | 1 398 | 1 571 |
| 2b. Gross regional product | 7 603 | 8 369 | 9 356 | 10 366 | 12 566 | 14 830 | 15 683 | 17 610 | 19 578 | 22 408 |
| 2c. % of gross world product | ... | ... | ... | ... | ... | ... | ... | ... | ... | ... |
| **3. Absolute 1970–1989 PARE** | | | | | | | | | | |
| 3a. Per capita gross regional product | 1 365 | 1 429 | 1 497 | 1 536 | 1 505 | 1 549 | 1 598 | 1 673 | 1 749 | 1 763 |
| 3b. Gross regional product | 33 964 | 36 222 | 38 687 | 40 439 | 40 326 | 42 199 | 44 212 | 46 926 | 49 677 | 50 745 |
| 3c. % of gross world product | 0.48 | 0.49 | 0.50 | 0.49 | 0.48 | 0.49 | 0.49 | 0.50 | 0.51 | 0.50 |
| **4. Relative 1970–1989 PARE** | | | | | | | | | | |
| 4a. Per capita gross regional product | 666 | 732 | 803 | 878 | 938 | 1 061 | 1 163 | 1 300 | 1 458 | 1 601 |
| 4b. Gross regional product | 16 560 | 18 567 | 20 740 | 23 120 | 25 147 | 28 911 | 32 183 | 36 462 | 41 416 | 46 084 |
| 4c. % of gross world product | 0.48 | 0.49 | 0.50 | 0.49 | 0.48 | 0.49 | 0.49 | 0.50 | 0.51 | 0.50 |
| **5. Absolute 1980–1989 PARE** | | | | | | | | | | |
| 5a. Per capita gross regional product | 1 615 | 1 688 | 1 766 | 1 808 | 1 769 | 1 816 | 1 874 | 1 961 | 2 049 | 2 068 |
| 5b. Gross regional product | 40 176 | 42 787 | 45 635 | 47 595 | 47 410 | 49 472 | 51 845 | 54 986 | 58 222 | 59 531 |
| 5c. % of gross world product | 0.46 | 0.47 | 0.48 | 0.47 | 0.46 | 0.47 | 0.47 | 0.48 | 0.49 | 0.48 |
| **6. WA** | | | | | | | | | | |
| 6a. Per capita gross regional product | 693 | 749 | 828 | 925 | 1 053 | 1 230 | 1 324 | 1 445 | 1 527 | 1 661 |
| 6b. Gross regional product | 17 240 | 18 985 | 21 403 | 24 358 | 28 211 | 33 525 | 36 626 | 40 520 | 43 368 | 47 802 |
| 6c. % of gross world product | 0.54 | 0.54 | 0.53 | 0.50 | 0.51 | 0.54 | 0.55 | 0.54 | 0.49 | 0.47 |

| | 1980 (11) | 1981 (12) | 1982 (13) | 1983 (14) | 1984 (15) | 1985 (16) | 1986 (17) | 1987 (18) | 1988 (19) | 1989 (20) | Averages 1970–89 (21) | 1970–79 (22) | 1980–89 (23) |
|---|---|---|---|---|---|---|---|---|---|---|---|---|---|
| | 2 355 | 2 405 | 2 130 | 1 813 | 1 853 | 1 827 | 1 812 | 1 968 | 2 112 | 2 382 | 1 661 | 1 143 | 2 065 |
| | 854 090 | 891 536 | 807 132 | 702 334 | 733 166 | 738 791 | 748 162 | 829 604 | 908 883 | 1 045 974 | 595 720 | 365 472 | 825 967 |
| | 7.37 | 7.61 | 6.94 | 5.92 | 6.01 | 5.87 | 5.02 | 4.83 | 4.76 | 5.22 | 5.85 | 6.00 | 5.78 |
| | 3 346 | 3 661 | 3 701 | 3 549 | 3 686 | 3 775 | 3 915 | 4 057 | 4 140 | 4 278 | 3 002 | 1 937 | 3 830 |
| | 1 163 989 | 1 302 575 | 1 346 817 | 1 320 965 | 1 402 189 | 1 467 739 | 1 555 345 | 1 646 319 | 1 715 793 | 1 809 988 | 1 032 453 | 591 735 | 1 473 172 |
| | ... | ... | ... | ... | ... | ... | ... | ... | ... | ... | ... | ... | ... |
| | 1 815 | 1 793 | 1 743 | 1 667 | 1 693 | 1 718 | 1 749 | 1 760 | 1 739 | 1 724 | 1 661 | 1 549 | 1 741 |
| | 658 373 | 664 812 | 660 477 | 645 831 | 669 833 | 694 687 | 722 221 | 742 089 | 748 548 | 757 227 | 595 720 | 495 030 | 696 410 |
| | 6.34 | 6.28 | 6.19 | 5.89 | 5.84 | 5.85 | 5.91 | 5.87 | 5.67 | 5.57 | 5.85 | 5.74 | 5.92 |
| | 1 799 | 1 946 | 2 013 | 1 991 | 2 094 | 2 183 | 2 267 | 2 347 | 2 397 | 2 473 | 1 682 | 1 065 | 2 166 |
| | 652 619 | 721 353 | 762 940 | 771 237 | 828 552 | 882 575 | 935 995 | 989 377 | 1031 494 | 1086 239 | 603 392 | 340 546 | 866 238 |
| | 6.34 | 6.28 | 6.19 | 5.89 | 5.84 | 5.85 | 5.91 | 5.87 | 5.67 | 5.57 | 8.33 | 5.59 | 10.33 |
| | 2 158 | 2 129 | 2 068 | 1 978 | 2 007 | 2 036 | 2 073 | 2 087 | 2 062 | 2 042 | 1 975 | 1 848 | 2 065 |
| | 782 572 | 789 465 | 783 713 | 766 300 | 794 309 | 823 022 | 856 050 | 879 963 | 887 318 | 896 960 | 708 252 | 590 536 | 825 967 |
| | 6.19 | 6.13 | 6.04 | 5.75 | 5.70 | 5.71 | 5.78 | 5.74 | 5.55 | 5.44 | 5.71 | 5.61 | 5.78 |
| | 2 314 | 2 529 | 2 126 | 1 801 | 1 828 | 1 805 | 1 789 | 1 860 | 2 063 | 2 345 | 1 668 | 1 186 | 2 044 |
| | 839 202 | 937 619 | 805 901 | 697 664 | 723 526 | 729 819 | 738 461 | 784 246 | 887 935 | 1029 745 | 598 188 | 378 964 | 817 412 |
| | 7.29 | 7.95 | 6.91 | 5.89 | 5.92 | 5.77 | 5.02 | 4.71 | 4.74 | 5.25 | 5.92 | 6.25 | 5.78 |
| | 1 973 | 2 040 | 2 132 | 2 229 | 2 288 | 2 097 | 2 191 | 2 284 | 2 356 | 2 477 | 1 748 | 1 204 | 2 217 |
| | 57 521 | 60 278 | 63 842 | 67 668 | 70 432 | 65 483 | 69 423 | 73 462 | 76 947 | 82 148 | 50 633 | 32 546 | 68 720 |
| | 0.50 | 0.51 | 0.55 | 0.57 | 0.58 | 0.52 | 0.47 | 0.43 | 0.40 | 0.41 | 0.50 | 0.53 | 0.48 |
| | 1 826 | 1 975 | 1 985 | 1 976 | 2 149 | 2 031 | 2 062 | 2 137 | 2 163 | 2 256 | 1 620 | 1 053 | 2 064 |
| | 26 543 | 29 271 | 30 010 | 30 474 | 33 807 | 32 607 | 33 747 | 35 671 | 36 810 | 39 124 | 23 322 | 13 837 | 32 806 |
| | ... | ... | ... | ... | ... | ... | ... | ... | ... | ... | ... | ... | ... |
| | 1 749 | 1 827 | 1 846 | 1 880 | 1 903 | 1 935 | 1 937 | 1 943 | 1 956 | 1 966 | 1 748 | 1 567 | 1 901 |
| | 50 992 | 53 981 | 55 280 | 57 066 | 58 574 | 60 411 | 61 364 | 62 508 | 63 894 | 65 193 | 50 633 | 42 340 | 58 926 |
| | 0.49 | 0.51 | 0.52 | 0.52 | 0.51 | 0.51 | 0.50 | 0.49 | 0.48 | 0.48 | 0.50 | 0.49 | 0.50 |
| | 1 734 | 1 983 | 2 133 | 2 245 | 2 354 | 2 458 | 2 510 | 2 591 | 2 695 | 2 820 | 1 767 | 1 070 | 2 370 |
| | 50 547 | 58 572 | 63 856 | 68 147 | 72 453 | 76 750 | 79 527 | 83 338 | 88 045 | 93 518 | 51 197 | 28 919 | 73 475 |
| | 0.49 | 0.51 | 0.52 | 0.52 | 0.51 | 0.51 | 0.50 | 0.49 | 0.48 | 0.48 | 0.50 | 0.49 | 0.50 |
| | 2 058 | 2 137 | 2 156 | 2 190 | 2 210 | 2 246 | 2 252 | 2 266 | 2 281 | 2 294 | 2 045 | 1 842 | 2 217 |
| | 60 015 | 63 123 | 64 550 | 66 471 | 68 028 | 70 130 | 71 365 | 72 911 | 74 520 | 76 091 | 59 243 | 49 766 | 68 720 |
| | 0.47 | 0.49 | 0.50 | 0.50 | 0.49 | 0.49 | 0.48 | 0.48 | 0.47 | 0.46 | 0.48 | 0.47 | 0.48 |
| | 1 852 | 2 032 | 2 112 | 2 142 | 2 106 | 2 120 | 2 126 | 2 186 | 2 288 | 2 444 | 1 689 | 1 155 | 2 151 |
| | 54 008 | 60 036 | 63 233 | 65 012 | 64 827 | 66 187 | 67 373 | 70 310 | 74 728 | 81 061 | 48 941 | 31 204 | 66 678 |
| | 0.47 | 0.51 | 0.54 | 0.55 | 0.53 | 0.52 | 0.46 | 0.42 | 0.40 | 0.41 | 0.48 | 0.51 | 0.47 |

**Table A.6** Total and per capita gross regional product expressed in United States dollars using alternative conversion rates, and individual shares of gross world product, 1970−1989 [cont.]

| Country or area | 1970 (1) | 1971 (2) | 1972 (3) | 1973 (4) | 1974 (5) | 1975 (6) | 1976 (7) | 1977 (8) | 1978 (9) | 1979 (10) |
|---|---|---|---|---|---|---|---|---|---|---|
| **Latin America** | | | | | | | | | | |
| **1. MER** | | | | | | | | | | |
| 1a. Per capita gross regional product | 606 | 595 | 658 | 856 | 1 083 | 1 154 | 1 302 | 1 381 | 1 577 | 1 868 |
| 1b. Gross regional product | 158 172 | 159 343 | 180 856 | 241 071 | 312 971 | 341 710 | 395 049 | 429 435 | 501 900 | 608 760 |
| 1c. % of gross world product | 4.96 | 4.55 | 4.50 | 4.91 | 5.64 | 5.50 | 5.89 | 5.68 | 5.59 | 5.91 |
| **2. PPPs** [a] | | | | | | | | | | |
| 2a. Per capita gross regional product | 1 200 | 1 225 | 1 359 | 1 588 | 1 847 | 2 014 | 2 199 | 2 390 | 2 580 | 2 944 |
| 2b. Gross regional product | 312 736 | 327 624 | 372 929 | 447 054 | 533 370 | 596 216 | 666 947 | 742 506 | 820 862 | 958 738 |
| 2c. % of gross world product | ... | ... | ... | ... | ... | ... | ... | ... | ... | ... |
| **3. Absolute 1970−1989 PARE** | | | | | | | | | | |
| 3a. Per capita gross regional product | 1 295 | 1 343 | 1 402 | 1 483 | 1 546 | 1 564 | 1 619 | 1 657 | 1 688 | 1 757 |
| 3b. Gross regional product | 337 876 | 359 492 | 385 153 | 417 994 | 446 829 | 463 325 | 491 280 | 515 151 | 537 360 | 572 442 |
| 3c. % of gross world product | 4.76 | 4.86 | 4.94 | 5.04 | 5.27 | 5.39 | 5.43 | 5.46 | 5.46 | 5.63 |
| **4. Relative 1970−1989 PARE** | | | | | | | | | | |
| 4a. Per capita gross regional product | 632 | 688 | 752 | 848 | 964 | 1 072 | 1 178 | 1 287 | 1 407 | 1 595 |
| 4b. Gross regional product | 164 738 | 184 269 | 206 480 | 238 970 | 278 641 | 317 426 | 357 613 | 400 282 | 447 999 | 519 857 |
| 4c. % of gross world product | 4.76 | 4.86 | 4.94 | 5.04 | 5.27 | 5.39 | 5.43 | 5.46 | 5.46 | 5.63 |
| **5. Absolute 1980−1989 PARE** | | | | | | | | | | |
| 5a. Per capita gross regional product | 1 553 | 1 609 | 1 678 | 1 773 | 1 848 | 1 868 | 1 932 | 1 978 | 2 013 | 2 092 |
| 5b. Gross regional product | 405 156 | 430 833 | 460 980 | 499 670 | 534 076 | 553 313 | 586 289 | 614 960 | 640 743 | 681 682 |
| 5c. % of gross world product | 4.66 | 4.75 | 4.82 | 4.92 | 5.15 | 5.27 | 5.30 | 5.33 | 5.34 | 5.50 |
| **6. WA** | | | | | | | | | | |
| 6a. Per capita gross regional product | 588 | 606 | 728 | 986 | 1 268 | 1 174 | 1 330 | 1 387 | 1 582 | 1 939 |
| 6b. Gross regional product | 153 256 | 162 171 | 200 014 | 277 881 | 366 329 | 347 791 | 403 579 | 431 081 | 503 493 | 632 005 |
| 6c. % of gross world product | 4.80 | 4.65 | 4.99 | 5.71 | 6.57 | 5.64 | 6.01 | 5.72 | 5.67 | 6.18 |
| **Western Asia** | | | | | | | | | | |
| **1. MER** | | | | | | | | | | |
| 1a. Per capita gross regional product | 455 | 517 | 620 | 840 | 1 473 | 1 687 | 1 960 | 2 248 | 2 290 | 2 797 |
| 1b. Gross regional product | 46 303 | 54 161 | 66 988 | 93 529 | 169 079 | 199 459 | 238 591 | 281 565 | 295 269 | 371 557 |
| 1c. % of gross world product | 1.45 | 1.55 | 1.67 | 1.91 | 3.04 | 3.21 | 3.56 | 3.72 | 3.29 | 3.61 |
| **2. PPPs** [a] | | | | | | | | | | |
| 2a. Per capita gross regional product | 942 | 1 102 | 1 241 | 1 440 | 2 164 | 2 534 | 2 901 | 3 136 | 3 094 | 3 580 |
| 2b. Gross regional product | 92 059 | 110 933 | 128 752 | 153 985 | 238 532 | 287 994 | 339 693 | 378 175 | 384 403 | 458 676 |
| 2c. % of gross world product | ... | ... | ... | ... | ... | ... | ... | ... | ... | ... |
| **3. Absolute 1970−1989 PARE** | | | | | | | | | | |
| 3a. Per capita gross regional product | 2 232 | 2 409 | 2 609 | 2 762 | 2 941 | 2 958 | 3 240 | 3 317 | 3 157 | 3 143 |
| 3b. Gross regional product | 227 110 | 252 447 | 281 865 | 307 531 | 337 568 | 349 683 | 394 386 | 415 546 | 407 107 | 417 598 |
| 3c. % of gross world product | 3.20 | 3.41 | 3.61 | 3.71 | 3.98 | 4.07 | 4.36 | 4.40 | 4.14 | 4.11 |
| **4. Relative 1970−1989 PARE** | | | | | | | | | | |
| 4a. Per capita gross regional product | 1 088 | 1 235 | 1 399 | 1 579 | 1 834 | 2 026 | 2 358 | 2 578 | 2 632 | 2 855 |
| 4b. Gross regional product | 110 732 | 129 399 | 151 108 | 175 818 | 210 506 | 239 570 | 287 082 | 322 888 | 339 407 | 379 237 |
| 4c. % of gross world product | 3.20 | 3.41 | 3.61 | 3.71 | 3.98 | 4.07 | 4.36 | 4.40 | 4.14 | 4.11 |
| **5. Absolute 1980−1989 PARE** | | | | | | | | | | |
| 5a. Per capita gross regional product | 3 193 | 3 448 | 3 742 | 3 956 | 4 184 | 4 184 | 4 602 | 4 698 | 4 435 | 4 391 |
| 5b. Gross regional product | 324 877 | 361 346 | 404 209 | 440 488 | 480 164 | 494 713 | 560 141 | 588 510 | 571 872 | 583 309 |
| 5c. % of gross world product | 3.73 | 3.99 | 4.23 | 4.33 | 4.63 | 4.71 | 5.06 | 5.10 | 4.77 | 4.70 |
| **6. WA** | | | | | | | | | | |
| 6a. Per capita gross regional product | 460 | 521 | 621 | 837 | 1 421 | 1 647 | 1 951 | 2 232 | 2 285 | 2 738 |
| 6b. Gross regional product | 46 817 | 54 578 | 67 125 | 93 147 | 163 073 | 194 763 | 237 489 | 279 630 | 294 594 | 363 713 |
| 6c. % of gross world product | 1.47 | 1.56 | 1.68 | 1.92 | 2.92 | 3.16 | 3.54 | 3.71 | 3.32 | 3.56 |

| 1980 (11) | 1981 (12) | 1982 (13) | 1983 (14) | 1984 (15) | 1985 (16) | 1986 (17) | 1987 (18) | 1988 (19) | 1989 (20) | Averages 1970–89 (21) | 1970–79 (22) | 1980–89 (23) |
|---|---|---|---|---|---|---|---|---|---|---|---|---|
| 2 388 | 2 436 | 2 129 | 1 778 | 1 816 | 1 805 | 1 781 | 1 942 | 2 092 | 2 374 | 1 653 | 1 138 | 2 052 |
| 796 569 | 831 258 | 743 290 | 634 666 | 662 734 | 673 309 | 678 739 | 756 142 | 831 936 | 963 825 | 545 087 | 332 927 | 757 247 |
| 6.87 | 7.10 | 6.39 | 5.35 | 5.43 | 5.35 | 4.56 | 4.40 | 4.35 | 4.81 | 5.35 | 5.46 | 5.30 |
| 3 413 | 3 734 | 3 775 | 3 617 | 3 752 | 3 850 | 3 995 | 4 139 | 4 225 | 4 365 | 3 063 | 1 976 | 3 906 |
| 1 137 446 | 1 273 303 | 1 316 807 | 1 290 491 | 1 368 382 | 1 435 132 | 1 521 599 | 1 610 648 | 1 678 982 | 1 770 864 | 1 009 132 | 577 898 | 1 440 365 |
| ... | ... | ... | ... | ... | ... | ... | ... | ... | ... | ... | ... | ... |
| 1 821 | 1 790 | 1 734 | 1 649 | 1 675 | 1 700 | 1 734 | 1 745 | 1 722 | 1 704 | 1 653 | 1 547 | 1 728 |
| 607 380 | 610 831 | 605 197 | 588 765 | 611 259 | 634 276 | 660 857 | 679 580 | 684 654 | 692 035 | 545 087 | 452 690 | 637 483 |
| 5.85 | 5.77 | 5.68 | 5.37 | 5.33 | 5.35 | 5.41 | 5.38 | 5.19 | 5.09 | 5.35 | 5.25 | 5.42 |
| 1 805 | 1 942 | 2 003 | 1 970 | 2 072 | 2 160 | 2 247 | 2 327 | 2 372 | 2 445 | 1 675 | 1 065 | 2 148 |
| 602 072 | 662 781 | 699 084 | 703 091 | 756 099 | 805 825 | 856 468 | 906 039 | 943 449 | 992 720 | 552 195 | 311 628 | 792 763 |
| 5.85 | 5.77 | 5.68 | 5.37 | 5.33 | 5.35 | 5.41 | 5.38 | 5.19 | 5.09 | 5.37 | 5.31 | 5.40 |
| 2 166 | 2 129 | 2 060 | 1 960 | 1 990 | 2 018 | 2 059 | 2 073 | 2 044 | 2 022 | 1 968 | 1 848 | 2 052 |
| 722 557 | 726 342 | 719 163 | 699 829 | 726 282 | 752 892 | 784 686 | 807 052 | 812 797 | 820 869 | 649 008 | 540 770 | 757 247 |
| 5.71 | 5.64 | 5.55 | 5.25 | 5.21 | 5.22 | 5.30 | 5.27 | 5.08 | 4.98 | 5.23 | 5.13 | 5.30 |
| 2 354 | 2 572 | 2 128 | 1 772 | 1 805 | 1 779 | 1 761 | 1 833 | 2 045 | 2 337 | 1 666 | 1 189 | 2 034 |
| 785 194 | 877 584 | 742 668 | 632 652 | 658 699 | 663 632 | 671 088 | 713 935 | 813 207 | 948 684 | 549 247 | 347 760 | 750 734 |
| 6.82 | 7.44 | 6.37 | 5.34 | 5.39 | 5.25 | 4.56 | 4.28 | 4.34 | 4.83 | 5.44 | 5.73 | 5.31 |
| 3 280 | 3 384 | 3 543 | 3 407 | 3 199 | 3 155 | 3 295 | 3 768 | 4 179 | 4 584 | 2 798 | 1 559 | 3 604 |
| 449 633 | 479 403 | 519 087 | 516 478 | 501 252 | 510 138 | 548 869 | 645 928 | 736 359 | 829 471 | 377 656 | 181 650 | 573 662 |
| 3.88 | 4.09 | 4.46 | 4.36 | 4.11 | 4.05 | 3.69 | 3.76 | 3.85 | 4.14 | 3.71 | 2.98 | 4.02 |
| 4 139 | 4 406 | 4 576 | 4 728 | 4 745 | 4 886 | 4 691 | 4 798 | 4 913 | 4 997 | 3 771 | 2 299 | 4 703 |
| 547 700 | 602 879 | 648 219 | 693 353 | 719 583 | 765 099 | 757 165 | 797 242 | 839 466 | 877 035 | 491 047 | 257 320 | 724 774 |
| ... | ... | ... | ... | ... | ... | ... | ... | ... | ... | ... | ... | ... |
| 3 002 | 2 913 | 2 907 | 2 787 | 2 692 | 2 603 | 2 417 | 2 393 | 2 361 | 2 312 | 2 798 | 2 911 | 2 615 |
| 411 542 | 412 612 | 426 006 | 422 464 | 421 822 | 420 828 | 402 600 | 410 131 | 415 962 | 418 308 | 377 656 | 339 084 | 416 228 |
| 3.96 | 3.90 | 4.00 | 3.85 | 3.68 | 3.55 | 3.30 | 3.25 | 3.15 | 3.07 | 3.71 | 3.94 | 3.54 |
| 2 976 | 3 161 | 3 359 | 3 328 | 3 330 | 3 306 | 3 132 | 3 190 | 3 253 | 3 316 | 2 777 | 2 014 | 3 235 |
| 407 945 | 447 704 | 492 095 | 504 498 | 521 774 | 534 647 | 521 768 | 546 800 | 573 193 | 600 061 | 374 812 | 234 575 | 515 048 |
| 3.96 | 3.90 | 4.00 | 3.85 | 3.68 | 3.55 | 3.30 | 3.25 | 3.15 | 3.07 | 3.65 | 4.00 | 3.51 |
| 4 142 | 4 002 | 4 014 | 3 870 | 3 731 | 3 606 | 3 334 | 3 285 | 3 231 | 3 159 | 3 907 | 4 128 | 3 604 |
| 567 845 | 566 951 | 588 202 | 586 628 | 584 491 | 583 109 | 555 442 | 563 095 | 569 232 | 571 622 | 527 312 | 480 963 | 573 662 |
| 4.49 | 4.40 | 4.54 | 4.40 | 4.20 | 4.05 | 3.75 | 3.67 | 3.56 | 3.47 | 4.25 | 4.57 | 4.02 |
| 3 142 | 3 345 | 3 502 | 3 361 | 3 127 | 3 134 | 3 249 | 2 715 | 2 768 | 2 772 | 2 488 | 1 541 | 3 091 |
| 430 698 | 473 814 | 513 081 | 509 527 | 490 002 | 506 774 | 541 289 | 465 390 | 487 775 | 501 625 | 335 745 | 179 493 | 491 997 |
| 3.74 | 4.02 | 4.40 | 4.30 | 4.01 | 4.01 | 3.68 | 2.79 | 2.61 | 2.56 | 3.32 | 2.96 | 3.48 |

**Table A.6** Total and per capita gross regional product expressed in United States dollars using alternative conversion rates, and individual shares of gross world product, 1970−1989 [*cont.*]

| Country or area | 1970 (1) | 1971 (2) | 1972 (3) | 1973 (4) | 1974 (5) | 1975 (6) | 1976 (7) | 1977 (8) | 1978 (9) | 1979 (10) |
|---|---|---|---|---|---|---|---|---|---|---|
| **Asia (eastern, south−eastern, and southern)** | | | | | | | | | | |
| **1. MER** | | | | | | | | | | |
| 1a. Per capita gross regional product | 215 | 232 | 273 | 349 | 387 | 410 | 437 | 516 | 670 | 718 |
| 1b. Gross regional product | 427 151 | 471 029 | 568 773 | 742 460 | 841 063 | 909 525 | 987 267 | 1 188 043 | 1 571 876 | 1 713 456 |
| 1c. % of gross world product | 13.39 | 13.46 | 14.14 | 15.13 | 15.14 | 14.64 | 14.72 | 15.71 | 17.49 | 16.63 |
| **2. PPPs** [a] | | | | | | | | | | |
| 2a. Per capita gross regional product | 567 | 607 | 662 | 741 | 799 | 891 | 959 | 1 073 | 1 204 | 1 324 |
| 2b. Gross regional product | 602 389 | 660 052 | 736 166 | 843 796 | 930 118 | 1 060 526 | 1 165 286 | 1 331 243 | 1 525 214 | 1 712 328 |
| 2c. % of gross world product | ... | ... | ... | ... | ... | ... | ... | ... | ... | ... |
| **3. Absolute 1970−1989 PARE** | | | | | | | | | | |
| 3a. Per capita gross regional product | 557 | 568 | 592 | 623 | 612 | 625 | 640 | 667 | 697 | 718 |
| 3b. Gross regional product | 1 104 416 | 1 153 905 | 1 231 283 | 1 326 992 | 1 330 869 | 1 386 262 | 1 446 524 | 1 536 413 | 1 633 974 | 1 711 921 |
| 3c. % of gross world product | 15.54 | 15.59 | 15.78 | 15.99 | 15.70 | 16.12 | 15.98 | 16.28 | 16.62 | 16.84 |
| **4. Relative 1970−1989 PARE** | | | | | | | | | | |
| 4a. Per capita gross regional product | 271 | 291 | 317 | 356 | 382 | 428 | 466 | 518 | 581 | 652 |
| 4b. Gross regional product | 538 480 | 591 470 | 660 089 | 758 652 | 829 925 | 949 736 | 1 052 957 | 1 193 823 | 1 362 249 | 1 554 664 |
| 4c. % of gross world product | 15.54 | 15.59 | 15.78 | 15.99 | 15.70 | 16.12 | 15.98 | 16.28 | 16.62 | 16.84 |
| **5. Absolute 1980−1989 PARE** | | | | | | | | | | |
| 5a. Per capita gross regional product | 673 | 686 | 716 | 754 | 740 | 754 | 773 | 805 | 840 | 865 |
| 5b. Gross regional product | 1 335 053 | 1 394 349 | 1 489 898 | 1 605 613 | 1 608 495 | 1 672 951 | 1 747 790 | 1 854 908 | 1 969 661 | 2 063 250 |
| 5c. % of gross world product | 15.34 | 15.38 | 15.59 | 15.80 | 15.51 | 15.92 | 15.80 | 16.09 | 16.42 | 16.64 |
| **6. WA** | | | | | | | | | | |
| 6a. Per capita gross regional product | 215 | 232 | 276 | 348 | 387 | 410 | 437 | 516 | 670 | 718 |
| 6b. Gross regional product | 427 403 | 472 279 | 573 590 | 740 529 | 840 921 | 909 063 | 987 520 | 1 189 759 | 1 571 249 | 1 713 329 |
| 6c. % of gross world product | 13.39 | 13.54 | 14.32 | 15.23 | 15.07 | 14.75 | 14.72 | 15.78 | 17.69 | 16.75 |
| **Eastern Asia (excluding Japan)** | | | | | | | | | | |
| **1. MER** | | | | | | | | | | |
| 1a. Per capita gross regional product | 125 | 132 | 145 | 175 | 184 | 202 | 199 | 228 | 288 | 347 |
| 1b. Gross regional product | 108 152 | 117 214 | 132 301 | 163 449 | 174 659 | 195 824 | 196 377 | 228 584 | 292 767 | 356 342 |
| 1c. % of gross world product | 3.39 | 3.35 | 3.29 | 3.33 | 3.14 | 3.15 | 2.93 | 3.02 | 3.26 | 3.46 |
| **2. PPPs** [a] | | | | | | | | | | |
| 2a. Per capita gross regional product | ... | ... | ... | ... | ... | ... | ... | ... | ... | ... |
| 2b. Gross regional product | ... | ... | ... | ... | ... | ... | ... | ... | ... | ... |
| 2c. % of gross world product | ... | ... | ... | ... | ... | ... | ... | ... | ... | ... |
| **3. Absolute 1970−1989 PARE** | | | | | | | | | | |
| 3a. Per capita gross regional product | 183 | 192 | 195 | 209 | 211 | 223 | 224 | 240 | 264 | 280 |
| 3b. Gross regional product | 159 124 | 171 140 | 178 142 | 195 348 | 200 883 | 216 149 | 220 831 | 240 189 | 267 864 | 288 233 |
| 3c. % of gross world product | 2.24 | 2.31 | 2.28 | 2.35 | 2.37 | 2.51 | 2.44 | 2.55 | 2.72 | 2.83 |
| **4. Relative 1970−1989 PARE** | | | | | | | | | | |
| 4a. Per capita gross regional product | 89 | 99 | 105 | 120 | 132 | 153 | 163 | 186 | 220 | 255 |
| 4b. Gross regional product | 77 584 | 87 723 | 95 502 | 111 682 | 125 270 | 148 085 | 160 748 | 186 631 | 223 319 | 261 756 |
| 4c. % of gross world product | 2.24 | 2.31 | 2.28 | 2.35 | 2.37 | 2.51 | 2.44 | 2.55 | 2.72 | 2.83 |
| **5. Absolute 1980−1989 PARE** | | | | | | | | | | |
| 5a. Per capita gross regional product | 189 | 198 | 202 | 217 | 219 | 231 | 233 | 250 | 275 | 292 |
| 5b. Gross regional product | 164 132 | 176 608 | 183 997 | 202 055 | 208 131 | 223 756 | 229 740 | 250 071 | 278 646 | 299 938 |
| 5c. % of gross world product | 1.89 | 1.95 | 1.92 | 1.99 | 2.01 | 2.13 | 2.08 | 2.17 | 2.32 | 2.42 |
| **6. WA** | | | | | | | | | | |
| 6a. Per capita gross regional product | 125 | 132 | 145 | 175 | 183 | 202 | 199 | 228 | 289 | 347 |
| 6b. Gross regional product | 108 686 | 117 435 | 132 450 | 163 184 | 174 404 | 195 643 | 196 176 | 228 442 | 292 975 | 356 643 |
| 6c. % of gross world product | 3.41 | 3.37 | 3.31 | 3.36 | 3.13 | 3.17 | 2.92 | 3.03 | 3.30 | 3.49 |

| | 1980 (11) | 1981 (12) | 1982 (13) | 1983 (14) | 1984 (15) | 1985 (16) | 1986 (17) | 1987 (18) | 1988 (19) | 1989 (20) | Averages 1970–89 (21) | 1970–79 (22) | 1980–89 (23) |
|---|---|---|---|---|---|---|---|---|---|---|---|---|---|
| | 778 | 819 | 774 | 814 | 840 | 853 | 1 082 | 1 254 | 1 470 | 1 477 | 759 | 429 | 1 030 |
| | 1 888 083 | 2 024 640 | 1 949 542 | 2 088 594 | 2 192 525 | 2 263 019 | 2 921 354 | 3 446 792 | 4 113 537 | 4 212 680 | 1 826 071 | 9 42 064 | 2 710 078 |
| | 16.29 | 17.29 | 16.77 | 17.62 | 17.98 | 17.97 | 19.62 | 20.06 | 21.53 | 21.01 | 17.92 | 15.46 | 18.98 |
| | 1 495 | 1 670 | 1 760 | 1 853 | 1 997 | 2 057 | 2 129 | 2 245 | 2 430 | 2 615 | 1 544 | 898 | 2 047 |
| | 1 974 269 | 2 253 361 | 2 426 948 | 2 611 759 | 2 876 826 | 3 026 931 | 3 199 475 | 3 445 237 | 3 805 765 | 4 181 487 | 2 018 459 | 1 056 712 | 2 980 206 |
| | ... | ... | ... | ... | ... | ... | ... | ... | ... | ... | ... | ... | ... |
| | 740 | 760 | 774 | 799 | 834 | 867 | 887 | 923 | 972 | 1 002 | 759 | 631 | 861 |
| | 1 795 398 | 1 878 406 | 1 950 108 | 2 048 328 | 2 176 529 | 2 299 911 | 2 395 196 | 2 536 537 | 2 721 029 | 2 857 418 | 1 826 071 | 1 386 256 | 2 265 886 |
| | 17.28 | 17.74 | 18.29 | 18.67 | 18.98 | 19.38 | 19.61 | 20.07 | 20.63 | 21.00 | 17.92 | 16.09 | 19.27 |
| | 733 | 824 | 894 | 954 | 1 032 | 1 101 | 1 149 | 1 230 | 1 340 | 1 437 | 789 | 432 | 1 082 |
| | 1 779 707 | 2 038 162 | 2 252 638 | 2 446 068 | 2 692 267 | 2 921 954 | 3 104 162 | 3 381 795 | 3 749 561 | 4 098 952 | 1 897 866 | 9 49 205 | 2 846 527 |
| | 17.28 | 17.74 | 18.29 | 18.67 | 18.98 | 19.38 | 19.61 | 20.07 | 20.63 | 21.00 | 26.21 | 15.57 | 33.93 |
| | 891 | 914 | 930 | 958 | 999 | 1 036 | 1 059 | 1 099 | 1 157 | 1 192 | 911 | 762 | 1 030 |
| | 2 162 507 | 2 261 139 | 2 344 423 | 2 457 987 | 2 606 730 | 2 749 433 | 2 858 697 | 3 022 376 | 3 237 384 | 3 400 098 | 2 192 137 | 1 674 197 | 2 710 077 |
| | 17.10 | 17.55 | 18.08 | 18.43 | 18.71 | 19.08 | 19.29 | 19.72 | 20.24 | 20.62 | 17.67 | 15.89 | 18.98 |
| | 777 | 817 | 775 | 814 | 837 | 855 | 1 081 | 1 252 | 1 463 | 1 475 | 758 | 429 | 1 029 |
| | 1 884 886 | 2 021 102 | 1 953 031 | 2 086 706 | 2 185 432 | 2 268 692 | 2 919 127 | 3 441 403 | 4 095 063 | 4 206 391 | 1 824 374 | 9 42 564 | 2 706 183 |
| | 16.36 | 17.14 | 16.76 | 17.60 | 17.88 | 17.94 | 19.85 | 20.65 | 21.88 | 21.43 | 18.06 | 15.54 | 19.14 |
| | 387 | 372 | 367 | 387 | 399 | 392 | 396 | 445 | 547 | 610 | 326 | 205 | 434 |
| | 402 646 | 393 609 | 393 957 | 420 019 | 437 930 | 434 908 | 444 736 | 507 277 | 632 347 | 715 741 | 337 442 | 196 567 | 478 317 |
| | 3.47 | 3.36 | 3.39 | 3.54 | 3.59 | 3.45 | 2.99 | 2.95 | 3.31 | 3.57 | 3.31 | 3.23 | 3.35 |
| | ... | ... | ... | ... | ... | ... | ... | ... | ... | ... | ... | ... | ... |
| | ... | ... | ... | ... | ... | ... | ... | ... | ... | ... | ... | ... | ... |
| | ... | ... | ... | ... | ... | ... | ... | ... | ... | ... | ... | ... | ... |
| | 291 | 303 | 321 | 349 | 387 | 425 | 457 | 499 | 545 | 559 | 326 | 223 | 418 |
| | 302 737 | 320 361 | 345 010 | 379 354 | 425 416 | 470 955 | 512 834 | 568 414 | 629 690 | 656 165 | 337 442 | 213 790 | 461 094 |
| | 2.91 | 3.03 | 3.24 | 3.46 | 3.71 | 3.97 | 4.20 | 4.50 | 4.77 | 4.82 | 3.31 | 2.48 | 3.92 |
| | 288 | 329 | 371 | 417 | 479 | 540 | 592 | 665 | 751 | 802 | 354 | 154 | 531 |
| | 300 092 | 347 607 | 398 533 | 453 016 | 526 221 | 598 331 | 664 631 | 757 829 | 867 709 | 941 265 | 366 677 | 147 830 | 585 523 |
| | 2.91 | 3.03 | 3.24 | 3.46 | 3.71 | 3.97 | 4.20 | 4.50 | 4.77 | 4.82 | 3.57 | 2.52 | 3.99 |
| | 302 | 315 | 334 | 363 | 402 | 440 | 473 | 518 | 565 | 580 | 338 | 231 | 434 |
| | 314 343 | 332 855 | 358 224 | 393 987 | 441 319 | 487 450 | 531 542 | 589 553 | 653 114 | 680 781 | 350 012 | 221 707 | 478 317 |
| | 2.49 | 2.58 | 2.76 | 2.95 | 3.17 | 3.38 | 3.59 | 3.85 | 4.08 | 4.13 | 2.82 | 2.10 | 3.35 |
| | 387 | 373 | 368 | 387 | 399 | 393 | 396 | 443 | 545 | 613 | 326 | 205 | 434 |
| | 402 841 | 394 522 | 394 865 | 420 437 | 438 297 | 435 656 | 444 809 | 504 628 | 629 667 | 719 633 | 337 570 | 196 604 | 478 535 |
| | 3.50 | 3.35 | 3.39 | 3.55 | 3.58 | 3.45 | 3.02 | 3.03 | 3.36 | 3.67 | 3.34 | 3.24 | 3.38 |

**Table A.6** Total and per capita gross regional product expressed in United States dollars using alternative conversion rates, and individual shares of gross world product, 1970–1989 [cont.]

| Country or area | 1970 (1) | 1971 (2) | 1972 (3) | 1973 (4) | 1974 (5) | 1975 (6) | 1976 (7) | 1977 (8) | 1978 (9) | 1979 (10) |
|---|---|---|---|---|---|---|---|---|---|---|
| **Japan** | | | | | | | | | | |
| **1. MER** | | | | | | | | | | |
| 1a. Per capita gross regional product | 1 953 | 2 186 | 2 844 | 3 809 | 4 172 | 4 481 | 4 981 | 6 070 | 8 453 | 8 725 |
| 1b. Gross regional product | 203 736 | 231 017 | 304 763 | 414 049 | 459 614 | 499 774 | 561 703 | 691 304 | 971 322 | 1 010 979 |
| 1c. % of gross world product | 6.39 | 6.60 | 7.58 | 8.44 | 8.28 | 8.05 | 8.37 | 9.14 | 10.81 | 9.81 |
| **2. PPPs [a]** | | | | | | | | | | |
| 2a. Per capita gross regional product | 2 763 | 3 029 | 3 483 | 4 055 | 4 335 | 4 750 | 5 173 | 5 751 | 6 553 | 7 388 |
| 2b. Gross regional product | 288 275 | 320 183 | 373 269 | 440 736 | 477 554 | 529 754 | 583 325 | 654 908 | 752 990 | 856 052 |
| 2c. % of gross world product | ... | ... | ... | ... | ... | ... | ... | ... | ... | ... |
| **3. Absolute 1970–1989 PARE** | | | | | | | | | | |
| 3a. Per capita gross regional product | 6 892 | 7 095 | 7 584 | 8 067 | 7 863 | 7 968 | 8 258 | 8 609 | 8 967 | 9 354 |
| 3b. Gross regional product | 719 052 | 749 924 | 812 782 | 876 796 | 866 126 | 888 644 | 931 154 | 980 399 | 1 030 417 | 1 083 879 |
| 3c. % of gross world product | 10.12 | 10.13 | 10.42 | 10.57 | 10.22 | 10.33 | 10.29 | 10.39 | 10.48 | 10.66 |
| **4. Relative 1970–1989 PARE** | | | | | | | | | | |
| 4a. Per capita gross regional product | 3 360 | 3 637 | 4 066 | 4 612 | 4 903 | 5 459 | 6 011 | 6 689 | 7 476 | 8 495 |
| 4b. Gross regional product | 350 588 | 384 397 | 435 731 | 501 271 | 540 113 | 608 815 | 677 808 | 761 789 | 859 062 | 984 314 |
| 4c. % of gross world product | 10.12 | 10.13 | 10.42 | 10.57 | 10.22 | 10.33 | 10.29 | 10.39 | 10.48 | 10.66 |
| **5. Absolute 1980–1989 PARE** | | | | | | | | | | |
| 5a. Per capita gross regional product | 8 726 | 8 982 | 9 601 | 10 213 | 9 955 | 10 088 | 10 455 | 10 900 | 11 353 | 11 843 |
| 5b. Gross regional product | 910 374 | 949 461 | 1 029 044 | 1 110 090 | 1 096 581 | 1 125 091 | 1 178 911 | 1 241 259 | 1 304 587 | 1 372 273 |
| 5c. % of gross world product | 10.46 | 10.47 | 10.77 | 10.92 | 10.57 | 10.71 | 10.66 | 10.77 | 10.87 | 11.07 |
| **6. WA** | | | | | | | | | | |
| 6a. Per capita gross regional product | 1 953 | 2 185 | 2 844 | 3 809 | 4 172 | 4 481 | 4 981 | 6 070 | 8 453 | 8 725 |
| 6b. Gross regional product | 203 736 | 231 015 | 304 761 | 414 046 | 459 611 | 499 779 | 561 699 | 691 304 | 971 313 | 1 010 979 |
| 6c. % of gross world product | 6.38 | 6.62 | 7.61 | 8.51 | 8.24 | 8.11 | 8.37 | 9.17 | 10.94 | 9.88 |
| **South–eastern Asia** | | | | | | | | | | |
| **1. MER** | | | | | | | | | | |
| 1a. Per capita gross regional product | 133 | 141 | 149 | 195 | 259 | 277 | 315 | 362 | 408 | 451 |
| 1b. Gross regional product | 38 109 | 41 257 | 44 805 | 60 174 | 81 711 | 89 442 | 104 063 | 121 967 | 140 727 | 158 559 |
| 1c. % of gross world product | 1.19 | 1.18 | 1.11 | 1.23 | 1.47 | 1.44 | 1.55 | 1.61 | 1.57 | 1.54 |
| **2. PPPs [a]** | | | | | | | | | | |
| 2a. Per capita gross regional product | 385 | 420 | 453 | 517 | 609 | 673 | 751 | 848 | 966 | 1 134 |
| 2b. Gross regional product | 89 855 | 100 679 | 111 238 | 130 281 | 157 224 | 178 075 | 203 379 | 234 769 | 273 683 | 328 424 |
| 2c. % of gross world product | ... | ... | ... | ... | ... | ... | ... | ... | ... | ... |
| **3. Absolute 1970–1989 PARE** | | | | | | | | | | |
| 3a. Per capita gross regional product | 299 | 312 | 323 | 344 | 357 | 364 | 385 | 406 | 427 | 444 |
| 3b. Gross regional product | 85 603 | 91 389 | 97 132 | 105 967 | 112 546 | 117 544 | 127 089 | 136 967 | 147 040 | 156 330 |
| 3c. % of gross world product | 1.20 | 1.23 | 1.25 | 1.28 | 1.33 | 1.37 | 1.40 | 1.45 | 1.50 | 1.54 |
| **4. Relative 1970–1989 PARE** | | | | | | | | | | |
| 4a. Per capita gross regional product | 146 | 160 | 173 | 197 | 222 | 249 | 280 | 316 | 356 | 403 |
| 4b. Gross regional product | 41 737 | 46 844 | 52 072 | 60 582 | 70 183 | 80 530 | 92 511 | 106 426 | 122 588 | 141 969 |
| 4c. % of gross world product | 1.20 | 1.23 | 1.25 | 1.28 | 1.33 | 1.37 | 1.40 | 1.45 | 1.50 | 1.54 |
| **5. Absolute 1980–1989 PARE** | | | | | | | | | | |
| 5a. Per capita gross regional product | 342 | 357 | 370 | 394 | 409 | 417 | 441 | 466 | 489 | 510 |
| 5b. Gross regional product | 97 986 | 104 728 | 111 397 | 121 501 | 129 017 | 134 731 | 145 706 | 157 021 | 168 552 | 179 342 |
| 5c. % of gross world product | 1.13 | 1.16 | 1.17 | 1.20 | 1.24 | 1.28 | 1.32 | 1.36 | 1.40 | 1.45 |
| **6. WA** | | | | | | | | | | |
| 6a. Per capita gross regional product | 125 | 135 | 150 | 193 | 254 | 276 | 315 | 361 | 408 | 448 |
| 6b. Gross regional product | 35 704 | 39 681 | 44 966 | 59 594 | 80 250 | 89 003 | 104 060 | 121 809 | 140 495 | 157 702 |
| 6c. % of gross world product | 1.12 | 1.14 | 1.12 | 1.23 | 1.44 | 1.44 | 1.55 | 1.62 | 1.58 | 1.54 |

|  |  |  |  |  |  |  |  |  |  | Averages |  |  |
| 1980 | 1981 | 1982 | 1983 | 1984 | 1985 | 1986 | 1987 | 1988 | 1989 | 1970–89 | 1970–79 | 1980–89 |
| (11) | (12) | (13) | (14) | (15) | (16) | (17) | (18) | (19) | (20) | (21) | (22) | (23) |
|---|---|---|---|---|---|---|---|---|---|---|---|---|
| 9 068 | 9 914 | 9 129 | 9 883 | 10 440 | 10 973 | 16 125 | 19 467 | 23 265 | 23 046 | 9 642 | 4 825 | 14 180 |
| 1 059 262 | 1 166 972 | 1 082 496 | 1 179 976 | 1 254 408 | 1 325 996 | 1 958 373 | 2 374 979 | 2 850 008 | 2 834 232 | 1 121 748 | 534 826 | 1 708 670 |
| 9.14 | 9.97 | 9.31 | 9.95 | 10.28 | 10.53 | 13.15 | 13.82 | 14.92 | 14.13 | 11.01 | 8.78 | 11.97 |
| 8 262 | 9 201 | 9 918 | 10 388 | 10 987 | 11 363 | 11 817 | 12 635 | 13 748 | 14 955 | 8 138 | 4 761 | 11 335 |
| 965 063 | 1 083 037 | 1 176 113 | 1 240 278 | 1 320 152 | 1 373 093 | 1 435 150 | 1 541 438 | 1 684 193 | 1 839 159 | 946 736 | 527 705 | 1 365 767 |
| ... | ... | ... | ... | ... | ... | ... | ... | ... | ... | ... | ... | ... |
| 9 691 | 9 988 | 10 197 | 10 446 | 10 901 | 11 350 | 11 571 | 12 026 | 12 661 | 13 229 | 9 642 | 8 065 | 11 200 |
| 1 132 044 | 1 175 737 | 1 209 109 | 1 247 217 | 1 309 764 | 1 371 514 | 1 405 259 | 1 467 178 | 1 550 984 | 1 626 984 | 1 121 748 | 893 917 | 1 349 579 |
| 10.90 | 11.10 | 11.34 | 11.37 | 11.42 | 11.56 | 11.51 | 11.61 | 11.76 | 11.96 | 11.01 | 10.37 | 11.48 |
| 9 607 | 10 838 | 11 778 | 12 474 | 13 484 | 14 420 | 14 996 | 16 034 | 17 447 | 18 978 | 9 884 | 5 507 | 14 021 |
| 1 122 150 | 1 275 732 | 1 396 685 | 1 489 400 | 1 620 118 | 1 742 459 | 1 821 208 | 1 956 090 | 2 137 247 | 2 333 900 | 1 149 944 | 610 389 | 1 689 499 |
| 10.90 | 11.10 | 11.34 | 11.37 | 11.42 | 11.56 | 11.51 | 11.61 | 11.76 | 11.96 | 11.19 | 10.40 | 11.51 |
| 12 270 | 12 646 | 12 910 | 13 225 | 13 801 | 14 370 | 14 649 | 15 226 | 16 030 | 16 749 | 12 207 | 10 211 | 14 180 |
| 1 433 253 | 1 488 572 | 1 530 825 | 1 579 073 | 1 658 262 | 1 736 441 | 1 779 165 | 1 857 559 | 1 963 664 | 2 059 885 | 1 420 219 | 1 131 767 | 1 708 670 |
| 11.33 | 11.55 | 11.81 | 11.84 | 11.90 | 12.05 | 12.01 | 12.12 | 12.28 | 12.49 | 11.45 | 10.74 | 11.97 |
| 9 068 | 9 914 | 9 129 | 9 883 | 10 440 | 10 974 | 16 125 | 19 462 | 23 256 | 23 052 | 9 641 | 4 825 | 14 180 |
| 1 059 257 | 1 166 993 | 1 082 509 | 1 179 966 | 1 254 397 | 1 326 018 | 1 958 373 | 2 374 372 | 2 848 852 | 2 834 971 | 1 121 697 | 534 824 | 1 708 571 |
| 9.20 | 9.90 | 9.29 | 9.95 | 10.26 | 10.49 | 13.32 | 14.25 | 15.22 | 14.45 | 11.10 | 8.82 | 12.08 |
| 554 | 602 | 611 | 586 | 594 | 564 | 533 | 561 | 627 | 698 | 455 | 276 | 594 |
| 199 108 | 221 115 | 229 286 | 224 851 | 232 923 | 226 078 | 218 090 | 234 310 | 267 490 | 303 645 | 161 886 | 88 082 | 235 689 |
| 1.72 | 1.89 | 1.97 | 1.90 | 1.91 | 1.80 | 1.46 | 1.36 | 1.40 | 1.51 | 1.59 | 1.45 | 1.65 |
| 1 327 | 1 513 | 1 588 | 1 716 | 1 839 | 1 807 | 1 879 | 2 001 | 2 174 | 2 405 | 1 336 | 691 | 1 843 |
| 392 801 | 457 766 | 491 218 | 542 408 | 593 865 | 595 868 | 632 830 | 687 606 | 762 300 | 860 064 | 391 217 | 180 761 | 601 673 |
| ... | ... | ... | ... | ... | ... | ... | ... | ... | ... | ... | ... | ... |
| 462 | 480 | 483 | 502 | 516 | 510 | 518 | 536 | 564 | 598 | 455 | 369 | 519 |
| 166 180 | 176 174 | 181 327 | 192 829 | 202 455 | 204 507 | 211 864 | 223 823 | 240 571 | 260 374 | 161 886 | 117 761 | 206 010 |
| 1.60 | 1.66 | 1.70 | 1.76 | 1.77 | 1.72 | 1.73 | 1.77 | 1.82 | 1.91 | 1.59 | 1.37 | 1.75 |
| 458 | 520 | 558 | 600 | 638 | 648 | 671 | 714 | 777 | 858 | 478 | 255 | 652 |
| 164 728 | 191 157 | 209 457 | 230 272 | 250 428 | 259 819 | 274 574 | 298 408 | 331 506 | 373 505 | 169 965 | 81 544 | 258 385 |
| 1.60 | 1.66 | 1.70 | 1.76 | 1.77 | 1.72 | 1.73 | 1.77 | 1.82 | 1.91 | 1.65 | 1.39 | 1.76 |
| 530 | 550 | 553 | 575 | 590 | 583 | 591 | 612 | 645 | 684 | 521 | 423 | 594 |
| 190 611 | 201 901 | 207 782 | 220 825 | 231 627 | 233 831 | 242 106 | 255 778 | 274 910 | 297 524 | 185 344 | 134 998 | 235 689 |
| 1.51 | 1.57 | 1.60 | 1.66 | 1.66 | 1.62 | 1.63 | 1.67 | 1.72 | 1.80 | 1.49 | 1.28 | 1.65 |
| 547 | 600 | 612 | 586 | 593 | 564 | 532 | 554 | 619 | 689 | 452 | 274 | 591 |
| 196 738 | 220 452 | 229 783 | 225 027 | 232 693 | 226 098 | 217 626 | 231 468 | 264 180 | 299 936 | 160 863 | 87 326 | 234 400 |
| 1.71 | 1.87 | 1.97 | 1.90 | 1.90 | 1.79 | 1.48 | 1.39 | 1.41 | 1.53 | 1.59 | 1.44 | 1.66 |

**Table A.6**   Total and per capita gross regional product expressed in United States dollars using alternative conversion rates, and individual shares of gross world product, 1970−1989 [*cont.*]

| Country or area | 1970 (1) | 1971 (2) | 1972 (3) | 1973 (4) | 1974 (5) | 1975 (6) | 1976 (7) | 1977 (8) | 1978 (9) | 1979 (10) |
|---|---|---|---|---|---|---|---|---|---|---|
| **Southern Asia** | | | | | | | | | | |
| 1.   **MER** | | | | | | | | | | |
| 1a.   Per capita gross regional product | 106 | 110 | 114 | 135 | 157 | 153 | 150 | 172 | 192 | 211 |
| 1b.   Gross regional product | 77 155 | 81 542 | 86 904 | 104 788 | 125 078 | 124 484 | 125 124 | 146 187 | 167 059 | 187 575 |
| 1c.   % of gross world product | 2.42 | 2.33 | 2.16 | 2.14 | 2.25 | 2.00 | 1.87 | 1.93 | 1.86 | 1.82 |
| 2.   **PPPs** [a] | | | | | | | | | | |
| 2a.   Per capita gross regional product | 309 | 322 | 331 | 351 | 371 | 433 | 455 | 519 | 574 | 594 |
| 2b.   Gross regional product | 224 259 | 239 190 | 251 659 | 272 779 | 295 341 | 352 696 | 378 582 | 441 567 | 498 541 | 527 852 |
| 2c.   % of gross world product | ... | ... | ... | ... | ... | ... | ... | ... | ... | ... |
| 3.   **Absolute 1970−1989 PARE** | | | | | | | | | | |
| 3a.   Per capita gross regional product | 194 | 190 | 188 | 191 | 190 | 201 | 201 | 210 | 217 | 206 |
| 3b.   Gross regional product | 140 638 | 141 452 | 143 228 | 148 881 | 151 314 | 163 926 | 167 449 | 178 859 | 188 652 | 183 480 |
| 3c.   % of gross world product | 1.98 | 1.91 | 1.84 | 1.79 | 1.79 | 1.91 | 1.85 | 1.90 | 1.92 | 1.80 |
| 4.   **Relative 1970−1989 PARE** | | | | | | | | | | |
| 4a.   Per capita gross regional product | 94 | 98 | 101 | 109 | 118 | 138 | 146 | 163 | 181 | 187 |
| 4b.   Gross regional product | 68 571 | 72 506 | 76 784 | 85 116 | 94 359 | 112 306 | 121 890 | 138 977 | 157 280 | 166 625 |
| 4c.   % of gross world product | 1.98 | 1.91 | 1.84 | 1.79 | 1.79 | 1.91 | 1.85 | 1.90 | 1.92 | 1.80 |
| 5.   **Absolute 1980−1989 PARE** | | | | | | | | | | |
| 5a.   Per capita gross regional product | 224 | 220 | 217 | 221 | 219 | 232 | 232 | 243 | 250 | 238 |
| 5b.   Gross regional product | 162 562 | 163 553 | 165 460 | 171 967 | 174 767 | 189 372 | 193 433 | 206 558 | 217 876 | 211 698 |
| 5c.   % of gross world product | 1.87 | 1.80 | 1.73 | 1.69 | 1.68 | 1.80 | 1.75 | 1.79 | 1.82 | 1.71 |
| 6.   **WA** | | | | | | | | | | |
| 6a.   Per capita gross regional product | 109 | 113 | 120 | 133 | 159 | 153 | 151 | 174 | 191 | 211 |
| 6b.   Gross regional product | 79 277 | 84 148 | 91 413 | 103 705 | 126 657 | 124 639 | 125 584 | 148 204 | 166 466 | 188 004 |
| 6c.   % of gross world product | 2.48 | 2.41 | 2.28 | 2.13 | 2.27 | 2.02 | 1.87 | 1.97 | 1.87 | 1.84 |
| **Europe** | | | | | | | | | | |
| 1.   **MER** | | | | | | | | | | |
| 1a.   Per capita gross regional product | 1 880 | 2 065 | 2 394 | 2 947 | 3 198 | 3 666 | 3 757 | 4 185 | 5 007 | 5 854 |
| 1b.   Gross regional product | 1 320 645 | 1 461 772 | 1 706 360 | 2 116 321 | 2 312 383 | 2 669 071 | 2 752 770 | 3 084 453 | 3 712 233 | 4 364 651 |
| 1c.   % of gross world product | 41.40 | 41.77 | 42.43 | 43.12 | 41.64 | 42.97 | 41.03 | 40.78 | 41.31 | 42.36 |
| 2.   **PPPs** [a] | | | | | | | | | | |
| 2a.   Per capita gross regional product | 3 055 | 3 324 | 3 654 | 4 123 | 4 550 | 4 940 | 5 444 | 5 943 | 6 631 | 7 497 |
| 2b.   Gross regional product | 1 002 472 | 1 097 044 | 1 213 025 | 1 376 198 | 1 526 770 | 1 665 892 | 1 843 976 | 2 020 981 | 2 263 566 | 2 567 728 |
| 2c.   % of gross world product | ... | ... | ... | ... | ... | ... | ... | ... | ... | ... |
| 3.   **Absolute 1970−1989 PARE** | | | | | | | | | | |
| 3a.   Per capita gross regional product | 4 038 | 4 160 | 4 308 | 4 561 | 4 674 | 4 711 | 4 908 | 5 044 | 5 187 | 5 338 |
| 3b.   Gross regional product | 2 837 157 | 2 944 232 | 3 071 558 | 3 274 867 | 3 380 084 | 3 429 341 | 3 595 550 | 3 717 829 | 3 845 752 | 3 979 962 |
| 3c.   % of gross world product | 39.93 | 39.77 | 39.37 | 39.47 | 39.88 | 39.87 | 39.73 | 39.40 | 39.11 | 39.14 |
| 4.   **Relative 1970−1989 PARE** | | | | | | | | | | |
| 4a.   Per capita gross regional product | 1 969 | 2 132 | 2 310 | 2 607 | 2 915 | 3 227 | 3 573 | 3 919 | 4 324 | 4 847 |
| 4b.   Gross regional product | 1 383 311 | 1 509 158 | 1 646 658 | 1 872 268 | 2 107 809 | 2 349 461 | 2 617 281 | 2 888 825 | 3 206 216 | 3 614 362 |
| 4c.   % of gross world product | 39.93 | 39.77 | 39.37 | 39.47 | 39.88 | 39.87 | 39.73 | 39.40 | 39.11 | 39.14 |
| 5.   **Absolute 1980−1989 PARE** | | | | | | | | | | |
| 5a.   Per capita gross regional product | 4 859 | 5 003 | 5 180 | 5 479 | 5 608 | 5 636 | 5 868 | 6 027 | 6 195 | 6 376 |
| 5b.   Gross regional product | 3 414 118 | 3 540 433 | 3 692 880 | 3 934 444 | 4 055 644 | 4 103 134 | 4 298 970 | 4 442 357 | 4 593 037 | 4 753 854 |
| 5c.   % of gross world product | 39.23 | 39.05 | 38.64 | 38.72 | 39.10 | 39.05 | 38.87 | 38.53 | 38.28 | 38.34 |
| 6.   **WA** | | | | | | | | | | |
| 6a.   Per capita gross regional product | 1 886 | 2 043 | 2 339 | 2 853 | 3 174 | 3 604 | 3 755 | 4 163 | 4 898 | 5 754 |
| 6b.   Gross regional product | 1 324 764 | 1 446 175 | 1 667 478 | 2 048 651 | 2 294 911 | 2 623 366 | 2 751 271 | 3 068 245 | 3 631 518 | 4 290 642 |
| 6c.   % of gross world product | 41.51 | 41.46 | 41.63 | 42.12 | 41.13 | 42.57 | 41.00 | 40.69 | 40.89 | 41.95 |

| | 1980 (11) | 1981 (12) | 1982 (13) | 1983 (14) | 1984 (15) | 1985 (16) | 1986 (17) | 1987 (18) | 1988 (19) | 1989 (20) | Averages 1970−89 (21) | 1970−79 (22) | 1980−89 (23) |
|---|---|---|---|---|---|---|---|---|---|---|---|---|---|
| | 250 | 261 | 256 | 270 | 268 | 270 | 287 | 308 | 332 | 321 | 228 | 152 | 284 |
| | 227 068 | 242 944 | 243 803 | 263 749 | 267 264 | 276 037 | 300 156 | 330 226 | 363 691 | 359 071 | 204 995 | 122 590 | 287 401 |
| | 1.96 | 2.08 | 2.10 | 2.22 | 2.19 | 2.19 | 2.02 | 1.92 | 1.90 | 1.79 | 2.01 | 2.01 | 2.01 |
| | 679 | 767 | 798 | 851 | 965 | 1 036 | 1 083 | 1 138 | 1 243 | 1 325 | 758 | 433 | 1 003 |
| | 616 405 | 712 559 | 759 617 | 829 073 | 962 809 | 1 057 970 | 1 131 495 | 1 216 193 | 1 359 272 | 1 482 263 | 680 506 | 348 247 | 1012 766 |
| | ... | ... | ... | ... | ... | ... | ... | ... | ... | ... | ... | ... | ... |
| | 214 | 221 | 225 | 235 | 239 | 247 | 253 | 259 | 274 | 280 | 228 | 199 | 247 |
| | 194 436 | 206 134 | 214 662 | 228 927 | 238 894 | 252 935 | 265 239 | 277 123 | 299 784 | 313 896 | 204 995 | 160 788 | 249 203 |
| | 1.87 | 1.95 | 2.01 | 2.09 | 2.08 | 2.13 | 2.17 | 2.19 | 2.27 | 2.31 | 2.01 | 1.87 | 2.12 |
| | 212 | 240 | 260 | 280 | 296 | 314 | 328 | 345 | 377 | 402 | 235 | 136 | 310 |
| | 192 737 | 223 666 | 247 964 | 273 380 | 295 501 | 321 345 | 343 749 | 369 469 | 413 100 | 450 282 | 211 280 | 109 441 | 313 119 |
| | 1.87 | 1.95 | 2.01 | 2.09 | 2.08 | 2.13 | 2.17 | 2.19 | 2.27 | 2.31 | 2.06 | 1.86 | 2.13 |
| | 247 | 256 | 260 | 271 | 276 | 285 | 292 | 298 | 316 | 323 | 263 | 230 | 284 |
| | 224 299 | 237 812 | 247 592 | 264 103 | 275 522 | 291 711 | 305 883 | 319 485 | 345 696 | 361 907 | 236 563 | 185 725 | 287 401 |
| | 1.77 | 1.85 | 1.91 | 1.98 | 1.98 | 2.02 | 2.06 | 2.08 | 2.16 | 2.19 | 1.91 | 1.76 | 2.01 |
| | 249 | 257 | 258 | 268 | 260 | 275 | 285 | 309 | 322 | 314 | 227 | 154 | 282 |
| | 226 050 | 239 136 | 245 874 | 261 276 | 260 045 | 280 920 | 298 319 | 330 936 | 352 365 | 351 851 | 204 243 | 123 810 | 284 677 |
| | 1.96 | 2.03 | 2.11 | 2.20 | 2.13 | 2.22 | 2.03 | 1.99 | 1.88 | 1.79 | 2.02 | 2.04 | 2.01 |
| | 6 445 | 5 837 | 5 724 | 5 608 | 5 350 | 5 439 | 7 174 | 8 660 | 9 369 | 9 640 | 5 267 | 3 515 | 6 938 |
| | 4 832 453 | 4 400 329 | 4 338 583 | 4 273 138 | 4 096 901 | 4 186 057 | 5 546 558 | 6 726 020 | 7 308 980 | 7 552 403 | 3 938 104 | 2 550 066 | 5 326 142 |
| | 41.70 | 37.58 | 37.32 | 36.04 | 33.59 | 33.24 | 37.25 | 39.14 | 38.26 | 37.66 | 38.66 | 41.84 | 37.30 |
| | 8 376 | 9 013 | 9 640 | 9 984 | 10 664 | 11 023 | 11 518 | 12 165 | 13 040 | 14 050 | 7 964 | 4 928 | 10 955 |
| | 2 877 875 | 3 105 198 | 3 329 913 | 3 457 244 | 3 700 637 | 3 833 630 | 4 014 150 | 4 248 597 | 4 563 400 | 4 926 874 | 2 731 759 | 1 657 765 | 3 805 752 |
| | ... | ... | ... | ... | ... | ... | ... | ... | ... | ... | ... | ... | ... |
| | 5 422 | 5 434 | 5 488 | 5 594 | 5 714 | 5 821 | 5 950 | 6 070 | 6 269 | 6 433 | 5 267 | 4 697 | 5 821 |
| | 4 065 519 | 4 096 975 | 4 159 692 | 4 262 585 | 4 375 982 | 4 479 617 | 4 600 792 | 4 714 478 | 4 890 319 | 5 039 790 | 3 938 104 | 3 407 633 | 4 468 575 |
| | 39.14 | 38.70 | 39.01 | 38.86 | 38.16 | 37.75 | 37.67 | 37.31 | 37.07 | 37.05 | 38.66 | 39.55 | 38.00 |
| | 5 375 | 5 896 | 6 339 | 6 680 | 7 068 | 7 395 | 7 712 | 8 092 | 8 638 | 9 227 | 5 275 | 3 197 | 7 254 |
| | 4 029 989 | 4 445 418 | 4 805 006 | 5 090 285 | 5 412 888 | 5 691 192 | 5 962 603 | 6 285 498 | 6 738 831 | 7 229 554 | 3 944 331 | 2 319 535 | 5 569 127 |
| | 39.14 | 38.70 | 39.01 | 38.86 | 38.16 | 37.75 | 37.67 | 37.31 | 37.07 | 37.05 | 54.47 | 38.06 | 66.39 |
| | 6 472 | 6 482 | 6 542 | 6 664 | 6 805 | 6 934 | 7 088 | 7 234 | 7 471 | 7 671 | 6 292 | 5 627 | 6 938 |
| | 4 852 589 | 4 887 202 | 4 958 974 | 5 077 930 | 5 211 611 | 5 336 263 | 5 480 466 | 5 618 487 | 5 828 182 | 6 009 717 | 4 704 515 | 4 082 887 | 5 326 142 |
| | 38.36 | 37.93 | 38.24 | 38.08 | 37.41 | 37.03 | 36.98 | 36.66 | 36.45 | 36.44 | 37.92 | 38.75 | 37.30 |
| | 6 427 | 5 881 | 5 720 | 5 605 | 5 433 | 5 502 | 6 977 | 8 353 | 9 311 | 9 577 | 5 219 | 3 466 | 6 891 |
| | 4 818 741 | 4 433 824 | 4 335 639 | 4 270 563 | 4 160 957 | 4 234 072 | 5 394 390 | 6 488 065 | 7 263 606 | 7 503 724 | 3 902 530 | 2 514 702 | 5 290 358 |
| | 41.84 | 37.60 | 37.20 | 36.03 | 34.03 | 33.49 | 36.68 | 38.94 | 38.81 | 38.24 | 38.63 | 41.46 | 37.41 |

**Table A.6**   Total and per capita gross regional product expressed in United States dollars using
alternative conversion rates, and individual shares of gross world product,
1970−1989 [*cont.*]

| Country or area | 1970 (1) | 1971 (2) | 1972 (3) | 1973 (4) | 1974 (5) | 1975 (6) | 1976 (7) | 1977 (8) | 1978 (9) | 1979 (10) |
|---|---|---|---|---|---|---|---|---|---|---|
| **Western Europe** | | | | | | | | | | |
| **1.   MER** | | | | | | | | | | |
| 1a.  Per capita gross regional product | 2 238 | 2 515 | 3 006 | 3 779 | 4 228 | 4 919 | 5 092 | 5 744 | 7 039 | 8 533 |
| 1b.  Gross regional product | 832 087 | 940 355 | 1 130 147 | 1 428 414 | 1 606 455 | 1 878 049 | 1 952 215 | 2 211 060 | 2 719 520 | 3 307 998 |
| 1c.  % of gross world product | 26.08 | 26.87 | 28.10 | 29.11 | 28.92 | 30.24 | 29.10 | 29.23 | 30.27 | 32.10 |
| **2.   PPPs** [a] | | | | | | | | | | |
| 2a.  Per capita gross regional product | 3 055 | 3 324 | 3 654 | 4 123 | 4 550 | 4 940 | 5 444 | 5 943 | 6 631 | 7 497 |
| 2b.  Gross regional product | 1 002 472 | 1 097 044 | 1 213 025 | 1 376 198 | 1 526 770 | 1 665 892 | 1 843 976 | 2 020 981 | 2 263 566 | 2 567 728 |
| 2c.  % of gross world product | ... | ... | ... | ... | ... | ... | ... | ... | ... | ... |
| **3.   Absolute 1970−1989 PARE** | | | | | | | | | | |
| 3a.  Per capita gross regional product | 5 903 | 6 063 | 6 271 | 6 607 | 6 727 | 6 723 | 6 986 | 7 159 | 7 352 | 7 596 |
| 3b.  Gross regional product | 2 194 186 | 2 266 644 | 2 357 813 | 2 497 703 | 2 555 855 | 2 566 647 | 2 678 486 | 2 755 719 | 2 840 653 | 2 945 046 |
| 3c.  % of gross world product | 30.88 | 30.62 | 30.22 | 30.10 | 30.15 | 29.84 | 29.60 | 29.20 | 28.89 | 28.97 |
| **4.   Relative 1970−1989 PARE** | | | | | | | | | | |
| 4a.  Per capita gross regional product | 2 878 | 3 108 | 3 362 | 3 777 | 4 195 | 4 606 | 5 085 | 5 562 | 6 129 | 6 899 |
| 4b.  Gross regional product | 1 069 818 | 1 161 839 | 1 264 021 | 1 427 957 | 1 593 822 | 1 758 425 | 1 949 730 | 2 141 247 | 2 368 262 | 2 674 514 |
| 4c.  % of gross world product | 30.88 | 30.62 | 30.22 | 30.10 | 30.15 | 29.84 | 29.60 | 29.20 | 28.89 | 28.97 |
| **5.   Absolute 1980−1989 PARE** | | | | | | | | | | |
| 5a.  Per capita gross regional product | 7 324 | 7 520 | 7 780 | 8 197 | 8 340 | 8 317 | 8 639 | 8 851 | 9 089 | 9 390 |
| 5b.  Gross regional product | 2 722 560 | 2 811 597 | 2 925 116 | 3 098 506 | 3 169 021 | 3 175 047 | 3 312 372 | 3 407 266 | 3 511 663 | 3 640 329 |
| 5c.  % of gross world product | 31.29 | 31.01 | 30.60 | 30.49 | 30.55 | 30.22 | 29.95 | 29.55 | 29.27 | 29.36 |
| **6.   WA** | | | | | | | | | | |
| 6a.  Per capita gross regional product | 2 238 | 2 512 | 2 975 | 3 759 | 4 221 | 4 897 | 5 085 | 5 735 | 7 004 | 8 475 |
| 6b.  Gross regional product | 832 041 | 939 019 | 1 118 673 | 1 420 884 | 1 603 613 | 1 869 595 | 1 949 630 | 2 207 884 | 2 705 969 | 3 285 794 |
| 6c.  % of gross world product | 26.07 | 26.92 | 27.93 | 29.22 | 28.74 | 30.34 | 29.06 | 29.28 | 30.47 | 32.12 |
| **Eastern Europe** | | | | | | | | | | |
| **1.   MER** | | | | | | | | | | |
| 1a.  Per capita gross regional product | 1 477 | 1 562 | 1 710 | 2 023 | 2 057 | 2 285 | 2 293 | 2 480 | 2 796 | 2 952 |
| 1b.  Gross regional product | 488 558 | 521 417 | 576 212 | 687 907 | 705 927 | 791 022 | 800 555 | 873 393 | 992 713 | 1 056 653 |
| 1c.  % of gross world product | 15.31 | 14.90 | 14.33 | 14.02 | 12.71 | 12.73 | 11.93 | 11.55 | 11.05 | 10.25 |
| **2.   PPPs** [a] | | | | | | | | | | |
| 2a.  Per capita gross regional product | ... | ... | ... | ... | ... | ... | ... | ... | ... | ... |
| 2b.  Gross regional product | ... | ... | ... | ... | ... | ... | ... | ... | ... | ... |
| 2c.  % of gross world product | ... | ... | ... | ... | ... | ... | ... | ... | ... | ... |
| **3.   Absolute 1970−1989 PARE** | | | | | | | | | | |
| 3a.  Per capita gross regional product | 1 943 | 2 030 | 2 118 | 2 285 | 2 402 | 2 492 | 2 626 | 2 732 | 2 831 | 2 891 |
| 3b.  Gross regional product | 642 971 | 677 588 | 713 744 | 777 165 | 824 230 | 862 694 | 917 064 | 962 110 | 1 005 098 | 1 034 915 |
| 3c.  % of gross world product | 9.05 | 9.15 | 9.15 | 9.37 | 9.72 | 10.03 | 10.13 | 10.19 | 10.22 | 10.18 |
| **4.   Relative 1970−1989 PARE** | | | | | | | | | | |
| 4a.  Per capita gross regional product | 948 | 1 040 | 1 136 | 1 307 | 1 498 | 1 707 | 1 912 | 2 123 | 2 360 | 2 626 |
| 4b.  Gross regional product | 313 493 | 347 319 | 382 638 | 444 311 | 513 987 | 591 037 | 667 551 | 747 578 | 837 954 | 939 848 |
| 4c.  % of gross world product | 9.05 | 9.15 | 9.15 | 9.37 | 9.72 | 10.03 | 10.13 | 10.19 | 10.22 | 10.18 |
| **5.   Absolute 1980−1989 PARE** | | | | | | | | | | |
| 5a.  Per capita gross regional product | 2 090 | 2 183 | 2 279 | 2 458 | 2 584 | 2 681 | 2 825 | 2 939 | 3 046 | 3 111 |
| 5b.  Gross regional product | 691 558 | 728 836 | 767 764 | 835 938 | 886 623 | 928 088 | 986 599 | 1 035 091 | 1 081 374 | 1 113 525 |
| 5c.  % of gross world product | 7.95 | 8.04 | 8.03 | 8.23 | 8.55 | 8.83 | 8.92 | 8.98 | 9.01 | 8.98 |
| **6.   WA** | | | | | | | | | | |
| 6a.  Per capita gross regional product | 1 489 | 1 519 | 1 629 | 1 846 | 2 014 | 2 177 | 2 296 | 2 443 | 2 607 | 2 807 |
| 6b.  Gross regional product | 492 723 | 507 155 | 548 805 | 627 767 | 691 298 | 753 772 | 801 641 | 860 361 | 925 549 | 1 004 848 |
| 6c.  % of gross world product | 15.44 | 14.54 | 13.70 | 12.91 | 12.39 | 12.23 | 11.95 | 11.41 | 10.42 | 9.82 |

|  |  |  |  |  |  |  |  |  |  | Averages | | |
|---|---|---|---|---|---|---|---|---|---|---|---|---|
| 1980 | 1981 | 1982 | 1983 | 1984 | 1985 | 1986 | 1987 | 1988 | 1989 | 1970−89 | 1970−79 | 1980−89 |
| (11) | (12) | (13) | (14) | (15) | (16) | (17) | (18) | (19) | (20) | (21) | (22) | (23) |
| 9 603 | 8 506 | 8 141 | 7 857 | 7 523 | 7 762 | 10 611 | 13 139 | 14 199 | 14 651 | 7 491 | 4 728 | 10 207 |
| 3 734 740 | 3 318 249 | 3 184 345 | 3 081 511 | 2 957 347 | 3 058 525 | 4 189 880 | 5 199 002 | 5 629 319 | 5 819 821 | 2 908 952 | 1 800 630 | 4 017 274 |
| 32.23 | 28.34 | 27.39 | 25.99 | 24.25 | 24.28 | 28.14 | 30.25 | 29.46 | 29.02 | 28.55 | 29.54 | 28.13 |
| 8 376 | 9 013 | 9 640 | 9 984 | 10 664 | 11 023 | 11 518 | 12 165 | 13 040 | 14 050 | 7 964 | 4 928 | 10 955 |
| 2 877 875 | 3 105 198 | 3 329 913 | 3 457 244 | 3 700 637 | 3 833 630 | 4 014 150 | 4 248 597 | 4 563 400 | 4 926 874 | 2 731 759 | 1 657 765 | 3 805 752 |
| ... | ... | ... | ... | ... | ... | ... | ... | ... | ... | ... | ... | ... |
| 7 702 | 7 708 | 7 757 | 7 867 | 8 047 | 8 238 | 8 442 | 8 655 | 8 959 | 9 260 | 7 491 | 6 737 | 8 263 |
| 2 995 530 | 3 006 855 | 3 034 183 | 3 085 427 | 3 163 378 | 3 246 062 | 3 333 578 | 3 424 606 | 3 552 084 | 3 678 585 | 2 908 952 | 2 565 875 | 3 252 029 |
| 28.84 | 28.40 | 28.46 | 28.13 | 27.59 | 27.36 | 27.30 | 27.10 | 26.93 | 27.04 | 28.55 | 29.78 | 27.66 |
| 7 635 | 8 364 | 8 960 | 9 394 | 9 953 | 10 466 | 10 941 | 11 539 | 12 346 | 13 284 | 7 459 | 4 571 | 10 294 |
| 2 969 351 | 3 262 584 | 3 504 892 | 3 684 550 | 3 912 952 | 4 124 005 | 4 320 300 | 4 565 798 | 4 894 751 | 5 276 912 | 2 896 287 | 1 740 963 | 4 051 610 |
| 28.84 | 28.40 | 28.46 | 28.13 | 27.59 | 27.36 | 27.30 | 27.10 | 26.93 | 27.04 | 28.18 | 29.65 | 27.59 |
| 9 517 | 9 522 | 9 582 | 9 718 | 9 938 | 10 175 | 10 426 | 10 692 | 11 069 | 11 443 | 9 264 | 8 343 | 10 207 |
| 3 701 293 | 3 714 309 | 3 748 047 | 3 811 449 | 3 906 916 | 4 009 045 | 4 117 026 | 4 230 676 | 4 388 468 | 4 545 512 | 3 597 311 | 3 177 348 | 4 017 274 |
| 29.26 | 28.83 | 28.90 | 28.58 | 28.04 | 27.82 | 27.78 | 27.60 | 27.44 | 27.56 | 28.99 | 30.16 | 28.13 |
| 9 602 | 8 532 | 8 168 | 7 865 | 7 536 | 7 765 | 10 545 | 12 997 | 14 391 | 14 655 | 7 485 | 4 709 | 10 214 |
| 3 734 460 | 3 328 046 | 3 195 186 | 3 084 718 | 2 962 493 | 3 059 657 | 4 163 961 | 5 142 553 | 5 705 694 | 5 821 421 | 2 906 564 | 1 793 310 | 4 019 819 |
| 32.42 | 28.22 | 27.41 | 26.02 | 24.23 | 24.20 | 28.31 | 30.86 | 30.48 | 29.66 | 28.77 | 29.57 | 28.43 |
| 3 042 | 2 974 | 3 147 | 3 223 | 3 058 | 3 002 | 3 586 | 4 008 | 4 378 | 4 486 | 2 863 | 2 174 | 3 499 |
| 1 097 712 | 1 082 079 | 1 154 238 | 1 191 627 | 1 139 554 | 1 127 532 | 1 356 678 | 1 527 018 | 1 679 661 | 1 732 582 | 1 029 152 | 749 436 | 1 308 868 |
| 9.47 | 9.24 | 9.93 | 10.05 | 9.34 | 8.95 | 9.11 | 8.89 | 8.79 | 8.64 | 10.10 | 12.30 | 9.17 |
| ... | ... | ... | ... | ... | ... | ... | ... | ... | ... | ... | ... | ... |
| ... | ... | ... | ... | ... | ... | ... | ... | ... | ... | ... | ... | ... |
| 2 965 | 2 996 | 3 068 | 3 183 | 3 254 | 3 285 | 3 350 | 3 385 | 3 488 | 3 524 | 2 863 | 2 442 | 3 252 |
| 1 069 989 | 1 090 120 | 1 125 509 | 1 177 158 | 1 212 604 | 1 233 555 | 1 267 214 | 1 289 872 | 1 338 235 | 1 361 205 | 1 029 152 | 841 758 | 1 216 546 |
| 10.30 | 10.30 | 10.56 | 10.73 | 10.58 | 10.40 | 10.38 | 10.21 | 10.14 | 10.01 | 10.10 | 9.77 | 10.35 |
| 2 939 | 3 251 | 3 544 | 3 802 | 4 025 | 4 173 | 4 341 | 4 513 | 4 806 | 5 055 | 2 916 | 1 679 | 4 056 |
| 1 060 638 | 1 182 834 | 1 300 114 | 1 405 736 | 1 499 936 | 1 567 187 | 1 642 303 | 1 719 700 | 1 844 080 | 1 952 642 | 1 048 044 | 578 572 | 1 517 517 |
| 10.30 | 10.30 | 10.56 | 10.73 | 10.58 | 10.40 | 10.38 | 10.21 | 10.14 | 10.01 | 10.20 | 9.85 | 10.34 |
| 3 190 | 3 224 | 3 301 | 3 425 | 3 501 | 3 534 | 3 604 | 3 642 | 3 753 | 3 791 | 3 081 | 2 627 | 3 499 |
| 1 151 296 | 1 172 893 | 1 210 927 | 1 266 482 | 1 304 695 | 1 327 218 | 1 363 440 | 1 387 811 | 1 439 715 | 1 464 206 | 1 107 204 | 905 540 | 1 308 868 |
| 9.10 | 9.10 | 9.34 | 9.50 | 9.36 | 9.21 | 9.20 | 9.06 | 9.00 | 8.88 | 8.92 | 8.60 | 9.17 |
| 3 005 | 3 039 | 3 109 | 3 207 | 3 216 | 3 127 | 3 252 | 3 531 | 4 061 | 4 356 | 2 771 | 2 093 | 3 396 |
| 1 084 281 | 1 105 778 | 1 140 453 | 1 185 845 | 1 198 464 | 1 174 415 | 1 230 429 | 1 345 512 | 1 557 911 | 1 682 303 | 995 966 | 721 392 | 1 270 539 |
| 9.41 | 9.38 | 9.78 | 10.00 | 9.80 | 9.29 | 8.37 | 8.08 | 8.32 | 8.57 | 9.86 | 11.89 | 8.99 |

**Table A.6**    Total and per capita gross regional product expressed in United States dollars using
alternative conversion rates, and individual shares of gross world product,
1970−1989 [*cont.*]

| Country or area | 1970 (1) | 1971 (2) | 1972 (3) | 1973 (4) | 1974 (5) | 1975 (6) | 1976 (7) | 1977 (8) | 1978 (9) | 1979 (10) |
|---|---|---|---|---|---|---|---|---|---|---|
| **Oceania** | | | | | | | | | | |
| **1.  MER** | | | | | | | | | | |
| 1a.  Per capita gross regional product | 2 481 | 2 782 | 3 269 | 4 528 | 5 369 | 5 638 | 5 878 | 5 756 | 6 691 | 7 366 |
| 1b.  Gross regional product | 47 353 | 54 120 | 64 795 | 91 399 | 110 293 | 117 765 | 124 715 | 123 981 | 146 211 | 163 285 |
| 1c.  % of gross world product | 1.48 | 1.55 | 1.61 | 1.86 | 1.99 | 1.90 | 1.86 | 1.64 | 1.63 | 1.58 |
| **2.  PPPs** [a] | | | | | | | | | | |
| 2a.  Per capita gross regional product | 3 147 | 3 392 | 3 739 | 4 217 | 4 572 | 4 977 | 5 282 | 5 445 | 6 020 | 6 672 |
| 2b.  Gross regional product | 57 634 | 63 294 | 71 072 | 81 606 | 90 034 | 99 631 | 107 374 | 112 339 | 125 972 | 141 605 |
| 2c.  % of gross world product | ... | ... | ... | ... | ... | ... | ... | ... | ... | ... |
| **3.  Absolute 1970−1989 PARE** | | | | | | | | | | |
| 3a.  Per capita gross regional product | 6 562 | 6 757 | 6 905 | 7 054 | 7 136 | 7 138 | 7 223 | 7 126 | 7 318 | 7 357 |
| 3b.  Gross regional product | 125 245 | 131 431 | 136 840 | 142 371 | 146 575 | 149 100 | 153 251 | 153 482 | 159 911 | 163 088 |
| 3c.  % of gross world product | 1.76 | 1.78 | 1.75 | 1.72 | 1.73 | 1.73 | 1.69 | 1.63 | 1.63 | 1.60 |
| **4.  Relative 1970−1989 PARE** | | | | | | | | | | |
| 4a.  Per capita gross regional product | 3 200 | 3 464 | 3 702 | 4 033 | 4 450 | 4 891 | 5 258 | 5 537 | 6 101 | 6 681 |
| 4b.  Gross regional product | 61 066 | 67 369 | 73 360 | 81 395 | 91 404 | 102 149 | 111 555 | 119 258 | 133 318 | 148 107 |
| 4c.  % of gross world product | 1.76 | 1.78 | 1.75 | 1.72 | 1.73 | 1.73 | 1.69 | 1.63 | 1.63 | 1.60 |
| **5.  Absolute 1980−1989 PARE** | | | | | | | | | | |
| 5a.  Per capita gross regional product | 8 008 | 8 243 | 8 424 | 8 605 | 8 709 | 8 710 | 8 813 | 8 690 | 8 919 | 8 965 |
| 5b.  Gross regional product | 152 842 | 160 342 | 166 939 | 173 676 | 178 890 | 181 917 | 186 980 | 187 166 | 194 908 | 198 731 |
| 5c.  % of gross world product | 1.76 | 1.77 | 1.75 | 1.71 | 1.72 | 1.73 | 1.69 | 1.62 | 1.62 | 1.60 |
| **6.  WA** | | | | | | | | | | |
| 6a.  Per capita gross regional product | 2 477 | 2 749 | 3 219 | 4 162 | 5 462 | 5 782 | 6 003 | 5 935 | 6 612 | 7 432 |
| 6b.  Gross regional product | 47 268 | 53 479 | 63 804 | 84 010 | 112 185 | 120 767 | 127 373 | 127 829 | 144 483 | 164 737 |
| 6c.  % of gross world product | 1.48 | 1.53 | 1.59 | 1.73 | 2.01 | 1.96 | 1.90 | 1.70 | 1.63 | 1.61 |
| **Australia and New Zealand** | | | | | | | | | | |
| **1.  MER** | | | | | | | | | | |
| 1a.  Per capita gross regional product | 2 968 | 3 336 | 3 922 | 5 443 | 6 480 | 6 809 | 7 112 | 6 968 | 8 119 | 8 935 |
| 1b.  Gross regional product | 45 621 | 52 206 | 62 464 | 88 171 | 106 682 | 113 797 | 120 507 | 119 602 | 141 079 | 157 162 |
| 1c.  % of gross world product | 1.43 | 1.49 | 1.55 | 1.80 | 1.92 | 1.83 | 1.80 | 1.58 | 1.57 | 1.53 |
| **2.  PPPs** [a] | | | | | | | | | | |
| 2a.  Per capita gross regional product | 3 563 | 3 850 | 4 264 | 4 809 | 5 230 | 5 705 | 6 062 | 6 248 | 6 928 | 7 677 |
| 2b.  Gross regional product | 54 774 | 60 245 | 67 896 | 77 900 | 86 094 | 95 339 | 102 727 | 107 255 | 120 382 | 135 035 |
| 2c.  % of gross world product | ... | ... | ... | ... | ... | ... | ... | ... | ... | ... |
| **3.  Absolute 1970−1989 PARE** | | | | | | | | | | |
| 3a.  Per capita gross regional product | 7 872 | 8 114 | 8 298 | 8 492 | 8 590 | 8 614 | 8 739 | 8 640 | 8 884 | 8 954 |
| 3b.  Gross regional product | 121 008 | 126 965 | 132 149 | 137 554 | 141 415 | 143 949 | 148 086 | 148 301 | 154 380 | 157 496 |
| 3c.  % of gross world product | 1.70 | 1.72 | 1.69 | 1.66 | 1.67 | 1.67 | 1.64 | 1.57 | 1.57 | 1.55 |
| **4.  Relative 1970−1989 PARE** | | | | | | | | | | |
| 4a.  Per capita gross regional product | 3 838 | 4 159 | 4 449 | 4 855 | 5 357 | 5 901 | 6 361 | 6 713 | 7 407 | 8 131 |
| 4b.  Gross regional product | 59 000 | 65 080 | 70 845 | 78 641 | 88 186 | 98 620 | 107 795 | 115 233 | 128 707 | 143 029 |
| 4c.  % of gross world product | 1.70 | 1.72 | 1.69 | 1.66 | 1.67 | 1.67 | 1.64 | 1.57 | 1.57 | 1.55 |
| **5.  Absolute 1980−1989 PARE** | | | | | | | | | | |
| 5a.  Per capita gross regional product | 9 607 | 9 899 | 10 124 | 10 360 | 10 485 | 10 510 | 10 664 | 10 537 | 10 829 | 10 912 |
| 5b.  Gross regional product | 147 676 | 154 897 | 161 222 | 167 810 | 172 607 | 175 646 | 180 695 | 180 865 | 188 181 | 191 939 |
| 5c.  % of gross world product | 1.70 | 1.71 | 1.69 | 1.65 | 1.66 | 1.67 | 1.63 | 1.57 | 1.57 | 1.55 |
| **6.  WA** | | | | | | | | | | |
| 6a.  Per capita gross regional product | 2 968 | 3 301 | 3 865 | 4 998 | 6 605 | 7 002 | 7 274 | 7 194 | 8 025 | 9 041 |
| 6b.  Gross regional product | 45 628 | 51 654 | 61 557 | 80 959 | 108 725 | 117 021 | 123 265 | 123 483 | 139 449 | 159 031 |
| 6c.  % of gross world product | 1.43 | 1.48 | 1.54 | 1.66 | 1.95 | 1.90 | 1.84 | 1.64 | 1.57 | 1.55 |

| | 1980 (11) | 1981 (12) | 1982 (13) | 1983 (14) | 1984 (15) | 1985 (16) | 1986 (17) | 1987 (18) | 1988 (19) | 1989 (20) | Averages 1970–89 (21) | 1970–79 (22) | 1980–89 (23) |
|---|---|---|---|---|---|---|---|---|---|---|---|---|---|
| | 8 378 | 9 234 | 8 719 | 8 633 | 9 103 | 8 096 | 8 562 | 10 240 | 12 281 | 12 978 | 7 554 | 5 040 | 9 683 |
| | 188 480 | 210 793 | 202 029 | 203 086 | 217 392 | 196 295 | 210 724 | 255 830 | 311 445 | 333 975 | 168 698 | 104 392 | 233 005 |
| | 1.63 | 1.80 | 1.74 | 1.71 | 1.78 | 1.56 | 1.42 | 1.49 | 1.63 | 1.67 | 1.66 | 1.71 | 1.63 |
| | 7 424 | 8 089 | 8 270 | 8 694 | 9 152 | 9 478 | 9 763 | 10 256 | 10 782 | 11 420 | 7 274 | 4 788 | 9 390 |
| | 159 841 | 176 700 | 183 325 | 195 571 | 208 921 | 219 584 | 229 533 | 244 692 | 261 002 | 280 435 | 155 508 | 95 056 | 215 961 |
| | ... | ... | ... | ... | ... | ... | ... | ... | ... | ... | ... | ... | ... |
| | 7 466 | 7 488 | 7 316 | 7 591 | 7 858 | 8 039 | 8 109 | 8 299 | 8 458 | 8 614 | 7 554 | 7 055 | 7 948 |
| | 167 966 | 170 940 | 169 516 | 178 572 | 187 666 | 194 905 | 199 587 | 207 353 | 214 495 | 221 676 | 168 698 | 146 129 | 191 267 |
| | 1.62 | 1.61 | 1.59 | 1.63 | 1.64 | 1.64 | 1.63 | 1.64 | 1.63 | 1.63 | 1.66 | 1.70 | 1.63 |
| | 7 401 | 8 125 | 8 450 | 9 065 | 9 720 | 10 213 | 10 510 | 11 065 | 11 655 | 12 357 | 7 564 | 4 774 | 9 930 |
| | 166 498 | 185 478 | 195 813 | 213 246 | 232 134 | 247 620 | 258 663 | 276 450 | 295 573 | 317 993 | 168 922 | 98 898 | 238 947 |
| | 1.62 | 1.61 | 1.59 | 1.63 | 1.64 | 1.64 | 1.63 | 1.64 | 1.63 | 1.63 | 2.33 | 1.62 | 2.85 |
| | 9 097 | 9 125 | 8 917 | 9 252 | 9 576 | 9 792 | 9 880 | 10 107 | 10 299 | 10 487 | 9 208 | 8 605 | 9 683 |
| | 204 653 | 208 298 | 206 615 | 217 642 | 228 691 | 237 429 | 243 155 | 252 519 | 261 177 | 269 873 | 205 622 | 178 239 | 233 005 |
| | 1.62 | 1.62 | 1.59 | 1.63 | 1.64 | 1.65 | 1.64 | 1.65 | 1.63 | 1.64 | 1.66 | 1.69 | 1.63 |
| | 8 195 | 9 271 | 9 383 | 8 894 | 9 242 | 8 774 | 8 890 | 9 648 | 12 374 | 13 321 | 7 654 | 5 049 | 9 859 |
| | 184 350 | 211 627 | 217 423 | 209 224 | 220 718 | 212 724 | 218 801 | 241 058 | 313 796 | 342 814 | 170 923 | 104 593 | 237 253 |
| | 1.60 | 1.79 | 1.87 | 1.76 | 1.81 | 1.68 | 1.49 | 1.45 | 1.68 | 1.75 | 1.69 | 1.72 | 1.68 |
| | 10 196 | 11 321 | 10 709 | 10 634 | 11 251 | 9 998 | 10 542 | 12 650 | 15 247 | 16 178 | 9 214 | 6 073 | 11 939 |
| | 181 585 | 204 206 | 195 687 | 196 869 | 211 064 | 190 030 | 202 998 | 246 813 | 301 372 | 323 833 | 163 087 | 100 729 | 225 446 |
| | 1.57 | 1.74 | 1.68 | 1.66 | 1.73 | 1.51 | 1.36 | 1.44 | 1.58 | 1.62 | 1.60 | 1.65 | 1.58 |
| | 8 585 | 9 392 | 9 624 | 10 127 | 10 689 | 11 101 | 11 442 | 12 053 | 12 695 | 13 472 | 8 421 | 5 472 | 10 979 |
| | 152 883 | 169 411 | 175 858 | 187 473 | 200 506 | 210 996 | 220 345 | 235 163 | 250 926 | 269 679 | 149 044 | 90 765 | 207 324 |
| | ... | ... | ... | ... | ... | ... | ... | ... | ... | ... | ... | ... | ... |
| | 9 125 | 9 170 | 8 965 | 9 331 | 9 685 | 9 930 | 10 031 | 10 289 | 10 492 | 10 704 | 9 214 | 8 508 | 9 800 |
| | 162 505 | 165 394 | 163 825 | 172 752 | 181 678 | 188 749 | 193 160 | 200 741 | 207 386 | 214 255 | 163 087 | 141 130 | 185 044 |
| | 1.56 | 1.56 | 1.54 | 1.57 | 1.58 | 1.59 | 1.58 | 1.59 | 1.57 | 1.57 | 1.60 | 1.64 | 1.57 |
| | 9 045 | 9 950 | 10 356 | 11 143 | 11 980 | 12 616 | 13 000 | 13 717 | 14 458 | 15 354 | 9 229 | 5 758 | 12 242 |
| | 161 085 | 179 461 | 189 240 | 206 296 | 224 727 | 239 799 | 250 335 | 267 635 | 285 777 | 307 347 | 163 342 | 95 513 | 231 170 |
| | 1.56 | 1.56 | 1.54 | 1.57 | 1.58 | 1.59 | 1.58 | 1.59 | 1.57 | 1.57 | 1.59 | 1.63 | 1.57 |
| | 11 119 | 11 175 | 10 929 | 11 374 | 11 804 | 12 098 | 12 222 | 12 530 | 12 776 | 13 031 | 11 232 | 10 379 | 11 939 |
| | 198 019 | 201 565 | 199 704 | 210 575 | 221 425 | 229 955 | 235 350 | 244 482 | 252 531 | 260 850 | 198 800 | 172 154 | 225 446 |
| | 1.57 | 1.56 | 1.54 | 1.58 | 1.59 | 1.60 | 1.59 | 1.60 | 1.58 | 1.58 | 1.60 | 1.63 | 1.58 |
| | 9 990 | 11 363 | 11 539 | 10 959 | 11 426 | 10 863 | 11 000 | 11 943 | 15 380 | 16 608 | 9 349 | 6 094 | 12 174 |
| | 177 912 | 204 960 | 210 851 | 202 890 | 214 343 | 206 476 | 211 832 | 233 024 | 303 996 | 332 444 | 165 475 | 101 077 | 229 873 |
| | 1.54 | 1.74 | 1.81 | 1.71 | 1.75 | 1.63 | 1.44 | 1.40 | 1.62 | 1.69 | 1.64 | 1.67 | 1.63 |

**Table A.6**    Total and per capita gross regional product expressed in United States dollars using
alternative conversion rates, and individual shares of gross world product,
1970–1989 [*cont.*]

| Country or area | 1970 (1) | 1971 (2) | 1972 (3) | 1973 (4) | 1974 (5) | 1975 (6) | 1976 (7) | 1977 (8) | 1978 (9) | 1979 (10) |
|---|---|---|---|---|---|---|---|---|---|---|
| **Other Oceania** | | | | | | | | | | |
| **1.  MER** | | | | | | | | | | |
| 1a.  Per capita gross regional product | 466 | 503 | 599 | 810 | 885 | 950 | 985 | 1 002 | 1 147 | 1 338 |
| 1b.  Gross regional product | 1 732 | 1 914 | 2 331 | 3 228 | 3 611 | 3 967 | 4 208 | 4 380 | 5 132 | 6 123 |
| 1c.  % of gross world product | 0.05 | 0.05 | 0.06 | 0.07 | 0.07 | 0.06 | 0.06 | 0.06 | 0.06 | 0.06 |
| **2.  PPPs** [a] | | | | | | | | | | |
| 2a.  Per capita gross regional product | 971 | 1 012 | 1 030 | 1 175 | 1 220 | 1 298 | 1 373 | 1 467 | 1 575 | 1 808 |
| 2b.  Gross regional product | 2 860 | 3 049 | 3 176 | 3 707 | 3 940 | 4 292 | 4 647 | 5 084 | 5 591 | 6 570 |
| 2c.  % of gross world product | ... | ... | ... | ... | ... | ... | ... | ... | ... | ... |
| **3.  Absolute 1970–1989 PARE** | | | | | | | | | | |
| 3a.  Per capita gross regional product | 1 141 | 1 174 | 1 205 | 1 209 | 1 265 | 1 234 | 1 209 | 1 185 | 1 236 | 1 222 |
| 3b.  Gross regional product | 4 238 | 4 466 | 4 691 | 4 818 | 5 161 | 5 151 | 5 165 | 5 180 | 5 531 | 5 591 |
| 3c.  % of gross world product | 0.06 | 0.06 | 0.06 | 0.06 | 0.06 | 0.06 | 0.06 | 0.05 | 0.06 | 0.05 |
| **4.  Relative 1970–1989 PARE** | | | | | | | | | | |
| 4a.  Per capita gross regional product | 556 | 602 | 646 | 691 | 789 | 845 | 880 | 920 | 1 030 | 1 109 |
| 4b.  Gross regional product | 2 066 | 2 289 | 2 515 | 2 754 | 3 218 | 3 529 | 3 760 | 4 025 | 4 611 | 5 078 |
| 4c.  % of gross world product | 0.06 | 0.06 | 0.06 | 0.06 | 0.06 | 0.06 | 0.06 | 0.05 | 0.06 | 0.05 |
| **5.  Absolute 1980–1989 PARE** | | | | | | | | | | |
| 5a.  Per capita gross regional product | 1 391 | 1 432 | 1 468 | 1 472 | 1 540 | 1 502 | 1 471 | 1 441 | 1 503 | 1 484 |
| 5b.  Gross regional product | 5 166 | 5 444 | 5 717 | 5 866 | 6 282 | 6 271 | 6 286 | 6 301 | 6 727 | 6 792 |
| 5c.  % of gross world product | 0.06 | 0.06 | 0.06 | 0.06 | 0.06 | 0.06 | 0.06 | 0.05 | 0.06 | 0.05 |
| **6.  WA** | | | | | | | | | | |
| 6a.  Per capita gross regional product | 442 | 480 | 577 | 765 | 848 | 897 | 962 | 994 | 1 125 | 1 247 |
| 6b.  Gross regional product | 1 640 | 1 826 | 2 247 | 3 051 | 3 459 | 3 746 | 4 108 | 4 346 | 5 034 | 5 706 |
| 6c.  % of gross world product | 0.05 | 0.05 | 0.06 | 0.06 | 0.06 | 0.06 | 0.06 | 0.06 | 0.06 | 0.06 |

Note:  Gross regional product is expressed in millions of United States dollars.
Three dots (...) indicate that the data are not available.

a        Regional totals are comprised of countries with available PPPs only.

| | | | | | | | | | | Averages | | |
|---|---|---|---|---|---|---|---|---|---|---|---|---|
| 1980 (11) | 1981 (12) | 1982 (13) | 1983 (14) | 1984 (15) | 1985 (16) | 1986 (17) | 1987 (18) | 1988 (19) | 1989 (20) | 1970–89 (21) | 1970–79 (22) | 1980–89 (23) |
| 1 471 | 1 375 | 1 295 | 1 241 | 1 235 | 1 196 | 1 443 | 1 648 | 1 801 | 1 774 | 1 211 | 887 | 1 459 |
| 6 895 | 6 587 | 6 343 | 6 218 | 6 328 | 6 266 | 7 726 | 9 018 | 10 074 | 10 141 | 5 611 | 3 663 | 7 560 |
| 0.06 | 0.06 | 0.05 | 0.05 | 0.05 | 0.05 | 0.05 | 0.05 | 0.05 | 0.05 | 0.06 | 0.06 | 0.05 |
| 1 870 | 1 915 | 1 918 | 2 034 | 2 068 | 2 064 | 2 160 | 2 192 | 2 268 | 2 369 | 1 757 | 1 313 | 2 099 |
| 6 957 | 7 289 | 7 468 | 8 098 | 8 415 | 8 588 | 9 188 | 9 530 | 10 076 | 10 757 | 6 464 | 4 292 | 8 637 |
| ... | ... | ... | ... | ... | ... | ... | ... | ... | ... | ... | ... | ... |
| 1 165 | 1 158 | 1 162 | 1 161 | 1 169 | 1 175 | 1 200 | 1 208 | 1 271 | 1 298 | 1 211 | 1 211 | 1 201 |
| 5 461 | 5 545 | 5 691 | 5 820 | 5 988 | 6 156 | 6 426 | 6 612 | 7 109 | 7 421 | 5 611 | 4 999 | 6 223 |
| 0.05 | 0.05 | 0.05 | 0.05 | 0.05 | 0.05 | 0.05 | 0.05 | 0.05 | 0.05 | 0.06 | 0.06 | 0.05 |
| 1 155 | 1 256 | 1 342 | 1 387 | 1 446 | 1 493 | 1 555 | 1 611 | 1 751 | 1 862 | 1 205 | 820 | 1 501 |
| 5 414 | 6 017 | 6 574 | 6 950 | 7 407 | 7 821 | 8 328 | 8 815 | 9 797 | 10 646 | 5 581 | 3 385 | 7 777 |
| 0.05 | 0.05 | 0.05 | 0.05 | 0.05 | 0.05 | 0.05 | 0.05 | 0.05 | 0.05 | 0.05 | 0.06 | 0.05 |
| 1 415 | 1 406 | 1 411 | 1 410 | 1 418 | 1 427 | 1 457 | 1 468 | 1 546 | 1 578 | 1 473 | 1 475 | 1 459 |
| 6 634 | 6 733 | 6 911 | 7 066 | 7 266 | 7 474 | 7 804 | 8 037 | 8 646 | 9 023 | 6 822 | 6 085 | 7 560 |
| 0.05 | 0.05 | 0.05 | 0.05 | 0.05 | 0.05 | 0.05 | 0.05 | 0.05 | 0.05 | 0.05 | 0.06 | 0.05 |
| 1 374 | 1 392 | 1 342 | 1 264 | 1 245 | 1 192 | 1 301 | 1 468 | 1 752 | 1 814 | 1 176 | 852 | 1 425 |
| 6 439 | 6 667 | 6 572 | 6 334 | 6 376 | 6 247 | 6 969 | 8 034 | 9 800 | 10 370 | 5 448 | 3 516 | 7 381 |
| 0.06 | 0.06 | 0.06 | 0.05 | 0.05 | 0.05 | 0.05 | 0.05 | 0.05 | 0.05 | 0.05 | 0.06 | 0.05 |

**Table A.7** Number of countries or areas included in cross–classification of regional groups and population quarters and eighths, based on per capita gross domestic product

| Conversion rate and population group | Africa Total | Sub–Saharan | Northern | Northern America | Latin America and Caribbean Total | Caribbean | Latin America | Asia Total | Western |
|---|---|---|---|---|---|---|---|---|---|
| **1970** | | | | | | | | | |
| **Market rate** | | | | | | | | | |
| Poorest quarter | 14 | 14 | 0 | 0 | 1 | 1 | 0 | 10 | 1 |
| Second quarter | 11 | 10 | 1 | 0 | 0 | 0 | 0 | 4 | 1 |
| Third quarter | 27 | 23 | 4 | 0 | 35 | 15 | 20 | 20 | 10 |
| fifth eighth | 19 | 16 | 3 | 0 | 13 | 6 | 7 | 10 | 3 |
| sixth eighth | 8 | 7 | 1 | 0 | 22 | 9 | 13 | 10 | 7 |
| Fourth quarter | 1 | 0 | 1 | 2 | 7 | 6 | 1 | 6 | 4 |
| seventh eighth | 1 | 0 | 1 | 0 | 4 | 3 | 1 | 3 | 1 |
| richest eighth | 0 | 0 | 0 | 2 | 3 | 3 | 0 | 3 | 3 |
| Total | 53 | 47 | 6 | 2 | 43 | 22 | 21 | 40 | 16 |
| **PARE** | | | | | | | | | |
| Poorest quarter | 5 | 5 | 0 | 0 | 0 | 0 | 0 | 6 | 0 |
| Second quarter | 7 | 7 | 0 | 0 | 1 | 1 | 0 | 7 | 0 |
| Third quarter | 39 | 34 | 5 | 0 | 31 | 12 | 19 | 14 | 7 |
| fifth eighth | 34 | 30 | 4 | 0 | 15 | 6 | 9 | 11 | 5 |
| sixth eighth | 5 | 4 | 1 | 0 | 16 | 6 | 10 | 3 | 2 |
| Fourth quarter | 2 | 1 | 1 | 2 | 11 | 9 | 2 | 13 | 9 |
| seventh eighth | 2 | 1 | 1 | 0 | 8 | 6 | 2 | 8 | 6 |
| richest eighth | 0 | 0 | 0 | 2 | 3 | 3 | 0 | 5 | 3 |
| Total | 53 | 47 | 6 | 2 | 43 | 22 | 21 | 40 | 16 |
| **1980** | | | | | | | | | |
| **Market rate** | | | | | | | | | |
| Poorest quarter | 13 | 13 | 0 | 0 | 1 | 1 | 0 | 11 | 0 |
| Second quarter | 17 | 16 | 1 | 0 | 0 | 0 | 0 | 3 | 1 |
| Third quarter | 20 | 16 | 4 | 0 | 29 | 11 | 18 | 13 | 6 |
| fifth eighth | 14 | 12 | 2 | 0 | 18 | 9 | 9 | 6 | 1 |
| sixth eighth | 6 | 4 | 2 | 0 | 11 | 2 | 9 | 7 | 5 |
| Fourth quarter | 3 | 2 | 1 | 2 | 13 | 10 | 3 | 13 | 9 |
| seventh eighth | 2 | 2 | 0 | 0 | 12 | 9 | 3 | 7 | 5 |
| richest eighth | 1 | 0 | 1 | 2 | 1 | 1 | 0 | 6 | 4 |
| Total | 53 | 47 | 6 | 2 | 43 | 22 | 21 | 40 | 16 |
| **PARE** | | | | | | | | | |
| Poorest quarter | 11 | 11 | 0 | 0 | 0 | 0 | 0 | 8 | 0 |
| Second quarter | 15 | 14 | 1 | 0 | 1 | 1 | 0 | 6 | 1 |
| Third quarter | 24 | 20 | 4 | 0 | 31 | 11 | 20 | 13 | 6 |
| fifth eighth | 18 | 16 | 2 | 0 | 10 | 5 | 5 | 7 | 2 |
| sixth eighth | 6 | 4 | 2 | 0 | 21 | 6 | 15 | 6 | 4 |
| Fourth quarter | 3 | 2 | 1 | 2 | 11 | 10 | 1 | 13 | 9 |
| seventh eighth | 3 | 2 | 1 | 0 | 10 | 9 | 1 | 7 | 5 |
| richest eighth | 0 | 0 | 0 | 2 | 1 | 1 | 0 | 6 | 4 |
| Total | 53 | 47 | 6 | 2 | 43 | 22 | 21 | 40 | 16 |
| **1989** | | | | | | | | | |
| **Market rate** | | | | | | | | | |
| Poorest quarter | 19 | 18 | 1 | 0 | 2 | 0 | 2 | 6 | 0 |
| Second quarter | 5 | 5 | 0 | 0 | 0 | 0 | 0 | 2 | 0 |
| Third quarter | 26 | 22 | 4 | 0 | 28 | 10 | 18 | 17 | 6 |
| fifth eighth | 19 | 18 | 1 | 0 | 9 | 2 | 7 | 13 | 4 |
| sixth eighth | 7 | 4 | 3 | 0 | 19 | 8 | 11 | 4 | 2 |
| Fourth quarter | 3 | 2 | 1 | 2 | 13 | 12 | 1 | 15 | 10 |
| seventh eighth | 3 | 2 | 1 | 0 | 12 | 11 | 1 | 12 | 8 |
| richest eighth | 0 | 0 | 0 | 2 | 1 | 1 | 0 | 3 | 2 |
| Total | 53 | 47 | 6 | 2 | 43 | 22 | 21 | 40 | 16 |
| **PARE** | | | | | | | | | |
| Poorest quarter | 22 | 21 | 1 | 0 | 1 | 1 | 0 | 10 | 1 |
| Second quarter | 10 | 10 | 0 | 0 | 0 | 0 | 0 | 4 | 1 |
| Third quarter | 18 | 14 | 4 | 0 | 28 | 8 | 20 | 12 | 5 |
| fifth eighth | 11 | 10 | 1 | 0 | 10 | 3 | 7 | 6 | 1 |
| sixth eighth | 7 | 4 | 3 | 0 | 18 | 5 | 13 | 6 | 4 |
| Fourth quarter | 3 | 2 | 1 | 2 | 14 | 13 | 1 | 14 | 9 |
| seventh eighth | 3 | 2 | 1 | 0 | 13 | 12 | 1 | 11 | 7 |
| richest eighth | 0 | 0 | 0 | 2 | 1 | 1 | 0 | 3 | 2 |
| Total | 53 | 47 | 6 | 2 | 43 | 22 | 21 | 40 | 16 |

| Eastern | Japan | South-eastern | Southern | Europe Total | Western | Eastern | Oceania Total | Australia and New Zealand | Other Oceania | Total |
|---|---|---|---|---|---|---|---|---|---|---|
| 0 | 0 | 4 | 5 | 0 | 0 | 0 | 0 | 0 | 0 | 25 |
| 1 | 0 | 1 | 1 | 0 | 0 | 0 | 1 | 0 | 1 | 16 |
| 4 | 0 | 4 | 2 | 10 | 5 | 5 | 7 | 0 | 7 | 99 |
| 2 | 0 | 3 | 2 | 0 | 0 | 0 | 4 | 0 | 4 | 46 |
| 2 | 0 | 1 | 0 | 10 | 5 | 5 | 3 | 0 | 3 | 53 |
| 0 | 1 | 0 | 1 | 18 | 16 | 2 | 4 | 2 | 2 | 38 |
| 0 | 1 | 0 | 1 | 6 | 4 | 2 | 1 | 0 | 1 | 15 |
| 0 | 0 | 0 | 0 | 12 | 12 | 0 | 3 | 2 | 1 | 23 |
| 5 | 1 | 9 | 9 | 28 | 21 | 7 | 12 | 2 | 10 | 178 |
| 1 | 0 | 1 | 4 | 0 | 0 | 0 | 0 | 0 | 0 | 11 |
| 0 | 0 | 4 | 3 | 0 | 0 | 0 | 0 | 0 | 0 | 15 |
| 3 | 0 | 3 | 1 | 9 | 3 | 6 | 8 | 0 | 8 | 101 |
| 2 | 0 | 3 | 1 | 2 | 0 | 2 | 6 | 0 | 6 | 68 |
| 1 | 0 | 0 | 0 | 7 | 3 | 4 | 2 | 0 | 2 | 33 |
| 1 | 1 | 2 | 0 | 19 | 18 | 1 | 4 | 2 | 2 | 51 |
| 1 | 0 | 1 | 0 | 10 | 9 | 1 | 2 | 1 | 1 | 30 |
| 0 | 1 | 1 | 0 | 9 | 9 | 0 | 2 | 1 | 1 | 21 |
| 5 | 1 | 10 | 8 | 28 | 21 | 7 | 12 | 2 | 10 | 178 |
| 0 | 0 | 4 | 7 | 0 | 0 | 0 | 0 | 0 | 0 | 25 |
| 1 | 0 | 0 | 1 | 0 | 0 | 0 | 1 | 0 | 1 | 21 |
| 3 | 0 | 4 | 0 | 9 | 3 | 6 | 7 | 0 | 7 | 78 |
| 2 | 0 | 3 | 0 | 1 | 0 | 1 | 6 | 0 | 6 | 45 |
| 1 | 0 | 1 | 0 | 8 | 3 | 5 | 1 | 0 | 1 | 33 |
| 1 | 1 | 2 | 0 | 19 | 18 | 1 | 4 | 2 | 2 | 54 |
| 1 | 0 | 1 | 0 | 6 | 5 | 1 | 3 | 1 | 2 | 30 |
| 0 | 1 | 1 | 0 | 13 | 13 | 0 | 1 | 1 | 0 | 24 |
| 5 | 1 | 10 | 8 | 28 | 21 | 7 | 12 | 2 | 10 | 178 |
| 1 | 0 | 4 | 3 | 0 | 0 | 0 | 0 | 0 | 0 | 19 |
| 0 | 0 | 0 | 5 | 0 | 0 | 0 | 1 | 0 | 1 | 23 |
| 3 | 0 | 4 | 0 | 9 | 3 | 6 | 7 | 0 | 7 | 84 |
| 2 | 0 | 3 | 0 | 1 | 0 | 1 | 5 | 0 | 5 | 41 |
| 1 | 0 | 1 | 0 | 8 | 3 | 5 | 2 | 0 | 2 | 43 |
| 1 | 1 | 2 | 0 | 19 | 18 | 1 | 4 | 2 | 2 | 52 |
| 1 | 0 | 1 | 0 | 9 | 8 | 1 | 3 | 1 | 2 | 32 |
| 0 | 1 | 1 | 0 | 10 | 10 | 0 | 1 | 1 | 0 | 20 |
| 5 | 1 | 10 | 8 | 28 | 21 | 7 | 12 | 2 | 10 | 178 |
| 0 | 0 | 2 | 4 | 0 | 0 | 0 | 0 | 0 | 0 | 27 |
| 1 | 0 | 0 | 1 | 0 | 0 | 0 | 0 | 0 | 0 | 7 |
| 2 | 0 | 6 | 3 | 6 | 0 | 6 | 8 | 0 | 8 | 85 |
| 2 | 0 | 4 | 3 | 1 | 0 | 1 | 5 | 0 | 5 | 47 |
| 0 | 0 | 2 | 0 | 5 | 0 | 5 | 3 | 0 | 3 | 38 |
| 2 | 1 | 1 | 1 | 22 | 21 | 1 | 4 | 2 | 2 | 59 |
| 2 | 0 | 1 | 1 | 9 | 8 | 1 | 3 | 1 | 2 | 39 |
| 0 | 1 | 0 | 0 | 13 | 13 | 0 | 1 | 1 | 0 | 20 |
| 5 | 1 | 9 | 9 | 28 | 21 | 7 | 12 | 2 | 10 | 178 |
| 0 | 0 | 4 | 5 | 0 | 0 | 0 | 0 | 0 | 0 | 33 |
| 1 | 0 | 0 | 2 | 0 | 0 | 0 | 1 | 0 | 1 | 15 |
| 2 | 0 | 4 | 1 | 3 | 0 | 3 | 7 | 0 | 7 | 68 |
| 1 | 0 | 3 | 1 | 1 | 0 | 1 | 5 | 0 | 5 | 33 |
| 1 | 0 | 1 | 0 | 2 | 0 | 2 | 2 | 0 | 2 | 35 |
| 2 | 1 | 2 | 0 | 25 | 21 | 4 | 4 | 2 | 2 | 62 |
| 2 | 0 | 2 | 0 | 11 | 7 | 4 | 1 | 1 | 0 | 39 |
| 0 | 1 | 0 | 0 | 14 | 14 | 0 | 3 | 1 | 2 | 23 |
| 5 | 1 | 10 | 8 | 28 | 21 | 7 | 12 | 2 | 10 | 178 |

**Annex B.** List of countries and areas by region and subregion

# Africa

## Sub—Saharan Africa

| | | |
|---|---|---|
| 1 Angola | 17 Gambia | 33 Reunion |
| 2 Benin | 18 Ghana | 34 Rwanda |
| 3 Botswana | 19 Guinea | 35 Sao Tome—Principe |
| 4 Burkina Faso | 20 Guinea—Bissau | 36 Senegal |
| 5 Burundi | 21 Kenya | 37 Seychelles |
| 6 Cameroon | 22 Lesotho | 38 Sierra Leone |
| 7 Cape Verde | 23 Liberia | 39 Somalia |
| 8 Central African Republic | 24 Madagascar | 40 South Africa |
| 9 Chad | 25 Malawi | 41 Swaziland |
| 10 Comoros | 26 Mali | 42 Togo |
| 11 Congo | 27 Mauritania | 43 Uganda |
| 12 Côte d'Ivoire | 28 Mauritius | 44 United Rep. of Tanzania |
| 13 Djibouti | 29 Mozambique | 45 Zaire |
| 14 Equatorial Guinea | 30 Namibia | 46 Zambia |
| 15 Ethiopia | 31 Niger | 47 Zimbabwe |
| 16 Gabon | 32 Nigeria | |

## Northern Africa

| | | |
|---|---|---|
| 1 Algeria | 3 Libyan Arab Jamahiyira | 5 Sudan |
| 2 Egypt | 4 Morocco | 6 Tunisia |

# Northern America

| | |
|---|---|
| 1 Canada | 2 United States of America |

# Latin America and Caribbean

## Latin America

| | | |
|---|---|---|
| 1 Argentina | 8 Ecuador | 15 Nicaragua |
| 2 Belize | 9 El Salvador | 16 Panama |
| 3 Bolivia | 10 French Guiana | 17 Paraguay |
| 4 Brazil | 11 Guatemala | 18 Peru |
| 5 Chile | 12 Guyana | 19 Suriname |
| 6 Colombia | 13 Honduras | 20 Uruguay |
| 7 Costa Rica | 14 Mexico | 21 Venezuela |

## Caribbean

| | | |
|---|---|---|
| 1 Anguilla | 9 Dominican Republic | 16 Netherlands Antilles and Aruba |
| 2 Antigua and Barbuda | 10 Grenada | 17 Puerto Rico |
| 3 Bahamas | 11 Guadeloupe | 18 Saint Kitts and Nevis |
| 4 Barbados | 12 Haiti | 19 Saint Lucia |
| 5 Bermuda | 13 Jamaica | 20 Saint Vincent and the Grenadines |
| 6 British Virgin Islands | 14 Martinique | 21 Trinidad and Tobago |
| 7 Cuba | 15 Montserrat | 22 United States Virgin Islands |
| 8 Dominica | | |

# Asia

## Eastern Asia

| | | |
|---|---|---|
| 1 China | 3 Korea, Republic of | 5 Mongolia |
| 2 Hong Kong | 4 Korea, DPR | 6 Japan |

## South–eastern Asia

| | | |
|---|---|---|
| 1 Brunei Darussalam | 5 Malaysia | 9 Thailand |
| 2 Cambodia | 6 Myanmar | 10 Viet Nam |
| 3 Indonesia | 7 Philippines | |
| 4 Lao People's Dem. Rep. | 8 Singapore | |

## Southern Asia

| | | |
|---|---|---|
| 1 Afghanistan | 4 India | 7 Pakistan |
| 2 Bangladesh | 5 Maldives | 8 Sri Lanka |
| 3 Bhutan | 6 Nepal | |

## Middle East

| | | |
|---|---|---|
| 1 Bahrain | 7 Jordan | 13 Syrian Arab Republic |
| 2 Cyprus | 8 Kuwait | 14 Turkey |
| 3 Democratic Yemen [a] | 9 Lebanon | 15 United Arab Emirates |
| 4 Iran (Islamic Rep. of) | 10 Oman | 16 Yemen [a] |
| 5 Iraq | 11 Qatar | |
| 6 Israel | 12 Saudi Arabia | |

# Europe

## Western Europe

| | | |
|---|---|---|
| 1 Austria | 8 Greece | 15 Norway |
| 2 Belgium | 9 Iceland | 16 Portugal |
| 3 Denmark | 10 Ireland | 17 Spain |
| 4 Finland | 11 Italy | 18 Sweden |
| 5 France | 12 Luxembourg | 19 Switzerland |
| Germany [b] | 13 Malta | 20 United Kingdom |
| 6 Fed. Rep. of Germany | 14 Netherlands | 21 Yugoslavia [c] |
| 7 German Dem. Rep. | | |

## Eastern Europe

| | | |
|---|---|---|
| 1 Albania | 4 Hungary | 7 former USSR |
| 2 Bulgaria | 5 Poland | |
| 3 Czechoslovakia | 6 Romania | |

# Oceania

## Australia and New Zealand

| | |
|---|---|
| 1 Australia | 2 New Zealand |

## Other Oceania

| | | |
|---|---|---|
| 1 Cook Islands | 5 New Caledonia | 9 Tonga |
| 2 Fiji | 6 Papua New Guinea | 10 Vanuatu |
| 3 French Polynesia | 7 Samoa | |
| 4 Kiribati | 8 Solomon Islands | |

Note:    Rule divisions within the listings indicate approximate quartile divisions of world population. Where quartile divisions fall within a large country or area, it is shaded.

a    On 22 May 1990 Democratic Yemen and Yemen merged to form a single State. Since that date they have been represented as one Member with the name "Yemen".

b    Through accession of the German Democratic Republic to the Federal Republic of Germany with effect from 3 October 1990, the two German states have united to form one sovereign State.

As from the date of unification, the Federal Republic of Germany acts in the United Nations under the designation Germany.

c    Data provided for Yugoslavia are for periods prior to 1 January 1992 and refer to the Socialist Federal Republic of Yugolavia which was composed of six republics. Data provided for Yugoslavia after that date refer to the Federal Republic of Yugoslavia which is composed of two republics (Serbia and Montenegro).

## Annex C    Technical notes

### 1. Gini index

Even though the Gini index is described as a ratio between two areas in the chart of the Lorenz curve, several equivalent formulas are used for Gini index calculations. The formula used in the present study is based on one of the coefficients of dispersion, namely the so-called absolute deviation, which is the average of the absolute values of the differences between pairs of values of all variables. In the analysis of the present study this should be interpreted as the weighted average of the absolute values of the differences between per capita GDP of all pairs of countries.

To arrive at an area ratio between 0 and 1 compatible with the Lorenz chart, the weighted average is divided by a number twice the level of per capita gross world product:

$$G = \frac{g}{2\bar{x}}$$

where: $\bar{x}$ = gross world product per capita and

$$g = \frac{1}{n^2} \sum_{1}^{k} i \sum_{1}^{k} j f_i f_j |x_i - x_j|$$

where: n = number of data (here: total world population)
k = number of classes (here: number of countries)
f = weights (here: population of countries)
x = income (here: per capita GDP of countries).

The Gini index is equal to 0 if the numerator is 0, i.e., if there is perfect equality; in this case x−y = 0 for each x end y. If there is perfect inequality g = 2x, and the Gini index equals 1.

### 2. Spearman's coefficient of rank correlation

The coefficient is calculated on the basis of the following formula:

$$r_s = 1 - \frac{6 \sum D^2}{n(n^2 - 1)}$$

where:
D = rank difference for any country
n = number of countries

### 3. Decomposition of standard deviation

Since one of the formulas for standard deviation ($\sigma$) of grouped data is

$$\sigma = \sqrt{\frac{\sum f_i (x_{ij} - \bar{x})^2}{n}}$$

and

$$x_{ij} - \bar{x} = (x_{ij} - \bar{x}_j) - (\bar{x} - \bar{x}_j)$$

it can be proven that

$$\sigma = \sqrt{\sigma_W^2 + \sigma_B^2}$$

Therefore

$$1 = \frac{\sigma_W^2}{\sigma^2} + \frac{\sigma_B^2}{\sigma^2}$$

where the symbols, traditionally used in income distribution, represent:

$\sigma$ = standard deviation of income related to the population as a whole (here: standard deviation of per capita GDP of all countries in the world)

$x_{ij}$ = income of unit "i" of group "j" (here: per capita GDP for country "i" belonging to region "j")

$\bar{x}_j$ = weighted average income of group "j" (here: per capita gross regional product for region "j")

$\bar{x}$ = weighted average income for the whole population (here: per capita gross world product)

$\sigma_W$ = standard deviation of income within the groups (here: standard deviation of per capita GDP within regions)

$\sigma_B$ = standard deviation of average income of groups (here: standard deviation of per capita gross regions products)

$\sigma_B^2 / \sigma^2$ = percentage of the differences caused by the differences between the groups.